Centro interuniversitario per la storia delle università italiane

Studi

7

Peter Denley

STUDIO IN LATE MEDIEVAL
NAISSANCE SIENA

CLUEB

Denley, Peter
    Commune and Studio in Late Medieval and Renaissance Siena / Peter Denley. – Bologna : CLUEB, 2006
    XVIII-497 p. ; ill. ; 27 cm
    (Centro interuniversitario per la storia delle università italiane : Studi / 7)
    ISBN 88-491-2646-8

CLUEB
Cooperativa Libraria Universitaria Editrice Bologna
40126 Bologna - Via Marsala 31
Tel. 051 220736 - Fax 051 237758
www.clueb.com

Finito di stampare nel mese di novembre 2006
da Legoprint - Lavis (TN)

Contents

PREFACE XI

ABBREVIATIONS AND CONVENTIONS XIII

LIST OF FIGURES XV

LIST OF TABLES XVII

INTRODUCTION 1
1. 'Una delle principali corone della nostra città' 1
2. The state of research 9
3. The sources 15
   a. The main communal institutions 17
   b. The *Savi dello Studio* 20
   c. The colleges of doctors and the chancellor of the *Studio* 21
   d. The student-university 23
   e. The Casa della Sapienza 23
   f. Other institutions 27
   g. Other universities 27
   h. Miscellaneous 27

PART ONE
COMMUNE AND *STUDIO*

I. ORIGINS AND GROWTH 31
1. The *Studio* to 1357 31
2. From 1357 to 1408 46
3. The fifteenth century: continuity 56

II. COMMUNAL ADMINISTRATION 65
1. 'Onore e utile' 65
2. The *Savi dello Studio* 69
3. The *Savi* and other bodies 76
4. Other officials 81

III. RESOURCES AND CONTRIBUTORS 87
1. Introduction 87
2. The budget 88
3. Expenditure: wages 98
4. Sources of income 99
5. The clergy and the hospital of S. Maria della Scala 101

IV. TIMES AND PLACES 109
1. The academic year 109
2. Interruptions 113
3. Venues for teaching 115

V. THE ORGANISATION OF TEACHING 121
1. Introduction 121
2. Structures 122
3. Policy: the profile of the *Studio* 129
4. 'La margarita della scientia' 131
5. Hierarchies of teaching 137

PART TWO

THE TEACHERS

I. CONTRACTS AND COMPETITION 149
1. The hiring of teachers 149
2. Conditions of service 155
3. Absenteeism, substitution, leave 158
4. Payment 169
5. The academic market 174
6. Siena and other *studi* 178

II. THE FORMATION OF A LOCAL TEACHING FORCE 183
1. Academic salaries and careers 183
2. From *forenses* to *cives* 190
3. The colleges of doctors 195

III. TEACHERS AND THE COMMUNITY 209
1. Teachers in public life 209
2. Teachers and factional politics 219
3. Social status 223

PART THREE

THE STUDENTS

I. THE STUDENT POPULATION 231
1. Introduction 231
2. The status of foreign students 231
3. Recruitment and retention 236
4. 'Tanta varietà de linghua et de paesi et de nationi' 239
5. Sienese students 245

II. THE STUDENT-UNIVERSITY 249
1. Introduction 249
2. The student university to the 1420s 250
3. The issue of statutes 253
4. The rector 257
   a. The method of choosing the rector 258

    b. Eligibility and conditions of office 261
    c. Status and formal role 263
    d. Functions and jurisdiction 265
    e. Problems and controversies 267
    f. The vice-rector 270
5. The operation of the university 271

III. THE STUDENT EXPERIENCE 279
1. Introduction 279
2. Material considerations 279
3. Student lectureships 282
4. Degrees 286
5. 'Le consuetudini de' studenti' 290
6. Identities and collectivities 293

PART FOUR
THE CASA DELLA SAPIENZA

I. THE GROWTH OF A NEW TYPE OF COLLEGE 299
1. Origins 299
2. From *domus pauperum scholarium* to the charging of fees 305
3. Admission 310

II. LIFE IN THE COLLEGE 325
1. Statutes and deliberations 325
2. Discipline and daily life 331

III. ADMINISTRATION 339
1. Layers of government: the comune and the *Savi dello Studio* 339
2. The rector 340
3. The *Camarlengo* 353
4. Other personnel 357

IV. THE ESTATE: FINANCE 361
1. From Misericordia to Sapienza: the estate 361
2. The comune and the finances of the Sapienza 370

V. BUILDINGS AND PROJECTS 381
1. The buildings 381
2. A library? 386
3. Plans for a new college 388

CONCLUSION 403

BIBLIOGRAPHY 409

INDEX OF PERSONAL NAMES 457

INDEX OF PLACE NAMES AND INSTITUTIONS 489

PREFACE

The origin of this work is an Oxford D.Phil. thesis submitted over two decades ago. This sought to reconstruct the history of the University of Siena from its official foundation charter to the fall of the republic, on the basis of extensive archival research. The context was the comparative history of Italian universities, and my research only focused on Siena when it became apparent just how rich were the unpublished and indeed in many cases undiscovered sources for that university. The thesis was very much an 'interim report'; to say that I had bitten off more than I could chew is an understatement, but in this case it is also a part of the explanation – along with my continuation of comparative work and digressions into other areas of research – for the long delay in the appearance of this book. In the intervening period I have examined a much wider range of sources, and a considerably larger volume of material, than for the original study, and a fuller and richer picture for the Quattrocento at least has become possible. Meanwhile, of course, much research has been done both on Sienese history and Italian universities in the period, which has helped sharpen the context and enrich the present work. Though this is a return to the same theme, it is both substantially expanded in terms of depth and documentation, and fundamentally revised in all respects; and while its essential approach is not dissimilar and its broad thrust still recognisable, it is now a very different work.

This publication was originally planned as part of a cluster of research projects. It complements the joint volume of Giovanni Minnucci and Leo Košuta (respectively publishing and analysing notarial documents of the fifteenth century, and a range of documents of the period 1531-1542),[1] and is a sequel to that of Paolo Nardi, which traces the development of Sienese higher education up to the foundation charter of 1357.[2] My debt to these scholars will be abundantly clear. Though the work now appears in another series, my aims have not changed; what I have tried to do is to build on the work of these and other scholars to offer a systematic overview based on the immense range of evidence for the period. This is part of the reason for the density of the references, which some will doubtless find disconcerting. On this, a word of explanation is necessary. The fact that this work appears with an Italian publisher, but in English, in a sense places it between two different academic cultures, and I have tried to keep in mind two different audiences. For specialists in Italian university history and in Sienese his-

---

[1] G. Minnucci and L. Košuta, *Lo Studio di Siena nei secoli XIV-XVI*. Orbis Academicus, Saggi e Documenti di Storia delle Università, 3/Saggi e Documenti per la Storia dell'Università di Siena, 1 (Milan, 1989).

[2] P. Nardi, *L'insegnamento superiore a Siena nei secoli XI-XIV*. Orbis Academicus, Saggi e Documenti di Storia delle Università, 6/Saggi e Documenti per la Storia dell'Università di Siena, 2 (Milan, 1996).

tory I have tried to present, as fully and clearly as possible, conclusions about how the university came to be sustained and administered, exploring the factors peculiar to Siena as well as those common to other *studi* in the rapidly changing university system of late medieval Italy. I have attempted to do this in full detail, which has entailed thorough documentation of the very rich archival evidence. At the same time, conscious of how obscure this whole area is among scholars of medieval Italy in the English-speaking world, I have deliberately erred on the side of more rather than less explanation, especially of terminology that has different meanings in Italy than in the northern European university world with which such readers may be more familiar. This hybridity is undoubtedly less than satisfactory. I can imagine that specialists will find many passages excessively 'divulgative', while generalists will doubtless tire of the detail and the weight of the footnotes. It is a question of attempting balance where perhaps balance cannot exist. All I can do is request indulgence and patience on the part of both groups.

Many people have already demonstrated these qualities in abundance, and my gratitude to them is matched only by my profound regret at having kept them waiting for so long. My debts are of course many. Several scholars have played key roles in the completion of this book. It was Domenico Maffei who, after reading my original thesis, invited me to participate in the collaborative publication project described above. I am immensely grateful for his support, encouragement and patience. Paolo Nardi read parts of an earlier draft, made helpful suggestions, and facilitated my research in the Circolo Giuridico in Siena; his generosity and enthusiasm have been invaluable. The late Philip Jones, my D.Phil. supervisor, set high standards, asked trenchant questions and gave unobtrusive but real support. Without the inspiration, advice and when necessary strictures of these three the book would have been much the poorer. A number of individuals and institutions have made publication possible. I am most grateful to Gian Paolo Brizzi and his colleagues on the board of the Centro Interuniversitario per la Storia delle Università Italiane for offering to host the volume in their series; given the extraordinary energy and standards of this institution this is a great honour. The Isobel Thornley Bequest Fund has generously contributed towards the cost of publication, and I have also benefited from a British Academy Grant for research (1982). I am grateful to Westfield Medieval Studies for permission to rework some of the material in my article 'Academic Rivalry and Interchange: the Universities of Siena and Florence', which first appeared in *Florence and Italy. Renaissance Studies in Honour of Nicolai Rubinstein*, eds. P. R. Denley & C. M. Elam. Westfield Publications in Medieval Studies, 2 (London, 1989), pp. 193-208. In Siena, the staff of the Archivio di Stato have been tireless in their assistance on a variety of matters, as have those of the Biblioteca Comunale, the Archivio Arcivescovile and the Circolo Giuridico; this has been matched by the helpfulness of librarians in London, particularly of the Warburg Institute and the British Library, as well as the inter-library loan team at Queen Mary University of London. Over the decades I have also benefited from discussions with, and received expert advice, encouragement, material, references, and palaeographical or linguistic help from Mario Ascheri, Nello Barbieri, Bob Black, Laurence Brockliss, Howard Burns, Giuliano Catoni, Maria Assunta Ceppari Ridolfi, Jonathan Davies, Veronica Denley, Rosemary Devonshire-Jones, Sonia Fineschi, John Fletcher, Dieter Girgensohn, Michael Kiene, Leo Košuta, Ubaldo Morandi, Giovanni Minnucci, Fabrizio Nevola, Giulio Prunai, Nicolai Rubinstein, Charles Schmitt, Luca Trapani, Patrizia Turrini, Daniel Waley and Diana Webb. The forbearance of my colleagues at Queen Mary has been exceptional. Last but not least, the support of Silvia Sovič though the tortuous birth of this work has been beyond measure.

London
August 2006

ABBREVIATIONS AND CONVENTIONS

Unless otherwise stated, references to unpublished sources are to archival series in the Archivio di Stato di Siena.

Repeated bibliographical references are given in abbreviated form; they can be found in full in the bibliography. The most frequently cited works, and those referred to for convenience by the name of the author alone or by an abbreviation of the title that does not respect its alphabetical position in the bibliography, are listed below.

All dates are given in modern style unless otherwise stated.

AAS	=	Archivio Arcivescovile di Siena
ASS	=	Archivio di Stato di Siena
BAI	=	C. BAI, 'Documenti per la storia dello Studio senese dal 1450 al 1475', unpublished *tesi di laurea*, Università degli Studi di Siena, Facoltà di Giurisprudenza, anno accademico 1993-94, relatore P. Nardi.
Balìa	=	ASS, *Balìa*
BCS	=	Biblioteca Comunale di Siena
Bicch.	=	ASS, *Biccherna*
BSSP	=	*Bullettino Senese di Storia Patria*
CATONI, *Pergamene*	=	G. CATONI et al., *Le Pergamene dell'Università di Siena e la 'Domus Misericordiae'. Seminario di Archivistica* (Siena, 1975-6).
CG	=	ASS, *Consiglio Generale*
Chartularium	=	G. CECCHINI and G. PRUNAI (eds.), *Chartularium Studii Senensis* (Siena, 1942).
Conc.	=	ASS, *Concistoro*
DENIFLE, *Entstehung*	=	H. DENIFLE, *Die Entstehung der Universitäten des Mittelalters bis 1400* (Berlin, 1885). The Sienese entry, pp. 429-52, has been translated in *I tedeschi nella storia dell'Università di Siena*, ed. G. Minnucci (Siena, n.d.), pp. 13-31.
Dipl.	=	ASS, *Diplomatico*
DBI	=	*Dizionario biografico degli Italiani* (Rome, 1960-).
EUBEL	=	K. EUBEL, *Hierarchia Catholica Medii Aevi*, I-II (Monasterii, 1913-14).
FERRERI	=	T. FERRERI, 'Documenti per la storia dello Studio senese dal 1475 al 1500', unpublished *tesi di laurea*, Università degli Studi di Siena, Facoltà di Giurisprudenza, anno accademico 1995-96, relatore P. Nardi.
GAROSI	=	A. GAROSI, *Siena nella Storia della Medicina, 1240-1555* (Florence, 1958).
KOŠUTA, 'Documenti'	=	L. KOŠUTA, 'Documenti per la Storia dello Studio senese dal 1531 al 1542', in G. MINNUCCI and L. KOŠUTA, *Lo Studio di Siena nei secoli XIV-XVI*. Orbis Aca-

		demicus, Saggi e Documenti di Storia delle Università, 3/Saggi e Documenti per la Storia dell'Università di Siena, 1 (Milan, 1989), pp. 317-578.
MINNUCCI, 'Documenti'	=	G. MINNUCCI, 'Documenti per la Storia dello Studio senese (Secoli XIV-XVI)', in G. MINNUCCI and L. KOŠUTA, *Lo Studio di Siena nei secoli XIV-XVI*. Orbis Academicus, Saggi e Documenti di Storia delle Università, 3/Saggi e Documenti per la Storia dell'Università di Siena, 1 (Milan, 1989), pp. 9-314.
MINNUCCI, *Lauree*, I	=	G. MINNUCCI, *Le lauree dello Studio senese alla fine del secolo XV*. Quaderni di 'Studi senesi', 51 (Milan, 1981).
MINNUCCI, *Lauree*, II	=	G. MINNUCCI, *Le lauree dello Studio senese all'inizio del secolo XVI (1501-1506)*. Quaderni di 'Studi senesi', 55 (Milan, 1984).
MINNUCCI, *Lauree*, III	=	G. MINNUCCI, *Le lauree dello Studio senese all'inizio del secolo XVI*, II *(1507-1514)*. Quaderni di 'Studi senesi', 56 (Milan, 1985).
MINNUCCI and MORELLI, *Lauree*, IV	=	G. MINNUCCI and P. G. MORELLI, *Le lauree dello Studio senese nel XVI secolo. Regesti degli atti dal 1516 al 1573*. Bibliotheca Studii Senensis, 5 (Siena, 1992).
MINNUCCI and MORELLI, *Lauree*, V	=	G. MINNUCCI and P. G. MORELLI, *Le lauree dello Studio senese nel 16. secolo: regesti degli atti dal 1573 al 1579*. Università degli Studi di Siena, Dipartimento di Scienze Storiche, Giuridiche, Politiche e Sociali: Istituto Storico Diocesano di Siena (Siena, 1998).
Mis.	=	ASS, *Casa della Misericordia*
NARDI, *Insegnamento*	=	P. NARDI, *L'insegnamento superiore a Siena nei secoli XI-XIV*. Orbis Academicus, Saggi e Documenti di Storia delle Università, 6/Saggi e Documenti per la Storia dell'Università di Siena, 2 (Milan, 1996).
Not.	=	ASS, *Notarile ante-cosimiano*
'Ordini'	=	'Ordini del vivere de li scholari'; rules for the Casa della Sapienza, c.1416-18. In *Mis.* 1, ff. 47r-49v; ed. CATONI, 'Genesi', pp. 177-82 (see Table 7, pp. 328-9).
PIANIGIANI	=	A. PIANIGIANI, 'Documenti per la storia dello Studio senese nella prima metà del Quattrocento', unpublished *tesi di laurea*, Università degli Studi di Siena, Facoltà di Giurisprudenza, anno accademico 1991-92, relatore P. Nardi.
PRUNAI, I	=	G. PRUNAI, 'Lo studio di Siena dalle origini alla "migratio" bolognese (sec. XIII-1321)', *BSSP*, 56 (1949), pp. 53-79.
PRUNAI, II	=	G. PRUNAI, 'Lo studio senese dalla "migratio" bolognese alla fondazione della "Domus Sapientiae" (1321-1408)', *BSSP*, 57 (1950), pp. 3-54.
PRUNAI, III	=	G. PRUNAI, 'Lo studio senese nel primo quarantennio del principato Mediceo', *BSSP*, 66 (1959), pp. 79-160.
RASHDALL	=	H. RASHDALL, *The Universities of Europe in the Middle Ages*, eds. F. M. Powicke and A. B. Emden. 3 vols. (Oxford, 1936 edn.).
Sale	=	ASS, *Quattro Maestri del Sale*
Scala	=	ASS, *Ospedale di S. Maria della Scala*
Statuti	=	ASS, *Statuti di Siena*
Studio	=	ASS, *[R.] Università degli Studi*
ZDEKAUER	=	L. ZDEKAUER, *Lo Studio di Siena nel Rinascimento* (Milan, 1894, repr. Bologna, 1977).
ZDEKAUER, *Documenti*	=	L. ZDEKAUER, *Documenti per servire alla storia dello Studio di Siena, 1240-1789* (Siena, 1896); extract from *L'Unione universitaria*, 3 (1896).
ZDEKAUER, *Origini*	=	L. ZDEKAUER, *Sulle Origini dello Studio Senese* (Siena, 1893).

LIST OF FIGURES

1a   Funeral monument of Guglielmo di Ciliano and Niccolò Aringhieri da Casole, fourteenth century   39

1b   Funeral monument of Guglielmo di Ciliano and Niccolò Aringhieri da Casole; detail.   40

2a   Seal of Federico Petrucci, early fourteenth century.   41

2b   Seal of Biagio Montanini, early fourteenth century   44

2c   Seal of Giovanni di Niccolò di Mino Vincenti, second half of fourteenth century   49

3   Bull of pope Gregory XII confirming the privilege of the emperor Charles IV and extending it to include theology   55

4   Size of the teaching force at Siena, Pisa and Bologna, 1473-1500   62

5   Classroom scene, from Ambrogio Lorenzetti, *The Effects of Good Government*, fresco, 1338.   69

6   Presentation of the Sienese flag in Piazza Tolomei, in front of S. Cristoforo, one of the churches used for university lectures. 116

7   A university lecture, mid-fifteenth century. 142

8a   Seal of Angelo degli Ubaldi of Perugia, who taught law in Siena in the mid-fifteenth century 179

8b   Signature and seal of Pietro Luti, who taught law in the second half of the fifteenth century 189

9   Opening of Giovanni Battista Caccialupi, *De modo studendi*, written in Siena in the 1460s. 195

10   Seal of the college of doctors of law 200

11   Signature and seal of Mariano Sozzini 221

12a   The mace of the *Studio*, c. 1440. 275

12b The mace of the *Studio* – detail   275

12c The mace of the *Studio* – detail   275

13   Seal of the *Studio*, possibly eighteenth century   276

14   'Ordini del vivere de li scholari', c. 1415-6   326

15   Concentration of Casa della Misericordia/Casa della Sapienza property   367

16   Plan of central Siena   382

17   Ground plan of the Sapienza area   382

18   The Casa della Sapienza in 1595. From Francesco Vanni, *Pianta di Siena*   383

19   Groundplan of the Casa della Sapienza, c. 1679   383

20a Giuliano da Sangallo, first designs for a Casa della Sapienza   392

20b Giuliano da Sangallo, more detailed designs for a Casa della Sapienza   393

21   Giovanni Battista da Sangallo, copy of Giuliano da Sangallo's designs   394

22   G. A. Pecci, cross-section of Giuliano da Sangallo's design   394

23   Francesco di Giorgio Martini, possible design for a Casa della Sapienza in Siena   395

24a Assistant of Francesco di Giorgio Martini, lower-floor plan for a Casa della Sapienza   396

24b Assistant of Francesco di Giorgio Martini, upper-floor plan for a Casa della Sapienza   396

24c Assistant of Francesco di Giorgio Martini, variant upper-floor plan for a Casa della Sapienza   397

24d Assistant of Francesco di Giorgio Martini, variant upper-floor plan for a Casa della Sapienza   397

List of Tables

1   Size of the teaching force, 1450-1500   60

2   Expenditure on *Studio* salaries   91

3   Profile of the subjects taught   127

4   Leading Sienese families in the *Studio*   194

5   Statistics from the list of matriculated students in 1533   240

6   Known admissions to the Casa della Sapienza (first twenty-five years)   312

7   'Ordini del Vivere' of the Casa della Sapienza compared with the 'Constitutiones' of the Collegio Gregoriano, Perugia   328

8a The largest Casa della Misericordia properties in 1318   367

8b The largest Casa della Sapienza properties in 1451   367

INTRODUCTION

1. *'Una delle principali corone della nostra città'*[1]

The protagonists of this study may appear unlikely and, by currently fashionable criteria, unprofitable objects of investigation. When we think of the Italian Renaissance, and the cities that gave birth to it, Siena is not the place to which our first thoughts are usually directed. Florence, Rome and Venice would certainly take precedence; so too, probably, would Milan, Naples, Mantua, Ferrara and Urbino. The popular perception, at least in the English-speaking world, is that Siena, while possessed of a splendid medieval civic tradition, was by the fifteenth century something of an oddity, a cultural backwater which almost self-consciously and deliberately 'opted out of the Renaissance' in favour of traditional forms of artistic expression.[2] Similarly when we consider the great intellectual transformations of the period, we do not think of the universities first but rather of the humanists, working, according to the conventional view, outside the institutional framework of higher education, sometimes attacking that framework, and certainly building their own intellectual network in parallel to it. Were the universities not 'enemies of humanism',[3] bastions of conservatism and established structures? This attitude is only one aspect of a wider phenomenon, namely the fall from grace of university history as an area of interest to mainstream 'Anglo-Saxon' medievalists, whose current preoccupations have

---

[1] *CG* 224, f. 326v, 16 Feb 1450, ed. A. Garosi, *Siena nella storia della medicina, 1240-1555* (Florence, 1958), doc. 62, pp. 530-1; see below, p. 65.

[2] To this might be added the view that fifteenth-century Siena also 'opted out of modernity' in the sense of experiencing economic decline, having eschewed new investment opportunities in favour of an extensive *rentier* foundation for oligarchic power; M. Ascheri, *Renaissance Siena (1355-1559)* (Siena, 1993), p. 9; G. Pinto, 'Signori della finanza: le grandi compagnie bancarie', in *Storia di Siena, I. Dalle origini alla fine della repubblica*, eds. R. Barzanti, G. Catoni and M. De Gregorio (Siena, 1995), pp. 69-78; Idem, '"Honour" and "Profit": Landed Property and Trade in Medieval Siena', in *City and Countryside in Late Medieval and Renaissance Italy: Essays Presented to Philip Jones*, eds. T. Dean and C. Wickham (London, 1990), pp. 81-91 (pp. 89-90); S. Tognetti, '"Fra li compagni palesi et li ladri occulti". Banchieri senesi del Quattrocento', *Nuova Rivista Storica*, 88 (2004), pp. 27-102, questioning the pessimistic view (p. 30 esp.), as does G. Piccinni, 'Cultura, società, Università a Siena nel Medioevo', in *Cultura e Università a Siena. Epoche, argomenti, protagonisti*, ed. B. Baccetti (Siena, 1993), pp. 11-17 (p. 11 on Siena's 'vocazione terziaria').

[3] A view that can be traced back to Rashdall's much-quoted pronouncement that 'universities, at least in Italy, were above all things places of professional study, and their professors were long the enemies of humanism.' H. Rashdall, *The Universities of Europe in the Middle Ages*, eds. F. M. Powicke and A. B. Emden, 3 vols. (Oxford, 1936 edn.), II, pp. 50-1.

found few resonances in what tends to be seen as an arcane and technical subject.[4] Putting Siena and university history together – and then focusing explicitly on the institutional angle within that subject – might be seen as an act of historiographical perversity, a wilful attempt to ignore current trends and explore precisely those recesses of the late middle ages that had seemed destined to be consigned to the dustbin, not the record, of history.

Needless to say, this is not my view. The role of Italian universities in the culture of the period has come to be reassessed. The close interdependence of humanists and the university world is better appreciated now,[5] as are the reasons why it sometimes appears otherwise.[6] So is the fundamental importance of the Italian universities in providing professional expertise for all aspects of public life – government, diplomacy, the legal system and the cultural world that developed in tandem with it. As to Siena, it has been amply demonstrated that the old picture of a Quattrocento of isolationism and decline is wide of the mark.[7] To the extent that it persists it is a consequence of a cultural positivism of the Great Ideas, Great Texts and Great Art variety, more preoccupied with the evaluation of achievement than with the explanation of its roots, and thus slow to acknowledge the profound extent to which the history of the Italian city-states is integrated and interdependent.[8] Proud formulations of

---

[4] A glance at the immensely wide-ranging programmes of the international conferences of medievalists at Kalamazoo or Leeds over the last decade demonstrates the extent to which university history has become all but invisible, especially to younger generations of historians in the English-speaking world. The continental tradition is very different. The student movement of 1968 has been diagnosed as a catalyst in the revival of interest in medieval universities; P. RENZI, 'Studium Generale: aurea mediocritas? Riflessioni sul caso senese', *Nuova Rivista Storica*, 79 (1995), pp. 303-20 (p. 303).

[5] The first seriously to challenge this view was P. O. KRISTELLER, *Die italienischen Universitäten der Renaissance*. Schriften und Vorträge des Petrarca-Instituts Köln, 1 (1953); repr. in his *Studies in Renaissance Thought and Letters*, IV (Rome, 1996), pp. 97-113. P. F. GRENDLER, 'Renaissance Humanism, Schools, and Universities', in *L'étude de la Renaissance. Nunc et cras. Actes du colloque de la Fédération internationale des Sociétés et Instituts d'Étude de la Renaissance (FISIER), Genève, septembre 2001*, eds. M. Engammare, M.-M. Fragonard, A. Redondo and S. Ricci (Geneva, 2003), pp. 69-91, has argued that the perception of the wrongness of this antagonistic paradigm was one of the spurs to the growth of research on Italian universities (p. 84). Among the many writers who have contributed to the revision of this traditional view see particularly M. ASCHERI, 'Giuristi, umanisti e istituzioni del Tre-Quattrocento. Qualche problema', *Annali dell' Istituto Storico italo-germanico in Trento*, 3 (1977), pp. 43-73; C. VASOLI, 'L'università e gli umanisti', in *L'università e la sua storia. Origini, spazi istituzionali e pratiche didattiche dello* Studium *cittadino. Atti del Convegno di Studi (Arezzo, 15-16 novembre 1991)*, ed. P. Renzi (Siena, 1998), pp. 149-69; J. DAVIES, *Florence and its University during the Early Renaissance* (Leiden, 1998), ch. 6; A. SOTTILI, 'Zum Verhältnis von Stadt, Staat und Universität in Italien im Zeitalter des Humanismus, dargestellt am Fall Pavia', in *Die Universität in Alteuropa*, eds. A. Patschovsky and H. Rabe. Konstanzer Bibliothek, 22 (Konstanz, 1994), pp. 43-67; and IDEM, 'Università e Umanesimo', in *Acta conventus neo-latini Abulensis. Proceedings of the Tenth International Congress of Neo-Latin Studies (Avila, 4-9 August 1997)*, ed. R. Green et al. Arizona Center for Medieval and Renaissance Studies, Medieval Texts and Studies, 227 (Tempe, Az., 2000), pp. 603-10. For a more fundamental recasting of the problem, see L. AVELLINI, 'Università e umanesimo', in *L'Università in Europa dall'Umanesimo ai Lumi*, eds. G. P. Brizzi and J. Verger (Milan, 2002), pp. 20-35; and cf. G. P. BRIZZI and A. DE BENEDICTIS, 'Le università italiane', in the same volume, pp. 36-72 (pp. 36-9).

[6] Notably the insecurity displayed by some humanists working within the universities, their need to establish reputations through personalised 'causes', and rhetorical exercises such as the *dispute delle arti* that have sometimes been mistaken for vehicles for such antagonisms. A key work is A. GRAFTON and L. JARDINE, *From Humanism to the Humanities: Education and the Liberal Arts in Fifteenth- and Sixteenth-Century Europe* (London, 1986), esp. chs. 1 and 2.

[7] For overviews, see J. HOOK, *Siena. A City and its History* (London, 1979), ch. 8; M. ASCHERI, *Siena nella storia* (Milan, 2000), ch. 4; K. CHRISTIANSEN, 'Painting in Renaissance Siena', in K. CHRISTIANSEN, L. B. KANTER and C. B. STREHLKE, *Painting in Renaissance Siena 1420-1500* (New York, 1988), pp. 3-32; C. B. STREHLKE, 'Art and Culture in Renaissance Siena', in op. cit., pp. 33-60; and D. NORMAN, *Painting in Late Medieval and Renaissance Siena* (New Haven, Ct., and London, 2003), chs. 4 and 5.

[8] Cf. reflections on this in P. BURKE, 'Decentering the Renaissance: the Challenge of Postmodernism', in *At the Margins. Minority Groups in Premodern Italy*, ed. S. Milner (Minneapolis, Mn., 2005), pp. 36-49.

the city's identity (and subsequent recastings of it, right down to those of the contemporary tourist industry) can obscure the fact that Sienese writers, artists and architects were closely connected with those elsewhere, and that there was a high degree of mobility and interchange. The city's place in Renaissance culture is much more profitably assessed in this light.

Siena's university, or *Studio*, was central to these interconnections. The patience and stamina with which Siena nurtured this institution is typical of its cultural policy. In addition to its obvious functions as provider of educational opportunities and professional expertise for citizens, the *Studio* played a cardinal role in developing the profile of the city on the Italian and indeed the European stage, attracting teachers from across Italy and students from all over the continent. What Siena lacked because, as a republic, it did not have a court,[9] it was partly able to make up for through its university, thanks not least to its central geographical location, specifically with its position on the Via Francigena and its proximity to Rome.[10]

As my title indicates, this study focuses on a relationship, and it is appropriate to say something here about its protagonists. On one hand we have the creator and sponsor of the *Studio*. The commune of Siena had a long tradition of cultural accomplishment, all of it wrought painstakingly. By persistent attention to all aspects of its spiritual, cultural, economic and political health, Florence's smaller southern neighbour managed to carve out for itself a distinctive role in the peninsula's history. Two characteristics in particular should be emphasised for our purposes. The first might be described as technical; a programmatic administration of the city which brought the authorities directly into play in all aspects of public life, including the spheres of art, building, town and country planning, ceremonial, and literary and intellectual patronage. Siena's skills in administration have been diagnosed as one of its distinctive features, emulated by other states;[11] so too is the extent to which the city's large projects transcended political differences, over a long period of time.[12] The formidable and coherent body of legislation that was the direct legacy of this government bears witness to a pattern of continual, laboured but relentless experimentation which permitted the republic to endure to the end of the fifteenth century, with comparatively little of the turbulence experienced elsewhere in the peninsula. The second characteristic might be described as presentational. Some of the best known as-

---

[9] P. PERTICI, 'La furia delle fazioni', in *Storia di Siena*, I, pp. 383-94 (p. 388) defined the *Studio* as 'il principale veicolo di promozione culturale, in assenza di una corte'.

[10] On the significance of Siena's position on the Via Francigena, as attested by the numbers of students from elsewhere, RENZI, '*Studium Generale: aurea mediocritas?*', p. 311; more generally, R. STOPANI, *La Via Francigena. Una strada europea nell'Italia del Medioevo* (Florence, 1988).

[11] 'Pochi numericamente, di fatto i Senesi di allora coltivavano essenzialmente la scienza dell'amministrazione, nel pubblico e nel privato, che li portava ad esempio ad avere un ospedale che fu il modello per quello di Milano e un collegio della Sapienza anch'esso oggetto di ammirazione.' M. ASCHERI, 'Siena centro finanziario, gioiello della civiltà comunale italiana', in *Le Biccherne di Siena. Arte e finanza all'alba dell'economia moderna*, ed. A. Tomei (Bergamo, 2002), pp. 14-21 (p. 20); and IDEM, *Renaissance Siena*, p. 13 ('Siena had created a new occupation, that of administrator'); cf. PICCINNI, 'Cultura, società, Università', referring to Siena's 'accumulo di sapere amministrativo e politico', and citing as an example the *Tavola delle Possessioni* of the early fourteenth century, the first European cataster (p. 12). On the impact on this specialism on the historical documentation, see P. CAMMAROSANO, *Tradizione documentaria e storia cittadina. Introduzione al 'Caleffo Vecchio' del Comune di Siena* (Siena, 1988).

[12] The Sienese 'sapevano riconoscere i progetti boni, e sapevano portarli avanti nonostante il cambiamento di "regime"'. M. ASCHERI, *Siena e la città-stato del medioevo italiano* (Siena, 2004), p. 8. Among the many such projects, one of the more neglected (because least visible) is the ambitious and comprehensive scheme of underground irrigation, with almost 25 km of tunnelling, that was developed through the later middle ages and virtually completed by the early fifteenth century; cf. esp. D. BALESTRACCI et al., *I bottini. Acquedotti medievali senesi* (2nd ed. Siena, 1985); D. BALESTRACCI, D. LAMBERINI and M. CIVAI, *I bottini medievali di Siena* (Siena, n.d.); and for a finely contextualised study, M. P. KUCHER, *The Water Supply System of Siena, Italy. The Medieval Roots of the Modern Networked City* (New York and London, 2005).

pects of Siena's 'cultural heritage' – the public image of Sienese government as reflected in the political iconography of Ambrogio Lorenzetti's frescoes in the Palazzo Pubblico,[13] the civic rituals whose legacy is the highly visible *palio*, now perceived as *doyen* of Italian civic festivals and ever the object of intense interdisciplinary study[14] – are self-conscious statements of civic individuality and purpose, carefully conceived and finely calibrated (and, in the case of the *palio*, constantly reinvented down to the present). A similar point can be made about the *Studio*, whose creation and sustenance was constantly described in terms of the honour and reputation that it would bring to the city. If the legacy of this Sienese creation is not particularly visible, or of limited popular interest – something that could actually be said of most university centres that failed to bequeath the architectural heritage of Oxford and Cambridge – that does not make it any less important to our understanding of Siena's history.

Siena has long been recognised as a pioneer in the history of universities, in that it appeared to have been the first instance of a town attempting to found its own *Studio* without the blessing of a higher authority; and it has also been judged to be an extreme instance of a university run by the town.[15] Yet it is unhelpful to look at the *Studio* as if it had been no more than an instrument of the commune. The reality was that, in order to create and maintain a successful university in the thirteenth, fourteenth or fifteenth centuries, it was necessary to take full cognisance of what was going on elsewhere; to satisfy expectations and conform to recognised practice; in other words, to offer a level, range and quality of education that would be accepted by teachers, students and the rest of society, not just in Siena itself, but elsewhere in Italy, and indeed – in an age of international migration of students – beyond the confines of the peninsula. So in a sense the second protagonist of the title is not just the *Studio* of Siena, but also the whole concept of what a university should consist of and how it should be organised. But this concept was in almost permanent flux.[16] When the Sienese made their initial attempts, in the thirteenth century, first to attract teachers at the higher level and then to open a *studium generale*, they were up against the huge reputation of the university of Bologna, but also against a handful of other towns or rulers that were attempting to break the apparent hegemony of that centre. Some of these were doing so in explicit imitation of Bologna, where the often anarchic interplay between the interests of students, teachers and local powers were still in the process of forging a complex constitutional framework for the developing *Studio*. Others were taking a very different approach, one which was more centralised, even authoritarian.[17] By the early fifteenth century, as Siena's

---

[13] References (insofar as these frescoes have relevance to the *Studio*) below, p. 68 n. 23.

[14] Cf. most recently G. PARSONS, *Siena, Civil Religion and the Sienese* (Aldershot, 2004).

[15] Below, p. 32 for the verdicts of Rashdall and Denifle in the late nineteenth century; more recent evaluations in M. ASCHERI, 'Istituzioni e governo della città', in *Storia di Siena*, I, pp. 327-40 (p. 334); and IDEM, 'Città e Università a Siena: il presente in prospettiva storica', in *Università in Europa. Le istituzioni universitarie dal Medio Evo ai nostri giorni. Strutture, organizzazione, funzionamento. Atti del Convegno Internazionale di Studi, Milazzo 28 Settembre – 2 Ottobre 1993*, ed. A. Romano (Soveria Mannelli, Catanzaro – Messina, 1995), pp. 115-27 (revised version of his 'Società, cultura e Università: una proposta tra passato e presente', in *Cultura e Università a Siena*, pp. 61-7).

[16] There are very few general histories of Italian universities in the late middle ages. Since E. COPPI, *Le Università Italiane nel Medioevo* (2nd edn., Florence, 1880), only M. BELLOMO, *Saggio sull'Università nell'Età del Diritto Comune* (Catania, 1979), focusing strongly on Bologna, and for the later part of the period P. F. GRENDLER, *The Universities of the Italian Renaissance* (Baltimore, Md., 2002), have attempted this herculean task. For a survey of recent developments in the field, see P. R. DENLEY, 'Medieval and Renaissance Italian Universities and the Role of Foreign Scholarship', *History of Universities*, 19/1 (2004), pp. 159-81 (esp. pp. 159-62).

[17] The best-known example is Naples, founded by Frederick II in 1224; but the organisation at Rome, Salerno and Arezzo in the thirteenth century also appears to have been fundamentally different from that of Bologna. I propose to deal more fully with the topic of 'models' in future; for now, see P. R. DENLEY, 'Recent Studies on Italian Universities of the

repeated efforts were finally rewarded with success, the situation was very different. The *Studio* of Bologna had certainly won the battle for status, in the sense that its antiquity, precedence and authority in constitutional matters were accepted, and rivals were no longer seeking overtly to destroy it. In reality, though, it was only one of a dozen universities, all increasingly directed by the prevailing local power, and locked in intense competition with each other for teachers, students and status. The competition took place within a framework of carefully defined conventions, but ones which were also changing thanks to that same competitive impulse.

The present study focuses on Siena's engagement with this system. It is an engagement which operated in both directions; as well as adopting the necessary structures and mechanisms, the Sienese, through constant experimentation, contributed important new elements which were influential in changing the framework. It is this two-way traffic of ideas and practices which drew me, as a historian of universities rather than of Siena, to the subject. The importance of the Italian university world as a whole emerges at every stage and through all aspects of the *Studio*'s history. Its long gestation, from the first initiative in the 1240s, through a series of 'revivals', a brief migration to Siena of the *Studio* of Bologna in 1321, an eventual imperial charter in 1357, and finally the attainment of stability in the second and third decades of the fifteenth century, have to be seen above all in the context of Siena's models and rivals. The same is true of the attraction and retention of teachers and students; while arguably the biggest element in its long-term success, the creation of the Casa della Sapienza, a college with a peculiarly secular framework, with well-connected, fee-paying students from all over Europe, constitutes Siena's unique contribution to that system.

The theme of 'commune and *Studio*' is not as straightforward as it may seem. First, it should not be assumed that the relationship is one of contraposition. The 'town and gown' paradigm, of which it is redolent, rather points in that direction. The phrase is widely used as shorthand for the relationship of two distinct bodies, somehow thrust together, that had to find a way to coexist. This assumption is appropriate, if at all, to the earliest phase of university history, when rights were being fought over, teachers and students were threatening walkouts, and wholesale and often bloody conflicts between the academic community and its urban hosts were not uncommon.[18] But although this way of studying university history has a long pedigree,[19] it may not be the most productive approach for the later medieval period.[20] Far from being opponents, the two participants in the relationship are often not even clearly separable.[21] This is not surprising. Italian universities at the time were constitutionally 'incomplete'.[22] Apart from formal ceremonies such as the start of the academic year, they never came to-

---

Middle Ages and Renaissance', *History of Universities*, 1 (1981), pp. 193-205 (p. 198), and IDEM, 'The University of Siena, 1357-1557', unpublished D.Phil. thesis, University of Oxford, 1981, pp. 35-7.

[18] P. R. DENLEY, 'Trasgressioni e rivolte studentesche', in *Le Università dell' Europa: Gli uomini e i luoghi, secoli XII-XVIII*, eds. G. P. Brizzi & J. Verger (Milan, 1993), pp. 81-103 (esp. pp. 83-93) (translated and modified version 'Students in the Middle Ages', in *Universitates e Università*. Atti del Convegno, Bologna 16-21 novembre 1987 [Bologna, 1995], pp. 119-24).

[19] E.g. J. PAQUET, 'Bourgeois et universitaires a la fin du Moyen Age', *Le Moyen Age*, ser. 4, 16 (1961), pp. 325-40.

[20] Cf. esp. I. MATSCHINEGG, 'Student Communities and Urban Authorities', *Medium Aevum Quotidianum*, 48 (2003), pp. 29-36 (pp. 32-3) on the limitations of the conflictual paradigm for medieval university history.

[21] Trombetti Budriesi has rightly defined 'città e Studio' as a 'binomio difficilmente scindibile'; A. L. TROMBETTI BUDRIESI, *Gli statuti del collegio dei dottori, giudici e avvocati di Bologna (1393-1467) e la loro matricola (fino al 1776)*. Deputazione di Storia Patria per le Province di Romagna. Documenti e Studi, 23 (Bologna, 1990), p. 23.

[22] For what follows see P. R. DENLEY, 'Communities within Communities: Student Identity and Student Groups in Late Medieval Italian Universities', in *Studenti, università, città nella storia padovana*. Atti del convegno di studi, 6-8 febbraio 1998, eds. F. Piovan and L. Sitran Rea (Padua, 2001), pp. 721-44 (esp. pp. 721-8).

gether, and there was no practical embodiment of their identity or even a meeting of representatives covering the whole *studio*. The university had no hierarchy that covered all its members, and even the definition of its membership is problematic. Students – or at least, in most cases, non-citizen students – could form a body or bodies (a *universitas*, and in some cases *nationes* within that), though the operation of these suggest that by the fifteenth century they were often compromises between a half-remembered, half-invented tradition of autonomy on the one hand, and the pragmatic realities of what they were allowed to do on the other. The most dynamic force was that of the local authorities, whether as paymasters of the teachers, as instigators of the competition with rivals, or as regulators of the whole institution. The key theme of the period was localisation and 'domestication'.[23] It is surely significant that teachers did not form a body parallel to that of the students. Separate colleges of doctors for different subjects emerged, but these were not usually inclusive of all teachers, let alone formally representative of them; they were hybrid bodies with functions and membership that transcended *studio* boundaries, and they often became bastions of local privilege. Teachers were more and more closely involved in government and civic life – teaching was only one of their activities – and thus even if the *studio* as a whole was not involved in politics, individual members of it certainly could be. As with the apparent dichotomy of 'church and state', there is a great danger of simplification, and for some similar reasons; very often we find the same people, or at the very least their relatives, on both sides of the divide.[24]

The imbalance in this relationship, the institutional weakness of the Sienese *Studio*, and its close dependence on the commune, also mean that we cannot avoid seeing the former overwhelmingly through the eyes of the latter. This is a familiar problem to those studying the Italian universities,[25] but one that is particularly acute in the case of Siena because the key documents that elsewhere have been the natural starting-points for research into the internal workings of the university, and those that would most help us assess the extent of its independence, are missing. Teachers can be studied in some detail because, as communal employees, they turn up with great frequency in communal records. However, evidence of collective activity, either through the colleges of doctors or otherwise, is exceptionally sparse. Statutes and minutes of the colleges of doctors of law and arts/medicine have not survived for the fifteenth century;[26] nor, for most of the century, have the records of the degrees they awarded. For the student university before 1500 the situation is even direr; the statutes, matriculation registers and (with only fragmentary exceptions) the minutes of meetings are all missing. What we have instead is a strikingly detailed, and largely complete, record of how the commune administered its *Studio*. This record strongly suggests an exceptional degree of intervention and control of all dimensions of the *Studio*'s life, including supposedly

---

[23] The memorable definition of J. Le Goff, 'Les universités et les pouvoirs publics au moyen âge et a la Renaissance', *XIIe Congrès International des Sciences Historiques, Vienne, 29 Août – 5 Septembre 1965. Rapports, III: Commissions* (Vienna, n. d.), pp. 189-206 (p. 202) [tr. as 'The Universities and the Public Authorities in the Middle Ages and the Renaissance' in his *Time, Work, and Culture in the Middle Ages* (Chicago, Il., 1980), pp. 135-49, 321-4].

[24] Below, Chapter II.3. This general point was well captured by L. Zdekauer, *Sulle Origini dello Studio Senese* (Siena, 1893), p. 23: 'Lo Studio non era un ornato esteriore della città, ma un organo della sua vita.'

[25] On the difficulty of seeing both town and gown at same time in the documents, C. Frova, 'L'università e la città: elementi per una discussione', in *L'università e la sua storia*, pp. 15-28, esp. pp. 18-19 ('Non stupisce che l'immagine dell'università e degli universitari che queste fonti [giudiziari] restituiscono sia fortemente condizionata dal punto di osservazione cittadino'), and p. 22 on the particular case of Siena. On other kinds of inherent bias in the evidence – for example, leaving us with more information on foreign than on local students, and within that category more on some groups than on others – see below, pp. 240 and 244.

[26] For a handful of exceptions to this generalisation see below, pp. 205-6.

autonomous elements such as the colleges and the student university.[27] Nonetheless it presents a fundamental methodological problem. Are we looking at weak separate institutions, or are we just not seeing them because of the distortions of what has survived? Is the fact that so much has not survived in itself an indication of the weakness of these institutions? All this takes us into the perilous territory of when absence of evidence can be taken as evidence of absence. This is a heuristic conundrum that will perhaps not be resolved satisfactorily unless further evidence, such as missing statutes, comes to light.

My response to this conundrum has been the only one possible short of abandoning the subject altogether; to attempt to make a virtue out of necessity. In default of key documents such as statutes, we are forced not to start from the theoretical basis of how things were supposed to work, but from the practical basis of how they actually worked. The mitigating factor is the great wealth of the records that do survive. The extent of communal intervention means that we can learn a great deal about very many aspects of university life, albeit from a partial and in a sense external viewpoint. The approach of this study has therefore been, as it were, anatomical. I have tried to unearth the inner workings of the *Studio*, basing my conclusions inevitably on what we have, which is mainly the commune's unceasing flow of deliberations, measures, contracts for teachers, and instructions to the various elements that made up the *Studio* on all possible subjects. These records, in all their minutiae, illustrate the realities of the academic market, the careers of teachers, the organisation of teaching, and to a lesser extent the environment offered to students. They occasionally cast indirect light on the relationship between the various elements of the university; and they illuminate the attitudes of the sponsors and paymasters of the *Studio* to their creation, not only when they declaim, in formal terms, the value of maintaining a centre of higher education and training for their offspring and for students from outside the territory, but also when they take difficult decisions to ensure the best possible operation of that centre within the constraints of the moment.

This approach is of course not failsafe, and I have tried to be open about those areas in which my conclusions are bound to remain tentative or speculative. An obvious tool that can assist with the problems and distortions of missing evidence is knowledge of what was happening elsewhere. But there are limitations and dangers in this too. As will be seen, I have made constant comparisons with other universities. The purpose of this is to provide the background against which Siena's record can be assessed. I have, however, been wary of the temptation to use evidence of practices in other universities, especially Bologna, to fill the gaps in what we can know about practices in Siena. It is true that there is a considerable degree of homogeneity, imposed by the competitive nature of the university system, especially when it comes to academic matters such as syllabus, timetabling and examinations. But as I have argued elsewhere,[28] uncritical recourse to what Fioravanti rightly refers to as the 'precario

---

[27] To assert that the extent of control in Siena was exceptional is not, of course, to suggest that it was unique. Morelli observed, *à propos* the civic documentation for the University of Bologna, 'come il governo cittadino si occupasse con estrema precisione non solo dello Studio, ma entrasse nel merito di questioni di stretta competenza di organismi che avevano loro specifiche costituzioni.' G. MORELLI, 'I Collegi di Diritto nello Studio di Bologna fra XIV e XVII secolo. Considerazioni preliminari', *Il Carrobbio*, 8 (1982), pp. 248-58 (p. 252). Similar incursions into traditionally 'independent' domains are evident in the relationship between Lorenzo de' Medici's *Ufficiali dello Studio* and Pisa after 1472, the intrusions of Venice in Padua and the Visconti and then the Sforza of Milan in Pavia, to name but a few. See P. R. DENLEY, '*Signore* and *Studio*: Lorenzo in a Comparative Context', in *Lorenzo the Magnificent: Culture and Politics*, eds. M. Mallett and N. Mann (London, 1996), pp. 203-216; and G. SILVANO, 'Stato, territorio e istituzioni: lo Studio generale a Padova, Pavia e Pisa al tempo di Lorenzo il Magnifico', in *La Toscana al tempo di Lorenzo il Magnifico. Politica economia cultura arte*. Convegno internazionale di Studi, Firenze, Pisa, Siena 5-8 novembre 1992 (Pisa, 1996), III, pp. 981-94.

[28] DENLEY, 'Recent Studies', pp. 199-200.

argomento di analogia'[29] is what has inhibited progress in our understanding of the institutional history of the Italian universities and perpetuated the stereotypical view of Bologna as a model which spawned student universities and student power everywhere. If such reasoning can be justified in some areas, it is dangerous in others. Comparative deductions on the basis of statutes are particularly unsound, because such documents give an inherently static picture – whereas, as has been seen, the dynamism of the Italian university system was one of its key features. Extreme caution is therefore necessary in the use of evidence from other *studi*, and I have usually taken the view that it is better to be inconclusive than wrong.

Some limitations of this study ought to be mentioned. I have sought to show how a late medieval *studio* actually operated. The purpose of this approach is to provide the underpinning necessary for the study of other aspects of university history. Traditionally research has divided the subject into the institutional, the prosopographical and the intellectual (though increasingly the best studies are those which transcend these categories). I see the first of these subdivisions as the necessary preliminary to the other two. My excursions into prosopography in this study are limited. Though the reader will find a large number of individuals cited, and their careers discussed in some detail, I have deliberately stopped short of formal prosopographical analysis. The time for that is not yet ripe, though I hope that the work constitutes a contribution towards what I am convinced must be a collaborative enterprise if it is to succeed.[30] The work has even less pretension to be an intellectual history of the *Studio*. I am certainly not competent to write that – but then I would argue, as have others before me,[31] that such a history is beyond the reach of any individual historian. Within those parameters I have also confined myself to the university proper, and not covered pre-university education. Although teachers of grammar and *abacus* were also employed by the commune and hired, paid and regulated by the same communal bodies, often at the same time as those at university level – to the extent that it is often difficult to disentangle the two, and to be sure at which level a teacher of grammar was being appointed – this is planned as the subject of a separate study.

A final point concerns the chronological focus of the work. Although I begin with a chapter on the history of the *Studio* to 1357, this is largely because the context is essential, rather than because it is the main focus of my research. My archival investigations begin with the award of a charter by the emperor Charles IV in 1357. The *terminus ad quem* is less clear-cut. My original intention was to cover the whole of the republican period. For practical reasons the full, systematic trawl of archival material has not been taken beyond 1500, although I have made soundings beyond that and hope that I have taken account of all the major known documents of the commune's administration down to the end of Sienese independence. The work thus focuses primarily on the century and a half from the first demonstrable external validation of the *Studio* to the rise of Pandolfo Petrucci at the end of the fifteenth century – and within that, given the state of the records, above all from the second decade of the fifteenth century, when the *Studio*'s continuity became assured. A plea can perhaps be made in defence of the lesser focus on the first half of the sixteenth century. First, the institutional history of

---

[29] G. FIORAVANTI, 'Le "arti liberali" nei secoli XII-XV', in *L'Università di Siena. 750 anni* (Milan, 1991), p. 265.

[30] Documented lists of the rectors of the *Studio*, and of students admitted to the Sapienza, in the fifteenth century were prepared during the course of this research, but further work on the identification of individuals is needed before they can be published.

[31] L. ZDEKAUER, *Lo Studio di Siena nel Rinascimento* (Milan, 1894, repr. Bologna, 1977), p. XI; P. NARDI, 'Lo Studio di Siena nell'età rinascimentale: appunti e riflessioni', *BSSP*, 99 (1992), pp. 249-65 (pp. 249-50) (earlier version, without notes, 'Lo Studio di Siena nell'età rinascimentale', in *Cultura e Università a Siena*, pp. 19-26).

those years has received or is receiving attention from other scholars.[32] Second, the history of the *Studio* in that phase of its existence is so intimately bound up with the political history of the republic in its last decades that it is perhaps best evaluated by historians more familiar with that period. All I can hope is that I have provided some of the institutional background for such a fuller appreciation. As I make clear at the end of the book, it seems to me that the key developmental stages for the *Studio* had all been laid during the history of the republic, and most of that had taken place by the end of the fifteenth century. It will be for future scholarship to decide whether that instinct is correct.

2. *The state of research*

Interest in the history of the *Studio* from its origins through to the renaissance dates back to the republican period itself.[33] There is no easily definable point at which memorialisation can be deemed to have turned into history-writing; the testimonies of alumni such as Pius II,[34] and the funeral orations for teachers by Agostino Dati,[35] in the fifteenth century are followed seamlessly by Sigismondo Tizio's early sixteenth-century descriptions of fifteenth-century teachers (some of whom he had known personally as a student, others by reputation), in his *Historiae senenses*.[36] The decline and eventual fall of the republic led to a hiatus, bringing, as they did, new preoccupations. But in the seventeenth century a new interest in the *Studio*, along with other aspects of the city's historical traditions, is evident.[37] By the end of the century the form this took, an intense interest in collecting materials, had significant results as far as the *Studio* is concerned. Under the auspices of two enthusiastic sponsors and practi-

[32] For the period 1531 to 1542, L. KOŠUTA, 'Documenti per la Storia dello Studio senese dal 1531 al 1542', in G. MINNUCCI and L. KOŠUTA, *Lo Studio di Siena*; for work on the rest of the century see below, n. 63.

[33] What follows is not intended as a full bibliographical review, but rather to highlight the principal areas in which research has been conducted and the factors which have constrained it. For a full account of earlier publications see G. MINNUCCI, 'Rassegna bibliografica sulla storia dello Studio senese dalle origini fino alla prima metà del Cinquecento', *Studi senesi*, 93 (1981), pp. 425-45; and IDEM, 'Bibliografia sulla storia dello Studio senese dalle origini fino al XVI secolo', in *I tedeschi nella storia dell'Università di Siena*, ed. G. Minnucci (Siena, 1988), pp. 159-65; for the major recent additions see below, pp. 13-15.

[34] Below, p. 59 n. 191.

[35] A. DATI, *Opera* (Senis, 1503), *Orationes, Liber V, Orationes III-VI*, ff. 97v-100v (Mariano Sozzini, Tommaso Docci, Pietro de' Rossi, Bartolo di Tura).

[36] This immense history is only now being edited; vol. I.I.I ed. M. Doni Garfagnini, *Rerum Italicarum Scriptores Recentiores*, 6 (Rome, 1992); vol. I.II.I ed. G. Tomasi Stussi, *RISR*, 10 (Rome, 1995), and vol. III.IV ed. P. Pertici, *RISR*, 12 (1998). Tizio's references to members of the *Studio* were collected (from the copy in BCS, *mss.* B.III.6-15) by G. A. PECCI, *Zibaldone per la Storia dell'Università di Siena* (1749; BCS, *ms.* B.IV.28, ff. 6r-20r); and see also P. PICCOLOMINI, *La vita e l'opera di Sigismondo Tizio, 1458-1528* (Siena, 1903), pp. 33-8, 83, 133. Tizio apart, the official and semi-official chroniclers of the republic's history say relatively little about the *Studio*. Such lack of interest in reporting the affairs of the local *ateneo* is common enough among Italian chroniclers, even in major university towns such as Bologna and Padua. The other exception, interestingly, is the chronicle of another academic, B. ZAMBOTTI, *Diario ferrarese dall'anno 1476 sino al 1504*, a cura di G. Pardi, in *Rerum Italicarum Scriptores*[2] (Bologna, 1928-1937), t. XXIV, parte VII.

[37] The seventeenth-century *Relazione di tutti i privilegi, ch'è stato concesso dell'excelso Concistoro sanese à tutti i Castelli...della Città, e Stato di Siena dall'anno MCCC. in quà* (BCS, *ms.* A.III.19) includes a brief sketch of the history of the Sapienza and the *Studio* (ff. 188r-198r); the *Miscellanea istorica* in BCS, *ms.* A.V.1 includes a (very selective) list of teachers paid by the *Biccherna* between 1322 and 1450, ff. 25r-27r. They appear to be in the hand of Isidoro UGURGIERI AZZOLINI, author of *Le Pompe Sanesi o vero relazione degli huomini e donne illustri di Siena e suo Stato*, 2 vols. (Pistoia, 1649), a biographical compendium not surpassed before the late nineteenth century – though it is complemented by the mine of information that is G. GIGLI, *Diario Sanese* (Lucca, 1723).

tioners of scholarship, Uberto Benvoglienti and Galgano Bichi, inventories and transcripts were made of documents relating to the *Studio* and the Sapienza, principally by the indefatigable archivist and palaeographer canon Antonio Sestigiani.[38] These volumes are important even now because of the subsequent destruction of parts of the corpus of documents; these collectors knew material that we no longer have.[39] They were followed by attention to the main communal archival series, soon resulting in a compilation of the names of rectors[40] and the transcription of lists of lecturers.[41] This extension of the range of sources to be taken into account is best evident in the *Zibaldone per la Storia dell'Università di Siena* by Giovanni Antonio Pecci (1749), a preliminary to a history of the *Studio* which was never completed.[42] Sporadic attempts to collate material continued for a while. Giovacchino Faluschi compiled similar lists in the late eighteenth century;[43] a further, and according to the last scholar to have seen it much more substantial, effort at the collection of material, a manuscript compiled by or

---

[38] These consist principally of a *repertorium* and transcriptions of documents in the Sapienza, the majority of which go back to its earlier incarnation as hospital of the Misericordia; ASS, *ms.* B.82, entitled *Repertorio di Strumenti Antichi della Sapienza*, and BCS, *mss.* A.VII.1-5; description in G. GAROSI (ed.), *Inventario dei manoscritti della Biblioteca Comunale di Siena*, 3 vols. (Florence, 1978-86), II, pp. 134-5, and copies in ASS, *mss.* B.31-33 (see also *mss.* B.66-7, C.51 *ter*, and the later, typed *ms.* B.98). These volumes were compiled by Sestigiani between 1695 and 1700, for Galgano Bichi. He also made a copy, for Uberto Benvoglienti, of BCS, *ms.* C.IV.26, itself a copy of the statute book of the Casa della Misericordia/Casa della Sapienza, which had ended up in the hospital of S. Maria della Scala. On this book see below, pp. 25-7. Sestigiani also knew, and compiled indices for, the volumes of deliberations of the *Savi dello Studio* (below, n. 84). Sestigiani's is also the hand responsible for the survey of documents concerning the *Studio*'s migration in 1420 to Corsignano, in *Archivio Sergardi-Biringucci*, *ms.* A.II, ff. 256r-258v (see below, pp. 113-4). On the strengths and weaknesses of Sestigiani's scholarship, ARCHIVIO DI STATO DI SIENA, *Guida-Inventario dell'Archivio dello Stato* [Pubblicazioni degli Archivi di Stato, 5 (vol. I, Rome, 1951), 6 (vol. II, Rome, 1951), 92 (vol. III, Rome, 1977)], II, p. 13; G. CATONI et al., *Le Pergamene dell'Università di Siena e la 'Domus Misericordiae'. Seminario di Archivistica* (Siena, 1975-6), p. 8; and G. HANLON, 'The Decline of a Provincial Military Aristocracy: Siena 1560-1740', *Past and Present*, 155 (May 1997), pp. 64-108 (p. 70). The Benvoglienti collection includes further, more selective summaries of the Misericordia/Sapienza documents (BCS, *mss.* C.V.7 and C.V.16).

[39] See below, pp. 16-17.

[40] ASS, *ms.* A.119, a catalogue of rectors of the Casa della Misericordia and the *Studio*, made on the order of Galgano Bichi in 1725. This has been checked against the fuller list of documentation compiled for this study, and while it inevitably has many omissions the information that is included is highly accurate. A few of the gaps are filled by the much more cursory list of G. A. PECCI, *Rettori dello Spedale della Misericordia, Rettori dello Studio, e della Casa della Sapienza dal 1273 al 1757* (BCS, *ms.* A.IX.2, ff. 64r-83v [new foliation], esp. ff. 73r-76v).

[41] ASS, *mss.* A.140-44, transcriptions by or for Bichi of *ruoli di dottori leggenti* from 1513 to 1725. This was the first such transcription since the work of Ugurgieri Azzolini (above, n. 37).

[42] BCS, *ms.* B.IV.28. In both this and his *Memorie storico-critiche della Città di Siena che servono alla Vita Civile di Pandolfo Petrucci* (Siena, 1755-60, repr. 1988), Pecci blamed the authorities' refusal to let him borrow materials from the *Studio*'s and other archives for his failure to complete it; G. CATONI, 'Introduzione' to *Archivio Storico dell'Università di Siena. Inventario della Sezione storica* (Siena, 1990), pp. XI-XXV (pp. XI-XII). Other unpublished materials covering the republican period include a brief analytical sketch by A. B. FANCELLI, *Origine dello Studio Sanese* (BCS, *ms.* A.XI.29, ff. 2r-20r; copy in *Studio* 126, ff. 2r-21v [new foliation]), which appears to be the first attempt at a systematic description of the *Studio*; miscellaneous notes in *Studio* 127 (including some in the hands of Sestigiani and Fancelli), esp. *filza* XXI, nos. 2 and 3, no foliation (the latter is entitled *Memorie della Pia Casa della Misericordia detta La Sapienza...* and was ordered by Firmano Bichi in 1738, the former is a variant of it); entries on the *Studio* and the *Sapienza* in ASS, *ms.* D.131, *Attinenze d'Antichità* (pp. 35-6, 45-7, 51-2, 65-7, 177-8); and *Notizie relative all'Università di Siena* by Ansano Luti, written in 1799-1800, in BCS, *ms.* A.III.33: *Raccolta degli Autori Senesi* (ff. 86r-93r).

[43] These were collected into a single volume by Ettore Romagnoli in 1835; BCS, *ms.* E.VI.9 (G. FALUSCHI, *Disordinate Memorie per formare la Storia dello Studio, e Università di Siena*). Faluschi was the author of a *Breve relazione delle cose notabili della Città di Siena* (Siena, 1784, rev. 1815), and compiler of archival *spogli* (e.g. BCS, *mss.* E.VI.17-19), but also one of the perpetrators of the infamous *scarto* of material from Sienese archives in 1779; E. CASANOVA, *Archivistica* (2nd. ed. Siena, 1926, and in *La biblioteca di ARCHIVI*, http://archivi.beniculturali.it), p. 156.

on behalf of Luigi De Angelis in the early nineteenth century, is now lost.[44] With rare exceptions[45] the work of the mid-nineteenth century is undistinguished; the *Risorgimento* writers who did take their researches as far as publication were more interested in glorifying the role of Siena than in using the formidable body of material that had already been assembled.[46]

The late nineteenth-century growth of university history as a subject for research had a significant though limited impact on Siena. The period saw the publication of what is still the only general history of the *Studio* in the fifteenth century, and the starting-point for current research, Lodovico Zdekauer's *Lo Studio di Siena nel Rinascimento*, published in 1894.[47] Born in Prague and educated there and in Vienna and Munich, this prolific scholar settled permanently in Italy in 1882 at the age of twenty-seven, living in Rome, Venice, Pistoia and Florence, then teaching the history of law in Siena for eight years (1888-96) before moving to Macerata where he held a similar post until 1923, shortly before his death.[48] Zdekauer's interests ranged from archaeology (a brief initial flirtation) to epigraphy, the history of games and gambling, public and private life, dowries, and commerce; his pioneering work on central Italian trade is only now being appreciated. He was also an indefatigable archival scholar whose publications include editions of statutes and other documents of various cities, especially Pistoia, Siena, and a number of other towns in Tuscany and the Marches.[49] Zdekauer's his-

---

[44] A two-volume manuscript of transcribed notices and documents, including deliberations of the *Consiglio Generale*, the *Concistoro*, the *Balìa* and the *Biccherna*, initiated by De Angelis, was purchased in the 1870s by Arnold Luschin von Ebengreuth (A. LUSCHIN VON EBENGREUTH, review of Zdekauer in *Göttingische gelehrte Anzeige*, n.s. 12 [1895], pp. 965-71 [pp. 970-1]; cf. PRUNAI, 'Lo studio senese dalla "migratio"' (n. 47 below), p. 27 n. 3, but does not feature in his *Nachlaß* in the Universitätsbibliothek Graz (kindly confirmed to me by the compiler of the catalogue, Dr Thomas Csanády), although it must have been used in the compilation of his manuscript collection on, and register of, German students in Italy (*Nachlaßsammlungen*, nos. 2024-5). This may well be the manuscript De Angelis himself refers to in his *Biografia degli Scrittori Sanesi* (Siena, 1824, repr. Bologna, 1976), p. 7 n. 2. De Angelis's only publication specifically on the *Studio*, *Discorso storico sull'Università di Siena ai Signori Commissari per l'Organizzazione della Pubblica Istruzione nei Dipartimenti Francesi Cisalpini* (Siena, 1831, repr. 1840), was for political rather than historical purposes (see MINNUCCI, 'Rassegna bibliografica', pp. 425-6).

[45] E.g. L. BANCHI, 'Alcuni documenti che concernono la venuta in Siena nell'anno 1321 dei lettori e degli scolari dello Studio bolognese', *Giornale Storico degli Archivi Toscani*, 5 (1861), pp. 237-47, 309-31.

[46] E.g. C. F. CARPELLINI, *Sulla origine nazionale e populare delle università di studi in Italia, e particolarmente della università di Siena* (Siena, 1861); L. MORIANI, *Notizie sulla Università di Siena* (Siena, 1873). The partisanship of the writers of this period is the exception; for the most part the historiography of the Sienese *Studio* has been remarkably free of campanilism.

[47] The only other scholarly attempt at such a study is that of Giulio Prunai, whose history of the university from its origins to the end of the sixteenth century was published in incomplete form; the chapter on the period 1408-1557 was lost in transit between prisoner-of-war camps. G. PRUNAI, 'Lo studio di Siena dalle origini alla "migratio" bolognese (sec. XIII-1321)', *BSSP*, 56 (1949), pp. 53-79; IDEM, 'Lo studio senese dalla "migratio" bolognese alla fondazione della "Domus Sapientiae" (1321-1408)', *BSSP*, 57 (1950), pp. 3-54; IDEM, 'Lo studio senese nel primo quarantennio del principato Mediceo', *BSSP*, 66 (1959), pp. 79-160.

[48] The obituary of L. CHIAPPELLI, 'Lodovico Zdekauer', *Archivio Storico Italiano*, 82 (1924), pp. 159-74, who knew Zdekauer well, is the most authoritative; see now also P. NARDI, 'La carriera accademica di Lodovico Zdekauer storico del diritto nell'Università di Siena (1888-1896)', *Studi senesi*, 100 (1988), Suppl. II, pp. 751-81, and M. MORONI, *Lodovico Zdekauer e la storia del commercio nel medio Adriatico*. Quaderni monografici di "Proposte e ricerche", 22 (Ancona, 1997), esp. pp. 12-16 for the pre-Macerata period, and with an updated bibliography (pp. 42-50).

[49] MORONI, op. cit. The most significant of his Sienese publications, apart from those on the *Studio*, are 'Il Constituto dei Placiti del Comune di Siena', *Studi senesi*, 6 (1889), pp. 152-206, and 'Il Constituto dei consoli del Placito del Comune di Siena. II Parte', *Studi senesi*, 9 (1892), pp. 35-75; his edition of *Il Constituto del Comune di Siena del 1262* (Milan, 1897); *La vita privata dei senesi nel dugento* (Siena, 1896), and *La vita pubblica dei senesi nel dugento* (Siena, 1897), tr. together as *The Life of Old Siena* (Siena, 1914), and repr. Bologna, 1973; and *Il mercante senese nel dugento* (Siena, 1900). He was a key figure in the emergence of a number of local publishing initiatives, most notably the *Bullettino Senese di Storia Patria*, where he was a dominant figure for a number of years; D. BALESTRACCI, 'Appunti per una storia del "Bullettino Senese di Storia Patria": la metodologia e i contenuti', *BSSP*, 84-85 (1977-8), pp. 290-319 (pp. 297-300, 302, 306, 318).

tory of the *Studio* bears all the hallmarks of that breadth, placing it expertly in both the Sienese context and that of university practice as understood at the time. The work was judged at the time to be 'veramente delle migliori che siansi scritte sulle nostre università e forse la migliore di quelle pubblicate in Italia per pazienza e novità di ricerche, vastità di coltura, abilità e freschezza di esposizione'.[50] It was based, too, on wide archival knowledge; the selection of documents he published, in the appendix to his history and in articles on the *Studio*,[51] demonstrates a full sense of the range of sources available. He also warned that the publication of the documentation in communal administrative sources was an essential prerequisite to further study (while remaining doubtful that the internal workings of the *Studio* could be illuminated much further short of fresh discoveries of missing documents).[52] But his own subsequent attempt at a 'storia documentata' never saw the light of day.[53]

Since Zdekauer, research on the Sienese *Studio* has lagged behind that elsewhere, and for precisely the reason that he cited. As has been said, Zdekauer was writing in the era when the groundwork for Italian university history was being laid. The octocentenary celebrations of the University of Bologna in 1888 was a particular occasion for what became a flurry of research,[54] resulting in the publication of editions of statutes and other key records,[55] and also of registers,[56] compendia,[57] and indeed full chronological collections of documents.[58] No such enterprise was successful in Siena at the time.[59] A prime reason for this failure was the sheer volume and disparateness of the material. It was 1942 be-

---

[50] See NARDI, op. cit., p. 780.

[51] L. ZDEKAUER, *Documenti per servire alla Storia dello Studio di Siena, 1240-1789* (Siena, 1896); extract from *L'Unione universitaria*, 3 (1896), and IDEM, 'Dai protocolli d'uno scriba *Universitatis Studii Senensis*, 1437-41', *BSSP*, 12 (1905), pp. 318-26.

[52] ZDEKAUER, pp. V-VI and X-XI.

[53] ZDEKAUER, p. IX; IDEM, *Documenti*, p. 3. The manuscript was last seen in 1912 (PRUNAI, III, p. 79n).

[54] Fuller references in DENLEY, 'Recent Studies', p. 193 and n. 1; and see W. TEGA (ed.), *Lo Studio e la Città. Bologna 1888-1988* (Bologna, 1987), part I.

[55] E.g. for Bologna, C. MALAGOLA, *Statuti delle Università e dei Collegi dello Studio bolognese* (Bologna, 1888), and the comparative study of H. DENIFLE, 'Die Statuten der Juristen-Universität Bologna vom Jahre 1317-47 und deren Verhältniß zu jenen Paduas, Perugias, Florenz', *Archiv für Literatur- und Kirchengeschichte des Mittelalters*, 3 (1887), pp. 196-408; U. DALLARI, *I Rotuli dei Lettori legisti e artisti dello Studio di Bologna dal 1384 al 1799* (Bologna, 1888-1924), 4 vols.; E. FRIEDLÄNDER and C. MALAGOLA (eds.), *Acta Nationis Germanicae Universitatis Bononiensis* (Berlin, 1887, repr. Bologna, 1988); for Padua, H. DENIFLE, 'Die Statuten der Juristen-Universität Padua vom Jahre 1331', *Archiv für Literatur- und Kirchengeschichte des Mittelalters*, 6 (1892), pp. 309-562. For Florence, the octocentenary had been anticipated by A. GHERARDI, *Statuti della Università e lo Studio Fiorentino* (Florence, 1881).

[56] E.g. G. PARDI, *Titoli dottorali conferiti dallo Studio di Ferrara nei secc. XV e XVI* (Lucca, 1900, repr. Bologna, 1970). IDEM, 'Titoli dottorali conferiti nello Studio di Lucca nel sec. XV', *Studi Storici*, 8 (1899), pp. 3-14.

[57] A. GLORIA, *Monumenti della Università di Padova (1222-1318)* (Venice, 1884, repr. Bologna, 1972); IDEM, *Monumenti della Università di Padova (1318-1405)*, 2 vols. (Padua, 1888, repr. Bologna, 1972).

[58] E.g. A. ROSSI, 'Documenti per la storia dell'Università di Perugia', *Giornale di Erudizione Artistica*, 4-6 (1875-77); G. MARIOTTI, *Memorie e documenti per la storia dell'Università di Parma nel Medio Evo* (Parma, 1888); A. SOLERTI, 'Documenti riguardanti lo Studio di Ferrara nei Secoli XV e XVI conservati nell'Archivio Estense', *Atti della Deputazione Ferrarese di Storia Patria*, 4.ii (1892), pp. 7-65; R. MAIOCCHI, *Codice diplomatico dell'Università di Pavia*, 2 vols. in 3 (Pavia, 1905-15). For Florence, GHERARDI, *Statuti*, included the edition of over four hundred documents covering the years 1320 to 1472. The *Chartularium Studii Bononiensis*, 15 vols. (Bologna, 1909-88) must be considered a project apart given its exhaustive publication of all documents relating to members of the university.

[59] Apart from Zdekauer's work, the only publication Siena has to show from these years is the work of a pair of undergraduates, who published a compendium of notices about teachers; F. COSELSCHI and D. CAPORALI, 'Appunti biografici e bibliografici sui giureconsulti senesi', *Studi senesi*, 1 (1884), pp. 81-96, 204-18 and 321-6, and 2 (1885), pp. 141-51 and 335-41, and the even less scholarly P. COLOMBINI, *Cenni Storici sulla Università di Siena* (Siena, 1891).

fore Siena got its counterpart to the collections for other universities, with the publication of the first volume of the *Chartularium Studii Senensis* in 1942 by Giovanni Cecchini and Giulio Prunai. This comprehensive edition of the documentation of the *Studio* from the earliest days to the obtention of an imperial charter in 1357, according to the long-established editorial criteria for such collections,[60] has formed the basis for subsequent research on that period.[61] Unfortunately no further volumes of the *Chartularium* have been published,[62] and indeed it is not difficult to see why. The relevant sources are scattered over a wide range of archival series, and the process of discovery is far from complete. Moreover, from the mid-fifteenth century onwards the scale of the documentation is such that this would be a huge task, running into many volumes.

Since the publication of the *Chartularium* scholars have prudently opted for a segmented approach. Some studies have focused on specific periods. Paolo Nardi's volume *L'insegnamento superiore a Siena nei secoli XI-XIV*, which traces the development of Sienese higher education up to the foundation charter of 1357, provides for the first time a thorough conspectus of higher education in Siena during the years of the origins of the *Studio* and the long and tortuous process leading up to the attainment of a foundation charter.[63] Leo Košuta's publication of the documents for 1531 to 1542 is thematic in structure, and while it does not claim to be exhaustive, it comes closest to continuing the enterprise of the *Chartularium*.[64] Others have concentrated on disciplines, approaching them in very different ways. Among studies of the history of law in the period, two biographies stand out, Paolo Nardi's on Mariano Sozzini and the late Roberta Bargagli's on Mariano's son Bartolomeo; again, both scholars have added significantly to the published documentation as well as to our understanding of the *Studio*.[65] The extensive work on the history of medicine in republican Siena, *Siena nella storia della*

---

[60] For an evaluation see CAMMAROSANO, *Tradizione documentaria*, pp. 20-1. As he pointed out, the volume is not a cartulary in the strict sense of the publication of a collection of documents originally compiled as such, but rather a compilation of disparate sources. In form and structure the *Chartularium* is very close to that of Maiocchi for Pavia, equally inaccurately entitled a *Codice diplomatico* (above, n. 58).

[61] Cf. NARDI, *Insegnamento*, which has also added significantly to the documentation (appendix, pp. 215-40).

[62] Prunai and Sandro De' Colli did compile a card-index of teachers and students in preparation for subsequent volumes. I am most grateful to Prof. Prunai, Dott. Ubaldo Morandi and Prof. Giuliano Catoni for making this available to me.

[63] See also P. NARDI, 'Comune, Impero e Papato alle origini dell'insegnamento universitario in Siena (1240-1275)', *BSSP*, 90 (1983), pp. 50-94, and 'Dalle origini al 1357', in *L'Università di Siena. 750 anni*, pp. 9-26; for related studies see below, pp. 31 *seq.*, esp. nn. 1, 6, 19 and 20. These and PRUNAI, I and II are the only overall profiles of the *Studio* as such, for specific periods, in the republican era apart from my 'Dal 1357 alla caduta della repubblica', in *L'Università di Siena. 750 anni*, pp. 27-44. The fifteenth century *Studio* is also evaluated in P. NARDI, 'Lo Studio di Siena nell'età rinascimentale'. The *Studio* at the end of the republican period and in the first decades of Medicean rule are covered in P. NARDI, 'Note sulla scuola giuridica senese negli anni della caduta della Repubblica', *Studi senesi*, 87 (1975), pp. 195-220; D. MARRARA, *Lo Studio di Siena nelle riforme del granduca Ferdinando I (1589 e '91)* (Milan, 1970); G. CASCIO PRATILLI, *L'Università e il Principe. Gli Studi di Siena e di Pisa tra Rinascimento e Controriforma*. Accademia Toscana di Scienza e Lettere 'La Colombaria', Studi, 38 (Florence, 1975); and G. CATONI, 'Le riforme del Granduca, le "serre" degli scolari e i lettori di casa', in *L'Università di Siena. 750 anni*, pp. 45-66; it will be revisited in J. DAVIES, *Culture and Power: Tuscany and its Universities, 1540-1609* (Leiden, forthcoming); and L. TRAPANI, 'Statuti senesi concernenti lo Studio', in *Gli statuti universitari: tradizione dei testi e valenze politiche*. Convegno Internazionale di Studi, Messina, 14-17 aprile 2004 (in press), part 3. I am most grateful to Dott. Trapani for allowing me a preview of this work.

[64] KOŠUTA, 'Documenti'. The organisation of the material is thematic rather than chronological, and excludes some categories of document (see pp. 320-8).

[65] P. NARDI, *Mariano Sozzini giureconsulto senese del Quattrocento*. Quaderni di 'Studi senesi', 32 (Milan, 1974); R. BARGAGLI, *Bartolomeo Sozzini giurista e politico (1436-1506)*. Quaderni di 'Studi senesi', 92 (Milan, 2000); and EADEM, 'Documenti senesi per la biografia di Bartolomeo Sozzini (1436-1506)', *BSSP*, 99 (1992), pp. 266-323. A further monograph in this vein is E. MECACCI, *La biblioteca di Ludovico Petrucciani docente di diritto a Siena nel Quattrocento*. Quaderni di 'Studi senesi', 50 (Milan, 1981).

medicina, by Alcide Garosi, a practising doctor enthused by history, attracted some criticism when it was published in 1958, and is certainly not without shortcoings, especially in terms of editorial accuracy,[66] but the fact remains that he uncovered a great deal of material, much of which has still not been absorbed by subsequent scholars. In his series of studies on the literary culture of Siena in the fifteenth century, Gianfranco Fioravanti has taken a different approach, illuminating it from manuscript rather than archival evidence but shedding valuable light on the history of the *Studio* in the process.[67]

Yet others have focussed on specific types of record or aspects of the *Studio*'s history. Giovanni Minnucci has worked tirelessly on the publication of the extant records of degrees.[68] Since the *bastardelli* of the notaries of the episcopal chancery recording these only survive from the end of the fifteenth century, this still leaves a major hole in our knowledge which only anecdotal or accidentally surviving evidence can begin to fill,[69] but we at least have a clearer idea of the practice. He has also published and analysed the volumes of a number of other notaries, including two who at some stage had formal roles in the *Studio* in the later fifteenth century.[70] Between them the documents published by Minnucci form an invaluable prosopographical source, as well as offering important information about administrative practice and the daily life of the *Studio*. A start has been made on the immense task of collating material on the contracts of teachers, in the shape of three *tesi di laurea* supervised by Paolo Nardi in the 1990s.[71] A less productive area, despite rich documentation, has been the study of

[66] Cf. the review of G. CANTUCCI GIANNELLI in *BSSP*, 65 (1958), pp. 179-81. Garosi's work on Sienese doctors of medicine also includes, most substantially, 'Alcuni documenti sulla vita di Ugo Benzi', in *Atti del IV Congresso Nazionale della Società Italiana di Storia delle Scienza Mediche e Naturali (Roma, 1933)* (Siena, 1934), pp. 89-135, over which he locked horns with D. P. LOCKWOOD, *Ugo Benzi, Medieval Philosopher and Physician, 1376-1439* (Chicago, Il., 1951) (see GAROSI, pp. 214-20), and 'La vita e l'opera di Francesco Casini Archiatro di sei papi', *BSSP*, 42 (1935), pp. 277-378; and more generally, *Inter artium et medicinae doctores* (Florence, 1963). Since Garosi's researches there has been little work on Sienese medicine in the republican period; but see now A. WHITLEY, 'Concepts of Ill Health and Pestilence in Fifteenth-Century Siena', unpublished Ph.D. thesis, Warburg Institute, University of London, 2005.

[67] Esp. G. FIORAVANTI, 'Alcuni aspetti della cultura umanistica senese nel '400', *Rinascimento*, 19 (1979), pp. 117-67, and IDEM, 'Pietro de' Rossi: Bibbia ed Aristotele nella Siena del '400', *Rinascimento*, 20 (1980), pp. 87-159; both repr. in his *Università e città. Cultura umanistica e cultura scolastica a Siena nel '400* (Florence, 1981); IDEM, 'Classe dirigente e cultura a Siena nel '400', in *I ceti dirigenti nella Toscana del Quattrocento. Atti del V e VI Convegno: Firenze, 10-11 dicembre 1982; 2-3 dicembre 1983* (Florence, 1987), pp. 473-84; IDEM, 'Le "arti liberali"', pp. 255-71; IDEM, 'Maestri di grammatica a Siena nella seconda metà del Quattrocento', *Rinascimento*, 33 (1993), pp. 193-207, repr. in *Umanesimo a Siena. Letteratura, Arti Figurative, Musica*. Atti del convegno, Siena, 5-8 Giugno 1991, eds. E. Cioni and D. Fausti (Siena, 1994), pp. 11-27. Less work has been done on the teaching of theology in Siena, despite the existence of both statutes and minutes of meetings of the college of doctors of theology. The former were published by L. BERTONI, 'Il "Collegio" dei teologi dell' Università di Siena e i suoi statuti del 1434', *Rivista di Storia della Chiesa in Italia*, 21 (1968), pp. 1-56. The neglect may perhaps be ascribed to the peculiar relationship of theology to the *Studio* in Siena as elsewhere in Italy; see below, pp. 125-6.

[68] G. MINNUCCI, *Le lauree dello Studio senese alla fine del secolo XV*. Quaderni di 'Studi senesi', 51 (Milan, 1981); IDEM, *Le lauree dello Studio senese all'inizio del secolo XVI (1501-1506)* and *II (1507-1514)*. Quaderni di 'Studi senesi', 55 and 56 (Milan, 1984 and 1985); G. MINNUCCI and P. G. MORELLI, *Le lauree dello Studio senese nel XVI secolo. Regesti degli atti dal 1516 al 1573* (Siena, 1992); EIDEM, *Le lauree dello Studio senese nel 16. secolo: regesti degli atti dal 1573 al 1579*. Università degli Studi di Siena, Dipartimento di Scienze Storiche, Giuridiche, Politiche e Sociali: Istituto Storico Diocesano di Siena (Siena, 1998).

[69] See below, p. 22.

[70] See below, pp. 21-2.

[71] A. PIANIGIANI, 'Documenti per la storia dello Studio senese nella prima metà del Quattrocento', unpublished *tesi di laurea*, Università degli Studi di Siena, Facoltà di Giurisprudenza, anno accademico 1991-92, relatore P. Nardi; C. BAI, 'Documenti per la storia dello Studio senese dal 1450 al 1475', unpublished *tesi di laurea*, Università degli Studi di Siena, Facoltà di Giurisprudenza, anno accademico 1993-94, relatore P. Nardi; T. FERRERI, 'Documenti per la storia dello Studio senese dal 1475 al 1500', unpublished *tesi di laurea*, Università degli Studi di Siena, Facoltà di Giurisprudenza, anno accad-

the Casa della Sapienza. Giuliano Catoni's pioneering studies of this institution[72] have not really been followed up, apart from a *tesi di laurea* on admissions to the college from the 1470s,[73] and more recently interest in the college by those studying its predecessor, the Casa della Misericordia,[74] and by historians of architecture.[75]

Taken together, these and other pieces of work constitute a substantial advance in our understanding of the *Studio*. This is evident in the works published in connection with the celebration in 1991 of the 750th anniversary of the university (a date selected, as is often the way in these matters, on somewhat tenuous historical grounds), which include a formidable *de luxe* publication as well as volumes of conference proceedings.[76] It remains the case, though, that the copious but disparate nature of the unpublished records is still holding scholars back. Further progress on this front really requires systematic work on the sources, and the scale of the problem means that this will only happen through teamwork. An important step in this direction was the prosopographical project on teachers and students at the universities of Perugia and Siena begun in the late 1990s under the direction of Carla Frova, Paolo Nardi and the late Paolo Renzi. The resumption of this project is warmly to be welcomed.[77]

3. *The sources*

As has been indicated, the biggest problem for the study of the Sienese *Studio* has actually been that the evidence is at once superabundant and very fragmented.[78] No one body held sway over the whole *Studio*; constant but nuanced shifts in power could result in changes in practice year by year. For many aspects of *Studio* life it is therefore necessary to connect or cross-refer fragments of evidence to build up a picture. To take just one example; the custom of publishing *rotuli* or lecture lists was clearly followed,

emico 1995-96, relatore P. Nardi. Between them these students have gone through the deliberations of the *Concistoro* for whole of the fifteenth century and transcribed those records relating to teachers' contracts (and in the case of the second two, more than that). All three *tesi* can be consulted in the Archivio di Stato di Siena. In quoting them I have given archival references as well, after double-checking where our transcriptions have differed, and I have silently corrected errors in dating, foliation and transcription as appropriate.

[72] G. CATONI, 'Genesi e ordinamento della Sapienza di Siena', *Studi senesi*, 85 (1973), pp. 155-98; IDEM, *Pergamene*; and IDEM, 'Il Comune di Siena e l'amministrazione della Sapienza nel secolo XV', in *Università e società nei secoli XII-XVI, Pistoia 20-25 sett. 1979*. Centro italiano di Studi di Storia e d'Arte: Nono Convegno Internazionale (Pistoia, 1982), pp. 121-29.

[73] M. BONAFACCIA, 'La "Domus Sapientiae" di Siena ed i suoi studenti nei secoli XV-XVI', unpublished *tesi di laurea*, Università degli Studi di Siena, Facoltà di Giurisprudenza, anno accademico 1988-89, relatore P. Nardi.

[74] M. ASCHERI and P. TURRINI (eds.), *La Misericordia di Siena attraverso i secoli. Dalla Domus Misericordiae all'Arciconfraternita della Misericordia* (Siena, 2004).

[75] See M. CIAMPOLINI, 'Casa della Sapienza', in *L'Università di Siena. 750 anni*, pp. 312-5; IDEM, 'La Domus Misericordiae dalle origini ai giorni nostri: vicende costruttive e decorazione', in *La Misericordia di Siena*, cit., pp. 135-55; and below, pp. 388-402.

[76] *L'Università di Siena. 750 anni*; CIONI and FAUSTI (eds.), *Umanesimo a Siena*; M. BROGI (ed.), *Il diritto a studiare: residenze universitarie a Siena tra passato e futuro. Atti del convegno, Siena, 6-7 dicembre 1991* (Siena, 1995); BACCETTI (ed.), *Cultura e Università a Siena*. A further multi-author volume on the University of Siena is the forthcoming issue of *Annali di Storia delle Università italiane*, 10 (2006).

[77] *Maestri e scolari a Siena e Perugia, 1250-1500. Una prosopografia dinamica del corpo accademico e studentesco*. Ricerche di prosopografia elettronica curate da Carla Frova, Paolo Nardi, Paolo Renzi, at www.unisi.it/docentes.

[78] The survey of sources that follows is given in the hope that it will clarify for the reader the basis on which the present research has been conducted, and to enable an assessment of the methodological soundness or otherwise of my conclusions. A full list of volumes consulted can be found in the bibliography, pp. 404-14.

but the actual lists survive only sporadically. Sometimes they were transcribed into communal records, sometimes not. Usually, to answer the simple question of who taught what and when, and for what salary, it is necessary to put together a whole sequence of documents: contracts of hire (mostly biennial); instructions for payment (issued thrice yearly); actual records of payment (also thrice yearly); and reports of particular circumstances such as permitted absences, fines etc. The lack of formal lists means more work for the researcher, but also ultimately a more thorough picture. The quality of coverage also varies considerably over time. For the late fourteenth century the omissions are all too evident; none of the main communal series has the level of detail or consistency for us to make confident claims that all teachers are known to us, while evidence of other aspects of the *Studio* is virtually nonexistent. For the early fifteenth century the picture is already improved, and greatly so for the later part of the century, especially the 1470s and 1480s, but the documents are still not exhaustive.[79] Even in 1451 there is external evidence of negotiations about the hiring of a teacher that have not left traces in these series.[80] This must have been unusual. Yet such *lacunae* remind us to exercise caution about excessive confidence, and specifically against too much reliance on a statistical approach.[81]

The major part of the documentation for the *Studio* is in the archival series of the main communal bodies, preserved in the Archivio di Stato di Siena. For the documentation relating directly to the *Studio* or elements within it, the story is more complex. Apart from degree records in the Archivio Arcivescovile di Siena, the bulk of it is now in two series in the Archivio di Stato di Siena: the *Università degli Studi* (referred to here simply as *Studio*), and the *Domus Misericordiae* or *Casa della Misericordia*.[82] The history of how the documents in these series reached their present locations has been traced by Giuliano Catoni, and is important not least because the various inventories and *spogli* made at various stages give us clear and sometimes detailed indications of documents that have been lost.[83] The division between the two series essentially reflects the practice over the centuries. Material pertaining to the *Studio* and that pertaining to the Casa della Misericordia (which was converted into the Casa della Sapienza in the early fifteenth century) were kept separately, albeit in the same place, the Sapienza, until the eighteenth century.[84] In 1741 it was decided to merge the administration of the college and the university, and consequently their archives. The decision caused controversy, and there was an at-

---

[79] Cf. the example of Niccolò Tedeschi, known from his own writings to have been teaching in Siena throughout the 1420s but not recorded as such in the main communal series before 1424; below, p. 59 n. 191.

[80] The case of Giovanni Matteo Ferrari da Grado, discussed below, p. 187 n. 38.

[81] Where it is possible this can be of considerable interest, as the study of D. ZANETTI, 'A l'Université de Pavie au XVᵉ siècle: les salaires des professeurs', *Annales: Economies, Sociétés, Civilisations*, 17 (1962), pp. 421-33 [Italian tr. in his *Fra le antiche torri: scritti di storia pavese* (Pavia, 2000), pp. 103-17] demonstrates. We are still some way from being in a position to replicate such studies for Siena.

[82] There is a small amount of material from the student-university and the colleges of doctors in the *Notarile ante-cosimiano* series, and several petitions from the *Savi dello Studio* in the *Scritture Concistoriali* (see below, pp. 21, 23 and 205-6).

[83] CATONI, *Pergamene*, pp. 3-8; cf. IDEM, 'Introduzione' to *Archivio Storico dell'Università di Siena*, and 'L'inventario dell'archivio storico dell'Università di Siena', in *La storia delle università italiane. Archivi, fonti, indirizzi di ricerca*, ed. L. Sitran Rea. Contributi alla Storia dell'Università di Padova, 30 (Trieste, 1996), pp. 103-7.

[84] At the end of the seventeenth century Sestigiani compiled indices to two of the volumes of *Deliberazioni dei Savi* (*Studio* 2 and 3; beside the hand, his authorship is confirmed by Santi Landi in ASS, *ms.* C.51 *bis*, f. 14v), but omitted them from his comprehensive *Repertorio di Strumenti Antichi della Sapienza* (ASS, *ms.* B.82). The printed *Indice dei Cartoni esistenti nell'Archivio della Venerabil Casa della Sapienza* of 1732 (*Studio* 127, no. 1) lists twenty-five boxes, all of which relate predominantly to the Sapienza; Santi Landi, *maestro della Sapienza*, described the contents of the same boxes, substantially unchanged in structure, in his more detailed *Indice...delle filze, e Deliberazioni che sono nell'Armario dipinto coll'Arme della Sapienza* (ASS, *ms.* C.51 *bis*) of 1777 (with additions to 1783), but also included, in a separate list, extensive summaries of a number of volumes that are now in the *Studio* series.

tempt in 1779 to separate the documents out again. Though this was not officially agreed, there did follow a separation of 'political' and 'economic' material,[85] which appears to have facilitated the destruction, in 1790, of the majority of the 'economic' documents.[86] In 1816 what was left of these records was transferred to the new University buildings, and in 1860 the older part, including all the records of the republican period, moved again to the new Archivio di Stato,[87] to be divided into the two series mentioned above.

The description of the sources which follows has been arranged pragmatically, partly according to content and partly according to the emanator or location of the source. Any more sophisticated typology would have pre-empted questions about the constitutional arrangements of the *Studio*, which are discussed in more detail in the appropriate chapters below.

a. *The main communal institutions*

The direct administration of many aspects of the *Studio* by the main organs of government means that the backbone of materials for its history is formed by the records of these bodies, all of which are in the Archivio di Stato di Siena. Together they constitute our chief guide to legislation, to the commune's relationship with the teachers, to admissions to the Casa della Sapienza, and to the general health of the enterprise. In the absence of statutes of the colleges and the student-university they are also an important source of information for the history of those bodies.

i) As will be seen, the main legislative bodies were all closely involved in the life of the *Studio* in different ways. The two main councils – the *Consiglio Generale del Comune* (or *Consiglio della Campana*), and later the *Consiglio del Popolo* which in time took over the majority of its political functions – were the broadest bodies in the republic.[88] The principal executive body, the *Concistoro*, consisting

---

[85] *Studio* 16, ff. 5v, 15 Jun, 7r, 29 Jul, 8r, 24 Nov 1779, and 12r, 17 Mar 1780; further information on the state of the archive in the years following Landi's inventory in *Studio* 38 and *Studio* 39.

[86] CATONI, *Pergamene*, pp. 3-4; IDEM, 'Introduzione', pp. XIV-XV; ASS, *Governatore* 929, no. 356.

[87] CATONI, as n. 83. Much of the post-republican material formed the core of the Archivio dell'Università, on which, apart from Catoni, see also M. SCALI, A. LEONCINI and N. SEMBOLONI, 'L'Archivio dell'Università di Siena', *Annali di Storia delle Università italiane*, 3 (1999), pp. 231-3. The archive contains just one volume from the fifteenth century, a file of legal *consilia* (*Manoscritti varî*, 1: *Recollectiones diversorum doctorum / Consilia / Allegationes*), on which see M. ASCHERI, 'Scheda di due codici giuridici senesi', *Studi senesi*, 83 (1971), pp. 125-46.

[88] The *Consiglio del Popolo*, as the body of which all those who had held office were automatically members, effectively became a senate, while the *Consiglio Generale* retained the largely formal role of approving measures passed by the *Consiglio del Popolo*. The deliberations of both were recorded in the same volumes, the series known as *Consiglio Generale*. The elucidation of this distinction has been the work especially of M. ASCHERI, 'Siena nel rinascimento: dal governo di "popolo" al governo nobiliare', in *I ceti dirigenti nella Toscana del Quattrocento*, pp. 405-30; expanded version in his *Siena nel Rinascimento. Istituzioni e sistema politico* (Siena, 1985), pp. 9-108 (pp. 32-4, 57-69); IDEM, 'Assemblee, democrazia comunale e cultura politica: dal caso della Repubblica di Siena (secc. XIV-XV)', in *Studi in onore di Arnaldo d'Addario*, ed. L. Borgia, F. De Luca, P. Viti and R. M. Zaccaria (Lecce, 1995), IV/I, pp. 1141-55; repr. with minor changes in *Contributi alla storia parlamentare europea (secoli XIII-XX)*, ed. M. S. Corciulo. Atti del 43° Congresso ICHRPI, Camerino, Palazzo Ducale 14-17 Luglio 1993. Studies presented to the International Commission for the History of Representative and Parliamentary Institutions, 78 (Camerino, 1996), pp. 77-99; IDEM, 'La Siena del "Buon Governo" (1287-1355)', in *Politica e cultura nelle repubbliche italiane dal Medioevo all'Età moderna. Firenze – Genova – Lucca – Siena – Venezia*, eds. S. Adorni Braccesi and M. Ascheri. Annuario dell'Istituto storico italiano per l'età moderna e contemporanea, 53-4 (Rome, 2001), pp. 81-107 (pp. 101-2), and for a brief summary IDEM, *Siena nella storia*, pp. 92-3. Ascheri's work is an important addition to the still useful overview in ARCHIVIO DI STATO DI SIENA, *Archivio del Consiglio Generale del Comune di Siena. Inventario*. Pubblicazioni degli Archivi di Stato, 9 (Rome, 1952), 'Introduzione', pp. VII-XXI. The *Consiglio Generale* was never reduced to a rubber-

of priors who held office for two months, meeting together with the 'ordini' or key office-holders of the state,[89] made all the detailed decisions and largely controlled the agenda of the *Consiglio del Popolo*; while the *Balìa*, originally a succession of *ad hoc* committees set up to override the normal constitutional procedures on specific issues, but which soon became semi-permanent and the centrepiece of government, increasingly took over the main political decisions.[90] Between them these bodies controlled most aspects of the organisation of teaching, from the hiring of doctors to the budget, the academic calendar and occasionally even the forms of lecture and disputation. They also legislated on matters concerning students, and intervened regularly in individual cases concerning members of the *Studio*. The intricate, often tense and constantly changing relationship between these bodies[91] means that tracing and understanding decisions can be complicated. The series of deliberations of the three archival series left by these bodies has been consulted for the entire period 1357-1500; the *Consiglio Generale* series (which contains measures approved by both it and the *Consiglio del Popolo*) has been consulted to 1559.

ii) The *Concistoro*'s and the *Balìa*'s deliberations can very usefully be supplemented by recourse to minor series in their archives. Correspondence has survived for both, in collections of formal letters to the Sienese authorities (*Carteggio*) and transcriptions of outgoing communications (*Copialettere*). Taken together, these series contain a great deal of information relating to the recruitment of teachers and recommendations of students, as well as correspondence with diplomats and others, which occasionally includes information about negotiations, not to mention impressions about the health and situation of the Sienese *Studio* and the Italian university world generally. The *Concistoro* records also include a number of other series, most important among which are the *Scritture Concistoriali*, a miscellaneous collection including records of business put to the *Concistoro*, proposals by special commissions and subordinate bodies such as the *Savi dello Studio*, and petitions from individuals.[92] These have proved a rich addition to our knowledge of the operation of the *Studio*. Again, these series, and others, have been consulted up to 1500.[93]

---

stamping body, however; R. TERZIANI, 'L'instaurazione del regime oligarchico-signorile (1487-1488)', in *Siena e il suo territorio nel Rinascimento, III/Renaissance Siena and its Territory, III*, ed. M. Ascheri (Siena, 2000), pp. 195-208 (pp. 195-6), and more generally IDEM, *Il governo di Siena dal Medioevo all'Età moderna. La continuità repubblicana al tempo dei Petrucci (1487-1525)*. Documenti di Storia (Siena, 2002), p. 4. For a comparative dimension see C. SHAW, 'Counsel and Consent in Fifteenth-Century Genoa', *English Historical Review*, 116 (2001), pp. 834-62 (esp. pp. 840-1, 852-3 on Siena).

[89] ARCHIVIO DI STATO DI SIENA, *Archivio del Concistoro del Comune di Siena. Inventario*. Pubblicazioni degli Archivi di Stato, 10 (Rome, 1952), introduction (by G. CECCHINI), pp. IX-XXIV; D. P. WALEY, *Siena and the Sienese in the Thirteenth Century* (Cambridge, 1991), pp. 48-50, 56-7; TERZIANI, *Il governo di Siena*, p. 49.

[90] On this body, ARCHIVIO DI STATO DI SIENA, *Archivio di Balìa. Inventario*. Pubblicazioni degli Archivi di Stato, 26 (Rome, 1957), introduction (by G. PRUNAI and S. DE' COLLI), pp. IX-LXXXI; revised/abridged version with minor modifications as 'La Balìa dagli inizi del XIII secolo fino alla invasione francese (179)', *BSSP*, 65 (1958), pp. 33-96; for a survey of the constitution at the end of the fifteenth century see TERZIANI, *Il governo di Siena*, ch. I.1.

[91] In so far as this concerned the *Studio* it is discussed below, pp. 76-8. A detailed analysis is in M. GINATEMPO, *Crisi di un territorio. Il popolamento della Toscana senese alla fine del medioevo* (Florence, 1988), pp. 66-73.

[92] Of the various sub-series of the *Scritture Concistoriali* the most important for our purposes are: *Proposte dei Savi*, a series containing the proposals of special commissions which operated outside the *Concistoro*'s filter of business put to the *Consiglio del Popolo* (these are discussed, and partly edited, in C. SHAW, 'Provisions following "Proposte generali" 1436 and 1456', in *Siena e il suo territorio nel Rinascimento, III*, pp. 109-52); *Ufficiali del Comune*, which includes petitions to officials; *Luoghi pii e Studio*, which includes many petitions from the *Savi dello Studio*; *Particolari*, from individuals; and the miscellaneous series of *Scritture Concistoriali* proper. Leo Košuta first drew my attention to the great value of this series, and of the miscellaneous *Carte varie*, for the *Studio*'s history.

[93] The series *Lettere senza data* has also been consulted.

ii) Parallel to the daily deliberations of these bodies are periodic attempts to codify reforms, or at least to make the many legislative changes more systematically accessible. These results of these initiatives are the volumes in the series of *Statuti di Siena*. These volumes vary considerably in importance. Some of the earlier ones are fully-fledged urban statutes; others, including all those between the statutes of 1338-9 and 1544, are either elucidations of specific areas of practice (e.g. on office-holding) or attempts to capture and cross-reference the constant stream of legislation emanating from the authorities.[94] The value of these volumes for our purposes lies not so much in any fresh information they might contain (though it has certainly helped to fill some *lacunae*, as not all the measures they collect have survived in the main series), as in the context that they provide; seeing *Studio* measures alongside those concerning other bodies and other officials makes it easier to compare the treatment of the *Studio* with other civic enterprises. Above all, the fact of their transcription in these volumes is an indication of the importance that was ascribed to certain specific measures. All the volumes pertaining to the period to 1500 have been consulted.

iv) The financial records of the commune are also abundant, though much less complete. The main financial office of the commune, the *Biccherna*, was responsible for the payment of all communal employees, including all teachers and *Studio* officials.[95] Its records are thus an invaluable adjunct to those of the other three main communal series for the reconstruction of the *Studio* payroll from year to year. The *Entrate e Uscite* of this office have been consulted to 1500, as have the *Memoriali*, the *Significazioni* and a number of other subsidiary series which help to fill the many gaps. Other financial offices with occasional responsibilities for, or relationships with, the *Studio* include the *Gabella Generale* and the *Quattro Maestri del Sale*. The nature of these relationships is discussed below;[96] the records pertaining to these offices have been con-

---

[94] The functions of these collections are discussed in M. ASCHERI, 'Statuti, legislazione e sovranità: il caso di Siena', in *Statuti, città, territori in Italia e Germania tra Medioevo ed età moderna*, eds. G. Chittolini and D. Willoweit. Annali dell'Istituto storico italo-germanico, Quaderni, 30 (Bologna, 1991), pp. 145-94; repr. as 'Legislazione, statuti e sovranità', in *Antica Legislazione della Repubblica di Siena*, pp. 1-40. Individual volumes (*Statuti* 26-37) are described in D. CIAMPOLI, 'Le raccolte normative della seconda metà del Trecento', in *Antica Legislazione*, cit., pp. 121-36. *Statuti* 36 was edited by A. LISINI, *Provvedimenti economici della Repubblica di Siena nel 1382* (Siena, 1895), *Statuti* 37, the 'Libro della Pace', by M. GUERRINI, 'Provvedimenti congiunturali 1385-1386', in *Siena e il suo territorio nel Rinascimento II*, eds. M. Ascheri and D. Ciampoli (Siena, 1990), pp. 71-97; a register of measures in *Statuti* 38 was published by D. CIAMPOLI, 'Una raccolta di provvisioni senesi agli albori del XV secolo: il "libro della catena"', *BSSP*, 86 (1979), pp. 243-83, and a similar register for *Statuti* 40 was published by E. BRIZIO, 'Leggi e provvedimenti del Rinascimento (1400-1542): Spoglio di un registro archivistico (*Statuti di Siena 40*)', in *Antica Legislazione*, cit., pp. 161-200. Excerpts of *Statuti* 39 have been edited by F. NEVOLA, 'Cerimoniali per santi e feste a Siena a metà Quattrocento. Documenti dallo Statuto di Siena 39', in *Siena e il suo territorio nel Rinascimento, III*, pp. 171-84; *Statuti* 44 has been edited by M. A. CAMBI and M. QUARTESAN (eds.), 'Gli uffici del Comune di Siena e le incompatibilità, 1433', in *Siena e il suo Territorio nel Rinascimento, II*, cit., pp. 121-49. Apart from these last four the volumes relating to the fifteenth century await systematic study, though some, notably *Statuti* 41, the 'Tesoretto', are well known to historians; see M. ASCHERI, 'Introduzione: Lo Statuto del Comune di Siena del 1337-1339', introduction to D. CIAMPOLI, *Il Capitano del popolo a Siena nel primo Trecento. Documenti di Storia*, 1 (Siena, 1984), pp. 7-21 (esp. pp. 14-21). *Statuti* 49-52 constitute a formal collection of statutes and have been published by M. ASCHERI (ed.), *L'ultimo statuto della Repubblica di Siena (1545)*. Accademia Senese degli Intronati, Monografie di storia e letteratura senese, 12 (Siena, 1993).

[95] On this office, ARCHIVIO DI STATO DI SIENA, *Archivio della Biccherna del Comune di Siena. Inventario*. Pubblicazioni degli Archivi di Stato, 12 (Rome, 1953), introduction (by G. CECCHINI), pp. IX-XXV; W. M. BOWSKY, *The Finance of the Commune of Siena, 1287-1355* (Oxford, 1970), esp. ch. 1; most recently, C. ZARRILLI, 'Amministrare con arte. Il lungo viaggio delle Biccherne dagli uffici al Museo', in *Le Biccherne di Siena*, pp. 22-34.

[96] Pp. 99-101.

sulted as appropriate. Full use has also been made of another source; from the establishment of the office of the *Regolatori* in the mid-fourteenth century, Siena had superb auditing procedures in the form of annual accounts or *Revisioni* for all the commune's major officials and projects.[97] These give an excellent overview of both expenditure on *Studio* salaries and the financial situation of the Casa della Sapienza.

v) Less use has been made of the other major general series of the commune, including the fiscal and the judicial. There is no doubt that these series contain material relating to the teachers, and less frequently the students, of the *Studio*. Most obviously, the *Lira*, the series of tax assessments made periodically of Sienese citizens and subjects, contains valuable information about the economic condition of these individuals.[98] The series has been consulted fully for the fifteenth century, though since the focus of the present work is institutional rather than prosopographical, the information gleaned has not yet been analysed systematically, and is only presented here where it relates to the institutional history of the *Studio*. I have also drawn the line at judicial records; series such as the *Mercanzia*, the *Podestà*, the *Curia del Placito* and the *Esecutore e Capitano di Giustizia* have only been consulted where there were specific indications elsewhere that a relevant case had been heard in one of these courts.[99] The scale of the task in these under-researched *fondi*, and the low probability of returns compared with the effort involved, meant that they had to be excluded from systematic research.

b. *The* Savi dello Studio

The *Savi dello Studio* were the executive officials of the university; six citizens, communally appointed, for a year.[100] The documentation associated with them is dispersed in a variety of locations. Very little survives before the 1470s. The main series is of *Deliberazioni*, a series which begins in 1473. The *Deliberazioni* have been studied for the remainder of the republican period, but with particular emphasis on *Studio* 2, the volume covering the late fifteenth century. This is a far from complete record, with some lengthy periods when there are no entries.[101] To this series must be added the records of the

---

[97] The fundamental study is G. CATONI, 'I "Regolatori" e la giurisdizione sui contabili nella repubblica di Siena', *Critica Storica*, 12 (1975), pp. 46-70; and see S. MOSCADELLI, 'Apparato burocratico e finanze del Comune di Siena sotto il Dodici (1355-1368)', *BSSP*, 89 (1982), pp. 29-118 (pp. 64 *seq.*), and W. CAFERRO, *Mercenary Companies and the Decline of Siena* (Baltimore, Md., and London, 1998), pp. xviii and 146-9. A full flavour of the range of their activities is given by the summary of *Regolatori* 1, their statute book, by G. CHIRONI, 'Il testo unico per l'ufficio dei Regolatori, 1351-1533', in *Siena e il suo Territorio nel Rinascimento, II*, pp. 183-220 (and see M. ASCHERI, 'Presentazione' to the same volume, p. xvi). A comparable series in Florence appears to be the account books of the *Camera del Comune*, on which see esp. A. MOLHO, 'The State and Public Finance: a Hypothesis Based on the History of Late Medieval Florence', in *The Origins of the State in Italy 1300-1600*, ed. J. Kirshner (Chicago, Il., 1995), pp. 97-135 (pp. 110-13).

[98] A useful introduction is GINATEMPO, *Crisi di un territorio*, pp. 27 *seq.*; studies include G. CATONI and G. PICCINNI, 'Alliramento e ceto dirigente nella Siena del Quattrocento', in *I ceti dirigenti nella Toscana del Quattrocento*, pp. 451-61, and EIDEM, 'Famiglie e redditi nella *Lira* senese del 1453', in *Strutture familiari, epidemie, migrazioni nell'Italia medievale*, eds. R. Comba, G. Piccinni and G. Pinto (Naples, 1984), pp. 291-304.

[99] It has to be said that these forays have proved to be overwhelmingly fruitless. Cases involving student discipline were in any case mostly dealt with by the *Studio*'s internal authorities. See below, p. 290.

[100] Their role is discussed below in Chapter I.2.

[101] These become more obvious in the sixteenth century; below, p. 26 n. 139. In the late fifteenth century the gaps are often of weeks, occasionally of months.

Quattro Maestri del Sale, under whose aegis the *Savi* were placed, at least temporarily, in 1429,[102] and which therefore occasionally include their deliberations.[103] Fragments of notes of the *Savi*'s deliberations have also survived in a volume of their notary in the 1470s, Ser Lorenzo di Lando Sborgheri, edited by Minnucci.[104] This also includes correspondence (e.g. recommendations of students addressed to the *Savi*), notes of advice and petitions by the *Savi* to the *Concistoro*, and details of their administration of the Sapienza's estate. Similar documents survive elsewhere in the *Studio* series,[105] as well as in the *Scritture Concistoriali* mentioned above. Taken together these documents gives a detailed picture of the everyday life of the *Studio* below the level at which the main communal decision-making bodies were involved.

c. *The colleges of doctors and the chancellor of the* Studio

Although, as has been seen, the colleges of doctors did not represent or include all teachers, and were not limited to university activities, they were an important element of the *Studio*. For Siena the records of these colleges are dismally poor. For the main two within the *Studio*, the college of doctors of law and that of the doctors of medicine and arts, the loss is almost total; we have statutes for neither before the sixteenth century, nor do the minutes of their meetings survive in anything but the most fragmentary form.[106] The reconstruction of the activities of these through almost exclusively communal documents is bound to be unsatisfactory. The exception to this gloomy picture is the much more peripheral college of the doctors of theology, which functioned along very different lines as a sort of federation of religious institutions with teaching responsibilities. For this we do have both a set of statutes, promulgated in 1434, and a record of deliberations from 1472 onwards.[107]

These losses are particularly acute because they rob us of much information about the degrees awarded. In Siena, as elsewhere, the doctorate was awarded formally by the representative of the chancellor, the bishop, after examination by the appropriate college of doctors. While the deliberations of the theologians give us a record of degrees from 1472 (a record which is additionally useful because it includes details of examinations for the baccalaureate and incorporations in the college),[108] for the rest

---

[102] See below, p. 100 n. 57.

[103] *Sale* 20-25; and cf. U. MORANDI, 'L'Ufficio della Dogana del Sale in Siena', *BSSP*, 70 (1963), pp. 62-91 (p. 69). The relationship between the two series is unclear. For 1483-4 there is a degree of overlap, with parallel records of deliberations recorded in the *Sale* register (*Sale* 21, ff. 208r-217v, 28 Jul 1483 to 13 Jun 1484) and in *Studio* 2 (ff. 94v-101r) The *Sale* entries are rougher and less chronologically consistent; they are sometimes briefer, sometimes fuller than the more formal version; both books include several measures not recorded in the other (*Sale* 21, f. 208v, 24 Sept, 209r, 7 Nov, 209v, 10 Nov; *Studio* 2, f. 99r).

[104] *Not.* 694; ed. G. MINNUCCI, 'Documenti per la Storia dello Studio senese (Secoli XIV-XVI)', in MINNUCCI and KOŠUTA, *Lo Studio di Siena*, pp. 9-314 (docs. II-4 to II-19 and II-31 to II-53, pp. 77-88 and 97-125, and cf. p. 32 n. 75). The deliberations largely echo those recorded in *Studio* 2, which is partly in Lorenzo's hand, but also add significantly to them, especially where there are chronological gaps in that volume. A further such fragment is in *Not.* 886, ff. 152r-154r, a volume of Ser Alessandro di Niccolò della Grammatica, notary of the *Savi* and the *Studio* in 1483.

[105] *Studio* 19 is a short miscellany of letters to the *Savi* from 1441 to 1569.

[106] See below, pp. 205-6.

[107] BCS, *ms.* A.XI.1; description in GAROSI, *Inventario*, III, pp. 254-5.

[108] The few theology degrees recorded in the *bastardelli* of the chancellor at the end of the fifteenth century (MINNUCCI, *Lauree*, I, nos. 1, 33, 49, 103, 104, 110) and in other notarial records (MINNUCCI, 'Documenti', doc. I-8, pp. 59-61, 29 Mar 1490) have precise parallels in the records of degrees awarded by the college of doctors of theology (BCS, *ms.* A.XI.1, ff. 19v, 27r, 39r, 40r, 41v, 42r, 43v).

we are thrown back on the books kept by notaries, either of a college or of the episcopal *curia*. The notaries of the chancery appear to have begun to record the degrees awarded in a series of *bastardelli* only in 1484, though even then there was some initial discontinuity, with no entries from 1487 to 1495. All the degrees in these volumes from 1484 to 1579 have been edited in *regesto* form by Minnucci and Morelli.[109] Minnucci also published the contents of a volume of the notary Ser Feliciano di Ser Neri regarding the *Studio*, which (for reasons that are still not clear) includes a handful of degree records dated mostly from 1489 to 1493.[110] For the early fifteenth century, the survival and recuperation of degree information is very hit-and-miss. Only two notaries known to have worked in the chancery in that period are also known to have recorded degrees. One was Ser Antonio da Calci, for whom a volume of *rogiti* survives for the years 1409-23.[111] Zdekauer published or referred to some of the degrees in this volume; a few more remain unpublished.[112] The other was Ser Giacomo Nuccino, from whose *atti* Zdekauer published a number of extracts.[113] Unfortunately this volume has not been seen since Zdekauer's day and must be presumed lost. Beyond that, the best hope is in the notarial series in the Archivio di Stato, where Minnucci found a handful of degrees from the late fourteenth and early fifteenth centuries.[114] This period of fragmentary evidence is however followed by a veritable drought; for the central decades of the century, and specifically between 1428 to 1472, which arguably included the most florid epoch in the history of the *Studio*, we have next to nothing. One happy discovery is that of the names of degree candidates who paid their dues to the Opera del Duomo in the 1440s, due to be published by Paolo Nardi.[115] A variety of pointers – measures granting degree candidates special privileges,[116] autobiographical information,[117] the consolidated results of scholarship,[118] and anecdotal evidence[119] – gives us some further clues as to what we are missing. Some of the

---

[109] AAS, 6435-40 (*Protocolli degli atti di laurea*, 1484-1579); See above, p. 14 n. 68.

[110] *Not.* 858; the records of these degrees are edited in MINNUCCI, 'Documenti', docs. I-7 to I-21, pp. 57-74. Ser Feliciano di ser Neri was notary of the 'Universitas scholarium' in 1480, and these records appear in the same volume as those of his work for that body. Several of them were drawn up not by Ser Feliciano but by the notary of the *curia*, Ser Leonardo di Antonio Gesti, whose single volume in the Archivio di Stato, *Not.* 799, also includes much *Studio* material.

[111] AAS, 4420 (*Notai e cancellieri della curia:* Protocollo dei rogiti di Ser Antonio di Gandino da Calci, 1409-23).

[112] See below, p. 199 nn. 134-5.

[113] ZDEKAUER, *Documenti*, part II, docs. 1-11, 15-17, pp. 15-20; he describes the volume as 'Atti di Curia dal 1427 al 1428'.

[114] MINNUCCI, 'Documenti', docs. I-1 to I-6, pp. 47-57; and IDEM, 'A Sienese Doctorate' (see below, p. 51 n. 133).

[115] P. NARDI, 'Una fonte inedita delle lauree senesi nel secolo XV: i libri di amministrazione dell'Opera del Duomo', *Annali di storia delle Università italiane*, 10 (2006, forthcoming). I am most grateful to Professor Nardi for kindly letting me have a preview of this article.

[116] See below, pp. 207 and 289.

[117] An example is the statement of the Pistoiese medical doctor Polidoro Bracali in his *Ricordi* that he had taken his degree in Siena on 28 Feb 1449; ZDEKAUER, *Origini*, pp. 22-3; also recorded in the Opera del Duomo documents published by NARDI, op. cit.

[118] For example, the *Repertorium Germanicum*, VIII. *Verzeichnis der in den Registen und Kameralakten Pius' II. vorkommenden Personen, Kirchen und Orte des Deutschen Reiches, seiner Diözesen und Territorien, 1458-1464*, 2 vols., eds. D. Brosius and U. Scheschkewitz (Tübingen, 1993) lists five Germans as having obtained a degree in Siena; Borchardus de Anderten, who obtained a licence in canon law on 20 Dec 1460 (no. 551, p. 86), Johannes Blasoyss de Oelper who obtained a licence on 30 Dec 1460 (no. 2529, p. 376), Wilhelmus de Reichenau, promoted on 5 Mar 1464 (no. 5894, p. 825), and Dethardus Sleter (no. 914, p. 133) and Johannes de Weissenbach (no. 3830, pp. 549-50) who took doctorates on unspecified dates.

[119] See for example Agostino Dati's eulogy of the eminent physician Bartolo di Tura, stating that he had been *promotor* of over eighty students during his career; DATI, *Opera, Orationes, Liber* V, *Oratio* VI, ff. 99v-100v (at 100r); cf. ZDEKAUER,

original certificates – the vital piece of paper or parchment taken away by students – will have ended up in other European archives, public or private,[120] and more may well turn up.[121] But short of the discovery of college deliberations, the prospects are not rosy, and the chance of us recovering a full record must be presumed gone forever.

d. *The student-university*

The records of the student university have if anything undergone even greater devastation than those of the colleges of doctors. A normally functioning *Studio* with a student-university could be expected to have a set of statutes and a book in which students' names were inscribed when they 'matriculated' or became members of the university. Though there is evidence that statutes were drawn up, they have not survived,[122] nor have any matriculation records before 1533. The latter deficiency is far from un-usual for Italian universities; there are various obvious explanations for why records pertaining to students, particularly 'foreign' students, went astray so frequently.[123] But the loss of statutes is a serious problem for the reconstruction of the institution's history, which has again had to be performed through communal sources.[124] The only exception to this sad state of affairs is the survival of a booklet of a notary of the student university, Ser Feliciano di Ser Neri, for 1480. Minnucci has published the contents of this slim volume, which briefly records meetings and decisions of the rector and his *consiliarii* as well as some ceremonial occasions.[125] This source provides significant clues to the operation of the student university at that time, though its brevity and uniqueness means that it raises as many is-sues as it solves.

e. *The Casa della Sapienza*

The records of Siena's most particular contribution to the university system, its residential college, are extensive because it was built on the considerable foundations of its predecessor, the Casa della Miseri-

---

p. 98; and G. PICCINNI, 'Tra scienza ed arti: lo Studio di Siena e l'insegnamento della medicina (secoli XIII-XVI)', in *L'Uni-versità di Siena. 750 anni*, pp. 145-58 (p. 148).

[120] No systematic list of these has been compiled, though some have been signalled or reproduced; e.g. the certificate *in utroque* of Tarugio di Bernardino Tarugi of Montepulciano of 1507, in the archive of the Secchi Tarugi family in Montepul-ciano (*Storia di Siena*, I, p. 367).

[121] An example is the certificate of a doctorate in arts and medicine of Francesco di Bartolomeo Angeli de Cassianis plebensis, awarded on 9 Aug 1525. This appears in MINNUCCI and MORELLI, *Lauree*, IV, no. 74, pp. 41-2; the original is in the East Sussex Record Office, Lewes, Ashburnham *ms.* 2978. I am most grateful to Dr Daniel Waley, who found this while cataloguing the Ashburnham collection, for informing me of its existence, and to Mr Christopher Whittick of the Record Office for supplying a reproduction of the certificate.

[122] A set of rubrics, in *Studio* 100, assumed by Zdekauer to be of the Sienese student-university, is discussed below, pp. 255-6.

[123] One appears to be the phenomenon of student rectors taking documents with them on departure. The only consolation in this is the prospect that these might occasionally turn up in archives elsewhere. For an example of such a discovery, G. PACE, 'Nuovi documenti su Hinrich Murmester, *rector iuristarum* dello Studio di Padova nel 1463. Con un *consilium* di Angelo degli Ubaldi', *Quaderni per la Storia dell'Università di Padova*, 32 (1999), pp. 223-38. On this issue see also below, p. 273 and n. 226.

[124] See below, Chapter III.2.

[125] *Not.* 858; the relevant documents were published by MINNUCCI, 'Documenti', docs. II-20 to II-30, pp. 88-97 and cf. pp. 34-6.

cordia, in its heyday one of the largest property owners within the republic. But the change of function of the institution creates some complications for the historian. On one hand, the hospital and college phases of the institution are not always easily separable in the records, especially in matters relating to the house's estate and finances, in which the one was treated as the legal continuation of the other. On the other hand, as the Sapienza took off, it soon became a natural centre for the university as a whole, so its organisational structures rapidly became intertwined with those of the university. Yet neither its antique but continued status as a pious institution nor its more recently created role within the *Studio* protected it from communal regulation and control; it was above all seen as a creation and a responsibility of the republic. The history of the Sapienza thus has to be traced through many of the sources that have just been described – those of the communal decision-making bodies and the *Savi dello Studio* – as well as through documents belonging to the institution itself.

Of the documents in the Misericordia/Sapienza archive, three volumes call for specific comment here. The first relates to the possessions of the institution. The great bulk of the archive relates to the estate, and most of it is concerned with the preceding period.[126] It has been used for comparative purposes. However the centrepiece for the history of the estate in our period is a single volume, *Casa della Misericordia* 36. The first part of this is a *catasto* or inventory, made in 1451, of all the possessions of the Sapienza. Bound with it are several contracts dated from the mid-fifteenth century to the early sixteenth.[127] It is the main source for such contracts to survive from the fifteenth century. The volume has thus been of particular value in piecing together the economic position of the Sapienza.

The second document of particular relevance is a volume in the Biblioteca Comunale di Siena, *ms.* A.XI.12, in which students in the Sapienza were supposed to sign for and list the items (furniture, bedding etc.) they received on taking up a place in the college.[128] This volume begins in 1470; it has been known since the nineteenth century and has been used by many scholars.[129] Apart from its interest as a collection of (in some cases) original student handwriting, its value for the prosopography and daily life of the college is self-evident. It has also rather deflected attention onto the late-fifteenth-century history of the Sapienza, since no such record survives for the previous period. That, however, rather sidelines

---

[126] These have been surveyed and described by Catoni; see above, p. 16 n. 83.

[127] The two parts must have been bound together in the eighteenth century; Sestigiani lists the contracts of the second half, in chronological order as they appear in the volume today (ASS, *ms.* B. 82, ff. 151r-155r), but the entry for the *catasto* is made by Landi who found the entire volume in 1751 (*ibid.*, f. 14v). On the date of the *catasto* see below, p. 363 n. 20.

[128] The names of the students entering between 1470 and 1495 were extracted and published by ZDEKAUER, doc. XXIII, pp. 180-90, and the full list, to 1547, is now in BONAFACCIA, 'La "Domus Sapientiae"', pp. 74-194, with biographical *schede* on pp. 195-301. The *ms.* is described by GAROSI, *Inventario*, III, p. 266, and in more detail by F. WEIGLE, *Die Matrikel der Deutschen Nation in Siena, 1573-1738*. Bibliothek des Deutschen Historischen Instituts in Rom, 22-3 (Tübingen, 1962), pp. 24-5 (and by BONAFACCIA, pp. 67-73). The volume escaped the attention of Sestigiani and subsequent archivists, from which it can be concluded that it probably left the Sapienza quite early on. The practice of issuing property to entrants 'per inventario' already existed in 1435 (*Mis.* 1, f. 82r, 17 Sept), and we know from a late seventeenth-century inventory of the college's archive that such a register was kept from at least 1441 (ASS, *ms.* B.82, f. 10v, and see CATONI, *Pergamene*, p. 4, and 'Introduzione', p. XV; on the *ms.* see above, p. 10 n. 38). The inventory lists five such volumes, covering the period 1441-1505. The relationship of these volumes to BCS, *ms.* A.XI.12 – which runs from 1470 to 1547, and which is clearly original, with students writing their own entries – is as yet unclear. The surviving volume does not look as if it is a rebinding of previously separate ones.

[129] Apart from ZDEKAUER, see R. J. MITCHELL, *The Laurels and the Tiara. Pope Pius II, 1458-1464* (London, 1962), p. 74; EADEM, *John Free. From Bristol to Rome in the Fifteenth Century* (London, 1955), pp. 26-7, and EADEM, 'English Student Life in Early Renaissance Italy', *Italian Studies*, 7 (1952), pp. 62-81 (p. 74).

the fact that admissions were controlled by the *Concistoro* and the *Consiglio del Popolo*, and whose series thus contain the names of a great number of students admitted to the Sapienza year on year.

The third volume, *Casa della Misericordia* 1, has a different kind of significance. It is a statute book of 130 pages of good parchment, with a wood cover, and a red leather spine[130] bearing the (later) inscription *Statuti della Casa della Misericordia delli Scolari, Bolle e Privilegi. Dal 1345 a tutto il 1521*. The first forty-five pages are the statutes and amendments, first in the vulgar and then in Latin, of the old Casa della Misericordia, which in 1416 became the Casa della Sapienza, a residential college of the university. There follow, from f. 47r to f. 49v, the 'Ordini del vivere' of the new Sapienza, drawn up in the opening years of the college, which were published by Catoni in 1973;[131] from f. 63r to f. 78v, copies of the eight bulls regarding the *Studio* and the Sapienza by Gregory XII in 1480 (first in Italian then in Latin, with a digest in Italian on ff. 59r-60r); and a bull of Pius II (ff. 97r-100r).[132] Interspersed on other pages of this volume is a collection of transcriptions, and sometimes vernacular translations, of measures passed by the *Consiglio Generale*, the *Concistoro*, the *Balìa* and the *Savi dello Studio* concerning both the Sapienza and the *Studio*.[133] That the volume was considered significant in earlier times is evidenced by the fact that there are no fewer than three copies of it,[134] one of which was in

---

[130] From this, presumably, derives the description of it as a 'statutello rosso' by the compiler of *Mis.* 36, f. 6r (1451); cf. CATONI, 'Genesi', p. 171. Bound in with the original manuscript is a full *spoglio* in the hand of the ubiquitous Sestigiani. I am not competent to judge whether this involved the destruction and replacement of the original binding.

[131] CATONI, 'Genesi', pp. 177-82.

[132] The Italian versions of the bulls of Gregory in this volume (on which see below, p. 55) were published by D. BARDUZZI, *Documenti per la storia della R. Università di Siena* [Siena, 1900], pp. 24-34 (as was the bull of Pius II, pp. 34-8, though he transcribed this from the version in *Capitoli* 5 ['*Caleffetto*'], ff. 127r-130r). The inclusion of copies of general privileges of the *Studio* in books that pertain only to a component of it is not unusual. One example is the statute-book of the Bolognese college of doctors, lawyers and advocates, which begins with a series of privileges to the *Studio*; TROMBETTI BUDRIESI, *Gli statuti del collegio dei dottori*, who comments (p. 2) that this is 'in ossequio allo spirito di una consolidata tradizione di autonomia universitaria'. Another is the post-republican statute-book of the Sienese college of doctors of law, which opens with the privilege of the emperor Charles IV of 1357 (*Studio* 40; on this document see below, pp. 199-201). But the case of *Mis.* 1 is slightly different, as this collection soon became the *de facto* book of measures regarding the whole *Studio*; see below, p. 26.

[133] This *ad hoc* agglomeration of measures in a book that began with the institution's statutes is nothing unusual. A close parallel is the statute book for the Sapienza's closest comparator, the Collegio Gregoriano or Sapienza Vecchia in Perugia; Biblioteca Augusta di Perugia, *ms.* 1239, on which see below, pp. 326 *seq*.

[134] They are:
1) BCS, *ms.* C.IV.26, a manuscript copied by Sestigiani for the *erudito* Uberto Benvoglienti (1668-1733), on which see CATONI, 'Genesi', pp. 171-2 n. 75.
2) ASS, *ms.* C.51, transcribed from C.IV.26 by Tommaso Mocenni, another priest who like Sestigiani worked for Bichi (see DE ANGELIS, *Biografia degli Scrittori Sanesi*, p. 131), in 1725. Mocenni's introduction confirms that Sestigiani was the copyist of *ms.* C.IV.26. Also from this year is the transcription of the bulls of Gregory XII and Pius II in ASS, *ms.* D.88, *Miscellanea di cose spettanti alla Città, e Stato di Siena*, ff. 51r-74r, made from 'un libro di Statuti, et Ordinamenti, et altro spettanti allo Spedale della Misericordia, Leggi Casa della Sapienza di Siena, il quale libro si conserva nell'Archivio della medesima', which I take to be C.IV.26.
2) *Mis.* 2, possibly transcribed by Santi Landi in 1776 (a note in *Mis.* 1, after f. 130v, attributes it to him, and the hand may well be his, but he only admits to the index; see C.51 *bis*, f. 13r). Textual evidence confirms this tradition, and also that *Mis.* 2 was copied from C.51.
Two of these copies were found in the Sapienza archive by Landi – one assumes the last two, as the first has ended up in the Biblioteca Comunale along with the original (see C.51 *bis*, f. 13r). One reason for the sequence of copies may be that *Mis.* 1 itself was moved at some stage to the archive of the hospital of S. Maria della Scala (according to C.IV.26, f. 161v, and C.51, front page; and cf. CATONI, loc. cit.). Sestigiani, who compiled the index now bound with the original as well as being the author of the copy in C.IV.26, omitted it from his *Repertorio di Strumenti Antichi della Sapienza*, compiled in 1695 (ASS, *ms.* B.82). It is not clear how it got there. G. PICCINNI, 'L'Ospedale di Santa Maria della Scala di Siena. Note sulle origini dell'assistenza sanitaria in Toscana (XIV-XV secolo)', in *Città e servizi sociali nell'Italia dei secoli XII-XV. Dodicesimo convegno di studi. Centro Italiano di Storia e d'Arte, Pistoia* (Pistoia, 1990), pp. 297-324 (p. 319) argued

fact used by Zdekauer and another by a more recent historian;[135] but lack of reference to the original meant that neither appears to have realised that it was a contemporary collection. What this demonstrates is that, along with the estate books of the old Casa della Misericordia, the statute book of the hospital was taken over as well, and was thereafter intended and regarded as the statute book of the Sapienza,[136] as the inscription on the last page, *liber capitulorum domus sapientie*, shows.[137]

The measures copied date from 1386 to 1521. A new book was called for in 1475,[138] but did not materialise until 1533,[139] after, mysteriously, the *Consiglio del Popolo* had granted the *Concistoro* and the *Savi* 'authoritatem reficiendi statuta et capitula Sapientie iam perdita'.[140] The differences in handwriting and the order of the documents show that it was not always filled in at the date of the respective measure, but that there was some backdating.[141] It is also clear that the collection is by no means exhaustive – for example, compilation was discontinued between 1425 and 1433. Nor do the contents amount to a major discovery, as most of the deliberations have always been available in the communal records (though they have never been used to the full), as well as in the three copies. The importance of the volume is rather the very fact of its existence, and the nature of the resolutions it contains. Though it began as the statute book of the Misericordia and then became that of the Sapienza, it soon came to incorporate the major communal legislation concerning the whole *Studio*. This is unsurprising; the jurisdiction of the *Savi* covered both, the Sapienza rapidly became the centre of the

that this indicated a close connection between the two institutions, a theme that is explored below, pp. 105-7; the only other relevant archival evidence I have found – and it is a straw in the wind – is a decision of 1519 by the *Savi dello Studio* to write to the rector and *Camarlengo* of the hospital asking them to return the account books of the Sapienza or face legal action (*Studio* 3, f. 2r, 5 Jan).

[135] MARRARA, *Lo Studio di Siena*, esp. pp. 92-102, used the second of these copies, ASS, *ms.* C.51, Zdekauer the first, BCS, *ms.* C.IV.26 (misquoting it as C.IV.6, p. 161; his comment on p. 162 makes it clear that he did not know or recognise *Mis.* 1 as the 'missing' original, which he describes as a *ms.* of the Scala). Apart from Barduzzi, who published the bulls (and recognised the volume for what it is; op. cit., p. 34), the first scholar to return to the original was Catoni who published ff. 47r-49v (CATONI, 'Genesi', pp. 177-82. See also his discussion of it, p. 171 n. 75). I have made use of all three copies as well as the original, but only refer to them where variants are significant.

[136] Cf. *Mis.* 1, f. 130v; cf. f. 105r, and *CG* 236, f. 127v, 28 Jun 1475, where a book was ordered 'perché li statuti d'essa casa sonno molti, et ordinati in diversi tempi, et con longhi Proemi che è tedio el leggerli, et sono implicati con quelli quando era Casa di Spedale' – which seems an apt description of *Mis.* 1. There are contemporary references to the volume; the compiler of *Mis.* 36 (1451) described it as the 'statutello rosso de la Casa' (see above, n. 130). However, the 1459 inventory of the college in *Studio* 128 (on which see below, pp. 384-6) lists 'un libricciuolo degli ordini de la Casa' that was kept in the sacristy of the chapel (f. 2r; ed. CATONI, 'Genesi', p. 188), a description which would appear to relate to a smaller volume.

[137] On 'constitutiones' as the standard Sienese term for statutes, see ASCHERI, *Siena e la città-stato*, pp. 68, 80.

[138] See n. 136 above.

[139] *Studio* 109, which however was also used, as was *Studio* 110 (1541) for the deliberations of the *Savi*; hence the discontinuity in the series of *deliberazioni dei Savi* (*Studio* 3 ends in 1530, *Studio* 4 records deliberations from mid-1534 to mid-1541, and *Studio* 5 resumes in 1549).

[140] *CG* 243, ff. 185v-186r, 28 Sept 1531; ed. KOŠUTA, 'Documenti', doc. I-1, p. 333. Košuta speculated (n. 2) that the statutes might have been destroyed in the fire to which the *Savi* allude in a letter of 28 Mar 1527 (*CG* 242, f. 187v, and *Conc.* 963, f. 18r-v), but this does not refer to the destruction of documents. It is therefore more likely that the statutes had been mislaid, or had already been transferred to the Scala (above, p. 25 n. 134). Košuta knew *Mis.* 1 but did not believe that they were the missing statutes (p. 489, n. 1). He also published (doc. XXII, loc. cit.) a fragment from the second half of the sixteenth century excerpting a measure from the 'Liber capitulorum vel statutorum Sapientie' which he dated to the late fourteenth century by its content (it relates to the office of *Senator*), but which is clearly not referring to *Mis.* 1.

[141] Witness not least the fact that the volume contains measures pertaining to the *Studio* of 1387; and see below, pp. 340 n. 13 and p. 346 n. 75. There must however have been periods when the transcription was made almost immediately. A *Consiglio del Popolo* measure of 10 May 1437 was amended by the *Concistoro* on 27 May, but the transcribed version does not take account of this (*CG* 219, ff. 136v-137v, 10 May; *Conc.* 428, ff. 16v-17r, 27 May 1437; *Mis.* 1, ff. 83r-85r).

Studio, and by the mid-fifteenth century the two terms are often used in formulaic conjunction or even interchanged.[142] The contents of this statute book is demonstration of both the integral role of the Sapienza in the *Studio*, and the extent to which both were directed and controlled by the city's authorities.

f. *Other institutions*

The *Studio* had a sometimes contentious relationship with the hospital of S. Maria della Scala, and also with the clergy, since both were ordered to subsidise it in the late fourteenth century and reluctantly continued to do so into the fifteenth. Its relationship with the hospital was more complex, operating as it did on several levels.[143] The deliberations of its chapter, and a number of estate books, have been examined to this end, as have some of the records of other hospitals and pious institutions. More detailed investigation of ecclesiastical sources would undoubtedly be profitable.

g. *Other universities*

The intensely competitive nature of the Italian university system means that a full consideration of the history of any one *Studio* must entail reference to the records of its rivals. This has been a particular feature of the research for this book, not least as it took place alongside research on the system as a whole. No claim is laid to comprehensiveness, but the main published sources for Bologna, Perugia, Florence, Pisa, Padua, Pavia, Ferrara and Rome have been consulted amongst others, and in a few cases archival material has also been quoted. Comparisons of practice are not just of interest to today's scholars; they were frequently being made by the university administrators of the time.[144] Aside from this the most direct relevance of such use of the records of other *studi* is to fill in the details of the many teachers and students whose careers were peripatetic.

h. *Miscellaneous*

Beyond the institutional sources discussed above, a number of other series and types of material should briefly be mentioned.

---

[142] See below, pp. 80 and 339 n. 7. Perhaps typical of the confusion in the minds of both contemporaries and subsequent archivists is the fact that a booklet in *Not.* 858, published by MINNUCCI, 'Documenti', docs. II-20 to II-30, pp. 88-97, is entitled 'Bastardello dell'offitio della Sapientia per uno anno', whereas it is in fact that great rarity, the record of the notary of the student university, Ser Feliciano di Ser Neri (see above, pp. 22-3).

[143] See below, pp. 105-7.

[144] An unusually detailed example is the summary of Sapienza practice made for the Florentine/Pisan authorities in the late fifteenth century; Archivio di Stato di Firenze, *Studio Fiorentino e Pisano, 1357-1568* (formerly *Repubblica: Ufficiali dello Studio*) 7, ff. 67r-72v, ed. A. VERDE, *Lo Studio fiorentino 1473-1503* (5 vols., Florence and Pistoia, 1973-94), V, pp. 44-48, dating it to 1487 by connecting it with a deliberation of that year by the *Ufficiali dello Studio* 'quod provisor eat Senas ad videndum Sapientiam et sumendum capitula ut nunc sit exemplum et ad videndum facultatem [...]' (p. 44). The summary reveals practices not known otherwise through surviving documentation. KOŠUTA, 'Documenti', p. 323, was thus not right to dismiss this document as 'senza grande interesse'.

i) The *Fondo diplomatico* of the Archivio di Stato contains a great variety of documents, private letters, contracts etc. I have made use of it where the various *spogli* have indicated specific references to the *Studio*.

ii) Reference has already been made to the notarial series (*Notarile ante-cosimiano*). A pragmatic rather than an exhaustive approach has been taken here. Minnucci's researches have shown just how valuable these volumes can be, but my choice among the nine hundred or so volumes covering the period 1357 to 1500 has been dictated by the confines of the topic; apart from some preliminary random sampling, I have examined only the records of those notaries who are known to have had some formal connection with the *Studio* or one of its components. There can be no doubt that a full trawl would yield a great deal more information about individual members of the *Studio*.

iii) Private archives undoubtedly contain material relating to the *Studio*. Here I have only followed references given by previous scholars.

iv) A number of references to the *Studio* have come to light in 'literary' sources, be they letters of students, the testimony of teachers, the evidence of chroniclers and historians, or even the popular image of the Sapienza as presented in literary works. These have been acknowledged and used where appropriate, but I do not claim to have investigated them systematically.

PART ONE
COMMUNE AND *STUDIO*

I

ORIGINS AND GROWTH

1. *The* Studio *to 1357*

The obscurity in which the origins of the Sienese *Studio* are wrapped is not unusual, any more than is the way in which the evidence (or lack of it) has been used by successive generations of scholars in the service of the historiography of the moment.[1] The author of the first scholarly monograph on the *Studio*, Lodovico Zdekauer, suggested great similarities with the spontaneous growth of Bologna. He held that the cathedral and lay schools of the eleventh and twelfth centuries, and the tradition of law teaching in particular, crystallised in an attempt at organisation with the self-assertion of the commune in the thirteenth.[2] But the stimulus to such organisation was of course competition; and it is no accident that the first regular notices of teachers date from the 1240s, when the emperor Frederick II was trying to discredit and weaken the Bolognese *Studio*.[3] Siena, like Bologna, was able to take advantage of the papal-imperial struggles to obtain assistance from both the supreme authorities for their own enterprise. In 1246 King Frederick of Antioch, the illegitimate son of Frederick II and his vicar in Tuscany, forbade the Sienese to study at Bologna, and the commune immediately sent out messages to Bologna recalling the Sienese contingent there, as well as inviting students from all over Tuscany to

[1] P. NARDI, 'Introduzione ad una ricerca sulle origini dello Studio di Siena', *Studi senesi*, 94 (1982), pp. 348-61. The long tradition of higher education in Siena, and the history of the *Studio* up to its official recognition as a *studium generale* in 1357, are the subjects of NARDI, *Insegnamento*; see also IDEM, 'Comune, Impero e Papato'. Other works on this period include ZDEKAUER, *Origini*, and PRUNAI, I; see also H. DENIFLE, *Die Entstehung der Universitäten des Mittelalters bis 1400* (Berlin, 1885), pp. 429-46. The majority of the documents that have come to light for the period were published in *Chartularium*; see also some additions by NARDI, *Insegnamento*, Appendice, pp. 215-40.

[2] ZDEKAUER, *Origini*, esp. pp. 8-12. 'Lo Studio non è uscito dalla scuola ecclesiastica medioevale, nè dalla scuola notarile: la libertà politica lo ha creato, riassumendo le tradizioni di tutte e due, e gli ha impresso un carattere nuovo' (p. 14); 'La libertà Senese e lo Studio generale della città hanno origine comune' (p. 9).

[3] PRUNAI, I, p. 60; NARDI, *Insegnamento*, pp. 53-6; IDEM, 'Comune, Impero e Papato', pp. 51-2, and pp. 55-8 esp. on Frederick's academic policy generally. This is not the place to rehearse the many and much-debated aspects of Frederick II's attitude to universities, his foundation of the University of Naples and the conflicts with Bologna; but for broad overviews see esp. J. VERGER, 'La politica universitaria di Federico II nel contesto europeo', in *Federico II e le città italiane*, eds. P. Toubert and A. Paravicini Bagliani (Palermo, 1991), pp. 129-43; and cf. F. BRUNI, 'Provocazioni sulla politica culturale di Federico II', in *Nel segno di Federico II. Unità politica e pluralità culturale del Mezzogiorno*. Atti del IV Convegno Internazionale di Studi della Fondazione Napoli Novantanove (Napoli, 30 settembre-1 ottobre 1988) (Naples, 1989), pp. 93-109; repr. in his *Testi e chierici del Medioevo* (Genoa, 1991), pp. 71-89 (esp. pp. 74-5).

the new *Studio*.[4] In 1250 the salaries to be paid to the teachers were laid down in the statutes of the commune.[5] In 1252 Siena was reconciled with Innocent IV, who granted to the 'universitas magistrorum et doctorum Senis regentium ac ipsorum scolarium ibidem degentium' exemptions from all communal taxation and military service, and appointed the bishop as conservator of the privilege.[6] In 1262 and 1274 there were further privileges in the communal statutes; exemptions for specific teachers as well as for any masters of grammar at Bologna who were willing to defect to Siena, and safeguards for teachers and scholars alike.[7]

Then in 1275, five years after the Guelph assumption of power and in a year of increased teaching activity, there is a communal measure that has caused much controversy. On 18 July of that year the *Consiglio Generale*, the town's supreme legislative body, passed a resolution 'super habendo, reducendo et fundando generali studio licterarum in civitate Senarum', guaranteeing the safety of all students, providing for the salaries of teachers and setting up a body of *sapientes* to supervise the running of the *Studio* and to safeguard the interests of its members.[8] For the nineteenth-century students of the constitutional history of universities this was a unique event. Denifle wrote: 'Diese Beschlüsse der Commune von Siena bilden ein einzigartiges Factum in der Geschichte der mittelalterlichen, speciell der italienischen Universitäten.'[9] For Rashdall,

> The attempt of the city in 1275 to erect a *studium* by a distinct executive and legislative act represents the first attempt of the kind in the history of the Italian city-republics; and it remains the only instance (except in the early secessions from Bologna) in which the attempt was made without any effort or intention to apply for a Bull of erection.[10]

How singular was this resolution? The use of the word 'reducere' may not be that significant;[11]

---

[4] *Chartularium*, docs. 3 and 4, p. 6, Aug-Sept 1246. King Enzo was also involved in the campaign. The invitation was repeated in 1248 (doc. 5, p. 7, Sept), 1249 (doc. 6, p. 7, Sept) and 1264 (doc. 15, p. 12, Nov). See also NARDI, *Insegnamento*, p. 60, and ZDEKAUER, *Origini*, p. 16.

[5] *Chartularium*, doc. 8, p. 8, June; cf. ZDEKAUER, *Origini*, p. 17, and NARDI, *Insegnamento*, p. 60. The payments, in the Biccherna records, are 'secundum formam capituli constituti'.

[6] *Chartularium*, doc. 10, pp. 9-10, 29 Nov; also ed. DENIFLE, *Entstehung*, p. 430 n. 868; and cf. R. DAVIDSOHN, 'Documenti del 1240 e del 1251 relativi allo Studio Senese', *BSSP*, 7 (1900), pp. 168-70. It is also now reproduced in facsimile in *L'Università di Siena. 750 anni*, p. 11. Neither the *Chartularium* nor Denifle included the last line which appoints the bishop as conservator. See also NARDI, *Insegnamento*, pp. 63-6, and IDEM, 'Dalle origini al 1357', p. 9.

[7] *Chartularium*, docs. 13-14, pp. 10-11 (1262) and 21, pp. 13-15 (1274); ZDEKAUER, p. 24 and in IDEM, *Il Constituto del Comune di Siena*, p. 410. The 1262 privileges for 'magister Tebaldus' were granted 'quia vituperium est comuni et populo quod Ar[e]tini ipsium civem nostrum tenent in eorum terra' (*Chartularium*, p. 11). The 1274 measures again came at a moment of crisis in the Bolognese *Studio*, which resulted in migrations to Padua and Paris, on which see now G. MILANI, 'La memoria dei *rumores*. I disordini bolognesi del 1274 nel ricordo delle prime generazioni: note preliminari', in *Le storie e la memoria. In onore di Arnold Esch*, eds. R. Delle Donne and A. Zorzi (Florence, 2002), pp. 271-93. For this period generally see NARDI, *Insegnamento*, pp. 67-73.

[8] *Chartularium*, doc. 24, pp. 16-9, 18-20 July; also DENIFLE, *Entstehung*, p. 431 n. 871. See PRUNAI, I, pp. 66-7; ZDEKAUER, *Origini*, p. 19.

[9] DENIFLE, *Entstehung*, p. 433; words taken over almost verbatim by Zdekauer: 'Questa deliberazione costituisce un fatto unico nella storia delle Università medioevali' (loc. cit.). On Denifle's connections with Italian scholars, NARDI, 'Introduzione', pp. 353-55.

[10] RASHDALL, II, p. 34. As MINNUCCI, 'Rassegna bibliografica', p. 432, has pointed out, Rashdall's account derives largely from that of Denifle.

[11] M. BELLOMO, 'Scuole giuridiche e università studentesche in Italia', in *Luoghi e metodi di insegnamento nell'Italia medioevale (secoli XII-XIV)*, eds. L. Gargan and O. Limone (Galatina, Lecce, 1989), pp. 121-40 (pp. 131-2) argues (in the context of the foundation of the University of Naples) that 'reducere' can be understood as similar to 'ordinare', without implying the previous existence of the institution. This is also the view of G. M. VARANINI, 'Come si progetta uno *Studium*

however, an assessment is complicated by the fact that the measure speaks of 'etiam constitutiones factas ab imperatore super facto Studii Generalis'. From this phrase derives the tradition, which reappears in the fourteenth century and is followed by seventeenth- and eighteenth-century Sienese writers, of some sort of imperial blessing for the *Studio* dating back to Frederick II.[12] The Risorgimento historian Carpellini, who found both the 1246 and the 1275 documents, took a less obvious line. Reading 'etiam' in the phrase quoted above as 'contra', he saw the Sienese as rebelling against an unknown imperial instruction, and used the point as evidence for his thesis of the independent and indigenous origins of the Sienese *Studio*, as he argued for others in Italy.[13] The major scholars of the late nineteenth century who wrote on the subject, Denifle and Zdekauer, adopted Carpellini's mis-reading without question, and Siena's reputation for uniqueness has therefore not a little to do with paleographical error. Even Barduzzi, who corrected the reading, did not appreciate its significance and continued to adhere to the 'independence' theory.[14]

An opposing view, equally favourable to Siena although in a different way (stressing the *Studio*'s antiquity and pedigree rather than its originality), was put by Sanesi in 1901 in a review of Barduzzi's work.[15] Sanesi interpreted the phrase to mean that there had already been an imperial foundation, probably of 1240 and by implication preceding even the first document referring to communally-paid teachers in Siena, dated 26 December 1240.[16] The 'lost charter' theory did not gain immediate acceptance – the finder of the 1240 document, Davidsohn, did not agree with it – but in due course it was elaborated by Prunai,[17] who posited a charter of 1245/6, which he thought might have been lost or destroyed during the upheavals of 1269-70 when the Guelphs came to power.[18] The belief was taken up by the authoritative writers on Bologna, De Vergottini and Rossi, in the 1950s, and thus became elevated to the status of a tradition.[19]

Much of the argument for a lost charter is circular. The unilateral gesture posited by advocates of the 'independent foundation' theory could not have happened, therefore it did not happen; such a foundation had so little hope of survival that it would not have been contemplated; and neither Enzo nor Frederick of Antioch could conceivably have encouraged students to leave Bologna for a centre which did not have the status of *studium generale*.[20] It is a view which already by the early fourteenth

generale. Università, società, comune cittadino a Treviso (1314-1318)', in *L'Università medievale di Treviso* (Treviso, 2000), pp. 11-46 (p. 18), discussing a very similar Trevisan resolution of 1263 or earlier, 'super studio scolarium in civitat Tarvisii reducendo et perseverando' (p. 17).

[12] For this whole issue, see NARDI, 'Introduzione ad una ricerca'.

[13] CARPELLINI, *Sulla origine nazionale*, esp. pp. 65-70.

[14] NARDI, 'Introduzione ad una ricerca', pp. 353-7.

[15] G. SANESI, 'Rassegna bibliografica dei documenti per la storia della Università di Siena', *Archivio Storico Italiano*, ser. 5, 27 (1901), pp. 376-87.

[16] Ibid., pp. 382, 385.

[17] PRUNAI, I, pp. 60-7.

[18] Ibid., p. 65.

[19] G. DE VERGOTTINI, 'Lo Studio di Bologna, l'Impero, il Papato', in *Studi e Memorie per la storia dell' Università di Bologna*, n.s., 1 (1956), pp. 19-95, repr. in his *Scritti di storia del diritto italiano*, ed. G. Rossi. Seminario giuridico della Università di Bologna, 74 (Milan, 1977), vol. II, pp. 695-792; G. ROSSI, '"Universitas scholarium" e Comune', in *Studi e Memorie per la storia dell'Università di Bologna*, n.s., 1 (1956), pp. 173-266; on these see also NARDI, 'Introduzione ad una ricerca', pp. 348-9. De Vergottini promised a full study on the origins of the Sienese *Studio*, which did not materialise (NARDI, loc. cit.).

[20] PRUNAI, I, pp. 63-4. King Enzo was Leicht's candidate for the authorship of the 'lost charter'; P. S. LEICHT, 'Discorso inaugurale per l'inizio del VIII centenario della R. Università', in *Senarum universitatis...ineunte octavo vitae suae saeculo* (Siena, 1942), p. 35.

century would have been entirely plausible, and indeed the strongest evidence for such a belief is not the 1275 document, which could be referring to the emperor Frederick Barbarossa's Authentic *Habita*,[21] but a resolution of the *Concistoro* on 31 December 1347 which mentions

> privilegia contenta in scripta domini Frederigi, videlicet quod prohibiti audire iura civilia possint illa au-dire; et quod venientes ad Studium Senense et inde recedentes non pregraventur, et cetera. Ista duo privi-legia, si possibile erit, etiam habeantur…[22]

It is hard not to see the 'lost charter' view as suffering from an excess of constitutionalism. Howev-er much scholars have speculated, no actual bull of foundation from this period has ever been un-earthed, and the only evidence for it is still the 1246 document, which in time clearly came to form the basis of a tradition of imperial intervention and allowed the Sienese to claim not only a degree of antiquity but the right to 're-establish' something that they believed had existed.[23] Even that process is elusive, but one original and important point has come out of this sometimes arid *querelle*. Paolo Nar-di's investigation of the issue led him to a detailed examination of the changing significance of the concept of *studium generale* in the thirteenth century as articulated by the pre-eminent lawyers of the age, and he has given us a much clearer picture of it.[24] From this crucial work it emerges that the term

---

[21] NARDI, *Insegnamento*, p. 72. The Authentic has inevitably been studied exhaustively, most authoritatively by W. STELZER, 'Zum Scholarenprivileg Friedrich Barbarossas (Authentica 'Habita')', *Deutsches Archiv fur Erforschung des Mittelal-ters*, 34 (1978), pp. 123-65, who has shown that it dates from 1155 and not 1158 as has often been maintained (pp. 124-5, 146-53); though K. ZEILLINGER, 'Das erste roncaglische Lehensgesetz Friedrich Barbarossas, das Scholarenprivileg (Authen-tica Habita) und Gottfried von Viterbo', *Römische Historische Mitteilungen*, 26 (1984), pp. 191-217 dates it one year earlier, attributing it to the Diet of Roncaglia.

[22] *Chartularium*, doc. 403, pp. 526-8 (p. 528); previously published by ZDEKAUER, pp. 139-40 (p. 140); see NARDI, 'Comune', p. 68, who also explains the superiority of Zdekauer's transcription (the one quoted here). This reference could certainly not be to the Authentic *Habita*, which famously did not mention any specific *studio*; on the other hand it might be construed as referring to Frederick of Antioch rather than Frederick II. Cf. also NARDI, *Insegnamento*, pp. 207-8.

[23] One might add that the bolstering of the belief in an older authority is not unknown at the time. After all, Bologna's reaction to growing competition in the 1220s, with a secession to Padua in 1222 and then the emperor Freder-ick II's foundation of the University of Naples in 1224, included the forging of the so-called 'Privilegio Teodosiano', giv-ing the University an imperial foundation charter dating back to 423AD. This and an additional 'notitia' were used for-mally by the commune of Bologna in 1271. See esp. G. FASOLI and G. B. PIGHI, 'Il privilegio teodosiano. Edizione criti-ca e commento', *Studi e memorie per la storia dell'Università di Bologna*, n.s., 2 (1961), pp. 55-94; G. FASOLI, 'Il falso privilegio di Teodorico II per lo Studio di Bologna', in *Fälschungen im Mittelalter. Internationaler Kongreß der Monumen-ta Germaniae Historica, München, 16. – 19. September 1986. Teil I: Kongreßdaten und Festvorträge, Literatur und Fälschung*. Monumenta Germaniae Historica, Schriften, 33.i (Hannover, 1988), pp. 627-41, and EADEM, 'La compo-sizione del falso diploma Teodosiano', *Studi e memorie per la storia dell'Università di Bologna*, n.s. 3 (1961), pp. 77-94, repr. in her *Scritti di storia medievale*, eds. F. Bocchi, A. Carile and A. I. Pini (Bologna, 1974), pp. 583-608; A. I. PINI, 'Federico II, lo Studio di Bologna e il "Falso Teodosiano"', in *Federico II e Bologna*. Deputazione di Storia Patria per le Province di Romagna: Documenti e Studi, 27 (Bologna, 1996), pp. 27-60, repr. in *Il pragmatismo degli intellettuali. Origini e primi sviluppi dell'istituzione universitaria*, ed. R. Greci (Turin, 1996), pp. 67-89; more generally cf. A. L. GABRIEL, 'Translatio Studii. Spurious Dates of Foundation for some Early Universities', in *Fälschungen im Mittelalter*, pp. 601-26, and now C. F. WEBER, 'Ces grands privilèges: The Symbolic Use of Written Documents in the Foundation and Institutionalization Processes of Medieval Universities', *History of Universities*, 19/1 (2004), pp. 12-62 (esp. pp. 23-29). This last writer stresses (pp. 23-24) that the practice of founding universities by bull or charter dates only from the early thirteenth century (Naples 1224, Toulouse 1233), and coexists with the process of retrospective validation of older insti-tutions. It could be argued that the aspiration to found a local university without prior licence, although unusual, was thus not unprecedented.

[24] P. NARDI, 'Le origini del concetto di "Studium generale"', *Rivista internazionale di diritto comune*, 3 (1992), pp. 47-78; also in *L'università e la sua storia*, pp. 29-58. The original pagination is referred to here. That this work grew out of his Sienese investigations is made clear at the end of his 'Introduzione' (1982), p. 360.

was barely in currency among civilians before 1240;[25] that the use of *studium* among canonists before that time was far more geared to the concept of study than to the institutions at which it took place;[26] that the use of the term *studium generale* indicating an institution was applied to schools of theology before acquiring a secular aspect;[27] and that when it did begin to be used to denote what we call universities, in the mid-to-late 1240s, the term is found in papal, not imperial, documents, and without being defined.[28] To an extent these conclusions render the hunt for a mythical and lost imperial charter for a *studium generale* in Siena superfluous and even anachronistic. The reason the – much less formal – imperial action of 1246 had to be invested retrospectively with such significance is rather that by 1275 such definitions did matter in a way that they had not in 1246. Nardi also argued that the Sienese institution fell into an intermediate category, between internationally accepted *studia generalia* on the one hand and *studia* in places that were not cities on the other.[29]

Nardi's observations take the matter as far as it can usefully be taken. His conclusions are in tune with, and fill in the detail for, Rashdall's instinctive verdict on the 1275 document that 'the necessity of a foundation-Bull was at this time not sufficiently recognised to prevent the attempt being made; but it was becoming too well-established for the attempt to succeed.'[30] And of course it was no surprise to either Rashdall or Denifle, given the constitutionalist approach that they shared, that the attempt was a failure. Denifle was one of many to emphasise that it was this lack of a charter that continued to bedevil every initiative of this *Studio* until 1357.[31] The problem of recognition – and in particular the absence of authority to award the *licentia ubique docendi*, an increasingly significant factor[32] – dominated its history until 1357.

For four and a half decades after the 1275 resolution there are modest but frequent notices regarding education in Siena: salary payments for around six, sometimes as many as ten, teachers a year,[33] ranging from 10 to 58 *lire* per annum,[34] and various redactions of the statutes which amplified the privileges of 1274.[35] There is a degree of stability, but nothing to suggest that the *Studio* had signifi-

---

[25] NARDI, 'Le origini del concetto di "Studium generale"', pp. 52-3.

[26] Ibid., pp. 54-68.

[27] Ibid., pp. 71-2.

[28] Ibid., pp. 72-4. On the fluidity of the term in this period see also P. NARDI, 'Dalle *Scholae* allo *Studium generale*: la formazione delle università medievali', in *Studi di storia del diritto medioevale e moderno*, ed. F. Liotta (Bologna, 1999), pp. 1-32, esp. pp. 20-32; and IDEM, '*Licentia ubique docendi* e Studio generale nel pensiero giuridico del secolo XIII', *Studi senesi*, 112 (2000), pp. 554-65, and in *A Ennio Cortese*. Scritti promossi da D. Maffei e raccolti a cura di I. Birocchi, M. Caravale, E. Conte and V. Petronio, II (Rome, 2001), pp. 471-77.

[29] NARDI, *Insegnamento*, pp. 13-14, and also 60-61.

[30] RASHDALL, II, p. 33.

[31] DENIFLE, *Entstehung*, p. 431.

[32] This aspect in particular is stressed by NARDI, *Insegnamento*, pp. 95 and 148-50.

[33] This puts the Sienese operation in this period within the second half of Grendler's arbitrary but workable definition of an Italian university as 'a teaching institution that awarded doctorates and had a minimum of six to eight professors'; GRENDLER, *Universities of the Italian Renaissance*, p. 5.

[34] The most common salary was 25 *lire*, which became the statutory norm for teachers of law. *Chartularium*, doc. 61, pp. 41-3 (1286 statutes), esp. pp. 42-3; cf. NARDI, *Insegnamento*, p. 85; and PRUNAI, I, p. 76.

[35] Published in *Chartularium*, docs. 61, pp. 41-3 (1286); 64, pp. 45-8 (1287); 68, pp. 50-2 (1288); 91, pp. 64-6 (1295); 94, pp. 68-70 (1296); 96-7, pp. 71-7 (1300-2); and 125, pp. 103-6 (1309-10), for which see also M. S. ELSHEIKH (ed.), *Il costituto del Comune di Siena volgarizzato nel MCCCIX-MCCCX* (Siena, 2002), dist. I, cap. 95 (vol. I, pp. 94-5), dist. IV, caps. 13-19 (vol. II, pp. 167-70). Cf. NARDI, *Insegnamento*, pp. 85 and 91-2; PRUNAI, I, p. 78, DENIFLE, *Entstehung*, p. 437.

cantly more than a local 'catchment area'.[36] However that certainly did not mean that Sienese academic activity was conducted in isolation. For much of the second half of the thirteenth century, and beyond, Sienese students and teachers continued regularly to frequent other *studi*, notably Bologna, but also Arezzo;[37] and the traffic (of teachers, at least) was in both directions.[38] Of the non-Sienese teachers who are found in Siena for varying periods of time,[39] few appear to have been top-flight;[40] in the thirteenth century the only scholar of truly international repute whose teaching in Siena can be established is the medical scholar Petrus Hispanus, later to become pope John XXI.[41] Yet the almost continuous presence of non-Sienese teachers, together with the activity of Sienese teachers elsewhere, had a significant influence both on intellectual traditions in Siena and on Sienese aspirations for a fully-fledged *studio*.[42] Contacts with the main academic centres can be said to have whetted the appetite at the periphery, a process that can be seen with increasing clarity in the opening years of the fourteenth century.[43]

[36] A statute of 1286 (*Chartularium*, doc. 61, pp. 41-3) which exempted grammar teachers 'qui tent scholares et docent scholares et morantur cum scholaribus in hospitio' from night-watch duties in wartime implies the presence of non-citizen students, but these may well have been from the *contado* (cf. NARDI, *Insegnamento*, p. 85). Zdekauer considered it unlikely that there were *scholares forenses* in Siena before 1321 as the phrase does not occur (p. 9). He may be right for the late thirteenth century (though there is evidence of the presence of foreign scholars in 1240; NARDI, 'Comune', p. 62). However, there is also clear evidence, if not incontrovertible proof, of the presence of foreign students in 1306 (NARDI, *Insegnamento*, p. 101).

[37] For example, the well-known case of Tebaldo, a Sienese grammarian, who taught in Siena in the 1240s, left for the revived *Studio* of Arezzo by 1251 (along with several Sienese students), but returned in the 1260s to teach for a further period. NARDI, *Insegnamento*, pp. 52-3, 60, 66, 67-70, IDEM, 'Comune', pp. 82-4, and IDEM, 'Dalle origini', p. 10; *Chartularium*, docs. 2, 5, 13, 15, 17-21, 25, 26; P. R. DENLEY, 'Governments and Schools in Late Medieval Italy', in *City and Countryside*, pp. 93-108 (p. 96). On Tebaldo and more generally on the relationship between the *Studi* of Siena and Arezzo in the thirteenth century, H. WIERUSZOWSKI, 'Arezzo as a Centre of Learning', *Traditio*, 9 (1953), pp. 321-91, repr. in her *Politics and Culture in Medieval Spain and Italy* (Rome, 1971), pp. 387-474 (esp. pp. 415-18); and more generally R. BLACK, *Studio e scuola in Arezzo durante il medioevo e il Rinascimento* (Arezzo, 1996), pp. 99-108. Sienese students were particularly in evidence in Bologna in the 1260s (NARDI, *Insegnamento*, pp. 67-70), and in 1301 a Sienese, Fredo Tolomei, became rector of the citramontane law university (ibid., p. 95); for details, see P. ROSSI, 'Fredo Tolomei rettore della Università dei legisti citramontani dello Studio bolognese nel 1301. Documenti e notizie', *Studi senesi*, suppl. to 5 (1888), pp. 187-204.

[38] Examples are the grammarians Guidotto da Bologna, hired and paid for teaching in 1278 and again in 1281 and 1282 (NARDI, *Insegnamento*, pp. 74-6; *Chartularium*, docs. 30, 32-3, 42, 44, 48); Bandino d'Arezzo, who taught in Siena almost continuously from 1287 to 1296 and again from 1302 to 1308 (NARDI, *Insegnamento*, pp. 88-90 and 97-8; *Chartularium*, docs. 65, 67, 70, 72, 74, 76-7, 79-82, 86-7, 89, 93; DENLEY, 'Governments and Schools', p. 96. His son took over his teaching); and Guicciardo di Bondo of Bologna, who taught there from 1306 to about 1311 and again in 1314-5 (NARDI, *Insegnamento*, pp. 103-4; *Chartularium*, docs. 107, 109-110, 116, 122, 128-9, 131-2, 134-5).

[39] Other foreign teachers in the period include the philosopher Nicholaus 'de Anglia' (1278-82: see NARDI, *Insegnamento*, pp. 76-7; *Chartularium*, docs. 30-1, 34-5, 38-9, 45-6, 49), and another Englishman, the grammarian Giovanni (1297-1301 – the only teacher on the payroll at the time; NARDI, *Insegnamento*, p. 92; *Chartularium*, doc. 95, pp. 70-1, 28 Nov 1298).

[40] Suggestions that the famed Bolognese rhetorician Guido Faba taught in Siena in the 1240s are not proven (NARDI, *Insegnamento*, pp. 63-5 for a review of the issue); likewise the sixteenth-century lawyer Diplovatatius's claims that the famous jurists Jacopo di Belviso and Oldrado da Ponte taught in Siena in the early fourteenth century have not been substantiated (NARDI, *Insegnamento*, pp. 98-9).

[41] He taught in Siena at some stage between 1245 and 1250. See NARDI, *Insegnamento*, pp. 56-8, 60-62 and 77-8 on his relations with Siena and for references to the copious literature.

[42] The relative paucity of expert teachers should not, of course, be taken to suggest that Siena was short of professional men in the areas traditionally covered by higher education. Tax records of 1285 indicate the presence of fifteen judges and seventeen doctors, and no fewer than ninety-seven notaries; WALEY, *Siena and the Sienese*, p. 18 (and pp. 86-8 on the status of lawyers). The figures given for 1311 in the anonymous 'Arti esercitate in Siena nel 1311', *Miscellanea storica senese*, 4 (1896), pp. 57-9, giving eleven judges, twenty doctors and only thirty-two notaries, may not be reliable.

[43] The interdict placed on Bologna in 1306 led to a minor exodus which brought the eminent medical doctor Dino del Garbo of Florence to Siena, together with his colleague Braccino da Pistoia and a number of scholars (NARDI, *Insegnamento*,

These contacts and relationships must have played a part in the sequence of events in 1321 that was temporarily to lift the profile of Siena onto an altogether higher level. In March of that year a student, Jacopo of Valencia, was executed at Bologna for the attempted abduction of the daughter of a notary, and the students who had been his accomplices – the incident had escalated into a substantial 'town-gown' brawl – were severely punished. Outraged at the breach of their privileges, the majority of teachers and students left in protest for Imola, there to be courted by various towns wishing to play host to Italy's most important *studio*.[44] Siena was not the most obvious candidate, but a plausible one given its long history of higher education and the contacts between it and Bologna. The commune spared no pains at this unique opportunity. On 8 May the *Consiglio Generale* voted to raise 6,000 florins for the enterprise.[45] The next day 500 florins were assigned for the expenses and clothing of the rector, and the costs of transporting the books and other possessions of scholars.[46] By 11 May, 4,000 florins had been raised, and it was decided that the remaining 2,000 were to be supplied from the coffers of the *Biccherna*, the chief financial office of the commune.[47] The communal records for the months that followed are dense with measures, large and small, testifying to the scale of the enterprise and the vigour and attention to detail with which it was pursued. Ambassadors were sent all over Italy to announce the move, while pressure appears to have been put on Florence to dissuade it from pressing its own candidature for the transfer.[48] Privileges equal to those of the citizens of Siena (and in some cases even superior to them) were granted to all teachers and scholars who decided to come,[49] and considerable effort and intrigue was applied to the problems of what could be

pp. 99-103. Dino stayed for at least three years). The following decade also saw the involvement with Siena of one of the most distinguished lawyers and intellectuals of the age, Cino da Pistoia, who briefly became a communal official. The contacts forged between eminent lawyers and the Sienese 'establishment' proved important foundations for the future of the *Studio* (NARDI, *Insegnamento*, p. 109).

[44] These included Padua, Perugia and Florence; see NARDI, 'Dalle origini', p. 14 and n. 30 for references. The definitive account is still F. FILIPPINI, 'L'esodo degli studenti da Bologna nel 1321 e il "Polifemio Dantesco"', *Studi e Memorie per la storia dell'Università di Bologna*, 6 (1921), pp. 105-85; see also A. FAVARO, 'Nuovi documenti intorno all'emigrazione dei professori e degli scolari dello Studio di Bologna nel 1321', *Atti e Memorie, R. Deputazione di Storia Patria per le Provincie di Romagna*, ser. 3, 10 (1892), pp. 313-23; on the Sienese angle, NARDI, *Insegnamento* (p. 113-50, with full bibliography), publishing some important new documents on the episode (Appendice, esp. docs. 2-8, pp. 218-30); BANCHI, 'Alcuni documenti'; and PRUNAI, II, pp. 8-17.

[45] *Chartularium*, doc. 150, pp. 128-33, 8 May; NARDI, *Insegnamento*, p. 115.

[46] *Chartularium*, doc. 151, pp. 133-6, 9 May; NARDI, *Insegnamento*, p. 116.

[47] *Chartularium*, doc. 152, pp. 136-8, 11 May; NARDI, loc. cit. BOWSKY, *Finance*, p. 300 gives the total Biccherna expenditure for 1321 as £165,030/15/2. At an exchange rate of £3/6/0 per florin (that used for the payment of teachers in the first half of 1322; *Chartularium*, doc. 174, pp. 207-8, 1 Jan – 4 Aug 1322) this means that the sums voted would have been constituted about 17% of the total expenditure for the year.

[48] This is how FILIPPINI, 'L'esodo', p. 128, interprets the report of the ambassadors to Imola mentioning the commune's order that Agnolo di Messer Grifolo attend the 'parlamento' summoned in Florence (*Chartularium*, doc. 157, pp. 155-7); cf. also E. SPAGNESI, 'I documenti costitutivi dalla provvisione del 1321 allo statuto del 1388', in *Storia dell'Ateneo Fiorentino. Contributi di Studio,* I (Florence, 1986), pp. 109-45. That the Bolognese crisis led to Florence's decision to open its *Studio* that year is undeniable, though it is also to be qualified by the growing evidence that the project had been brewing previously; see most recently P. FIORELLI, 'Una data per l'Università di Firenze', in *Le vie della ricerca. Studi in onore di Francesco Adorno*, ed. M. S. Funghi (Florence, 1996), pp. 491-6. For the context of the relations between Siena and Florence in matters of higher education policy P. R. DENLEY, 'Academic Rivalry and Interchange: the Universities of Siena and Florence', in *Florence and Italy. Renaissance Studies in Honour of Nicolai Rubinstein*, eds. P. R. Denley & C. M. Elam. Westfield Publications in Medieval Studies, 2 (London, 1989), pp. 193-208 (p. 194).

[49] NARDI, *Insegnamento*, p. 117; offences against members of the universities of law or medicine were to attract double the penalty that would have been due for those against a citizen. *Chartularium*, 154, pp. 143-6, 11 May 1321.

described as the medieval equivalent of a 'hostile takeover'; the acquisition of books which the commune of Bologna was trying to impound[50] (many in retaliation for debts that migrant scholars had run up in Bologna),[51] and attempts to persuade those who had remained in Bologna to join the tide of defectors.[52]

By the second half of 1321 the initiative appeared crowned with success. Along with Padua, Siena proved to be the main beneficiary of the Bolognese exodus; effectively a 'replica' of the *Studio* of Bologna was established.[53] In all, 2,600 florins were spent on the wage-bill for 1321-22; twenty-two teachers were appointed, at salaries frequently exceeding 200 florins.[54] The operation brought to Siena eminent teachers such as the lawyers Paolo dei Liazari of Bologna, Cino da Pistoia and Bonaccorso Bonaccorsi of Florence, and two of the greatest medical doctors of the day, Dino del Garbo of Florence (who had also taught there a few years earlier)[55] and Gentile da Foligno, as well as a substantial if unquantifiable student population, whose rights and interests were protected by the wholesale recognition and incorporation of the constitution of the student-universities. Yet the enterprise was short-lived. Two years later not much was left of it; the Bolognese had achieved a reconciliation, the masters and students had mostly returned,[56] and only a handful of teachers remained. Dino del Garbo, finishing his commentary on Avicenna in 1325, stated that he had begun it in Siena but finished it in Florence 'propter illius Studii diminutionem et annihilationem'.[57] The failure is no surprise to historians, nor would it have been to contemporaries. The poaching of a university had never entirely succeeded, and the *Studio* of Bologna, like those of Paris and Oxford, had survived showdowns more dramatic and long-lasting than the 1321 *migratio*.[58] The very autonomy of the *Studio*, guaranteed by the commune, had facilitated its return to Bologna,[59] but it could not have been otherwise; the masters and students would not have settled for anything less.

[50] NARDI, *Insegnamento*, 119-20; IDEM, 'Dalle origini', p. 16; *Chartularium*, doc. 157, pp. 155-7, 25 May 1321; PRUNAI, II, p. 12. See also E. MECACCI, 'Lo Studio e i codici', in C. BASTIANONI et al., *Lo Studio e i testi. Il libro universitario a Siena (secoli XII-XVII). Catalogo della mostra coordinato da Mario Ascheri, Siena, Biblioteca Comunale, 14 settembre – 31 ottobre 1996* (Siena, 1996), pp. 17-38 (pp. 23-24).

[51] NARDI, *Insegnamento*, pp. 123-4.

[52] NARDI, *Insegnamento*, p. 125; PRUNAI, II, p. 13.

[53] See below, pp. 250-1.

[54] The highest paid, the decretalist Paolo dei Liazari, was hired for 400 florins. The series of payments for the academic year 1321-22 is published in *Chartularium*, docs. 160-89, pp. 158-232 *passim*; for an analysis, NARDI, *Insegnamento*, pp. 126-9. Nardi's verdict on the efficacy of the operation was that 'Fu soprattutto l'impegno profuso dal governo dei Nove, risoltosi a retribuire alcui autorevoli maestri in modo adeguato ai loro meriti, a provocare una notevole fioritura delle scuole senesi' (p. 113).

[55] See above, n. 43.

[56] NARDI, *Insegnamento*, pp. 144-8; PRUNAI, II, pp. 14-15. On the Bolognese campaign to achieve a settlement see P. KIBRE, *Scholarly Privileges in the Middle Ages. The Rights, Privileges, and Immunities, of Scholars and Universities at Bologna, Padua, Paris, and Oxford* (London, 1962), pp. 35-6.

[57] NARDI, *Insegnamento*, p. 148 (and pp. 99-101, 169-71); N. SIRAISI, *Taddeo Alderotti and his Pupils. Two Generations of Italian Medical Learning* (Princeton, 1981), p. 58 (and on Dino more generally, pp. 55-64). Dino's remark is often repeated (e.g. ZDEKAUER, p. 13; DENIFLE, *Entstehung*, p. 490); but he had already left Siena before the academic year 1323-4.

[58] Elegantly summarised in E. BRAMBILLA, 'Genealogie del sapere. Per una storia delle professioni giuridiche nell'Italia padana (secoli XIV-XVI)', *Schifanoia*, 8 (1989), pp. 123-50, and in *Forme ed evoluzione del lavoro in Europa: XII-XVIII secc. Atti della 'Tredicesima Settimana di Studio', 2-7 maggio 1981*, ed. A. Guarducci. Istituto Datini di Prato (Florence, 1991), pp. 733-86 (p. 146 n. 14 of earlier version); and cf. DENLEY, 'Trasgressioni e rivolte studentesche', pp. 83-8.

[59] This is elaborated further below, pp. 250-1.

Fig. 1a – Funeral monument of Guglielmo di Ciliano and Niccolò Aringhieri da Casole, fourteenth century. Goro di Gregorio (Siena, University courtyard).

It is perhaps more fruitful to ask what consequences the episode had for Siena, and the answer is complex. Siena's brief experience of the academic limelight brought it contacts and connections which yielded lasting benefits to the city's own store of intellectual expertise and may have helped to focus that expertise on the *Studio* itself. In the short term the Bolognese *migratio* appears to have brought some Sienese lawyers into teaching or helped advance their university careers. Guglielmo da Ciliano, a judge who is recorded as having represented Siena on an embassy to Pisa in 1318, was already teaching in June 1321 and subsequently acted as replacement for two of the 'visiting' teachers until 1324, one at the full 'foreigner's' salary of 200 florins.[60] Neri Pagliaresi is also recorded as having been paid for lectures in June 1321, the first time, as far as can be seen, that a member of this prominent family, with a tradition of legal expertise, was engaged in teaching.[61] In the longer term, the involvement of

---

[60] Though little is known about his teaching activity, he was immortalised in the tomb by Goro di Gregorio that stands in the Rectorate of the University (Figs. 1a and 1b). R. BARTALINI, 'Goro di Gregorio e la tomba del giurista Guglielmo da Ciliano', *Prospettiva. Rivista di storia dell'arte antica e moderna*, 41 (1985), pp. 120-38, who discusses his teaching and publishes extracts of the relevant documents (pp. 26, 36); NARDI, *Insegnamento*, pp. 122 and n. 30, 153 n. 7 esp.; *Chartularium*, docs. as quoted in BARTALINI, cit.

[61] NARDI, *Insegnamento*, pp. 68 n. 4 (pointing out that there is no evidence that Jacopo Pagliaresi taught in the mid-thirteenth century), 122 n. 29; *Chartularium*, docs. 160, pp. 158-63, 6-30 Jun 1321 (p. 162), and 185, pp. 223-5, 30 Jun 1322 (p. 224).

Fig. 1b – Funeral monument of Guglielmo di Ciliano and Niccolò Aringhieri da Casole; detail.

eminent communal figures in the university, and of teachers in communal affairs, may have helped place the *Studio* at the centre of the town's intellectual life in a way that is not perceptible earlier.[62] But there must also have been an element of frustration that this growing expertise could not find a satisfactory domestic outlet. The careers of the two most notable Sienese lawyers of the day illustrate the point. Among the highest-paid teachers of 1321 – at 260 florins – was the Sienese canonist Federico Petrucci, who had studied at Bologna in the second decade of the century, and then taught there and at Padua.[63] He remained in Siena for a while after the exodus, although on a substantially reduced salary – 150 florins in the academic years 1324-5 and 1325-6, and as little as 150 *lire*, or about 40 florins, from 1327-8 to 1329-30. By 1333 he had unsurprisingly moved to Perugia, where his career flourished.[64] In the next generation Giovanni di Neri Pagliaresi's career shows a not dissimilar pattern. He is known to have been studying in Bologna in 1333, and first made a name for himself teaching at Perugia (from 1339). In that year the Sienese made strenuous efforts to coerce him into returning to teach, with diplomatic pressure on one hand and the threat of a huge fine on the other; he remained in Perugia and avoided the fine by getting his father Neri to accept the Sienese contract on his behalf, but it was another twenty years before he was persuaded to return.[65]

---

[62] See for example the much-debated question of intellectual influences on Ambrogio Lorenzetti's *Allegory of Good and Bad Government* in the Sala della Pace; below, p. 68 and n. 23; and NARDI, *Insegnamento*, p. 199 on this and on other instances of *Studio* teachers' involvement in government in the period.

[63] GLORIA, *Monumenti della Università di Padova (1222-1318)*, para. 414, p. 340.

[64] *Chartularium*, docs. 169-308, *passim*; P. NARDI, *Insegnamento*, pp. 161-3, and 190-1; IDEM, 'Contributo alla biografia di Federico Petrucci con notizie inedite su Cino da Pistoia e Tancredi da Corneto', *Scritti di storia del diritto offerti dagli allievi a Domenico Maffei*, ed. M. Ascheri. Medioevo e Umanesimo, 78 (Padua, 1991), pp. 153-80.

[65] NARDI, *Insegnamento*, pp. 122 and n. 29, 204 esp.; *Chartularium*, doc. 375, pp. 480-3, 27 Apr 1430; for a summary biography see MINNUCCI, 'Documenti', p. 275, and below, p. 174 n. 239.

Fig. 2a – Seal of Federico Petrucci, early fourteenth century (Arezzo, Museo statale di arte medioevale e moderna, inv. no. 16076).

Most of all, the experience of 1321 gave the Sienese renewed ambitions and stiffened their resolve to make a success of their *Studio*. The regime of the time was, after all, that of the *Nove*, whose art of government, patronage and urban renewal was as explicit and articulate at the time as it became legendary in posterity. A university for the education of its youth, for the enrichment of intellectual life and for the advancement of the international reputation of the city was considered as indispensable as the many other projects, spiritual and physical, with which the community was to be enhanced.[66] One factor in persuading the teachers and students to leave Siena in 1323 – though only one – had probably been the lack of official status of the Sienese *Studio*.[67] At any rate the commune perceived this to be the fundamental problem, and henceforward determined efforts were made to obtain a foundation privilege. An interdict on Bologna in 1338 aroused fresh hopes and repeated attempts were made, and sums expended, at the *curia*, to no avail.[68] Further attempts there in 1347-48 proved equally fruit-

---

[66] For an overview, W. M. BOWSKY, *A Medieval Italian Commune. Siena under the Nine, 1287-1355* (Berkeley and Los Angeles, Ca., 1981), esp. ch. 7; for a more detailed survey, D. BALESTRACCI and G. PICCINNI, *Siena nel Trecento. Assetto urbano e struttura edilizia* (Florence, 1977). The emphasis on the period of the Nine is perhaps more evident in the writings of non-Italian scholars; more work on other medieval regimes, and in particular on the fifteenth century, is redressing the balance. See in particular P. PERTICI, *La città magnificata. Interventi edilizi a Siena nel Rinascimento. L'ufficio dell'Ornato (1428-1480)* (Siena, 1995); P. TURRINI, *"Per honore et utile de la città di Siena". Il comune e l'edilizia nel Quattrocento* (Siena, 1997). This is not the place for an extensive bibliography, but for a broader overview see also *Storia di Siena*, I. On the use of the term 'Government of the Nine' see the reservations of ASCHERI, 'La Siena del "Buon Governo"'.

[67] This is the unequivocal diagnosis of NARDI, *Insegnamento*, pp. 148-50, echoing a long line of predecessors. Other factors were political unrest in Siena (pp. 144-5) and the inability to compete financially in the academic salary market (pp. 148-50).

[68] *Chartularium*, docs. 349, pp. 432-5, 29 May 1338; 353, pp. 442-4, 4 Jan 1339; 355-9, pp. 445-56, 20 Jan – 19 Feb 1339; 363, pp. 460-3, 26 Feb 1339; cf. PRUNAI, II, pp. 18-20, and above all NARDI, *Insegnamento*, pp. 194-201, and IDEM, 'Dalle origini', p. 19-21. Fear of competition, or at least the undoing of the project 'a malis convicinis invidis dicti boni' led to an insistence on secrecy; *Chartularium*, doc. 349, pp. 432-5, 29 May 1338 (pp. 433-4), DENIFLE, *Entstehung*, p. 446, and

less,[69] and from that point onwards the cumulative effect of plague and political crisis precluded any more such initiatives for a while; for the next decade Siena had even to do without any law teaching.[70] Only after Charles IV's arrival in Italy and the overthrow of the *Nove* in 1355 was the much-desired formal recognition finally received. A delegation was sent to Prague in the summer of 1357,[71] and in August the emperor granted Siena 'Studii generalis privilegium...in iure civili et canonico et medicinis, philosophia, loyca, gramatica et quavis alia facultate'. This privilege included imperial protection for the students and exemption from various duties, and appointed the bishop the conservator of the *Studio* with the right to grant degrees.[72] The charter was followed by communal legislation; first, a meas-

quoted as part of a wider picture in F. REXROTH, *Deutsche Universitätsstiftungen von Prag bis Köln. Dir Intentionen des Stifters und die Wege und Chancen ihrer Verwirklichung im spätmittelalterlichen Territorialstaat*. Beischrifte zum Archiv für Kulturgeschichte, 34 (Cologne – Weimar – Vienna, 1992), p. 100. AGNOLO DI TURA DEL GRASSO, *Cronaca Senese*, in *Rerum Italicarum Scriptores*[2], vol. XV, part VI (Bologna, 1933-5), pp. 255-564 (p. 523) recorded that 'Papa Benedetto scomunicò li scolari de lo studio di Bologna, e per questo tutti li detti scolari si partiro e grande parte di detti scolari venero a li studii in Siena del mese d'ottobre'. But they certainly did not stay very long, and the judgement of J. POLZER, 'Ambrogio Lorenzetti's *War and Peace* Murals Revisited: Contributions to the Meaning of the *Good Government Allegory*', *Artibus et historiae. Rivista internazionale di arti visive e cinema*, 45 (2002), pp. 63-105 (pp. 64, 76) that this and the 1321 episode were important elements in the creation of the Lorenzetti frescoes is not based on evidence. Padua, Siena's chief rival in 1321, had similar aspirations of benefiting from Bologna's difficulties; A. FAVARO, 'Contribuzioni alla storia dello Studio di Padova intorno alla metà del secolo XIV', *Atti dell'Accademia di scienze, lettere ed arti in Padova*, 36 (1920), pp. 31-40, esp. pp. 33-4.

[69] *Chartularium*, docs. 403, pp. 526-8, 31 Dec 1347 (previously published by ZDEKAUER, doc. III, pp. 139-40); NARDI, *Insegnamento*, Appendice, doc, 13, pp. 238-40, 8 Feb 1348, a document which eluded the compilers of the *Chartularium*. See also W. M. BOWSKY, 'The Impact of the Black Death upon Sienese Government and Society', *Speculum*, 39 (1964), pp. 1-34 (p. 13); PRUNAI, II, pp. 20-21; and GAROSI, pp. 160-3.

[70] P. NARDI, 'Carlo IV di Boemia e l'Università di Siena', in *Siena in Praga. Storia, arte, società...* Catalogo della mostra, eds. A. Pazderová and L. Bonelli Conenna (Prague, 2000), pp. 50-53 (p. 51); and more generally BOWSKY, op. cit., pp. 14 *seq*.

[71] P. ROSSI, 'Carlo IV di Lussemburgo e la Repubblica di Siena (1355-1369)', *BSSP*, 37 (1930), pp. 5-39, 179-242 (p. 35). As the charter mentions, the delegation included Antimo degli Ugurgieri, a Sienese who was teaching at Padua. The *Biccherna* payments to teachers for the first half of 1357 make it clear that there was no teaching of the higher subjects in Siena at the time; *Chartularium*, doc. 424, pp. 555-6, 30 Jul 1357.

[72] *Chartularium*, doc. 427, pp. 560-3, 16 Aug (with references to previous editions), and see now P. NARDI, with collaboration by G. MINNUCCI and M. BROGI, 'Siena', in *Charters of Foundation and Early Documents of the Universities of the Coimbra Group*, eds. J. M. M. Hermans and M. Nelissen (Groningen, 1994), pp. 24-5. Cf. also NARDI, *Insegnamento*, pp. 210-11; DENIFLE, *Entstehung*, p. 427; PRUNAI, II, pp. 22-3; ZDEKAUER, pp. 20-1; G. MINNUCCI, 'La Chiesa e le istituzioni culturali senesi tra Medioevo e Rinascimento', in *Chiesa e vita religiosa a Siena dalle origini al Grande Giubileo. Atti del Convegno di studi (Siena 25-27 ottobre 2000)*, eds. A. Mirizio and P. Nardi. Istituto Storico Diocesano di Siena, Testi e Documenti, 4 (Siena, 2002), pp. 217-28 (esp. 217-8 on the implications of the charter for the relationship between the university and the ecclesiastical hierarchy); also P. ROSSI, 'Carlo IV di Lussemburgo', esp. pp. 33-6. On imperial relations with Siena, in the broader regional political context, see also N. RUBINSTEIN, 'The Place of the Empire in Fifteenth-Century Florentine Political Opinion and Diplomacy', *Bulletin of the Institute of Historical Research*, 30 (1957), pp. 125-35.

There is a tradition that the charter was confirmed by the emperor Sigismund in 1433; MORIANI, *Notizie sulla Università di Siena*, pp. 17-8; DENIFLE, *Entstehung*, p. 452, who states that this document was in the Fondo Diplomatico in the Archivio di Stato di Siena; repeated by D. BARDUZZI in the introduction to his 'Brevi notizie sulla R. Università di Siena', in *Monografie delle Università e degli Istituti Superiori*, 1 (Rome, 1911), pp. 469-80 (repr. Siena, 1912, as a separate booklet). No trace of a separate charter for the *Studio* has come to light in Siena, nor is one mentioned in the old but systematic surveys of imperial charters for universities; M. MEYHÖFER, 'Die kaiserlichen Stiftungsprivilegien für Universitäten', *Archiv für Urkundenforschung*, 4 (1912), pp. 291-418; G. KAUFMANN, 'Die Universitätsprivilegien der Kaiser', *Deutsche Zeitschrift für Geschichtswissenschaft*, 1 (1889), pp. 118-65; and A. VON WRETSCHKO, 'Universitäts-Privilegien der Kaiser aus der Zeit von 1412-1456', in *Festschrift Otto Gierke zum siebzigsten Geburtstag* (Weimar, 1911), pp. 793-816. It is more likely that Barduzzi was referring to the general confirmation Sigismund gave to Siena after his stay in Siena in 1432-3; W. ALTMANN (ed.), *Die Urkunden Kaiser Sigmunds (1410-1437)*, in *Regesta Imperii*, ed. J. F. Böhmer, XI, 2 vols. (Innsbruck, 1897-1900), vol. 2, p. 248, no. 9691, 29 Sept 1433; cf. ASCHERI, 'Legislazione, statuti e sovranità', p. 21 n. 78. This was one of a great number of confirmations of charters of Charles IV; J. ASCHBACH, *Geschichte Kaisers Sigmund's*, 4 vols. (Hamburg, 1838-45), vol. 4, p. 119. This document is recorded as lost by Altmann (loc. cit., working on the imperial registers) but it is in fact in

ure recalling all Sienese who were studying abroad and forbidding Sienese teachers to leave the town for another *studio* (on the draconian penalty of 5,000 florins), then a further measure which gave the rector unusually wide jurisdiction over scholars and teachers, foreign and Sienese alike.[73]

Why had the road to official *studium generale* status taken so long?[74] The *Leitmotiv* was rivalry with Bologna; the anti-papal campaigns of the 1240s, the exodus of 1321 and the interdicts on Bologna in 1306 and 1338 were all moments at which the Sienese reacted to difficulties in the *alma mater studiorum* by pushing their claims. In the first half of the fourteenth century the focus of these initiatives increasingly became the papacy, whose approval was seen as the *sine qua non* of success; yet this was precisely the stumbling-block. Girgensohn has speculated that Siena's failure to get a bull out of the Avignon papacy may have been connected with a fear of competition, not just with Bologna, but also with Perugia – in other words, with the two functioning universities in the Papal State.[75] In fact this was part of a broader picture of intensifying competition in the region. In addition to Arezzo (a competitor since the thirteenth century, by now languishing, but by no means out of the picture)[76] and Perugia (a *studium generale* since 1308),[77] the Sienese now had to reckon with the aspirations of Pisa (founded in 1343 with a papal bull)[78] and Florence (likewise, in 1349).[79] In none of their efforts did the Guelph city of Siena have much luck with the popes, not because of any innate hostility but be-

---

Dipl., Riformagioni, Leone, no. 13. It makes no specific reference to the *Studio*. It is possible that the misunderstanding of Moriani and others derives from the fact that Pecci chose to make this entry on the subject in his *Zibaldone per la Storia dell'Università di Siena*: 'L'imperatore Sigismondo primo per suo particolar privilegio conferma ai Sanesi per benefizio, e tranquillità delli stati loro tutto ciò, che avea loro concesso della Bolla d'oro. Dato in Mantova il 29 settembre 1433' (BCS, *ms.* B.IV.28, f. 25v). In the margin he cites what is still the location for the document: 'Nel Cassone di Balìa, Cassetta decta di Leone, n.° 13'.

[73] *Chartularium*, docs. 431, pp. 567-9, 19 Oct, and 432, pp. 570-2, 24 Nov (the latter was previously published by Zdekauer, doc. IV, pp. 141-2); cf. Nardi, *Insegnamento*, pp. 211-14; Denifle, *Entstehung*, p. 448; Prunai, II, p. 23.

[74] Renzi, '*Studium generale*: *aurea mediocritas*?' observed that this was 'un arco di tempo assai lungo, per le nostre unità di misura, e invece non particolarmente straordinario per i tempi dell'amministrazione e del governo delle università medievali' (p. 306). On the protracted nature of the process of applying for and obtaining a bull in this period, H. Diener, 'Die Hohen Schulen, ihre Lehrer und Schüler in den Registern der päpstlichen Verwaltung des 14. und 15. Jahrhunderts', in *Schulen und Studium im sozialen Wandel des hohen und späten Mittelalters*, ed. J. Fried. Vorträge und Forschungen / Konstanzer Arbeitskreis für mittelalterliche Geschichte, 30 (Sigmaringen, 1986), pp. 351-74 (esp. pp. 354-5).

[75] D. Girgensohn, review of Nardi, *Insegnamento*, in *Annali di storia delle università italiane*, 1 (1997), pp. 219-220 (p. 220). The University of Rome can be omitted from the equation at this time, as at this stage it was effectively in abeyance; C. Frova and M. Miglio, '"Studium Urbis" e "Studium Curiae" nel Trecento e nel Quattrocento: linee di politica culturale', in *Roma e lo Studium Urbis. Spazio urbano e cultura dal Quattro al Seicento*. Atti del convegno, Roma, 7-10 giugno 1989. Pubblicazioni degli Archivi di Stato, Saggi, 22 (Roma, 1992), pp. 26-39. The *Studium Curiae* and the *Studium Urbis*, far from being distinct institutions as traditionally viewed in the literature, are now thought to be different terms for the same university, reflecting the joint responsibility for it; G. Adorni, 'L'Archivio dell'Università di Roma', in the same volume, pp. 389-430; Eadem, 'Statuti del Collegio degli Avvocati Concistoriali e Statuti dello Studio Romano', *Rivista internazionale di diritto comune*, 6 (1995), pp. 293-355; Eadem, 'L'Università di Roma e i suoi archivi', in *La storia delle università italiane*, pp. 109-31; and Grendler, *Universities of the Italian Renaissance*, pp. 56-7.

[76] Black, *Studio e scuola in Arezzo*, docs. 4-11, pp. 185-193 (1312-1345).

[77] G. Ermini, *Storia dell'Università di Perugia* (Florence, 1971 edn.), I, pp. 25-9; Rashdall, II, p. 41; Denifle, *Entstehung*, pp. 536 *seq*. The bull in this instance followed full communal recognition, as at Siena: and in 1355 Perugia obtained a further confirmatory charter from Charles IV. See p. 45 below.

[78] C. Fedeli, *I documenti pontifici riguardanti l'Università di Pisa* (Pisa, 1908), pp. 85-88. See M. Tangheroni, 'L'età della Repubblica (dalle origini al 1406)', in *Storia dell'Università di Pisa*, I. *1343-1737* (Pisa, 1993), pp. 5-32 (esp. pp. 13-16).

[79] Gherardi, *Statuti*, appendix, part I, doc. VI, pp. 116-9 (31 May 1349). On the detrimental effect on Siena of this growing competition, Nardi, 'Carlo IV', p. 51; also Denley, 'Academic Rivalry', pp. 194-5.

Fig. 2b – Seal of Biagio Montanini, early fourteenth century (Rome, Museo di Palazzo Venezia,
Collezione Tagliavini, no. 7).

cause their priorities lay elsewhere.[80] That left only one other option,[81] and what ultimately helped
bring about the much-sought approval was the accession of an emperor who saw no problems with
such proliferation of universities. Charles IV's 'academic policy' has never really been considered as a
whole,[82] though a case could be made for its existence and even its enlightened nature. It began with
the most concrete and durable achievement, the foundation of the University of Prague (1348), in
which the emperor took a close interest, but it also entailed a long list of foundation charters in Italy

---

[80] NARDI, *Insegnamento*, pp. 142, 145-6, and IDEM, 'Dalle origini', p. 17, stressing that John XXII's intervention in
favour of Bologna in early 1322 had been critical in undoing the *migratio*; and *Insegnamento*, pp. 150, 201 on the papal response to the 1338 initiative. By contrast RENZI, '*Studium generale: aurea mediocritas*?', p. 309, took the view that the absence of the papacy from Italy 'ha veramente favorito la relativa autonomia e il consolidamento amministrativo dello Studio
senese'. Certainly Italian universities were not a high priority within papal policy towards universities; cf. D. QUAGLIONI,
'La cultura', in IDEM (ed.), *La crisi del Trecento e il papato avignonese (1274-1378)* (Cinisello Balsamo, 1994), pp. 367-80
(esp. pp. 372-4). But it would in any case be dangerous to be too mechanistic in interpreting the respective roles of pope
and emperor in founding universities. Notwithstanding R. SCHMIDT, 'Päpstliche und kaiserliche Universitätsprivilegien im
späten Mittelalter', in *Das Privileg im europäischen Vergleich*, II, eds. B. Dolemayer and H. Mohnhaupt. Ius Commune,
Sonderhefte, 93 (Frankfurt, 1997), pp. 143-54, the academic policy of both authorities has yet to be studied comparatively
and exhaustively.

[81] 'Wollte man sich nicht an den Papst wenden – aus Gründen, die in erster Linie mit den inneren Verhältnissen Italiens
zusammenhingen, aber auch mit der Tatsache, daß sich das Papsttum im französischen Exil befand – so blieb nur der
Kaiser.' R. SCHMIDT, 'Begründung und Bestätigung der Universität Prag durch Karl IV. und die kaiserliche Privilegierung
von Generalstudien', in *Kaiser Karl IV., 1316-1378. Forschungen über Kaiser und Recht*, ed. H. Patze (Neustadt/Aisch,
1978), and *Blätter für deutsche Landesgeschichte*, 114 (1978), pp. 695-719; repr. in IDEM, '*Fundatio et confirmatio universitatis'. Von den Anfängen deutscher Universitäten* (Goldbach, 1998), pp. 1*-25* (p. 21*).

[82] The best survey is P. NARDI, 'Relations with Authority', in *A History of the University in Europe*, I. *Universities in the
Middle Ages*, ed. H. De Ridder-Symoens (Cambridge, 1992), pp. 77-107 (pp. 97-9).

and elsewhere: Cividale (1353),[83] Arezzo[84] and Perugia[85] (1355), Siena (1357), Pavia (1361),[86] Florence (1364),[87] Geneva[88] and Orange[89] (1365), and Lucca (1369).[90] Of course it could not be claimed that his interest in these had any depth – indeed, the more obvious conclusion is that his bestowal of such charters was indiscriminate, motivated by political and/or financial considerations, and therefore unsurprisingly limited in terms of success.[91] But one should perhaps not exaggerate the political value

[83] P. S. LEICHT, 'Il primo tentativo di costituire un'Università nella Venezia orientale', *Memorie storiche forogiuliesi*, 6 (1910), pp. 1-14 (edition, pp. 13-14, and comment, pp. 9-13); IDEM, 'Sull'Università di Cividale', *Memorie Storiche Forogiuliesi*, 8 (1912), pp. 311-3; R. SALOMON, 'Eine vergessene Universitätsgründung', *Neues Archiv der Gesellschaft für ältere deutsche Geschichte*, 37 (1912), pp. 810-7 and additional note, 879-80 (edition pp. 816-7).

[84] BLACK, *Studio e scuola in Arezzo*, p. 195.

[85] ERMINI, *Storia*, I, pp. 31-33; statutes published by V. BINI, *Memorie Istoriche della Perugina Università degli Studi* (Perugia, 1816, repr. Bologna, 1977), pp. 207-8, and ROSSI, 'Documenti per la storia dell'Università di Perugia', docs. 96-7.

[86] MAIOCCHI, *Codice diplomatico dell'Università di Pavia*, I, doc. 1, pp. 7-9.

[87] GHERARDI, *Statuti*, appendix, part I, doc. XXIX, pp. 139-40 (2 Jan 1364).

[88] RASHDALL, II, p. 329.

[89] RASHDALL, II, p. 185.

[90] RASHDALL, II, p. 328; DENIFLE, *Entstehung*, pp. 649-52; P. BARSANTI, *Il pubblico insegnamento in Lucca dal sec. XIV alla fine del sec. XVIII* (Lucca, 1905), esp. pp. 83-4; and see now J. DAVIES, 'A "Paper University"? The *Studio lucchese*, 1369-1487', *History of Universities*, 15 (1997-9), pp. 261-306. On these foundations generally see also NARDI, *Insegnamento*, pp. 210-11; IDEM, 'Carlo IV', p. 51. The texts of these charters have been compared by several scholars. The privilege for Prague is technically not a foundation charter (which came from the pope) and is in any case highly specific to the university in which Charles took the closest interest, and derivative from older imperial writings (see esp. SCHMIDT, 'Päpstliche und kaiserliche Universitätsprivilegien', pp. 144-6). Of the remainder the first, for Cividale, is substantially different from the rest (see P. S. LEICHT, 'Sull'Università di Cividale'), and it is actually the first imperial foundation given that Naples was founded by Frederick II in his capacity as king of Sicily; cf. F. TRAUTZ, 'Die Reichsgewalt in Italien im Spätmittelalter', *Heidelberger Jahrbücher*, 7 (1963), pp. 45-81 (p. 67; pp. 66-69 generally on emperors and university foundations in the late middle ages). The Sienese charter takes significantly from that granted to Perugia (REXROTH, *Deutsche Universitätsstiftungen*, p. 103). M. KUBOVÁ, 'University založené Karlem IV. (Die von Karl IV. gegründeter Universitäten)', *Acta Universitatis Carolinae – Historia Universitatis Carolinae Pragensis*, 11 (1971), pp. 7-31 demonstrates the particular textual closeness of the four charters for the central Italian universities, Lucca, Perugia, Siena and Florence (apart from the comparative table inset between p. 12 and p. 13 I have relied on the abstract in German, pp. 30-31), and M. MEYHÖFER's older analysis of the manuscript tradition ('Die kaiserlichen Stiftungsprivilegien') shows the Sienese charter to have been influential in the drawing up of subsequent charters. But if the texts have been analysed the full background is still neglected. Schmidt's appeal of 1978 that 'Die Universitätsprivilegien Karls IV. für diese italienischen [und burgundischen] Universitäten bedürfen dringend einer speziellen eingehenden Untersuchung' ('Begründung', p. 18*) has not yet been taken up. NARDI, 'Relations with Authority', pp. 97-9 makes the point that the emperor's charters merely 'confirmed the regulations established long ago, predominantly by the church, and repeated the organization of the *studia generalia* as modelled mainly by the church' (p. 97) – an observation borne out in the case of Siena by Charles IV's tacit confirmation of Innocent IV's appointment of the bishop of Siena as conservator of teacher and student privileges (above, p. 32). Charles' French education and close relations with the papacy may well explain this feature, which also puts his charters, and indeed his educational policy, in a more positive perspective than the traditional one of papal-imperial rivalry for spheres of influence.

[91] Three of the measures, for Cividale, Geneva and Lucca, did not result in active universities; the fate of Orange was not much better (RASHDALL, II, pp. 184-6). See NARDI, 'Dalle origini', p. 22 on Charles's need for money as a factor. For an overview of the historiography of Charles IV, particularly as boosted by the sixth centenary of his death, K. WALSH, '"Böhmens Vater – Des Reiches Erzstiefvater?" Gedanken zu einem neuen Bild Kaiser Karls IV.', *Innsbrucker Historische Studien*, 3 (1980), pp. 189-210; on how the denigration of him built up systematically in the later middle ages, B. FREY, *Pater Bohemias – Vitricus Imperii. Böhmens Vater, Stiefvater des Reichs. Kaiser Karl IV. in der Geschichtsschreibung* (Berne, 1978). The critical view is largely sustained by E. SCHUBERT, *König und Reich. Studien zur spätmittelalterlichen deutschen Verfassungsgeschichte* (Göttingen, 1979), while the more positive line is adopted by F. SEIBT, *Karl IV. Ein Kaiser in Europa 1346 bis 1378* (Munich, 1978). On Charles and the intellectual world, F. KAVKA, 'Politics and Culture under Charles IV', in *Bohemia in History*, ed. M. Teich (Cambridge, 1998), pp. 59-78, and S. H. THOMSON, 'Learning at the Court of Charles IV', *Speculum*, 25 (1950), pp. 1-20.

of these charters to the emperor either. The most thorough recent discussion of Charles' political relations with Italian powers, while exploring his dealings with Siena in fine detail, fails to mention the
1357 charter.[92] It may have been part of the alliance with the new regime of the *Dodici* (1355-68), but
was surely not a key component. Whatever the motivation, Charles's foundation charters opened up
the field to further competition. It was an irony, but a politically understandable one, that the success
which eluded the *Nove*, who had done so much for the *Studio*, was in the end granted only to the
regime that replaced them.[93]

2. *From 1357 to 1408*

The communal documents of 1357 display a clear and understandable sense of achievement. Yet the
charter could hardly have come at a less auspicious moment. The political and economic crisis of the
mid-fourteenth century, the constant changes of government in the Italian city-states in this period
and the ever-present threat of destabilising (and ruinously expensive) military campaigns need no
elaboration here. It was a lean period for universities generally[94] and for Italian universities in particular.[95] Apart from Pavia, the other Italian foundations of the middle decades of the century came to
very little. Such *studi* as managed to operate did so very much on a localised basis. Political and other
uncertainties discouraged attendance at any but the most established universities, i.e. Bologna, Padua
and Perugia, and only in the 1380s and 1390s did Pavia, under determined patronage, and shortly af-

---

[92] E. WIDDER, *Itinerar und Politik. Studien zur Reiseherrschaft Karls IV. südlich der Alpen*. Forschungen zur Kaiser- und
Papstgeschichte des Mittelalters, Beihefte zu J. F. Böhmer, *Regesta Imperii*, 10 (Cologne/Weimar/Vienna, 1993).

[93] Noted by (amongst others) BOWSKY, *A Medieval Italian Commune*, p. 278. Ironies apart, the outcome was the result
of continued or at least repeated efforts, and it is no accident that these were renewed by the incoming regime. This I take
to be at least part of the sense of the acute observation of RENZI, '*Studium generale: aurea mediocritas?*', p. 306, that the century of attempts was a period 'nel quale le relazioni fra autorità politiche cittadine, organizzazioni professionali e istituzioni
assistenziali trovano un equilibrato momento di convergenza nel modo di amministrare e promuovere lo Studio cittadino'.

[94] Cf. A. GOURON, 'La crise des Universités françaises à la fin du XIVᵉ siècle', in *Atti del Simposio Internazionale
Cateriniano-Bernardiniano*, Siena, 17-20 aprile 1980, eds. D. Maffei and P. Nardi (Siena, 1982), pp. 907-15; IDEM, 'À l'o-
rigine d'un déclin: les universités méridionales au temps du Grand Schisme', in *Genèse et débuts du Grand Schisme d'Occident*. Colloques internationaux du C.N.R.S, 586 (Paris, 1980), pp. 175-84. The present work eschews the long-running debate about the impact of the Black Death on higher education, in which the worst consequences of attempting to pinpoint
the constellation of factors in the 'fourteenth-century crisis' on a single cause are apparent; a useful corrective is W. J.
COURTENAY, 'The Effects of the Black Death on English Higher Education', *Speculum*, 55 (1980), pp. 676-714, finding an
increase in the number of students at Oxford after the plague. A. BORST, 'Crisis and Reform in the Universities of the Late
Middle Ages', in his *Medieval Worlds. Barbarians Heretics and Artists* (tr. Cambridge, 1991), pp. 167-81, has sought to locate
the roots of the university crisis in the earlier half of the century, with the rash of foundations and the indiscriminate licences for theology faculties playing a part.

[95] C. FROVA, 'Crisi e rifondazione nella storia delle piccole università italiane durante il medioevo', in *Le università minori in Europa (secoli XV-XIX)*. Convegno Internazionale di Studi, Alghero, 30 Ottobre – 2 Novembre 1996, eds. G. P.
Brizzi and J. Verger (Soveria Mannelli, Catanzaro, 1998), pp. 29-47 (esp. pp. 32 *seq.*) is a useful survey. On the vicissitudes
of Florence in the late fourteenth century see G. C. GARFAGNINI, 'Città e Studio a Firenze nel XIV secolo: una difficile convivenza', *Critica storica*, 25 (1988), pp. 182-201, and in *Luoghi e metodi di insegnamento*, pp. 101-20 (esp. pp. 110 *seq.*); G.
BRUCKER, 'Florence and its University, 1348-1434', in *Action and Conviction in Early Modern Europe*, eds. T. K. Rabb and J.
E. Seigel (Princeton, 1969), pp. 220-36; repr. in his *Renaissance Florence: Society, Culture and Religion* (Goldbach, 1994),
pp. 189*-205*; DENLEY, 'Academic Rivalry', pp. 195-6; on similar problems at Pisa, TANGHERONI, 'L'età della Repubblica',
esp. pp. 28 *seq.*; and finally and most revealing of the detailed political problems, T. E. MORRISSEY, 'Padua in Crisis and
Transition Around 1400', paper for International Congress of the Historical Sciences, Oslo 2000, published on
www.oslo2000.uio.no/A10/A1016/group~2/Morrissey.pdf (downloaded on 7 April 2004).

terwards Florence, begin to grow and develop wider reputations.[96] The commune of Siena, in regular political turmoil and crippled by the cost of warfare, was simply not equipped to follow up the legislation of 1357 even if circumstances had been more favourable.[97] That year, in the lead-up to the obtention of the charter, the budget for teaching contracts had been established at 2,000 florins,[98] but in 1360 the statute prohibiting teachers from leaving Siena was also repealed.[99] The abandonment of this might well have been the pragmatic acceptance of at least temporary lack of success; the previous year the Florentines, reviving their own *Studio*, had hired the Sienese canonist Cerretano de' Cerretani.[100] It may also be connected with a financial downturn; Moscadelli, who has done much to restore the reputation of the regime of the *Dodici*, has pointed out that the financial situation was not bad in the initial years, but deteriorated from 1358, precipitating into crisis in 1360.[101] War with Perugia and raids of mercenary companies were responsible, and the amounts of money required to ward (and on subsequent occasions to buy) them off put the budget of the *Studio* entirely in the shade.[102] In 1361 the siege of Bologna by Bernabò Visconti renewed hopes in Siena, as on so many previous occasions, that they might profit from Bologna's difficulties. A further resolution was passed, increasing the budget to 3,000 gold florins and restoring the task of appointing teachers to the *Savi*, the officials responsible for the *Studio*;[103] attempts were also made to woo Bolognese teachers.[104] In August 1362 the invitation to students was renewed and their privileges repeated.[105] The academic year 1362-3 saw

[96] MAIOCCHI, *Codice diplomatico dell'Università di Pavia*, I, to which should be added esp. A. BELLONI, 'Giovanni Dondi, Albertino da Salso e le origini dello studio pavese', *Bollettino della Società Pavese di Storia Patria*, 82 (1982), pp. 17-47, and EADEM, 'Signorolo Omodei e gli inizi della scuola giuridica pavese', *Bollettino della Società Pavese di Storia Patria*, 85 (1985), pp. 29-39, demonstrating that there was more activity in the early years than Maiocchi had thought.

[97] On the political vicissitudes of the fourteenth century see below; a brilliant crisp synthesis is in G. CATONI, 'La faziosa armonia', in A. FALASSI and G. CATONI, *Palio* (Siena, 1982), pp. 225-72 (pp. 230-4); see also *Storia di Siena*, I, esp. S. MOSCADELLI, 'Oligarchie e Monti' (pp. 267-78). Narrative and 'divulgative' accounts are in L. FUSAI, *La Storia di Siena dalle origini al 1559* (Siena, 1987), and U. CAGLIARITANO, *Storia di Siena* (Siena, 1977). On the economic background, PINTO, '"Honour" and "Profit"'; on the impact of warfare on the finances of the city in particular see now CAFERRO, *Mercenary Companies*.

[98] *Chartularium*, doc. 426, pp. 558-9, 28 Jul; it was increased from an earlier sum of 1,200 florins, voted only weeks earlier; doc. 425, pp. 556-8, 3 Jul. On the *Studio* in the period covered in this section, see PRUNAI, II, and for a briefer but more up-to-date summary MINNUCCI, 'La Chiesa e le istituzioni culturali', pp. 220-2. A much more detailed analysis of the teachers of the period is in L. TRAPANI, 'Docenti senesi dalla fondazione dello Studio generale all'istituzione della facoltà teologica (1357-1408)', *Annali di storia delle Università italiane*, 10 (2006, forthcoming). I am most grateful to Dott. Trapani for generously allowing me to see this important work.

[99] *CG* 165, f. 33v, 4 Dec 1360.

[100] GHERARDI, *Statuti*, appendix, part II, doc. XIV, pp. 290-1 (1-5 Oct 1358). On the ongoing competition with Florence over teachers, DENLEY, 'Academic Rivalry', pp. 196-9.

[101] MOSCADELLI, 'Apparato burocratico', pp. 87-95. On the *Dodici* see also V. L. WAINWRIGHT, 'Conflict and Popular Government in Fourteenth Century Siena: il Monte dei Dodici, 1355-1368', in *I ceti dirigenti nella Toscana tardo comunale*. Atti del III Convegno: Firenze, 5-7 dicembre 1980 (Florence, 1983), pp. 57-80; and J. LUCHAIRE, *Documenti per la storia dei rivolgimenti politici del Comune di Siena dal 1354 al 1369* (Lyons, 1906). On the political and financial aspects of the early years of this regime see also G. CHERUBINI, 'I mercanti e il potere a Siena', in *Banchi e mercanti di Siena* (Rome, 1987), pp. 161-220; repr. in his *Scritti toscani. L'urbanesimo medievale e la mezzadria* (Florence, 1991), pp. 71-115 (pp. 98-101).

[102] MOSCADELLI, loc. cit.; M. BORGOGNI, *La guerra tra Siena e Perugia (1357-1359): appunti su un conflitto dimenticato* (Siena, 2003); and cf. CAFERRO, *Mercenary Companies*, pp. 19, 44, 51, 55, 113 etc.

[103] *CG* 168, f. 4r-v, 19 Jul; ZDEKAUER, doc. V, p. 143 (and cf. pp. 16-17). On the *Savi* see below, pp. 69 *seq*.

[104] 'Et enim ex novitatibus et offensione facta civitati Bononie, per dominem Barnabovem Mediolani dominum, potuerunt haberi doctores famosissimi in qualibet scientie facultate, qui aliis temporibus haberi nullatenus potuissent' (loc. cit.). See *Bicch.* 241, f. 95v, 8 Nov 1361, for the payment of a messenger to Bologna.

[105] *CG* 169, f. 38r, 23 Aug. This was also a better year financially; MOSCADELLI, 'Apparato burocratico', p. 102.

nine university teachers on the payroll, the highest number since the charter.[106] In 1363 plague struck again, accompanied by another mercenary incursion, which the Sienese rebuffed, but at great cost.[107] In 1364 the clergy were made to contribute 1,200 florins towards the *Studio* salaries in exchange for a voice in the election of the teachers;[108] but in April 1365 matters came to a head. On 25 April the regime decided as an economy measure to pay only a proportion of each teacher's salary.[109] Three days later the *Concistoro* heard expert advice to the effect that it was impossible to sustain salary payments, and dismissed all the foreign teachers.[110] The next year hiring of teachers began again, though on a minimal scale.[111] This was the last such initiative before the *Dodici* were toppled, in August 1368.

The regime of the *Riformatori* (1368-85) saw a series of crises during which the revitalisation of the *Studio* was not even seriously attempted.[112] As far as the higher subjects are concerned the period is almost totally devoid of signs of activity. Medical teaching was virtually non-existent. The distinguished Sienese doctor Francesco Casini, who had been contracted to teach in 1366,[113] was by now furthering his career elsewhere (and proving of considerable diplomatic value to Siena in the process),[114] and although several medical doctors were employed by the commune for a variety of purposes there is no evidence

---

[106] *Conc.* 26, ff. 74r, 11 Jan 1363, 75v-6r, 19 Jan, 77v; *Bicch.* 243, ff. 105r, 11 Jan, 123r, 13 Mar, 132v, 20 Apr, 133r, 26 Apr, and 138v, 30 Apr; *Bicch.* 596, ff. 103r-105v, 12 Jan-26 Apr; *CG* 170, f. 11v, 3 Feb 1363, partially edited by GAROSI, doc. 97, p. 547. The teachers included the lawyers Francesco Tegrini da Pisa, hired at 250 florins (*CG* 170, f. 54v, 20 Oct), Francesco di Betolo da Perugia (100 florins) and, later, Alessandro del Antella of Florence (300 florins). The total expended on teachers' salaries was slightly over 1,025 florins. The list included a teacher of *notaria*, Baldinaccio da Gubbio (paid on 19 Jan; *Conc.* 26, ff. 75v-76r); and there is also a letter from the lawyer Giovanni di Neri Pagliaresi inviting an unnamed teacher to accept a lectureship in this subject, which Minnucci suggests is probably of this year (MINNUCCI, 'Documenti', doc. II-1, p. 75 and n. 1). The commune also employed a master of *abaco* (*Bicch.* 243, f. 112r, 4 Feb), and several doctors in non-teaching roles, including a 'medico d'occhio' (*Bicch.* 243, f. 134v, 29 Apr: cf. also f. 153v, 30 Jun, and *CG* 171, f. 123v, 18 Dec 1364).

[107] MOSCADELLI, 'Apparato burocratico', pp. 104-5.

[108] *CG* 171, ff. 31r-v, 27 Mar, and 111r-v, 26 Nov, ed. ZDEKAUER, doc. VI, pp. 144-6; and below, p. 102.

[109] *Bicch.* 3, f. 75r, 25 Apr (also in *Statuti* 31, f. 140r-v and *Statuti* 32, f. 118r). The *Concistoro* was authorised by the *Consiglio Generale* to hire one grammarian, one teacher of logic and two doctors of medicine, one 'fisicus' and one 'cerusicus', at the lowest salary possible.

[110] *Conc.* 31, f. 58v, 28 Apr, ed. GAROSI, 'La vita e l'opera di Francesco Casini', p. 297 n. 1 but with erroneous reference and date. The notes of FALUSCHI, *Disordinate Memorie...* in BCS, *ms.* E.VI.9, f. 19v, record that one teacher, Niccolò de' Cambioni da Prato, was retained as adviser and reformer of statutes and was therefore allowed to keep his lectureship as well. This does not appear in the *Concistoro* deliberation. The notice may have resulted from confusion with another document; Niccolò de' Cambioni was hired in December 1366 (*CG* 175, f. 63r), and his contract was renewed a year later (*CG* 177, f. 35v, 20 Dec 1367), in a measure in which his other functions are also mentioned.

[111] *Conc.* 37, ff. 13r, 12 Jan, and 16r-v, 18 Jan 1366. In August the *Consiglio Generale* hired the Sienese doctor of medicine Francesco Casini, and authorised the *Concistoro* to hire one grammarian, one lawyer and one doctor of medicine; *CG* 175, ff. 28v-29r, 28 Aug 1366, partially edited in GAROSI, doc. 65 p. 532. Two further appointments were made in December; *CG* 175, ff. 57v, 11 Dec, and 63r.

[112] The most detailed, if somewhat roseate, study of the regime is A. RUTIGLIANO, *Lorenzetti's Golden Mean. The Riformatori of Siena, 1368-1385* (New York, 1991).

[113] See n. 111 above; payments for teaching in *Bicch.* 247, f. 193v (new foliation), 9 Nov 1368; *Bicch.* 248, ff. 150v, 20 Oct, and 204r, 31 Dec 1369.

[114] See his correspondence with the *Concistoro*; *Conc.* 1783-1800 and 1808, *passim*. He was explicitly in the commune's pay for diplomatic activity in 1384 (*Conc.* 124, f. 36, Sept-Oct 1384; *Bicch.* 269, ff. 37v-38r, 19-20 Oct, and 57v, 26 Dec; *Bicch.* 270, ff. 145r-v, 19-20 Oct, 188v, 26 Dec [all new foliation]), but the apparent attempt to include some teaching in his contract came to nothing and was cancelled (*Conc.* 125 f. 21r-v, 24 Jan 1385). On Casini see GAROSI, 'La vita e l'opera di Francesco Casini'; further pointers in MINNUCCI, 'Documenti', p. 251; on his and his brother Antonio's activity at the papal *curia*, P. NARDI, 'Siena e la Curia pontificia nel 1378', in *La Roma di santa Caterina da Siena*, ed. M. G. Bianco. Quaderni della Libera Università 'Maria SS. Assunta', 18 (Rome, 2001), pp. 49-66; also below, pp. 54-5.

Fig. 2c – Seal of Giovanni di Niccolò di Mino Vincenti, second half of fourteenth century (Rome, Museo di Palazzo Venezia, Collezione Corvisieri, sezione italiana, inv. no. 9529/568).

that they were given any teaching.[115] The lawyers employed for various purposes by the commune, previously an easy source of teaching expertise, were strikingly not given lectureships, with few exceptions. In 1369 Buvalello de' Buvalelli da Bologna, the *maggior sindaco* and *giudice d'appellagioni* in the commune, was granted a contract to teach civil law (and awarded citizenship); the teaching was simply added to his existing posts, a short-term, *ad personam* appointment which hardly indicates a policy.[116] A teaching contract was again linked with the granting of citizenship, to the lawyer Francesco di Neri Gherardini da Rapolano, in 1372, at his own request; in return for this honour he was to lecture without salary 'omnibus audire volentibus'.[117] But he appears to have got out of the teaching; the following year he was in the employment of the queen of Naples.[118] The most consistent trace of law teaching comes in the shape of another communal official, the Sienese Giovanni di Niccolò di Mino Vincenti. He taught civil law briefly in 1373,[119] and some time after October 1381, when the *Consiglio Generale* resolved to hire a civil-

---

[115] PRUNAI, II, pp. 44-7 for a summary, p. 45 for those he claims were teaching between 1368 and 1385. It has not been possible to confirm the teaching activities of any of those he lists for the period. Cf. also PICCINNI, 'Tra scienza ed arti', p. 146 on these individuals.

[116] *Statuti* 35, ff. 14r-15r, 6 Dec. A year later he had been replaced in these civic offices; *CG* 181, f. 8v, 26 Jan 1371.

[117] *CG* 182, ff. 114v-115v, 24 Oct; cf. PRUNAI, II, p. 40.

[118] *Conc.* 1783, no. 107h, 24 Jan 1374; see A. GIORGI, 'Il carteggio del Concistoro della Repubblica di Siena (Spogli delle lettere: 1251-1374)', *BSSP*, 97 (1990), pp. 193-573 (pp. 464-5). In 1379 he became a Franciscan; C. PIANA, 'Il traduttore e commentatore della Divina Commedia fra Giovanni Bertoldi da Serravalle O.F.M. baccalario a Ferrara nel 1379 ed altri documenti per la storia degli Studi francescani', *Analecta Pomposiana. Studi di storia religiosa delle diocesi di Ferrara e Comacchio*, 7 (1982), pp. 131-83 (pp. 146-9), and cf. *Conc.* 1800, no. 61, 1380; in 1381 he was granted tax relief (*CG* 191, f. 66r, 17 Oct).

[119] *Bicch.* 251, f. 143v, 9 Aug. The documentation of previous years makes no reference to his teaching (*Conc.* 61, f. 27r, 11 Oct 1371, appointing him *advocatus comunis*; *Bicch.* 249, ff. 121v [new foliation], 142r, 157r, 27 Apr 1372, *Bicch.* 250, f. 199r, 20 Nov 1372); neither do several subsequent salary payments (*Bicch.* 252, f. 46r [new foliation], 17 Mar 1374, *Bicch.* 254, f. 29r and *Bicch.* 255, f. 18r [no foliation], both 2 Aug 1374). On Vincenti see PRUNAI, II, p. 40, and MINNUCCI, 'Documenti', p. 277.

ian,[120] he was reappointed, though by October 1382 he was sacked again on financial grounds.[121] What the regime did maintain was education at a more basic level. There is a regular provision throughout of grammarians and abacus teachers, on average two of each,[122] and although it is difficult to be sure, it is likely that the grammarians were teaching at the pre-university rather than the elementary level.[123]

An attempt at a fresh start was made in 1386, shortly after the fall of the government of the *Riformatori* and the installation of a coalition regime, the 'governo dei Dieci Priori'.[124] The regime began with a package of 'austerity' measures[125] but soon showed that the *Studio* was to be a priority. On 23 December 1386 it was decided to re-found it, and to that effect a body of citizens was elected to put forward reforms.[126] Their proposals, presented and accepted on 23 January 1387, re-instated the *Savi*, empowering them to sign teachers up for three-year periods, and fixed the budget at 2,500 florins, to which the clergy and the hospital of S. Maria della Scala were to contribute.[127] In March, arrangements were made to re-cruit from Bologna, Perugia and Padua, and the *Savi dello Studio* were authorised to hire teachers as they pleased.[128] This was followed later in the year by expenditure on the renting of schools and the provision of furniture, and the lifting of duties on the goods of any teachers and scholars who wished to come to Siena.[129] By the end of 1387 fourteen lectureships had been offered, six to Sienese and eight to non-Sienese teachers, and as far as can be seen most were accepted.[130] The foreign teachers included the canon-ist Pietro d'Ancarano, hired at 150 florins,[131] and the civilian Tommaso de' Covoni of Florence (155 florins);[132] early the next year the canonist Guglielmo di Cellolo da Perugia was also signed up at the un-precedented salary of 500 florins.[133] Another subsequent appointment was the Paduan physician Mar-

---

[120] *CG* 191, f. 67v, 17 Oct 1381.

[121] He was paid for teaching from 1 Jan 1382; *Bicch.* 264, f. 172r, 23 May; *Bicch.* 428, f. 119v (new foliation), Jun; *Bicch.* 265, f. 178v, 3 Dec 1382. His dismissal was part of a package of economy measures; *Statuti*, 36, f. 4v, 14 Oct 1382, ed. A. LISINI, *Provvedimenti economici della Repubblica di Siena nel 1382* (Siena, 1895), p. 21. In 1385 Francesco Casini was also sacked from his 100-florin contract (*Conc.* 125, f. 21r-v, 24 Jan 1385).

[122] In 1379 an appointment was made on the grounds that there was only one remaining grammar teacher (*CG* 189, f. 89v, 9 Nov); similarly the resolution to hire both a grammarian and an abbacist in 1384 was taken at a time when there was at most one grammarian on the books (*CG* 193, f. 85v, 10 Jan).

[123] The 1369 contract of Pietro di Chello, 'gramatice professor', was to read 'gramatice ordinarie et rettoricam extra-ordinarie' for a salary of 50 florins (*CG* 179, f. 96v, 28 Dec 1369); both the terminology and the pay suggest a university or pre-university level appointment. Grammarians and abacus teachers, though administered in the same way, were re-garded and paid differently. For a discussion of this issue see below, p. 136; on ordinary and extraordinary lectureships, see below, pp. 137-40.

[124] The term used by E. BRIZIO, 'L'elezione degli uffici politici nella Siena del Trecento', *BSSP*, 98 (1991), pp. 16-62 (p. 50).

[125] GUERRINI, 'Provvedimenti congiunturali'. The government of the *Popolo* has remained among the least researched of the period. On the crises in Siena from 1385 and 1419 see CHERUBINI, 'I mercanti e il potere', pp. 76-7.

[126] *CG* 195, f. 110v, 23 Dec (and see below, p. 210). For the election, *Conc.* 134, f. 28v, 22 Dec.

[127] *CG* 195, f. 115r-v, 23 Jan, ed. GAROSI, p. 194, n. 1; copy in *Mis.* 1, f. 50r-v; and see ZDEKAUER, pp. 25-6. Further legislation in 1388-9 defined the status and mode of election of the *Savi*. Below, p. 70.

[128] *Conc.* 136, ff. 4v, 4 Mar, and 21v, 16 Apr, ed. GAROSI, 'La vita e l'opera di Francesco Casini', p. 297 nn. 2-3 but with erroneous dates.

[129] *Conc.* 139, ff. 49v-50r, 16 Oct, and f. 62r, 27 Oct. On the 1387 measures see also GAROSI, p. 194.

[130] *Conc.* 139, f. 50r, 16 Oct (the Sienese teachers); *Conc.* 139, f. 91r-v, 18 Sept, and *Conc.* 140, f. 51r, November (the foreigners).

[131] *Conc.* 140, f. 51r, November 1387; payment in *Bicch.* 460, f. 10r (1388); cf. MINNUCCI, 'Documenti', pp. 305-6. On Ancarano in Siena see also I. BAUMGÄRTNER, 'Stadtgeschichte und Consilia im italienischen Spätmittelalter', *Zeitschrift für historische Forschung*, 17 (1990), pp. 129-54 (p. 144), and below, p. 51 and n. 133.

[132] *Conc.* 140, f. 51r, November 1387; the original contract was for 250 florins (*Conc.* 139, f. 91r-v, 18 Sept) but the sum appears to have been reduced; payment in *Bicch.* 460, f. 10v (1388).

silio Santasofia, the biggest catch apart from the lawyers.[134] This was a substantial coup in university circles, and both Florence and Pavia soon tried to lure him away, the Florentines succeeding first but soon losing him in turn to Giangaleazzo Visconti.[135] In fact the period of activity of the *Studio* was again short-lived. In October 1389 Tommaso de' Covoni's contract was revoked;[136] in March 1390 payment of salaries was suspended because of war (though the commune begged the teachers to continue nonetheless, promising payment after the end of fighting).[137] By October Ancarano had gone;[138] in fact the *Studio* closed for a year, and by January 1391 three teachers of medicine had been laid off.[139] From 1390 onwards payments are once again only made to grammar and abacus teachers and to medical doctors for non-teaching work.

The abeyance in which the *Studio* languished for much of the 1390s was something about which little could be done. The financial crisis was all-engulfing; little more than hand-to-mouth solutions could be contemplated.[140] The most to which the authorities aspired was provision of grammar teaching; in 1395, 100 florins were voted for the employment of a grammarian 'acciò che chi vuole studiare in grammatica non rischia per manchamento di maestro'.[141] In the same year the civilian Giovanni di Francesco Bellanti was released from a 100-florin fine for having taught in Bologna, another recognition of the state of affairs.[142] Yet there are some initiatives, albeit on a very modest scale. In 1396 a petition to refound the *Studio*, with two-thirds of the funding to come from the bishop, the clergy, and the hospitals of S. Maria della Scala and the Misericordia and the rest from the commune, was defeated by thirty-eight votes to twenty-two.[143] However, there was a recognition that the economic interests

---

[133] *CG* 196, f. 50v, 26 Feb 1388; cf. Minnucci, 'Documenti', pp. 257-8. Minnucci was the first to identify this as the Sienese period of Guglielmo di Cellolo, who appears, along with Pietro d'Ancarano, as *promotor* of the first extant degree for Siena, awarded on 25 April. Minnucci published this in 'Documenti', doc. I-1, p. 47, and Idem, 'A Sienese Doctorate' in Canon Law from 1389', in *The Two Laws. Studies in Medieval Legal History Dedicated to Stephan Kuttner*, eds. L. Mayali & S. A. J. Tibbetts. Studies in Medieval and Early Modern Canon Law, 1 (Washington, 1990), pp. 202-8; Italian version, with additions and revisions, 'Una laurea senese in diritto canonico del 1389', *Annuario dell'Istituto Storico Diocesano di Siena* (1994-5), pp. 151-60. The Italian version corrects the impression given in the English (doubtless a consequence of translation) that Ancarano and Cellolo had been present at the *Consiglio Generale* and *Concistoro* deliberations of 1386 and 1387. On the significance of the 1387 revival see also G. Minnucci, 'Professori e scolari giuristi nello Studio di Siena dalle origini alla fine del XV secolo', in *L'Università di Siena. 750 anni*, pp. 111-30 (pp. 114-5). The operation seems also to have netted Benedetto da Piombino, who was a member of the examining college of doctors in May 1390; loc. cit., and Idem, 'Documenti', doc. I-2, pp. 47-8, and p. 238; on him see below, p. 162 n. 137.

[134] Payment in *Bicch.* 460, f. 10v, 1388; the details are not sufficiently specific for the calculation of the annual salary, and details of the contract itself have not come to light. On this appointment see T. Pesenti, *Marsilio Santasofia tra Corti e università. La carriera di un 'Monarcha medicinae' del Trecento*. Contributi alla Storia dell'Università di Padova, 35 (Treviso, 2002), pp. 223-6, speculating that 'la prospettiva di essere il rifondatore della medicina accademica senese', as well as the salary, were the attractions of Siena rather than political factors. The Mantuan Antonio 'de Guaçiis' planned to move from Bologna to study in Siena because of this new appointment (loc. cit.). Below, p. 238.

[135] Pesenti, *Marsilio Santasofia*, pp. 226-34 on the details of this conflict, to which add *Conc.* 147, f. 11v, 12 Jan 1389, releasing him from his contract after pressure had been brought to bear on the government by Giangaleazzo Visconti. Cf. also E. Spagnesi, *Utiliter Edoceri. Atti Inediti degli Ufficiali dello Studio Fiorentino (1391-96)* (Milan, 1979), pp. 17, 61-3.

[136] *CG* 196, f. 123v, 20 Oct.

[137] *Conc.* 154, f. 17v, 23 Mar.

[138] Cf. his letter to the *Concistoro* from Venice; *Conc.* 1828, no. 4, 12 Oct.

[139] *Conc.* 159, f. 6v, 9 Jan. The commune retained only two doctors for medical purposes.

[140] Caferro, *Mercenary Companies*, esp. pp. 156-65 (and 129-30 for background).

[141] *CG* 197, f. 141r, 21 May, also in *Conc.* 2111, f. 92r.

[142] *CG* 197, f. 138r, 28 Apr; cf. Prunai, II, p. 41 (confusing his name), and on this figure generally Minnucci, 'Documenti', p. 274, and also below, pp. 52 n. 150, 53 n. 152, 164 n. 155, 167 n. 182 and 191 n. 78.

[143] *Conc.* 2111, f. 126v, 23 Apr; and see below, p. 102.

of the community were served by persuading Sienese students to stay at home,[144] and by encouraging people from the *contado* to come and study in the town.[145] In December of that year it was decided to hire a town surgeon with the condition that, should six or more students demand it, he had to lecture as well.[146] 1396 was also the year in which the comune hired Giovanni di Buccio da Spoleto to teach grammar and rhetoric as well as a *lectura Dantis*, a decision which demonstrates that, despite the circumstances, the authorities had not lost sight of intellectual ambitions in respect of their *Studio*.[147]

In 1398 a more modest attempt was made to reconstitute the *studio generale* 'come altra volta fu'. It was recognised that in the circumstances of the time this could not be achieved overnight,[148] so a committee of four was appointed for a period of two years to make reforms and contracts. They were authorised to hire a total of nine teachers, with a total budget of 600 florins.[149] Over the following months seven fresh teachers were signed up, almost all Sienese (whose lower salaries meant that little more than half of the budget was spent).[150] The next year the commune took advantage of political

---

[144] See Bishop Mormille's proposal for a college, 1393, ed. ZDEKAUER, doc. VIII, pp. 148-9 (see below, p. 300); and cf. CAFERRO, *Mercenary Companies*, pp. 161-2.

[145] A measure was passed to permit them to study in Siena free of the risk of reprisal – a sort of local version of the imperial authentic *Habita* (above, p. 34); *CG* 198, f. 31r, 22 Oct 1396.

[146] *Conc.* 2111, f. 124r; approved 16 Dec (edited by ZDEKAUER, doc. IX, p. 150); cf. *CG* 198, ff. 34v-35r, 18 Dec.

[147] *Conc.* 191, f. 6r, 4 May. His letter of acceptance is *Conc.* 1837, no. 39, 5 May (on permanent exhibition in the Archivio di Stato di Siena). Giovanni di Buccio's career at Siena was to last half a century. On this appointment see P. ROSSI, 'La "Lectura Dantis" nello Studio Senese: Giovanni da Spoleto maestro di rettorica e lettore della "Divina Commedia" (1396-1445)', *Studi giuridici dedicati ed offerti a Francesco Schupfer nella ricorrenza del XXV anno del suo insegnamento, II. Studi di Storia del diritto italiano* (Turin, 1898, repr. Rome, 1975), pp. 153-74 (the two documents above are edited in the appendix); P. NARDI, 'Appunti sui maestri e gli studi giovanili di San Bernardino da Siena', *Istituto Storico Diocesano di Siena. Annuario 1992-93* (Siena, 1993), pp. 201-222, esp. pp. 208-12, and G. ARBIZZONI, 'Giovanni da Spoleto (Giovanni di ser Buccio da Spoleto)', *DBI*, 56 (2001), pp. 227-30 include extensive and up-to-date references for this figure. Once again, the 'shadow of Florence' is evident in this initiative. A *lectura Dantis* had been initiated in 1373 (Boccaccio); Filippo Villani had held it from 1392 (cf. SPAGNESI, *Utiliter Edoceri*, p. 56), and it continued in the fifteenth century with Giovanni Malpaghini (1412) and thereafter Giovanni Gherardi da Prato. 1396 is of course famously also the year in which Emanuel Chrysoloras was appointed to teach Greek (though in the event this took place outside the *Studio*; DAVIES, *Florence and its University*, p. 15). In the context of the competition between the two cities it is difficult not to be struck by the closeness in time of these appointments. The negotiations of Chrysoloras's contract took place began in February 1496 (see GHERARDI, *Statuti*, appendix, part II, docs. 100-1, 103, pp. 364-5, 367-8); Giovanni di Buccio's appointment, made in May, began immediately, in contrast to the more frequent habit of hiring people in advance for the following academic year (below, pp. 149-51) and the salary, of 100 florins (the same as Boccaccio's), was virtually unprecedented for a teacher of grammar and rhetoric, let alone one so young. Chronology aside, it is difficult not to see the establishment by Siena of a Dante lectureship as a clearly directed bid for the intellectual stage – though it was certainly not unique, as Giovanni had previously lectured on Dante in Bologna and then Pistoia (ARBIZZONI, op. cit., p. 227). This may help explain the terms of the appointment (see also below, pp. 136-7).

[148] 'per le tempi forti delle guerre che sono stati e sono non si potrebbe così di presente a uno tracto riformarsi come si richiede'; *Conc.* 206, f. 51v, Nov (also *Conc.* 2111, ff. 209v-210r and *Conc.* 2112, f. 3r).

[149] As above, and *CG* 198, f. 95r, 27 Nov; PRUNAI, II, p. 52.

[150] The main hirings were made on 24 Jan 1399 (*Conc.* 207, f. 16r), and involved five teachers. Giovanni Bandini was given an ordinary lectureship in civil law; on 1 Dec the *Concistoro* ordered an investigation into what he had actually taught (*Conc.* 212, f. 11r); they found it to be 'ad satisfactionem auditorum et scolarum' and ordered that he be paid for a full year (f. 22v, 26 Dec; cf. ff. 15r, 12 Dec, and 43v, 27 Dec; and *Bicch.* 286, f. 38r, 9 Oct for an interim payment subject to his declaring 'ch'esso abi letto e abi auti almeno sei iscolari'). On this teacher see A. BELLONI, *Professori giuristi a Padova nel secolo XV. Profilo bio-bibliografico e cattedre*. Ius commune, Sonderhefte, 28 (Frankfurt a. M., 1986), p. 92 n. 86; WHITLEY, 'Concepts of Ill Health and Pestilence', pp. 49-51; MINNUCCI, 'Documenti', p. 271; and below, pp. 200 and 252 n. 17. Giovanni Bellanti was given an extraordinary lectureship in civil law; Mignanello di Leonardo Mignanelli was to teach the *Volumen* and *notaria* (cf. payment in *Bicch.* 285, f. 55r, 28 Jun; for a brief profile cf. MINNUCCI, 'Documenti', p. 290). Antonio Tani was to teach canon law (his salary was confirmed in 22 Oct as 80 florins, *Conc.* 211, f. 16r; the record of the payment has him as 'Misser Antonio de tomo da chianciano calonaco di Siena' and shows that his contract started on the same day as its

opportunity; the treaty whereby Siena surrendered to Giangaleazzo Visconti placed on him the obligation to provide for the *Studio* to the tune of 3,000 florins annually.[151] The 1400 and 1401 records
show roughly the same small number teaching as before the treaty (though with quite a bit of
turnover of personnel),[152] but in January 1402, with the duke's obligation clearly not honoured and
the financial crisis deepening, the *Studio* was closed by the *Consiglio Generale*, 'che pochissimi scolari
anno o non neuno, perchè si può dire spesa perduta, et è vergogna e danno gravissimo di nostro comuno'.[153]

Giangaleazzo's death and the rapid disintegration of his empire left Siena, like other states, once more
to its own devices. In 1403 there began the regime now commonly referred to as tripartite. It was to

approval, 24 Jan: *Bicch.* 286, f. 44v, 27 Nov), as was Niccolò Sozzini (also at 80 florins by October; *Conc.* 211, f. 16r, 22
Oct; he was to teach *decretalium*, *Conc.* 212, f. 5v, 13 Nov; and cf. payment in *Bicch.* 285, f. 55v, 28 Jun, also revealing the
conditions of the contract, and *apotissa* for his salary in *Conc.* 212, f. 41v, 26 Nov. For a profile see MINNUCCI, 'Documenti', pp. 293-4). Two further appointments were made that year; Tommaso da Amelia, *doctor utriusque iure*, to an extraordinary lectureship (*Conc.* 212, f. 5v, 13 Nov; he had already taught Decretals as a substitute for Sozzini when the latter had
been a prior in July and August, 8v, 22 Nov), and Pasquino di Simone to teach *notaria* at a salary of 40 florins (*Conc.* 211,
f. 16r, 22 Oct; on him see MINNUCCI, 'Documenti', p. 298). These are in addition to the continuing employment of Giovanni da Spoleto, whose contract was renewed this year for a further two years (*Conc.* 211, f. 16r, 22 Oct).

[151] *CG* 199, f. 49r, 6 Oct 1399, published in S. FAVALE, 'Siena nel quadro della politica viscontea nell'Italia centrale',
BSSP, n.s., 7 (1936), pp. 315-82, doc. 6 (esp. p. 379); see also ZDEKAUER, p. 30, and IDEM, *Origini*, p. 22; also *Dipl., Riformagioni*, 11 Dec 1399, and *Capitoli*, 107 (1399); also recorded in *Annali Sanesi* (1385-1422). *Rerum Italicarum Scriptores*, XIX (Milan, 1731), coll. 387-428 (col. 416), and TOMMASO MONTAURI, *Cronaca Senese*, eds. A. Lisini and F. Iacometti, *Rerum Italicarum Scriptores*,[2] XV, 6 (Bologna, 1931-9), p. 753. The following year Perugia made a similar pact
with Giangaleazzo, who undertook to pay 2,000 florins a year on teachers; H. M. GOLDBRUNNER, 'Die Mailändische
Herrschaft in Perugia (1400-1403)', *Quellen und Forschungen aus italienische Archiven und Bibliotheken*, 45 (1972), pp.
397-475 (p. 457; Visconti also undertook to protect the Perugian Casa della Sapienza, 457-8); and ERMINI, *Storia*, I, p.
192. The pact was made on the advice of lawyers representing the *Studio*'s college of jurists; H. M. GOLDBRUNNER, 'Die
Übergabe Perugias an Giangaleazzo Visconti (1400)', *Quellen und Forschungen aus italienische Archiven und Bibliotheken*,
42/43 (1964), pp. 285-369 (p. 329). On the *signoria* of Giangaleazzo over Siena, M. A. CEPPARI, 'La signoria di Gian
Galeazzo Visconti', in *Storia di Siena*, I, pp. 315-26. On the history of Siena's relations with Giangaleazzo (including its
impact on the *Studio*) see, in addition to FAVALE, op. cit., PESENTI, *Marsilio Santasofia*, pp. 224-6, 236, and G. COLLINO,
'La guerra veneto-viscontea contro i Carraresi nelle relazioni di Firenze e di Bologna col Conte di Virtù', *Archivio Storico
Lombardo*, 37 (1909), pp. 5-58, 315-86.

[152] Mignanello Mignanelli continued to teach until the end of January 1402 (*Conc.* 215, f. 18v, 19 Jun 1400; *Bicch.*
439, f. 233v, 1400; *Conc.* 220, f. 34r, 26 Apr 1401, ed. PIANIGIANI, doc. 4, pp. 24-5; *Bicch.* 440, f. 10v, 1401; *Bicch.* 287, f.
56v, 6 Mar 1402). Niccolò Sozzini was paid for teaching only in 1400 (*Conc.* 218, f. 39v, 29 Dec; *Bicch.* 439, f. 207v). Giovanni Bellanti, another of those given an extraordinary lectureship in 1399, replaced Antonio da Amelia in an ordinary
morning lectureship on the Digest (*Conc.* 215, f. 6v, 9 May 1400, ed. PIANIGIANI, doc. 1, p. 22) and continued to be paid
until 1402 (*Conc.* 220, f. 32r, 30 Mar 1401, ed. PIANIGIANI, doc. 3, p. 24; *Conc.* 222, f. 39, 23 Aug 1401, ed. PIANIGIANI,
doc. 5, pp. 25-6; *Conc.* 223, ff. 20r, 28 Oct 1401, ed. PIANIGIANI, doc. 7, pp. 27-8, and 34v, Sept-Oct 1401, ed.
PIANIGIANI, doc. 9, pp. 29-30; *Biccherna* 440, f. 92v [new foliation]; *Conc.* 225, f. 42v, Feb 1402; *Bicch.* 287, f. 55v, 28 Feb
1402; *Bicch.* 441, ff. 61v, 71v [new foliation]. There were also some new appointments. Bartolomeo di Cola da Castiglione
Aretino, canonist, was paid for an extraordinary lectureship he had had since the start of the academic year 1400-1 (*Conc.*
220, f. 31v, 17 Mar 1401, ed. PIANIGIANI, doc. 2, p. 23). Pietro Bonazini was paid for *notaria* teaching since 20 January
1401 (*Conc.* 223, f. 33v, Sept-Oct 1401, ed. PIANIGIANI, doc. 8, pp. 28-9). On 22 Sept 1401 three apparently new teachers
were hired; Francesco di Ser Nini and Mariano di Ser Jacopo (for ordinary lectureships in medicine), and Bartolomeo, vicar
of the bishop of Siena (an ordinary lectureship in canon law). Finally Giovanni di Buccio da Spoleto was reappointed
(*Conc.* 223, f. 10r, ed. PIANIGIANI, doc. 6, pp. 26-7).

[153] *CG* 200, ff. 60v-61r, 27 Jan (also in *Conc.* 2112, f. 8r). One grammarian and one *maestro d'abaco* were however to be
retained. On the failure of the *Studio* to retain even the relatively undistinguished teachers it had over this period see
NARDI, 'Appunti sui maestri', pp. 214-6. Perugia's experiment with Visconti rule led to very similar consequences for its
Studio; after an initial boost in 1400, closure by 1403 (GOLDBRUNNER, 'Die Mailändische Herrschaft', p. 449).

outdo that of the *Nove* in longevity, though there was little sign of that at the outset.[154] The *Studio* struggled on for another decade in the same stop-go fashion as before. Peace with Florence was concluded in 1404 and the new government turned to the revitalisation of Siena's amenities. Citing the almost total devastation of the Italian universities because of war and the political situation, it refounded the *Studio* with a budget of 3,000 florins.[155] It was decided to hire no fewer than twenty teachers, including such luminaries as the physician Jacopo da Forlì, at a salary of 650 florins (an immense sum at the time, particularly for a non-lawyer) and the jurists Paolo di Castro and Giovanni Nicoletti da Imola (both at 270 florins).[156] Sienese doctors and students were again recalled,[157] and for the academic year 1405-6 a student rector was appointed.[158] This was over-optimistic; in December 1406 the aspiration was still 'studium refirmare et reformare',[159] and a few months later the number of examiners required for degrees in medicine had to be reduced from seven to four 'considerata paucitate doctorum medicine'.[160]

However the *Studio*'s fortunes were by now finally on the turn. Two critical and interconnected developments in 1408 ensured its future. The first was papal intervention. The election of Gregory XII to the Roman obedience in November 1406 was welcomed by the Sienese,[161] and especially by their representative in Rome, the physician Francesco Casini, who urged that his native city offer to host a council to resolve the schism.[162] The fact that Francesco's nephew Antonio was bishop of Siena was an additional bonus.[163] The outcome of the diplomatic activity was that the pope came to Siena on 4

---

[154] Overviews are: Ascheri, *Siena nel Rinascimento*, Saggio I: 'Dal governo di "Popolo" al governo nobiliare' (pp. 9-108); and Idem, 'Siena nel primo Quattrocento: un sistema politico tra storia e storiografia', in *Siena e il suo territorio nel Rinascimento, I*. Documenti raccolti da M. Ascheri and D. Ciampoli. Documenti di Storia, 4 (Siena, 1986), pp. 1-53. On the first years of the regime see also Ciampoli, 'Una raccolta di provvisioni', esp. pp. 246-53, and T. Terzani, 'Siena dalla morte di Gian Galeazzo Visconti alla morte di Ladislao d'Angiò Durazzo', *BSSP*, 67 (1960), pp. 3-84.

[155] 'Veduto che di presente quasi in tutte le città dove era lo Studio per le guerre e per altre differentie, in tutto sono guasti e tolti via'. *CG* 201, f. 166r-v, 21 Nov 1404, partially ed. by Garosi, doc. 54, pp. 526-7; copies in *Mis.* 1, ff. 50v-51r, and *Statuti* 38, f. 23r; and see Terzani, 'Siena dalla morte', p. 26; Ciampoli, 'Raccolta', p. 231; and Catoni, 'Genesi', p. 160, who saw this as a deliberate attempt to be different from the previous regime. Cf. *CG* 205, ff. 135v-136r, 28 June 1412: 'cognoschasi chiaramente che se mai fu habilitata affare lo Studio è al presente, quando tutti gli Studii d'Italya e degli altri paesi so rotti e quasi mancanti ...' (see below p. 56 n. 175).

[156] *Conc.* 235, ff. 46r-47v, 3 Feb 1405, ed. Pianigiani, doc. 11, pp. 31-7. The records of payments for these years are not extant, so it is difficult to see how many of these appointments materialised. On Paolo di Castro, G. D'Amelio, 'Castro, Paolo di', in *DBI*, 22 (1979), pp. 227-33, and for additional information and references Minnucci, 'Documenti', p. 299; on Giovanni Nicoletti see Belloni, *Professori giuristi a Padova*, pp. 89-90, 236-42; cf. also D. and P. Maffei, *Angelo Gambiglioni giureconsulto aretino del Quattrocento* (Rome, 1994), pp. 10 *seq.* on both figures.

[157] *Conc.* 238, f. 31v, 21 Aug 1405. Cf. Garosi, pp. 228-9.

[158] *Conc.* 239, f. 14r, 16 Nov 1405 ('Franciscus de Catelonia studens in iure canonico'); and see below, pp. 252, 258 and 267.

[159] *Conc.* 245, f. 31r, 17 Dec, ed. Pianigiani, doc. 14, pp. 39-40.

[160] *Conc.* 247, f. 18r, 8 Apr 1407, ed. Pianigiani, doc. 16, pp. 41-42.

[161] The fullest description is still A. Lisini, 'Papa Gregorio XII e i senesi', *La Rassegna Nazionale*, 91 (1 Sept. 1896), pp. 97-117, 280-321. On the wider diplomatic context see also A. Landi, *Il papa deposto (Pisa 1409). L'idea conciliare nel grande schisma* (Turin, 1985).

[162] On Casini's diplomatic activity see Lisini, 'Papa Gregorio XII', pp. 99, 293-4, 297 n. 1, 308-9, and Landi, op. cit., pp. 79, 84-5. He was contracted to teach at the newly revitalised *Studium Urbis*, but when it closed in January 1407 he proposed to the Sienese that he and three others should transfer to Siena, bringing students with them. *Conc.* 1864, f. 56, 13 Jan 1407; cf. Lisini, p. 296 n. 1. On the short-lived reform of the *Studium Urbis* of 1406 – which did not outlast its instigator, Innocent VII – see C. Frova, 'L'Università di Roma in età medievale e umanistica con una nota sulle vicende istituzionali in età moderna', in *L'Archivio di Stato di Roma*, ed. L. Lume (Florence, 1992), pp. 247-61 (p. 249).

[163] Minnucci, 'La Chiesa e le istituzioni', pp. 219-20, including further references. Antonio became the official recipient of the privileges that followed; below, n. 166.

September 1407 and remained there for three months, during which the city inevitably became a temporary centre of international attention.[164] Again, it may be that the moment seemed right in other ways; the Florentine *Studio* had closed in 1407.[165] In any case, the payoff for Siena came some months later. In May 1408 Gregory XII issued no fewer than eight privileges in favour of the university.[166] Three of them confirmed the privileges of *studium generale* (and extended them to clerics),[167] and a fourth added theology to the subjects that might be taught. In all this there are strong echoes of the intervention of Charles IV.[168] The inclusion of theology and the extension of privileges to clerics completed the process initiated in 1357, and with them Siena had finally achieved the dual blessing, as it were, of pope and emperor. But there was more, for this beneficence brought closer a second development. The other four bulls founded and provided for a *sapienza* or college, for thirty poor students, in the old hospital of the Misericordia, a project that had been brewing for two decades. It is no exaggeration to say that these measures were decisive for the future of the *Studio*.[169]

Fig. 3 – Bull of pope Gregory XII confirming the privilege of the emperor Charles IV and extending it to include theology (Archivio di Stato di Siena, *Diplomatico, Riformagioni*, 17 May 1408).

[164] On the connections between Sienese and others fostered during this period, P. NARDI, 'Umanesimo e cultura giuridica nella Siena del Quattrocento', *BSSP*, 88 (1981), pp. 234-53 (esp. pp. 237-8); and PERTICI, *La città magnificata*, p. 31.

[165] BRUCKER, 'Florence and its University', pp. 223-4.

[166] *Mis.* 1, ff. 72r-78v (Latin), and 63r-71r (Italian). The vernacular versions were published from this *ms.* by BARDUZZI, *Documenti*, pp. 24-34. The originals are in the *Fondo Diplomatico*; and cf. Archivio Segreto Vaticano, *Reg. Lat.* 131, f. 196r-v. See also CATONI, 'Genesi', pp. 162-3; and LISINI, 'Papa Gregorio XII', pp. 294-7. On the negotiations for the privileges, BERTONI, 'Il "Collegio" dei teologi', pp. 2-3. In January 1409 a payment of 40 florins was made to the bishop of Siena in respect of these privileges (*Bicch.* 293, f. 47v: 'per più brevileghi ci rechò per lo studio e chosa de la sapienza de la nostra città').

[167] Although the extension of privileges to include dispensation from residence for beneficed clergy had according to ZDEKAUER (p. 19) been an important reason for the quest of *studium generale* status, it was only achieved at this stage. But BERTONI, 'Il "Collegio" dei teologi', p. 4 is mistaken in asserting that the dispensation only applied to teachers; see the bull of 9 May 1408 published by BARDUZZI, *Documenti*, pp. 33-4.

[168] The parallels are actually quite striking; first the visit, then the privileges, then the rejection by Siena – which, just as it had booted the emperor out in an undignified manner in 1368, now repaid Gregory by switching allegiance, a little more than a year after the bulls, to the newly elected Alexander V. Cf. LISINI, 'Papa Gregorio XII', p. 320; LANDI, *Il papa deposto*, p. 205.

[169] See below, part IV.

3. *The fifteenth century: continuity*

The brief cultural and political centrality of Siena in the months of Gregory XII's stay in the city, coupled with the privileges he granted the *Studio*, raised aspirations once more. Although we are poorly informed about 1407, there is evidence that a number of distinguished lawyers were in Siena, some of them teaching, during the period of the pope's stay, and the hirings that followed these privileges include Onofrio Bartolini of Perugia, Giovanni Nicoletti da Imola and Raffaele Fulgosio.[170] Yet this revival, too, soon proved to be fragile. Once again political events pushed the enterprise off the agenda; an invasion of Sienese territory by Ladislas of Durazzo in April 1409 set in motion a series of crises.[171] On 31 May 1409 the hospital of S. Maria della Scala asked to be released from its contribution to the *Studio* as it was in decline and the commune's money could better be spent against Ladislas; and on 3 June the *Consiglio Generale* sacked all Sienese teachers because, it was alleged (in a much quoted phrase), there were so few students that teachers were reduced to lecturing to their servants to make up the numbers.[172] Later in the year total closure was narrowly avoided at the petition of the rector and the students.[173] From 1409 to 1412 there was little activity, and an outbreak of plague in 1411 reduced it further.[174] In June 1412 the *Studio* was reopened[175] (though only after the *Concistoro* had sent the proposal back to the *Consiglio Generale* on the grounds that it had been very narrowly lost),[176] but by Sep-

---

[170] *Conc.* 255, f. 29v, 31 Jul 1408, ed. PIANIGIANI, doc. 18, pp. 43-4; cf. D. and P. MAFFEI, *Angelo Gambiglioni*, p. 12 n. 7 on the activities of these at Siena. The continued or renewed teaching of Paolo di Castro is attested not in communal records but by the man himself: 'Et ita dico et consulo ego Paulus de Castro utriusque iuris doctor actu legens Senis mo.cccc.viii. … de mense nouembris'; D. MAFFEI, E. CORTESE, A. GARCÍA Y GARCÍA, C. PIANA and G. ROSSI, *I codici del Collegio di Spagna di Bologna.* Orbis Academicus. Saggi e documenti di storia delle università, 5 (Milan, 1992), p. 233. He was also a member of the college of doctors in law that year, examining a candidate on 4 May; ZDEKAUER, doc. X.2, pp. 153-4. The alleged Sienese teaching of Prosdocimo Conti in this period (BELLONI, *Professori giuristi a Padova*, p. 303; the suggestion originates from I. FACCIOLATI, *Fasti Gymnasii Patavini* [Padua, 1757], II, p. 26) has never been substantiated from communal evidence, any more than has speculation that he might have taught at a later stage, either between 1422 and 1425 or in 1432-3; see respectively B. KOHL, 'Conti, Prosdocimo' in *DBI*, 28 (1983), pp. 463-5 (p. 464) and R. CESSI, 'La biblioteca di Prosdocimo de' Conti', *Bollettino del Museo Civico di Padova*, 12 (1909), pp. 140-8 (p. 143), repr. in his *Padova Medioevale. Studi e Documenti*, collected and re-edited by D. Gallo, 2 vols. Scritti Padovani, 2 (Padua, 1985), II, pp. 729-42.

[171] On the politics, TERZANI, 'Siena dalla morte'; more generally GINATEMPO, *Crisi di un territorio*, pp. 261-66 esp.; and S. K. COHN, JR., *Death and Property in Siena, 1205-1800* (Baltimore, Md., 1988), p. 49 esp. on the vicissitudes of the period as described in chroniclers' accounts.

[172] 'quia est paucissimus numerus studentium fiuntque expositum ipsis magnificis dominis quod maior pars legentium non habeant quasi scolares, sed pro complendo numeri multi legunt in parte ipsorum propriis famulis'. *Conc.* 260, f. 25r, 31 May, ed. PIANIGIANI, doc. 21, pp. 45-7, and *CG* 204, f. 14r-v, 3 Jun (also *Statuti* 38, ff. 79r-v, 81r); GAROSI, p. 52; ZDEKAUER, p. 37; CATONI, 'Genesi', p. 163; CIAMPOLI, 'Raccolta', pp. 251, 282-3; TERZANI, 'Siena dalla morte', pp. 51-2; PICCINNI, 'Tra scienza ed arti', p. 147.

[173] *Conc.* 262, f. 22r, 24 Sept 1409.

[174] *Annali Sanesi* (1385-1422), cols. 422-4.

[175] *CG* 205, ff. 135v-136r, 28 June, published in CATONI, 'Genesi', p. 164 n. 38; copies in *Mis.* 1, ff. 52v-53r, and *Statuti* 41, f. 124r (partial). Cf. GAROSI, p. 23, and TERZANI, 'Siena dalla morte', p. 65. A notary was sent out to sign contracts with teachers, *Conc.* 1609, f. 59r, 28 Jul 1412. The June document observes that 'tutti li Studii dItalya e degli altri paesi so' rotti et quasi mancanti', which well expressed current sentiment but may not have been entirely accurate. Padua may well have been an exception; teaching, and payment for it, were thought by R. CESSI, 'L'invasione degli Ungari e lo Studio di Padova (1411-1413)', *Atti e Memorie, R. Accad. Di Scienze, lettere ed arti in Padova*, n.s., 27 (1910-11), pp. 237-55, repr. in his *Padova Medioevale*, II, pp. 665-80 (pp. 677-8), to have continued relatively undisturbed under Venetian rule despite the threat posed to the republic by the forces of Ladislas of Naples. This positive view has however been questioned by D. GIRGENSOHN, 'Per la storia dell'insegnamento giuridico nel Quattrocento: risultati raggiunti e ricerche auspicabili', *Quaderni per la storia dell'Università di Padova*, 22-23 (1989-1990), pp. 311-9 (p. 313).

[176] *Conc.* 278, f. 28v, 23 June.

tember much of its financial provision had been diverted to the repair of the town walls, and the *Studio* was effectively closed.[177] A fresh attempt was made on 10 October 1414, when the decree of June 1412 was repeated almost verbatim.[178] This time, however, the announcement was followed up with a development of substance; on 1 February 1416 the Casa della Sapienza finally opened its doors.[179]

It is no coincidence that the long period of stop-go ended at the same time as the opening of the new college. The fundamental importance of this institution will be explored in Part IV; what it meant in terms of guaranteeing continuity and a focus for the *Studio* as a whole will also become apparent. But there were other factors too. The list of teachers hired, albeit for brief periods, since the late 1380s is a promising sign, for it suggests to us that, if the Sienese were only able to maintain the stream of funding, there was no shortage of eminent scholars ready to participate and perhaps even keen to play a prominent role in the revitalisation of their subject in Siena.[180] The *studi* of Italy were in a melting-pot; none were immune from the instability of the times, and teachers had to make career decisions accordingly. Crises were both dangers and opportunities; there was a substantial pool of teachers who yearned for more secure employment. Moreover, the need for trained professionals was as strong as ever, and given favourable circumstances, the demand for university teaching would be there too; and it is above all the changing political climate of Italy that eventually made this growth possible. Nor are these positive signs confined to Italy. For many, the ending of the Schism removed the barriers to studying abroad, and enabled a resumption of the *peregrinatio academica* that had previously been so characteristic of the university world,[181] while happily the episode that brought it about, the Council of Constance, had played a vital role in bringing academics together, forging informal networks of intellectual exchange and patronage.

A few years later Siena had the opportunity to see at first hand the benefits of this exciting new mechanism for conducting international affairs, when it found itself in the role of host of a church council from July 1423 to February 1424 following the outbreak of plague in Pavia, where it had origi-

---

[177] *CG* 205, ff. 156-7, 159, 30 Sept, quoted in TURRINI, *"Per honore et utile"*, p. 24; the payment by the hospital of S. Maria della Scala due to the *Studio* was to be made instead to the *operai delle mura*. See below, p. 106. Cf. TERZANI, 'Siena dalla morte', p. 63. *Cronaca Senese*, p. 772 (Cronaca di Tommaso Montauri) recorded that 'e' Sanesi sospesero lo Studio per due anni, che di poco era ordinato; e di questi denari si murasse le mura della città'; and cf. the account of a writer who had himself taught at the *Studio*, G. BANDINI, *Historia senensis ab anno MCCCCII usque ad annum MCCCCXXII, auctore Johanne Bandino de Bartholomeis....* in *Rerum Italicarum Scriptores*, XX (Milan, 1731), cols. 5-64 (col. 13); also FIORAVANTI, 'Pietro de' Rossi', p. 126 n. 3. Whether or not this amounted to formal closure, that was its practical effect; in 1413 the only teachers apart from grammarians were lecturers in *Institutiones* – the humblest of the law chairs – and *notaria* (*Conc.* 286, ff, 30v, 32r, 30 Oct; also *CG* 206, f. 93r, 13 Oct 1413). Is it perhaps an indication of the ongoing sense of precariousness that two degrees awarded in 1412 include phrases stressing the compatibility of Sienese procedures with those elsewhere? The *puncta* assigned to the two candidates were 'iuxta consuetudinem in talibus observatam Bononie, Padue, Perusii, Rome, Senis, Pisis, Papie et in quibuscumque aliis Ytalicis Studiis et Universitatibus'; the licence granted included 'cathedram adscendendi, legendi, regendi, disputandi, interpretandi, componendi et alios benemeritos magistrandi, Parisiis, Bononie, in Montepesulano plago, Padue, Rome, Neapoli, Tholose, Pisis, Avinionis et ubique locorum et – citra mare et ultra mare'. *Not.* 292, ff. 63r-64v, 22-23 Dec 1412, ed. MINNUCCI, 'Documenti', doc. I-3, pp. 48-52 (pp. 50-51).

[178] *CG* 206, f. 206r, 10 Oct (also in *Mis.* 1, f. 80r, *Statuti* 41, f. 213v, *Statuti* 47, ff. 212v-213r, and *Conc.* 2113, ff. 34v-35r). On the other measures of the succeeding weeks, CATONI, 'Genesi', p. 165. Yet again, Florentine competition may have been a factor, as the *Studio* there had been reopened the previous year; BRUCKER, 'Florence and its University', p. 224; GHERARDI, *Statuti*, appendix, part I, doc. XCI, p. 186 (30 Mar 1413); DENLEY, 'Academic Rivalry', pp. 195-6.

[179] See below, p. 305.

[180] A point made by PESENTI, *Marsilio Santasofia*, pp. 225-6.

[181] Cf. C. FROVA, 'Martino V e l'università', in *Alle origini della nuova Roma: Martino V (1417-1431)*, eds. M. Chiabò, G. D'Alessandria, P. Piacentini and C. Ranieri (Rome, 1992), pp. 187-203 (p. 194).

nally been convened.[182] While hardly a distinguished council in itself – indeed, it was aborted before it could even grow in size – it briefly placed the city centre-stage, this time in a more formal way, and for longer, than had the residence in Siena of Gregory XII. It was also very much a meeting dominated by academics,[183] and brought a delegation from the University of Paris as well as many scholars in the employment of major figures.[184] The *Studio's* opening ceremony of the academic year (18 Oct 1423) was held in the presence of many council members,[185] and several members of the *Studio*, both Sienese and foreign, participated in the council.[186] One such was the Sienese canon Pietro d'Antonio de' Micheli, a university figure since 1421 and subsequently a leading Sienese diplomat.[187] Another was Johannes von Azel, canon of Hildesheim, hired to teach in Siena by the beginning of 1423,[188] and involved in the negotiations to bring the council to Siena.[189] The prominent Scottish churchman Andrew

---

[182] The definitive work is W. BRANDMÜLLER, *Das Konzil von Pavia-Siena 1423-4*, 2 vols. Vorreformationsgeschichtliche Forschungen, 16; Vol. I, *Darstellung* (Münster, 1968), 2nd ed. in the series *Konziliengeschichte*, Reihe I: Darstellungen, ed. W. Brandmüller (Paderborn etc., 2002) (references are to this edition), now tr. as *Il Concilio di Pavia-Siena 1423-1424. Verso la crisi del conciliarismo* (Siena, 2004); Vol. II, *Quellen* (Münster, 1974). See also IDEM, 'Il concilio di Siena del 1423-24', in *Chiesa e vita religiosa a Siena*, pp. 389-406; and N. MENGOZZI, 'Martino V e il concilio di Siena', *BSSP*, 25 (1918), pp. 247-314.

[183] The proposal of the Italian and French nations that members should have at least the rank of doctor or a licentiate in theology seems to have been adopted; M. C. MILLER, 'Participation at the Council of Pavia-Siena, 1423-1424', *Archivum historiae pontificiae*, 22 (1984), pp. 389-406 (p. 397). On the importance for universities of this decision, L. BOEHM, 'Libertas Scholastica und Negotium Scholare. Entstehung und Sozialprestige des akademischen Standes im Mittelalter', in *Universität und Gelehrtenstand 1400-1800*, eds. H. Rössler and G. Franz. Deutsche Führungsgeschichte in der Neuzeit, 4 (Limburg/Lahn, 1970), pp. 15-61 (p.33); repr. in *Geschichtsdenken, Bildungsgeschichte, Wissenschaftsorganisation. Ausgewählte Aufsätze von Laetitia Boehm anläßlich ihres 65. Geburtstag*, eds. G. Melville, R. A. Müller and W. Müller. Historische Forschungen, 56 (1996), pp. 607-46; on the prominence of universities in the movement generally, R. W. SWANSON, *Universities, Academics and the Great Schism* (Cambridge, 1979).

[184] 'El patriarca e li anbasciatori de l'università di Parigi veneo a Siena a dì 13 di febraio [1424]; erano 6 dottori e fu lo' fatto grande onore da' cortigiani del concilio, e anco el comuno di Siena lo' fe' grande onore'; (Tommaso Montauri), *Cronaca Senese*, p. 802. Cf. BANDINI, F. T. (Francesco Tommaso di Giovanni Bandini de' Bartolomei), *Historia Senensis*, in *Rerum Italicarum Scriptores*, XX (Milan, 1731), cols. 23-26 (23-4); for their participation BRANDMÜLLER, *Konzil*, I, *ad indicem*. The rector of the Roman *Studio*, Guillelmus Brillet, was also a member of the Council (BRANDMÜLLER, *Konzil*, I, p. 402; MILLER, 'Participation', p. 401).

[185] 'E' dottori dello studio di Siena co' li scolari férono el siermone nella sala del conseglio, andovi molti vescovi e prelati del concilio, a dì 18 di ottobre'; *Cronaca Senese*, cit., p. 801. In November, 115 students participated in university elections (*Conc.* 347, f. 7r, 7 Nov 1423, and cf. BRANDMÜLLER, *Konzil*, I, p. 143 n. 2).

[186] BRANDMÜLLER, *Konzil*, I, pp. 229-30, and II, 290 on how the Sienese university members got caught up in the split of the Italian nation in February 1424.

[187] MILLER, 'Participation', p. 400. He is found engaged in a *disputatio* in 1321 (ZDEKAUER, p. 49 n. 1), and was offered a lectureship with effect from the academic year 1421-2, on condition that he obtained his degree by then; *Conc.* 330, f. 19v, 13 Feb 1421. See esp. MINNUCCI, 'Documenti', pp. 300-1; on his diplomatic career also W. BRANDMÜLLER, 'Die Römischen Berichte des Pietro d'Antonio De' Micheli an das Concistoro von Siena im Frühjahr 1431', *BSSP*, 73-75 (1966-8), pp. 146-99, and IDEM, 'Der Übergang vom Pontifikat Martins V. zu Eugen IV.' *Quellen und Forschungen aus italienischen Archiven und Bibliotheken*, 47 (1967), pp. 596-629. Another figure who was influential in bringing the council to his native Siena (cf. BRANDMÜLLER, *Konzil*, I, pp. 127-9), though he died soon after, was the general of the Franciscan order, Angelo Salvetti, who had been offered a teaching contract at the *Studio* in 1420 (see below, p. 155 n. 50).

[188] MILLER, 'Participation', p. 400 (with references); *Conc.* 1621, f. 6r, 11 Jan 1423; and C. SCHUCHARD, *Die Deutschen an der päpstliche Kurie im späten Mittelalter (1378-1447)*. Bibliothek des Deutschen Historischen Instituts in Rom, 65 (Tübingen, 1987), p. 81. His contract was renewed for two years, at 125 florins, in 1425 (*Conc.* 356, f. 19v, 22 Jun, ed. PIANIGIANI, doc. 69, pp. 90-1) and he was recommended to the pope by the *Concistoro* later that year (*Conc.* 1626, f. 43r-v, 15 Oct).

[189] *Conc.* 1622, f. 2r-v, 1-2 Jul 1423. BRANDMÜLLER, *Konzil*, I, pp. 133-4 (and IDEM, 'Il concilio', p. 204), recounts the 'unglaublichen Gewaltritt' of this figure from Pavia through Siena to Rome in seven days to announce the decision to move the council. He was paid for teaching despite his absence on this mission (*Conc.* 345, f. 15v, 3 Aug 1423; BRANDMÜLLER, *Konzil*, I, p.133 n. 28).

of Hawyk had come to Siena in the middle of a dynamic career to study canon law, and was rector of the university for the academic year 1423-4; he was an influential figure in the council.[190] Finally the participants included Niccolò Tedeschi, the most celebrated canonist of his age, whose presence in Siena is first recorded in 1419 and then regularly since 1421, and who remained there for over a decade, deeply influential both in the formation of canon law studies at Siena and in the reorganisation of the *Studio* itself, as will be seen.[191] Although some of the shine of the episode came off rapidly with the closure of the council in February 1424, and even more when the *Concistoro* ordered that the city gates be locked to prevent its departure,[192] the longer-term impact on Siena in academic terms is not in doubt.[193]

---

[190] MILLER, 'Participation', p. 403; BRANDMÜLLER, *Konzil*, I, pp. 64 n. 75 and 298 n. 18, II, pp. 359, 392, 394-5 and 397-8; D. E. R. WATT, *A Biographical Dictionary of Scottish Graduates to AD 1410* (Oxford, 1977), p. 257. He came to Siena with a baccalaureate from Florence (*Dipl., Arch. Gen.*, 6 Apr 1321), and was aiming to become bishop of Aberdeen (*Conc.* 1620, f. 1v, 1 Jan 1422); he was studying in Siena by July 1423 (*Conc.* 1622, f. 5r, 6 Jul; cf. also *Conc.* 1624, f. 5r, 15 Jul 1424, letter to Cardinal Arnaldo de Via requesting a benefice on his behalf). The council also included Peter of Perpignan, a student of medicine in Siena, while another medical student, Juan Almaçán from Sagunto, acted as notary (BRAND-MÜLLER, *Konzil*, I, p. 210 n. 35).

[191] MILLER, 'Participation', p. 406; BRANDMÜLLER, *Konzil*, I, p. 294; for bibliography see MINNUCCI, 'Documenti', p. 293. He clearly taught at the *Studio* for most of this period. Enea Silvio Piccolomini records of him 'Senis ad decem annos canones legit' (*Enee Silvii Piccolomini, postea Pii PP II, De viris illustribus*, ed. A. van Heck. Biblioteca Apostolica Vaticana, Studi e Testi, 341 [Vatican City, 1991], p. 3), which is clearly an approximation, as is his report of Tedeschi's salary (see below). Certainly he was a member of the college of doctors of law, since he was present at most of the degrees in law recorded for the period; witness at that of Angelus Andree Bernardini de Guidonibus of Perugia, 4 Jan 1419 (AAS 4420, f. 151r-v), presenter of Valentius Angelelli of Narni, 31 May 1421 (loc. cit., ff. 194r-195v), witness to Filippo Balducci, 7-8 Nov 1424 (*Not.* 325, ff. 40v-44r, ed. MINNUCCI, 'Documenti', doc. I-5, pp. 54-6), *promotor* of Giovanni da Prato, 7 Feb 1428 (see below, p. 202 n. 158), examiner of Giovanni Riczari, 29 Mar 1428 (*Not.* 326, f. 63r-v, ed. MINNUCCI, 'Documenti', doc. I-6, pp. 56-7). There is also no shortage of evidence of his legal activities in Siena, including his work for the commune; M. ASCHERI, 'Nicola "el monaco" consulente, con edizione di due suoi pareri olografi per la Toscana', in *Niccolò Tedeschi (abbas panormitanus) e i suoi Commentaria in Decretales*, ed. O. Condorelli (Rome, 2000), pp. 37-68 (esp. pp. 40-3), and see *Bicch.* 302, ff. 36r, 52r, and *Conc.* 321, f. 36v, 31 Aug and 31 Dec 1419. It is less clear, however, when exactly he began teaching. His printed works include reference to a *quaestio* disputed by him on 29 Jan 1422 (ZDEKAUER, p. 49 n. 1). Though the *Concistoro* records for these years include decisions regarding the hiring of teachers, they do not mention him in this role until a letter to the pope on his behalf, dated 27 May 1424, in which his teaching is described as having brought glory to the city; *Conc.* 1623, ff. 52v-53r, and cf. N. MENGOZZI, 'La crise religieuse du XV siècle – Martino V ed il concilio di Siena (1418-1431)', *BSSP*, 25 (1918), pp. 247-314 (pp. 298-9). The first proof of a teaching contract dates from 1424, for the period from which we have *Biccherna* volumes in which the payment of teaching salaries is recorded; he was paid from December 1424 (*Bicch.* 307, ff. 38v, 12 Dec, 52 *lire*, and 45v, 31 Dec, 668 *lire*; *Bicch.* 456, ff. 39v, 21 Mar 1425, 400 *lire*, and 30 Apr, 240 *lire*, 84v, 31 Aug, 300 *lire*, 86v, 9 Sept, 80 *lire*, and 99v, 24 Dec, 440 *lire*). His contract was renewed for two years on 14 Apr 1428 at a salary of 750 florins (*Conc.* 372, f. 27v; he accepted; this is as close as the records come to support Enea Silvio Piccolomini's statement that 'stipendium ei octingentorum aureorum in anno fuit', *De viris illustribus*, loc. cit.) and again in May 1429 (*Conc.* 379, ff. 10r, 14 May, and 16v, 16 May, with the additional clause that he was to follow the rector of the *Studio* and 'scolares nobiles' but to precede the rector of the Casa della Sapienza' in 'honoribus'). Payments are recorded again in 1430 (*Bicch.* 310, ff. 11r, 13 Mar, 41r, 12 Jun, and 69v, 28 Dec, 250 fl. each for the three *terzarie* of the academic year 1429-30). On 5 Mar 1431 he was given leave of absence for fifteen days to travel to meet the pope, with no loss of salary provided that he arranged a substitute (*Conc.* 391, f. 5v); on 4 Jun that year he was released from his contract and the remaining 225 florins of his salary were to be paid (*Conc.* 392, f. 44r). A replacement for his lectures was, however, only arranged in April 1433 (Mariano Sozzini; see below, p. 167 n. 176).

[192] BRANDMÜLLER, *Konzil*, I, pp. 273-92, and IDEM, 'Il concilio', pp. 212-4.

[193] On the importance of the Council for the development of the *Studio*, MINNUCCI, 'La Chiesa', p. 223; NARDI, *Mariano Sozzini*, pp. 8-9. A similar impact can be traced for the Council of Ferrara (1438) on the *Studio* there; BARGAGLI, *Bartolomeo Sozzini*, p. 8. The seven-month residence in Siena of Eugenius IV and the *curia* in 1443 caused a similar resurgence in *Studio* activity.

Table 1 – Size of the teaching force, 1450-1500

Academic Year	Average of *apotisse*[1]	Lists of lectureships[2]
1450-1	17.00	
1451-2	24.33	
1452-3	15.67	
1453-4	12.67	
1454-5	9.33	
1455-6	10.67	
1456-7	12.67	
1457-8	9.33	
1458-9	21.00	23
1459-60	23.00	
1460-1	24.33	
1461-2	26.00	
1462-3	16.33	
1463-4	24.00	
1464-5	27.67	
1465-6	34.67	
1466-7	31.00	
1467-8	26.33	
1468-9	33.00	
1469-70	25.00	
1470-1	36.00	
1471-2	28.00	
1472-3	26.00	
1473-4	35.67	
1474-5	38.67	
1475-6	45.67	
1476-7	33.67	
1477-8	28.67	
1478-9	0.00	
1479-80	12.00	
1480-1	29.67	30
1481-2	32.00	
1482-3	20.00	
1483-4	27.00	
1484-5	29.00	
1485-6	33.67	
1486-7	34.33	
1487-8	39.67	30
1488-9	35.50	42
1489-90	36.67	
1490-1	47.50	36
1491-2	48.33	
1492-3	41.50	45
1493-4	45.33	
1494-5	33.00	38
1495-6	21.33	
1496-7	35.33	
1497-8	36.67	
1498-9	41.67	39
1499-1500	46.00	

[1] The data in this column represents the average number of doctors over the three annual lists of instructions to pay salaries, adjusting for delayed payments and the occasional missing list. Pre-university teachers have been excluded from the calculations even where they appear in the lists. Data is taken from the records of the *Concistoro*, eds. BAI and FERRERI, *passim*.

[2] Information from lists in the *Concistoro* and *Balìa* records intended to represent the full teaching force (similar to the formally published *rotuli*). Details in Table 3, below, pp. 127-8.

This narrative will not be pursued into the mid and late fifteenth century; the *Studio* in that period will be observed from a number of angles in the chapters that follow. But it is perhaps appropriate to try to give a sense of what is meant here by stability and continuity. The most obvious indicator is the roll-call of leading figures. The 1420s and 1430s saw a large number of eminent teachers finding their way to Siena, if only briefly in many cases. The *Studio* of these years included, besides Niccolò Tedeschi, lawyers of the calibre of Antonio Roselli of Arezzo, Guasparre Sighicelli of Bologna, Sallustio Buonguglielmi, Benedetto Barzi and Baldo Bartolini of Perugia, and Lodovico Pontano of Rome; the physician Pietro Giovannetti of Bologna, the humanist Filelfo and the theologian-philosophers Paolo Veneto, Andrea Biglia and Gabriele da Spoleto. The later part of the century sees the same localisation that has been observed for other universities, but always with a sprinkling of academic stars from elsewhere; Francesco Accolti, Giovanni Battista Caccialupi da San Severino, Lancilotto and Filippo Decio in law, Alessandro Sermoneta in medicine. The period also saw the emergence of native Sienese teachers, both as the backbone of the teaching force and as leading lights – Pietro de' Pecci, Tommaso Docci, Mariano and Bartolomeo Sozzini in law, Bartolo di Tura Bandini in medicine, Agostino Dati in rhetoric, Pietro de' Rossi in philosophy and theology – and by the later part of the century a host of perhaps less distinguished names, but nonetheless ones whose presence ensured the credentials of a *Studio* which could continue to attract large numbers of foreign students. This flow of students, attracted by a number of factors, including particularly the Casa della Sapienza, is another key reason for the determination to keep the *Studio* going through thick and thin.

Another obvious indication of health is the size of the *Studio*. Unambiguous figures are difficult to compile. For comparative purposes the simplest measure to take would be the one by which the Sienese themselves would have wanted to be judged, the *rotoli* or lists of teachers published at the beginning of the academic year (or their equivalent in the communal minutes). But these are rare before the late fifteenth century, and express aspiration rather than reality. A better indicator is the number of those paid for teaching, for which there is consistent data from 1450 (Table 1).[194] From these figures it is evident that by the second half of the fifteenth century the Sienese university was a substantial, ongoing institution. If we set aside the fact that we are comparing different types of information, some crude comparisons can be made. The Sienese lists are, of course, shorter than those of the largest Italian *studi* of the period, Bologna, Pavia and Padua.[195] They are, however, very similar to those for Pisa in the late fifteenth century (Fig. 4). The Florentine *Studio*, reopened in its new location in 1473, overtook Siena by 1479,[196] but was smaller again between 1486-7 and 1492-3. Between 1473-4 and 1500-1, Siena had the larger payroll in sixteen academic years, Pisa for eight.[197]

[194] Figures for earlier years can be compiled from individual records of payment that survive in the *Biccherna*, together with other sources. A full statistical profile will only be possible after further prosopographical research. Comparison of the payment figures with those of the full *rotolo*-type lists (Table 1, col. 3) make it clear that not all those appointed actually taught – though there are also years in which the number paid is greater than that in the formal list, suggesting either that these lists are not complete or that subsequent appointments were made. This will never be an exact science.

[195] For Bologna, cf. DALLARI, *I Rotuli*, I, and the summary table for the years 1473-1503 in VERDE, *Lo Studio fiorentino*, I, pp. 294-5 (and see Fig. 4); for Pavia, ZANETTI, 'A l'Université de Pavie', table facing p. 428. The few surviving lecture lists for Padua, analysed by GRENDLER, *The Universities of the Italian Renaissance*, pp. 23-31, suggest that it comes in third place, but still well ahead of Siena.

[196] We have no data for Siena for 1478-9, suggesting that the *Studio* was closed; see below, p. 63.

[197] The situation may have been not that different earlier in the century. *Biccherna* payments are made to twenty-six teachers in the second half of 1424 and twenty-seven in the first half of 1425 (see Table 2 below, p. 95, for references). DAVIES, *Florence and its University*, p. 2, gives the average number of teachers in Florence as nineteen in the period 1413-23, eight in 1423-8 and twenty-seven in 1428-32.

A crucial factor in this happy outcome is the comparative stability of Sienese government in the period. The regime that began in 1403 turned out to be one of the longest in duration, and, despite reversals, one of the most cohesive. During its lifetime, the importance of keeping the *Studio* going was never seriously questioned. An indicator of this is the determined way in which the authorities faced and overcame all threats to its survival. The frequent recurrence of plague could cause disruption, but from 1417 onwards this was always dealt with by temporary relocation within Sienese territory.[198] The *Studio* also recovered quickly on other occasions when its stability was jeopardised. In the early 1430s there was a danger of decline – shortage of funds at a time of warfare led to an overall reduction in salaries in 1431, which was followed by the departure of several teachers and a dramatic increase in absenteeism[199] – but the situation was soon back to normal. There was a decline in the early

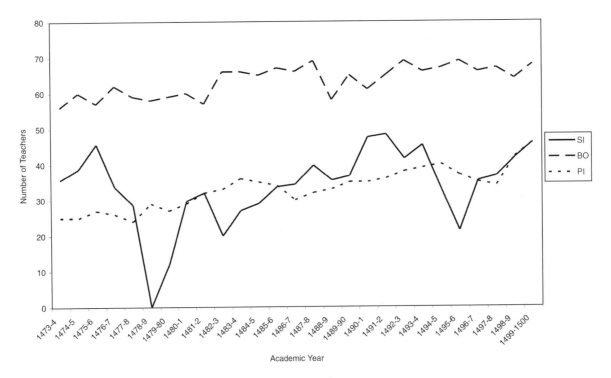

Fig. 4 – Size of the teaching force at Siena, Pisa and Bologna, 1473-1500.

Sienese data represents the averages of the *apotisse* (see Table 1, p. 60). Pisan and Bolognese data is from *rotoli*, and is taken from VERDE, *Lo Studio fiorentino*, I, pp. 293-5. Teachers based in Florence have not been included in the Pisa data. The figures for Bologna do not include student lectureships, which is reasonable given that they were a form of subsidy rather than real teaching posts (see below, p. 283 n. 41).

---

[198] Below, pp. 113-5.

[199] See below, pp. 184-5. There was in fact an unsuccessful move to close the *Studio* for three years because of the war, on 29 Jul 1431 (*CG* 216, f. 63v; the motion was defeated by 163 votes to 110). The financial crisis was not confined to the *Studio*; it was felt by the biggest landowner, the hospital of S. Maria della Scala as well; G. PICCINNI, 'La strada come affare. Sosta, identificazione e depositi di denaro di pellegrini (1382-1446)', in G. PICCINNI and L. TRAVAINI, *Il Libro del Pellegrino*

1450s, in the last stages of warfare before the Peace of Lodi,[200] but after Siena's own political crisis of 1456 the re-formed government soon made the revival of the *Studio* a priority.[201] Another financial crisis appears to have occurred in 1462,[202] while there appears to have been no teaching in the academic year 1478-9 because of war.[203] None of this amounted to serious threats to the future existence of the enterprise. The tradition of the *Studio* – embodied physically in the Casa della Sapienza, and also in the numbers of teachers and students present – became established to the point where its discontinuation became unthinkable.

The very length of the *Studio*'s odyssey appears to have become one of the guarantors of its continuity. The impulse towards 'renovatio', observable in the reforms and initiatives that followed each change of regime in the fourteenth century, continued in the fifteenth century and beyond.[204] By the time of its final flowering, after all the false starts, the will to guarantee the *Studio* appears to have become not just fixed in the political psyche, but a priority.[205] In this sense the *Studio* did indeed 'transcend politics'.[206] But the reasons for this are practical as well as idealistic. The positioning of Siena in a respectable central role (if not a dominant one) among the political echelons of Italy, and the blossoming of the *Studio*, are two sides of same phenomenon. If Siena's temporary political eminence helped boost the *Studio* at the time of the church council, it could equally be argued that the *Studio* was instrumental in helping Siena to find itself a niche. The many instances of recommendations for students, and their subsequent careers, detailed in the chapters that follow, show how this reciprocal process could operate.

(Siena 1382-1446). Affari, uomini, monete nell'Ospedale di Santa Maria della Scala (Napoli, 2003), pp.1-81 (esp. p. 19). Nor was Siena the only *Studio* to feel the pinch that year; Florence saw the sacking of some teachers (GHERARDI, *Statuti*, appendix, part 1, doc. 132, pp. 240-1, 11 Oct; and see p. LII). The 1431 crisis appears to have led Bologna into an attempt at revival; 'Cronaca A', *Corpus Chronicorum Bononiensium*, in *Rerum Italicarum Scriptores*, 18/1, p. 53 ('et per chasone delle guerre, ch'eno circumstante, credese che'l studio de Fiorenza, de Siena, de Padoa et de Pavia se desviarono per tale modo che quello de Bologna se refermarà bene; et speremo che non passarà Nadale che qui haveremo più de cinquecento scolari').

[200] See Table 1 above, p. 60. Niccolò Nanni observed in his tax declaration of 1453 'quanti sieno e ghuadagni di quegli che si doctorano ne lo studio et città vostra, anco questo è noto che piccolissimi sono perché e tempi sono stati e sono contrari agli studii, et molto più s'apparechiano et saranno ne' tempi bisognara usare la lira, et così tutti studianti sono partiti' (*Lira* 145, n. 46).

[201] 'Renovatione studii' is the agenda in 1458; *Conc.* 552, f. 12r, 15 Sept, ed. BAI, doc. 111, p. 92. Cf. *Balìa* 10, ff. 122v-123v, and *Statuti* 40, f. 133r-v, 13 Sept 1458: 'Et essendo per le guerre passate e altre cagioni in parte manchato; et hora ritrovandosi quieta, con salubrità d'aere, si cognosce manifestamente che prestissimo lo studio si magnificarebbe e diventarebbe copioso nella vostra città. Et sicondo le informationi che anno e detti Savi dello Studio, per lettere d'avisi da Bolognia, ferrara, perugia e altri luoghi, Immediate si sentissero facte le condotte oportune, Infiniti scolari verieno qua, loco aptissimo allo studio e gratissimo alli scolari.' The proposal was to return to contracts as made 'quando lo studio era famoso'. Cf. the measure designed for the 'conservationem et restaurationem Studii' in 1478 (*Conc.* 668, f. 8v, 8 Jan, ed. FERRERI, doc. 59, p. 51).

[202] *CG* 229, ff. 196r-7r, 9 Apr. 1462; below, p. 101 n. 65.

[203] I have found no specific references to the impact of the political situation on the *Studio*; all the normal sources simply dry up. It is perhaps significant that on 4 Mar 1479 the long-serving doctor of medicine, Alessandro Sermoneta, writing from Pisa, requested permission to teach elsewhere; *Balìa* 498, no. 59, ed. L. ZDEKAUER, 'Lettere volgari del rinascimento senese', *BSSP*, 4 (1897), pp. 237-86 (letter XXXXI, pp. 284-5), and below, p. 181 n. 289.

[204] See n. 201 above, and below, pp. 65-8.

[205] Antonio Bichi, giving an *Oratio coram generali Collegio Studii Senensis* shortly before 1457, praised the regime for continuing to maintain the Studio in times of war; FIORAVANTI, 'Pietro de' Rossi', p. 126 n. 1.

[206] On this theme see also below, pp. 216 *seq*.

II

COMMUNAL ADMINISTATION

1. *'Onore e utile'*

To Rashdall 'the most remarkable feature of this university is the closeness of its dependence on the town'.[1] Papal or imperial authority notwithstanding, from the 1270s to the fall of the republic resolutions passed in the *Consiglio Generale* or the *Consiglio del Popolo* were worded on the basis that the *Studio* was the creation and responsibility of the commune.

The preambles to these measures give some of the reasons why the commune so valued the *Studio*. The committee appointed to propose reforms in 1450 termed it 'una delle principali corone de la nostra città';[2] reformers of 1463 described it as 'la gloria fama utile et honore a la città'.[3] 'Onore' and 'utile' are recurrent themes of these statements,[4] as they are for other Sienese projects.[5] The honour and nobil-

---

[1] RASHDALL, II, p. 34.

[2] *CG* 224, f. 326v, 16 Feb, ed. GAROSI, doc. 62, pp. 530-1. The terms continue to be used after the fall of the republic; the *Studio* is described as 'principalissimo ornamento della città, a cui portava grande utile et reputatione' (1583), and 'principale splendore della città' (1587); PRUNAI, III, pp. 95, 97.

[3] *CG* 229, f. 379r-v, 21 Jun (f. 379r). Cf. the preamble to a measure of 13 Sept 1458: 'Considerata la fama honore e utilità quale sempre a riportata la vostra città ne' tempi passati, che chiaramente si comprende essa città nostra per lo studio essere nobilitata e locuplectata', *Balìa* 9, f. 110r, and also *Balìa* 10, ff. 122v-123r, and *Statuti* 40, f. 133r-v.

[4] 'Item veduto quanto lo studio sia et d'honore et d'utile ala città nostra' (*CG* 219, f. 117r, 25 Feb 1437; = *Conc.* 2114, f. 103r, ed. SHAW, 'Provisions following "Proposte generali"', p. 121, giving the date as 1436; on this see below, p. 299 n. 1); 'In prima considerato l'onore e utile che la vostra M. città conseguisse per lo studio quando è florido' (*Balìa* 6, f. 143r, 27 Jan 1458; also *Balìa* 7, ff. 142v-153r, and *Statuti* 40, f. 131r-v). The *Balìa* in 1488 considered the *Studio* 'essere uno di quelle cose che rechano a la nostra città utile et honore' (*Conc.* 730, ff. 26v-30r, 9 Jun, ed. FERRERI, doc. 281, pp. 245-51 [p. 246]). 'Et è noto a ciascuno che [*sic*] quanto utile et honore sia estata et sia lo detto studio ala città nostra' (*Conc.* 2139, no. 104, f. 187r-v, 16 Jan, n.d. but probably mid-1490s judging by its position in the collection). It is 'membro honorevole e utile a la uostra Eccelsa Republica' (*CG* 243, f. 244v, 14 Dec 1533, ed. KOŠUTA, 'Documenti', doc. I-4, pp. 335-6). The consequences of failure are also expressed in the opposite terms; the 'grandissima declinatione' of the *Studio* which had begun in the 1520s would, if it continued unchecked, result in 'non poco detrimento et infamia della vostra republica'; *CG* 242, ff. 98v-100r, 3 Apr 1526 (f. 98v).

[5] So much so that it forms the title of P. TURRINI, *"Per honore et utile"*; and cf. EADEM, 'Lo Stato senese e l'edilizia pubblica e privata nel '400: un'introduzione archivistica', in *Siena e il suo territorio nel Rinascimento, III*, pp. 185-94 (p. 185); and PICCINNI, 'L'Ospedale', p. 297 and n. 1, quoting a measure of 1433 where it is observed of the hospital 'fa grande honore ala nostra città et àlle, per li tempi passati, prestato buona et grande fama fra tutte le nationi de' christiani'. On the theme of *honor* at the heart of public projects, ASCHERI, *Siena nel Rinascimento*, pp. 24-5.

ity accruing to a city in possession of such a fount of culture was self-evident; 'la scienzia è quella chosa che onora la città è cittadini d'essa, et per la quale si vive in grandeza sì di virtù et sì ancho di richeze, chome manifestamente si vede.'[6] More specific reasons are also cited. A *studio* attracted wise men[7] and the influx of foreigners enriched the city financially,[8] brought qualified people into office,[9] spread the fame of Siena[10] and gave it contacts and influence.[11] More practically it provided the means of educating the sons of citizens at elementary and higher levels,[12] and of setting them on career paths,[13] especially as many Sienese could not afford the luxury of studying in other towns[14] or of seeking professional

[6] *CG* 206, f. 206r, 10 Oct 1414 (also in *Mis.* 1, f. 80r, *Statuti* 41, f. 213v, *Statuti* 47, ff. 212v-213r, and *Conc.* 2113, ff. 34v-35r); quoted in ZDEKAUER, p. 36 (mis-dated 1419), and FIORAVANTI, 'Pietro de' Rossi', p. 130. Cf. *CG* 168, f. 4r-v, 19 Jul 1361 (ed. ZDEKAUER, doc. V, p. 143): 'civitatem quanlibet omni magnanimitate florere virtutibus ac lucris et honoribus quibuscumque ex Studio generali', and *CG* 171, f. 31r-v, 27 Mar 1364 (ed. ZDEKAUER, doc. VI, pp. 144-5): 'quanta sit utilitas quantaque nobilitas et honorificentia, que provenit ex Studio generali civitatibus'.

[7] *CG* 168, f. 4r-v, 19 Jul 1361 (ed. ZDEKAUER, doc. V, p. 143): 'Hic venient moraturi Senis viri sapientes'.

[8] *CG* 205, ff. 135v-136r, 28 Jun 1412, ed. CATONI, 'Genesi', p. 164 n. 38 (and above, p. 56 n. 175 for other versions): 'peroché tutti e cittadini ne guadagnano et bonificano tutte l'arti et le cabelle et entrate del comune et molti denari forestieri ne vengono nella nostra città, sì come s'è veduto per experientia chiaramente ne' tempi passati quando c'è stato lo Studio'; or the assertion that 'per questa via de li scolari molti denari si lassano in Siena' (*CG* 240, f. 72r, 26 Jan 1486, ed. BARGAGLI, 'Documenti senesi', doc. 72, pp. 312-3, and see EADEM, *Bartolomeo Sozzini*, p. 101 and n. 47). The 1533 proposal (above, n. 4) also referred to 'l'utile deli denari che giornalmente li studenti spendono'.

[9] The need for an expert lawyer to advise the commune is given as a reason for a *condotta* in 1366 (*CG* 175, f. 63v, 24 Dec; cf. PRUNAI, II, pp. 39-40); the lack of expertise is the justification for an (unsuccessful) attempt to revitalise the *Studio* in 1396 (*Conc.* 2111, f. 126v, 23 Apr 1396, and see above, pp. 51-2). On the increasing number of offices for which a degree was required and the problems this presented, below, pp. 216 *seq.*

[10] Cf. Martino di Pietro of Portugal's petition (*CG* 232, f. 23v, 22 Oct 1467) to be admitted to the Casa della Sapienza because the *Studio* of Siena was very famous in his country 'peroché tutti quasi li doctori che sono in quello regno sono doctorati nel vostro studio' (= also *Conc.* 2138, no. 107, f. 176r). See below, pp. 231, 241 and 299; and the 1533 proposal (as above, n. 4), which includes the phrase: 'oltre a l'honore, riputatione e fama che ne riporta essa vostra Città per tutto il mondo'.

[11] In 1480 an expansion of the *Studio* was proposed 'a la quale cose ne sete confortati etiam dal summo pontifice, et molti R[everendissi]mi S[igno]ri Car[dinal]i che hanno studiato nel vostro studio, et etiam da la M[aes]tà del Re'; *Conc.* 2123, ff. 19r-20r, 2 Jun (f. 19r), on which document see below, p. 89 n. 24. In 1533 a petition was presented to the *Consiglio del Popolo* asking that the *Studio* be preserved 'tal che molti principi e signori, ecclesiastici e temporali sonno stati pronti in esserli favorevoli come si fussero stati de proprii vostri cittadini, sol per havere studiato nela vostra Città'; *CG* 243, f. 244v, 14 Dec, ed. KOŠUTA, 'Documenti', doc. I-4, pp. 335-7 (p. 336). Earlier that year the record of the election of the rector includes a similar endorsement of the value of the 'alumnus factor': 'perché per il passato apertamente si è conosciuto, oltre al utile, di quanti honori sia stato sempre ala Città nostra lo Studio che in essa si ritrova, per esserci concorsi infiniti scolari a studiare, quali di poi partitosene dottorati e ritornati ala patria loro e andati in altri luoghi, hanno molto la fama d'esso ampliata.' *Conc.* 2208, no foliation, 23 Jun 1533, ed. KOŠUTA, 'Documenti', doc. XII-1a, p. 417.

[12] 'Sapientum multitudo, Salomone testante, erit sanitas toti urbi' (1361; as n. 6 above). It was common practice for grammarians who taught at elementary level to come under the organisation and pay of the *Studio*. Cf. VERDE, *Lo Studio fiorentino*, III, pp. 1005 *seq.*, and below, p. 136.

[13] 'e inoltre che li vostri figli diventano ripieni di littere, quali li sono scala ale prelature e altre dignità', 1533 (as above, n. 4).

[14] 'Si darebbe materia a nostri cittadini che studiassero et diventassero valenti, la qual chosa non possono fare per non avere il modo d'andare a studiare nelle terre altrui, dove si sta con grandi disagi et spese'; 28 Jun 1412, cit. (n. 8 above). Cf. the proposal of Bishop Mormille for a Casa della Sapienza, *Conc.* 2171, fasc. 42 (1392), ed. ZDEKAUER, doc. VII, p. 147, but December 1393: 'ad ciò che di gli uomini si facciano valenti, e chi vuole studiare e non può, per non andare per l'altrui terre', and the commune's response, *CG* 107, f. 88v, 12 Jan 1394, ed. ZDEKAUER, doc. VIII, pp. 148-9: 'acciò che i cittadini possino fare studiare e' loro figliuoli, però che molti cittadini potranno a casa loro fare studiare e' loro figliuoli, dove e' non so' possenti a mandarli a Bologna nè altrove per la spesa grande che l'occorrirebbe' (for correct dating see below, p. 300 nn. 5 and 9); also a petition by the rector and scholars for more teachers, citing 'utilitate et favore vestrorum civium et subditorum pauperum qui non possunt ad aliena studia se transferre', *Conc.* 2136, no. 48, 7 Oct, n.d. but either 1407 or1408; and a measure of 1415, when the Sapienza was to be founded so that Sienese could study 'sine eundo ad terras alienas cum gravibus expensis' (*Mis.* 1, f. 51v, 12 Aug 1415). The problem had been identified in 1278: 'nec expediat cives talium civitatum

advice from outside the city.[15] These last reasons are most frequently voiced; but it is clear that the Sienese viewed the domestic and international aspects of the *Studio* as closely linked, and the principal effort was expended in attracting foreign teachers and students, which was seen as the key to its success.

None of these reasons are in the slightest unusual,[16] and indeed elsewhere they can often be found listed together in documents of foundation and measures relaunching universities.[17] The formulaic nature and function of some of these phrases is undoubted, and they frequently echo the self-interested arguments made by members of the university itself, particularly on the many solemn occasions of the academic calendar in which these are routinely and perhaps even ritually expressed.[18] However, the fact that the legislators had ready access to the rhetoric employed within and by the *Studio* itself does not make the *topoi* any less real.[19] In Siena, besides appearing together at moments of attempted re-foundation (1412) or reassessment and reform (1450), these justifications are frequently articulated separately, in the preambles to specific measures.[20] The sometimes stylised or repetitive nature of these phrases does not detract from what they reveal, namely a strong belief in the commune's role as sponsor of education and in the many-faceted value of that education, both for the reputation and for the prosperity of the city.[21] This formed an integral part of the ideology that accompanied government in

ad terras causa proficiscendi pergere alienas'; *Chartularium*, doc. 31, pp. 22-4, 2 Sept (p. 23). The argument is also a familiar one in other centres. The 1429 reopening of the Florentine *Studio* was partly motivated by a desire to limit the outflow of bullion due to the many Florentines studying elsewhere; GHERARDI, *Statuti*, appendix, part I, doc. CXVII, pp. 210-14, 15 Mar, discussed in A. MOLHO, *Florentine Public Finances in the Early Renaissance, 1400-1433* (Camb., Ma., 1971), pp. 134-5 (and see below, p. 279 n. 3).

[15] 'Et tutti gli uomini della nostra città e del nostro contado non anno li spendii a mandare loro cose a Padova o a Bologna'; the measure of 10 Oct 1414 (as n. 6 above).

[16] On the utilitarian justifications of state-sponsored higher education, J. VERGER, 'Les universités européennes à la fin du XVᵉ siècle', in *Les échanges entre les universités européennes à la Renaissance*, eds. M. BIDEAUX and M.-M. FRAGONARD (Geneva, 2003), pp. 11-22, and P. J. JONES, *The Italian City-State. From Commune to Signoria* (Oxford, 1997), esp. pp. 450-1; for Roman and Neapolitan comparisons (both special cases because of papal and imperial interests), FROVA, 'L'università e la città', pp. 22-4. Similar rhetoric in Arezzo has been described as having become 'uno standard ideologico dell'amministrazione'; P. RENZI, '"Ché più si spara et dimenticha in uno dì che non se impara in dieci": Arezzo, lo *Studio* che abbiamo perduto', *Nuova Rivista Storica*, 85 (2001), pp. 39-60 (p. 44).

[17] For example, a petition to Leonello d'Este in 1442 for the re-foundation of the Ferrarese *Studio* gives a list of reasons almost identical to the above. F. BORSETTI, *Historia almi Ferrariae Gymnasii* (Ferrara, 1735), pp. 47-9, tr. in L. THORNDIKE, *University Records and Life in the Middle Ages* (New York, 1944), pp. 333-4. Similar utilitarian arguments predominate in the 1459 petition for the foundation of the university of Basel, stressed in the influential review of S. STELLING-MICHAUD, 'Quelques remarques sur l'histoire des universités à l'époque de la renaissance', in *Les Universités Européennes du XIVᵉ au XVIIIᵉ siècle. Actes du Colloque International à l'occasion du VIe Centenaire de l'Université Jagellonne de Cracovie, 6-8 Mai 1964*. Commission Internationale pour l'Histoire des Universités, Etudes et Travaux, 1 (Geneva, 1967), pp. 71-83 (p. 75), on which see also S. DE ROSA, 'Studi sull'Università di Pisa. I, Alcune fonti inedite: Diari, lettere e rapporti dei bidelli (1473-1700)', *History of Universities*, 2 (1982), pp. 97-125 (pp. 98-9), and WEBER, 'Ces grands privilèges', pp. 23 *seq.* (with full references to the sources and literature). The point about Siena's non-uniqueness in this respect is also made by FIORAVANTI, 'Pietro de' Rossi', p. 130.

[18] See esp. FIORAVANTI, 'Pietro de' Rossi', pp. 125-7 and 130.

[19] 'Il fatto che la retorica sullo Studio si identifichi con la retorica nello Studio, monotona, ma abbondante, regolare ed istituzionalizzata (lodi delle discipline, discorsi di dottorato, orazioni inaugurali dei vari corsi etc.) è anch'esso indizio di un più regolare funzionamento, di uno spazio e di una importanza reali acquistati da questa istituzione nella vita della Siena quattrocentesca.' (Ibid., pp. 127-8). The evidence alongside the rhetoric for the earlier period convinced BOWSKY, *A Medieval Italian Commune*, p. 278, that 'Sienese support for the university stemmed from a genuine desire to augment communal glory and attain intellectual eminence and renown.'

[20] They also precede the internal practices of the university, since they can be found as early as the thirteenth century.

[21] 'La coerenza della scuola con la città si esprime naturalmente nella consapevolezza che c'è un nesso necessario tra formazione scolastica, attività di governo, esercizio di compiti tecnici a servizio delle amministrazioni cittadine, svolgimento di

Siena (as elsewhere, though arguably more so), with its many physical and other manifestations,[22] and with a coherent didacticism to back it up. These beliefs are most famously exemplified in Ambrogio Lorenzetti's frescoes depicting good and bad government, painted between 1337 and 1340 and adorning the Sala della Pace, meeting-place of the *Nove* in the Palazzo Pubblico;[23] but they were remembered and perpetuated or revitalised through repeated changes of regime. Success in the *Studio* enterprise, as in others, brought honour to the city; failure would bring shame.[24]

attività economiche da parte dei ceti produttivi socialmente emergenti'. FROVA, 'L'università e la città', p. 22; and cf. EADEM, 'Processi formativi istituzionalizzati nelle società comunali e signorili italiane: una politica scolastica?', in *Culture et idéologie dans la genèse de l'état moderne*. Collections de L'École française de Rome, 82 (Rome, 1985), pp. 117-31.

[22] A point made with great clarity by ASCHERI, *Siena nel Rinascimento*, pp. 24-5.

[23] As is well known, the frescoes include a classroom scene, with a teacher, prominent in the central part of *The Effects of Good Government* (see Fig. 5). In his wide-ranging exploration of the concrete Sienese realities behind the frescoes, M. SEIDEL, *Dolce vita. Ambrogio Lorenzettis Porträt des Sieneser Staates*. Vorträge der Aeneas-Silvius-Stiftung an der Universität Basel, 33 (Basel, 1999), pp. 26-9; It. tr. in IDEM, *Arte italiana del Medioevo e del Rinascimento* (Venice, 2003), has argued that it depicts a university lecture rather than an elementary schoolroom, and also that its inclusion is connected to the renewed efforts of the Sienese to trigger another Bolognese *migratio* in 1338-9, precisely the period during which Lorenzetti was painting. The other scholar to have treated this subject, U. FELDGES-HENNING, 'The Pictorial Programme of the Sala della Pace: a New Interpretation', *Journal of the Warburg and Courtauld Institutes*, 35 (1972), pp. 145-62, had speculated that this was a lecture in medicine, or possibly law (pp. 153-4). The frescoes also depict the Seven Liberal Arts, together with philosophy, in medallions unusually placed underneath the main compositions of *The Allegory of Good Government* and *The Effects of Good Government*. Attempts to link the cycle with specifically scholastic thought and even directly with members of the *Studio*, such as it was, in the 1330s have not met with much success; see NARDI, *Insegnamento*, pp. 158-9 (n. 29) and 199 (n. 45). The debate over the significance of the frescoes is beyond the scope of this work. It can be followed in: N. RUBINSTEIN, 'Political Ideas in Sienese Art: the Frescoes by Ambrogio Lorenzetti and Taddeo di Bartolo in the Palazzo Pubblico', *Journal of the Warburg and Courtauld Institutes*, 21 (1958), pp. 179-207; repr. in his *Studies in Italian History in the Middle Ages and the Renaissance*, ed. G. Ciappelli, 3 vols. (Rome, 2004-), I, pp. 61-98; IDEM, 'Le allegorie di Ambrogio Lorenzetti nella Sala della Pace e il pensiero politico del suo tempo', *La Diana. Annuario della Scuola di Specializzazione in Archeologia e Storia dell'Arte dell'Università degli Studi di Siena*, I (1995), pp. 33-46 (without notes); full version in *Rivista Storica Italiana*, 109 (1997), pp. 781-802; repr. in his *Studies in Italian History*, I, pp. 347-64; C. FRUGONI, 'Il governo dei Nove a Siena e il loro credo politico nell'affresco di Ambrogio Lorenzetti', *Quaderni Medievali*, 7 (1979), pp. 14-42, and 8 (1979), pp. 71-103, revised version in EADEM, *A Distant City* (tr. Princeton, 1991), ch. 6 and appendix; Q. SKINNER, 'Ambrogio Lorenzetti and the Portrayal of Virtuous Government', in his *Visions of Politics*, II (Cambridge, 2002), pp. 39-92, revised version of 'Ambrogio Lorenzetti: the Artist as Political Philosopher', *Proceedings of the British Academy*, 72 (1986), pp. 1-56 (briefer version in *Malerei und Stadtkultur in der Dantezeit. Die Argumentation der Bilder*, eds. H. Belting and D. Blume [Munich, 1989], pp. 85-103; translated, abridged and revised version as '*Il Buon Governo di Ambrogio Lorenzetti e la teoria dell'autogoverno repubblicano*', in *Politica e cultura nelle repubbliche italiane*, pp. 21-42); IDEM, 'Ambrogio Lorenzetti on the Power and Glory of Republics', in his *Visions of Politics*, II, pp. 93-117, revised version of 'Ambrogio Lorenzetti's *Buon Governo* Frescoes: Two Old Questions, Two New Answers', *Journal of the Warburg and Courtauld Institutes*, 62 (1999), pp. 1-28; R. STARN, 'The Republican Regime of the "Room of Peace" in Siena, 1338-40', *Representations*, 18 (1987), pp. 1-32; revised and expanded version in R. STARN and L. PARTRIDGE, *Arts of Power: Three Halls of State in Italy, 1300-1600* (Berkeley and Los Angeles, Ca., 1992), Part I, pp. 9-80 (see esp. pp. 38-40 on the theme of culture in the frescoes); M. M. DONATO, 'La "bellissima inventiva": immagini e idee nella Sala della Pace', in *Ambrogio Lorenzetti. Il Buon Governo*, ed. E. Castelnuovo (Milan, 1995), pp. 23-41 (see esp. pp. 26 *seq.* on the 'efficacia comunicativa della pittura politica del Trecento'), and among her many other articles see esp. 'Ancora sulle "fonti" nel *Buon Governo* di Ambrogio Lorenzetti: dubbi, precisazioni, anticipazioni', in *Politica e cultura nelle repubbliche italiane*, pp. 43-79, and 'Il princeps, il giudice, il "sindacho" e la città. Novità su Ambrogio Lorenzetti nel Palazzo Pubblico di Siena', in *Imago urbis. L'immagine della città nella storia d'Italia*, eds. F. Bocchi and R. Smura (Rome, 2003), pp. 389-416. The relationship of the frescoes to the statutes compiled between 1337 and 1339 is discussed in M. ASCHERI, 'Legislazione, statuti e sovranità', in *Antica Legislazione della Repubblica di Siena*, pp. 1-40 (pp. 17-25).

[24] An early example is the petition of Maestro Ventura, son of Tebaldo, to be exempted from military service because if he was called up students would leave, 'quod esset destructio studii dicte artis et potius redundaret ad detrimentum civitatis et vituperium Comunis Senarum'. *Conc.* 2311, no foliation, n.d. (an archival annotation suggests 1261); NARDI, *Insegnamento*, p. 90.

Fig. 5 – Classroom scene, from Ambrogio Lorenzetti, *The Effects of Good Government*, fresco, 1338 (Siena, Palazzo Pubblico, Sala della Pace).

2. *The* Savi dello Studio

The chief means by which the commune exercised control over the *Studio* was the body of *Savi* or *Riformatori dello Studio*. The phenomenon of the temporary delegation of business to specially appointed officials, some of which subsequently developed into permanent offices, is ubiquitous among medieval Italian communes.[25] This is true of university administration as well as other areas of government, especially in those cases where communes had aspirations to control these emergent institutions.[26] That is what occurred with the *Savi dello Studio* in Siena, as elsewhere, though the process of evolution was gradual. The legislation of 1275 appointed two *syndici* 'ad faciendum conventiones, promissiones, obligationes et pacta rectoribus, dominis, magistris, scholaribus, staççonen-

[25] Cf. D. P. WALEY, *The Italian City-Republics* (London, 1978 edn.), pp. 31-2; BOWSKY, *A Medieval Italian Commune*, pp. 80-4.

[26] In Perugia *sapientes* were granted authority on an *ad hoc* basis in the year of the foundation bull, 1308, and they were formally established as *Studio* regulators in 1322; ERMINI, *Storia*, I, pp. 25, 39-40, and cf. G. CECCHINI, *Archivio di Stato di Perugia. Archivio Storico del Comune di Perugia. Inventario*. Pubblicazioni degli Archivi di Stato, 21 (Rome, 1956), pp. XXVII-III. In Padua, according to the statutes of 1331, the *Tractatores Studii* nominated and paid the doctors but they were formally elected by the students; RASHDALL, II, p. 17; DENIFLE, 'Statuten', pp. 417-22; D. GALLO, *Università e signoria a Padova dal XIV al XV secolo* (Trieste, 1998), pp. 26-8. In Florence by 1366 they were already usurping many of the functions of the rectors (RASHDALL, II, p. 60; GHERARDI, *Statuti*, appendix, part 1, doc. XLV, p. 153, 26 Nov), and their full panoply of powers was laid down in 1385 (GHERARDI, op. cit., doc. LVIII, pp. 162-4, 14 Jul).

sis, qui venerint ad legendum, regendum et docendum in civitate Senensi'.[27] Special envoys were entrusted with the negotiations at Imola over the 1321 migration, though they appear not to have been given any formal title. The only mention of such a title appears in one of the 1321 documents in which payment was made to 'Ser Iohanni Naddi notario, offitiali comunis Senensis et sapientum electorum super Studio',[28] terminology which hardly implies the existence of a formal magistrature.[29] The term does not recur for a number of years. The communal statutes of 1337-9 gave the *Concistoro* the power to hire teachers and indeed to increase their salaries in conjunction with 'officiales seu prudentes super Studio' – the first clear suggestion of a magistrature.[30] In 1347 a special body of three men, one for each *terzo* of the city, was appointed, 'qui sint officiales super Studio generali habendo in dicta civitate', i.e. for the specific task of setting up the *Studio*.[31] On 24 June 1357 – the year of the obtention of the charter – a special committee of six 'super procurando Studio generali' was established, to hold office for six months, which could be extended.[32] On 3 July, when their election was held – they were chosen by the *Consiglio Generale* from a list of eighteen names proposed by the *Concistoro* – there was no longer a mention of the length of their office, but their powers were defined as including the hiring of teachers and the expenditure of up to 1,200 florins.[33] By 19 October there are indications that the office was intended as the permanent executive for the *Studio*; the *Savi* were to enforce the statute that no Sienese could study elsewhere, and these powers were given to those 'electi et deputati, et in posterea eligendi'.[34] Yet their authority was soon reined in again; from 1359 they could only hire upon the express instruction of the *Concistoro*.[35] Only in the 1380s did the office become more clearly defined. The 're-founding' of the *Studio* in 1386-7 again saw the *Savi* being put in charge of teachers' contracts, powers which were amplified in 1388 owing to the pressure of work in the *Concistoro*.[36]

The method whereby the *Savi* were to be elected was further defined in the fifteenth century. In 1412 they were elected by the *Concistoro*, two for each *Monte* (the groupings of families that by this time had hardened into political factions).[37] In 1419 the *Concistoro* and the current *Savi* elected eighteen citizens, whose names were then put to the *Consiglio del Popolo* for scrutiny to produce the final

[27] *Chartularium*, doc. 24, pp. 16-19, 18-20 Jul.

[28] *Chartularium*, doc. 160, pp. 158-63, 6-30 Jun (p. 161); cf. NARDI, *Insegnamento*, p. 136.

[29] The date is interesting, however; it coincides closely with the first establishment of such an office in Perugia. See n. 26 above.

[30] Published in NARDI, *Insegnamento*, doc. 12, pp. 236-8 (p. 237); cf. also p. 199.

[31] *Chartularium*, doc. 402, p. 526, 20 Nov; cf. NARDI, *Insegnamento*, p. 207. They were not, therefore, in charge of the *Studio* itself, as Zdekauer implied (p. 52 and n. 3), but were appointed to obtain a charter.

[32] *Chartularium*, doc. 423, pp. 552-55 (p. 553); and cf. NARDI, *Insegnamento*, pp. 209-10.

[33] *Chartularium*, doc. 425, pp. 556-8; NARDI, loc. cit.

[34] *Chartularium*, doc. 431, pp. 567-69.

[35] Below, p. 77 n. 105.

[36] *CG* 195, f. 115r-v, 23 Jan 1387, ed. GAROSI, p. 194, n. 1; copy in *Mis.* 1, ff. 50r-v; ZDEKAUER, pp. 25-6, and *Conc.* 144, f. 8v, 6 Jul 1388; and see above, p. 50.

[37] 28 Jun; as n. 8 above. On the *Monti* and their role in Sienese politics see esp. MOSCADELLI, 'Oligarchie e Monti', pp. 267-78; CATONI, 'La faziosa armonia', esp. pp. 230-5; A. K. ISAACS, 'Magnati, comune e stato a Siena nel Trecento e all'inizio del Quattrocento', in *I ceti dirigenti nella Toscana tardo comunale*, pp. 81-96; EADEM, 'Popolo e monti nella Siena del Primo Cinquecento', *Rivista Storica Italiana*, 82 (1970), pp. 32-80 (pp. 49 *seq.*, esp. p. 53 n. 37); D. MARRARA, *Riseduti e nobiltà. Profilo storico-istituzionale di un'oligarchia toscana nei secoli XVI-XVIII*. Biblioteca del 'Bollettino Storico Pisano', Collana Storica, 16 (Pisa, 1976), ch. 1.

six.[38] In 1427 a more methodical approach was introduced to cover all 'extraordinary offices', of which this had been one since at least early in the century.[39] Henceforth such positions were to be filled by a three-stage process whereby a list of 198 members of the *Consiglio del Popolo*, sixty-six per *Monte*, was compiled, then reduced by scrutiny to sixty, and finally by the same process to six.[40] Like most such communal posts, the appointment was for one year,[41] beginning on 1 January,[42] and no *Savio* could serve for two successive years.[43] By the 1440s the *Savi* were expected to meet twice a week.[44] The Casa della Sapienza soon became their regular meeting-place.[45] Later in the century there is evidence of formal agendas,[46] of memoranda left for their successors,[47] and of officials in their employ.[48]

The evolution of the office of the *Savi* must be seen in the context of the extraordinarily complex Sienese electoral system of the time.[49] This is perhaps best illustrated by the string of qualifications that accompanied the measures described above defining *vacazioni*, the rules about ineligibility for office. Reforms of these rules were not new.[50] By the early fifteenth century the division between 'ordi-

---

[38] *Mis.* 1, f. 81r, *Statuti* 41, f. 54r, *Statuti* 40, f. 15r-v, *Statuti* 47, f. 54r, 19 Jun 1419. The mechanism is similar to that adopted in 1357.

[39] *Conc.* 2112 (Proposte dei Savi, 1400-1412), f. 103v, n.d. but 'circa al 1410' pencilled. The grouping of such offices continued (below, p. 75 n. 86).

[40] *Conc.* 369, f. 36r, *Statuti* 41, f. 198r, 9/20 Sept 1427; cf. *Statuti* 47, ff. 182v-183r, 197r; ZDEKAUER, p. 36 and n. 1. In 1459 two more officials from a fourth *Monte*, that of the *Gentilhuomini*, were to be added (*CG* 228, ff. 93-6, 25 Apr), but there is little evidence that this happened other than the apparently exceptional existence of eight *Savi* in 1484 (*Not.* 879, no. 42, 13 Jun). The representatives of the *Gentilhuomini* replaced those of the *Riformatori* in 1501 (*CG* 241, f. 97v, 22 Dec), and from then on there were endless permutations until 1531 when the number was finally increased to eight (*CG* 243, f. 152r, 20 Jan 1531). The method of selection was simplified in 1496; *Conc.* 781, f. 17r-v, 23 Dec, ed. FERRERI, doc. 376, p. 359.

[41] 28 Jun 1412 (as n. 8 above).

[42] In 1419 the beginning of the office was moved to 1 April; as n. 38 above, and cf. G. CHIRONI, 'Il testo unico per l'ufficio dei Regolatori, 1351-1533', in *Siena e il suo Territorio nel Rinascimento, II*, pp. 183-220 (n. 208/1, p. 200; 23 Jun 1419). In 1437, 1 January again became the beginning of the term of office, to make it easier for the teachers' contracts to be made in time (*CG* 219, ff. 146v-147v [new foliation], 10 May, ed. ZDEKAUER, doc. XVIII, pp. 169-71, and cf. pp. 59-60; copies in *Statuti* 41, ff. 255v-256r, and *Mis.* 1, ff. 83r-85v). This relative stability is in contrast to the situation in Florence; DAVIES, *Florence and its University*, pp. 10-11.

[43] 1419; as n. 38 above.

[44] In 1444 they were instructed to meet once a week, on Friday mornings, for Casa della Sapienza business in addition to their other obligations; *Conc.* 471, f. 38r, 18 Aug 1444 (= *Conc.* 2115, ff. 129v-130r). In 1456 the *Consiglio Generale* decided that they should meet twice weekly; *Mis.* 1, f. 94r, 10 Sept 1456. An earlier measure stipulating that they were to meet twice a week, on Mondays and Thursdays, in the Casa della Sapienza (*Conc.* 2115, f. 91r), is dated 1443 by archivists but I have not found corroborative evidence. The minutes of the *Savi*'s meetings, preserved from 1473 (*Studio* 2-6), despite *lacunae* (see above, pp. 20-1) suggest that they normally met with at least this frequency throughout the year.

[45] In 1475 the Sapienza is described as 'eorum solita residentia' (*Not.* 694, f. 14r, 4 Jan; published in MINNUCCI, 'Documenti', doc. II-17, p. 87; cf. a similar phrase in *Studio* 2, f. 18r, 26 Aug 1474). Other venues were not unknown; in 1498 meetings were held at the premises of the archbishop (*Sale* 24, f. 164r, 29 Mar) and the *Nove di Custodia* (*Sale* 24, f. 169v, 22 Dec).

[46] An example is *Not.* 694, f. 28r, n.d., published in MINNUCCI, 'Documenti', doc. II-53, p. 122.

[47] *Not.* 694, f. 4r, n.d., published in MINNUCCI, 'Documenti', doc. II-35, pp. 101-2.

[48] See below, pp. 84-5.

[49] A detailed study is E. BRIZIO, 'L'elezione degli uffici politici nella Siena del Trecento', *BSSP*, 98 (1991), pp. 16-62; and see EADEM, 'L'elezione della Signoria: provvedimenti inediti (1371-1398)', in *Antica Legislazione della Repubblica di Siena*, ed. M. Ascheri (Siena, 1993), pp. 136-59.

[50] See for example MOSCADELLI, 'Apparato burocratico', pp. 70-2 on the reforms of 1355, demonstrating how the rules could be manipulated for political purposes.

nary' and 'extraordinary' offices had become a matter of segregation; nobody holding an 'ordinary', salaried post could hold an 'extraordinary' one. This was designed to prevent excessive accumulation of honours and power in the hands of individuals, and its repetition and amendment suggests that it continued to be a contentious issue.[51] But the bundling together of the *Savi dello Studio* with other offices did not cater adequately for the particular functions of this committee, and more was necessary. First, there was the need to prevent members of the *Studio* from becoming its managers. From 1425 teachers and students were not eligible for the office,[52] a measure that by and large was observed.[53] Secondly, there was the problem that the kind of person best suited to the office would also be in demand elsewhere. The authorities therefore had to make exceptions in order to fill the post; for example, in 1389 it was declared that the *vacazioni* which went with many communal posts were suspended in the case of the *Savi*,[54] though once in office they could not take up posts or embassies which would take them out of Siena.[55]

The problem with which the authorities were grappling was that faced in all *studi* where the role of paymaster of teachers had been assumed by the government; how to find the expertise necessary to make the right choices of teachers, and how to run an organisation of people who were by defini-

[51] *Conc.* 2112, f. 103v (as above, n. 39); *Statuti* 44, ff. 6r, 13r, publ. in CAMBI and QUARTESAN, 'Gli uffici', pp. 128, 140; on the whole issue of *vacazioni* see also M. ASCHERI's introduction to the same volume, pp. xiv-xv. The regulations were modified in 1451 (CHIRONI, 'Il testo unico', p. 213) and restored again in 1457; *Balìa* 2, f. 189v, and *Balìa* 3, f. 188r, 20 Feb (from 18 Feb), and *Statuti* 44, f. 22r, 18 Feb 1457 (not edited by Cambi and Quartesan). Cf. also *CG* 407, ff. 1r-11v, a compendium of regulations for the elections to communal posts written in 1457, with emendations to 1472.

[52] *CG* 210, f. 175v, *Statuti* 41, ff. 67r, 169r (new foliation), 5 Feb; published by GAROSI, doc. 60 p. 529, with erroneous date. I take 'doctore' in this document to mean teacher rather than person with degree, given the context of the phrase and the fact that there is no explicit evidence before 1533 of a bar on graduates holding the office. It is not unusual for non-teaching doctors to hold the office; e.g. in 1471 (*CG* 234, f. 61r, 22 Dec) two of the *Savi*, Battista de' Bellanti and Niccolò di Nanni Severini, were graduates who had taught at the *Studio* earlier in their careers (on Bellanti see MINNUCCI, 'Documenti', esp. pp. 236-7). The measure was incorporated in the *Statuto delle Vacazioni* compiled in 1433; CAMBI and QUARTESAN, 'Gli uffici', p. 140 (and cf. *Conc.* 2395, ff. 25v-26r). A *Savio* who was subsequently drawn for a salaried office, however, could accept it. Another version of this document, in *Statuti* 45, f. 20r, unfortunately not dated, has the additional note that 'chi fosse Cavaliere o doctore ab antiquo s'è costumato che possa esser de' Savii predicti non obstante lo esser doctore'. In 1533, however, the *Savi* have to be 'non dottori, né attinenti a Dottori in 4.° grado' (*CG* 243, f. 246r, 26 Dec; names only published by KOŠUTA, 'Documenti', doc. I-5, pp. 337-8). Relatives of teachers could be *Savi*, as with Francesco Marretta, brother of the teacher Girolamo, in 1483 (*CG* 239, f. 67r, 23 Dec 1482), and Alessandro Borghesi, a *Savio* in 1489 (*Balìa* 36, f. 74v, 1 Jan), at a time when four Borghesi were on the payroll as lecturers.

[53] E.g. Angelo Fondi, drawn as *Savio* in 1499, was deemed ineligible as he was teaching (*CG* 241, f. 58r, 23 Dec; on this figure, see below, pp. 215-6). Pietro de' Micheli, however, was elected despite this prohibition (*CG* 224, c190r, 13 Dec 1448). In 1443 the *Concistoro* directed that his *polizza*, which had been torn up because he was a doctor (teacher), be reinserted in the election bags (*Conc.* 467, f. 23r, 7 Nov), and at his death in 1449 his position as *Savio* was awarded to his son Antonio (*Conc.* 498, f. 37r, 22 Feb; *CG* 224, f. 211v, 5 Mar). Previous to this legislation, with a predominance of foreign teachers, this was probably not an issue – although in 1387 two *Savi*, Mino Vincenti and Marco di Giovanni, appointed to the office in February, were offered teaching contracts in October (*Conc.* 135, f. 13v, 2 Feb, and *Conc.* 138, f. 50r, 16 Oct). Non-contemporaneous holding of the office by teachers appears not to have been a problem. Pertici has pointed out that Francesco di Jacopo Tolomei was a *Savio* in 1446 and hired to teach canon law in 1450; P. PERTICI (ed.), *Tra politica e cultura nel primo Quattrocento senese. Le epistole di Andreoccio Petrucci (1426-1443)* (Siena, 1990), p. 95 n. 1.

[54] *CG* 196, f. 95r-v, *Statuti* 41, f. 41v and *Statuti* 47, f. 41v, 22 Jan; cf. *Statuti* 30, f. 38r, 18 Jun. The 1357 committee 'eligendorum super procurando Studio generali', to hold office for six months, had also been chosen without limitation of *vacazioni*. *Chartularium*, doc. 423, pp. 552-55, 24 Jun 1357 (p. 553).

[55] *Statuti* 41, f. 82v, 18 Jun. The ban on *Savi dello Studio* becoming ambassadors is found again in the mid-fifteenth century; CAMBI and QUARTESAN, 'Gli uffici', p. 144 (undated marginal annotation, but probably not much later than the previous one which is dated 1442).

tion almost bound to be better educated than themselves. The complex election procedure was no guarantee of ideal results, while the annual rotation of office meant that there was little opportunity to gain experience of the particular problems of the *Studio*.[56] A few men were of course chosen more than once. Ser Niccolò Dardi, for example, the chancellor of the commune, was a *Savio* in 1423, 1427 and 1430 and was elected in 1429 as one of a special commission to treat with rebellious scholars, although he was found to be ineligible for the appointment.[57] Nanni Biringucci was also a *Savio* in both 1423 and 1427,[58] and his son Pietro was appointed in 1461 after a spell as rector of the Casa della Sapienza.[59] Agostino di Niccolò Borghesi held the post four times, in 1435, 1444, 1446 and 1458;[60] Mino Bargagli and Gheri Bulgarini both held it three times.[61] These were all eminent Sienese figures, as were Castellano Utinelli, a frequent notary of the *Concistoro* and *Savio* in 1412,[62] Cristoforo d'Andrea, chancellor of the republic for most of the period between 1404 and 1419 and *Savio* in 1415,[63] and the leading Sienese humanist Barnaba, *Savio* in 1438.[64] It has been pointed out that members of magnate families, though excluded from formal participation in the political process since 1277,[65] were not debarred from middle-ranking offices such as this, and these citizens could be found among the *Savi dello Studio*, or on special commissions for the *Studio*, at critical moments such as the attempts of 1347 and 1357 to obtain recognition.[66] The presence of such eminent figures lends special interest to the view of the *Studio* as being run by the elite,[67] a line of enquiry invited by comparison with other centres.[68] A case in point is the tenure of the prominent political and cultural

---

[56] Florentine moves (1418, 1458) to make the office last for three years were presumably an attempt to respond to this as well as a bid for political control. DAVIES, *Florence and its University*, pp. 11-12.

[57] *Conc.* 343, ff. 6r, 6 Mar, 12v, 18 Mar, and 37v, 21 Apr 1423; *Conc.* 367, f. 5r, 7 Mar 1427; *Conc.* 379, f. 23r, 14 Jun 1429; *CG* 215, f. 30v, 15 Mar 1430.

[58] As note 57 above. He had previously been a *Camarlengo* of the Sapienza (below, p. 354 n. 138).

[59] *CG* 229, f. 150, 17 Dec, and below, pp. 344-5.

[60] *CG* 218, f. 141r, 12 Apr 1435; *CG* 222, f. 82r, 6 Dec 1443; *CG* 223, f. 88v, 3 Dec 1445; *CG* 228, f. 23r, 27 Dec 1457.

[61] *CG* 223, f. 88v, 3 Dec 1457; *CG* 225, f. 278r, 23 Mar 1452; *CG* 226, f. 170v, 23 Dec 1453 (Bargagli); *CG* 234, f. 246v, 22 Dec 1472; *CG* 237, f. 239v, 2 Dec 1477; *CG* 238, f. 193v, 20 Dec 1480 (Bolgarini).

[62] *Conc.* 278, f. 31r, 28 Jun; cf. CATONI, 'Genesi', p. 164 n. 39; and ASCHERI, *Siena nel Rinascimento*, p. 43 n. 63.

[63] CATONI, 'Genesi', p. 166; and ASCHERI, *Siena nel Rinascimento*, loc. cit.; on him see also MINNUCCI, 'Documenti', p. 244. Notaries are frequent occupiers of the office.

[64] *CG* 403, f. 319r; NARDI, 'Lo Studio di Siena nell'età rinascimentale', p. 255.

[65] WALEY, *Siena and the Sienese*, ch. 4, and BOWSKY, *A Medieval Italian Commune*, pp. 63 *seq.* on this and the continued influence of these families thereafter.

[66] D. MARRARA, 'I magnati e il governo del Comune di Siena dallo statuto del 1274 alla fine del XIV secolo', in *Studi per Enrico Fiumi* (Pisa, 1979), pp. 239-76. The 1347 special commission included an Ugurgieri and a Marescotti (op. cit., p. 259 n. 93; and *Chartularium*, doc. 402, p. 526, 20 Nov 1347); the *Savi* of 1357 included a Tolomei and a Gallerani (MARRARA, 'I magnati', p. 264 n. 116; *Chartularium*, doc. 433, pp. 572-3, 5 Dec), while the enactment of the protectionist measures of that year was inspired by a Malavolti (MARRARA, 'I magnati', p. 265 n. 117; *Chartularium*, doc. 431, pp. 567-9, 19 Oct).

[67] E.g. the observations of A. LEONCINI, 'I simboli dell'Università di Siena', *Annali di Storia delle Università italiane*, 4 (2000), pp. 123-38; rev. vn. 'I simboli dell'Università di Siena dal XIV al XX secolo', in *Siena e il suo territorio nel Rinascimento, III*, pp. 235-58 (pp. 241-2).

[68] See in particular DAVIES, *Florence and its University*, esp. pp. 51-2, 78-82, 86-90 and 127-30; and cf. G. PETTI BALBI, '*Felix Studium viguit*: l'organizzazione degli studenti e dei dottori a Parma del Quattrocento', in *Università in Europa. Le istituzioni universitarie*, pp. 37-50, stressing that the *Riformatori* of 1414 were all from the elite of Parma.

figure Francesco di Bartolomeo Petrucci, 'Checco Rosso', of the office in 1426.[69] It has been pointed out that the humanist Antonio Beccadelli, il Panormita, took the opportunity to introduce his colleague and friend Giovanni Aurispa to Petrucci's son Antonio in the hope that his father would arrange a lectureship.[70] However, this can easily be taken too far. In many years the list of the *Savi* did not include such figures, and when they are found they are in a minority. It would be too easy to assume that educated men made most of the running on these committees; the fact is that we know relatively little about how they operated, though it is clear that in making recommendations regarding teachers they must have sought and listened to advice from those in the know, both within and outside the *Studio*.

In the administrative records it is perhaps inevitably the drawbacks of the system that stand out. Most in evidence is the burden, which in Siena was arguably greater than in many other republics, of having to fill such a large number of offices not only servicing a highly sophisticated internal system of government but also controlling a subject territory that was disproportionate in size to the population that sought to govern it.[71] The result was frequent vacancies, pluralism and absenteeism. The administration of the *Studio* did not escape these problems. If any of the elected *Savi* turned out to be unavailable – and this officially meant those in full-time office, members of the *Concistoro* or incumbents in other high positions – another name was drawn from the *bossoli* or bags;[72] but the number of names it contained was limited, and for this or other reasons the *Savi* were often not up to full complement. In 1435 there were only four *Savi*,[73] in 1409 and 1436 only three,[74] and in 1430 at one stage only two;[75] In 1444 only one official was elected because the *bossoli* contained no other names;[76] in 1451 only four were elected,[77] in 1463 five,[78] in 1464 two,[79] in 1465 again one,[80] in 1523 two.[81] The *Concistoro* could make a variety of *ad hoc* arrangements to deal with these shortcomings. In 1409 the three *Savi* were given full authority,[82] in 1430 the *Savi*, again numbering three, were to conduct their business in conjunction with the *Concistoro*,[83] while in 1435 a fresh

---

[69] *Conc.* 361, f. 16r, 22 Mar; NARDI, 'Lo Studio di Siena nell'età rinascimentale', p. 252 and n. 10.

[70] NARDI, op. cit., pp. 252-3; FIORAVANTI, 'Alcuni aspetti della cultura umanistica senese', p. 145 n. 3.

[71] On this see ASCHERI, *Renaissance Siena*, pp. 13-14; IDEM, 'Istituzioni e governo della città', p. 337; and M. GINATEMPO, 'Potere dei mercanti, potere della città: considerazioni sul "caso" Siena alla fine del medioevo', in *Strutture del potere ed élites economiche nelle città europee dei secoli 12-16*, ed. G. Petti Balbi (Naples, 1996), pp. 191-221 (esp. p. 207).

[72] Two examples of *Libri dei Bossoli*, with the lists of names of candidates for the office of *Savi*, survive; *CG* 434 (1474; names on ff. 1r, 5r, 9r) and *CG* 438 (1480; additional names for the new Monte degli Aggregati, ff. 51r-53r).

[73] *Conc.* 415, f. 13v, 21 Mar, and *CG* 218, f. 134v, 23 Mar.

[74] *Conc.* 261, f. 17v, 20 Jul 1409, ed. PIANIGIANI, doc. 23, pp. 47-8 (they were given full authority); *Conc.* 421, ff. 23r-v, 28 Mar, and 32v, 12 Apr 1436; *CG* 219, f. 11v, 31 Mar 1436.

[75] *CG* 215, ff. 55v, 12 Jul; when one of these died a replacement was appointed (f. 65r, 10 Sept 1430).

[76] *CG* 222, f. 230v, 6 Nov.

[77] *CG* 225, f. 239v, 18 Dec (there was a fresh election on 23 March 1452; *CG* 225, f. 267r).

[78] *CG* 230, f. 65v, 17 Dec.

[79] *CG* 230, f. 222v, 20 Dec.

[80] *CG* 231, f. 50v, 22 Dec.

[81] *CG* 241, f. 302r, 23 Dec.

[82] *Conc.* 261, f. 17v, 20 Jul.

[83] *CG* 215, ff. 55v, 12 Jul. There is no sign in the Sienese records of the Florentine practice of entrusting a 'duty' official on a weekly basis with everyday business (VERDE, *Lo Studio fiorentino*, I, p. 3).

election was held for the two vacancies.[84] In 1452 and 1465 fresh lists of candidates were drawn up,[85] and it may be that these shortages led to the practice in the later fifteenth century whereby the *Savi dello Studio* were given priority over the other extraordinary offices in the selection process.[86] Finally at the end of the fifteenth century the *Balìa* is found taking an increasingly directive role in the resolution of these problems, holding fresh elections for vacant posts.[87]

Even when the full number of *Savi* had been elected, their activity and attendance were not guaranteed. Despite the 1389 measure barring *Savi* from embassies, the more eminent holders of the office would naturally on occasion be given such commissions, and other business – or occasionally, one suspects, simply lack of interest – could keep the *Savi* from performing their functions. In 1417 a substitute was appointed for one member who was away from Siena,[88] but when in 1419 not one of the six was available the *Concistoro* performed their duties for them until the return of three of them and then gave these three full powers.[89] In 1477 the *Concistoro* validated the election of candidates for the rectorate of the Casa della Sapienza, made by only two *Savi*[90] – three were *podestà* or other officials in the employ of the commune, while a fourth was absent from Siena on business to do with the plague[91] – and later appointed two substitutes.[92] In 1422, another moment when only two of them were present in the city, the *Concistoro* eventually ruled that the *Savi* were not to leave the town during their period of office, on pain of a 100-*lira* fine.[93] On another occasion, in 1440, the *Concistoro* forbade them to leave the palace until they had made up their minds on a *condotta*;[94] and in 1443 a 10-*lira* fine was threatened unless they appeared before them.[95] Sometimes, too, there is evidence, or at least there are allegations, of inefficiency or corruption. In 1442 the *Consiglio del Popolo* reduced the budget of the *Studio* because it was being wasted on undistinguished *condotte*, and even on hiring students instead of

---

[84] *CG* 218, ff. 138v and 141v, 12 Apr.

[85] *Conc.* 513, f. 22r-v, 21 Mar 1452; *Conc.* 590, f. 6v, 7 Jan 1465.

[86] *CG* 239, f. 149r, 4 Dec 1483, according to which the first six names extracted from the *bossolo* were to be *Savi dello Studio*, the next six the *Savi* of the hospital of the Scala and the six thereafter to be *Savi* of the Opera del Duomo. This hierarchy is maintained in the reforms of 1487, ed. TERZIANI, 'L'instaurazione del regime oligarchico-signorile' (see p. 204), and in a measure of 1494 (*Conc.* 769, f. 12v, 18 Dec, ed. FERRERI, doc. 348, pp. 331-2); cf. also *CG* 241, ff. 37r, 28 Dec 1497, and 44v, 19 Dec 1498, *CG* 243, ff. 28v-29r, 28 Jan 1529, and 151r, 18 Jan 1531. The system bears close comparison with that established in Florence at the end of the fifteenth century; VERDE, *Lo Studio fiorentino*, I, p. 266-7 n. 6, quoting N. RUBINSTEIN, 'I primi anni del Consiglio Maggiore a Firenze (1494-1499)', *Archivio Storico Italiano*, 112 (1954), pp. 151-94, 321-47 (pp. 334-46).

[87] *Balìa* 35, f. 27r, 23 Aug 1487; *Balìa* 36, f. 74v, 1 Jan 1489; *Balìa* 39, ff. 79v-80r, 11 Jan 1494; *Balìa* 40, ff. 113v-114r, 4 Jan 1496.

[88] *Conc.* 306, f. 23r, 13 Feb. Absence could of course be on *Studio* business, as that of Barnaba in 1438, sent to Lombardy to attempt to lure the great Catone Sacco from Pavia; NARDI, 'Lo Studio di Siena nell'età rinascimentale', p. 255, and below, p. 152.

[89] *Conc.* 322, ff. 3v, 2 Sept, ed. PIANIGIANI, doc. 42, pp. 66-7, and 5r, 5 Sept 1419.

[90] *Conc.* 666, f. 38r, 26 Oct, ed. FERRERI, doc. 51, p. 45, and *Conc.* 2117, f. 202v, same date; the *Consiglio del Popolo* also validated it (*CG* 237, f. 210r [new foliation], 26 Oct).

[91] *Conc.* 2187, no foliation, n.d.

[92] *Conc.* 667, ff. 15r, 23 Nov, and 22r, 4 Dec 1477, ed. FERRERI, docs. 54-5, pp. 47-8.

[93] *Conc.* 341, ff. 7r, 11 Nov, and 19r, 10 Dec.

[94] *Conc.* 447, f. 23v, 11 Aug. Cf. the threat of a fine of eight florins each if they did not hire a teacher, *CG* 224, ff. 68r-v, 6 Oct 1447.

[95] *Conc.* 466, f. 41v, 12 Oct. Ironically, when they did turn up, no decisions were taken because of the absence of the *ordini di città* (loc. cit.). On the *ordini* see above, p. 18.

doctors.[96] In 1447 reforms were passed 'a ciò che s'attenda a conducere e doctori per le loro virtù et per essere reputati valenti et non per altrui rispecti'.[97] Another attempt was made in 1475,

> veduto l'ordine di condurre e doctori essere trasordinato, et non servarsi la legge a ciò laudabilmente ordinata; et per consuetudine ciascuno si fa preporre ali ordini nel tempo lo piace aspettando vi sia l'amico, donde ne seguita che gli salari non sono bene partiti.

It was stipulated that *condotte* could only be made in the months of May, June and July, and that a committee of *Savi* who ignored this ruling would have to pay that teacher's salary out of their own pockets.[98]

3. *The* Savi *and other bodies*

As has been seen, the *Savi* were initially given responsibility for the hiring of teachers. This, however, put them straight into a potentially sensitive area; and while it was accepted that the *Savi*'s knowledge and views were essential, the making of decisions was another matter, and *condotte* were soon felt to be too important to be left to them. In practice, control over *condotte* also became a bone of contention between the key bodies of the republic, in games of power-play which often, one suspects, had little to do with academic appointments at all. The conflict was essentially between two levels of government. Specialist committees such as the *Savi* traditionally worked with and for the *Concistoro*, the republic's executive, meeting with them and making relevant decisions in conjunction with them.[99] The *Concistoro* also managed the business of the two large assemblies, the *Consiglio Generale*, and subsequently the *Consiglio del Popolo*; with few exceptions,[100] only matters forwarded by it could be discussed in the larger assemblies.[101] This gave rise to tensions, with the *Consiglio* attempting to reserve for itself important business. The reservation of the power to hire teachers usually reflected a desire of the *Consiglio del Popolo* to exercise direct control over such an important – yet not explicitly political – aspect of the status and fortunes of Siena, and as the *Consiglio* became less effective politically this was one of the remaining areas in which it could assert itself.[102] Yet the engagement of the *Consiglio* on individual *condotte* was a heavy-handed expedient, and invariably had to be abandoned. Thus there is a long se-

---

[96] *CG* 221, f. 95v, 26 Mar, ed. GAROSI, doc. 67, pp. 533-4: 'Veduto ch'egl'è provveduto... fiorini 3600, e questo fu ordinato per avere dottori famosissimi et de autorità per dare ragione che de li scolari ce venissero assai comprendasi oggi dì e detti danari non spenderse come fu la intenzione di chi ordinò, ma piuttosto desutilmente, perché si vede che se conducono a le volte scolari piuttosto per compiacere che per necessità a le letture, per modo che se spendano l'anno le centinaia di fiorini in esse condocte che non besognarebbero' (see below, p. 89).

[97] *CG* 223 f. 229v, 20 Feb; GAROSI, doc. 61, pp. 529-30.

[98] *CG* 236, f. 128r-v; *Mis.* 1, ff. 105v-106r, 28 Jun. Cf. *CG* 243, f. 244v, 14 Dec 1533, and below, pp. 109 and 149-51.

[99] 'Il "Concistoro" è un luogo ove ci si riunisce, ma anche un "modo" di riunirsi, per decidere provvedere governare; perciò la sua composizione è variabile...' ASCHERI, *Siena nel Rinascimento*, p. 32 n. 44.

[100] These are discussed in C. SHAW, 'Provisions following "Proposte generali"', pp. 109-10; and see above, p. 18 and n. 92.

[101] On the development and the different roles of these two, see above, p. 17 n. 88.

[102] On the relationship between the two, ARCHIVIO DI STATO DI SIENA, *Guida-Inventario*, I, pp. 172 *seq.*; ARCHIVIO DI STATO DI SIENA, *Archivio del Concistoro*, Introduzione (G. Cecchini), pp. IX-XXIV; S. MOSCADELLI, 'Recenti studi su Siena medievale', *Archivio Storico Italiano*, 145 (1987), pp. 81-98 (pp. 89-90); M. ASCHERI, 'Istituzioni', pp. 334-6. The conflict over which body should control the hiring of teachers goes back to the thirteenth century, as is pointed out by TRAPANI, 'Statuti senesi concernenti lo Studio', and NARDI, *Insegnamento*, p. 83.

ries of definitions and re-definitions of the power to make *condotte* in which the *Savi* were little more than pawns. In the measures of 1357 the *Consiglio Generale* had resolved that a body of *Savi* should recommend appointments of teachers, which would have to be agreed by the *Concistoro*, the main executive body of the regime.[103] This was in contrast to the previous practice of restricting teachers' appointments to the *Consiglio Generale*,[104] and two years later the task was again reserved by the latter body;[105] but in 1361 it was returned to the *Concistoro* who employed the *Savi* as executives.[106] From 1364 the *Savi*, plus one representative of the clergy, were supposed to make the choice of teachers within the limits imposed by the *Concistoro*; in practice, though, these decisions were often made by the *Concistoro*.[107] From 1412 there were repeated attempts by the *Consiglio del Popolo* to reserve at least the *condotte* of Sienese citizens;[108] and while this was intended as a defence against favouritism it could also be cumbersome and contentious. In 1431 all foreign *condotte* were reserved to the *Consiglio del Popolo*, and were to run for only one year at a time.[109] This was also the case for citizens. The measure was, not surprisingly, grossly impracticable,[110] and in 1437 it was repealed.[111]

Matters came to a head in the 1440s. In 1447, expressing continuing dissatisfaction with the existing system, the *Consiglio del Popolo* decided that all citizen *condotte*, and all renewals of foreign *condotte* after an initial period of two years, would have to come before them, and heavy fines were threatened for *condotte* that were made illegally.[112] Yet even this was too cumbersome. On 16 February 1450 the *Consiglio del Popolo* heard a recommendation by 'certi cittadini electi a fare le provisioni', which analysed the decline of the *Studio*, at a time when all the external indications were good for Siena, explaining it above all in terms of the lack of eminent foreign teachers. The commission specifically blamed the measures of 1447 which denied these teachers any security of tenure.[113] A compromise was reached whereby the renewals of contracts could be effected by the *Concistoro*, but increases in salary had to be referred to the *Consiglio del Popolo*.[114] Thereafter the control of the *Consiglio* waned.

---

[103] *Chartularium*, doc. 425, pp. 556-8, 3 Jul.

[104] *Bicch.* 1, f. 315v, 10 Jun 1357 (not published in the *Chartularium*).

[105] *CG* 163, f. 43v, 27 Nov 1359, and *Statuti* 33, ff. 22v-23r. A version of the measure is also found in the statutes of the Biccherna for 1363; *Bicch.* 3, ff. 24v-25r, May 1363, suggesting that it was considered of some importance that it be re-iterated.

[106] See above, p. 47.

[107] *CG* 171, f. 3lr-v, 27 Mar, ed. ZDEKAUER, doc. VI, pp. 144-5.

[108] See n. 8 above, and below pp. 191-2. It was relinquished again, to the *Concistoro* and *Savi*, in 1419; *Statuti* 41, f. 192r; ASCHERI, *Siena nel Rinascimento*, pp. 36-7 n. 53.

[109] *CG* 215, f. 36v; *Statuti* 41, f. 231r, 23 Feb; ASCHERI, loc. cit; and cf. *Conc.* 390, f. 12r, 19 Jan.

[110] In 1433 there was an instance of the *Consiglio del Popolo*, unable to agree on the contracts for citizen teachers, leaving it to the *Savi* to make decisions and refer them back; *Conc.* 2176, no foliation, 19 Sept.

[111] *CG* 219, ff. 146v-147v (new foliation), 10 May, ed. ZDEKAUER, doc. XVIII, pp. 169-71, and cf. pp. 59-60; copies in *Statuti* 41, ff. 255v-256r, and *Mis.* 1, ff. 83r-85v: 'veduto quanta difficultà e perdimento di tempo' the one-year rule has caused, *condotte* of *cittadini* can now be made for two years. See below, p. 155. But the *Concistoro* was still referring some foreign *condotte* to the *Consiglio del Popolo* in 1440; *Conc.* 447, ff. 18v, 1 Aug, ed. PIANIGIANI, doc. 207, p. 239 (renewals of the Dominican Battista da Fabriano in a chair of theology and philosophy, and Jacomo da San Gimignano in logic; and cf. 23r, 9 Aug, ed. PIANIGIANI, doc. 210, pp. 241-2).

[112] 20 Feb (as n. 97 above). See also GAROSI, p. 239.

[113] 'Tali doctori famosi forestieri, s'intende che le condotte loro non si possono fare per vigore de le riformagioni vostre se non per due anni e poi a le riferme bisogna capitare al consiglio parendo alloro impossibile esser mai rifermi avendo a passare al Consiglio del popolo' (*CG* 224, f. 318r, 16 Feb 1450, ed. GAROSI, doc. 62, pp. 530-1).

[114] Loc. cit. There is an example in 1495 of the *Consiglio del Popolo* reducing a teacher's salary (*CG* 241, f. 8r, 23 Jun).

In 1476 it was stipulated that *condotte* of citizens which entailed salaries of over 100 florins had to be approved by the *Consiglio*, a measure which rather implies that their authority over *condotte* of citizens generally had been ignored, as was indeed the case.[115] In 1481 the *Balìa* removed even those rights and vested them in the *Concistoro*,[116] and although this latter body remained constitutionally in overall charge until 1544, in practice the *Savi* took orders from the newer *Balìa*, among whose records the lists of hired teachers are also to be found from the end of the fifteenth century onwards.[117]

The struggles between the *Consiglio del Popolo* and the *Concistoro* about control over the *condotte* were a running sore that could threaten the stability of the whole operation. When matters were left to the *Concistoro* this tended to run much more smoothly, as the relationship between that body and the *Savi* was always close and flexible. The *Concistoro* would delegate decisions about *condotte*, as well as their execution, when it was too busy,[118] when confidentiality was of the essence,[119] or when these decisions were not likely to be controversial. It could delegate some areas and reserve others, and, because of the ease with which the *Savi* could be summoned and the frequency of joint meetings, this sharing of duties could be tuned and altered regularly. The period immediately after the re-launching of the *Studio* in 1414 is a good example of this flexibility. In 1414 the *Savi* were empowered to hire foreign but not Sienese teachers;[120] in 1415 they were again to hire Sienese.[121] In 1419 they were again given only citizen *condotte*,[122] in 1421 only foreign ones,[123] in 1422 again both,[124] and in 1423 fresh *condotte* were dealt with by the *Savi* and renewals by the *Concistoro* – the usual pattern thereafter.[125]

---

[115] *Studio* 2, f. 37v, 12 Jan; cf. the defensive assertion in *Conc.* 640, f. 21r, 30 May 1473, ed. BAI, doc. 340, pp. 336-7, that the *Concistoro* have 'in pertinentibus ad Studij conservationem et augmentum tantam auctoritatem quantam habet Consilium Generale'. The *Concistoro*'s deference to the *Consiglio del Popolo* thereafter is illustrated by its reference of the salaries of Francesco Accolti and Giovanni Battista Caccialupi to the *Consiglio* (*Conc.* 675, f. 9v, 11 Mar 1479, ed. FERRERI, doc. 79, p. 67; *Conc.* 678, f. 8r, 20 Sept 1479, ed. FERRERI, doc. 85, p. 71). *Condotte* of citizens by the *Concistoro* reappear as early as 1454 (*Conc.* 528, f. 54r, 14 Oct), ed. BAI, doc. 45, pp. 55-6. The document GAROSI published (doc. 59, p. 529, *CG* 235, f. 269, 21 Oct 1474 – not 1424 as he has it) which reserved for the *Consiglio Generale* the *condotte* of 'doctori medici' almost certainly refers not to teachers at all but to medical doctors.

[116] *Balìa* 24, ff. 88v-90v, 30 Jun (f. 90v), eds. F. PUCCINOTTI, *Storia della Medicina* (Florence, 1870), II.1, pp. CLXIII-CLXVIII (p. CLXVII), and repr. (without acknowledgement) by A. ILARDI, 'Ordinamenti del magistrato di Balìa di Siena ai lettori del pubblico studio', in *Atti del XXI congresso internazionale di storia della medicina, Siena (Italia), 22-28 settembre 1968* (Rome, 1969), pp. 164-70 (pp. 166-70; see p. 169); copy in *Mis.* 1, ff. 107r-109v (f. 109r). After the coup of 1487 the *Balìa* took over all *condotte*; *Balìa* 35, f. 104v, 5 Oct, and cf. BARGAGLI, *Bartolomeo Sozzini*, pp. 145-6.

[117] On the continuing importance of the *Consigli*, TERZIANI, 'L'instaurazione del regime', pp. 195-6.

[118] E.g. *Conc.* 144, f. 8r, 6 Jul 1388; *Conc.* 258, f. 4v, 3 Jan 1409.

[119] In 1425 *condotte* were reserved to the *Concistoro* and the *Savi* 'salvo che quando venisse chaso, che s'avesse ad condurre alcuno doctore famoso forestiero, el quale fusse di fuore di Siena in alcuno Studio forestiero, in quel caso se ne possa fare remissione ne' Savi dello Studio se parrà a' Signori e Gonfalonieri' (*Statuti* 41, f. 67v, and *Statuti* 47, f. 168v, 5 Feb).

[120] *Conc.* 292, f. 27r, 16 Oct.

[121] *Conc.* 298, ff. 29r-v, 16-17 Oct, ed. PIANIGIANI, doc. 30, pp. 54-6, and 31r, 20 Oct 1415. In 1416 both types were explicitly delegated to them; *Conc.* 304, f. 62v, 26 Oct.

[122] *Conc.* 321, f. 24r, 25 Aug.

[123] *Conc.* 330, f. 13r-v, 21-2 Jan.

[124] *Conc.* 339, f. 5v, 8 Jul, ed. PIANIGIANI, doc. 54, pp. 77-8.

[125] *Conc.* 347, f. 22r, 1 Dec; cf. *Conc.* 358, f. 27v, 9 Oct 1425. In 1433 the *Savi* were permitted to re-hire Mariano Sozzini for a different lectureship than previously, but not to fix his salary without the approval of the commune (*Conc.* 407 f. 15v, 29 Nov 1433, eds. NARDI, *Mariano Sozzini*, doc. 13, p. 120, and PIANIGIANI, doc. 152, p. 177). Occasionally the *Concistoro* delegated final choices between candidates to the *Savi*; e.g. *Conc.* 372, f. 50r-v, 28 Apr 1428, ed. PIANIGIANI, doc. 90, pp. 114-5 (between Polo da Lucca and Antonio Roselli for medicine, and Jacopo de Fornaria and the abbot of Reggio for canon law), and *Conc.* 447, f. 16v, 27 Jul 1440, ed. PIANIGIANI, doc. 206, pp. 238-9 – between Benedetto Barzi

Some of these measures are *ad hoc* solutions, others declarations, however short-lived, of principle; the point is that it was a workable partnership. What seems to have alarmed the *Consiglio del Popolo* was the fact that these delegations of authority threatened to give the office of the *Savi* something more than an executive function. To some extent this became inevitable as the powers of the *Savi* increased. However the *condotte* were arrived at, the decision as to which chair should be filled by which appointee, and the allocation of rooms to those teachers, were the exclusive province of the *Savi*; they were in charge of the day-to-day supervision of academic life, of the lecture programme[126] and of student affairs, and were given wide powers over the running of the Casa della Sapienza, as will be seen. Yet this delegation was never intended as a handing over of control over the *Studio*, and the controversy over *condotte* shows this. It is also shown by the fact that at all stages in this period of the *Studio*'s history, whenever it was felt that reforms of the system were necessary, special commissions, and not the *Savi*, were appointed to make proposals.[127] In the first half of the fifteenth century, the period when the question of control was particularly acute, such commissions were set up no fewer than ten times in twenty-eight years.[128] Occasionally they were set up on the initiative of private citizens.[129] The habit of adding people to the process could spread in other ways. Sometimes special commissions were set up to deal with specific *condotte* instead of the *Savi*,[130] and sometimes experts were brought in to help the *Savi* with specific tasks.[131]

The making of recommendations for reform was not usually considered to be part of the *Savi*'s functions, which could fairly be described as executive and advisory, and only in well-delineated areas more than that.[132] By the late fifteenth century some of these functions, too, were gradually supersed-

---

and Antonio da Pratovecchio. On the latter, see Nardi, *Mariano Sozzini*, pp. 21 n. 14, 42 and 69, and now P. Griguolo, 'Antonio Mincucci da Pratovecchio e il Monastero della Vangadizza', *Quaderni per la Storia dell'Università di Padova*, 36 [2003], pp. 101-8.).

[126] Of the many examples, cf. *Conc.* 566, f. 27r, 30 Jan 1461, ed. Bai, doc. 164, p. 137; the *Savi* have discretion as to the lectureship to be given to Borghese Borghesi.

[127] E.g. the appointment of six 'provisionarii pro Studio', *Conc.* 688, f. 10r, 10 Jan 1478, ed. Ferreri, doc. 60, pp. 51-2, and the following year of three *provisionarii* to draw up provisions on the *condotte*, *Conc.* 678, ff. 20v, 21 Oct, and 21r, 22 Oct 1479, ed. Ferreri, doc. 88, pp. 74-5. In 1480 the *Giudice delle Riformagioni*, Giovanni Battista Caccialupi, was asked to come forward with proposals, despite the fact that he was also teaching at the *Studio*. P. Nardi, 'Giovanni Battista Caccialupi a Siena: Giudice delle Riformagioni e docente nello Studio', *Studi senesi*, 109 (1997), pp. 83-124 (p. 111), and for the proposals that resulted see below, p. 89 and n. 24.

[128] *Conc.* 379, f. 23r, 14 Jun 1429; *Conc.* 386, f. 32r, 3 Aug 1430, ed. Pianigiani, doc. 123, pp. 151-3 (*condotte* are made by the *Concistoro* 'nec non tribus Sapientibus Studij cum quibus tribus Sapientibus negotia Studij'); *Conc.* 408, f. 3lr, 24 Feb (and *Conc.* 409, f. 8r, 7 Mar) 1434; *Conc.* 416, f. 18v, 20 May 1435; *CG* 219, f. 117r, 25 Feb 1437; *Conc.* 450, f. 36r, 4 Feb 1441; *Conc.* 496, f. 4r, 3 Sept 1448; *CG* 224, f. 318r, 16 Feb 1450 (ed. Garosi, doc. 62, pp. 530-1); *Mis.* 1, ff. 93r-95r, 10 Sept 1456; *Balìa* 3, ff. 72r, 78r, 88r, 111v, 132v, 1457.

[129] *CG* 243, f. 244v, 26 Dec 1533.

[130] *Conc.* 206, f. 51v, Nov 1398; *Conc.* 260, f. 23v, 29 May 1409; *Conc.* 286, f. 26v, 23 Oct 1413.

[131] In 1490 the *Balìa* decreed that seven citizens should be elected to help the *Concistoro* and the *Savi* with the *condotte*; *Conc.* 743, f. 6v, 16 Jul, ed. Ferreri, doc. 301, pp. 272-3, and *Conc.* 744, f. 7v, 7 Oct, ed. Ferreri, doc. 306, pp. 278-9 (six were elected). In 1497 three men were elected to join the *Savi* in the task of selling some Sapienza property; *Balìa* 41, f. 103v, 8 Feb. One of those elected was Jacopo del Germonia, an eminent public figure who also taught in the *Studio* (though not that year); Minnucci, 'Documenti', pp. 265-6.

[132] The *Savi* kept much of the clerical work, for example of issuing authorities of payment for minor lectureships, for school-teachers and for the officials of the *Studio* (e.g. *Studio* 2, ff. 104v, 23 Aug, and 105r, 13 Sept 1484; 109v, 17 May 1485; 123r, 11 Feb, 123v, 21 Mar, and 124r, 22 Mar 1488; *Sale* 24, f. 160v, 29 Dec 1497) at a time when their decision-making powers had been largely removed. In 1472 they were authorised to allow substitute teachers for up to three lectures, but the authorisation of the *Concistoro* was required for longer periods, as it was for the release of teachers from their con-

ed. Most of the political power of the *Concistoro* was taken over by *Balìe*, a series of special committees which by this time had assumed the characteristics of a quasi-permanent institution, to the extent that they are often referred to as a single body, the *Balìa* (and leave an archival source with this name). This institution also took an increasing interest in *condotte*.[133] The *Savi* did not have the same direct access to the *Balìa* as it had to the *Concistoro*, but had to communicate with it by means of written memoranda; its decision-making role was thus further compromised.[134] The control of the *Savi* over the Casa della Sapienza – embodied in their occasional denomination as *Savi dello Studio e della Sapienza*[135] or even *Savi della Sapienza*[136] – remained, but even this was partially reduced by the emergence of the *Camarlengo* who in 1491 acquired the right to sit and vote with them,[137] and they continued to be closely supervised in this role.[138] Finally in 1533 the functions of the *Savi* were divided between two bodies. The task of hiring teachers was given to four *Deputati sulle Condotte*, while the *Savi* were left with the Sapienza and the supervision of the students.[139] In the 1545 statutes of the republic, the office of *Savi* was restricted to members of the Senate, *riseduti* (members of the restricted group of families eligible for high office) and a few others who had been specially elected to that body.[140]

The Sienese *Savi dello Studio* were a key body in the administration of the *Studio*. Their membership was drawn entirely from the political class, as elsewhere, and they became the main interface between commune and *Studio*. But their office was kept under tight control. They never quite achieved the power of their counterparts in Florence/Pisa in the late fifteenth century, though that is arguably

tracts (*CG* 234, f. 180r, 1472). An unusual but unsurprising role is that of pacifiers in a dispute between two Spanish students; *Not.* 335, ff. 150v-152r, 20 Aug 1440, ed. MINNUCCI, 'Documenti', doc. III-227, pp. 196-7; and cf. IDEM, 'La Casa della Sapienza', in *Storia di Siena*, I, pp. 357-70 (pp. 364-5). (The students do not appear to have been members of the Casa della Sapienza.) The *Savi*'s natural connections with the legal world meant that they were sometimes consulted on the appointment of the *Giudice delle Riformagioni* and the judge of appeals, both posts which had to be filled by non-Sienese lawyers; *CG* 239, f. 126r, 9 Sept 1483 (the *Savi* are consulted on these appointments); *Conc.* 703, f. 16r, 14 Dec 1483, ed. FERRERI, doc. 188, p. 159 (they join the *Concistoro* in electing the judge of appeals; and again four months later, *Conc.* 705, f. 20r-v, 21 Apr 1484, ed. FERRERI, doc. 196, p. 165. However the following year they are no longer involved in the choice of the *Giudice delle Riformagioni*; *CG* 239, f. 165r-v, 23 Jan 1484).

[133] E.g. in 1487 the *Balìa* ruled that the *Concistoro* could not make any contracts for longer than a year (*Conc.* 726, f. 28v, 15 Oct, ed. FERRERI, doc. 256, pp. 218-9); in 1492 the *Balìa* appointed three of its members to examine all contracts to be made (*Balìa* 37, f. 22r, 5 Jul). On the development of the *Balìa* see ARCHIVIO DI STATO DI SIENA, *Archivio di Balìa*; introduction by G. Prunai and S. De' Colli, pp. IX-LXXXI, and PRUNAI and DE' COLLI, 'La Balìa'; also D. L. HICKS, 'The Sienese Oligarchy and the Rise of Pandolfo Petrucci, 1487-97', in *La Toscana al tempo di Lorenzo*, III, pp. 1051-72 (pp. 1056-7).

[134] In 1493 the *Balìa* appointed two of its members to be *Savi dello Studio*, and stipulated that the existing *Savi* were to make no decisions except in the presence of these two (*Balìa* 38, ff. 29v, 4 Jan, and 33v, 9 Jan); in 1495 the *Balìa* gave the *Savi* authority to make a range of decisions over a period of fifteen days (*Balìa* 40, f. 103r, 26 Dec). An example of the precision with which the *Savi*'s role could be prescribed is the reform of 1481 stating that they have precedence over the *Camarlengo di Gabella* but had to defer to the *Regolatori*; *Balìa* 24, f. 90r, 30 Jun 1481, eds. PUCCINOTTI, *Storia della Medicina*, p. CLXVII, and ILARDI, 'Ordinamenti', p. 169; copy in *Mis.* 1, f. 109r.

[135] *Mis.* 1, f. 85v, 18 Apr 1438; *CG* 236, f. 126r, 28 Jun 1475, and below, p. 339 n. 7.

[136] *CG* 241, f. 44r, 19 Dec 1498.

[137] *Mis.* 1, f. 115r, 13 Jun, and below, p. 357.

[138] For example the 'liber in quo descripta sunt bona misericordie' (possibly the present *Mis.* 36, on which see above, p. 24) was kept by the *Balìa* or the *Concistoro* (*Studio* 2, f. 47v, 14 Oct 1476).

[139] *CG* 243, ff. 248r-250v, 28 Dec, ed. KOŠUTA, 'Documenti', doc. I-6, pp. 338-41.

[140] In ASCHERI, *L'ultimo statuto*, rubrics I-24, p. 14, and I-200, p. 113, and MARRARA, *Lo Studio di Siena*, pp. 297-303 (and cf. pp. 91-8, and IDEM, *Riseduti e nobiltà*, pp. 90 n. 10 and 91); see also CASCIO PRATILLI, *L'Università e il Principe*, pp. 14-6. For a similar process of decline of the role of the *Savi* at Perugia, cf. ERMINI, *Storia*, I, pp. 202-3.

because of the exigencies of government by distance rather than any peculiarities of the universities of territorial states.[141] The insistence on keeping the most important decisions regarding teaching contracts within the more explicitly political organisms, from the fifteenth century through to the fall of the republic, suggests that this is a continuous concern. The key appointments were a matter for the rulers, too important to be left to the administrators.

4. *Other officials*

The smooth operation of the *Studio* depended on a number of other officials as well. Foremost among these was the *bidello*, the chief regular official of the *Studio* as a whole (as opposed to the *Savi* who held authority over it, and the rector who was a short-term appointment and a student). In one of his last contributions to the history of the Bolognese *Studio* the late Antonio Ivan Pini explored the history of this office – or rather these offices, for at Bologna each component of the *Studio* (the *universitates*, the nations, the colleges of doctors and the faculty of theology) had its own *bidello*, as did individual teachers.[142] In Siena there is no evidence of such proliferation in the fifteenth century.[143] Although there is some ambiguity of terminology, especially in the late fourteenth century, these are, as with other aspects of the *Studio*, signs of its new and as yet undeveloped state, and perhaps of lack of continuity, rather than of a proliferation of officials.[144] Moreover, although the office of 'bidello generale' has close connections with the student university thanks to the influence of the Bolognese

[141] DENLEY, '*Signore* and *Studio*', esp. 204-8, 210-11; SILVANO, 'Stato, territorio e istituzioni', esp. pp. 992-3; and see below, pp. 404 *seq.*

[142] A. I. PINI, 'Per una storia sociale dell'università: i bidelli bolognesi nel XIII secolo', *Annali di storia delle università italiane*, 1 (1997), pp. 43-75; and IDEM, 'Il mondo universitario: professori, studenti, bidelli', in *Ceti, modelli, comportamenti nella società medievale (secc. XIII – metà XIV)* (Pistoia, 2001), pp. 123-45. Cf. also G. FASOLI, 'I bidelli: sotto la cattedra c'erano anche loro', *Saecularia Nona. università di Bologna 1088-1988*, 3 (1988), pp. 50-53, and for Padua, M. BILANOVICH DAL ZIO, 'Bidelli, cartolai e miniatori allo Studio di Padova nel secolo XV', *Quaderni per la Storia dell'Università di Padova*, 6 (1973), pp. 59-72 (esp. pp. 59-62). For an overview of research on Italian *bidelli* that is slightly more positive than Pini about what has been accomplished, DE ROSA, 'Studi sull'Università di Pisa'. The distinction between the *bidello generale* and *bidelli speciali* appears to be a function of size. Pavia has it; see MAIOCCHI, *Codice diplomatico dell'Università di Pavia*, II.1, doc. 194, pp. 123-4, 7 Oct 1412 (and cf. doc. 197, p. 126, 13 Oct), showing that in addition to the *bidellus generalis* there is a special *bidello* 'ad gubernationem scolarum studii'; and P. ROSSO, 'Presenze studentesche e collegi pavesi nella seconda metà del Quattrocento', *Schede umanistiche*, n.s. (1994), n. 2, pp. 25-42 (n. 27 and n. 7). However, Perugia also had the distinction (ERMINI, *Storia*, I, pp. 340-2), and there are references to the *bidello generale* in Florence (SPAGNESI, *Utiliter edoceri*, p. 115).

[143] The only moment at which I am aware of there being more than one such officer is in 1478, when the long-serving Ser Jacopo is given three months' leave on 21 Mar (*Conc.* 669, f. 17r, and see n. 153 below), on the same day that mention is made of 'Ser Philippus bidellus'; f. 16v. The earliest evidence of more than one *bidello* comes with the approval of the statutes of the college of doctors of medicine in 1511, in which it was stipulated that the college was to elect its own official; *Balìa* 253, ff. 335v-345v, 13 Oct; Rubric 7, f. 338v (on these statutes see below, p. 206). Even then, however, the names of *bidelli* reported as present at degree ceremonies (MINNUCCI, *Lauree*, III, and MINNUCCI and MORELLI, *Lauree*, IV) do not suggest that different individuals are in fact appointed.

[144] E.g. the same official, Simone di Neri, was described as 'bidello...studii' (*Bicch.* 242, f. 137r [new foliation], 20 Dec 1362) and as 'bidello del rettore de lo studio e de' dottori' (*Bicch.* 243, f. 137r, 29 Apr 1363); Domenico di Francesco appears first as 'bidello sopra le schuole de lo studio' (*Bicch.* 460, g. 10v, 1388) and then as 'bidello istato dello studio generale' (*Regolatori* 4, f. 221r, 1389). The variation persists in the fifteenth century; Ser Filippo di Angelo di Pietro is both 'bidello de la Sapienzia' (*Bicch.* 338, f. 154r, 6 May 1483; cf. *Sale* 21, f. 208r, 28 Jul 1483) and 'bidello Universitatis studii' (*Not.* 879, no. 20, 28 Jul 1483), as is Ser Gilio di Pietro in 1490 (*Bicch.* 344, f. 75r [new foliation], 17 Apr; *Not.* 858, f. 30r).

'model',[145] at Siena this was a communally salaried post. It may be that the missing statutes of the student university included details of the *bidello*'s office and functions, but as usual we have to make do with communal deliberations. It is likely that the student university chose the official,[146] but it appears to have required confirmation by the *Concistoro*, which intervened in this as in so many matters pertaining to that body.[147] In 1452 the appointment of Ser Jacopo Celli as 'bidello Generalis Studii' by the *Concistoro* and *Savi* was accompanied by one of the few surviving measures regulating his office. To counter threats from students that he would be sacked, his office, hitherto usually for two years,[148] was extended to three years, during which he could not be removed.[149] In practice, though, the striking feature of this official is continuity. Always a Sienese citizen or subject, and in the fifteenth century always a notary,[150] his appointment by the student body may have been more a formality than the result of active student initiative,[151] since *bidelli* could hold office for substantial periods. Ser Bartolomeo di Checho di Binduccio da Asciano was *bidello* from 1428 until at least 1449.[152] Ser Jacopo Celli is first heard of in this role in 1451 and held the post continuously until at least 1475.[153] Ser Filippo

---

[145] See below, p. 273.

[146] E.g. below, n. 149; *Not.* 858, ff. 11r-12r, 22 Mar 1481, ed. MINNUCCI, 'Documenti', doc. II-31, pp. 96-7.

[147] See below, Chapter III.2.

[148] *Conc.* 430, f. 7r, 11 Sept 1437; *Conc.* 439, f. 23v, 9 Apr 1439; *Conc.* 462, f. 57r-v, 27 Feb 1443; *Conc.* 507, f. 44v, 27 Oct 1450. But some one-year appointments were made; *Conc.* 475, f. 28v, 24 Apr 1445; *Conc.* 493, f. 25r, 12 Apr 1448.

[149] *Conc.* 517, f. 9r-v, 7 Nov 1452, ed. BAI, docs. 35-37, pp. 32-35 (and see pp. xiii-xiv): 'acciochè ogni domino di nuovo non s'abbi a consumare nelle pratiche da farsi per essere confermato et ogni dì non sia minacciato non facendo il perché d'esser casso o vero di mutar bidello'. One cannot but be struck by the fact that only the previous year the bedel and notary of the university of jurists at Padua had successfully petitioned for the extension of their contracts in perpetuity, for apparently similar reasons; M. P. RIGONI, 'Una conferma in ruolo a metà del XV secolo: il notaio e il bidello generale dell'Università giurista', *Quaderni per la Storia dell'Università di Padova*, 6 (1973), pp. 163-7. As Bai points out, the Sienese measure does not seem to have been implemented or at least not to have lasted for long; subsequent documents refer to the *bidello*'s contract as being for two years (*Conc.* 544, f. 12r, 30 May 1457; *Conc.* 552, f. 14v, 23 Sept 1458; *Conc.* 582, f. 28v, 17 Oct 1463). Earlier it had been a one-year appointment; cf. *Conc.* 475, f. 28v, 24 Aug 1445.

[150] As at Bologna; cf. PINI, 'Il mondo universitario', pp. 44, 49; IDEM, 'Per una storia', p. 143. A late fourteenth-century *bidello*, Domenico di Francesco, was a *cartaio* (*Bicch.* 460, f. 10v, 1388, and *Regolatori* 4, f. 221v, 1389). At the end of the fifteenth century Ser Gilio di Pietro was described as 'notario et bidello universitatis studii' (*Not.* 858, ff. 29r-30r, 24 Sept 1490, 27r-28r, 8 May 1492, 32r-33r, 2 May 1493, ed. MINNUCCI, 'Documenti', docs. I-9, I-11 and I-12, pp. 61-7; Not 799, no foliation, 18 May 1491); less ambiguously (since the first of these might be considered a declaration of occupation rather than office) his successor, Ser Filippo di Antonio, is described as 'bidelli et notarii studii' (*Not.* 801, f. 29r and 29v, 1495?).

[151] However, in 1440 a *bidello* was sacked by the rector, and this was confirmed by the *Concistoro* (*Conc.* 449, f. 8v, Nov).

[152] *Bicch.* 309, ff. 39v, 53r (1428-9), *Bicch.* 310, f. 65v, 6 Dec 1430 (and ff. 44r, 36r); *Bicch.* 311, f. 147v, 24 Oct 1433; *Studio* 127, no. 3, 8 Apr 1433; *Bicch.* 312, ff. 71v, 5 Nov, and 87r, 30 Dec 1438; *Conc.* 475, f. 28r, 24 Apr 1445. Bartolomeo was also the *bidello* responsible from 1440 to 1449 for collecting and passing on the *4-lire* payments due to the Opera del Duomo from students who were taking their degree; NARDI, 'Una fonte inedita delle lauree senesi'.

[153] *Bicch.* 319, ff. 69v, 6 May, and 96v, 15 Sept 1451; *Bicch.* 320, ff. 81v, 15 Sept, and 87v, 10 Oct 1451; *Conc.* 509, f. 70r, 1451 (*apotissa*); *Conc.* 517, f. 9r-v, 7 Nov 1452, ed. BAI, docs. 35-37, pp. 32-35; *Bicch.* 321, f. 202v, 19 May 1453; *Conc.* 527, f. 5r, 3 Jul 1454, ed. BAI, doc. 60, p. 51 (and also p. xiii); *Conc.* 544, f. 12r, 30 May 1457 (renewal of appointment); *Conc.* 552, f. 14v, 23 Sept 1458 (renewal for two years); *Conc.* 582, f. 28v, 17 Oct 1463 (renewal for two years); *Conc.* 593, f. 38v, 22 Aug 1465; *Bicch.* 327, f. 114v, Jun 1466; *Bicch.* 328, f. 182r, 30 Jan 1470; *Bicch.* 329, ff. 175v, 14 Jan, and 190r, 22 Apr 1471; *Bicch.* 330, ff. 32v (and 264r), 28 Feb, 153v (and 271v), 4 Jun, and 283v, 4 Oct 1472; *Bicch.* 331, ff. 149v, 18 May, and 164r, 6 Sept 1473; *Gabella* 24, f. 155v, 17 Mar 1474. On 6 Feb 1474 he was sacked, and banished to Bologna for ten years (*Conc.* 644, f. 31r-v, 6 Feb), for reasons that are unclear but connected with his son and a benefice; four days later he was reinstated (f. 34v, 10 Feb, and cf. f. 43r, 21 Feb). He was given three months' leave in 1475 on condition that he found a substitute to be approved by the *Concistoro* (*Conc.* 651, f. 24r, 1 Apr, and again on 30 Oct, when a journey to Rome is mentioned; *Conc.* 654, f. 40r). By 1478, when the threat of exile to Bologna is again made, he

d'Agnolo di Pietro is known to have been *bidello* from at least 1481, and possibly 1478, until his death in 1488.[154] His successor but one, Ser Filippo d'Antonio, held this office from 1495 well into the next century.[155] The office attracted a modest salary of 20 florins,[156] sometimes paid annually,[157] later more usually in *terzarie*.[158]

The functions of the *bidello* were protean. He had his own premises, which judging from Bolognese comparisons and the multiplicity of his duties must have been used for a variety of purposes;[159] in 1545 his *bottega* was certainly large enough to accommodate public disputations.[160] He had a responsibility for the lecture rooms used by teachers, and was periodically given oversight of their refurbishment.[161] He was closely involved in the administration of teaching; receiving the doctors' acceptance of their contracts,[162] passing on the instructions of the *Savi*, ordering teachers to teach,[163] drawing up the *rotolo* or list of lectures,[164] organising disputations,[165] monitoring the satisfactory attendance of lecturers, keeping the list of absences which would result in fines being deducted from their salaries,[166] announcing holidays,[167] and occasionally being involved in the payment of salaries.[168] His

has retired from the office (*Conc.* 669, ff. 16v, 18 Mar, 17r, 21 Mar, and 32v, 14 Apr). He was still alive in 1484 (*Not.* 658, no. 11, 26 Apr; a sale). His association with the office persisted into posterity, with his children bearing the epithet ('Scipione Ser Jacobi bidelli', *Conc.* 766, f. 19r, 19 Jun 1494; cf. Marianus, *Conc.* 779, f. 8r, 16 Aug 1496, and Jacoba, BCS, *ms.* C.III.2, *Obituario di S. Domenico*, f. 120v, buried 3 Nov 1499).

[154] *Conc.* 669, f. 16v, 21 Mar 1478 mentions a 'Ser Philippus bidellus'. Surer notices are in *Bicch.* 335, f. 54v, 6? Jan 1481 (= *Bicch.* 336, f. 317r); *Bicch.* 336, f. 322r, 1 Aug 1481; *Bicch.* 338, ff. 151r, 26 Feb, and 154r, 6 May 1483; *Sale* 21, ff. 208r, 28 Jul, and 214v, 1483 (*apotissa*); *Not.* 879, nos. 14, 10 Jul, and 20, 28 Jul 1483; *Bicch.* 338, f. 169r, 13 Feb 1484; *Bicch.* 339, ff. 59r, 5 Feb, 61r, 8 Apr, and 70v, 15 Nov 1485; *Bicch.* 340, ff. 79r, 27 Jan, 85v, 9 Jan 1487(=1438), and 89r, 15 Sept 1487; *Bicch.* 341, ff. 97v, 10 Mar, and 102r, 21 May 1488. Filippo then died, and was buried on 22 May 1488; *Studio* 2, f. 124r.

[155] *Not.* 801, f. 29r and 29t, 1495?; *Sale* 23, f. 93v, 21 Apr 1496; *Sale* 24, ff. 155r, 24 Apr 1497, and 163v, 17 Feb 1498; *Sale* 25, f. 84v, 22 Dec 1518. He appears regularly as witness to degrees from 14 Feb 1496 to 16 Feb 1522; MINNUCCI, *Lauree*, I, pp. 31 *seq.*, *passim*; IDEM, *Lauree*, II and III, *passim*; MINNUCCI and MORELLI, *Lauree*, IV, *passim* to p. 35.

[156] References as in nn. 144, 153 and 154 above. On one occasion he is paid slightly more, 85 *lire*, 'pro pensione'; *Conc.* 466, ff. 54v, 28 Oct, 62r and 64r, 31 Oct 1443. In 1339 it had been 25 *lire*, paid in two instalments; ZDEKAUER, p. 137.

[157] E.g. *Conc.* 360, f. 35r, 14 Feb 1426.

[158] *Studio* 127, no. 2, 8 Apr 1433 (two *terzarie*).

[159] It included the storage of administrative documents and university texts, ceremonial items and robes; it was 'un po' ufficio, un po' bottega, un po' deposito'. PINI, 'Per una storia sociale', p. 51; IDEM, 'Il mondo universitario', p. 142.

[160] *Studio* 22, no foliation.

[161] E.g. *Bicch.* 460, f. 10v, 1388, 'Domenico di franciescho chartaio + bidello alecto sopra le schuole de lo studio'; *Conc.* 370, f. 19v, 4 Dec 1427, the *bidello* is to make an inventory of chairs and lecterns in the Sapienza (cf. CATONI, 'Genesi', p. 168).

[162] *Conc.* 581, f. 18v, 29 Jul 1463.

[163] *Balìa* 11, f. 48r, 21 Dec 1478.

[164] *Studio* 2, f. 124r, 23 Jul 1488: 'Pier Ieronimo bidello' is paid 'pro conficiendo rotolo doctorum'. On the *rotolo* see below, pp. 110-11.

[165] *Balìa* 24, f. 89r-v, 30 Jun 1481, eds. PUCCINOTTI, *Storia della Medicina*, p. CLXV-VI, and ILARDI, 'Ordinamenti', pp. 167-8; copy in *Mis.* 1, f. 107v-108r. In the 1545-6 *rotolo* the *bidello* is charged with putting out the benches for disputations and remaining till the end to ensure full attendance by the doctors. *Studio* 22, no foliation.

[166] *Conc.* 595, f. 45v, 30 Dec 1465; the *apotisse* were to be made 'secundum squadram portandam per bidellum'. On the imposition and administration of fines, below, pp. 159 *seq.*

[167] *Studio* 22, *rotolo* of 1545-6, no foliation.

[168] E.g. *Conc.* 669, f. 16v, 21 Mar 1478. In 1494 it was he who summoned the newly-established 'collegio doctorum legentium'; *Not.* 1019, no foliation, 23 Jun. Below, p. 173.

involvement with the accounting of teachers' salaries could land him in hot water. Ser Jacopo Celli was challenged by Mansueto Mansueti of Perugia over this in 1465; the case was sent to the *Giudice delle Riformagioni*, Giovanni Battista da Caccialupi, for a ruling,[169] but was still running between their heirs over a decade later.[170] On several occasions the *bidello* travelled on *Studio* business, at least once to recruit teachers.[171] He had responsibilities towards the students, and while we have few illustrations of these it is reasonable to assume that, as elsewhere, they were wide-ranging,[172] and included the need to deal with students of diverse origins and linguistic backgrounds.[173] He played a specific role within the colleges of doctors, often summoning or being present at meetings,[174] and regularly being present and acting as witness at examinations,[175] for which he was entitled to a fee;[176] and from 1440 onwards he assumed responsibility for the collection of graduands' payments to the Opera del Duomo.[177] Though Sienese evidence has not come to light for the practice, elsewhere *bidelli* had specific responsibilities connected with the provision of texts and making available written records of disputations.[178] Finally he had an important function in the Casa della Sapienza, reading out orders from the *Savi*,[179] and removing those students that the *Savi* or *Concistoro* had decided to deprive of their places.[180]

As in any medieval organisation, notaries were needed to oil the wheels at various levels. At various stages the *Savi* had their own notary[181] (just as they could employ other people for miscellaneous

---

[169] *Conc.* 593, f. 39v, 23 Aug.

[170] *Conc.* 1693, f. 109r-v, 27 Apr 1478; *Conc.* 1694, ff. 35v-36r, 25 Apr 1480.

[171] *Conc.* 380, f. 8r, 8 Jun 1429; *Conc.* 421, ff. 45v-46r, 27 Apr 1436; *Conc.* 498, f. 5v, 5 Mar 1449 (and f. 31v, 15 Apr; a substitute is elected); *Bicch.* 320. f. 87v, 10 Oct 1451 (£32/0/0 was paid 'per suo salario di dì xvi andò e ste per fatti de lo studio a trovare dottori con uno cavallo'). A further expedition was to Perugia, and though its purpose is not stated it is likely to have been the same; *Conc.* 527, f. 5r, 3 Jul 1454, ed. BAI, doc. 60, p. 51 (and also p. xiii).

[172] E.g. he is found announcing rectoral elections on the instructions of the *Concistoro*; *Conc.* 380, f. 8r, 8 Jun 1429.

[173] *Conc.* 517, f. 9r, 7 Nov 1452, ed. BAI, doc. 36, pp. 33-34; 'et maxime avendo conversare con tanta varietà de linghua et de paesi et de nationi'.

[174] E.g. *Not.* 589, ff. 108v-109v, 30 May 1466, in attendance at the meeting of the college of doctors of arts and medicine; *Not.* 801, f. 29r-v, 1495, meeting of the college of doctors of law for a degree ceremony 'ad requisitione bidelli'. On the colleges see below, pp. 195 *seq.*

[175] MINNUCCI, *Lauree*, I, *passim*; IDEM, 'Il conferimento dei titoli accademici nello Studio di Siena fra XV e XVI secolo. Modalità dell'esame e provenienza studentesca', in *Università in Europa*, pp. 213-26; revised version in MINNUCCI and MORELLI, *Lauree*, V, pp. ix-xxviii.

[176] *Conc.* 517, f. 9r, 7 Nov 1452, ed. BAI, doc. 37, pp. 34-35 (and pp. xiii-xiv).

[177] Above, n. 152.

[178] On the importance of *bidelli* in the world of university texts and books, L. GARGAN, 'Libri, librerie e biblioteche nelle università italiane del Due e Trecento', in *Luoghi e metodi di insegnamento*, pp. 221-46 (esp. pp. 237-9).

[179] E.g. *Not.* 886, ff. 153r-154r, 6 Oct 1483.

[180] E.g. *Conc.* 569, f. 19r, 22 Jul 1461.

[181] In 1425 this was the same as the notary of the *Studio*; cf. *Conc.* 355, f. 13r, 22 Mar, and *Conc.* 358, ff. 16v-17r, 22 Sept 1425 (also *Bicch.* 456, f. 39r, 16 Apr, and *Bicch.* 358, ff. 16v-17v, 22 Sept). Thereafter, however, when a notary of the *Savi* is specified he is a different person from the notary of the *Studio* (e.g. in 1451 Ser Francesco di Domenico is *notaio* of the *Savi*, Ser Simone di Iacomo di Ghieri da Radicondoli is notary of the university, *Bicch.* 320, f. 87v, 1 Oct; in 1472 Ser Giovanni di ser Mariano was *notaio* of the *Savi* [*Bicch.* 330, f. 32v, 28 Feb and 12 Apr], while Ser Cecci di Bernardo di Matteo di Salvi was *Notaio dello Studio* [*Bicch.* 330, f. 57v, 30 Apr]. The exception is Ser Magius Bargalius, who is paid for his services as *notaio* of the *Savi* on 1 Jan 1497 [*Sale* 24, ff. 151r] but as *Notaio dello Studio* both before and after that [*Sale* 23, f. 99r, 19 Dec 1496 and *Sale* 24, f. 163v, 17 Feb 1498]). At those times when payments were effected through the offices of the *Sale* and the *Paschi* (see below, p. 100 n. 47), they shared a notary with them (*Conc.* 2114, f. 21v, 10 May 1433). Such figures were of course involved in a range of other activities; Ser Giacomo Nuccino was described as 'notarius publicus, et iudex ordinarius senen., nec non officialis, et scriba dictorum sapientum, et reformatorum dicti almi studii senen., et gubernatorum dicte domus sapientie senen.' (*Mis.* 1, f. 82v, 14 Sept. 1435).

tasks).[182] The colleges of doctors[183] and the student-university also required the services of a notary. The latter was commonly described as the *notaio dello studio*, a figure appointed by the student-university[184] but paid for by the commune. His salary was more modest than that of the *bidello*,[185] as was that of the *puntatore* (whose pay was lower still),[186] and the *famegli* who were employed from time to time.[187] Even the bell-ringers who triggered the *Studio*'s daily timetable are mentioned in the sources.[188] Finally the commune employed messengers or officials to other towns to publicise the *Studio* and to recruit teachers.[189]

---

[182] In 1424 they employed a *barisello* to collect dues from the clergy and others (*Conc.* 1623, f. 58v, 7 Jun). In the late fifteenth century they also had a *fameglio*, Galgano di Caterino (paid 8 *lire* for his labours in this capacity for a *terzaria* in 1471-2, *Bicch.* 330, f. 32v, 15 Apr; 16 *lire* on 3 Nov 1487, *Bicch.* 340, f. 92r; 8 *lire* on 17 Oct 1490, *Bicch.* 344, f. 75r [new foliation]; 12 *lire* each on 19 Jan, 9 Jun and 25 Sept 1492, *Bicch.* 347, ff. 127v, 135v, and 143v). Galgano seems to have covered a multiplicity of roles; he is described as *fameglo de lo studio* in 1474 (*Gabella* 24, ff. 41r, 125v, and *Bicch.* 332, f. 13r, 4 Feb) and 1476 (*Studio* 2, f. 41v, 3 Apr), as *famulus universitatis studii* in 1483 (*Sale* 21, f. 208r, 28 Jul), as servant of the Sapienza in 1479 (below, p. 358 n. 187), and as *famulus palatii* in 1476 and 1485, in which capacity he was involved in the determination of teachers' fines for absences during this period (below, p. 160 nn. 113 and 120). In 1489 the *Savi* have a different servant, Giovanni di Jachomo (paid 7 *lire* on 6 Nov, *Bicch.* 343, f. 162v).

[183] The statutes of the college of doctors of medicine drawn up in 1511 stipulate the method of electing a notary and his functions. His term of office was up to the college, and he was paid for each examination for which he drew up the documents (*Balìa* 253, ff. 335v-345v, 13 Oct, Rubric 6, ff. 338r-v).

[184] Below, pp. 273-4.

[185] Below, p. 99.

[186] Below, loc. cit.

[187] See note 182 above.

[188] *Bicch.* 456, f. 9r, 3 Mar 1425; see also *Bicch.* 309, ff. 39v and 68r 1428-9, and *Bicch.* 310, f. 65v, 1430.

[189] Below, p. 151.

III

RESOURCES AND CONTRIBUTORS

1. *Introduction*

'Il più utile denaio che voi spendiate, si è quello dello Studio.' This was the view of San Bernardino, himself a former student at the university and an influential voice in Siena, as elsewhere, in the 1420s.[1] The funding of Italian universities has been described as their 'problema esistenziale',[2] and in Siena, too, financial issues dominate the deliberations of the authorities regarding the *Studio*. For the fifteenth century, at least, it could be said that Siena's sustained commitment to the financing of its *Studio* was the chief cause of its continuity and hence ultimately to its guaranteed success. There were of course fluctuations in the amount that the authorities were prepared to spend on teachers, and instances where the growth of the *Studio* was stunted because of short-term financial retraction; but on the whole the record is good, and certainly so if it is compared to that of two neighbours, Florence and Rome.[3]

[1] The statement is in a sermon preached in Siena in 1425, especially to the teachers and students of the *Studio*; it is published in C. CANNAROZZI (ed.), *Le prediche volgari di San Bernardino. Predicazione in Siena* (Florence, 1958), II, pp. 293-307 (p. 301). Bernardino had already given such sermons in Padua and in Florence; D. PACETTI, 'La necessità dello studio: predica inedita da S. Bernardino', *Bullettino di Studi Bernardiniani*, 2 (1936), pp. 301-21 (p. 302), for comparisons; and cf. M. STICCO, *Pensiero e poesia in S. Bernardino da Siena* (Milan, 1945 edn.), pp. 131 *seq.*, 143; and I. ORIGO, *The World of San Bernardino* (London, 1963), esp. pp. 189-93. He returned to the theme in the cycle of sermons preached in the Piazza del Campo in 1427, urging the continuation of the *Studio*: 'Non lo lassate partire da Siena, cittadini sanesi, che voi non comprendete l'utile e l'onore che ve ne viene di chi [di qui] a poco tempo. Ponete mente a Bologna, il nome e l'utile e l'onore: così vi seguitarà a voi, se voi vel saprete mantenere…'; BERNARDINO DA SIENA, *Prediche Volgari sul Campo di Siena, 1427*, ed. C. Delcorno, 2 vols. (Milan, 1989), XXXVIII 120, 24 Sept (p. 1132). His enthusiasm for the *Studio* did not extend to condoning the commune's taxation of the clergy for this purpose (see below, pp. 103-4). On Bernardino's studies in Siena see now esp. NARDI, 'Appunti sui maestri'; and the older L. DI STOLFI, 'De S. Bernardini Senensis formatione scientifica', *Antonianum*, 20 (1945), pp. 245-66; for another example of his influence, below, p. 233, and on his position as patron of the university, p. 276.

[2] M. C. ZORZOLI, 'Interventi dei Duchi e del Senato di Milano per l'Università di Pavia (secoli XV-XVI)', *Studi senesi*, 92 (1980), pp. 128-49 (p. 133).

[3] The financial problems of these two *studi* are highlighted by BRUCKER, 'Florence and its University', and D. S. CHAMBERS, 'Studium Urbis and the *Gabella Studii*', in *Cultural Aspects of the Italian Renaissance*, ed. C. Clough (Manchester, 1976), pp. 68-110; repr. in his *Individuals and Institutions in Renaissance Italy* (Aldershot, 1998), Ch. II.

2. *The budget*

The impressive financial commitment to the hosting of the Bolognese *migratio* in 1321, discussed above,[4] was of course exceptional. But a relatively stable concept of what it was appropriate to spend on the *Studio* emerges soon after the obtention of its charter in 1357. At the reopening of the *Studio* in 1361 the maximum amount that could be spent on teachers' salaries was fixed at 3,000 gold florins.[5] This sum almost immediately proved to be over-ambitious. In 1364 the commune decided, controversially, to impose a tax on the clergy to help attain it.[6] In the following year money ran out all the same, and the teaching force was sacked.[7] With the revival in 1386-7 a maximum of 2,500 florins was stipulated,[8] yet in 1398 only 600 florins were voted.[9] However the initial figure of 3,000 obviously represented a target; it was the figure agreed in the treaty with Giangaleazzo Visconti.[10] In 1404 – still a period in which the *Studio* was barely in existence – it is mentioned again.[11] In 1406 there is an increase to 3,500 florins.[12] In 1409 the hospital of S. Maria della Scala refused to pay its contribution, and all local teachers were sacked.[13] In 1412 the 3,000 maximum was again repeated.[14] In 1416, when the *Studio* finally got under way, the *Savi* reached the limit before they had filled all of the *cattedre* and 300 florins were voted to fill the remaining five with local (cheaper) teachers.[15] The following year the

---

[4] Pp. 37-8.

[5] *CG* 168, f. 4r, 19 Jul, ed. ZDEKAUER, doc. V, p. 143. The gold florin had reached about 70 *soldi* by the mid-fourteenth century; full tables are given by C. M. CIPOLLA, *Studi di Storia della Moneta. I movimenti dei cambi in Italia dal secolo XIII al XV* (Pavia, 1948), pp. 132-214, and P. SPUFFORD, *Handbook of Medieval Exchange*. Royal Historical Society Guides and Handbooks, 13 (London, 1986), pp. 1-25. By the fifteenth century all salaries except those of *maestri d'abaco* and officials such as the *bidello* were agreed and announced in florins, as at other *studi*, and paid at 80 *soldi* per florin despite the continuing devaluation of *moneta piccola* charted by CIPOLLA (pp. 62-4). In the later fifteenth century these figures are sometimes given in ducats. This may be connected with the fact that Siena had started to coin ducats; G. TODERI, 'Le Monete della repubblica di Siena (1180-1559)', in B. PAOLOZZI STROZZI, G. TODERI and F. VANNEL TODERI, *Le monete della repubblica senese* (Milan, 1992), pp. 283-403 (p. 317); D. PROMIS, *Monete della repubblica di Siena* (Turin, 1868), pp. 36, 50; cf. CIPOLLA, p. 64. However, the term appears to be used in exactly the same way as the florins at a fixed rate of exchange. As with the *fiorino di suggello*, which appears eventually to have become a unit of account, in which salaries of teachers and communal officials were fixed in Florence, the effect of this was to devalue the salaries of the teachers in real terms by maintaining a fictional rate of exchange lower than the actual value. N. RUBINSTEIN, 'Die Vermögenslage florentiner Humanisten im 15. Jahrhundert', in *Humanismus und Ökonomie*, ed. H. Lutz. Mitteilungen der Kommission für Humanismusforschung, 8 (Weinheim, 1983), pp. 107-19 (pp. 113-4). The *fiorino di suggello* was also known in the Laurentian period, when referring to teachers' salaries, as the *fiorino di studio* (examples in VERDE, *Lo Studio fiorentino*, II, pp. 15, 192, 196, 209-10, 213, 300, 350, 552, 555, 567, 575, 589, 598, and cf. pp. 3-4). On the problems of interpreting Sienese financial information using the different systems of coinage, A. K. CHIANCONE ISAACS, 'Fisco e politica a Siena nel Trecento', *Rivista Storica Italiana*, 85 (1973), pp. 22-46 (pp. 28-9).

[6] *CG* 171, ff. 31r-32v, 27 Mar, and 111r, 26 Nov, ed. ZDEKAUER, doc. VI, pp. 144-5 (and see p. 21); and below, p. 102.

[7] *Conc.* 31, f. 58v, 28 Apr 1365.

[8] *CG* 195, f. 115r-v, 23 Jan 1387, ed. GAROSI, p. 194 n. 1; copy in *Mis.* 1, f. 50r-v. The hospital of S. Maria della Scala was obliged to contribute in addition to the clergy (below, pp. 105 *seq.*).

[9] *CG* 198, f. 95r, 27 Nov.

[10] *CG* 199, f. 49r, 6 Oct 1399; ZDEKAUER, p. 30, and IDEM, *Origini*, p. 22.

[11] *CG* 201, ff. 165v-166r, and *Mis.* 1, f. 50v-51r, 21 Nov.

[12] *CG* 202, f. 84r-v, 17 Feb.

[13] *Conc.* 260, f. 25r, 31 May, ed. PIANIGIANI, doc. 21, pp. 45-7; *CG* 203, f. 14v, 3 Jun 1409 (ed. GAROSI, doc. 55, p. 527, giving the date as 1408).

[14] *CG* 205, f. 135v, and *Mis.* 1, ff. 52v-53r, 28 Jun.

[15] *Conc.* 305, f 18v, 2 Dec; *CG* 207, f. 245r, 20 Dec, ed. GAROSI, doc. 56, pp. 527-8.

shortfall was 1,500 florins,[16] and in 1418, 500.[17] At this point it was apparently decided to try to increase the annual budget, not, however, out of the communal funds, but with a tax on the clergy. The new limit was 3,600 florins, a third of which was to be provided by the clergy and the hospital. It is not clear whether that decision was implemented,[18] but 3,600 remained the basic figure for some time thereafter, although there were some fluctuations.[19] In 1425 the hospital was exempted from its contribution,[20] and from 1427 so was the clergy;[21] the commune then had to bear the full brunt of the cost. Less enthusiastic voices now began to be heard in the *Consiglio del Popolo*. In 1442 the budget was reduced to 2,800 florins,

> veduto ch'egli è provveduto... fiorini 3600, e questo fu ordinato per avere dottori famosissimi et de autorità per dare ragione che de li scolari ce venissero assai et comprendasi oggi dì e detti danari non spenderse come fu la intenzione di chi ordinò, ma piuttosto desutilmente.[22]

That appears to have been a temporary measure; in 1456 it was again 3,600 florins.[23] The authorities must subsequently have reverted to 3,000 florins, since in 1480 the *Savi* proposed an expansion of the *Studio*, with a restoration of the 3,600-florin budget 'come era prima a la ultima la quale reduce la somma a fl. tremila'.[24] In 1481 the budget was again 3,600 florins,[25] and it appears to have remained at that level, theoretically at least, until 1533.[26]

Compared with the overall Sienese budget this sum, while not of course amounting to a major outlay, was by no means negligible. There are few indications of the total size of the Sienese budget. Bowsky's work on the finances of the commune, which stopped two years before the period under consideration, shows a range of figures for expenditure from 30,426 *lire* (1290) to 277,555 *lire* (1344)

---

[16] BCS, *ms.* C.V.16, no foliation, Feb 1417.

[17] *Conc.* 316, ff. 27r, 19 Oct, and 31r, 25 Oct; *CG* 208, f. 114r, 22 Oct, ed. GAROSI, doc. 57, p. 528.

[18] *Statuti* 40, f. 15v (margin gives 8 Mar 1419); copy in *Statuti* 41, f. 54v, n.d., and GAROSI, pp. 232-3. This collection also reports the measure as being 'in libro de XLV'. However, *Regolatori* 1, ff. 113r-116r (reg. of CHIRONI, 'Il testo unico', p. 200) records that the 'Balìa dei 45' on 23 Jun 1419 agreed a budget of 3,000 florins.

[19] In 1420 another 400 florins were voted (*CG* 209, f. 28v, 8 Mar), and again in 1422, for 2 years; *CG* 209, f. 220r, 21 Jun (and *Conc.* 338, ff. 3v, 5 May, and 30r, 18 Jun, ed. PIANIGIANI, doc. 53, pp. 76-7).

[20] Below, p. 106. In September of that year proposals to confirm the budget, to give the *Savi* discretion as to its use and to introduce student lectureships, were defeated (*Conc.* 2113, f. 155v, 25 Sept).

[21] Below, pp. 103-4.

[22] *CG* 221, f. 87, 16 Mar, ed. GAROSI, doc. 67, pp. 533-4; and cf. *Bicch.* 2, f. 269v, *Conc.* 2115, f. 6v. There had been an attempt the previous year to increase the budget by 300 florins; *Conc.* 2138, no. 9, f. 16r, 9 May 1441. The outcome is not recorded.

[23] *Conc.* 2138, no. 39, f. 62r (approved on 13 Jul); the sum is referred to as 'che ordinato è per forma di statuto'.

[24] *Conc.* 2123, f. 19r, 2 Jun. The *Savi* pointed out that this sum included 'maistri di schola che viene a levare de la somma ordinata più che mille fl.' Without the proposed increase 'non venghano potersi provedere come sarebbe la intentione de reggimento. Notificando che in tucti e loci dove sonno studii la spesa è cresciuta per che si danno e salari magiori che non solevano; onde è impossibile provedere con quella somma fu deliberato'. The proposal, which appears to have come from Giovanni Battista Caccialupi (above, p. 79 n. 127), was approved for forwarding to the *Consiglio del Popolo*.

[25] *Balìa* 24, f. 90v, 30 Jun, eds. PUCCINOTTI, *Storia della Medicina*, p. CLXVII, and ILARDI, 'Ordinamenti', p. 169; copy in *Mis.* 1, f. 109r.

[26] In 1484 the *Concistoro* decided that the sum would not include the salary of Alessandro Sermoneta, who had been hired by the *Balìa*; *Conc.* 707, f. 10v, 15 Jul. As his salary was 500 florins (*Conc.* 709, f. 27r, 30 Dec, ed. FERRERI, doc. 290, pp. 259-60), this exception was of some significance. The list of appointments for 1488 shows the authorities to be working to a budget of 3,300 florins (*Conc.* 730, ff. 26v-30r, 9 Jun 1488, ed. FERRERI, doc. 281, pp. 245-51), though I have not found a measure in the intervening period that changed it to that sum. In 1533 it was decided that the budget be raised by 1,000 florins (*CG* 243, ff. 244r-245r; 244v, 14 Dec, ed. KOŠUTA, 'Documenti', doc. I-4, pp. 335-7).

per half-year, rarely falling below 100,000 *lire* after 1313.[27] If expenditure continued at such levels after the fall of the *Nove*, the *Studio* wage-bill would have accounted for between 2% and 5% of the total, which seems unlikely.[28] Ginatempo's more recent research on this and the subsequent period, taking into account the money raised not just by the *Biccherna* but also the *Ufficio di Gabella*, suggests considerable fluctuation from year to year.[29] What can perhaps be said is that by Italian standards the provision was not ungenerous. Though never reaching the budget of Pavia,[30] in the amount that they were prepared to spend the Sienese measure favourably against neighbouring *studi*. In the fourteenth century the Perugians were working on an allocation of 2,000 florins from 1366, reduced to 1,500 from 1379 to 1385;[31] in the pre-Medicean period the Florentines' budget oscillated mainly between 1,500 and 2,000 florins, occasionally less, in only one instance reaching 3,000 (in 1385).[32] And it is clear that, on the occasions at the end of the fourteenth century and the beginning of the fifteenth when the Sienese *Studio* was closed or virtually closed, the reasons behind this action were lack of funds coupled with a general – and justified – view that it had been a failure. There are few signs in the records of the *Consiglio Generale* and the *Consiglio del Popolo* of the hostility towards the *Studio* which occasionally surfaced in Florence.[33] On this basis the commune's record of financial support can be judged positively.

[27] BOWSKY, *Finance*, pp. 298-304. Bowsky makes no mention of the 1321 episode when payments to the *Studio* totalled about a fifth of the total budget of the commune.

[28] RUTIGLIANO, *Lorenzetti's Golden Mean*, p. 95 gives the income of the commune as 300,000 florins in 1371. Had the *Studio* been operational at the time its official budget would have accounted for 1% of this. Notwithstanding such crude estimates, there is every reason to subscribe unreservedly to the laconic observation on university payrolls of D. LINES, *Aristotle's Ethics in the Italian Renaissance (ca. 1300-1650): The Universities and the Problem of Moral Education* (Leiden, 2002), p. 98 that 'interpreting budget percentages is problematic'.

[29] M. GINATEMPO, *Prima del debito. Finanziamento della spesa pubblica e gestione del deficit nelle grandi città toscane (1200-1350 ca.).* Biblioteca Storica Toscana, 38 (Florence, 2000), pp. 118-22, 130.

[30] BRUCKER, 'Florence and its University', p. 225 n. 20, calculating from ZANETTI, 'A l'Université de Pavie', table facing p. 428.

[31] ERMINI, *Storia*, I, pp. 31, 71. Giangaleazzo Visconti's treaty with Perugia agreed, like that with Siena, to pay the *Studio*'s wage bill, and the sum agreed was 2,000 florins (p. 192). The budget rose steadily in the fifteenth and sixteenth centuries (pp. 262-74). Even the original figure was substantially more than the budget for the small *Studio* of Turin, which operated on a budget of 1,000 florins; E. BELLONE, 'I primi decenni della Università di Torino: 1406-1436', *Studi piemontesi*, 12 (1983), pp. 351-69 (p. 362).

[32] BRUCKER, 'Florence and its University', pp. 222-5. The revival of the Florentine *Studio* at Pisa brought with it substantial increases. In what can be seen as a bid to outdo communal universities the budget was raised to 6,000 florins in 1472, the year before its launch; cf. SILVANO, 'Stato, territorio e istituzioni', pp. 988-91. Up to 9,000 florins was spent annually in the thirty years studied by VERDE (*Lo Studio fiorentino*, V, pp. 6-7); the government provided 8,300 florins but recouped 5,000 ducats from its taxation of the clergy (DAVIES, *Florence and its University*, pp. 76-7).

[33] BRUCKER, loc. cit.

Table 2 – Expenditure on *Studio* salaries

Data has been collected from the reports of the *Regolatori*. Unless otherwise stated, figures from this source are as given in the documents. In years for which these are missing or suspect, where possible a total has been calculated from entries from the *Biccherna* or the *Gabella*. The *Regolatori* included pre-university teachers and *Studio* officials in their summary reports; for the sake of consistency these are included in the calculated totals as well.

Year/Semester	Total	Description	Reference
1359 (1)	£254/19/12		*Bicch.* 239, f. 43r–v
1359 (2)	No records		
1360 (1)	£262/12/4		*Bicch.* 240, ff. 66r, 68v, 74r–v, 80v
1360 (2)	No records		
1361 (1)	No records		
1361 (2)	12.5 fl.		*Bicch.* 241, ff. 62v; + £17/2/1 embassy re *Studio*, 95v
1362 (1)	£221/11/10	'a dottori e medici salariati'	*Regolatori* 2, f. 28v
1362 (2)	£773/7/8	'a medici giudici per loro salaro e pigioni di case per la balia e di comandamento de savi dello studio'	*Regolatori* 2, f. 32v
1363 (1)	£6,862/15/8		*Bicch.* 243, ff. 105r, 123r, 132v, 133r, 134r, 137r, 138v, 153v
1363 (2)	£2,218/0/0	'a dottori e medici salariati per lo comune'	*Regolatori* 2, f. 68v
1364 (1)	£3,545/17/0	'a doctori in decretali e in legge e in medicina'	*Regolatori* 2, f. 78r
1364 (2)	£1,990/4/2	'a dottori e medici salariati per lo comune'	*Regolatori* 2, f. 133v
1365 (1)	No records		
1365 (2)	200 fl. + £1,203/10/0		*Bicch.* 245, ff. 43v, 61v, 88r, 89v, 97r
1366 (1)	No records		
1366 (2)	No records		
1367 (1)	No records		
1367 (2)	No records		
1368 (1)	£884/0/0	'a dottori medici e maestri'	*Regolatori* 3, f. 131r
1368 (2)	£306/0/0		*Bicch.* 247, ff. 143v, 193r
1369 (1)	£229/10/0		*Bicch.* 417, ff. 6r, 84r, 85v
1369 (2)	£190/0/0		*Bicch.* 248, ff. 137v, 150v, 193r, 201r
1370 (1)	No records		
1370 (2)	No records		
1371 (1)	No records		
1371 (2)	No records		
1372 (1)	55 fl. + £102/0/0		*Bicch.* 249, ff. 142r, 146v, 157r
1372 (2)	£291/2/6		*Bicch.* 250, ff. 198v, 199r, 218r

1373 (1)	No records	
1373 (2)	£347/10/0	
1374 (1)	£332/10/0	*Bicch.* 251, ff. 143v, 210v *Bicch.* 252, ff. 41v, 46r-v, 67v, 68v; *Bicch.* 253, ff. 159v, 168v, 169r, 217r, 218v
1374 (2)	50 fl.	*Bicch.* 254, f. 29r; *Bicch.* 255, f. 144r
1375 (1)	£182/0/0	*Bicch.* 418, ff. 45r, 80r, 115v, 133r
1375 (2)	No records	
1376 (1)	No records	
1376 (2)	£70/0/0	*Bicch.* 257, ff. 47v, 48v; cf. *Bicch.* 457, ff. 12v, 16r
1377 (1)	£236/5/0	*Bicch.* 258, ff. 113r, 130r, 146v; cf. *Bicch.* 420, ff. 142r-v, 153v, 186r, 191v
1377 (2)	£100/0/0	*Bicch.* 259, ff. 48v, 49v; cf. *Bicch.* 421, ff. 161v, 185r
1378 (1)	50 fl. + £15/16/0	*Bicch.* 422, ff. 64v, 108r
1378 (2)	£50/0/0	*Bicch.* 260, f. 80v; cf. *Bicch.* 423, f. 183v
1379 (1)	50 fl.	*Bicch.* 424, ff. 46v, 63r
1379 (2)	£50/0/0	*Bicch.* 261, f. 175r
1380 (1)	62.5 fl.	*Bicch.* 425, ff. 47r, 54r, 68v
1380 (2)	£90/12/6	*Bicch.* 262, ff. 112r, 184r, 198v; cf. *Bicch.* 426, ff. 47r, 94r
1381 (1)	62.5 fl. (= £231/5/0)	*Bicch.* 263, ff. 28v, 56v; cf. *Bicch.* 427, ff. 63v, 64r, 107r
1381 (2)	No entries	*Bicch.* 459, 604
1382 (1)	100 fl. (=£360/0/0)	*Bicch.* 264, ff. 112r, 150r, 172r; cf. *Bicch.* 428, ff. 60r, 94v, 119v
1382 (2)	£202/18/4	*Bicch.* 265, ff. 178v, 180r
1383 (1)	25 fl.	*Bicch.* 429, f. 82v
1383 (2)	No entries	*Bicch.* 267
1384 (1)	No entries	*Bicch.* 268, 605
1384 (2)	£161/5/0	*Bicch.* 269, f. 32v, and *Bicch.* 270, ff. 130r, 145r
1385 (1)	No records	
1385 (2)	£209/13/0	*Bicch.* 271, ff. 28r, 39v, 53v, 54r; cf. *Bicch.* 272, ff. 118r, 142r, 173r, 175r, and *Bicch.* 430, ff. 63r, 105v, 134v
1386	No records	
1387	No records	

1388 (1)	£2,733/0/0	'a iudici e doctori medici e altri maestri salariati per lo comune di Siena sopra lo Studio'	*Regolatori* 4, f. 182v
1389 (1)	1,086 fl. + £13/17/1	'a docti [*sic*] dello studio'	*Regolatori* 4, f. 237r bis
1389 (2)	974 fl. + £8/2/0	'dottori che leggono per lo studio'	*Regolatori* 4, f. 258v
1390 (1)	757 fl. + £120/2/10	'più dottori del generale studio per vigore di loro stantiamenti'	*Regolatori* 4, f. 292v
1390 (2)	425 fl. + £5/14/8	'a quegli dello studio'	*Regolatori* 4, f. 323r
1391 (1)	£1,083/6/0	'a più dottori de lo studio di Siena'	*Regolatori* 4, f. 355v
1391 (2)	£373/6/8	'a maestri dello studio per loro salaro'	*Regolatori* 4, f. 397r
1392 (1)	£168/0/0	'a mag[ist]ri di gramatica et altri doctori per lo facto dello studio'	*Regolatori* 4, f. 426v
1392 (2)	No entries		*Bicch.* 434
1393 (1)	£338/4/0 (calculated)	[Abacus & grammar teacher]	*Regolatori* 5, ff. 8v, 9r
1393 (2)	Figure subsumed		
1394 (1)	£320/1/4 (calculated)	[Abacus & grammar teacher]	*Regolatori* 5, f. 36r
1394 (2)	Figure subsumed		*Regolatori* 5, f. 49r
1395 (1)	£382/10/0	'a maestri de la gramatica e dell'abaco'	*Regolatori* 5, f. 69v
1395 (2)	£708/6/6	'a Maestro Nofrio e a Maestro Gilio e a Ser Andrea de le riformagioni'	*Regolatori* 5, f. 83v
1396 (1)	5 fl. + £542/19/0	'a maestri di Grammatica e del abbaco e al notaio de le Riformagioni'	*Regolatori* 5, f. 104r
1396 (2)	79 fl. + £283/17/2	'al m° de la Gramatica, e m° del albaco e a Ser Andrea de le Riformagioni'	*Regolatori* 5, f. 125r
1397 (1)	£700/13/4	'a Maestri della Gramatica e a Ser Andrea de le Riformagioni, Maestro Gilio Maestro del albaco'	*Regolatori* 5, f. 146r
1397 (2)	132 fl. + £18/4/0	'Maestri di gramatica e d'albaco + altri offitiali salariati come appare a libro di Sco. Augustino…'	*Regolatori* 5, f. 161r
1398 (1)	119 fl. + £12/6/8	'a Ser Andrea not. de le riformagioni per lo studio'	*Regolatori* 5, f. 201v
1398 (2)	132 fl.	'A Ser Andrea di giusto not. rif. + a maestro giovanni di Ser Buccio Maestro di Gramatica + a maestro giglio di ceccho maestro dell'albaco'	*Regolatori* 5, f. 224r
1399 (1)	200 fl. + £19/1/10	'A maestro Johann. Da Spoleto Maestro di gramatica, + a Maestro Giglio Maestro del Albaco + a ser Andrea … not. dele reformagioni + a ser Johanni xpofori Not.° dele reformagioni'	*Regolatori* 5, f. 233r
1399 (2)	54 fl.	A maestro gilio di Cechi M° dell'albaco e a maestro Johi. Di ser guido da Spuleto e a ser Joh. Cristofani …'	*Regolatori* 5, f. 252r
1400 (1)	118 fl.	'al nor° delle riformagioni al maestro di grammatica e dell'abaco'	*Regolatori* 5, f. 273v
1400 (2)	No entries		*Bicch.* 464
1401 (1)	153 fl. + £15/15/5	'al maestro de la gramatica e del albaco, + a ser Giovanni Cristofani de le riformagioni'	*Regolatori* 5, f. 298v
1401 (2)	106 fl. + £21/1/0	'a maestri di gramatica e altri doctori'	*Regolatori* 5, f. 323v
1402 (1)	93 fl. + £7/9/0	'dottori + medici provisionati a leggere ne la citta di Siena'	*Regolatori* 5, f. 338r
1402 (1)	165 fl. + £18/9/0	'al notaio de le riformagioni + a doctori + maestri di gramatica e albaco'	*Regolatori* 5, f. 339v
1402 (2)	220 fl. + £420/10/0	'a precti et a Maestri dell'albaco + de la gramatica et a doctori + a più altre persone'	*Regolatori* 5, f. 346v
1403 (1)	Figure subsumed		*Regolatori* 5, f. 361r
1403 (2)	No records		

Year	Amount	Description	Reference
1404 (1)	66fl. + £114/12/0	'a maestro gilio di cecco del albaco e a maestro giovanni di Ser buccio maestro di gramatica'	*Regolatori* 5, f. 386v
1404 (2)	300 fl. + £583/8/8	'a Ser Johani Xpofori, e a maestri di gramatica, dalbaco, e altre persone'	*Regolatori* 5, f. 404v
1405 (1)	70 fl. + £14/0/0	'al notaio de le riformagioni + al maestro de la gramatica e dell albaco'	*Regolatori* 5, f. 415v
1405 (2)	347 fl. + £684/18/0	'a doctori e maestri dello studio'	*Regolatori* 5, f. 428r
1406 (1)	601 fl. + £282/0/6	'a doctori de lo studio + a Ser Giovanni Xpofani e ad altri salariati'	*Regolatori* 5, f. 451r
1406 (2)	1,032 fl. + £125/1/0	'a dottori de lo studio a Ser Giovanni Xpofani e altri salariati'	*Regolatori* 6, f. 5v
1407 (1)	1,569 fl. + £107/14/8	'dottori e altre persone salariati per lo studio'	*Regolatori* 6, f. 23v
1407 (2)	1,255 fl. + £128/1/4	'a doctori de lo studio + el salario di Ser Giovanni Xpofori et altre spese'	*Regolatori* 6, f. 32v
1408 (1)	923 fl. + £109/8/0	'a doctori per lo studio'	*Regolatori* 6, f. 46v (new foliation)
1408 (2)	1,375 fl. + £345/1/8	'al notaio de le riformagioni et a maestri di gramatica + d'albaco + dottori per cagione dello studio'	*Regolatori* 6, f. 59r
1409 (1)	803 fl. + £361/13/10	'a Dottori dello Studio'	*Regolatori* 6, f. 78v; *Regolatori* 6, f. 82r
1409 (2)	806 fl. + £233/18/0	'a dottori maestri di gramatica maestro d'albaco + notaio de le riformagioni'	*Regolatori* 6, f. 93v
1410 (1)	250 fl. + £12/13/0	'a dottori e ad altri per lo studio'	*Regolatori* 6, f. 114v
1410 (2)	200 fl. + £139/16/4	'a maestri di gramaticha e a quello della albacho, e a ser giovanni xpofori'	*Regolatori* 6, f. 137r
1411 (1)	106 fl. + £74/18/0	'a maestri della gramatica e del albacho'	*Regolatori* 6, f. 151r
1411 (2)	Figure subsumed		*Regolatori* 6, f. 170r
1412 (1)	119 fl. + £46/18/0	'a dottori e maestri di scuole'	*Regolatori* 6, f. 187r (new foliation)
1412 (2)	135 fl. + £33/0/4	'a dottori not. de le Riformagioni maestri di scuola'	*Regolatori* 6, f. 194v (new foliation)
1413 (1)	73 fl. + £142/7/10	'a maestri di schuole'	*Regolatori* 6, f. 214v (new foliation)
1413 (2)	182 fl. + £51/2/4	'a maestri della schuola dela gramatica e dell abbaco per loro provisioni'	*Regolatori* 6, f. 226v
1414 (1)	235 fl. + £10/19/0	'a più lettori e maestri di schuola per loro salari'	*Regolatori* 6, f. 240v
1414 (2)	112 fl. + £46/0/0	'A doctori et maestri di schuola'	*Regolatori* 6, f. 256v (text has L. LXLVI)
1415 (1)	130 fl. + £11/10/0	'a più persone maestri di gramatica + d'albaco'	*Regolatori* 6, f. 281v
1415 (2)	£632/2/2	'a più persone medici maestri di scuola di gramatica e d'albaco e notari'	*Regolatori* 6, f. 292v
1416 (1)	211 fl. + £167/12/4	'a più maestri di scuola e doctori'	*Regolatori* 6, f. 318r
1416 (2)	280 fl. + £162/13/4	'A dottori Maestri di scuole di gramatica + salari di notari'	*Regolatori* 6, f. 328r
1417 (1)	1,405 fl. + £1,718/4/6	'a più dottori e maestri dello studio'	*Regolatori* 6, f. 357v
1417 (2)	190 fl. +£4,041/9/4	'a più doctori + maestri di studio'	*Regolatori* 6, f. 372r
1418 (1)	1,230 fl. + £4,566/11/8	'a più doctori et maestri di squola'	*Regolatori* 6, f. 402v
1418 (2)	49 fl. + £5,618/19/8	'a Maestri di scuola e doctori de lo studio'	*Regolatori* 6, f. 413v
1419 (1)	No entries		*Bicch.* 301, 451
1419 (2)	No entries		*Bicch.* 302, 452
1420 (1)	No entries		*Bicch.* 303, 473
1420 (2)	No entries		*Bicch.* 304, 453
1421 (1)	No records		
1421 (2)	No records		

Year	Amount	Description	Reference
1422 (1)	No records		
1422 (2)	No records		
1423 (1)	No records		
1423 (2)	No entries		*Bicch.* 305
1424 (1)	No entries		*Bicch.* 306, 454
1424 (2)	£8,836/10/6		*Bicch.* 307, ff. 29r-46r; cf. *Bicch.* 455, ff. 57r, 70r, 81v, 84r
1425 (1)	£14,143/13/8		*Bicch.* 456, ff. 9r, 39v, 50v, 56r, 78v, 84v, 86v, 92r, 99v, 111r; cf. *Bicch.* 308, f. 72v
1425 (2)	No records		
1426 (1)	No records		
1426 (2)	No records		
1427 (1)	No records		
1427 (2)	No records		
1428	£13,920/1/4	'per cagione de lo studio a più doctori e maestri di scuola di gramatica'	*Regolatori* 7, f. 41v
1429	£14,083/7/10	'a lo studio di n.ro comune'	*Regolatori* 7, f. 72v
1430	£13,139/13/10	'per cagione de lo studio generale del comune di Siena a più doctori maestri e più persone condocte al dicto studio'	*Regolatori* 7, f. 111r
1431	£12,897/17/0	'per le spese del generale studio facte in detto anno in salari di dottori Rectore + altre spese	*Regolatori* 7, f. 147r
1432	£4,661/13/6	'A lo studio per salari di doctori + maestri + altre spese'	*Regolatori* 7, f. 204r
1433	£4,540/0/0	'nel generale studio di nostro Comuno'	*Regolatori* 7, f. 243v
1434	No records		
1435	£12,035/15/2	'per le spese del generale studio in salari di dottori, e altre spese a esso studio'	*Regolatori* 8, f. 25r
1436	£10,397/18/2	'a più doctori forestieri e cittadini condocti a leggiere nel generale studio di Siena'	*Regolatori* 8, f. 63v
1437	£10,033/12/0	'a più doctori forestieri e cittadini condotti a legiare nel generale studio di Siena'	*Regolatori* 8, f. 89r
1438	£12,386/13/3	'a più doctori conducti al generale studio di Nostro comune cioe cittadini e forestieri'	*Regolatori* 8, f. 140r
1439	£12,226/0/10	'al generale studio del comune di Siena cioe a più doctori ed altri'	*Regolatori* 8, f. 187r
1440	£14,684/0/9	'a più + più doctori salariati del comune et che anno lecto nel decto tempo nello Studio di Siena'	*Regolatori* 8, f. 224v
1441	£11,832/6/9	'al generale studio del nostro comuno'	*Regolatori* 8, f. 265r
1442	Figure subsumed		*Regolatori* 8, f. 328v
1443	£8,978/9/2	'a più doctori chome appare a debito al generale studio'	*Regolatori* 8, f. 461r
1444	£11,653/0/4	'a più dottori chome appare a debito al generale studio'	*Regolatori* 8, f. 497v
1445	No records		
1445	No records		

Year	Records / Amount	Description	Reference
1447	£12,002/18/6		*Bicch.* 315, f. 17v and 316, f. 181v (details 2v, 10r, 18r, 21v, 39v, 50v, 52v, 59v, 65r, 71r, 74v, 84r, 86v)
1448	£7,079/1/38 (records incomplete after August)		*Bicch.* 317, ff. 278r, 283r-v, 289v, 300r-332v
1449	Fragment only		
1450	No records		
1451	£10,022/15/1		*Bicch.* 320, ff. 3r, 6v, 15v, 57v, 62v, 66r, 77r, 79v, 81v, 87v, 98v, 109r
1452	No records		
1453	£10,6948/8		*Bicch.* 321, ff. 157r, 161r, 163v, 169v, 176v, 197v, 202v, 207r, 210r, 216v, 225r, 232r, 239r
1454	No records		
1455	No records		
1456	£9,029/3/4		*Bicch.* 322, ff. 317v-358r
1457	No records		
1458	No records		
1459	£12,396/13/4		*Bicch.* 323, ff. 155r-184r
1460	No records		
1461	No records		
1462	No records		
1463	Fragment only		
1464	Figure subsumed		*Bicch.* 324
1465	Figure subsumed		*Regolatori* 9, f. 23r
1466	Figure subsumed		*Regolatori* 9, f. 39r
1467	Figure subsumed		*Regolatori* 9, ff. 97r, 99v
1468	Figure subsumed		*Regolatori* 9, f. 143r
1469	£17,730/9/5	'a dottori et altri salarii per lo Comune di Siena come se M' di schuole dell'albacho bidelli et altri'	*Regolatori* 9, ff. 168v, 173v
1470	Figure subsumed		*Regolatori* 9, f. 207v
1471	£17,735/4/6	'a più persone a doctori e altri salari come se maestri di scuola dalbaco bidegli et altre persone che sono creditori per lo libro de doctori'	*Regolatori* 9, f. 254v
1472	£14,491/6/6	'a più doctori di leggi civile et canonica et a doctori di medicina Et maestri di squole + altri condocti allo studio'	*Regolatori* 9, f. 310r
1473	£13,747/12/0	'a più doctori di leggie civile et chanonico et a dottori di medicina et a naestri di schuole et altri condotti allo studio'	*Regolatori* 9, f. 365v
1474	£13,565/13/8		*Regolatori* 9, f. 400r
1475	No records		*Gabella* 24, ff. 50r-66r, 125r-133v; *Bicch.* 332, ff. 7r, 8r, 13r
1476	£20,949/5/4		*Bicch.* 333, ff. 301r-333v
1477	No records		

Year	Amount	Description	Reference
1478	No records		
1479	No records		
1480	No records		
1481	£14,506/0/0		*Bicch.* 336 ff. 53r-76v, 312r-332v
1482	No records		
1483	£12,576/3/4		*Bicch.* 338 ff. 150r-167v
1484	Incomplete records		
1485	£11,106/6/8		*Bicch.* 339 ff. 57r-74v
1486	No records		
1487	£16,968/18/4		*Bicch.* 340 ff. 79r-94r
1488	£12,978/18/6	'a più e più doctori et altre persone condocte'	*Regolatori* 10, f. 64v
1489	£11,780/1/8	'a più doctori'	*Regolatori* 10, f. 53v
1490	£13,535/14/7	'a più + più doctori e altre persone condocte'	*Regolatori* 10, f. 74v
1491	£8,336/14/6	'a più doctori e altri persone conducte'	*Regolatori* 10, f. 127r
1494	£2,961/17/6 + £8,195/5/4	'a più doctori e maestri condocti et a più altri condocti .... come apare a sua auscita di dco ser Antonio depositario'	*Regolatori* 10, f. 164r-v
1495	£10,866/6/10	'a li doctori condocti a llegere et altri condocti'	*Regolatori* 10, ff. 165v, 166v (cf. *Bicch.* 347)
1496/7?	£22,408/13/0	'le condocti di più doctori come si vede al libro di Santo Austino'	*Regolatori* 10, f. 196r (given as Jan-Dec 1495)
1500	£10,310/15/0	'per salari di doctori e medici e m.i di schuola et altri'	*Regolatori* 10, f. 239r

3. Expenditure: wages

The figures decided on by the commune – which are of course a maximum – give little indication of how much was actually spent from year to year; and here the incompleteness of records is an added problem, although it takes different guises in different periods. Teachers' contracts are no infallible guide, both because the hiring of a teacher did not necessarily mean that he then taught,[34] and because he might have had periods of absence, fines etc. which would have reduced his salary.[35] In any case the records before the mid-fifteenth century are clearly incomplete. Records of actual payments of salaries, in the *Biccherna*, represent the reality but are also patchy; the sum of those that do survive is helpful. Gaps can partly be filled by the instructions by the *Concistoro* for the *terzarie* of teachers to be paid (*apotisse*); these feature regularly at the end of *Concistoro* volumes (one for each of the two-month periods of office) from the 1450s onwards, but they too tend not to take account of fines, and do not always give amounts.[36] The most helpful source is the series of *Revisioni* of the *Regolatori*, a body set up towards the end of the regime of the 'Nine' with a wide range of functions including the auditing and overseeing of communal accounts.[37] A conspectus of the surviving entries for the *Studio* is presented in Table 2, with completions from other sources where possible. Another complication of these figures is that the administration of the *Studio* included responsibility for pre-university teaching, and the total figures do not of course isolate these sums (which occasionally subsume payments to non-*Studio* officials as well). The figures are usually (but not always) given in *lire*, *soldi* and *denari*, while salaries (with the occasional exception of those of some of the pre-university level teachers) were stipulated in *fiorini d'oro*, which, despite the name, from the mid-1420s were fixed at 4 *lire* or 80 *soldi* each; interpretation of these figures thus has to allow for the fact that two currencies are in operation. Notwithstanding these qualifications, the evidence suggests that for much of the fifteenth century the *Studio* was operating not far off the budget allocated. It is also evident that the authorities were developing realistic expectations regarding the discrepancy between the number of those who were hired and the number of those who actually taught. In 1488 a meticulous calculation was made with the drawing up of the payroll to ensure that the budget was not exceeded.[38] However, in the years following that, teachers were regularly hired in excess of that limit in the knowledge that the actual bill would not match those aspirations.

---

[34] Two examples: the annotated *Balìa* copy of the 1480-1 *rotolo* shows that no fewer than eight out of the thirty *condotte* advertised were declined (*Balìa* 20, ff. 57r-58v, 2 Aug 1480). In 1450-1, twenty-eight *condotte* were recorded (*Conc.* 507, ff. 40r, 43r-v, 23 Oct 1450, ed. Pianigiani, doc. 303, pp. 335-7; *Conc.* 508, f. 21r-v, 20 Nov 1450, ed. Pianigiani, doc. 304, pp. 337-9) but by the second *terzaria* only twenty teachers were being paid (*Conc.* 510, f. 20v, 21 May 1451, ed. Bai, doc. 8, pp. 6-8), and by the third only seventeen (*Conc.* 511, f. 29r, 19 Aug 1451, ed. Bai, doc. 12, pp. 11-12). However, these did not result simply in savings for the commune, but rather the reabsorption of sums laid out for those who had not accepted *condotte* in the payments to other teachers. The problem is highlighted in, amongst others, K. Park, 'The Readers at the Florentine Studio according to Comunal Fiscal Records (1357-1380, 1413-1446)', *Rinascimento*, 20 (1980), pp. 249-310 (p. 249), and see below, Chapter III.1.1.

[35] In theory these could be quite fierce; 390 *puncte* were recorded for two *terzarie* in 1537-8, which at 10 *lire* each would in theory have saved 975 florins, although of course by that reckoning some teachers would have lost more than their salary. It is difficult to believe that such large sums were saved. In fact fines were frequently excused or reduced. For the 1537-8 *puncte*, and for a full discussion of this problem, below, pp. 159 *seq.*

[36] A clear definition of the *apotisse* is in Bargagli, *Bartolomeo Sozzini*, p. 19 n. 38.

[37] See above, p. 20.

[38] *Conc.* 730, ff. 26v-30r, 9 Jun 1488, ed. Ferreri, doc. 281, pp. 246-51.

Teachers' pay constituted the overwhelming part of the total budgetary requirement. The salaries of the officials of the *Studio* were further regular expenses. The rector of the university was paid a salary by the commune; after the 1321 influx, salaries of 100 florins are recorded for each of the three rectors,[39] though by 1339 the single rector is paid only 50 florins,[40] and this appears to have remained the figure throughout the fifteenth century[41] (although from the mid-1420s he was also customarily awarded a lectureship).[42] The rector of the Sapienza was normally paid out of Sapienza resources, although there were occasions when he was paid by the commune.[43] The commune also paid the salary of the *bidello* (20 florins,)[44] the *notaio dello studio*,[45] the *puntatore*,[46] and even the bell-ringers.[47] A more variable figure was the expense of sending messengers or officials to other towns to publicise the *Studio* and to recruit teachers.[48] Finally *Studio*-earmarked funds could also be used to pay others who occasionally came under the *Savi*'s purview, such as medical practitioners (whether or not they also taught), and surveyors (who might or might not also be teachers of arithmetic and/or geometry).[49]

4. *Sources of income*

How did the commune find these sums? The early records suggest that they came simply out of general expenditure. The paymaster of the teachers was traditionally the *Camarlengo di Biccherna*; from the earliest times salary and rent payments are found in the *Biccherna* archive, the contribution of the clergy was made via his office,[50] and his role in this respect was described in the communal statutes as late as 1424.[51] All this implies, from what we know of Sienese financial organisation, that payments were

---

[39] *Chartularium*, docs. 161, pp. 163-7, 8 Jun 1321 to 14 Jan 1322 (p. 164); 164, pp. 172-4, 11 Aug 1321; 184, pp. 221-3, 25 Jun 1322; 190, pp. 232-3, 9-27 Aug 1322 (p. 233); 192, p. 235, 20 Aug 1322; 194, pp. 238-9, 28 Sept 1322, also ed. ZDEKAUER, doc. I^A, no. 2, pp. 134-5.

[40] *Chartularium*, doc. 369, pp. 472-4, 20-31 Dec, ed. ZDEKAUER, doc. I^B, pp. 136-8 (p. 137).

[41] *Conc.* 526, f. 54v, 11 Apr 1454; *Studio* 2, ff. 75v, 24 Jul 1481, and 91v, 16 Apr 1483 (all *terzarie* of £66/13/4). This is twice the salary usually awarded for a lectureship (below, pp. 282-3).

[42] Below, p. 262.

[43] *Conc.* 400, f. 35r, 5 Oct 1432; *Studio* 2, f. 105v, 2 Nov 1484.

[44] *Conc.* 360, f. 35r, 14 Feb 1426 (annual); *Studio* 127, no. 2, 8 Apr 1433 (2 *terzarie*); cf. *Conc.* 475, f. 28v, 24 Aug 1445 (*condotta*). On one occasion he is paid slightly more, 85 *lire*, 'pro pensione'; *Conc.* 466, ff. 54v, 28 Oct, 62r and 64r, 31 Oct 1443. In 1339 it had been 25 *lire*, paid in two instalments; ZDEKAUER, p. 137.

[45] In 1425 his salary was 9 fl. (*Conc.* 355, f. 13r, 22 Mar), but later it was 54 *lire* (*Conc.* 401, f. 57v, 22 Dec 1432, payment of 18 *lire*; *Studio* 127, no. 3, 8 Apr 1433, payment of 18 *lire terzarie* of his full salary of 54 *lire*). Below, pp. 273-4.

[46] In 1440 the salary of this figure was 12 *lire* (*Conc.* 447, f. 29r, *Mis.* 1, f. 57r, 20/23 Aug) and in 1442 it was doubled (*Conc.* 461, f. 5r, 6 Nov). Below, pp. 159-60.

[47] *Bicch.* 456, f. 9r, 3 Mar 1425; four *lire* are paid for the previous two months 'a chierici di duomo che suonano la campana a lo studio'.

[48] Below, p. 151.

[49] E.g. in the 1460s Giovanni di Lorenzo de' Giustini da Roma was hired to practice medicine on the recommendation of the *Savi*; it was decided that he was to be paid out of *Studio* funds (*CG* 230, ff. 29v-298r, 24 Jun 1465, and cf. *Conc.* 592, f. 66r, 30 Jun, and *Conc.* 2138, no. 77, ff. 125r-126v). This arrangement was still in place in 1468 (*CG* 232, ff. 81v-82r, 23 Feb). On this figure see below, p. 211 n. 14.

[50] *CG* 171, f. 31, 27 Mar 1364 (ZDEKAUER, doc. VI, pp. 144-5); we can assume that the 'camerario' (p. 145, ll. 2-3) is the *Camarlengo di Biccherna*. On the functions of this official, ARCHIVIO DI STATO DI SIENA, *Archivio della Biccherna*, pp. XII *seq.*, XXI-XXIII, and more generally BOWSKY, *Finance*, ch. I.

[51] *Statuti* 41, f. 60v, 25 Aug.

made out of general funds. In the fifteenth century this practice was gradually altered.[52] In 1407 the authorities drew on the *gabella dei contratti* to pay salaries.[53] In 1412 the first signs of a new approach appear in the decision that the budget of 3,000 florins was to be divided; half would come directly from the commune, the rest was up to the *Concistoro* and the *Savi* to raise 'per quello modo che alloro parrà et piacerà.[54] In 1417 the 1,500-florin shortfall was to be met partly from payments from various debtors[55] and partly from the *gabella del vino*.[56] This soon became established as a regular pattern; in the reorganisation that took place probably in 1419 the 2,000 florins contributed by the commune were to come from this source, and a reserve source, the *gabella dei paschi*, was named to cover any amounts the *gabella del vino* could not provide.[57] This localisation of funds has parallels in other *studi*. In Padua the ox tax, wagon tax and prostitutes' tax were earmarked for the *Studio*;[58] in Rome it was the *gabella del vino*, which was increased and administered by the *Reformatores Studii*, and soon became known as the *gabella studii*.[59] By contrast, Perugia earmarked various different funds at different stages – the *gabella del vino*, the *gabella dei contratti*, the *gabella del sale* and others.[60] Siena seems to have followed the second pattern; the source of the funds allocated could continue to change. In 1420 the *gabella dei contratti* was again obliged,[61] and in 1437 the *gabella di Asciano* was added.[62] These two were still the main sources in 1458.[63] Other taxes were also obligated from time to time,[64] and it was

---

[52] The hegemony of the *Biccherna* was already in question towards the end of the 'government of the Nine', and the *Dodici* (1355-68) had increasingly made use of other offices. MOSCADELLI, 'Apparato burocratico', esp. pp. 57 *seq*.

[53] *Conc.* 250 f. 21r, 24 Oct 1407. I. ZOLLER, 'I medici ebrei laureati a Siena negli anni 1543-1695', *La rivista israelitica* (1913-15), pp. 60-70, 100-10 (p. 60) states that Jews were forced to buy salt in Grosseto to an extent that would generate 2,000 florins for the *Studio Communal* on 14 Feb 1407. I have been unable to find the evidence to substantiate this in the *Mention* records; nor is there any record of it, or any other direct connection between taxes on the Jews and the *Studio*, in the authoritative work of S. BOESCH GAJANO, 'Il Comune di Siena e il prestito ebraico nei secoli XIV e XV', in *Aspetti e problemi della presenza ebraica nell'Italia centro-settentrionale (secoli XIV e XV)*. Quaderni dell'Istituto di Scienze Storiche dell'Università di Roma, 2 (Rome, 1983), pp. 177-225.

[54] *CG* 205, f. 135v, and *Mis.* 1, ff. 52v-53r, 28 Jun.

[55] *Conc.* 311, f. 28r, 11 Dec.

[56] *Conc.* 306, f. 31v, 26 Feb, and *Conc.* 307, f. 3v, 5 Mar 1417. In 1419, 1,000 *lire* came from this source (*Conc.* 322, ff. 15r and 29r, 18 Oct).

[57] *Conc.* 318, f.14v, 25 Jan, ed. PIANIGIANI, doc. 40, pp. 64-5, and *Statuti* 41, f. 54v. See also p. 89 n. 18 above, and cf. *CG* 207, f. 28r, 8 Mar 1420. The *gabella del vino* was paying in 1424; *Bicch.* 455, ff. 68r, 70r, 81v, 90r. The designation of the *gabella dei paschi* as a reserve source foreshadowed another development; in 1429 the *Savi* were placed under the office of the *Quattro Maestri del Sale e dei Paschi* (*Statuti* 41, ff. 2l6v-217r; and cf. *Statuti* 47, f. 215v), sharing their notary and on occasion leaving traces in their archive (see above, p. 21).

[58] G. DE SANDRE, 'Dottori, Università, Comune a Padova nel '400', *Quaderni per la Storia dell'Università di Padova*, 1 (1968), pp. 15-47 (pp. 17-8).

[59] CHAMBERS, 'Studium Urbis', pp. 70-3. Not, of course, that this change of name protected it from the depredations of the pope or others who wished to spend it on other things; op. cit., p. 77; C. MANTEGNA, *Lo* Studium Urbis *nei Diversa Cameralia dell'Archivio Segreto Vaticano. Nuova edizione di documenti universitari romani (1425-1517)* (Rome, 2000), pp. 19-20, 38-40; and F. GUIDI BRUSCOLI, *Benvenuto Olivieri. I* mercatores *fiorentini e la camera apostolica nella Roma di Paolo III Farnese (1534-1549)* (Florence, 2000), pp. 190-4 (esp. p. 191).

[60] ERMINI, *Storia*, I, p. 71.

[61] *Conc.* 329, f. 31v, 31 Dec. The reference is to the *gabella delle scritture*, which I take to be another name for the *gabella dei contratti*, since I know of no other reference to a distinct tax of this name.

[62] *CG* 219, ff. 146v-147v (new foliation), 10 May, ed. ZDEKAUER, doc. XVIII, pp. 169-71 (p. 170); copies in *Statuti* 41, ff. 255v-256r, and *Mis.* 1, ff. 83r-85v.

[63] *Balìa* 6, f. 143r-v, 27 Jan; also *Balìa* 7, ff. 142v-143r, and *Statuti* 40, f. 131r-v. The *gabella di Asciano* was specified as the source of Giovanni Battista Caccialupi's salary on 29 Dec 1457 (*Balìa* 6, ff. 111v-112r).

[64] E.g. in 1483 the *gabelle* of Orbetello and Paganico contributed, alongside that of Asciano, to the salary of Lancilotto

also not unknown for specific funds, debts or transactions to be designated for the payment of individuals or groups on particular occasions.[65] A logical consequence was that the function of paymaster also shifted from the general financial overseer, the *Camarlengo di Biccherna*, to a more specialised official, the *Camarlengo di Gabella*. This is by no means a clear-cut development. The *Camarlengo di Gabella* is first found making payments to teachers in 1407, and then again in 1416, 1420 and 1421.[66] From 1424 to 1432 this duty reverted to the *Camarlengo di Biccherna*;[67] in 1435 it is again the *Camarlengo di Gabella*,[68] whose role is finally recognised in 1437;[69] but instructions of 1443 state that either could be designated.[70] In 1475 both offices were jointly involved in helping the Sapienza in its financial difficulties;[71] in 1480 they acted together in paying salaries,[72] after which date teachers' salary payments make brief appearances again in the records of the *Biccherna*; but this seems exceptional, as in 1481 it is again the *Camarlengo di Gabella* who is officially in charge.[73]

5. *The clergy and the hospital of S. Maria della Scala*

These were regular sources. Occasionally 'externally' found funds might be used, as with the opportunity of driving a bargain with Giangaleazzo Visconti and making him pay the *Studio*'s wage-bill (an

---

Decio (*Balìa* 404, f. 242, 29 Dec, and cf. *Balìa* 31, f. 15r, 27 Nov); in 1492 the *gabella delle castagne* was obligated for the salary of Lutio Bellanti (*Balìa* 58, f. 21v, 21 Dec).

[65] E.g. in 1409 the amount owed to the commune by the heirs of Nanni Ranucci was assigned to Pietro di Antonio Bonazini in payment of his salary for his lectureship in *notaria* (*Conc.* 260, f. 26v, 31 May, ed. PIANIGIANI, doc. 22, p. 47); in 1459 debts written in the 'libro di 5 stelle' were assigned to teachers (*CG* 228, f. 149v, 6 Sept, and cf. *Conc.* 558, f. 6v. Other debts were assigned specifically to Francesco Accolti), and similar decisions were made in 1462 (*CG* 229, ff. 196r-197v, 9 Apr; 'libbri di quattro et di cinque stelle'; and cf. *Conc.* 573, f. 23r, 6 Apr) and 1482 (*CG* 239, f. 3r, 10 Jan; 'libri stellarum'). On a couple of occasions the authorities resorted to unusual measures to ensure that the teachers were paid. In 1420 the *Camarlengo di Gabella* was ordered not to pay for any building work until the 200 florins still due to teachers was paid (*Conc.* 325, ff. 15v-16r, 2 Apr), while in 1455 the entrance fees to the Sapienza were commandeered in settlement of the salary of the rector of the *Studio* (*Conc.* 530, f. 41r, 25 Jan, and 71v, 12 Feb; ten entrants had forced loans imposed on them). In 1458 an attempt to regularise procedures was made with the creation of a *cassetta de' dottori*, and the end of the century saw the further step of the creation of a *depositarius* for teachers' salaries; on these see below, pp. 172-3. The innovations were no guarantee of stability. In 1462 the *Savi* reported that the debts to doctors amounted to 5,000 florins (*CG* 229, ff. 196r-197r, 9 Apr). This was the equivalent of arrears of five *terzarie*. The situation was not helped by the fact that the diversion of resources described above could, exceptionally, work in the other direction as well; in 1458, 75 florins were borrowed from money earmarked for the *Studio* salaries to pay for an embassy to pope Pius II (*Conc.* 553, f. 29v, 7 Dec), while in 1460, 200 florins due to the pope were taken from the same fund (*Conc.* 2180, no foliation, 26 May).

[66] *Conc.* 250, f. 21r, 24 Oct 1407; *Conc.* 301, f. 26v, 22 Apr 1416, ed. PIANIGIANI, doc. 32, p. 57; *Conc.* 326, f. 3r, 2 May 1420; *Conc.* 330, f. 15v, 25 Jan 1421 (the *Camarlengo dei Paschi* paid the *Camarlengo di Gabella* who in turn paid the doctors); *Conc.* 330, f. 23v, 26 Feb 1421; *Conc.* 331, f. 26r, 23 Apr 1421 (the funds came from the *Biccherna* but were paid by the *Camarlengo di Gabella*).

[67] *CG* 210, f. 133r, 25 Aug 1424; *Conc.* 398, f. 3v, 2 May 1432, ed. PIANIGIANI, doc. 132, pp. 162-3 (cf. *Conc.* 400, f. 35r, 5 Oct 1432, and *Studio* 127, no foliation, 8 Apr 1433).

[68] *Conc.* 418, f. 2v, 2 Sept.

[69] As n. 62 above; and cf. *Conc.* 460, f. 52v, 29 Oct 1442.

[70] *Conc.* 462, f. 57r, 27 Feb.

[71] *CG* 236, f. 126, and *Mis.* 1, f. 105r, 28 Jun. The *Quattro di Biccherna* themselves and the *Esecutori di Gabella* were involved.

[72] *Studio* 2, f. 69v, 15 Dec.

[73] As p. 89 n. 25 above. Only on 28 March of that year the *Camarlengo di Biccherna* had paid the rector of the *Studio* for his teaching (*Studio* 2, f. 72v). The *Camarlengo di Gabella* was still in charge of teachers' salaries in 1545 (*Studio* 22, no foliation). On the growth of his power, ARCHIVIO DI STATO DI SIENA, *Guida-Inventario*, I, pp. 223-6.

agreement, it must be said, that was probably never put into effect).[74] But there was another very significant source that the authorities attempted, very controversially, to tap. From the initial move in
1364 through to the third decade of the fifteenth century, repeated and partly successful attempts
were made to tax first the clergy and then the hospital of the Scala and other 'pious institutions'. The
process is revealing.

Secular taxation of the clergy, overriding their traditional privileges and challenging the fundamental distinction between the separate jurisdictions of the spiritual and the secular world, has a long and
contentious history, and it was to play an important role in the history of certain Italian universities.[75]
In Siena the story begins in 1364, when on 27 March the *Consiglio Generale* resolved that the Sienese
clergy should contribute an unspecified amount towards the wage bill of the *Studio*. The commune
had taken the advice of at least one doctor of theology and three doctors of law, who affirmed that this
measure would not lead to any danger of excommunication; it had obviously also been discussed with
representatives of the clergy, who objected on the grounds that it was unfair that they should have to
contribute without having a say in the choice of teachers, and as a sop to this they were given one vote
in addition to the six of the *Savi* in this matter.[76] On 26 November that year the clergy 'volunteered'
1,200 gold florins towards the cost of the *Studio*.[77] Although they thus agreed to the measure, it was
clearly not popular, and had to be restated and reimposed, in varying detail, whenever the authorities
wished to obtain fresh income. This happened during the course of the revival of the *Studio* in 1386-
7, when the commune again ordered the clergy to contribute, this time adding the hospital of S.
Maria della Scala.[78] In 1396 there was an unsuccessful proposal to refound the *Studio*, which tried to
pass on no less than two-thirds of the wage bill to the bishop, the clergy and two hospitals, the Scala
and the Casa della Misericordia.[79] The principle of sharing the cost of salaries was clearly in operation,

[74] Above, pp. 52-3.

[75] This is as yet an under-researched topic. There is an earlier, non-Italian precedent; from 1300, ecclesiastical taxes were
used to pay teachers' salaries at the university of Salamanca; RASHDALL, II, pp. 81-2, and A. GARCÍA Y GARCÍA, 'Los difíciles
inicios (siglos XIII-XIV)', in *La Universidad de Salamanca*, ed. M. Fernández Alvarez et al., 3 vols. (Salamanca, 1989-90), I.
Trayectoria histórica y proyecciones, pp. 13-34 (p. 22). My attention was drawn to this by Prof. Kate van Liere through the
STUDIUM university history discussion list (studium@listserv.cc.kuleuven.ac.be).

[76] *CG* 171, f. 31r, 27 Mar 1364 (ZDEKAUER, doc. VI, pp. 144-5), and GAROSI, p. 168.

[77] *CG* 171, f. 9lr, 26 Nov 1364 (ZDEKAUER, doc. VII, pp. 145-6). The marginal annotation summarising the March
document, 'Quod clerici habeant unam vocem in electione Sapientum Studii et eligere possint, quos voluerint', is surely
window-dressing, though it convinced Zdekauer. His interpretation of the documents, that in March the commune offered
the clergy a say in the choice of teachers and in November the clergy in return 'si offrono spontaneamente a rilevare il Comune dalle spese di certi corsi' does not bear closer examination; the first decision explicitly stated that the clergy were to
contribute, which implies that the clergy's letter of November was little more than a face-saving device. No evidence has
come to light suggesting that the clergy were in practice ever consulted on teaching appointments, still less given an actual
vote. The curious eighteenth-century history of the Sienese *Studio* in *Studio* 126 appreciated this point (f. 3v). This whole
episode is still not fully understood, and would probably benefit from being studied in the context of the financial crisis of
that year and its impact on relations with the church; cf. R. C. TREXLER, '*Ne fides comunis diminuatur*. Papal Authority and
Communal Sovereignty at Florence and Siena, 1345-1380', *Rivista di Storia della Chiesa in Italia*, 39 (1985), pp. 448-501,
and 40 (1986), pp. 1-25; repr. in his *Church and Community 1200-1600. Studies in the History of Florence and New Spain*
(Rome, 1987), pp. 357-439 (esp. pp. 368-72).

[78] *CG* 195, f. 115r-v, 23 Jan 1387, ed. GAROSI, p. 194 n. 1; copy in *Mis.* 1, f. 50r-v. The clergy were contributing in
1399 (*Conc.* 211, f. 16r, 22 Oct), as were S. Maria della Scala and various pious institutions in 1405 (*Conc.* 238, f. 31v, 21
Aug).

[79] *Conc.* 2111, f. 126v, 23 Apr. The proposal accused them of wasting their charity ('fanno le mosine assai deboli dando
el loro a gente vile e da pocho' – a revealing interpretation of the concept).

though in a more discriminatory fashion; in 1399 it was decided that the clergy should pay half of the salaries of two canon lawyers but not of the teacher of *notaria*.[80]

The first evidence recording the clergy's contribution covers a short period, 1405-9, after which the political crisis and the renewed struggle to keep the *Studio* open appears to have taken over.[81] When fresh attempts were made in 1412 the *Consiglio Generale* stated that the commune would only pay half of the total 3,000-florin bill but left the *Concistoro* and *Savi* to decide on how to raise the rest.[82] Renewed pressures on the clergy and pious institutions accompanied the various attempts to revive the *Studio*. A tax on the clergy collected in 1412 appears to have raised about 1,600 *lire*;[83] a similar tax in 1414 raised £2,613/14/8.[84] A further 'presta' was collected in 1416,[85] and again in 1418 when the *Concistoro* wrote to several people to help with the collection.[86] Later that year here was a fresh offensive; the *Concistoro* appealed to the pope for permission to raise 600 gold florins from the clergy for as long as the *Studio* lasted, and this was conceded;[87] shortly afterwards, probably in the following year, it was decreed that 600 florins were to come from the clergy, 500 from S. Maria della Scala and 100 from the *opera del Duomo*.[88] It is not clear, however, from the surviving financial records whether the clergy's contribution actually materialised after this date.[89] What is clear is that the intervention of San Bernardino in 1427 killed off the policy. While this future patron of the *Studio* did plenty to encourage support for the institution, clerical taxation was a step too far. He attacked the practice in a sermon given in the Piazza del Campo on 29 September,[90] and a month later a petition from the clergy

---

[80] *Conc.* 211, f. 16r. 22 Oct 1399.

[81] The clerical contributions listed are: in 1405, £1770/18/0 (after costs, £1756/18/0) (*Lira* 411, 'El libro de la presta del chericato', Oct 1405; confirmed in *Regolatori* 6, f. 56r, 24 Dec 1408); in 1407, 1589 fl. (after £11/10/0 costs) (*Regolatori* 6, f. 55v, Dec 1408). For 1408 the situation is less clear; the auditors' books contain two entries: £1607/19/3 (£1597/9/3 after costs) from the clergy (*Regolatori* 6, f. 82r, 30 Aug 1409, which also calculates that at the exchange rate of £0/78/4 this amounted to 408 fl. and £0/9/9), and for the first semester, 831 fl. £188/18/6 from both clergy and the hospital (*Regolatori* 6, f. 59r). The last entry is for the first semester of 1409, i.e. just before the crisis, in which the clergy are recorded as having contributed 415 fl. and £11/19/0 (*Regolatori*. 6, f. 78v).

[82] *CG* 205, f. 135v, and *Mis.* 1, ff. 52v-53r, 28 Jun. See above, pp. 56-7.

[83] Though the purpose of this tax is not explicitly declared, it is difficult to imagine what else it could have been; that is what the clergy were being taxed for at the time. *Conc.* 2173, *filza* for 1412, no foliation, 7 May to 7 Jun.

[84] *Conc.* 2173, conserved, despite its date, in the *filza* for 1413, no foliation.

[85] *Lira* 414. There are no totals and not all of the list of those contributing appear to have paid.

[86] *Conc.* 1615, ff. 24, 2 Mar (to the bishop of Massa), 26r, 9 Mar (to Tommaso da Bordello of Perugia, vicar general of the bishop of Arezzo), and 22 Apr (to the *podestà* of Asciano).

[87] *Conc.* 316, f. 30r, 23 Oct, and *Conc.* 317, ff. 3v, 4 Nov, and 14v, 27 Nov, ed. PIANIGIANI, doc. 38, pp. 61-2. According to the eighteenth-century history in *Studio* 126 the bishop of Sovana was granted a two-year exemption. ASS, *ms.* B.22, a *spoglio* of the *Fondo Diplomatico, Riformagioni*, refers (no. 2056) to a bull of Pope John XXIII dated 15 May 1414 authorising the commune to tax the clergy up to 10,000 florins. This document is now lost. The status of this papal claimant, at this juncture of the Schism, obviously means that the privilege would have had little weight; it is nonetheless interesting that it was sought and obtained.

[88] See above, p. 89 n. 18.

[89] It may be significant that while the *Biccherna* records list payments from the hospital of S. Maria della Scala for 1424 and 1425 (see n. 118 below), none are listed for the clergy. A petition in 1427 referred to arrears; below, n. 119. In 1424 the *Savi dello Studio* employed a *barisello* to collect dues 'tam a clericis quam aliis' (*Conc.* 1623, f. 58v, 7 Jun).

[90] 'Ho udito che so' certe chiese, che so' tanto venute al debile, che non possono pagare quello che l'è stato imposto che paghino per lo Studio. Io vi dico che voi non fate bene a farli pagare, e saretene anco pagati per iudicio di Dio ché non che voi le doviate far pagare, ma eziandio sete tenuti di trarle di debito. Sapete che vi dico? A la barba l'avete! O se elle so' tanto debili, che elle non possono reggiare il prete, come lo' ponete anco gravezza?' BERNARDINO DA SIENA, *Prediche Volgari sul Campo di Siena*, ed. C. Delcorno, XLIII 116, 29 Sept (p. 1297).

to be released from this obligation was successful.[91] Another attempt was made in 1440 to obtain papal permission to tax the clergy to the tune of 500 or 600 florins,[92] but there is no evidence that it was successful, any more than was the attempt in 1495 to obtain a five-year *decima* yielding 3,000 ducats.[93]

The clerical contribution has to be seen in the context of the long tradition of papal and ecclesiastical support for education. In Siena this could take many forms,[94] including the series of papal measures favouring the *Studio*,[95] clerical and specifically mendicant participation in teaching,[96] and help with the project to found the Casa della Sapienza (as will be seen).[97] The bishop of Siena had a special role. As the *Studio*'s chancellor, the nominal awarder of degrees, and at least initially court of appeal,[98] he had a natural interest in its running, though little actual control, and the commune and *Savi* only rarely came to resent his intrusion, although he may sometimes have defended students against communal interference.[99] It was the bishop who acted as advocate to the pope and helped obtain privileges,[100] the bishop who came forward with the offer of the Casa della Misericordia for conversion to a college for students (and then helped win it privileges and assets),[101] and who was often approached by the commune for other favours and help with matters such as the procurement of teachers.[102] Moreover, it might be observed that he did not demand, and certainly did not receive, very much in return. The concession to the clergy in 1364 of a voice alongside the *Savi* in the appointment of teachers appears to have remained a dead letter. Similarly the Casa della Misericordia was handed to the commune for transformation into the Casa della Sapienza without any expectation of even vestigi-

---

[91] *CG* 211, f. 83v, 29 Oct. The petition used the same argument made by Bernardino – poverty – adding that 'questa prestanza o vero debito vecchio è la cagione che non si truova rectori'.

[92] *Conc.* 446, f. 30r, 30 May. S. Maria della Scala, the Opera del Duomo and the mendicant orders were to be exempted.

[93] *Balìa* 40, f. 60r, 14 Nov (and cf. f. 90r, 10 Dec).

[94] MINNUCCI, 'La Chiesa e le istituzioni' is a recent discussion of this theme.

[95] These range from Innocent IV's original privilege (above, p. 32) to Gregory XII's eight bulls of 1408 (pp. 55, 304 and 361), Martin V's and Nicholas V's bulls in favour of the Sapienza estate (below, p. 362) and Pius II's bull of 1459 allowing clergy who studied in Siena the privilege of benefice (*Mis.* 1, ff. 97r-100r; *Capitoli* 5, ff. 127r-130r, 22 Apr 1459, ed. BARDUZZI, *Documenti*, pp. 34-8). One of the few writers to take account of this latter bull is N. MENGOZZI, 'Il pontefice Paolo II e i senesi', *BSSP*, 21-5 (1914-18) (21, pp. 463-4).

[96] Below, pp. 134-5.

[97] Below, pp. 300-1.

[98] *Chartularium*, doc. 427, pp. 560-3, 16 Aug 1357. See also BERTONI, 'Il collegio dei teologi', p. 1.

[99] As in 1447, when the bishop claimed jurisdiction over a cleric, Federicus Johannes Corradi of Nürnberg, detained by the *podestà* for being armed at night; ZDEKAUER, *Documenti*, no. 49, pp. 29-30, 5 Aug. It is not beyond question, however, that this concerns a student; he is described just as *clericus*.

[100] See for example the role of Antonio Casini in obtaining the eight bulls from Gregory XII (above, pp. 54-5); On 2 Jan 1409 he presented them to Siena, *Conc.* 258, f. 4r, and cf. CATONI, 'Genesi', p. 163, and P. BROGINI, 'La trasformazione della Casa della Misericordia in Casa della Sapienza', in *La Misericordia di Siena*, pp. 121-33 (p. 123). Casini was paid for his labours by the commune (above, p. 55 n. 166). In 1422 the bishop was in Rome negotiating for the grant of *incerte* and other fiscal favours from Martin V (*Conc.* 1620, ff. 38v-39r, 12 Mar, and 69v, 10 May; and cf. the his report on negotiations, *Conc.* 1901, no. 6, 25 Apr, and also *Conc.* 1903, no. 49, 17 Jun 1423), and the following year the commune asked him to plead on behalf of the commune for the privilege of exemption from residence for beneficed clergy who were studying civil law or medicine (*Conc.* 1621, f. 6r, 11 Jan 1423).

[101] Below, pp. 300-1.

[102] E.g. in 1415 the *Concistoro* wrote to the bishop asking for help in hiring teachers (*Conc.* 1612, ff. 63r, 13 Jun, and 78r, 13 Jul). The results were not positive. On 10 Jan 1416 they wrote again complaining that he was obstructing their efforts (*Conc.* 1613, f. 5r).

al control; Bishop Mormille agreed in his letter of 1393, proposing the Sapienza, that its control would remain in the hands of the commune,[103] and although in 1422 the bishop was offered the opportunity of putting some students in the Sapienza, in recognition of his efforts to obtain papal approval for a further transfer of assets,[104] there is no evidence that this was taken up, and there is no further evidence of clerical influence on its administration. But disinterested episcopal support was one thing, clerical taxation quite another. A tax on the clergy was not a new move for the commune, which attempted it for various purposes.[105] However, the extent and the regularity of this tax was seen as unacceptable, and it proved both unpopular and indeed, according to the lower clergy who actually had to pay the tax, unsustainable. But the episode was significant, both for the revenue it produced over a critical period in the *Studio*'s history and for the precedent that it constituted. The Florentines took the idea to heart in particular; from 1426 the idea of a similar tax for the Florentine *Studio* gained momentum, and the precedent of Siena was quoted explicitly by the Florentines in their attempt to persuade the pope to allow them the same.[106] In the Laurentian period they were much more successful than the Sienese, obtaining an annual 5,000 ducats and renewing it over decades. Silvano deemed Florence's success in this respect to be a characteristic of the administration of universities by emergent territorial states,[107] and the greater success of the Florentines in achieving a regular and high level of clerical subsidy may well be a function of Florence's greater political weight and territorial extent. But if Florence reaped the benefit, Siena modelled the way.

The exploitation of the other major source, the hospital of S. Maria della Scala, took place at the same time and with the same eventual outcome. It was less controversial but harder to sustain because opposition to it was more readily focused; both the rector and the chapter of the hospital, which met regularly, could speak on its behalf. As Siena's richest pious institution, the Scala had long been considered an appropriate source to tap for communal projects and needs.[108] The 1386-7 measure referred to above nominated the hospital as a contributor for the first time.[109] The obligation is men-

---

[103] Catoni, *Pergamene*, p. 33 suggested that his concern was primarily to keep the Misericordia estate intact. For another example of Mormille's cooperation with the commune see N. Mengozzi, *Il feudo del vescovado di Siena* (Siena, 1911, repr. 1980), pp. 67-70. The commune also legislated on degrees, over which the bishop's control was also purely nominal, as in other *studi* (below, pp. 286 *seq.*). It is not possible, then, to agree with Zdekauer that the foundation of the Sapienza increased the influence of the church on the university as well as increasing its stability (pp. 31-5, esp. p. 34).

[104] *Conc.* 337, f. 8r, 10 Mar, and *Conc.* 1620, f. 39r, 12 Mar (letter to the bishop, revealing that all he was being offered was the right to nominate one student in canon and one in civil law).

[105] Caferro, *Mercenary Companies*, pp. 109-11; F. A. D'Accone, *The Civic Muse. Music and Musicians in Siena during the Middle Ages and the Renaissance* (Chicago, 1997), p. 32 n. 68.

[106] Gherardi, *Statuti*, appendix, part I, doc. 112, p. 207 (18 Nov); cf. Zdekauer, p. 60 n. 1.

[107] Silvano, 'Stato, territorio e istituzioni', pp. 990-1. Davies, *Florence and its University*, pp. 75-6 has a full account of the clerical levy at Florence, and cf. Idem, 'Studio, Stato and State: the University of Florence and the Medici from Party Bosses to Grand Dukes', paper to the International Commission of the History of Universities session at the 19th International Congress of Historical Sciences, Oslo, 6 to 13 August 2000, published on www.oslo2000.uio.no/A10/A1016/group-2/Davies.pdf (downloaded on 7 April 2004), which takes the theme further while stressing its fundamental importance. Documents pertaining to the raising of the tax in and immediately after the Laurentian period are published in Verde, *Lo Studio fiorentino*, V, pp. 16-30. Cf. also Denley, 'Academic Rivalry', pp. 201-2, and for the previous period G. Brucker, 'A Civic Debate on Florentine Higher Education (1460)', *Renaissance Quarterly*, 34 (1981), pp. 517-33; repr. in his *Renaissance Florence: Society, Culture and Religion* (Goldbach, 1994), pp. 207*-223* (pp. 519, 526).

[108] Ginatempo, *Prima del debito*, pp. 73 *seq.*; Piccinni, 'La strada come affare', pp. 17-19); S. R. Epstein, *Alle origini della fattoria toscana. L'ospedale della Scala e le sue terre (metà '200 – metà '400)* (Florence, 1986), pp. 26-8, 258-61; Caferro, *Mercenary Companies*, pp. 83, 110-11.

[109] Above, n. p. 88 n. 8.

tioned again in 1405,[110] and we know that the hospital was contributing in the years 1406-8.[111] In 1409 the rector and brothers of the hospital famously objected, first on the grounds that it could ill afford the payment and secondly because, it alleged, the *Studio* was virtually non-existent anyway. It was released from its obligation and the *Studio* was all but closed.[112] The attempted revival of the *Studio* in June 1412 appears not to have changed the situation much; although the commune aimed to find half of the 3,000-florin budget from unspecified other sources,[113] as has been seen, this initiative came to nothing, and by September the hospital's contribution to the *Studio* was diverted to the construction of new city walls.[114] With the revival of the *Studio* the obligation was renewed, and from 1417 we know that the hospital was having to sell property in order to keep up with the monthly payments.[115] Eventually a series of partial exemptions was obtained. The amount due was reduced in August 1418,[116] and again by 200 florins, for a three-year period, in 1420 because poor harvest, bad weather and rising costs had weakened the hospital's position.[117] Payments were certainly made in 1424 and 1425,[118] but that year the hospital was released from its contribution,[119] and thereafter no attempts to reinstate it on a regular basis were made.[120]

---

[110] *Conc.* 238, f. 31v, 21 Aug, ed. GAROSI, p. 228 n. 3; money raised from the hospital (as well as the clergy) was to be spent on refurbishing classrooms as well as on salaries.

[111] There are two sets of figures, those from the records of the hospital itself and those of the *Regolatori*. For 1406 the hospital accounts record a payment of 90 fl. and £18/0/0 (*Scala* 517, f. 8v, 16 Jun); for 1407 the hospital accounts have two payments, 80 fl. and £16/0/0 (loc. cit., 23 Mar), and 1,874 fl. and £300/4/6 (f. 85v), while the *Regolatori* accounts have 838 fl. and £6/4/0 for the first semester (*Regolatori* 6, f. 23r), and 750 fl. and £58/0/0 for the second (f. 32r; the text gives 550 fl., the marginal annotation 750 fl.). For 1408 the *Regolatori* accounts record a total of 831 fl. and £188/18/6 from the hospital and the clergy together (*Regolatori* 6, f. 59r), but the hospital accounts have only a single payment, of 50 fl., made directly to a *Studio* teacher, Pietro Bonazini (*Scala* 517, f. 85v, 14 Mar).

[112] See above, p. 88 n. 13. Previous obligations still had to be met, however, and there was still some dispute over this in July; *Conc.* 261, f. 17v, 20 Jul 1409, and *Scala* 22, f. 96v, 21 Jul (when the chapter resolved to look for funds 'per pagare la minore quantità che si può per lo studio'). This episode is well-known (though usually misdated, following Garosi, to 1408), but there is an aspect of it that has not been explored. The bulls of Gregory XII (7 May 1408) transferring the property of the Casa della Misericordia to the proposed Casa della Sapienza included the condition that, if the project were to fail, the bishop of Siena was to decide what to do with these resources (*Mis.* 1, ff. 73r-74r, Italian version ff. 64r-65v, ed. BARDUZZI, *Documenti*, pp. 25-7); they also united all hospitals within the territory, with the exception of the Scala, to the new Sapienza (*Mis.* 1, ff. 74r-75r, Italian version ff. 65v-67v, ed. BARDUZZI, *Documenti*, pp. 27-9), thus creating – or rather rebuilding (since the Misericordia was second only to the Scala in the *Tavola delle Possessioni*; see below, pp. 363 *seq.*) – a substantial rival. Could the weakness of the *Studio* in 1409 have offered an incentive to the hospital, not just to get rid of the fiscal burden that it resented, but to kill off the Sapienza project as well?

[113] Above, p. 88 n. 14.

[114] Above, pp. 56-7.

[115] *Scala* 22, f. 162v, 17 Feb 1417; *Patrimonio Resti*, 2189, ff. 145v-146r, 16 Nov 1417; *Scala* 22, ff. 169r, 23 Aug 1418, and 172r, 12 Aug 1419.

[116] *CG* 208, f. 105v, 19 Aug, ed. ZDEKAUER, p. 32 n. 1 (and *CG* 2113, f. 127v). It was reduced by 350 florins a year to 62 *lire* a month. Around 1419 it was still officially supposed to be 500 florins (above, p. 103).

[117] *CG* 209, f. 90r, 30 Dec; copy in *Scala*, 65, no foliation, ed. EPSTEIN, *Alle origini*, p. 27 n. 107. The reduction was still in effect in 1425, when the measure abolishing the Scala's contribution stated that it was 300 florins annually. Below, n. 119.

[118] The *Biccherna* books record two sums of 400 *lire* (*Bicch.* 307, f. 6v, 22 Dec 1424, and *Bicch.* 456, f. 140r, 21 Mar 1425), and one of 880 *lire* (*Bicch.* 308, f. 8r, 1425).

[119] *CG* 210, f. 197r, 26 May 1425. The petition describes it as 'uno debito incomportabile'.

[120] The attempt in 1440 to obtain papal permission to tax the clergy specifically exempted the hospital, the Opera del Duomo and the mendicant orders (*Conc.* 446, f. 30r, 30 May 1440). In 1514 the hospital was ordered to contribute eight *moggia* of grain to the Casa della Sapienza; it was just one of many institutions instructed to help the ailing college (*Mis.* 1, ff. 117v-118r, 26 Jan) (below, p. 378).

The relationship between these two large institutions of the fifteenth century, the young, prestigious *Studio* and the venerable hospital, one of the oldest institutions of the republic, is complex and has not yet been fully explored. There are close institutional parallels, especially given the way the commune steadily encroached on the hospital's internal government in the late fourteenth century.[121] There is the financial relationship between the new and demanding body and the commune's chief milch-cow, described here; there is the intricate relationship between the two great institutional landowners, the hospital and the Casa della Sapienza, which will be discussed in due course;[122] there is the question of the respective status of the two bodies, and occasionally perhaps an imitative and/or a competitive element between them in matters of communal ritual, to which we will also return;[123] and finally there is the highly elusive medical connection. Piccinni and Balestracci have pondered this relationship, and stressed the need for further research,[124] while rightly warning us not to expect too much; after all, however prestigious, the hospital's function, as in all hospitals of the period, was caritative first, medical second, and the salaries offered by the hospital were hardly such as to attract high-profile and high-status university teachers.[125] Yet detailed comparison between the lists of those hired by the two institutions suggest that they were absolutely right to stress the connection;[126] the hospital regularly hired university men, and a substantial number of teachers did accept hospital appointments, as will be seen.[127] The slow pace with which the university world and the world of hospitals converged after our period is indicative of the huge gap, in terms of function as well as of prestige, between them; but some moves in this direction are already discernible in the fifteenth century.[128]

[121] EPSTEIN, *Alle origini*, ch. 1; A. K. ISAACS, 'Lo spedale di Santa Maria della Scala di Siena nell'antico stato senese', in *Spedale di Santa Maria della Scala. Atti del Convegno Internazionale di Studi, 20-22 novembre 1986* (Siena, 1988), pp. 19-29 (pp. 24-5); P. DI TORO and R. DI PIETRA, *Amministrazione e contabilità nel XV e XVI secolo. Lo Spedale senese del Santa Maria della Scala attraverso i libri contabili*. Storia delle Istituzioni e del Pensiero Ragioneristico, 4 (Padua, 1999), p. 48.

[122] Below, pp. 370, 372-4.

[123] Below, pp. 227 n. 128 and 264.

[124] 'Un capitolo ancora aperto è quello che concerne la funzione che l'ospedale ricopre nella formazione dei giovani medici e degli scolari che studiano medicina presso lo Studio e in genere il rapporto tra teoria e pratica medica.' PICCINNI, 'L'Ospedale di Santa Maria della Scala', p. 318; and cf. also EADEM and L. VIGNI, 'Modelli di assistenza ospedaliera tra Medioevo ed Età Moderna. Quotidianità, amministrazione, conflitti nell'ospedale di Santa Maria della Scala di Siena', in *La società del bisogno. Povertà e assistenza nella Toscana medievale*, ed. G. Pinto (Florence, 1989), pp. 131-74 (pp. 154-8).

[125] Both these points are made in D. BALESTRACCI and G. PICCINNI, 'L'ospedale e la città', in D. GALLAVOTTI CAVALLERO, *Lo Spedale di Santa Maria della Scala in Siena. Vicenda di una committenza artistica* (Pisa, 1985), pp. 21-42 (p. 21).

[126] 'In Siena, during the fifteenth century, the same masters who were teaching medicine in the *Studium* treated sick people in the hospital of Santa Maria della Scala.' D. BALESTRACCI, 'The Regulation of Public Health in Italian Medieval Towns', in *Die Vielfalt der Dinge. Neue Wege zur Analyse mittelalterliche Sachkultur. Internationaler Kongress Krems an der Donau, 4. bis 7. Oktober 1994. Gedenkschrift In Memoriam Harry Kühnel* (Vienna, 1998), pp. 345-57 (p. 355); cf. PICCINNI, 'L'Ospedale', p. 318, and EADEM and VIGNI, 'Modelli di assistenza', p. 156.

[127] Below, p. 211 and n. 15.

[128] Beyond the evidence of university teachers in the hospital, there is fragmentary evidence of the Scala accommodating students, possessing, acquiring and selling academic books (law as well as medicine), and offering junior posts as 'coadiutore' from which the recipients could progress up to a full position; PICCINNI, 'L'Ospedale', loc. cit., and below, pp. 280 n. 8 and 281 n. 15.

IV

TIMES AND PLACES

1. *The academic year*

Not least of the commune's tasks was to ensure that the *Studio* opened on the right date. By the four-teenth century the academic year was supposed to begin on the feast of St. Luke's, 18 October, as was the practice in Italian *studi*;[1] but on several occasions this proved impossible. In 1417 it began on 1 November because of plague;[2] in 1422 it was delayed till 22 November;[3] in 1429 to 3 November because the teaching programme had only been published on 22 September and there had been a major dispute over the rectorate;[4] in 1430 again till 1 November,[5] in 1437 till 11 November,[6] and in 1440 by a few days 'cum scolares plures venturi sint'.[7] But the aspiration to open on 18 October, 'come si costumava antiquamente, et come si observa nelli studi bene istituiti', was not abandoned.[8]

---

[1] *CG* 195, f. 115r-v, 23 Jan 1387, ed. GAROSI, p. 194 n. 1; copy in *Mis.* 1, f. 50r-v, 23 Jan 1387. This itself represents a slide from an earlier timetable. In 1275 it had been declared that teachers were to appear in Siena eight days before Michaelmas, 29 Sept (*Chartularium*, doc. 24, pp. 16-19; ZDEKAUER, *Origini*, p. 19). The 1252 statutes of Bologna had stipulated 8 October; D. MAFFEI, 'Un trattato di Bonaccorso degli Elisei e i più antichi statuti dello Studio di Bologna nel manoscritto 22 della Robbins Collection', *Bulletin of Medieval Canon Law*, 5 (1975), pp. 73-101 [repr. in his *Studi di storia delle università e della letteratura giuridica* (Goldbach, 1995), pp. 23*-51* with additions pp. 524*-6*], p. 94. See also BELLOMO, *Saggio sull'Università*, pp. 200-1. The thirteenth-century Bolognese jurist Odofredo had announced '...Incipiam super Dig. vetus octava die vel circa post festum S. Michaelis...Codicem semper incipiam circa festum S. Michaelis per XV. dies vel circa'. F. C. VON SAVIGNY, *Geschichte des Römischen Rechts im Mittelalter*, 6 vols (Heidelberg, 1815-31), III, pp. 501-2.

[2] *Conc.* 310, ff. 29r, 16 Oct, and 33r-v, 23 Oct.

[3] *Conc.* 341, f. 7r, 11 Nov, ed. PIANIGIANI, doc. 57, pp. 79-80. Doctors were to appear by 20 November.

[4] *Conc.* 381, f. 24r, 11 Oct; cf. f. 14r, 22 Sept. On the rectorate see below, Chapter III.2.4.

[5] *Conc.* 387, f. 11v, 18 Sept. Contracts, however, were to run from 11 October; f. 12r, eds. NARDI, *Mariano Sozzini*, doc. 8, p. 118, and PIANIGIANI, doc. 124, pp. 153-4.

[6] *Conc.* 430, f. 25v, 12 Oct.

[7] *Conc.* 448, f. 33r, 17 Oct. The late middle ages seems to have seen a general slide of the beginning of the academic year. By the end of the fifteenth century Perugia opened in early November (ERMINI, *Storia*, I, pp. 432-4 and 275-6). On the length of the academic year generally see also BELLOMO, *Saggio sull'Università*, pp. 200-1, and ERMINI, *Storia*, I, pp. 432-4. The teaching of theology within the religious orders began on 30 Sept; BERTONI, 'Il "Collegio" dei teologi', pp. 14-16, and Rubric 36 of the 1434 statutes, p. 47.

[8] *Balìa* 24, f. 88v, 30 Jun 1481, eds. PUCCINOTTI, *Storia della Medicina*, p. CLXIV, and ILARDI, 'Ordinamenti', p. 167; copy in *Mis.* 1, f. 107r.

The opening of the *Studio* depended on preparations having been made on time. Crucial to this was the fixing of the contracts for teachers, and moreover doing so in good time for the announcement of these to reach students from outside Siena who might be persuaded to come. To this end the practice of drawing up and publicising a list of all teachers hired, known as a *rotolo*, grew up among the Italian *studi*. The custom seems to have originated in Bologna in the late fourteenth century and became common early in the fifteenth.[9] It appears to have had a dual function, representing the formal record of all the contracts issued, as well as serving as an advertisement to potential students. The *rotolo* first appears in Siena in the 1420s, the period when the *Studio* was adopting so many of the practices of the Italian system.[10] The first known reference to a *rotolo* dates from 1429, when the *Concistoro* approved a list and had it sent out;[11] in 1437 it was ordered that the list be completed by 16 August, Siena's patronal festival, to give students from far away time to choose Siena and come,[12] and by 1447 this appears to have been the norm.[13] Thereafter mentions of the *rotolo*, though infrequent, suggest that it was a routine affair.[14] The actual text of these *rotuli* is often elusive. Originals seldom survive (as publicly displayed notices they were, after all, a form of consumable), and in Siena they were only copied into the records of the *Savi* or the *Balìa* from the late fifteenth century onwards.[15]

[9] On *rotuli* generally see P. R. DENLEY, 'Career, Springboard or Sinecure? University Teaching in Renaissance Italy', *Medieval Prosopography*, 12:2 (Autumn 1991), pp. 95-114 (esp. pp. 99-101). In the second half of the fifteenth century the largest universities appear to have issued their *rotuli* to coincide roughly with the opening of the academic year. Bologna's were usually published in September or October (only four in August and one in July in the fifteenth century; DALLARI, *I Rotuli*, I, *passim*). The Pavian *rotuli*, which like the Bolognese first appear at the end of the fourteenth century, were issued by the duke accompanied by a formal letter of promulgation, and were usually associated with the operation of opening the academic year. They were thus mostly published in October or November, though by the 1480s and 90s it was quite common for the publication to slip to well into the academic year, suggesting that the creation of a 'definitive' list with legal status was by now considered more important than the need for an advance recruiting tool. MAIOCCHI, *Codice diplomatico dell'Università di Pavia*, II.1-2, *passim*, and Biblioteca Civica 'Bonetta' di Pavia, *ms.* II.39 (R. MAIOCCHI, *Regesto e trascrizione di documenti universitari pavesi del secolo XV*), *passim*; A. SOTTILI (ed.), *Documenti per la storia dell'Università di Pavia nella seconda metà del '400*, I. *(1450-1455)*. Fonti e studi per la storia dell'Università di Pavia, 21 (Milan, 1994), docs 32, pp. 445 (20 Oct 1452) and 195-6, pp. 188-94 (17 and 21 Oct 1455). For Padua too few survive to allow generalisation; for what is known see BELLONI, *Professori giuristi a Padova*, pp. 45-52. Elsewhere the competitive edge could depend on earlier publicity. For pre-Laurentian Florence *rotuli* do not survive, but the fixing of contracts operated on the same sort of timetable as in Siena (cf. DAVIES, *Florence and its University*, p. 29); the *rotuli* from 1473 to 1500 were issued predominantly in spring or summer (VERDE, *Lo Studio fiorentino*, I, pp. 296-375), though September/October lists reappear from the end of the 1480s.

[10] Below, pp. 199-200, 253-5.

[11] *Conc.* 381, f. 14r, 22 Sept 1429. The formality of the term is still unclear; in 1433, after some controversy over the contracts of citizens, the *Consiglio del Popolo* ordered the *Savi* to make a *rotolo* of citizens as necessary (*Conc.* 2176, no foliation, 11 Sept).

[12] '…maximamente perché li scolari da longa ne possino avere notitia al tempo, che abilmente possano venire al nostro studio'. *CG* 219, f. 136v, 10 May 1437, ed. ZDEKAUER, doc. XVIII, pp. 169-71; copies in *Mis.* 1, f. 83r, and *Statuti* 41, f. 255v. There is a close parallel with the practice at Perugia, where in 1434 it had been stipulated that *condotte* were to be offered in May and June for the coming academic year, with teachers' responses due by August; ERMINI, *Storia*, I, p. 243.

[13] *CG* 223, f. 229r, 20 Feb 1447, ed. GAROSI, doc. 61, pp. 529-30 (and see p. 239) – 'a ciò ch'e' savi de lo Studio possino avere facto el ruotolo a Santa Maria come è ordinato'. Though it does not mention a *rotolo*, similar considerations of timing may have been at work in the proposal in 1456 to reform mechanisms for payment, which refers to letters to students in other *studi*; *Conc.* 2138, no. 39, f. 62r, 1456 (approved 13 July).

[14] E.g. approval of the *rotolo* by the *Savi*, 18 October 1497 (*Sale* 24, f. 157v), and 4 Nov 1498 (*Sale* 24, f. 167r); an approval of a teacher's contract as declared in the *rotolo*, *Conc.* 484, f. 28v, 21 Oct 1446; payments to the notary of the *Studio* for drawing it up, *Studio* 2, ff. 7v, 23 Dec 1473 (6 *grossi*), 46v, 24 Aug 1476 (max. £1/9/0), 89r, 20 Sept 1482 (33 *soldi*).

[15] No originals have come to light for the fifteenth century, and only two are known from the republican period; that of 1537-8 (*Studio* 21, no. 12, 5 Sept 1537, ed. L. KOŠUTA, 'Documenti', doc. XI-4, pp. 405-9; he points out, p. 395, that it bears traces of having been pinned up), and that of 1545-6 (*Studio* 22, no foliation). Even these, it should be said, are poor relations

Nor do we know much about the circulation of the *rotuli* to other *studi*,[16] but there is no shortage of evidence of their public circulation within Siena; as well as being read out at the opening of the academic year,[17] they were posted in key locations for the university, where they became a point of reference,[18] and the sequence and hierarchy of names had real implications, as will be seen.[19]

If the preparation of the *rotolo* came to be seen in Siena as an indispensable preliminary, the start of the academic year was marked by another formal process, the opening ceremony. A rare account of such a ceremony dates from 1473. The teachers and students of the university gathered in the Sala del Consiglio of the Palazzo Comunale, where they were joined by the members of the *Concistoro*; after mass and an oration, the *rotolo* was read out.[20] As elsewhere the oration was considered to be a highlight of these ceremonies. This could be given by a lecturer or an important figure in Siena; Andrea Biglia gave it in 1429 or 1430,[21] Filelfo in 1435,[22] Agostino Dati may have given it in 1455 or thereabouts.[23]

of the splendidly formal and richly illuminated parchment *rotuli* published in Bologna (Archivio di Stato di Bologna, *Assunteria di Studio: Riformatori dello Studio: Rotuli dei lettori originali 1438-1800*. The lists of names published from these by DALLARI, *I Rotuli*, do not begin to give an idea of the status and significance of these documents). Formally the closest we actually have to a *rotolo* for circulation is *Not.* 694, f. 23r, n.d., ed. MINNUCCI, 'Documenti', doc. II-49, pp. 119-21. This groups lectureships by subject, subdivided by type and time of lecture, in the conventional hierarchical order. It is however a scrap of paper (in a *bastardello* volume), and is annotated in ways suggesting it is a working document rather than one intended for publication. For the preceding period they can be 'reconstructed' through the records of the *condotte* in the *Concistoro* and other collections, though the habit of labelling payment lists as 'rotuli' is confusing and unhelpful, and of course neither these nor the advertisement of a teacher in a *rotolo* means that the teacher actually took up the invitation. PARK, 'The Readers at the Florentine Studio', p. 249; below, pp. 153-4, and above, p. 98 n. 34; and GRENDLER, *Universities of the Italian Renaissance*, p. 165.

[16] On the other hand the nature of the system opens the possibility that Sienese *rotoli* might turn up in the archives of other *studi* or towns. The Pavian *rotoli* of 1480-1 and 1482-3 are for example preserved in the Archivio di Stato in Florence among *Studio* papers (*Studio Fiorentino e Pisano, 1357-1568*, 7, ff. 61r-63v, 79r-81v, ed. VERDE, *Lo Studio fiorentino*, I, pp. 384-92).

[17] Cf. the granting of permission to the *bidello* to read it out in the *sala pubblica* of the *Consiglio* (*Studio* 3, f. 22v, 26 Oct 1520); instructions that the completed *rotolo* be shown first to two priors and then presented to the *Concistoro* 'more solito' (*Studio* 3, f. 28v, 1521).

[18] E.g. in 1480 the list of lectures 'quas affigit in locis publicis et consuetis' was the basis on which checks were made on whether they were being given; *Not.* 858, f. 4v, 23 Apr 1480, ed. MINNUCCI, 'Documenti', doc. II-23, pp. 90-1 (though the term *rotulus* does not appear here).

[19] Below, pp. 129 and 137 *seq.*

[20] *Conc.* 642, f. 26r, 18 Oct, ed. BAI, doc. 347, p. 343 (and see p. xiii). There is also the opening ceremony of 1423-4, held in presence of the ecclesiastical council; above, p. 58.

[21] *De laudibus disciplinarum*, published in K. MÜLLNER (ed.), *Reden und Briefe italienischer Humanisten: ein Betrag zur Geschichte der Pädagogik der Humanismus* (Vienna, 1899, repr. Munich, 1970, ed. B. Gerl, Humanistische Bibliothek. Abhandlungen und Texte), pp. 64-70. R. SABBADINI, 'Andrea Biglia milanese, frate agostiniano del secolo XV', *Rendiconti del R. Instituto Lombardo di Scienze e Letteratura*, 39 (1906), pp. 1087-1102 (p. 1095) dated it 18 Oct 1430 through the reference to Niccolò Tedeschi in the text; the year is plausible, but that year the opening of the *Studio* was delayed to 1 Nov (*Conc.* 387, ff. 11v-12r, 18 Sept 1430 – which refers to the fact that there was to be a *sermo* but without naming the speaker). F. MARLETTA, 'Note all'Epistolario del Panormita', *La Rinascita*, 5 (1942), pp. 516-26 (p. 523) preferred 1429 as fitting better given that he taught in Siena in 1429-30 but not the following academic year. This dating is followed by the anonymous author of the entry for Biglia in *DBI*, 10 (1968), pp. 413-5 (p. 414), but not by G. FIORAVANTI, 'Formazione e carriera di un domenicano nel '400: l'autobiografia di Simone Bocci da Siena (1438-1510)', in *Studio e studia: le scuole degli ordini mendicanti tra XIII e XIV secolo*. Atti del XXIX convegno internazionale, 'Società Internazionale di Studi Francescani di Assisi' e del 'Centro Interuniversitario di Studi Francescani', n.s., 12 (Spoleto, 2002), pp. 339-64 (p. 364 n. 54).

[22] ZDEKAUER, p. 6; the reference should be *Conc.* 418, f. 2v, 2 Sept 1435.

[23] ZDEKAUER, loc. cit.; the oration he believes to have been given to inaugurate the academic year is in DATI, *Opera, Orationes, Liber* III, *Oratio* XVI, ff. 77v-78r. This is one of many orations given by Dati within the university environment (e.g. *Liber* I, ff. 46r-51r, *Orationes* XV-XXXIII; *Liber* III, *Orationes* XVII-XX, ff. 78r-79v, like this one for inaugurations of rectors or vice-rectors; and the funeral orations for colleagues in *Liber* V, *Orationes* III-VI, ff. 97v-100v). Bernardino Tom-

The rector was also expected to give an oration on taking office, and if (as was considered desirable) that occasion coincided with the opening of the *Studio*, this could form part of the ceremony.[24] Teaching proper began the day after,[25] and was supposed to continue until the feast of S. Lorenzo (10 August)[26] in the case of all but the doctors of medicine, who (from 1481 at least) were to teach till the feast of S. Giovanni (24 June).[27] It is possible that this too had been flexible; the *Savi* occasionally made arrangements for the summer vacation in July,[28] and by the mid-sixteenth century the end of the academic year had come forward to 23 June.[29] Apart from special vacations for state occasions or to mark political change,[30] there were also some extended breaks during the year. Two in particular are discussed in the documents. One, for carnival, was universal in Italian universities and widely popular among students. Carnival celebrations had a tendency to get out of hand in some *studi*, both in terms of the length of the break and the unruliness which accompanied it – though there is less evidence of this in Siena than in some other centres.[31] The other was more typically Sienese; teaching was regularly interrupted in May to allow visits to the spas in the Sienese territory for which the republic was renowned.[32] These breaks were customary, and it was only in the sixteenth century that they appear to have become formalised. In 1510-11 the academic year lasted from 3 November to 22 July and there were five vaca-

---

masi gave it in 1475 (*Studio* 2, f. 32r, 21 Aug), and there are two other references to inaugural orations in the *Concistoro* records (*Conc.* 341, f. 7r, 11 Nov 1422, ed. PIANIGIANI, doc. 57, pp. 79-80; *Conc.* 387, ff. 11v-12r, 18 Sept 1430). A lot of information has been assembled by FIORAVANTI, 'Alcuni aspetti', and more recently IDEM, 'Formazione e carriera', pp. 361-3, based particularly on the collection in the Biblioteca Braidense, *ms.* A.F.IX.32, on which see also BARGAGLI, *Bartolomeo Sozzini*, p. 17 n. 34. On Italian academic orations see now esp. the discussion in D. GIRGENSOHN, 'Studenti e tradizione delle opere di Francesco Zabarella nell'Europa centrale', in *Studenti, università, città*, pp. 127-76 (pp. 156-60).

[24] *Conc.* 400, f. 40r, 11 Oct 1432; the rector, 'Johannes de francia' (cf. f. 41v, 13 Oct, ed. PIANIGIANI, doc. 138, p. 167, and cf. p. 267 n. 166 below) 'faciat sua solemna et sermonem in sala consilio more consueto'. The record does not indicate whether there was another oration at this ceremony. Below, p. 263.

[25] *Studio* 2, f. 6r, 9 Oct 1473.

[26] CG 234, f. 180r-v, 3 Aug 1472 'prout antiquius erat consuetus'; and the 1481 reform (as p. 109 n. 8 above). Cf. Perugia (ERMINI, *Storia*, I, p. 276).

[27] The 1481 reform (as p. 109 n. 8 above). There is no sign of this earlier date for medical teachers in the reforms of 1472 (*CG* 234, f. 180r-v, 3 Aug). The 1481 exemption applied to 'medici pratici o teorici', though in the 1510 *calendario* only *pratici* are mentioned; P. PICCOLOMINI, 'Istruzioni di Giacomo Todeschini-Piccolomini al figlio Enea (1499-1500) e Calendario dello Studio Senese nel 1510', *BSSP*, 10 (1903), pp. 107-16 (p. 115): 'li medici pratici da S. Giovanni in là non possino essere punctati', evidence that the nativity (24 June), rather than the martyrdom (29 Aug), is meant, and that the reason for the shorter medical year was probably climatic.

[28] *Conc.* 321, f. 12v, 20 Jul 1419; *Conc.* 429, ff. 14r, 17 Jul, and 17r, 23 Jul 1437; *Conc.* 435, f. 9r, 8 Jul 1438. On the other hand in 1442 it was decided to hold the elections for the rectorate on 24 August rather than in September because thereafter students would be on vacation (*Conc.* 459, f. 38r-v, 7 Aug 1442).

[29] *Studio* 22, *rotolo* of 1545-6, no foliation.

[30] E.g. the suspension of lectures for the visit of the emperor Frederick III and his future spouse Eleonora of Portugal in 1452 (*Conc.* 513, f. 66v, 18 Apr, ed. BAI, doc. 26, p. 25; and cf. also CATONI, 'Genesi', p. 176); the closure of the *Studio* from 25 Jun to 5 Jul 1480 for the celebrations of the removal of the *Riformatori* from the regime (*Not.* 858, f. 6v, 25 Jun, ed. MINNUCCI, 'Documenti', doc. II-26, pp. 92-3).

[31] There is evidence for the carnival break in *Conc.* 758, f. 9r, 8 Feb 1493, ed. FERRERI, doc. 327, p. 308, and *Sale* 24, f. 162v, 21 Jan 1498. Contrast the numerous episodes that exercised the *Ufficiali dello Studio* in Florence/Pisa in the late fifteenth century; VERDE, *Lo Studio fiorentino*, IV, pp. 46, 332, 656-8, 770-2, 792-7, 883, 1025, 1068, 1106-7 and 1193, 1424; and see DENLEY, 'Communities within Communities', p. 742.

[32] In 1478 several teachers were granted a month's leave to go to the spas (*Conc.* 669, ff. 9v, 10 Mar, ed. FERRERI, doc. 64, pp. 54-5, 15r, 17 Mar, ed. FERRERI, doc. 66, pp. 56-8, and 36r, 21 Apr, ed. FERRERI, doc. 69, pp. 59-60). In 1480 the rector and his *consiliarii* were responsible for fixing 'vacationes balneorum presentis annis'; they declared them to begin with immediate effect (7 Apr) and to end on 26 Apr (*Not.* 858, f. 3r-v, ed. MINNUCCI, 'Documenti', doc. II-21, pp. 89-90); in 1496 the *Savi* fixed them as from 8 May until Pentecost (*Sale* 23, f. 93v, 21 Apr). On Sienese spas see also below, p. 323 n. 193.

tions; three weeks at Christmas, a fortnight each at Carnival, Easter and in mid-May, and seven days at Pentecost.[33] In 1533 it was decided that this was excessive.[34] The Carnival vacation was to be limited to the fifteen days before Lent; the spring vacation usually given 'per cagione di bagni' was discontinued since it was not customary at other *studi*, and spring was considered the best time for study.[35] Finally the *rotolo* of 1545-6 gives a complete list of all holidays. Between 18 October and 23 June there was a break from S. Lucia (13 December) till Epiphany (6 January), another of fifteen days for Carnival, finishing on Ash Wednesday, and a third in Easter week, plus Easter Monday. Twenty-two other feast-days are listed, and in addition all Thursdays (in March, Fridays) in weeks in which no such day fell were also designated *festivi*,[36] though some teaching was scheduled for these days.[37] The academic calendar was closely related to the dates on which teachers were supposed to be paid (Christmas, Easter, and the end of the academic year). For this purpose the academic year was divided into three *terzarie*,[38] which had a largely administrative function, but which also appear to have functioned as 'terms'.[39] The 1538 records of *puncte* suggest that in that year there were thirty-five teaching days in the second *terzaria* and thirty-one in the third.[40]

2. *Interruptions*

The many signs of stability in the *Studio* from the second decade of the fifteenth century do not mean that it flourished without interruptions. The most frequent reason was plague, which became a recurrent threat for which the authorities soon developed a standard strategy.[41] Plague had struck two years after the opening of the Sapienza, just before the beginning of the academic year 1417-8; the *Studio* was suspended for the whole of October 1417, and reopened in Montalcino at the beginning of November, returning to Siena before Christmas.[42] It is significant that by this time transfer rather than closure was the preferred measure, notwithstanding the cost, which was borne by the commune.[43] In 1420

---

[33] Piccolomini, 'Istruzioni di Giacomo Todeschini-Piccolomini', p. 115. The May vacation is also mentioned in 1525 (*Studio* 3, f. 45v, 5 May).

[34] 'E non faccino tante vacationi, quante ch'hora si costumano. Con torre via ancora molte mangiarie...'; *CG* 243, ff. 244r-245r, 14 Dec 1533, ed. Košuta, 'Documenti', doc. I-4, pp. 335-7.

[35] *CG* 243, ff. 248r-250v, 28 Dec 1533, ed. Košuta, 'Documenti', doc. I-5, pp. 338-41. Teachers who were in need of treatment could go to the baths with concistorial approval.

[36] *Studio* 22, *rotolo* of 1545-6, no foliation. This goes back to the 1252 statutes of Bologna (Rubric II, Maffei, 'Trattato', pp. 93-4), and is made more explicit in the 1317-47 fragment; cf. Bellomo, *Saggio sull'Università*, p. 201.

[37] Below, p. 140.

[38] This goes back at least to the city statutes of 1337-9; Nardi, *Insegnamento*, doc. 12, pp. 236-8.

[39] Cf. the decision in 1498 to allocate lectureships according to whether a specific individual was going to read for at least half a *terzaria*. See below, p. 141 n. 130.

[40] *Studio* 20, no foliation. At the end of the sixteenth century a minimum academic year of ninety days was specified. Prunai, III, p. 107.

[41] On the practical impact of plague in Siena, see still Garosi, pp. 425 *seq.*, and now Whitley, 'Concepts of Ill Health and Pestilence', esp. chs. I and II.

[42] *Conc.* 310, ff. 29, 16 Oct, 33r-v, 23 Oct, *Conc.* 311, f. 28r, 11 Dec; *Conc.* 1614, ff. 174r, 17 Oct, and 199r, 11 Dec, setting teachers until 19 December to return. Some teachers were still inactive in January; *Conc.* 312, f. 6r, 7 Jan 1418. The authorities had already explored contingency plans for the removal of the *Studio* as early as August; Massa was sounded out before they settled on Montalcino. *Conc.* 1614, f. 150v, 30 Aug, and, for correspondence with Montalcino, ff. 155r, 6 Sept, and 163r, 18 Sept 1417.

[43] The transfer of the *Studio* of Pavia to Piacenza in 1398 was a recent example; as with Siena, there were problems in

there was a more serious outbreak. Preparations were made for the event of plague in March, when a doctor was sent into the Sienese countryside to choose a suitable site for the *Studio*.[44] The plague lasted all summer, with the *Studio* in Corsignano, and although the commune's intentions were to provide a safer haven for it, famine, ill-discipline and resentment between students and villagers reached a dangerous level, and when the commune, in an attempt to defuse the situation, recalled it there came the reply that the scholars would rather abandon the *Studio* altogether than return to Siena before the epidemic was over.[45] In the 1424 outbreak – which some blamed for the abrupt closure of the church council[46] – the authorities were more cautious; the initial request by the *Savi* for the transfer of the *Studio* was defeated, and the transfer, to Montalcino, was only approved when the plague was more widespread. Even so one teacher, Paolo da Venezia, had to be forced to go by the threat that he would lose his salary.[47] Plague necessitated the transfer of the *Studio* on other occasions: for example in 1430, when the disruption lasted from June to November and the *Studio* moved first to Lucignano Val di Chiana and then, when plague reached that town in August, elsewhere;[48] and in 1436, when the *Studio* again transferred to Lucignano,[49] and again refused to return prematurely.[50] In 1448 plague during the summer led to the suspension of the *Studio* in October 'attendentes quod doctores conducti ac etiam scolares pro maiori parte sunt absentes a civitate propter aeris corruptionem'.[51] These disruptions were an

persuading members of the university to return, and in fact although Pavia reopened its doors in 1402 it was another decade before the numbers of students returned to previous levels; P. VACCARI, *Storia dell'Università di Pavia* (Pavia, 1957 edn.), pp. 47 *seq.*; MAIOCCHI, *Codice diplomatico dell'Università di Pavia*, I, pp. 408-11, and II, pp. 10-20; E. NASALLI ROCCA DI CORNELIANO, *Il trasferimento dello Studio visconteo di Pavia a Piacenza dal 1398 al 1402* (Milan, 1927). Migration for a different reason is evidenced by the meanderings of the newly-created *Studio* of Turin through Chieri and Savigliano, as each town in turn proved unwilling to support its cost; E. BELLONE, 'L'Università di Torino a Chieri (1427-1434) e a Savigliano (1434-1436)', *Studi piemontesi*, 14 (1985), pp. 23-33, and IDEM, 'I primi decenni'. And migration continued to be an option later in the century; the *Studio* of Florence/Pisa underwent similar upheavals at the end of the fifteenth century, due to plague in 1479-80 (to Pistoia), 1482 and 1486 (to Prato), and the rebellion of Pisa in 1495 (the *Studio* moved to Prato until plague hit it in 1497, and then to Florence); VERDE, *Lo Studio fiorentino*, IV, pp. 345-7, 357-76, 439-43, 613-21, 1186-99, 1246-57; and R. BLACK, 'Higher Education in Florentine Tuscany: New Documents from the Second Half of the Fifteenth Century', in *Florence and Italy*, pp. 209-222 (pp. 213-4).

[44] *Conc.* 325, f. 9v, 16 Mar, and see *CG* 209, f. 28r, 8 Mar 1420.

[45] The correspondence is in *Archivio Sergardi-Biringucci*, ms. A.II, docs. 2-9, n.d. and 2 Sept – 9 Nov 1420. Excerpts were published by ZDEKAUER, doc. XI, pp. 156-9. See also MITCHELL, *The Laurels and the Tiara*, pp. 35-8, and below, p. 241.

[46] BRANDMÜLLER, *Konzil*, p. 251. For the fuller picture see IDEM, 'Il concilio', esp. pp. 210-4.

[47] *Conc.* 350, ff. 14r, 28 May, 18v, 9 Jun, 19r, 10 Jun, ed. PIANIGIANI, doc. 65, pp. 86-7 (he was not to be allowed to live in the convent of S. Agostino, presumably the venue for the rest of the teachers, 'cum sit scandalosus') and 22r, 20 Jun (the threat of loss of salary is renewed). On this 'migration' see also correspondence in *Conc.* 1623, f. 60v, 12 Jun, and *Conc.* 1624, f. 8v, 27 Jul. On Paolo da Venezia, below, p. 134 n. 75.

[48] *Conc.* 385, ff. 38r-v, 18-9 Jun, 39r, 21 Jun, and 41r, 23 Jun; *Conc.* 1634, ff. 58v-59r, 23-24 Jun (correspondence); *Conc.* 386, ff. 15r, 13 Jul, and 33r, 4 Aug; *Conc.* 387, ff. 11v-12r, 18 Sept, partially ed. PIANIGIANI, doc. 124, pp. 153-5; cf. A. LIBERATI, 'Lucignano di Val d'Arbia. Ricordi e documenti', *BSSP*, 45 (1938), pp. 48-67 (p. 52 n.2). The plague had the consequences of affording two Sienese teachers, Mariano Sozzini and Bartolomeo Borghesi, the opportunity of going to Padua; NARDI, *Mariano Sozzini*, p. 22.

[49] *Conc.* 421, ff. 22v, 26 Mar, and 24r, 28 Mar; cf. *Conc.* 1646, f. 35r, 31 Mar.

[50] *Conc.* 421, f. 40r, 24 Apr. On 18 May Filelfo was allowed to leave Siena 'cum nullus sit hic scolarus'; *Conc.* 422, f. 22r, ed. L. DE FEO CORSO, 'Il Filelfo in Siena', *BSSP*, 47 (1940), pp. 181-209, 292-316 (doc. 2, p. 300; and cf. p. 190).

[51] *Conc.* 496, f. 33v, 22 Oct, ed. GAROSI, doc. 76, p. 538 (and see p. 263 on the episode); cf. *Conc.* 495, f. 44v, 29 Aug, ed. GAROSI, doc. 76, pp. 537-8, *Conc.* 496, f. 25r, 12 Oct, *CG* 224, f. 188r, 22 Nov, and *Conc.* 498, f. 18v, 24 Jan 1449, ed. GAROSI, doc. 78, p. 538, authorising the transfer of the *Studio* to Radicondoli, Casole or Asciano; cf. C. CORSO, 'Araldi e canterini nella Repubblica Senese del '400', *BSSP*, 62-63 (1955-56), pp. 140-60 (p. 144). Other occasions of plague were 1450, when the *Savi* requested permission to hire Sienese teachers to replace the *forenses* who had not turned up (*CG* 225, f. 73v, 20 Oct); 1457, when there were not enough scholars in the Sapienza because of plague, and it was difficult to find someone will-

endemic feature of university life, and did not necessarily lead to closure. In 1462 the *Savi* lamented of the *Studio* 'come sarebbe stato florida e bello in questo anno se la peste non l'avesse interrocto', though they drew comfort from the prospect of attracting students from Perugia, which had also been affected.[52] Yet benefiting from the misfortunes of others in this respect was not without risk; when Perugia was hit by plague in 1465 the Sienese were urged to take steps to prevent students from Perugia from coming to Siena and bringing the infection with them.[53]

3. *Venues for teaching*

Evidence about where lectures were held is as scanty for Siena as it is for all the Italian *studi*.[54] The authorities occasionally got involved in providing, or paying for, or improving the venues for teaching. For the early period the contracts for teachers are quite informative about this; we know that in the thirteenth century the *Studio* used the churches of S. Vincenti, S. Vigilio and, in the wake of the 1321 influx, S. Cristoforo.[55] From at least 1338 S. Pietro d'Ovile was also used,[56] and this continued

ing to take on the rectorate (*Conc.* 546, f. 17r, 1 Oct, and cf. *Balìa* 6, f. 32r, 24 Oct. Mariano Sozzini again left and was reluctant to return; NARDI, *Mariano Sozzini*, p. 84 n. 61); 1462, when the authorities contemplated moving the *Studio* to Casole (*Conc.* 575, ff. 5r, 4 Jul, and 40v, 8 Aug), and later in the year, ordering teachers and scholars to return, lamented of the *Studio*, 'come sarebbe stato florido e bello in questo anno se la peste non l'avesse interrotto' (*Conc.* 577, ff. 43v-44r, 24 Dec); 1464, when grammar, rhetoric, poetry and arithmetic schools were closed (*Conc.* 586, f. 40r-v, 11-12 Jun. On the plague disruption caused to the *Studio* by the epidemic of 1463-5 see BARGAGLI, *Bartolomeo Sozzini*, pp. 35-6); 1478, when the *Concistoro* allowed a teacher of medicine to come and go as he pleased while plague was rife (*Conc.* 672, ff. 41v-42r, 26 Oct; see also *Conc.* 2187, no foliation, n.d., archived with documents of 1477). The epidemic of 1486, by contrast, which struck in June and lasted for several months (see D'ACCONE, *The Civic Muse*, pp. 246-7), appears not to have had a substantial impact on the *Studio*. Nor did the epidemics of 1480, which disrupted government (C. SHAW, 'Politics and Institutional Innovation in Siena, 1480-1498 (II)', *BSSP*, 104 [1997], pp. 194-307 [p. 198]), apart from the effect it had on rents (*Studio* 2, f. 67r-v, 7 Jul).

[52] *Conc.* 577, f. 43v, 24 Dec. Plague had, after all, brought the Council from Pavia to Siena in 1423.

[53] *Conc.* 2012, no. 99, 29 Mar, and *Conc.* 2010, no. 21, 4 Apr. On the impact of plague on the Sapienza see below, p. 319 n. 159. Other reasons for the disruption of teaching included one further case of *force majeure*, of teaching being suspended for eight days in 1430 when the *curia* had burned down (*Conc.* 385, f. 38v, 19 Jun 1430), and one of breakdown; the serious troubles over the organisation of the student-university in 1429 caused considerable delay in the opening of the *Studio* (above, p. 109 n. 4, and below, p. 259).

[54] At the first major conference on Italian university history, held in Pistoia in 1979, the concluding round table found the venues of study in Italian universities before the fifteenth-century spate of building to be one of the most vexing problems in their history. *Università e società nei secoli XII-XVI, Pistoia 20-25 sett. 1979.* Centro italiano di Studi di Storia e d'Arte: Nono Convegno Internazionale (Pistoia, 1982), pp. 576-8.

[55] PRUNAI, I, pp. 74-5, in some detail; I. MORETTI, 'L'architettura delle sedi universitarie', in *L'Università di Siena. 750 anni*, pp. 275-300 (pp. 275-8); BALESTRACCI and PICCINNI, *Siena nel Trecento*, p. 154 n. 47; A. LIBERATI, 'Chiese, monasteri, oratori e spedali senesi (Ricordi e notizie)', *BSSP*, 46-68 (1939-61): 64 (1957), p. 188. The practice of teaching in churches, familiar from Bologna (F. CAVAZZA, *Le scuole dell'Antico Studio bolognese* [Milan, 1896]), was also in evidence in Florence as late as 1394 (SPAGNESI, *Utiliter Edoceri*, p. 171) and continued in Siena until the sixteenth century with theology being taught in the cathedral (PRUNAI, III, p. 107).

Fig. 6, overleaf, is one of a series of five scenes representing Sienese political events, originally perhaps part of a *cassone*, now all dispersed, and as yet insufficiently researched. It is usually assumed to be from the school of Vecchietta, but the attribution by Everett Fahy to Vecchietta's brother, Giovanni di Pietro, has been questioned on the basis that not enough is known about this artist. M. BOSKOVITS, *Tuscan Paintings of the Early Renaissance* (tr. Budapest, 1968), nos. 10-11; full discussion by V. Tátrai in P. CSÉFALVAY (ed.), *Christian Museum Esztergom* (tr. Budapest, 1993), pp. 236-7. P. A. RIEDL and M. SEIDEL (eds.), *Die Kirchen von Siena* (Munich, 1985-), vol. 2.1.2, p. 354-5, were the first to ask topographical questions about this painting, and have argued that it depicts the Piazza Tolomei. Other contemporary illustrations of the square and the church of S. Cristoforo are published in vol. 2.2, figs. 338-9 and 341.

[56] NARDI, *Insegnamento*, p. 203; *Chartularium*, docs. 352, p. 440, 4 Dec 1338, 367-70, pp. 467-78, 1339; LIBERATI, 'Chiese, monasteri, oratori e spedali': *BSSP*, 64 (1957), pp. 198-9.

Fig. 6 – Presentation of the Sienese flag in Piazza Tolomei, in front of S. Cristoforo, one of the churches used for university lectures. Mid-15th century, possibly school of Vecchietta (Esztergom, Kereszteny Muzeum, 55.161). See p. 115, n. 55.

throughout the period;[57] by the mid-fifteenth century its links with the *Studio* appear to have extended.[58] Apart from S. Pietro d'Ovile, in the fourteenth century the use of churches was overshadowed by the more common practice of hiring rooms in private houses,[59] though churches continued to be used for theology teaching and canon law lectures.[60] We know about the use of private houses in the thirteenth and fourteenth centuries largely because at that stage it was not infrequent for teaching con-

[57] Giovanni Pagliaresi and Francesco di Bettolo Coppoli da Perugia were teaching there in 1365; *Bicch.* 236, n. 98r, 31 Dec, and PRUNAI, II, p. 31; ZDEKAUER, p. 18 n. 2; MINNUCCI, 'Documenti', pp. 252 and 275.

[58] A formal document with the seal of the university was drawn up in 1447 'apud ecclesiam Sancti Petri de Ovile' (ZDEKAUER, *Documenti*, no. 54, p. 31, and see below, p. 275). G. MACCHI, *Memorie* (ASS, *ms.* D.111, f. 200r) observed that the church of S. Desiderio 'è servita un qualche tempo...per li Dottori e filosofi', but gave no indication of dates.

[59] PRUNAI, I, pp. 74-5, and II, pp. 30-1; MORETTI, loc. cit.

[60] Alessandro da Bologna taught in the cathedral in 1471 (*Conc.* 631, f. 4v, 4 Nov 1471, ed. BAI, doc. 318, p. 313 confirms Prunai's conjecture; loc. cit; and MORETTI, loc. cit.).

tracts to include subsidies for rents.[61] This practice declined shortly after the official approval of the university by Charles IV – there are few traces other than for pre-university teachers (who came under the same administrative umbrella),[62] and the last of these that has been found dates from in 1424[63] – so we are deprived of a valuable source of information about the locations of teaching rooms.

The fifteenth century witnessed the biggest change in practice. The opening of the Casa della Sapienza provided the university for the first time with a natural focus for teaching. Its predecessor, the Casa della Misericordia, was clearly already being used for teaching in the same way as were churches,[64] though there is no information about the number of rooms available for this purpose. Despite the fact that this was never a declared function of the Sapienza, its value as a centre for teaching must have been obvious from the outset. Such information as survives about the maintenance of these teaching rooms suggests that this could be carried out at the commune's rather than the Sapienza's expense.[65] Since the Sapienza was essentially a residential not a teaching college,[66] this is unsurprising; the Sapienza was doubling up as a location for the *Studio*'s teaching. It was of course only one of these. Little is known about the capacity of the Sapienza – an inventory made in 1459 only covers the private rooms[67] – but it was clearly not able to provide more than a proportion of the rooms necessary.[68] But in any case there is little indication that that was a priority. In the 1470s the shortage of student accommodation in the college led to the suggestion that some of the first-floor classrooms be converted into rooms for students; the teaching rooms are described as 'di superchio'.[69] Only in the 1490s, with plans for a new Sapienza to be built next door, do we see the emergence of the idea that teaching could be concentrated further on this natural centre.[70]

The handful of decisions we have regarding teaching to be located in the Sapienza suggests that

[61] The usual practice in this period was for the teacher to hire a room and for the commune to pay him a fixed sum 'per sua pigione' – the standard rate was 25 *soldi* a year – which might or might not correspond to the rent. NARDI, *Insegnamento*, pp. 98, 106; PRUNAI, as n. 59; *Chartularium*, docs. 67, p. 49, 29 Dec 1288; 70, p. 53, Jun 1289; 74, p. 56, Jun 1290; 79, p. 58, 31 Dec 1291; 82, p. 59, 31 Dec 1292; 93, pp. 67-8, Dec 1296 (p. 67); 98, p. 77, Jun 1302; 101, p. 79, 31 Dec 1302; 104, p. 82, 30 Jun 1305; 110, pp. 89-90, 30 Jun 1307; 123, pp. 99-100, 30 Jun 1309; 126, pp. 106-7, 6 Apr 1310; 131, pp. 110-11, 31 Dec 1310; etc.

[62] Lawyers and doctors of medicine were paid for salaries and 'pigioni di case' on the authority of the *Savi* in 1362, second semester (*Regolatori* 2, f. 32v), 1363 (f. 68v) and 1368 (*Regolatori* 3, f. 131r); in 1365 the rector of S. Pietro d'Ovile was paid rent for the rooms used by Giovanni Pagliaresi and Francesco da Perugia (above, n. 57).

[63] *Conc.* 348 f. 5r, 7 Jan.

[64] Cf. the order of 1407 that the halls of the Casa della Misericordia usually used for teaching be cleared for the doctors (*Conc.* 250, f. 21r, 24 Oct 1407, and below, p. 304 and n. 35). It had been the practice for the Casa della Misericordia to retain a *maestro di grammatica* to teach young inmates. CATONI, *Pergamene*, p. 17, and below loc. cit.

[65] Cf. the instruction by the *Concistoro* in 1427 that an inventory be made of 'omnibus bancis et catedris que sint in scolis sapientie' (*Conc.* 370, f. 19v, 4 Dec. Cf. CATONI, 'Genesi', p. 175); and the ordering of new *cattedre* for 'scolis novis sapientie' (marginal annotation) in 1441, to be paid for 'expensis comunis' (*Conc.* 454, f. 50v, 16 Oct 1441). But in 1467 it was decided that the 52-ducat entrance fee for the German student Johannes Brensset should be used 'pro bancis reficiendis conficiendis et murandis in scolas' (*Conc.* 605, f. 20v, 24 Jul; the work was ordered in *Conc.* 606, f. 28v, 12 Oct).

[66] Below, esp. Chapter IV.5.1.

[67] For a discussion of this, CATONI, 'Genesi', p. 168, and below, pp. 384-5.

[68] The 1545 *rotolo*, one of the few to stipulate the times of lectures, shows that at least eight classrooms would have been necessary by that stage; *Studio* 22, no foliation. But see PRUNAI, III, pp. 82 and 107.

[69] *Not.* 694, f. 4r, n.d., ed. MINNUCCI, 'Documenti', doc. II-35, pp. 101-2, a note of the *Savi* for their successors, not dateable, though its position in the collection strongly suggests this decade. There is no evidence that it was implemented.

[70] Below, pp. 388 *seq.*

these rooms were used predominantly for the less prestigious and the ancillary subjects and topics.[71] Certainly this has to be seen as part of a hierarchical game; some lecture rooms were considered better and more prestigious than others, and competition for them thus formed part of the process whereby a teacher made his career in a competitive environment.[72] Unfortunately the records of controversies about who should get which lecture room tell us little specific about the venues themselves. Only slightly more can be gleaned from the other source for such information, measures to ensure their maintenance. Although it does not appear that the commune paid rent for these rooms in the fifteenth century,[73] it does frequently take responsibility for their upkeep and furnishing.[74] There appears

[71] The Sapienza appears to have been used mostly for teaching within arts and medicine. The appointment of a student, Mag. Giovanni di Donato da Arezzo, to an unsalaried lectureship in logic in the Sapienza on the same day that he was awarded a place in the college (*Conc.* 415, f. 10r, 10 Mar 1435) is unusual and suggests basic teaching, perhaps mainly aimed at his peers. In 1439 and again in 1444 Francesco di Sante/Santi da Roma was appointed to teach medicine 'cum hoc quod debeat legere in Domo Sapientie aliter non habeat salarium' (*Conc.* 441, f. 61v, 29 Aug 1439, ed. Pianigiani, doc. 201, p. 231-3). 'M. Bartolomeo siculo', from his title presumably another teacher of arts/medicine (it has not been possible to identify him further from other records), was appointed to teach an unspecified subject in 1499 (*Sale* 24, f. 172v, 8 Aug). The only teacher of law mentioned in the sources is Bernardino Luti, who was appointed in 1474 to read *Institutiones*, one of the most basic texts, 'in scholis sibi deputandis…sine aliqua mercede aut salario' and in concurrence with three other teachers (*Studio* 2, f. 13v, 14 Mar 1474, ed. Bai, Appendix, doc. 13, p. 386, giving 'secundo' instead of 'sine'). On the other hand not all Sapienza lectures were low-profile; Niccolò Borghesi, a key figure in the *Studio* and in political life, was teaching there in 1492 (*Balìa* 37, f. 97r, 29 Oct 1492). A possible special case is the theology teaching of the Augustinian 'M. Antonius basilij' in 1445; a condition of his modestly rewarded appointment (15 florins) was 'quod legat in domo sapientie et non in conventu'; *Conc.* 477, f. 13r, 15 Jul 1445, ed. Pianigiani, doc. 257, pp. 289-90 (p. 288). The appointment raises the question whether the authorities had come to feel it appropriate to provide some moral instruction for the inmates of the college in the form of theology lectures, as is evident elsewhere. On the other hand this is the only such evidence, so perhaps it would be a mistake to make too much of it. Finally, I have no explanation for the condition attached to the appointment of the maverick humanist Porcelio de' Pandoni that specifically prohibited him from reading in the Sapienza; *Conc.* 489, f. 7r-v (and *Conc.* 2177, no foliation), 8 Jul 1447, ed. F. Marletta, 'Per la biografia di Porcelio Pandoni (Note e Documenti)', *La Rinascita*, 3 (1940), pp. 842-81 (doc. 2, p. 878); *CG* 224, f. 30r[new], and *Dipl., Riformagioni*, 14 Jul 1447; and *Conc.* 489, f. 37r, 24 Aug 1447, ed. Pianigiani, doc. 274, p. 305, and Marletta, op. cit., doc. 3, p. 879; and see also below, p. 137.

[72] Below, pp. 137 *seq.* Cf. the instruction of 1476 that teachers were to be given them 'secondo il grado del loro dottorato' (*Studio* 2, f. 47v, 14 Oct 1476). An example of this pecking order in operation is a decision of 1440; Bartolomeo Bellanti was excused his *condotta* because of illness, and the *Concistoro* decided that either Filippo [Lazzari] da Pistoia or Mariano Sozzini could inherit his schoolroom (*Conc.* 448, f. 30r, 11 Oct, ed. Pianigiani, doc. 214, pp. 246-7), a measure which demonstrates at least one case of a particular school being associated with a particular discipline; and cf. the 'differentia scole' between Antonio Giordano da Venafro and Alessandro Petrucci in 1495; *Sale* 23, f. 98r (new foliation), 14 Nov, ed. Zdekauer, doc. XXV, pp. 193-5 (p. 195).

[73] There may well be records of payment of rents for classrooms in other archival series.

[74] This goes back at least to the 1321 influx (*Chartularium*, doc. 161, pp. 163-7, esp. p. 166, 8 Jan 1321 to 14 Jan 1322). In 1338 and 1339 the commune spent further sums on providing tables and benches (*Chartularium*, docs. 352, pp. 440-1, 4-31 Dec 1338; and 367, pp. 467-8, 30 Jun 1339; Zdekauer, p. 14 n. 3). Such payments are found again in 1361 (*Regolatori* 2, f. 34r-v; 108 florins are spent on 'fare le squole e aconciare le chase de' dottori'). Money is regularly spent at moments of attempted relaunch of the *Studio*. In 1387, 66 florins were voted 'ad facere cathedras pro doctoris et banchis pro scolaribus' (*Conc.* 139, f. 50r, 16 Oct 1387; and cf. the *bidello*'s accounts, *Regolatori* 4, f. 221r, 15 Apr 1389). In 1405 the pious institutions were ordered to prepare and pay for the schools, *cattedre* and *banche* (*Conc.* 238, f. 31v, 21 Aug, ed. Garosi, p. 228 n. 3). Cf. also *Conc.* 316, f. 25r, 14 Oct 1418 (resolution to make all benches and *cattedre* for the *Studio* at the commune's expense); *Conc.* 318, f. 15r, 25 Jan 1419 (another general renewal for all schools); *Conc.* 323, f. 12r, 22 Nov 1419 (furnishing of 'scolas notaie'); *Conc.* 379, f. 29r, 25 Jun 1429; *Conc.* 454, f. 50v, 16 Oct 1441 (*cattedre* for new Sapienza schools; see above); *Conc.* 486, f. 56v, Feb 1447 (a loan of furniture to a teacher); *Conc.* 566, f. 4r, 5 Jan 1461 (benches for the school of Agostino Dati); *Conc.* 606, f. 28v, 12 Oct 1467 (benches for the Sapienza); *Conc.* 641, f. 3v, 4 Jul 1473 (six to eight *banche* are required for schools in S. Vigilio). Other measures providing explicitly for the schools of pre-university teachers have not been listed here.

always to have been a degree of flexibility and inventiveness about such matters.[75] But ultimately, beyond what was provided by the authorities, it appears to have remained very much up to the teacher to make suitable arrangements for his teaching. After all, lectures took place behind closed doors, and their regulation could by and large be left to the lecturers, with the authorities – in the first instance, the *Savi* – intervening only when there were conflicts. The only general concern voiced by the commune comes as late as 1545, when teachers were required to 'ritener scuola in luoghi honesti et non sospetti acciò li scolari non si venghino a svagliolare et pigliare gattivi costumi et mali exempli'.[76] Public disputations were another matter, as will be seen; here visibility was all, to the extent that at one stage the teachers were even ordered to conduct these nightly contests in the Piazza del Campo.[77]

---

[75] This is perhaps best typified by the fact that in 1423 one of the schools was converted into a residence for the cardinal of S. Eustachio during the Council, and returned to the evicted teacher only after some delay (*Conc.* 346, f. 21r, 30 Oct 1423; *Conc.* 348, f. 14v, 4 Feb 1424). In 1488 Benedetto da Cingoli was excused his fine for not having taught on the grounds that no teachers' chair had been available (*Conc.*, doc. 267, p. 229).

[76] *Studio* 22, no foliation.

[77] *Studio* 2, f. 48v, 31 Oct 1476; see below, p. 144 and n. 154.

V

THE ORGANISATION OF TEACHING

1. *Introduction*

In the late medieval universities most of what pertained to teaching – the syllabus for each discipline, and the pathway through that syllabus, right through to the examination and conferment of degrees – was largely dictated by conventions. These conventions were enshrined in statute in some of the older universities, a fact which augmented their value as possible models for more recent foundations. (In the case of Italy that meant predominantly Bologna, though other major *studi* could also have an influence.) They passed into the system through custom and legislation (such as the stipulation of foundation bulls or charters prescribing the Bolognese 'model') and were maintained and updated through the constant mobility of teachers and students alike, which ensured that news of innovations or fresh developments elsewhere percolated through. The establishment of a new *studio* in competition with existing ones would only work if the new bidder could convince the academic world generally that what they had to offer was respectable and would lead to a degree that was considered valid. This *de facto* mechanism of quality assurance (to use the unfortunate technical language of our times) ensured that, in respect of teaching as in other aspects, the Italian universities of the late middle ages had a high degree of homogeneity.[1]

This is just as well for us, because if we hope to look to the surviving documentation for an understanding of how teaching was organised and practised in Siena we are in for a major disappointment. In the early days of the officially constituted *Studio* the authorities were content to stipulate that teaching was to proceed 'sichondo lo studio di Bologna',[2] and Gregory XII's 1408 bulls included

---

[1] This is the corollary of the commonality of the skills and training that were being imparted. Ascheri observed of the legal system: 'La conseguenza di questi caratteri generali del sistema...è che così come lo studente trovava un insegnamento sostanzialmente identico, nei metodi e nei contenuti, ovunque si muovesse in Europa, i professori a loro volta potevano essere non "locali", perché venivano chiamati ad insegnare non in base ad una loro presunta approfondita conoscenza del diritto locale, bensì per la loro capacità di dare technice interpretative e dottrine generali, "spendibili" poi ovunque, conseguita la laurea, sul "mercato comune" del diritto europeo...di fronte a qualunque possibile diritto locale. Insomma, l'insegnamento poteva rivolgersi ad un pubblico tanto più ampio ed eterogeneo proprio per la massima generalità e "astrattezza" (da contenuti locali) del suo oggetto. Lo Studio si poteva definire "generale" proprio perchè i suoi titoli e la formazione che esso conferiva avevano riconoscimento formale e importanza pratica ovunque.' M. ASCHERI, 'La scuola giuridica senese in età moderna', in *L'Università di Siena. 750 anni*, pp. 131-44 (p. 131).

[2] *Bicch.* 460, f. 10r-v, 1388. The earliest teacher known to have defected from Bologna was to teach 'iuxta morem illius civitatis'; *Chartularium*, doc. 13, pp. 10-11 (1262); PRUNAI, II, p. 26.

the wish 'che nel decto Studio tucte le buone consuetudinj et le rigorose examinationj le quali s'osservano negli Studi di Bologna et di Parigi al tucto s'osservino'.[3] Unfortunately, however, we do not have the one document which might possibly have told us more precisely how in due course these conventions were implemented. One of the practices to be inherited was that the detailed regulations regarding the syllabus were incorporated in the statutes of the *universitas scholarium*. This harks back to the days when student-universities had some actual power, which may have been the case in thirteenth-century Bologna but which was much less true of more recent foundations. However, the fact that later compilations of statutes in Bologna continued to include these details ensured that the practice was followed elsewhere as well. In Siena these statutes appear to have been compiled in the 1420s,[4] but since they have not survived we are thrown back on searching for corroboration or otherwise of the standard practices through sporadic references in occasional legislation. Perhaps it is precisely because these conventions were so fixed, and the dangers of tampering with them so obvious, that there is so little information.[5] The commune limited itself largely to enforcing the regularity of teaching[6] and, more unusually, to trying to ensure that students attended the lectures they organised.[7]

2. *Structures*

As in other Italian universities, the organisation of teaching in Siena is best viewed as divided into three disciplines or clusters of disciplines; law (which included both canon and civil law), 'arts and medicine' (which included most of the other subjects taught), and (a little later and on an entirely different organisational basis) theology. However, it would be entirely wrong to think of all three of these as 'faculties'. The legal and constitutional sense of this term as a formal embodiment of teachers and students is a phenomenon of northern Europe, and above all of Paris; in Italy the term is overwhelm-

---

[3] *Mis.* 1, ff. 68r-69r (Latin), and 76r-v (*volgare*), ed. BARDUZZI, *Documenti*, p. 31. The inclusion of Paris is more than a formality, not least because theology is allowed for the first time at Siena in this very bull; below, p. 126.

[4] Below, pp. 253 *seq.* In 1399 Niccolò Sozzini was paid having taught 'sicondo la forma et capitoli de lo studio gienerale da Siena' (*Bicch.* 285, f. 55v, 28 Jun). In the absence of corroborative evidence it would be wrong to take this as implying that there was a formal and detailed set of regulations by that date.

[5] See D. BUZZETTI, 'La Faculté des arts dans les universités de l'Europe méridionale. Quelques problèmes de recherche', in *L'enseignement des disciplines à la Faculté des arts (Paris et Oxford, XIIIe-XVe siècles). Actes du colloque international*, eds. O. Weijers and L. Holtz. Studia Artistarum: Études sur la Faculté des arts dans les Universités médiévales, 4 (Turnhout, 1997), pp. 457-66 (pp. 462-4) for perceptive comments on the limitations of administrative documents for information on what was actually taught.

[6] E.g. orders that lessons were to be held daily unless the *bidello* announced otherwise; they were to be read in strict order, none being omitted (*Conc.* 584, ff. 23v-24r, 3 Feb 1464, ed. BAI, doc. 205, pp. 178-9; *Mis.* 1, f. 100v, 20 Mar 1473; *Studio* 22, *rotolo* of 1545, no foliation).

[7] The rule stipulating a minimum of five students, a relic from the student boycott in Bologna, was seen to place the teachers at an unfair disadvantage, and in 1510 the *Balìa*, tightening up on the habit of extended vacations and on the *puncta* system in general, punished students as well for taking unauthorised vacations or obstructing teaching. PICCOLOMINI, 'Istruzioni di Giacomo Todeschini-Piccolomini', pp. 115-6; see also pp. 111-12. Cf. p. 333 n. 58 below, but contrast with Perugia (ERMINI, *Storia*, I, p. 105). The complaints of Simone Bocci, a Dominican who taught briefly in Siena in the 1470s, about how much teachers had to do to persuade enough students to attend lectures (and about how the behaviour of competitive teachers ensured that it was impossible to opt out of this circus) makes it clear that there was a problem (FIORAVANTI, 'Formazione e carriera di un domenicano', pp. 357-8; and below, pp. 142-3).

ingly used to denote disciplines (as in its modern German derivative, *Fach*).[8] In Siena, as elsewhere, this can be demonstrated by the wide variety of combinations in which the term is found: to describe individual subjects ('facultà di ragione canonica' and 'facultà di ragione civile',[9] 'studens…in facultate notarie',[10] 'facultate oratoria',[11] 'grammaticali facultate'[12]); occasionally to refer to combinations of such subjects ('facultate medicine, philosophie et logice');[13] to cover all subjects in blanket provisions;[14] or to allow a measure to apply to other disciplines not listed[15] – the sense in which it appears in the foundation charter of Charles IV[16] and the bulls of Gregory XII.[17] But this is not just a matter of terminology. The absence of any term to cover what we today would regard as a faculty reflects the

---

[8] A. MAIERÙ, 'La terminologie de l'universitè de Bologne de médecine et des arts: "facultas", "verificare"', in *Vocabulaire des écoles et des méthodes d'enseignement au moyen âge*. Actes du colloque Rome 21-22 octobre 1989, ed. O. Weijers. Études sur le vocabulaire intellectuel du moyen âge, 5 (Turnhout, 1992), pp. 140-56; repr. in *Miscellanea Domenico Maffei dicata: historia, ius, studium*, eds. A. García y García and P. Weimar (Goldbach, 1995), 2, pp. 393-409; rev. and tr. as Chapter 3 of his *University Training in Medieval Europe*, tr./ed. D. N. Pryds (Leiden, 1994) (p. 77 on how this was the case for Siena as well). On the use of the term in the thirteenth century, O. WEIJERS, *Terminologie des universités au XIIIe siècle*. Lessico Intellettuale Europeo, 39 (Rome, 1987); and cf. NARDI, 'Dalle *Scholae* allo *Studium generale*', p. 12.

[9] *Conc.* 2137, no. 57, ff. 107r-108r, 24 Jan 1478 (a failed proposal for reform). Cf. the declaration privileging law students in the Casa della Sapienza in 1422: 'considerato che le Facultà di ragione canonica e di ragione civile sono quelle, che fanno venire in grande dignità e stato quelli che li seguitano… e più honore riportano a la città che niuna altra Facultà in che l'uomo studi' (*Mis.* 1, f. 53v, 14 Dec). ZDEKAUER, doc. XIII, pp. 161-2, edited this measure from the seventeenth-century copy in BCS, *ms.* C.IV.26 (on which see above, p. 25 n. 134), and reproduced the mistranscription in that manuscript of 'la Faculftà' for 'le Faculftà'. The 1511 statutes of the college of doctors of medicine, which appears to have taken over many of the functions of the older *Arte dei Medici e Speziali*, even refers to 'aromataria facultate' (*Balìa* 253, ff. 335v-345v, 13 Oct, Rubric 19, f. 343r-v).

[10] *Conc.* 2141, no. 6, 15 Jul 1406.

[11] *Conc.* 589, f. 35v, 22 Dec 1464.

[12] *Conc.* 530, ff. 73v-74r, 8 Jun 1455. In 1395 Antonio di Ser Salvi da San Gimignano was elected 'ad lecturam gramatice facultatis'; *Conc.* 186, f. 18v, 16 Aug. Individual 'faculties' could be listed in combination; cf. the hiring in 1430 of Simonetto di San Lupidio 'catedram tenendum in facultate loyce et in facultate filosofie'; *Conc.* 386, f. 19r, 18 Jul 1430, ed. PIANIGIANI, doc. 122, pp. 150-1.

[13] *Conc.* 592, f. 38v, 30 May 1465, ed. BAI, doc. 221, pp. 195-200 (p. 197). MAIERÙ (op. cit., pp. 79-81) has speculated that towards the end of the middle ages the term *facultas* may have acquired a more specific significance at Bologna as a subject or combination of subjects in which it was possible to obtain a degree. It is difficult to find any support for this hypothesis from the Sienese evidence; although the evidence for degrees before the late fifteenth century is minimal, what we do have suggests degrees were only awarded for the minimum standard combinations (see below, p. 25). It should be said that most of the Sienese examples quoted here are from mid-to-late fifteenth-century decisions of the *Concistoro* to make teaching contracts in batches; these are listed thematically and in the hierarchical sequence to be expected in a *rotulus*. In the case above, however, lest it be assumed that the heading 'facultate medicine philosophie et logice' means the whole arts/medicine branch of the *Studio*, it should be pointed out that the next heading is 'In geometria et astrologia' (and the previous one 'In iure civile'); the insertion of the term *facultate* is casual not institutional. A similar list for 1469 (*Conc.* 616, f. 22r-v, 2 Jun, ed. BAI, doc. 292, pp. 276-8) decides on contracts in 'infrascriptis facultatibus', then groups them in three categories, 'In iure canonico', 'In medicina' and 'In philosophiam et loyca'. The closest I have found to Maierù's suggested sense of the word is the stipulation in the Casa della Sapienza reforms of 1422 (above, n. 9) that to be admitted to the college students had to have studied for two years 'in quella Faculftà, che studiasse a esso tempo'.

[14] *Not.* 694, f. 31r-v, Jul-Sept 1474?, ed. MINNUCCI, 'Documenti', doc. II-56, pp. 123-4: 'hanno sollecitato solidare le conducte in tutte le facultà'.

[15] The delegation of power to the *Savi* in 1361 entitles them to 'conducere ad legendum in civitate Senarum doctores in scientiis legalibus iuris canonici et civilis, medicine et aliis facultatibus quibuscumque'; *CG* 168, f. 4r-v, 19 Jul 1361, ed. ZDEKAUER, doc. V, p. 143. In 1405 doctors could be hired in civil law, canon law, medicine, grammar 'et aliis facultatibus'; *Conc.* 235, f. 27r, 28 Jan, and *Conc.* 237, f. 9v, 14 May 1405.

[16] Above, p. 42 and n. 72.

[17] BARDUZZI, *Documenti*, p. 31.

fact that the major groupings, law and arts/medicine, actually did not have any corporate existence in Italian universities. In Siena as elsewhere there were colleges of doctors which correspond to the three-fold division; but those for law and arts/medicine were hybrid organisations which had, as far as the university was concerned, the specific function of examining students and awarding degrees (they also had other, communal, functions); their membership included non-teachers but, most significantly for our argument here, did *not* include all those who did teach. There is no sense in which these even represented, let alone incorporated, all those active in the disciplines they covered,[18] and they had no responsibility for teaching; it is therefore no surprise that they never spoke on behalf of the teachers (let alone the students) of these disciplines. At the level of student organisation the picture is no clearer. Whereas at Bologna the evolutionary process had produced separate student-universities for law[19] and for arts/medicine, in Siena, as in the majority of smaller Italian centres, a single university was created. Within this, there is a limited sense in which 'subject' identity played a role; in 1435, for the purposes of the rotation of the rectorate, three *facultates* were to be taken into account, canon law, civil law and medicine.[20] However this was repeatedly challenged by those who preferred the principle of rotation by geographical origin, so even within the student-university the significance of the disciplines is far from obvious.[21]

For law and arts/medicine it is virtually impossible to find any legal or institutional sense in which the concept of a faculty was meaningful. Indeed, even to say that the *Studio* was divided into these groupings is almost to invite expectations of institutionalisation that had not yet taken place. The practical distinction commonly made between the two groups is looser and more pragmatic; it reflects the groupings of the professions for which students were to be trained. The intrinsic closeness of canon and civil law made it natural that they should be brought together; the substantial number qualifying in both laws (and the not insignificant number whose teaching crossed over between them as well) is evidence of this. The connection between medicine and 'arts' may be less obvious to those more familiar with the northern European system. It arises from the way in which the arts developed as propaedeutic to medicine in southern Europe; and these too are reflected in biographical terms, with many instances of teachers working their way up through junior teaching posts in logic or natural philosophy to the (by and large) more prestigious medical lectureships.[22] Once the structural links (dictated by the exigencies of medical training) had been established, this 'subject grouping' then served as the gateway into universities for the teaching of other 'arts' – astrology, rhetoric, poetry, ultimately 'humanitas'. As is well known, this was the least formalised end of the university syllabus, and hence the area where experimentation could most easily flourish. Crossovers between these groupings

---

[18] Above, p. 6, and DENLEY, 'Communities within Communities', pp. 723-9.

[19] Actually two, one citramontane and one ultramontane, in practice all but merged by the fifteenth century. RASHDALL thought that the universities of jurists remained theoretically distinct in the fourteenth century, albeit sharing statutes, assemblies and possibly a seal (I, p. 176); the 1252 fragment however refers unequivocally to 'universitas tam ultramontanorum quam citramontanorum' (rubrics IV and I, MAFFEI, 'Trattato', pp. 93-4), and the only vestige of duality in the 1317-47 statutes is the fact that there are two rectors, who were however empowered to act on one another's behalf (rubric 12, MALAGOLA, *Statuti,* p. 15; DENIFLE, 'Statuten', pp. 269-71).

[20] *Conc.* 419, f. 9v, 13 Jan; and see below, pp. 258 *seq.* This was also the basic division in the unsuccessful reform proposal of 1478, which sought to cap the lecture list at ten canonists, ten civilians and about twelve teachers of arts/medicine; below, pp. 130-1.

[21] Below, pp. 258-9, 267-8.

[22] Cf. MAIERÙ, 'La terminologie', in his *University Training*, pp. 74-6 on the links (as well as the differences) between arts and medicine in the Italian system.

were rare,[23] and never extended to the degree level; indeed, the validity of the groupings is reflected in the degrees it was possible to take. In Siena, students in law took degrees in canon or civil law, or both; students in arts/medicine took degrees in medicine, more rarely in arts,[24] or in both; students in theology could take a degree in theology. In Siena, right up to 1579, no evidence has come to light of any other combinations.[25] Indeed, given that the 'examining boards', the colleges of doctors, reflected the same three-fold division, it could hardly have been otherwise. These boards (of which more later) were the closest to the embodiment of that division.

The exception to all that has just been said is the third grouping, theology. This formed a faculty in the full, northern, sense of the term, and it is no accident that this is the only discipline in which the word *facultas* is used in its modern sense – as shorthand for the organisation – since it was taken from the Parisian model when theology teaching was finally incorporated into the Italian university system (via Bologna, even though it was not the earliest university to be granted the privilege).[26] The regular members of the orders who taught within the federation of religious houses were not normally paid for their labours, and the authorities made no claims on them in that capacity; like their north European counterparts, the Italian faculties of theology are to all extent and purposes self-regulating bodies.[27]

The teaching of theology in Siena followed exactly the same pattern. The Dominicans had a *studium particulare* in Siena by 1305, and taught philosophy and arts by 1311, logic by 1331.[28] The Fran-

---

[23] But see below, p. 132. This does not, of course, mean that it was impossible for students who had a previous training in arts to progress to law, as in the case of 'Magr. Ambroxius Artium doctor de Ungaria scolaris in Iure canonico', admitted to the Sapienza in 1474 (*Conc.* 647, f. 15r, 29 Jul; cf. his entry in BCS, *ms.* A.XI.12, f. 21v, new foliation; ZDEKAUER, doc. XXIII, p. 183, the location of which suggests that he may not have taken up the place until 1477).

[24] Only seven degrees in arts or philosophy are recorded in the extant documentation; MINNUCCI, 'Il conferimento', Tavola I, p. xxiii.

[25] This is in marked contrast to Pisa, where by the second half of the sixteenth century students were enrolling for a variety of narrower subjects as well as in new combinations of them; surgery, philosophy, logic, humanism, mathematics, philosophy and theology, arts and law, humanism and law, arts and mathematics, and Hebrew. C. B. SCHMITT, 'The Faculty of Arts at Pisa at the Time of Galileo', *Physis*, 14 (1972), pp. 243-72 [repr. in his *Studies in Renaissance Philosophy and Science* (London, 1981), Ch. IX], p. 252 n. 39.

[26] Cf. A. PARAVICINI BAGLIANI, 'La fondazione dello "Studium Curiae": una rilettura critica', in *Luoghi e metodi di insegnamento*, pp. 57-81, repr. in IDEM, *Medicina e scienze della natura alla corte dei Papi nel Duecento*. Centro italiano di Studi sull'alto medioevo (Spoleto, 1991), pp. 363-90, and in *Il pragmatismo degli intellettuali*, pp. 125-45 on Innocent IV's use of *facultas* for theology, never for law (for which the term *scholae* is reserved); and see G. CREMASCOLI, 'La facoltà di teologia', in *Luoghi e metodi di insegnamento*, pp. 181-200. I also elaborate on this in DENLEY, 'Medieval and Renaissance Italian Universities', pp. 169-70. For a full treatment of this matter, which has largely become an issue because of Kristeller's misunderstanding of the constitutional position of these faculties, see A. POPPI, 'Il dibattito sull'esclusione della teologia dal ruolo universitario nello Studio di Padova (1363-1806). Un aggiornamento', in IDEM, *Ricerche sulla teologia e la scienza nella scuola padovana del Cinque e Seicento*. Saggi e testi, n.s. 1 (27) (Soveria Mannelli, Catanzaro, 2001), pp. 7-22.

[27] See MAIERÙ, 'La terminologie', in his *University Teaching*, pp. 78-9 on the consequent interchangeability of the terms *facultas* and *universitas* when applied to theology. This interchangeability appears to cover the term *collegium* as well. The Bolognese institution is referred to as *collegium universitatis theologorum* (loc. cit.), while in Padua the statutes of 1406 of the 'theologice facultatis' are replaced in 1424 by those of the 'collegii theologorum universitatis paduane'; A. POPPI, *Statuti dell' "Universitas theologorum" dello Studio di Padova (1385-1784)*. Contributi per la Storia dell'Università di Padova, 36 (Treviso, 2004), pp. 12 and 19.

[28] M. D'ALATRI, 'Panorama geografico, cronologico e statistico sulla distribuzione degli *Studia* degli ordini mendicanti: Italia', in *Le Scuole degli ordini mendicanti (secoli XIII-XIV)*. Convegni del Centro di Studi sulla Spiritualità Medievale, 17 (Todi, 1978), pp. 49-72 (pp. 56-9).

ciscans[29] and Augustinians[30] had *studia generalia* in Siena in the fourteenth and fifteenth centuries. The Servites in Siena were paying teachers from outside the order at the end of the thirteenth century, though probably at a more elementary level.[31] The teaching of the Carmelites at this stage is more obscure. Gregory XII's 1408 authorisation of theology as one of the subjects to be taught and examined in the *studium generale*[32] presented the opportunity for these separate centres of teaching to be aggregated so that the members of the orders would be able to receive the doctorate. Nothing is known of how this was initially achieved, but by 1434 statutes were drawn up, from which we can see the full extent of its functions.[33] These statutes are of the *universitas theologorum*, and are clearly close in structure to the Bolognese and therefore the Parisian 'model'. All theologians over a certain level[34] were members; the university was headed by a dean, and controlled and legislated over the syllabus and the calendar, the incorporation of scholars at all levels,[35] the moral life of its members, the reverence students were to accord their superiors, and the examination process. This largely self-regulating body left very little scope for intervention by the commune. The teaching of the religious houses was a matter for the hierarchy within their own orders,[36] and the communal authorities limited themselves to supporting candidates within those hierarchies,[37] or asking that they might teach within the Sienese *Studio*.[38] There was no attempt to intervene in membership or examining matters as was the case with the colleges of doctors in law and arts/medicine.[39] The only significant area of interaction was that the authorities drew substantially on members of the religious orders as suppliers of teachers for the 'secular' *Studio*, to teach both theology (which will be discussed below) and other subjects; metaphysics and logic within the arts, but also canon law.[40]

[29] Op. cit., pp. 62, 67; C. PIANA, 'Il traduttore' (p. 150 on the uncertainty surrounding the precise date at which the Franciscan school at Siena became a *studium generale*). On the Franciscan contribution to the Sienese *Studio* see op. cit., pp. 165-75; and more generally B. ROEST, *A History of Franciscan Education (c.1210-1517)* (Leiden, 2000).

[30] D'ALATRI, 'Panorama', p. 69.

[31] Op. cit., p. 70.

[32] As n. 17 above.

[33] BCS, *ms.* A.XI.9, ed. BERTONI, 'Il "Collegio" dei teologi', pp. 36-56. Bertoni surmises that there must have been earlier statutes; the 1651 revision of the 1434 statutes, in *Sanctiones reformatae collegii theologorum senensis universitatis* (Siena, 1651), refers to 'antiquiora statuta' and to statutes promulgated by Martin V. He also deduces from the 1434 statutes themselves, particularly from the rubrics forbidding the questioning or attempted reform of them and the initial absence of full representation of all religious houses on the panel that drafted them, that the measure was only achieved after considerable conflict (pp. 5-6).

[34] At Siena, bachelors, *biblici* and incorporated students; BERTONI, 'Il "collegio" dei teologi', p. 9.

[35] From 1472 we have, in a 'libro sacrae Theologicae facultatis', the record of all incorporations made; BCS, *ms.* A.XI.1.

[36] Cf. the appointment of Fr. Bernardino of Siena to teach the Bible in 1480, in a letter written by the general of the Carmelite order on 11 May 1478 and issued on 21 May 1480; B. SZABÓ-BECHSTEIN, 'Die Sieneser Urkunden der Staatsbibliothek Preussischer Kulturbesitz Berlin (12.-18. Jh.). Die Fonds S. Leonardo al Lago, S. Salvatore di Lecceto, S. Maria del Carmine und Piccolomini', *Quellen und Forschungen aus Italienischen Archiven und Bibliotheken*, 55-6 (1976), pp. 159-99 (p. 171).

[37] E.g. *Concistoro* letters to the rector-general of the Augustinians, one asking that Matteo da Siena to a lectureship on the Sentences (*Conc.* 1639, f. 182r, 30 Nov 1432), another recommending Francesco Franci for the same post (*Conc.* 1641, f. 113v, 24 Nov 1433), a third asking him to prolong the post of Giovanni di Matteo as the whole university wanted him (*Conc.* 1648, f. 4r, 5 Jan 1438).

[38] *Conc*, 1677, f. 168r, 24 Oct 1459; the general of the Augustinians is asked to allow Gregorio da Spoleto to teach philosophy in the *Studio* (he was already teaching 'in conventu'). This may well be the teacher FIORAVANTI, 'Formazione e carriera di un domenicano', p. 357 n. 40, thought might be a mistake for Gabriele da Spoleto.

[39] See below, Chapter II.2.3.

[40] See below, pp. 134-5, and esp. n. 80.

Table 3 – Profile of the subjects taught

The entries below include details from formal *rotuli* where available, and (more frequently in the fifteenth century) lists of teachers hired where those lists are clearly intended to cover the whole payroll. Contracts that were awarded or renewed individually or in smaller batches have not been included for the purpose of this exercise. Total figures should be interpreted with caution. Where they can be compared with the number of teachers paid, this is often significantly lower (see Table 1, p. 60 above).

Year	Total	Law			Arts/Medicine					Theology	School-teachers	Reference
		Total	Canon	Civil	Total	Medicine	Philosophy, Logic	Astrology/ Astronomy/ Mathematics[1]	*Humanitas*			
1404	18	6	2	4[2]	7[3]	2	1	1	1	2	3	*Conc.* 235, ff. 46r-47v, ed. PIANIGIANI, doc. 11, pp. 32-7.
1458-9	23	12[4]	5	5	10	6	3		1	1		*Conc.* 552, ff. 16r-17r, ed. BAI, doc. 113, pp. 93-7.
1480-1	30[5]	16	9	7	15							*Balìa* 20, ff. 57r-58v
1487-8	30	17			9						4	*Conc.* 726, ff. 28v-30r, ed. FERRERI, docs. 266-270, pp. 218-22.
1488-9	42	24	9	15	18		13[6]	1	4	7		*Conc.* 730, ff. 26v-30r, ed. FERRERI, doc. 281, pp. 245-51.
1490-91	36	18	6	12	17		14	1	2		1	*Conc.* 744, ff. 9v-11r, ed. FERRERI, docs. 307-8, pp. 279-82.
1492-3	45	22	8	14	21	10	8	1	2		2	*Balìa* 37, ff. 48r-50r, ed. ZDEKAUER, doc. XXIV, pp. 191-3.
1494-5	38	15[8]	5	9	22[9]	7	5	1	2	1	2	*Conc.* 768, ff. 14r-15v, ed. FERRERI, doc. 345, pp. 326-8.
1498-9	39[10]	23			14				1			*Conc.* 791, ff. 5r-v and 9v-10r, ed. FERRERI, docs. 393-5, pp. 377-80.
1500-1	54	31	18	13	18	9	4	1	4	3	2	*Balìa* 46, ff. 111v-113v, ed. G. MONDOLFO, 'Il ruolo dello Studio Senese del 16 ott. 1500', *BSSP*, 4

1519-20	64	30	8	22	27	21		1	5		7	*Studio* 3, f. 6r-v.
1521-2	42	20	5	15	20	16		1	3		2	*Studio* 3, ff. 28v-29v.
1524-5	53[11]	22	5	17	19	16		1	2		4	*Studio* 3, ff. 33r-34v.
1531-2	54	27	6	21	22	16		1	5		5	*Conc.* 2209, no foliation, ed. KOŠUTA, 'Documenti', doc. XI-2, pp. 397-9.
1533-4	57	24	7	17	28	21		1	6		5	*Conc.* 2209, no foliation, ed. KOŠUTA, 'Documenti', doc. XI-1, pp. 399-402.
1535-6	59	25	5	20	28	22		1	5		6	*Studio* 17, ff. 16v-18r, ed. KOŠUTA, 'Documenti', doc. XI-3, pp. 402-5.
1537-8	47	18	3	15	24	12	7	1	4		5	*Studio* 21, no. 2, ed. KOŠUTA, 'Documenti', doc. XI-4, pp. 405-9.
1539-40	52	25	7	18	22	10	7	1	4		5	*Studio* 17, ff. 64r-66r, ed. KOŠUTA, 'Documenti', doc. XI-5, pp. 409-13.
1541-2	48	22	6	16	21	10	8	1	3		5	*Studio* 20, no foliation, ed. KOŠUTA, 'Documenti', doc. XI-6, pp. 413-16.
1545-6	51	28	8	20	16	8	4	1	3	2	5	*Studio* 22, no foliation.
1548-9	46										6	*Studio* 127, no foliation.

1 Until 1520, astrology; from 1521 to 1538, astronomy; from 1539, mathematics.
2 One of these was teaching 'Institutiones et notarie'.
3 Two teachers cross categories.
4 Two may teach either canon or civil law.
5 Eight teachers did not accept the *condotte* offered
6 Includes 'teologia et filosofia'.
7 Theology subsumed with philosophy.
8 In one case the subject is not stated.
9 In six cases the subject is not stated.
10 Subjects are not specified in this list. The figures have been compiled on the basis of what is known about these teachers.
11 Eight renewed; subject not stated.

3. *Policy: the profile of the* Studio

In the absence of statutes, what can we glean about the Sienese attitude to the provision of teaching in the various disciplines, and to their relative status and interrelationship? It would perhaps be a mistake to expect to find a consistent academic policy, a modern concept which implies more planning and continuity than is in evidence for much of the period. The overwhelming need was to keep the teaching going, keep up with developments elsewhere and perhaps seize opportunities to steal a march on rivals; and since so much of this was a matter of following established practices which did not require spelling out, the details of decisions made and the thinking behind them are to a large extent concealed from view.

Since there are no statutes, and few clues in the legislation, or in the decisions made, we are forced back on other indicators. The best starting-point is the listing of teachers, either when they are being hired or when they are being paid. The *rotuli* are of particularly interest, because with their formal and public functions they are intended as indicators of hierarchy and status (and the inclusion of salaries only adds to their value). They are all the more useful for this purpose because, in common with all the other Italian *studi* except Bologna (where two separate *rotuli* were published for law and arts/medicine), the *rotuli* listed all teachers in one strict hierarchy (which reflects in the first instance the notional hierarchy of disciplines).[41] Unfortunately the originals of these are also rare in Siena,[42] but there are lists in the volumes of the *Concistoro* and the *Balìa*, particularly for the late fifteenth century, which resemble them in structure and have broadly similar formal purposes (see Table 3). Where it is evident, the hierarchy is usually unambiguous. When theology features on the list, it is normally given pride of place.[43] Next come the laws; canon law first, then civil law. Within these, the key texts or types of lecture always come first, followed by the supplementary ones. Then come medicine and arts; medicine first, again with the internal hierarchy of theory first, practice next, and surgery after that. The 'arts' are less obviously hierarchical, though metaphysics and logic tend to precede poetry and rhetoric. Astrology and *notaria* tend to appear at the end of the lists, just ahead of the names of school grammar and abacus teachers.

It took time for the *Studio* to grow to the point where all these subjects were taught at a level of depth which implied stability. As has been seen,[44] for decades Siena struggled to attain just basic coverage of a range of disciplines; from the official foundation until the third decade of the fifteenth century the authorities struggled to retain a basic level of teaching that was little different to that of the century before Charles IV's charter. As the *Studio*'s fortunes finally took their irreversible turn for the better in the 1420s, with richer and more sustained provision of teaching, and a regular

---

[41] An exception to this, also copied from other places, is that for much of the fifteenth century the rector of the university was listed first. On the *apotisse* this practice endured until 1468; *Conc.* 609, f. 42v, 27 Apr, ed. BAI, doc. 276, pp. 255-6. By the sixteenth century there is another change; although the lists continue to respect the separation between law and arts/medicine, within those two the seniority and prestige of individual *sedie* is also taken into account. For example, the 1545-6 *rotolo* lists ordinary morning lectureships in canon law, then ordinary morning lectureships in civil law, then canon law *de sero*, ordinary civil law *de sero*, extraordinary civil law *de mane* and *de sero*, canon law *ad sextum*, and finally *Institutiones* (*Studio* 22, no foliation).

[42] Above, p. 110.

[43] See below, pp. 134-5. An exception is the list of 1488-9, when theology and philosophy are grouped together (see Table 3, pp. 127-8, for reference).

[44] Above, Chapter I.1.1.

flow of non-Sienese teachers and students, signs emerge of more specialisation, and the need to cover all aspects of the major disciplines taught was also made explicit. For example, the appointment of a newly-graduated teacher of *Sextus et Clementinae* in 1438 was justified on the grounds that the lack of such a teacher brought shame on the *Studio* and was a deterrent to potential students.[45] Although there were occasional previous 'policy' decisions that there should be a certain number of teaching posts,[46] the crystallisation of this in the language can only be traced as far back as the 1430s; reforms of 1437 established that 'in ciascuna sedia di qualunche facultà se metta uno doctore Ciptadino'.[47] The *sedia* is not defined in the document, and is clearly a term that was widely understood,[48] indicating a specialised category of teaching within the broad subject groupings; something quite specific within law and often medicine (e.g. indicating the actual texts taught, the status and time of the lecture), or in the case of minority and fringe disciplines simply the subject of the lecture (e.g. astrology, *notaria*). That this view of what should be taught was becoming much clearer and less flexible than before is indicated by references to *sedes vacantes* in measures of the years following this reform.[49]

The concept of a fixed minimum number of *sedie* that had to be filled, subjects that had to be covered, is a significant step. It did not, however, relate very directly to the question of the total size of the payroll. As will be seen, by the time of the 1437 legislation it was common practice to fill all but the most marginal *sedie* with more than one teacher, in response to existing demand or in anticipation of assumed demand. This left the field wide open (subject only to financial restrictions), and made it possible for the authorities to seize opportunities that arose to hire famous teachers. Of course, there was little point in having more teachers of the same subject than warranted by student demand, but the flexibility did amount to upward pressure. An unsuccessful attempt to limit the total payroll was made in 1478,[50] when a number of complaints were voiced: that the budget had been exceeded;[51] that this was to the detriment of young doctors who, denied opportunities or good

---

[45] *Conc.* 437, f. 35v, 16 Dec, ed. PIANIGIANI, doc. 194, pp. 223-5; 'quod hoc redindat in vilipendium ipsius Studij et dannum ex eo quod multi scolares venirent in ciuitate Senarum qui non veniunt'. The appointee was Malatesta de' Cattani da Burgo, rector of the Sapienza, who was about to graduate and who was to take up his appointment on 1 January on condition that he resigned the rectorate first. The need to cover basic teaching may also have been the motivation for the condition added to the contract of Luca de Callio in 1442 to teach civil law, that he should in addition to his basic contract (a *lettura universitaria* for the minimum salary of 25 florins) teach *Institutiones* without a salary (*Conc.* 459, f. 45r, 30 Aug 1442, ed. PIANIGIANI, doc. 231, pp. 261-2; a correction from the original contract, in which he was to teach civil law *extraordinarie* for 30 florins, *Conc.* 459, f. 32v, 29 Jul, ed. PIANIGIANI, doc. 230, p. 261; it is possible that they had not realised that he did not have a degree). On this individual see also below, p. 140 and n. 120.

[46] Above, Chapter I.1.2 and see n. 48 below.

[47] *CG* 219, f. 146v-147v (new foliation), ed. ZDEKAUER, doc. XVIII, pp. 169-71; *Mis.* 1, f. 83v; *Statuti* 41, ff. 255v-256r, 10 May.

[48] The first Sienese reference to *sedie* that I know of is in *CG* 207, f. 245r, 20 Dec 1416, ed. GAROSI, doc. 56, pp. 527-8: 'Quinque sedes in eo adhuc deficiant, videlicet una de iure canonico, una in practica medicine, una in cerugia, una in lectura voluminis et una in loica'. 300 florins per year could be expended on filling these vacancies.

[49] *CG* 224, ff. 68r-v, 6 Oct 1447; cf. *Conc.* 437, f. 35v, 16 Dec 1438, ed. PIANIGIANI, doc. 194, pp. 223-4, and *Conc.* 484, f. 32r, 27 Oct 1446. A parallel to this is the reform ordered by pope Nicholas V for Bologna in 1450, stipulating the number of chairs to be filled for each subject and category of lectureship; M. CAVINA, *Dottrine giuridiche e strutture sociali padane nella prima età moderna. Carolus Ruinus (1456-1530) eminentis scientia doctor* (Milan, 1988), pp. 109-112.

[50] *Conc.* 2139, no. 57, ff. 107r-108r, 24 Jan.

[51] 'Veduto quanto sia disordine venuto nelle condocte de doctori et la inobservantia della leggie di non passare el numero de denari lassato per le conducte da farsi per le ordini vostri. Et questo inobservantia per la grande multiplicatione di dottori di proximo facti' (loc. cit.).

salaries, would leave to try to establish careers elsewhere;[52] and that if the current trend continued, aside from the waste of money involved, it would be difficult to adapt the existing teaching provision.[53] The proposal to limit the payroll to ten canonists, ten civilians and twelve teachers in arts/medicine[54] was perhaps too crude – we do not know why it was rejected – but three years later a major reform was passed, in which for the first time the future profile of the *Studio* was laid down.[55] The number of lecturers was fixed at a maximum of twenty-seven: six canonists, six civilians, four doctors of medicine, four of philosophy, two of rhetoric, two of theology, one of astrology and two of logic. Yet whatever the intentions of the legislators, the size of the lecture list oscillated substantially. In terms of proportions, the profile of lectureships produces a not unconventional picture. The largest number of lectureships is consistently in civil law, but the balance between law and arts/medicine is fairly even, much as in Laurentian Pisa and Bologna (though not pre-Laurentian Florence, or Ferrara),[56] and it would seem, as far as can be judged, that these proportions are reflected in the number of students.[57]

4. *'La margarita della scientia'*[58]

The administrative records give us some limited insights into the changing nature of the disciplines, though a full picture can of course only be attained through specialist knowledge of those disciplines. The most high-profile subject, law, was also undoubtedly the chief engine of Siena's rise to fame in the first half of the fifteenth century. The presence, fleeting in some cases, more lasting in others, of eminent lawyers like Pietro Ancarano, Paolo di Castro, Raffaele Fulgosio, Onofrio Bartolini, and a few years later Niccolò Tedeschi and Benedetto Barzi, and then the growth of indigenous talent such as Tommaso Docci, Mariano Sozzini, Pietro de' Pecci, and Battista Bellanti, all ensured that Siena's legal training was of comparable standards to that elsewhere. The highly structured nature of the law course is perhaps the reason why so little detail survives in communal records; surviving evidence, for example, of the urgency in 1438 of filling a gap in the provision by hiring a teacher of *Liber Sextus* and

---

[52] '...li denari del comuno non sonno utilmente collocati, et etiam decto guadagno in consequentia nuoce a qualche doctore giovane che andando fuore et exercitandosi facilmente potarebbe e fama et robba aquistare' (loc. cit.).

[53] 'Et veduto che se ne conduca assai in magior numero la qual cosa è dannosa al comuno per li salari disutili e non necessari, et etiam fa che è impossibile adactare le cathedre per tanta multiplicatione' (loc. cit.).

[54] An insert adds one lectureship in astrology and one in *eloquentia* to the original ten (loc. cit.).

[55] *Balìa* 24, f. 90v, 30 Jun 1481, eds. PUCCINOTTI, *Storia della Medicina*, p. CLXVIII, and ILARDI, 'Ordinamenti', p. 170; copy in *Mis.* 1, f. 109v. A clause detailing the length of each lecture lists fifteen categories: *ragione canonica, ordinaria, mattina: ragione canonica, ordinaria, sera: Sesto: Clementine: ragione civile, ordinaria, mattina: ragione civile, ordinaria, sera: Istituta*, 'o altra extraordinaria': *medicina, ordinaria, mattina: medicina pratica, ordinaria, sera: logica, ordinaria*: 'qualunque altra extraordinaria': *physica: teologia: rettorica: astrologia*. Such details often do appear on *condotte*, but equally the details are often left to the *Savi*; for most of the fifteenth century, many *condotte* state simply that the specific *lettura* would be allocated by the *Savi*. For the terminology here and in what follows, see below, pp. 137 *seq.*

[56] For Florence/Pisa, cf. DAVIES, *Florence and its University*, pp. 27-8, 334, and the tables in VERDE, *Lo Studio fiorentino*, I, pp. 293-5; for Bologna, the lists in DALLARI, *I Rotuli*, I; for Ferrara, a recent work is S. CHIELLINI, 'Contributo per la storia degli insegnamenti umanistici dello studio ferrarese', in *La rinascita del sapere. Libri e maestri dello studio ferrarese*, ed. P. Castelli (Venice, 1991), pp. 210-45.

[57] Below, pp. 239 *seq.*

[58] The phrase appears in the bulls of Gregory XII, Italian translation in *Mis.* 1, f. 68r (and cf. 63r), ed. BARDUZZI, *Documenti*, p. 30, and cf. p. 24.

Clementinae, mentioned above, just confirms the pattern that is known from elsewhere.[59] When we do hear about the syllabus in any detail it is always the ancillary lectureships that require the attention of the authorities, and then mostly the *Institutiones*. Indeed, of the various supplementary texts that completed the law syllabus, this is the only one to be regularly specified.

The teaching of the notarial arts requires comment, as it was an exception to the neat separation between subject groupings to which reference was made earlier. Obviously *notaria* was closely linked with, and propaedeutic to, the study of law;[60] on the other hand it was historically also part of the constellation of the arts of writing and expression. For what it is worth, the sparse information for Siena suggests that there may have been a shift, over time, from the traditional connections of *notaria* with arts to those with law. In the fourteenth century we find rhetoric and *notaria* being taught by the same person,[61] while by the early fifteenth century the pairing of *notaria* with the *Institutiones* is evident.[62] What does not seem to have changed is the relatively humble status of the subject; despite its connection with law and the likely source of demand for it, the lectureship in *notaria* was always placed towards the bottom of the hierarchy.[63]

Medical teaching in Siena developed, as in most *studi*, somewhat in the shadow of law. It was not that Siena lacked famous doctors, from Pietro Ispano, later pope John XXI, in the thirteenth century, through the brief sojourns of Dino del Garbo and Gentile da Foligno during the Bolognese diaspora, to Pietro Lapini, Bartolo di Tura and later Alessandro Sermoneta in the fifteenth century – though the most distinguished Sienese medical authority of all, Ugo Benzi, made his career chiefly away from his birthplace.[64] However, there is no doubt that in number, status and salary, as well as fame, these appointments mostly took second place to law. Contracts for teachers of medicine accompanied those for lawyers in most years in which the *Studio* functioned up to the early fifteenth century. But in years of dearth it is unsurprising to find people being hired to act as doctors, treating the sick, as well as teaching.[65] In one late fourteenth-century case citizens petitioned for a town surgeon to be hired, with the condition that he would be required to teach if six students wished to attend his lectures.[66] This kind of dual contract persists occasionally throughout the fifteenth centu-

---

[59] Above, p. 130 and n. 45.

[60] The *notaria* teaching of Pietro di Antonio Bonazini in 1406 was to be timetabled on days when there were no lectures in civil law, a decision which must reflect the requirements of the students or at least what was intended for them (*Conc.* 244, f. 37r, 30 Oct, ed. PIANIGIANI, doc. 13, p. 38).

[61] In 1359 a teacher of *notaria* and rhetoric was hired (*CG* 163, f. 24r-v, 27 Sept).

[62] *CG* 206, f. 93r, 13 Oct 1413 (two unnamed doctors are to be hired 'ad notariam et institutum'); *Conc.* 367, f. 16v, 28 Mar 1427, ed. PIANIGIANI, doc. 79, pp. 99-100 ('Dominum Pietrum ser Antonii [= Bonazini] ad Institutiones et notariam'). A similar change is evident in Bologna, where *notaria* was listed among *artisti* from the early fourteenth century till 1457 and among *legisti* thereafter (DALLARI, *I Rotuli*, I, p. 48; cf. SORBELLI, *Storia*, p. 236). Brizzi (BRIZZI and DE BENEDICTIS, 'Le università italiane', p. 38) sees this as indicative of the impact of humanism on the organisation of teaching.

[63] Another indication of the much more humble status of the subject, at least earlier on, was that the contract of Baldaccio degli Ubaldi of Gubbio, teacher of *notaria* in 1363, despite having the title 'dominus' (usually an attribute of doctors of law), was stipulated in *lire* like those of grammar and abacus teachers (*Conc.* 26, f. 75v, 19 Jan), whilst the salaries of all the other teachers were as usual stipulated in florins (cf. f. 74r).

[64] Below, pp. 220-1. Unfortunately, despite Garosi's very full history of medicine in Siena, our understanding of actual teaching is minimal. For example, his outline of the syllabus (p. 237) is entirely derived from other *studi* and has no support from Sienese sources.

[65] Below, pp. 210-11.

[66] *Conc.* 2111, f. 124r, 16 Dec, n.d. but archived under 1396, ed. ZDEKAUER, doc. IX, p. 150, and cf. PICCINNI, 'Tra scienza ed arti', p. 146. This is an unusual reversal of the standard principle enshrining the power of boycott, namely that a teacher who failed to attract a minimum number of students to his lectures was deemed not to have taught and fined accordingly. See below, p. 158.

ry.[67] This, combined with the growing importance of surgery and its rise in status within the medical hierarchy,[68] means that we know more about pratical medicine generally than about the teaching of theoretical medicine[69] – though even here there remain many unanswered questions, for example regarding the relationship of those who taught at the *Studio* and other medical doctors in the city, and specifically the whole relationship between the *Studio* and the Hospital of S. Maria della Scala.[70]

An area of particular interest to the authorities was anatomy. The growing importance of public dissection for teaching purposes in Italian universities is well known, and reaches our records for two reasons; the ethical and the logistical. The commune had to be involved in the delicate matter of approving the dissection of individual criminals after their execution, since no teacher would dare to commit himself to this without authorisation. And since demand for this form of teaching constantly outstripped supply, the commune was inevitably drawn, in a university with weak autonomous structures, into the contentious issue of how to apportion places at these events when they took place. There are several requests, by the college of doctors or by the students, for the cadavers of condemned criminals,[71] and indications that competition among students for a place at what was after all a comparatively rare occasion was as intense as elsewhere.[72]

[67] See for example the *Savi*'s recommendation to the *Concistoro* that Jacopo di Galgano Faccalume be rehired for three years 'quanto sia utile havere qualche cerusico docto docto et experto in quella facultà sì per la lectura sì etiam per la pratica per li casi che di continuo occorrono a li vostri cittadini et maxime quando concorrisse tempo di pestilentia'. *Not.* 694, f. 13r-v, Jun-Jul 1474?, ed. MINNUCCI, 'Documenti', doc. II-42, pp. 111-12 (additional corroboration of his proposed date is *Conc.* 647, ff. 24r and 25r, 20 Aug 1474, sending 'proposita super Recordio Sapientum studii quantum ad conductum Magistri Jacobi Galgani Ser Jacobi fachalume' to the *Consiglio del Popolo*). For more examples see below, pp. 210-11.

[68] On the relationship of surgery to academic medicine, SIRAISI, *Taddeo Alderotti*, pp. 108-10, and on medicine in Italian universities generally see, still, C. B. SCHMITT, 'Thomas Linacre and Italy', in *Linacre Studies*, ed. F. Maddison (Oxford, 1977), pp. 36-75 [repr. in his *The Aristotelian Tradition and Renaissance Universities* (London, 1984), ch. XII] (pp. 55-9).

[69] In the fourteenth century it is notable that the hiring of a surgeon was given at least the same priority as that of a physician (and since the contracts often included an obligation to heal the sick it is perhaps not surprising, particularly at the low points of the *Studio*'s existence, that they adhered to this, often retaining a surgeon even when there were no resources for a physician).

[70] Below, p. 211.

[71] In 1428 the rector and other scholars requested the body of 'quidam de candia', who was due to be hanged, on behalf of the *universitas scholarium* (*Conc.* 371, f. 9v, 9 Jan; see GAROSI, p. 257). In 1446 a request was made that the body of Arigus de Bramante de Alamania be made available to the College of Medical Doctors for anatomy 'secundum statuta dicti Collegii et Studi senensis' (*Conc.* 480, f. 5v, 5 Jan 1446, ed. GAROSI, p. 257 n. 3). The body of Piero di Francesco di Tagliacozzo was given to the doctors in 1457 (*Balìa* 2, f. 127r, and *Balìa* 3, f. 128r, 11 Jan). The names of executed criminals in the opening pages of BCS, *ms.* A.IX.46, published anonymously and without reference in 'Elenco nominativo dei giustiziati in Siena dall'anno 1476 al 1491', *BSSP*, 29 (1922), pp. 100-111 (p. 100) (on the *ms.*, cf. P. TURRINI, 'Le cerimonie funebri a Siena nel basso Medio evo: norme e rituale', *BSSP*, 110 [2003], pp. 53-102 [p. 99 n. 103]), includes, in 1476, an entry for 'Giovanni Polo, parmigiano, fu impiccato adì ... per lo Magnifico Capitano di Giustizia, e fu dello suo corpo fatto per li Medici notomia'. He was the only one of the 127 criminals in the list to be described as receiving this treatment. One not in the list was 'T. de Mutina', whose body was granted in 1490, on petition of Arcangelo di Giovanni and other doctors of medicine (*Conc.* 740, f. 3r, 13 Jan, ed. GAROSI, p. 257 n. 257). Finally in the successful petition of medical students for the body of one Baccio in 1498 it emerges that statutes (which have not come to light) stipulated that a cadaver was to be granted for this purpose every three years (*Conc.* 789, f. 2v, 2 Mar). All of these requests were made in the winter months, for obvious reasons, and four of the five criminals were certainly from outside Siena (the origins of the fifth, Baccio, are not given), which is in line with regulations in Bologna and practice elswhere, and would appear to support the hypothesis of K. PARK, 'The Criminal and the Saintly Body: Autopsy and Dissection in Renaissance Italy', *Renaissance Quarterly*, 47:1 (1994), pp. 1-33, that poverty and foreign-ness rather than criminality were the main criteria for selection for dissection. On anatomy in Siena see also GAROSI, pp. 255-8, and PICCINNI, 'Tra scienza', p. 149; ZDEKAUER, pp. 83-4; C. CHŁEDOWSKI, *Siena* (Berlin, 1913), II, pp. 141-2; in Perugia ERMINI, *Storia*, I, p. 178; on Padua L. PREMUDA and G. ONGARO, 'I primordi della dissezione anatomica in Padova', *Acta medicae historiae patavina*, 12 (1965-66), pp. 117-42, and J. J. BYLEBYL, 'The School of Padua: Humanistic Medicine in the Sixteenth Century', in *Health, Medicine and Mortality in the Sixteenth Century*, ed. C. Webster (Cambridge, 1979), pp. 335-70 (pp. 354-7); and generally SIRAISI, *Taddeo Alderotti*, pp. 111-3 (esp. p. 113 on the difficulties of getting bodies and the regulations about who attended), SCHMITT, 'Thomas Linacre and Italy', pp. 64-6, and C. H. TALBOT, 'Medicine', in *Science in the Middle Ages*, ed. D. C. Lindberg (Chicago, 1978), pp. 391-428 (pp. 409-10).

[72] *Conc.* 466, f. 42r, 13 Oct 1443 (the new rector of the Sapienza was to have precedence 'in sexionibus'). The 1511

The study of medicine is inseparable from that of some of the other subjects that came under 'arts'. For the reasons described above, we are tantalisingly far from knowing (from administrative records at least) what exactly was involved in contracts to teach philosophy and logic. The interest of the authorities is in hiring the teacher, not in stipulating what exactly they were supposed to read. However it can be noted that, as elsewhere, there is considerable mobility between lectureships of medicine, philosophy and logic, a feature which only emphasises the extent to which these last two were considered ancillary and propaedeutic to the study of the first.[73] As elsewhere, there is a tendency among those who begin their careers in Siena to start by teaching logic and/or philosophy and then to move on to medicine.[74] Although Sienese administrative records give us no indication of it, the 'biological' flavour of the (mainly Aristotelian) philosophy texts prescribed in the 1405 statutes of Bologna makes it clear how this could be, and as argued above, there is no reason to imagine that Siena might have deviated from the general pattern. Indeed, there are strong reasons to assume that it did not; Grendler has pointed to the fact that the Sienese treated logic as an introductory subject only.[75]

A feature that merits attention is the important use the Sienese made of resident members of the religious orders to undertake much of this basic teaching. Alongside the young careerists, those who started teaching logic or philosophy and worked their way up to the lectureships in medicine, the payroll regularly includes representatives of this by and large more stable population which was readily available and less likely to be assertive in respect of salary demands.[76] For most of them this would have been a sideline to the subject in which they were primarily engaged, theology. As has been seen, the teaching of theology for 'professional' theologians took place within the *studi* of the orders and was entirely beyond the remit of the commune. It is thus the least visible subject from the point of view of communal records, though since the college of doctors of theology was the most developed of all, the record of its meetings are also the richest, giving frequent and detailed information about all the examinations held and the people involved – a valuable prosopographical tool.[77] But this was not the whole story; as elsewhere,[78] theology did feature on the *rotolo*, usually at its head, as in most

statutes of the college of the doctors of medicine include provisions for the arrangements at anatomy sessions, of which no more than one could take place per year without special permission (*Balìa* 253, ff. 335v-345v, 13 Oct, Rubric 20, ff. 343v-344r).

[73] C. B. SCHMITT, 'Science in the Italian Universities in the Sixteenth and Seventeenth Centuries', in *The Emergence of Science in Western Europe*, ed. M. P. Crosland (London, 1975), pp. 35-56 [repr. in his *The Aristotelian Tradition*, ch. XIV] (p. 37): 'Medicine was indeed the primary purpose for the existence of the arts faculties; logic and philosophy were mere propaedeutic studies to give students the necessary background for medical subjects'.

[74] Examples in Chapters II.1 and II.2. See also GAROSI, pp. 236-7; FIORAVANTI, 'Le "arti liberali"', pp. 256, 263-9, pointing out that the careers of Ugo Benzi, Francesco Casini, Bartolo di Tura, Alessandro Sermoneta, Bernardo Lapini and other distinguished Sienese doctors of medicine all began in this way, and that only Sermoneta left any significant philosophical writings). On the mobility of teachers in this respect, SIRAISI, *Taddeo Alderotti*, pp. 114-5 esp; cf. SCHMITT, 'Thomas Linacre and Italy', pp. 49-50, showing that the tendency at Padua was for teachers to start with philosophy and graduate to medicine.

[75] GRENDLER, *Universities of the Italian Renaissance*, p. 256. The only logician of substance to teach at Siena was Paolo da Venezia in the 1420s; op. cit., p. 250 for fuller references. On logic as preparatory to philosophy, FIORAVANTI, 'Le "arti liberali"', pp. 256, 263-9.

[76] For examples see FIORAVANTI, 'Formazione e carriera di un domenicano'; on the general point, IDEM, 'Pietro de' Rossi', pp. 139 *seq*.

[77] See p. 126 n. 35 above.

[78] C. PIANA, *La facoltà teologica dell' Università di Firenze nel Quattro e Cinquecento*. Spicilegium Bonaventurianum, 15 (1977), esp. pp. 32-3.

studi, and indeed had done so in Siena before the institution of the faculty.[79] Theology would have been of interest to students of canon law;[80] equally, its inclusion might have the moral purpose of offering the prospect of theological study of a limited nature to all students. The subject with closest affinity was of course philosophy, though without more detailed description it is difficult to know what exactly that entailed.[81] Grendler has argued that the Sienese authorities appear to have treated theology and metaphysics as interchangeable, in the fifteenth century hiring a teacher for one or the other but not both.[82]

An anomaly that was also fitted in under the umbrella of 'arts' was astrology, which appears with regularity, almost invariably in the form of just one, modestly paid, teacher of humble origins.[83] The other significant area within arts consists, of course, of those subjects which by the end of our period were coming to be known as 'humanità'. The teaching of *grammatica, eloquentia, retorica* and *poesia* appears at various stages and in varying combinations. Three well-known characteristics are found in Siena, as elsewhere. First, this is largely a separate tradition, with a separate career path, from the teaching of philosophy and logic.[84] These latter were, as has been seen, closely linked to medicine, even if some of its practitioners might venture into the disciplines of communication.[85] The teachers of the grammatical and rhetorical arts seldom had a career in one of the other university disciplines, and some, the classic type of

---

[79] *Chartularium*, doc. 337, p. 416, 24 Apr 1336.

[80] NARDI, *Mariano Sozzini*, p. 12. The Camaldolese Antonio Berti, abbot of S. Maria della Rosa, taught canon law from 1470s into the early sixteenth century; in 1495 he took a degree in theology. The *Balìa* measure granting him citizenship, incorporating him in the *monte dei Nove*, and appointing him *avvocato fiscale...in causis spiritualibus*, describes him as learned in both 'professione sacrorum canonis' and 'oratoria facultate et humanitatis studiis' (*Balìa* 18, ff. 47v-48r, 26 Jul 1480), though there is no evidence that he taught 'humanitas'. On this important figure see MINNUCCI, 'Documenti', esp. pp. 222-3. See also below, p. 140 n. 124.

[81] The Augustinian humanist Andrea Biglia, who moved to Siena in 1429 and appears to have remained there until his untimely death in 1435, was hired to teach philosophy and subsequently also theology on feast days; *Conc.* 381, f. 8r, 13 Sept 1429, ed. PIANIGIANI, doc. 115, pp. 143-4 (a one-year contract for moral and natural philosophy, at 90 florins); payment of first and third *terzarie* in *Bicch.* 310, f. 3r, 15 Jan, and 65v, 16 Nov 1430; *Conc.* 406, ff. 27v-28r, 18 Oct 1433, ed. PIANIGIANI, doc. 150, pp. 175-6 (contract for theology teaching at 30 florins in addition to his salary for the teaching of philosophy. I have not been able to find corroboration of the claim in 'Biglia, Andrea', *DBI*, 10, p. 414 that in 1430 the contract was renewed and an obligation to teach theology on feast days added); *Conc.* 412, f. 62v, 23 Oct 1434, ed. PIANIGIANI, doc. 161, pp. 187-8 (one-year contract for moral philosophy, 25 florins); *Conc.* 414, f. 26r, 12 Feb 1435 (his contract, which is for *diebus festivis*, is raised to 30 florins); *Conc.* 417, ff. 27r, 23 Aug, ed. PIANIGIANI, doc. 172, p. 198, and 30v, 29 Aug 1435 (his contract is renewed for two years). Biglia died of the plague on 27 September. He was a member of the college of theology in 1434 (BERTONI, 'Il "Collegio" dei teologi', p. 43). Cf. MARLETTA, 'Note all'Epistolario', pp. 523-5. I have found no evidence to support the assertion of FIORAVANTI, 'Le "arti liberali"', p. 261 that he taught rhetoric.

[82] GRENDLER, *Universities of the Italian Renaissance*, pp. 380-1. But in the 1420s two *religiosi* were contracted to teach theology and natural philosophy, the Franciscan Angelo Salvetti in 1420 (see below, p. 155 n. 50) and the Augustinian Gabriele da Spoleto in 1426 (*Conc.* 361, f. 20r, 30 Mar, ed. PIANIGIANI, doc. 74, p. 95, and cf. NARDI, *Mariano Sozzini*, p. 12 n. 53 for further references; also PIANA, *La facoltà teologica*, p. 33 on both cases); and in 1488 five members of religious orders are hired to teach theology and philosophy; *Conc.* 730, f. 29r, ed. FERRERI, doc. 281, pp. 245-51 (p. 249). On the relationship between teaching in *conventi* and holding public chairs in arts, see F. BUZZI, 'La teologia tra Quattro e Cinquecento. Istituzione scolastica, indirizzi e temi', *Cheiron. Materiali e strumenti di aggiornamento storiografico. Rivista semestrale del Centro di ricerche storiche e sociali Federico Odorici*, 33 (2000), pp. 17-78 (pp. 28-9).

[83] On astrology in Siena GAROSI, pp. 249-53 *seq.*; GRENDLER, *Universities of the Italian Renaissance*, p. 425, and for Italy generally see the introductory bibliography in SCHMITT, 'Faculty of Arts', p. 259 n. 81.

[84] See the recent verdicts (among many) of T. PESENTI, 'Arti e medicina: la formazione del curriculum medico', in *Luoghi e metodi di insegnamento*, pp. 155-77 (p. 176); R. BLACK, *Humanism and Education in Medieval and Renaissance Italy: Tradition and Innovation in Latin Schools from the Twelfth to the Fifteenth Century* (Cambridge, 2001), pp. 28-33; and LINES, *Aristotle's Ethics*, pp. 5-7.

[85] E.g. Bernardo Lapini, teacher of medicine and philosophy, as poet known as l'Ilicino (his family was from Montalci-

humanist, were largely dependent on teaching salaries and patronage for their livelihood. Their marginality may have made them precarious in terms of career security, and this brings us to the second feature, namely that at least some of the teaching of these subjects may have been at the more preparatory level. As in most other Italian *studi*, the commune placed the administration of grammar schools, as well as what grammar teaching there might have been in the *Studio* proper, under the control of the *Savi*. This produces a special difficulty in interpreting the evidence, as it is very often not possible to be sure at which level the teachers cited were operating.[86] This problem is compounded by continuing uncertainty about the role of grammar teaching in Italian universities – it seems to have been limited to a preparatory role for the other courses, but the small number of grammar teachers in most universities (not to mention everything that we know about student careers) makes it impossible that this was a substantial part of the course to be taken by all.[87] As well as paying and controlling both, the Sienese authorities often grouped university teachers of grammar and schoolmasters in the same category in other respects. In the 1440s a maximum of 180 florins was fixed for grammar teachers, a budget which in 1448 paid for three masters and two *repetitores*.[88] These *repetitores* feature frequently under grammar teachers;[89] they were normally paid by the teacher out of his salary, although the amount would be fixed by the *Savi* and *Concistoro* who also chose them.[90] This did not always go to plan; in 1448 the *Concistoro* resorted to refusing Porcelio's salary until he had paid his *repetitores*.[91] Porcelio, however, was probably not typical; despite an exceptional salary and several special concessions which were made to hire this celebrity, his career in Siena was short and as unsatisfactory as it was elsewhere.[92]

The marginality of these disciplines had one positive aspect (as it turned out); they were largely unregulated. This is the third feature, and meant that, in contrast to the rigid structures of the established disciplines, universities were free to experiment and innovate.[93] To a limited extent this also finds its way into communal decisions. In Siena an early example of this is the institution in 1396 of a *lectura Dantis*, with the appointment of Ser Giovanni di Buccio da Spoleto who continued to teach in Siena for half a centu-

---

no); FIORAVANTI, 'Maestri di grammatica', p. 15 of reprint in *Umanesimo a Siena*, pp. 11-27, and C. CORSO, 'L'Ilicino (Bernardo Lapini)', *BSSP*, 64 (1957), pp. 3-108.

[86] Contrast Perugia, however, where the two had grown apart by the fourteenth century; ERMINI, *Storia*, I, p. 184-5.

[87] Cf. esp. R. G. C. MERCER, *The Teaching of Gasparino Barzizza, with Special Reference to his Place in Paduan Humanism*. Modern Humanities Research Association, Texts and Dissertations, 10 (1979), pp. 11-12. SIRAISI, *Arts and Sciences*, p. 24 suggested that the status of master of grammar might have been conferred by individual masters, as in the case of rhetoric at Bologna in the 1220s. This might account for the almost total lack of surviving evidence about students taking these subjects as preliminary to arts and medicine degrees, let alone law degrees.

[88] *Conc.* 494, f. 28v, 18 Jun. The maximum was exceeded in the previous year, by Porcelio (on whom below, p. 137); *Conc.* 489, ff. 7r-v, 8 Jul, and 37r, 24 Aug 1447, ed. PIANIGIANI, doc. 274, pp. 304-6.

[89] The earliest reference that has come to light of a *repetitore* is of 1419; *Conc.* 321, f. 4v, 5 Jul 1419.

[90] *Conc.* 411, f. 17r, 13 Jul 1434, ed. PIANIGIANI, doc. 167, pp. 182-3; but see *Conc.* 465, f. 15r, 26 Jul 1443, ed. PIANIGIANI, doc. 240, p. 271, when a 'repetitor seu magr. gramatice' was paid directly by the commune. The salary here as elsewhere was 25 florins.

[91] *Conc.* 492, f. 10r, 10 Jan, ed. PIANIGIANI, doc. 281, pp. 314-5. On the role of *repetitores* cf. BELLOMO, *Saggio sull'Università*, pp. 230-1.

[92] *CG* 224, f. 30r, 14 Jun 1447; *Conc.* 489, ff. 6v, 7 Jul, 7r-v, 8 Jul, 37r, 24 Aug (ed. PIANIGIANI, doc. 274, pp. 305-6) and 40r, 28 Aug (ed. PIANIGIANI, doc. 275, pp. 306-7); *Conc.* 490, ff. 8r, 8 Sept, and 9v, 11 Sept 1447 (ed. PIANIGIANI, doc. 276, p. 307); also *Dipl., Riformagioni*, 14 Jul 1447. The series is published in MARLETTA, 'Per la biografia di Porcelio Pandoni', pp. 878-81. On Porcelio in Rome, E. LEE, *Sixtus IV and Men of Letters* (Rome, 1978), pp. 185-7, and CHAMBERS, 'Studium Urbis and the *Gabella Studii*', p. 85.

[93] Among the many to comment on this, A. BUCK, 'Die "studia humanitatis" im italienischen Humanismus', in *Humanismus im Bildungswesen des 15. und 16. Jahrhunderts*, ed. W. Reinhard. Deutsche Forschungsgemeinschaft: Mitteilung XII der Kommission für Humanismusforschung (Winheim, 1984), pp. 11-24 (p. 23).

ry.[94] The qualitative shift appears to come in the 1430s, with the four-year lectureship of Filelfo, which to the circle of his humanistic supporters in Siena must have seemed to herald a new dawn and a new direction.[95] As is well known, of course it did no such thing; after Filelfo's departure no humanist of similar stature taught at the university.[96] However his presence does appear to have left a determination that the new subjects should be represented, and so alongside the regular provision of modest teachers of grammar, we see a regular provision of at least one, and sometimes more than one, teacher of something more than that, either *oratoria* or poetry or some combination of these. Attempts to get a figure from outside Siena were infrequent and not always successful – the hiring of Porcelio was perhaps a particularly unfortunate experience – but continuity was assured by a more successful practice, the appointment of the chancellor of the republic to a lectureship.[97] A final illustration of how innovation was possible in this area is the repeated effort made in the late fifteenth century to introduce the teaching of Greek in Siena. Though the leading authority on humanism in Siena, Gianfranco Fioravanti, has stated that after Filelfo 'per tutto il '400 non sembra esserci più stato a Siena un insegnamento di greco',[98] the administrative records tell of two appointments at school level; in 1478 a Greek, Andromacus, was hired 'ad docendas latinas et grecas literas discere volentes',[99] and in 1490 Pietro da Pisa was to teach Greek to anyone who wanted it.[100]

5. *Hierarchies of teaching*

The 'hierarchy of disciplines' is a key feature. As important to our understanding of the hierarchy of, and interconnections between, disciplines is the hierarchy of posts within each discipline, through which career paths can be understood.

The most basic distinction is the classification of lectureships in the largest disciplines as ordinary or extraordinary. This is now well-covered ground, but ground which is still shrouded in uncertainties, since what we are seeing is a complex process of evolution.[101] Again, what little information there is

---

[94] *Conc.* 191, f. 6r, 4 May 1396; *Conc.* 199, f. 18v, 14 Oct 1397; ROSSI, 'La "Lectura Dantis"'. As has been seen (above, p. 52), it is likely that this was instituted in imitation of, or in competition with, Florence. It has to be said that the *lectura Dantis* did not feature in his subsequent appointments, which were for grammar, rhetoric and *auctores*. It is not impossible that this part of his teaching was included in the initial appointment because he had already lectured on the Florentine poet elsewhere (above, loc.cit.). There seems to be little subsequent interest in this chair in Siena. E. BULLETTI, 'Angelo Salvetti (c. 1350-1423) in documenti dell'Archivio di Stato di Siena', *Archivum Franciscanum Historicum*, 54 (1961), pp. 26-93 (p. 28) thought that Angelo Salvetti may have lectured on Dante in the cathedral in 1408, but did not provide documentation.

[95] DE FEO CORSO, 'Il Filelfo in Siena', esp. pp. 185-8; and cf. FIORAVANTI, 'Le "arti liberali"', pp. 260-1; IDEM, 'Maestri di grammatica', pp. 11-12.

[96] NARDI, 'Umanesimo e cultura giuridica', has pointed out that this does not fairly represent Siena's engagement with humanism, which has to be seen both through the various figures who passed through the city (and the *Studio*) and the connections and friendships of Sienese intellectuals. Further observations in P. ORVIETO, 'Siena e la Toscana', in *Letteratura italiana. Storia e geografia*, II.2 (Turin, 1987-9), pp. 203-34 (pp. 206-9).

[97] Below, pp. 215-6.

[98] FIORAVANTI, 'Le "arti liberali"', p. 261.

[99] *Conc.* 668, f. 46r, 25 Feb, ed. FERRERI, doc. 62, pp. 53-4. Records for the year, which are patchy, do not demonstrate whether he came, let alone whether he was paid.

[100] *Conc.* 744, f. 10v, 11 Oct, ed. FERRERI, doc. 307, pp. 279-81. He was also to read in the Sapienza on holidays; this is another case in which it is not clear to which level of teaching an appointment was being made.

[101] A point stressed in the useful evaluation of A. BELLONI, 'L'insegnamento giuridico nelle università italiane', in *Luoghi e metodi di insegnamento*, pp. 143-52 (p. 143). For recent work on this subject see also EADEM, *Professori giuristi a Padova*, esp. pp. 43-4, 77-9; cautiously reviewed in GIRGENSOHN, 'Per la storia dell'insegnamento giuridico'; A. MAIERÙ, 'Gli Atti

for Siena tends to confirm the views of recent scholars on the general practice, and in some respects adds to the picture.[102] The original distinction between ordinary and extraordinary chairs appears, at least in law (from which the system was copied for medicine), to have reflected the importance of the lecture within the syllabus; it bears at least some relationship, and originally perhaps a strong one, to the distinction between 'ordinary' and 'extraordinary' texts.[103] But these terms also soon acquired a number of other connotations. The first and most obvious of these relates to the extent of coverage provided. The ordinary lectures tended to constitute the meat of the course, while the extraordinary lectures in some cases supplemented them with texts of lesser importance, and in others repeated in more cursory fashion ground covered in other years of the course.[104] That the ordinary lectures in Siena were intended to be more thorough and comprehensive is also suggested by the fact that in 1481 all of them except *medicina pratica la sera* were declared to be of two hours' duration, while extraordinary lectures were all one hour.[105]

The second connotation relates to pay and status. The original distinction soon translated into the fact that ordinary lectureships tended to be better paid, or at least on a better scale, than extraordinary ones,[106] and of higher status. It was a natural consequence of the importance of the status of the appointment that ordinary lecturers tended to be more important, and better paid, than extraordinary lecturers.[107] The division was also one of rungs in the career hierarchy.[108] An ordinary lectureship was a

---

scolastici nelle Università italiane', in *Luoghi e metodi di insegnamento*, pp. 247-87; English tr. as Chapter 2 of his *University Training in Medieval Europe*, pp. 45-54; and useful remarks in F. E. ADAMI, 'L'insegnamento del diritto canonico nello Studio di Ferrara tra il XV e il XVI secolo', *Annali di storia delle università italiane*, 8 (2004), pp. 37-60 (pp. 39-43).

[102] Brief recent summaries in MINNUCCI, 'Documenti', p. 39, and FERRERI, pp. xvi-xvii; and for the later period MARRARA, *Lo Studio di Siena*, pp. 20-1 n. 47.

[103] For an elucidation of the distinction cf. the contract at Bologna for Alessandro Tartagni da Imola; 'Habeantur ideo forsan lecturae ordinarie et extraordinarie sive librorum ordinarium sive extraordinarium'; A. SABATTANI, *De vita et operibus Alexandri Tartagni de Imola*. Quaderni di Studi senesi, 27 (Milan, 1972), p. 32, quoted in A. L. TROMBETTI BUDRIESI, 'L'esame di laurea presso lo Studio bolognese. Laureati in diritto civile nel secolo XV', in *Studenti e università degli studenti dal XII al XIX secolo*, eds. G.P. Brizzi and A.I. Pini. *Studi e memorie per la storia dell'Università di Bologna*, n.s., 7 (Bologna, 1988), pp. 137-91 (p. 159 n. 62). Cf. also the 1480 and 1483 *rotuli* for Pavia which include appointments 'ad lecturam extraordinariam ordinariorum iuris civilis de mane', i.e. extraordinary lectures on 'ordinary' material (VERDE, *Lo Studio fiorentino*, I, pp. 385 and 389). A similar distinction also appears in Siena in 1426 (*Conc.* 361, f. 18r, 25 Mar) and 1427 ('extraordinarias ordinariorum'; *Conc.* 2196, no foliation, n.d.). Both texts classified as ordinary and those designated extraordinary could be central to the syllabus, and at least one of the extraordinary civil law texts, the *Institutiones*, was considered basic to the subject (BELLONI, 'L'insegnamento giuridico', pp. 147-9). But the closeness of the two concepts is still reflected in sixteenth-century Padua, where it was stipulated that students of arts and medicine had to have heard all the ordinary lectures before taking a degree (SCHMITT, 'Thomas Linacre and Italy', p. 46).

[104] BELLOMO, *Saggio sull'Università*, pp. 203-5. Cf. also the 1405 Bolognese statutes of Medicine and Arts, Rubric 78, ed. MALAGOLA, *Statuti*, pp. 274-7. Both VON SAVIGNY, *Geschichte*, III, p. 250 and RASHDALL, I, p. 206 argued the now outdated view that while the division of texts between ordinary and extraordinary lectureships is related to their importance in the syllabus in the case of civil law, in canon law this was quite arbitrary, which they adduced as evidence that subject-matter was not initially the main criterion for the distinction. This was certainly not the case in either Bologna or Padua by the fifteenth century; BELLONI, *Professori giuristi a Padova*, pp. 43-4.

[105] *Balìa* 24, f. 89r, 30 Jun, eds. PUCCINOTTI, *Storia della Medicina*, p. CLXIV, and ILARDI, 'Ordinamenti', p. 167; copy in *Mis.* 1, f. 107v. There is also an ordinary lectureship in logic. Rhetoric, however, is not defined as ordinary or extraordinary, but is of two hours' duration as well. Cf. VON SAVIGNY, loc. cit.

[106] Below, Chapter II.2.1.

[107] It now seems probable that salaries, when introduced, were first given to ordinary rather than extraordinary lecturers; BELLOMO, *Saggio sull'Università*, p. 162.

[108] Famously, in fifteenth-century Bologna the ordinary chairs of law were reserved to members of the College of Doctors (see esp. BRAMBILLA, 'Genealogie del sapere'). In the 1405 statutes of Arts and Medicine at Bologna only doctors who were *conventuati* could hold ordinary lectureships (rubric 42, ed. MALAGOLA, *Statuti*, p. 254); in Padua, for ordinary lectureships in medicine, three years' experience or the holding of a similar position elsewhere was required. SIRAISI, *Arts and*

sign of having arrived academically; unsurprisingly teachers who reached this level tended to stay longer in post than those who held extraordinary lectureships, who in many cases can be assumed to be hopeful of promotion.[109] As a general trend this can broadly be said to be true for Siena, though there are some exceptions. Although experience was certainly required for the best-paid ordinary posts, extraordinary lectureships might also be held by senior as well as junior men,[110] and in view of the lighter work-load involved they might hold attractions for those with other responsibilities or nearing retirement.[111] What is clear is that in Siena the distinction was to be translated into an altogether harsher economic fact; ordinary lectureships were to be filled first, so that if money should run out these lectures would not be affected.[112]

What the ordinary/extraordinary distinction did not refer to was the time of the lecture. An earlier pattern of ordinary lectures in the morning and extraordinary lectures in the evening[113] seems to have been on the way out by or during the course of the fifteenth century.[114] Siena had both types of lecture in both morning and evening;[115] the only distinctive feature is that theoretical medicine was taught in the mornings and practical medicine in the evenings.[116] Teaching was in fact spread fairly evenly over both morning and evening; the hours stipulated in 1545 include three in the morning ('ore I-III') and four in the evening ('ore XIX-XXII').[117] Far from retaining a natural focus on ordinary morning lectures, Siena participated in a trend in the opposite direction. Intervening in a dispute between two teachers at the newly reopened university at Pisa in 1474, Rodolfo Baglioni wrote to Lorenzo de' Medici that in the *Studi* of Bologna and Siena 'la lectione della sera forse è reputata la prima, actento che li più valenti doctori leggono la sera';[118] and there is further anecdotal evidence to support this perception.[119] There were finer gradations too, with, for example, lecture times of greater or lesser prestige.

Sciences, p. 30; C. B. SCHMITT, 'The University of Pisa in the Renaissance', *History of Education*, 3 (1974), pp. 3-17 [repr. in his *Reappraisals in Renaissance Thought* (London, 1989), Ch. IX], p. 7; BYLEBYL, 'The School of Padua', pp. 343-4, 353.

[109] In Padua, 'core' ordinary teachers tended to have longer careers at the *Studio*; BELLONI, 'L'insegnamento giuridico', p. 152. The same appears broadly true at Siena, though no statistical analysis has been performed.

[110] This was admitted by VON SAVIGNY, *Geschichte*, III, pp. 247-8.

[111] Below, pp. 140 and 167-8.

[112] *Balìa* 24, f. 90v, 30 Jun 1481 (and as n. 105 above for full references); and see below, p. 172 n. 221.

[113] It used to be thought, and may well have been true in the case of early Bologna, that this was the principal distinction between ordinary and extraordinary lectures. VON SAVIGNY, *Geschichte des Römischen Rechts*, III, pp. 243-50; cf. SCHMITT, 'The Faculty of Arts at Pisa', p. 252 n. 42. For a full overview of the problem, RASHDALL, I, pp. 205-7; DALLARI, *I Rotuli*, II, pp. VI-VII; A. SORBELLI, *Storia dell'Università di Bologna* (Bologna, 1940), I, pp. 86-7.

[114] In Padua it is still evident in the early fifteenth century but has more or less disappeared by the sixteenth; BELLONI, *Professori giuristi a Padova*, pp. 77-9. At Bologna, on the other hand, there were several exceptions to this division by the mid-fifteenth century, while in late fifteenth-century Florence/Pisa it is as hard to detect as it is in Siena.

[115] ZDEKAUER, p. 109, is incorrect in holding to the traditional view.

[116] *Studio* 22, *Rotolo* of 1545-6, no foliation; GAROSI, docs. 110-1, pp. 553-4 (1550-1).

[117] *Studio* 22, loc. cit. These hours refer to the beginning of lectures. If some lasted for two hours the timetable might indeed have covered more hours of the day. On the practice of time-keeping in Siena, N. BARBIERI, 'Note di cronologia: le ore a Siena dal XIV al XVIII secolo', *BSSP*, 90 (1983), pp. 148-51; for the fuller Italian context, P. DOMINICI, 'La misura del tempo. Storia delle ore del giorno in Italia: dalle horae temporariae romane alle ore attuali di tempo universale coordinato', *Sapere*, 51:12 (Dec 1985), pp. 29-39; and on time-keeping and education more generally, G. DOHRN-VAN ROSSUM, *History of the Hour. Clocks and Modern Temporal Orders* (tr. Chicago, Il., 1996), esp. pp. 251-60.

[118] Publ. in A. FABRONI, *Laurentii Medicis magnifici vita* (Pisa, 1784), II, pp. 83-5. One of the teachers was the celebrated Sienese jurist Bartolomeo Sozzini.

[119] BARGAGLI, *Bartolomeo Sozzini*, p. 63 n. 41. The trend was eventually followed at Padua too; BELLONI, *Professori giurist a Padovai*, pp. 88-104 (she cautiously observes, p. 79, that, as at Bologna in the early sixteenth century, 'la cattedra mattutina cedette lentamente il primato a quella pomeridiana').

This is illustrated by a letter of 1441 by Guidantonio da Montefeltro, the Count of Urbino, asking that the young doctorand Luca de Callio be given a lectureship either immediately after the main morning ordinary lectures or immediately before the main afternoon ordinary lectures.[120]

As elsewhere, a third type of lecture was that given on feastdays (i.e. at least once a week).[121] This was usually the type allocated to peripheral subjects such as surgery[122] and astrology,[123] but such posts could also be allocated in combination with a regular lectureship,[124] or used to accommodate the wishes of senior or older teachers of mainstream legal and medical subjects who wished to do less teaching, but who the authorities decided were nonetheless a valuable asset (a sort of pre-retirement arrangement).[125] Individual exceptions aside, in terms of status these lectureships were the lowest in the pecking order, apart from student lectureships, to which we will return.[126]

The categories of teaching post, the hierarchy within them and the hierarchy of disciplines are still not the whole story. A feature of late medieval Italian universities is the system of competition within these categories. A sizeable *studio* would need more than one teacher in at least the major *sedie* if it was to satisfy student demand. The authorities and paymasters, however, chose to highlight the fact that such teachers were in competition by insisting that the teachers in the same *sedia* taught *in concurrentia*, meaning that they were timetabled against each other, obliged to give identical lectures at the same time. Concurrence was initially a matter of appointing pairs, though major *sedie* could have three, four or even more teachers allocated, in a strict order of seniority which was reflected in the salaries of the appointees.[127] Where the syllabus allowed any choice, the decision of what to teach was

---

[120] *Conc.* 1949, no. 96, 24 Dec; if this is the same Luca de Chalgli who took his degree in December 1443 (NARDI, 'Una fonte inedita delle lauree senesi'; and see above, p. 130 n. 45, and below, pp. 177 n. 265 and 188), the request was somewhat premature. Cf. DAVIES, *Florence and its University*, pp. 32-3 for parallels in Florence, and BELLONI, *Professori giuristi a Padova*, pp. 74-6 for a detailed illustration of the timetable at Padua. The appointment of students close to graduation – especially rectors or vice-rectors – to extraordinary lectureships is not unusual; below, p. 262 n. 115, and cf. DAVIES, loc. cit., and BELLONI, op. cit., pp. 57-8 (edition of the relevant rubric of the Paduan law statutes of 1445/63).

[121] Above, p. 113.

[122] GAROSI, docs. 110-1, pp. 553-5 (1550-1). This is standard practice elsewhere too. Cf. Perugia; ERMINI, *Storia*, I, pp. 167-8.

[123] The 1481 reform (as p. 138 n. 105). In the sixteenth century it was felt that lectures on feast days had got out of hand; there was a call in 1532 for the abolition of all of them (described as 'inutili') apart from that of Filippo Decio (*Conc.* 2007, no foliation, n.d., ed. KOŠUTA, doc. I-3, pp. 334-5), and a reform was passed the following year to restrict lecturing on these days to theology; *CG* 243, f. 248r-250v, 28 Dec 1533, ed. KOŠUTA, doc. I-6, pp. 338-41 (p. 240). The theologian was, however, to have a concurrent.

[124] Examples include Andrea Biglia, hired to teach moral philosophy and subsequently theology on feast days as well (above, p. 135 n. 81); Mariano Sozzini, hired to teach *Decretum* on feastdays and *Liber sextus et clementinae* on ordinary days (*Conc.* 369, f. 16r, 27 Sept 1427, eds. NARDI, *Mariano Sozzini*, Doc. 3, pp. 115-6, and PIANIGIANI, doc. 80, pp. 100-2); and Antonio Berti, hired on 15 Jul 1474 to an ordinary chair plus a lectureship on *Decretum* on feastdays (*Conc.* 647, f. 9r). There is also the enigmatic wording of the appointment of Giovanni da San Gimignano, a canon lawyer, 'ad lecturam extraordinariam diebus festis et aliis extraordinariis' (*Conc.* 565, f. 46r, 30 Dec 1460, ed. BAI, doc. 161, p. 134).

[125] Below, pp. 167-8 and 185 n. 22.

[126] Below, pp. 282-5.

[127] Cf. the 1389 statutes of Perugia, which show the pairing to be optional according to the wishes of scholars: 'In iure civili eligi debeant duo doctores ad ordinaria concurrentes, et concurrere ambo simul de mane, seu alter eorum de mane, et alter de sero secundum voluntatem et electionem scolarium… Alij duo eligi debeant in iure civili similiter ad extraordinaria concurrentes modo et ordine antedicto... In medicinalibus vero eligantur et eligi debeant duo doctores medici concurrentes ad lecturam physice...' etc. (ROSSI, 'Documenti per la storia dell' Università di Perugia', doc. 242; cf. ERMINI, *Storia*, I, p. 48). BELLONI, *Professori giuristi a Padova*, pp. 33, 80-7, emphasises that at Padua a pairing was envisaged, although the late fifteenth century saw the emergence of 'tertii loci', 'letture di infimo grado riservate ai cittadini padovani, soprattuto ai giovani che dovevano apprendere ad insegnare' (p. 84).

taken by the senior and highest paid teacher, and the others had to take the same texts. These academic beauty contests – which have been hailed by a recent scholar as more efficient and just than certain present-day practices[128] – were certainly in evidence in Siena by the 1420s.[129] Though the early examples we have do not suggest that there was a limit to the number of concurrents,[130] in 1433 two was stipulated as a maximum.[131] That appears to have remained the norm for the rest of the century,[132] though it clearly was no longer the case in the mid-sixteenth century.[133]

[128] GIRGENSOHN, 'Per la storia dell'insegnamento giuridico', p. 312.

[129] In 1424 Leonardo Roselli da Arezzo was contracted to teach medicine *in nonis* in concurrence with Girolamo da San Miniato (*Conc.* 349, f. 14r, 24 Mar 1424, ed. PIANIGIANI, doc. 64, pp. 84-6; and cf. GAROSI, p. 233); and cf. n. 130 below.

[130] The allocation of lectureships was often left to the *Savi* (e.g. *Conc.* 730, ff. 26r-30r [27r], 9 Jun 1488, ed. FERRERI, doc. 281, pp. 245-51: 'da deputarsi et ordinarsi le concurrenti et sedie...per li spectabili Savi de lo Studio'), who had control of the details of timetabling, and this means that before the beginning of the series of their *deliberazioni* in 1473 we know relatively little about this process, except for those occasions when they are referred up (or claimed by higher authority) because of disputes or the status of the individuals concerned. However, the arrangements arrived at shortly before the beginning of the academic year in 1427 are a good illustration of the mechanisms and factors involved. It is complex, but can be traced because of the fortuitous survival of records of two separate stages in the process. On 27 Sept, six Sienese doctors of civil law were hired (*Conc.* 369, f. 16r, ed. PIANIGIANI, doc. 80, pp. 100-2). Although the *Savi* were, unusually, given the responsibility of deciding on their salaries (with the proviso that none was to exceed 30 florins), comparison of the record of the following day (f. 17r, ed. PIANIGIANI, doc. 81, pp. 102-3) with a rougher but more detailed note (*Conc.* 2186, no foliation, n.d.; misfiled with records of 1476) shows that the allocation of lectureships was made jointly by the *Concistoro* and the *Savi*. First, all six names were scrutinised and the two receiving the largest number of votes, Bartolomeo Borghesi and Giovanni di Urbano Giovanelli, were appointed concurrents to one of the *Studio*'s star lecturers, Benedetto Barzi da Perugia, in an evening lectureship. The remaining four were then scrutinised again, and Jacopo di Nanni di Jacopo di Griffolo was chosen unanimously as concurrent to the rector of the Sapienza, Filippo da Lucca. The last three names were scrutinised for a third time, the two most popular candidates, Battista Bellanti and Tommaso Docci, being appointed to an extraordinary morning lectureship to be given after the ordinary morning one, and finally the lecturer least voted for throughout, Antonio di Lorenzo Lanti, receiving the lectureship in 'volumen at institutiones'. This appeared to settle the matter, but a few days later the whole issue was back in the *Concistoro*. It appears that Barzi was not satisfied with the arrangements, since on 2 Oct he was allowed to choose a third concurrent, alongside the two already appointed, from the next two in the voting order; he chose Docci, and Bellanti was then assigned as concurrent for the ordinary morning lectureship held by Sallustio da Perugia and Pietro de' Pecci (*Conc.* 369, f. 18v, 2 Oct 1427, ed. PIANIGIANI, doc. 82, pp. 103-5). These were not the only instances of concurrence that year; at the same time Roberto Cavalcanti of Florence, the rector of the *Studio* (cf. *Conc.* 367, f. 5r, 7 Mar, and *Conc.* 368, f. 16v, 31 Jul 1427), was appointed concurrent to Mariano Sozzini in the lectureship of *Liber Sextus* and *Clementinae* (*Conc.* 369, f. 16r, eds. NARDI, *Mariano Sozzini*, Doc. 3, pp. 115-6, and PIANIGIANI, doc. 80, pp. 100-2).

A further instance of the hierarchical aspect of concurrence is the juggling of positions that occurred among the lawyers in 1498. Alessandro Petrucci, Matteo Ugurgieri and Girolamo Sergardi were to teach *ordinarie* in the evening, and Simone Borghesi was to do the same in the morning. However, if Francesco Borghesi was reading in the evening slot for at least half a *terzaria*, Sergardi was to be moved to the morning to make way. *Sale* 24, f. 162r, 5 Jan.

[131] *Conc.* 406, f. 22r, 9 Oct.

[132] E.g. legislation of 1479 stipulated that the names of four doctors were to be put forward 'pro qualibet facultate'; the two with the most votes were to be hired to teach in concurrence (*Conc.* 678, ff. 22v-23r, 24 Oct, ed. FERRERI, doc. 90, pp. 76-7). In the detailed reforms of 1481, concurrence is recognised as a desirable principle which should be implemented wherever possible ('In ciascheduna sedia ordinaria sia concurrentia, et quando ci sieno tanti Doctori che sieno conducti che si possi dare concurrentia, et alli extraordinari anco in quello sia concurrentia'), but the numbers fixed per subject make it clear that only two concurrents per *sedia* are envisaged (*Balìa* 24, f. 89v, 30 Jun, eds. PUCCINOTTI, *Storia della Medicina*, p. CLXVI, and ILARDI, 'Ordinamenti', p. 168; copy in *Mis.* 1, f. 108r).

[133] Cf. the *rotoli* of 1537-8, 1539-40, and 1541-2, eds. KOŠUTA, 'Documenti', docs. XI-4 to XI-6, pp. 405-16 (in which up to seven teachers are found in concurrence); and that of 1545-6 (*Studio* 22, *Rotolo*, no foliation), in which it is stipulated that in each category the first lecturer on the list was to decide on the subject-matter (which he was to announce by 8 October on pain of a 20-florin fine) and his concurrents had to adopt his choice. In the late sixteenth century two months' notice was required in order to give *concorrenti* and also students time to prepare (PRUNAI, III, p. 107).

Fig. 7 – A university lecture. Sienese miniaturist, mid-fifteenth century (BCS, *ms.* F.III.8, f. 1r).

Concurrence appears to have been popular with students, and was certainly seen as such by the authorities. In 1454 the *Savi*, proposing additional appointments in civil law, argued that 'altrimenti la facultà di ragion civile arebbe troppo gran mancamento in modo che li scolari che ci sono non avendo concurrentia non si fermarebbero'.[134] Performance in these competitive stakes would influence the prospects of a renewal of one's contract, one's salary, and one's reputation;[135] and in the context of the stipulation that teachers had to have a minimum of five students,[136] could have more immediate consequences as well. The late Agostino Sottili described the concurrence system as 'strumento indispensabile per garantire un buon livello didattico' and 'uno dei cardini su cui si basavano i rapporti didattici tra professori e studenti'.[137] It was certainly not to the taste of all teachers. While they had to play the game, and some demonstrated great adeptness at it, negotiating for a higher rank in the pecking order, trying to stipulate who their concurrent(s) would be,[138] or trying to gain exemption from concurrence,[139] others were clearly disillusioned. In his unusual autobiography the Sienese Dominican Si-

---

[134] *Conc.* 2138, no. 29, f. 44r, 24 Oct.

[135] An illustration of its function is the appointment in 1474 (*Studio* 2, f. 13v, 14 Mar, ed. BAI, Appendix, doc. 13, p. 386) of Bernardino Luti to teach *Institutiones* in the Sapienza, 'ora decimanona', without salary but in concurrence to three teachers, Antonio di Bastiano (Tinellocci), Bartolomeo di Tofo Sansedoni and Alessandro de' Tommasi, who undoubtedly were being paid (*Conc.* 645, ff. 32v-33r, 13 Apr 1474, ed. BAI, doc. 351, pp. 346-8).

[136] This applied to all contracts, but was also explicitly incorporated in the measure of 27 Sept 1427 described above (n. 124). On this condition, its origins and application at Siena see below, p. 158.

[137] A. SOTTILI, '*Aemulatio*: la concorrenza tra i professori all'Università di Pavia nel Quattrocento', in '*Parlar l'idiom soave*'. *Studi di filologia, letteratura e storia della lingua offerti a Gianni A. Papini*, ed. M. M. Pedroni (Novara, 2003), pp. 107-19 (pp. 115, 117).

[138] See above, n. 130.

[139] In 1497 Piermarino da Foligno, hired to teach in the mornings, was told he must not teach the same subject that Angelo Fondi taught in the evening (*Sale* 24, f. 153v, 20 Feb). Since both were teachers of oratory, a subject for which there was normally no fixed syllabus, this is presumably an attempt to enhance variety more than a matter of personal standing. For further examples of the complex competitive instincts and the managerial issues involved in the concurrence system see the documents in VERDE, *Lo Studio fiorentino*, IV, pp. 31-3, 143, 261, 410, 430, 818, 863-4, 874, 1103.

mone Bocci, describing his brief teaching career at the Sienese *Studio*, lamented that teachers sometimes had to resort to bribery, lending books and taking students out to dinner to maintain good relations, and those who did this eagerly suborned students away from those who refused to engage in
this humiliating practice.[140]

Closely related to the principle of concurrence was the authorities' interest in ensuring that teachers held public disputations. Disputation had always occupied a key place in the structures of university teaching.[141] The Italian system had for some time made salaried lectureships conditional on an obligation on each teacher to hold a disputation, usually once a year, at which concurrents, other colleagues and students could question them.[142] Such academic exercises – often called *palæstrae* – were
not always as appreciated by the teachers as by the students, and the fact that those who had taught
for a long period (varying between twenty and twenty-five years) were granted an exemption from this
indicates that it was considered an unwelcome obligation.[143] In Siena the interest of the authorities in
this practice is long-standing,[144] but is evident above all from the mid-1470s. On 17 June 1474 the
Concistoro resolved that each doctor was to conduct a public disputation once a year.[145] A detailed
schedule was drawn up giving the sequence of all those who were to perform; three names a month
from November through to June.[146] The following summer those who had failed to dispute were not

---

[140] FIORAVANTI, 'Formazione e carriera di un domenicano', pp. 357-8 (and above, p. 122 n. 7). Simone cites the case of
Battista da Fabriano who he says was short of the minimum number of pupils on several occasions because of such behaviour by rival teachers.

[141] And of course of medieval culture more broadly. 'La *disputatio* è infatti un elemento fondamentale della vita culturale
delle città italiane del XV secolo: si disputa in pubblico, in chiesa e in piazza, e sono dispute collegate alla vita universitaria,
ma anche alla predicazione…' (FIORAVANTI, op. cit., pp. 348-9). Of the rich and extensive literature see particularly M.
BELLOMO (ed.), *Die Kunst der Disputation. Probleme der Rechtsauslegung und Rechtsverwendung im 13. und 14. Jahrhundert*.
Schriften des Historischen Kollegs, 38 (Munich 1997); M. BELLOMO, *I fatti e il diritto. Tra le certezze e i dubbi dei giuristi
medievali (secoli XIII-XIV)*. I libri di Erice, 27 (Rome, 2000), esp. chs. 5-8, 12; O. WEIJERS, *La "disputatio" dans les Facultés
des arts au Moyen Age* (Turnhout, 2002). For a survey of exceptional breadth see K. CHANG, 'From Oral Disputation to
Written Text: the Transformation of the Dissertation in Early Modern Europe', *History of Universities*, 19/2 (2004), pp.
129-87 (pp. 129-45). In the Sienese administrative records there are few references to disputation as a teaching tool; an exception is the contract of Oliverius Pisanelli (arts and medicine) which included the condition 'che sia obligato fare o far
fare a suoi scolari ogni due mesi una disputa pubblica a la Costarella o vero a' cartari come si costuma'. *Conc.* 744, f. 10r, 11
Oct 1490, ed. FERRERI, doc. 307, pp. 279-81 (p. 280).

[142] This appears in the 1432 statutes of the university of jurists of Bologna, which are known to reflect earlier practice
(rubrics 45-46 in the edition of MALAGOLA, *Statuti*, pp. 107-9. The tradition goes back to the twelfth century but was formalised in the wake of the introduction of salaried lectureships; BELLOMO, *Saggio sull'Università*, p. 232). The practice is also evident in Padua, in the jurist statutes of 1331 (DENIFLE, 'Die Statuten der Juristen-Universität Padua', pp. 475-6) and
1445/63 (BELLONI, *Professori Giuristi a Padova*, pp. 58-60); in the 1387/8 statutes of Florence (GHERARDI, *Statuti*, rubr. 53,
p. 67); and in the 1457 law statutes of Perugia (ERMINI, *Storia*, I, pp. 453-5). MAIERÙ, *University Training*, pp. 62-5 is a
useful overview, completed by IDEM, 'Ancora sugli atti scolastici nelle università italiane', in *Studi sulle società e le culture del
Medioevo per Girolamo Arnaldi*, eds. L. Gatto and P. Supino Martini (Florence, 2002), pp. 307-26 (pp. 313-20).

[143] The Bolognese law statutes of 1432 exempted those who had taught for twenty-four years (MALAGOLA, *Statuti*, Book
2, Rubr. 114, p. 148). The legal right of exemption was stressed, unsurprisingly, by the lawyers themselves; S. DI NOTO
MARRELLA, *Doctores. Contributo alla storia degli intellettuali nella dottrina del diritto comune*, 2 vols. Pubblicazioni della Facoltà di Giurisprudenza, Università degli Studi di Parma, n.s. 18-19 (Padua, 1994).

[144] E.g. the order that all teachers perform them in *Conc.* 490, f. 22v, 3 Oct 1447, ed. PIANIGIANI, doc. 277, pp. 308-11.

[145] *Conc.* 646, ff. 38v-39r, ed. BAI, doc. 349, pp. 352-3.

[146] *Not.* 694, f. 21r, n.d., ed. MINNUCCI, 'Documenti', doc. II-47, pp. 117-8. Minnucci suggested that this had to be
from the period 1471 to 1474 since it includes the name of Bernardo Lapini, who is known to have taught at Siena in that
period. He thought 1472 most likely since all the teachers listed appear in the 1472 *rotolo*. In fact they do not; Placido
di Aldello de' Placidi, Cristoforo di Domenico, and Giovanni di Antonio do not seem to have taught that year. Comparison
with the *apotisse* given in the *Concistoro*'s records for the period suggests that the schedule was for the academic year 1474-5.

paid.[147] The same obligation was placed on new teachers as and when they were hired,[148] though by 1476 some leniency had crept into the system.[149] At the same time, though, a more demanding form of disputation was being introduced. The 1460s and 1470s saw the rise of a new version of these exercises, with a somewhat more ambiguous purpose than the strictly pedagogical; public disputation in *circuli* or circular format. The first known reference to this new practice is in the statutes of the university of arts and medicine in Padua, dated around 1465.[150] The *circuli* appear to have spread rapidly in the mid-1470s. In Bologna they were made a condition of appointments in the *rotoli* of 1474;[151] Florence made them a requirement for the teachers at Pisa in 1476[152] (and drew some opposition from one of the leading lawyers teaching there, Felino Sandei, who claimed that the practice was unknown elsewhere).[153] Siena also saw the appearance of this new phenomenon in 1476, when the *Savi* decided that all doctors were to appear in the Piazza del Campo immediately after their official lectures, in full academic dress, there to hold disputations for half an hour.[154] In 1481 more detailed pro-

Five teachers on the list, Francesco da Vergelle, Giacomo Aretino, Girolamo del Maretta, Girolamo Piccolomini and Mag. Prospero, appear only from 1474-5 (*Conc.* 649, ff. 31v-32r, ed. BAI, doc. 358, pp. 358-60). It is true that two, Bernardo Lapini and Niccolò di Lazaro, were no longer teaching, but they had taught the previous year (*Conc.* 645, f. 26r-v, ed. BAI, doc. 354, pp. 350-1), and may well feature on the list in the expectation that they would continue. A similar advance calendar of disputations survives for 1477 in the records of the deliberations of the *Savi*; *Studio* 2, f. 58v, 16 Jun 1477, in which the schedule is fixed up to the following May.

[147] *Conc.* 653, f. 45r, 29 Aug 1475, ed BAI, doc. 363, pp. 366-8. They were eventually paid with the next batch once they had fulfilled their obligations; *Conc.* 655, f. 40r, 24 Dec 1475, ed. BAI, doc. 368, p. 373, giving 16 Nov.

[148] *Conc.* 655, f. 13r, 16 Nov 1475, ed. BAI, doc. 366, pp. 370-1; Felice da Pieve di Cadore hired to teach medicine 'cum hac conditione: quod in tempore dicte sue conducte debeat facere unam disputationem publicam'. A note of the *Savi* to their successors, recommending that all new contracts include this condition, which was 'cosa molto laudabile et utile a li scolari', is unfortunately not precisely dateable, though it is found in a collection of documents relating to the mid-1470s. The note acknowledges that it might be difficult for medical doctors who also practice to fulfil this obligation, and recommends that they are excused (*Not.* 694, f. 4r, ed. MINNUCCI, 'Documenti', doc. II-35, pp. 101-2).

[149] E.g. the *Concistoro*'s decision that Lodovico da Spoleto was to be paid despite not having disputed (*Conc.* 657, f. 15v, 18 Mar 1476, ed. FERRERI, doc. 5, p. 4); and their ruling later that year that, since the *Savi* had not assigned deadlines for disputations that year, 'iudicando non esse utiles', doctors who had not yet disputed were not to be penalised (*Conc.* 657, f. 44r-v, 26 Aug 1476, ed. FERRERI, doc. 23, p. 21).

[150] Cf. MAIERÙ, 'Ancora sugli atti scolastici', pp. 320-3, pulling together what is known of this new phenomenon.

[151] DALLARI, *I Rotuli*, I, p. VIII; MAIERÙ, loc. cit.

[152] VERDE, *Lo Studio fiorentino*, IV, p. 9, April 1476. For Pavia the first evidence is Giason del Maino's funeral oration for Girolamo Torti in 1484, which makes it clear that it was customary by then. SOTTILI, 'Aemulatio', pp. 115, 117.

[153] VERDE, *Lo Studio fiorentino*, IV, pp. 219-20, 1 May 1476. Resistance continued; on 17 Mar 1491 the *bidello* complained to the *Ufficiali dello Studio* in Florence that while the teachers of arts and medicine were cooperating, the lawyers were claiming that they were not obliged to attend (op. cit., p. 925), and the *Ufficiali* were still trying to enforce the practice in 1496 (p. 1251, 20 Nov).

[154] *Studio* 2, f. 48v, 31 Oct; cf. ZDEKAUER, p. 108 (giving the date as 1475). There is no indication prior to 1476 that this custom was in operation. The doctors were to appear 'in campo fori', the term used for the Piazza del Campo since the late twelfth century; M. TULIANI, 'Il Campo di Siena. Un mercato cittadina in epoca comunale', *Quaderni medievali*, 46 (Dec 1998), pp. 59-100 (pp. 63-4, 83, 85). The significance of the measure may go beyond the obvious point that these communally-salaried employees were to give public displays of their erudition in the central communal arena, something that I have stressed before (DENLEY, 'Dal 1357 alla caduta della repubblica', p. 38). The Campo was used for a wide range of activities, both commercial and ceremonial (TULIANI, op. cit., pp. 72 *seq.*, HOOK, *Siena*, ch. 5, and F. J. D. NEVOLA, 'Urbanism in Siena [*c*.1450-1512]. Policy and Patrons: Interactions between Public and Private', unpublished Ph.D. thesis, University of London, 1998, pp. 77-80). This measure places the doctors alongside the traders and artisans, but also the notaries, who had their own tables (NEVOLA, loc. cit.). Like the iconography of Lorenzetti's *Good Government*, this measure was making a point about the integration of the *Studio* among the activities of the city – indeed, giving it a physical reality. How the doctors reacted to this equation with a predominantly artisanal activity must remain a matter for speculation. The

visions were made, this time by the *Balìa*. From the opening of the *Studio* until Christmas (for doctors of medicine and arts till Carnival) all doctors were to attend 'Circuli Disputatori' *in piazza* every evening; they would take it in turns, in the order in which their names appeared on the *rotolo*, to defend one or more *conclusioni* (to a maximum of three) against other doctors. They could have a student propose these but in that case the doctor had to reply at least to objections raised by his *concurrente*. Doctors of more than twenty-five years' standing were excused disputation, but had to attend to ensure that the event was fairly conducted, and to add dignity to the proceedings. The *bidello* was to check that all doctors were present; a fine of 10 *lire* was imposed on those who failed to come.[155]

The immediate fate of the daily *circuli* is not clear. There are no further direct references to it in the rest of the fifteenth century. In the 1545-6 *rotolo* the measures were repeated (the phrasing suggests that the practice had fallen into disuse), with some amendments, notably that the disputations were to be held for the first *terzaria* (i.e. until Christmas) only.[156] However, the regular annual disputations certainly continued. Their value was reaffirmed in 1488: 'li disputatori sonno quelli che fanno molto lo ingiegno acuto'.[157] Both types, while responding to a fashion in Italian universities, also reflected a local appetite for public displays of what the university was doing and where the commune's expenditure was going. The fact that lawyers were to hold their *circuli* in a public *piazza* is indicative of this. In fact the tradition of making public displays of *Studio* activity goes quite a way further back. Some lectures, such as those on Dante, were designated public in the *condotte*, and were clearly aimed at a wider audience.[158] Some disputations may have attracted a public audience; the session of 'quaestiones disputatae' between Giovanni Battista Caccialupi and Mariano Sozzini on 1 April 1459 was held in the presence of 'plurimi oratores et reuerendi prelati auditores et aduocati et alii infiniti notabiles curiales',[159] while the (probably unusual) public debate between the jurist Francesco Accolti and the Dominican Simone Bocci took place in the cathedral.[160] The public nature, even the theatricality, of disputations must have responded to a deeper wish. Unlike so many occupations, what teachers and students got up to in their daily activity was normally hidden to view, behind closed doors. Public disputations, even more than public lectures, took the lid off this secrecy.

---

subsequent measure of 1481 (below, n. 155) refers to disputations 'in piazza', but there is no further information about the location of these.

[155] *Balìa* 24, f. 89v, 30 Jun, eds. PUCCINOTTI, *Storia della Medicina*, p. CLXV, and ILARDI, 'Ordinamenti', p. 168; copy in *Mis.* 1, f. 108r. A month earlier the Savi had ordered the doctors to obey the regulations on disputations; *Studio* 2, f. 73v, 26 May 1481. On *circuli* in Siena see also FIORAVANTI, 'Le "arti liberali"', p. 269.

[156] *Studio* 22, *Rotolo* of 1545-6, no foliation. The exemption was now for doctors with twenty years' teaching and the fine was 5 *lire*; the disputations in medicine were to be held 'in buttiga del bidello' rather than in the *piazza*. The annual obligation to give a public disputation or repetition was also confirmed; these were to take place 'nel tempo de le vacationi' in the *scuole di Sapienza*.

[157] *Conc.* 730, ff. 26v-30r, 9 Jun, ed. FERRERI, doc. 281, pp. 246-51 (p. 250). The order of precedence at disputations was also of significance; cf. the decision that Antonio Giordano da Venafro was to be considered of equal rank to the vicerector of the *Studio*, *Conc.* 753, f. 18v, 27 Apr 1492, ed. FERRERI, doc. 321, p. 300.

[158] *Conc.* 191, f. 6r, 4 May 1396; and see above, p. 52. It is less clear what is meant when in 1440 two civilians were hired expressly to lecture publicly; one was to lecture on the *Decretum* and the other, who was also given a normal *lettura*, on an unspecified subject; *Conc.* 444, f. 22r, 27 Jan 1440.

[159] MAFFEI et al. (eds.), *I codici del Collegio di Spagna*, p. 586.

[160] FIORAVANTI, 'Formazione e carriera di un domenicano', p. 349. The visit to Siena of the famous theologian Fernandino of Cordoba on 12 August 1446, and the public debates he held on theological matters, apparently led to the suspension of the *Studio* because of the great crowds he drew; FIORAVANTI, 'Pietro de' Rossi', pp. 154-6, and IDEM, 'Polemiche antigiudaiche nell'Italia del Quattrocento: un tentativo di interpretazione globale', in *Atti del VI Congresso internazionale dell'Associazione Italiana per lo Studio del Giudaismo* (Rome, 1988), pp. 75-91 (p. 83).

PART TWO
THE TEACHERS

I

CONTRACTS AND COMPETITION

1. *The hiring of teachers*

The most important task of any authority in Italy hosting a *studio* was to ensure a stable and distinguished supply of teachers. 'Li doctori si tirano dietro li scolari', declared one Sienese petition;[1] another asserted specifically that eminent foreign teachers 'sonno la ragione d'acoltare gli scolari e rendere lo studio famoso'.[2] The fortunes of such an enterprise depended more than anything else on the success of this operation. At the same time it was the most complex task the commune had to face regarding the *Studio*; it required expertise and immediate decisions because in this Siena was in direct competition, year after year, with the other *studi* of Italy. The volatility of the market can scarcely be exaggerated. In a system where to benefit from higher education, even to obtain a degree, there was no need to remain at the same *studio* for the entire period of study,[3] the eminence of teachers signed up at the various centres could play an important part in students' decisions as to where to pursue their academic career – decisions which could be altered not just from year to year but even more frequently than that. A *studio* was thus evaluated on its ongoing reputation for having good teachers. A specific draw could be the attraction of big names, which was spread by word of mouth just as much as through formal announcements and lists. However, the shelf-life of such a reputation could be very short indeed.

For practical reasons the authorities tended to prefer fixing *condotte* in batches. This made it easier to plan the academic provision for the coming year in a coherent manner, and also to manage the aspirations of doctors, treating them in relation to each other. Of course this was not always possible; shortages, sudden departures necessitating immediate replacements, advance notice that teachers were not renewing their contracts, and the exigencies in particular of the 'top end' of the market could all necessitate more frequent decisions. However, planned and cyclical batch hirings remained the ideal.

---

[1] *Conc.* 2139, no. 69, f. 128r, 1 Feb 1482. Cf. the observations made by reformers in 1458 (*Balìa* 9, f. 110r, 13 Sept 1458; also *Balìa* 10, ff. 122v-123v, and *Statuti* 40, f. 133r-v): 'Et sicondo le informationi che anno e detti Savi dello Studio, per lettere d'avisi da Bolognia, ferarra, perugia e altri luoghi, immediate si sentissero facte le condotte oportune, infiniti scolari veriano qua, loco aptissimo allo studio e gratissimo alli scolari.' Cf. the *Savi*'s belief in 1456 that with the right *condotte* 'la maggior parte degli scolari sonno a Bologna e a Perugia verrieno nel vostro studio'; *Conc.* 2138, no. 39, 13 Jul, quoted in CATONI, 'Il Comune di Siena e l'amministrazione della Sapienza', p. 128 (with a different date; see below, p. 171 n. 22).

[2] *CG* 224, f. 326v (new foliation), 16 Feb 1450 (GAROSI, doc. 62, pp. 530-1, and see pp. 239-40).

[3] Below, pp. 236-8.

It was also sensible because there was a certain seasonality to the exercise. Academic exigencies made it sensible for contracts to be expressed in academic years and to begin in October wherever possible; and the intense competition between *studi* meant that the timely announcement of the lecture list for the following year, before students made the decision to go elsewhere, was essential. Market forces, and specifically the *rotolo* system described above,[4] thus forced Siena to reorganise its periods of hiring teachers. In the fourteenth century the custom had been to hire new teachers in November and December and to confirm existing *condotte* in June and July;[5] in practice, though, it was the spring or later which saw the most activity, autumn *condotte* usually being a sign of failure to hire enough teachers earlier in the year. The perceived need to get a list out by August, or at the latest September, imposed a time-limit on the signing of *condotte*.[6] This was why the beginning of the *Savi*'s year of office was put back to January in 1437, and *condotte* not completed by them before the end of June were to be made in conjunction with the new *Concistoro* of July, so that the *rotolo* could be published by 16 August.[7] This remained the aspiration until the last few years of the century. Reforms of 1458, following political upheaval, laid down that the *Savi* were to bring proposed contracts to the *Concistoro* by 15 May, and that there should be two meetings of the *Concistoro* and *Savi* in May and June, the first to take place within ten days of receipt of the proposals. No individual could be voted on more than three times at each meeting. Should the two meetings fail to reach agreement on any individuals, up to two further meetings could be held in July on the same basis, after which the list was to be closed. A teacher who did not accept a *condotta* could not be hired for the coming year – all this 'acciò che per l'inportunità, amicitia o parentele non si esca dell'onesto'.[8] These principles remained in effect for some time, finding their way into collections of statutes in 1476.[9] In 1475 it was stipulated that *condotte* were to be made only in the months of May, June and July, any made outside this period being at the personal expense of the *Savi*.[10] But this timetable increasingly proved unrealistic. Though in 1480 the *Savi* expressed concern to the *Concistoro*, on 2 June, that other *studi* had already issued their *rotoli* for the coming year, and urged immediate action,[11] in 1482 a number of lectureships had still not been filled by mid-October, and the *Balìa* authorised the *Concistoro* and *Savi* to issue further contracts by the end of the month 'non obstante quod sit elapsus tempore conducendi'.[12] In this period, late summer and autumn *condotte* appear to become the norm; that year they were made in small batches from August to October.[13] In 1483 the *Balìa* again approved an extension of the period for *condotte*,[14] and there was a similar extension in 1487.[15] In 1490 all *condotte* were made in one sitting, in early October, at short notice, in a last-minute attempt to fix the teaching arrangements for the

---

[4] See above, pp. 110-11.

[5] ZDEKAUER, p. 57, PRUNAI, II, p. 28.

[6] Above, p. 110.

[7] See above, loc. cit.

[8] *Balìa* 9, f. 110r, 13 Sept; see also *Balìa* 10, ff. 122v-123v, and *Statuti* 40, f. 133r-v.

[9] *Conc.* 2395 ('Statuto delle Vacazioni'), ff. 45v-46r; *Statuti* 46, ff. 44v-45r.

[10] *Mis.* 1, f. 105v, 28 Jun (and see p. 76 above).

[11] *Conc.* 2123, ff. 19r-20r, 2 Jun (on which see above, p. 89 n. 24).

[12] *Balìa* 26, f. 118r, 15 Oct; cf. also *Studio* 2, f. 89r, 20 Sept.

[13] *Conc.* 695, ff. 10r, 12 Aug, 11r, 17 Aug, *Conc.* 696, ff. 8r, 20 Sept, 19r-v, 16 Oct, 20r, 17 Oct, 21v, 20 Oct 1482 (ed. FERRERI, docs. 149-57, pp. 126-34).

[14] *Balìa* 30, f. 45v, 19 Sept; fifteen days were granted.

[15] *CG* 240, ff. 154v-155r, 23 Sept.

new academic year,[16] and this appears to have become the pattern.[17] The notion of a May-June season, with a second round in July-August, was still the accepted one as late as 1525;[18] only after this, when the number of foreign teachers had fallen drastically, could the authorities permit themselves a laxer timetable, establishing September as the month for all *condotte*.[19]

Condotte took time because of the various levels of approval on which the Sienese insisted, as well as because of distance and problems of communication.[20] The choice of teachers was in the first instance a matter for the *Savi*, but, as has been seen, unless specifically given permission to do otherwise they had to refer these choices and the proposed salaries to the *Concistoro*, who in turn had to seek approval, for many *condotte*, from the *Consiglio del Popolo*.[21] This done, the offer would be made to the teacher – a messenger sent, in the case of a foreign doctor, with a simple offer and no powers of negotiation. Frequently a foreign student would be chosen for the task, often a compatriot of the teacher proposed.[22] Sienese diplomats might also be enlisted to help,[23] as might other distinguished citizens, be it from the academic world or the political. In the course of Siena's repeated attempts to woo the

---

[16] *Conc.* 744, f. 7v, 7 Oct (election of a special committee of citizens charged with the *condotte*), 9v-10v, 11 Oct, 10v-11v, 12 Oct, ed. FERRERI, docs. 306-7, pp. 279-82. Such was the perceived need for speed that the *Concistoro*'s servants divided up the list of doctors to be notified; they were to reply within three days. It is again perhaps more than a coincidence that the *Studio* of Florence/Pisa also published its *rotolo* uncharacteristically late that year (16 Oct), as it had done the previous year (21 Oct); VERDE, *Lo Studio fiorentino*, I, pp. 337-42.

[17] In 1494 the whole batch of two-year contracts were made on 7 and 8 October (*Conc.* 768, ff. 14r-15v, ed. FERRERI, doc. 345, pp. 326-8); in 1496 they were made in two batches, on 9/10 and 17 November (*Conc.* 781, ff. 4v-5r, 7r-v, ed. FERRERI, docs. 374 and 375, pp. 356-8); in 1497 the *rotolo* – for this was effectively the purpose of the exercise – was approved on 18 October (*Sale* 24, f. 157v), and in 1498 on 4 Nov (*Sale* 24, f. 167r).

[18] *CG* 242, ff. 42v-43r, 11 Sept 1425.

[19] *CG* 243, f. 246r, 26 Dec.

[20] Cf. FERRERI, p. xi on the length of such negotiations.

[21] Above, pp. 76 *seq.* Proposals could also fail; in 1464 the *Concistoro* decided not to approve the nominations by two grammarians of repetitors (*Conc.* 590, f. 39v, 13 Feb 1465, ed. BAI, doc. 216, p. 191).

[22] E.g. in 1438 Miss. Biagio da Castro was paid 24 *lire* for such a mission to Padua; *Biccherna* 312, f. 47r, 14 Jun, ed. F. MARLETTA, 'Un episodio della vita di Andrea Barbazza', *Archivio Storico Messinese*, 40-49 (1939-48), pp. 23-34 (p. 31 n. 42), speculating that the teacher might have been Lodovico (Petrucciani) da Terni. However, Petrucciani was already on the Sienese payroll (*Conc.* 425, f. 25v, 16 Dec 1436, and cf. MECACCI, *La biblioteca di Ludovico Petrucciani*, p. 8). In 1445 'dns. Iohannes Giliachi de Francia' (Savoy) was sent to Lombardy to negotiate with one or two 'doctores forenses et famosos' (*Conc.* 477, ff. 37r, 27 Aug, and 44v, 27 Aug); cf. MARLETTA, op. cit., p. 32, erroneously giving 1444, and again speculating that one of them may well have been Martino Garati da Lodi. This hypothesis may be no better founded; while Garati has been identified on the basis of manuscript evidence as teaching in Siena by 25 Oct 1445 (D. MAFFEI, 'Il trattato di Martino Garati per la canonizzazione di San Bernardino da Siena', *Studi senesi*, 100 [1988], pp. 580-603 [p. 582 n. 3], repr. in his *Studi di storia delle università*, pp. 253*-276*, and see MECCACI, op. cit., p. 9 n. 40), it has not been noticed that his contract had already been signed before the summer; *Conc.* 476, f. 15r, 29 May 1445 (on his Sienese period see also I. BAUMGÄRTNER, *Martinus Garatus laudensis. Ein italienischer Rechtsgelehrter des 15. Jahrhunderts*. Dissertationen zur Rechtsgeschichte, 2 [Cologne and Vienna, 1986], pp. 39-45). In 1463 the law student Agostino Curradi of Alessandria was paid 60 *lire* for a thirty-day mission to Lombardy on *Studio* business (*Conc.* 581, ff. 33r, 55r, 31 Aug). In 1483 the *Savi* paid 'Domini Andree florentino' four ducats for negotiations with Lancilotto Decio (*Studio* 2, f. 97v, 29 Dec, and cf. f. 95v, 14 Nov, both ed. FERRERI, p. xi n. 2); it is not clear whether or not he was a student. Occasionally the *bidello* was chosen (above, p. 84), and on one occasion one of the *Savi* went on such a mission himself (*Conc.* 239 f. 23v, 9 Apr 1439). It has not always been possible to identify the messenger; Ser Pietro di Giovanni Cecchini, sent 'ad conducendum doctores' in 1412 (*Conc.* 1609, f. 59r, 28 Jul) may have been a notary but there is no information on whether he had a specific *Studio* connection. On the sending of such messengers see also below, p. 285 n. 55.

[23] For example, Niccolò di Nanni de' Piccolomini was sent 'ad alcune parti dove fussero doctori' to attempt to recruit one or two civilians (*Conc.* 1696, f. 67r, 14 May 1483). The deliberate vagueness was doubtless for security (see below, p. 152). In 1463 the *Concistoro* allowed the *Savi* to send an unnamed citizen on a recruitment mission for ten or twelve days (*Conc.* 580, f. 33r, 10 Jun); shortly after the *condotta* of an unnamed but famous lawyer was approved by the *Consiglio del Popolo* (*CG* 229, f. 379r-v, and *Conc.* 580, f. 49r, 21 Jun, ed. BAI, docs. 188-9, pp. 163-5).

distinguished jurist Catone Sacco from Pavia, first in 1438-9 the humanist Barnaba di Nanni (who was one of the *Savi* at the time),[24] and then in 1441-2 no less a figure than the future saint Bernardino,[25] were involved, while in the exceptional case of Bartolomeo Sozzini, whom Siena tried for many years to get back from Florence at the end of the century, Pandolfo Petrucci himself was active, appropriately enough given Sozzini's close relationship to Lorenzo de' Medici.[26] Such operations had of course to be kept secret from the authorities of the *studio* from which the teacher was to be lured.[27] The reply might not be immediate, and although there was occasionally the suspicion that a student was dallying at the commune's expense,[28] the journey plus negotiations at the end of it regularly took from ten days to two or three weeks, and sometimes longer.[29]

If the teacher accepted, the contract could be drawn up; if on the other hand he attempted to negotiate a higher salary or special conditions the whole procedure would have to be repeated. Sometimes the *Savi* tried to preempt this by sending a preliminary messenger – or by using an existing envoy of the commune – to sound out the teacher they had in mind to see what sort of salary he would consider;[30] that took time as well. Sometimes such negotiations could turn into protracted exercises in brinkmanship; the operation to get Alessandro Sermoneta to return from Padua in the early 1480s took two and a half years.[31] Teachers already in Siena could cause difficulties too. In 1467, after a year in service, Alberto Cattani of Bologna was offered a three-year contract on a rising salary scale; he refused it and it was withdrawn, leaving him little better off than previously.[32]

---

[24] NARDI, 'Lo Studio di Siena nell'età rinascimentale', pp. 255-6, esp. n. 18; an exhaustive account now in P. ROSSO, 'Catone Sacco. Problemi biografici. La tradizione delle opere', *Rivista di Storia del Diritto Italiano*, 73 (2000), pp. 237-338 (pp. 254-7). Cf. also below, p. 186.

[25] ROSSO, 'Catone Sacco', pp. 258-9; A. SOTTILI, 'Università e cultura a Pavia in età visconteo-sforzesca', *Storia di Pavia*, 3:2. *Dal Libro Comune alla fine del principato indipendente 1024-1535* (Milan, 1990), pp. 359-451 (pp. 388-9).

[26] BARGAGLI, *Bartolomeo Sozzini,* p. 201; and on Sozzini's relationship with Lorenzo see also EADEM, 'Bartolomeo Sozzini, Lorenzo de' Medici e lo Studio di Pisa (1473-1494)', in *La Toscana al tempo di Lorenzo*, III, pp. 1165-71. On Bartolomeo Sozzini see also below, pp. 222-3.

[27] E.g. *Conc.* 538, f. 50r, 24 Jun 1456; the *Savi* may send two people where they wish to agree *condotte* 'pro honore et utilitate Studii et ut res secrete procedat'. A similar operation took place in 1458; *Conc.* 550, f. 12r, 15 Sept, ed. BAI, doc. 109, p. 91.

[28] *Conc.* 500, f. 33v, 13 Jun 1449 (it was decided that a messenger's salary would cease after seventeen days).

[29] E.g. in 1428, Maestro Cola da Sicilia was sent to Bologna for fourteen days (*Conc.* 375, ff. 12v, 14 Sept, 26r and 42v, 1 Oct). In 1434 a student spent twenty-two days on a mission to Padua (*Conc.* 412, f. 63r, 23 Oct 1434); Messer Niccolò Cavallo de Sicilia was paid for twenty-two days in 1445 (*Conc.* 477, f. 28r, 12 Aug, and *Conc.* 478, f. 11r, 18 Sept). An extreme case is Messer Pace da Ascoli who spent over two months on a mission to Rome in 1433 (*Conc.* 407, ff. 3v and 37r, 4 Nov, and cf. *Bicch.* 311, f. 147r, 13 Nov).

[30] E.g. *Conc.* 375, f. 29r, 8 Oct 1428 (the *Concistoro* writes to one of the commune's orators in Florence to find out how much Lodovico Pontano would accept as a salary); *Conc.* 461, f. 31r, 28 Nov 1444 (enquiries are made in Pavia as to the chances of getting Catone Sacco to teach in Siena).

[31] The *Concistoro* resolved to try to get him back on 1 Feb 1482; he had had a two-year lectureship in Padua with Sienese approval (*Conc.* 2139, no. 69, f. 128r). A year later he was absolved from the penalties for not returning and offered a five-year contract (*Balìa* 28, ff. 65v, 24 May, and 72r, 30 May 1483). This was subsequently postponed for another year but coupled with the threat of confiscation of his property if he did not accept (*Balìa* 29, f. 7r, 4 Jun 1483). The contract was finally agreed on 30 Jul 1484 (*Balìa* 32, f. 29r). Sermoneta has attracted particular interest because of his library; A. GAROSI, 'I codici di medicina del maestro Alessandro Sermoneta', *Rivista di Storia delle Scienze Mediche e Naturali*, 28 (1937), pp. 225-32, and E. MECACCI, 'Contributo allo studio delle biblioteche universitarie senesi (Alessandro Sermoneta – Giorgio Tolomei – Domenico Maccabruni)', *Studi senesi*, 97 (1985), pp. 125-78; more generally see also M. ROTZOLL, 'Appunti su un "magister" del secondo Quattrocento: Alessandro Sermoneta da Siena', *Quaderni del raggruppamento tosco-umbro-emiliano di storia della medicina* (1987), pp. 87-99, and particularly WHITLEY, 'Concepts of Ill Health and Pestilence', ch. VI, pp. 213-65.

[32] *Conc.* 605, f. 21r, 24 Jul. A Bolognese chronicle for Sept 1467 refers to the appointment of 'Alberto de Sinibaldo Catanio dotore de leze, el quale in quello tempo ligea a Siena, conducto da quella comunitade; et fu incontinenti revocato' (*Corpus chronicorum bononiensium*, in *Rerum italicarum scriptores*, XVIII/1, vol. iv, *Cronaca A*, p. 383, ll. 25-9).

Even when agreement was reached, care had to be exercised in stipulating the correct terms in the contract and getting approval from the competent authorities according to the regulations of the moment. As these were complex and constantly changing, mistakes could happen, and on several occasions *condotte* were revoked because they had not been made properly.[33] The *Savi* were threatened with various penalties for such mistakes,[34] but they continued to occur, and these officials were in any case by no means always responsible. On one occasion the notary of the *Concistoro* refused to enter two *condotte* in the register, the *Libro di S. Agostino*, on the grounds that the *Consiglio del Popolo* had not been consulted; the *Concistoro* threatened to fine him if he continued to disobey their order.[35]

Above all, the authorities tried to discourage negotiation and speed up the process by insisting on short deadlines for a response. To start with this was an individual matter. Teachers were given varying periods within which to accept; a fortnight was not untypical but some offers were valid for as little as three days' time).[36] Eventually legislation regulated the periods; in 1463, teachers offered contracts were to accept within ten days.[37] When in 1472 the *Consiglio del Popolo* reduced this to eight days,[38] four prestigious teachers failed to respond in time, but the principle was upheld.[39] Of course, teachers could and did refuse contracts, though sometimes they did so just in hope of a better deal. Attitudes to such behaviour varied; in 1456 Andrea Barbazza was denied the pay rise he had been offered,[40] but the famous grammarian Cantalicio's *condotta* was held over for a year when in 1475 he was unable to accept it.[41] In 1449 Mag. Teodorico di Piemonte, having failed to accept a contract within the stipulated fifteen days, was told he could still have it provided he presented himself to the *Concistoro* (which he did).[42] And in 1433 at least three teachers were successful in holding out for higher salaries.[43] Failure

---

[33] E.g. *Conc.* 354, f. 10r, 17 Jan 1425; *Conc.* 443, f. 8r-v, 10 Nov 1439, ed. PIANIGIANI, doc. 203, pp. 234-5; *Conc.* 479, f. 19r, 29 Nov 1445; *Conc.* 615, f. 42r, 29 Apr 1469, ed. BAI, doc. 291, pp. 275-6.

[34] *CG* 223, f. 229v, 20 Feb 1447 (GAROSI, p. 239); the *Savi* were subject to a 20-florin fine for invalid *condotte*. See above, p. 76. In reforms of 1458 it was stipulated that *condotte* not made through due process would be invalid and the perpetrators, including the notary, would be fined 100 florins (*Balìa* 9, f. 110r, 13 Sept 1458; also *Balìa* 10, ff. 122v-123v, and *Statuti* 40, f. 133r-v). This was repeated in the operation to hire teachers in 1488, in which procedures were tightened up (*Conc.* 730, ff. 26v-30r, 9 Jun 1488, ed. FERRERI, doc. 281, pp. 245-51).

[35] *Conc.* 413, f. 27r, 13 Dec 1434. On the various stages in the process of hiring teachers at Perugia, ERMINI, *Storia*, I, p. 77.

[36] *Conc.* 488, f. 54r, 28 Jun 1447, ed. PIANIGIANI, doc. 272, pp. 302-4 (offer of a *condotta* to Giovanni Burgi, who had fifteen days in which to accept); *Conc.* 452, f. 37v, 26 Jun 1441, ed. PIANIGIANI, doc. 225, pp. 257-8 (Malatesta di Borgo has three days to accept).

[37] *Conc.* 581, f. 18v, 29 Jul, ed. BAI, doc. 193, p. 168. This was repeated in 1465 (*Conc.* 592, f. 39r, 30 May, ed. BAI, doc. 222, p. 200) and 1467 (*Conc.* 604, f. 56r, 18 Jun, ed. BAI, doc. 241, pp. 237-8, and *Conc.* 605, f. 21r, 25 Jul, ed. BAI, doc. 244, p. 242). In 1490, however, doctors were given three days from notification to accept their *condotte*; *Conc.* 744, f. 11v, 12 Oct, ed. FERRERI, doc. 309, pp. 283-5.

[38] *CG* 234, f. 180r, 3 Aug.

[39] *Conc.* 2139, no. 24, f. 43r-v, 22 Sept; petition by the *Savi* to allow the four, Alessandro Sermoneta, Borghese Borghesi, Guidantonio Buoninsegni and Bulgarino Bulgarini, to be given contracts. The *Savi* pointed out that there was a shortage of teachers ('essendo il vostro studio questo anno con qualche mancamento di lettioni'), both because some had refused contracts and because of the new measure which was considered unreasonable. Their petition appears not to have been successful; Borghese Borghesi did teach that year (*Conc.* 640, f. 5v, 7 May 1473, ed. BAI, doc. 337, p. 333; *Conc.* 641, f. 32v, 27 Aug 1473, ed. BAI, doc. 343, p. 329), but Alessandro Sermoneta and Guidantonio Buoninsegni had to wait until the following August for contracts; *Conc.* 641, ff. 25v-26r, 20 Aug, and 31r, 25 Aug 1473, ed. BAI, docs. 341-2, pp. 337-8 (Sermoneta) and 33r, 27 Aug 1473, ed. BAI, doc. 344, p. 340 (Buoninsegni).

[40] *Conc.* 539, f. 11r, 9 Jul.

[41] *Conc.* 655, f. 13r, 16 Nov, ed. BAI, doc. 316, p. 370.

[42] *Conc.* 500, ff. 17v, 22 May, 41v, 24 Jun, and *Conc.* 501, f. 13v, 13 Jul, ed. PIANIGIANI, docs. 291-3, pp. 324-6.

[43] Francesco de Mansuetis of Perugia declined a salary of 360 florins and three days later was hired for 380 florins; the

to turn up after accepting a *condotta* was of course the worst possible offence, being insulting as well as disruptive. The best-known example was Andrea Barbazza, whose image was painted in the Piazza del Campo, the Piazza Tolomei and the Casa della Sapienza in 1445 after he accepted a *condotta* of 475 florins but failed to turn up.[44] A similar penalty had been imposed on Guasparre Sighicelli da Bologna, for defecting to Florence in 1429.[45] Earlier penalties for such breach of contract included banishment.[46]

canonist Giovanni da Sicilia got his raised from 70 to 80 florins; and the canonist Manuel of Catalonia got his up from 25 to 35 florins (*Conc.* 406, ff. 26r, 15 Oct, and 28v, 18 Oct 1433, ed. PIANIGIANI, docs. 149-50, pp. 174-6).

[44] *Conc.* 478, f. 37r, 27 Oct, ed. A. MOCENNI, 'Pene ai traditori', *Miscellanea Storica Senese*, 1 (1893), pp. 23-4 (and see also *Conc.* 478, ff. 7v, 10 Sept, 16v, 29 Sept, and *Conc.* 479, f. 13v, 20 Nov); ZDEKAUER, pp. 12, 58 n. 3; IDEM, 'Dai protocolli', p. 325; PRUNAI, II, p. 54. The punishment was lifted on 9 Dec (*Conc.* 479, f. 24r). Cf. F. LIOTTA, 'Barbazza, Andrea', in *DBI*, 6 (1964), pp. 146-8; and A. L. TROMBETTI BUDRIESI, 'Andrea Barbazza tra mondo bolognese e mezzogiorno d'Italia', in *Scuole, diritto e società nel mezzogiorno medievale d'Italia*, ed. M. Bellomo. Settimana di Studio Erice, 1983, 1 (Catania, 1985), pp. 289-324 (p. 309). The sanction did not prevent the Sienese from offering, and Barbazza from accepting, a contract some years later; *Conc.* 527, f. 26v, 21 Jul 1454, ed. BAI, doc. 61, pp. 51-2, and see p. 153 and n. 41 above; NARDI, *Mariano Sozzini*, p. 81. Barbazza has the possibly unique distinction of having been thus punished in two *studi*; Ferrara also commissioned a *pittura infamante* of him. G. SECCO-SUARDO, 'Lo Studio di Ferrara a tutto il secolo XV', *Atti della Deputazione Ferrarese di Storia Patria*, 6 (1894), pp. 11-294 (pp. 110-11), and cf. TROMBETTI BUDRIESI, op. cit., p. 309 n.74. The story does not stop there; he also got into trouble in Bologna for accepting *condotte* elsewhere; C. PIANA, *Il "Liber Secretus Iuris Caesarei" dell'Università di Bologna, 1451-1500*. Orbis Academicus. Saggi e Documenti di Storia delle Università, 1 (Milan, 1984), p. 59*.

[45] He was threatened with this indignity should he leave Siena (*Conc.* 381, f. 8r-v, 13 Sept, ed. PIANIGIANI, doc. 115, pp. 143-4, and 9v, 14 Sept 1429). The ensuing correspondence with the *Savi* of the Florentine *Studio*, and from Guasparre himself, shows their fears were fully justified (*Conc.* 381, f. 24r, 11 Oct 1429; GHERARDI, *Statuti*, appendix, part 2, docs. 160-1 and 164, pp. 411-3, 17 and 23 Sept and 7 Nov respectively; and see ZDEKAUER, p. 61, and below, p. 176 n. 246). The punishment was carried out; *Bicch.* 309, f. 80v, 31 Dec 1429 details payment of the painter. Two years earlier the Sienese had politely declined to release him back to Bologna (*Conc.* 1629, f. 29r, 26 Sept 1427, and see the original request of the papal legate to Bologna, the cardinal of Arles, *Conc.* 1913, no. 6, 17 Sept, pointing out that Guasparre was in contempt of Bologna's own protectionist legislation). On this figure see LINES, *Aristotle's Ethics*, p. 403, speculating about identification with Gaspare Sighicelli; the 1427 Sienese document, referring to his provenance, San Giovanni in Persiceto, confirms it. Cf. also IDEM, 'Natural Philosophy in Renaissance Italy: the University of Bologna and the Beginnings of Specialization', *Early Science and Medicine*, 6 (2001), pp. 267-323 (pp. 289-90). M. ASCHERI, *Dedicato a Siena* (Siena, 1989), p. 62, and IDEM, 'Un trittico da Siena nel Quattrocento', in *Excerptiones iuris. Studies in Honor of André Gouron*, eds. B. Durant and L. Mayali. Studies in Comparative Legal History (Berkeley, Ca., 2000), pp. 17-34 (p. 25 n. 32) has found a similar punishment for Lodovico Pontano in 1428 for preferring a Florentine offer, but has not published the references. Other cases of eminent men punished in this way because of their breach of agreement with Siena (coupled, of course, with their absence) include the eminent reformer, preacher, anti-humanist and now cardinal Giovanni Dominici, painted in 1409 (*Conc.* 261, f. 33v, 17 Aug). The use of this device for recalcitrant academics goes back certainly to Bologna, where Paolo de' Liazari was thus threatened as a traitor if he did not return from Siena in 1321 (NARDI, *Insegnamento*, pp. 124-5, 225-6; quoted in SEIDEL, *Dolce vita*, p. 27). On this punishment more generally, D. FREEDBERG, 'Infamy, Justice, and Witchcraft: Explanation, Sympathy, and Magic', in his *The Power of Images: Studies in the History and Theory of Response* (Chicago & London, 1989), pp. 246-82, 480-85; S. Y. EDGERTON, *Pictures and Punishment: Art and Criminal Prosecution during the Florentine Renaissance* (Ithaca, N.Y., 1985).

[46] *Conc.* 2306, fasc. 17, no. 5, 15 Apr ?, letter from Raynaldus de Camerino, teacher at Padua, protesting at being banished for not accepting a *condotta*. Rainaldo's negotiations for a Sienese post took place in spring 1425; see D. GALLO, 'Lauree inedite in diritto civile e canonico conferite presso lo Studio di Padova (1419-1422, 1423, 1424, 1428)', *Quaderni per la Storia dell'Università di Padova*, 20 (1987), pp. 1-50 (p. 50), and cf. BELLONI, *Professori giuristi a Padova*, p. 326. He was offered a contract again in 1434 (*Conc.* 413, f. 6r *bis*, 9 Nov), for 350 florins, but there is no evidence that he took it up. The case of Ugo Benzi (below, pp. 220-1) is exceptional as the threat of banishment and confiscation of goods was connected with his status as a member of the disgraced *Dodici* more than with his teaching.

2. *Conditions of service*

The length of teaching contracts varied, but within guidelines established from time to time by the *Consiglio Generale* or the *Consiglio del Popolo*. The pre-1357 documents gathered in the *Chartularium Studii Senensis* do not include many *condotte*. What has survived suggests no particular pattern; terms could be from six months to five years, with the longer ones tending to be found at the humbler end of the scale.[47] Zdekauer thought that a two-year period had become the norm by the fourteenth century, but this may well be too early.[48] Perugia had a system of three-year *condotte*,[49] and in 1387 this was instituted in Siena as well;[50] but in 1428 a maximum two-year term was established 'come si costuma in tucti e buoni Studii di ytalia'. The reasons given are indicative of a trend; longer *condotte* were impractical

> perché le condotte de' Doctori che si fanno per longo tempo si vede chiaro essi Doctori non tenere que' debiti modi che terrebero se avessero el freno dell'aversi ad riconducere in più breve tempo.[51]

The anxieties of the authorities on this score culminated in a further reduction, in 1431, of the maximum term for foreign doctors to one year,[52] as seems already to have been the practice for Sienese doctors;[53] but the regulation was tacitly abandoned in 1434,[54] and in 1437 the citizen *condotte* were also extended to two years 'veduto quanta difficultà e perdimento di tempo' they had caused.[55] From then on, two years remained the norm, although some one-year contracts persisted, either at the request of the teacher or because of caution on the part of the authorities.[56] In the 1460s, however, longer contracts started to creep back in as a way of attracting or keeping high-fliers. The trend appears to have begun with the operation to secure an anonymous lawyer in 1463; the *Consiglio del Popolo* was

[47] E.g. *Chartularium*, docs. 53, pp. 33-5, 9 May 1285 (five years, *chirurgia*), 107, pp. 85-6, 3 Dec 1306 (four years, grammar), and 139, pp. l20-2, 29 Dec 1316 (three years, grammar).

[48] ZDEKAUER, p. 57.

[49] ERMINI, *Storia*, I, p. 66. In practice the terms were often longer still, including regular appointments for ten or more years (n. 71).

[50] *CG* 195, f. 115r-v, 23 Jan, ed. GAROSI, p. 194 n. 1; copy in *Mis.* 1, f. 50r-v. In 1420 the Franciscan Angelo Salvetti was signed for a five-year contract to teach theology and moral philosophy (*Conc.* 329, f. 14v, 22 Nov, eds. BULLETTI, 'Angelo Salvetti', doc. 24, pp. 78-9, and PIANIGIANI, doc. 44, pp. 69-70). This was perhaps a special case, honouring a distinguished citizen; in any case the contract was short-lived, since the following year Salvetti became general of the Franciscan order.

[51] *CG* 212, f. 117r, *Bicch.* 2, f. 240r, *Statuti* 41, f. 204r, *Statuti* 47, f. 203r, 27 Feb. In Perugia, in 1440, one-year terms became standard, with the exception of two eminent foreigners who might have two- or three-year terms. The exception was removed in 1514, and the reasons given are very similar to those given in Siena (ERMINI, *Storia*, I, p. 257).

[52] *Conc.* 390, f. 12r, 19 Jan 1431; *CG* 216, f. 36v; *Statuti* 41, f. 231r, 23 Feb 1431.

[53] Cf. *Conc.* 387, ff. 11v-12r, 18 Sept 1430.

[54] See two-year *condotte* in *Conc.* 409, ff. 36r and 44r, 23 Apr; *Conc.* 412, ff. 43v, 5 Oct, and 62v, 23 Oct 1434.

[55] *CG* 219, f. 157v (new foliation), 29 May, ed. ZDEKAUER, doc. XVIII (appended to measure of 10 May, p. 171); copies in *Statuti* 41, f. 255v, and *Mis.* 1, f. 85r.

[56] E.g. *Conc.* 381, f. 12v, 18 Sept 1429; Dns. Ricciardus de Fonte was to be hired for two years if he was willing, otherwise for one year. (Ricciardus had previously taught at Bologna in 1427-8, having been elected by the university of students to a lectureship on the *Decretum diebus festivis*; DALLARI, *I Rotuli*, IV, p. 54.) There are also some shorter contracts, usually last-minute replacements. Messer Silvestro was hired in April 1425 for the remainder of the academic year (*Conc.* 355, f. 3lr, 28 Apr); Giovanni da Sermoneta was hired in December 1437 for the remainder of the current academic year and the next one (*Conc.* 431, f. 23r, 20 Dec); and cf. the 1457 decision that a logician could be hired for the remainder of the academic year (*Balìa* 2, f. 182r, 14 Feb). The canonist Filippo Farfalla was renewed for a year only in 1470 (*Conc.* 65, f. 7v, 8 Nov, ed. BAI, doc. 209, pp. 299-300). The only regular exceptions to this were the five-year *condotte* of elementary-level teachers such as Gilio dell'Abbaco (*Conc.* 2142, no. 8, 21 Jul and 8 Aug 1414) and Pietro dell'Abbaco (e.g. *CG* 210, f. 7r-v, 5 Feb 1425; *Conc.* 385, f. 33r, 9 Jun 1430; *Conc.* 441, f. 59v, 27 Aug 1439). Such longer contracts for schoolmasters were traditional; four were given four-year contracts in 1392 (*Conc.* 166, ff. 6v, 17 Mar, 7r, 21 Mar, and 17v, 24 Apr).

told that he would not consider coming for less than a four-year contract.[57] Once the rule had been breached, this privileged treatment soon became extended on an individual basis to eminent foreigners. Alberto Cattani of Bologna was offered a three-year contract in 1467;[58] the medical doctor and reader in surgery Giovanni di Lorenzo de' Giustini da Roma[59] and the Dominican Alessandro da Bologna[60] were offered four-year contracts in 1471, Francesco Accolti's was increased from two to six years in 1472,[61] and Pietro Sacco da Verona was offered the choice of a contract of anything from two to six years in 1474.[62] By the 1480s citizen teachers, and foreigners whose Sienese sojourn had acquired some permanency, were also benefiting. The most extreme example, which perhaps led the process, was Giovanni Battista Caccialupi, who received four-year contracts in 1466 and 1470, a contract of six years in 1474 and one of ten years in 1480.[63] Subsequent recipients of offers of longer contracts were Bulgarino Bulgarini (four years in 1480),[64] Bartolomeo Sozzini (five years, in 1482 and 1483),[65] Alessandro Sermoneta (five years in 1483),[66] Jacopo Faccalume (four years in 1482 or 1483, apparently extended on renewal to six years),[67] Rico Richi (four years, 1483),[68] and Lutio Bellanti (three years in 1487).[69] The authorities finally clamped down on the practice again in 1488, making all *condotte* of two years' length,[70] though teachers clearly did not give up negotiating for longer terms.[71]

A *condotta* was an individual contract between commune and teacher. It stipulated the salary, the period for which the contract was to run, and often also the specific *lettura* allotted to the teacher, as

[57] *CG* 229, f. 379r-v, 21 Jun. The attractions were that he would read twice a day, once in civil and once in canon law; and 'sarà ragione che molti scolari forestieri e persone nobili verranno a studiare nella città vostra.'

[58] *Conc.* 605, f. 21r, 24 Jul, ed. BAI, doc. 243, p. 241; and see above, p. 152.

[59] *CG* 234, f. 53r, and *Conc.* 631, f. 28r, 10 Dec 1471; and see *Conc.* 631, f. 39v, 23 Dec, and below, p. 211 n. 14.

[60] *Conc.* 629, f. 40r-v, 27 Aug, ed. BAI, doc. 317, p. 312, and *CG* 234, f. 21v, 28 Aug 1471. He was to lecture in the cathedral (*Conc.* 631, f. 4v, 4 Nov 1471, ed. BAI, doc. 318, p. 313).

[61] *CG* 234, f. 236r, 14 Dec.

[62] *Conc.* 645, f. 34v, 14 Apr; the result was a six-year contract (f. 36r-v, 16 Apr, ed. BAI, doc. 353, p. 349).

[63] *Conc.* 599, f. 51v, 28 Aug 1466; *Conc.* 622, f. 33v, 7 Jun 1470, ed. BAI, doc. 303, p. 291; *Conc.* 645, f. 36r, 16 Apr 1474, ed. BAI, doc. 352, pp. 348; *Conc.* 682, f. 21r, 25 May 1480, ed. FERRERI, doc. 100, p. 86; NARDI, 'Giovanni Battista Caccialupi a Siena', pp. 108-10. The fact that Caccialupi combined his chair with the office of *Giudice delle Riformagioni*, as well as the length of his service to Siena, are explanations for this special treatment; the 1466 and 1470 contracts were for both posts.

[64] *Regolatori* 59, f. 6r, 4 Aug 1488 (restoration of rights of rebels in 1480).

[65] *Balìa* 26, f. 107v, 25 Sept 1482, ed. BARGAGLI, 'Documenti senesi', doc. 20, p. 287, and cf. EADEM, *Bartolomeo Sozzini*, p. 93; *Balìa* 28, f. 72r, 30 May 1483, ed. EADEM, 'Documenti senesi', doc. 42, p. 300, and *Balìa* 29, f. 43v, 15 Jul 1483, ed. EADEM, op. cit., doc. 51, pp. 302-3.

[66] *Balìa* 28, f. 72r, 30 May, ed. BARGAGLI, op. cit., doc. 42, p. 300. On Sermoneta see also above, p. 152 n. 31.

[67] *Conc.* 2309, no foliation, 1 Jun 1486 (his petition for renewal of his four-year contract). The renewal does not specify the length (*Conc.* 718, f. 15v, 5 Jun 1486, ed. FERRERI, doc. 236, p. 201). A fresh appeal for renewal by Faccalume to the *Consiglio del Popolo* was approved on 28 Jan 1487 (*CG* 240, f. 111r-v), but again the length is not given. His heirs claimed in 1489 that he had had a six-year contract (*CG* 240, f. 212r, 24 Aug). On Faccalume see also MINNUCCI, 'Documenti', p. 265.

[68] *Balìa* 31, f. 6r, 10 Nov.

[69] *Balìa* 35, f. 28r-v, 25 Aug.

[70] *Conc.* 730, ff. 26v-30r, 9 Jun, ed. FERRERI, doc. 281, pp. 245-51. This list included Jacopo Faccalume whose contract had previously been for longer.

[71] The idea of longer contracts was certainly not dead. The Servite Emmanuele petitioned for a five-year contract in 1498 'che de tanto tempo altre volte è stato provisto', and in order that he might be granted the conditions of other teachers who were in orders: 'e che el vogliano pareggiare circa il salario e condocta ad altri Religiosi legenti la medesima facultà in decta università e studio' (*Conc.* 2139, no. 114, f. 204r, 3-9 Jan 1498).

well as occasionally the place in which he was to hold lectures, and other conditions. Only a handful of original contracts survive,[72] but the majority are known to us through their authorisation by the competent body. Many of these were routine and uniform, so much so that long-established teachers, and occasionally younger ones also, would often begin their term of teaching before their contracts were actually signed; the back-dated contract is a frequent occurrence,[73] as elsewhere, and there were clearly years in which renewals were little more than a formality.[74] As the contract was individual it was possible to vary the terms considerably within the standardised framework. In one of the many attempts to persuade Bartolommeo Sozzini back to Siena he was, perhaps uniquely, offered the equivalent of a 200-florin 'signing fee' in 1482.[75] In 1466 the Bolognese civilian Alberto Cattani was expected to bring with him ten students on taking up his lectureship.[76] One teacher, Floriano Sampieri, was to receive help in finding accommodation;[77] other special treatment accorded included permission for Jacopo Faccalume to start teaching whenever he liked,[78] and for Cola da Gaeta, a doctor who was treating plague victims in the city, to decide whether or not to teach.[79] Special conditions, or conditions which we may assume were general but which are specifically stipulated in these records, are a guide to the preoccupations of the authorities. Easily the most frequent of these is the stipulation that a teacher must accept the *condotta*, appear in Siena and begin to teach within a short period – often within the month – for the contract to be valid.[80] The 1275 're-foundation' required that the teachers arrive eight days before the opening of the *Studio*.[81] Once the academic year had begun the authorities were keen that late *condotte*

---

[72] Examples of full texts of contracts in *Concistoro* 2180, no foliation (Andrea Barbazza, 14 Jul 1456, and Angelo da Perugia, 11 Aug 1456); above, pp. 153-4.

[73] Similarly, disputes over salaries did not necessarily hold up teaching; Mansueto da Perugia was evidently teaching, and being paid for doing so, in 1462 despite a failure of the authorities to agree on his salary for that and the previous year (*Conc.* 577, ff. 32r, 13 Dec, and 36v, 16 Dec; and cf. *Conc.* 575, f. 39r, 4 Aug, ed. BAI, doc. 181, p. 157, for payment).

[74] In 1474 the entire list of lawyers and doctors of medicine was confirmed for another year by the *Savi*. *Not.* 694, f. 27r, 15 Oct, ed. MINNUCCI, 'Documenti', doc. II-12, pp. 84-5.

[75] *Balìa* 26, f. 108r, 25 Sept, ed. BARGAGLI, 'Documenti senesi', doc. 20, p. 287. The payment was 'pro dannis per eum passis et eius benemeritis erga rem publicam Senensem', but would only be forthcoming 'casu quod acceptet supradictam conductam'.

[76] *Conc.* 599, f. 12r, 12 Jul. Presumably he did; he was paid for the next academic year; *Conc.* 601, f. 34v, 20 Dec 1466, *Conc.* 603, f. 49r, 24 Apr, *Conc.* 606, f. 3v, 4 Sept 1467, ed. BAI, docs. 248 (p. 225), 257 (p. 232) and 265 (p. 243).

[77] *Conc.* 345, f. 9v, 14 Jul 1423, ed. PIANIGIANI, doc. 59, pp. 81-2. In 1424 he was exceptionally given the house normally reserved for the *Giudice d'Appellazione* (*Conc.* 352, f. 14v, 18 Sept).

[78] *Conc.* 681, f. 11r, 22 Mar 1480, ed. FERRERI, doc. 97, p. 83.

[79] *Conc.* 587, ff. 5r, 7 Jul, and 9r, 14 Jul 1464, ed. BAI, docs. 209-10, pp. 184-5. A similar dispensation was given to Jacopo di Giovanni d'Arezzo in 1478; since he was experienced in the treatment of plague, he was given *carte blanche* to come and go during his two-year contract (*Conc.* 672, ff. 41v-42r, 26 Oct, ed. FERRERI, doc. 74, pp. 62-3. On him see also MINNUCCI, 'Documenti', p. 266).

[80] *Conc.* 437, f. 30v, Dec 1438. In 1450, Lodovico Petrucciani was required to arrive within eight days and to begin teaching within fifteen (*Conc.* 507, f. 43v, 23 Oct); in 1459, Bartolomeo de Erculanis of Bologna and Nicola da Sirmione were to appear within fifteen days of notification or their contracts would be annulled (*Conc.* 558, f. 33r, 20 Oct, ed. BAI, docs. 122-3, pp. 106-7). The batch of *condotte* offered on 30 and 31 May 1465 were subject to a ten-day acceptance period (two doctors were given exemptions), and in this case the annotations to the record indicate that all but one were in fact accepted within the period (*Conc.* 592, ff. 37v-39r, 30-31 May, ed. BAI, docs. 221-3, pp. 195-202). This was of course much easier with resident teachers whose contracts were being renewed, or with citizen contracts. Busy or absent teachers could mandate a representative to accept a *condotta* on their behalf, as did Francesco Accolti in 1466 (*Conc.* 598, f. 32r, 7 Jun; accepted by Niccolò d'Angelo da Siena, 21 Jun).

[81] ZDEKAUER, *Origini*, p. 19; *Chartularium*, doc. 24, pp. 16-9, 18-20 Jul. In Bologna in 1252 doctors were required to give their deposit of 25 *lire* three weeks before the beginning of the academic year (MAFFEI, 'Un trattato di Bonaccorso degli Elisei', p. 94).

should take effect immediately, and insisted on the teachers moving at no notice at all. The pretensions of the commune on this score were often not met. On occasion the period was extended,[82] and frequently when teachers did arrive late they were forgiven and their salary paid in full nevertheless.[83]

3. *Absenteeism, substitution, leave*

Once the teachers were hired there was the further and not inconsiderable problem of keeping them in Siena and at work. The communal records and the series of *deliberazioni dei Savi* reflect the extent to which this was a preoccupation. Teachers were, as in other *studi*, required to read daily except on feast days,[84] for which special lectures were arranged;[85] only illness was accepted as an excuse, and that had at one stage to be ratified by no less than the *Capitano del Popolo*.[86] Stipulations about regularity of teaching must have been quite detailed, although the statutes containing them – possibly as elsewhere student-university statutes – have not survived. Teachers were to teach at the allotted time,[87] they were not to omit any lessons other than those permitted by the statutes,[88] and in addition they had to have present a minimum number of students. This Bolognese import, the legislation granting the students the right of boycott, must have been adopted in Siena at an early stage, though there is some variation in the level at which the number was fixed. In 1399 Mignanello Mignanelli and Niccolò Sozzini were paid their salaries because they had the minimum of six students.[89] In 1402, however, the lawyer Giovanni di Guccio da Rapolano was paid because he had read with at least ten scholars present.[90] That the principle was still considered valid is shown by the complaint made in 1409 by the hospital of S. Maria della Scala that to make up numbers teachers were reading to their own servants.[91] The first actual legislation we have is of 1428, when a minimum of five students was declared.[92] In 1440 it was briefly altered to six again,[93] but in 1442 it returned to five,[94] the form in

---

[82] E.g. *Conc.* 509, f. 34r, 31 Jan 1451.

[83] *Conc.* 140, f. 5r, 6 Nov 1387; *Conc.* 413, f. 28r, 15 Dec 1434 (the case of Filelfo).

[84] E.g. *Conc.* 372, f. 35r, 20 Apr 1428; *Conc.* 437, f. 30v, Dec 1438; *Studio* 22, 1545 *rotolo*, no foliation.

[85] Above, p. 140.

[86] *Balìa* 24, f. 89v, 30 Jun 1481, eds. Puccinotti, *Storia della Medicina*, p. CLXVI, and Ilardi, 'Ordinamenti', p. 168; copy in *Mis.* 1, f. 108v.

[87] *Mis.* 1, f. 100v, 20 Mar 1473.

[88] *Conc.* 584, ff. 23v-24r, 3 Feb 1464, and see below, p. 257.

[89] *Bicch.* 285, ff. 55r (Mignanello – 'con patti e modi chome si contiene ne la sua lezione cioè che almeno die avere 6 scolari che almeno entrino…'), 55v (Sozzini – 'com pacto espresso che esso debba continovamente [*sic*] 6 scolari altrimenti la detta condocta è nulla'), 28 Jun. Later that year Giovanni Bandini was to be paid 'quando avea fatto fede ch'eso abi letto e abi auti almeno sei iscolari' (*Bicch.* 286, f. 38r, 9 Oct). Mignanelli and Sozzini were paid again in 1400 having had 'sufficientem numerum scolarium' (*Conc.* 218, f. 39v. Sozzini's receipt is dated 29 Dec, Mignanelli's is undated but lies between documents dated 18 Dec and 24 Dec). The notion that six students constituted a quorum is further illustrated by the 1396 proposal that the commune hire a surgeon. If six students demanded it he would also be required to teach (*Conc.* 2111, f. 124r, 1396, ed. Zdekauer, doc. IX, p. 150). The measure was passed on 18 Dec (*CG* 198, ff. 34v-35r).

[90] *Conc.* 225, f. 42r, 23 Feb, ed. Pianigiani, doc. 10, p. 30.

[91] See above, p. 56. In 1450 the statutes stipulated that the audience had to be 'scolari cappati e audienti' which would presumably have made this sort of abuse slightly more difficult (*Conc.* 507, f. 36v, 19 Oct, and *CG* 225, f. 74r, 20 Oct).

[92] *Conc.* 375, f. 22v, 28 Sept.

[93] *Conc.* 447, f. 29r, *Mis.* 1, f. 57r, 20/23 Aug.

[94] *Conc.* 461, ff. 4v-5r, 6 Nov.

which it was enshrined in the legislation of 1450.[95] But the power of boycott could be abused, especially by the non-cooperative or the indigent, and eventually in 1510 the *Balìa* threatened the students with penalties for non-attendance as well.[96]

Failure to comply with these stipulations led to a fine or *punctum*.[97] This could be severe. In 1428 teachers were to be fined a whole month's salary on each occasion on which they had an insufficient number of students.[98] In 1442 it was fixed at 10 *lire* and 10 *soldi*,[99] still a considerable sum, and one which would indeed have been harsher than the deduction of a month's salary for the lowest-paid teachers. In 1445 this became simply 10 *lire*,[100] and by 1464 that sum was the standard fine for all contraventions.[101] Enforcement of the regulations developed in time. Whereas in 1399 teachers were paid on making a sworn declaration that they had taught in accordance with the terms of their contracts,[102] a larger and more complex payroll demanded greater supervision. In the Bolognese system, scholars or indeed anyone could make secret denunciations. In Siena evidence for this is scanty, but the imposition of fines appears to have been carried out by a special official, the *puntatore*. Initially at least this was a minor functionary of the palace, and it is important to note that he was a communal, not a university, official, not surprisingly given that he acted on behalf of the paymasters. This 'spauracchio dell'insegnamento', as Zdekauer called him,[103] was to our knowledge first appointed in 1440, at a salary of 12 *lire* per annum.[104] Two years later the salary was doubled and in addition the *puntatore* was to receive 10 *soldi* for every fine he imposed.[105] He was to appear in the *scolae*, check on numbers attending and on the punctuality of the teachers,[106] and present his fines to the *Camarlengo di Biccherna* who would give him his 10 *soldi* and enter 10 *lire* against the name of the offending teacher for each fine.[107] At a later stage a book of fines seems to have been kept,[108] although only a few fragments have survived,[109] and for the most part it is necessary to rely on the deliberations of

---

[95] *Conc.* 507, f. 36v, 19 Oct, and *CG* 225, f. 74r, 20 Oct 1450. It was still expected in 1467; the *revisore* (see below) was to check whether teachers had read and had had 'debitum numerum scolarium' (*Conc.* 607, f. 22r, 16 Nov).

[96] See above, p. 122 n. 7.

[97] Not to be confused with the *puncta* or breaks in the texts on the syllabus whereby the progress of the teachers was regulated. On the various meanings of the term in the university context, BELLOMO, *Saggio sull'Università*, pp. 205 *seq.*, 255.

[98] *Conc.* 375, f. 22v, 28 Sept.

[99] *Conc.* 461, ff. 4v-5r, 6 Nov.

[100] *Conc.* 477, ff. 13v-14r, 17 Jul.

[101] *Conc.* 584, ff. 23v-24r, 3 Feb; and cf. *Studio* 2, f. 36v, 9 Dec 1475.

[102] See the case of Giovanni Bandini (above, n. 89), and also *Bicch.* 286, f. 44v, 27 Nov 1399; Antonio Tani da Chianciano is paid for teaching canon law 'quando arà fatto fede abi letto sicondo la forma de la sua lezione'.

[103] ZDEKAUER, p. 108.

[104] The institution was established in August and the first *puntatore* appointed in October (*Conc.* 447, f. 29r, *Mis.* 1, f. 57r, 20/23 Aug; *Conc.* 448, ff. 35v-36r, 21 Oct). We cannot be sure that such a system was not in operation earlier, though it clearly was not in 1399 when a notary was instructed to make inquiries as to whether a teacher had been giving lessons or not (*Conc.* 212, f. 11r, 1 Dec, and 22v, 26 Dec). Also in 1428, fines were still to be paid by the teachers before the *apotisse* for their salaries were given, whereas later fines were deducted automatically (*Conc.* 375, f. 22v, 28 Sept).

[105] *Conc.* 461, f. 5r, 6 Nov 1422.

[106] Loc. cit.; also *Conc.* 477, f. 12r, 14 Jul 1445. In the *rotolo* of 1545-6 this was stipulated as a daily obligation (*Studio* 22, no foliation).

[107] *Conc.* 477, ff. 13v-14r, 17 Jul 1445. In 1483 these fines were passed to the office of the *Gabella*, the paymasters at the time. *Studio* 2, f. 92r, 27 May.

[108] *Mis.* 1, f. 100v, 20 Mar 1473.

[109] Some are in *Notarile* 858 (no foliation) and *Studio* 20. See below, pp. 162-3.

the *Concistoro* or the *Savi*, as well as on salary payments, for evidence. Despite the regulations, there was some fluidity about this job. In the later fifteenth century he was described by a variety of alternative titles – *ricercatore*,[110] *revisore*,[111] *inquisitore*,[112] *scrutator*,[113] *exploratore sive requisitore*,[114] as well as *puntatore*.[115] Towards the end of the century *Studio* officials did get involved in enforcement,[116] though the office of *puntatore* continued into the sixteenth century.[117] But it also appears that this official, whatever his title or powers, was, at least by the late fifteenth century, seen as an adjunct to the traditional mechanisms of secret denunciation, both in universities and in communal life generally. Secret denunciation of delinquent teachers was encouraged in 1464 (a quarter of the fine was to be given to the anonymous informant),[118] and in 1472 this was increased to a third; the informant would be allowed to keep his cut even if the fine was lifted. At the same time the two mechanisms were brought together; the records were to be kept by a *custos secretum*, or even more than one.[119] In a further measure of 1475 it is evident that this was the new role of the *ricercatore*, whose identity was now to be kept secret.[120]

The repeated modifications of the *puntatore's* job may be connected to the career of the first individual we know to have held the office, one Giovanni da Napoli. His activities were subject to frequent correction by the *Concistoro*. In July 1443 a teacher was excused two of his three fines; in one case it had been alleged that he had had an insufficient number of scholars, which he claimed was not the case, and in the other he had changed classrooms 'propter immunditiam quandam in solitis scolis factam'.[121] In October another four teachers were excused, with no reasons given,[122] in Decem-

[110] *Bicch.* 326, ff. 75v, 151v, 26 Mar 1465 (Ser Filippo d'Agnolo da Prato 'ricercatore de'lletture de' dottori') *Conc.* 606, ff. 3v-4r, 4 Sept 1467, ed. BAI, doc. 245, p. 243 (Pasquino Menci); *Conc.* 637, ff. 2v-3r, 2 Nov 1472 (two are appointed); *Conc.* 654, f. 40r, 30 Oct 1475, ed. BAI, doc. 345, p. 369 (the *Savi* were to elect 'unum recercatorem secretum ad lustrandum et perquirendum si legentes in Studij Senensi faciunt eorum debitum secundum formam Statutorum'). The appointment of *recercatores* to make *pontature* in a non-*Studio* context in 1413 (*Bicch.* 2, ff. 217v-218v, 22 Mar) makes it clear that there was nothing special about this terminology.

[111] *Conc.* 607, f. 22r, 16 Nov 1467, ed. BAI, doc. 246, f. 244. The term was used of the same Pasquino, above, n. 110, 'revisorem deputandum ad puntandum doctores legentes et perquirendum si legunt'.

[112] *Conc.* 607, f. 82r, 29 Dec, ed. BAI, doc. 269, p. 247; again, used of Pasquino.

[113] *Conc.* 702, f. 25v, 3 Oct 1483, ed. FERRERI, doc. 181, pp. 154-5; Galgano di Caterino is *scrutator studii*. The same man had performed this role in 1476 (*Conc.* 657, f. 14v, 18 Mar, ed. FERRERI, doc. 4, p. 3), and in 1485, when he was still doing it, he was described as *famulus palatii* (*Conc.* 715, f. 9r, 17 Nov, ed. FERRERI, doc. 221, p. 186). On him see above, p. 85 n. 182.

[114] *Conc.* 724, f. 32v, 29 Jun 1487, ed. FERRERI, doc. 247, p. 211.

[115] The term is still – or again – in use in 1494 (*Conc.* 765, ff. 13v-14r, 29 Apr, ed. FERRERI, doc. 339, p. 321; a fine is cancelled 'salvo tamen iuris puntatoris pro sua quarta parte consueto'), though it is perhaps significant that in 1498 the person appointed to this post was described as 'deputatus…super puntaturis doctorum', and subsequently 'famulus studii' rather than *puntatore* (*Sale* 24, f. 164r, 13 Mar, and 164v, 29 Mar).

[116] Loc. cit. In 1492 the 'bidellus sapientie' (a mistake for the *bidello* of the *Studio*?) was to check whether a grammar teacher was teaching the prescribed texts (*Balìa* 37, f. 50r, 13 Aug).

[117] *Studio* 19, no foliation, n.d., but judging by the hand probably sixteenth century: 'Bartolomeo di Pier atonio [*sic*] sarto ha inteso che il luogo del Pontatore è vacato' and applied for it.

[118] *Conc.* 584, ff. 23v-24r, 3 Feb, ed. BAI, doc. 205, pp. 178-9.

[119] *CG* 234, f. 180r-v, 3 Aug.

[120] *Conc.* 654, f. 40r, 30 Oct, ed. BAI, doc. 345, p. 369 (see n. 110 above). But the secrecy does not appear to have been intended to last for long; the following year it becomes clear that a palace official, Galgano di Caterino Rotellino, had been in charge of the operation (see n. 113).

[121] *Conc.* 465, f. 12r, 22 Jul.

[122] *Conc.* 466, f. 46r, 18 Oct.

ber another two,[123] and in November Giovanni was found to have fined a teacher who was no longer on the payroll.[124] Giovanni was doubtless overenthusiastic about his duties;[125] but from what can be gleaned from the deliberations of the *Savi* in particular it is clear that the frequency of fines is all but matched by the frequency of their cancellation. The desire to get teachers back to work could outweigh considerations of discipline and authority. Fines could be cancelled if the offending teacher made up the lectures he had missed.[126] Sometimes the 'honesta ragione'[127] for absence – the cause of the great majority of fines – is given as an obvious excuse; the teacher had been unable to get a free classroom,[128] had had permission from the *Savi*,[129] had skipped three lessons just before carnival,[130] had been at a spa,[131] had been ill, or engaged in public affairs.[132] On other occasions no explanation is given,[133] and in the late fifteenth century these pardons are often done in batches, giving the appearance of amnesties.[134] A certain laxity or tolerance must have been considered advisable when the

[123] *Conc.* 467, f. 36r, 30 Dec.

[124] *Conc.* 467, f. 16v, 28 Nov. An even clearer example of the authorities having egg on their faces is the case of Bernardino Guelfi, who in 1520 was paid his salary despite the fact that he had not taught; this was deemed to be not his fault, as the previous *Savi* had omitted to appoint him to a *lettura* (*Studio* 3, f. 16v, 1 Jan).

[125] It is not known for how long he held this office, but he was a long-standing communal employee; in 1465 he marked forty-two years of service to the *palazzo pubblico* (CG 230, ff. 237v-238r, 20 Jan).

[126] *Conc.* 578, f. 22r, 25 Jan 1463, eds. NARDI, *Mariano Sozzini*, doc. 49, pp. 143-4, and BAI, doc. 186, pp. 162-3; and *Sale* 23, f. 95r, 8 Jul 1496.

[127] *Conc.* 584, ff. 23v-24r, 3 Feb 1464, ed. BAI, doc. 205, pp. 178-9.

[128] *Conc.* 728, f. 12v, 24 Jan 1488, ed. FERRERI, doc. 267, pp. 228-9; Benedetto da Cingoli had missed four lessons because 'non potuit habere sedem'.

[129] *Conc.* 728, ff. 12v-13v, 24 Jan 1488, ed. FERRERI, docs. 268-9, pp. 229-30. Francesco da Ciglione had missed ten lessons, the Carmelite Bernardino had missed one.

[130] *Conc.* 770, f. 22v, 13 Feb 1495, ed. FERRERI, doc. 352, pp. 337-8.

[131] *Sale* 23, f. 95r, 8 Jul 1496.

[132] *Conc.* 726, f. 27v, 13 Oct 1487, ed. FERRERI, doc. 254, p. 217 (Bartolomeo Compagnini was excused his *puncte* because he was ill); *Conc.* 777, f. 16r-v, 21/22 Apr 1496, ed. FERRERI, doc. 345, pp. 349-50 (five doctors who did not teach through illness, and three who had been 'pro re publica impediti', were paid their salaries). In 1498 Cennino di Maestro Niccolò had his fines lifted as he had been absent on communal business (*Sale* 24, f. 166r, 6 Jul), and in 1499 the Franciscan Manuele had his fines cancelled for both reasons, 'quod ipse erat occupatus in rebus publicis et in egritudine' (*Conc.* 794, f. 23v, 26 Feb, ed. FERRERI, doc. 401, p. 385). Antonio Giordano da Venafro was also excused his fines ('occupatus in rebus publicis') on the same day. Fines could also be waived at the end of a contract or on renunciation of a contract, as was the case with Giovanni di Ser Donato d'Arezzo, doctor in art and medicine (*Conc.* 613, f. 34r, 30 Dec 1468, ed. BAI, doc. 284, p. 268). If this is the same man he had not been so fortunate a decade previously, when he had been fined for missing fifty of his seventy-five teaching days (*Conc.* 549, f. 27r, 27 Apr 1458, ed. BAI, doc. 106, p. 89).

[133] Placido Placidi and Guidantonio Buoninsegni's excuses were accepted as 'iustis et rationabilibus' (*Conc.* 607, f. 22r, 16 Nov 1467, ed. BAI, doc. 267, pp. 245-6); Mag. Oliviero di Michele's excuses, though not described, were similarly accepted on 2 Nov 1468 (*Conc.* 613, f. 3r, ed. BAI, doc. 282, p. 265); Ferrandus of Portugal, *cerusico*, and Magister Jordanus had their fines expunged without explanation on 20 Apr 1473 (*Conc.* 639, f. 25v, ed. BAI, doc. 333, pp. 328-9; Ferrandus's absence was declared to have been legitimate).

[134] On 29 Dec 1467 four teachers were absolved of their *puncte*; Bulgarino Bulgarini, Giovanni di Mariano di Ser Bindotto, Lodovico da Spoleto and Francesco di Meo Peri (*Conc.* 607, f. 82r, 29 Dec, ed. BAI, doc. 269, p. 247). In that academic year three others had their fines cancelled; Placido Placidi and Guidantonio Buoninsegni, whose excuses were accepted as 'iustis et rationabilibus' (*Conc.* 607, f. 22r, 16 Nov, ed. BAI, doc. 267, pp. 245-6), and Pietro Sacco da Verona (*Conc.* 609, f. 42v, 18 Apr 1468). In 1476 teachers unjustly fined were to have their fines cancelled (the measure does not give names or numbers); *Conc.* 656, f. 5r, 6 Jan 1476, ed. FERRERI, doc. 1, p. 1. An example of a bulk cancellation is in *Studio* 2, ff. 40v-41r, 20 Mar 1476. The *Savi* listed eight teachers who were to be penalised: Guidantonio Buoninsegni (number of *puncte* not specified); then a list of seven, all of whom had not taught: Filippo Francesconi (eighteen *puncte*), 'Dominum seu magistrum' Alessandro da San Gimignano, Augustinian (two *puncte*), Bartolomeo Sansedoni (three), Pietro de' Spinelli (one), Maestro

chief concern of the *Savi* was to get teachers back to work and when their bargaining position was not very strong; it may well also be an indicator that certain teachers were receiving preferential treatment. The importance of a teacher to the *Studio* could outweigh any offence he may have committed. This was made explicit in the case of Lodovico Pontano da Roma, whose fine of 350 florins, imposed on 26 November 1428, was lifted on 23 April 1434 'considerato quantum lectura…sit utilis Studio Senensi'.[135] The only element that appears to have remained unchanged, at least by end of the century, was the *puntatore*'s cut.[136]

What was the extent of absenteeism? Clearly it could be a recurrent problem. In addition to the individual cases mentioned above, there is occasional evidence in the fifteenth century of teachers who had contracts but did not teach, at least for a period. The danger of assuming from lists of contracts that all who were hired then carried out their duties is most clearly illustrated by the presence of Benedetto Barzi in both Sienese and Florentine lists for a number of years.[137] In 1462 three eminent teachers, Mariano Sozzini, Borghese Borghesi and Mansueto da Perugia, were not initially paid their first *terzaria* because they had not lectured.[138] The fact that they were offered cancellation of their fines provided they made up the lessons they had omitted is revealing, and it may be no coincidence that a measure of 1464 lamented that 'per ogni minima cosa et ogni minimo impedimento la maggior parte de' doctori lassano molte volte l'anno le molte lectioni'.[139] In a record of voting for the payment

Barbetta (three), Giovanni da Montalcino (two), Matteo da Grosseto (twenty). In 1477 six teachers had their fines cancelled by the *Savi* on the same day; the Augustinian Maestro Alessandro (five *puncte*), Guidantonio Buoninsegni (number of *puncte* unspecified, Francesco Accolti (two), Jacopo di Bastiano Tinellocci (two), Bernardino Luti (number not specified), Bartolommeo Sansedoni (number not specified) (*Studio* 2, ff. 55v-56r, 18 Apr). Another example is the confirmation in 1483 of the fines of four teachers; Jacopo da Germonia had twenty-seven *puncte*, Borghese Borghesi and Lutio Luti each had fifteen, and Arcangelo di Giovanni di Maestro Domenico eight (*Conc.* 702, f. 25v, 3 Oct, ed. FERRERI, doc. 181, pp. 154-5). The *Concistoro* declared that, should the fines exceed the amount due for a *terzaria*, the excess would be discounted. (Borghesi was subsequently excused as the absences had been due to his brother's illness and death; *Conc.* 705, f. 29r, 21 Apr 1484, ed. FERRERI, doc. 197, p. 166.) In 1485 ten teachers had their fines confirmed in one batch (this was becoming standard practice). The most serious offenders were Alessandro Sermoneta who had forty-six *puncte*, Borghese Borghesi with eleven, and Francesco Ciglioni with ten; *Conc.* 715, f. 9r, 17 Nov, ed. FERRERI, doc. 221, pp. 186-7. (Borghesi's were again subsequently lifted; the *Concistoro* accepted that he had been ill and had arranged a substitute, *Conc.* 716, f. 29v, 21 Feb 1486, ed. FERRERI, doc. 228, pp. 193-4). In 1494 the *Concistoro* records include a list of five doctors who had been fined, including the rector who attracted twenty-five *puncte* (*Conc.* 765, parchment addition to inside back cover, ed. FERRERI, doc. 341, p. 324). One of those penalised, Bindino di Tommaso, was subsequently excused three of his four *puncte* on the grounds that the lectures had fallen just before carnival the previous year (*Conc.* 770, f. 22v, 13 Feb 1495, ed. FERRERI, doc. 352, pp. 337-8). The most striking example is the blanket cancellation of all fines of all doctors; *Sale* 24, f. 168v, 6 Dec 1498; cf. *Studio* 3, ff. 38v-39r, 18 May 1524 (thirteen teachers absolved of their fines), 45v-46r, 6 May 1525 (nine teachers absolved).

[135] *Conc.* 409, f. 36v, 23 Apr, ed. imperfectly by PIANIGIANI, doc. 166, pp. 180-1.

[136] In 1472 this was raised from 10 *soldi* out of the 10-*lire* fine (i.e. 5%) to a third (*CG* 234, f. 180r, 3 Aug 1472), though by the end of the century it was a quarter (*Conc.* 765, ff. 13v-14r, 29 Apr 1494, ed. FERRERI, doc. 339, p. 321; a fine was cancelled 'salvo tamen iuris puntatoris pro sua quarta parte consueto').

[137] Below, pp. 186-7 and n. 29. On Barzi see D. MAFFEI, 'Una nuova fonte per la biografia di Benedetto Barzi da Perugia (1379 ca. – 1459). Con precisazioni su Benedetto da Piombino', *Index. Quaderni camerti di studi romanistici / International Survey of Roman Law*, 22: Omaggio a Peter Stein (1994), pp. 511-28; repr. in his *Studi di storia delle università*, pp. 235*-252*. Whether this was wishful thinking or an advertising ploy is debatable. The appearance of the name of Mariano Sozzini on the *rotuli* in the 1530s was judged by KOŠUTA, 'Documenti', p. 396 (and cf. pp. 397, 400, 410, 414), to be a case of the latter.

[138] *Conc.* 577, f. 47r, 4 Aug, ed. BAI, doc. 185, p. 161; BARGAGLI, *Bartolomeo Sozzini*, p. 34 and n. 33. The authorities eventually relented on condition that the teachers made up the lessons they had missed; see above, p. 161 n. 126.

[139] *Conc.* 584, ff. 23v-24r, 3 Feb, ed. BAI, doc. 205, pp. 178-9; also discussed in BARGAGLI, *Bartolomeo Sozzini*, p. 34. For a similar perception of a widespread problem in Padua in 1424, V. LAZZARINI, 'Crisi nello Studio di Padova a mezzo il Quattrocento', *Atti dell'Istituto Veneto di Scienze Lettere ed Arti, Classe di Scienze Morali e Lettere*, 109 (1950-51), pp. 201-11 (pp. 204 *seq.*). In 1478 the *Balìa* had to order all doctors to get on with their teaching (*Balìa* 11, f. 48r, 21 Dec).

of teachers dateable to 1497-8 – an exceptional period of crisis perhaps – twenty-five out of the forty-seven doctors on the list are recorded as not having taught for a whole *terzaria*.[140] By the mid-sixteenth century absenteeism was clearly becoming chronic. In 1532 the *collegio di dottori leggenti* complained about those who 'sotto finti colori non leghono la metà del tempo',[141] and in 1533 a body of 'cittadini zelanti della Conservazione dello Studio' reported that salaries were 'male distribuiti, e non secondo le fadighe, e alcuni sotto varii pretesti non leggevano, e havevano il salario in danno di quelli, che si affadigavano'.[142] Cascio Pratilli felt that by the mid-sixteenth century it must have been usual for the *rotolo* to include teachers 'nominalmente iscritti nei ruoli' as well as those who actually taught.[143] Certainly it was not uncommon elsewhere for teachers not to fulfil all their obligations. The complete series of *puncta* for late fifteenth-century Bologna shows frequent absences of many teachers for weeks or months at a time, almost as if, for some, a *condotta* was an optional way of adding to income as and when necessary, rather than an occupation in itself.[144] It is difficult to be sure of the situation in Siena. Some lists of *puncte* in the late 1530s, the only period for which totals survive, show great disparity. The year 1537-8 shows a fair degree of absenteeism. A total of 390 *puncte* are recorded. Of forty-three teachers in the second *terzaria* and forty-five in the third, only ten have no *puncte*, ten have two, another ten have between three and eight, seven have between ten and seventeen, and five have thirty or over. Of those five, three were absent for most or all of one of the two *terzarie*, while the other two barely put in an appearance. It is noticeable that those with the highest record of absenteeism were from the middle ranks of the payroll; none of the very highest or lowest paid teachers were fined very much.[145] On the other hand the first two *terzarie* of 1538-9 reveal only ten teachers who received *puncte* at all (plus one who ceased teaching halfway through the second *terzaria*), and only one of these, a regular absentee in the previous year, had more than ten.[146]

No teacher was to omit to teach without permission, and this general prohibition was sometimes repeated in specific contracts.[147] Yet leave was frequently given, for a great variety of reasons. A fre-

---

[140] *Conc.* 2139, no. 110, ff. 201r-202r, n.d. but relating to the academic year 1497-8; dateable by the payment of the vice-rector, Filippo de Scalandrini.

[141] *Conc.* 2007, no foliation, Nov 1532, ed. Košuta, doc. I-3, pp. 334-5. On this body see below, p. 173.

[142] CG 243, f. 244v, 14 Dec, ed. Košuta, doc. I-4, pp. 335-7.

[143] Cascio Pratilli, *L'Università e il Principe*, p. 201 – and see p. 11, n. 3, and pp. 13 *seq*. This has been described by Grendler, review of Minnucci and Košuta, *Lo Studio di Siena* in *Renaissance Quarterly*, 43 (1990), pp. 836-8 (p. 837) as 'deceptive advertising'. Cf. Pavia, where teachers were found to have been dictating lessons and failing to attend disputations; Zorzoli, 'Interventi dei Duchi', p. 148.

[144] Archivio di Stato di Bologna, *Assunteria di Studio: Riformatori dello Studio: Appuntazioni dei Lettori, 1465-1512*. An interesting case of frequent absenteeism is outlined by H. S. Matsen, 'Alessandro Achillini (1463-1512) as Professor of Philosophy in the "Studio" of Padua (1506-1508)', *Quaderni per la Storia dell'Università di Padova*, 1 (1968), pp. 91-109 (esp. pp. 94-5, 102-3, 105-8). A similar point is made in relation to Rome in the fifteenth century by Frova, 'Crisi e rifondazione', p. 31, where a contract could be little more than a form of benefice. A number of lecturers also missed whole *terzarie* at Pisa; Verde, *Lo Studio fiorentino*, V, pp. 7-16.

[145] *Studio* 20, no foliation. *Puncte* could be given for a host of reasons, of course, but absenteeism seems to have been the most frequent, and when teachers were close to being given the maximum number possible it is perhaps safe to assume that this was the reason.

[146] Loc. cit. He had nineteen *puncte* in the first *terzaria* and was replaced for the second.

[147] E.g. the Franciscan Luca, 'sacre theologie professori' (*Conc.* 348, f. 27r, 23 Feb 1424); and Gabriele da Spoleto (*Conc.* 377, f. 28v, 15 Feb 1429), on whom Nardi, *Mariano Sozzini*, p. 12, Idem, 'Appunti sui maestri', p. 217, and P. Vian, 'Garofoli, Gabriele', *DBI*, 52 (1999), pp. 368-70. Cf. also the contract of Giovanni di Ser Donato d'Arezzo; permission for him to miss teaching had to be obtained from the *Concistoro* itself (*Conc.* 534, ff. 56v-57r, 28 Oct 1455).

quent one was taking the waters at one of Siena's spas, particularly in May, when as has been seen there was also a break in teaching for this purpose.[148] The standard period for leave, as with communal offices, was eight days, and this was often granted in the summer months without the specification of any reason;[149] longer periods of ten days,[150] fifteen days,[151] twenty days,[152] one month,[153] or even indefinite leave,[154] were not unknown. Variants on this are the occasions when a teacher's other commitments are recognised and his 'teaching load' alleviated, naturally with a drop in salary.[155] When the reason for absence was personal and the teacher a non-Sienese, there were obviously risks in granting leave, and the authorities were aware of them; Francesco Pontano, teacher of arts and rhetoric, was granted leave in 1422 on condition that if he failed to return within the permitted fifteen days he would be fined without any further payment of salary due, and without any prospect of being reinstated. He did overstay his leave, but when the commune refused to have him back several students forced it to back down by threatening to depart as well.[156] On another occasion the *Concistoro* was so fearful of the prospect of Florence enticing one of their teachers, Guasparre Sighicelli da Bologna, away that they refused him leave altogether despite the fact that his request came in the middle of the summer vacation.[157]

The reasons for leave of absence were sometimes personal and were often not given; frequently however they were a consequence of the teachers' inevitable involvement with communal affairs, and in this sense the commune can be said to have been its own worst enemy. A teacher who was elected prior,[158] or *gonfaloniere*,[159] or member of a *balìa*,[160] or *podestà* in the Sienese *contado* or elsewhere,[161]

---

[148] E.g. Bartalo di Tura (who had a house in the spa community of Petriolo) was given three days leave for this reason, *Conc.* 556, f. 7r, 8 May 1459, and below, p. 323 n. 193; Giovanni Battista Caccialupi was given a month, subsequently extended into a second month (*Conc.* 669, ff. 15r, 17 Mar, 36r, 28 Apr (leave was also given to Francesco Nini), 40r, 29 Apr 1478, ed. FERRERI, docs. 66, p. 58, 69-70, pp. 59-60. In the mid-sixteenth century there is an instance of a medical attestation for a teacher; *Conc.* 2221, no foliation, 1541, ed. KOŠUTA, 'Documenti', doc. XXIV, 1541.

[149] E.g. *Conc.* 193, f. 11r, 30 Sept 1396, and *Conc.* 216, f. 15v, 21 Jul 1400 (both Giovanni di Buccio da Spoleto); *Conc.* 321, f. 12v, 20 Jul 1419 (Ugo Benzi; he may go to Florence for the permitted period, as stipulated in his contract); *Conc.* 351, f. 20v, 10 Aug 1424 (the lawyer Antonio Roselli, allowed to return to his native Arezzo during the vacation).

[150] *Conc.* 427, f. 37r, 12 Apr 1437 (Abroardus de Camerino, doctor of law).

[151] *Conc.* 338, f. 3v, 5 May 1422 (Francesco da Roma), *Conc.* 435, f. 32v, 13 Aug 1438 (Angelo de' Narducci da Perugia).

[152] *Conc.* 372, f. 13r, 18 Mar 1428 (Antonio de Aretio, grammar teacher, unpaid leave).

[153] *Conc.* 466, f. 12r, 10 Sept 1443 (Filippo da Pistoia). In 1462 the highly-paid Mansueto da Perugia obtained one month's leave without salary (*Conc.* 574, f. 17r, 19 May) at the request of Braccio Baglioni of Perugia (*Conc.* 2003, no. 59, 15 May, and cf. the *Concistoro*'s reply, *Conc.* 1680, f. 64v, 19 May), and in the summer was given leave for the rest of the vacation (which might well be connected with the outbreak of plague); *Conc.* 575, f. 37r, 4 Aug.

[154] *Conc.* 337, f. 43r, 25 Apr 1422 (Lorenzo d'Arezzo).

[155] E.g. *Conc.* 244, f. 37r, 30 Oct 1406 (Giovanni de' Bellanti). In 1495 Niccolò Borghesi's salary was reduced from 300 to 250 florins and the condition imposed that he read personally (*CG* 241, f. 7v, 23 Jun 1495). He was chancellor at the time.

[156] *Conc.* 338, f. 3v, 5 May, *Conc.* 339, f. 13r, 29 Jul, and *Conc.* 340, f. 26r, 31 Oct.

[157] See above, p. 154 and n. 45.

[158] *Conc.* 212, f. 8v, 22 Nov 1399 (Niccolò Sozzini); *Conc.* 467, f. 5r, Nov 1443 (Galgano Borghesi); *Conc.* 488, f. 14r, 11 May 1447 (Bartolomeo Salimbeni).

[159] *Conc.* 465, f. 7r, 8 Jul, and *Conc.* 467, f. 5r, Nov 1443 (Pietro de' Micheli).

[160] *Conc.* 403, f. 2v, 2 Mar 1433 (unnamed 'doctoribus de balia'); *Conc.* 525, f. 36r, 24 Mar 1454 (Tommaso Docci and Bartolo di Tura).

[161] *Conc.* 387, f. 12r, 18 Sept 1430 (Pietro di Ser Antonio Bonazini); *Conc.* 418, ff. 3r, 2 Sept, 13r, 23 Sept 1435 (Bartolomeo Borghesi); *Conc.* 425, f. 7r, 10 Nov 1436 (Tommaso Docci).

could obviously not continue to fulfil the daily requirements of his teaching contract. Still less could a doctor who was chosen – as they so naturally were – for an embassy or mission;[162] while medics were often sent to attend and treat *signori* (or their relatives) with whom Siena was anxious to maintain cordial relations – a professional service, but, like that of lawyer-ambassadors, also a diplomatic function.[163] These offices could be heaped upon eminent citizens to the virtual exclusion of teaching. Between 1431 and 1455 Tommaso Docci was almost annually on missions or in office, and was constantly on advisory commissions;[164] Pietro de' Micheli was in almost continual service from 1442 to 1446 while holding a *lettura*.[165] On very few occasions do *Concistoro* records show the interests of the *Studio* being put first, with the teacher excused office rather than teaching. Two such instances are cases where the office was a *podesteria* in Sienese territory, for which the appointee was presumably not considered indispensable.[166] The conflict of priorities, between keeping the *Studio* staffed with the best

[162] *Conc.* 259, f. 17v, 1 Apr 1409 (Francesco Casini); Conc 287, f. 3v, 1 Nov 1413 (Pietro de' Pecci, sent off as orator to Florence and to the pope the day after the ratification of his *condotta*; *Conc.* 286, f. 32r, 30 Oct); *Conc.* 390, ff. 16v, 29 Jan (Pietro – de' Micheli?), and 18v, 3 Feb 1431 (Giovanni da Chianciano); *Conc.* 401, f. 13v, 9 Nov 1432 (Pietro de' Micheli); *Conc.* 402, ff. 2v-3r, 1 Jan 1433 (Tommaso Docci, orator to the pope); *Conc.* 403, f. 4v, 4 Mar 1433, *Conc.* 456, f. 18r, 17 Jan and *Conc.* 457, f. 77r, Apr 1442 (Pietro de' Micheli); *Conc.* 458, *apotissa*, no foliation, n.d. but May-Jun 1442 (Giovanni de' Mignanelli), etc. Lorenzo Lanti, who after years of peregrination had successfully petitioned the *Consiglio del Popolo* for a *condotta* in 1474 (*CG* 235, ff. 206v-207r, 28 Apr), was the Sienese ambassador in Rome in 1482; he wrote from there requesting that it be extended for the coming year (*Balìa* 506, no. 40, 12 Nov). See also below, p. 216.

[163] Giovanni da Sermoneta was repeatedly given permission to absent himself in the service of the *signore* of Piombino, mainly to treat his mother (*Conc.* 390, f. 25v, 12 Feb 1431; *Conc.* 433, f. 3r, 3 Mar 1438; *Conc.* 449, f. 2v, 2 Nov 1440; *Conc.* 461, f. 44v, 11 Dec 1442. She was subsequently treated by Bartolo di Tura, who received similar permission to absent himself from teaching; *Conc.* 473, f. 23r, 26 Nov 1444, as he did in 1447 for the treatment of another *signore*, *Conc.* 488, f. 14r, 11 May 1447), and once to treat the *condottiere* Gattamelata (*Conc.* 448, f. 8v, 13 Aug 1440); in 1438, Pietro Giovanetti was allowed to go to Bagni di Petriolo to treat the cardinal of Siena (*Conc.* 434, f. 2r-v, 1 May). See also GAROSI, p. 307.

[164] Docci was twice *Capitano del Popolo* (*Conc.* 480, f. 1r, 1 Jan 1446; *CG* 226, f. 20v, and *Conc.* 517, f. 1r, Nov-Dec 1452), three times member of a *balìa* (*Conc.* 402, ff. 68v-69v, 21 Feb – twice – and *Conc.* 404, f. 2r, 1 Jun 1433, *Conc.* 525, f. 30r, 20 Mar, *Conc.* 529, f. 67v, 8 Dec 1454), twice member of the *Concistoro* (*Conc.* 472, f. 41v, 14 Oct 1444, *Conc.* 474, f. 2v, 1 Jan 1445, *Conc.* 522, f. 2r, 1 Sept 1453), three times *podestà* of a commune in the *contado* (*Conc.* 393, f. 32r, 23 Jul 1431, *Conc.* 396, f. 73r, 26 Feb 1432, *Conc.* 422, f. 61v, 30 Jun 1436, *Conc.* 425, f. 7r, 10 Nov 1436, *Conc.* 469, f. 6v, 7 Mar 1444), orator to the pope in 1432 (*Conc.* 401, f. 25v, 19 Nov 1432, *Conc.* 402, ff. 2v-3r, 1 Jan, 43r, 2 Feb 1433; *Conc.* 403, ff. 10r, 12 Mar, 56v, 28 Apr 1433), to the *signore* of Piombino in 1439 (*Conc.* 442, ff. 18v, 26 Sept, 22r, 3 Oct, 22v, 4 Oct, 39v and 66v-67r, 27 Oct 1439) and to the king of Aragon in 1447 (*Conc.* 490, ff. 33r, 16 Oct, 49r, 31 Oct 1447). He was sent on six missions in the *contado*, was once a syndic of the *podestà*, once an *allibratore* and member of no fewer than thirty commissions of varying importance and duration. By the end of this period it was rare for him not to be on any commission of importance. He was excused office because of teaching once (*Conc.* 1938, no. 50, 24 Jul 1437), and in 1452 he was excused a fine for non-attendance at the *Consiglio del Popolo* because he had been teaching (*Conc.* 2122, no. 57, 3 Nov). In 1455 he was made eligible for the *podesteria* of Buonconvento despite his name having originally been excluded because of his teaching; this was in recognition of the work he had done for the *Balìa* (*Conc.* 530, f. 50v, 31 Jan). See P. NARDI, 'Docci, Tommaso', in *DBI*, 40 (1991), pp. 339-44; IDEM, 'Enea Silvio Piccolomini, il cardinale Domenico Capranica e il giurista Tommaso Docci', in *Studi in memoria di Mario E. Viora*. Biblioteca della Rivista di storia del diritto italiano, 30 (Rome, 1990), pp. 539-47; and MINNUCCI, 'Documenti', pp. 311-2.

[165] *Conc.* 456, f. 18v, 17 Jan 1442 (he is orator to Lombardy); *Conc.* 457, f. 77r, Apr 1442 (his leave is extended until the end of May); *Conc.* 463, f. 24v, 22 Mar 1443 (he is excused teaching because he is in charge of the arrangements for honouring the pope); *Conc.* 465, f. 7r, 8 Jun 1443 and *Conc.* 467, f. 5r, Nov 1443 (he is *gonfaloniere*); *Conc.* 469, ff. 16v, 21 Mar, 25v, 4 Apr 1444 (his *lettura* is annulled for the rest of the academic year with effect from Easter, as he is ambassador to Ferrara); *Conc.* 477, f. 12r, 14 Jul 1445 (he is on an embassy to the king of Aragon); *Conc.* 481, f. 5v, 6 Mar 1446 (he is given thirty days' leave to go to the baths); *Conc.* 481, ff. 27v-28r, 26 Mar 1446 (another commission, for which an indefinite period of leave is given). On his earlier diplomatic activity cf. BRANDMÜLLER, 'Die Römischen Berichte'. Cf. also the example of Mariano Sozzini, well-documented by NARDI, *Mariano Sozzini*, and below, pp. 221-2.

[166] *Conc.* 418, f. 3r, 2 Sept 1435 (Bartolomeo de' Borghesi is excused his appointment as *podestà* of Magliano so that he can teach. Strangely, though, he was replaced as *podestà* by another teacher, Bartolo di Tura; *Conc.* 420, f. 29r, 23 Feb 1436). Cf. also *Conc.* 425, f. 7r, 10 Nov 1436. In 1462 it was decided that Giovanni di Domenico, newly elected *podestà* of Radicofani, should continue to teach and have a substitute in the administrative post instead (*Conc.* 577, f. 29v, 10 Dec).

teachers, and using the same expertise for the commune, was felt to be problematic for both the authorities and the individuals concerned. The commune struggled through legislation to achieve a balance,[167] while the teachers concerned complained about the interruptions,[168] but rarely hesitated to accept the prestigious offers of important missions and commissions. The problem was especially acute in Siena for two reasons. The city's strategic position meant that intense diplomatic engagement was a constant and unavoidable necessity, while the size and configuration of Siena's *contado* meant that a disproportionate amount of effort had to go into lower-status administrative posts there, many at considerable distance from the city.[169] Teachers were by and large much keener to avoid the latter.

None of this meant that teaching stopped. Substitutes were arranged, despite their prohibition by the statutes (and by individual contract) other than in cases of illness.[170] Where these were allowed, it was initially for the teacher to find a substitute[171] and pay him out of his own salary,[172] although his choice had to be approved by the *Savi* before his departure.[173] Later in the fifteenth century there may have been a tendency for substitution to be organised by the commune,[174] and certainly for the authorities to wish to exercise greater control over the process.[175] Even this system, however, was not fail-

Teaching could be a valid excuse for non-attendance at meetings; Goro Lolli's fine for absence from the *Consiglio del Popolo* was lifted for this reason (*Conc.* 538, f. 21r, 17 Apr 1456), and later that year he was allowed to absent himself from the *Balìa* on days he was teaching, except Sundays (*Balìa* 1, f. 41r, 17 Oct).

[167] E.g. excusing doctors (as well as *cavalieri*) from the scrutiny for the offices of *Camarlengo* of the *Biccherna*, *Sale e Paschi*, and *Gabella* (*Statuti* 41, f. 198r, 1427) and a large number of lesser posts (f. 198v); see ASCHERI, *Siena nel Rinascimento*, p. 21 n. 14. In 1441 the repetition of the famous 'statuti Bernardiniani' measure, ordering that everyone was to work, exempted 'Cavalieri doctori notari et altri alla università de' giudici e notari della città di Siena sottoposti né per studenti che portino cappa o habito scholasticho'. In 1450 the ban on doctors holding office was reiterated: 'non possino exercitare alcuno altro offitio o benefitio né essi usare o fruire né alcuna delegatione di Comune di Siena acceptare né exercitare durante il tempo dele loro condotte, né etiandio le presenti condotte o da farsi rifiutare o rinuntiare, ma s'intenda solamente dovere potere exercitare le loro condotte a lectioni ale quali saranno deputati et non più là.' (*Conc.* 507, f. 36v, 19 Oct, ed. PIANIGIANI, doc. 302, pp. 333-5). See also below, pp. 212 *seq.*

[168] 'Sienese humanists' complaints demonstrate the difficulty of belonging to the leading political groups; they were often appointed to offices far from the city in the distant Maremma – a serious detriment for their studies and for their beloved "otia"'. ASCHERI, *Renaissance Siena*, p. 14. The same could be said of university teachers as a whole (and indeed has been said of artists; HOOK, *Siena*, pp. 102-3).

[169] ASCHERI, *Renaissance Siena*, p. 13.

[170] *Conc.* 393, f. 67v, 23 Aug 1431, ed. PIANIGIANI, doc. 129, pp. 158-60; *CG* 224, f. 68r-v, 6 Oct, and *Conc.* 490, f. 22v, 3 Oct 1447, ed. PIANIGIANI, doc. 277, pp. 308-11; G. MONDOLFO, 'Il ruolo dello Studio Senese del 16 ott. 1500', *BSSP*, 4 (1897), pp. 412-17 (p. 415).

[171] *Conc.* 337, f. 43r, 25 Apr 1422; *Conc.* 387, f. 12r, 18 Sept 1430, ed. PIANIGIANI, doc. 124, p. 154 (Pietro di Ser Antonio Bonazini, who had a *podestaria*, to pay out of his own salary for a substitute to be approved by the *Savi*); *Conc.* 390, f. 25v, 12 Feb 1431. In January 1456 Benedetto da Cingoli, grammarian, was given leave until Easter provided he put in a *schambio* (*Conc.* 536, f. 7v, 9 Jan).

[172] *Conc.* 401, f. 13v, 9 Nov 1432 (Pietro de' Pecci).

[173] *Conc.* 584, ff. 23v-24r, 3 Feb 1464, ed. BAI, doc. 205, pp. 178-9.

[174] Substitution arrangements directed by the *Concistoro* could be quite complex: e.g. *Conc.* 463, f. 24v, 22 Mar 1443 (Galgano di Agostino Borghesi is to stand in for Pietro de' Micheli); *Conc.* 465, f. 7r, 8 Jul 1443, ed. PIANIGIANI, doc. 238, p. 270 (Malatesta di Borgo and Galgano Borghesi replace Pietro de' Micheli who has become *gonfaloniere*); *Conc.* 467, f. 5r, 7 Nov 1443, ed. PIANIGIANI, doc. 254, p. 274 (Niccolò da Pistoia substitutes Galgano Borghesi, Bindo di Giovanni substitutes Pietro de' Micheli), etc. In 1472 it was decided that the *Savi* could approve a substitute for up to three lectures, but would need the *Concistoro*'s approval for more than that (*CG.* 234, f. 180r, 3 Aug 1472). The 1500-1 *rotolo* prohibited substitution without the permission of the *Consiglio del Popolo*, on penalty of a 50-*lire* fine. MONDOLFO, 'Il ruolo dello Studio Senese', p. 415.

[175] For example, in May 1465 Galgano Borghesi, who had been elected *podestà* of Montalcino for six months from 1 July, was offered a two-year renewal of his contract on condition that the *Consilium* allowed him a substitute for his lectures from 18 Oct to the end of the calendar year (*Conc.* 592, f. 37v, 30 May, ed. BAI, doc. 220, p. 196).

safe. The substitute was usually a more junior man, for whom the teaching might be a stepping-stone;[176] sometimes it was a colleague of equal standing who took on additional lectures,[177] occasionally necessitating 'promotion' and a further substitution.[178] There were occasionally difficulties in forcing the teacher to find an acceptable substitute[179] – on one occasion no doctor could be found and a student was appointed[180] – and it was not unknown for the substitute himself to be sent off in turn by the commune, leaving the lectureship vacant.[181]

The problems associated with keeping the teaching going can appear overwhelming, and to focus on them exclusively would be excessively negative. In the same way that substitution could provide opportunities for young and aspiring lecturers, at the other end of the career span the commune could demonstrate itself a considerate employer. Those who had risen to such positions of eminence that their service elsewhere was deemed more important than their daily lectures, and those whose longevity of service was considered to have earned them some privileges and respite, were rewarded. Niccolò Borghesi was offered a reduced teaching load in 1495 because he held the chair in conjunction with the chancellorship;[182] in 1428 Pietro de' Pecci was excused teaching 'propter casum eminentem persone sue', but accorded the same privileges as an active teacher.[183] A pension was offered to Giovanni

---

[176] The substitution of the young Mariano Sozzini for Niccolò Tedeschi in 1433 is perhaps the best-known example; *Conc.* 403, f. 48v, 24 Apr, ed. NARDI, *Mariano Sozzini*, doc. 12, p. 119 (and pp. 24-5), and PIANIGIANI, doc. 144, pp. 170-1. The following November he was appointed to an ordinary lectureship; *Conc.* 407, f. 15v, 29 Nov, ed. NARDI, op. cit., doc. 13, p. 120, and PIANIGIANI, doc. 152, p. 177. Mariano's son Bartolomeo began in a similar way; his first teaching 'break' after receiving his doctorate was as substitute for Galgano Borghesi. *Conc.* 564, f. 17v, 2 Oct 1460, ed. BAI, doc. 154, p. 129; and cf. BARGAGLI, *Bartolomeo Sozzini*, p. 17.

[177] For example, when Bernardino was *Capitano del Popolo* in 1472, Gregorio d'Alessandria was his substitute, while the lawyer Ugo Bellanti, a member of the *Concistoro*, was replaced by Niccolò di Ser Angelo Guidoni (*Conc.* 637, ff. 2v-3r, 2 Nov). During the illness of Filippo Francesconi in 1475, Antonio Berti substituted for him during the second *terzaria* (*Conc.* 665, f. 45, 30 Dec); that he continued with his own contract is clear from the *apotisse* for that *terzaria* (*Conc.* 657, f. 37r-v, 9 Apr 1476, ed. FERRERI, doc. 12, pp. 11-13). In 1482 Giovanni Battista Caccialupi was charged with giving the lectures of his concurrent, Guidantonio Buoninsegni, who had been elected *Capitano del Popolo* (*Conc.* 697, ff. 2v-3r, 4 Nov, ed. FERRERI, doc. 160, p. 136).

[178] In 1468 Domenico di Ser Francesco was given a two-year contract substituting for Borghese Borghesi during his tenure of the office of *Capitano del Popolo*, and he in turn was substituted by Niccolò di Ser Lazaro Benedetti (*Conc.* 609, f. 40v, 13 Apr, ed. BAI, doc. 275, pp. 254-5).

[179] *Studio* 2, f. 89v, 17 Nov 1482.

[180] *Conc.* 395, f. 60r, 18 Dec 1431, ed. PIANIGIANI, doc. 130, p. 161 (Giovanni Mignanelli in place of Battista Bellanti 'non obstante quod dictus d. Johannes non sit doctor'. On Mignanelli see MINNUCCI, 'Documenti', pp. 274-5).

[181] E.g. *Conc.* 458, Apotisse (no foliation), May/Jun 1442 (Giovanni Mignanelli, on a mission from 28 Apr to 14 May). D'ACCONE, *The Civic Muse*, p. 448 describes Siena's policy of granting musicians paid leave of absence as 'liberal'. There are certainly instances of similar generosity towards teachers, but it is accompanied by anxiety over excessive loss of teaching hours, or more likely covered by the substitute system. One has also to gauge the level of absenteeism in comparison with other *studi*. A. B. COBBAN, 'Elective Salaried Lectureships in the Universities of Southern Europe in the Pre-Reformation Era', *Bulletin of the John Rylands University Library of Manchester*, 67 (1984-85), pp. 662-87 (esp. pp. 670-5) saw this as the specific affliction of the 'southern universities'; 'the network of substitute lecturers seems to have been fairly basic to the running of many southern European universities in the pre-Reformation era' (p. 674). His evidence, drawn more from Spain and southern France than from Italy, stresses the role played by tenure in this development; tenured teachers had little incentive to be scrupulous about their teaching commitments. Since this was not an Italian problem it should perhaps not surprise us to find this issue kept in perspective.

[182] *CG* 241, f. 8r, 23 Jan. His salary was reduced from 300 to 150 florins, 'legendo però lui personalmente le lectioni'. In 1406 Giovanni Bellanti had been allowed to reduce his load to one hour a day (*Conc.* 244, f. 37r, 30 Oct, ed. PIANIGIANI, doc. 13, p. 38).

[183] *Conc.* 375, f. 36v, 23 Oct, ed. PIANIGIANI, doc. 102, pp. 128-9.

di Buccio da Spoleto, who had taught since 1396, half a century later.[184] Long-serving foreign teachers could be rewarded with citizenship,[185] as could humbler men from the Sienese *contado* or beyond who pledged to teach in Siena.[186] Foreigners and citizens alike could also expect testimonial letters of recommendation,[187] and, as has been seen, exemptions from the obligation to dispute.[188] The comune could also graciously accept the possibility that a teacher might want to leave.[189]

---

[184] *CG* 223, ff. 110v-111r, 11 Feb 1446, ed. ROSSI, 'La "Lectura Dantis"', doc. VI (erroneously giving 1445); see NARDI, 'Appunti sui maestri', p. 202 n. 4, and above, p. 52. On pension and retirement arrangements for teachers see above, pp. 139-40 and below, p. 185 n. 22.

[185] Gabriele Fabritio da Perugia was made a citizen in 1466, though with the conditions that he purchase property worth at least 500 florins in Sienese territory within the year, and that he could not hold office for twenty-five years, or become a member of the college by virtue of his citizenship (*CG* 231, ff. 88v-89r, 7 Feb, and cf. *Conc.* 596, f. 31r, 7 Feb); Gregorio d'Alessandria was made a citizen in 1474 (*CG* 235, ff. 218v-219r, 18 May). Lodovico da Spoleto, a long-serving teacher who had become a member of the college of doctors in 1466, was aggregated into the regime as a member of the *monte* of the *Popolo* in 1479 (*Conc.* 678, ff. 2r, 2 Sept, 4r-v, 10 Sept, ed. FERRERI, docs. 83-4, pp. 69-71, and 20v, 21 Oct; cf. Lodovico's letters of acceptance, *Conc.* 2043, nos. 30, 12 Sept, and 32, 22 Oct). It was not necessary to be so long-serving to be offered this privilege. Baverio de' Maghinardi de' Bonetti was made a citizen after five years of teaching; *Conc.* 498, f. 17v, 22 Jan 1449, ed. L. MÜNSTER, *Baverio Maghinardo de' Bonetti, medico imolese del Quattrocento: la vita, i tempi, il pensiero scientifico* (Imola, 1956), Appendice, Documenti senesi, doc. 9, p. 111 (and see *Conc.* 2174, no foliation, and *Conc.* 498, f. 13v, 15 Jan); on his teaching see below, p. 188); Alberto Cattani was offered it 1468, before leaving for Bologna (*CG* 232, ff. 173v-174r, and *Conc.* 612, ff. 9v-10r, 11 Sept). See also below, p. 205.

[186] E.g. Simone da Campiglia (Pisa) (*CG* 172, f. 45r, 21 Apr 1365 – 'intentio sui est pueros docere et scolas retinere cum ipse sit bonus gramaticus'). Two teachers are in fact recorded as teaching without salary in return for citizenship; Francesco di Neri Gherardini da Rapolano (*CG* 182, ff. 114v-115r, 24 Oct 1372; cf. ZDEKAUER, p. 18 and PRUNAI, II, p. 40) and Jacopo di Lippo da S. Miniato (*Chartularium*, doc. 298, pp. 369-75, 2 Dec 1328). Cf. also the case of Onofrio Bartolini of Perugia, below, p. 176. A number of doctors of medicine who do not appear to have taught also obtained this privilege; cf. Naldo da Colle, *medico fisico*, *Chartularium*, doc. 102, pp. 79-81, 25 Feb 1303(=1304); Onesto di Bartolomeo da Montepulciano, granted citizenship on 21 Jan 1317 (W. M. BOWSKY, 'Medieval Citizenship: the Individual and the State in the Comune of Siena', *Studies in Medieval and Renaissance History*, 4 [1967], pp. 195-243 [pp. 213-4]; in 1326 he was given exemption from various taxes because there was a shortage of physicians in Siena); M.º Leonardo da S. Miniato, 'il quale è molto riccho' (*CG* 165, f. 3r-v, 3 Jan 1360); Domenico da Chianciano, *medico* (*CG* 172, f. 4v, 12 Jan 1365 and GAROSI, pp. 534-5); Ser Francesco da Abbadia S. Salvatore, surgeon (*CG* 171, f. 59r, 31 May 1364). On citizenship in Siena generally BOWSKY, op. cit., and on the fee involved, BALESTRACCI and PICCINNI, *Siena nel Trecento*, pp. 30-1. It is worth remembering that it is of course university lawyers themselves who frame and debate the issues of citizenship; e.g. W. M. BOWSKY, 'A New *Consilium* of Cino of Pistoia (1324): Citizenship, Residence and Taxation', *Speculum*, 42 (1967), pp. 431-41; J. KIRSHNER, 'Paolo di Castro on Cives ex Privilegio: a Controversy over the Legal Qualifications for Public Office in Early Fifteenth-Century Florence', in *Renaissance Studies in Honor of Hans Baron*, eds. A. Molho and J. A. Tedeschi (Florence, 1971), pp. 227-64; and IDEM, '*Civitas sibi faciat civem*: Bartolus of Sassoferrato's Doctrine on the Making of a Citizen', *Speculum*, 48 (1973), pp. 694-713.

[187] See p. 178 and n. 266.

[188] Above, p. 145.

[189] This was the case with the departure of Paolo di Castro and Giovanni da Imola in 1410 (*Conc.* 265, f. 34r, 15 Apr, ed. PIANIGIANI, doc. 25, pp. 49-50), the grammarian Domenico da Arezzo in 1417 (*Conc.* 308, f. 13r, 24 May (ed. PIANIGIANI, doc. 34, pp. 58-9), Cristoforo Castiglione in 1418 (*Conc.* 317, f. 4r, 7 Nov, ed. PIANIGIANI, doc. 35, pp. 59-60; the cardinal of Piacenza had written and he was going to teach elsewhere), the theologian Gabriele da Spoleto in 1429 (*Conc.* 380, f. 5r, 4 Jul 1429, ed. PIANIGIANI, doc. 112, p. 141; he had been made bishop of Lucera), and Pietro Giovannetti in 1425 and again in 1439, both times recalled to his native Bologna (*Conc.* 358, f. 11v, 13 Sept 1425, ed. PIANIGIANI, doc. 70, pp. 91-2; letters of request from the archbishop of Arles and the city of Bologna in *Conc.* 1908, nos. 20, 7 Aug, and 38, 7 Sept; replies in *Conc.* 1626, f. 34r, 22 Sept; *Conc.* 441, f. 32r, 1 Aug 1439, ed. GAROSI, doc. 58.i, p. 528, and PIANIGIANI, doc. 199, pp. 229-30; *apotisse* f. 51r, 21 Aug, ed. GAROSI, doc. 58.ii, p. 529). In one such case the authorities appear not to have waited to be asked; Mattia Lupi of San Gimignano, reader in grammar and poetry, was offered release from his contract should he want it (*Conc.* 346, f. 14r, 13 Oct 1423, ed. PIANIGIANI, doc. 62, pp. 83-4). For further examples see below, p. 176 n. 253 and p. 177. Not all departures were handled so smoothly. That of Giovanni Battista Caccialupi, which appeared harmonious, was followed by what NARDI, 'Giovanni Battista Caccialupi', pp. 117-9 described as the 'squallido episodio' of the authorities reallocating the outstanding amount of his salary to his successor.

4. *Payment*

A final – but essential – part of the commune's task was of course to ensure and control the payment of teachers' salaries. In the fourteenth century salaries were usually paid twice a year,[190] as indeed they had been in the thirteenth century,[191] but by the mid-fifteenth century Siena had gone over to the system customary among Italian universities of three instalments a year.[192] Contracts were entered in a book, the *Libro di S. Agostino*, which was kept first in the office of the *Gabella* and subsequently that of the *Biccherna*.[193] On receipt of the *apotissa* or instructions for payment from the *Concistoro* and the *Savi*,[194] the *Camarlengo di Biccherna*, or whoever was responsible for the *Studio* salaries at the time, would pay each teacher the amount stipulated less any fines due. From the mid-fifteenth century onwards, foreign teachers' salaries were also subject to a levy that went to communal projects, which led to some ill-feeling and protests.[195] Short delays – of a few months – were not uncom-

[190] E.g. *Bicch.* 247, f. 193v, 9 Nov 1368; *Bicch.* 248, f. 150r, 20 Oct 1369; *Conc.* 83, f. 76v, 27 Feb 1377; *Bicch.* 420, f. 153r, 1377. But a teacher of *notaria* was granted the privilege of two or three-monthly payments in 1401 (*Conc.* 220, Apotisse, no foliation, 18, 21, 30 Mar, 27 Apr), and M.° Gilio, master of abacus, was paid at two-monthly intervals (*CG* 199, f. 176r-v, 17 Feb. This is still the case in 1414; *Conc.* 2142, no. 8, 21 Jul and 8 Aug 1414). Pietro (Moreschi) dell'Abaco was paid on a monthly basis as late as 1468 (*Balìa* 6, f. 170r, 28 Feb); on him, N. ADAMS, 'The Life and Times of Pietro dell'Abaco, a Renaissance Estimator from Siena (active 1457-1486)', *Zeitschrift für Kunstgeschichte*, 48 (1985), pp. 384-95).

[191] E.g. *Chartularium*, docs. 61, p. 42 (1286), 64, p. 47 (1287), 94, p. 69 (1296), and cf. NARDI, *L'insegnamento*, p. 85.

[192] The regulation is in *CG* 223, f. 229v, 20 Feb 1447 (GAROSI, p. 560), but already in 1430 it can be seen from the terms of a *condotta* to be customary; *Conc.* 384, f. 4v, 4 Mar. Cf. *Conc.* 477, f. 13r, 15 Jul 1445.

[193] *Bicch.* 307, f. 29r, 1424: 'a libri di sancto aghustino che sta in chabella'. *Conc.* 556, f. 28r, 30 May 1459, ed. BAI, doc. 118, p. 101 implies that by that date it was kept in the *Biccherna*. It certainly was by 1483; *Conc.* 699, f. 33r-v, 29 Apr, ed. FERRERI, doc. 168, p. 143 (and cf. p. xvii) and GAROSI, doc. 94, p. 545, and *Conc.* 700, f. 33v, 26 Jun, ed. FERRERI, doc. 175, p. 148. The first reference to the *Libro di S. Agostino* I have found dates from 1396 (*Regolatori* 5, f. 125r), when payments to a grammar teacher, an abachist and the notary of the *Riformagioni* are noted 'chome apare per lo libro di Sancto Agostino'. It seems to have been, or become, the generic term for the *Studio* payroll account book, replaced when full by another book of the same name (*Bicch.* 307, f. 30v, 1424 refers to the 'libro nuovo di santo aghustino'; and cf. the ordering of a fresh book, *Balìa* 821, f. 28r, 11 Dec 1505), and the usage remains unchanged until it is replaced by the *Libro di S. Girolamo* in 1544. No book of either title has survived. The book is occasionally referred to by teachers as the 'libro de' dottori'; cf. Angelo degli Ubaldi's letter about the salary he was owed (*Conc.* 2138, no. 45, f. 75r, 12 Sept 1460). On a similar book and procedure in Florence/Pisa, VERDE, *Lo Studio fiorentino*, II, pp. 1-2.

[194] From around 1450 details of the *apotisse* for teachers are recorded in the *Concistoro* records, at the end of each volume, where the practice had long been to list *apotisse* of officials on communal business (above, p. 98). The original *apotisse*, which were slips of paper, seldom survive, but there are a couple of examples, complete with seals, in *Conc.* 2306, fasc. 29, nos. 27, 7 Apr 1469 (M.° Pietro di Bastiano Tinellocci), and 29, 7 Mar 1470 (Miss. Alessandro Aringhieri). A teacher who lost his *apotissa* might obtain a duplicate, as did the lawyer Mariano di Paolo Berti, five years after the issue of the original, on 9 Aug 1487 (annotation to *Conc.* 697, f, 35r, 24 Dec 1482, ed. FERRERI, doc. 162, p. 138). Officials of the *Studio*, pre-university teachers and occasionally student lecturers usually received their *apotisse* directly from the *Savi*. The receipt of instructions to pay did not necessarily mean that payment was instant. In those years for which we have the records (in the *Biccherna* or the *Gabella*), it is clear that payments to individuals were spread over days, weeks or even months. In one year, 1474, all teachers received their salaries in a series of small instalments stretching over the year (cf. the amounts due, recorded in *Gabella* 24, ff. 50r-66r and 125r-133v, and *Bicch.* 332, ff. 7r, 8r and 13r, with the actual payments, in *Bicch.* 332, ff. 150r-193v).

[195] This first appears to my knowledge in 1458; three *condotte* of non-Sienese teachers made on 16 June are 'cum retentione Cabelle' and one explicitly 'cum retentione Cabelle opere' (*Conc.* 550, f. 14v, ed. BAI, docs. 108-110, pp. 90-92). Angelo degli Ubaldi da Perugia protested in October of that year that he was being harassed by the *Camarlengo* of the *Opera* for payment and asserted that he was exempt; the matter was referred to Giovanni Battista Caccialupi in his capacity as *Giudice delle Riformagioni* (*Conc.* 552, f. 31r, 20 Oct). Other examples of the levy include *Conc.* 565, f. 22r, 24 May 1459, ed. BAI, doc. 117, pp. 99-100; salaries are 'nitidis omni gabella, excepta ea qua solvitur per forenses tantum Opere Maioris Ecclesie Cathedralis'. In 1463 it is 'cum debita retentione Cabelle Turri et Opere' (*Conc.* 583, ff. 25r, 25 Nov, 30v-31r, 6? Dec 1463, ed. BAI, docs. 199-200, pp. 172-4). The most distinguished protester was Francesco Accolti, who in 1466 pointed out that he had not known that 170 *lire* of his 850-florin salary were to be retained for this purpose according to the re-

mon,[196] though they were more likely to occur in the case of a teacher who had finished his contract.[197] Some were for the most trivial of reasons – such as the absence from Siena of the notary of the *Concistoro*, meaning that the *apotisse* had not been transcribed into the *Libro di S. Agostino*[198] – but most of the time one suspects the usual combination of sluggish bureaucracy and shortage of funds, the one disguising the other. Individual teachers who had some complaint could appeal to the *Concistoro* which would appoint someone to arbitrate;[199] if the commune's debt was of some standing, compensation might be paid.[200] In one year, 1464-5, when payment of all teachers' salaries was set back, this is clearly related to the advent of plague, which affected teaching as well.[201] In the second half of the fifteenth century there are signs that delayed payment could amount to a substantial problem that threatened to compromise the success of the *Studio* – or at least, it was adduced as a factor. In 1459 Francesco Accolti, by then teaching in Ferrara, was described in a letter from Francesco Sforza on his behalf as 'creditore grossamente';[202] in 1460 Angelo de Ubaldis of Perugia claimed he was owed over a thousand florins,[203] another Perugian, Mansueto Mansueti, was also owed the large part of his 500-florin salary in 1463.[204] A reputation of slow payment or non-payment was not good to acquire.[205] Pietro Sacco da Verona initially refused a 600-florin offer to return

cent 'legge della torre'. His eminence ensured that the *Savi* took his case to the *Consiglio del Popolo*, where he was granted an exemption (*CG* 231, f. 252r-v, 23 Dec). The following year Pietro Sacco da Verona was also excused the tax (*CG* 232, f. 41r, and cf. *Conc.* 607, ff. 50r, 7 Dec, and 76r, 23 Dec). The tax is revealed here to be at the rate of 2 *soldi* per *lira* or ten per cent. By 1471 the tax is again for the Duomo (*Conc.* 627, ff. 20v-21r, 27 Mar, ed. BAI, doc. 313, pp. 306-7). In 1488 it was payable to the *Monte di Pietà*, but was a less stinging 4*d.* per *lira* or 1/60th (*CG* 240, f. 177r, 10 Jun), and it was targeted at all non-citizens: 'qualunche forestiere fusse condotta in qualunche facultà dal Comune di Siena sia obligato pagare al cam.o de la pietà dx. 4 per lire…'. The rector was exempted (*Conc.* 767, f. 3v, 5 Jul 1494, ed. FERRERI, doc. 343, p. 325).

[196] E.g. *Bicch.* 417, f. 84r, 1369, when Pietro di Chello had to wait three months for settlement of his salary.

[197] Cf. the case of Floriano Sampieri, below, pp. 176-7. In 1513 about ten per cent of the amounts due was withheld from the first *terzaria* (*Studio* 21, no. 7). 'Final' short payments were particularly difficult to resolve. There are instances of the heirs of deceased teachers having to petition for the due amounts; cf. the cases of Mariano Sozzini (*Conc.* 656, f. 30r, 24 Feb 1476, ed. FERRERI, doc. 3, pp. 2-3 – this is almost a decade after his death), and Jacopo Faccalume (*CG* 240, f. 212r, 24 Aug 1489; his heirs appeal to the *Consiglio del Popolo* for help in extracting payment for his salary).

[198] *Conc.* 385, ff. 23v-24r, 28 May 1430, ed. PIANIGIANI, doc. 121, pp. 149-50.

[199] E.g. *Conc.* 139, f. 37v, 5 Oct 1387; Maestro Niccolò di Giglio da Città di Castello, grammar teacher, claims he has not been paid for the upkeep of his school. Three members of the Sienese judiciary who are also doctors of law are appointed and find in his favour. A dispute over the salary of the lawyer Agapito di Matteo da Perugia ended up before the courts (*Studio* 127, ff. 70r-73v, n.d.; cf. *Conc.* 2301, fasc. 13, 2 Nov, no year, and fasc. 14, 13 Dec, no year); the complaint of another Perugian, Angelo degli Ubaldi, in 1480 that the *Camarlengo dell'Opera* was pursuing him for his dues to that body was put to the *Giudice delle Riformagioni* for resolution (*Conc.* 552, f. 31r, 20 Oct).

[200] E.g. Antonio d' Arezzo, teacher of grammar, complained on 14 Sept 1428 that he had still not been paid his salary for 1425; he was given 48 florins instead of the 35 outstanding in recompense for the time that had elapsed (*Conc.* 375, ff. 12v, 14 Sept, 14r, 16 Sept, 17v, 22 Sept 1428).

[201] BARGAGLI, *Bartolomeo Sozzini*, pp. 35-6 and n. 36.

[202] *Conc.* 1993, no. 77, 22 Mar (1458=9). Accolti himself had written from Ferrara about the payment of his salary two and a half years earlier (*Balìa* 490, no. 84, 13 Sept 1456), and again the next year (*Conc.* 1991, no. 61, 21 Dec 1457).

[203] *Conc.* 2138, no. 45, f. 75r, 12 Sept; he claimed that he had been forced to accept a contract in Padua, in a hurry; £4,406/6/8 were outstanding after four years of teaching in Siena. He asked for at least 200 ducats from the *cassetta* of the *gabella dei contratti*, despite the regulations, and for the rest in the form of 'uno assegnamento sopra e paschi'. The *Concistoro* decided he should be paid from the *entrate* of the *paschi* by the end of December.

[204] *Conc.* 2006, no. 10, 3 May (letter from the *priori* of Perugia); *Conc.* 2138, no. 66, f. 108r, n.d. (*Savi dello Studio* to *Concistoro*. He has received only 70 florins. The *Savi* recommend that the *paschi* be obligated again.).

[205] On a similar phenomenon in Bologna, where in the 1450s it was observed that delays in payment were causing teachers, especially eminent ones, to leave, see A. DE COSTER, 'Vreemde docenten en burgerschapsverlening te Bologna (15de eeuw)', *Bulletin van het Belgisch Historisch Instituut te Rome / Bulletin de l'Institut historique Belge de Rome*, 70 (2000), pp. 59-

to Siena in 1474 because he was not happy with the arrangements for the payment of his salary;[206] Guidantonio Buoninsegni was paid in 1482 for salary arrears dating back to 1477 and 1478,[207] Francesco Nini and Ambrogio Luti experienced similar delays,[208] while Francesco Accolti, writing once more to the *Balìa* from Pisa in November 1482, shortly after the coup in Siena, enquired politely whether the political situation was now calm enough for him to be paid the arrears that he and the Florentine authorities had repeatedly written about – or at least the 921 florins or thereabouts due him from the *Paschi* and the *Gabella*.[209] A special case was the group of citizen teachers exiled in the 1480s, who had to wait years for payment.[210]

Given that it was mostly financial constraints that led to these delays, it is not surprising to find the authorities mostly responding in an *ad hoc* manner, committing specific funds or debts to individual teachers who successfully argued that they had been unfairly treated, whose needs seemed particularly pressing, or whose retention was considered a priority. The *Concistoro* made special arrangements to pay Angelo degli Ubaldi's arrears in 1460.[211] Similar arrangements were made to pay established and key teachers; Giovanni Battista Caccialupi in 1474,[212] Bulgarino Bulgarini in 1488,[213] and a growing number of teachers in the 1490s: Lutio Bellanti in 1492,[214] Giovanni Antonio Alato da Ascoli[215] and Pietro Bellanti[216] in 1493, the Dominican Bartolomeo da Sicilia in 1496,[217] Cristoforo da

---

143 (p. 135). On the other hand E. LEE, 'Humanists and the "Studium urbis", 1473-1484', in *Umanesimo a Roma nel Quattrocento*, eds. P. Brezzi and M. De Panizza Lorch (Rome, 1984), pp. 127-46 (esp. pp. 138-42) shows that in Rome such problems were not necessarily real deterrents to teachers – perhaps because they were widespread throughout the university world?

[206] *Conc.* 645, f. 34r-v, 14 Apr; he refused 'perché non sonno ordenati unde si habbino e suoi pagamenti'. The *Concistoro* resolved to obligate the *gabella* and the *casse comuni* for 100 *lire* a month each, and the *condotta* was approved on 16 Apr, f. 36r-v, ed. BAI, doc. 353, p. 349 (making it clear that by '*casse comuni*' was meant the '*capsettina doctorum*'). The initial offer was made in November 1473 (*Conc.* 643, ff. 12r, 15 Nov, and cf. f. 28v, 30 Nov, when the *Concistoro* decided to find a way of paying him). Sacco's response to the firmer offer (*Not.* 694, f. 40r-v, 31 May 1474, ed. MINNUCCI, 'Documenti', doc. II-6, p. 82) was elusive – Minnucci describes it as 'piuttosto sibillina' (p. 37) – but he eventually accepted in August, *Not.* 694, f. 42r-v, 15 Aug 1474, ed. MINNUCCI, 'Documenti', doc. II-11, p. 84. Sacco's hesitation may well have been based on his previous experience; in 1467 the *Concistoro* had had to exempt him from the *cabella turri* (see above, n. 195) (*Conc.* 607, ff. 50r, 7 Dec, and 76r, 23 Dec), and further special arrangements to pay him were made in 1468 (*CG* 232, f. 179r-v, 25 Sept). Alessandro Sermoneta hinted at late payment as one reason for his reluctance to return from Padua in the early 1480s ('et per me non è rimasto aspectare quanto aspectare dovevo'; *Balìa* 519, no. 34, 21 Jul 1484. He was also unhappy at the disparity between the salaries of lawyers and doctors of medicine).

[207] *Conc.* 695, f. 32v, August, ed. FERRERI, doc. 152, pp. 129-30.

[208] *Conc.* 699, f. 33r, 29 Apr 1483, ed. FERRERI, doc. 167, pp. 141-2 (salaries due since 1478).

[209] *Balìa* 506, no. 42, 12 Nov.

[210] In 1487 and 1488 compensation was paid to those teachers who had been banished in 1482 and had thus been unable to teach; Giovanni Battista Santi (*Conc.* 726, f. 29r, 15 Oct, and *Conc.* 727, f. 17v, 27 Nov 1487, ed. FERRERI, docs. 257, p. 220, and 262, pp. 223-4), Mariano Berti (*Conc.* 725, f. 30r, 9 Aug 1487, and *Conc.* 726, f. 29r, 16 Oct 1487, ed. FERRERI, docs. 249, p. 212, and 256, p. 219), Francesco Borghesi (*Conc.* 726, f. 28r, 15 Oct, and *Conc.* 727, ff. 28v-29r, 20-23 Dec 1487, ed. FERRERI, docs. 255, p. 217, and 263, pp. 224-5), Bulgarino Bulgarini (*Conc.* 731, f. 16r, 11 Aug 1488, ed. FERRERI, doc. 284, p. 253), Arcangelo Toti (*Conc.* 731, f. 16r, 11 Aug 1488, ed. FERRERI, doc. 285, p. 254) and Bartolomeo di Tofo Sansedoni (*Conc.* 732, f. 6r, 16 Sept 1488, ed. FERRERI, doc. 287, p. 257).

[211] Above, n. 203.

[212] *Conc.* 645, ff. 37v-38r, 17 Apr (he was to be paid from the *Gabella* of Asciano, with supplements from those of Paganico and Orbetello), and 48v, 29 Apr 1474 (Montalcino was substituted for Orbetello).

[213] *Balìa* 36, f. 33r, 15 Oct; *gabelle* from San Quirico, Vignone, Paganico and Orbetello were obliged. Bulgarini was a member of the *Balìa* at the time that it voted this payment to him.

[214] *Conc.* 2139, no. 94, f. 172r, 16 Apr.

[215] *Balìa* 39, ff. 48v, 23 Oct, and 53r, 4 Nov 1493.

[216] *Balìa* 39, ff. 48r, 23 Oct, and 71r, 18 Dec 1493.

[217] *Balìa* 41, f. 3v, 1 Sept.

Chianciano[218] and Antonio Giordano da Venafro[219] in 1497, and a number of teachers in 1498.[220] But delayed payments were also recognised as being a problem that could affect the *Studio* as a whole. A proposal of 1456 to tighten up on the control of the funds earmarked for the payment of salaries blamed delays in payment for the fact that prospective teachers were refusing *condotte* and existing ones were planning to leave.[221] It is not clear what became of this proposal at the time, but reforms were effected in a *Balìa* measure of 1458. Recognising that the *Studio* had been diminished 'in parte per essere mal pagati li doctori e altri condocti e leggenti', this measure instituted a *cassetta* for the moneys earmarked for teachers' salaries, with two keys, one to be held by the *Camarlengo di Gabella* and the other by the *Savi dello Studio*.[222] At least three *Savi* were to meet with the *Camarlengo* every two months to check that the latter had deposited the due amounts. This was an attempt to stave off the diversion of resources, but on its own it was not enough; the authorities frequently had to commit specific taxes and offices to the *Studio* in order to meet the wage-bill.[223] Later in the fifteenth century there is a further development; the creation in 1488 of the office of *depositarius*, who was 'banchiere per lo collegio delli doctori', and whose task was to receive the income for the *Studio* salaries and to

[218] *Balìa* 41, f. 180r-v, 7 Jun 1497. He was to be paid on a monthly basis.

[219] *Balìa* 41, ff. 218v, 17 Aug, 248r, 31 Oct 1497. He was made citizen and *riseduto* weeks later; *Balìa* 43, f. 22r-v, 14 Dec 1497.

[220] *Balìa* 43, ff. 52r-v, 12 Jan (Ugo Sermini; and cf. 244v, 21 Oct), 67r-v, 9 Feb (Bartolommeo Sozzini), 89r, 13 Mar (Giovanni Battista di Messer Sante), 98r, 29 Mar (Bulgarino Bulgarini), and 242v, 8 Oct (Buoninsegna Buoninsegni). In two of these cases specific *gabelle* were earmarked (the *Gabella di Asciano* for Giovanbattista, that of Orbetello for Ugo); in each case, however, a commission of three was established to ensure that the funds would be available. Pandolfo Petrucci was a member of two of these (for Ugo Sermini and Bartolommeo Sozzini). Delayed payments were a complaint of teachers from the religious orders as well. The autobiography of the Dominican Simone Bocci claims that Francesco da Savona (the future pope Sixtus IV) and Gregorio da Spoleto were owed money after many years; two Dominicans, Francesco da Nardò and Giordano da Bergamo, made the commune's debt to them over to the prior of S. Domenico in return for a 40% payment. FIORAVANTI, 'Formazione e carriera di un domenicano', p. 357.

[221] The *Savi* 'truovano che la principale cagione che ritarda li doctori ad volersi conduciare è la fama che già è corsa de pagamenti che non si fanno più secondo lo usato et non observarsi in cio alcuna promessa. Et non tanto che loro credino poter avere degli altri eccellenti, ma quelli che ci sono non provedendosi altrimenti sono in proposito di non volere piu stare.' *Conc.* 2138, no. 39, 13 Jul, quoted in CATONI, 'Il Comune di Siena e l'amministrazione della Sapienza', p. 128 (giving the date as 1465; correct dating removes what he saw as the paradox that in 1465 the finances were in a healthier state). Similar complaints were made by or on behalf of grammar teachers on a number of occasions. In 1472 a petition of grammarians for more regular payment by *terzaria* defines the importance of punctuality of payment succinctly. The current shortage of grammar teachers was entirely due to the backlog in payment: 'Et al presente c'è mancamento di maestri el quale difecto solo nascie dal non essere pagati a debiti tempi...'. They ask to be paid 'in tre paghe come gia si costumava interamente di terzaria in terzaria, et non sicondo a la distributione + rata di quello si truovavano in mano i camarlenghi di cabella che pagano per lira + per soldo cosi a deti maestri come a doctori; che quando interamente sieno pagati ne succedeva che si trovava copia di maestri e staranno con manco salario che non hanno fatto per lo presente' (*CG* 234, f. 199v, and *Mis.* 1, f. 101r, 25 Sept). A similar diagnosis was made in the late 1480s; the 'manchamento grave di maestri di schuola' was 'perché non sonno pagati delloro salario et condocta, et quelli pochi che ci sonno si partano et voglianosi partire per dicta cagione di non essare pagati' (petition from *Savi* to *Concistoro*, *Conc.* 2139, no. 83, f. 153r, n.d. but between documents of 1487 and 1488). It seems that, in the perennial struggle for payment of salaries, the lowest on the ladder were also the last to be satisfied.

[222] *Balìa* 6, f, 143r-v, 27 Jan; also *Balìa* 7, ff. 142v-143r, and *Statuti* 40, f. 131r-v. The proposed reform goes back to 1456 (*Conc.* 2138, no. 39, 13 Jul), but the outcome is not clear. The box was soon being referred to as the 'cassettina attribuita a salari dei doctori' (*Conc.* 2138, no. 66, f. 108r, n.d. but from position in file around 1363), and 'casettina de' doctori'.

[223] Above, pp. 100-1.

distribute them in accordance with contracts.[224] The *depositarius* kept accounts that were inspected by the *Regolatori*,[225] and instantly became an important figure.[226]

The introduction of the *depositarius* was soon followed by another, closely related innovation; the emergence of a forum for teachers (distinct from the colleges which were responsible for examination and the award of degrees), to control and negotiate on matters relating to salaries and their payment. A joint meeting of 'doctoribus tam legum quam medicine vz. maiore parte ipsorum' on 3 Feb 1494[227] appears to be the first indicator of this change.[228] It was called to discuss a proposal of Antonio Berti, prior of the college of law, 'pro conficiendo novo depositario', and established a system of election. The meeting coincided with a crisis in payment; the commune had been unable to pay any teachers for their first *terzaria* and ended up paying two together in March of that year.[229] A few months later the same group, this time described as 'collegio doctorum legentium', met, having been summoned by the *bidello*, to consider the salary situation, and agreed to accept debts in place of arrears.[230] The problems did not go away; with their newly-discovered collective voice the doctors complained again in the autumn, about both the low proportion of their salaries that was paid at the last distribution and the commune's failure to implement the traditional pay rise for the new academic year, and threatened not to accept their contracts.[231] The new 'college' would not disappear conveniently. It is found again electing the *depositarius* in 1498[232] and 1499, though the latter was quickly annulled by the *Balìa* which replaced it by a system involving three of their members, one of whom was Pandolfo Petrucci.[233] Despite this obvious attempt at political control, the college was there to stay. In the sixteenth century it was clearly a formal part of the *Studio*; in 1532, at another moment of widespread discontent, the *Collegio dei dottori leggenti* is found petitioning the *Concistoro* with a number of proposals, both about how payments should be regulated and on wider issues such as ensuring that only citizens who have taken their degree in Siena would be eligible for lectureships.[234]

---

[224] *Balìa* 36, ff. 27r-28r, 2 Oct.

[225] E.g. *Regolatori* 10, ff. 64v (1488), 164r-v (1494), 165v (1495). For much of the 1490s the office was held by Ser Antonio Campani (see also *Balìa* 45, f. 74r, 22 Aug 1499). He could be given orders by the comune (e.g. *Balìa* 43, ff. 267v, 15 Dec, and 270v, 17 Dec 1498; *Balìa* 45, f. 124r, 8 Nov 1499).

[226] Bologna had had a *depositarius doctorum* for some time.

[227] *Not.* 1018, no foliation, 3 Feb. It is described as a meeting of 'doctoribus tam legum quam medicine vz. maiore parte ipsorum'. Another document of the same date (loc. cit.), summarising the meeting more briefly, refers to it as one of 'doctoribus legentibus'.

[228] There is however the unexplained terminology of *Conc.* 669, f. 16v, 21 Mar 1478, ed. FERRERI, doc. 67, p. 58, ordering 'quod Magister Jacobus Filippi de Asinalonga Prior seu Camerarius Universitatis doctorum et Ser Filippus bidellus solvant Magistro Jacobo Galgani ciuis ratam sive distributionem'.

[229] *Conc.* 765, ff. 4v-5v, 7 Mar, ed. FERRERI, doc. 337, pp. 317-20.

[230] *Not.* 1019, no foliation, 23 Jun.

[231] *Conc.* 768, ff. 24v-25r, 31 Oct, ed. FERRERI, doc. 347, pp. 329-31 (and see p. xiii); and cf. *Conc.* 2191, no foliation, n.d. 350 florins were made available for sharing out between ten doctors in consequence of the protest (for the original appointments see *Conc.* 768. ff. 14r-15r, 8-9 Oct, ed. FERRERI, doc. 345, pp. 326-8). Contrast with 1480, when eight out of thirty did not accept *condotte* offered, but there is no evidence of collective action (*Balìa* 20, ff. 57v-59r, 2-3 Aug).

[232] *Not.* 1019, no foliation, 23 Aug.

[233] *Balìa* 43, f. 283v, 16 Jan. The *Balìa* decided instead that the prior was to elect three who would decide how the *depositarius* was to be elected; also that three members of the same *Balìa*, one of whom was Pandolfo Petrucci, were to produce measures regarding the contracts and payment of doctors.

[234] *Conc* 2007, no foliation, Nov 1532, ed. KOŠUTA, 'Documenti', doc. I-3, pp. 334-5.

The payment of salaries is bound to appear problematic; the documentation mostly points up issues and moments of disfunction and confrontation. Yet although there were many cases of individual dissatisfaction, some warnings to the authorities that the *Studio* was in danger of suffering, and occasional crises affecting the whole teaching body,[235] on the whole the record is positive, and certainly no worse than the commune's treatment of other employees, or than in other *studi*.[236] Regular payment of teachers' salaries was regarded as one of the top priorities among the commune's obligations.[237] Only in the sixteenth century was there any major disturbance of the *Studio*'s activity because of delays in payment. In 1532 the teachers went on strike, resuming work only when they had been promised payment; in 1533 less than half of the amount due had been paid and they stopped teaching again, resuming only after extensive reforms. Payment was only one of their grievances, however, the other being the imbalance in the teaching load, and the measures passed were more concerned with reforming the way in which *condotte* were made, and with the regularity of teaching, than with salaries.[238] In fact these, rather than questions of salary, seem to have been the main causes of discontent in the system throughout the period.

5. *The academic market*

Financial instability aside, perhaps the chief danger to the system lay in the competitive designs of other *studi*. As has been seen, the Sienese, like other Italian university authorities, forbade the departure of Sienese doctors[239] or indeed any doctors currently teaching,[240] and in theory imposed a fine

---

[235] E.g. the suspension of salaries (because of war) in 1390, accompanied by a plea by the *Concistoro* to continue teaching nonetheless (*Conc.* 154, f. 7v, 23 Mar); the collective complaint in 1409 of foreign teachers that their salaries were overdue, a matter which received prompt attention (*CG* 204, f. 25v, 19 Jul).

[236] Cf. GRENDLER, *Universities of the Italian Renaissance*, p. 101 on the situation at Ferrara.

[237] As in 1407, when special funds are allocated 'ut possint satisfacere doctoribus legentibus in facultatibus secundum ordine et modos datos' (*Conc.* 250, f. 21r, 24 Oct 1407). Cf. pp. 99-101 above. In 1420 the *Camarlengo di Gabella* was told not to pay for any building work until the 200 florins' worth of outstanding teachers salaries had been paid off (*Conc.* 325, ff. 15v-16v, 2 Apr; and cf. *Conc.* 326, f. 3r, 2 May, and *Studio* 126, f. 3r-v).

[238] *CG* 243, ff. 244v, 14 Dec, 246r, 26 Dec, ed. KOŠUTA, 'Documenti', doc. I-5, and I-6, pp. 337-41. For earlier, similar strike threats in Pavia, ZANETTI, 'A l'Université de Pavie', p. 428; SOTTILI (ed.), *Documenti per la storia dell'Università di Pavia*, I, doc. 71, p. 85; and P. ROSSO, 'Problemi di vita universitaria pavese nella seconda metà del Quattrocento: i professori', *Bollettino della Società Pavese di Storia Patria*, 45 (1993), pp. 67-93 (pp. 89-90).

[239] Deliberation of *Consiglio Generale* of 12 Feb 1339, *Chartularium*, doc. 358, pp. 451-3. The measure was not eventually included in the collection of statutes known as the 'statuto del Buon Governo', apparently because it conflicted with existing law; see NARDI, *Insegnamento*, pp. 197-8. Nardi points out (p. 200) that this measure negated one of the cardinal principles of the imperial Authentic *Habita*, that recognising the freedom of movement of teachers and scholars, though it too had precedent in Roman law, given that what was at stake was a contract between teacher and employer. This may also help to explain how easily the principle could come to be applied to all teachers in the commune's employ, not just Sienese citizens (see below, n. 240). The issue was not academic; at the same time Siena was struggling in its attempt to get back Giovanni di Neri Pagliaresi, a Sienese citizen, who had left to study at Bologna and who was teaching at Perugia from at least 1339. He was probably helped in Perugia by another Sienese lawyer, the more famous Federico Petrucci, who was teaching there. Siena was not able to do anything about Petrucci because of his eminence, but they threatened Pagliaresi with the 1339 measure and a 1,000 florin fine. In the end his father undertook the teaching in his place, to avoid the fine. Pagliaresi himself never returned (NARDI, *Insegnamento*, pp. 204-5, and see above, p. 40). The measure was enshrined in the legislation following the obtention of the imperial charter; *Chartularium*, doc. 431, pp. 567-9, 19 Oct 1357. Cf. ZDEKAUER, p. 16.

[240] *CG* 220, f. 13r, 12 Feb 1439, renewed in 1473 (*Conc.* 640, f. 21r, 30 May, ed. BAI, doc. 340, pp. 336-7), and cf. *Studio* 2, f. 2r, 12 May 1473, ed. BAI, appendix, doc. 19, pp. 376-7 reminding Bartolomeo Sozzini of this measure (discussed

of 1,000 florins against offenders.[241] But such offenders were often as not forgiven when they returned,[242] and there is a regular stream of approved departures, the details of which show the futility of trying to retain teachers against their will or that of important people or powers. In the early stages Siena could not expect to hold on for long to teachers of the eminence of Marsilio Santasofia or Cristoforo Castiglioni;[243] even so it often required the intervention of the government or *signore* of a rival town, rather than merely the *Savi*'s opposite numbers, to prise them away. Higher authorities – cardinals, kings, popes – occasionally helped as well,[244] and when combined with the request of the teacher concerned such demands were difficult to resist.[245] The diplomatic refusal was a fine-

in BARGAGLI, *Mariano Sozzini*, p. 52). The implication – often made explicit in the contracts – was that Siena claimed first option on the renewal of *condotte* (as at Florence; VERDE, *Lo Studio fiorentino*, II, pp. 1-2). Cf. *Conc.* 255, f. 13r-v, 10 Jul 1408, when a teacher was refused permission to leave at the end of the academic year. A commission found in his favour, however; *Conc.* 256, ff. 19v, 8 Oct, 20r-v, 10 Oct.

[241] See the measures of 1339, 1439 and 1473 (nn. 239 and 240 above). In 1429, however, a fine of 500 gold florins was stipulated in *Conc.* 379, ff. 8v-9r, 12 May 1429. The raising of this penalty to 5,000 florins in 1357, just after the promulgation of the imperial charter (n. 239), must be regarded as exceptional.

[242] E.g. *Chartularium*, doc. 375, pp. 480-3, 27 Apr 1340; Giovanni di Neri Pagliaresi's fine was to be cancelled on his return from Perugia (but see p. 40 above). Cf. the case of Benedetto Barzi, below, pp. 186-7, esp. n. 29.

[243] The former was allowed to leave at the request of Giangaleazzo Visconti (*Conc.* 147, f. 11v, 12 Jan 1389; cf. SPAGNESI, *Utiliter Edoceri*, pp. 17, 61-3 esp.), the latter at the request of the cardinal of Piacenza (*Conc.* 317, f. 4r, 6 Nov 1418, ed. PIANIGIANI, doc. 35, pp. 59-60); and cf. A. MARONGIU, 'Protezionismi scolastici e stipendi professoriali', in *Studi in onore di Amintore Fanfani*, 6 vols. (Milan, 1942), VI, pp. 313-28; repr. in his *Stato e Scuola. Esperienze e problemi della scuola occidentale* (Milan, 1974), pp. 251-65 (p. 259, n. 17).

[244] E.g. the request of the king of Portugal for the release of Sallustio Buonguglielmi of Perugia, 1423 (below, n. 253); at the request of Cardinal Colonna the decretalist Giovanni Minocci was released to go and teach in Bologna in 1436 (*Conc.* 425, f. 25v, 16 Dec, and cf. Minocci's letter to the *Concistoro*, *Conc.* 1937, no. 35, 21 Nov 1436); the cardinal of Nicaea requested the release of Mariano Sozzini to help revive the *Studio* of Bologna in 1450 (*Conc.* 1966, no. 63, 13 Jul); the *Signoria* of Florence asked for Francesco Accolti in 1472 (*Conc.* 2029, no. 95, 18 Mar; the writer is the chancellor, Bartolomeo Scala); and see also nn. 243 and 245.

[245] Cf. n. p. 154 and n. 45 above, and *Conc.* 470, f. 39r, 1 Jun 1444; the Florentine *Signoria* ask for Filippo da Lucca (*Conc.* 1955, no. 51, 31 May 1444), who also asks to leave; the *Concistoro* release him from his *condotta*, which was due to run until 17 Oct 1445, with immediate effect. He had been elected to the office of *Riformatore* in his native Lucca (see *Conc.* 1662, f. 59v, 1 Jun – the *Concistoro*'s reply to the Florentine *Signoria*). An example of success in resisting such pressure is the case of the apostolic protonotary Lodovico Pontano. Pope Eugenius IV requested his return after his two-year teaching contract (*Dipl., Riformagioni*, 4 Nov 1435). The *Concistoro* first resisted (letters to pope in *Conc.* 1645, ff. 40r, 8 Oct, 44r, 17 Oct – the *Concistoro* wish to hold on to Lodovico for fear of 'totalis desolationis studii' – and 52r, 1 Nov), though meanwhile the *Consiglio del Popolo* decided to sack him (*Conc.* 419, f. 4v, 6 Nov; report of decision on 15 Oct). The *Concistoro* started to look for a replacement (*Conc.* 419, f. 6v, 7 Nov), and on 21 November Lodovico came to them in person to explain that he wanted to continue to teach if papal dispensation could be obtained. The rector of the *Studio* also presented a petition from the university of scholars to the effect that many scholars would leave if he did, and the *Concistoro* revoked his leave subject to the agreement of the pope (*Conc.* 419, f. 19v; see also below, p. 278 n. 258). Papal permission for him to teach for a further year was duly obtained (*Conc.* 1935, no. 36, 10 Dec 1435; letter of Cardinal Domenico Capranica), and Lodovico accepted a new *condotta* (*Conc.* 419, f. 48r, 27 Dec). The following year, however, he was the subject of a fresh 'transfer bid', this time by King Alfonso; *Conc.* 1936, no. 2, 27 Mar 1436, ed. N. F. TARRAGLIA, *Storia della lotta tra Alfonso V d'Aragona e Renato d'Angiò* (Chianciano, 1908), doc. 24, pp. 302-3. This was politely refused on the grounds that Lodovico was indispensable to the *Studio* (*Conc.* 1646, f. 44v, 24 Apr 1436). There is also a case of a request from the rector of a *studio* writing – Berengarius de Comitibus de Catelonia, 'Rector Incliti Studii Perusini', requesting that Magister Petrus, *artium ac medicine doctor*, a Sienese teacher, who has been ordered back to Siena within a month, might stay at Perugia to teach. Petrus had appealed to the *universitas scolarium* for support (*Conc.* 2301, fasc. 26, 16 Jan, no year given. The subject to be taught is not given). Cf. also the letter from the *doge* of Venice insisting that the Sienese allow Pietro Sacco to leave in order to take up his contract at Padua, *Conc.* 2027, no. 2, 3 Oct 1471.

ly-tuned art,[246] though it did not always work, and of course the Sienese could find themselves at the receiving end of similar treatment.[247] The prospect of losing eminent teachers, however, could provoke sharp, and occasionally extreme, reactions from the commune. The refusal of the Sienese to release Guasparre da Bologna to the Florentines in 1429 caused anger,[248] as had their seizure in the previous year of the books of a law student, Lodovico Pontano, who had turned down a *condotta* in Siena in favour of one in Florence.[249] And violation of agreements could always lose teachers. Onofrio Bartolini of Perugia, hired in 1408,[250] was imprisoned in June 1409 in reprisal for an attack on some Sienese merchants in Perugia, despite the immunities granted to foreign teachers;[251] he was released on production of guarantors to the tune of 1,000 gold florins, and eventually to make amends the Sienese offered him and his descendants citizenship, which he accepted, but that was not surprisingly the last they saw of him.[252]

Of course these examples of mismanagement and failure are far from the whole picture. There are many more instances where the authorities are flexible and part company with their teachers with reasonably good grace.[253] Compromises could be worked out. Floriano Sampieri from Bologna was absolved from his *condotta* in September 1424 on condition that he stayed until a replacement could be

---

[246] See the letter to the king of Sweden and Norway politely declining his request for Pietro Lapini on the grounds of his necessity for the *Studio* (*Conc.* 1612, ff. 92v, 26 Aug, and 93v, 27 Aug 1415, reproduced in GAROSI, facing p. 132; cf. PICCINNI, 'Tra scienza ed arti', p. 147); or the refusal in 1427 to release the Dominican Guasparre back to Bologna (see below, p. 154 n. 45). The cardinal of Piacenza, who wanted Battista da Fabriano for his personal service at the Council of Ferrara, was told that this would lead to the detriment of the *Studio* (*Conc.* 1650, f. 9v, 27 Jan 1438). Even Pope Eugenius IV's request for the Sienese to allow Mariano Sozzini to accept a chair at the University of Vienna was politely rejected (*Conc.* 1661, f. 60v, 6 Nov 1443, ed. NARDI, *Mariano Sozzini*, doc. 29, pp. 127-8, and see pp. 62-3).

[247] E.g. the Perugian refusal to release the doctor of arts Mateolo de Baltasaris, *Conc.* 1880, no. 57, 13 Oct 1412; or Filippo Maria Visconti's refusal to release Catone Sacco on the grounds that it would cause 'maxima dicti studii deformatione' (*Conc.* 1943, no. 67, 4 Jul 1439, and see above, p. 154 n. 24).

[248] Above, p. 154 n. 45.

[249] As p. 162 n. 135 above. The seizure of the books of a defecting teacher was clearly common; the sanction was applied to the Dominican theologian Leonardo da Perugia in 1458 (letters of intercession by Cardinal Domenico Capranica, *Balìa* 494, no. 40, 12 Jan, and the *Priori* of Perugia, *Conc.* 1991, no. 72, 21 Jan). The Bolognese did the same; see letter of *Concistoro* to them protesting that Pietro da Verona, whom they had hired, was unable to get his books out (*Conc.* 1661, f. 43v, 3 Oct 1443). This Sienese hiring of Pietro Sacco (*Conc.* 465, f. 29r, 24 Aug 1443, ed. PIANIGIANI, doc. 242, pp. 272-3) has not previously been noticed in the literature on him. It was a two-year contract to teach philosophy, but the following year he was released (*Conc.* 472, f. 37r, 10 Oct), returning to Bologna to take up a chair in medicine (DALLARI, *I Rotuli*, I, p. 21).

[250] *Conc.* 255, ff. 29v-30r, 31 Jul.

[251] *Conc.* 260, f. 34r, 9 Jun.

[252] *Conc.* 260, ff. 38v, 13 Jun, 39v, 14 Jun, 44v, 18 Jun, *CG* 204, f. 25v, 19 Jul, *Conc.* 261, ff. 16v, 18 Jul, 27v, 3 Aug. Cf. PRUNAI, II, p. 41. On Bartolini cf. R. ABBONDANZA, 'Bartolini, Onofrio', *DBI*, 6 (1964), pp. 617-22. The extremities of such reactions are perhaps best illustrated by the case of a Sienese teacher, Bartolomeo Sozzini, who had left Siena to teach at Ferrara. With his transfer to the newly reopened Florentine *Studio* at Pisa, the Sienese authorities determined to try to win him back, and Sozzini was simultaneously threatened with the protectionist legislation of thirty-five years previously, precisely quoted, and offered a contract with the highest salary ever given to a Sienese teacher (*Conc.* 640, f. 8v, 13 May 1473, ed. BAI, doc. 338, p. 335; *Studio* 2, f. 2r-v, 12 and 14 May 1473, ed. BAI, appendix, docs. 1-2, pp. 376-8; cf. BARGAGLI, *Bartolomeo Sozzini*, p. 52, and see below, pp. 222-3).

[253] E.g. *Conc.* 218, f. 4v, 8 Nov 1400 (the physician Marco di Giovanni is given permission to go to read medicine at Perugia); *Conc.* 259, f. 12v, 19 Mar 1409 (Ugo Benzi, who may go to Pisa; cf. below, p. 220); *Conc.* 260, f. 22v, 27 May 1409 (Benzi again; he may teach wherever he wants); *Conc.* 343, f. 32v, 26 Apr 1423 (Sallustio Buonguglielmi of Perugia is released; even the king of Portugal has written asking for this); *Conc.* 358, f. 11v, 13 Sept 1425, ed. PIANIGIANI, doc. 70, pp. 91-2 (Pietro Giovannetti of Bologna, released on petition of the governor general of Bologna, the cardinal archbishop of Arles); and above, pp. 168 n. 189 and 175 n. 244.

found;[254] in the meantime he was given prestigious lodgings[255] (although admittedly it took the commune fifteen months after his departure to pay him the balance of his salary).[256] Another teacher was given permission to leave on condition that he could be recalled if the *Savi* had need of him;[257] yet another was excused one year of his two-year *condotta*.[258] Teachers could also effectively be loaned to another *studio* for a fixed term.[259] There were occasions when the authorities were happy to lose a teacher, such as Luca da Perugia, teacher of medicine, who was allowed to leave 'cum non sit utilis'.[260] Some left as a result of dissatisfaction.[261] Illness was of course accepted automatically as a reason for terminating a *condotta*,[262] as was in most cases a prestigious appointment or communal service.[263] And invitations to Sienese teachers to accept *condotte* in other *studi* had advantages; Siena, too, could export learning and gain by reputation. It is therefore by no means unusual for the protectionist laws to be waived for Sienese teachers as well.[264] Siena, after all, was playing the same game, sending secret messengers to entice teachers, using diplomatic influence. Totally effective protectionism would have isolated universities and made them entirely local institutions; mobility and flexibility were the order of the day. And the process was reciprocal in another sense; cardinals, patrons and governments would not hesitate to write to the commune recommending someone for a teaching post.[265] In turn, Siena

[254] *Conc.* 352, f. 6r, 6 Sept; *Conc.* 353, ff. 6r, 10 Nov, 21r, 27 Dec. This was also in response to a request from the governor of Bologna for his return. The *Concistoro* agreed to this subject to the finding of a suitable replacement (*Conc.* 1624, f. 40v, 9 Oct).

[255] *Conc.* 352, f. 14v, 18 Sept. Cf. the summary of the situation in a report in *Conc.* 2307, fasc. 25, no. 7, 24 Sept [n.d.].

[256] *Conc.* 361, f. 5r, 4 Mar 1426. For his complaint see *Conc.* 2307, fasc. 25, no. 7, n.d.

[257] *Conc.* 496, f. 7v, 11 Sept 1448 (Mattiolo da Perugia, teacher of medicine).

[258] *Conc.* 472, f. 28r, 28 Sept 1444 (Bindo di Ser Giovanni Bindi, lawyer).

[259] Buoninsegna Buoninsegni was permitted to teach in Perugia in 1498 on that basis, but the *Balìa* had to flex its muscles to get him back a year later (*Balìa* 415, f. 153r, 17 Nov, and *Balìa* 45, f. 134r-v, 28 Nov 1499).

[260] *Conc.* 410, f. 21r, 31 May 1434. Giovanni Antonio di Paolo and Placido Placidi were similarly released – a euphemism? – from their contracts in 1477 (*Conc.* 665, f. 49r, 25 Aug, ed. FERRERI, doc. 49, p. 44, and *Conc.* 666, f. 42r, 30 Oct, ed. FERRERI, doc. 53, p. 46 respectively).

[261] E.g. Ser Nerio de Monte Piscario, *presbiter* and grammar teacher, who renounced his contract 'quia non fuit neque est satisfactus de salario et mercede sua' (*Sale*, 24, f. 164v, 29 Mar 1498).

[262] *Conc.* 317, f. 32v, 29 Dec 1418 (Antonio Roselli); *Conc.* 323, f. 7v, 10 Nov 1419 (the canonist Lorenzo da Arezzo); *Conc.* 437, f. 3v, 4 Nov 1438 (Tommaso Docci is told by his doctors that he will die if he continues to teach); *Conc.* 448, f. 30r, 11 Oct 1440, ed. PIANIGIANI, doc. 214, pp. 246-7 (Battista Bellanti).

[263] Cf. p. 165 n. 169 above, and *Conc.* 251, f. 3r, 1 Nov 1407 (Mag. Guilielmus Anglius is released from his *condotta* because he is 'conductus ad servitia comunis senarum' – the nature of the service is not specified); *Conc.* 494, ff. 34r, 20 Jun, 38r, 29 Jun 1448, ed. PIANIGIANI, doc. 286, pp. 318-9 (Goro Lolli, who is elected *podestà* of Grosseto). Gabriele da Spoleto was released on appointment to the bishopric of Lucera (*Conc.* 380, f. 5r, 4 Jul 1429, ed. PIANIGIANI, doc. 112, p. 141).

[264] E.g. *Conc.* 467, f. 7r, 11 Nov 1443 (Giovanni Mignanelli is allowed to accept a *condotta* in Rome); *Conc.* 503, f. 28r, 15 Dec 1449 (Battista Bellanti has permission to teach in Bologna); and the case of Ugo Benzi below, pp. 220-1.

[265] The Florentines recommended Tommaso de' Arrighini da Pontremoli, bishop of Brugnato, for a lectureship in canon law in 1427 (*Conc.* 1912, no. 40, 25 Jun); cf. three letters, from Guidantonio da Montefeltro, the cardinal of S. Croce and Cardinal Colonna, recommending Luca de Callio for a *lettura* in civil law in 1441 (*Conc.* 1949, nos. 96, 24 Dec, and 99, two of 31 Dec respectively); more locally, the letters of the bishop of Arezzo recommending Fabiano d'Antonio da Monte San Savino for a lectureship in law in 1450 (*Studio* 19, no foliation, 12 Nov, ed. ZDEKAUER, p. 42 n. 1; and *Conc.* 1967, no. 35, 7 Dec 1450; for possible identification with the 'Fabiano del Monte' who took his degree in Siena between 24 Jul 1445 and 13 Jun 1446 see NARDI, 'Una fonte inedita delle lauree senesi'); Cardinal Francesco Todeschini Piccolomini, the cardinal archbishop of Siena, recommending Niccolò, a teacher of philosophy, for a lectureship in 1474 (*Not.* 694, f. 36r-v, 12 Jul, ed. MINNUCCI, 'Documenti', doc. II-9, pp. 83-4); Cardinal Orsini recommending Niccolò Baglioni of Perugia, prior of the Gerosolimitans and doctor of canon law, for a *lettura* (*Conc.* 2302, fasc. 3, no. 33, 25 Sept, no year given). A less formal

could be active in helping those who had taught for them in the furtherance of their own careers,[266] and often continued to cultivate good relations with them after they had left.[267] The academic market used the diplomatic system; it was also part of it.

6. *Siena and other* studi

A definitive picture of Siena's performance on the academic market – to pursue the metaphor for a little longer – would entail prosopographical investigation that is beyond the scope of this study. It would not only require analysis of the role that a spell of teaching in Siena played in the subsequent careers of the many who passed through, but also a series of bilateral studies of the relationships between Siena and other university towns. There are some indications that this could be a profitable exercise. The substantial number of teachers from Perugia who were employed in Siena at some stage in the fifteenth century – Onofrio Bartolini,[268] Benedetto Barzi,[269] Sallustio Buonguglielmi,[270] Mattiolo Mattioli,[271] Angelo degli Ubaldi,[272] Mansueto[273] and Francesco de' Buonriposi,[274] Baldo Bartolini ('Baldo Novello')[275] and others who appear briefly in the lists[276] – was not reciprocated.[277] Perugia clearly provided a useful source of foreign teachers, including the intellectual heirs and even biological descendants of the two great Perugian lawyers of the fourteenth century, Bartolo da Sassoferrato and

---

attempt at persuasion was Poggio Bracciolini's letters to Berto Ildebrandi, chancellor of Siena, and Bartolomeo della Grazia recommending Benedetto Accolti for a lectureship in 1440; POGGIO BRACCIOLINI, *Lettere*, II. *Epistolarum familiarorum libri*, ed. H. Harth (Florence, 1984), II, pp. 363-5, 367-9; and cf. R. BLACK, *Benedetto Accolti and the Florentine Renaissance* (Cambridge, 1985), pp. 56-7. Lorenzo de' Medici wrote to the *Balìa* on 27 Jun 1485 recommending the canonist Stefano d'Arezzo for a lectureship; *Balìa* 524, no. 36, 27 Jun; publ. in LORENZO DE' MEDICI, *Lettere*, VIII, ed. H. Butters (Florence, 2001), letter 763, p. 227. (Judging from the *Balìa* and *Concistoro* records for that year and the next, the recommendation does not appear to have had the desired outcome.)

[266] E.g. the commune's efforts on behalf of Niccolò Tedeschi in 1424; letters to the pope, the college of cardinals, the bishop of Siena, and Malatesta dei Malatesti, *Conc.* 1623, ff. 52v-53r, 27 May; excerpts ed. in N. MENGOZZI, 'La crise religieuse du XV siècle – Martino V ed il concilio di Siena (1418-1431)', *BSSP*, 25 (1918), pp. 247-314 (p. 298); letter of recommendation to the king of Portugal in 1492 on behalf of Emanuel of Portugal, who is returning home after years of teaching theology in Siena (*Balìa* 411, ff. 61v-64r, 12 Mar).

[267] In 1490 Filippo Decio, now teaching in Pisa, was happy to accept a case from the Sienese; *Balìa* 543, no. 38, 1 Jun 1490. Decio had taught in Siena in 1484-7 for an initial salary of 200 florins, subsequently raised to 280 florins, at the same time as his then more famous brother Lancilotto was being paid 600 florins (see FERRERI, docs. *ad annum*) and was to end his career in Siena in the sixteenth century (for details see KOŠUTA, 'Documenti', pp. 500-1).

[268] See p. 176 above.

[269] See below, pp. 186-7.

[270] P. MARI, 'Buonguglielmi, Sallustio', *DBI*, 15 (1972), pp. 237-41 (and above, p. 175 n. 244, p. 176 n. 253, and below, p. 187).

[271] See below, p. 190.

[272] See below, p. 190.

[273] See below, p. 190, and above, p. 162.

[274] See p. 153 n. 43 above; for identification see *Maestri e scolari* (as p. 15 n. 77 above).

[275] The presence of this important figure in Siena, a speculation of ERMINI, *Storia*, I, p. 507, is confirmed by the payment of his salary, 200 *lire* for a *terzaria* (i.e. 150 florins annually), in *Bicch.* 316, f. 65r, 13 Sept 1447. On his later career, VERDE, *Lo Studio fiorentino*, II, pp. 64-5, and BARGAGLI, *Bartolomeo Sozzini*, pp. 59-60, 62, 66-7.

[276] See pp. 164 n. 151, 168 n. 185, 170 n. 199, 177.

[277] After Federico Petrucci and Giovanni di Neri Pagliaresi in the early fourteenth century the only Sienese names of substance to appear in the Perugian lists are those of Francesco Casini, who it has been speculated may have taught there at various points between 1374 and 1403 (see F.-C. UGINET, 'Casini, Francesco', *DBI*, 21 [1978], pp. 356-9. He was offered a salary of

Baldo degli Ubaldi; the Umbrian *studio* was a resource for the Sienese, as well as a model, until the late fifteenth century. A similar attempt at a 'balance-sheet' with Bologna shows a different pattern, first because the opportunities for non-citizens to teach in Bologna were always strictly limited, and secondly because although the Sienese made infrequent attempts to hire Bolognese teachers, these were usually countered with draconian measures to prevent those teachers from leaving.[278] Similar exercises for Pavia and Padua would take us pretty much directly into the wider study of relations between the states. Nothing moved without the agreement of the duke of Milan and the *Serenissima* respectively – and indeed, nothing much did move for most of the fifteenth century.

Fig. 8a – Seal of Angelo degli Ubaldi of Perugia, who taught law in Siena in the mid-fifteenth century (Archivio dell'Università di Siena, *ms.* 1, f. 74r).

Such exercises may be helpful as a way of assessing the status of Siena and its *Studio*, but there is an artificiality about them, because they fall into the trap of treating organisations as if they had personalities. The Sienese authorities, like others, were opportunistic about competition, assessing and taking their chances cannily, weighing up the state of play, perhaps sometimes hiring and advertising more in hope than in expectation.[279] The identity of the rivals was a secondary consideration from an academic point of view, though it might not be that from a political perspective. However there is one competitor that stands out as different. Mention has been made at several points of the close rivalry with Florence, and the close correspondence of initiatives for reform.[280] This invites the question of how the 'academic market' specifically between these two actually operated. The question is interesting not

445 florins in 1400, but it is not clear whether he accepted; ERMINI, *Storia*, I, pp. 273 n. 135, 556, and GOLDBRUNNER, 'Die Mailändische Herrschaft', p. 421), and Buoninsegna Buoninsegni, who taught there in 1489 (ERMINI, p. 565) and 1498-9 (see n. 259 above). Buoninsegni was one of the more mobile of Sienese teachers in this period, doing two spells at Pisa as well. For details see the summary in MINNUCCI, 'Documenti', p. 241, and the entry in *Maestri e scolari* (as p. 15 n. 77 above).

[278] The extreme example is the threat of the death penalty and the confiscation of goods issued to Bartolomeo de Herculanis in 1459 for having accepted a teaching post from the Sienese; PIANA, *Il "Liber Secretus Iuris Caesarei"*, pp. 33*34*, 50* (and on a similar threat to Barbazza in 1452, p. 50*).

[279] Cf. the cynical report by an unidentified writer in Bologna in *Conc.* 2304, fasc. 11, no. 1, 5 Oct, no year given: 'A questi dì sono facte qua più condocte di dottori valenti parmi più tosto per dare nome a questo studio et conforto a li scolari che speranza che alcuno ce ne venga. Et sono questi, Misser Mariano Sozini, Misser Benedecto Barzi, Miss. Cato da Pavia, et uno medico che si dice essare molto valente...'. Its provenance and archival location aside, there is not enough in this document to allow us to determine whether it refers to the *Studio* of Bologna or to that of Siena.

[280] See pp. 37, 43, 47, 50-1, 52 n. 147, 55, 57 n. 178, 152, 154 n. 45, 192 n. 88, and DENLEY, 'Academic Rivalry', from which the following paragraphs are drawn, with amendments.

least, of course, because eventually Siena was drawn fully and irreversibly into the orbit of the major Tuscan power in the next century, and the *Studio* with it.

A number of celebrated teachers of Italian and indeed international standing feature in the lists of both Florence and Siena. In the fourteenth century these include the physicians Dino del Garbo of Florence and Marsilio Santasofia of Padua; in the fifteenth century the Sienese physician Ugo Benzi, the lawyers Paolo di Castro, Benedetto Barzi of Perugia, Lodovico Pontano, Antonio Roselli and Francesco Accolti of Arezzo, Filippo and Lancilotto Decio of Milan and the Sienese Bartolommeo Sozzini, the theologian Andrea Biglia and the humanist Francesco Filelfo. This list, not unimpressive in itself, shows a degree of commonality at the highest level of the profession which is perhaps unexceptional for two neighbouring *studi* given that such levels of distinction and reputation are achieved chiefly by mobility; most 'great names' of the Italian universities are of peripatetic teachers. More interesting for the present purposes is to note the direction and circumstances of the movements of these teachers from one *studio* to another. In the fourteenth century movement from one town to another can certainly be seen as an indication of the relative state of competing universities. Thus the 1320s see the Florentines Dino del Garbo and Tommaso Corsini teaching in Siena, albeit briefly. In the Florentine revival of 1359 onwards three Sienese were attracted to Florence, the brothers Giovanni and Francesco di Bartolomeo and Cerretano Cerretani. In the wake of Florentine decline after 1366, by contrast, Niccolò da Prato moved from Florence to Siena. The competitive climate of the late 1380s, however, set the pattern for the future. Although both *studi* were making strenuous efforts to attract teachers, the attractions of Florence were naturally stronger. Two teachers, Marsilio Santasofia and Niccolò da San Miniato, were lured there from Siena.

These trends were perpetuated in the fifteenth century, with the difference that was made by Siena's preeminence in the early part of the century. A comparison of Florentine and Sienese records of teachers who began their careers in the first half of the fifteenth century has identified twenty-six teachers who appear in both *studi*. Analysis of their careers reveals an unexpected pattern. Of the Florentines who taught in both, one from Florence itself and eight from subject towns began their careers in Florence and at some stage moved to Siena.[281] Four of these do not appear to have returned, and three, Francesco Accolti, Filippo Lazzari da Pistoia and Giovanni di Donato da Arezzo, made most of the remainder of their careers in Siena.[282] There are also three Florentine subjects who began their academic careers in Siena before moving to Florence: Antonio di Giovanni Roselli da Arezzo, teacher of medicine, whose presence in the Sienese college of doctors dates back to 1409, and two from Florence itself who first obtained lectureships in Siena as students, Zanobi Guasconi and Roberto Cavalcanti (who was also rector of the Sienese *Studio*).[283]

Native Sienese teachers, by contrast, barely feature in the Florentine list. There is the famous case of Ugo Benzi, described below,[284] and there is Giovanni di Mignanello Mignanelli, who appears to have begun teaching in Florence before returning to a chair in Siena. No other Sienese are common to

---

[281] They are Antonio di Rosello Roselli (civilian), Francesco Accolti, Filippo Lazzari da Pistoia, Leonardo Roselli, Timoteo da Pistoia, Girolamo da San Miniato, Giovanni di Donato da Arezzo and Taddeo di Giovanni da Firenze.

[282] Francesco Accolti had been a student at Siena.

[283] A similar case, albeit not yet a Florentine subject, was Filippo da Lucca, who in 1416 was among the first students to be admitted to the Sienese Sapienza, and who then began in Siena a teaching career that took back and forth between the two universities for two decades. Finally, it should be added that there are two Florentine subjects, Giovanni Boscoli and Bartolomeo di Cristoforo da Arezzo, who taught at Siena in the late 1420s but who do not appear to have taught at Florence (though the former was a member of the college of doctors of law there in 1437; DAVIES, *Florence and its University*, p. 166).

[284] See pp. 220-1.

both *studi* in the documents known to date.[285] The largest group, the twelve teachers who are neither Florentine nor Sienese, contains the most distinguished names and also the most revealing pattern. Three, Andrea Biglia, Baldo Bartolini of Perugia and Francesco Filelfo, taught first in Florence (and as Filelfo fled from there to Siena for political reasons his case must be considered exceptional). The other nine – Paolo di Castro, Benedetto Barzi, Lodovico and Francesco Pontano, Angelo degli Ubaldi and Sallustio Buonguglielmi da Perugia, Giovanni da Sermoneta, Guasparre da Bologna and Filippo da Lucca – all taught in Siena first, and all spent more time teaching in Siena than they did in Florence. Like other *studi*, Florence obtained its high-profile teachers from elsewhere. Siena was an obvious and convenient source, but at this level the traffic was clearly one-way.

The pattern of Florence drawing on the Sienese *Studio* for teachers – though not the reverse – continued after the move to Pisa in 1473. By this stage, though, it was native Sienese who were being recruited, apart from Francesco Accolti, who left Siena once more for a chair in Pisa (1479-84). Verde lists eight Sienese teachers, of varying degrees of eminence, who taught in Pisa; Alessandro da Sermoneta (who by then had been granted Sienese citizenship), Bartolommeo Sozzini, Bulgarino dei Bulgarini, Francesco Nini, Buoninsegna dei Buoninsegni, Francesco da Vergelle, and the philosophy teachers Galgano and Oliviero.[286] The first four of these were highly distinguished and among the best paid at Pisa, and it is with pardonable exaggeration that a Sienese reported from Pisa in 1484 that together they were holding up the Pisan *Studio*.[287]

The much more richly documented last decades of the fifteenth century provide ample evidence that this fundamental antagonism persisted. Florence's recruitment drive of 1473 is well-charted; the main efforts were directed at the larger *studi*,[288] but Siena was affected too. In 1474 a correspondent of Lorenzo de' Medici, reporting that he had heard of Francesco Nini's willingness to transfer to Pisa, opined that if this was achieved on top of the already effected transfer of Alessandro da Sermoneta 'non dubito che si guasterà penitus lo Studio delli artisti in Siena et tutti convoleranno qui'.[289] The Sienese for their part redoubled their efforts in the same year to keep Giovanni Battista Caccialupi da San Severino 'maximamente havuto respecto a lo studio di Pisa'.[290] Despite a political rapprochement with Florence in 1483 which led to a proposal in Siena to allow Florentine and Sienese subjects access to each others' *studi* 'durante la presente lega',[291] by early 1484 the competition over teachers had been renewed.[292] And the mistrust is evident on both sides. In 1489 difficulties over the *condotte* of Bar-

---

[285] Mention should be made of Andrea and Sozzino Benzi, sons of Ugo Benzi, who both taught at Florence. Both left Siena with their father and consequently never taught there.

[286] The plan to hire a ninth, Arcangelo, in 1491 (VERDE, *Lo Studio fiorentino*, IV, p. 935), does not seem to have come to anything.

[287] Sozzini and Alessandro Sermoneta are described as 'li fondatori dello Studio di Pisa' (*Balìa*, 520, c. 66r, 30 Oct 1484).

[288] BRUCKER, 'A Civic Debate', p. 526; LORENZO DE' MEDICI, *Lettere*, I, ed. R. Fubini (Florence, 1977), pp. 464-65.

[289] VERDE, *Lo Studio fiorentino*, IV, pp. 63-64 (27 Jun 1474); quoted in FIORAVANTI, 'Le "arti liberali"', p. 269. In 1479 Sermoneta was allowed to teach wherever he wanted except Florence (*Balìa* 15, f. 66r, 20 Aug), following his petition from Pisa, written on 4 May of that year, for permission to teach outside Siena (*Balìa* 498, no. 59, ed. ZDEKAUER, 'Lettere volgari del rinascimento senese', letter XXXXI, pp. 284-5).

[290] *CG* 235, ff. 180v-181r, 23 Mar 1474. The petition of students of the Sapienza in 1475 for the removal of its rector, Bernardino da Cortona, smacks strongly of anti-Florentine sentiment; below, p. 350.

[291] See below, p. 246 n. 117.

[292] See the highly coloured language of the proposal to win back Bartolommeo Sozzini, *CG* 239, f. 192r-v, 4 Apr 1484 (he is described as 'el fiore di tutti li studii di Italia ... Et pisa si tiene vivo solo con la reputatione del Sozino'); and the letter

tolommeo Sozzini and Francesco Nini led the *procuratore* at Pisa to suspect that the Sienese 'si sieno acchordati a sollevare tutto questo Studio'.[293]

It is right to view the relations between these universities in competitive terms since the documents make it abundantly clear that that was how they saw themselves. But such a view gives only one, rather sensationalist, side of the picture, and tends to emphasise the role of the famous and highly-paid teachers at the expense of the majority which sustained the regular activity of a *studio*. Siena's move in the fifteenth-century towards greater reliance on local teachers[294] had consequences for the nature of competition; it was soon appreciated that releasing teachers to other universities gained them fame and experience which in due course would benefit their own *Studio*. That there were risks involved was clear, but there were academic as well as diplomatic advantages to be gained from granting requests for teachers. The flow of teachers to and from Florence, which in the case of teachers under contract involved the approval of the authorities, suggests that these authorities used and developed this possibility, and perhaps also saw Florence as an opportunity to help teachers in their careers under the conditions of semi-controlled proximity. Certainly the Sienese who wrote to the Florentine *Ufficiali dello Studio* in 1488 to recommend Francesco da Vergelle for a teaching post at Pisa were showing a different aspect of inter-university relations than that evident in the more spectacular, and hence better documented, cases of disagreement.[295]

from a Sienese at Pisa recommending the return of Sienese teachers there in similar tones, *Balìa* 520, f. 66r, 30 Oct 1484. See below, pp. 222-3.

[293] VERDE, *Lo Studio fiorentino*, IV, p. 805 (30 Jun 1489). A further attempt to lure a Sienese teacher, Camillo Pasquali, to Pisa was proposed in 1491; op. cit., p. 1021 (21 Dec).

[294] Below, pp. 190 *seq*. The detailed analysis by DAVIES, *Florence and its University*, pp. 52-61, suggests that such a trend was not obviously replicated in Florence; he found considerable variation between subjects, with an overall predominance of local teachers in law and theology but the opposite in medicine and arts.

[295] *Conc.* 1700, no foliation, 5 Jul and 27 Oct 1488 (and on him see MINNUCCI, 'Documenti', p. 250). The protection of citizen teachers employed in other *studi* is a regular subject of correspondence between cities.

II

THE FORMATION OF A LOCAL TEACHING FORCE

1. *Academic salaries and careers*

The figures mentioned in the previous chapter show that, as has been noted for other universities, the salaries paid for these lectureships varied enormously. With a base salary usually of 20 or 25 florins,[1] and star performers achieving often many hundreds of florins, it was not uncommon for payroll lists to include teachers who were earning twenty, thirty or more times as much as the lowest-paid.[2] Often the lion's share of the money available was used up on a handful of 'names'; in the early 1450s in fact a little under half of the total expenditure went on just two teachers.[3] On the other hand the lowest salaries scarcely differentiated their recipients from manual labourers, and survival on these salaries alone meant that a substantial proportion of the pay would go on food and clothing.[4] Also as elsewhere, salaries varied considerably from subject to subject. Lawyers were paid higher salaries than doctors of medicine of corresponding eminence and experience in virtually all cases, and within that category civilians tended to be better paid than canonists, at least at the higher end of the scale.[5] Grammarians, whether teaching at the university or at elementary level – and they are often difficult to dis-

---

[1] On currency equivalents, see above, p. 88 n. 5. Comparison with other *studi* has to take into account the variety of currencies. A good example is the letter of Alessandro Sermoneta, responding from Padua to an offer of the Sienese of a *condotta* of 400 florins; 'Et qui o fiorini 650 che sono più di fiorini 800 de V.' (*Balìa* 519, no. 34, 21 Jul 1484). For a recent attempt to compare and evaluate musicians' salaries and status in Siena see D'ACCONE, *The Civic Muse*, pp. 250-5, 532-5, 540-1.

[2] A. ZANNINI, 'Stipendi e status sociale dei docenti universitari. Una prospettiva storica di lungo periodo', *Annali di storia delle università italiane*, 3 (1999), pp. 9-39 (pp. 18-19) makes considerable use of this measure for the sixteenth century.

[3] Benedetto Barzi, from 1448, and Francesco Accolti from 1451 both earned 550 florins a year. Below, pp. 186 and 189. Cf. ZANETTI, 'A l'Université de Pavie', pp. 432-3.

[4] Although the fifteenth century has scarcely been studied, it has been shown that in 1340-1 a *maestro* in the building trade earned on average 2.064 florins a month. D. BALESTRACCI, '"Li lavoranti non cognosciuti". Il salariato in una città medievale (Siena 1340-1344)', *BSSP*, 82-83 (1975-6), pp. 67-157 (p. 117, and cf. p. 126 *seq.*, esp. pp. 141-3). For Florentine comparisons, R. A. GOLDTHWAITE, *The Building of Renaissance Florence. An Economic and Social History* (Baltimore, Md., 1980), Appendix 3, pp. 436-9. Martines estimated that it cost about 20 florins a year to keep a student at university in the fifteenth century; below, p. 279 n. 3. On the inadequacy of the lowest salaries, PARK, 'The Readers at the Florentine Studio', pp. 252 and 271, and on the modest living standards of most teachers ZANETTI, 'A l'Université de Pavie', pp. 432-3. On the other hand the top range of the sort of salaries attained by citizen teachers placed them roughly at the level of all but the highest-paid communal officials. The salary of a *maggior sindaco* in the mid-fourteenth century ranged from 100 to 200 florins. BOWSKY, 'The Impact of the Black Death', p. 34, and IDEM, *Finance*, p. 316.

[5] Cf. ZANETTI, 'A l'Université de Pavie', p. 425, LEE, *Sixtus IV and Men of Letters*, p. 151 n. 2, and most published *rotoli*.

tinguish because both were administered by the *Savi* – could expect much more modest sums, even if they were eminent humanists; while theologians, being mostly regular clergy, were usually given only a token salary.

Salaries appear to have been almost the only aspect of the *Studio* that was not regulated. The statutes of 1309-10 fixed the salaries of law teachers at 25 *lire*,[6] as did those of the 'buon governo' in 1337-9.[7] After that, however, they were not stipulated in law with any intention to bind successive administrations. This is not surprising or significant. Where it was regulated, as at Pavia, the regulations were frequently ignored;[8] a *studio* in need of eminent teachers had to maintain flexibility. Besides, in the cases of long-serving teachers, salaries tended to rise naturally, possibly giving career prospects in some cases better than the Pavian regulations would have allowed. Sienese teachers do not come out too badly even in periods when the *Studio*'s finances and general state of health were unstable. New teachers, or teachers with fresh degrees, began at a salary of 20, 25 or 30 florins according to the financial position;[9] a rise was virtually automatic even though not embodied in regulations or contracts. The clearest cases of this can be seen in the third, fourth and fifth decades of the fifteenth century, when increasingly the local teaching force was coming to provide a backbone of continuity for the ever-volatile foreign element. Seven lawyers, Battista Bellanti, Tommaso Docci, Mariano Sozzini, Bartolomeo Borghesi, Giovanni Giovanelli, Jacopo de' Griffoli and Antonio Lanti, were all hired by the *Studio* in 1427 for 30 florins a year.[10] In 1428 Bellanti, Borghesi and Sozzini were given rises of 8 florins, Docci a rise of 6 and Griffoli of 4.[11] In 1429 salaries were increased dramatically; Bellanti's, Borghesi's and Sozzini's to 70 florins, Docci's to 60 and Griffoli's to 50.[12] Within two years financial

---

[6] ELSHEIKH (ed.), *Il costituto*, dist. IV, rubr. 17, vol. 3, p. 169. Others were not fixed (rubr. 16, pp. 168-9).

[7] NARDI, *Insegnamento*, p. 237. These salaries have to be seen in the context of *collectae*, fees which teachers could charge their students (op. cit., p. 91). This was the original system, which salaried lectureships began by complementing in the thirteenth century, replacing it entirely by the fifteenth. There are few references in Siena to *collectae*, and none known to me in the period under investigation here.

[8] ZANETTI, 'À l'Université de Pavie', p. 424. The regulations of 1384 declare that a canon or civil lawyer should receive 30 florins for the first two years, 40 for the next two and 60 thereafter; doctors of medicine should receive 30 for the first four years and 50 thereafter; surgeons 25 for the first four years and 40 thereafter. MAIOCCHI, *Codice diplomatico dell'Università di Pavia*, I, pp. 98-9 (15 Oct 1384). On the regulation of salaries and contracts in late fourteeth-century Pavia (and their ineffectiveness) cf. also ZANNINI, 'Stipendi e status sociale', pp. 15-16, and P. ROSSO, 'I "Rotuli" dell'Università di Pavia nella seconda metà del Quattrocento: considerazioni sull'entità degli stipendi assegnati al corpo docente', *Schede umanistiche*, 10:1 (1996), pp. 23-49 (esp. pp. 27 *seq.*). On the attempts by Nicholas V to fix categories of lectureship, with salary bands, at Bologna in 1448 and 1450 see TROMBETTI BUDRIESI, *Gli statuti del collegio dei dottori*, pp. 81-3, 87-90 (edition of the two measures); also CAVINA, *Dottrine giuridiche*, pp. 112-4; A. DE COSTER, 'Vreemde docenten en burgerschapsverlening te Bologna (15de eeuw)', *Bulletin van het Belgisch Historisch Instituut te Rome / Bulletin de l'Institut historique Belge de Rome*, 70 (2000), pp. 59-143 (p. 78); and EADEM, 'La mobilità dei docenti: Comune e Collegi dottorali di fronte al problema dei lettori non-cittadini nello Studio bolognese', in *Studenti e dottori nelle università italiane (origini – 20. secolo: atti del Convegno di studi, 25-27 novembre 1999*, eds. G. P. Brizzi and A. Romano (Bologna, 2000), pp. 227-41 (p. 230).

[9] The starting salary of Bartolomeo Sozzini (below, pp. 222-3) of 35 florins was exceptional, an indicator of his ability and perhaps also the reputation of his father. For Bologna, BRAMBILLA, 'Genealogie del sapere', pp. 131-1, 133-4 has noted that lower salaries were either devices for getting one's degree costs paid (in the case of student lectureships) or, with *straordinarii*, more a sign of belonging than a real wage.

[10] *Conc.* 369, f. 16r, 27 Sept, ed. PIANIGIANI, doc. 80, pp. 100-2. Sozzini had had a student lectureship in 1425; *Conc.* 355, f. 6v, 8 Mar 1425, eds. NARDI, *Mariano Sozzini*, doc. 2, p. 115, and PIANIGIANI, doc. 68, pp. 89-90.

[11] *Conc.* 375, f. 24v, 29 Sept.

[12] *Conc.* 379, f. 22v, 14 Jun, ed. PIANIGIANI, doc. 111, pp. 138-40; confirmed in 1430, *Conc.* 387, f. 12r, 18 Sept, ed. PIANIGIANI, doc. 124, pp. 153-5.

crisis threatened to overwhelm the *Studio*; many foreign doctors, including Niccolò Tedeschi, left, and salaries fell back to roughly earlier levels – 30 florins for Bellanti, Borghesi and Sozzini, 25 for Giovanelli – where they remained for four years.[13] Those teachers who remained through this period, however, were rewarded. In 1435 Bellanti, Borghesi, Docci and Sozzini saw their salaries rise to 60 florins and Giovanelli's rose to 40;[14] in 1437 Sozzini and Docci were receiving 100;[15] in 1441 they and Bellanti were receiving 110;[16] in 1445, 145 florins;[17] in 1451 Docci and Sozzini were getting 160;[18] and finally in 1465 Sozzini's salary reached 250 florins,[19] only at this stage exceeding the salary of the most eminent Sienese teacher of his student days, Pietro de' Pecci, who in 1426 and 1428 was earning 175 florins.[20] The important point about these eminent figures was that they had worked their way up in Siena. It was much rarer by this stage for an already eminent Sienese lawyer to be assumed by the *Studio*, the only example perhaps being Pietro de' Micheli, who heads the list of Sienese lawyers in the *Studio* throughout the early part of Sozzini's career with a salary of 125 florins in 1426, 150 in 1429, 50 in 1431, 100 in 1435, 150 in 1442 and 160 in 1445.[21] It was rarer still for teachers of arts and medicine to receive anything like such a salary, although not infrequent for them to remain for many years in Sienese service. During the period of the tripartite regime the highest figure was attained, in one of the longest and most distinguished careers in the *Studio*, by Bartolo di Tura. Bartolo too worked his way up. He is first found teaching logic in 1426 for a salary of 20 florins; in 1428 he taught natural philosophy, and in 1429 his salary was 40 florins. It fell again in 1431 (from when he taught medicine) to 20 florins, rose to 40 in 1433, to 50 in 1435, to 90 in 1437, to 100 in 1441, to 135 in 1444, to 145 in 1450, to 160 in 1451, to 200 in 1461 and finally to 250 in 1467.[22]

---

[13] *Conc.* 393, f. 67r-v, 23 Aug 1431, ed. PIANIGIANI, doc. 129, pp. 158-60; confirmed in *Conc.* 399, f. 63v, 28 Aug 1432, eds. NARDI, *Mariano Sozzini*, doc. 11, p. 119 and PIANIGIANI, doc. 136, pp. 165-6 (Giovanelli's was restored to 30 florins). A commission had been set up to negotiate lower salaries with the teachers (*Conc.* 392, f. 44r, 4 Jun, and *Conc.* 393, f. 25v, 16 Jul 1431).

[14] *Conc.* 417, f. 8v, 12 Jul, eds. ZDEKAUER, doc. XVII, pp. 167-8, and PIANIGIANI, doc. 167, pp. 193-4. Borghesi died later that year (for a profile see MINNUCCI, 'Documenti', pp. 233-4).

[15] *Conc.* 428, ff. 28v-29r, 13 Jun, ed. PIANIGIANI, doc. 183, pp. 211-3.

[16] *Conc.* 451, f. 25r, 11 Apr, eds. NARDI, *Mariano Sozzini*, doc. 25, p. 125, and PIANIGIANI, doc. 219, pp. 251-2. Bellanti's salary later increased to 120 florins; *Conc.* 453, f. 16v, 19 Jul, ed. PIANIGIANI, doc. 226, p. 258.

[17] *Conc.* 475, f. 27v, 24 Apr, eds. NARDI, *Mariano Sozzini*, doc. 30, pp. 128-9, and PIANIGIANI, doc. 255, pp. 287-8. Cf. *Conc.* 507, f. 40r, 23 Oct 1450.

[18] *Conc.* 510, f. 20v, 21 May, ed. BAI, doc. 8, pp. 6-8.

[19] *Conc.* 592, ff. 37v-38r, 30 May, eds. NARDI, *Mariano Sozzini*, doc. 50, p. 144, and BAI, doc. 221, pp. 195-200. This was the highest salary offered to a Sienese citizen to date; it was matched by an offer of the same amount to Bartolomeo Sozzini in 1473 in an attempt to get him back from Florence. Below, p. 222.

[20] *Conc.* 361, f. 16r, 22 Mar 1426; *Conc.* 372, f. 7r, 8 Mar 1428, ed. PIANIGIANI, doc. 87, pp. 108-10. On Sozzini's career see esp. NARDI, *Mariano Sozzini*, and also A. SATTA MEUCCI, 'Per un'interpretazione di due lettere di Enea Silvio Piccolomini', *BSSP*, 81-82 (1975-6), pp. 393-404, and M. P. GILMORE, 'Pius II and Mariano Sozzini 'De Sortibus'', in *Enea Silvio Piccolomini: Papa Pio II*. Accademia Senese degli Intronati: Atti del Convegno per il Quinto Centenario della morte ed altri scritti raccolti da Domenico Maffei (Siena, 1968), pp. 187-194. On Pecci see MINNUCCI, 'Documenti', pp. 304-5.

[21] *Conc.* 361, f. 16r, 22 Mar 1426; *Conc.* 372, f. 7r, 8 Mar 1428, ed. PIANIGIANI, doc. 87, pp. 108-10; *Conc.* 379, f. 22v, 14 Jun 1429, ed. PIANIGIANI, doc. 111, pp. 138-40; *Conc.* 387, f. 12r, 18 Sept 1430, ed. PIANIGIANI, doc. 124, pp. 153-5; *Conc.* 393, f. 67v, 23 Aug 1431, ed. PIANIGIANI, doc. 129, pp. 158-60; *Conc.* 399, f. 63v, 28 Aug 1432, eds. NARDI, *Mariano Sozzini*, doc. 11, p. 119, and PIANIGIANI, doc. 136, pp. 165-6; *Conc.* 417 f. 8v, 12 Jul 1435, eds. ZDEKAUER, doc. XVII, pp. 167-9, and PIANIGIANI, doc. 167, pp. 193-4; *Conc.* 451 f. 25r, 11 Apr 1445, ed. NARDI, *Mariano Sozzini*, doc. 25, p. 125.

[22] *Conc.* 364, f. 31v, 19 Oct 1426, ed. PIANIGIANI, doc. 77, pp. 97-8; *Conc.* 373, f. 29r, 4 Jun 1428, ed. PIANIGIANI, doc. 91, pp. 116-7; *Conc.* 380, f. 16r, 19 Jul 1429, ed. PIANIGIANI, doc. 113, pp. 141-2; *Conc.* 387, f. 12r, 18 Sept 1430, ed. PIANIGIANI,

Such figures, rarely attained by Sienese teachers, were quite common among foreigners, among whom there are many examples of salaries greatly exceeding the limits for citizens. It could be argued that foreigners needed to be compensated for their additional expenses and additional job insecurity; and also of course for the fact that, as foreigners, they were unlikely to be made members of the relevant college of doctors and therefore would not receive the fees and emoluments for examinations that their citizen counterparts could expect.[23] The highest salary recorded in Siena in the first half of the fifteenth century is that agreed for Lodovico Pontano in 1433; 800 florins per annum, subsequently modified in 1434 to a two-year contract of 700 florins for the first year and 800 for the second.[24] In this sort of bracket, though, the Sienese were out of their depth; Pontano, who had probably studied in Siena and who had been the subject of Sienese attentions since he took up a teaching post in Florence in 1428,[25] in the event remained for less than two years, wooed by the *curia* and the Aragonese court.[26] The next highest lawyer's salary offered, 600 florins, was not sufficient to persuade Catone Sacco to abandon Pavia for Siena; the Sienese tried to lure him on several occasions without success.[27] These two were both civilians, as was Benedetto Barzi da Perugia, who was first hired in 1425,[28] was at a salary of 450 florins from 1430,[29] left for

---

doc. 124, pp. 153-5; *Conc.* 393, f. 67v, 23 Aug 1431, ed. PIANIGIANI, doc. 129, pp. 158-60; *Conc.* 400, f. 43r, 14 Oct 1432, ed. PIANIGIANI, doc. 139, pp. 167-8; *Conc.* 406, f. 23v, 10 Oct 1433, eds. GAROSI, doc. 101, p. 548, and PIANIGIANI, doc. 148, pp. 173-4; *Conc.* 413, f. 28r, 15 Dec 1434, ed. PIANIGIANI, doc. 165, pp. 191-2; *Conc.* 417, f. 8v, 12 Jul 1435, eds. ZDEKAUER, doc. XVII, pp. 167-9, and PIANIGIANI, doc. 167, pp. 193-4; *Conc.* 428, f. 29r, 13 Jun 1437, ed. PIANIGIANI, doc. 183, pp. 211-3; *Conc.* 451, f. 25r, 11 Apr 1441, eds. NARDI, *Mariano Sozzini*, doc. 25, p. 125, and PIANIGIANI, doc. 219, pp. 251-2; *Conc.* 471, f. 26r, 29 Jul 1444, ed. PIANIGIANI, doc. 250, p. 280; *Conc.* 507, f. 43r, 26 Oct 1450, ed. PIANIGIANI, doc. 303, pp. 335-7; *Conc.* 509, ff. 21v-22r, 18 Jan 1451, ed. BAI, doc. 1, pp. 1-2; *Conc.* 567, f. 52r, 28 Apr 1461, eds. GAROSI, doc. 109, pp. 552-3, and BAI, doc. 169, pp. 141-2; *Conc.* 604, ff. 53v-54r, 17 Jun 1467, eds. GAROSI, doc. 86, pp. 541-2, and BAI, doc. 260, pp. 235-7; and on Bartolo di Tura generally, GAROSI, pp. 261-9, G. PRUNAI, 'Bandini, Bartalo (Bartolo di Tura)', *DBI*, 5 (1963), pp. 106-7, and FIORAVANTI, 'Pietro de' Rossi', pp. 133-4. On the other hand semi-retirement, or at any rate a lightening of the teaching load after long service, is not unknown, and in 1544-5 teachers of thirty years' standing were entitled to opt out of half their teaching (dist. I, rubr. 60, eds. MARRARA, *Studio*, p. 298, and ASCHERI, *L'ultimo statuto*, p. 34; and cf. TRAPANI, 'Statuti senesi concernenti lo Studio', pp. 9-10), as well as being exempt from disputation after twenty or twenty-five years at various stages (above, p. 145). This accounts for some drops in salary, a phenomenon more observable in Pavia (ZANETTI, 'A l'Université de Pavie', p. 430).

[23] See below, pp. 202 *seq.*

[24] *Conc.* 405, f. 9r, 8 Jul 1433, ed. PIANIGIANI, doc. 197, pp. 172-3; *Conc.* 409, f. 36r, 23 Apr 1434, ed. PIANIGIANI, doc. 166, pp. 180-2. As has been seen, Enea Silvio Piccolomini's report that Niccolò Tedeschi received a salary of 800 florins appears to be a slight exaggeration, but he did reach 750 florins in the last years of his career in Siena (above, p. 59 n. 191).

[25] *Conc.* 375, ff. 29r, 8 Oct, 35v, 21 Oct, 36r, 22 Oct, 36v, 23 Oct (last two ed. PIANIGIANI, docs. 101-2, pp. 127-9); GHERARDI, *Statuti*, appendix, part 2, docs. 152-5, pp. 407-9 (23 Nov 1428 to 4 Jan 1429); NARDI, *Mariano Sozzini*, pp. 35-6.

[26] An initial appointment as apostolic protonotary resulted in a petition from the rector to the effect that his departure would be disastrous for the *Studio* and would lose it many students. The pope waived the appointment but Siena was not able to withhold Pontano from the king of Aragon who requested him in 1436 (*CG* 219, f. 18v, 23 Apr). See NARDI, *Mariano Sozzini*, p. 36.

[27] *Conc.* 439, f. 23v, 9 Apr 1439 (500 fl. proposed) (cf. *Conc.* 1652, no foliation, 8 Jun 1439, letter to the duke of Milan asking for him; *Conc.* 1943 no. 67, 4 Jul 1439, Filippo Maria Visconti's reply); *Conc.* 459, f. 51v, 26 Aug 1442 (600 fl.); *Conc.* 461 f. 31r, 28 Nov 1442. The Sienese had invited him in 1438 but he was refused permission to leave Milan. In October 1439 his salary was however increased from 400 to 460 florins by special decree; MAIOCCHI, *Codice Diplomatico dell'Università di Pavia*, II.i., docs. 512, p. 387 (12 Aug 1438), 518, p. 390 (1 Oct 1439), 522, p. 394 (1439-40 *rotolo*). See also ZORZOLI, 'Interventi dei Duchi', pp. 133-4 n. 17, and above, pp. 152 and 176 n. 247.

[28] *Conc.* 359, f. 49r, 27 Dec. The salary is not stipulated. He was made a member of the college in 1427 (*Conc.* 369, f. 18v, 2 Oct, ed. PIANIGIANI, doc. 82, pp. 103-5). There is no evidence that he was hired in 1409 as claimed in PRUNAI, II, p. 41, on the basis of a secondary tradition. See also above, p. 162 n. 137.

[29] *Conc.* 383, f. 6r, 5 Jan 1430; *Sale* 20, f. 91r, 1432/3, ed. ZDEKAUER, doc. XIV, p. 164; *Conc.* 405, f. 4r, 3 Jul 1433, ed. PIANIGIANI, doc. 146, pp. 171-2; *Conc.* 410, f. 29v, 12 Jun 1434. Strangely *condotte* continued to be offered, in terms (at

Florence in 1435, passed to Ferrara in 1443, returned to Siena in 1448 with a *condotta* of 550 florins and remained there at that salary until 1454.[30] Two more civilians, Sallustio Buonguglielmi da Perugia[31] and Giovanni de' Guasconi da Bologna,[32] taught for 500 florins, though neither for very long. In 1445, 475 florins were offered to Andrea Barbazza who accepted but failed to come, as has been seen.[33] The next highest law salary actually paid in the first half of the century was to Filippo Lazzari of Pistoia, who was hired for 350 florins in 1436[34] and obtained 450 florins in 1438[35] (he was unsuccessful in negotiating a further raise in 1442.[36] Non-lawyers could expect less again. Apart from Jacopo da Forlì who in 1405 received an annual salary of 650 florins 'cum pacto quod non habeat concurrentem civem vel alium',[37] salaries in the first half of the century did not exceed 400 florins.[38] Filelfo, obviously an exception, received 350 florins;[39] Giovanni da Sermoneta was hired in 1425 at 265 florins and reached a salary of 300 by 1437;[40] and Baverio

least in the 1436 offer) implying a simple continuation of his current salary, when he is known to have been paid by the Florentine *Studio* from 1435 to 1440 (PARK, 'The Readers at the Florentine Studio', pp. 292-6; *Conc.* 424, f. 11v, 15 Sept 1436; *Conc.* 434, f. 33v, 5 Jun 1438, ed. PIANIGIANI, doc. 189, pp. 218-9); a warning that it is possible to deduce more than is justified from these invitations. He was invited again in 1440 (*Conc.* 447, ff. 16v, 27 Jul, ed. PIANIGIANI, doc. 206, pp. 238-9, 21v, 6 Aug, ed. PIANIGIANI, doc. 209, p. 241, 29r, 23 Aug 1440, ed. PIANIGIANI, doc. 211, pp. 243-4), but taught again in Florence from 1441 to 1443 (PARK, 'The Readers at the Florentine Studio', pp. 298-9).

[30] *Conc.* 491, f. 43v, 27 Dec 1447, ed. PIANIGIANI, doc. 278, pp. 311-2 (the *condotta* – no salary is given); *Conc.* 497, f. 29v, 18 Dec 1448 (first *terzaria* – again no figure is given); *Conc.* 500, f. 15v, 19 May 1449 shows the third *terzaria* to have been 183 florins; £733/6/8 is paid to him thrice yearly in the lists of *apotisse* from 1450 to 1454. ZDEKAUER, p. 56, mistakenly believed that the 900 florins offered in 1438 were for one year only whereas they were for two. For further information on Barzi's career, MAFFEI, 'Una nuova fonte per la biografia di Benedetto Barzi'. Neither ERMINI, *Storia*, I, p. 505, nor the anonymous author of 'Barzi, Benedetto', *DBI*, 7 (1965), pp. 20-5, is aware of the full extent of his Florentine and Sienese teaching.

[31] *Conc.* 371, f. 22r, 27 Jan 1428.

[32] *Conc.* 384, f. 4r, 4 Mar 1430, ed. PIANIGIANI, doc. 120, pp. 148-9.

[33] Above, p. 154.

[34] He was originally offered a contract in 1435, for 300 florins (*Conc.* 417, f. 20r, 4 Aug, eds. ZDEKAUER, doc. XVII, pp. 167-9, and PIANIGIANI, doc. 169, p. 196). It is not clear whether this sum was annual or for the two years of his contract. That autumn Florence offered him 150 florins (GHERARDI, *Statuti*, appendix, part 2, doc. 184, p. 441, 11 Oct; cf. ZDEKAUER, p. 173). It is not clear which offer, if either, he accepted. On 21 Aug 1436 the Concistoro authorised the Savi to hire him at 200 florins; in the event he was given 350 (*Conc.* 424, f. 17r, 23 Sept, ed. PIANIGIANI, doc. 178, p. 203).

[35] *Conc.* 434, f. 18v, 16 May, ed. PIANIGIANI, doc. 188, pp. 217-8; and see ZDEKAUER, doc. XIX, p. 174.

[36] *Conc.* 459 f. 20v, 17 Jul, and see his acceptance, 23r, 18 Jul, ed. PIANIGIANI, doc. 229, pp. 260-1. The remainder of his salary was paid to his father after his death; *CG* 224, f. 166v, 8 Jun 1444, *Conc.* 470, ff. 12v, 10 May, 44r, 4 Jun (though he had ceased to teach in May 1443). The words 'mille conductus aureis' appear on his tombstone in Pistoia which ZDEKAUER (p. 56) interpreted literally to mean that he was paid an annual salary of 1,000 florins at Siena, but there is no evidence of this.

[37] *Conc.* 235, f. 46v, 3 Feb, ed. PIANIGIANI, doc. 11, pp. 31-7 (pp. 33-4).

[38] Giovanni Matteo Ferrari da Grado was apparently courted in 1451; he stipulated that he wanted an ordinary lectureship at 400 florins, which was agreed, but he did not come. H.-M. FERRARI, *Une chaire de médecine au XVᵉ siècle. Un professeur à l'Université de Pavie de 1432 a 1472* (Paris, 1899), pp. 40-43; and cf. ROSSO, 'Problemi di vita universitaria', p. 74. I have not found traces of this episode, which was conducted through an intermediary, in the Sienese archives.

[39] *Conc.* 413, f. 5v, 6 Nov 1434; 300 had failed to lure him (*Conc.* 412, f. 71r, 29 Oct, ed. PIANIGIANI, doc. 163, p. 190). He was also given 400 *lire* in advance and when he nonetheless arrived late he was excused; *Conc.* 413, f. 28r, 15 Dec 1434, ed. PIANIGIANI, doc. 165, pp. 191-2. On his career in Siena, DE FEO CORSO, 'Il Filelfo in Siena', cf. FIORAVANTI, 'Alcuni aspetti della cultura umanistica senese', p. 146.

[40] Giovanni was teaching in 1416 (when no salary is mentioned); *Conc.* 301, f. 26v, 22 Apr, ed. PIANIGIANI, doc. 32, p. 57. The *condotta* of 1425 is a curious one; four years at 265 florins, scaled, 253 florins for the first three years, 300 for the fourth. *Conc.* 354, f. 10r, 18 Jan 1425, ed. PIANIGIANI, doc. 67, pp. 88-9. In 1429 it was renewed for two years at 275 florins; *Conc.* 377, f. 32r, ed. PIANIGIANI, doc. 107, pp. 133-5. Cf. also *Conc.* 404, f. 39r, 13 Jun 1433; *Conc.* 417, ff. 10v, 12r, 14 Jul 1435, ed. PIANIGIANI, doc. 168, p. 195; *Conc.* 431, f. 23r, 20 Dec 1437, ed. PIANIGIANI, doc. 185, pp. 214-5,

Bonetti of Bologna was hired at 250 florins in 1443 and reached 300 by 1447.[41]

It was not just at the top of the scale, however, that foreigners had the advantage. It was quite possible for the starting salaries for teachers who had only just obtained their degrees to be considerably higher than those of citizens, and for their salaries to rise more rapidly. In 1427 Roberto de' Cavalcanti of Florence was offered a starting salary of 40 florins[42] (having previously had a 25-florin lectureship as rector of the *Studio*);[43] in 1429 another former student, Cola da Sicilia, was given a starting salary of 50 florins.[44] Luca de Callio, one of the four student lecturers in 1442 for a salary of 25 florins,[45] was given a two-year contract in 1443 at a salary of 65 florins, to start as soon as he had taken his degree.[46] The possibility of such rapid increases was implied in the not infrequent staggering of a salary within a *condotta*, such as that of Timoteo da Pistoia in 1423, to teach philosophy at a salary of 80 florins for the first year and 100 for the next two.[47] Foreign teachers were more likely to be able to negotiate their salaries, whether men of the reputation of Filelfo or grammarians like Giovanni da Spoleto who in 1405 rejected an offer of 100 florins, settling eventually at 125.[48] They could more readily dictate special terms such as advance payments,[49] or even in one case a favour of the commune; in 1437 Pietro de' Giovanetti of Bologna accepted a *condotta* on condition that he could have a certain student put in the Sapienza.[50] On the other hand intransigence in negotiation could backfire. Tommaso de' Covoni of Florence, a civilian who was in 1389 being paid 300 florins per annum, was refused an increase in salary; after much negotiation which involved the Sienese orator in Florence he in fact accepted a two-year *condotta* at 300 florins the first year and 250 the second.[51] In an even stranger episode Filippo da Lucca, another civilian, was offered 350 florins in 1439, and refused in the hope of a higher offer; displeased with this attitude, the commune did indeed vote a higher salary, 450 florins, but offered it to someone else, Antonio Roselli, instead. Filippo must have repented, for shortly after-

and on Giovanni da Sermoneta generally GAROSI, pp. 258-9. There is also an offer to 'Magr. Ant. de Rossellis de Aretio' of 300 florins 'ad lecturam medicine ordinariam de mane' (*Conc.* 412, f. 67r, 26 Oct 1434, ed. PIANIGIANI, doc. 162, p. 189), though there is no sign that it was accepted. On this figure see above, pp. 78 n. 125, 177 n. 262, and 180.

[41] *Conc.* 465, f. 16r, 30 Jul 1443, eds. MÜNSTER, *Baverio Maghinardo de' Bonetti*, Appendice, Documenti senesi, doc. 1, pp. 109-10, and PIANIGIANI, doc. 241, pp. 271-2 (giving as 'Ranerio'), and cf. *Conc.* 1661, f. 14r, 2 Aug; renewed at 275 florins in 1445 (*Conc.* 475, ff. 25v, 20 Apr 1445, eds. MÜNSTER, op. cit., doc. 2, p. 110, and PIANIGIANI, doc. 254, pp. 265-6, and 30r, 27 Apr. The authorities had fixed a ceiling of 280 florins, *Conc.* 475, f. 23r, 16 Apr, but in the event agreed on 275 for both Baverio and a lawyer). In 1447 he was rehired at 300 florins (*Conc.* 487, f. 25v, 27 Mar 1447). On him see above, p. 168 n. 185, MÜNSTER, op. cit., pp. 31-5, and also U. STEFANUTTI, 'Bonetti, Baverio Maghinardo de', *DBI*, 11 (1969), pp. 792-4.

[42] *Conc.* 369, f. 16r, 27 Sept, ed. PIANIGIANI, doc. 80, pp. 100-2.

[43] *Conc.* 367, f. 5r, 7 Mar, and cf. *Conc.* 368, f. 16v, 31 Jul 1427.

[44] *Conc.* 377, f. 32v, 21 Feb, ed. PIANIGIANI, doc. 107, pp. 133-5; see below, p. 152 n. 29.

[45] *Conc.* 459, f. 45r, 20 Aug, ed. PIANIGIANI, doc. 231, p. 262. On student lecturers below, pp. 282-5.

[46] *Conc.* 467, f. 20v, 4 Dec, ed. PIANIGIANI, doc. 245, pp. 275-6. Initially he had been offered 30 florins and a two-year contract but this had to be reduced because he had not taken his degree. *Conc.* 459, f. 32v, 29 Jul 1442, ed. PIANIGIANI, doc. 230, p. 261.

[47] *Conc.* 345, f. 8r, 10 Jul, ed. PIANIGIANI, doc. 58, p. 81. Cf. the case of Lodovico Pontano, p. 186 above.

[48] *Conc.* 235, f. 46r, 3 Feb.

[49] *Conc.* 166, f. 17v, 24 Apr, and *Conc.* 167, f. 24r, 20 Jun 1392 (the grammar teacher Nofrio), and see n. 39 above.

[50] Conc 427, f. 12v, 11 Mar.

[51] *Conc.* 151, f. 10v, 14 Sept 1389, *Conc.* 153, ff. 3r, 2 Jan, 8r, 8 Jan, 9r, 10 Jan, 54r, 12 Jan 1390; GHERARDI, *Statuti*, appendix, part 2, doc. 186, p. 354 (25 Nov 1389).

wards Roselli's contract was revoked and Filippo was engaged at only 300 florins.[52] By and large, though, it was the commune that lost out, bowing to the inevitable demands for a raise unless they had a good alternative lecturer, putting up with the vagaries and unreliability of the academic high-fliers and devoting considerable energies to often hopeless enterprises like the luring or retaining of men like Catone Sacco or Lodovico Pontano. Foreigners could get away with more, arriving late or leaving early, and when they broke their contracts were virtually impossible to punish. They were inevitably the most volatile part of the system, and it was only a matter of time before pressures began to mount in favour of citizen *condotte* to offset this unpredictability.

Fig. 8b – Signature and seal of Pietro Luti, who taught law in the second half of the fifteenth century (Archivio dell'Università di Siena, *ms.* 1, f. 54r).

The second half of the fifteenth century sees a shift as well, reflecting perhaps the fact that the disparity in terms of reputation between foreign and local citizens was not always that clear-cut. In the 1450s and 1460s large sums were still being offered to foreigners; Francesco Accolti d'Arezzo, appointed in 1451 (having been wrested from Ferrara), was receiving 550 florins in the early 1450s for an extraordinary chair in canon law, a high figure for that subject.[53] He returned to Ferrara in 1457, still owed substantial amounts of his Sienese salary.[54] The Sienese tried to tempt him back with an offer of 700 florins in 1459,[55] a sum offered again in 1460 and 1461, without success.[56] By the time the

---

[52] *Conc.* 441, ff. 22v, 25 Jul, 30r, 30 Jul, ed. PIANIGIANI, docs. 197-8, pp. 226-8 (and see below, p. 203 n. 165). Roselli had taught in Siena in 1423-4 (*Conc.* 346, f. 13v, 13 Oct 1423; *Conc.* 348, f. 25r, 25 Feb 1424; *Conc.* 349, f. 14r, 24 Mar 1424, ed. PIANIGIANI, doc. 64, pp. 84-6; *Conc.* 351, f. 20v, 10 Aug 1424). On Roselli see NARDI, *Mariano Sozzini*, esp. pp. 9-10 and n. 39, etc., BELLOMO, *Saggio sull'Università*, p. 257 and n. 66, and MINNUCCI, 'Documenti', pp. 224-5.

[53] *Conc.* 512, f. 48v, 23 Dec 1451, ed. BAI, doc. 22, pp. 17-18; *Conc.* 515, f. 61v, 17 Aug 1452, ed. BAI, doc. 31, pp. 28-30 (with erroneous figure); *Conc.* 518, f. 21r, 24 Jan 1453, ed. BAI, doc. 45, p. 40; *Conc.* 519, f. 32v, 4 Apr 1453, ed. BAI, doc. 50, p. 44; *Conc.* 522, f. 23v, 19 Sept 1453, ed. BAI, doc. 56, p. 48; *Conc.* 525, f. 55r, 11 Apr 1454; *Conc.* 526, f. 35r, 27 May 1454; *Conc.* 528, f. 61v, 19 Oct 1454, ed. BAI, doc. 68, p. 57; *Conc.* 530, f. 75r, 17 Feb 1455, ed. BAI, doc. 72, p. 60; *Conc.* 533, ff. 24, 18 Jul, and 38r, 8 Aug 1455, ed. BAI, docs. 77-8, pp. 63-5; *Conc.* 534, f. 19v, 19 Sept 1455, ed. BAI, doc. 79, p. 66; *Conc.* 535, f. 27v, 30 Dec 1455, ed. BAI, doc. 82, p. 68; *Conc.* 537, f. 19r, 14 Apr 1456, ed. BAI, doc. 83, p. 70; *Conc.* 540, f. 7v, 7 Sept 1456, ed. BAI, doc. 89, p. 75; *Conc.* 541, f. 23r, 24 Dec 1456, ed. BAI, doc. 93, p. 79; *Conc.* 544, f. 8r, 17 May 1457, ed. BAI, doc. 96, p. 81; *Conc.* 545, f. 32r, 27 Aug 1457, ed. BAI, doc. 103, p. 86.

[54] Above, pp. 170-1.

[55] *Conc.* 556, f. 22r, 24 May, ed. BAI, doc. 117, pp. 99-100.

[56] *Conc.* 562, f. 7r, 8 May 1460, ed. BAI, doc. 131, p. 114; *Conc.* 566, f. 33r-v, 7 Feb 1461, ed. BAI, docs. 165-7, pp. 137-40. He accepted this last offer, but did not appear.

Sienese persuaded him to return, in 1467, it took an offer of 850 florins, raised in 1470 to 900 florins, as far as has been ascertained the highest salary of the fifteenth century.[57] 700 florins were also offered in 1456 to Andrea Barbazza, the Sicilian jurist who a decade earlier had been shamed in paint for reneging on his contract.[58] The 1456 attempt at revival also included offers of contracts of 500 florins to the civilian Benedetto Accolti[59] and 450 florins to the canonist Angelo degli Ubaldi da Perugia,[60] as well as offers of 500 florins to the teachers of medicine Mattiolo da Perugia[61] and Niccolò da Sirmione.[62] The policy continued, with offers of 450 florins to Benedetto Capra da Perugia (law) and Pietro Sacco da Verona (medicine) in 1458.[63] Mansueto da Perugia (law) was earning 500 florins in 1462,[64] and in 1483 the Sienese hired the celebrated lawyer Lancilotto Decio at a salary of 600 florins.[65] But the balance was no longer so one-sided. Giovanni Battista Caccialupi's salary was raised to 600 florins in 1474,[66] and as a long-standing teacher who was eventually made a citizen his recompense has to be seen in a different light. By the end of the century there were some impressive salaries for local teachers, as will be seen.[67]

2. *From* forenses *to* cives

The differences between career patterns of foreign and citizen teachers are self-evident. What has not yet been demonstrated is the change in attitude on the part of the authorities. In the early fifteenth century there was a rapid shift from the assumption that the bedrock of the *Studio* was to be teachers from outside the town, to almost precisely the opposite view. The development can be traced through the legislation as well as through contracts, which should help us to understand the rationale for this, perhaps the most crucial step in the process of 'domestication' of late medieval Italian universities.[68]

The question of whether foreign or citizen teachers should be employed arose relatively early in the history of the *Studio*, most notably as a result of the great Bolognese exodus of 1321. Previous to this,

---

[57] *Conc.* 598, ff. 32r, 7 Jun, and 46-v, 23 Jun 1466; *CG* 231, f. 252r-v, 23 Dec 1466; *Conc.* 621, f. 27v, 10 Apr 1470, ed. Bai, doc. 300, pp. 287-8.

[58] *Conc.* 539, f. 16v, 14 Jul, ed. Bai, doc. 86, pp. 71-2; above, p. 154.

[59] *Conc.* 539, f. 45r, 10 Aug, ed. Bai, doc. 88, pp. 73-4; above, p. 178 n. 265.

[60] Loc. cit.

[61] Loc. cit.

[62] *Conc.* 539, f. 17r, 14 Jul, ed. Bai, doc. 87, pp. 72-3.

[63] *Conc.* 552, f. 16r, 25 Sept, ed. Bai, doc. 113, pp. 93-7.

[64] *Conc.* 573, f. 32v, 27 Apr, ed. Bai, doc. 178, pp. 152-4 (instructions for payment). His salary was a matter of contention; it was not approved for two years (*Conc.* 577, ff. 36v, 16 Dec, and 43v-44r, 24 Dec), and he did not read for the first *terzaria* of 1462-3 (*Conc.* 577, f. 47r, 28 Dec 1462, ed. Bai, doc. 183, pp. 159-60), but he was present and paid again in 1465 (*Conc.* 593, f. 33r, 17 Aug, ed. Bai, doc. 227, pp. 204-5). The civilian Francesco da Crema was also offered 500 florins in 1462, but the offer was revised to 300 florins (*Conc.* 573, ff. 14r, 18 Mar, and 23r, 6 Apr, ed. Bai, docs. 175 and 177, pp. 150-2).

[65] *Balìa* 31, f. 5r, 7 Dec. On this contract see also Nardi, 'Giovanni Battista Caccialupi', p. 117 and n. 71.

[66] Op. cit., pp. 107-8.

[67] Below, p. 193.

[68] See Denley, 'Career, Springboard or Sinecure?', pp. 109-12, and for parallels in Padua, De Sandre, 'Dottori, Università, Comune', pp. 27-9.

the regulations had been slanted in favour of citizens; a foreigner had to be a *doctor iuris* in order to teach, whereas a Sienese citizen only had to be *iuris peritus*.[69] Foreign teachers were regularly hired, but as in many *studi* of the time they were modestly paid, the statutory salary being 25 *lire*.[70] The arrival in 1321 of other foreign teachers, far from altering these modest salaries, seems to have served to underline the contrast between the high-fliers and the regulars, and may well have opened up the possibility of having citizens in the humbler but more regular role. Not long after, in 1339, Sienese doctors were for the first time forbidden to go and teach outside Siena, at a penalty of 1,000 *lire*.[71] This protectionist measure was repeated after the *Studio* obtained its diploma from Charles IV.[72] Three years later, however, the restrictions on leaving were lifted,[73] and in 1361, with the siege of Bologna reopening the possibilities of recruitment (or so they thought), the commune decided to devote funds exclusively to the hiring of foreign teachers.[74] In the re-launching of the *Studio* in 1387, however, a decision was taken which set the pattern for some time to come. The *Savi* set out to hire foreign doctors, but were relatively unsuccessful. On 16 October, two days before the opening of the *Studio*, it was decided that six *cives* could be hired for a total expenditure of 300 florins.[75] The citizen teacher as 'stopgap' had appeared. It remained for many decades a reserve expedient. In 1409, when crisis again curtailed the activities of the *Studio*, the Sienese teachers only were sacked.[76] When the *Studio* picked up again in 1414, the *Savi* were empowered to hire all teachers except resident ones, for whom the *Concistoro*'s approval was required.[77] The *condotta* offered to Ugo Benzi in 1415 had to be dealt with by the *Consiglio del Popolo* as a special case.[78] In that same year, again just before the opening of the *Studio*, it was reported that the foreigners who had been hired had failed to turn up, and as a result citizens were to be hired for a total of 400 florins, with none to be given a salary exceeding 50 florins.[79] In 1416 the *Savi* reported that with the 3,000-florin budget they were still left with five *cattedre* to fill; a further 300 florins were approved for the hire of citizens 'qui possint haberi pro multo minori pretio quam forenses'.[80] In 1418 the *Savi* were given discretion as to whether to hire *cives* or *forenses*;[81] and the fol-

[69] NARDI, *L'insegnamento*, pp. 91-2.

[70] *Chartularium*, doc. 61, pp. 41-3 (1286).

[71] *Chartularium*, doc. 358, pp. 451-3, 12 Feb 1338(=1309); ZDEKAUER, p. 58; the legislation is referred to as late as 1473 (ZDEKAUER, p. 59). See above, p. 174.

[72] *Chartularium*, doc. 431, pp. 567-9, 19 Oct 1357.

[73] *CG* 165, f. 33v, 4 Dec 1360.

[74] *CG* 168, f. 4r-v, 19 Jul; ZDEKAUER, doc. V, p. 143; the *Savi* are appointed but may not 'salariare aliquem civem Senensem'.

[75] *Conc.* 139, ff. 49v-50r, 16 Oct.

[76] *CG* 204, f. 14v, 3 Jun; GAROSI, doc. 55, p. 527 (given as 1408).

[77] *Conc.* 292, f. 27r, 16 Oct.

[78] *CG* 207, f. 29r, 16 May. Zdekauer seems to have been mistaken in stating that the same procedure applied to Giovanni Bellanti in 1404; his *condotta* is made by the *Concistoro* with the *Savi*, *Conc.* 235, f. 47r, 28 Feb 1405, ed. PIANIGIANI, doc. 11, pp. 31-7 (pp. 35-6).

[79] *Conc.* 298, f. 29r-v, 16-17 Oct, ed. PIANIGIANI, doc. 30, pp. 54-6.

[80] *Conc.* 305, f. 18v, 2 Dec, *CG* 207, f. 244r, 20 Dec, ed. GAROSI, doc. 56, pp. 527-8. The persistence of the perception that foreigners cost more is seen in 1465; the contract of Borghese Borghesi was renewed on the basis that 'non acceptando lui bisognarebbe condurre a detta sedia uno doctore forestiero nel quale spendareste fior. 400 et più'; *CG* 230, f. 302r-v, 28 Jun.

[81] *Conc.* 317, f. 17v, 2 Dec, ed. PIANIGIANI, doc. 39, pp. 62-3; on 5 Dec the *Concistoro* however stepped in to decide for them that foreigners were preferable (f. 18v).

lowing year saw the first explicit statutory declaration that *cives* may be hired on a regular basis.[82] In 1422 this had the consequence that it was now foreigners who could be hired to fill the vacancies.[83]

A further shift in the direction of citizen *condotte* is evident in the 1430s. The general drop in salaries in 1431 that accompanied the crisis of the time and the consequent loss of confidence in the *Studio*[84] may well have been responsible for increased difficulty in getting distinguished foreigners to teach. A measure of 1434 decreed that any citizen doctor of law who wished to volunteer for a *condotta* would be accepted at a salary of 20 florins, more if a specially appointed commission so decided.[85] Later in the year there were still vacancies in the *sedie* or chairs usually reserved for foreigners, and the *Concistoro* debated whether or not to fill these with citizens.[86] In September 1435 the *Savi* reported to the *Consiglio del Popolo* that so far, 'propter carestiam denariorum', it had not been possible to elect foreigners, but that one chair in civil law would remain vacant unless the council changed its mind (which it did).[87] Further evidence of the difficulties is found in the following year; Tommaso Docci was to teach despite his election to the *podesteria* of Asciano because of the difficulty there had been in getting foreign doctors.[88] In 1437, 'veduto che, mancando a le volte e' Doctori forestieri, e' ciptadini sonno el reparo e'l supplemento del nostro Studio', a citizen was to be placed in each *sedia* of each faculty, and for the first time citizen *condotte* were to be for two years because the one-year system had proved cumbersome.[89]

The change of 1437 was made possible because by this time Siena was beginning to reap the results of the decade of continuous teaching under a constellation of eminent teachers, in the form of a growing amount of native talent, eager and impatient to begin their careers (and of course prevented by law from doing so elsewhere). The consequence of the change was dramatic. Within three years a special step had to be taken to exclude public officials from lectureships for three years, since many of them were allegedly neglecting their duties because they hoped to be given a lectureship or the rectorate of the Sapienza.[90] The predominance of *forenses* was in fact never recovered, and with an established regular citizen element pressures on the authorities became inevitable. In 1441 an extra 300 florins were approved in addition to the 1,000 already budgeted for citizen teachers, in a measure that declared them to be much better value, and more reliable, than foreigners.[91] The following year saw an

---

[82] *Statuti* 40, f. 15r, *Statuti* 47, f. 191r; ZDEKAUER, p. 59.

[83] *Conc.* 339, f. 5r, 8 Jul, ed. PIANIGIANI, doc. 54, pp. 77-8. The practice in this period was to hire foreign and citizen teachers in separate batches; cf. *Conc.* 374, f. 11v, 23 Jul 1428, ed. PIANIGIANI, doc. 94, pp. 119-20, and partial ed. in NARDI, *Mariano Sozzini*, doc. 4, p. 116; *Conc.* 387, ff. 12r, 18 Sept, and 32v, 25 Oct 1430, ed. PIANIGIANI, docs. 124-5, pp. 153-6. The importance of non-citizen appointments was of course still recognised, and in 1431 the *Consiglio del Popolo* reserved them to itself; *Conc.* 390, f. 12r, 19 Jan 1431, ed. PIANIGIANI, doc. 127, p. 158.

[84] Above, pp. 62 and 184-5.

[85] *Conc.* 411, f. 25v, 20 Jul. Another reason seems to have been that many citizens had ceased to teach and were increasingly involved in communal affairs. The preceding year had seen several releases from *condotte*, and on 11 Sept 1433 the *Consiglio del Popolo* had had to order the *Savi* to draw up the *rotolo* of citizen teachers as the operation to hire them had failed (*Conc.* 2176, no foliation).

[86] *Conc.* 413, f. 13v, 17 Nov.

[87] *CG* 218, f. 191v, 14 Sept. In the same year there is evidence that the distinction remained an important one in the eyes of the authorities; the validity of Benedetto da Volterra's *condotta* was questioned because since it had been made he had acquired Sienese citizenship (*Conc.* 415, f. 19r, 10 Mar).

[88] *Conc.* 425, f. 7r, 10 Nov 1436. The document refers to unsuccessful attempts to get doctors from Bologna, Florence and Perugia.

[89] *CG* 219, f. 136v, 10 May (ZDEKAUER, doc. XVIII, pp. 169-171).

[90] *CG* 220, f. 178r, 21 Sept 1440.

[91] '...et perché si dice e dottori forestieri fanno venire più scolari alla vostra città benché spesse volte non riescha, et volendo provedere a riempire le decte sedie di dottori forestieri sarebbe di necessità di spendare asai più quantità di denari

(unsuccessful) attempt to make it harder for foreign graduates of the Sienese *Studio* to be given ordinary lectures by stipulating that they had to have had their degree for three years.[92] By the late 1440s the situation was clearly getting out of hand. Allegations of favouritism led to the *Consiglio del Popolo* deciding to take both foreign and citizen *condotte* back under its direct control,[93] and to outlaw the tenure of office by teachers;[94] and in 1450 the same body, revising the arrangements yet again, blamed the whole failure of the *Studio* on the lack of famous foreign doctors.[95] 1472 saw an attempt at a pay freeze for citizen doctors,[96] but by 1476 it was simply attempting to limit the scale of abuse by declaring that no Sienese could accept a *condotta* of over 100 florins without its agreement.[97]

By the end of the century the transition was virtually complete. Very few foreigners appear in the lists of the teachers, and their presence is transitory. In the 1480-1 list only one outsider, Giovanni Battista Caccialupi da San Severino, appears, and even he was a Sienese citizen by then.[98] In the 1492-3 list there are only four identifiable foreigners, in the 1494-5 list there is only one.[99] At the same time high salaries became much rarer. In the 1480-1 list the only exceptional salary is Caccialupi's, 700 florins; the highest after that is 250 florins (Bulgarino de' Bulgarini and Francesco Nini).[100] In 1492-3 only three salaries were over 200 florins; Bulgarino and Francesco were earning 600, Arcangelo di Giovanni 690.[101] In 1494-5 the highest salary was 200 florins.[102] The 1500-1 list includes six salaries over 200 florins, the highest being 300;[103] and in 1513-4 Alessandro Petrucci appears to have been paid 250 florins.[104] The other sixteenth-century lists that have been examined, however, all have an upper limit of 200 florins. The 'career structure' becomes more defined, teachers build longer careers in the *Studio*, salaries are more rigidly scaled, dominant families feature recurrently (see Table 4).[105] The same hierarchical system that has been noted in sixteenth-century Pavia[106] has set in.

che non si spende, e alcuna volta si conducano assai dottori forestieri con grande salario che non sonno valenti tanto quanto n'avete nella vostra città, E pertanto avendo voi molti cittadini dottori, E quali sonno valentissimi e non sonno condotti per manchamento di non potere spendare ne' dottori cittadini se no mille fiorini, Et potendosi spendare qualche denaro più verebbe a dire che essi dottori vostri valenti saranno condotti, Et lo studio vostro arà sua perfectione' (*Conc.* 2138, no. 9, f. 16r, 9 May).

[92] *Conc.* 2115, f. 4v, 15 Feb 1442. This was clearly an attempt to protect young Sienese at the beginning of their careers from direct competition from non-Sienese, and needs to be evaluated in the context of policy towards students. It should also be seen in the context of the restrictive measures habitual at Bologna; above, p. 179.

[93] *CG* 223, f. 229r, 20 Feb 1448, ed. GAROSI, doc. 61, pp. 529-30 (and see p. 239).

[94] *Conc.* 490, f. 22v, 3 Oct 1447, ed. PIANIGIANI, doc. 277, pp. 308-11.

[95] *CG* 224, ff. 318v-319r, 16 Feb 1450; GAROSI, doc. 62, pp. 530-1. A limit of 1,000 florins per annum was placed on the amount to be spent on *cives* (*Conc.* 507, f. 36v, 19 Oct, and *CG* 225, f. 73v, 20 Oct 1450).

[96] *Conc.* 635, f. 37v, 13 Aug, ed. BAI, doc. 326, pp. 321-2.

[97] *Studio* 2, f. 37v, 12 Jan.

[98] *Balìa* 20, f. 58r, Aug 1480.

[99] ZDEKAUER, doc. XXIV, pp. 191-3.

[100] As n. 98 above. On these two see MINNUCCI, 'Documenti', pp. 240-1 and 254.

[101] As n. 99 above.

[102] *Conc.* 768, ff. 24v-25r, 31 Oct 1494, ed. FERRERI, doc. 347, pp. 329-31.

[103] MONDOLFO, 'Il ruolo dello Studio Senese', pp. 415-7.

[104] *Studio* 21, no. 7, 5 Jan 1514.

[105] Cf. M. ASCHERI, 'Repubblica, principato e crisi del diritto comune a Firenze. Dalla motivazione delle sentenze all'edizione delle Pandette', *Annali della Facoltà di Lettere e Filosofia dell'Università di Siena*, 6 (1985), pp. 117-40 (p. 136 and n. 50).

[106] ZORZOLI, 'Interventi dei Duchi', pp. 144-5.

Table 4 – Leading Sienese families in the *Studio*

Family	No. of teachers active mainly 1357-1480	No. of teachers active mainly 1480-1557	No. of students mentioned 1357-1557
Bellanti	3	3	-
Benvoglienti	-	5	-
Borghesi	5	11	4
Buoninsegni	1	7	4
Cerretani	-	2	3
Docci	1	3	1
Luti	2	4	2
Maccabruni	1	3	1
Malavolti	-	4	1
Piccolomini	-	3	3
Sozzini	3	3	1
Tantucci	-	4	1
Tolomei	1	2	2
Ugurgieri	-	3	-
Umidi	-	3	-

This table has been prepared on the basis of a card-index of teachers and students compiled by G. Prunai and S. De Colli in preparation for subsequent volumes to the *Chartularium* (see above, p. 13). I am most grateful to Prof. Prunai, to Dott. Ubaldo Morandi, then Director of the Archivio di Stato di Siena, and to Prof. Giuliano Catoni for making this available to me, and merely pass on their warnings that the index makes no claim to completeness.

The legislation of the 1430s led to a decisive tipping of the scales. Local teachers moved at a stroke from being the back-up to constituting the mainstay of the *Studio*. Yet this change, dramatic though it appears to have been, disguises a truth that is at the same time more mundane and more complex. The relationship between *forenses* and *cives* was and remained symbiotic. It was the continued – or rather, recurring – presence of eminent teachers, from the 1380s to the 1430s – Paolo di Castro, Giovanni Nicoletti da Imola, Niccolò Tedeschi, in medicine Marsilio Santasofia – that first stimulated and then helped consolidate the growth of an indigenous teaching force, generations which, led by Pietro de' Pecci, Mariano Sozzini, Pietro Lapini and others, then spawned the ranks of their successors. Foreigners were the leaven, the means of intellectual fertilisation. If administrative documents tend not to labour the point, it is well understood by the protagonists themselves. Caccialupi, whose treatise *De modo studendi* was written in Siena and largely based on his years of teaching there, devoted a substantial part of the work to a recitation of the names and works of generations of law teachers.[107] Writers' accounts of their student days, and the debts they acknowledge to their teachers,[108] are more than commonplaces

---

[107] J. B. CACCIALUPUS, *De modo studendi et vita doctorum tractatus* (Venetiis, 1472); accessible now in G. B. CACCIALUPI, *Modus studendi in utroque iure*, Intr/tr. S. di Noto Marrella (Parma, 1995); a critical edition is promised in A. FRIGERIO, 'Umanesimo del diritto: il "De modo in iure studendi" di Giovanni Battista Caccialupi', *Annali dell'Istituto storico italo-germanico in Trento / Jahrbuch des italienisch-deutschen historischen Instituts in Trient*, 30 (2004), pp. 35-48, which also surveys recent views on the significance of this work. Cf. also esp. D. MAFFEI, 'Giovanni Battista Caccialupi biografo', *Zeitschrift der Savigny-Stiftung für Rechtsgeschichte. Kanonistische Abteilung*, 83 (1997), pp. 392-400.

[108] Well-known examples are Enea Silvio Piccolomini's tributes to his teachers, Antonio Roselli and Pietro de' Pecci (*De viris illustribus*, pp. 30, 42), and Girolamo Agliotti's memoir of his time in Siena, which coincided with that of Piccolomini; HIERONYMUS ALIOTTI, *Epistolae et opuscola*, 2 vols. (Arezzo, 1769), 2, pp. 349-51 (and see ZDEKAUER, pp. 48 n. 4, 97).

and handy biographical clues for historians; they are real tributes to the transmission of knowledge, skill, and the right and duty to impart them. In a broad sense the 1437 legislation marks a point of transition and of transmission. It is a key moment in the process that Nardi has evaluated as follows:

> Soprattutto l'Università si era potuta giovare dell'impegno dispiegato dalla classe dirigente senese nel potenziare gli insegnamenti delle diverse discipline, chiamando ad impartirli docenti autorevoli ed in qualche caso autentici luminari, che non si erano sottratti ai doveri accademici, ma anzi avevano lasciato tracce profonde nella formazione dei loro scolari e favorito la crescita di un ambiente intellettuale cittadino di notevole livello e, quindi, di una classe dirigente colta e preparata.[109]

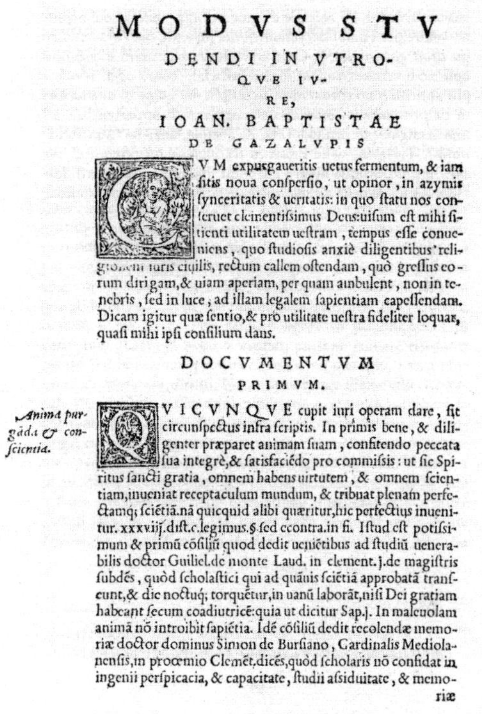

MODVS STV
DENDI IN VTRO-
QVE IV-
RE,
IOAN. BAPTISTAE
DE GAZALVPIS

CVM expurgaueritis uetus fermentum, & iam sitis noua consperſio, ut opinor, in azymis ſynceritatis & ueritatis: in quo ſtatu nos conſeruet clementiſsimus Deus: uiſum eſt mihi ſitienti utilitatem ueſtram, tempus eſſe conueniens, quo ſtudioſis anxiè diligentibus religionem iuris ciuilis, rectum callem oſtendam, quò greſſus eorum dirigam, & uiam aperiam, per quam ambulent, non in tenebris, ſed in luce, ad illam legalem ſapientiam capeſſendam. Dicam igitur quæ ſentio, & pro utilitate ueſtra fideliter loquar, quaſi mihi ipſi conſilium dans.

DOCVMENTVM
PRIMVM.

Anima purgāda & conſcientia.

QVICVNQVE cupit iuri operam dare, ſit circunſpectus infra ſcriptis. In primis bene, & diligenter præparet animam ſuam, confitendo peccata ſua integrè, & ſatisfaciēdo pro commiſsis: ut ſic Spiritus ſancti gratia, omnem habens uirtutem, & omnem ſcientiam, inueniat receptaculum mundum, & tribuat plenam perfectamq; ſciētiā. nā quicquid alibi quæritur, hic perfectius inuenitur. xxxviij. diſt. c. legimus. § ſed econtra. in fi. Iſtud eſt potiſsimum & primū cōſiliū quod dedit ueniētibus ad ſtudiū uenerabilis doctor Guiliel. de monte Laud. in clement. j. de magiſtris ſubdēs, quòd ſcholaſtici qui ad quāuis ſciētiā approbatā tranſeunt, & die noctuq; torquētur, in uanū laborāt, niſi Dei gratiam habeant ſecum coadiutricē: quia ut dicitur Sap. j. In maleuolam animā nō introibit ſapiētia. Idē cōſiliū dedit recolendæ memoriæ doctor dominus Simon de Burſiano, Cardinalis Mediolanenſis, in procemio Clemēt. dicēs, quòd ſcholaris nō confidat in ingenii perſpicacia, & capacitate, ſtudii aſsiduitate, & memoriæ

Fig. 9 – Opening of Giovanni Battista Caccialupi, *De modo studendi*, written in Siena in the 1460s (from Lyon, 1547 edition).

3. *The colleges of doctors*

What was the institutional impact of this localisation? How far did Sienese teachers develop mechanisms to represent and defend their interests? This is a very complex issue, largely because there is no expression of the collectivity of teachers, at least until the emergence of the 'collegio dei dottori leggenti' of the end of the fifteenth century, discussed above, which took specific responsibility for negotiating salaries.[110] What we do have is the thorny problem of the Sienese colleges of doctors.

[109] Nardi, 'Giovanni Battista Caccialupi', p. 95.

[110] Above, p. 173.

In the Italian system, colleges were powerful bodies, of considerable significance for both *studio* and town. The key to their importance within the *studio* lies in their power to award degrees – power with which they emerge in Bologna by the end of the thirteenth century, as a clear counterweight to the collective bargaining power claimed by students.[111] As degree-awarders, colleges controlled the transmission of expertise and knowledge.[112] But they also played a critical role for the town, since from their earliest days they also acted as focal points for expertise on which it could draw. The constitutional position of these bodies was far from simple. They were hybrids; not all teachers were necessarily members, and not all members taught.[113] By the fourteenth century, and certainly the fifteenth, in the majority of Italian *studi* membership of these colleges was confined to citizens, and such colleges could then increasingly constitute an elite, with wide-ranging powers – offering expert *consilia*, acting as a pool from which expertise could be drawn for advice, and (in the case of colleges of doctors of law) appointing to, sometimes even supplying nominees for, judicial positions within the town.

Intensive research on these colleges over recent decades has focused attention on the socio-political aspect of these bodies, and has also stressed the complexity of their history.[114] Different towns developed different traditions, reflecting different local situations. The main distinction that is usually noted is that between the 'closed' or 'exclusive' system of a fixed number of citizen members, and the 'open' or 'inclusive' system in which such limits disappeared, and non-citizens were also admitted. The extreme and perhaps 'archetypal' instance of the closed system is the Colleges of Doctors of Canon and Civil Law in Bologna. These had a fixed number of *numerarii* and eventually a smaller number of *supernumerarii*, with a strict hierarchy of places determined by the date of admission to the college. It was not uncommon for there to be a waiting-list as well, which could be manipulated by the college. This system made it possible for the colleges to develop a hereditary dimension, with all that that implied for the role of the college in urban life. These colleges acquired extensive control over various aspects of the university, including not just the award of degrees (and manipulation of the number awarded) but also the reservation of key lectureships to themselves.[115] But the most significant indicator of the extent of their influence is financial. Following pope Eugenius IV's dedication of funds from the *gabella grassa* to teachers' salaries (1433), the College of Doctors in Civil Law is found administering this process;[116] and not long after this change we note the appearance of a startling innovation,

---

[111] MORELLI, 'I Collegi di Diritto', pp. 252-3; more generally BELLOMO, *Saggio sull'Università*, pp. 239-41.

[112] A process aptly characterised in the title of the seminal article by BRAMBILLA, 'Genealogie del sapere'. For theoretical reflections on this topic see S. VAN DAMME, 'Enseignants et société (XIIIᵉ-XIXᵉ siècle). Problèmes posés par la construction des identités "professionnelles"', *Cahiers d'histoire. Révue d'histoire critique*, 71 (1998), pp. 5-12.

[113] The inclusion of non-teachers is seen by Morelli as initially to make up numbers (op. cit., p. 252).

[114] A key work is BRAMBILLA, 'Genealogie del sapere', now substantially expanded in EADEM, *Genealogie del sapere. Università, professioni giuridiche e nobiltà togata in Italia (XIII-XVII secolo). Con un saggio sull'arte della memoria*. Early Modern: Studi di storia europea protomoderna, 19 (Milan, 2005), which reached me too late for close consideration here. Also of relevance is J. DAVIES, 'Elites and Examiners at Italian Universities during the Late Middle Ages', *Medieval Prosopography*, 21 (2001), pp. 191-209.

[115] MORELLI, 'I Collegi di Diritto', pp. 253-4.

[116] V. COLLI, 'Cattedre minori, letture universitarie e collegio dei dottori di diritto civile a Bologna nel secolo XV', in *Sapere e/è potere. Discipline, dispute e professioni nell'Università medievale e moderna. Il caso bolognese a confronto*, 3 vols. (Bologna, 1990): III. *Dalle discipline ai ruoli sociali*, ed. A. De Benedictis, pp. 135-55 (pp. 144-5); cf. also A. DE BENEDICTIS, *Repubblica per contratto. Bologna: una città europea nello Stato della Chiesa*. Annali dell'Istituto storico italo-germanico, Monografie, 23 (Bologna, 1995), pp. 152-3; EADEM, 'Luoghi del potere e Studio fra Quattrocento e Cinquecento', in *L'Università a Bologna. Personaggi, momenti e luoghi dalle origini al XVI secolo*, ed. O. Capitani (Milan, 1987), pp. 205-27 (esp. 206-7); and A. I. PINI, 'I maestri dello Studio nell'attività amministrativa e politica del Comune bolognese', in *Cultura uni-*

nominal lectureships worth the exact cost of graduation, awarded to favoured individuals. The use of communal funds for the subsidy of degrees for the scions of the patriciate (or at least the 'academic patriciate') was a considerable achievement.[117] Yet notwithstanding the growth of their control over university matters, their privileged social status and involvement in urban politics led to the colleges of doctors of law becoming effectively detached from the *Studio*, a mechanism of access to the 'nobiltà togata' and by the same token an obstacle to social mobility.[118]

The clearest example of the open system is Pavia, which, as a university for the whole of the territorial state of Milan and subject to its control, was ordered to include *forenses*, or at least to subjects of that state, provided they had either been resident in Pavia for a year or were teaching there for the year.[119] But here and elsewhere it is questionable whether the distinction between the two models is that clear-cut, or at least that significant in terms of the realities of status, power and control. The Pavians soon found mechanisms of compensation for this apparent loss of exclusivity. Non-citizens, while eligible to join the college, had a lesser role, most specifically not being paid for participation in the normally lucrative business of awarding degrees,[120] and they were not eligible for membership of the *Collegio dei giudici* of the city, to which most local advisory functions were increasingly reserved.[121] A similar argument could be made for the situation in Padua. Here the initially closed system in the College of Doctors of Law was opened up, first by an increase in the number of members from twelve to twenty-five and then to thirty, and later by total freedom of cooptation, including that of *forenses* who were teaching.[122] This had taken place by 1382, well before the subjection of Padua to Venetian rule. Yet it hardly affected the privileged status of the elite, which found its expression in the *Collegio dei giudici*, entirely reserved to citizens and the heart of the Paduan intellectual aristocracy;[123] and since under the Venetians the university appears to have been treated as a form of compensation for the patriciate for loss of political control,[124] the fact that this power was not focused specifically on the College of Doctors of Law makes little difference to their position.[125]

The argument that the differences between the two systems was not actually so great can be developed further. In many university colleges of doctors[126] the distinction between full members – *numerarii* – and

---

versitaria e pubblici poteri a Bologna dal XII al XV secolo. Atti del 2° convegno, Bologna, 20-21 maggio 1988, ed. O. Capitani (Bologna, 1990), pp. 151-78 (pp. 175-6).

[117] BRAMBILLA, 'Genealogie del sapere', pp. 130-31; COLLI, 'Cattedre minori', pp. 144-5.

[118] BRAMBILLA, 'Genealogie del sapere', pp. 125-6; cf. COLLI, 'Cattedre minori', p. 151, who stresses the increasing divergence between the careers of 'teachers' and college members.

[119] BRAMBILLA, 'Genealogie del sapere', esp. pp. 135-40; ZORZOLI, *Università, dottori, giureconsulti*, pp. 153-5. On the implications of this status in a comparative context see SILVANO, 'Stato, territorio e istituzioni'.

[120] ZORZOLI, *Università, dottori, giureconsulti*, p. 153 n. 39.

[121] BRAMBILLA, 'Genealogie del sapere', p. 138; M. C. ZORZOLI, 'Il Collegio dei giudici di Pavia e l'amministrazione della giustizia (Le basi normative, dallo Statuto visconteo alle Nuove Costituzioni)', *Bollettino della società pavese di storia patria*, 81 (1981), pp. 55-90; and EADEM, 'Alcune considerazioni sui collegi dei giuristi nella Lombardia dall'antico regime', *Annali di storia moderna e contemporanea*, 7 (2001), pp. 449-75.

[122] GALLO, *Università e signoria*, p. 66.

[123] GALLO, op. cit., p. 67.

[124] DE SANDRE, 'Dottori, Università, Comune'.

[125] Two centuries later this anomaly was resolved when the *Collegio dei giudici* was subsumed under College of Doctors of Law; GALLO, *Università e signoria*, p. 68. Venice did insist on Venetians being able to be members of the College of Arts and Medicine (p. 72).

[126] Colleges of doctors were not confined to functioning university towns. Towns which had acquired *studium generale* status for their universities, but which either no longer operated the university or had so-called 'paper' universities, could

additional members – *supernumerarii* – helped to maintain a sense of rank and to keep both real status and, equally importantly, revenue in the hands of the elite. It is also worth pointing out that Bologna, too, developed a college to represent teachers, the *Collegio dei Dottori, Giudici e Avvocati*, a body which emerged in the late thirteenth century out of a desire for a professional organisation that did not include notaries, and which by the fifteenth century included all teachers of law, and was thus able to negotiate and administer finances on behalf of the 'professoriate'. The role of this body went beyond the disciplines and professions it formally represented; the late fourteenth-century statutes of the college makes it clear that it was responsible for the distribution of all *Studio* salaries, with participation for this purpose by representatives from arts and medicine. In this respect the college effectively became an association of *dottori dello Studio*, and its prior was deemed the equal, for ceremonial purposes, to the priors of the colleges of canon and civil lawyers.[127]

This lengthy preamble has been necessary because in the case of Siena, once again, the colleges are wrapped in obscurity and we have to pick up clues where we can. The core of the problem is that, for the main disciplines that concern us, law and arts/medicine, in contrast to the situation in many Italian *studi*, no statutes survive from before the sixteenth century; and – apart from degree certificates – only a handful of documents of these colleges themselves have come to light, mostly in the *Archivio notarile*.[128] It is therefore necessary to attempt to reconstruct the practice of the time from the evidence of communal records; and this brings with it the added complication, as usual, that most of the measures we have are ones that interfere with that practice, modifying or challenging it. The ensuing picture of weakness may not be a full reflection of the actual situation. But it is probably more accurate than the 'reconstruction' of the Sienese colleges largely on the basis of what happened elsewhere, or what happened later.[129]

The oldest and most important of the colleges was that of doctors of law. The creation of the *Studio* introduced the possibility of a new body alongside the *Arte dei Giudici e Notai*, whose statutes go back to the beginning of the fourteenth century.[130] The practice of consulting the doctors of law as a group certainly goes back at least to the period of the Bolognese influx; in 1324 the *Consiglio Generale* received a *consilium* 'a doctoribus iuris canonici et civilis forensibus de studio et iudicibus potestatis et prudentibus advocatis civitatis sen.'.[131] The 1357 bull of foundation implied the need for formal colleges; although the right to grant degrees was vested in the bishop, there was no other way of examining and awarding degrees without losing all semblance of credibility. However, through the decades of the *Studio*'s precarious existence in the late fourteenth century there is very little evidence of how these bodies functioned and what continuity they might have had. This is not an argument against their existence – for example, it has been argued that the Bolognese colleges were the most stable and important of university bodies[132] – just an argument for caution. The only two records of degrees being

---

have such bodies as well (e.g. Treviso, Lucca, Pisa in the first half of the fifteenth century). I have excluded them from the present discussion – despite the considerable body of literature on them – only out of considerations of compatibility.

[127] Trombetti Budriesi, *Gli statuti del collegio dei dottori,* esp. pp. 38-9; Morelli, 'I Collegi di Diritto', p. 256; Brambilla, 'Genealogie del sapere', pp. 132-3.

[128] See above, pp. 21-4.

[129] Archivio di Stato di Siena, *Guida-Inventario*, II, p. 236 is largely a fictional reconstruction of how the colleges were organised, partly based on later, documented, organisation. Many of these points were taken from Zdekauer, pp. 38 and 64 esp., but few can be substantiated. The same is true of Prunai, III, pp. 134-5.

[130] G. Catoni (ed.), *Statuti Senesi dell'Arte dei Giudici e Notai del Secolo XIV*. Fonti e studi del *Corpus membranarum italicarum*, 8 (Rome, 1972), dating these between May 1303 and May 1306 (see pp. 11-13); G. Prunai, 'I notai senesi del XIII e XIV secolo e l'attuale riordinamento del loro archivio', *BSSP*, 60 (1953), pp. 78-109.

[131] Bowsky, *Finance*, p. 96.

[132] L. Paolini, 'La laurea medievale', in *L'Università di Bologna. Personaggi, momenti e luoghi dalle origini al XVI secolo,*

awarded which have come to light for the fourteenth century – a year apart, both recorded by the same notary, both in canon law – show a college of eight in one case and six in another, with a total of eleven canonists involved.[133] But this comes in the wake of a revival, and there are certainly periods in which it is difficult to believe that there were enough qualified people to mount an examination. Both documents list the promotors and the doctors who awarded the degrees; neither refers to a 'college'.

Evidence of a more solid body emerges from early in the fifteenth century, roughly corresponding to the revival of the *Studio* as a whole. Antonio Pace de' Carapelli d'Aquila's degree in civil law (1409) was awarded by an examining body of eleven 'doctoribus utriusque iuris Collegii Senensis',[134] although this figure is not equalled in the three further civil law degrees that have come to light for the following three, much leaner, years.[135] Yet the growing profile of expert lawyers in Siena that accompanied the development of the *Studio* was beginning to pay off in terms of recognition of the college. In 1418 members of the Strozzi family of Florence wrote to the 'Spectabilis et egregiis viris iuris utriusque doctoribus excellentissimo Senarum collegio' on a legal matter,[136] and in 1423 the college was asked to adjudicate in a dispute between Ancona and Venice, which must be an indication of its prestige at the time.[137] The eminence of the individual members of the college may also account for a new role it was given within the town; in 1421 it became the court of appeal against decisions of the *Podestà* in cases worth more than 25 florins, and received a fee of 2% of the value of the case.[138] The experiment was short-lived, however; it was perceived as unfair and prone to abuse, with votes being bought and cases not being given proper consideration, and a year later the function was transferred to the *Maggior Sindaco*.[139]

The clearest indication that the college was taking more permanent and more organised shape is the fact that, at some stage during the early years of continuity, statutes were compiled. This too is a curious and elusive story. As has been said, no statutes survive for our period. However, statutes drawn

---

ed. O. Capitani (Milan, 1987), pp. 133-55 (p. 145), quoted by DAVIES, *Florence and its University*, p. 37 (also in IDEM, 'Elites and Examiners', p. 192) who nicely glosses: 'Students, teachers, and administrators came and went, but the members of the colleges of doctors remained.'

[133] *Not.* 231, f. 9r-v, 25 Apr 1389, ed. MINNUCCI, 'Documenti', doc. I-1, p. 47 (degree of Bartolo da Perugia), and cf. IDEM, 'A Sienese Doctorate'; *Not.* 231, ff. 70v-71r, 11-12 May 1390 (degrees awarded to two Benedictines, 'Nicolaus olim Benedicti de Caltararis' and 'Buccius quondam Nicolay de Collestefano'), ed. MINNUCCI, 'Documenti', doc. I-2, pp. 47-8.

[134] AAS, 4420 (*Notai e cancellieri della curia*: Protocollo dei rogiti di Ser Antonio di Gandino da Calci, 1409-23), ff. 10v-12r, ed. ZDEKAUER, doc. X.2, pp. 153-4. Zdekauer has miscopied the indiction (VIIII) as VIII and thus has 1408 for 1409.

[135] AAS, 4220, ff. 15v-17v, 4-5 Jul 1410 (degree of Francesco di Ser Matteo da San Miniato, with seven examiners); 23r-25r, 18-19 Aug 1410 (degree of Almerico, son of Messer Filippo Corsini of Florence, also with seven examiners); 84r-85r, 24 Feb 1412 (degree of Filippo d'Antonio del Frignano, awarded by only four examiners). These degrees are referred to by ZDEKAUER, p. 155 n. 1, but still lie unpublished.

[136] *Studio* 41, no foliation, 2 Sept; and see ZDEKAUER, p. 64. This is the only document from our period in the *fondo* of the *Collegio dei Giureconsulti*. It should be pointed out that the title *Collegio dei Giureconsulti* is not used in the fifteenth century, but as no other term is consistently used it has been adopted here. The variety of terminology is perhaps further evidence of the flexible approach of the commune to the bodies of the *Studio*.

[137] *Conc.* 1902, nos. 35, 21 Jan (from the cardinal of Siena), and 37, 22 Jan (from the *Anziani* of Ancona). This role continued; cf. a case concerning Bartolomeo di Antonio da Perugia, heard by the Sienese college, concerning which the *priori* of Perugia wrote to the *Concistoro*; *Conc.* 1953, no. 74, 14 Sept 1443.

[138] *CG* 209, f. 98r, 28 Feb.

[139] *CG* 209, ff. 226v-227r (new foliation), and *Maggior Sindaco* 2 *bis*, ff. 31v-32r, 1 Aug 1422, ed. in L. PAGNI and S. VACCARA, 'Un Magistrato scomodo: il Maggior Sindaco nello statuto del 1422', in *Siena e il suo territorio nel Rinascimento*, eds. M. Ascheri and D. Ciampoli (Siena, 1986), pp. 251-336 (pp. 318-9).

Fig. 10 – Seal of the college of doctors of law (Siena, Museo Civico, inv. no. 49).

up soon after the fall of the republic[140] offer a partial if complicated insight into what had been before. First of all, they are a revision of 'fragmenti antiquarum constitutionum a Niccolao siculo Abbate Panormitano in senensi Gimnasio nostro tunc legente, Petro Pecci, Iohanne Bandineo, et Mignanello de Mignanellis collegi nostri Doctoribus compilatis'.[141] This phrase dates the lost original at least to the period 1419 to 1431, the period of Niccolò Tedeschi's presence in Siena,[142] and probably to the beginning of that period, since Giovanni Bandini is not heard of in Siena after 1418.[143] It also places it at the beginning of what we know to have been a period of organisation and codification in the *Studio* generally. Moreover, in drafting the revised statutes the compilers helpfully indicate in most cases under the rubric whether the statute is old or new. Unfortunately this cannot be taken at face value to mean that all those labelled 'Const. vetus' are verbatim transcriptions of the early fifteenth century statutes. Some of the terminology is clearly from a later date; the amounts to be paid to the college for the doctoral examination or for admission to the college are prescribed in 'scutos',[144] the doctors are to

---

[140] 'Constitutiones Sanensis Collegii Iureconsultorum' in *Studio* 40, ff. 7r-31v. The measures were passed on 31 Jan 1566 (f. 8r). This is a later copy.

[141] *Studio* 40, f. 7r.

[142] Above, p. 59.

[143] F. Zazzera, *Della Nobiltà dell'Italia*, 2 vols. (Naples, 1615-28), II, n.p., under 'Tommasi', gives his death as 1420; cf. Minnucci, 'Documenti', p. 276. On this figure see above, p. 52 n. 150, and below, p. 252 n. 17.

[144] Const. 10, ff. 18v-22r.

take an oath of allegiance to the 'Princeps',[145] and the rubric forbidding procurators from representing the college has a preamble of what for the 1420s would have been an unusually Platonic flavour (as well as referring to 'Gymnasii Bibliothecam').[146] However it would not be unreasonable to assume that these were updates to the earlier compilation, which would at least tell us that statutes existed which covered matters including the number of numerary and supernumerary members,[147] what constituted a quorum,[148] the order of seniority,[149] payment for degrees and admission,[150] the oath of loyalty,[151] what members should wear,[152] that they were not to be represented by a procurator,[153] that the college had a seal,[154] and arrangements regarding the 'scriba colegii'.[155]

Such is our limited knowledge of this institution that it is difficult even to estimate its size. The clause in the 1566 statutes concerning this is one of the 'old' ones, and stipulates that there should be twelve *numerari*, but in the late 1420s and 1430s the number appears to have been thirteen.[156] The clause also gives the maximum number of *supernumerari* as nineteen, but we have no way of checking

---

[145] Const. 12, ff. 22v-23r.

[146] Const. 15, ff. 24r-26r. The first instances I have found in Sienese administrative documents of the fashionable humanistic use of 'gymnasium' to denote the *Studio* are late fifteenth century: *Studio* 2, f. 2r, 12 May 1473, ed. BAI, Appendix, doc. 19, pp. 376-7; cf. *Conc.* 699, f. 8v, 17 Mar 1483, ed. FERRERI, doc. 164, pp. 139-40; *CG* 239, f. 239r, 1 Dec 1484; *Conc.* 721, f. 11r, 14 Dec 1486, ed. FERRERI, doc. 239, p. 204. This of course does not prove anything, since the term had been used in this sense in Florence since the 1420s; J. HANKINS, 'The Myth of the Platonic Academy of Florence', *Renaissance Quarterly*, 44 (1991), pp. 429-75 (p. 434 and n. 15), though there too it became much more common later in the century. The issue of a possible library of the Sapienza (the only candidate for this description) is discussed below, pp. 386-8.

[147] Const. 10, esp. ff. 20v-21r.

[148] Const. 2, f. 9v.

[149] Const. 4, ff. 11v-12r.

[150] Consts. 8, f. 18r-v, and 10, ff. 18v-22r.

[151] Const. 12, ff. 22v-23r.

[152] Const. 14, ff. 23v-24r.

[153] Const. 15, ff. 24r-26r.

[154] Const. 22, f. 30r. The matrix of the college's seal does survive (Fig. 10); art historians have dated it to the early fifteenth century. G. BASCAPÉ, 'Sigilli Universitari Italiani', in *Studi Storici in Memoria di Mons. Angelo Mercati*, Fontes Ambrosiani XXX (Milan, 1956), pp. 43-72; repr. in IDEM, *Sigillografia: il sigillo nella diplomatica, nel diritto, nella storia, nell'arte*, 3 vols. (Milan, 1969-94), I, pp. 303-42 (Tav. VIII, 1, and see p. 314; also op. cit., p. 148); see also E. CIONI, *Il Sigillo a Siena nel Medioevo. Catalogo della mostra di Siena 25 febbraio – 19 marzo 1989* (Siena, 1989), no. 30; and L. BORGIA and F. FUMI CAMBI GADO, 'I sistemi emblematici e le Università europee con particolare riferimento all'Ateneo senese', in *L'Università di Siena. 750 anni*, pp. 559-73 (pp. 564-5). The seal depicts St. Nicholas, whose association with the innocent may have given him a legal connection, and who, jointly with St. Catherine of Alexandria, was honoured by the *universitas scholarium* in 1440 (below, p. 276; and see LEONCINI, 'I simboli dell'Università di Siena', p. 238). Whether these indications are sufficient to allow the conclusion that St. Nicholas was the patron of the college of doctors is perhaps another matter. In the 1511 statutes of the college of doctors of medicine, he is referred to as 'patroni et advocati doctorum omnium et scolarium' (*Balìa* 253, ff. 335v-345v, 13 Oct, *proemium*, f. 336v, and cf. Rubric 13, f. 341r-v).

[155] Const. 23, f. 30r-v.

[156] Below, p. 202. In any case, the number was comparable with that of colleges of doctors of law in other *studi*. In this period Florence had a quota of fourteen numerary members but accepted an unspecified number of supernumeraries (DAVIES, *Florence and its University*, p. 39). Perugia, also with a maximum of fourteen, closed the doors to foreigners in 1429 (ERMINI, *Storia*, I, p. 291-2). Ferrara fixed the maximum at fourteen numeraries and eight supernumeraries; V. CAPUTO, 'Gli statuti del collegio ferrarese dei dottori utriusque iuris (sec. XV)', *Annali dell'Università di Ferrara. Sezione di scienze giuridiche*, 2 (1952-3), pp. 1-99 (p. 34). Bologna, with separate colleges of canon and civil law (twelve numerary and three supernumerary for the canonists, sixteen and three respectively for the civilians; BELLOMO, *Saggio sull'Università*, p. 254 nn. 46 and 47), and with the particular situation described above, is a less useful comparator; the same is true of Padua, which had moved to an open policy by the late fourteenth century (loc. cit.).

whether this was the case in the original statute. Those of the records of degree awards which actually list the members of the college who took part in the examination can give only a rough indication; it cannot be assumed that all members of the college were always present (indeed, discrepancies in certificates issued within a short time of each other confirm that they were not), but it was equally possible that some names were registered *in absentia*.[157] Eighteen members of the college (two *promotores*, thirteen other Sienese and three *forenses*) awarded Giovanni da Prato his degree in canon law in 1428,[158] twenty-nine participated in the examination of the civilian Gianfrancesco Carboni da Santa Vittoria in 1489 (again with two promotors; the college was entirely Sienese).[159] These figures may be part of a trend, but they are hardly sufficient to permit any confident assertions.

Given the total absence of degree certificates between 1429 and 1484, as well as statutes that are unequivocally from the period, in order to learn anything significant about the college's inner workings we are forced, once again, back onto communal measures. These include frequent decisions that an individual law teacher was to be given a place in the college. Between 1427 and 1439 there are seven such orders relating to a total of ten people. All but one of these was for a foreigner who was teaching in Siena at the time.[160] The remaining order placed four Sienese, doctors but as far as we know not teachers, in the college as supernumeraries, unusually leaving it to the college and the *Savi* to decide jointly on their precise status.[161] Several points become clear from these instructions. The first is that the system of numerary and supernumerary members was in operation here as elsewhere. In 1427 Benedetto Barzi was made the fourteenth member; in 1435 Antonio da Pratovecchio was put in the college 'cum hoc quod sit supernumerarius ultra xiii doctores qui ad presens sunt in collegio'.[162] Secondly, the membership of these *forenses* was considered to be qualitatively different from that of the citizen members. The granting of a college place was either recognition of eminence[163] or a special condition of a *condotta*;[164] in one case it appears part of the compromise outcome of difficult negotia-

---

[157] Cf. LOCKWOOD, *Ugo Benzi*, p. 173, and below, pp. 220-1.

[158] See n. 160.

[159] *Not.* 858, f. 23r-v, ed. MINNUCCI, 'Documenti', doc. I-7, pp. 57-9; and see below, n. 169.

[160] *Conc.* 369, f. 18v, 2 Oct 1427, ed. PIANIGIANI, doc. 82, pp. 103-5, and cf. *Conc.* 2175, no foliation (Benedetto Barzi); *Conc.* 407, f. 23r, 14 Dec 1433 (Lodovico Pontano); *Conc.* 411, f. 54v, 18 Aug 1434 (Antonio da Pratovecchio); *Conc.* 412, f. 43r, 5 Oct 1434, ed. PIANIGIANI, doc. 160, p. 186 (Matteo Feliziano); *Conc.* 425, f. 25v, 16 Dec 1436 (Angelo de' Narducci da Perugia); *Conc.* 441, f. 30r, 30 Jul 1439, ed. PIANIGIANI, doc. 198, pp. 227-8 (the civilian Filippo da Lucca). It is clear from degrees awarded that these were not the only instances of foreign teachers obtaining places in the college, merely the ones in which the *Concistoro* ordered it. The examiners for the canon law degree awarded to Giovanni da Prato in 1428 includes not just Benedetto Barzi, who had been placed in the college four months earlier by the *Concistoro*, but also Sallustio Buonguglielmi of Perugia and Roberto Cavalcanti of Florence. ZDEKAUER, *Documenti*, part II, doc. 1, pp. 15-16, 7 Feb 1427 (which I take to mean 1428, as Zdekauer's usual practice was to record the *stile senese*; also because of the presence of Barzi who was placed in the college on 2 Oct 1427. The volume in from which Zdekauer published the document has not come to light; see above, p. 22).

[161] *Conc.* 418, f. 12v, 23 Sept 1435; Conte di Costantino, Baldassare Vettori, Jacopo Tolomei and Paolo di Antonio may enter the 'collegium ad examinandum doctorum fiendos in studio Sen.' as supernumeraries; the college, together with the *Savi*, are to decide what their precise status is to be.

[162] See n. 160. The 1566 compilation has twelve as the number of *numerarii* in the 'Const. vetus'; if this had not been altered since the original statutes this suggests an increase of one.

[163] The cases of Benedetto Barzi, Lodovico da Roma, Antonio da Pratovecchio; above, n. 160.

[164] Matteo Feliziano, above, n. 160. In this respect Siena appears to develop along lines similar to those of Pavia, where *forenses* could be coopted provided they had either been resident for a year or were teaching for a year. ZORZOLI, *Università, dottori, giureconsulti*, p. 153 n. 39, quoting the statutes of 1395.

tions over a contract.[165] But the understanding (sometimes made explicit) was that membership lasted only as long as the teaching contract[166] (whereas Sienese doctors, if practice elsewhere is anything to go by, would have been members for life),[167] and it is also made clear that the assumption of foreigners was not to prejudice the position of citizen members.[168] They could not become numeraries; the order for Antonio da Pratovecchio is followed by a general condition that if any doctor of the college is absent, *forenses* cannot take their place as this would prejudice the number of citizen doctors in the college.[169] Finally, by the late fifteenth century it appears to be the practice that citizens with a doctorate had a right to membership.[170]

Our knowledge of the college of lawyers virtually ends there. We know next to nothing about the fees chargeable at degrees in the fifteenth century. The 1566 statutes suggest that supernumerary members could receive examination fees, and indeed there would have been little point in putting *forenses* in otherwise. We also know that in the late fifteenth century the college could be called upon to advise the commune on political matters.[171] The *Collegio dei Medici* is similarly elusive for the fifteenth century. As with the College of Doctors of Law, it arose at a time when there was already an older body, the *Arte dei Medici e Speziali*,[172] though we know nothing about the subsequent relationship between the two in the fifteenth century. The social status of medical doctors and grammarians was clearly inferior to that of legists, and this appears to be reflected in the position of their organisation as well, at least from the little we can tell. Although it was just as active in awarding degrees, it appears to have been less developed than the college of doctors of law.[173] It also appears that the au-

---

[165] Filippo da Lucca in 1439 (above, n. 160). He had previously rejected a salary of 350 florins; the *Concistoro* had invited Antonio Roselli in his place, at a salary of 450 florins; this had then been revoked, and Filippo settled for the lower sum of 300 florins (see above, pp. 188-9). The place in the college granted five days later has to be seen in this context.

[166] Matteo Feliziano, above, n. 160: 'intelligatur esse durante eius conducta de collegio doctorum Senensium'. A similar condition must have applied to the granting of places in the college of doctors of arts and medicine; Pietro Giovanetti received this honour twice, in 1423 and 1437 (below, n. p. 204 and n. 175).

[167] For example see the number of degrees at which Bartolomeo Sozzini took part, long after he had ceased to be a teacher at the *Studio*; below, p. 223 n. 103.

[168] The allocation of a place to Filippo da Lucca (above, n. 160) is made 'non privando civibus'.

[169] See above, n. 160. It is not clear when a limit was placed on the number of supernumeraries. The 1566 statutes suggest it was nineteen, but it also gives a total ceiling of forty for the college. This is less than clear, even laying aside the uncertainties of the date of the measure (*Studio* 40, f. 20v). As far as concerns the question of the relationship of citizens to *forenses*, though, the matter soon became academic; at the civil law degree of Gianfrancesco Carboni da Santa Vittoria in 1489, twenty-nine members of the college were present, all but one Sienese (and that one, Antonio Berti, had been teaching in Siena since the 1470s). See n. 159 above, and MINNUCCI, 'Documenti', pp. 222-3.

[170] In 1387 Bernardino da Lucignano Val di Chiana claimed the right to be a member of the college now that he had taken his degree; Lucignano citizens had the right to be treated as Sienese citizens. The college had resisted; the measure is unfinished so we do not know what the *Concistoro* resolved (*Conc.* 727, f. 22v, 4 Dec).

[171] Cf. the *Concistoro*'s letter to the cardinal of Siena in 1480 on the league that had been concluded: 'parere havendo inteso dal collegio de li doctori nostri come essa liga dal principio fu perfecta' (*Conc.* 1694, f. 74v, 10 Jun).

[172] In 1389 there was a *consiglio* of *medici* in Siena, with its own rector; *Not.* 231, f. 10r, 28 Apr, ed. MINNUCCI, 'Documenti', doc. III-19, p. 131.

[173] The first extant record of a degree dates from 19 Jun 1409; AAS, *ms.* 4420 (see above, p. 199 n. 134), f. 7, ed. ZDEKAUER, doc. X.1, pp. 151-3 (Angelo di Francesco Bruogi da San Gimignano, in philosophy and arts). Seven members of the college of arts and medicine examined the candidate. This was clearly the statutory minimum, since two years earlier it had been reduced from seven to four 'considerata paucitate doctorum medicine' (*Conc.* 247, f. 18r, 8 Apr 1407, ed. PIANIGIANI, doc. 16, pp. 41-2). The next records of the award of degrees to survive, to Johannes Dodonis of Rotterdam and Nicolaus Ffabri of Žagan in Poland (*Not.* 292, ff. 63r-64v, 22-23 Dec 1412, ed. MINNUCCI, 'Documenti', doc. I-3, pp. 48-51) and Ippolito di Ser Niccolò da San Gimignano (*Not.* 292, ff. 195r-196v, 2-2 Apr 1414, ed. MINNUCCI, 'Documenti', doc. I-4, pp. 51-54) do not give the names or numbers of members of the college, which itself is unusual.

thorities were more willing to intervene in the college's affairs, even when this interference was resisted. Ten cases have come to light for the fifteenth century of the *Concistoro* (or more rarely the *Consiglio del Popolo* or the *Balìa*) ordering that an individual be placed in the college.[174] Again, these offer interesting clues. The first striking point is the inconsistency of terminology. A 1423 instruction placed Pietro Giovanetti in the college of arts and medicine, the term also used when he was given a place once more in 1437.[175] But in 1425 Domenico da Ragusa was placed 'in collegio medicine civitatis sen.'.[176] This might be thought to be just an abbreviative term,[177] but in the same year Timoteo da Pistoia was placed in the college of arts.[178] In 1466 it was decreed that Lodovico da Spoleto was to be a member 'sia del Collegio dell'arti et del Collegio di medicina'.[179] This fluidity is unlikely to be explicable just by poor drafting; such vagueness would only be possible in a situation where the body or bodies concerned were anything other than regular and high-profile.[180]

The second feature relates to the type of member. All but one of the 'intromissions' of the first half of the century are of foreigners.[181] In contrast to the college of doctors of law, those granted a place in the college of medicine/arts appear to be granted full rights; Giovanetti 'sit de numero', Timoteo da Pistoia was to be a full member, with the same status and rights as examiner.[182] There is also the suggestion that a place in the college was automatic for teachers; in 1425 Domenico da Ragusa was hired and therefore put in the college.[183] The evidence is far from overwhelming, but if this was the case that would have placed some strain on the concept of the college as bastion of citizen privileges, at least in the third and fourth decades of the fifteenth century when there were so many foreign teachers in Siena. The order for Timoteo da Pistoia in 1424, which states that he was to be a full member of the

---

[174] *Conc.* 343, f. 17v, 29 Mar 1423 (Pietro Giovanetti); *Conc.* 357, f. 4v, 3 Jul 1425 (Domenico da Ragusa); *Conc.* 358, f. 24r, 3 Oct 1425, ed. PIANIGIANI, doc. 72, pp. 92-4 (Timoteo da Pistoia, artium doctor); *Conc.* 427, f. 20r, 22 Mar 1437 (Pietro Giovanetti again); *Conc.* 452, f. 37r, 26 Jun 1441 (Andrea di Bartolomeo); *Conc.* 503, f. 31r, 20 Dec 1449, ed. PIANIGIANI, doc. 296, pp. 328-9 (Lodovico da Spoleto); *Conc.* 646, f. 27r, 5 Jun 1474 (Gregorio d'Alessandria); *CG* 237, f. 271r-v, and *Conc.* 2160, no. 39, 26 Feb 1478 (M. Felice di Giovanni de' Tagoni of Castello della Pieve); *Balìa* 24, f. 76r, 28 Jun 1481 (M.º Latino di Niccolò de' Ranuccini).

[175] *Conc.* 343, f. 17v, 29 Mar 1423; *Conc.* 427, f. 20r, 22 Mar 1437.

[176] *Conc.* 357, f. 4v, 3 Jul; GAROSI, p. 285 n. 3.

[177] Cf. n. 181 below.

[178] *Conc.* 358, f. 24r, 3 Oct, ed. PIANIGIANI, doc. 72, pp. 92-4; the fuller text, in *Conc.* 2113, f. 160r, declares that he is to be 'de collegio et inter doctores collegii artium'.

[179] *CG* 231, f. 82r-v, 31 Jan; for fuller details see above, p. 168 n. 185, and below, n. 187. We know that the two disciplines were represented by a single college at the time because that body's eventual approval of his membership is one of the few documents of the college itself we have; below, n. 187. Finally in 1474 Gregorio d'Alessandria was put in 'collegio doctorum et professorum artium ed medicine' (*Conc.* 646, f. 27r, 5 Jun 1474), a description which, though not to my knowledge reflected in any document of the college itself, has some validity; 'professor' was a title given to an advanced scholar who did not have a degree, and this was the period in which rhetoric was not infrequently taught by such people. Above, pp. 135-7.

[180] On the other hand it has to be said that the 1511 statutes of the college refer interchangeably to both 'artium et medicine collegio' and 'medicorum collegio' (e.g. *Balìa* 253, ff. 341v and 342r, 13 Oct).

[181] The exception is the Sienese Andrea di M.º Bartolomeo. He had violated the town's protectionist legislation by obtaining his degree from Florence (*Conc.* 452, f. 5r, 4 May 1441). It was decided (by the *Concistoro* and the college of doctors of medicine) that he may not enter the college for two years. This was confirmed by the *Concistoro* on 26 June (*Conc.* 452, f. 37r); but the *Concistoro* also decided at that point that at the end of the two years Andrea was to be admitted to the college even if it was full (*Conc.* 453, f. 53r, 28 Aug).

[182] *Conc.* 358, f. 24r, 3 Oct 1425, ed. PIANIGIANI, doc. 72, pp. 92-4 (he is 'artium doctor'); the fuller text, in *Conc.* 2113, f. 160r, declares that he is to be a full member of the college of arts (*sic*), with the same status and rights as examiner, and with no objections from the members being entertained.

[183] As n. 176 above.

college, with the same status and rights as examiner, adds that no objections from the college to his membership would be entertained.[184] In the second half of the century all the subjects of such communal orders were originally non-Sienese doctors who had become citizens.[185] This suggests a change in practice, and indeed raises the possibility that in the intervening period the college had closed its doors to foreigners, and/or that membership for citizens had become a matter of right.[186] Perhaps most significantly, there is now clear evidence of resistance to these orders by the college, resistance which also appears to grow with time. The order placing Lodovico da Spoleto, now a citizen, in the college for the second time (1466) was approved but then delayed because of fears that the college of doctors of medicine might refuse (they agreed, but only five months later).[187] In 1474 Gregorio d'Alessandria, having been granted citizenship, was given a place; the college's recalcitrance lasted three months and culminated in an order that the eight members appear before the *Concistoro*.[188] The longest-running dispute was over Giovanni di Michele Contugio da Volterra; the *Consiglio del Popolo* granted him citizenship and a place in the college in 1480. The college refused, and on Contugio's appeal in 1490 the *Concistoro* referred the matter to the *Savi* and the *Giudice degli Appellagioni*, Antonio Giordano da Venafro.[189]

Beyond this there is really very little evidence of the activity of the college in the fifteenth century. No references to statutes have come to light in this period. We hear of the college requesting and obtaining the body of a condemned man for dissection in 1446.[190] In 1464 and 1466 meetings are recorded; in 1464 the college of doctors of arts and medicine met under their prior, Bernardi di Pietro Lapini, to ap-

---

[184] Above, n. 178.

[185] See nn. 187-9 below.

[186] In 1478 Maestro Felice di Giovanni de' Tagoni of Castello della Pieve, having lived in Siena for many years and obtained his degree there, successfully petitioned the *Consiglio del Popolo* for citizenship, and was made a member of the college of arts and medicine 'come li altri doctori di dette facultà' (*CG* 237, f. 271r-v, and *Conc.* 2160, no. 39, 26 Feb 1478). The widening of college membership to include all those with degrees, or elsewhere the appearance of colleges with a wider remit than examining (e.g. Bologna; see above, p. 196) perhaps account for the expression used by the early sixteenth century to denote a person with a 'proper' degree; 'dottore di collegio e non di privilegio' (*CG* 241, ff. 333r, 333v, 335r, 13 Nov 1524). On the other hand the concept of a limited number must have persisted at least for a while, if the opinion of the anonymous late fourteenth-century treatise on doctoral privileges published by I. BAUMGÄRTNER, '*De privilegiis doctorum. Über Gelehrtenstand und Doktorwürde im späten Mittelalter*', *Historisches Jahrbuch*, 106 (1986), pp. 298-332 is anything to go by. Quoting Baldus, the writer says 'consului in civitate Senarum, cum essent duo doctores novelli et unus volebat prius recepi quam alter inter collegium medicorum. Ego consului, quod praeferatur ille, qui est filius doctoris per praemissa, et ita fuit obtentum.' (p. 326; *Vat. lat.* 5607 version).

[187] In a petition of 31 Jan (*CG* 231, f. 82r-v) Lodovico da Spoleto asks to be put in the college, in old age; he was a citizen, had taught for twenty-five years, married fourteen years ago and had no intention of leaving again; as citizen, he requested a place in both colleges of arts and medicine (he had already been placed in the college in 1449, presumably as an accompaniment to his teaching; *Conc.* 503, f. 31r, 20 Dec, ed. PIANIGIANI, doc. 296, pp. 328-9). The petition was approved (forwarded initially by the *Concistoro*; *Conc.* 596, f. 18r, 23 Jan), but put on hold the following day (f. 18v). The College of Arts and Medicine approved his membership on 30 May (*Not.* 589, ff. 108v-109v).

[188] *Conc.* 646, f. 27r, 5 Jun, repeated ff. 30v-31r, 9 Jun; citizenship had been granted on 18 May (*CG* 235, ff. 218v-219r). The college failed to implement this decision, and were ordered to do so again on 5 October (*Conc.* 648, f. 20r-v), and when they continued to disregard the instruction the eight members were ordered to appear in person before the *Concistoro* to be told again (f. 23r-v). On Gregorio see MINNUCCI, 'Documenti', pp. 261-2.

[189] *Conc.* 740, f. 4v, 12 Jan (and *Conc.* 741, f. 5r, 16 Mar for his full name; on identification see MINNUCCI, 'Documenti', p. 277). Not all such intromissions are recorded as being opposed. In 1481 Latino di Niccolò de' Ranuccini was granted citizenship and a place in the college of arts and medicine, as well as being placed in the *monte degli aggregati* – by the *Balìa* (*Balìa* 24, f. 76r, 28 Jun). Whether the college's compliance – which can only be assumed – has anything to do with the fact that the order came from the more authoritative *Balìa* can only be a matter for speculation.

[190] *Conc.* 480, f. 5v, 5 Jun; see above, p. 133. But it is perhaps interesting that in 1427 this was granted to the student-university; *Conc.* 371, f. 9v, 9 Jan 1427.

prove the application of Girolamo di Andrea del Marretta to be examined for the doctorate in arts,[191] and in 1466 to discuss the proposed membership of Lodovico da Spoleto.[192] Both meetings were held in the church of S. Desiderio, which in the 1466 document is described as 'eorum consueta residentia'. The main piece of information about the college in the republican period comes from the early sixteenth century, in the form of a set of statutes approved by the *Balìa* in 1511.[193] This was discovered recently by Antonia Whitley who summarised its contents in her Ph.D. dissertation.[194] The statutes were drawn up by five doctors of medicine,[195] approved by the college and now authorised by the regime.[196] They are a comprehensive statement of how the college was to operate, with detailed regulations concerning the election or appointment of the prior[197] and other officials of the college,[198] the conduct and cost of examinations[199] and of anatomy sessions,[200] and the approval and licensing of medical practitioners.[201] Two features stand out for our purposes. First, the statutes confirm that by this time only Sienese could be full members of the college.[202] Secondly, the rubrics governing medical practice in Siena strongly suggest that with this measure the college took over some of the functions previously carried out by the *Arte dei Medici e Speziali*; not only was it to examine all those wishing to practice medicine within Sienese territory, but it was also to license apothecaries and prescribe their activities.[203]

The exception to this sorry tale of ignorance is theology. Modelled as it was on the northern system, the statutes of this college, drawn up in 1434, contain extremely detailed regulations about syllabus, teaching, organisation, procedure and discipline, and are really an equivalent of faculty statutes.[204] But as has been seen, this body could be described as 'semi-detached' from the *Studio*, and has little relationship with the authorities.

---

[191] *Not.* 589, ff. 67r-68r, 7 Jun. On him see MINNUCCI, 'Documenti', p. 269.

[192] *Not.* 589, ff. 108v-109r, 30 May, and 109v, n.d.

[193] *Balìa* 253, ff. 335v-345v, 13 Oct; the *proemium*, ff. 336r-v, is inserted. The measure approving the statutes is on ff. 335v and 337r; the statutes themselves begin on f. 337r.

[194] WHITLEY, 'Concepts of Ill Health and Pestilence', Appendix VI.2, pp. 388-90. The comments that follow are based on a study of the text, but I have not been able to investigate the full context of the decision to promulgate these statutes, as the systematic archival trawl on which this research is based ended at 1500.

[195] They were: Alexander Tancii de Tanciis, Hieronimus Johannis Vici de Bindis, Carolus Augustini de Pinis, Marianus Crescentii Petri de Goris and Antonius Cristophori Petri Dni. Johannis Cristophori (f. 336r).

[196] Loc. cit., ff. 335v-337r.

[197] Rubric 1, f. 337r. The prior was chosen by lot from among those who had been members of the college for at least six years. He was to hold office for four months.

[198] Rubric 2, f. 337r-v on the *consiliarii*; Rubric 3, f. 337v on the *camerarius*; Rubric 6, f. 338r-v on the notary; Rubric 7, f. 338v on the *bidello* (on whom see above, pp. 81 *seq.*). In addition, Rubric 8 (ff. 338v-339r) laid down the procedure for meetings, Rubrics 3 (f. 337v) and 24 (f. 345r) laid down the standards of documentation to be maintained, and the latter rubric also provided for a gold or silver seal. (The extant seal of the college postdates the republic; LEONCINI, 'I simboli dell'Università di Siena', pp. 250-1.)

[199] Rubric 4, f. 337v on the method of choosing a prior for examinations; Rubrics 10-14, ff. 339r-341v.

[200] Rubric 20, ff. 343v-344r (and see above, p. 133).

[201] Rubrics 16-18, ff. 342r-343r.

[202] Rubric 15, ff. 341v-342r. In addition, five-sixths of the college had to agree to a candidate's admission.

[203] Rubric 19, f. 343r-v. The college of doctors of medicine at arts at Padua had similar control over the licensing of surgeons; e.g. G. ZONTA and A. BROTTO, *Acta graduum academicorum gymnasii patavini ab anno 1406 ad annum 1450*, 3 vols (Padua, 2nd ed. 1970), II, no. 1563, p. 130 (5 Jan 1442).

[204] They are published and analysed by BERTONI, 'Il "Collegio" dei teologi'; see above, pp. 125-6. Collective activity by theologians is not unheard of before this date; the proceedings against Baroccino Barocci for heresy in 1321 involved disputations with 'quasi tutti i dottori e di sacra teologia' as well as 'd'altre facultà', though there is no suggestion of a formal or-

The relationship between the communal authorities and the colleges of doctors was complex, and not just characterised by these usually successful attempts to control them. Certainly there are many decisions of the commune which would have pleased or at least financially favoured members, such as the frequent permission for students to have more than the normal number of *promotores*,[205] or the permission granted to members of the colleges to receive their share of student fees for degrees *in absentia*.[206] It is also interesting that in the one instance that has come to light of permission being granted for a student to have a *promotor* who is not a member of the college, it was clearly stated that it is granted only because the college has agreed to it.[207] Nonetheless communal interference with the most basic privilege of a college, that of determining its own membership, struck typically at the root of the doctors' power.[208] The decision of the *Balìa* in 1488 that the rector of the Sapienza should receive a free degree also struck at their rights, though in a more conventional way.[209] The authorities would also intervene in cases of disputes within a college, such as that in 1492 in the college of arts and medicine over who was the legitimate prior.[210] There is even a case of the commune enforcing attendance by members of a college, deciding in 1445 that failure to attend after a summons had been issued by the prior carried a penalty of 25 *lire*.[211] It may also be an indication of the paucity of the college's corporate power or functions that there are few signs of the officials which guilds or colleges might normally possess, *notai* or *bidelli* mentioned in degree certificates or other formal documents pertaining to the college being invariably those of the *curia* or of the *Studio*.[212]

---

ganisation (AGNOLO DI TURA DEL GRASSO, *Cronaca Senese*, pp. 389-90). It is not entirely clear to me that the mid-fifteenth-century *consilium* produced by 'sacre almeque Universitatis Senensis' relating to the controversy between Franciscan Conventuals and Spirituals is in fact from the college of doctors of theology (referred to interchangeably as *collegium* and *universitas*; see above, p. 125 n. 27) as opposed to the *studium generale* of the Franciscans in Siena; C. PIANA, 'Scritti polemici fra Conventuali e Osservanti a metà del '400 con la partecipazione di giuristi secolari', *Archivum Franciscanum Historicum*, 72 (1979), pp. 37-105 (p. 92 n. 2, and cf. pp. 77-9).

[205] Below, p. 289.

[206] E.g. permission in 1448 to Giorgio Andreucci, chancellor of the republic, to receive the regular emoluments from the granting of degrees despite his absence on communal business (*Conc.* 492, f. 25r, 29 Jan); and cf. *Conc.* 598, f. 2v, 1 May 1466 (a similar privilege to Niccolò Severini, Bartolomeo Salimbene and Borghese Borghesi, at least two of whom appear to have been away on official business; 4r, 2 May, 18v, 22 May); *Conc.* 658, f. 26v, 8 Jun 1476 (Lodovico Petroni and Niccolò Severini); *Balìa* 17, f. 33v, 3 Dec 1479 (Niccolò di Nanni Severini again, this time because he was *podestà* of Montalcino); *Balìa* 18, f. 20r, 24 Jan 1480 (Lodovico da Spoleto); *Balìa* 38, f. 109v, 26 Apr 1493 (Arcangelo di Domenico, at Bagno Vignoni in the service of the wife of the ruler of Piombino – presumably an error for Arcangelo di Giovanni di Domenico).

[207] *Conc.* 455, f. 47v, 19 Dec 1441. The candidate was 'D. Guglielmo ciscar de Valentia', so this must have been the college of doctors of law. He was permitted to have Giorgio Bardassini as *promotor* – not a name that has come up in any other *Studio* context.

[208] There seem ultimately to have been as many methods of admission to colleges in Italy as there were *studi* – from those in which election (of suitably qualified doctors) was exclusively the privilege of the college, like Perugia (ERMINI, *Storia*, I, p. 291) to those, like Parma, in which certain doctors had a right to a supernumerary place; U. GUALAZZINI, *Corpus Statutorum Almi Studii Parmensis* (Milan, 1978 ed.), p. CCVI. The whole subject would repay full comparative study, in which Siena would be condemned, through lack of evidence, to pay a minor part.

[209] *Balìa* 26, f. 66v, Dec (Achille di Ser Michele, student of arts and medicine). Below, p. 351. The 1511 statutes of the doctors of medicine are revealing in this respect. Rubric 13 (*Balìa* 253, f. 341r-v) admits the practice of granting a degree to a poor student once a year, on the feast of St. Nicholas ('Ut caritas omnium suprema virtutum in nostro Medicorum Collegio vigeat'), but all that is involved is lower rates for the many fees that a doctorand had to pay.

[210] *Conc.* 752, ff. 25v-26r, 28 Feb. The candidates are Magr. Lucas and Magr. Boninsigna de Boninsignis.

[211] *Conc.* 475, f. 8r, 12 Mar. Strangely the college is not specified.

[212] Contrast Perugia (ERMINI, *Storia*, I, p. 288).

III

TEACHERS AND THE COMMUNITY

1. *Teachers in public life*

When they were teaching, lawyers and doctors of medicine were exercising only one of their possible roles within the community. The shift from a foreign to a local predominance within the teaching force is reflected closely in the other functions they had – as professional advisers, purveyors of expertise, and men of natural influence. One only has to contrast the frequency with which the commune consulted non-Sienese lawyers in the thirteenth and fourteenth centuries with the fifteenth-century habit of increasingly using Sienese doctors as ambassadors, of sending cases and appeals to panels of lawyers or to the predominantly Sienese college of doctors of law, and of involving individual lawyers in communal administration. Here too, legislation and contracts can help to trace the development.[1]

The incidental, non-teaching, functions of university teachers, though supposedly limited by statute, grew parallel to the growth of an indigenous group of qualified men, stimulated this growth and were at all times closely linked to it. Daniel Waley has demonstrated how influential lawyers were in Sienese public affairs in the thirteenth century.[2] In the period of the *Nove* the formal advice of the foreign teachers and the judges and advocates of the town might be sought, as in 1324 over

---

[1] For what follows, there are helpful comparative points from Bologna in PINI, 'I maestri dello Studio'.

[2] WALEY, *Siena and the Sienese*, pp. 86-9. On the history of lawyers in town affairs generally, E. CORTESE, 'Legisti, canonisti e feudisti: la formazione di un ceto medievale', in *Università e società*, pp. 195-281; A. PADOA SCHIOPPA, 'Sul ruolo dei giuristi nell'età del diritto comune: un problema aperto', in *Il diritto comune e la tradizione giuridica europea. Atto del convegno di studi in onore di Giuseppe Ermini, Perugia, 30-31 ottobre 1976*, ed. D. Segolini. Università degli Studi di Perugia, Annali della Facoltà di Giurisprudenza, n.s., 6/1 (Perugia, 1980), pp. 155-66; and see esp. a number of studies of Bologna; PINI, 'I maestri dello Studio'; H. G. WALTHER, 'Die Anfänge des Rechtsstudiums und die kommunale Welt Italiens im Hochmittelalter', in *Schulen und Studium im sozialen Wandel des hohen und späten Mittelalters*, ed. J. Fried. Vorträge und Forschungen / Konstanzer Arbeitskreis für mittelalterliche Geschichte, 30 (Sigmaringen, 1986), pp. 121-62; IDEM, 'Learned Jurists and their Profit for Society – Some Aspects of the Development of Legal Studies at Italian and German Universities in the Late Middle Ages', in *Universities and Schooling in Medieval Society*, eds. W. J. Courtenay and J. Miethke (Leiden, 2000), pp. 100-26 (esp. 100-12); M. VALLERANI, 'The Generation of the "Moderni" at Work: Jurists between School and Politics in Medieval Bologna (1270-1305)', and G. MILANI, 'Bologna's two Exclusions and the Power of Law Experts', both in press (*Europäisches Forum junger Rechtshistorikerinnen und Rechtshistoriker, Osnabrück, 22-25 May 2002*), and online on 'Reti Medievali' ('Library' section of www.retimedievali.it); and see also DE BENEDICTIS, *Repubblica per contratto*, pp. 151-5. On the relationship of teaching to other professional activities generally, see the observations of J. VERGER, *Men of Learning in Europe at the End of the Middle Ages* (tr. Notre Dame, In., 2000), pp. 84 *seq.* and 103; and P. F. GRENDLER, 'The Universities of the Renaissance and Reformation', *Renaissance Quarterly*, 57 (2004), pp. 1-42 (pp. 11-12).

the commune's right to collect taxes;[3] or a smaller group of foreign doctors might be consulted.[4] In-dividual teachers such as Cino da Pistoia are also recorded as having given formal advice to the com-mune during the period of their *condotte*,[5] and when indigenous expertise was available that was of course exploited as well; a payment to the Sienese Federigo Petrucci in 1328 was made 'per suo salario d'un anno de' leggiare in decretali et di consigliare el comune'.[6] The link is also made explicit in the *condotta* of Niccolò da Prato in 1366, the justification of which is that 'esse necessarium haberi in civitate sen. hominem sufficientem legum doctorem praticum et expertum in consulendo negotiis comunis sen.',[7] and even more so in the double appointments of Buvalello de' Buvalelli of Bologna in 1369 ('legge e sia avocato del vostro comune')[8] and of Giovanni di Niccolò di Mino Vincenti as 'avochato del comuno di Siena e dotore a legiare ragione civile per lo chomuno di Siena' in 1372.[9] One cannot help noting the coincidence that plans to re-launch the *Studio* in December 1386 followed, by only a month, a charge of 240 ducats by the doctors of Bologna for legal advice on a dispute between Siena and Florence.[10] At the end of the century the need for local expertise was given explicitly as a reason for trying to revive the *Studio*.[11] The possibilities of using lecturers for other practical purposes were of course not confined to law. Doctors of medicine – who might also be used as ambassadors[12] – were also consulted formally in times of plague or other diseases,[13] and again this might have been a motive for hiring them; there are a number of *condotte*, right through the fifteenth century, which stipulate medical as well as teaching duties, at least in time of

---

[3] *Statuti* 23, f. 62r: 'cum habitum sit consilium per dominos tabule in presentia notarii reformationum comunis Sen. a doctoribus iuris canonici et civilis forensibus de studio et iudicibus potestatis et prudentibus advocatibus civitatis sen. …', cit. in BOWSKY, *Finance*, p. 96. Cf. *Chartularium*, doc. 281, p. 359, 31 Mar 1322.

[4] E.g. *Chartularium*, doc. 323, p. 394, 3 Sept 1332 – six doctors have given a *parere*.

[5] BOWSKY, 'A new *Consilium* of Cino of Pistoia', pp. 195-6.

[6] *Chartularium*, doc. 289, p. 364, 26 Feb 1327(=1328), and ZDEKAUER, p. 13 n. 2 (the version quoted here is that of the *Chartularium*); cf. *Chartularium*, doc. 308, p. 384, 27 Feb 1329(=1330). On Petrucci see most usefully NARDI, 'Contributo alla biografia di Federico Petrucci' (on his teaching and service to the comune esp. pp. 168-75).

[7] *CG* 175, f. 63v, 24 Dec; and cf. PRUNAI, II, pp. 39-40. TRAPANI, 'Docenti senesi' gives extensive biographical details of the teachers of the period, and stresses the heavy engagement of many of them in communal affairs.

[8] *Statuti* 35, ff. 14v-15r; and above, p. 49.

[9] *Bicch.* 251, f. 143v, 9 Aug 1373, and see above, p. 49 n. 119. Another example of this dual function is Giovanni da Rapolano (*Conc.* 139, f. 50r, 16 Oct 1387) whose cases were however suspended the following year when he was sent on an embassy (*Conc.* 144, f. 8r, 7 Jul 1388).

[10] *Conc.* 134, f. 17r, 28 Nov.

[11] 'Conciosia cosa che la città di siena sia molto diminuita di buoni e sufficienti huomini, et dessi sufficienti huomini cie n'abbia maggiore carestia che fusse mai, poiché questa città fu hedificata vedendo che se bisogna nuovo consiglio si vuole fare capo a forestieri, perché ci a pochi cittadini experti, et è veduto per gli decti savi quanto e nostri vicini che ano lo studio sono tucto di bonificati di buoni huomini, perché d'esso studio ciaschuna persona n'a utile e honore et a li huomini fanno e loro figlioli artefici, e vengono da pocho che se ci fusse studio potrebbero cum picola spesa essare da pur assai perché acciò che la decta città ci escha di buoni huomini'; *Conc.* 2111, f. 126v, 23 Apr 1396 (failed proposal to refound the *Studio*, with two thirds of the funding to come from the bishop, the clergy, the hospital of S. Maria della Scala and the Casa della Misericordia). See above, pp. 51 and 102. The prescience of this is highlighted in 1419 by the payment, made out of communal funds for a *consilium* to the commune, to seven doctors, Paolo di Castro, Sallustio Buonguglielmi and Angelo da Perugia, Niccolò Tedeschi, and the Sienese Mignanello Mignanelli, Pietro de' Pecci and Antonio da Batignano. All but the last of these had taught or were teaching at the *Studio* (*Conc.* 321, f. 36v, Jul-Aug 1419, and *Bicch.* 302, ff. 36r, 31 Aug, and 52r, 31 Dec).

[12] See above, pp. 48 and 165-6.

[13] ZDEKAUER, *Origini*, pp. 15-6.

plague.[14] A number of those who taught medicine in the *Studio* are also found in the employment of the hospital of S. Maria della Scala, which appointed a physician and a surgeon each year (and by the end of the fifteenth century had expanded the medical team to include assistants for both).[15]

[14] An obligation to perform as doctor in time of plague was a condition of the contract of Lodovico da Spoleto in 1457 (*Conc.* 543, f. 16v, 26 Mar 1457, ed. BAI, doc. 94, pp. 79-80), as it was for Jacopo di Galgano Faccalume in 1474 (*Not.* 694, f. 13r-v, 15, ed. MINNUCCI, 'Documenti', docs. II-42 and II-43, pp. 111-12, and see n. 154). During the 1448 plague epidemic there is an example of a doctor, M.° Elias, being hired to visit the sick and later being given a *condotta* in the *Studio*; *CG* 224, f. 188r, 22 Nov 1448; cf. GAROSI, pp. 241-2; and *Conc.* 497, ff. 17r, 24 Nov, and 21r, 6 Dec; see also C. CORSO, 'Araldi e canterini nella Repubblica Senese del '400', *BSSP*, 62-63 (1955-56), pp. 140-60 (pp. 144-5). In 1482 Giovanni d'Arezzo was hired for two years, at a salary of 150 florins, to treat plague victims and, when there was no plague, to teach (*Balìa* 26, f. 19r, 27 Jun). Unusually the *Savi* and *Concistoro*'s order for *apotisse* of 1 Apr 1475 is for 'Doctoribus Magistris et aliis conductis ad legendum et medendum' (*Conc.* 651, f. 24r, ed. BAI, doc. 359, p. 360). This is likely to refer only to teachers who also had a responsibility for medical care; Jacopo Faccalume (see above) is on the list, but Giovanni da Roma, hired the previous year for two years by the *Consiglio del Popolo* 'ad medicandum in chyrurgia' (*CG* 235, ff. 183r, 184v, 23 Mar 1474), and presumably still in the commune's employ during the period covered by the order (cf. *Conc.* 649, f. 38v, 30 Dec 1474, granting him eight days leave, his third such concession that year; *Conc.* 647, f. 9r, 16 Jul, and *Conc.* 648, f. 11v, 20 Sept, both for ten days), is not. (He is probably identifiable with Giovanni di Lorenzo de' Giustini da Roma, hired 'a medicare in cerusia' by the *Consiglio del Popolo* in 1465, *CG* 230, ff. 297v-298r, 24-25 Jun, at the behest of the *Savi*, who 'hanno giudicato che la condotta sua de farsi de farsi sarebbe non tanto utilissima ma necessarissima. E perché l'officio loro insieme con le M.S.V. Et altri ordini della città non ann[o] auctorità di potere fare condocto se non di chi si conducesse nel alcune lectura'. Giovanni at some stage petitioned for a lectureship; *Conc.* 2138, f. 125r, n.d., ed. WHITLEY, 'Concepts of Ill Health and Pestilence', Appendix I.7, p. 315. The earliest evidence that he was successful is from 1471 (see above, p. 156 n. 59). Another example of a 'medico condotto' who was clearly not teaching is 'Antonius magistri Jacobi Vite de Senis, who appeared before the *Concistoro* on 4 Nov 1463 asserting that he had been hired 'ad providendum ut pestis cesset et cetera' for the month; he was confirmed in the role, *Conc.* 583, f. 6v, ed. BAI, doc. 197, p. 171.) On the role of such teachers see V. NUTTON, 'Continuity or Rediscovery? The City Physician in Classical Antiquity and Mediaeval Italy', in *The Town and State Physician in Europe from the Middle Ages to the Enlightenment*, ed. A. W. Russell. Wolfenbütteler Forschungen, 17 (Wolfenbüttel, 1981), pp. 9-46, and, notwithstanding its title, R. PALMER, 'Physicians and the State in Post-Medieval Italy', in op. cit., pp. 47-61.

[15] The decisions of appointments are recorded in the *Deliberazioni* of the hospital's chapter; those relating to the period under consideration are *Scala* 20-25. Some of these names are listed in WHITLEY, 'Concepts of Ill Health and Pestilence', Appendix III.3, pp. 336-42. In what follows, references to teaching periods, where not given, are to the *apotisse* issued by the *Concistoro*, eds. PIANIGIANI, BAI and FERRERI, *passim*. Of the thirty-six doctors appointed by the chapter of the hospital between 1401 and 1500, twenty-four were teachers at the *Studio*. Twelve of these are described as physicians, six as surgeons; the rest are simply *medici*. The list includes some of the more eminent and long-standing *Studio* figures, who accepted such annual appointments for brief periods. The great majority were Sienese; apart from Mattiolo da Perugia, who taught briefly at the *Studio* in 1447-8, and again in 1456 (above, p. 190), and who was appointed at the hospital in 1447 (*Scala* 23, f. 137r, 9 Oct), and Serafino da Camerino, who taught in 1451 (*Conc.* 511, f. 29v, 20 Aug, ed. BAI, doc. 16, pp. 13-14), was appointed at the Scala in the same year (*Scala* 24, f. 24r, 6 Jul 1452, renewal of his contract for one year), but left within months (*Conc.* 517, f. 17v, 15 Nov 1452; he is offered a renewal of his teaching contract but rejects it; by 28 May 1453 he has left for Rome, *Scala* 24, f. 31v), the only foreigners were teachers who settled in Siena for long periods; Giovanno di Ser Donato da Arezzo, who taught from 1449 to 1486, and was doctor at the hospital in 1459 (*Scala* 24, f. 103v, 27 Mar), 1466 (f. 173r, 13 Dec) and 1480 (f. 281r, 28 Mar), and Lodovico da Spoleto, who eventually acquired citizenship, who taught from 1442 to 1482 (see above, p. 205), and was at the Scala in 1453 (f. 31v, 28 May) and 1454 (f. 39r, 28 Mar). A third foreigner, Gregorio d'Alessandria (taught 1464 to 1492), was nominated as a reserve in 1465 (f. 162r-v, 30 Dec) but in the event appears not to have been needed (f. 173r, 13 Dec 1466). Of the Sienese, there appear to be several patterns which this dual service could take. A number of doctors accepted an appointment at the hospital early in their teaching career. These tended to be minor figures, most with brief careers in the *Studio*. Giovanni di Francesco Nini, a member of a medical family (FIORAVANTI, 'Formazione e carriera di un domenicano', pp. 343-4) actually began his public career at the hospital in 1444 (*Scala* 23, f. 79r, 9 Jun; and cf. ff. 93r, 5 Jan, and 101r, 30 Mar 1445, and ff. 128v-129r, 27 Jan 1447), before securing a lectureship (*Conc.* 475, f. 27v, 24 Apr 1445). He was appointed town physician at Città di Castello in 1447 (release from his teaching on 24 Jun, *Conc.* 488, f. 51r, ed. PIANIGIANI, doc. 271, p. 302, and from the hospital on 26 Jun, *Scala* 23, f. 134v), but returned to teach in Siena in 1451, continuing until 1456. Andrea di Maestro Bartolomeo taught from 1440 to 1444, and held a four-month appointment at the Scala in 1444 (*Scala* 23, f. 79r, 9 Jun). The surgeon Francesco di Ser Jacopo di Ser Mino di Tura was appointed to both a hospital and a teaching job in 1460 (*Scala* 24, f. 116v, 27 Mar; *Conc.* 563, f. 22r, 11 Aug, ed. BAI, doc. 141, p. 121) but disappears from the *Studio* records after

And *maestri dell'abaco*, although not part of the university organisation, were regularly hired to perform as surveyors as well as teachers.[16]

The dangers of teachers taking on extra-curricular activities are and were obvious.[17] In 1427 the commune made doctors ineligible for the offices of *Camarlengo* of the *Biccherna*, the *Gabella* and the *Sale e Paschi*,[18] in 1435 a collective contract stipulated that none of the teachers to whom it applied could have any other salary in the commune,[19] and in 1437 it was decided that 'niuno ciptadino, el quale fosse condotto et avesse accettato a leggere, possa exercitare alcuno offitio di Comune, ordi-

1461 (the last reference is a payment for the first *terzaria* of 1461-2, *Conc.* 571, f. 29v, ed. BAI, doc. 174, p. 150). Cristoforo di Ser Domenico taught from 1474 to 1479, and was *coadiutore* to the doctors at the Scala in 1477 (*Scala* 24, f. 264v, 26 Nov). Biagio Smeraldi began teaching and work at the hospital in 1498 (*Balìa* 43, f. 52v, 11 Jan; *Scala* 25, f. 56r, 7 Aug) and Lodovico da Gubbio began teaching in 1498 (*Conc.* 791, f. 9v, 27 Jul, ed. FERRERI, doc. 394, p. 378) and work at the hospital in 1500 (*Scala* 25, f. 67r, 26 Mar). (The careers of these two have not been followed through post-1500). One might speculate that for these doctors the attractions would have been the practical experience they gained as well as the second salary from the Scala, which, however modest, would have been an important addition to their low pay at the university (e.g. Lodovico da Gubbio earned 40 florins as teacher, 17 florins at the hospital). For some, a stint at the hospital was done in mid-career or later. Francesco Nini is found at the hospital in 1411 (*Scala* 22, f. 120r, 5 Dec), and teaching in 1401 (*Conc.* 223, f. 10r, 22 Sept, ed. PIANIGIANI, doc. 6, pp. 26-7) and again in the 1420s (*Conc.* 334, f. 9v, 12 Sept 1421, ed. PIANIGIANI, doc. 50, pp. 73-4; *Conc.* 358, f. 24r, 3 Oct 1425, ed. PIANIGIANI, doc. 72, p. 93; *Conc.* 377, f. 32r, 21 Feb 1429, ed. PIANIGIANI, doc. 107, pp. 133-5. On him see MINNUCCI, 'Documenti', pp. 251-2). Mariano di Ser Jacopo Manni, who taught in 1401 (*Conc.* 223, f. 10r, 22 Sept, ed. PIANIGIANI, doc. 6, pp. 26-7), was employed by the hospital in 1435 and 1436 (*Scala* 23, ff. 2v, 21 Apr 1435, and 10r, 26 Mar 1436). Giovanni da Sermoneta, who taught between 1416 and 1442, accepted a Scala appointment in 1438 (f. 28r, 26 Mar). Bartolo di Tura, whose distinguished teaching career spans from 1426 to 1468 (above, p. 185), was appointed by the Scala in 1444 (f. 78v, 2 Jun), though it is not clear whether he accepted (the appointment a week later of three further doctors for four months each, f. 79r, 9 Jun, rather implies that he did not). For such a figure, a period of service at the hospital may well have been considered a social or pious obligation (though of course there were many more teachers who do not appear in the Scala's records at all). But a handful of teachers accepted such posts more than once, in some cases developing long-standing connections with the institution. Sinibaldo di M. Bartalaccio of Montalcino taught from 1429 at the *Studio*, and was *fisico* at the Scala from 1439 until his death in 1444 (*Scala* 23, ff. 35v, 26 Mar 1429, 39v, 26 Mar 1440, 43v, 26 Mar 1441, 52r bis, 26 Mar 1443); he appears to have stopped teaching in 1442. Giovanni di Domenico taught from 1440 to 1467 and was hired by the hospital in 1444 (*Scala* 23, f. 79r, 9 Jun), 1445 (f. 101v, 30 Mar), 1457 (*Scala* 24, f. 83r, 17 Jun) and again in 1465 (f. 162r, 30 Dec). Jacopo di Galgano di Ser Jacopo Faccalume, who taught continuously from 1459 until his death in 1491, was the hospital's surgeon in 1462 (*Scala* 24, f. 131v, 23 Jun) and 1463 (f. 141r, 11 May); in 1465 he worked as physician as well (f. 154v, 16 Mar), and reappears at the hospital in 1480 (f. 284r, 15 Sept); his contemporary and rival Jacopo di Filippo da Sinalunga taught from 1465 to 1496, working at the hospital first as an assistant in 1466 (*Scala* 24, f. 172v, 24 Dec) and again in 1480 (f. 281r, 28 Mar), 1490 (*Scala* 25, f. 12r, 16 Jun) and finally 1496 as a principal (f. 38r, 29 Feb). Andrea di Francesco Marretta taught from 1487 to 1498 and served at the Scala in 1489 as assistant (f. 5v, 27 Feb), in 1492 at three-quarters of the salary of a principal (f. 21r, 26 Mar), and in 1496 as one of the principals (f. 38r, 29 Feb). Guasparre Berti began teaching logic in 1490 (*Conc.* 744, f. 10r, 11 Oct, ed. FERRERI, doc. 307, pp. 279-81) and accepted a hospital appointment as *coadiutore* in 1496 (*Scala* 25, f. 38r, 29 Feb) and then a full post in 1498 (f. 56r, 7 Aug). Finally there are two doctors who made brief appearances in the lecture lists but more substantial contributions to the hospital; Benedetto di Ser Lazaro, who taught in 1451-2 (contract in *Conc.* 511, f. 29v, 20 Aug, ed. BAI, doc. 15, p. 13), and who was hired by the hospital in 1450 (*Scala* 24, f. 4r, 12 Nov), 1453 (f. 34v, Oct or Nov), 1455 (f. 55r, 13 Aug) and 1457 (ff. 75r, 18 Feb, and 83r, 17 Jun), and Cipriano di Simone da Radicondoli, who taught briefly in 1445 (*Conc.* 477, f. 13r, 15 Jul, ed. PIANIGIANI, doc. 257, pp. 289-90) but who is found in the Scala as surgeon for six months in 1446 (*Scala* 23, f. 120v, 27 Apr) and again in 1449, as *fisico* (f. 153v, between 13 Feb and 5 Mar) and 1450 (*Scala* 24, f. 2r, 31 May).

[16] E.g. *Chartularium*, doc. 133 pp. 112-5, 30 Aug 1312 (Maestro Gerardo dell'Abbaco); *Conc.* 359, f. 6v, 5 Nov 1425 (Pietro dell'Abaco is sent to Sovana); *Conc.* 375, f. 18r, 9 Dec 1428 (he has been in Talamone). On this phenomenon, see M. BIAGIOLI, 'The Social Status of Italian Mathematicians, 1450-1600', *History of Science*, 27 (1989), pp. 41-95 (pp. 42-3).

[17] See above, Chapter II.1.3.

[18] *Statuti* 41, f. 198r.

[19] *Conc.* 417, f. 9r, 12 Jul, ed. ZDEKAUER, doc. XVII, p. 168.

nario et extraordinario, ne la ciptà o fuore de la ciptà cum salario o senza salario, durante la sua con-dotta'.[20] In 1440 the reverse was applied, making communal officials ineligible for *condotte* or for the rectorate of the Sapienza;[21] and in 1447 the ban on teachers holding office explicitly included ambas-sadorships.[22] These restrictions would have suited those lecturers who preferred to teach undisturbed and had previously had to be forced to accept such posts,[23] but it must have been a strain for the commune (which relied extensively on prestigious teachers for this role), and a disappointment for many other teachers who would have regarded such appointments as a privilege.[24] By and large the ban does appear to have been upheld, with a handful of exceptions. In 1465 Borghese Borghesi was elected to be one of the *Quatttro Maestri dei Paschi et Sale*. He accepted the office because his teach-ing contract had expired, but his teaching was considered 'necessaria perché a una bellissima scuola' and his *sedia* was 'uno delle principali del vostro studio'; and since he had no concurrent, failure to hire him would lead to 'grande interructione dello studio' which could only be remedied by hiring a foreign teacher for at least 400 florins. An exemption was made so he could be rehired while holding office.[25] By 1481 such exemptions appear to have become more regular; Ugo di Battista Bellanti, re-questing one from the *Consiglio del Popolo* in 1481, pointed out that it had become regular practice for recent *balìe* to allow teachers to accept podestariates.[26] The following year Guidantonio Buonin-segni was granted permission to accept the podestariate of Sovana despite his teaching contract; he was allowed to put his brother into the post for three months while he continued with his teaching.[27] In 1491 the legislation itself was relaxed; in addition to the offices of *Capitano del Popolo* and *Gon-falonieri Maestri* (which could be accepted by placing a substitute in the teaching for the relevant two months, to be approved by the *Concistoro* and *Savi*) a teacher could now be *consigliere del Capitano*, one of the *Nove de' Paschi*, the *Nove del Vino*, the *Ventiquattro*, the *Nove de la Guardia* and the *Nove*

---

[20] *CG* 219, f. 157v (new foliation), 29 May, ed. ZDEKAUER, doc. XVIII, p. 171; copies in *Mis.* 1, f. 85r, *Statuti* 41, f. 255v, *Statuti* 44, f. 20r, and *Statuti* 47, f. 254v. The sole exceptions were the offices of *Capitano del Popolo* and *Gonfalonieri Maestri*. Cf. ERMINI, *Storia*, I, p. 63 n. 63 for Perugian parallels. At Padua such segregation resulted from the barring of citi-zens from lectureships; J. K. HYDE, *Padua in the Age of Dante* (Manchester and New York, 1966), p. 124.

[21] *CG* 220, f. 178r, 21 Sept.

[22] *Conc.* 490, f. 22r, 3 Oct, and *CG* 224, f. 68r-v, 6 Oct.

[23] Cf. *Conc.* 454, f. 42v, 9 Oct 1441, when the penalty for refusal was fixed at 100 *lire*, and *Conc.* 457, f. 32r, 20 Mar, *Conc.* 459, ff. 24r-v, 19 Jul, and 25v, 21 Jul, 1442, when Messer Paolo di Martino was so fined but eventually excused, and the fine was ultimately reduced to 50 *lire*. Examples of teachers who cited teaching commitments as a reason for not taking up office include Tommaso Docci (above, p. 165 n. 164), and in 1440 Giovanni Mignanelli, who obtained a certificate from the *Regolatori* exempting him from the podestariate of Lucignano Val di Chiana on the grounds of his teaching post (*Conc.* 2177, no foliation, 29 Oct). A similar 'certificate of vacation' was granted by the *Regolatori* to Tommaso Docci and Francesco Patrizi in 1441 (loc. cit.), and cf. also the case of Sinibaldo Bartalacci, given a similar certificate on 25 Feb 1441 (loc. cit.). On the other hand Niccolò Nanni, also teaching at the time, was permitted to apply for a *podestaria* (loc. cit., Feb 1441). The restriction could work the other way. Jacopo di Pietro Tolomei, in the *cerna* for a podestariate, had regularly been drawn only to be disqualified because he was teaching; in 1442 he successfully appealed to be released from the 'in-tollerabile fadigha desso leggiare' which had resulted 'in grandi et in diverse infirmitadi et da dubitare di pegio sopra la sua sanità', and to be given the first podestariate that became vacant (*Conc.* 2148, no. 21). On this figure, possibly the father of the poet of the same name, see C. DIONISOTTI, 'Jacopo Tolomei fra umanisti e rimatori', *Italia medioevale e umanista*, 6 (1963), pp. 137-76 (p. 138), and MINNUCCI, 'Documenti', pp. 267-8.

[24] A point well made by L. MARTINES, *Power and Imagination: City-States in Renaissance Italy* (London, 1980), p. 269.

[25] *CG* 230, f. 302r-v, 28 Jun. On this teacher see C. GENNARO, 'Borghese, Borghese', *DBI*, 12 (1970), pp. 583-4.

[26] *CG* 238, f. 240r, 28 Sept. He himself wanted to accept such office 'per alcuni suoi bisogni, et maxime per potere sat-isfare le dote d'una sua figliuola, ha maritata'.

[27] *Balìa* 26, f. 122r, 22 Oct 1482. On him see also MINNUCCI, 'Documenti', p. 262.

del Ornato, as well as accepting ambassadorships.[28] Finally in 1494 the principle of ineligibility was largely abandoned; teachers who were *de regimine* and who were elected to an office could accept it and had to choose a suitable substitute either for the office or for the lectureship, to be approved by the *Capitano del Popolo* and the *Gonfalonieri*.[29]

A separate category must be those cases in which the expertise of an individual was prized, to the extent that it was considered appropriate for him both to hold office and to teach – much in the tradition seen to have existed in the fourteenth century. In 1480 the Portuguese Pedro Vasques was both teaching and holding the post of *Giudice degli Appelli*;[30] while in the same year Antonio Berti, abbot of S. Maria della Rosa, was made a citizen, a member of the *Nove*, and 'advocatum fiscalem et consistorii…in causis spiritualibus'.[31] The most outstanding example of the combination of public office with a lectureship in the fifteenth century was Giovanni Battista Caccialupi da San Severino, who began a long and distinguished teaching career in Siena by adding a *lettura* to his post as *Giudice delle Reformazioni* in 1452, and who remained in Siena for over three decades.[32] At the end of the century Antonio Giordano da Venafro is also found in both communal office and teaching – he apparently arrived in Siena in 1482, graduated there,[33] began his career as a teacher in 1486,[34] was *Giudice delle Appellagioni* from 1488 to 1494[35] and *Giudice delle Riformagioni* by 1494,[36] and of course from 1497 became the trusted lieutenant of Pandolfo Petrucci, eventually reaching political heights that no other teacher achieved. The regularity and fluidity of such cross-overs are embodied in the way in which the *Savi dello Studio* were consulted in the late fifteenth century over senior judicial appointments.[37]

---

[28] *Conc.* 2395, ff. 36v-37r; *Statuti* 45, f. 32r-v; *Statuti* 46, f. 36r.

[29] *Balìa* 39, f. 162v, 9 Jun. In 1533 the practice was sanctioned by a measure to the effect that 'quelli, che fussero condotte, e non tenessero scuola pubblica, perdesseno il salario, per quel tempo, che non la tenessero, eccettuato però i casi d'infirmità o d'assenza per la Republica' (*CG* 243, f. 246r, 26 Dec). On the evils of the substitution convention, M. Ascheri, 'Le novelle: una fonte per la storia di Siena', in M. A. Ceppari Ridolfi, E. Jacona and P. Turrini, *Schiave ribaldi e signori a Siena nel Rinascimento* (Siena, 1994), pp. 201-10 (p. 208). On the interruptions of office to the work of artists, Hook, *Siena*, pp. 102-4.

[30] See below, p. 348 n. 84.

[31] *Balìa* 20, ff. 47v-48r, 26 Jul.

[32] *Conc.* 415, f. 81r-v, 23 Aug, *CG* 226, f. 3r, 23 Aug 1452, ed. Nardi, 'Giovanni Battista Caccialupi', pp. 92-3. The dual role was not necessarily easy, certainly if his own protestations are to be believed. In 1462, requesting a pay rise on his behalf, the *Savi* reported him complaining that he was treated as a citizen when it came to his salary but as a foreigner in all other respects: 'Ven dire che avendo lecto gia circa dieci anni nel vostro studio la lectione ordinaria che è la più fadighosa, e sempre quasi in concorrentia de famosissimi doctori… Et tucti questi anno avuti grandi salari di 550 chi 400 chi 300 fiorini e più, E lui già parechie anni avea servito per fx. 200. Le pare essere nel piccolo salario trattato come cittadino, e nel altre cose come forestiere, e danne la colpa a se medesmo per essere troppo rimesso, e humano ne le sue cose, e non importuno a domandare come fanno molti altri. Dice anco che per affectione a la V. città non ha mai date orecchie alli inviamenti grandi e honorevoli Li sono occorsi' (*Conc.* 577, ff. 43v-44r, 24 Dec).

[33] M. De Gregorio, 'Giordano, Antonio', *DBI*, 55 (2000), pp. 258-9. On Giordano see also C. De Frede, 'Un docente di diritto civile nel Rinascimento: Antonio Giordano da Venafro', in *Sodalitas. Scritti in onore di Antonio Guarino* (Naples, 1984), 8, pp. 3805-16.

[34] *Conc.* 721, f. 13v, 21 Dec, ed. Ferreri, doc. 240, p. 205.

[35] *Conc.* 729, f. 23r, 28 Apr 1488; *Balìa* 39, f. 139v, 22 Apr 1494.

[36] *Conc.* 773, f. 5v, 5 Jul 1495 a *Giudice delle Riformagioni* has to be elected for a year, since Giordano is absent. In 1496 both his tenure of this post and his teaching contract are renewed for three years (*Balìa* 41, ff. 22v-23r, 14 Oct 1496); both renewed, this time for six years, *Balìa* 43, f. 181v, 23 Jun 1498.

[37] *CG* 239, f. 126r, 8 Sept 1483 (the *Savi* are consulted over the election of the *Giudice delle Appellagioni*); *Conc.* 703, f. 16r, 14 Dec 1483, ed. Ferreri, doc. 188, p. 159 (they participate in the election); *Conc.* 705, f. 20r-v, 21 Apr, ed. Ferreri, doc. 196, p. 165 (they are present for his renewal). Compare with the *Savi*'s role in the appointments of medical doctors,

The other exception to the general principle was the very specific one of chancellors of the republic. There has been little focus to date on this office in Siena.[38] Appointed, as elsewhere, for their rhetorical and literary skills, chancellors were key cultural figures in the community, and it would have been surprising not to find them in relationship to the *Studio*. Giorgio Andreucci, chancellor in the mid-fifteenth century, was a doctor of law and member of the college of doctors, though he does not appear to have taught.[39] From the middle of the century, however, it became common for the chancellor also to have a *lettura* in the *Studio*. The first known case of this dual role is Agostino Dati, who was chancellor and lecturer in 1455, and again in 1458.[40] Niccolò di Bartolomeo Borghesi petitioned to be allowed to continue teaching rhetoric during his chancellorship in 1467 on the grounds that 'grande numero di scholari lo strenghano ad seguire il libro principiato'.[41] After another term as chancellor in 1479[42] he returned to teaching.[43] A victim of the political upheavals of the 1480s, he was out of Siena for several years, but in 1487 he was given a five-year contract and a salary of 300 florins to teach 'opus humanitatis et moralem phylosophiam' in the *Studio*, combined with the secretaryship of the republic and the duty of writing the annals of Siena.[44] Pietro Fondi also combined the two, in 1464,[45] and again in 1468,[46] whereas in 1477 he was awarded a lectureship as a reward for his labours as chancellor.[47] His son Angelo also held both in 1495.[48] Another humanist who held both the chancellorship and a *Studio* post was Giovanni Antonio di Nastoccio Saracini, chancellor in 1487 and

above, p. 211 n. 14; and cf. Florence, where the election of the *Giudici Collaterali del Podestà*, the *Giudice della Mercanzia* and the *Giudice delle Appellazioni* were at one stage chosen by the *Ufficiali dello Studio* (VERDE, *Lo Studio fiorentino*, I, p. 3).

[38] A recent discussion is TERZIANI, *Il governo di Siena*, pp. 10-14; see also M. ASCHERI, 'Siena senza indipendenza: Repubblica continua', in *I libri dei leoni: la nobiltà di Siena in età medicea, 1557-1737*, ed. M. Ascheri (Siena, 1996), pp. 9-69 (p. 57). In contrast to Florence, the chancellorship in Siena was a six-month post in the fourteenth century, and although it was at some stage extended to an annual post, there is still the consequence that, while eminent orators and humanists are found as chancellors, they have repeated but short periods of office. 1396 saw a petition to extend the period to a year 'conciosiacosa che della Cancellaria di Siena escono meno famose lettere che di cancellaria d'Italia, e questo avenga per lo spesso mutare de' Cancellieri' (*Conc.* 2111, f. 125r, 28 Dec). The reform of the office in 1442 has it as a one-year appointment (*Conc.* 2115, ff. 49r-50r). Much remains to be done on this subject.

[39] See above, p. 207 n. 206.

[40] ARCHIVIO DI STATO DI SIENA, *Archivio di Balìa. Inventario*, pp. 417-20; 'Serie dei Cancellieri di Balìa e dei Segretari delle Leggi della Repubblica di Siena'. The series is incomplete. Dati was on the *Studio* payroll during both of these periods; *Conc.* 535, f. 27v, 30 Dec 1455, ed. BAI, doc. 82, p. 69, and *Conc.* 553, f. 35r, 14 Dec 1458, ed. BAI, doc. 115, p. 98. An anonymous chancellor, requesting that the conditions of the post be defined, argued that he should be allowed to continue with his lectureship at a salary of 100 florins; *Conc.* 2180, n.d., archived under 1460 ('Le chose si dimandandano[sic] andando secondo la leggie del cancelliere').

[41] *Conc.* 2138, no. 99, f. 163r, 29 Jan; the petition was approved by the *Consiglio del Popolo*, CG 231, f. 270r-v, 18 Feb. His namesake and relative, Niccolò d'Andrea Borghesi, was also chancellor, in 1492-3.

[42] *Archivio di Balìa. Inventario*, loc. cit. He was awarded an additional 20 ducats for outstanding work as chancellor, *Balìa* 18, f. 5r, 3 Jan 1480.

[43] Payments from the academic year 1480-81; *Conc.* 685, f. 17r, 20 Dec 1480, ed. FERRERI, doc. 114, p. 98.

[44] *Balìa* 35, ff. 37v-38r, 10 Sept. The contract was renewed in for a further two years; *Balìa* 35, f. 52v, 18 Aug 1492. In 1495, when the secretaryship had come to an end, his teaching-only salary was reduced (CG 241, f. 8r, 23 Jun; *Balìa* 40, f. 58v, 13 Nov). On this important Sienese figure see now C. SHAW, *L'ascesa al potere di Pandolfo Petrucci il Magnifico, Signore di Siena (1487-1498)* (Siena, 2001), pp. 38-40 and *ad indicem*; also below, p. 220.

[45] *Conc.* 589, f. 35r-v, 22 Dec.

[46] CG 232, f. 60r-v, 22 Jan; he petitioned the *Consiglio del Popolo* on the same grounds, and indeed in exactly the same terms, as had Niccolò Borghesi the previous year (above, n. 41).

[47] *Conc.* 665, f. 38r, 31 Jul.

[48] *Balìa* 40, f. 38r, 22 Oct. He had been teaching from 1491; *Conc.* 751, f. 14r, 20 Dec, ed. FERRERI, doc. 318, p. 297.

1488,[49] and lecturer from 1487 to 1490;[50] and finally Lorenzo Lanti held both the office and a lectureship, briefly, in 1482.[51] The dual role had clearly become standard practice; the only restriction was that chancellors were not supposed to accept a second salary for their teaching.[52] It is notable that not all of these were graduates; neither Pietro nor Angelo Fondi had a degree, and nor did Niccolò Borghesi in the early days of his teaching. Apart from students close to the end of their studies, these men of letters were the only non-doctors to teach on a communal salary.

This natural desire to have eminent men advise and represent the commune did not merely lead to the temptation of pluralism. Increasingly key posts in the administration and especially in the judiciary were reserved to those with degrees, and sometimes experience was also stipulated.[53] As early as 1383 the *senator* of the commune had to employ a judge who had to be a *legum doctor* and to swear that this was the case.[54] The post of *Giudice delle Riformagioni*, initiated in 1451 and given to Giovanni Battista Caccialupi, was to be held by a foreign doctor.[55] In 1414 both the *Giudice dell' Appellagione* and the *Giudice de' Pupilli* had to have degrees;[56] from 1431 the latter had to have held a degree for four years.[57] The 'collaterals' or expert advisors of officials such as the *Capitano di Giustizia* had to have held a degree for five years,[58] although we know of this stipulation principally through the commune's readiness to waive it;[59] from 1451 this provision applied to the *Giudice della Mercanzia* as

---

[49] *Archivio di Balìa. Inventario*, loc. cit.

[50] *Conc.* 726, f. 29r, 16 Oct 1487, ed. FERRERI, doc. 258, p. 221 (*condotta*); *Conc.* 730, f. 29r, 9 Jun 1488, ed. FERRERI, doc. 281, p. 249 (*condotta* in 'Arte oratoria'); *Conc.* 744, f. 11r, 12 Oct 1490, ed. FERRERI, doc. 307, p. 282 (*condotta* 'In humanitatibus').

[51] He taught civil law in 1464 (*Conc.* 585, f. 16r-v, 15 Mar 1464, ed. BAI, doc. 206, p. 181), from 1474 (*Conc.* 649, ff. 31v-32r, 22 Dec, ed. BAI, doc. 358, p. 359) to 1479 (*Conc.* 674, f. 14r, 5 Feb 1479, ed. FERRERI, doc. 76, p. 64), and was hired again in 1482 (*Conc.* 696, f. 8r, 20 Sept, ed. FERRERI, doc. 154, p. 131), a year in which he was chancellor (as he was again in 1485; *Archivio di Balìa. Inventario*, loc. cit.), as well as being sent to Rome on an embassy (*Conc.* 693, f. 20v, 8 Apr, ed. FERRERI, doc. 141, p. 120). On Lanti see also MINNUCCI, 'Documenti', p. 281.

[52] *Statuti* 45, f. 27r-v, and *Statuti* 46, f. 32r-v, n.d.: 'Vacatione del Cancelliere del Comune'. An earlier version (*Statuti* 44, f. 15v, n.d.), has no mention of the possibility of the chancellor also teaching.

[53] An early sign of this is found in the 1309-10 statutes of the commune, which stipulate that 'neuno giudice forestiere sia overo essere possa ad alcuno officio de la città, da inde a due anni, poscia che sarà tornato da lo Studio'; ELSHEIKH (ed.), *Il costituto*, I, p. 352; Dist. I, rubric 501. Despite the editor's capitalization of 'Studio' I take this to mean that two years must elapse after completion of study, rather than being a specific reference to the Sienese university.

[54] *CG* 192, f. 38r, 11 Jan; and cf. *Conc.* 2111, ff. 27r-28r, 13 Sept 1385. However it is notable that in 1384 'D. Vivianus de Portunaonis foroliviensis' (Pordenone), a mere 'civilis iuris eximium professorem', was recommended for the post of *Giudice delle Appellagioni*; *Conc.* 1815, no. 85, *ult.* Feb.

[55] TERZIANI, *Il governo di Siena*, pp. 18-19, and NARDI, 'Giovanni Battista Caccialupi a Siena', pp. 87-91.

[56] *CG* 206, ff. 184v-185r, 21 Jul.

[57] *CG* 216, f. 27r, 4 Feb. The four-year rule was still in operation in 1471; *Conc.* 2077, no. 7, 8 Oct, letter of recommendation from Scipio de Rubertis of Ferrara asking that Guasparre Fontano da Modena be made *Giudice de' Pupilli* despite having had a degree for three years rather than the required four. A similar request in 1485, on behalf of a Messer Cipriano Antonini da Foligno, was supported by Giulio Cesare da Varano, *signore* of Camerino, on the grounds of his 'longa pratice et experientia delli officii' (*Balìa* 524, no. 4, 3 Jun), and by Lorenzo de' Medici (*Balìa* 524, no. 12, 7 Jun, ed. LORENZO DE' MEDICI, *Lettere*, VIII, ed. H. Butters [Florence, 2001], no. 758, p. 221). By 1487 the requirement for the *Giudice dell'Appellagione* was five years, as it was for most other offices (below, n. 58); *Conc.* 2311, no foliation, 19 May.

[58] *CG* 241, ff. 333r-336v (esp. 333v), 13 Nov 1524. Both the *Capitano di Giustizia* and his collateral had to be 'dottori di collegio e non di privilegio', i.e. the degrees had to be awarded through the proper academic processes and not through, for example, counts palatine (ff. 333r, 335r). The *Capitano* had to be 'huomo di grande qualità', preferably 'conte, o signore o almeno cavaliere' and the collateral, who was also to be *iudex* on the *Corte de' Pupilli*, had to be over twenty-five.

[59] *Conc.* 1940, no. 22, 28 Apr 1438; Cardinal Colonna, writing from Ferrara on behalf of Giorgio d'Alato, asking for an exemption on the grounds of his expertise. The *Concistoro*'s renewal three year's later of his appointment and of the exemp-

well.[60] The only office for which doctors were apparently ineligible was that of *Ufficiali della Mercanzia*.[61] These offices were only open, however, to citizens of towns in which the Sienese degree was recognised; protectionism encroached here also.[62] With the institution of the *Rota* at Siena in 1503 the demand for foreign doctors continued, and indeed was formalised further; the city was always to employ a total of five foreign judges, with degrees of three years' standing,[63] and as late as 1529 the *Giudici della Rota* had to include foreign doctors.[64]

Other functions regularly performed by doctors included the syndication of the outgoing *podestà*, which also became reserved to *dottori di collegio*,[65] and less formally the re-drafting of communal statutes.[66] More generally, doctors' advice was regularly sought and heard in the *Consiglio Generale* and the *Consiglio del Popolo* from the fourteenth century onwards,[67] and their frequent appearance on, not to say domination of, special commissions of every description is apparent throughout the fifteenth

tion (*Conc.* 450, f. 60v, 23 Feb 1441) indicates that he became collateral of the *Capitano di Giustizia*. A similar exemption, for the same post, was accorded to Benedetto da Lucca in 1445 (*Conc.* 475, ff. 13v, 22 Mar, and 15r, 24 Mar), and was requested for Natimbene de' Valenti da Trevi in 1463 (*Conc.* 2007, nos. 46, 48, 10 Dec, and 52, 15 Dec. The outcome is not clear), and granted for Antonio de Caputis da Castello in 1465 (*CG* 230, f. 271r, 19 Apr). Not surprisingly however the commune reacted sharply to any subterfuge or false declarations. In 1440 the commune approved a request by the *Capitano di Giustizia*-elect that his nominee as collateral, Luigi d'Aversa, be appointed despite the fact that he had not held his degree for the stipulated five years. Shortly afterwards, however, it came to light that Luigi was in fact only *licentiatus* and had only become *cavaliere* after the *Capitano*'s letter of request had been written. Luigi was given a 50-*lire* fine, payable within four days, and was banned from all future office. The fine was lifted and the ban reduced to ten years after the intervention of various people, one of whom declared that Luigi was 'satis simplex persona' who 'non fecit predicta animo commictendi falsum'; *Conc.* 444, ff. 10r, 13 Jan, 43v-44v, 23 Feb, 46v-47r, 26 Feb 1440. The outcome of a similar case, that of Misser Jacomo Castello da Brescia, who turned out not to have the degree he had claimed, is not known (*Conc.* 2311, no foliation, n.d.). The laxity about checking credentials implied by these cases is perhaps not surprising given that the growth in importance of the degree was a relatively recent trend. Similar legislation at Mantua stipulated the *studi* from which appointees could have their degree; D. S. CHAMBERS and T. DEAN, *Clean Hands and Rough Justice. An Investigating Magistrate in Renaissance Italy* (Ann Arbor, Mi., 1997), p. 271.

[60] *Statuti* 40, f. 23v, 28 Oct 1451.

[61] *CG* 241, ff. 335v-336r, 13 Nov; cit. in ISAACS, 'Popolo e monti', p. 66.

[62] *CG* 219, f. 147r (new foliation), 10 May 1437, ed. ZDEKAUER, doc XVIII, p. 171; copies in *Mis.* 1, f. 83v; *Statuti* 41, f. 256v; and see ZDEKAUER, p. 60 on the significance of this clause which seems to have been directed at Florence in particular. On the increasing importance of the degree qualification for office, G. CENCETTI, 'La laurea nelle università medievali', *Studi e memorie per la Storia dell'Universita di Bologna*, 16 (1943), pp. 247-73 (p. 272) [repr. in his *Lo Studio di Bologna. Aspetti Momenti e Problemi (1935-1970)*, eds. R. Ferrara, G. Orlandelli and A. Vasina (Bologna, 1989), pp. 77-93].

[63] *Statuti* 40, ff. 160r-163v, 11 Dec; cf. M. ASCHERI, 'La Rota della Repubblica di Siena nel secolo XVI', in *Case Law in the Making. The Techniques and Methods of Judicial Records and Law Reports*, ed. A. Wijffels. Comparative Studies in Continental and Anglo-American Legal History, 17/1 (Berlin, 1997), pp. 183-97 (esp. p. 186); and A. K. ISAACS, 'Politica e giustizia agli inizi del Cinquecento: l'istituzione delle prime Rote', in *Atti di convegni di grandi tribunali e rote nell'Italia di antico regime*, eds. M. Sbriccoli and A. Bettoni. Pubblicazioni della Facoltà di Giurisprudenza, Università di Macerata, 4 (Milan, 1993), pp. 341-86, pointing out that these '*forenses*' often included doctors from the then subject town of Montepulciano, and also a high proportion of graduates of the Sienese *Studio*, politically connected with the regime.

[64] *CG* 243, f. 38r, 25 Feb.

[65] An early example is *Conc.* 208, f. 2v, 1 Mar 1399. It was reserved to *dottori di collegio* in 1495; *CG* 241, f. 14r, 5 Jul. For a full discussion of the procedure of syndication, M. A. CEPPARI RIDOLFI, 'Il sindacato degli ufficiali del Comune di Siena nel Trecento', in *Scrivere il medioevo. Lo spazio, la santità, il cibo. Un libro dedicato a Odile Redon*, eds. B. Laurioux and L. Moulinier-Brogi (Rome, 2001), pp. 77-94.

[66] *CG* 210, f. 217v, 12 Sept, and *Conc.* 359, ff. 6v-7r, 6 Nov 1425.

[67] E.g. Francesco Accolti and Giovanni Battista Caccialupi to make provisions in 1476 (*Conc.* 656, f. 20v, 6 Feb, ed. FERRERI, doc. 2, p. 2); Caccialupi, Borghese Borghesi and Bulgarino Bulgarini writing a 'scritto' in 1482 (*Conc.* 693, f. 6r, 9 Mar, ed. FERRERI, doc. 140, p. 120). ISAACS, 'Popolo e monti', p. 66, found that doctors were frequently entrusted with the task of presenting recommendations of the *Concistoro* to the *Consiglio del Popolo* in the early sixteenth century.

century. Doctors were occasionally members of the *Concistoro* in the fifteenth century,[68] and Isaacs found that between 1524 and 1530 over a third of the *Capitani del Popolo*, and over a quarter of the *Officiali di Balìa e Conservatori della Libertà*, were doctors, mostly of law.[69]

Finally, doctors often practised privately whilst teaching. It is of course difficult to be sure from communal records of the extent of this, but an occasional indication is given when a teacher was sent on communal business and both his *lettura* and his current cases were suspended. This happened twice with Tommaso Docci, who is revealed as being involved in five cases in January 1433 and three in September 1434.[70] As one of the most eminent lawyers in Siena at the time, Docci is probably atypical; but teachers clearly had plenty of opportunity to supplement their income in this way. The only restriction was that teachers were not allowed to take on cases against the commune.[71] Even foreign teachers could be given permission to practise while teaching, provided they matriculated into the guild of *giudici e notai*.[72] Medical doctors were of course also able to combine private consultations with their teaching duties.[73]

Far from being incompatible with their university commitments, private practice brought teachers into contact with real cases that might hold considerable theoretical interest. The rich literature of *consilia* is witness to this.[74] Ultimately the extent to which law teachers could also conduct private practice is discernible above all through legal sources.[75] Analysis of the relationship between these sides of lawyers' careers is well beyond the scope or competence of the present work; but it should be pointed out that such 'outside' activities were both an indicator of the reputation of Siena's *Studio* and a ve-

---

[68] See GAROSI, p. 305. There is also the unusual case of Giorgio Andreucci, who was a prior in Sept-Oct 1436 while a student (*Conc.* 424, front page). W. M. BOWSKY, 'The *Buon Governo* of Siena (1287-1355): a Medieval Italian Oligarchy', *Speculum* (1962), p. 374, remarked on the lack of teaching doctors in office during the government of the Nine, despite Tommasi's assertion that there were some (p. 370). But Tommasi's assertion concerned *dottori*, i.e. graduates. The separation of teachers and executive office, which seems to have been intended at the outset, would not have applied to all men with qualifications. By the fifteenth century this too had changed.

[69] ISAACS, 'Popolo e monti', p. 66.

[70] *Conc.* 402, f. 3r, 1 Jan 1433; *Conc.* 412, ff. 13r and 14v, 9 Sept, and 15v, 10 Sept 1434. On Docci's many commitments see also above, p. 165.

[71] *Conc.* 417, f. 9r, 12 Jul 1435, ed. ZDEKAUER, doc. XVII, pp. 167-9, penalty 100 florins; and cf. *Conc.* 2117, f. 189r, n.d. but in a file of *Proposte dei Savi, 1450-83*: decision 'che niuno doctore condotto con salario nel comune di Siena, overo alcuno doctore o giudice il quale fusse condotto con alcuno offitiale desso comune di Siena, possa né debba per alcuno modo dare in scriptura alcuno consiglio contra el comune di Siena... sotto pena di fl. L...'. The measure is repeated in 1495 (*Conc.* 773, f. 5r, 6 Jul 1495, ed. FERRERI, doc. 341, p. 345, and cf. *Conc.* 2311, no foliation, for the original proposal). This measure also banned doctors of law from entering the *palazzo* of the *Podestà*, or talking to other doctors there, except when participating in a case.

[72] *CG* 209, f. 85r, 15 Nov 1420, ed. ZDEKAUER, doc. XII, p. 160, and see p. 39; also discussed in FIORAVANTI, 'Alcuni aspetti della cultura umanistca senese', p. 166. The permission was given after plague had severely reduced the number of lawyers available, and was valid for eight years.

[73] For examples see above, p. 165.

[74] These included professional advice to the commune on political matters, as illustrated recently by *consilia* which have, significantly, ended up in the Archivio di Stato, in *Conc.* 2315; ASCHERI, 'Un trittico da Siena', pp. 23-30; and more broadly see also IDEM, 'I "consilia" dei giuristi: una fonte per il tardo Medioevo', *Bullettino dell'Istituto Storico Italiano per il Medio Evo*, 105 (2003), pp. 305-34; IDEM, 'Le fonti e la flessibilità del diritto comune: il paradosso del *consilium sapientis*', in *Legal Consulting in the Civil Law Tradition*, eds. M. Ascheri, I. Baumgärtner and J. Kirshner. Studies in Comparative Legal History (Berkeley, Ca., 1999), pp. 11-53; IDEM, 'Il *consilium* dei giuristi medievali', in *Consilium. Teorie e pratiche del consigliare nella cultura medievale*, eds. C. Casagrande, C. Crisciani and S. Vecchio. Micrologus' Library, 10 (Florence, 2004), pp. 243-58; and BAUMGÄRTNER, 'Stadtgeschichte und Consilia'.

[75] Mariano Sozzini is an obvious example, charted by NARDI, *Mariano Sozzini*, pp. 76-78.

hicle for its enhancement. The fact that Lorenzo de' Medici sought the formal opinion of Bartolomeo Sozzini, Bulgarino Bulgarini and Francesco Accolti in 1478 in the wake of the Pazzi conspiracy[76] is an example of this. That applies equally to the *consilia* and practical work of medical doctors.[77]

2. *Teachers and factional politics*

The close involvement of a number of teachers in key aspects of government – which by the end of the fifteenth century entailed the holding not just of 'technical' posts but also more political ones – leads inevitably to the question of how political life impinged on the *Studio* and vice versa. It should be said straight away that we are not talking about the wholesale involvement of the university in politics. As should be clear by now, the structure of the *Studio* made that quite impossible, while it has also been seen that regimes of all colours were agreed on the importance of maintaining the university. The individual level was another matter. By the mid-fifteenth century the *Studio* was rapidly becoming a focus for the activities and aspirations of a number of patrician families. This could include noble families formally barred from political office, but it also included a number of families that were politically active, most notably members of the *Nove*, the *monte* that included the highest proportion of lawyers.[78] The instability of the 1480s certainly collected a few *Studio* casualties. Placido di Aldello Placidi was executed for treason in 1483;[79] and in the late 1480s teachers who had

---

[76] Bargagli, *Bartolomeo Sozzini*, pp. 77-81 (further bibliography on p. 79 n. 76).

[77] Above, pp. 165, 176 n. 246, and 218.

[78] D. L. Hicks, 'Sienese Society in the Renaissance', *Comparative Studies in Society and History*, 2 (1959-60), pp. 412-20 (p. 419) [tr. as 'Caratteristiche socio-economiche delle famiglie senesi aggregate ai monti tra 400 e 500', in *La caduta della Repubblica di Siena*, ed. E. Pellegrini (Siena, n.d.), pp. 53-60] found that for the first half of the fifteenth century the doctors who appear in communal records as officials, ambassadors, members of the *Concistoro* or of commissions reveal a predominance of members of the *Nove* and the *Popolo*, while at the end of the century the lists of lecturers show a predominance of the *Nove* and *Riformatori*. It is also significant that of those teachers who were members of *monte* families (i.e. members of the groups eligible for political office) in the early sixteenth century, the great majority were lawyers; Isaacs, 'Popolo e Monti', p. 67.

P. Pertici, 'Una "coniuratio" del reggimento di Siena nel 1450', *BSSP*, 99 (1992), pp. 9-47 (pp. 14-15) (and cf. Eadem [ed.], *Tra politica e cultura nel primo Quattrocento senese. Le epistole di Andreoccio Petrucci (1426-1443)* [Siena, 1990], p. 10), has suggested that the *cenacolo* 'nell'ambito dello Studio' known to subsequent writers as the 'Accademia Grande' may, with its predominance of *Noveschi*, have contributed to the political upheavals of 1450 and 1456. Little is known about this enigmatic body (a full summary is in P. Turrini, 'Lodovico Petroni, diplomatico e umanista senese', *Interpres*, 16 [1997], pp. 7-59 [pp. 58-9]), and it has yet to be subjected to the scrutiny that has been given to other 'back projections' of the academy movement such as the Platonic Academy of Florence (see J. Hankins, 'The Invention of the Platonic Academy of Florence', *Rinascimento*, 41 [2001], pp. 3-38 for a recent survey of the controversy by one of its main protagonists). The main authority for this is Gigli, *Diario Sanese*, I, pp. 222-4, whose account seems very obviously a subsequent ordering of evidence from the period from the perspective of his sixteenth- and seventeenth-century sources. The idea of a pre-sixteenth century Sienese academy has been disputed by C. Mazzi, *La Congrega de' Rozzi di Siena nel secolo XVI*, 2 vols. (Florence, 1881), II, pp. 383-8. But in any case there is little evidence in Gigli that this gathering was specifically *Novesco* in sentiment in the years with which we are concerned. More relevantly for our purposes, it is difficult to demonstrate that this 'Academy' operated specifically in a *Studio* context. The pre-sixteenth-century names inscribed in the 'tabelloni' of the Accademia degli Intronati are a roll-call of eminent Sienese cultural figures, some of whom taught in the *Studio*, some of whom did not (Turrini, loc. cit.; and F. Sbaragli, '"I tabelloni" degli Intronati', *BSSP*, 49 [1942], pp. 177-213, 238-67 [pp. 188-9]); no contemporary evidence for their meetings have come to light. On present evidence it would not be easy to go beyond the assertion that some of the conspirators were *Novesco* individuals who also taught at the *Studio*.

[79] Bargagli, *Bartolomeo Sozzini*, p. 37 n. 43. On Placidi see also Minnucci, 'Documenti', pp. 306-7.

been exiled or had had their careers otherwise interrupted were still claiming their salaries.[80] Only with the advent of Pandolfo Petrucci was there a real attempt to take closer control of the *Studio* and to use appointments in an obviously political way. *Studio* teachers were prominent in both sides of the struggle for power, the most prominent being Niccolò Borghesi, whose teaching salary oscillated according to his political status,[81] and Antonio Giordano da Venafro, Petrucci's chief minister.[82] Once Petrucci was firmly installed, in 1500-1, at least four of the teachers on the *rotolo* were closely associated with his regime.[83]

The *Studio* of course survived these upheavals. Other teachers replaced the suspect and the disgraced, and though there were years of shortage the institution proved resilient. The impact of changes in political fortunes was perhaps more subtle. Arguably the three most eminent Sienese university men of the fifteenth century all had their academic careers profoundly shaped by political factors. The most serious case was the loss of Ugo Benzi, one of the most distinguished teachers of medicine of his age.[84] A member of the discredited *monte* of the *Dodici*, Benzi had taught at Siena from 1405 to 1409 when he left under suspicion of having conspired against the government, though the Sienese agreed – at a time of crisis for the *Studio* itself – to grant him an honourable discharge.[85] In 1414 the Sienese helped Florence to wrest Benzi from Parma, and by September 1416 he was back at the Sienese *Studio*.[86] When however he was approached by the Florentines in 1421 there was resistance; he was given leave on 13 February, it was revoked in March when he was refused permission to leave the town 'sotto gravissime pene' which probably consisted of being declared rebel and having his property confiscated;[87] in April, eighty-two citizens met to discuss his case and eventually, after pleadings from Florence, in May he was given leave to accept the Florentine *condotta* for a two-year period only.[88] Benzi did not return to teach in Siena, although the commune did attempt once more to get him back,[89] and thereafter maintained what amounted to little more than the fiction that he was under their jurisdiction, authorising his transfer to Milan in 1428;[90] and the request of his sons for Flo-

[80] Above, p. 171. On the events of these years see esp. A. K. Isaacs, 'Cardinali e "spalagrembi". Sulla vita politica a Siena fra il 1480 e il 1487', in *La Toscana al tempo di Lorenzo*, III, pp. 1013-50; and C. Shaw, 'Politics and Institutional Innovation'.

[81] E.g. *Conc.* 772, ff. 20v-21v, 23 Jun 1495; Shaw, *op. cit.*, pp. 286-7; Eadem, *L'ascesa al potere, passim*; and Hicks, 'The Sienese Oligarchy', p. 1066. See also G. Chironi, 'Nascita della signoria e resistenze oligarchiche a Siena: l'opposizione di Niccolò Borghesi a Pandolfo Petrucci (1498-1500)', in *La Toscana al tempo di Lorenzo*, III, pp. 1173-95.

[82] De Frede, 'Un docente di diritto civile'.

[83] Mondolfo, 'Il ruolo dello Studio Senese', p. 413. On Petrucci and the *Studio*, Pecci, *Memorie storico-critiche della Città di Siena*, I, pp. 220-1. Philippa Jackson's Ph.D. thesis (Warburg Institute, University of London) on Petrucci's cultural policy is eagerly awaited.

[84] On Benzi, see the anonymous entry for 'Benzi, Ugo', *DBI*, 8 (1966), pp. 720-3; Nardi, *Mariano Sozzini*, p. 11, and Lockwood, *Ugo Benzi*; G. Federici Vescovini, 'Medicina e filosofia a Padova tra XIV e XV secolo: Jacopo da Forlì e Ugo Benzi da Siena (1380-1430)', in her *"Arti" e filosofia nel sec. XIV* (Florence, 1983), pp. 231-78; and further references in Minnucci, 'Documenti', p. 313.

[85] *Conc.* 259, f. 12v, 19 Mar, and *Conc.* 260, f. 22v, 29 May 1409; see also Lockwood, *Ugo Benzi*, p. 173. Garosi, p. 216, disputes this.

[86] Lockwood, *Ugo Benzi*, pp. 176-8.

[87] Thus the résumé of his case in *Conc.* 372, f. 27r, 14 Apr 1428, ed. Pianigiani, doc. 88, pp. 111-3.

[88] *Conc.* 330, f. 19v, 13 Feb; *Conc.* 331, ff. 9r, 13 Mar, 23r, 14 Apr, ed. Pianigiani, docs. 46-8, pp. 70-2; *Conc.* 332, ff. 4r, 3 May, 5r, 7 May, ed. Pianigiani, doc. 49, p. 73; Lockwood, *Ugo Benzi*, p. 179.

[89] See the peremptory letter in *Conc.* 1629, f. 22v, 4 Sept 1427. The possibility of his return after the original two years was certainly discussed; see his letter to the *Concistoro* of 12 January 1423 (*Conc.* 1902, no. 32).

[90] As n. 87; Lockwood, *Ugo Benzi*, p. 183.

Fig. 11 – Signature and seal of Mariano Sozzini (Archivio dell'U-niversità di Siena, *ms.* 1, f. 76v).

rentine citizenship, in 1447, stating that their father 'propter partialitates, coactus fuit deserere patri-am', places the blame for this on the Sienese authorities.[91]

Less dramatic, but undoubtedly significant, was the effect of their *monte* affiliation on the two great Sienese lawyers Mariano Sozzini and his son Bartolomeo. Two recent biographies make this abundantly clear. As a member of the *Dodici*, Mariano's career was always going to be conditioned by suspicions about his loyalties. In his case, though, this manifested itself in a firm resolution to keep him in Siena where the regime could keep a check on him, which either meant getting him to teach in Siena or, at certain moments, detaining him or sending him out of the city *a confino*.[92] A request from the pope to allow him to take up a lectureship at the University of Vienna was refused,[93] and even vis-its to Ferrara, where he had connections with his brother-in-law and fellow *dodicino* Ugo Benzi and his circle, were regarded with distrust. When he was ill in 1436 he was permitted to go there to receive treatment from Benzi only on condition that he agreed to come back when the *Savi* summoned him,[94] and in 1451 he was allowed only twenty days to visit Ferrara at the request of Borso d'Este, and

[91] GHERARDI, *Statuti*, appendix, part 2, doc. 193, pp. 453-4 (9 to 14 Jun); ZDEKAUER, pp. 61-2. There has been heated debate about the significance of this series of events. Lockwood claimed that Garosi had exaggerated the effect of Siena's shoddy treatment of Benzi, suggesting that it was just a hiccough in a thirty-five-year career which spanned six universities, and classed the episode among 'routine academic bickerings'(*Ugo Benzi*, p. 18). Benzi did after all return to Siena briefly in 1439 for personal reasons, and was received with great honour and even allowed to act as *promotor* in an examination; nonetheless the fact remains that the Sienese never won him back to their *Studio*. Despite the extraordinary reaction of Garosi (pp. 197 *seq.*) to this criticism the question of the interpretation of these events is perhaps a storm in a teacup. It could be argued that Benzi was never Sienese by more than citizenship. His degree was from Pavia, he studied there and at Bologna, taught in Parma and Padua before returning briefly to Siena, and after his Florentine sojourn returned to Padua by 1429, before settling in Ferrara and becoming the personal physician of Niccolò d'Este. G. FIORAVANTI and A. IDATO, introduction to their edition of U. BENZI, *Scriptum de somno et vigilia*, Università degli Studi di Siena; Bibliotheca Studii Senensis, 3 (Florence, 1991), pp. I-II stress the political motivation of the regime's original treatment of Benzi.

[92] NARDI, *Mariano Sozzini*, pp. 28-9, 40-41, 64-6.

[93] Above, p. 176 n. 246.

[94] *Conc.* 423, f. 54v, 18 Aug, ed. NARDI, op. cit., doc. 16, p. 121 (and see p. 41).

only during the non-teaching period of August.[95] Mariano was highly unusual as having reached such a state of eminence with only the briefest of periods of teaching elsewhere;[96] almost all the 'big names' achieve such heights through mobility. Mariano's biographer, Paolo Nardi, was in no doubt that his career was kept in check by this restrictive policy.[97]

Bartolomeo's career – now the subject of a full study by the late Roberta Bargagli – was initially held back by the same distrust. Although his rapid rise through the ranks of Sienese teachers began in 1459 before his graduation, and was sustained for over a decade,[98] the hostility of those who remembered the *Dodici* as opponents of the regime persisted, and may have contributed to his decision to leave for Ferrara in 1472.[99] But if the stigma of *Dodici* affiliation helped bring about Sozzini's departure, thereafter the tables were turned completely. Sozzini's reputation, already exceptional, was now coloured by his abandonment of Ferrara, within a year and in contentious circumstances,[100] to participate as a key figure in the relaunch by Lorenzo de' Medici of the Florentine *Studio* at Pisa. Siena's efforts to get him back, both then and many times subsequently, were destined to failure in the face of Laurentian might; indeed, if anything it was the brilliant lawyer who was the chief beneficiary of these bitter and protracted negotiations.[101] Sozzini is almost emblematic of the fast-track academic superstar of the late fifteenth century, constantly playing on his marketability in a tortuous relationship with Florence that, despite perennial attempts to walk out, and culminating even in a period of imprisonment, left him in their continuous employ for over two decades. But if Sozzini never returned to teaching in Siena, that contrasts with an equally long and intense engagement with Sienese politics. After the political earthquake of 1482 in particular, he played an increasingly central role on the scene, influencing the formulation of policy, negotiating between the Sienese government and Lorenzo and helping to bring about a reconciliation between the two, belonging to the *Balìa*, later taking a leading role in negotiations with the invading French, and on several occasions holding the highest offices of state.[102] Among academics of the time he has the rare distinction of having had a full political career whilst teaching, and the probably unique one of doing so in one town while keeping up a

---

[95] *Conc.* 510, f. 43v, 22 Jun, ed. NARDI, op. cit., doc. 35, p. 134 (and see p. 80). The fear must have been that he would end up accepting a teaching post there.

[96] On his teaching in (and relations with) Ferrara and Florence in the 1430s, see NARDI, op. cit., pp. 32-51.

[97] NARDI, op. cit., pp. 28-9, and cf. BARGAGLI, *Bartolomeo Sozzini*, p. 8.

[98] As a student he was given a two-year contract to teach *Institutiones* on 6 Aug 1459; *Conc.* 557, f. 35v, eds. BAI, doc. 70, p. 104, and BARGAGLI, 'Documenti senesi', doc. 3, p. 276; the following year, presumably on graduation, he moved to a contract for the unusually high starting salary of 35 florins (*Conc.* 563, f. 23v, 13 Aug 1460, ed. BAI, doc. 152, pp. 127-8); in 1463 this rose to 60 fl. (*Conc.* 581, f. 16v, 25 Jul, ed. BARGAGLI, 'Documenti senesi' doc. 7, pp. 278-9), and thereafter steadily to 150 florins (*Conc.* 608, f. 21r, 20 Jan 1468, ed. BAI, doc. 261, pp. 250-1, confirmed on 3 Aug 1470, *Conc.* 623, f. 24v, ed. BAI, doc. 304, pp. 291-4); for full details of his Sienese teaching career see BARGAGLI, *Bartolomeo Sozzini*, pp. 14-17, 30-6, 42-5.

[99] BARGAGLI, *Bartolomeo Sozzini*, esp. pp. 44-5, 55-6.

[100] Op. cit., pp. 52-3, 56-7.

[101] On the three-cornered fight between Ferrara, Florence and Siena over Sozzini in 1473, BARGAGLI, *Bartolomeo Sozzini*, pp. 52-7; she argues that internal divisions within the Sienese regime contributed to its failure to retain him (see also above, p. 152). Negotiations resumed in 1482-5 (op. cit., pp. 92-102), and again in 1489 (pp. 160-2), involving the efforts of Pandolfo Petrucci (cf. SHAW, *L'ascesa al potere*, pp. 43-4). One more attempt was made when Sozzini had transferred to Padua, in 1499 (p. 201).

[102] BARGAGLI, *Bartolomeo Sozzini*, esp. pp. 115-47, 181-5; SHAW, *L'ascesa al potere*, pp. 62-4, 67, 74-5, 79-81; and on his diplomatic career, M. GATTONI DA CAMOGLI, *Pandolfo Petrucci e la politica estera della Repubblica di Siena (1487-1512)* (Siena, 1997), esp. pp. 27, 56, 70, 75.

teaching career in another, under a different jurisdiction. A final irony is that, as a leading university figure not teaching in the Sienese *Studio*, he could be consulted on university matters in a way that his erstwhile colleagues could not.[103]

3. *Social status*

The standing and respect accorded to teachers can be traced through communal documents to a greater extent than might be imagined, because social status was a matter of formal regulation as well as perception. In the thirteenth century, in order to attract foreign teachers, and to offer them protection and compensation for the fact that they would be living away from home and at a disadvantage with respect to citizens,[104] the commune had granted them the standard array of privileges associated with a *studio*; exemption from military and night watch duties, safe-conduct, freedom of movement for books and personal belongings, occasional permission to bear arms, and some fiscal privileges.[105] These were not forgotten in the fifteenth century[106] – the free movement of books, the 'tools of the trade',[107] was particularly valued – but with the transition to a more local and citizen-based professoriate, other more specific exemptions were added. In 1441 doctors were exonerated from the general obligation of citizens to work, along with *cavalieri*, members of the guild of judges and notaries, and students 'che portano cappe et habito scholastico' (this is often referred to as the law against *scioperati*).[108] The measure was coupled with another, the curious and short-lived experiment in social engineering whereby nobody between the ages of thirty and fifty-five was permitted to hold office

---

[103] In 1487, after the coup, his advice was sought on reform of the *Studio*'s organisation (*Balìa* 35, ff. 44v, 25 Sept, and 48v, 5 Oct 1487; cf. BARGAGLI, *Bartolomeo Sozzini*, pp. 145-6). He remained a member of the college of doctors of law, which was a life position, throughout his years of absence, and is found as *promotor* for a number of doctorates over the years at moments when he was back in Siena; op. cit., p. 222.

[104] BOWSKY, 'Medieval Citizenship', esp. p. 223; cf. ZANETTI, 'A l'Université de Pavie', p. 433 n. 1.

[105] These are very similar to the privileges accorded to students, discussed below, pp. 232 *seq.* See also ZDEKAUER, pp. 25-6, *Chartularium*, docs. 10, pp. 9-10, 29 Nov 1252; 13, pp. 10-11 (1262); 61, pp. 41-3 (1286); 96, pp. 71-4 (1300-2); 97, pp. 74-7 (1300-2); 125, pp. 103-6 (1309-10); 329, p. 400, 29 Jan 1333(=1334); *Conc.* 139, f. 62r, 27 Oct 1387, and NARDI, *Insegnamento*, pp. 85 and 236-8. In Bologna the exemption from military service was granted to the whole 'education sector' and to clergy and 'conversi sine tonsura'; R. GRECI, 'Professioni e "crisi" bassomedievali: Bologna tra Due e Quattrocento', in *Disuguaglianze: stratificazione e mobilità sociale nelle popolazioni italiane dal secolo 14. agli inizi del secolo 20.: relazioni e comunicazioni presentati da autori italiani al 2. Congré 'Hispano Luso Italià' de demografia hitòrica: Savona, 18-21 novembre 1992* (Bologna, 1997), pp. 707-29 (p. 724).

[106] *Conc.* 406, f. 16r-v, 24 Sept 1433; and *Conc.* 2141, no. 25, 1 Oct 1409 (Giovanni da Spoleto, teacher of grammar and rhetoric, has been taxed unfairly and wants to be exempt from the *lira* like other doctors). There is an example of these privileges being extended in 1435, when Baldassare Vettori was exceptionally permitted to sell and remove from Sienese territory one hundred pigs (*Conc.* 418, f. 14v, 27 Sept 1435).

[107] VERGER, *Men of Learning*, pp. 69-70.

[108] *Conc.* 453, ff. 29v-30r, 10 Aug; *Statuti* 44, ff. 21v-22r, 11 Aug. The *Statuti* 44 version has 'habito ecclesiastico', which led. C. FALLETTI-FOSSATI, *Costumi senesi nella seconda metà del secolo XIV* (Siena, 1881, repr. Bologna, 1980), p. 48 to see this as applying to 'gli Studenti e gli Ecclesiastici'. A similar measure in 1425 (*Statuti* 41, f. 71r, the 'statuta bernardiniana'), had exempted only students (ASCHERI, *Siena nel Rinascimento*, p. 50 n. 81). The requirement was repeated in 1481, when the exempted categories were 'Cavalieri, Dottori, e Notai, e studenti che attualmente vadino alle pubbliche scuole, e chi passasse l'età d'anni 60'; *Balìa* 24, ff. 93v-94r, 7 Jul, partial edn. in SHAW, 'Politics and Institutional Innovation', in *BSSP*, 103 (1996), p. 35. This has been quoted by PECCI, *Memorie storico-critiche della città di Siena*, p. 19n, and following him B. AQUARONE, *Gli ultimi anni della storia repubblicana di Siena (1551-1555)* (Siena, 1869), p. 47 and ASCHERI, *Siena nel Rinascimento*, loc. cit., as a measure of 1482.

(other than membership of the *Consiglio del Popolo*) 'se non a donna o veramente sposa' or was a widower or father of a legitimate child. Doctors were the only 'social' category to be exempted from this.[109]

The bracketing of doctors with *cavalieri* in the 1441 law against *scioperati* is no accident. In the late middle ages these two groups are increasingly seen as close in terms of social status, a closeness which is explicitly argued in the legal literature.[110] In Siena, as elsewhere, this is best illuminated by following the legislation, especially (though not only) sumptuary legislation, in the promulgation of which Siena was one of the most prolific of Italian cities.[111] As elsewhere, by far the most common groups to be ex-

---

[109] As n. 108. The experiment was quietly abandoned in January 1443 (*Conc.* 462, f. 25r, 25 Jan). ASCHERI, *Siena nella storia*, p. 90. An attempt to encourage citizens between the ages of twenty-eight and fifty to marry had been made in 1405, though doctors were not exempted at that stage. It was abandoned the following year as excessive. F. DONATI, 'Provvisioni della Repubblica sopra i matrimoni', *Miscellanea Storica Senese*, I (1893), pp. 167-8.

[110] DI NOTO MARRELLA, *Doctores*, and P. GILLI, *La Noblesse du droit. Débats et controverses sur la culture juridique et le rôle des juristes dans l'Italie médiévale (XIIᵉ-XVᵉ siècles)*. Études d'histoire médiévale, 7 (Paris, 2003) are both, in their different ways, fundamental and exhaustive; BAUMGÄRTNER, '"De privilegiis doctorum"' is wide-ranging. See also A. VISCONTI, 'De nobilitate doctorum legentium in studiis generalibus', in *Studi di storia e diritto in onore di Enrico Besta per il 40. anno del suo insegnamento* (Milan, 1939), III, pp. 219-41; G. BORELLI, '"Doctor an miles": aspetti della ideologia nobiliare nell'opera del giurista Cristoforo Lanfranchini', *Nuova Rivista Storica*, 73 (1989), pp. 151-68; A. DE BENEDICTIS, 'Retorica e politica: dall'*Orator* di Beroaldo all'ambasciatore bolognese nel rapporto tra *republica* cittadina e governo pontificio', in *Sapere e/è potere*, III, pp. 411-38 (p. 415); S. GASPARRI, *I 'milites' cittadini. Studi sulla cavalleria in Italia*. Istituto Storico Italiano per il Medioevo. Nuovi Studi Storici, 19 (Rome, 1972), esp. p. 67; H. DE RIDDER-SYMOENS, 'Rich Men, Poor Men: Social Stratification and Social Representation at the University (13ᵗʰ-16ᵗʰ Centuries)', in *Showing Status: Representations of Social Positions in the Late Middle Ages*, eds. W. Blockmans and A. Janse. Medieval Texts and Cultures of Northern Europe, 2 (Turnhout, 1999), pp. 159-75 (esp. p. 169); J. LE GOFF, 'Alle origini del lavoro intellettuale in Italia. I problemi del rapporto fra la letteratura, l'università e le professioni', in *Letteratura italiana*, I. *Il letterato e le istituzioni* (Einaudi, Turin, 1982), pp. 649-79 (pp. 668-9, 675 on the process of separation of intellectuals from manual workers that underpinned this parallel); BRAMBILLA, 'Genealogie del sapere' (esp. p. 127 on the innate parallels between the investiture of doctors and that of the nobility). On the theme of lawyers writing on nobility, D. DONATI, *L'idea di nobiltà in Italia. Secoli XIV-XVIII* (Rome, 1988), ch. 1, pp. 3-28 (and pp. 52-62, 81-3 on the concepts in Siena).

[111] C. KOVESI KILLERBY, *Sumptuary Law in Italy 1200-1500* (Oxford, 2002), surveying Italian sumptuary legislation from origins to 1500, puts Siena in equal third position along with Bologna and after Florence and Venice (pp. 27-30, 34). On Italian sumptuary legislation see above all the many works of M. G. MUZZARELLI; general survey in her 'Le leggi suntuarie', in *Storia d'Italia, Annali 19: La moda*, eds. C. M. Belfanti and F. Giusberti (Turin, 2003), pp. 185-220; EADEM (ed.), *La legislazione suntuaria secoli XIII-XVI. Emilia-Romagna*. Pubblicazioni degli Archivi di Stato, Fonti 41 (Rome, 2002); EADEM, *Gli inganni delle apparenze. Disciplina di vesti e ornamenti alla fine del Medioevo* (Turin, 1996) (pp. 106-111 on Siena); EADEM, 'Prestigio, vesti e "discernenza di persone"', in *I giochi di prestigio. Modelli e pratiche della distinzione sociale*, ed. M. Bianchini; Special issue of *Cheiron: materiali e strumenti di aggiornamento storiografico*, 31-32 (1999), pp. 171-86; EADEM, 'La disciplina delle apparenze. Vestiti e ornamenti nella legislazione suntuaria bolognese fra XIII e XV secolo', in *Disciplina dell'anima, disciplina del corpo, disciplina della società tra medioevo ed età moderna*, ed. P. Prodi (Bologna, 1994), pp. 757-84; also EADEM, '"Contra mundanas vanitates et pompas": aspetti della lotta contro i lussi nell'Italia del XV secolo', *Rivista di Storia della Chiesa in Italia*, 40 (1986), pp. 371-90. On sumptuary legislation in Siena see especially M. A. CEPPARI RIDOLFI and P. TURRINI, *Il mulino delle vanità. Lusso e cerimonie nella Siena medievale* (Siena, 1993), and on the legislation relating to funerals, P. TURRINI, 'Le cerimonie funebri a Siena nel basso Medio evo: norme e rituale', *BSSP*, 110 (2003), pp. 53-102 (esp. pp. 67-84); older works are C. BONELLI-GANDOLFO, 'La legislazione suntuaria senese negli ultimi centocinquant'anni della Repubblica', *Studi senesi*, 35 (1919), pp. 243-75, 334-98; E. CASANOVA, 'La donna senese del Quattrocento nella vita privata', *BSSP*, 8:1 (1900), pp. 3-93; A. LISINI, 'Le leggi prammatiche durante il governo dei Nove, 1287-1355', *BSSP*, 37 (1930), pp. 41-70; and C. MAZZI, 'Alcune leggi suntuarie senesi del secolo XIII', *Archivio Storico Italiano*, ser. 4, 5 (1880), pp. 133-44, and on the legislation as relating to doctors/teachers, also BOWSKY, *A Medieval Italian Commune*, esp. pp. 67-72. On doctors and sumptuary law see esp. O. CAVALLAR and J. KIRSHNER, '"Licentia navigandi... prosperis ventibus aflantibus". L'esenzione dei "doctores" e delle loro mogli da norme suntuarie', in *A Ennio Cortese*, I, pp. 204-27; on academic dress as professional identifier, in the context of others, I. TURNAU, *European Occupational Dress* (Warsaw, 1994), ch. 5; and on the iconography of academic dress, A. VON HÜLSEN-ESCH, 'Kleider machen Leute. Zur Gruppenrepräsentation von Gelehrten im Spätmittelalter', in *Die*

empt from sumptuary regulations were knights and doctors.[112] In Siena we can in fact see the impact of the arrival of the university. The thirteenth and fourteenth century Sienese legislation often exempts 'judges, medical doctors, and doctors in any faculty' from the restrictions imposed on the rest of the population. In the first systematic formulation of these laws in 1330s, only these (and their wives) could wear clothing made of the finer materials, embroidered shoes, bejewelled belts and silver buttons, and could have substantially more spent on their funerals.[113] Scholars are agreed that the motivation for these exemptions, here as elsewhere, was the desire to recognise and retain the comparatively few individuals within these categories,[114] and since foreigners were generally exempt from all such restrictions this meant the retention and rewarding of home-grown experts by placing them on a par with their non-citizen counterparts.

With the consolidation of the university comes an interesting change of terminology. By the fifteenth century these categories have been replaced; usually no specific mention is made of judges or medics, just doctors alongside *cavalieri*.[115] This may reflect the fact that judges certainly had to have degrees by this stage (though the same cannot be said of all categories of medical practitioner). It seems also to have reflected a consolidation of the status of graduate, as a definition replacing the previous range of exempted categories. But we also see attempts at more complex social ranking, as elsewhere (though not to the same extent as in Bologna or, in an even more sophisticated measure, in Savoy).[116] If doctors and *cavalieri* were set apart, their equivalence was still disputed; they might share certain exemptions, but in other cases the order of precedence between them is clearly stated, and in

Repräsentation der Gruppen. Text – Bilder – Objekte, ed. O. G. Oexle (Göttingen, 1998), pp. 225-57. Finally for a more general overview of the issues surrounding sumptuary legislation see A. HUNT, *Governance of the Consuming Passions* (Basingstoke, 1996).

[112] KOVESI KILLERBY, *Sumptuary Law*, pp. 84-9, with a statistical exercise which, whatever the problems it raises, amply bears this out. She finds forty-six exemptions for knights, thirty for doctors of medicine, and twenty-three for doctors of civil and canon law; the majority of other exemptions are for categories which are variants of these.

[113] CEPPARI RIDOLFI and TURRINI, *Il mulino delle vanità*, esp. pp. 64-98, and rubrics VII, IX, XI, XX, XXI, XXII and XXXIX. BONELLI-GANDOLFO, 'La legislazione suntuaria senese', p. 360 points out that wives of *dottori* and *cavalieri* had privileges not given even to wives of 'magistrati supremi'; quoted in CAVALLAR and KIRSHNER, '"Licentia navigandi"', p. 216. In Bologna, according to the 1288 statutes, teachers of civil law shared with the nobility the right to be buried in scarlet; the significance of this is emphasised by CORTESE, 'Legisti, canonisti e feudisti', pp. 227-8.

[114] M. ASCHERI, 'Tra vanità e potere: donne, lusso e miti (di ieri e di oggi)', in CEPPARI RIDOLFI and TURRINI, *Il mulino delle vanità*, pp. IX-XX (p. XVI); IDEM, *Siena nella Storia*, pp. 94-6, and IDEM, *Siena nel Rinascimento*, pp. 50-1; BOWSKY, loc. cit.; MUZZARELLI, 'Le leggi suntuarie', pp. 193-4.

[115] For example, in 1405 a limit on what could be spent on embassies was declared not to apply to doctors or *cavalieri* (*Statuti* 38, f. 37v; cf. ASCHERI, *Siena nel Rinascimento*, p. 69); a measure of 1412 exempts 'donne de' chavalieri et doctori come nele provisioni vecchie si contiene' (MAZZI, 'Alcune leggi', p. 143, and cf. CAVALLAR and KIRSHNER, '"Licentia navigandi"', p. 216); in 1434 the limitations on the size of banquet that could be held were removed 'pro militibus doctoribus et comitibus' (*Conc.* 408, f. 9r, 16 Jan). But measures of 1411 to contain and control behaviour in the face of plague exempted knights, *giudici*, *medici* and communal officials; CG 205, f. 27v, 12 Jul, ed. L. BANCHI, 'Provvisioni della Repubblica di Siena contro la peste degli anni 1411 e 1463', *Archivio Storico Italiano*, ser, 4, 14 (1884), pp. 325-32 (pp. 327-9), and cf. R. MUCCIARELLI, 'Igiene, salute e pubblico decoro nel Medioevo', in R. MUCCIARELLI, L. VIGNI and D. FABBRI, *Vergognosa immunditia. Igiene pubblica e privata a Siena dal medioevo all'età contemporanea* (Siena, 2000), pp. 13-84 (p. 75).

[116] MUZZARELLI, 'Prestigio', p. 180; N. BULST, 'La législation somptuaire d'Amédée VIII', in *Amédée VIII – Felix V premier duc de Savoie et pape (1385-1451. Colloque international, Ripaille-Lausanne, 23-26 octobre 1990*, eds. B. Andenmatten and A. Paravicini Bagliani (Lausanne, 1992), pp. 191-200. More comparable is the situation in Arezzo; L. BERTI, 'I capitoli "De vestibus mulierum" del 1460, ovvero "status" personale e distinzioni sociali nell'Arezzo di metà Quattrocento', in *Studi in onore di A. D'Addario*, IV, pp. 1171-214 (esp. pp. 1176, 1181, 1183-5).

the fifteenth century it is common to find a three-fold distinction of status in Siena.[117] In 1442, when it was decided how many men ambassadors might have as escort, *cavalieri* were allowed six, *dottori* five, others four.[118] Yet in a measure of 1471, doctors and *cavalieri* were exempted from the veto on wearing velvet,[119] and the same bracketing is found again in 1526, when *cavalieri* and *dottori* were permitted to wear gold chains and other luxury articles.[120] Other trends were also at work. The 1471 measure also gives exemptions just for *cavalieri* and those *allirati* over 3,000 *lire*, a new criterion for sumptuary distinctions,[121] while in 1525 the line drawn was purely between those who were of *riseduti* families and those who were not.[122]

A few doctors were actually knighted, Pietro de' Pecci being an early fifteenth-century example;[123] and the various tombstones to Sienese doctors[124] and the accounts of funeral ceremonies and orations which survive also testify to the esteem in which many were held.[125] The commune itself insisted that these doctors were seen to be important and active members of the community. For the ceremonial honouring of the pope in 1443 doctors were instructed to turn up 'in habitu solenni';[126] in 1444 they likewise played a prominent part in the mourning ceremony for the future Saint Bernardino.[127] In 1456, for the ceremony in honour of the newly created saint, in a measure which suggests a different

---

[117] Notaries had to list members of commissions in social order – *domini* first (*cavalieri, giudici,* doctors of law), *magistri* (doctor of medicine) and then those without titles; ISAACS, 'Popoli e monti', p. 67. Again, grammarians and others teaching less important subjects were accorded altogether humbler status.

[118] *CG* 221, f. 88v, 22 Mar 1442; *Statuti* 41, f. 194v, 26 Mar 1442 (see ASCHERI, *Siena nel Rinascimento*, p. 50 n. 81. For the closeness in social status of *doctores* and *milites*, P. J. JONES, *Economia e Società nell' Italia medievale* (Turin, 1980), pp. 73-4, and A. VON WRETSCHKO, *Die Verleihung gelehrter Grade durch den Kaiser seit Karl IV* (Weimar, 1910), p. 1.

[119] *Conc.* 2185, no foliation (filza for 1471); excerpts in BONELLI-GANDOLFO, 'La legislazione suntuaria', p. 260 n. 1. See also ASCHERI, *Siena nel Rinascimento*, p. 52 n. 83.

[120] ISAACS, 'Popoli e monti', p. 67.

[121] ASCHERI, op. cit., pp. 51-4. This is perhaps no more than a logical extension of the principle of *marcatura* – that people could buy exemption by paying a fine – that Siena had had since the fourteenth century.

[122] BONELLI - GANDOLFO, 'La legislazione suntuaria senese', p. 395.

[123] The ceremony at Pecci's knighthood cost 600 *lire* (*Conc.* 406, f. 48v, 27 Oct 1433). In the late fourteenth century Niccolo Aringhieri di Casole's sons were given the title of *conte* for his services to jurisprudence. C. CHŁEDOWSKI, *Siena* (Berlin, 1913), II, p. 138 *seq.* The medical doctor Lodovico da Spoleto was knighted (*Bicch.* 335, ff. 58v and 68r, 1481), as was the humanist Niccolò di Bartolomo Borghesi (f. 66r). Bartolus had argued that after having been a doctor for twenty years, one would automatically rise to the rank of count; O. CAVALLAR, S. DEGENRING and J. KIRSHNER, *A Grammar of Signs: Bartolo da Sassoferrato's "Tract on Insignia and Coats of Arms"*. Studies in Comparative Legal History (Berkeley, 1994), pp. 43-4. On the value of knighthood in fifteenth-century Siena, ASCHERI, op. cit. pp. 49-50, and 52 n. 83 for specific examples. Possession of a doctorate could still enhance knighthood. The rector of the hospital of the Scala was always to be a knight, or to receive a knighthood on taking office (ISAACS, 'Popolo e monti', p. 67); in 1427 his salary was fixed at 800 florins, to be raised to 850 if he also had a doctorate (*Scala*, 5934, no. 287).

[124] The best known of these are those of the fourteenth-century lawyers Niccolò Aringhieri and Guglielmo da Ciliano (Figs. 1a and 1b above, pp. 39-40), discussed in BARTALINI, 'Goro di Gregorio', pp. 120-38, and in M. PIERINI, *L'arca di San Cerbone* (Massa Marittima, 1995), pp. 21-2; cf. the summary by M. FOLCHI in *L'Università di Siena. 750 anni*, pp. 334-6.

[125] Cf. ZDEKAUER, p. 29. Agostino Dati's orations in memory of eminent teachers in the Sienese *Studio* are in his *Opera* (and see above, p. 111 n. 23). *Cronaca senese di Tommaso Fecini (1431-1479)*, in *Rerum Italicarum Scriptores²*, vol. XV, pt. VI (Bologna, 1939), p. 855, records for 1434: 'A dì 15 di giennaio morì maestro Mariano di ser Jacomo Manni, dottore in medicina, fu onorato di cataletto e portato da quattro istudianti tutti frati e preti e onoranza di cittadini e cera, e fu sotterrato in Duomo'. For comparisons see TURRINI, 'Le cerimonie funebri', esp. pp. 84-91.

[126] *Conc.* 462, f. 67r, 1 Jan.

[127] 'Venire debeant omnes milites doctores et graduati...similiter veniat universitas studii Civitatis sen.' (*Conc.* 470, f. 53v, 10 Jun).

classification from the social one mentioned above (it makes no reference to knights), civic officials had to donate eight *doppieri* or double-branched candlesticks and forty candles each, the rector and doctors of the *Studio* six *doppieri* each, and advisers of judges, notaries, the prior of the council of the *arte della lana* four to six each, depending on their rank.[128] These few accounts confirm the importance of doctors both in the integrative and in the socially distinctive aspects of communal ritual.[129] Visibility was important, but not exclusively about status; the commune's great insistence on the lecturers' duty to hold public disputations in the evenings in places as prominent as the Piazza del Campo[130] smacks of a determination to be seen to be getting their money's worth by demonstrating the activity of the *Studio*, at least as much as of serious academic aspirations.

[128] *Statuti* 39, ff. 76r-78r, 19 May, ed. F. NEVOLA, 'Cerimoniali per santi e feste a Siena', doc. 1, pp. 177-9; cf. M. BERTAGNA, 'Memorie Bernardiniane, I. Glorificazione senese di S. Bernardino', *BSSP*, 71 (1964), pp. 5-50 (pp. 37-8); also referred to in NARDI, 'Appunti sui maestri', p. 216 n. 55. Doctors are also found at public ceremonial events such as the funeral of the rector of the hospital of S. Maria della Scala (*Scala* 25, f. 49r, 3 Nov 1497; 'molti dottori'). A Dominican, 'Bartolomeo siculo', who was teaching at the *Studio* (*Balìa* 41, f. 3v, 1 Sept 1496) gave the funeral oration. On the other hand only one of the various contemporary accounts we have of the ceremonial for the visit of the emperor Frederick III and Eleonora of Portugal in 1452 mentions any specific role for doctors or for the *Studio*, and that, by Mariano Dati, suggests a relatively low-key presence. P. PARDUCCI, 'L'incontro di Federigo III imperatore con Eleonora di Portogallo', *BSSP*, 13 (1906), pp. 297-379 (pp. 351, 353, 354, 363); 14 (1907), pp. 35-96 (p. 87); general survey in F. J. D. NEVOLA, '"*Lieto e trionphante per la città*": Experiencing a Mid-Fifteenth-Century Imperial Triumph along Siena's *Strada Romana*', *Renaissance Studies*, 17:4 (2003), pp. 581-606.

[129] F. RICCIARELLI, 'Propaganda politica e rituali urbani nella Arezzo del tardo Medioevo', *Archivio storico italiano*, 162 (2004), pp. 233-58 (esp. pp. 240, 246 *seq.*). An oblique illustration of this is Tommaso Fecini's description of the masque during the celebrations for St. Catherine on 5 Jun 1444: 'Era in sul palco e' festaiuoli vestiti come inperadori, re, duchi, marchesi, cavalieri, signori e come dottori in legie, civigli e canonici, e in medicina come istrolagi, filosafi, musici, postici e in tutte le scienze.' *Cronaca senese di Tommaso Fecini* (as n. 125), p. 857. On the importance of ceremonial in Siena see, as well as the works of Nevola referred to above, PERTICI, *La città magnificata*, pp. 21-22.

[130] Above, pp. 144-5.

PART THREE
THE STUDENTS

I

THE STUDENT POPULATION

1. *Introduction*

If the main criterion of the success of a university was the ability to hire and retain teachers of sufficient merit, scarcely less important was the capacity to attract foreign students.[1] The former was a *sine qua non* for the latter, but other factors too could influence the decision of students as to where to study. The students themselves sometimes state what made them come to Siena, though as these declarations are usually found in petitions for favours or places in the Casa della Sapienza they must be treated with some scepticism.[2] Perhaps more relevant is the commune's own assessment of the reasons why students might or did choose Siena. A deliberation of 1450 declared that scholars came for peace, 'abundantia', 'sanità d'aere' and 'maxime per la vicinità de la Corte Romana'.[3] In exploring the issue of 'recruitment' (an inadequate modern equivalent), we need to look again at legislation (the attempts made by the commune to offer an attractive environment), at the individual cases which highlight the relations with other *studi*, and (to the much more limited extent possible) at the information which the records yield about the profile of the student population.

2. *The status of foreign students*

From the earliest times, Sienese legislation in favour of the students accompanied that relating to the *condotte* and to internal organisation, seeking to make conditions for the students as secure and attractive as possible. What Hyde called 'a *modus vivendi* whereby the students were given the privileges but

---

[1] 'Quanto ornamento sia havere una copia di scolari forestieri'; petition to hire Bartolommeo Sozzini, *CG* 239, ff. 192r-v, 4 Apr 1484; also *Conc.* 2139, no. 74, ff. 138r, 139v, ed. BARGAGLI, 'Documenti senesi', doc. 65, pp. 308-9.

[2] E.g. 'Nicholo di Lonenborche', applying for a place in the Casa della Sapienza on 12 Feb 1467, explains 'avendo lui inteso per insino nella città dove lui a studiato della gloriosa et laudabile fama della città vostro et dello studio vostro et delli famosissimi doctori legenti in esso studio'; *CG* 231, f. 267r-v (and *Conc.* 2138, no. 100, ff. 163r and 164v). The same year Martino di Pietro cited Siena's reputation in his native Portugal as his reason for choosing it 'per sua patria litteraria'; *CG* 232, f. 23v, 22 Oct (also *Conc.* 2138, no. 107, f. 176r). See above, p. 66.

[3] *CG* 224, f. 318r, 16 Feb, ed. GAROSI, doc. 62, pp. 530-1. Such statements are of course part of the rhetoric of petitions and deliberations, and cannot all be taken at face value. Cf. above, pp. 65-8.

not the burdens of citizenship'[4] is traceable through this legislation – both in the formal declarations that are repeated at key moments of re-opening or reform,[5] and in the more regular measures. As elsewhere, however, this approach leaves rather less defined the position of citizens who became students. We look at the student population through the optic of foreign students because that is precisely what the authorities of the time were doing. Only by the end of the fifteenth century (and especially in the early sixteenth century) do the voices and interests of Sienese students become more evident.

The most immediate requirement in support of the invitation sent out for students to come to Siena was a guarantee of rights, something which, though implicit in civil law since Frederick Barbarossa's Authentic *Habita* of 1155 in favour of students at a *studium generale*, had to be enshrined in local law as well. Foreigners were at the disadvantage of not having the same redress as citizens, and were in particular subject to the risk of *rappresaglia* or reprisal, the mechanism whereby redress for offences or debts could be exacted against fellow-citizens of a foreign offender or debtor.[6] It was therefore necessary to compensate for this if foreign students were to be persuaded to come in significant numbers. The safety of students was guaranteed in 1262, and this was repeated in 1274, in the 1286 statutes and in the various redactions of them thereafter.[7] They were considered to have rights equivalent to those of *cives assidui*, i.e. the punishment for an offence against them was equal to that for an offence committed against Sienese citizens.[8] In fact in 1321, for the brief period of the Bolognese migration, the punishment for offences against teachers or students in law or medicine was increased to double that of an offence against citizens.[9] That the effect of *rappresaglie* on students was far from abstract is demonstrated by a petition of 19 February 1339 to the *Consiglio Generale*. In view of the fact that

> nonnulli de civitate Senarum, pretextu represalliarum concessarum eisdem per comune Senense contra aliquas comunitates vel singulares homines ipsius comunitatis, nituntur et conantur atque intendunt reprehendere et capere in avere et personas scolares qui sunt de dictis comunitatibus

a re-statement of the students' privileges was called for and approved.[10] When this measure was incorporated into the city's statutes (the so-called 'Statuto del Buon Governo' of 1337-9), a 500-*lira* fine was stipulated in addition to compensation for the offended student.[11] Various repetitions of this

---

[4] J. K. HYDE, 'Universities and Cities in Medieval Italy', in *The University and the City: From Medieval Origins to the Present*, ed. T. Bender (New York, 1988), pp. 13-21 (p. 19).

[5] E.g. 1357 (above, pp. 42-3) and 1408, when Gregory XII confirmed to teachers and students 'tucti et ciaschedunj privilegij et indulgentie a' doctori e scolary a Bologna et Parigi studianti per la Sedia apostolica conceduti', including an exemption from the obligation to reside in benefices; BARDUZZI, *Documenti*, pp. 32-3 (and p. 55 above).

[6] On reprisals in Siena, BOWSKY, *A Medieval Italian Commune*, pp. 232-46; IDEM, 'Medieval Citizenship', p. 236; ASCHERI, *Siena nella storia*, pp. 104-6 (a late fourteenth-century instance).

[7] *Chartularium*, doc. 14, p. 12 (1262): 'quicumque venerit ad civitatem Senarum causa studendi, debeat custodiri in avere et persona et ipse et nuntii eius et a nemine offendi...'; cf. doc. 21, pp. 13-15 (1274) (p. 15) (and see NARDI, 'Comune, Impero e Papato', p. 88); for the 1286 statutes and subsequent redactions see above, p. 35 n. 35. The measure reappears in the 1309-10 vernacular statutes (Dist. IV, 14; ELSHEIKH, *Il costituto*, vol. 3, p. 168); it is also restated in the so-called 'Statuto del Buon Governo' of 1337-9, dist. 1, rubr. 359, ed. NARDI, *Insegnamento*, appendix, doc. 12, pp. 236-8 (p. 236), and was copied into the statute of the *Mercanzia* of 1342-3; Q. SENIGAGLIA, 'Lo statuto dell'Arte della Mercanzia senese (1342-1343)', *BSSP*, 16:1 (1909), pp. 211-71, and 16:2, pp. 67-290 (p. 228 of 16:2). A brief overview of the privileges of students in Siena is G. CATONI, 'I privilegi degli scolari nella Siena medievale e moderna', in *Il diritto a studiare*, pp. 9-18.

[8] 1309-10 statutes, Dist. IV, 84, ed. ELSHEIKH, vol. 3, p. 201; cf. TRAPANI, 'Statuti senesi'.

[9] *Chartularium*, docs. 153, pp. 139-43, and 154, pp. 143-6, both 11 May 1321; cf. NARDI, *Insegnamento*, p. 117.

[10] *Chartularium*, doc. 359, pp. 453-6, 19 Feb 1338(=1339) (p. 454).

[11] Published in NARDI, *Insegnamento*, appendix, doc. 12, pp. 236-8 (and cf. p. 198).

guarantee were found to be necessary, and in fact they frequently accompany invitations to the *Studio*, as well as being found on separate occasions.[12] The measure also had a localised variant; in 1396 it was agreed that scholars from the *contado* might come to Siena without having to be obliged for the debts of their commune.[13]

Students were a special category of the population. In the measures drawn up in 1425 (it is usually assumed at the instigation of San Bernardino), students and others engaged in study were the only able-bodied adult males to be excused from the duty to work;[14] and in 1555 even the emergency measures taken to expel all 'bocche inutili' from the city exempted the students, arranging safe-conducts for those who wished them, but not enforcing their departure.[15] Another mark of their special position was their exemption from most military and civic duties, and from most forms of direct taxation. Throughout the period there are repetitions, in various forms, of Innocent IV's exemption of the students 'a quibuslibet serviciis, talliis, et collectis ac omnibus et singulis angariis personalibus et realibus civitati Senarum',[16] though a significant exception was made of the *gabella* in 1404.[17]

It has been seen that in 1321 the commune offered to pay all travelling expenses of students coming to Siena (and that in that year it paid handsomely). Considerable subsidies were also made towards the accommodation of these students, mainly in the form of payments to masters who provided lodgings for their scholars.[18] The generosity of this campaign was of course not sustained, though there are subsequent measures supporting students in their problems with accommodation.[19] It is clear

---

[12] E.g. *CG* 169, f. 38r, 23 Aug 1362; *Statuti* 47, f. 105r, 3 Feb 1402 (addition in margin); *Balìa* 24, f. 90r, 30 Jun 1481, eds. PUCCINOTTI, *Storia della Medicina*, p. CLXVI-VII, and ILARDI, 'Ordinamenti', p. 169; copy in *Mis.* 1, f. 108v. This continued to be a real issue. In 1474 the state of reprisal declared against Perugia (*Conc.* 346, ff. 34r-36v, 13? Jun) specifically exempted students ('et nominatamente non si possi sine alcuna novità per cagione di dette represaglie contra scolari come di ragione comune et sicondo la dispositione delli statuti dela città di Siena'; f. 36r-v); and see the *Balìa*'s decision of 1492 to put a Genoese student in the Sapienza 'non obstantibus represalii contra Januenses' (*Balìa* 37, f. 15r, 23 Jun).

[13] *CG* 198, f. 31r, 22 Oct 1396.

[14] The exemption applies to 'alcuno studiante o in alcuna arte di Studio se exercitante'; CG 210, f. 201r, 8 Jun 1425 (also *Statuti* 47, f. 71r). See ZDEKAUER, p. 44, and A. CASTELLINI, 'Provvedimenti demografici dell'Antico Stato Senese', *BSSP*, n.s. 12 (1941), pp. 157-72 (161-62), and esp. ASCHERI, *Siena nel Rinascimento*, p. 50 n. 81 (also IDEM, 'Introduzione: Lo Statuto del Comune di Siena del 1337-1339', introduction to D. CIAMPOLI, *Il Capitano del popolo a Siena nel primo Trecento. Documenti di Storia*, 1 [Siena, 1984], pp. 7-21; p. 14 n. 28 on why the label 'Bernardinian statutes' is an exaggeration). The measure is repeated on various occasions, with the exemption including counts, knights, doctors and 'studianti che portano cappe o habito scholasticho'; *Conc.* 453, ff. 29v-30r, 10 Aug 1441 (30r); also *Statuti* 44, ff. 21v-22r ('habito ecclesiastico'; see above, p. 223); repeated on 13 Jul 1451, *Statuti* 40, ff. 26v-27r (and see FALLETTI-FOSSATI, *Costumi senesi*, p. 48), and on 7 Jul 1481 (above, p. 223 n. 108).

[15] See PRUNAI, III, p. 81, and CATONI, 'Le riforme del Granduca', p. 45.

[16] *Chartularium*, doc. 10, pp. 9-10, 29 Nov 1252. Cf. DAVIDSOHN, 'Documenti', pp. 169-70, and RASHDALL, II, p. 32. Tax exemptions, especially on books and wine, were confirmed in 1416; *Conc.* 303, f. 74v, 1 Aug; CATONI, 'Genesi', pp. 174-5.

[17] *CG* 201, f. 166r, 21 Nov 1404; *Mis.* 1, ff. 50v-51r. They had been exempted from the *gabella* on their personal possessions and clothes in 1387 (*Conc.* 139, f. 62r, 27 Oct, ed. ZDEKAUER, p. 26 n. 2). On the increasing importance of *gabelle* in Siena, BOWSKY, *Finance*, ch. VI. The non-exemption of students from this omnipresent tax must have gone some way to reducing the discrepancy between them and the Sienese citizens.

[18] Above, pp. 37-8. As late as 1474 the *Savi* were told to consider the availability of lodgings for students who come to Siena (*Conc.* 648, f. 23r, 10 Oct).

[19] An example is the communal subvention of 35 florins for a school and for accommodation of its students (*Conc.* 139, f. 50r, 16 Oct 1387). In 1423 the *Concistoro* decided 'quod [ipsi] sapientes Studii provideant et providere possint scolaribus presentibus et venturis ad Studium Senense de domis et stantiis opportunis, non accipiendo ecclesias nec domos ecclesie, cum competenti pensione et condecenti pretio' (*Conc.* 345, f. 8r, 10 Jul, and see CATONI, 'Genesi', p. 175 n. 86). In 1428 the *Savi* were empowered to ensure that students found accommodation 'pro iuxta pensione' (*Conc.* 375, f. 10r, 10 Sept), and an example of further measures is the deliberation of the *Savi* that, with the approval of the cardinal of Siena, clerics as

that the exemption from customs duty in respect of scholars' personal possessions, and in particular for books for their own personal use, as found in other Italian universities,[20] continued to be implemented.[21] Another privilege related to those with clerical status. The traditional right of clerics who were students to be absent from their livings – enshrined in canon law with Honorius III's bull *Super Speculam* (1219), but by no means an automatic feature of emergent *studi*[22] – was given to Siena in one of the bulls of Gregory XII in 1408 and confirmed in 1459 by Pius II.[23] The communal records that have been the focus of this investigation give little indication of how significant this privilege was for Siena, though it was not unknown for the commune to support students in the quest for a benefice.[24]

All these are 'standard' measures, defended in the legal tradition,[25] and it could be argued that, in announcing and repeating them, Siena was presenting its credentials and ensuring that students knew that they would have the same rights there as elsewhere. A student privilege with a long pedigree but changing fortunes was the right to bear arms in some circumstances. Traditionally towns hosting universities were extremely reluctant to concede any such rights to students. The main exception to this was the rectors, for whom the privilege was recognised but hedged with qualifications.[26] As far as the rest of the student population was concerned, the normal practice was that students could obtain the same permits to carry arms as citizens in cases where they feared for their safety.[27] Yet in Siena something more emerged, and may even have been enshrined in earlier laws which are now missing. In 1445 the authorities clamped down on the scandalous situation whereby 'per ciascuno di qualunche condictione si sia si porti l'armi contra la forma delli statuti', and explicitly denied students the possibility of seeking exemption from the ban.[28] In another clampdown, in 1469, it is clear that among those whose

well as citizens could put up scholars (*Balìa* 24, f. 90r, 30 Jun 1481, eds. PUCCINOTTI, *Storia della Medicina*, p. CLXVII, and ILARDI, 'Ordinamenti', p. 169; copy in *Mis.* 1, f. 109r). It is, however, surprising not to find more legislation on what elsewhere was a sensitive and often prominent issue. Cf. ERMINI, *Storia*, I, pp. 422-5, and BELLOMO, *Saggio sull'Università*, pp. 38-40, 96-101. See also below, pp. 280-1.

[20] L. GARGAN, 'Le note "conduxit". Libri di maestri e studenti nelle Università italiane del Tre e Quattrocento', in *Manuels, programmes de cours et techniques d'enseignement dans les universités médiévales*. Actes du Colloque international de Louvain-la-Neuve (9-11 septembre 1993), ed. J. Hamesse. Université Catholique de Louvain, Publications de l'Institut d'É-tudes Médiévales, Textes, Études, Congrès, 16 (Louvain-la-Neuve, 1994), pp. 385-401; IDEM, 'L'enigmatico "conduxit". Libri e dogana a Padova fra Tre e Quattrocento', *Quaderni per la Storia dell'Università di Padova*, 16 (1983), pp. 1-41. In Rome, student exemptions from taxes were reaffirmed by cardinal Riario in 1492; MANTEGNA, *Lo Studium Urbis*, pp. 57-8.

[21] The duty to be levied on academic books when imported to or exported from Siena without such exemption was laid down in 1478; 6*s.* for books in law or medicine, 3*s.* for books of *notaria* or grammar (*Gabella dei Contratti* 9, f. 10v). Books in transit were taxed at 4*s.* for the former category and 2*s.* for the latter (f. 21r).

[22] A. B. COBBAN, *The Medieval Universities: their Development and Organisation* (London, 1975), pp. 26-7.

[23] Above, pp. 54 and 104 n. 95.

[24] For example, in 1497 the *Balìa* wrote to the cardinal of Siena begging for a benefice for Hieronimo di Cristoforo Gabrielli to enable him to continue with his studies (*Balìa* 414, ff. 96v-97r, 12 Nov).

[25] KIBRE, *Scholarly Privileges*, esp. Chapter 1.

[26] Op. cit., pp. 47, 63-4.

[27] For the practice in thirteenth-century Siena, WALEY, *Siena and the Sienese*, p. 97. In 1291 such permits cost 36*s.*, and 131 were purchased in a few months. They were for defensive arms (i.e. armour) only. For the practice of allowing students this privilege in Padua, P. KIBRE, *Scholarly Privileges*, p. 59, and in Bologna, PIANA, *Il "Liber Secretus Iuris Caesarei"*, pp. 58*-60*. In Siena examples of grants of such licences to students are Paolo Peri, origin unknown, but not Sienese (*Conc.* 614, f. 34v, 20 Feb 1469), Paolo da Pisa (*Conc.* 639, f. 35r-v, 29 Apr 1473) and Giovanni Battista da San Gimignano (*Conc.* 661 f. 12v, 18 Nov 1476). The Bolognese and Sienese licences are all given for offensive as well as defensive arms.

[28] *Conc.* 2116, f. 7r-v, 14 Jul. This was followed by wide-ranging legislation against bearing arms (*CG* 223, ff. 247r-248v, 21 Apr 1447).

behaviour has led to the measure are 'alcuni [per essere] scolari e partecipi de li privilegi scolastici'. The ban on bearing arms was extended to all, 'non obstante qualunque privilegio scolastico', and in the justification for the measure it was spelt out 'che sia interesse publico et del vro. Studio, et grande etiamdio conforto di tucti quelli che vogliano bene vivere et che vogliano attendere etiam a li studi che quelli che non vogliano vivere honestamente siano gastigati'.[29] Yet the notion of privilege proved more durable. In 1498 the general ban on bearing arms exempted 'li scolari et rectori della università et Sapientia et loro famegli, cioè de' Rectori o nobilisti', who were allowed 'solamente armi non inhastanti'.[30] The social nuances of this measure are probably the clue to its rationale. A century later Grand Duke Ferdinand I allowed all students to bear both offensive and defensive weapons; the idea was to persuade noble Lombard students, who enjoyed this privilege at other *studi*, to come to Siena.[31]

Above all, of course, students had special rights in respect of jurisdiction. From the Authentic *Habita* to Innocent IV's appointment in 1252 of the bishop of Siena as conservator,[32] the students had a choice of three courts of appeal – the bishop, their rector, or their teacher. In 1429 this was modified, and the right of appeal to the *Concistoro* against the rector's judgment granted.[33] Yet although the process was gradually taken over by the commune (with the control it also won over the rector), the privilege of reserved jurisdiction continued to be valuable. In 1434 the rector successfully brought a suit against the *Capitano di Giustizia* because he had passed sentence on some students who had been caught out at night 'con l'armi in mano, e senz' Abito scolastico'; the *Consiglio del Popolo* ruled that the case was outside the *Capitano*'s competence, and that the *Concistoro* along with the *Savi dello Studio* could cancel his sentence.[34]

Was all this sufficient to attract and retain students? There were limitations to their rights and privileges as well. They were not allowed to roam the streets at night,[35] though if they were caught the penalties were no heavier than those for citizens provided they were unarmed.[36] One cannot be too

[29] *CG* 233, ff. 39v-40r, 10 Sept (also *Conc.* 2117, f. 69r-v). See also *CG* 233, f. 49v, and *Conc.* 618, f. 22v, 4 Oct.

[30] *Balìa* 253, ff. 56v-57r, 22 Nov. On 4 December it was clarified that this applies only to foreign students who were matriculated and who were attending classes; 'pedagoci' (schoolmasters) were not included (*Balìa* 43, f. 264r).

[31] Measure of 1591; cf. PRUNAI, III, p. 117; ARCHIVIO DI STATO DI SIENA, *Guida-Inventario*, II, p. 232. On the debate and local regulations on this issue see O. CAVALLAR, 'Ledere Rem Publicam. Il trattato *"De portacione armorum"* attribuito a Bartolo di Sassoferrato e alcune *quaestiones* di Martino da Fano', *Ius Commune*, 25 (1998), pp. 1-38. Jousting was after all part of what the nobility, and therefore also noble students, were supposed to do; E. CROUZET-PAVAN, 'A Flower of Evil: Young Men in Medieval Italy', in *A History of Young People in the West*, eds. G. Levi and J.-C. Schmitt (tr. Cambridge, Ma., 1997), pp. 173-221, esp. pp. 193-4.

[32] See above, pp. 32 and 34.

[33] *Conc.* 368, f. 22v, 14 Jun; below, p. 266.

[34] *CG* 218, f. 41v, 28 Jun; and *Conc.* 2176, no foliation, *ad annum*, *Consiglio del Popolo* deliberation of 13 Jun. Cf. *Studio* 2, f. 72r, 14 Apr 1481, when the *Savi* wrote to the *Podestà* and his *assessore* telling them not to interfere with cases in which scholars were concerned. Unfortunately the letter itself does not survive. The student privilege of jurisdiction appears to have been of no avail in cases against clerics. On 26 Aug 1444 the vicar of the bishop of Siena wrote to the *Podestà* to complain that he was trying 'Dns. Baptista magri. Iohannis' of Recanati, who was in minor orders, and who was accused of having attached the German servant of Lodovico of Barcelona, a student, with a knife, drawing blood. Normally student privileges were understood to cover their servants. AAS 4420 (see above, p. 199 n. 134), f. 39r, ed. ZDEKAUER, *Documenti*, part 2, doc. 43, pp. 26-28. On this case see also below, p. 266 n. 157.

[35] *Conc.* 380, f. 8r-v, 8-9 Jul 1429 (cf. ZDEKAUER, p. 54 n. 1); the Sienese were also forbidden to be out with foreign students. In 1422 the ban had been on students out 'de nocte sine lumine necque cum armis', contraveners being imprisoned pending punishment by the civic authorities (*Conc.* 336, f. 4r, 6 Jan). Exemptions were granted, though (e.g. *Conc.* 479, f.13r, 19 Nov 1445). On the curfew in Siena generally, BOWSKY, *A Medieval Italian Commune*, p. 119.

[36] *CG* 233, f. 49v, 4 Oct 1469; cf. *Statuti* 25, f. 354r.

sure how rigidly this curfew was enforced – the cases that survive in the records are mainly instances of armed students, which the authorities considered more serious.[37] In 1469 the ban was softened; *forestieri*, including students, could be out at night in groups of up to three, provided they carried a large lantern.[38] Students were also prevented by statute from holding office in the commune, and while similar prohibitions for the doctors were frequently broken, unsurprisingly this does often not seem to have been the case with their pupils.[39]

3. *Recruitment and retention*

The commune took a range of initiatives to persuade students to come. There were calculated public measures; the reappointment of Bartolommeo Sozzini in 1484 (over whom Florence/Pisa and Siena had competed intensely) was urged because of the dramatic impact it was expected to have on recruitment given the precarious state of other Italian *studi*.[40] There was advertisement through influential figures, such as the archbishop of Lisbon, to whom the *Concistoro* wrote in 1454 pointing out that, with the advent of peace, the Sienese *Studio* was restored, dynamic and open for business.[41] Other such letters hoped to recruit a specific privileged individual – the nephew of a pope or a cardinal,[42] or the son of Duke Albert of Saxony[43] – and from the mid-fifteenth century there appears to have been a specific interest in attracting noble students.[44] Yet other initiatives targeted a specific

---

[37] See the cases of 1434 (see n. 34 above), 1447 (ZDEKAUER, *Documenti*, no. 49, pp. 29-30, 5 Aug. The original has been lost; see above, p. 22), 1448 (*Conc.* 492, ff. 29r-v, 3 Feb, 30v-31r, 8 Feb) and 1461 (ASS, *ms.* C. 19, no. XLVII, in which the rector himself was allegedly involved). Below, p. 269.

[38] *CG* 233, f. 40r, 10 Sept (also *Conc.* 2117, f. 69v).

[39] *CG* 208, f. 121r, 19 Oct 1418. Cf. *Statuti* 41, ff. 90r, 186v; students were not allowed to become judges or notaries and then return to study, and communal officials were not allowed to hire students. But students who were also members of the *Consiglio del Popolo* were excused attendance when its meetings clashed with lectures on *feriali* (*Conc.* 337, f. 23v, 30 Mar 1422). But see below, p. 285.

[40] 'La qual cosa obtenendosi, vi potete indubitamente persuadere harete el fiore di tutti li Studii de Italia perché più è oggi el tempo che mai fusse a dì de viventi atteso che habiamo notitia tutti li Studii di Lombardia come e Padua, Pavia, Bologna et Ferrara, per le guerre et carestie essere quasi derelicti, et anco Perogia grandemente declinata, et Pisa si tiene vivo solo con la reputatione del Sozino, a cui tuti li scolari di quella facultà verranno dietro; et havendo el Sozino potete tenere certo più che trecento scolari forestieri harà lo Studio vostro, li quali venendo non possano fare non mettino in la città fiorini 15.000 l'anno, tutti in beneficio de vostri buttigari et cittadini' (*CG* 239, f. 192r-v, 4 Apr; also *Conc.* 2139, no. 74, ff. 138r, 139v, ed. BARGAGLI, 'Documenti senesi', doc. 65, pp. 308-9). Cf. *Balìa* 520, no. 66, 31 Oct 1484, letter of Bernardo Politi, on competition and the state of the *Studio*.

[41] *Conc.* 1675, f. 193v, 4 Jul.

[42] The news that the nephew of the pope was considering leaving the *Studio* of Perugia because of plague, reported to the *Concistoro* by Dns. Petrus Antonii, led them to decide to write to Antonio Casini, cardinal of S. Marcello, suggesting Siena as an alternative (*Conc.* 379, f. 29r-v, 25 Jun 1429, *Conc.* 380, f. 2v, 1 Jul, *Conc.* 1632, f. 58r, 30 Jun, and *Conc.* 1633, f. 8r, 18 Jul). Cf. *Balìa* 410, f. 171r, 11 Dec 1490, letter to Sinolfo, the Sienese orator in Rome, about the possibility that the nephew of the cardinal vice-chancellor, who was understood to be thinking of coming to Italy to study, might choose Siena. The orator replied that they were too late; none of his relatives 'in partibus' were due to come to Italy, but one of his Roman nephews had just left for Perugia. The appreciation of what they had missed would have been heightened by the information that he had taken a household of fifteen *bocche* to accompany him in his studies (*Balìa* 545, no. 57, 18 Dec).

[43] *Balìa* 411, ff. 20r-21r, 19 Jan, and 26v-27v, 29 Jan 1492. Cf. FRIEDLÄNDER and MALAGOLA, *Acta Nationis Germanicae*, pp. 239-40.

[44] See the recommendations of the *Savi* on how to revive the *Studio* in 1456, *Conc.* 2138, no. 39, f. 62r (approved 13 July), and the petition to hire an unnamed famous civilian 'che molti scolari forestieri e persone nobili verranno a studiare' (*CG* 229, f. 379r-v, 21 Jun 1463).

university with the intention of persuading students there to move to Siena. This venerable tradition is central to the growth of universities. It does not stop in the fifteenth century,[45] but by then such initiatives are not always what they seem. An example is the boast of the Sienese ambassador in Florence in 1428 that he had persuaded five, and possibly ten more, students to come to Siena.[46] Yet the 'protectionist norms' that made this theoretically a serious offence were only intermittently observed,[47] and it is surely significant that in the same year the Florentine *Signoria* wrote no fewer than four letters of recommendation to their Sienese counterparts in respect of Florentine subjects seeking preferment at the Sienese *Studio*.[48] Another serious competitor and attractive target was Perugia. When in 1459 the authorities in Perugia discovered a plot amongst the students of the Sapienza there to leave for Siena (after the deterioration of relations between town and gown), they expelled all the occupants and took over the college; the reaction, according to the Perugian chroniclers, led to a mass exodus which left Perugia almost emptied of its students.[49] There is no evidence in the Sienese administrative records that the Sienese authorities had played any part in this, but there is such evidence in correspondence of 1481, when the Sienese were planning a new Casa della Sapienza, and one of the persuasive factors was felt to be the opportunities afforded by the reported dissent among students at Perugia.[50]

All the competing *studi* were of course playing the same game,[51] and ultimately there was little that could be done to stop foreign students from leaving, either through dissatisfaction or because they simply wanted to move on. The protectionist legislation designed to prevent citizen and subject students from leaving in order to study elsewhere had its counterpart among the *forenses* – no students were supposed to leave without permission – but the only way to make this condition acceptable was

[45] For example, in 1428 emissaries were sent to Bologna and elsewhere to entice students (*Conc.* 374, ff. 26r, 1 Oct, 27v, 4 Oct).

[46] *Conc.* 1914, no. 66, 18 Sept; see BRUCKER, 'Florence and its University, 1348-1434', p. 235.

[47] BRUCKER, op. cit., p. 234.

[48] *Conc.* 1914, nos. 33, 4 Aug (recommending Giovanni, son of the famous medical doctor Pietro da Arezzo, for the rectorate of the university), and three requests for places in the Sapienza for students of civil law; Paolo di Ser Simone di Paolo, a Florentine (no. 2, 28 Mar; for his admission see p. 316 n. 123), Francesco di Antonio da Pescia (no. 36, 5 Aug), and Giovanni di Maestro Antonio da Pistoia (no. 93, 16 Oct, a recommendation backed up by pressure on the Sienese orators in Florence; see no. 96, 17 Oct). On the 'norme protezionistiche' (which appear to have been in abeyance in Florence at this time), see below, pp. 245-6; and on the close and often competitive relationship between the two *Studi*, DENLEY, 'Academic Rivalry'.

[49] ERMINI, *Storia*, I, pp. 415-6. The episode is discussed fully in M. SEBASTIANI, 'Il collegio universitario di San Gregorio in Perugia detto la Sapienza Vecchia', unpublished *tesi di laurea*, Università degli Studi di Perugia, Facoltà di Lettere e Filosofia, Anno Accademico 1966-67, pp. 86-90, and cf. A. FABRETTI (ed.), 'Cronaca della città di Perugia dal 1309 al 1491 nota col nome di Diario del Graziani', *Archivio Storico Italiano*, ser. I, 16 (1850), pp. 71-750 (p. 634).

[50] On 24 Dec Placido Placidi wrote to the *Concistoro*, 'Et perche ieri […] qua nuove che lo studio di perugia e tutto in arme per l'alarme occigioni et li scolari stanno sollevati, et dicesi che la maggior parte revolgiano venire a Siena' (*Conc.* 2045, f. 6v). This was referred to the orator Sinolfo in Rome: 'E tanto più ci pare di usarci sollecitudine quanto che intendiamo in lo studio di Perugia esser qualche rottura che facilmente la magior parte delli scolari che son là porieno venire qua' (*Conc.* 1695, f. 45r-v, 3 Jan 1482). In the same period, five German students who had set out for Perugia were diverted to Siena, where they obtained places in the Sapienza. One subsequently decided to return home but requested that his place be given to a brother of one of the others. See below, p. 314 and n. 110. On relations with Perugia see also above, n. 42.

[51] Cf. for example *Corpus Chonicorum Bononiensium*, Cronaca A: 'A dì 24 del predicto [= October 1431] se principiò in Bologna lo Studio in tucte le facultà; et per chasone delle guerre, ch'eno circumstante, credese che'l studio de Fiorenza, de Siena, de Padoa et de Parma se desviarano per tale modo che quello de Bologna se refermarà bene; et speremo che non passarà Nadale che qui haveremo più de cinquecento scolari'. *Rerum Italicarum Scriptores*, XVIII/I, vol. IV, p. 53.

to grant permission readily to those who requested it with good reason,[52] and the only real effort put into such protectionism was the attempt to get people who were studying in Siena to take their degree there rather than elsewhere – especially those who had obtained a place in the Sapienza, or a student lectureship.[53] To establish whether a student had moved, authorities would have to rely on hearsay and intelligence reports from other university towns,[54] and beyond protesting to their rivals there was little they could do.[55] The reasons for migration were ultimately often personal. There is no reason to suppose that the arts student Antonio Guacci of Mantua, who at some stage before 1394 expressed a wish to leave Bologna for Siena because he thought the teaching would be better there,[56] was more or less typical than the young humanist Giannantonio Campano, who set out from Naples for Siena in 1452, but ran into armed men in the Val d'Orcia and quickly decided that Perugia would be a more suitable place to study.[57] To cater for all tastes, to entice non-Sienese students and to build (and keep) a reputation, the Sienese had simply to make study at their university as attractive as possible in all senses.[58]

[52] Students wishing to leave and to take possessions with them would have to find guarantors; thus Messer Matteo di Rocca Contrada on 25 May 1480 (*Not.* 858, f. 6r, ed. MINNUCCI, 'Documenti', II-25, p. 92), and Mag. Hieronimus de Foligno on 6 Oct 1488 (*Not.* 1018, no foliation).

[53] See below, p. 289. The preference for students with Sienese degrees could be expressed in other ways too. In 1448 the ranking of two Pavian medical practitioners was reversed; although Carlo, having taken his degree one day before Elia, would normally have been regarded as the senior of the two, since he had left Siena (where he had been a student in the Sapienza) to obtain a degree in Florence, he was effectively demoted (*Conc.* 497, f. 17r, 24 Nov, ed. GAROSI, doc. 77, p. 538, and PIANIGIANI, doc. 287, pp. 319-21). Elia's Sienese career continued (*Conc.* 499, f. 42v, 29 Apr, 500, f. 18v, 23 May, *Bicch.* 318, f. 41v, 5 Jun and 29 Dec 1449), while of Carlo, who had been hired 'ad practicando medicine et ad medendo' on 31 Aug 1448 (*Conc.* 495, f. 47r), no more is heard. The situation was altogether more promising where the students in the Sapienza were concerned. Here the commune insisted on the students undertaking to remain until the completion of their course and degree, extracting payment in advance and, at one stage, a deposit at the student's arrival. Below, pp. 311 and 320.

[54] E.g. *Studio* 2, f. 96v, 22 Dec 1483; the *Savi* examine witnesses to see if some students have gone to Pisa.

[55] E.g. *Conc.* 1887, no. 18, 6 May 1415; the rector of the University of Arts and Medicine in Bologna complains to the commune of Siena that a Sienese student, Matteo di Cione, has left Bologna without permission and, more seriously, with the belongings of several of his fellow-students.

[56] He cites the presence at Siena of Marsilio Santasofia and 'in artibus…multi peritissimi doctores'. M. J. MONFRIN, 'Étudiants italiens a la fin du XIVe siècle', in *Mélanges d'archéologie et d'histoire, École Francaise de Rome*, 63 (1951), pp. 195-280 (pp. 261 *seq.*). Cf. C. PIANA, *Nuovi documenti sull' Università di Bologna e sul Collegio di Spagna*. Studia Albornotiana, 26 (1976), I, pp. 193-4 for a full discussion of this case; and see p. 51 n. 134 above.

[57] ERMINI, *Storia*, I, p. 600 gives the traditional version of this episode, relating the account of Campano's biographer, Ferni, of how, on entering the Val d'Orcia, he was set upon by robbers. F. DI BERNARDO, *Un vescovo umanista alla corte pontificio: Giannantonio Campano (1429-1477)* (Rome, 1975), pp. 41-5 demonstrates the literary context of Campano's original account and concludes that these were Florentine mercenaries rather than robbers, and it was the political climate that influenced his change of decision. This is also the view of F. R. HAUSMANN, 'Campano, Giovanni Antonio', *DBI*, 17 (1974), pp. 424-9. On Campano's subsequent career (including a later visit to Siena in 1459) see also G. IANZITI, *Humanist Historiography under the Sforzas. Politics and Propaganda in Fifteenth-Century Milan* (Oxford, 1988), pp. 54-66, 68.

[58] Many factors could influence students' choices. Johannes Ruysch, contemplating a return to Siena in April 1434, sung the praises of the *Studio* in a letter to his uncle sounding him out about funds for the projected transfer from the university of Turin, then at Chieri. By the end of June, however, he had heard from his brother Peter that, despite the presence in the Sienese *Studio* of Lodovico Pontano and the hope of the return of Niccolò Tedeschi, the city was in a bad way; there was a shortage of grain following the war with Florence, and the roads were infested with brigands and thieves. Ruysch decided to stay put. A. SOTTILI, 'Le lettere di Johannes Ruysch da Chieri e Pavia nel contesto dei rapporti tra umanesimo italiano e umanesimo tedesco', *Annali della Scuola Normale Superiore di Pisa*, Classe di Lettere e Filosofia, ser. 3, 19:1 (1989), pp. 323-412 (letters II, pp. 398-400, and V, pp. 404-7).

4. *'Tanta varietà de linghua et de paesi et de nationi'*[59]

The evidence about the students in Siena that emerges from institutional records is tantalisingly incomplete. Although there is a fair amount of anecdotal information which makes it possible, as elsewhere, to compile a substantial list of names,[60] there are no regular sources, such as matriculation lists, of the kind necessary for systematic prosopographical study. We will never be able to say much in quantitative terms about, for example, the social composition of the foreign student population, about how long students tended to stay in Siena, or (for the fifteenth century at least) about the proportion that took degrees, while the native student population is virtually a closed book. What follows is intended only as a provisional sketch of the most obvious features. The creation of a thorough biographical register would certainly enhance the picture, but it would still be essentially anecdotal.

Siena is no exception to the general uncertainty that remains over the size of Italian universities. There are only the sparsest of statistics. In 1423, 115 students are reported (though unfortunately not listed) as having voted on the provisions for the election of *consiliarii*;[61] in 1463, 361 votes were cast in the election of the rector;[62] and the 1533 matriculation list records a total of 242 students.[63] The first two of these figures may well not have included Sienese students, and in both cases there is of course no way of telling how many members of the university did not vote.[64] Bare and subject to the usual qualifications as these figures are, they should be considered a better guide than contemporary 'estimates',[65] and they do fit in with the general impression of the relative size of the *Studio* as measured by the size of the teaching staff. Perugia, clearly larger in the fourteenth century, had 142 matriculated students in 1339,[66] but does not show much sign of expansion, with 111 students voting in a rectoral election in 1443 and 172 matriculated in 1511.[67] Pisa at the end of the fifteenth century was clearly larger (judging simply by the number of students Verde has unearthed), as was Pavia, with 427 students voting in the rectoral elections of 1482.[68] These impressions are confirmed by an examination of the *rotoli* of these universities, which as far as can be ascertained seem to be a good guide to relative size.[69]

Analysis of the student population by subject is also fraught with difficulties. For the university as a whole the only breakdown available is, again, the matriculation list of 1533, which includes twenty

---

[59] *Conc.* 517, f. 9r, 7 Nov 1452, ed. BAI, doc. 36, pp. 33-5.

[60] Cf. the work of VERDE, *Lo Studio fiorentino*, III, who has amassed information on 1,296 students over thirty years, a proportion certainly unattainable for Siena.

[61] *Conc.* 347, f. 7r, 7 Nov (cf. CATONI, 'Genesi', p. 174 n. 85).

[62] *Conc.* 583, f. 33v, 10 Dec.

[63] *Studio* 17, ff. 89r, 101r-102r, 110r-v, 120r-v, 29-30 Jun, ed. KOŠUTA, 'Documenti', doc. XIII-2, pp. 425-32.

[64] Below, Chapter III.2.

[65] For example Girolamo Agliotti boasted that six hundred people had heard his eulogy of Aeneas Silvius, a number which would be useless as an estimate even if we could assume that it was exclusively composed of scholars. ZDEKAUER, p. 97.

[66] ROSSI, 'Documenti per la storia dell'Università di Perugia', doc. 64.

[67] ERMINI, *Storia*, I, p. 320; G. PARDI, 'Atti degli scolari dello Studio di Perugia dall' anno 1497 al 1515', *Bollettino della R. Deputazione di Storia Patria per l' Umbria*, 4 (1890), pp. 487-509 (pp. 490-1). Pardi's doubts as to whether this listed all students in the university are not difficult to resolve; the university would have been about the largest in Italy if the list represented only one year's entry.

[68] VACCARI, *Storia dell'Università di Pavia*, p. 74.

[69] See above, pp. 61-2.

students in canon law, ninety-five in civil law, sixty-nine in arts/medicine and fifty-eight in *humanitas* (see Table 5). It would be rash, however, to take this as wholly typical. The low number of canonists is surprising; there are markedly fewer canonists than civilians on the *rotoli*, but not so few as to confine the subject to the fringes of the *Studio's* activities. The explanation may lie in the practice of taking degrees *in utroque*, which accounts for the great majority of law degrees, but which entailed consecutive rather than simultaneous study; no students are recorded in the matriculation list as studying *in utroque*.[70] On the other hand, while civil law is easily the most popular subject, the virtual balance between law and arts/medicine is reflected in the proportions of the *rotoli*, and suggests a fundamentally different emphasis from that of, say, Pisa.[71] That this has not always been appreciated is probably due to the fact that the status of law, and the numbers studying civil law, have distorted the picture. The Casa della Sapienza had a deliberate policy, formulated at the outset and broadly maintained throughout the fifteenth century if not beyond, of taking mainly students of law.[72] Clearly many more students took degrees in law than in arts/medicine;[73] but this may be capable of a social explanation,[74] and meanwhile the meagre evidence available suggests that student numbers, like the number of lectureships, are not so weighted.

Table 5 – Statistics from the list of matriculated students in 1533

Provenance	Canon Law	Civil Law	Arts/Medicine	Humanitas	Total
Siena	5	22	16	48	91
Contado	1	9	7	3	20
Rest of Tuscany	3	11	6	-	20
Northern Italy	-	5	3	-	8
Papal States	3	21	17	3	44
Naples, Sicily, Sardinia	1	9	3	-	13
Iberia	4	7	2	-	13
Germany	1	2	-	-	3
Others/not identified	2	9	15	4	30
Total	20	95	69	58	242

From *Studio* 17, ff. 89r, 101r-102r, 110r-v, 120r-v, 29-30 Jun, ed. KOŠUTA, 'Documenti', doc. XIII-2, pp. 425-32.

[70] See the tables in G. MINNUCCI, 'Il conferimento dei titoli accademici', pp. xxiii-xxviii. Degrees *in utroque* were the overwhelming preference of the German students who took their degree in Siena; F. WEIGLE, 'Deutsche Studenten in Italien, II: Die Deutschen Doktorpromotionen in Siena, 1485-1804', *Quellen und Forschungen aus italienischen Archiven und Bibliotheken*, 33 (1944), pp. 199-251 (p. 211). It must of course also be remembered that the fact that someone took a degree in a *studio* does not necessarily imply that he had studied there.

[71] Cf. SCHMITT, 'The Faculty of Arts at Pisa', p. 252 and n. 37, showing a ratio of law to arts/medicine of over three to one for fifteenth- and sixteenth-century Pisa, measured by both degrees and matriculations at different stages. The Perugian matriculation list of 1339 gives 119 scholars in law, twenty-three in medicine (ROSSI, 'Documenti per la storia dell'Università di Perugia', doc. 64).

[72] Below, pp. 306-7. The first twenty-five years saw ninety-seven admissions in law, twenty-six in arts (and sixteen unspecified (see Table 6, below, p. 312); a list of members from the early 1470s shows thirty-five lawyers and twelve artists (*Not.* 694, f. 2ra-rd, ed. MINNUCCI, 'Documenti', doc. II-34, pp. 100-1).

[73] MINNUCCI, 'Il conferimento', Tavola I, p. xxiii.

[74] Below, p. 288.

Geographical distribution is again something for which only the tip of the iceberg can be seen. The 1533 matriculation list is the fullest snapshot, but it was drawn up at an untypical moment in the *Studio*'s history,[75] when ultramontanes were thin on the ground; it includes only sixteen of them (thirteen Iberians and three Germans),[76] and although there is no statistical evidence for other years it is most unlikely that this is representative. For the earlier period, approximate statistics can be compiled for the Sapienza for much of the fifteenth century, and through degree certificates from the end of the fifteenth century onwards we get an accurate profile of those who chose to take degrees in Siena. While it would be rash to assume that either of these necessarily gives samples that are representative of the student population as a whole, they are of interest in themselves.

That the ultramontane presence at the *Studio* was dominated by the Germans and the Iberians is amply demonstrated, both by the lists we have for the Sapienza[77] and by non-Sapienza evidence. From the early fifteenth-century revival onwards the Spanish students formed a substantial group (with an occasional reputation for rowdiness, as during the difficult months of 1420 when the *Studio* was transferred to Corsignano).[78] In the sixteenth century, during the military occupation of Siena, Spanish scholars found a way to take advantage of the wages paid to their soldier compatriots when they were absent, using them to help finance their studies;[79] they were also inevitably at the receiving end of anti-Spanish feeling, which caused divisions in the *Studio* along national lines.[80] On the other hand the links with Portugal were forged at the highest level,[81] and for a few years in the late fifteenth and early sixteenth century were very intense. The presence of the well-connected Luís Teixeira in Siena in the 1470s, traced in detail by Minnucci,[82] is only the best-known case; he was one of several in the period.[83] The Sapienza applicant who claimed in 1467 that almost all Portuguese who had degrees had obtained them in Siena[84] was clearly exaggerating, but his crude sales pitch does reflect the vigour of the tradition that had been established. Notarial records of 1509-10 show that there was still a sub-

---

[75] Above, p. 174.

[76] See Table 5 above.

[77] Below, pp. 310 *seq.*, esp. 324.

[78] Above, pp. 113-4; ZDEKAUER, doc. XI, pp. 156-9, 40-1. The dispute of 1429 may well have centred on the Spaniards as well (below, p. 259). G. MINNUCCI, 'Siena e l'Europa. Studenti stranieri a Siena fra XV e XVII secolo', in *Cultura e Università a Siena*, pp. 27-34 (p. 28), also discusses the conflict which developed within the Casa della Sapienza in 1440 as one between Spaniards and Sicilians; cf. IDEM, 'Documenti', doc. III-227, 20 Aug 1440.

[79] D. MAFFEI, 'Un documento spagnolo sulla ricettività studentesca senese nel Cinquecento', in *Scritti dedicati ad Alessandro Raselli*, 2 (Milan, 1971), pp. 953-58; and in MINNUCCI, 'Siena e l'Europa', p. 30, and ASCHERI, *Siena nella Storia*, p. 164.

[80] KOŠUTA, 'Siena', pp. 70-1 esp. Further information on the Spanish students in Siena in NARDI, *Mariano Sozzini*, p. 60 n. 21; J. ARRIZABALAGA, J. GARCIA-BALLESTER, F. SALMÓN, 'A propósito de las relaciones intelectuales entre la Corona de Aragón e Italia (1470-1520): los estudiantes de medicina valencianos en los estudios generales de Siena, Pisa, Ferrara y Padua', *Dynamis. Acta Hispanica ad Medicinae Scientiarumque Historiam Illustrandam*, 9 (1989), pp. 117-47; J. ARRIZA-BALAGA, 'Tradició medieval i cultura humanista en la medicina universitària: les activitats editorials de Francesc Argilagues i Guillem Caldentei per a les premses italianes de les acaballes del segle XV', in *Al tombant de l'edat mitjana. Tradició medieval i cultura humanista. XVIII Jornales d'Etudis Históricis Locals*, ed. M. Barceló Crespi (Palma de Mallorca, 2000), pp. 175-87.

[81] See pp. 175 n. 244, 236, 321 n. 182, 322 n. 185, and 323. On Portuguese law students at Siena see now G. MINNUCCI, 'Studenti giuristi portoghesi a Siena nella seconda metà del XV secolo', in *Amicitiae pignus. Studi in onore di Adriano Cavanna*, eds. A. Padoa Schioppa, G. di Renzo Villata and G. P. Massetto, 3 vols. (Milan, 2003), pp. 1477-88.

[82] Below, p. 323.

[83] Below, pp. 308 n. 72, 313 n. 97 and 99, 314 nn. 111 and 113, and 322 n. 185.

[84] Above, p. 66 n. 10.

stantial Portuguese student community in Siena, known to us through the banking contacts they used to ensure a flow of financial support from home.[85]

Perhaps the most important development was that by the late fifteenth century Siena was firmly established on the German circuit. Dotzauer ranks it with Bologna and Padua in popularity.[86] Allowing for the tendency of all those from north of the Alps to be lumped in indiscriminately as 'Germans', it is nonetheless the case that the German-speaking regions provide the largest proportion of ultramontanes. 175 Germans attended the Sapienza between 1470 and 1548.[87] They were easily the largest group of foreigners taking degrees, and accounted for about a fifth of all degrees between 1485 and 1600,[88] including half of the ultramontane doctorands in Siena recorded in surviving documents between 1484 and 1579.[89] They were also the only group to organise as a formal nation after the fall

---

[85] *Not.* 1020. I am most grateful to the erstwhile Director of the Archivio di Stato di Siena, Dott. Ubaldo Morandi, for sharing with me his card-index to the individuals who appear in this volume. Other examples of the conveyance of loans to Portuguese students are in V. RAU, 'Alguns estudiantes e eruditos portugueses em Italia no século XV', *Do Tempo e da Historia*, 5 (1972), pp. 29-99; Italian tr. 'Studenti ed eruditi portoghesi in Italia nel secolo XV', *Estudios Italiános em Portugal*, 36 (1973), pp. 7-73, and more widely on the phenomenon TOGNETTI, '"Fra li compagni palesi et li ladri occulti"', pp. 52-5; on its importance also A. BRILLI, 'L'Università e la presenza degli stranieri', in *L'Università di Siena. 750 anni*, pp. 541-7 (p. 543). A study of this characteristic is F. MELIS, 'Sul finanziamento degli allievi portoghesi del Real Collegio de España di Bologna nel XV secolo', *El Cardenal Albornoz y el Colegio de España*, ed. E. Verdera y Tuells, III. Studia Albornotiana, 13 (Bologna, 1973), pp. 417-34; repr. in *I mercanti italiani nell'Europa medievale e rinascimentale*, ed. L. Frangioni (Florence, 1990), pp. 19-33. A detailed example of the problems of a Portuguese studying in Pisa is in VERDE, *Lo Studio fiorentino*, III.2, pp. 895-7. A. D. DE SOUSA COSTA, 'Portugueses no Colégio de S. Clemente de Bolonha durante o século XV', in *El Cardenal Albornoz*, pp. 211-415, and IDEM, *Portugueses no Colégio de S. Clemente e Universidade de Bolonha durante o século XV*. Studia Albornotiana, 56 (Bologna, 1990) are full of references to the Sienese phases of Portuguese *alumni* of the Spanish College. On Portuguese in Italian universities see also V. RAU, 'Italianismo na cultura jurídica portuguesa do século XV', *Revista Portuguesa de História*, 12 (1969) (= Homenagem ao Doutor Paulo Merêa, I), pp. 185-206; and on the background to the Iberians in Italian *studi* see also E. VERONESE CESERACCIU, 'Spagnoli e portoghesi all'Università di Padova nel ventennio 1490-1510', *Quaderni per la Storia dell'Università di Padova*, 11 (1978), esp. pp. 40-1.

[86] W. DOTZAUER, 'Deutsches Studium in Italien unter besonderer Berücksichtigung der Universität Bologna. Versuch einer vorläufigen Zusammenstellenden Überschau', *Geschichtliche Landeskunde*, 14 (1976), pp. 84-130 (pp. 95-6), and IDEM, 'Deutsches Studium und deutsche Studenten an Europäischen Hochschulen (Frankreich, Italien) und die nachfolgende Tätigkeit in Stadt, Kirche und Territorium in Deutschland', in *Stadt und Universität im Mittelalter und in der früheren Neuzeit. 13. Arbeitstagung in Tübingen, 8.-10. 11. 1974*, eds. E. Maschke and J. Sydow. Stadt in der Geschichte. Veröffentlichungen des Südwestdeutschen Arbeitskreises für Stadtgeschichtsforschung, 3 (Sigmaringen, 1977), pp. 112-41 (p. 119). The conclusion – in common with WEIGLE, 'Deutsche Studenten in Italien, II', p. 200 – that Siena had overtaken Bologna in size is not supported by evidence and seems most unlikely.

[87] WEIGLE, 'Matrikel', p. 24, from BCS, *ms.* A.XI.12.

[88] WEIGLE, 'Deutsche Studenten in Italien, II', pp. 210, 241-6 esp.

[89] MINNUCCI, 'Il conferimento', Tavola III, pp. xxvii-xxviii. IDEM, *I tedeschi nella storia* collects and translates the main German studies pertaining to this theme, but they are focused almost entirely on the later period. SOTTILI, 'Le lettere di Johannes Ruysch', esp. pp. 364-72, and. P. ROSSO, 'Studenti di area germanica presso l'Università di Torino nel Quattrocento', *Schede umanistiche*, 15:2 (2001), pp. 35-55 (esp. pp. 43-49) explore the history of a group of students whose *peregrinationes* included a Sienese phase in the early 1430s. SOTTILI, 'Zum Verhältnis von Stadt, Staat und Universität', esp. p. 60, is also cogent on the attractions of Italian universities for Germans. Recent German work covering the role of Siena among other centres includes R. BECKER, 'Bildungskarrieren im Süden. Italienische Studienwege bayerische Bischöfe in der frühen Neuzeit (1448-1648)', *Römische Quartalschrift für christliche Altertumskunde und Kirchengeschichte*, 97 (2002), pp. 301-22; R. GRAMSCH, *Erfurter Juristen im Spätmittelalter: Die Karrieremuster und Tätigkeitsfelder einer gelehrten Elite des 14. und 15. Jahrhunderts* (Leiden, 2003); S. IRRGANG, *Peregrinatio Academica. Wanderungen und Karrieren von Gelehrten der Universitäten Rostock, Greifswald, Trier und Mainz im 15. Jahrhundert*. Beiträge zur Geschichte der Universität Greifswald, 4 (Stuttgart, 2002); and for the sixteenth century onwards C. ZONTA, 'La presenza degli slesiani nelle università europee e italiane dal XVI al XVIII secolo', in *Studenti, università, città nella storia padovana*, pp. 403-23 (esp. pp. 413-5); EADEM, *Schlesische Studenten an italienischen Universitäten. Eine prosopographische Studie zur frühneuzeitlichen*

of the republic.[90] Areas within and beyond the empire that we do not associate with 'Germans' are also represented. There is a modest but steady stream of Dutch students.[91] Over the centuries English[92] and Scottish[93] names appear sporadically; and there are occasional reports of Croatians,[94] Hungarians,[95] Czechs,[96] Poles[97] and Scandinavians.[98] The student with the furthest to travel must have been the Russian Martinus, whose presence in Siena extended over three years and who was a candidate for the rectorate of the Casa della Sapienza.[99]

Bildungsgeschichte. Neue Forschungen zur Schlesischen Geschichte, 10 (Cologne – Weimar – Vienna, 2004), esp. pp.81-2, 104-5; EADEM, 'Studenti stranieri in Italia: gli slesiani nell'età moderna', in *Studenti e dottori*, pp. 31-40. Many prosopographical studies, while recognising the importance of Siena on the German academic route, are unable to devote as much attention to it as they do to other centres precisely because so much remains unpublished and unresearched; and this is true of other areas as well.

[90] WEIGLE, 'Matrikel', loc. cit.

[91] A. TERVOORT, *The 'iter italicum' and the Northern Netherlands. Dutch Students and Italian Universities and their Role in the Netherlands' Society (1426-1575)*. Education and Society in the Middle Ages and the Renaissance, 21 (Leiden, 2005) has identified the six Dutch names that appear as students or witnesses at degrees in the late fifteenth century (CD appendix, nos. 28, 45, 166, 222, 481, 598, and see pp. 73-6 of the text), to which could be added Johannes Dodonis of Rotterdam, who took a degree in medicine on 22 Dec 1412 (*Not.* 292, ff. 63r-64r, ed. MINNUCCI, 'Documenti', doc. I-3, pp. 48-51), Jacomo Carusio of Utrecht (see below, p. 268 n. 170), and possibly 'Paulus de Danetria' (?= Daventria, i.e. Deventer?), a *sapientino* in 1492; *Not.* 694, f. 33r-v, 3 Jun, ed. MINNUCCI, loc. cit., doc. II-32, pp. 98-9. See also n. 93 below.

[92] E.g. Mag. Adovardus de Anglia, a *sapientino* in 1481 (*Conc.* 690, f. 39r, 23 Oct), on whom see MITCHELL, 'English Student Life'; John Bery, Austin hermit, in Siena at some stage between 1419 and 1423 (V. DAVIS, 'The English Medieval Clergy Database and University History', in *Computing Techniques and the History of Universities*, ed. P. R. Denley. Halbgraue Reihe zur historischen Fachinformatik, A30 [St. Katharinen, 1996], pp. 60-64 [p. 63]).

[93] Andrew of Hawyck, above, pp. 58-9. Alexander, son of King James and archbishop of St. Andrews, studied partly in Siena and partly in Rome between December 1508 and June 1509, though it is not clear whether this brought him into the ambit of the university; his presence is chiefly notable because it brought his tutor, Erasmus, to Siena; *Collected Works of Erasmus; Letters* (Toronto, 1974-), Vol. 2, pp. 145n, 151n, Vol. 8, p. 218, and Vol. 9, p. 319.

[94] Marin Držić, studied by L. KOŠUTA, esp. in 'Siena nella vita e nell'opera di Marino Darsa (Marin Držić)', *Ricerche slavistiche*, 9 (1961), pp. 67-121 is the known example; albeit without adding further names, C. BÉNÉ, 'Échanges universitaires dans l'Europe humaniste: l'exemple de la Croatie', in *Les échanges entre les universités européennes*, pp. 269-80 also saw Siena as one of the (secondary) Italian universities visited by Croatians. It is possible that some students described as Hungarians were in fact from the subject territory of Croatia.

[95] The Hungarian presence has a long tradition, from the many who transferred from Bologna in 1321 (NARDI, *Insegnamento*, pp. 119, 123-4, 140 n. 24; note the rectorate of 'Messer Jacomo da Ongaria'), through the unnamed Hungarian students who in the disturbances in 1420 following the temporary relocation of the *Studio* to Lucignano were described by a despairing official as 'dimoni senza catene' (ZDEKAUER, p. 41), to Ambrosio de Ungaria, doctor in arts and student of canon law, admitted to the Sapienza on 29 Jul 1474 (*Conc.* 647, f. 15r). Others are listed by E. VERESS, *Olasz egyetemeken járt magyarországi tanulók anya könyve és iratai, 1221-1864 (Matricula et acta Hungarorum in universitatibus Italiae studentium)*. Olaszországi magyar emlékek, 3 (Budapest, 1941), pp. 331-55. Cf. G. CATONI, 'Relazioni culturali fra la città di Siena e l'Ungheria nei secoli 14. e 15.', estr. from *'Ungheria d'oggi'. Atti del Convegno italo-ungherese di studi rinascimentali, Spoleto, 9-10 ottobre 1964*, pp. 1-4; K. PAJORIN, 'Enea Silvio Piccolomini ed i primi umanisti ungheresi', in *Rapporti e scambi: tra umanesimo italiano ed umanesimo europeo*, ed. L. Rotondi Secchi Tarugi. Istituto di Studi Umanistici Francesco Petrarca, Mentis Itinerarium, Caleidoscopio, 10 (Milan, 2001), pp. 649-56.

[96] See G. MINNUCCI, 'Studenti boemi laureati a Siena fra XV e XVII secolo', in *Siena in Praga*, pp. 54-58.

[97] Nicolaus Ffabri of Žagan, who took a degree in medicine on 22 Dec 1412 (*Not.* 292, ff. 63r-64r, ed. MINNUCCI, 'Documenti', doc. I-3, pp. 48-51); Niccolò Ghelde, admitted to the Casa della Sapienza in 1425 (see below, p. 307 n. 66).

[98] E.g. the Swedes studied by E. NYGREN, 'Ericus Olais och andra svenskars stidiebesök i Siena', *Kyrkohistorisk årsskrift*, I:19 (1918), pp. 118-26; IDEM, 'Ericus Olai', in *Svenskt Biografisket Lexikon* (Stockholm, 1917-), 14, pp. 216-42 (pp. 218-9); A. PILTZ (ed.), *Studium Upsalense, Specimens of the Oldest Lecture Notes Taken in the Medieval University of Uppsala*. Acta Universitatis Upsaliensis. Skrifter rörande Uppsala Universitet. C, Organisation och historia, 36 (Uppsala, 1977), pp. 15, 37-40, 49.

[99] He was granted a place in the Sapienza on 14 Jan 1484 for the full seven years (*Balìa* 31, f. 32r; his receipt for his room and furnishings is recorded in BCS, *ms.* A.XI.12, f. 39v; noted in ZDEKAUER, doc. XXIII, p. 185); the following

Compared to the Iberians and the Germans, the French appear to have been less strongly represented than might be expected. Although there is a reasonable presence in the first half of the fifteenth century[100] – including several candidates for the rectorate – by the end of the fifteenth century and in the early sixteenth, French students are less prominent, though still well represented in the statistics for degrees to 1579. The decline of French attendance at Italian universities is an old theme,[101] though it has been called into question recently.[102] Pending further research on Siena, it can merely be observed that French students may be less visible because they demonstrate less of a tendency towards collective activity; there are fewer instances in the evidence of them travelling together, forming a pressure group to obtain the rectorate, etc. In the same way that the evidence is biased towards foreigners, the proximity of France may well distort the picture; it may be that we see less of the French because coming to Siena to study was relatively problem-free.

For the citramontane student population the statistics from the Casa della Sapienza may be more typical. In his analysis of late-fifteenth century Sapienza students, Zdekauer rightly refrained from attempting complete statistics for the Italians as so many of them are not placeable, but a broad pattern can be discerned; by far the greatest number come from the Papal States (thirty-five at least, as well as five from Rome), while there is a steady intake from the south (one from Naples, six from Sicily – though there were many more Sicilians earlier in the fifteenth century) and from Tuscany (five from Pistoia, two from Lucca, and at least five others – none however from Florence), but fewer from northern Italy (one from Montferrat, one from Genoa, one from Verona).[103] The 1533 list (Table 5) shows a similar bias. Forty-four are ascertainably from the Papal States, eight from the south, five from Sardinia, twenty from Tuscany and eight from the north. Of those from the Papal States, a large proportion are from the Marche, and there is already in evidence the well-observed link between Siena and this area, and particularly with Macerata, which in the sixteenth century drew many teachers from Siena.[104] This composition clearly reflects academic geography as well as political conditions; Pisa/Florence was a strong rival in Tuscany, and there were even stronger competitors in the north, whereas in central Italy there was primarily Perugia to compete with, and it not surprisingly shared with Siena a large Marchesan intake.[105]

---

year he was a candidate for the rectorate of the college (*Conc.* 715, f. 9v, 17 Nov 1485, ed. FERRERI, doc. 222, p. 187, revealing that he was a canonist). In 1487 he featured in a dispute with a fellow-*sapientino*, Moscato da Spoleto, which was referred to the *podestà* (*Conc.* 725, f. 34v, 21 Aug), and he was still a member of the college in 1488 (*Not.* 967, no foliation). His career was thus not as distinguished as that at Bologna of his fellow-countryman Jurij Kotermak of Drogobyč, on whom see H. PESSINA LONGO, *Georgius de Russia, rettore a Bologna nel XV secolo*. Memorie e documenti dello Studio bolognese, 2 (Bologna,1988).

[100] Examples in pp. 285, 311 n. 96, 313, 315 n. 114, 316 n. 123, 320 n. 173, 321 n. 183, 339 n. 8, 345, 349 and 351.

[101] A. GOURON, 'The Training of Southern French Lawyers during the Thirteenth and Fourteenth Centuries', in *Post Scripta. Essays on Medieval Law and the Emergence of the European State in Honor of Gaines Post*, eds. J. R. Strayer and D. E. Queller. Studia Gratiana, 15 (1972), pp. 217-27 (esp. pp. 220-6), and cf. PARDI, 'Atti degli scolari', p. 493.

[102] N. BINGEN, 'Les étudiants de langue française dans les universités italiennes à la Renaissance: mise à jour du recensement et analyse des données', in *Les échanges entre les universités européennes*, pp. 25-43. Pavia still registered a significant French presence in the late fifteenth century; VACCARI, *Storia dell'Università di Pavia*, p. 75.

[103] ZDEKAUER, doc. XXIII, pp. 180-91 (and see pp. 96-7); see also below, p. 324.

[104] Two *marchigiani* became rectors at Siena within a few years; Evangelista (below, pp. 268-9) and Serafino (*Conc.* 484 f. 28v, 21 Oct 1446, and below, p. 284 n. 44), both from Camerino. On Macerata and Siena in the sixteenth century, A. MARONGIU, 'L'Università di Macerata nel periodo delle origini', *Annali della Università di Macerata*, 17 (1948); repr. in his *Stato e Scuola*, pp. 149-218, pp. 160, 168, 178 *seq*, 181, 199, 205 *seq.*, 211; and NARDI, 'Note sulla scuola giuridica senese', pp. 205-7.

[105] PARDI, 'Atti', p. 492.

Is this enough evidence to suggest the 'provincialisation' of the Sienese *Studio*? Certainly the Sicilians, Spaniards and Frenchmen appear less frequently in this list,[106] but on the other hand the German and Marchesan presence is if anything strengthened.[107] The real indicator of such provincialisation would of course be the proportion of the student population that was Sienese; and for this there is virtually no evidence at all. The only reasonably safe assertion of significance that can be made is that the *Studio* of Siena had established for itself a reputation, in certain areas such as Germany and the Marche, which survived the vicissitudes of the early sixteenth century and ensured a continuous, if perhaps slightly diminished, flow of students.

5. *Sienese students*

As elsewhere in Italy, the area which would perhaps be of most interest to the social historian of universities is, and will largely remain, hidden from sight. Local students barely appear in the legislation or in the formal *Studio* records. As far as statistics are concerned, the three main sources used above are little help. The Sapienza excluded local students. Minnucci's figures for degrees from 1485 to 1579 show that almost half the Italians who took degrees were Tuscans, which is clearly a measure of localisation, but the figures are not broken down beyond that.[108] The 1533 matriculation list is the only usable measure; out of a total of 242 students, eighty-eight were Sienese, and a further twenty-one from the *contado*. Strikingly, forty-seven Sienese citizens were 'enrolled' in *humanitas* (over four-fifths of the intake), most of them from *monte* families.[109] Since this is not a degree subject, we are looking at a different function of the university here. What this tells us is that half the citizens 'enrolled' were not aiming at the traditional vocational subjects towards which universities had conventionally been geared.

Only one measure was regularly directed towards Sienese students, that seeking to prevent them from studying elsewhere. Siena adopted the protectionist measures standard to most Italian *studi*,[110] with some additional refinements. The motive was expressed as early as 1278: 'nec expediat cives talium civitatum ad terras causa proficiscendi pergere alienas'.[111] The first formal measure in the period covered here followed hard upon Charles IV's diploma in 1357, forbidding Sienese students (and doctors) from attending other universities,[112] though this was relaxed again with the

---

[106] PRUNAI, III, p. 122.

[107] The Sapienza in 1541 is still quite evenly divided between Italians and foreigners (admittedly most of them Spaniards). Below, p. 324.

[108] MINNUCCI, 'Il conferimento', Tavola II, pp. xxiv-xxvi. For information on Sienese who took degrees in the fifteenth century, apart from the records for the 1440s being published in NARDI, 'Una fonte inedita delle lauree senesi' we are entirely dependent on anecdotal evidence.

[109] Cf. the social bias of the list of students enrolled in *humanitas* in Verde's Florence (*Lo Studio fiorentino*, III). The fact that the chairs in these subjects were retained in Florence after the refoundation of Pisa is highly significant. DENLEY, '*Signore* and *Studio*', pp. 214-5.

[110] The original study of this phenomenon was MARONGIU, 'Protezionismi scolastici e stipendi professoriali', and IDEM, 'Protezionismi scolastici e problemi universitari di ieri e di oggi', *Archivio giuridico* (1943), repr. in his *Stato e Scuola*, pp. 283-312. Examples of these in Italian *studi* are discussed in SOTTILI, 'Zum Verhältnis', p. 53; and SILVANO, 'Stato, territorio e istituzioni', pp. 992-3, claiming it as the hallmark of the territorial state.

[111] *Chartularium*, doc. 31, pp. 22-4, 2 Sept.

[112] *Chartularium*, doc. 451, pp. 567-69, 19 Oct.

crisis of the *Studio* in 1360.[113] However, subsequent reopenings of the *Studio* were backed by a re-call of all Sienese students who had left for other universities.[114] In 1425 the measure was extended to include all those under Sienese jurisdiction,[115] and this provision remained in force, more or less continuously (though with varying degrees of penalty),[116] until the fall of the republic.[117] Even more serious than studying elsewhere was going elsewhere to take a degree – a moment which was supposed to be prestigious for the commune and lucrative for the examiners). This too was pro-hibited, in a measure of 1451 which stated that no degrees were to be taken by Sienese at other universities without a pre-payment to the commune of 1,000 *lire*, on pain of a fine of 500 gold florins or well over double that amount.[118]

It is difficult to see how such legislation could have been enforced, relying as it must have done on hearsay and intelligence reports from other university towns[119] (and of course the Sienese were playing

[113] Above, p. 47; DENLEY, 'Academic Rivalry', p. 195; MINNUCCI, 'La Chiesa e le istituzioni', p. 220, pointing out that students did indeed leave.

[114] *Conc.* 238, f. 31v, 21 Aug 1405.

[115] *Conc.* 358, ff. 16v-17r, 22 Sept. Those already doing so were given one month in which to return.

[116] It is repeated in 1429 (*Conc.* 379, ff. 8v-9r, 12 May; a doctor or student who left Siena would be fined 500 florins); in 1464 (*Conc.* 584, f. 24r, 3 Feb, when students currently elsewhere were given two months to return, on penalty of a fine of 100 florins; the same penalty was payable by any citizen students who went to study elsewhere without permission from the *Consiglio del Popolo*; cf. BARGAGLI, *Bartolomeo Sozzini*, pp. 12 n. 19, 34-5); and in 1473, when the fine is re-stored to 1,000 florins (*Conc.* 640, f. 21r, 30 May). In 1491 teachers and students are giving *fideiussori* before leaving (*Studio* 127, no foliation, and *Not.* 968, no foliation). But the commune often relented. Giorgio di Tommaso Cecchi, a civil law student who in 1408 was threatened with a 1,000-florin fine if he left, was subsequently allowed to go (*Conc.* 255, f. 48r, 27 Aug, *Conc.* 256, f. 28r, 23 Oct. On him see MINNUCCI, 'Documenti', pp. 256-7). The 1425 measure was immedi-ately followed by a specific order that Bartolomeo Borghesi, who was known to be studying civil law elsewhere, return im-mediately; if he was in Florence he had five days in which to return, if in Bologna ten days. He eventually turned up al-most three weeks later and was excused his fine (*Conc.* 358, f. 18r, 24 Sept and 13 Oct). For theologians the punishment for breaking this law was even fiercer (BERTONI, 'Il "Collegio" dei teologi', p. 25), though clearly equally capable of being disregarded (e.g. in FIORAVANTI, 'Formazione e carriera di un domenicano', p. 348). The delicacy of these matters is nicely illustrated the case of Antonio da Fermo, who came to Siena with letters of recommendation from the cardinal of Fermo (*Conc.* 1437, no. 90, 25 Feb 1436) and Cardinal Colonna (*Conc.* 1437, no. 92, 27 Feb 1436). His problem was that, al-though he had begun his studies in Siena, he had then left to take his degree in Perugia; now he wished to be considered for the post of collateral.

[117] The exception is the highly unusual proposal in 1483, in the context of an alliance with Florence, of a 'free trade' agreement whereby Sienese subjects would be allowed to study at Pisa and Florentines at Siena (*Balìa* 404, f. 111v, 4 Jun 1483). It is not clear what became of the proposal, since later that year the *Savi* examined witnesses to see if some students had gone to Pisa (*Studio* 2, f. 96v, 22 Dec 1483); however, it is striking to find communal scholarship payments in Prato of 25 *lire* per annum to Giuliano di Ser Lorenzo di Giuliano Tani 'scholare allo Studio di Siena' from October 1494 to June 1496 (Archivio di Stato di Prato, *Archivio dei Ceppi, Ceppo Nuovo* 413, f. 276 l and r. I am most grateful to Dr Jonathan Davies for this reference). In 1511 the convention that Florentine and Sienese subjects could attend each other's universities was re-established (VERDE, *Lo Studio fiorentino*, V, p. 480). Again, it did not last, since in 1541 an agreement was made whereby Cosimo I gave Florentine subjects access to Siena until the *Studio* of Pisa reopened (*Capitoli* 5, f. 396v; PRUNAI, III, p. 81).

[118] *Conc.* 510, f. 51r-v, 30 Jun. The acting official was to receive a quarter of the fine, and the degree would also be deemed invalid in Siena. But here too the commune's bite was not always as fierce as its bark, as demonstrated by the case of Andrea di M.° Bartolomeo, who, having taken his degree in Florence, was in 1441 first barred from entering the *Collegio Medico* for life, but subsequently admitted within four months of the initial measure (See above, p. 204 n. 181). The 1511 statutes of the college of doctors of medicine stipulated that an entrant to the college had to pay double the admission charge (28 'aureos largos' instead of 14) if he had obtained his degree outside Siena (Rubric 15, *Balìa* 253, ff. 341v-342r).

[119] See p. 238 n. 55 above.

the same game, poaching students from other towns with similar legislation).[120] However draconian these measures, their value was probably limited. In fact no examples have come to light of such enormous fines actually being paid. However, those degree records from other universities which have been published or analysed to date contain a very low number of Sienese, and anecdotally too there seem to be far fewer Sienese in other Italian *studi*.[121] Whether this is more because of the legislation or whether the very existence of a thriving local university sufficed is a moot point.

---

[120] For example, emissaries were sent in 1428 to Bologna and elsewhere to entice students (*Conc.* 374, ff. 26r, 1 Oct, 27v, 4 Oct), and that year the Sienese ambassador in Florence reported that he had persuaded a number of students to come to Siena (see above, p. 237).

[121] Most of the instances of Sienese studying elsewhere date either from the late fourteenth century, when there was little hope of continuity of study in the city, or the early fifteenth, before that perception was overcome. Examples are Francesco di Giovanni di Bellanti, bishop of Grosseto, who had studied in Bologna (BCS, *ms.* I.III.2, *Obituario di S. Domenico*, f. 62v, 1417); possibly 'Ugolino di Piero da Siena' who appears as a witness in Florence in 1417 and who is described as a medical student (K. PARK, *Doctors and Medicine in Early Renaissance Florence* [Princeton, N.J., 1985], p. 61); and a number of other figures who had clearly decided to make their careers elsewhere. Mariano quondam Eustachii de Ubertinis de Senis, who was studying canon law in Bologna in 1436, took his degree in Ferrara in 1441, and subsequently became bishop of Forlì in 1446 and of Sarzana in 1449; PIANA, *Nuovi documenti*, p. 201. Lorenzo Casuli (da Casole?) da Siena taught surgery and obtained a degree in Padua; T. PESENTI, *Professori e promotori di medicina nello studio di Padova dal 1405 al 1509. Repertorio bio-bibliografico*. Contributi alla Storia dell'Università di Padova, 16 (Trieste, 1984), p. 70. And Giovanni Battista de' Malavolti took his degree and obtained citizenship in Bologna in 1494; PIANA, *Il "Liber Secretus Iuris Caesarei"*, pp. 356, 359, 364, 365, 366. The unusual case of the Jewish doctor Abramo da Montalcino, who received a degree in arts and medicine in Florence in 14 Mar 1472, probably does not fall in this category for a variety of reasons but not least since he is described as 'habitatorem Prati'; M. LUZZATI, 'Dottorati in medicina conferiti a Firenze nel 1472 da Judah Messer Leon da Montecchio a Bonaventura da Terracina e ad Abramo da Montalcino', in *Medicina e salute nelle Marche dal Rinascimento all'età napoleoica. Atti del Convegno, Ancona – Recanati, 28-30 maggio 1992*. Atti e Memorie per la storia Patria delle Marche, 97 (Ancona, 1994), pp. 41-53.

II

THE STUDENT-UNIVERSITY

1. *Introduction*

We turn now to one of the most vexed questions of Italian university history, the function of the 'student university'. These institutions are problematic and elusive from their very origins right through to their decline. Since I propose to deal with this topic extensively elsewhere,[1] I shall confine myself here to a brief summary of the issues, in order to provide the context for the particular complexities of the Sienese case.

For a long time, student universities were considered the key element that differentiated Bologna from Paris – and by consequence the 'southern' from the 'northern' universities, in that both became 'archetypes'. At Bologna, organisations of students, as opposed to those of masters, seem to have been the driving force in the institutionalisation of the *studium*.[2] According to the traditional view, because they paid the teachers collectively, as a 'guild of consumers'[3] they had control over the teachers and all those involved with the university, down to landlords and stationers. However, even staunch advocates of 'medieval student power'[4] recognise that it was at best transient, since communal salaries and communal control soon eroded a great deal of the bargaining power that they had. I am one of those who argue that it never amounted to that much anyway, representing only the height of what students could claim to have achieved in terms of autonomy.[5] From at least the fourteenth century, when

---

[1] For now, see DENLEY, 'Communities within Communities', esp. pp. 721-8; IDEM, 'The University of Siena', pp. 22-51.

[2] For a recent and eloquent summary, G. P. BRIZZI, 'Le università italiane', in *Le Università dell'Europa: dal Rinascimento alle riforme religiose*, eds. G. P. Brizzi and J. Verger (Milan, 1991), pp. 21-53; repr. as 'Le università italiane tra Rinascimento ed età moderna', in *Il pragmatismo degli intellettuali*, pp. 175-200 (pp. 178-9).

[3] HYDE, 'Universities and Cities', p. 19.

[4] The phrase became popular in the wake of the student movement of the 1960s; A. B. COBBAN, 'Medieval Student Power', *Past and Present*, 53 (1971), pp. 28-66. The idea was taken most seriously by W. STEFFEN, *Die studentische Autonomie im mittelalterlichen Bologna. Eine Untersuchung über die Stellung der Studenten und ihrer Universitas gegenüber Professoren und Stadtregierung im 13./14. Jahrhundert* (Berne, 1981).

[5] G. NICOLAJ, 'Forme di Studi medioevali. Spunti di riflessione dal caso aretino', in *Miscellanea Domenico Maffei dicata*, 3, pp. 183-217; repr. in *L'università e la sua storia*, pp. 59-91 questions whether Bologna ever became a 'modello canonico', at least at the time of its alleged influence, and warns of the danger of perpetually taking the Bolognese case as a departure point for comparison (p. 59). A thoughtful consideration of the fluidity of the situation is BELLOMO, 'Scuole giuridiche e università studentesche'.

salaried lectureships became almost universal, the student university must be seen as only one of several components of the university power-balance, alongside the chancellor, the increasingly powerful colleges of doctors and above all the town authorities.

If we accept this dynamic view we have also to describe in a more nuanced way the nature of Bologna's influence. Bologna's status as model is undoubted, in the sense that it was seen as the 'alma mater studiorum', to which other Italian universities referred; but they referred to it on all sorts of matters, not just the student universities: practices regarding teaching and syllabus; the organisation of the theology faculty, of colleges of doctors, and of residential colleges for students; issues of precedence and protocol. The influence of the Bolognese law statutes has long been known,[6] and they are of course the key ingredient in the idea of the 'archetype'. But the real nature of Bologna's influence seems to me to be rather broader; it is the notion that Bologna is the example of how to do things 'properly'. This, rather than a single specific form of organisation, was the critical feature. To be a reputable university, a *studio* was supposed to have bodies such as that of students, colleges of doctors, etc., even if in practice there was eventually a great deal of variety in the interpretation of these conventions and in the actual behaviour of these bodies.

The *Studio* of Siena was no exception here; indeed, given that its first moment of glory came in the form of an influx from Bologna, it is hardly surprising to find the Sienese imitating the Bolognese example. But Siena's rise as a *studium generale* clearly postdates the heyday of 'student power' (such as it was) and even of the *universitas scholarium*'s most significant period of influence. So the 'post-Bologna' question is: what role could a student body, deemed necessary for credibility and respectability, play in a *studio* created and run by a strongly interventionist local power? This is a central issue for our investigation, and also the most complex, since the methodological problem outlined in the introduction is at its greatest here. The transient nature of the student population may have contributed to the loss of evidence, but so too, arguably, may the weakness of the institution itself. Whatever the cause, we see the student university almost exclusively through the eyes of the commune.

2. *The student university to the 1420s*

The documentation reveals no trace of specifically student *universitates* before the Bolognese migration of 1321. Innocent IV's letter of 1252 was addressed to the 'universitas magistrorum et doctorum…ac ipsorum scolarium'.[7] It is equally clear that the 1321 migration brought student universities to Siena;[8] their rectors (three, one citramontane and one ultramontane in law, and one in arts and medicine) were paid by the commune for a few years thereafter,[9] and one of them was once even entrusted with the distribution of the teachers' communal salaries.[10] It is important to stress, though,

---

[6] The fundamental work is DENIFLE, 'Die Statuten der Juristen-Universität Bologna'.

[7] *Chartularium*, doc. 10, pp. 9-10 (29 Nov 1252). In other words, there is recognition of a legal corporation, but not one with the same membership as in Bologna, where the same year saw a redaction of statutes for the student-universities of canon and civil law (above, p. 109 n. 1). PRUNAI, II, p. 27, speculated that this might be evidence of Neapolitan influence, thinking presumably of the imperial activity of the 1240s, but there is no evidence to support this (see above, pp. 31-4).

[8] See NARDI, *Insegnamento*, esp. pp. 133 *seq.*; a brief summary in IDEM, 'Maestri e scolari: alle origini dello Studio', in *Storia di Siena*, I, pp. 141-54 (147); and IDEM, 'Dalle origini al 1357', pp. 16-17.

[9] Above, p. 99. The last such payment is in 1339; *Chartularium*, doc. 369, pp. 472-4, 20-31 Dec (p. 472); also ed. ZDEKAUER, doc. I^B, pp. 136-8 (p. 137).

[10] *Chartularium*, doc. 227, pp. 282-3, 4 Aug 1323.

that the sense of the documents is that the *Studio* of Bologna, or to be more precise the universities of scholars at Bologna, moved temporarily to Siena, as opposed to their members moving and constituting new universities; the rectors currently in office were taken on and paid by the commune of Siena, and the continuity is in spite of the fact that Siena did not have the status of *studium generale*. Indeed, it is arguable that the recognition and incorporation of the constitution of the Bolognese *Studio* was one of the weaknesses of the Sienese position. Allowed to see itself as the Bolognese *Studio* in exile, it could equally continue to negotiate its return; the very autonomy of the *Studio*, guaranteed by the commune, facilitated its return to Bologna.

The first evidence of properly Sienese constitutional arrangements that in some way reflected the 'model' dates from 1357 when, hard on the heels of the imperial diploma, the commune legislated to define the rector's jurisdiction.[11] This is a perplexing document, which Nardi has wisely described as 'una sorta di statuto'.[12] Despite its legal scope, it is clearly specific to the occasion; like the 1262 measures which were incorporated in the town's statute book but which includes privileges for maestro Tedaldo,[13] the 1357 measure names the rector, 'dominus Thomas de Ficechio'. It equally clearly marks a step away from the Bolognese precedent; there is only one reference to Bologna, granting the rector similar authority to his Bolognese counterparts in matters not covered by the measure. In practice the authority granted to the Sienese rector considerably exceeded that in Bologna, particularly in terms of his authority over the doctors (in which respect the Bolognese statutes of 1317-47 claim much, though we know that his authority was already being undermined). Far from symbolising student power in the Bolognese tradition, the measure does not mention him being elected by students; on the contrary, his appointment was approved by 'dominorum duodecim et ordinum civitatis Senarum', i.e. the regime, before his powers were confirmed by the *Consiglio della Campana*. Also in contrast to the Bolognese model (and for that matter to what had operated in Siena after the 1321 migration), there is reference to only one rector, and indeed at no stage thereafter do we find mention of anything other than a single student university.[14] But actually the document, however clear about the rector, tells us very little about the body over which he was to preside. Indeed, though it refers to him several times as 'rector Universitatis scolarium', he is also given 'potestatem...regendi Universitatem doctorum et scolarium'.[15]

Was this just casual drafting or loose expression? Or poor legal expertise, even? Or did the rector legally have authority over both? The answer must surely be that the system was as yet undeveloped and fluid. Confirmation of this comes with the realisation that this is recurrent; a similar inconsistency, and indeed ambiguity, is evident in the few references to the *universitas* between 1357 and the second decade of the fifteenth century. A payment in 1362, of which the original is now lost, appears to have described Corradino di Marchese as rector of both doctors and scholars,[16] while in 1389 Martino

---

[11] *Chartularium*, doc. 432, pp. 570-2, 24 Nov 1357; ZDEKAUER, doc. IV, pp. 141-2.

[12] NARDI, *Insegnamento*, p. 212.

[13] Above, p. 32 n. 7.

[14] There is one moment at which the possibility is raised of having two rectors, at the height of a conflict between ultramontanes and citramontanes in 1429; below, p. 259. The single *universitas scholarium* is not unusual in *studi* founded with the Bolognese model in mind; Florence and Perugia are close examples.

[15] As n. 11 above.

[16] BCS, *ms*. E.VI.9, 'Memorie relative allo Studio senese prese dalla Biccherna', 29 Apr 1362, no foliation. The original volume is missing. The same entry also refers to a payment for the 'bidello del Rettore de lo studio, e de' Dottori'.

da Genova is 'rectore scolarium et Studii Senensis'.[17] The ambiguities continue into the 1420s. The next reference to the body to come to light dates from 1405, when the *Savi* and *Concistoro* elect a 'rector scholarium',[18] and he is referred to in the same way in 1419,[19] but in 1420 the scholars and teachers, refusing to return to Siena after plague, actually styled themselves 'Vestra filia, Universitas doctorum et scollarium studii senensis',[20] and in 1422 – the last such instance to have been found – a student, Antonio 'vocatus Sciacha' de Sicilia', was granted safe-conduct at the behest of 'tota universitatis et doctorum et scolarium'.[21]

It is of course theoretically possible – but extremely unlikely, and unprecedented – for both the community of scholars and the larger community of teachers and scholars to have distinct legal personalities (which is what 'universitas' meant in juridical terms).[22] A much more likely explanation is the discontinuity in the life of the *Studio*, and *a fortiori* of the *universitas*. At the most basic level, the survival of the *Studio* entailed regular and continued hirings of teachers and the attraction of students. The appointment of a rector was perhaps a next step, in the more flourishing years. There is no sign that a separate *universitas* of students had any actual existence during the period. Interestingly, variation in terminology persists through the fifteenth century, but no longer relates directly to the doctors. That the rector of the scholars was at the same time considered to be rector of the *Studio* as a whole is evidenced repeatedly in fifteenth-century documents. In 1422, the same year as the last reference I have found to a university of doctors and scholars,[23] there is also a document referring to the rector as

---

[17] He appears as witness at the degree of Bartolo da Perugia, 25 Apr 1389; MINNUCCI, 'Documenti', doc. I-1, p. 47. Similar fluidity is evidenced in the fact that in 1390 the rector was a Sienese, Angelo Malavolti ('rector universitatis sen. studii'; *Conc.* 1827, no. 35, 4 Jul 1390). It is not clear whether this is the same as 'd. Angelo d. Iovannachi rectore Studii Senensis' who witnessed the degrees in canon law of two Benedictines on 11-12 May of the same year (ed. MINNUCCI, 'Documenti', doc. I-2, pp. 47-8).

There is one other reference to a Sienese rector; the teacher Giovanni Bandini (or Giovanni di Bandino Tommasi) is reported as having held the post. F. ZAZZERA, *Della Nobiltà dell'Italia*, II, n.p. (under 'Tommasi'), states 'Fu costui per le sue virtù, nella gioventù il primo Rettore creato dello studio di Siena, come si legge nel Proemio del Libro delle leggi di quello studio'. Uberto Benvoglienti quoted this unquestioningly in his introduction to the *Chronicon Senense* in 1729, while correcting other aspects of Zazzera's entry (A. DEI, *Chronicon Senense Italice scriptum ab Andrea Dei, et ab Angelo Turae continuatum…* in *Rerum Italicarum Scriptores*, XV [Milan, 1729]; p. 7). No archival evidence has been found to support this claim, and the interpretation of UGURGIERI AZZOLINI, *Le Pompe Sanesi*, I, p. 428, also quoting Zazzera but amending this point to 'tornò poi a Siena, nella cui Università fu honorato della prima Cattedra circa gli anni 1418', is more accurate. That is probably the best guess in the absence of further evidence on the other problematic aspect of the entry, the reference to the 'Libro delle leggi di quello studio'. Unless this refers to the missing statutes of the student university (on which see below), this must remain a mystery – though Bandini does appear in the preamble to the 1566 statutes of the college of doctors of law as one of the compilers of the original statutes of the college (*Studio* 40, f. 7r; see above, p. 200). Neither the 1540s legislation (below, pp. 270-1) nor that concerning the rectorate at the end of the sixteenth century (below, p. 403 n. 5) include any mention of Bandini.

[18] *Conc.* 239, f. 14r, 16 Nov 1405. Shortly after this he is for the first time referred to as 'rector studii' (f. 40v, 4 Dec). Below, p. 277.

[19] *Conc.* 322, f. 16r, 23 Sept.

[20] *Archivio Sergardi-Biringucci*, ms. A.II, no. 2, 11 Oct, ed. ZDEKAUER, doc. XI. 3, p. 159 (and see p. 41, and above, pp. 113-4).

[21] *Conc.* 337, f. 39v, 22 Apr (and cf. f. 43r-v, 25 Apr); on this figure see below, p. 278 n. 257.

[22] 'Universitas', *Lexikon des Mittelalters*, VIII (1997), cols. 1247-8. The term is found in Siena in reference to the *Studio* (e.g. *Conc.* 369, f. 18v, 2 Oct 1427, ed. PIANIGIANI, doc. 82, pp. 103-5; and *Conc.* 2175, no foliation, same date; the *Concistoro* and *Savi* order that Benedetto Barzi be admitted to the college of doctors of law 'non obstante quacumque dispositione Statutorum et ordinum universitatis Studij'), the colleges of doctors (e.g. *Not.* 589, f. 67r, 7 Jun 1464; reference to the 'collegium sive universitatis doctorum artium et medicine'), and of course guilds, or the commune itself ('comuni collegio et universitatis'; *Not.* 286, ff. 4r, 4 Mar, and 46r, 30 Dec 1423).

[23] Above, n. 21.

both 'rector studii' and 'rector universitatis studii';[24] in 1424 Antonio Cesso da Sicilia is described as 'rettore del gienerale studio de la città di Siena' in the record of his salary payment.[25]

Despite these ambiguities, the 1420s, with the great increase in the numbers of teachers and students alike, was clearly the time at which issues relating to the foreign students, and their representation and organisation, were played out. In 1423 the *Concistoro* legislated over the election of the rector and of his *consiliarii*, and in the same year a test case revived the question of his jurisdiction, while by the end of the decade the rotation of the rectorate, and the extent of his jurisdiction, were controversial issues.[26]

3. *The issue of statutes*

There is no getting away from the fact that the statutes of the student-university have vanished. The best we can do is to speculate as to the date and circumstances in which they may have been created, and to try to work out from other evidence what they might have contained.

There is no trace of statutes of a *universitas scholarium* as such before the 1420s. There is only the most tenuous hint of the existence of one element traditionally found in such statutes, namely the regulations about the syllabus, and nothing to connect that to a student-university.[27] The absence of statutes is not unusual – fourteenth-century Pisa and Florence both experienced an interim period between the foundation of the *Studio* and the promulgation of statutes[28] – and is often an indicator of fluidity.[29] The fifteenth century sees the promulgation of a number of sets of student-university statutes in Italian universities, in both initial and revised versions.[30] The act of compiling statutes is of

[24] *Conc.* 1620, ff. 13v-14r, 26 Jan; the *Concistoro*, writing to the rector, 'Dns. Antonius de Drepano' (Trapani), uses both forms. On this shift of terminology see below, p. 277.

[25] *Bicch.* 307, f. 36v; cf. 41v, and *Bicch.* 456, f. 50v, 1425. Andrew of Hawyck is described as 'Rectore Senensis Studii', *Not.* 325, f. 44r, 8 Nov 1424, ed. MINNUCCI, 'Documenti', doc. I-5, pp. 54-6 (p. 56). In 1495 the vice-rector is described as 'Vicerectore Studii Senensis et Universitatis scolarium'; *Conc.* 770, f. 23r, 13 Feb, ed. FERRERI, doc. 344, p. 339.

[26] Below, pp. 258-9.

[27] This is suggested by a shift in how these conditions were described. According to the records of payments of teachers in 1389 they were to teach 'sichondo lo studio di Bologna'; *Bicch.* 460, ff. 10r-11r, a phrase which would hardly have been included had the *Studio* had its own statutes at this stage. But by the end of the century such *condotte* referred to indigenous terms of employment; Niccolò Sozzini was to teach 'sicondo la forma et capitoli de lo studio gienerale da Siena, ed è tenuto d'osservare tucte quelle cose che disposti sono per forma de' detti statuti intorno a la detta letura' (*Bicch.* 285, f. 55r, 28 Jun 1399; cf. *Bicch.* 439, f. 207v, 1400, and the payment of Mignanello Mignanelli, f. 433v, 1400). If such regulations were laid down, the only evidence for them being perhaps part of student university statutes, as opposed to communally created ones, would be their subsequent disappearance! There is really not enough evidence for the 1390s to be sure of anything in this respect.

[28] M. TANGHERONI, 'L'età della Repubblica', pp. 19-20. Florence, founded in 1349, promulgated its first statutes in 1388 (GHERARDI, *Statuti*, pp. 11-104).

[29] A. GIEYZSTOR, 'Management and Resources', in *A History of the University in Europe*, I, pp. 108-43 (pp. 113-4).

[30] Bologna saw the first set we have of statutes of the university of artists drawn up in 1405, and a revision of the statutes of the university of jurists in 1432 (ed. MALAGOLA, *Statuti*, pp. 213-312 and 47-177 respectively); Parma has original statutes of jurists in 1414 (ed. U. GUALAZZINI, *Corpus Statutorum Almi Studii Parmensis* [Milan, 1978], pp. 73-190 [rev. edn. 1987]); Padua has revised statutes for jurists in 1463 (the edition of which is keenly awaited); Ferrara has original statutes for artists at some stage between 1474 and 1489 (ed. V. and R. CAPUTO, *L'Università degli Scolari di medicina e d'arte dello Studio ferrarese* [Ferrara, 1990], pp. 55-134); Florence revised the statutes for its single-subject university in 1478 (rubrics ed. VERDE, *Lo Studio fiorentino*, IV.1, pp. 10-11, and cf. BARGAGLI, *Bartolomeo Sozzini*, pp. 65, 81-2).

course a substantial exercise which can create an institution and give it identity, or just legitimacy – many are after all copied, either in the realistic assessment that others, older and better, should act as models (as we will see in the case of the Sienese Casa della Sapienza), or perhaps in a hasty quest for legitimacy. Certainly they do not always reflect contemporary realities,[31] even in Bologna itself. In sum, the most important feature of new statutes tends not to be their contents so much as the act and the moment of their promulgation.

We can perhaps come close to identifying the most likely moment at which statutes may have been compiled. As has been seen, there is a small number of late fourteenth-century references to statutes, all of the generic type that makes it impossible to be sure whether they refer to communal regulations about the *Studio*, or ones recognisably belonging to a student *universitas* in the legal sense. In the 1420s such references to statutes become more frequent, though they still refer to the *Studio* rather than to a student university; for example, a student is offered the rectorate in 1420 'secundum formam statutorum universitatis…studi'.[32] In 1423, when the method of election of the rector was established, and when the *Savi* were charged with proposing a method of election of the *consiliarii*, throughout the proceedings which follow (which include the approval of the 'congregatione studentium') no mention was made of existing statutes, even for the purpose of countermanding them.[33] In 1425 a rector undertook not to leave before syndication 'secundum formam statuti studii senensi';[34] but this could equally be referring to the commune's regulations governing the syndication of the rector, as ordered in 1419.[35] The most information comes towards the end of the decade. In 1428 the rector's jurisdiction was agreed 'secundum formam…statutorum universitatis dicti studii',[36] and in June 1429, when the *Concistoro* removed the students' traditional right to be judged by the bishop, their teacher, or the rector, the measure was entitled 'corrigendo statutum universitatis scolarium'.[37] In May 1429, in apparently the most explicit reference we have to statutes of a student university, the commune's protectionist legislation (forbidding either students or doctors from leaving Siena on pain of a 500-florin fine) was to be entered 'in volumine statutorum scolarium'.[38] But the significance of even this seemingly incontrovertible phrase is diminished when we turn to measures of only two months later; in July the *Concistoro* passed five measures – referred to as 'capitula…statutorum studii' and including two concerning the method and timetable of election of the new rector – which the *bidello* was instructed to publish 'pro scolas dicti studii',[39] and two of which were to be disseminated by public *banno*.[40] At no point in these deliberations is there reference to a book of statutes.[41]

---

[31] GIEYZSTOR, loc. cit.

[32] *Conc.* 1617, f. 59v, 6 May.

[33] Below, pp. 258-9.

[34] *Conc.* 357, f. 27r, 11 Aug.

[35] *Conc.* 322, f. 16r, 23 Sept.

[36] *Conc.* 376, f. 21r-v, 13 Dec.

[37] *Conc.* 379, f. 22r-v, 14 Jun.

[38] *Conc.* 379, ff. 8v-9r, 12 May (and cf. f. 22r-v, 14 Jun). ZDEKAUER, pp. 65-6, cited similar evidence for 1427, without giving references, but I have not found any and would assume that he was thinking of one of these measures.

[39] *Conc.* 380, ff. 7v-8r, 8 Jul.

[40] *Conc.* 380, f. 8v, 9 Jul.

[41] It ought to be pointed out that the author of the reference to 'volumine statutorum scolarium' (no mention of a *universitas*) might just conceivably have had in mind *Mis.* 1, in which statutes concerning the student-university were already being entered (e.g. p. 258 n. 79 below).

There can be little doubt that the 1420s were a period of development for the student body, and there is a considerable amount of information about it in the documents, which demonstrate clear moments of tension culminating precisely in 1429.[42] This led Zdekauer to locate in that period the one further piece of evidence that we must consider, one which he held to be of such significance that he made it the basis of his account of the student university in Siena. It is a fragment of nineteen rubrics, now preserved in the Archivio di Stato di Siena, *Studio* 100, which he published under the heading 'Riforma degli Statuti delle Università degli Scolari Citramontani et Ultramontani'. The document is concerned primarily with the citramontane and ultramontane rectors, the relationship between the two, their jurisdiction, salaries and rights (for example to promote to the first 'degree', the baccalaureate). It stipulates the functions of the *bedellus*, and that the statutes be kept 'in residencia Universitatis'. There are some variants on the original Bolognese 'model', such as the proportions of *consiliarii* in each 'nation'. Two of these had mysteriously to be citizens, and four foreigners.[43]

While Zdekauer's chronology cannot be faulted, the same cannot be said of his publication of the document, without comment or explanation, under the heading 'Riforma degli Statuti'. Zdekauer, still of the era of scholars for whom the constitution of a *studio* had to be the starting-point, rather assumed that this influence held good beyond that period.[44] It is in fact a one-sheet fragment, with no heading other than the word 'Ihesus' and the much later archivist's comment, underneath, 'Regolamenti circa i Rettori oltramontani d'una qualche arte (non si dice)' subsequently corrected to 'Regolamenti circa i Rettori oltramontani dello Studio di Siena'. It is more likely to be a draft than an official document (apart from anything else it consists only of rubrics, as Zdekauer says);[45] it nowhere mentions Siena and for all we know it could even be a digest of procedures in or suggestions from other *studi*, so abstract is its wording.[46] This is also suggested by its inherent contradictions; two references to universities in the plural,[47] two to a single university[48] (and one seal),[49] considerable ambiguity about the future number of rectors,[50] and the regulation of the number of *consiliarii* which would appear to make no sense at all.[51] There is no evidence elsewhere or later that these clauses were adopted; and in the case of Siena one is in a position to expect some traces in the communal documents of such a reform. Zdekauer gives no concrete evidence that the document belongs to this period; indeed it could be argued that the substance and terminology are more appropriate to the early fourteenth century situation, and are so discordant with what little we do know of the university's organisation in this period that he gets into considerable interpretative difficulty, deducing for example the continued existence

---

[42] It was also an intense period of statute-making and collecting in general in Siena; Ascheri, 'Statuti, legislazione e sovranità', pp. 180-1 (repr. as 'Legislazione, statuti e sovranità', pp. 27-8).

[43] Zdekauer, doc. XVI, pp. 166-7; see also pp. 65-8. The document is now in *Studio* 100, no. 1.

[44] Zdekauer, p. 66 esp.

[45] Zdekauer, pp. 65-6.

[46] E.g. each rector 'habeat integrum salarium a Dominis' (rubric III – the numbering is also Zdekauer's); the statutes are to be kept 'in residencia Universitatis' (rubric XIV).

[47] Rubrics XVI and XIX.

[48] Rubrics XIV and XV.

[49] Rubric XIII.

[50] Rubric XVIII, which, *pace* Zdekauer (p. 67), either contradicts the intentions of rubrics III-XIII or is simply badly worded.

[51] Rubric IX. Zdekauer's valiant attempt (p. 68) to explain this does not do away with the fact that it presupposed citizen *consiliarii* representing nations of both the citramontane and ultramontane universities. Citizen *consiliarii* do appear in 1430 (*Conc.* 387, f. 26r-v, 12 Oct), but not as formal representatives of these groups.

and distinctness of citramontane and ultramontane universities,[52] whereas the elections of rectors and the communal statutes relating to this office in the 1420s have no such distinction, nor do they give any evidence that there were ever actually two rectors after the early fourteenth-century Bolognese migration.[53] Moreover, the ineligibility of artists for the rectorate was not applied in Siena,[54] and the references in the document to a 'residencia Universitatis'[55] and to the rectors' promotions to the baccalaureate[56] find little echo in other documents before the last decades of the fifteenth century, though in the case of the latter it could be argued that this was a consequence of the measure itself.

So many features of this document are unique for the period, and run contrary to what little evidence we have, that in the absence of better credentials it must be regarded with suspicion. It is also questionable whether it can justly be described as a reform, drafted or adopted, of existing statutes. Zdekauer entitled it thus because in it – and elsewhere – he saw evidence of an older body of university statutes, now lost.[57] But there are very real problems about postulating missing statutes prior to this, not least, as has been seen, the difficulty of identifying a stage at which such statutes might have been drawn up, and the absence of any references to them in the surviving documentation.

So what might the missing book of statutes have contained? In the period following the 1420s there are a handful of references to statutes which unfortunately do not make the situation much clearer. The two most unambiguous are a note of 1489 in which the vice-rector, Henrighus di Sylberberg, declared that he had received, amongst other things, the 'libro statutorum antiquorum',[58] and a measure of 1472, regarding substitutes for teaching, which was recorded in the margin as 'positus in statutis Rectoris studii'.[59] So it is beyond dispute that there was a book which was supposed to be kept by the rector. But was this a formal statute of the student-university? The problem is that almost all the references we have to statutes of the students tell of the commune's interference in what should have been matters for that body; they appear either when the commune is enforcing or lending its authority to them or, more frequently, when it is adding to, altering or waiving them.[60] In 1463 two provisions were passed which the notary of the *Concistoro* tells us 'apparent manu mei in statutis dicti Studii'.[61] Even when it is a case of support or reinforcement, the statute in question often turns out to be one originally promul-

---

[52] ZDEKAUER, p. 66.

[53] Rubric I refers to the alternation of the citramontane and ultramontane rectors as *rector universalis*, common elsewhere. The term *rector generalis* does appear in Sienese documents (*Conc.* 407, f. 16v, 2 Dec 1433; *Conc.* 418, ff. 22v-23r, 18 Oct 1435. Zdekauer referred to such a description in 1423 but I have not found any such), but while Zdekauer saw in this (pp. 66-7) the implication that there were other rectors, we never hear of them. The particulars of the election procedure also make the existence of other rectors unlikely (below, pp. 258 *seq.*), as does the fact that in 1429 the possibility of electing two rectors just for that year is debated (*Conc.* 380, f. 17v, 21 Jul), but not put into practice (*Conc.* 381, f. 5r, 6 Sept). Below, p. 259.

[54] Rubric XVII; below, pp. 258 *seq.*

[55] Rubric XIV; below, p. 274.

[56] Rubric VII. On the baccalaureate, below, p. 287.

[57] The internal evidence is rubrics XIV ('quod Statuta Universitatis semper stent in residencia Universitatis') and XIX ('quod omnia et singula predicta scribantur in Statutis Universitarum' [*sic*]). But even if the document is what Zdekauer claims it is, these two rubrics may perfectly well be projecting those statutes rather than referring to existing ones. On the external evidence, above, pp. 253-4.

[58] *Studio* 127, no foliation, 4 Aug. Despite the formality this does not relate to the ceremonial of investiture; he had been vice-rector for over a year. Below, p. 265.

[59] *CG* 234, f. 180r, 3 Aug.

[60] A parallel is the book of statutes of the Casa della Sapienza, *Mis.* 1, which by the mid-fifteenth century included measures relating to teaching just as much as to the college itself; see above, pp. 25-7.

[61] *Conc.* 582, f. 28v, 17 Oct.

gated by the commune. This may well be the case with the determination of the rector's jurisdiction of 1428,[62] and is certainly true of the declaration in 1437 that the election of the rector was to take place 'secundum formam statutorum dicti universitatis', statutes which the commune had, it seems, imposed on the student university in 1423.[63] But perhaps the most striking feature is the way in which the commune did not hesitate to legislate over the *universitas*, instructing it to include the legislation forbidding students or doctors from leaving Siena in its statute-book,[64] removing at a stroke an important part of the rector's jurisdiction (the rubric in the records reads 'corrigendo statutum universitatis scolarium'),[65] or waiving the stipulation of the statutes that the election of the rector had to be announced one month in advance.[66] This interference with the statutes of the university places the legal significance of its status as a *universitas* very much in question. The extent of the commune's control is impressive. Strangely, the only area which it may have left to the student-university – to the extent that we know nothing about it – is the specification of the syllabus, the 'punctatio librorum' which stipulated how the texts were to be divided up. Although later communal legislation is ambiguous here, stating in 1464 simply that doctors could only omit *lectiones* where this was allowed 'per li Statuti dell'Università',[67] and in 1481 that teaching was to be 'secondo la forma delli statuti',[68] no such specific statutes have survived in communal records, and a similar measure in 1436 stating that doctors must read 'secundum formam statutorum sen. et universitatis scolarium'[69] points very much in that direction.

4. *The rector*

The problems raised by the question of the missing statutes are not untypical of those encountered in a study of the student-university in general. The communal legislation obviously provides a limited perspective, and one must be aware of these limitations. On the other hand, communal interference is interesting in itself, and there are several areas in which it reveals quite a lot about the university. Foremost among these is the rectorate, and a measure of the strength of the communal hold over the university is the way in which the rector was elected. The rectorate was seen as the key appointment in symbolic terms.[70] As well as being responsible for the *scolaresca* – he is described as their shepherd in the rhetoric[71] – he was the head of the whole *Studio*,[72] so that its fortunes could be described, un-

---

[62] See n. 306, and below, p. 265 and n. 149.

[63] *Conc.* 431, f. 22v, 19 Dec (with an ambiguity; three candidates were to be scrutinised 'in generali consilio scolarium universitatis studii senensi secundum formam statutorum dicte universitatis'); below, p. 258. Cf. *CG* 225, ff. 73v-74r, 20 Oct 1450; the rector was to be elected 'con quella autorità che se fosse electo secondo l'ordini e li statuti di decta università'.

[64] See above, p. 254 and n. 38.

[65] *Conc.* 379, f. 22r-v, 14 Jun 1429.

[66] *Conc.* 425, f. 20r, 8 Dec 1436 (derogation of 'statutum universitatis scholarium'); *Conc.* 442, f. 24r, 5 Oct 1439 ('Derogat. statutorum universitatis studii generalis').

[67] *Conc.* 584, ff. 23v-24r, 3 Feb, ed. BAI, doc. 225, pp. 178-9.

[68] *Balìa* 24, f. 88v, 30 Jun, eds. PUCCINOTTI, *Storia della Medicina*, p. CLXIII, and ILARDI, 'Ordinamenti', p. 166; copy in *Mis.* 1, f. 107r.

[69] *Conc.* 421, f. 40v, 24 Apr. For further examples of student involvement in such regulations, see p. 278.

[70] ZDEKAUER described the office as 'la pietra angolare dell'edificio' (p. 55).

[71] *Conc.* 528, f. 54v, 14 Oct 1454: 'viso quod pro anno futuro non invenitur aliquem velle de Rectore Studii, nisi habeat aliquod comodum, et viso quod oves sine pastore non bene se habent...'.

[72] An illustration of this formal role is the letter of pope Innocent VIII to the rector (rather than the communal authori-

doubtedly with exaggeration, as intricately bound up with his.[73] This historical dual function – the embodiment of both student representation (in an arguably vague sense) and the symbolic headship of the *Studio* itself – made the office of particular interest to the authorities, and it is no surprise to find them closely involved in the process of their creation.

a. The method of choosing the rector

The very few references to the rector in the late fourteenth century yield no evidence of how they were chosen,[74] but it is clear that the commune found its own way here. In 1405 the *Concistoro* and the *Savi* elected Dominus Franciscus de Catelonia *in rectorem scholarium*.[75] There is no mention of the students' or the university's role in this. Francesco was a student in canon law, and the following day the *Concistoro* stipulated that in future, 'ad hoc ut scandala non sequantur', the office was to rotate between subjects, starting with medicine and followed by civil and then canon law (an issue to which we will return).[76] In 1407, however, the 'universitas studii' was allowed to elect its own rector (who exceptionally might be married and not yet a doctor);[77] and in 1408 his term was renewed, by the *Consiglio Generale*, for another year, apparently with the approval of the university.[78]

In 1423 a new procedure was established; a shortlist of three candidates was to be drawn up by the *Concistoro*, the *Savi*, the outgoing rector and his *consiliarii*, and was voted on by the assembly of all matriculated students.[79] Interest in the role of the rector was clearly on the rise in the late 1420s, as was interest in the student university generally. For 1428 we have, unusually, several letters of recommendation for the rectorate.[80] But the continuation of the rotation of the rectorate by 'faculty' rather

---

ties or the college of doctors) requesting that Corrado Banghen be excused the fees for his doctorate in canon law (*Not.* 799, no foliation, 6 Apr 1489, ed. ZDEKAUER, *Documenti*, part 2, doc. 5, p. 40; see below, pp. 288-9).

[73] E.g. *Conc.* 614, f. 23v, 3 Feb 1469: 'Attendentes quantum honoris et utilitatis sit studium in civitate senarum, et caput dicti studii est rector dicti studii, sub cui...auctoritate scolares reguntur et gubernantur. Et viso quod est annus quando dictum studium et scolares ipsius no habuerunt nec habent Rectorem in maxima verecundiam et detrimentum nostre civitatis et studii predicti...'; cf. *Conc.* 597, f. 40r, 13 Apr 1466, where the continued vacancy of the rectorate is described as threatening the dissolution of the whole *Studio* ('et si studio...remaneret sine rectore esset dissolutio totale presentis studii').

[74] Even the initial decree of 1357 glosses over the issue of student participation, merely confirming that the choice of rector had been approved by the *Concistoro*; above, p. 251.

[75] *Conc.* 239, f. 14r, 16 Nov; and cf. f. 40v, 4 Dec, ed. ZDEKAUER, p. 54 n. 2 (his salary is ordered).

[76] *Conc.* 239, f. 14r, 17 Nov. Cf. ZDEKAUER, pp. 54-5 (giving the date as 16 Nov); see below, p. 267.

[77] *Conc.* 251, f. 12r, 16 Nov.

[78] *CG* 203, f. 133v, 23 Nov. The whole university is said to be satisfied with him. No name is given in this or the previous year's measure.

[79] *Conc.* 345, f. 16r, and *Mis.* 1, f. 54v, 4 Aug. 115 students voted in the ensuing election (*Conc.* 347, f. 7r, 7 Nov). MARRARA, writing on the sixteenth century, commented on the antiquity of this tradition (*Lo Studio di Siena*, p. 97 n. 368). Cf. ASCHERI, *Siena nel Rinascimento*, p. 122 and n. 26, placing this intervention in the context of the authorities' behaviour towards other institutions such as the hospital of S. Maria della Scala.

[80] The *priori* of Florence recommend their citizen 'Magistrum Johannem filium quondam famosi medicine doctoris magistri petri de Aretio', *Conc.* 1914, no. 33, 4 Aug 1428; Magister Antonius domini Johannis de Itro is recommended in two letters, *Conc.* 2305, fasc. 17, no. 13, 18 July (by the cardinal of Bologna), and *Conc.* 2302, fasc. 2, no. 25, 19 July (by the cardinal of S. Pietro ad Vincula). Neither of these have a year, but it is reasonable to assume they are both of 1428 since on 9 Aug of that year Antonio's was one of the three names to go forward; *Not.* 356, f. 31r-v, ed. MINNUCCI, 'Documenti', II-3, pp. 76-7. (The recommendation by the *priori* of Viterbo of 'Magistrum Oddonem petruccii', 1 Aug, *Conc.* 2305, fasc. 14, no. 14, has the wrong indiction for this year.)

than by geographical grouping promised trouble, and indeed in 1429 a prolonged and bitter quarrel erupted between the citramontanes and the ultramontanes over which group was to provide the next rector. The election was suspended,[81] the *Consiglio del Popolo* took up the matter,[82] and a series of commissions of citizens was appointed to negotiate with the two parties.[83] The suggestion that two rectors be elected was discussed,[84] and after a long summer, during which criminal charges were brought against several students[85] and further delays were incurred, an ultramontane rector was finally chosen in October.[86]

Despite these problems the two-stage, joint election, principle established in 1423, absolutely typical of Sienese electoral procedure, became the basic formula for subsequent elections.[87] The main embellishment was that by the mid-century six names were put forward, and the meeting of the *Concistoro* with the *Studio* representatives reduced this list to three before referring it back to the student university for a final vote.[88] The joint role of communal authority and *universitas* encapsulated in this measure persisted in one form or another for most of the century. The commune's role was both supervisory and participatory. The names of the candidates doubtless came from the student representatives, i.e. those with special involvement and knowledge of possible candidates, though there might be some variation here; in 1454 it was stipulated for the first time that the six names were provided by the rector and *consiliarii*,[89] but in 1463 the vice-rector and his *consiliarii* performed this task together with the *Savi*.[90] A further gesture towards student participation is also evident in the inclusion on a few occasions in the middle of the century of nine other students, alongside the rector or vice-rector's nine *consiliarii*, at the selection meeting.[91] The commune's participation in the reduction of the shortlist is perhaps largely symbolic, though no less important for that.[92] Communal officials, including the highest representatives of the state, were also often present at the final

---

[81] *Conc.* 380, f. 3v, 3 Jul (and see f. 5v, 6 Jul).

[82] *Conc.* 380, f. 6v, 7 Jul.

[83] *Conc.* 379, f. 23r, 14 Jun, *Conc.* 380, ff. 7r, 7 Jul, 14r, 16 Jul, 17v, 21 Jul (and see 8r, 8 Jul).

[84] *Conc.* 380, f. 17v, 21 Jul.

[85] *Conc.* 380, ff. 19r, 25 Jul, 22r, 28 Jul, 27v, 1 Aug. Zdekauer, p. 41.

[86] *Conc.* 381, f. 24v, 11 Oct (and see f. 5r, 6 Sept). Cf. 1451, when the *Concistoro* forced an election at a moment of factional dispute (*Conc.* 511*bis*, ff. 36v, 13 Oct, 49r, 30 Oct).

[87] Examples of regular elections are *Conc.* 368, f. 20v, 11 Aug 1427; *Conc.* 419, f. 59v, 31 Dec 1435; *Conc.* 431, f. 22v, 19 Dec 1437; *Conc.* 437, f. 8v, 9 Nov 1438; and *Conc.* 459, f. 50r, 24 Aug 1442. Occasionally the outgoing rector was absent, usually because he had left by the time of his successor's election. The 1447 decision to hold an election does not mention student participation in the drawing up of the shortlist (*Conc.* 490, f. 12v, 17 Sept 1447). Cf. *Conc.* 387, f. 26r-v, 12 Oct 1430 (*consiliarii cives* are included): 'ex justis et legittimis causes quod pro hac vice tam consiliarii cives universitatis dicti studii et ad vintiduorum consiliarorum possint intervenire in electione Rectoris dicti studi hodie fiendi'.

[88] *Conc.* 528, f. 61r, 19 Oct 1454.

[89] Loc. cit. Similarly in 1469 this was done by the vice-rector and his *consiliarii*; *Conc.* 614, ff. 25r, 4 Feb. On the peculiarities of this election see below, p. 261 n. 101.

[90] *Conc.* 583, f. 33v, 10 Dec.

[91] *Conc.* 431, f. 22v, 19 Dec 1437; *Conc.* 437, f. 8v, 9 Nov 1438; *Conc.* 459, f. 50r, 24 Aug 1442; *Conc.* 528, f. 61r, 19 Oct 1454; *Conc.* 583, f. 33v, 10 Dec 1463.

[92] There is also an occasion on which the expanded meeting of the *Concistoro*, *Capitano del Popolo*, *gonfalonieri*, rector, *Savi dello Studio* and representative scholars appear actually to make the final choice of rector from the shortlist of three, by-passing the customary second stage of the *universitas scholarium*. The wording is not conclusive and this may be a case of hasty drafting (*Conc.* 625, f. 45r, 23 Dec 1470).

meeting of the student university,[93] which, again significantly, took place in the *sala magna inferiore* of the *Palazzo della Signoria*.[94]

More important than the communal authorities' formal, perhaps token, involvement in the process of choosing candidates[95] was their role in organising the election and intervening when the process did not run smoothly, or when candidates were lacking.[96] Because they involved the *Concistoro* and *ordini* of the city, rectoral elections were ordered by the *Concistoro* and ultimately seen as their responsibility – which is interesting in what it says about the state of the student university itself. Though the outgoing rector or vice-rector was apparently responsible for organising the long-list of names to be put forward, he sometimes had to be instructed to do so and even threatened with penalties for delay.[97] Where there were no obvious candidates, or perhaps no university organisation to play its part, the *Concistoro* sometimes extended the period of office of the incumbent, sometimes as a short-term measure, occasionally simply granting him another year.[98] More drastic forms of intervention in the fifteenth century included one instance in which the *Concistoro* suspended the election because of the controversy surrounding the process,[99] one on which it declared a candidate to be

---

[93] *Conc.* 583, f. 33v, 10 Dec 1463 (members of the *Concistoro*, the *Capitano del Popolo* and the *gonfalonieri* attended); *Conc.* 591, f. 43r, 15 Apr 1465 (with the *gonfalonieri*). It is not stated whether they had voting rights in these assemblies, but the assumption must be that they did not, and that their presence was a symbolic formality or at most a mechanism of control.

[94] *Conc.* 534, f. 57r-v, 28 Oct 1455; *Conc.* 583, f. 33v, 10 Dec 1463; *Conc.* 591, f. 43r, 15 Apr 1465; *Conc.* 614, f. 26v, 7 Feb 1469.

[95] To which can be compared the interest taken by the Florentine *Ufficiali dello Studio* in rectoral elections; DAVIES, *Florence and its University*, pp. 23-4.

[96] For example, on 27 December 1481, some days after the term of office of the previous rector had expired, the *notaio* or *bidello* of the *Studio* was instructed to put up a notice advertising the vacancy; anyone wanting the office was to come forward by the end of the month, otherwise a vice-rector would be appointed (*Conc.* 691, f. 46v, ed. FERRERI, doc. 137, p. 118). It appears that only one candidate was found, since on 26 Jan 1482 the *Concistoro* and *Savi* dispensed with a formal election and appointed Dns. Francischus de Philippis of Montefalco (*Conc.* 692, f. 22v, ed. FERRERI, doc. 138, p. 119; his full name appears in the payment of Dec 1483 in *Sale* 21, f. 214v).

[97] E.g. *Conc.* 684, f. 22r, 19 Oct 1480, ed. FERRERI, doc. 108, p. 92; the vice-rector has one day in which to meet with his *consiliarii* and come up with the long-list of six candidates, on penalty of 100 ducats. There is an almost identical resolution in which the vice-rector faces the sack if he does not comply (*Conc.* 703, f. 13v, 6 Dec 1483, ed. FERRERI, doc. 185, p. 157).

[98] Dns. Giovanni da Barbanza was given a second year in office in 1432 (*Conc.* 400, f. 10v, 10 Sept); the office of Johannes Born [?] was extended for two months in 1435 (*Conc.* 418, ff. 22v-23vr 18 Oct), as was Bartolomeo da Genova's in autumn 1457 (*Balìa* 6, f. 14r, 28 Sept, *Conc.* 546, f. 17r, 1 Oct); in April 1458 it was decided that Bartolomeo could stay in office for as long as he liked (*Conc.* 550, f. 19v, 14 Apr); he was re-elected in November 1458 (*Conc.* 553, f. 21r, 28 Nov) and was still rector for much of 1459 (*Conc.* 557, f. 34r, 6 Aug, and *CG* 228, f. 141v, 13 Aug regarding his payment; the election of a vice-rector in October, for a six-month period, is the indication that he has finally given up office, *Conc.* 558, f. 32r, 17 Oct). The next rector to be appointed, Paolo da Prato (*Conc.* 560, f. 41v, 20 Apr 1460), had his term of office extended after eight months until the beginning of the following academic year, without recourse to an election procedure (*Conc.* 565, f. 46r, 30 Dec 1460). Filippo Boccaccini de Alamannis of Florence had at least three years in the post (first elected *Conc.* 591, f. 43r, 15 Apr 1465; reappointed *Conc.* 597 f. 40v, 13 Apr 1466 because despite advertisement no-one else wanted the job; reappointed again *Conc.* 603, f. 26v, 4 Apr 1467). Giovanni Pensio claimed in 1470 that at the time of his election it had been agreed that he might have another year as rector; this was granted (*Conc.* 620, f. 32r-v, 25 Feb; and see below, nn. 101 and 114, and p. 264). His successor, Ferdinando da Portogallo (elected 23 Dec 1470; *Conc.* 625, f. 45r) was also given a series of extensions, again without any recorded consultation of the student university (*Conc.* 633, f. 37r, 24 Apr 1472, one year's renewal; *Conc.* 639, f. 35v, 29 Apr 1473, another four months; *Conc.* 640, f. 21r, 30 May 1473, when this became a whole year; *Conc.* 645, f. 40v, 19 Apr 1474, reconfirmed for four months; *Conc.* 647, f. 31v, 30 Aug renewed until 18 Oct. He stood for re-election, *Conc.* 648, ff. 2v, 2 Sept, but appears not to have been successful, as a vice-rector was subsequently chosen; *Conc.* 648, ff. 24v, 15 Oct, 28v, 20 Oct). Domenico Mentebona da Roma was also given a second year in 1476 (*Conc.* 657, f. 31v, 4 Apr; original election in *Conc.* 652, f. 31v, 11 Jun 1475).

[99] Above, p. 259.

eligible,[100] two on which it suspended the regulations to allow Sienese students to vote,[101] two in which the authorities made the final choice of candidate without referring the shortlist back to the student university,[102] and one (in 1493) in which they simply imposed a candidate, the well-connected Matteo da Matera, granting him a uniquely high salary and organising an impressive inauguration ritual for him.[103]

b. Eligibility and conditions of office

The communal measures afford some insight into the changing requirements for the post. Many of the details of his appointment conform unsurprisingly to the pattern elsewhere. At the opening of the fifteenth century, as in the Bolognese 'model' and elsewhere, the rector was supposed to be a cleric, though we only know this from the instance in 1407 when the requirement was waived (along with the accompanying requirement of celibacy),[104] and in 1435 it was removed.[105] The 1407 'derogation' also allowed the rector not to have a degree; in fact, for all successive appointments that we know of, this appears to be the case, i.e. the rectors were students approaching the end of their studies (though some took their degree during their period of office).[106] Members of the Sapienza were ineligible.[107] The rectorate was an annual office, in theory coinciding with the academic year. The election of the rector was supposed to take place in September,[108] after one month's notice had been given.[109] It was sometimes

[100] *Conc.* 511, ff. 36r, 13 Oct, and 49r, 30 Oct 1451.

[101] *Conc.* 387, f. 26r, 12 Oct 1430; it was decided that Sienese students could participate in the shortlisting ('ex justis et legittimis causis quod pro hac vice tam consiliarii cives universitatis dicti studii et ad vintiduorum consiliariorum possint intervenire in electionem rectoris dicti studii'). In 1469 the election of the current vice-rector, Giovanni Pensio da Sicilia, as rector was achieved after the *Concistoro* had allowed both Sienese and non-matriculated students to vote (*Conc.* 64, f. 26v, 7 Feb).

[102] In 1450, in the wake of an outbreak of plague, the *Consiglio del Popolo* authorised the *Concistoro* and *Savi* to appoint a rector 'con quella autorità che se fosse electo secondo l'ordini e li statuti di decta università' (*CG* 225, f. 74r, 20 Oct; cf. *Conc.* 507, ff. 36v, 19 Oct, and 40r, 23 Oct); in 1470 the scrutinising committee – *Concistoro, Capitano del Popolo, gonfalonieri,* the outgoing rector (involved only in the first stage), the *Savi* and *consiliarii* – made the final choice (*Conc.* 625, f. 45r, 23 Dec).

[103] The election is in *Balìa* 38, f. 31r, 7 Jan 1493; cf. also ff. 56r, 1 Feb, 95v, 12 Apr; *Balìa* 39, ff. 38r, 30 Aug 1494, 51r, 31 Oct 1494, and 53v, 5 Nov 1494; *Not.* 968, no foliation, 18 Jul 1493; and *Balìa* 550, no. 54 for the letter of recommendation of Alfonso, duke of Calabria, 4 Dec 1493. Contrast the university's election of its own rector in two of the universities which came closest to Siena in the extent of communal control, Florence (VERDE, *Lo Studio fiorentino,* I, pp. 268-70) and Perugia (PARDI, 'Atti degli scolari', esp. pp. 493-4).

[104] *Conc.* 251, f. 12r, 16 Nov.

[105] *Conc.* 419, f. 59r, 30 Dec; ZDEKAUER, p. 37 n. 2. Cf. Perugia, where by the sixteenth century this regulation was waived; PARDI, 'Atti degli scolari', p. 493. On the traditional requirement, supported by Baldus and Bartolus, that the rector be a cleric, ERMINI, *Storia,* I, p. 89; GUALAZZINI, *Corpus Statutorum,* p. CXCVII; RASHDALL, I, pp. 181-2; and especially DENIFLE, *Entstehung,* pp. 187-91. Its relaxation has to be seen in the context of the widespread difficulties in filling the rectorate. On the other measures in this decision see below, p. 268.

[106] Several rectors took their degree during their period of office: e.g. *Conc.* 374, f. 17v, 9 Aug 1428; *Conc.* 411, f. 54v, 18 Aug 1434. On the requirement at Parma that rectors should not have degrees, GUALAZZINI, *Corpus Statutorum,* pp. CXCVIII, CLXXIV (the *licenza* was to be taken but not the *laurea*).

[107] This was incorporated in the 'Ordini del vivere' of the Casa della Sapienza, drawn up at or shortly after its opening (see below, pp. 325 *seq.*), clause 34 (my numbering; see below, Table 7, pp. 328-9 for references).

[108] *Conc.* 380, f. 8r, 8 Jul 1429; cf. *Conc.* 459, f. 38r-v, 7 Aug 1442.

[109] This was sometimes waived formally (*Conc.* 425, f. 20r, 8 Dec 1436; *Conc.* 442, f. 24r, 5 Oct 1439) as well as being ignored on many other occasions.

anticipated, more often delayed.[110] The authorities were concerned at the damaging effect of delay.[111] The growing frequency of extensions and renewals[112] make it clear that it was by no means always the case that competition for the post was intense. Equally, from the late 1450s a series of rectors were elected who held office for longer periods, of up to three or four years. On accepting the office the rector also swore that he would not leave until he had undergone syndication, a process also controlled by the communal authorities.[113] Like teachers he could, however, request and receive leave of absence, which in some cases lasted for significant periods of time (usually during periods of vacation); in such cases a deputy was found, either by the incumbent or, more frequently, by the *Concistoro*.[114]

From the 1430s the rector received a regular salary of 50 florins, payable initially by semester, later by trimester, but there is also a tradition, from about the same period, that the rector was given a lectureship, at a salary of 25 florins.[115] This is not an insignificant matter since the expense of

[110] Above, n. 87. When late elections took place they were often backdated to 18 October. There are several cases of spring elections; e.g. *Conc.* 652, ff. 29r, 8 Jun, and 31v, 11 Jun 1475 (Maestro Domenico Mentebona da Roma); *Conc.* 664, f. 9r, 8 May 1477 (Messer Francesco Cadichio dell'Aquila).

[111] It was feared that a delay in holding elections could lose the *Studio* good students (*Conc.* 459, f. 38r-v, 7 Aug 1442).

[112] The office of M.º Giovanni was extended for two months in 1435 (*Conc.* 418, ff. 22v-23r, 18 Oct); in December 1460 Paolo da Prato's term was prolonged until the beginning of the following academic year (*Conc.* 560, f. 46r, 30 Dec). Such extensions were invariably ordered by the *Concistoro* or the *Savi*, apparently without consultation of the university.

[113] *Conc.* 386, f. 15r, 16 Jul 1430. This promise is absent from the first known report of a (vice-)rectoral oath, made by 'Dns. Antonius mag.ri Francisci' on 20 Nov 1415 to the *Concistoro* (*Conc.* 299, f. 19r, 20 Nov. The later insertion of the term 'de Casinis sen.' is surely erroneous). The *Concistoro* determined that syndication should take place (e.g. *Conc.* 322, f. 16r, 23 Sept 1419) or gave permission for it (*Conc.* 375, f. 30r, 11 Oct 1428), though it seems that scholars may have actually done it; in 1419 two *forenses* and one Sienese were appointed (loc. cit.) and in 1437 the vice-rector was to choose them (*Conc.* 431, f. 11v, 27 Nov). Occasionally the rector was exempted (e.g. *Conc.* 368, f. 20r, 11 Aug 1427). At Perugia syndication was performed by scholars (PARDI, 'Atti degli scolari', p. 494), at Florence by public officials (BRUCKER, 'Florence and its University', p. 227).

[114] E.g. in 1462 the (unnamed) rector may leave because of plague (*Conc.* 575, ff. 40v-41r, 8 Aug); in 1464 Francesco da Urbino was given fifteen days' leave provided he put in a substitute (*Conc.* 587, f. 16v, 5 Aug); the rector in 1469 was given twenty days' leave to go to a spa (*Conc.* 616, f. 3v, 3 May). In 1470 Giovanni Pensio was given a month, with the substitute to be chosen by the *Concistoro* (*Conc.* 623, f. 34v, 18 Aug); others later received fifteen days (*Conc.* 636, f. 2r, 2 Sept 1472; *Conc.* 662, f. 5r, 9 Jan 1477), twelve days (*Conc.* 687, f. 27r, 18 Apr 1481, with a substitute of his choosing), or eight days (*Conc.* 698, f. 5r, 6 Jan 1483 – the rector could go to Chiusi on personal business – and *Conc.* 709, f. 28r, 30 Dec 1484 – for the vice-rector). Towards the end of the century there were longer periods, not all of which ended as planned. In 1487 the vice-rector was allowed to leave for the spas on health grounds; a substitute, Dns. Nicholaus alamannus, was found (*Conc.* 724, f. 4r, 6 May), but a few weeks later an unnamed vice-rector was installed for a four-month period (f. 32v, 29 Jun). In 1488 the German rector, Sigismund, was given forty-five days' leave (*Conc.* 728, f. 13r, 29 Jan), and never returned; his replacement, Henricus Sylberberg (appointed vice-rector on 5 Mar, *Conc.* 729, f. 5v) served for longer but was also granted generous leave, of one and a half months, in 1491 (*Conc.* 747, f. 10r, 6 Apr).

[115] The first unequivocal instance of a rector of the *Studio* being paid for a *lettura* rather than for his office is in 1425 (*Conc.* 359, f. 34v, 14 Dec, ed. PIANIGIANI, doc. 73, p. 94). As student lectureships became institutionalised, the rector began to receive one of these; *Conc.* 382, f. 7v, 13 Nov 1429, ed. PIANIGIANI, doc. 118, pp. 146-7; cf. *Bicch.* 309, f. 63v, 14 Oct 1429, payments to Antonio da Itri for both his rectorate (50 *lire*) and a lectureship (£336/8). By 1440 this was part of the form of his election according to the statutes of the *Studio* (*Conc.* 445, f. 41v, 23 Apr). Later in the century this practice appears to have become fused, at least for a while, with that of awarding student lectureships. Whereas in 1458 Bartolomeo da Genova was given a 'lecturam extraordinariam sue facultatis' (*Conc.* 548, f. 28v, 23 Feb, ed. BAI, doc. 105, p. 88), in 1460 Paolo da Prato was appointed to one of the student lectureships (*Conc.* 561, f. 41v, 20 Apr), as were 'Giorgio alamanno' in 1462 (*Conc.* 577, f. 37r, 16 Dec), Filippo Boccaccin de Alamannis of Florence in 1467 (*Conc.* 607, f. 21v, 16 Nov, ed. BAI, doc. 266, pp. 244-5), and Domenico Mentebona da Roma in 1476 (*Conc.* 660, ff. 60v-61r, 31 Oct); but not Ambrogio da Lucca in 1480, who received a 'conducta extraordinaria' (*Conc.* 685, f. 21v, 30 Dec, ed. FERRERI, doc. 115, p. 98; election on *Conc.* 684, ff. 22v-23r, 20 Oct, ed. FERRERI, docs. 109-10, pp. 92-4). On student lectureships see below, pp. 282 *seq.* The payment of the salary for the rectorate and that for an accompanying lectureship are clearly kept distinct in

the rectorate was perhaps the chief deterrent to potential candidates; in 1454 it was reported that no-one was interested in the job unless it attracted a salary,[116] and in the 1470s the *Savi* similarly recommended that the rector be given a higher salary and 'altre cose honorevoli' in order to attract a worthy incumbent.[117] It is interesting that in 1493 the rector, the privileged Matteo da Matera, was given 50 florins (in addition to a 150-florin lectureship) 'pro expensis fiendis in asumptione caputei'.[118]

c. Status and formal role

The rector's office began with a solemn ceremony of inauguration. Where possible this took place during the ceremonial opening of the academic year. He took an oath,[119] accepted the insignia of office, the *caputeus*,[120] and possibly the seal and mace,[121] and customarily delivered an inaugural oration.[122] The ceremony entailed the handing over of these insignia by his predecessor – which could be a problem if that individual had left,[123] or was reluctant to part with these symbols.[124] By the end of the century this ceremony could assume substantial proportions; the investiture of Matteo da Matera in 1493 took considerable organisation and involved a deputation of eight doctors riding on horseback to announce the ceremony, solemn music, and an oration in his honour.[125] Rectors had their own ceremonial obligations, which included entertainment. In 1436 we find a rector organising a *giostra* fifteen days before the end of his period of office.[126] In 1480 the notary of the *Studio* organised a banquet for the rector and his *consiglieri* 'ut moris est'.[127] Within the *Studio* the rector always

---

the *Biccherna* records of the 1430s and 1440s, less so thereafter. Ambiguity about the purpose of the rector's salary is not confined to Siena; cf. PARK, 'The Readers at the Florentine Studio', p. 275 n. 1.

[116] *Conc.* 528, f. 54v, 14 Oct. A *lectura universitatis* was therefore attached to the post.

[117] *Not.* 694, ff. 13r-v, ed. MINNUCCI, 'Documenti', doc. II-42, pp. 111-12 (who suggests a date of June or July 1474), and cf. 31r-v, ed. MINNUCCI, op. cit., doc. II-56, p. 124 (suggesting Jul-Sept 1474).

[118] *Balìa* 38, f. 31r, 7 Jan (and cf. *Balìa* 38, f. 21v, 21 Dec 1492).

[119] E.g. *Conc.* 357, f. 27r, 11 Aug 1425.

[120] *Conc.* 381, f. 24v, 11 Oct 1429; *Conc.* 507, f. 51v, 28 Oct 1450. Accepting the rectorate and accepting the *caputeus* became synonymous; *Conc.* 648, f. 28v, 20 Oct 1474.

[121] Below, pp. 274-6.

[122] Above, p. 112.

[123] *Conc.* 437, f. 33v, 10 Dec 1438 (the outgoing rector, wishing to leave early, renounced his part in the ceremony, the conferment of the *caputeus*, and a substitute was allowed). In 1489 the vice-rector, Henricus de Sylberberg, received the symbols of office from the bedel because his predecessor had left (*Studio* 127, no foliation, 4 Aug). It may have been customary to allow the outgoing rector to hang on to at least the *caputeo* for a short while after the end of his period of office; in 1468 Filippo Boccaccini de Alamannis of Florence was allowed to go about Siena for three more days 'cum capputeo et aliis prout soliti sunt ire alii Rectores dicti Studii' (*Conc.* 610, f. 2r, 1 May).

[124] *Conc.* 665, f. 12r, 10 Jul 1477. It also proved difficult to persuade the outgoing rector to leave the *caputeo* for his successor in 1465 (*Conc.* 593, f. 17r, 22 Jul).

[125] *Balìa* 38, ff. 31r, 7 Jan, and 195v, 12 Apr; *Conc.* 758, ff. 8v, 7 Feb, 9v, 13 Feb, 10r, 18 Feb, and 11r, 23 Feb, ed. FERRERI, docs. 326, 328-30, pp. 307-11, and above, n. 118.

[126] *Conc.* 420, f. 33r, 28 Feb. At Padua, one of the first duties of a new rector was to organise and pay for a banquet following his inception; those who failed to do this might organise an *astiludio* instead. E. MARTELLOZZO FORIN (ed.), *Acta graduum academicorum gymnasii patavini ab anno 1471 ad annum 1500*. Centro per la Storia dell'Università di Padova. Fonti per la Storia dell'Università di Padova. 17. 4 vols (Rome-Padua, 2001), I, pp. 26 *seq.*

[127] *Not.* 858, ff. 9v-10r, 30 Nov, ed. MINNUCCI, 'Documenti', doc. II-28, pp. 94-5.

took precedence;[128] his name appeared for a while at the head of the *rotolo*, and he had always to wear his insignia and to be accompanied by his 'famiglia'.[129] He was also expected to have suitably dignified lodgings, at which he was to conduct university business, and which appear to be distinct from the 'residentia universitatis'.[130] He represented the university, for example at the funeral of the teacher Borghese Borghesi in 1490.[131] And his status is also reflected in the matter of his doctorate. Since rectors were normally students close to the end of their period of study, they frequently ended up taking a degree in Siena (though in contrast to the practice with the rector of the Sapienza, this is not formally stipulated). There is no indication that they were exempt from examination fees, as at Bologna,[132] but rectors' doctorates could clearly be splendid occasions; two are recorded as including hired musicians,[133] and extra promotors might be permitted 'pro honore studii'.[134]

The dignity accorded him within the *Studio* was echoed at ceremonial moments in the city's life. He was prominent at the ceremony in honour of San Bernardino in 1456,[135] and present in the cathedral alongside the *Concistoro* on Palm Sunday in 1461.[136] In the procession for the creation of the rector of the hospital of S. Maria della Scala as *cavaliere* in 1477 he came immediately after the prior and preceded the members of the *Concistoro*;[137] and in a protocol for the procession of S. Maria on 16 August, unfortunately not precisely dateable, the outgoing rector is first, followed by the new *Podestà* and his collateral, the *Capitano di Giustizia* and his deputy, the outgoing *Podestà* and his collateral, and the incoming rector.[138]

Why did students volunteer for this post? It was undoubtedly onerous, but the commitment shown by a rector to his office of course had its rewards, not just in honour but in terms of future advancement. Giovanni Pensio was knighted[139] and made *Capitano di Giustizia* in 1471.[140] Francesco

---

[128] In 1429 a privilege accorded Niccolò Tedeschi lists the order of precedence as the rector of the *Studio*, the *scolares nobiles*, Tedeschi, the rector of the Sapienza, other doctors (*Conc.* 379, f. 10r, 14 May).

[129] *Conc.* 418, ff. 22v-23r, 18 Oct 1435.

[130] Gaming at the house of the rector was forbidden in 1419 (*Statuti* 40, f. 6v, 1 Jan; and cf. *Maggior Sindaco*, 2 *bis*, f. 24r, ed. L. PAGNI and S. VACCARA, 'Un Magistrato scomodo', p. 303. In 1473 business was transacted 'in domo dni. rectoris almi studii' (*Not.* 703, no. 36, ff. 72r-73r, 17 Dec), and in 1489 the degree of Corrado Banghen was conferred by the vice-rector in his residence (*Not.* 799, no foliation, 11 Apr; cf. ZDEKAUER, *Documenti*, part 2, doc. 5, p. 40). That this is not the permanent residence of the university is suggested by the order of 4 Jan 1484 that the (unnamed) rector leave his lodgings (*Conc.* 704, f. 2v, ed. FERRERI, doc. 191, pp. 161-2).

[131] *Conc.* 744, f. 6v, 25 Sept.

[132] PIANA, *Il "Liber Secretus Iuris Caesarei"*, p. 71*.

[133] Ceremonies in 1446 and 1538 described by D'ACCONE, *The Civic Muse*, pp. 468, 476, 521, 555, 560.

[134] *Conc.* 441, f. 22v, 25 Jul 1439, and see below, p. 289.

[135] Above, pp. 226-7.

[136] *Conc.* 567, f. 28r, 29 Mar.

[137] *CG* 237, ff. 104r *seq.*, 3 Feb.

[138] *Statuti* 41, f. 193r. According to the annotation in the right-hand margin the protocol dates from sometime between 1468 and 1536 and is therefore a curiously late addition to this volume. Zdekauer's view (p. 127) that the resolution of 1454 to waive the rector's precedence in favour of the Venetian ambassador (*Conc.* 526, f. 8r, 7 May) shows a decline in his status can be discounted; it was clearly a political expedient of the moment and in no way reflected on the rector of the *Studio*. In 1544-5 the rector was to follow the *priore* of the *Concistoro* and the *Capitano del Popolo* (MARRARA, *Lo Studio di Siena*, p. 96).

[139] *Conc.* 626, ff. 3r, 2 Jan, 33r, 10 Feb, 39r, 17 Feb, 41v, 19 Feb; and 45v, 24 Feb, ed. ZDEKAUER, doc. XX, p. 175 (giving 1470). Agostino Dati held an oration on the occasion (DATI, *Opera, Orationes, Liber* III, *Oratio* XXIII, f. 80r; and see FIORAVANTI, 'Pietro de' Rossi', p. 129 n. 2).

[140] *CG* 233, f. 244r, 11 Feb; *Conc.* 626, f. 46r, 25 Feb (cf. ZDEKAUER, loc. cit., note). He subsequently received a *bandiera*, worth 80 *lire* (*CG* 235, f. 81v, 16 Jul 1473).

Cadichio dell'Aquila received 'literas beneserviti' after completion of his rectorate in 1479;[141] he had been elected *podestà* during his office,[142] though the offer was subsequently withdrawn.[143] Francesco de' Filippis da Montefalco was knighted and elected *podestà* in 1483,[144] while Henrighus de Sylberberg, during a long period as vice-rector, was supported by the authorities in his quest for a prebend.[145]

d. Functions and jurisdiction

The rector's jurisdiction was, as elsewhere,[146] extensive. In 1357 the rector was granted 'plenam, liberam et absolutam potestatem et omnimodam iurisdictionem regendi universitatem doctorum et scolarium Studii generalis civitatis Senarum, tam civium quam forensium'. Doctors, citizen and foreign students alike were to take an oath of obedience to him, he could impose fines of up to 50 florins on doctors and 50 *lire* on students, and his jurisdiction was to cover civil cases between them of up to 50 *lire* in value.[147] In 1408 the rector was also given the right to be present at degree examinations.[148] There is a repeat of the 1357 definition of jurisdiction over civil cases in 1428,[149] and we know, from

---

[141] *Conc.* 676, ff. 9v-10r, 20 May.

[142] *Conc.* 2040, no. 11, 3 May 1478.

[143] *Balìa* 501, no. 37, 4 Feb 1480 (explanatory letter to Alfonso of Calabria).

[144] *Conc.* 701, ff. 6v-7r, 17 Jul. The following year he was given the symbols of *gonfaloniere* (on which 25 florins were spent), in recognition of his conduct as rector and as *podestà* (*CG* 239, f. 239r, 1 Dec 1484).

[145] *Balìa* 410, f. 58v, 12 Apr 1490. In a notarial document of 1504 he is described as 'canonicus et cantor wormatiensis' (*Not.* 801, f. 80v).

[146] The fundamental study of G. CENCETTI, 'Il foro degli scolari negli studi medievali italiani', *Atti e Memorie della R. Deputazione per l'Emilia e la Romagna*, 5 (1940), pp. 163-88 (esp. pp. 183 *seq.*) [repr. in his *Lo Studio di Bologna*, pp. 95-112], offered substantial evidence that the rectors' powers, in contrast to most other aspects of the student universities, were actually growing in the later middle ages. The Florentine statutes of 1387 grant the rector jurisdiction in cases up to 100 *lire* in value 'ubicumque arma non intervenerunt' (GHERARDI, *Statuti*, pp. 20, 23. In 1431 the 100-*lire* limit was abolished; p. 28). Those of the Artists in Bologna of 1405 grant it for cases of defamation and bodily harm (CENCETTI, op. cit., p. 183). At Ferrara in 1447 it was granted for all cases except theft, homicide and *lèse majesté*; VISCONTI, *Storia dell'Università di Ferrara* (Bologna, 1950), pp. 39-40. In such cases as exceeded the rectors' jurisdiction he nonetheless had the right to defend the accused student in the presence of the duke (BORSETTI, *Historia almi Ferrariae Gymnasii*, pp. 406 *seq.*). Cf. Pisa, where in cases punishable by death – the only ones outside rectoral jurisdiction – the rector had to be present at the trial. In Padua at one stage the rector's judgment could not be appealed against, though this law had later to be modified (CENCETTI, op. cit., pp. 186-7). Cencetti suggested that these increased powers argue a decline in the political effectiveness of the university, since no authority, least of all the Venetians, would grant such prerogatives unless they posed no danger. No other explanation is plausible in a period otherwise characterised by the tightening of local control over the universities. In fifteenth-century Pavia, however, these powers were reduced; ZORZOLI, 'Interventi dei Duchi', pp. 130-1.

[147] *Chartularium*, doc. 432, pp. 570-2, ZDEKAUER, doc. IV, pp. 141-2, 24 Nov; see also ZDEKAUER, p. 21, PRUNAI, II, p. 26. But even in Perugia communal officials had to swear to respect the rector as well (ERMINI, *Storia*, I, p. 194), and this part of the standard legislation seems not to have been adopted in Siena.

[148] ZDEKAUER, doc. X, p. 155, 6 May. This right was not always exercised; of the few records of degrees to survive from the period, only some report his presence.

[149] *Conc.* 376, f. 21r-v, 13 Dec. The jurisdiction is over cases involving 'scolares subditos universitatem dicti studi'. Elsewhere stationers and landlords came under the rector's jurisdiction. Although this is not spelt out here, such a practice would be the most likely explanation of the rector's declaration in 1452 that he was competent to judge the case of 'Maestro Giovanni di Filippo de' Catani da Milano studiante nello studio di Siena contra la divota figlia e cittadina nra. Mona Lisabetta donna che fu di checcho di iacopo di ser francesco bruni povarella vedova e mantellata' (*Conc.* 2152, nos. 122 and 123).

the *quaestio* debated in 1430 by Niccolò Tedeschi, that the issue of whether clerics were subject to rectoral jurisdiction was current and relevant.[150] Apart from these scant notices the main development seems to have been the reduction of the number of courts of appeal open to students. In 1429 two important alterations were made, one replacing the doctors as court of appeal with the *Podestà*, thus drastically amending the intentions of the Authentic *Habita*, and the other granting the right of appeal to the *Concistoro* against the rector's judgment.[151] The episcopal option seems also to have been exercised infrequently, though this impression may be a result of distortions in the surviving evidence. But it is the second action of 1429 that is the more significant. The *Concistoro* had already involved itself in disciplinary matters, on the one hand instructing the rector in 1423 to keep out of a quarrel between two students,[152] on the other acceding in 1424 to the rector's request first that a student be imprisoned and then that he be released,[153] and this mixture of cooperation and interference was to continue.[154] The scarcity of evidence makes it difficult to assert this with confidence, but it would seem that the commune could be relied upon to defend the rector's jurisdiction not least because it was increasingly able to control it.[155]

Actually, since no regular records of rector's judicial decisions have been found, we only know of cases which leaked beyond his jurisdiction. A violent incident in February 1430 between 'Maestro Girolamo da Ymola scolaro' and the well-known Sienese Dino di Bertoccio di Marzi ended up with the pacificatory action of the *Concistoro*, to whom the *Savi* reported it directly.[156] The rector's attempt in 1434 to keep the *Capitano di Giustizia* out of a case involving armed students out at night, alleging that that official had no competence over the case, resulted in the compromise of the *Concistoro* and *Savi* being given the matter for adjudication.[157] Even cases which clearly did fall within the rector's ju-

---

[150] ZDEKAUER, pp. 49-50. The result in Sienese law is not known, though it is clear that clerics were entitled to avail themselves of the privilege (the reason for the requirement that rectors be clerics was that otherwise they could not have such jurisdiction), and in fact in the same year there is a case of a student cleric declining the bishop's court in favour of that of the rector (ZDEKAUER, *Documenti*, part 2, no. 18b, p. 21, 12 Dec). There were also of course those who accepted episcopal jurisdiction (e.g. op. cit., no. 43, pp. 26-8, 26 Aug 1444; see n. 157 below).

[151] *Conc.* 368, f. 22v, 14 Jun. But a document of the following year refers to four courts of appeal, as if the *Podestà* had been added rather than substituted (ZDEKAUER, *Documenti*, part 2, no. 18a, p. 21, 6 Oct 1430), though there is no evidence of doctors acting in this capacity thereafter (nor, it must be admitted, before; this is not the sort of evidence that normally survives, and we are in complete ignorance as to how frequently students availed themselves of the privilege).

[152] *Conc.* 346, f. 18r, 25 Oct.

[153] *Conc.* 351, f. 14v, 22 Jul (the case of Mag. Jacobus Gothfredi de Roma; see below, p. 291 n. 96).

[154] E.g. in 1437 the rector and the *Podestà* were instructed to mount a joint investigation into some riotous student behaviour (*Conc.* 428, f. 7r, 10 May).

[155] The effective survival of only these two authorities as courts of appeal has close parallels in Perugia; ERMINI, *Storia*, I, pp. 334, 347. For an extreme case of co-operation cf. the Florentine arrangement, whereby the rector represented the *Ufficiali dello Studio* in Pisa, and civil cases between doctors and scholars were to be judged by the *Consoli del Mare*. VERDE, *Lo Studio fiorentino*, I, pp. 267 and 270.

[156] *Conc.* 2145, no. 59, 20 Nov 1433. Dino had been found guilty of assaulting Girolamo, but claimed he had been defending himself and his family from assault by a group of armed students. The outcome of his petition, almost four years after the event, is not recorded.

[157] *Conc.* 2146, no foliation, 13 Jun. An oddity is the case of 'Dns. Baptista mag.ri Iohannis de Racanata', a cleric in minor orders who is alleged to have attacked Johannes de Alamannia, a servant of the student Lodovicus of Barcelona. We hear of the case only because the vicar of the bishop protested about the fact that the *podestà* was trying it; ZDEKAUER, *Documenti*, part 2, doc. 43, pp. 26-8, 26 Aug 1444; the original is now lost (see above, p. 22). The vicar's claim to jurisdiction is understandable given the involvement of a cleric, but there is no explanation of how the case had got as far as the *podestà*; given that victim was a servant of a student, the rector might be expected to have a claim over the case as well. See above, p. 235 n. 34. Battista may well also have been a student; by 1448 he certainly was, being expelled from the Sapienza after another violent episode (see below, p. 290 n. 86).

risdiction – such as that between the teacher Gabriele Fabrizi da Perugia and a student, Niccolò da Recanati (1463) – might end up referred to the *Concistoro* on appeal.[158] Cases which involved the rector himself, either as individual or as representative of the student body or the *universitas studii*, were also referred.[159] And of course it must be recognised that rectoral protests over the intrusion of other authorities[160] are merely the formal way in which he stakes his juridical claim.[161]

The rector also had jurisdiction over and responsibility for the university's officials. He is found sacking the notary in 1428,[162] and nominating the notary and the *Camarlengo*, as well as confirming the *bidello*, in 1481,[163] though in practice the *Savi*, and even the *Concistoro*, were usually involved in these appointments. By the end of the century he is also found exercising his traditional right to award the title of *baccalarius*.[164]

e. Problems and controversies

In 1405 the *Concistoro* resolved 'quod sequenti anno sit Rector Studii unus studens in Medicina et tertio anno sit unus students in iure civili, et sic successive postea incipiat de novo in iure canonico, et sic sequatur; ad hoc ut scandala non sequentur'.[165] As Zdekauer pointed out, Siena thus made a break with the Bolognese system, prioritising subject over geographical origin as the principle of rotation. But this was optimistic. It clearly remained a dead letter for the following two and a half decades; although their disciplines are rarely listed, it is evident from their titles that all the rectors we know of in that period were lawyers. In 1431, however, it was declared that only canonists and medics would be eligible for election that year, and that if a canonist was elected the post was to be reserved for medics the following year.[166] This was clearly a period in which the rectorate was a continued matter of contention; in 1430 the *Concis-*

---

[158] *Conc.* 2181, no foliation, 4 Aug. Fabrizi is not referred to as a teacher in the document, but was on the teaching payroll that year (e.g. *Conc.* 581, f. 27r, 31 Aug, ed. BAI, doc. 194, pp. 169-70).

[159] There are two examples from the 1450s. In 1451 a dispute between the rector, Mag. Angelo di Paolo da Gubbio, and the legist Benedetto Barzi is sent first to the collateral and eventually directly to the *Capitano di Giustizia*, who was given four days to determine it (*Conc.* 510, f. 44r, 23 Jun, and *Conc.* 511, f. 33v, 25 Aug 1451), while in 1454 a lawsuit between the rector and foreign teachers, apparently concerning their salaries, was sent first to Mariano Sozzini and then, after the doctors declared themselves not satisfied with his impartiality, to the *Podestà* and *Capitano di Giustizia* (*Conc.* 527, ff. 22v, 16 Jul, and 29r, 24 Jul 1454, ed. BAI, doc. 63, pp. 53-4). In 1498 a case involving two students, the German Cristoforus Zbengh and the Portuguese Perus Gobboli, was heard by the *Giudice delle Appellagioni* because the vice-rector, Alvaro, also Portuguese, was representing his fellow-countryman (*Conc.* 2192, no foliation, 3 Aug).

[160] E.g. *Conc.* 770, f. 23v, 13 Feb 1495, ed. FERRERI, doc. 354, p. 339; the vice-rector protests at the *Podestà* of Grosseto's intrusion in the case of the arts student Paolus de Eversa.

[161] Cf. E. RIGONI, 'Il tribunale degli scolari dell'Università di Padova nel medioevo', *Memorie della R. Accademia di scienze, lettere ed arti i Padova*, n.s., 59:3 (1942-3), pp. 19-34, p. 20 (and more generally for insights into the nuanced relationship between the authority of the rector and that of the town magistrates at Padua).

[162] *Not.* 333, f. 24r-v, 26 Feb, ed. MINNUCCI, 'Documenti', doc. II-2, p. 76.

[163] *Not.* 858, ff. 11r-12r, 22 Mar, ed. MINNUCCI, 'Documenti', doc. II-30, p. 97.

[164] *Conc.* 707, f. 16r, 31 Jul 1484; an unnamed Dominican wishes to take the baccalaureate but there is no rector at the moment who could confer it. A substitute, 'egregium legum profexorem D.num 'nicolaum de montefalco', is appointed and empowered to act. Despite the implications of the phrasing here, the rector did not have a monopoly of this function, as the degree records published by Minnucci attest. See below, p. 287 and n. 64.

[165] *Conc.* 239, f. 14r, 16 Nov; ZDEKAUER, p. 55.

[166] *Conc.* 393, f. 55r, 12 Aug. In the event 'Johannis barbantis de alamannia' was elected. There is ambiguity in the records as to his title, his subject, and his nationality.

toro had intervened to allow Sienese students to participate, exceptionally, in the election,[167] while in 1434 it was decreed that in future no two consecutive rectors were to be from the same nation.[168] The principle of rotation was at least partially reaffirmed in 1435, with the decision to abrogate the statute that reserved the office to canonists and unmarried clergy; the next rector could be a civilian provided he was followed by a canonist.[169] And in fact the year after that, in 1437, a student of arts and medicine was elected.[170]

Whatever the intentions and antagonisms, for all the uncertainties and complications of filling the rectorate, the principle of choosing the rector by subject does continue for several decades; it is often not stated, and has to be deduced from the titles of candidates ('Dominus' for lawyers, 'Magister' for artists – which means that we cannot distinguish between canonists and civilians) or from additional evidence. Over the period 1429 to 1486 we know, through the communal records, of thirty-five elections. Twenty-three of these were of lawyers, eight of students in arts/medicine (three were just students in arts, in other words not advanced students), and four were mixed elections.[171] This latter phenomenon suggests resistance to the principle of rotation by subject, but it is difficult to know why this was or where it came from. It certainly does not appear to be the product of a desire to replace the system with one based on geographical origins. There are years in which all the candidates were citramontane,[172] and one in which they were all ultramontane,[173] and doubtless there were antagonisms – rectoral elections are excellent illustrations of the aptness of Daniel Waley's memorable phrase 'that forcing-house of xenophobia, the medieval university'[174] – but none that took the form (or were allowed to take the form) of explicit pressure on the format of elections. Zdekauer's implicit explanation for this was the hypothesis that there were two types of rector, the 'rettore generale' and, below him, a citramontane and an ultramontane rector. This extrapolation from his 'fragment'[175] is not borne out by any evidence known to me. Two measures including the expression 'rector generale' have come to light (not, however, in the documents to which he refers),[176] but these are more likely to be attributions of status than formal titles to distinguish the rector of the *Studio* from any others. Despite the discussions in 1429, no evidence that there were ever separate citramontane and ultramontane rectors has come to light, and they would be difficult to reconcile with everything else that is known about the student-university.

Whether or not their election had been contentious, several rectors proved less than satisfactory. An example of another type of problem came only a few years after the 1429-30 controversy. Evange-

---

[167] *Conc.* 387, f. 26r, 12 Oct.

[168] *Conc.* 413, f. 34r, 29 Dec.

[169] *Conc.* 419, f. 59r, 30 Dec; Zdekauer, p. 37 n. 2. Zdekauer saw this measure as linked with Rubric XVII of his 'statutes' (see above, pp. 255 *seq.*) which declared that no artist may be rector (p. 55). There is no mention of artists in the measure, but equally no mention of what was to happen the following year.

[170] *Conc.* 431, f. 22v, 19 Dec (Maestro Jacomo carusio de Traiecto, i.e. from Utrecht).

[171] *Conc.* 648, f. 2v, 2 Sept 1474; *Conc.* 703, ff. 14r, 7 Dec, and 14v, 9 Dec 1483, ed. Ferreri, docs. 186-7, pp. 157-8; *Conc.* 718, ff. 14v-15r, 3 Jun 1486, ed. Ferreri, doc. 235, p. 200. In the election of 1480 (*Conc.* 684, ff. 22v-23r, 20 Oct, ed. Ferreri, docs. 109-10, pp. 92-4), only one of the six shortlisted, 'Marianus spoletanus', has the title Magister (and indeed appears as Dominus in the second part of the proceedings when the list was whittled down to three). However, the researches of Minnucci, 'Documenti', p. 288 make it clear that he was indeed a student of medicine, making this a mixed election albeit with a strong bias towards the lawyers.

[172] E.g. *Conc.* 387, f. 26r-v, 12 Oct 1430; *Conc.* 540, ff. 17v, 12 Sept, and 25r, 25 Sept 1456; *Conc.* 583, ff. 33v, 10 Dec, and 40r, 13 Dec 1463; and *Conc.* 652, ff. 29r, 8 Jun, and 31v, 11 Jun 1475.

[173] *Conc.* 399, f. 63v, 28 Aug 1432.

[174] D. P. Waley and P. Denley, *Later Medieval Europe 1250-1520* (3rd edn. Harlow, 2001), p. 122.

[175] Above, pp. 255 *seq.*

[176] *Conc.* 407, f. 6v, 2 Dec 1433, *Conc.* 418, ff. 22v-23v, 18 Oct 1435 (referring to 'rectoris generalis studii', which could equally mean 'the rector of the *studium generale*').

lista da Camerino was chosen at the end of 1435,[177] but in April 1436 the *bidello* was sent to Perugia to confirm that he was coming,[178] and when in November he had still not appeared, another rector was elected.[179] On 22 March 1437 Evangelista was reinstated on the grounds that plague had prevented him from taking up the appointment,[180] and on 18 April he was given until 10 May to appear.[181] We do not know when he in fact arrived in Siena; the next information is that on 11 September he was imprisoned at the petition of his creditors, having been captured in flight.[182] Debt was a frequent risk for rectors,[183] and the possibility that they might be tempted to solve the problem by making a run for it occurred to the authorities just as much as to the luckless incumbents. In 1440 the rector was found to have incurred debts; measures were taken to prevent his flight.[184] Guasparre Pelliciai da Valentia left Siena shortly before the end of his term of office in 1456, owing money; he escaped from the clutches of troops that arrested him *en route*, and the authorities were left to fulminate about how his reputation ought to be blackened throughout the university system.[185] Escape was also the solution to other problems, and particularly when the rector was found to be, or was suspected of, committing exactly the offences for which he had the authority and the obligation to judge others. In 1448 the rector's leave was cancelled when he was alleged to be preparing to flee (he was described as 'traditore' and ended up in prison);[186] another, Mariano de' Vecchiani da Pisa, was fined 40 *lire* and had to provide guarantors after getting involved in a fight,[187] while on 25 July 1461 Paolo da Prato fled because he was under suspicion of having been at the head of a band of revellers, subsequently to protest his innocence from a safe distance.[188]

---

[177] *Conc.* 419, f. 59v, 31 Dec.

[178] *Conc.* 421, f. 45v, 27 Apr.

[179] *Conc.* 425, f. 15v, 29 Nov; a fresh election was held on 8 Dec (f. 20v). No explanation is given.

[180] *Conc.* 427, f. 20v, 22 Mar.

[181] *Conc.* 427, f. 42v, 18 Apr.

[182] *Conc.* 430, f. 6v, 11 Sept (and see 6r, 9 Sept). On 29 Oct he was threatened with removal from the rectorate if he did not pay his debts (f. 35r), and a fresh election was held on 19 Dec (*Conc.* 431, f. 22v; cf. also f. 11v, 27 Nov). Evangelista was released by agreement with his creditors on 4 Apr 1438 (*Conc.* 433, f. 26r). On this figure see also ZDEKAUER, 'Dai protocolli', pp. 321, 323. Irregularity in the tenure of the office continued; Agostino da Viterbo, elected on 10 Nov 1438 (*Conc.* 437, f. 9r), immediately took fifteen days' leave and then renounced office prematurely (*Conc.* 442, f. 3r, 2 Sept 1439); a vice-rector was appointed for one month (*Conc.* 442, f. 8v, 9 Sept).

[183] The first example I have found is Giovanni Milanesi da Prato, who was imprisoned in Staggia for debt and petitioned the *Concistoro* in 1418 for a safe-conduct to Siena so that he could resume his office (*Conc.* 1893, no. 3, 2 Apr).

[184] *Conc.* 449, f. 8v, 10 Nov. He is not named, either here or in documents recording his teaching appointment (*Conc.* 445, f. 41v, 23 Apr) or his election (*Conc.* 442, f. 27v, 11 Oct 1439), though the 'shortlist' on that occasion consisted of three civilians, Dns. Gabriel de Macerata, Dns. Stefanus de trentis de luccha and Dns. Johannes Arrigi? de Alamannia.

[185] 'dovarebbe essere publicato infame per tucti li studi d'italia'. The episode is known only through letters of the *Balìa* to the bishops of Siena and Chiusi (*Balìa* 397, ff. 177v-179v; 1-2 Oct 1456).

[186] *Conc.* 493, ff. 7v, 9 Mar (he was given fifteen days' leave 'ad balneis'), 10r, 13 Mar (revocation of leave), and 25r, 12 Apr (a vice-rector was appointed to cover the rest of his term unless he was released and wished to be restored to office). He is not named in these or other documents known to me.

[187] *Conc.* 522, f. 29r-v, 23 Sept 1453.

[188] *Conc.* 569, ff. 23r, 29 Jul, and 24v, 1 Aug 1461. He wrote to the *Concistoro* on 4 Aug passionately denying his involvement in the episode (*Conc.* 2000, no. 96), and obtained the support of the *Otto Difensori* of his native Prato (*Conc.* 2000, no. 98, 29 Jul, and *Conc.* 2001, no. 23, 2 Sept), the *Signoria* of Florence (*Conc.* 2001, no. 21, 2 Sept), and Piero di Cosimo de' Medici who describes him as a friend (*Conc.* 2001, no. 20, 1 Sept). For more on this episode see below, p. 292 n. 104.

f. The vice-rector

Conflicts over rectoral elections, with the commune repeatedly intervening to impose solutions, imply that the post was hotly contested. In fact there were, not infrequently, and increasingly towards the end of the fifteenth century, instances when rectors' periods of office were prolonged because no obvious alternative candidates presented themselves,[189] or when there were gaps, or when there was a drive to find out if anyone was interested in taking up the post.[190] Prestige came at a cost which not that many were willing to undertake. In the absence of a rector the commune reverted increasingly to the appointment of a vice-rector, who would hold slightly less authority but who also took on the job at slightly less expense.[191] Such an appointment was normally a temporary measure,[192] but it was also a way out of having to go through the difficulties and dangers of formal election, and in fact there are occasions when the *Concistoro* and the *Savi* simply appointed a vice-rector with no apparent consultation with the students.[193] The appointment of a vice-rector also avoided the great expense of the rectorate, which had got so many incumbents into difficulties, and so it was only one step from this to a more fundamental development, the eclipse of the rectorate. In 1435 the rector of the Sapienza was elected (by the customary process) vice-rector of the *Studio*,[194] and in 1480 the two offices were again held by the same man.[195] By the sixteenth century this had in fact become normal practice,[196] and the office of rector of the *Studio* was in terminal decline.[197] In the middle of the century this practice was formalised; according to the 1545 statutes of the republic, two types of rector might be elected, a *rector gymnasii* who was also *vicerector universitatis*, chosen by the Senate from a shortlist of three proposed by the members of the Sapienza, or a *rector universitatis et sapientiae*, elected by a complex procedure involving the non-Sienese scholars of the university as well.[198] These alternatives were to apply 'tunc et quando ab amplis-

---

[189] Above, p. 260 and n. 98.

[190] E.g. in 1466 the *Savi* reported to the *Concistoro* that they had advertised for a new rector, but without success. They warned 'Et si studio vr. remaneat sine rectore esset dissolutio totale presentis studii' (*Conc.* 597, f. 40v, 13 Apr).

[191] The first known vice-rector is Francesco di Ser Matteo da San Miniato, 'vicerectore Rectoris', who obtained his degree in 1410 (above, p. 199 n. 135). In 1415 Antonio di Maestro Francesco took the office (*Conc.* 299, f. 19r, 20 Nov 1415; and see above, p. 262 n. 113).

[192] *Conc.* 1617, f. 59v, 6 May 1420 (Gonsalvo d'Aragona is offered the rectorate or the vice-rectorate following the renunciation of the rectorate by Rainaldo da Sicilia on the death of his brother); *Conc.* 381, f. 24r, 11 Oct 1429 (a vice-rector is appointed pending resolution of the controversy over the rectorate 'ut universitas studii non remaneat sine aliquo rectore et gubernatore'); *Conc.* 442, f. 3r, 2 Sept 1439 (decision to elect a vice-rector following the resignation of the rector); *Conc.* 493, f. 25r, 12 Apr 1448 (election of Giovanni da Sicilia as vice-rector 'pro toto residuo temporis pro quo electus fuerat rector dicti studii'); *Conc.* 511 *bis*, f. 36v, 13 Oct 1451 (since the university had not called an election for a rector, the *Concistoro* order that of a vice-rector; on the stalemate among students see also f. 49r, 30 Oct).

[193] *Conc.* 403, f. 40v, 18 Apr 1433; *Conc.* 431, f. 11v, 27 Nov 1437; *Conc.* 497, f. 22r, 10 Dec 1448.

[194] *Conc.* 418, f. 8v, 14 Sept (Johannes de Catalonia).

[195] *Studio* 2, f. 68r, 23 Jul (the Portuguese Dnus. Gonsalvus Menendis de Silveira. The salaries for his two offices are kept separate; *Bicch.* 335, f. 53r, 4 Jan 1481). The two offices were combined again by Maestro Filippo Scalandrini da Bracciano in 1497 (*Conc.* 784, f. 12r, 9 Jun, ed. FERRERI, doc. 380, pp. 363-4; but see below, p. 346 n. 77).

[196] ASS, *ms.* A. 119 (BICHI, *Catalogo de Rettori della Casa della Misericordia*), under 1505, 1507, 1510, 1513, 1514, 1515, 1517, 1518, 1519; *Studio* 17, f. 3v, 1 Jul 1533, ed. KOŠUTA, 'Documenti', doc. XIII-3, p. 432; and see IDEM, 'Siena nella vita e nell'opera di Marino Darsa', pp. 69-71 for a detailed account of the election of 1541 in which a non-*sapientino* was chosen, though the explanation for this is rather speculative.

[197] Rectors were appointed in 1498 and 1499 (the rector of the Sapienza); ASS, *ms.* A. 119, *ad annum*. On similar developments at Bologna, RASHDALL, I, pp. 186-7.

[198] Below, pp. 272-3. The relevant statutes (in *Statuti* 49, dist. I, rubrics 196 to 199) were first published by MARRARA, *Lo Studio di Siena*, pp. 298-300, from a collection of 1544-5, and have now been edited in full in ASCHERI, *L'ultimo statuto*,

simo Senatu non esset electus alius specialis Rector Universitatis seu Sapientiae sive vicerector', but it is clear from the document that the most common form of election was expected to be the first.[199]

5. *The operation of the university*

The powers granted to either type of rector in the 1544-5 statutes were qualified by the stipulation that he could not act without his *consiliarii* and *camarlengo*;[200] but this is the first definition of the role of the *consiliarii* that we have, and in fact their only functions apparent through communal records are in connection with the election of the rector. The election of the *consiliarii* was regulated by the commune; nine were elected in all, three per subject (canon law, civil law, arts/medicine), but in 1435 it was decided that, in future, nine names per subject would be chosen by scrutiny, and the final selection would be made by lot.[201] In the sixteenth century this was refined; of the three *consiliarii* from each subject, one was to be from the Sapienza, one a member of the *universitas* and one a Sienese student.[202] But how such matters were conducted in practice is another matter. In 1481 the rector was instructed to decide which students were to be shortlisted,[203] and in 1491, when six scholars, including the vice-rector, elected the notary of the university, they were not even referred to as *consiliarii*, which rather suggests that the offices had not been filled.[204]

The most striking feature of the documentation is the omission of any reference to nations. The initial intention of the *Concistoro* in 1423 was that the *consiliarii* would be elected by nation, but no more is heard of this.[205] There is in fact no evidence that there were organised nations in the university, the only references to them being too generic to permit the assumption that specific bodies were intended.[206] The shadowy existence of nations in many *studi*[207] is thus even more accentuated in

---

pp. 111-3. But that need not necessarily be their date of origin; a vernacular version, identical for the most part but fuller in some details, appears, undated, at the end of *Studio* 109 (ff. 8r-10r), ed. KOŠUTA, 'Documenti', doc. II, pp. 349-50. They appear as 'Aggiunte posteriori', with the last date mentioned being 16 Dec 1533 (f. 6v; KOŠUTA p. 347). They are likely to be pre-1542, or they would have presumably been transcribed rather into *Studio* 110, compiled in that year.

[199] Dist. I, rubric 197, ed. ASCHERI, *L'ultimo statuto*, p. 112; cf. *Studi*o 109, ff. 9r-10r; as above, n. 198.

[200] *Studio* 109, f. 9r; as above, n. 198.

[201] *Conc.* 414, f. 9v, 13 Jan. In 1423, after consultation with the assembled body of students, the rector and the outgoing *consiliarii* elected three scholars per faculty to propose a method of election for the *Concistoro*'s approval, but we are not informed of the outcome (*Conc.* 347, ff. 3v, 3 Nov, 4v, 4 Nov, 7r, 7 Nov, and 7v, 9 Nov). The procedure was further regulated by the *Concistoro* in 1446 'ut tollantur scandala que segui possent intra scolares pro scrutinio consiliarios' (*Conc.* 485, f. 37v, 18 Dec).

[202] As above, p. 198. Sienese are already found as *consiliarii* in 1480; *Not.* 858, ff. 2r-v, 12 Mar, ed. MINNUCCI, 'Documenti', doc. II-21, p. 89, and 9v-10r, 30 Nov, MINNUCCI, op. cit., doc. II-28, pp. 94-5 (and see p. 34).

[203] *Conc.* 687, f. 9v, 12 Mar, ed. FERRERI, doc. 117, pp. 99-100.

[204] *Studio* 127, no foliation, 30 Aug.

[205] *Conc.* 347, f. 3v, 3 Nov.

[206] E.g. *Conc.* 380, f. 14r, 16 Jul 1429; *Conc.* 517, f. 63v, 30 Dec 1452. There is a petition to the *Concistoro* by the 'natione Chatelana che al presente si trovano nel vostro Mag.co studio', requesting the release of a Catalan student imprisoned after a falling-out with a Sienese citizen (*Conc.* 2147, no. 58, 30 Nov 1439). It is not evident that this means anything more than the *ad hoc* collective of Catalan students.

[207] A. SOTTILI, '"Sunt nobis Papie omnia iucunda": il carteggio tra Konrad Nutzel ed Anton Kress, prevosto di San Lorenzo a Norimberga', in *Filologia umanistica per Gianvito Resta*, eds. V. Fera and G. Ferraú. Medioevo e Umanesimo, 96 (Padova 1997), III, p. 1729-1765 (p. 1738) recently described the nations at Pavia as 'raggruppamenti degli studenti e italiani che si formavano e facevano sentire il loro peso soprattutto in occasione delle elezioni rettorali…Le nazioni compaiono

Siena. That the *consiliarii* were chosen by 'faculty', and that the rectorate continued to rotate between 'faculties' as opposed to national groupings, unusual for Italy,[208] are symptomatic of this lack of organisation. Despite the disturbances of 1429, in which the citramontanes and ultramontanes seem to have attempted to alter the system,[209] rotation by subject was restored within two years,[210] and, with the sole concession in 1434 that no rector could be succeeded by a student from the same 'natio seu provincia et reame',[211] it continued unaltered.[212]

The membership of the university seems to have undergone some changes over the period, though again evidence is minimal. The main development relates to the status of Sienese students. From 1357 these were subject to the jurisdiction of the rector, and had to take an oath of obedience.[213] We know from a measure of 1429 that they were strictly forbidden to vote in elections of the rector,[214] but as has been seen, in 1430 *consiliarii cives* were allowed a say in such an election.[215] A century later, however, Sienese students were matriculating in the university and electing *consiliarii*.[216] The position of Sapienza students within the university is less than clear. Florentine extrapolations of Sienese statutes, made apparently in 1487, include a rubric stating that the rector of the Sapienza was to have the same authority over the *sapientini* as the rector of the university had over the other students, which implies separation.[217] This is also evident in 1510, when a clear distinction is found between 'scolari di Sapientia' and 'Nobilisti et scolari de l'Università'.[218] The only surviving matriculation list, of 1533, includes both Sienese students and *sapientini*,[219] but a distinction drawn in the mid-sixteenth-century statutes between three groups of students, *universitari*, *sapientini* and Sienese, implies again that their membership was of a restricted nature.[220] The position only becomes unequivocally clear in the mid-

veramente sulla scena quando si tratta di eleggere il rettore.' Cf. also DENLEY, 'Communities within Communities', pp. 728 *seq*. The nations of course have a tendency towards invisibility because they did not deal directly with citizen bodies; cf. C. FROVA, 'L'Europa vista dai centri universitari italiani', in *Europa e Mediterraneo tra Medioevo e prima età moderna: l'osservatorio italiano*, ed. S. Gensini. Centro di studi sulla civiltà del tardo medioevo di San Miniato, 4 (Pisa, 1992), pp. 375-93 (pp. 385-6), but even allowing for this, the nations in Siena cannot be demonstrated to have had even the most meagre of existences before the organisation of the German nation in the late sixteenth century.

[208] In Perugia a six-year cycle for the rectorate was established between the nations or provinces of Rome, Sicily, Germany, the Marche, Tuscany and France (PARDI, 'Atti degli scolari', p. 492); in Florence it rotated between citramontanes and ultramontanes (VERDE, *Lo Studio fiorentino*, I, p. 268) but there was also the provision that the rector was to be an artist every third year (p. 270).

[209] Above, p. 259.

[210] *Conc.* 393, f. 55r, 12 Aug 1431.

[211] *Conc.* 413, f. 33v, 29 Dec.

[212] E.g. *Conc.* 306, f. 27v, 18 Oct 1433; *Conc.* 419, ff. 59r, 30 Dec, 59v, 31 Dec 1435; *Conc.* 466, f. 54v, 28 Oct 1443.

[213] Above, p. 251.

[214] *Conc.* 380, f. 8r, 8 Jul.

[215] *Conc.* 387, f. 26r-v, 12 Oct.

[216] As n. 198, and see below, p. 273.

[217] As above, p. 27 n. 144. According to the same document no *sapientino* could become rector of the *Studio* (loc. cit.).

[218] PICCOLOMINI, 'Istruzioni di Giacomo Todeschini-Piccolomini al figlio Enea', p. 116.

[219] *Studio* 17, ff. 89r, 101r-2r, 110r-v, 120r-v, 29-30 Jun, ed. KOŠUTA, 'Documenti', doc. XIII-2, pp. 425-32, and see above, pp. 239 *seq*. Doctors are also listed in the volume (ff. 78r-v); but so are other measures, and it would be a mistake to read anything into this. There is no suggestion that doctors belong to the university after 1422 (above, p. 252).

[220] As n. 198 above, and see below, p. 273. In Florence, subjects of the *contado* and district could vote for the rector while citizens were members of the university but had no vote (VERDE, *Lo Studio fiorentino*, I, pp. 269-70). The purpose of this, according to Verde, was to boost the prestige of the rector by increasing the size of the electorate.

sixteenth century regulations for the election of a rector of the *Studio* and the Sapienza. In these, the outgoing rector was to summon all the students who together elected four scholars, two of whom were to be of the Sapienza and two 'universales'; these four and the outgoing rector together were to choose three candidates whose names would then be put to the *Concistoro* for decision.[221] The *sapientini* thus had a say in the appointment of the rector (who was also their rector) as well as having their own *consiliarii*, while the rights of citizen students were confined to the second of these.[222]

The sketchiness of this picture is not least due to the loss of all but one matriculation list. That such a list was kept, and served as a control of who was entitled to vote in elections for the rector, is implied in references of the 1420s.[223] Such references reappear in the mid-sixteenth century,[224] and there is the list of 1533, but in between total silence prevails. The question inevitably arises of whether such a register was kept continuously, even during periods when no rectors were elected. As this is the kind of document that is least likely to have been preserved, it is ultimately unanswerable, but the almost universal disappearance of the matriculation lists of Italian *studi* before the sixteenth century[225] may, as well as being a matter of the non-survival of documents, also be capable of the additional explanation that such lists were not always kept.[226]

It comes as no surprise to find that, in Siena, the officials customarily associated with the student-universities are more than anything else under the control of the commune. The *bidello*, about whom there is most information, is a good illustration of this, as has been seen; he certainly had university functions, but even his appointment was a matter for the commune as much as for the student body.[227] Two officials are indisputably student-university appointments. The rector and *consiliarii* chose their notary,[228] who was eventually identifiable with the *notaio dello Studio*[229] (and who is some-

---

[221] As n. 198 above.

[222] There are interesting parallels with Perugia, where in the fifteenth century members of the two Sapienze were subscribing but non-voting members of the university (ERMINI, *Storia*, I, p. 321). This led to conflicts which seriously weakened the university and which resulted eventually in an elaborate structure of sixteen *consiliarii*, eight of whom were *universitari* and eight *sapientini* (op. cit., pp. 321-3; PARDI, 'Atti degli scolari', pp. 493-4).

[223] *Conc.* 345, f. 16r, 4 Aug 1423; *Conc.* 348, f. 25r, 22 Feb 1424; and cf. *Conc.* 534, f. 57r-v, 28 Oct 1455. In 1428 it was stipulated that only those *scolari matriculati* who had attended lectures regularly for the previous six months could vote (*Conc.* 375, f. 22v, 28 Sept).

[224] As n. 198 above.

[225] I know of only two matriculation lists before 1500, one for Perugia dating from 1339 (ed. ROSSI, 'Documenti per la storia dell'Università di Perugia', doc. 64), and an incomplete one for Parma from 1414 (ed. GUALAZZINI, *Corpus Statutorum*, pp. 191-3). A list of those voting in the rectoral elections of 1482 at Pavia has also survived (VACCARI, *Storia dell'Università di Pavia*, p. 74).

[226] I expressed strong scepticism about Italian matriculation lists generally in DENLEY, 'Career, Springboard or Sinecure?', esp. p. 98. DAVIES, *Florence and its University*, pp. 19-21 has found this view too pessimistic, and rightly points out that in Florence there is no shortage of evidence of the practice, even if the lists themselves do not survive. For Siena, even indirect references are remarkably few given the density of documentation overall. On the other hand it has to be accepted that matriculation lists, kept by non-citizen, migrant rectors who were in office for the briefest of periods, are just about the most likely form of document not to survive.

[227] Above, pp. 82-3.

[228] E.g. *Conc.* 599, f. 71v, 21 Jul 1466 (the *consiglieri* have complained that they have repeatedly requested the rector to hold the election to this post 'ut hactenus consuetum est et ex forma statutorum studii cavetur'. The *Concistoro* orders him to proceed within days); *Not.* 858, ff. 2r-v, 12 Mar 1480 (ed. MINNUCCI, 'Documenti', doc. II-21, p. 89), and 11v, 22 Mar 1481 (MINNUCCI, doc. II-30, p. 97); and cf. the election in 1541, ed. KOŠUTA, 'Documenti', doc. XV-1, p. 442.

[229] In 1425 the *notaio de l'università degli scholari* was Ser Petro di Lorenzo (*Bicch.* 456, f. 84v, 1 Sept), while the *notaio dello Studio*, who is also described as the *not. Savi*, was Ser Giovanni di Bindo (on this and other examples see above, p. 84 n. 181). There is a similar differentiation in 1428-9, with Ser Agostino di Martino di Conte the 'notaio de l'università degli

times described as *notaio e scriba*).[230] As in other matters, where there were problems with an appointment, the communal authorities would intervene.[231] The rector and *consiliarii* also appointed their own *camarlengo*.[232] The duties of this figure are not defined in surviving documents, but the fact of his existence implies assets and resources that needed administration.[233]

On the material and ceremonial side of the life of the student-university we again know disappointingly little. We cannot be sure, for example, where it met. The few surviving documents that pertain specifically to the *universitas scholarium* refer to various premises. There is a suggestion that the church of S. Pietro d'Ovile was used in the mid-fifteenth century.[234] On the other hand, by 1481 the rector and his *consiliarii* were meeting 'in eorum solita residentia in Sapientia'.[235] The mace of the *Studio* has survived, albeit in restored form (see Figs. 12a-c). Its creation in about 1440 is well documented, and makes it one of the oldest surviving maces of any European university.[236] The mace was carried by the *bidello* on formal occasions such as degree ceremonies; its association with the student-university is perhaps best attested by the fact that in 1489 the vice-rector, Henrighus de Sylberberg, acknowledged receipt of it.[237]

scholari' (*Bicch.* 309, ff. 39v and 69r) and Ser Franco di Stefano di Vanno notary of the 'università de lo studio' (*Bicch.* 309, f. 7r). The only other notary to be described as 'notaio dell'università degli scholari' is Antonio di Giovanni da Grosseto (*Bicch.* 316, f. 65r, 10 Oct 1447; *Bicch.* 317, f. 305v, 28 Feb? 1448. Slightly earlier, Ser Niccolò di Ser Galgano, 'notaio de l'università de lo studio', was also paid; *Bicch.* 316, f. 18 r, 1 or 2 Mar 1447). Thereafter the terms used are 'notaio dell'università de lo studio' (*Bicch.* 320, f. 87v, 1 Oct 1451, Ser Simone di Jacomo di Ghieri da Radicondoli, who is also described as 'notaio...de rectore de lo studio', f. 15v, 16 Mar 1451; *Bicch.* 321, f. 216v, 25 Jun 1453, Ser Simone di Bartolomeo Pocci; *Bicch.* 340, ff. 84r, 2 Apr, 86r, 22 Jun, and 91v, 22 Oct 1487 and *Bicch.* 341, f. 97r, 1 Mar 1488, Ser Lorenzo di Simone; *Bicch.* 344, ff. 75r, 17 Apr, and 80r [new foliations], 18 Aug 1490, *Bicch.* 345, f. 129r [old foliation], 11 Feb 1491 and *Bicch.* 346, f. 143v, 25 Sept 1492, Ser Jacomo di Benedetto), or simply 'notaio de lo studio' (*Bicch.* 323, f. 167r, 1459, Ser Giovanni di Ser Mariano; *Bicch.* 329, f. 176r, 15 Jan 1471, Ser Cristoforo di Ser Filippo [Cantoni], paid in arrears; *Bicch.* 329, f. 175v, 14 Jan 1471, Ser Bartalomeo di Filippo Ballati; *Bicch.* 330, f. 32v, 28 Feb and 12 Apr 1472; *Bicch.* 330, f. 57v, 30 Apr 1472, Ser Cecci di Bernardo di Matteo di Salvi, paid in arrears; *Bicch.* 331, f. 153v, 25 Jun 1473, Ser Cienni di Francesco Salviati; *Sale* 23, f. 99r, 19 Dec 1496 and *Sale* 24, f. 163v, 17 Feb 1498, Ser Magius Bargalius, who is also *notaio* of the *Savi, Sale* 24, ff. 151r, 1 Jan 1497). That both student-university and wider functions are covered by the same person is indicated in two instances; by the use of 'not. studii et universitatis scolariorum' to describe Ser Matteo mei francisci in 1443 (*Conc.* 462, f. 57r-v, 27 Feb), and by Ser Feliciano di Ser Neri's self-description as 'not. et scriba Universitatis et Studii' in 1480 (*Not.* 858, f. 2r-v, 12 Mar, ed. MINNUCCI, 'Documenti', doc. II-21, p. 89; he is also described as *notaio del rettore de lo studio, Bicch.* 335 f. 54v and *Bicch.* 336, f. 313r, 26 Jan 1481). The payment of Ser Paolo di Pietro as 'not.o universitatis' on 21 Aug 1475 (*Studio* 2, f. 32r) and as *notaio de lo studio* on 1 Aug 1476 (*Bicch.* 333, f. 320r) is further (though given the difference in dates not conclusive) evidence that the two terms had come to signify the same thing. On the fluidity of the terminology see below, p. 277.

[230] *Conc.* 462, f. 57r-v, 27 Feb 1443, and *Not.* 475, f. 2r, 1437, on which see ZDEKAUER, 'Dai protocolli', pp. 318-26.

[231] In 1421 a notary of the *universitas scolarium* was chosen; he protested that he was not worthy of the office and the *Savi* were instructed to decide whether he should take the office or not (*Conc.* 335, f. 6r, 8 Nov).

[232] *Not.* 868, ff. 11r-12r, 22 Mar 1481, ed. MINNUCCI, 'Documenti', doc. II-30, p. 97; and as above, n. 198.

[233] Other employees leave fleeting traces in the documents; e.g. *Bicch.* 309, f. 53r, 1428-9, payment to Francesco di Giovanni 'messo de l'università de lo studio' for four months' salary; *Bicch.* 310, f. 65v, 14 Nov 1430, where the same man is described as 'messo de Rettore de lo Studio' (and 36r where he is just 'messo dello studio').

[234] In 1447 a document bearing the seal of the university was drawn up 'apud ecclesiam Sancti Petri de Ovile'; ZDEKAUER, *Documenti*, part 2, doc. 54, p. 31.

[235] *Not.* 858, ff. 11r-12r, 18 Mar, ed. MINNUCCI, 'Documenti', doc. II-30, pp. 96-7.

[236] 'L'università delli scolari férono fare 2 pennoni di tronbe per onore dello studio, uno con Sancto Niccolò e uno con Sancta Caterina, e una maza d'ariento per lo bidello, la quale si opera a fare e' dottori e a loro offerte'. *Cronaca senese di Tommaso Fecini*, p. 852, 30 Apr 1440; LEONCINI, 'I simboli dell'Università di Siena', p. 238 (full discussion of the mace in pp. 236-45; reproductions in *Annali* version, pp. 125-8); and see also G. W. VORBRODT and I. VORBRODT, *Die akademischen Szepter und Stäben in Europa. Corpus Sceptrorum*, I.1 (Heidelberg, 1971), p. 232; reproductions on Plates 379 and 380.

[237] *Studio* 127, no foliation, 4 Aug 1489.

Fig. 12a – The mace of the *Studio*. Sienese silversmith, c. 1440 (Siena, Palazzo del Rettorato).

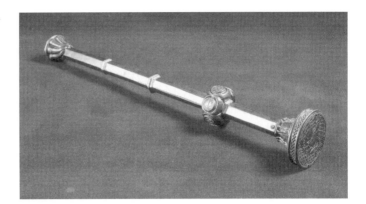

Fig. 12b – The mace of the *Studio* – detail.

Fig. 12c – The mace of the *Studio* – detail.

The information about the university's seal is even more tantalising. In 1406 it was ordered that the seal of the *Studio* be given to the rector by the *Camarlengo del Concistoro*,[238] but in 1414 two silver seals of the *Studio* were to be given to the *notaio* of its officials.[239] There are documents bearing traces of what may have been the university seal,[240] but no imprints before the *rotolo* of 1545-6.[241] This de-

---

[238] *Conc.* 242, f. 21r, 22 Jun 1406.

[239] *Conc.* 293, f. 4r, 2 Nov 1414; cf. CATONI, 'Genesi', p. 165 n. 41.

[240] Zdekauer alluded to the appearance of a seal on the document of 1447 referred to above (n. 234), but it has not been possible to find the original. The degree of Corrado Banghen, granted unusually by vice-rector Henricus de Sylberberg in 1489, has the marks of what must have been the university seal (*Not.* 799, no foliation, 11 Apr 1489, and see above, p. 264 n. 130).

[241] *Studio* 22, no foliation.

picts St. Catherine of Alexandria with her wheel, and thus adds weight to Bascapé's speculation that the seal of the *Studio* currently displayed in the Museo Civico (Fig. 13) was a remodelling of an earlier one.[242] The role of this saint (who had already long been associated with the protection of those engaged in or connected with learning)[243] as some sort of patron of the *Studio* in the fifteenth century is confirmed by evidence from 1440,[244] and again by a document of 1480, in which the notary of the *Studio* records the names of forty-two teachers and students who contributed offerings towards the celebration of her feast-day.[245] Earlier that year there is a similar document naming twenty-eight teachers and scholars who contributed to the feast-day of San Bernardino, this time described unequivocally as 'advocati et protectoris dicte Universitatis'.[246]

Fig. 13 – Seal of the *Studio*, possibly eighteenth century (Siena, Museo Civico, inv. no. 16).

[242] BASCAPÉ, 'Sigilli Universitari Italiani', Tav. X, 1 (and see p. 337); reproduction also in *L'Università di Siena. 750 anni*, p. 560. See also LEONCINI, 'I simboli dell'Università di Siena', p. 236; BORGIA and FUMI CAMBI GADO, 'I sistemi emblematici', pp. 563-4; and G. CATONI, 'Il Sigillo dell'Università di Siena', *Studenti &/a Siena. Periodico d'informazione della Azienda Comunale diritto allo Studio Universitario*, II:1 (15 gennaio 1991), p. 2.

[243] *Enciclopedia cattolica*, 3 (1949), cols. 1138-42. She was the patron of the lawyers at the University of Padua from at least 1377; S. BERNARDINELLO, 'Le orazioni per i santi protettori dell'Università di Padova', *Quaderni per la storia dell'Università di Padova*, 19 (1986), pp. 17-86 (p. 19).

[244] Above, n. 236.

[245] *Not.* 858, ff. 8r-9r, 23-24 Nov, ed. MINNUCCI, 'Documenti', doc. II-27, pp. 93-4 (and cf. p. 36). On the impact of Catherine in Siena, LEONCINI, 'I simboli dell'Università di Siena', p. 236, and A. WILSON TORDI (ed./tr.), *La festa et storia di Sancta Caterina. A Medieval Italian Religious Drama*. Studies in the Humanities: Literature – Politics – Society, 25 (New York, 1996), Introduction.

[246] *Not.* 858, ff. 5r-v, 13 May, ed. MINNUCCI, 'Documenti', doc. II-24, pp. 91-2, and cf. p. 36; also G. MINNUCCI, 'San Bernardino patrono dell'Università di Siena', *L'Osservatore romano*, 148 (28 Jun 1984), p. 7. As CATONI, 'Il Sigillo', points out, the coupling of St. Catherine of Alexandria and San Bernardino is not unique; both were considered protectors of the young, and of those who speak in public. This very specific reference to San Bernardino is, however, the only one formally connecting the Sienese saint with the university; unlike St. Catherine, whose association with the *Studio* continues, in the iconography at least, to the present. St. Catherine and St. Nicholas (above, p. 201 n. 154) should be regarded as the two chief objects of collective devotion in the *Studio*; they were the two honoured by the *universitas scholarium* in 1440 (above, n. 236), and according to the 1511 statutes of the college of doctors of medicine they were again the two to whom the student-university made regular oblations (*Balìa* 253, ff. 335v-345v, 13 Oct, Rubric 12, ff. 340r-341r), and this remained the case after the end of the republic (PRUNAI, III, p. 120).

These isolated but important notices are the only Sienese ones we have of the custom of *studi*, student-universities or nations having a patron saint, a largely underexplored topic.[247] It is of course a practice common to a variety of bodies in the period – guilds, confraternities – and its very mundanity may be the reason that we hear so little of it. But the wording of these documents – like that of others which deal with ceremonial, described above – highlights the general problem we have in trying to understand the scope and functions of the student-university. The terms used to describe the university are ambiguous, and that ambiguity is significant. The record of the 1423 negotiations on the method of electing *consiliarii*, for example, never uses the expression 'universitas', preferring 'consiliarorum studii' and even 'congregatio studentium',[248] and it is from this period onwards that the terms 'universitas studii' and indeed 'rector studii' are increasingly found where 'universitas scolarium' or 'rector scolarium' might previously have been used.[249] It is perhaps no surprise, then, that the legal status of the student-university becomes less clear in the fifteenth century, while it grew ever more subject to manipulation and overruling by local authorities.[250] In sum, so many of its theoretical functions were in practice taken over, or at the very least encroached upon, by the town authorities that it is difficult to see – at least from the communal records, which are basically the ones that we have – what was left of it.

To do so it is perhaps necessary to take a broader view than has been possible in this focused study of the institution over a century. Looking at the activities of the student-university in the turbulent years of the mid-sixteenth century described and documented by Leo Košuta, it is clear that a substantial achievement was probably to ensure the survival of mechanisms that could represent the students as and when necessary. The symbolic and judicial role played by the rector could continue even if his appointment was to a considerable extent manipulated by the *Concistoro*, and even if there were probably years in which the maintenance of the proper system of *consiliarii*, matriculation books and so on may well have eluded the university. Having a rector who could be expected to speak for the students (and also to have responsibility for their discipline) was by no means a problem for the authorities.[251] Apart from the years of the Bolognese migration, student power in Siena had probably never amounted to much, but the documents published by Košuta show the university acting as a focus of collective identity, able at times of pressure to come together and make demands, but equally capable of hosting festivals[252] and engaging in the theatrical experimentation for which it has become famous.[253]

As to that student power, perhaps it needs to be assessed in a different way. It has been observed that the true legacy of the 'Bolognese model', particularly as exported beyond the peninsula, was the tradition – emanating from (and particularly pronounced among) students of law, who were wealthier

---

[247] A summary of the state of knowledge is C. FROVA, 'Nazioni e culto dei santi nelle università medioevali', in *Comunità forestiere e 'nationes' nell'Europa dei secoli XIII-XVI*, ed. G. Petti Balbi (Naples, 2001), pp. 11-22.

[248] Above, p. 258 and n. 79.

[249] For examples see the shift in terms used to describe the notary, above, p. 273 n. 229. This quite literally foreshadows what has been described as the shift of emphasis from the 'Università degli Studenti' to the 'Università degli Studi', a phrase that appeared on the cover of BELLOMO, *Saggio sull'Università*, in 1979, and has since been the theme of a conference; A. ROMANO (ed.), *Dall'Università degli Studenti all'Università degli Studi* (Messina, 1991).

[250] As to the legal distinction between 'universitas scolarium' and 'universitas studii', the fifteenth-century legal writers, Siena's Caccialupi among them, gave the issue a wide berth. GUALAZZINI, *Corpus Statutorum*, pp. CXLI-II.

[251] Even in a *Studio* as autocratically governed as that of Pavia the duke of Milan availed himself of the rector's advice; SOTTILI (ed.), *Documenti per la storia dell'Università di Pavia*, I, doc. 162, pp. 162-3.

[252] See KOŠUTA, 'Documenti', Appendice III, pp. 569-78; IDEM, 'Siena nella vita e nell'opera di Marino Darsa'.

[253] See below, p. 295.

and more demanding than their counterparts in other subjects – that students should have a say in their choice of teachers.[254] This is also evident in Siena, though not in any formalised sense. Prunai thought that in the late fourteenth century there was a tradition that students could express a preference for specific teachers, and that if six or more students did so their choice would be respected.[255] Specific references to such a tradition in the fifteenth century have not come to light. However, there are signs of students' views being taken into account. I have found only one formal request by the rector and scholars of the university, for the hiring of teachers in addition to Paolo di Castro and Giovanni da Imola, who are not enough to satisfy demand;[256] and one petition, by 'certi scholari', for the retention of Tommaso Docci, who had been teaching for two years, despite the fact that he had not yet taken his doctorate.[257] Student preferences are most frequently not expressed in these direct ways, but are often adduced in support of the *Savi*'s wish to hire or keep a teacher,[258] and specifically as a reason for refusing to part with one at the request of other *studi*.[259] But if the students are not prominent in the choice of teachers in the fifteenth century, the notion that they should have a say appears to have survived, and in the sixteenth century reappears in the form of students proposing candidates for *condotte*,[260] and even of organising one themselves.[261]

[254] COBBAN, 'Medieval Student Power', esp. pp. 59-60. In Italy the most extreme manifestation of this tradition was in Padua, where it was a matter of contention with the Venetian authorities for much of the fifteenth century. See R. OHL, 'The University of Padua, 1405-1509: an International Community of Students and Professors', unpublished Ph.D. dissertation, University of Pennsylvania, 1980, pp. 72-8, and DENLEY, '*Signore* and *Studio*', p. 206.

[255] PRUNAI, II, pp. 27-8. In 1396 citizens petitioned for the hiring of a surgeon, who would be obliged to teach as well if six or more students demanded it (*Conc.* 2111, f. 124r-v, ed. ZDEKAUER, doc. IX, p. 150). Prunai's assertion is similar to Zdekauer's comment on this petition (p. 25) and appears to be based on it.

[256] *Conc.* 2136, no. 48, put to the *Consiglio Generale* on 7 Oct, no year given. These two were both hired in 1404 and again in 1408. There is no conclusive evidence that would help fix the date of this petition.

[257] *Conc.* 2144, no. 3, 20 Aug 1425. There are a few other petitions; the rector and scholars asking that the *Studio* be retained (Conc. 262, f. 22r, 24 Sept 1409); a petition from the rector and the universitas scolarium that the Studio be moved because of plague (*Conc.* 385, f. 38r, 18 Jun 1430; cf. also *Conc.* 1634, ff. 58v-59r, 23 and 24 Jun for the commune's response); students and teachers ('ad istantia tota universitatis et doctorum et scolarium') ask for a safe-conduct for 'Antonio vocatus Sciacha de Scicilia' (*Conc.* 337, ff. 39v-40r, 25 Apr 1422), a student in civil law who had been thrown out of town the previous year (Conc. 331, f. 14v, 29 Mar 1421, where his nickname is 'il Griacha'), on whom cf. ZDEKAUER, p. 41.

[258] E.g. *Conc.* 339, f. 13r, 29 Jul 1422, 'per certa secreta materia studii', which argues that if Francesco Pontano left the 'destructio et vastatio…senensis studio' would ensue because many students would follow him (cf. also *Conc.* 340, f. 26r, 31 Oct 1422). In 1435 the rector came to the *Concistoro* in person to present a petition from the whole *universitas scolarium* asking them to prevent Lodovico Pontano from leaving (*Conc.* 419, f. 19v, 21 Nov), because many students would follow him. Members of the *Concistoro* argued that this would result in the destruction of the *Studio* and revoked his licence. The petition is not quite what it seems; Lodovico himself also appeared, stating that he would prefer to continue teaching. Similar remarks apply to the proposal in 1495 to rehire Antonio Berti, the 'abbate Rosano', to prevent him leaving after thirty-six years of teaching without a pay rise; the students' satisfaction with his teaching, and disappointment at the prospect of his departure, are cited in support (*CG* 240, f. 286r-v, 23 Mar).

[259] Florence's request for Girolamo da S. Miniato was deflected on the grounds that it would result in 'maximo detrimento nostri studii, et cum displicentia scolarium studentium in facultate Medicine' (*Conc.* 1625, f. 43v, 21 Mar 1425); similar terms were used to keep Pietro de' Giovanetti (*Conc.* 1626, f. 17v, 24 Aug 1425).

[260] L. KOŠUTA, 'Aonio Paleario et son groupe humaniste et réformateur à Sienne (1530-1546)', *Lias*, 7 (1980), p. 49 n. 122.

[261] KOŠUTA, 'Documenti', doc. XIX, pp. 481-2. The students' say in the choice of teachers at Perugia, very strong in the early fourteenth century, was limited by the late fifteenth century (ERMINI, *Storia*, I, pp. 53-5), though as late as 1443 students were participating in a full election of a teacher; U. NICOLINI, 'Dottori, scolari, programmi e salari alla Università di Perugia verso la metà del sec. XV', *Bollettino della Deputazione di Storia Patria per l'Umbria*, 58 (1961), pp. 139-59 (doc. B, pp. 151-6). But even after that the rector was still to witness the payment of the teachers (ERMINI, p. 275), and the scholars retained their say in the choice of texts to be read (pp. 106, 444 *seq.*).

III

THE STUDENT EXPERIENCE

1. *Introduction*

No profile of a university would be complete without an attempt to describe what it was like to attend and study there; yet this is an area in which the institutional records that form the basis of the present work can offer the least help. Anecdote is a poor substitute for systematic sources, but for many aspects of the topic it is the only type of information that we have. It is therefore inevitable that for certain parts of this chapter we will draw more than usual on what is known generally about the Italian university world, to offer some comparative perspectives.

2. *Material considerations*

For those considering study at a university the fundamental question, as at all times, was cost. Although by the fifteenth century the practice of students paying fees for teaching (*collectae*) had disappeared,[1] the cost of not working, for all students, and for non-Sienese the cost of travel, lodging and sustenance, were major factors. For students who intended to take their studies as far as the doctorate – a minority, certainly – this was a substantial investment; law degrees could take six, seven or eight years, and the completion of both arts and medicine would take even longer.[2] We have no way of knowing what the cost actually was – the best that can be managed is intelligent guesswork[3] – but the

---

[1] Above, p. 184 n. 7.

[2] BARGAGLI, *Bartolomeo Sozzini*, p. 16; cf. DAVIES, *Florence and its University*, p. 21, and BELLOMO, *Saggio sull'Università*, pp. 246-8. In the absence of statutes it has not been possible to ascertain what the formal requirement was at Siena. At Bologna eight years was the minimum for a degree in civil law; TROMBETTI BUDRIESI, 'L'esame di laurea', p. 180.

[3] The Florentine proposal for a Sapienza in 1429 described the loss to the republic from students going elsewhere as follows: 'Troviamo fuori della città et provincia vostra circa ducento cinquanta scolari continuamente vivere, i quali traggono del nostro districto circa cinquemilia fiorini per anno' (GHERARDI, *Statuti*, appendix, part I, doc. CXVII, pp. 210-14 [p. 211], 15 Mar). The conclusion that it cost about 20 florins a year to keep a student at university in the fifteenth century has been quoted by L. MARTINES, *Lawyers and Statecraft in Renaissance Florence* (Princeton, N.J., 1968), pp. 90-1, and IDEM, *The Social World of the Florentine Humanists, 1390-1460* (London, 1963), p. 117, and has become the received wisdom (e.g. VERDE, *Lo Studio fiorentino*, II, p. 647), but it remains an isolated, albeit contemporary estimate.

preoccupation of students and the authorities with this issue is evident.[4] Of the various means by which students could obtain funds – parents, private patrons, bequests, living off income, finding tutoring work while studying,[5] loans from home[6] – perhaps the least appreciated to date is the practice, common to a number of Italian towns that were not themselves university centres, of awarding scholarships to promising (or well-connected) citizens to enable them to study at specified centres. Pisa appears to have been an early instance;[7] a number of Sicilians studying in Siena benefited from such arrangements; and in the late fifteenth century Prato and Lucca also enabled students to come to Siena in this way.[8] Another mechanism that is now beginning to be studied is the financial arrangements that could be made for transferring funds for students from their country of origin – a practice in which Siena, with its rich banking tradition, had a natural advantage.[9]

Once students had arrived in Siena the problems, far from going away, moved from the hypothetical to the very real. The most immediate issue was accommodation. For those not fortunate enough to have been granted a place in the Casa della Sapienza (or indeed, for those who arrived and then began to lobby for such a place) this meant living *a dozzina*,[10] at rents which do not appear to have been controlled by the authorities.[11] Again, this means that the subject is largely hidden from view, with the exception of students who are brought to the attention of the authorities for some reason.[12] The *Concistoro* intervened only when accommodation was perceived to be a serious or an acute problem,[13] or when well-born students demanded special treatment.[14] Some students were occasionally put up in pi-

---

[4] Above, pp. 66 n. 14, 233, and cf. *Conc.* 608, f. 18r, 19 Jan 1468; in response to a complaint from students about the costs of studying away from home, the *Concistoro* decided to put the issue to the *Consiglio del Popolo*.

[5] An example is Hieronimo de Rasimo of Narni, who acted as *repetitor* in the household of his patron (*Balìa* 555, no. 35a, 14 Feb 1495[=1496]); see below, p. 291 n. 97.

[6] See p. 242 above; and cf. the will of a citizen of Colle Val d'Elsa, including a bequest to his son 'ad studendum ad civitatem Senarum vel ad alia loca remota a dicta terra Collis ubi studium teneatur'; A. BROWN, *Bartolomeo Scala, 1439-1497, Chancellor of Florence. The Humanist as Bureaucrat* (Princeton, N.J., 1979), p. 5 n. 11.

[7] G. DEL GUERRA, *Rustichello da Pisa* (Pisa, 1955), p. 50.

[8] On Prato, see above, p. 246 n. 117; on Lucca, see BARSANTI, *Il pubblico insegnamento*, pp. 80-3 (nine students were subsidised to study in Siena between 1451 and 1492). Cf. P. TRIO, 'Financing of University Students in the Middle Ages: a New Orientation', *History of Universities*, 4 (1984), pp. 1-24. A variant of this is contribution towards the cost of a degree; cf. the decision of the commune of Assisi on 3 Jan 1479 to grant suitable Assisan citizens twenty-five ducats for this purpose provided they took their degree at Perugia, Siena, Bologna or Padua. C. PIANA, *Il "Liber Secretus Iuris Pontificii" dell'Università di Bologna, 1451-1500*. Orbis Academicus. Saggi e Documenti di Storia delle Università, 2 (Milan, 1989), p. 16*. An unusual form of subsidy was that accorded by the chapter of the hospital of S. Maria della Scala to a student who is described as 'buon gramatico et assai buon rethorico'. He wants to proceed to the study of canon law; the chapter decides that 25 florins a year can be spent on books for him (*Scala* 24, f. 71v, 4 Nov 1456).

[9] See above, p. 242.

[10] The phrase appears in the measures of 1481; *Balìa* 24, f. 90r, 30 Jun, eds. PUCCINOTTI, *Storia della Medicina*, p. CLXVII, and ILARDI, 'Ordinamenti', p. 169; copy in *Mis.* 1, f. 109r.

[11] The only indication of 'rent control' I have found for the fifteenth century is a resolution of 1428 to help scholars find lodgings, which stipulates that they 'habeat ipsas domos pro iuxta pensione' (*Conc.* 375, f. 10r, 10 Sept). The possibility that the missing student university statutes may have included regulations on this subject cannot be excluded. Contracts of rent survive in *Not.* 600, ff. 40r, 2 Jun 1470, and 49r-v, 22 Jan 1471.

[12] E.g. the eviction of the students living with Bartolomeo Petrucci in 1469 by the *Nove Ufficiali di Custodia*, 'ad evitandum omnia scandala'; ZDEKAUER, p. 105 and n. 2.

[13] They twice ordered the *Savi* to find more accommodation for students (*Conc.* 648, f. 23r, 10 Oct; *Conc.* 692, f. 16v, 21 Jan 1482).

[14] See the case of the Sicilian Domperus, who threatened to leave because of the poor conditions in the *Studio* (he was offered special lodgings of the *vicecancellarius*; *Conc.* 623, f. 39r, 20 Aug 1470); and the special arrangements made for Luís Teixeira, below, p. 323.

ous institutions;[15] others found lodgings with teachers, in a time-honoured practice.[16] This was only one of many aspects of the unequal relationship between teachers and students, which, as Zdekauer has shown, could extend to the borrowing of money[17] as well as of books.[18]

The next essential was the supply of texts. The trawl of communal legislation has added little to our knowledge of what has become a very specialised and much-researched area.[19] Students were served by a variety of sources. The libraries of the religious houses were clearly one, as was that of the Duomo, to which several fifteenth-century teachers left their collections.[20] The fifteenth century is too early to expect to find a university library, but perhaps more surprisingly, as will be argued below, it also seems most unlikely that the Casa della Sapienza possessed a formal library in this period.[21] As has been seen, teachers and students had the right to bring books with them free of duty, and in theory to remove them again when they left (if they left legally, without breaking the protectionist legislation).[22] Teachers and fellow-students certainly lent books, and occasionally had to resort to the law to get them back.[23] Beyond these possibilities, students were cast back on the traditional network of university stationers and *cartolai* for the borrowing and copying of texts. The world of these individuals is obscure. A number of them were foreigners, mostly Germans;[24] and the documents that inform us of the long-delayed introduction of printing in Siena – for which one of the main stimuli was the *Studio*[25] – accuse these

---

[15] In 1407 a scholar was received in the hospital of S. Maria della Scala, for the month of June only, at the request of the *Capitano del Popolo* (*Scala* 22, f. 64v, 27 May); in 1409 two scholars from Sarteano were given a room there (*Scala* 22, f. 96r, 1 Jul). See also PICCINNI, 'L'Ospedale', p. 319.

[16] E.g. *Conc.* 2181, no foliation, 14 Aug 1462; Tommaso Battista di Maestro Andrea da Pisa acknowledges a debt to 'M.º Alexandro artium et medicine doctore de senis' in respect of rent.

[17] Cf. *Not.* 660, no. 3, 30 Mar 1493; 'Dnus. Paulus de Plenzi de civitate competinensi de partibus alamanie alte studens sen.' acknowledges a debt to Lorenzo Luti of 15 gold ducats. Paulus had entered the Sapienza in 1490 (BCS, *ms.* A.XI.12, f. 56v; ZDEKAUER, doc. XXIII, p. 187, and BONAFACCIA, 'La "Domus Sapientiae"', p. 104); and cf. his oath of obedience to the statutes of the house on 3 Jun 1492, ed. MINNUCCI, 'Documenti', doc. II-32, pp. 98-9).

[18] Below, n. 23.

[19] See above all BASTIANONI et al., *Lo Studio e i testi*.

[20] ZDEKAUER, pp. 85-94 has given a full account of these libraries; see now also FIORAVANTI, 'Pietro de' Rossi', pp. 139 *seq.*; K. W. HUMPHREYS, *The Library of the Franciscans of Siena in the Late Fifteenth Century* (Amsterdam, 1978); and V. J. KOUDELKA, O.P., 'Spigolature dal Memoriale di Niccolò Galgani O.P. († 1424)', *Archivum Fratrum Praedicatorum*, 29 (1959), pp. 111-47.

[21] Below, pp. 386-8. This of course did not stop it from becoming an important centre for scholarship. Books could be taken out of the Sapienza with permission; e.g. *Sale* 6, f. 80r, 12 Aug 1432, ed. ZDEKAUER, doc. XIV, p. 163.

[22] Above, pp. 222 and 234. That an embargo of some sort was in effect can be deduced from the deliberation of 1450 that a Spaniard might take books out of Siena because he was not at the *Studio* (*Conc.* 507, f. 22r, 1 Oct. Cf. SPAGNESI, *Utiliter edoceri, passim*, and ERMINI, *Storia*, I, p. 465 for such legislation in Florence and Perugia respectively). The removal of books could be tricky; in 1434 two German students who had left Siena with the complication that one, Johannes de Lysura, was in debt, had to resort to a third party to retrieve them (SOTTILI, 'Le lettere di Johannes Ruysch', pp. 336-71; summarised with additional information in ROSSO, 'Studenti di area germanica', pp. 43-49).

[23] See Filippo Lazzari of Pistoia's letter of 1444, ed. ZDEKAUER, doc. XIX, pp. 172-3, and further material pp. 173-4; also MINNUCCI, 'Professori e scolari giuristi', p. 115. In 1476 the *Savi* ordered students who had borrowed books from teachers over the vacation to return them (*Studio* 2, f. 39r).

[24] A petition of 16 Dec 1474 names two German *magistros librorum* (*Conc.* 2312, no foliation). Miscellaneous references to scribes and copyists in G. SCAGLIA, *Francesco di Giorgio: Checklist and History of Manuscripts and Drawings in Autographs and Copies from ca. 1470 to 1687 and Renewed Copies (1764-1839)* (London, 1992), pp. 14-15, 246, 252-3.

[25] The three proposers of the enterprise, Lorenzo Cannucciari, Jacopo del Germonia and Luca di Niccolò Martini, all *Studio* teachers, justified the proposed introduction of printing with the reasoning that 'allo Studio della città vostra era molto commodo avere copia di libri assai'; *CG* 239, ff. 204v-205r, 21 May 1484, and see C. BASTIANONI and G. CATONI, *Impressum Senis. Storie di tipografi, incunaboli e librai* (Siena, 1988), pp. 17-19 and n. 35 for further references.

vested interests of having held it up out of fear of competition.[26] There is one document that may well be a stationer's inventory,[27] and if that is the case then we have at last some indication of the texts that were in circulation. However, it would be dangerous to expect it to shed that much light on what students read; Giovanni Battista Caccialupi already warned in the second half of the fifteenth century that the needs of the student in this respect were very different from those of the teacher.[28]

3. *Student lectureships*

For those who took their studies to the advanced stage, and aimed at professional careers, the fifteenth century saw a new attraction. Like other *studi* (and in competition with them), Siena developed the practice of offering lectureships at a modest salary to non-citizens near the end of their studies. Student lectureships went back at least as far as the 1317-47 jurist university statutes of Bologna, in which they were elective posts filled by the student university.[29] The Sienese declaration in 1423 that no rector or scholar of the Sapienza could receive a salary for a lectureship makes it clear that it was not unknown for students to teach.[30] In February 1425 it was stated that no non-doctor could be salaried,[31] but only a month later Mariano Sozzini, then still a 'scolarius in iure civili', was hired for a salary of 20 florins.[32] In September of that year, 'avuta informatione che in ciascuno altro studio…si costuma dare certe letture a scolari valenti vicini al dottorato…', a formal proposal was made to introduce four *letture*, which were to be chosen by the university of students and the six 'deputati sopra lo studio'. The proposal was lost,[33] but its introduction was inevitable if Siena wished to compete with other *studi*. When it came in 1428 it was justified, as ever, on utilitarian grounds: 'Et questo sarà grande utile per lo studio vostro perché molti scolari per speranza d'avere la decta lectura venendo a studiare ne lo studio vostro et facendo lo exame publico…Peroché questa legge e nello studio di bologna et negli altri famosi studi.' A total of 100 florins was to be set aside for four lectureships salaried at 25 florins each. Appointees had to take their degree in Siena within the year.[34] In contrast

---

[26] Bastianoni and Catoni , op. cit., pp. 11-12; G. Catoni, 'L'alchimia dei Monti', in *Repubblica di Siena (1400-1507)* (Milan, 2002), pp. 24-5.

[27] Below, pp. 386-8.

[28] J. B. Caccialupus, *De modo studendi*, f. 72r; tr. Di Noto Marrella, pp. 50-1. Essentially his advice at its most pithy was 'distrahit librorum multitudo'. Cf. Zdekauer, p. 85.

[29] Malagola, *Statuti*, rubr. 40, pp. 36-8 (38) – and see Bellomo, *Saggio sull'Università*, pp. 215-6. On the practice in fifteenth-century Bologna cf. Piana, *Il "Liber Secretus Iuris Caesarei"*, pp. 102*-109*.

[30] *CG* 210, f. 6lr, *Mis.* 1, f. 54r, 18 Aug. A student was given a *lettura* in 1429, though he was to be paid no salary until he had taken his degree (*Conc.* 377, f. 24r, 9 Feb, ed. Pianigiani, doc. 105, pp. 131-2). Unpaid lecturing by students was also not unknown; for example, in 1435 Magr. Giovanni di Donato da Arezzo was given a place in the Sapienza on condition that he read logic there with no salary (*Conc.* 415, f. 10r, 10 Mar 1435). Cf. Perugia, where this appears to have been more common, and was encouraged by the authorities provided such lectures did not clash with those of teachers (Ermini, *Storia*, I, p. 457).

[31] *CG* 210, f. 175v, 5 Feb, ed. Garosi, doc. 60, p. 529, copied in *Statuti* 41, ff. 67r, 169r, and 47, f. 168r-v.

[32] *Conc.* 355, f. 6v, 8 Mar, eds. Nardi, *Mariano Sozzini*, doc. 2, p. 115, and Pianigiani, doc. 68, pp. 89-90; and see the case of Tommaso Docci, above, p. 278.

[33] *Conc.* 2113, f. 155v, 22 Sept.

[34] *CG* 213, ff. 53v-54r, and *Conc.* 2137, no. 12, f. 17r, 10 Sept; see Zdekauer, p. 63 and n. 1. The proposals initially recommended six such appointments (and an expenditure of 150 florins), but only four were approved (*Conc.* 2137, f. 12r, 7 Sept). The first three appointments were made on 9 Dec (*Conc.* 376, f. 21r; Pianigiani doc. 104, pp. 130-1). For reiterations of the motive for their institution cf. *Conc.* 556, f. 50r, 23 Jun 1459, when it is considered advantageous to delay the appointments to attract more students to Siena in anticipation, and *Mis.* 1, f. 101r, 10 Sept 1472, when it is explicitly stated that the four *letture* had been introduced 'per induciare scolari ad venire nel vostro studio, et stare ne la ciptà a loro spese'.

to the proposals of three years earlier, however, there was now no mention of a student role in the allocation of the lectureships.[35] Within a year a fifth lectureship, awarded to the rector of the *Studio*, emerged.[36] For some time the length of the list oscillated between four and five, the fifth lectureship usually but not always going to the rector, and the salaries of all five being reduced to 20 florins to leave the total expenditure at 100 florins.[37] With the exception of a two-year suspension in the 1480s, the lectureships appear to have been awarded continuously until the fall of the republic.[38]

The popularity of these lectureships is well attested. There was undoubtedly competition for them, and they were incidentally one of the few opportunities for ultramontanes to obtain any sort of appointment in Italy.[39] But they could also be seen in a more negative light. One label by which they came to be known in Siena was 'letture morte',[40] which to Zdekauer indicated the scant academic regard in which they were held, and to others has suggested that they were basically scholarships which did not involve any actual teaching.[41] The appointments were not infrequently surrounded by contro-

---

[35] At no stage does there appear to have been any student participation in the procedure, nor, as at Bologna, is there evidence of the holding of formal disputations to help select students; H. S. MATSEN, 'Students' "Arts" Disputations at Bologna around 1500 Illustrated from the Career of Alessandro Achillini (1463-1512), *History of Education*, 6 (1977), pp. 169-181.

[36] *Conc.* 382, f. 7v, 13 Nov 1429, ed. PIANIGIANI, doc. 118, pp. 146-7.

[37] Five appointments were made in 1443 (*Conc.* 467, f. 36r, 30 Dec, ed. PIANIGIANI, doc. 246, pp. 266-7), 1445 (*Conc.* 479, f. 32v, 25 Dec, ed. PIANIGIANI, doc. 261, p. 293), 1461 (*Conc.* 571, f. 24r, 28 Nov; on this occasion the rector of the *Studio* was not included), 1464 (*Conc.* 589, f. 24r, 11 Dec), 1467 (*Conc.* 607, f. 21v, 16 Nov, ed. BAI, doc. 266, pp. 244-5), 1468 (*Conc.* 613, f. 31r, 23 Dec, ed. BAI, doc. 283, pp. 266-7), 1469 (*Conc.* 619, f. 42v, 27 Dec), and 1493 (*Studio* 2, f. 137r, 5 Jul). In 1459 only three appointments were made (*Conc.* 556, f. 50r, 23 Jun).

[38] *Balìa* 24, f. 90v, 30 Jun 1481, eds. PUCCINOTTI, *Storia della Medicina*, p. CLXVII, and ILARDI, 'Ordinamenti', p. 170; copy in *Mis.* 1, f. 109r: 'per due anni proximi s'intendino sospese quelle quattro letture extraordinarie che si davano a scolari, nelle quali si spendeva fiorini 100 l'anno'.

[39] Early examples of ultramontanes being given lectureships are 'Magister Ingerardus … de allamania artium doctor' (*Conc.* 386, f. 32v, 3 Aug 1430, ed. PIANIGIANI, doc. 123, pp. 151-3), the civilian Theodoricus de Spania (*Conc.* 441, f. 60v, 29 Aug 1439, ed. PIANIGIANI, doc. 201, pp. 231-3), the canonist 'Raffael catalanus' (*Conc.* 461, f. 58v, 16 Dec 1442), and 'Petrus de Michelibus de Chetelonia' (*Conc.* 479, f. 35v, 29 Dec 1445; he took the place of a 'Raphael de Cathelonia' who renounced the lectureship – *Conc.* 479, f. 32v, 25 Dec, ed. PIANIGIANI, doc. 261, pp. 292-3 – which raises the question of whether this is the same Raphael, and if so whether he was given a second lectureship). The unusual nature of this kind of appointment is confirmed by DE COSTER, 'Vreemde docenten', and EADEM, 'La mobilità dei docenti'. Her work demonstrates that at Bologna very few non-citizen students managed to teach beyond the doctorate, and these were almost all Italians.

[40] E.g. *Studio* 2, f. 62r, 20 Dec 1479; the *Savi* meet 'pro quatuor lectionibus mortuis dandis scolaribus ex forma consuetudinis scruptinandis in consistorio' (the first use of this expression to have been found. A shortlist of nine is drawn up; six are lawyers, including the vice-rector of the *Studio*, and three students of medicine. Four are ultramontanes); *Conc.* 687, f. 265v, 17 Apr 1481, ed. FERRERI, doc. 118, p. 100 ('lecturis scholasticis que dicuntur lecture mortue'); cf. *Sale* 23, ff. 96r, 19 Aug, and 97r-v, 22 Sept 1496 (ed. ZDEKAUER, doc. XXV, pp. 193-5, with old archival reference and incorrect year); *Sale* 24, ff. 163r, 21 Jan, 166v, 30 Oct 1498; *Balìa* 45, f. 98r, 8 Oct 1499. At an earlier stage circumlocutions are used to describe these appointments; for example, 'lecturas que dantur scolaribus non doctoratis' (*Conc.* 467, f. 36r, 30 Dec 1443, ed. PIANIGIANI, doc. 246, pp. 276-7).

[41] ZDEKAUER, p. 63; SOTTILI, 'Zum Verhältnis von Stadt, Staat und Universität', pp. 55-6 n. 52, following CATONI, 'Il Comune di Siena e l'amministrazione della Sapienza', p. 127. The theory has the indirect backing of practice in Bologna, where such lectureships were awarded to sons of the intellectual patriciate as, basically, a way of getting the commune to cover the costs of taking a degree (see esp. BRAMBILLA, 'Genealogie del sapere', pp. 130, 133). Corroborative evidence for this comes from the payment to 'Miss. Lupo de portoghalo scholare' 'per una delle iiij leture si dano senza farelo' (*Bicch.* 333, f. 332r, 11 Dec 1476). In other documents, however, the posts awarded in Siena have all the trappings of normal lectureships. On 23 Jun 1459 'M.° Guidone de Capranica scolare peritus in artibus' was hired to teach on feast days for 25 florins on condition that he took his degree; judging this condition to be useful as a way of attracting students to Siena ('multi scolares veniant cum dicta spe et postea restant in studio'), the *Concistoro* ordered that three further scholars 'diversis facultatibus' were to be hired on the same conditions 'ut moris est' (*Conc.* 556, f. 50r). In a contract of 1467 (*Conc.* 607, f. 21v, 16 Nov, ed. BAI, doc. 266, pp. 244-5) they are described as *extraordinarie*, and appointees had to read what they were told by the *Savi*. Moreover, Cosma da Arezzo, a scholar given such a *lettura* in 1493 (*Balìa* 39, f. 2r, 1 Jul) was subse-

versy and complaint. There were the inevitable disagreements over who should appoint such students – in 1476 the *Savi* actually proposed that three of the four lecturers should be appointed by themselves and the fourth by the *Concistoro*, a compromise unusual even by Sienese standards.[42] In 1442 a budget-cutting measure expressed dissatisfaction 'perché se vede che se conducono a le volte scolari piuttosto per compiacere che per necessità'.[43] It not infrequently happened that on completion of his term of office the outgoing rector would be given another year's lectureship, despite the intention that students should hold them for one year only;[44] and by the end of the fifteenth century two-year appointments were also not unknown.[45] The lectureships were designed to be additional and separate incentives from the Sapienza;[46] nonetheless we know of at least three rectors and one scholar of the Sapienza who held them, and a measure of 1472 admits that 'le letture si concedano spesse volte agli scolari de la Sapientia', and that the condition that the lecturer took his degree in Siena within the year was also often not fulfilled.[47] This condition was the one on which the authorities were most insistent; it was almost as if this was seen as a guarantee of a certain number of doctorates.[48] It is also ap-

quently given three fines or *puncte*, hardly possible if the award had been a mere bursary (*Conc.* 765, outside cover, Mar-Apr 1494, ed. FERRERI, doc. 341, p. 324). It may also be relevant that in 1470-1 one of these *letture* was given to a *religioso*, the Servite Bonifazio (*Bicch.* 326, p. 182r, 13 Mar).

[42] *Studio* 2, f. 47v, 14 Oct. For interventions of the *Balìa* in the process see below, p. 285 and nn. 50, 51-4.

[43] *CG* 221, f. 87r, 16 Mar; GAROSI, doc. 67, pp. 533-4. He misinterprets the document as meaning the suspension of such *letture* (p. 246).

[44] For example, Roberto Cavalcanti of Florence, *Conc.* 369, f. 16r, 27 Sept 1427, ed. PIANIGIANI, doc. 80, pp. 100-2 (though as this is at 40 florins it may have been considered a full lectureship – he was to read *in concurrentia* with Mariano Sozzini); *Conc.* 400, f. 10v, 10 Sept 1432, ed. PIANIGIANI, doc. 137, p. 166 (Johannes de Alamania; on his identity see above, p. 267 n. 166); *Conc.* 491, f. 50r, 31 Dec 1447, ed. PIANIGIANI, doc. 279, pp. 312-3 (Serafino da Camerino, whose status as rector is attested in his appointment to a *lettura* the previous year; *Conc.* 484, f. 28v, 21 Oct 1446; also cf. *Bicch.* 316, f. 39v, 9 Apr 1447).

[45] E.g. Cosma da Arezzo, n. 41 above, and below, nn. 49 and 50.

[46] In 1423, i.e. before the official introduction of the system, it was decreed that no Sapienza rector or scholar could hold any lectureship (*CG* 210, f. 60r; *Mis.* 1, f. 54r, 18 Aug), and this was not derogated in 1428. Before that it had been possible; in 1421 the rector of the Sapienza had been given a 'lectura sapientie' (*Conc.* 1619, f. 66v, 24 May. He was to read *Volumen*). The restriction was being applied in 1438, when the rector of the Sapienza, Malatesta de' Cattani di Borgo, was granted a lectureship in *Liber Sextus et Clementinae* on condition that he renounced the rectorate (*Conc.* 437, f. 35v, 16 Dec, ed. PIANIGIANI, doc. 194, pp. 223-5; see above, p. 130 and n. 45). In 1464 two students were declared ineligible for lectureships removed because they had places in the Sapienza (*Conc.* 589, f. 29v, 17 Dec, ed. BAI, doc. 213, pp. 187-8).

[47] *Mis.* 1, f. 101r, 25 Sept (and cf. *Conc.* 636, f. 15v, 23 Sept). The measure resolves 'quod nulla e quatuor lecturis scolariorum possit dari scolaribus sapientie vel pedagogis ymo dabant scolaribus qui steterint in studio sen. suis expensis pro annum, et quod non possit habere salarium nisi post eius doctoratum' (*Conc.* 636, loc. cit.). Filippo da Lucca was given a *lettura* concurrent with his second term as rector in 1426 (*CG* 211, f. 44v, and *Conc.* 2175, no foliation, 26 Mar – see ZDEKAUER, p. 99; *Conc.* 361, ff. 15v, 21 Mar, 18r, 25 Mar 1426, and cf. *Conc.* 373, f. 28r, 2 Jun 1428); so was Benedetto da Volterra in 1435 (*CG* 218, ff. 198v-199r, 23 Oct); Giovanni Battista da Lucca, 'scolari et presbitero domus sapientie', was appointed to a *lettura* on 20 Oct 1496 (*Sale* 23, f. 97r; ZDEKAUER, doc. XXV, p. 195); Conforto da Spoleto, another rector of the Sapienza, was given a 'lettura morta' at 25 florins on 18 Oct 1497 (*Sale* 24, f. 157v); and the same happened the following year to the new rector, 'Mag.co Dno. Alvero' (*Sale* 24, f. 166v, 30 Oct). By the late fifteenth century the entitlement of the Sapienza rector to a *lettura* seems to have been accepted (Archivio di Stato di Firenze, *Studio Fiorentino e Pisano, 1357-1568*, 7, f. 68r, ed. VERDE, *Lo Studio fiorentino*, V, p. 46, n.d. but dated by Verde to 1487. On this source see above, p. 27 n. 144).

[48] See p. 282 above, and *Conc.* 436, f. 37r, 24 Oct 1438 (Dns. Julianus de Squaquaris de Gaeta, lectureship in canon or civil law), ed. PIANIGIANI, doc. 112, pp. 220-1 (omitting this condition); *Conc.* 441, f. 60v, 29 Aug 1439, ed. PIANIGIANI, doc. 201, pp. 231-3 (Teodorico da Spagna; his lectureship in civil law cannot begin before he has taken his degree, which he must do before St. Luke's; he must also leave the Sapienza by then); *Conc.* 460, f. 20r, 21 Sept 1442, ed. PIANIGIANI, doc. 232, pp. 263-4 (a lectureship in logic for Lodovico da Spoleto, on whom see above, pp. 168 n. 185 and 204-6; he was to take his degree in arts by St. Luke's); *Conc.* 461, f. 58v, 16 Dec 1442 (Dns. Paulus Pontanus de Urbe, lectureship in civil or canon law; Magr. Ciprianus de Marcialla comitatus pisanorum, lectureship in philosophy; and Dns. Raffael cathelanus' lectureship in canon

parent that the restriction of these appointments to *forenses* was also occasionally flouted by the end of the century.[49]

Lectureships were the first rung of the academic ladder; they got students noticed. In this respect they could also be openings to appointments within the commune. A clear instance is the Roman civil law student Pietro da Capranica. In 1496 he was appointed to a student lectureship by the *Balìa*.[50] Two years later he appears as *Giudice dei Pupilli*.[51] In 1499 Stefano Macri of Savoy was appointed to a lectureship by the *Balìa* – the student lectureship quota apparently being full[52] – and shortly afterwards was made *Giudice delle Appellagioni*, on the same condition that attached to the lectureship, namely that he take his degree, in Siena, before taking up the post.[53] He held the office and the lectureship simultaneously,[54] but only took his degree in November 1500.[55]

---

law); *Conc.* 467, f. 36r, 30 Dec 1443, ed. PIANIGIANI, doc. 261, pp. 276-7 ('plurium scolarium non doctoratorum'; their appointments were conditional on their taking their degrees within a year, but were also without salary until such time as they did so); *Conc.* 479, f. 32v, 25 Dec 1445, ed. PIANIGIANI, doc. 261, pp. 292-3 (Raphael de Catelonia, again, lectureship in canon law, which he renounced – see above, n. 39; Johannes Mancini de Sicilia, canon law; and Benedictus de Farano in terris Rome, *in artibus*: 'nullum possint habere salarium nisi sint doctorati et fidem faciant de doctoratu'); *Conc.* 497, f. 22v, 10 Dec 1448, ed. PIANIGIANI, doc. 288, pp. 321-2 (Maestro Panunzio, lectureship in medicine); *Conc.* 503, f. 31r, 20 Dec 1449, ed. PIANIGIANI, doc. 296, p. 329 (Angelo di Pietro da Gubbio, lectureship *in artibus*; subsequent documents suggest that this was an error for Angelo di Paolo, later made rector); *Conc.* 636, f. 15v, 23 Sept 1472. Such conditions are also found in the second half of the century; in 1464, five students accepting lectureships were expected to leave a deposit or produce a guarantor to pledge that they would take their doctorates (*Conc.* 589, f. 24r, 11 Dec), and in 1467 it was stipulated that the four appointees were not to be paid until they had done so (*Conc.* 607, f. 21v, 16 Nov 1467, ed. BAI, doc. 266, pp. 244-5).

[49] In 1496 three of the four appointees to these 'letture morte' were Sienese subjects (*Sale* 24, f. 97r; ZDEKAUER, doc. XXV, p. 195, 20 Oct 1496; Ugo Sermini, Luca di Cristoforo da Asciano, Federico P.[*sic*] of Rocca di Val d'Orcia. The fourth was Giovanni Battista da Lucca, 'scolari et presbitero domus Sapientie'); a year later all four were Sienese (*Sale* 24, f. 163r, 21 Jan 1498; 'Antoniusmaria Bandini de Ptomasis', 'Lucas dominici presbitero de Asciano', 'Bernardinus pauli aurifici' – who died – and 'Ambrosius ser priami de cechinis'). The regulation can hardly be said to have atrophied, however; only in 1489 the *Concistoro* appointed 'unam ex quattuor lecturis, quas eis permissum est concedere scolaribus forensibus secundum formam Statutorum Comunis Senarum' (*Conc.* 735, f. 3r, 3 Mar, ed. FERRERI, doc. 291, p. 261). BARGAGLI, *Bartolomeo Sozzini*, pp. 15-16 and n. 29, suggested that Sozzini's appointment to teach *Istituzioni* in 1459, while he was still 'doctissimus scolarus', for 25 florins (*Conc.* 557, f. 35r, 6 Aug, eds. BARGAGLI, 'Documenti senesi', doc. 3, p. 276, and BAI, doc. 120, p. 104), was one of these student lectureships. It is possible that Sozzini's contract fell into this category, though this is not explicitly stated. Three other people were appointed at low salaries that year; another Sienese, Francesco di Meo Peri, 'artium doctor' (which does not of course rule out the possibility that he was also a student, of medicine) was appointed (on the same day as Sozzini, loc. cit.) to teach logic and moral philosophy, for 20 florins and later in the year Mariotto da Assisi was appointed to teach logic, and the Dominican Leonardo to teach astrology, both for 25 florins (*Conc.* 558, f. 33v, 20 Oct, ed. BAI, docs. 124-5, pp. 107-8). The status of these two is not clear; and the other anomaly is that all but the astrology appointment were for two years rather than one. If these were the student lectureships, one would have to conclude that the practice was in a state of flux at this stage. Bargagli also went along with Zdekauer's scepticism, and evidence from other *studi*, to suggest that these lectureships could occasionally be used for 'rimunerazione per scolari appartenenti ad eminenti famiglie cittadine' (*Bartolomeo Sozzini*, p. 16 n. 29, and cf. n. 41 above). The case of Sozzini apart, the evidence for this in the fifteenth century is limited. Of the seven appointees in 1496 and 1498 mentioned above, the only distinctive names are Tommasi and Sermini.

[50] *Balìa* 40, f. 118v, 8 Jan. The contract is for two years, the salary 25 florins annually, and he is to read *Institutiones*. The instructions for him to be paid (*Sale* 23, f. 86r, 19 Aug 1496, ed. ZDEKAUER, doc. XXV, p. 195) state unequivocally that this is a *lettura morta*. The salary appears to have been augmented, however; in 1497 he is paid 200 *lire* (40 florins) for the second year of the contract (*Balìa* 41, f. 197r, 11 Jul).

[51] *Sale* 24, f. 165v, 7 Jun 1498.

[52] The *Balìa* first tried to allocate one of the *letture morte* to a student, then backed off and awarded him a full lectureship instead (*Balìa* 45, f. 98v, 8 Oct, and 109v, 19 Oct 1499).

[53] *Balìa* 45, f. 128v, 19 Nov 1499.

[54] *Balìa* 46, ff. 103v, 12 Sept, 104r, 14 Sept.

[55] MINNUCCI, *Lauree*, I, doc. 109, p. 77, 13 Nov. On this figure see also IDEM, 'Documenti', p. 310. There were other means of currying favour with the authorities. The chief of these was acting as representative of the *Studio* elsewhere. Students

4. *Degrees*

The culmination of the period of study was the formal examination that led first to the licentiate and then, for those who could afford it, to the doctorate. This is another area in which our knowledge about the period to 1500 is frustrated by lack of evidence. Giovanni Minnucci has published, in register form and occasionally *in extenso*, the details of almost all the degrees awarded that have survived up to 1579,[56] but unfortunately this still leaves a huge gap, for most of the fifteenth century. That period is thus almost entirely incapable of any statistical evaluation. An exception is the 1440s, for which Paolo Nardi is publishing the recently discovered records of the payments of degree candidates to the Opera del Duomo.[57] From these documents some bare figures are possible, and give us an idea of the scale of what we must be missing for other decades. The records cover a period of just under nine years (20 April 1440 to 8 March 1449), and contain a number of gaps, including one of almost eighteen months.[58] In all, 134 students are recorded as having been examined and having paid their dues to the Opera. Reference to other *studi* suggests that Siena was thus running a healthy operation for its size,[59] and the figures are also comparable with those for the years from the end of the century onwards,[60] when the number of lectureships was substantially greater.[61] Equally, of course, it is a re-

must have been rewarded as effective envoys, for the phenomenon is quite common, and usually led to some sort of reciprocal favour. Cola da Sicilia was sent to Bologna for a fortnight in 1428 'pro habendibus scolaribus et aliis commissis'; on his return he took his degree and was given a 50-florin *condotta* (*Conc.* 375, ff. 12v, 14 Sept, 26r, 1 Oct, 42v, n.d., 1428; *Conc.* 377, f. 32v, 21 Feb 1429, ed. PIANIGIANI, doc. 107, p. 135). In 1435 Angelo di Jacopo d'Amelia, a student close to taking his law degree, was sent on two missions by the *Savi* (*Conc.* 417, *apotissa*, no foliation, 17 Aug, and cf. ff. 18v, 1 Aug, and 25r, 18 Aug; *Conc.* 418, ff. 9r, 16 Sept, and 23v, 18 Oct). Pace d'Ascoli spent two months in Rome in the summer of 1433 on behalf of the *Savi* and was rewarded with a place in the Sapienza (*Conc.* 407, ff. 3v, 37r, 4 Nov 1433), as were Angelo di Paolo da Narni (*Conc.* 408, f. 26r, 19 Feb 1434; *Conc.* 421, f. 27v, 3 Apr, and *Conc.* 424, f. 58r, 22 Sept 1436), and Antonio Gotto da Sicilia (*Conc.* 412, f. 63r, 23 Oct 1434; *Conc.* 428, f. 17v, 28 May 1437). The details of these embassies are rarely spelt out, and we know little of the standing of these men, but the commune's use of students in this way is an interesting aspect of the academic *mores* of the times. Students, as travellers, could also be used simply as general messengers (e.g. *Conc.* 1663, f. 35r, 22 Sept 1444; *Concistoro* to Niccolò Nanni: 'Noi aviamo ricevuto per le mani d'uno studiante che veniva qua vostra lettera').

[56] See above, p. 14 n. 68. In what follows I have relied heavily on Minnucci's researches; cf. also the summary in MINNUCCI, 'Il conferimento dei titoli accademici'.

[57] NARDI, 'Una fonte inedita delle lauree senesi'.

[58] The records were entered in batches by the *notaio dello Studio*, and this longest gap is presumably one of omission. However, since degree examinations appear often to have been held in clusters, and perhaps to have been confined to the teaching *terzarie*, it is not entirely clear which of these gaps represent lacunae in the records as opposed to periods in which there were no examinations. This problem of assessing the completeness of the documentation for degrees is evident in Bologna as well; cf. TROMBETTI BUDRIESI, 'L'esame di laurea', pp. 166-9.

[59] Statistics are not easy to come by short of calculation from the published records of the major *studi*. The number of degrees awarded in Siena in this period was clearly lower than those published for the substantially larger universities of Pavia, Padua and Bologna; cf. MAIOCCHI, *Codice diplomatico dell'Università di Pavia*, II, docs. 345, 358, 371, 384, 420, 434, 454, 500, 514, 521, 537, 580; ZONTA and BROTTO, *Acta graduum academicorum gymnasii patavini*; A. SORBELLI (ed.), *Liber Secretus iuris caesarei dell' Università di Bologna*, 2 vols. Universitatis Bononiensis Monumenta, 2-3 (Bologna, 1938-42); PIANA, *Il "Liber Secretus Iuris Caesarei"*, and IDEM, *Il "Liber Secretus Iuris Pontificii"*; and G. BRONZINO (ed.), *Notitia doctorum sive catalogus doctorum qui in collegiis philosophiae et medicinae bononiae laureati fuerunt ab anno 1480 usque ad annum 1800*. Universitatis Bononiensis Monumenta, IV (Milan, 1962), pp. 1-8; statistical analysis in TROMBETTI BUDRIESI, 'L'esame di laurea', pp. 169-76 (the figure for Siena on p. 176, table 8, suggesting a much lower rate, is misleading as it does not take account of the number of years for which there is no documentation).

[60] Over the eighty-seven years of degree awards covered by Minnucci's researches, 1,675 degrees are recorded (MINNUCCI, 'Il conferimento dei titoli accademici', p. xxiii), giving an average of 19.25 per year.

[61] See above, pp. 60-2.

minder that only a proportion of those who attended university at some stage actually went as far as to complete a qualification.[62]

The examination process at Siena was very much as elsewhere (it could not afford to be otherwise).[63] It is barely in evidence for the baccalaureate – which was more a title denoting status than a qualification,[64] and also very rare outside the faculty of theology.[65] The key hurdle was the twin one of the licentiate and the doctorate. These two were complementary but very different events. The examination element in the process was the licentiate, the moment at which a student came forward to be questioned by the college of doctors. The process was certainly laid down by custom, as some of the records for the early fifteenth century demonstrate.[66] The student would be admitted to the presence of the vicar of the chancellor and the appropriate college of doctors, usually in the episcopal palace, where he would be presented by his *promotor*, or *promotores*, and assigned *puncta* or set points from the canon of texts in his discipline. Shortly after, usually the following day, he would defend the propositions in those texts, 'privately', in front of the examining commission, which consisted of the college, with a prior selected for the occasion.[67] The verdict of the college was usually positive – considerable weight was clearly attached to the judgment of the presenting teacher or teachers that the candidate was ready – though failure was not unknown.[68]

---

[62] An extreme example, perhaps, is that of Avignon, for which J. VERGER, 'Le rôle social de l'Université d'Avignon au XVᵉ siècle', *Bibliothèque d'Humanisme et Renaissance*, 33 (1971), pp. 489-504 (p. 490), demonstrated that over the period 1430 to 1478 about 35% of law students became bachelors of arts, between 6% and 8% took the licence and only 3% the doctorate. Such precision is of course impossible in the absence of matriculation lists or precise figures of student numbers. The only alternative is recourse to informed guesswork. If one were arbitrarily to assume a student population in Siena of 250 (see above, p. 239) and, equally arbitrarily, that the average length of study required for a degree was seven years (see above, p. 279), then a 'full completion rate' would be 35.9 degrees per year. This of course ignores both the issue of migration between universities and the fact that students could take more than one degree. However, if such crude hypothetical estimates are even remotely close to the mark, comparison with the actual number of degrees (n. 60 above) would suggest that slightly over half those who attended the university took a degree of some sort.

[63] The fullest analyses are TROMBETTI BUDRIESI, 'L'esame di laurea', and A. SORBELLI, 'Sull'esame nell'Università durante il medioevo', introduction to his *Liber Secretus iuris caesarei*, vol. 2, pp. ix-clxii; see also the generic description, based primarily on practice at Bologna, in BELLOMO, *Saggio sull'Università*, pp. 253-63.

[64] See B. M. MARTI, *The Spanish College at Bologna in the Fourteenth Century* (Philadelphia, Pa., 1966), pp. 163-5 n. 26 for a summary; and ERMINI, *Storia*, I, pp. 467 *seq.* In Siena, as elsewhere, the baccalaureate could be bestowed without examination by means of presentation of the candidate to the college of doctors (MINNUCCI, 'Il conferimento dei titoli accademici', pp. xvi-ii).

[65] Apart from those in theology, the first Sienese record of a bachelor's degree to have survived is from 1504 (MINNUCCI, *Lauree*, II, no. 55, pp. 57-8; cf. WEIGLE, 'Deutsche Studenten in Italien, II', p. 210). Only a handful of bachelors' degrees survive from the Italian universities other than for theology; for examples, see MAIOCCHI, *Codice diplomatico dell'Università di Pavia*, I, no. 222, II, nos. 79, 115, and for baccalaureates in theology G. ZONTA and A. BROTTO, *La facoltà teologica dell'Università di Padova (secoli XIV e XV)* (Padua, 1922), docs. 2049, 2224, 2292, 2319, 2413, 2414, 2423, 2432, 2434. On the whole issue of bachelors' degrees in Italy see also A. SOTTILI (ed.), *Lauree Pavesi nella seconda metà del '400*, I (1450-1475). Fonti e studi per la storia dell'Università di Pavia, 25 (Milan, 1995), pp. 18, 20-22.

[66] Cf. the full records of the degrees of Angelo di Francesco Bruogi da San Gimignano, AAS 4420, ff. 7v-9r, 19 Jun 1409, ed. ZDEKAUER, doc. X.1, pp. 151-3; Johannes Dodonis of Rotterdam and Nicolaus Ffabri of Žagan in 1412, Ippolito di Ser Niccolò da San Gimignano in 1414, and Filippo da Lucca in 1424, ed. MINNUCCI, 'Documenti', docs. I-3 to I-5, pp. 48-56. The first three documents were drawn up by the same notary, Ser Antonio di Gandino da Calci. Naturally all use similar, often identical formulaic phrases, and those for Angelo Bruni and Ippolito have identical rhetorical passages, albeit at different points in the respective documents.

[67] This was not necessarily the prior of the college; the 1511 statutes of the college of doctors of medicine and arts stipulated a separate selection procedure for the prior of each examination (Rubric 4, *Balìa* 253, f. 337v).

[68] For examples see MINNUCCI, 'Il conferimento dei titoli accademici', pp. xi-xii n. 13, and pp. xiv-xv n. 23; also below, p. 351.

Despite the 'quality assurance' implied by success in this 'tremendum et rigorosum examen', the licence on its own was not enough to ensure the candidate's progress in the professional world. For those doors to be unlocked, it was increasingly necessary to have the big prize, the doctorate, the public ceremony in which the fact of the student having obtained the licence was acknowledged and transformed, by a powerful *rite de passage*, into reality. The many elements of this imposing event were laden with transactional significance. The assignment to the doctorand of symbols of learning, expertise and authority, by the official custodians of those prized attributes, was counterbalanced by gifts from the doctorand of a more immediately practical nature, namely hefty fees payable to everyone involved, and a banquet for participants, friends and well-wishers. A full doctorate was an expensive undertaking.[69] Full details for Siena are only known to us from the sixteenth century,[70] but the cost was clearly a deterrent to many. Those unable to afford it would stop at the licentiate, or wait until they could muster the resources to complete this ritual part of the process. Minnucci's work has revealed two such instances at the end of the fifteenth century, both Germans; Jodocus Jungmair, who received a licence in canon law in 1491 and a doctorate in 1503, and Johannes de Messchede, licensed *in utriusque* in 1494 and made doctor in 1500.[71] The latter case is interesting; at the time of his licentiate, Iohannes had negotiated a fee of 10 florins for his doctorate, and in the event he was required to swear that this was the agreed amount. This raises the whole question of what could be done for those who could not afford the doctorate. In the fifteenth century many Italian *studi* imposed a requirement on the colleges of doctors that they had to award a limited number of degrees – it might be as little as one a year – to a bright student who was declared to be *pauper*. Though there are some celebrated examples of such students,[72] the scheme does not appear to have been operated by the colleges with much enthusiasm – perhaps understandably, since this meant their members foregoing their remuneration.[73] Hard evidence for this practice has not emerged for Siena before the sixteenth century, though it is clear from the example just quoted that individuals could occasionally negotiate acceptable charges. Intervention from above could also effect a waiving of fees, as in the case of Corrado Banghen, awarded a doctorate in 1489 free of charge at the request

---

[69] MARTINES, *Lawyers and Statecraft*, pp. 89-91, estimated that a degree could cost 20, 30 or more florins. Cf. J. LE GOFF, 'Dépenses universitaires a Padoue', *Mélanges d'Archéologie et d'Histoire, École Française de Rome*, 68 (1956), pp. 377-95, tr. as 'Academic Expenses at Padua in the Fifteenth Century' in his *Time, Work, and Culture in the Middle Ages* (Chicago, Il., 1980), pp. 101-6, 309-18; BELLOMO, *Saggio sull'Università*, esp. p. 262; GUALAZZINI, *Corpus Statutorum*, p. CLXXXII.

[70] The 1511 statutes of the college of doctors of medicine and arts spell these out in minute detail. For a doctorate in medicine the candidate had to disburse 66 *lire* to the examiners, 6 *lire* to the *bidello*, 6 *lire* to the rector of the university and 2 *lire* to the same body 'pro oblationibus fiendis divo Nicolao diveque Catherine', 4 *lire* to the Opera del Duomo (as established in the fifteenth century), 6 *lire* to the representative of the chancellor, 10 *lire* for the certificate, 20 *soldi* to the notary and a further 13 *soldi* 'pro Cirotechis et collationibus'. Further charges could be demanded by the archbishop or his representative. Arts degrees were approximately two-thirds of this cost, and all these charges were simply accumulated for combined degrees (Rubric 12, *Balìa* 253, ff. 340r-341r). The 1566 statutes of the college of doctors of law have an even more detailed list of expenses (Rubric 10, *Studio* 40, ff. 18v-22r; and see above, pp. 201 and 203). For late sixteenth-century Siena see also PRUNAI, III, pp. 119, 121.

[71] MINNUCCI, 'Il conferimento dei titoli accademici', p. xv; IDEM, *Lauree*, I, no. 106, pp. 74-5, and *Lauree*, II, no, 49, p. 53. At Bologna there are many instances of such gaps, which could be much longer; TROMBETTI BUDRIESI, 'L'esame di laurea', p. 189 and n. 108.

[72] The most often quoted is the Bolognese degree in civil law granted in 1407 to Antonio Roselli (SORBELLI, *Liber Secretus iuris caesarei*, I, pp. 181-2, and II, p. LXX; and cf. BELLOMO, *Saggio sull'Università*, p. 257), who, of course, subsequently taught in Siena (above, pp. 187 n. 40, 188-9 and 203 n. 165).

[73] For parallels in Bologna, see TROMBETTI BUDRIESI, 'L'esame di laurea', p. 187 n. 106.

of the pope.[74] When evidence emerges for the formal practice of awarding degrees 'per amore dei', it is not quite what it seems; according to the 1511 statutes of the college of doctors of medicine and arts, payments to the examining doctors were waived in such cases, but most of the ancillary fees remained.[75]

What does stand out from the communal sources is the great eagerness of the authorities to have as many students as possible take their degree. The commune's commitment to this is evidenced by the number of times it tried to cajole student lecturers, and rectors and other members of the Sapienza to fulfil their obligation to take a degree within the time specified at the time of their appointment.[76] Such efforts were clearly aimed at getting the students to take the lucrative and prestigious doctorate, not just the licence; those who wanted just the licence had to swear not to go on to take the doctorate elsewhere.[77] As well as wielding sticks, the commune was happy to offer carrots; for those who did decide to take the doctorate, permission to have more than the stipulated number of *promotores* was granted frequently in the early fifteenth century, especially to lawyers;[78] it suited the doctors concerned, and made for a more splendid ceremony which reflected well on the *Studio* as a whole, not to mention its sponsors.[79] There were other incentives too. Nardi's analysis of the names of doctorands in the 1440s shows a significant number of individuals who went on to teach at the university. If it is a truism that a degree was the indispensable passport to a teaching career, it is perhaps less obvious, but equally clear, that a Sienese degree was a valuable opening for the specific pursuit of such a career in Siena.[80]

---

[74] *Not.* 799, no foliation, 11 Apr 1489, and cf. ZDEKAUER, *Documenti*, part 2, doc. V, p. 40 (edition of Innocent's letter of 6 Apr, in the same volume).

[75] Rubric 12, *Balìa* 253, f. 341r-v (and see above, p. 206). Such degrees can only be taken on the feast of St. Nicholas. The following year also sees the first such initiative in the Sapienza, when Bartolomeo Bolis, funding six student places, stipulated that they should each be given a payment of 100 *lire* towards the costs of the doctorate (below, p. 308).

[76] Above, p. 282, and below, pp. 320, 347 and 351. Serafino da Camerino, rector of the *Studio* in the academic year 1446-7, and given a further lectureship in 1447-8 (above, n. 44), had still not taken his degree by 15 Dec 1448; payment of his salary was made conditional on his providing a guarantor to vouch that he would do so within the required period (*Conc.* 497, f. 26v).

[77] MINNUCCI, 'Il conferimento dei titoli accademici', pp. xiv and xvi, citing examples from the late fifteenth century onwards. At Perugia, students taking the private examination had to promise to follow it with the public one, a source of endless friction and ultimately an ineffective measure (ERMINI, *Storia*, I, p. 120-2).

[78] E.g. *Conc.* 325, f. 11r, 20 Mar 1420 (a general dispensation, allowing doctorands to have three doctors to represent them, provided one is a citizen); *Conc.* 376, f. 28r, 27 Dec 1428 (Messer Piero da Pisa may have three *promotores*, one foreign and two citizen, despite the statutes); *Conc.* 408, f. 2v, 2 Jan 1434 (Messer Giovanni Minocci of Siena, the same conditions); and *Conc.* 411, f. 53r, 16 Aug 1434 (the protonotary Giorgio of Catalonia, taking a degree in canon law, 'possit accipere in promotores suos, ultra duos doctores, etiam si actualiter non legent in Studio'). Such dispensations are modest in comparison with the many that were commonly given to doctorands in civil law at Bologna by the end of the fifteenth century; TROMBETTI BUDRIESI, 'L'esame di laurea', pp. 180-91.

[79] Cf. *Conc.* 354, f. 10r, 18 Jan 1425 (Messer Zanobio may spend as much money on his degree as he wishes).

[80] It opened other doors as well, particularly as the *Studio* became more localised; in the 1511 statutes of the college of doctors of medicine and arts, admission to the college entailed a fee of 14 *aureos largos*, which, however, was doubled for those whose degree was not from Siena. Rubric 15, *Balìa* 253, ff. 341v-342r (and see above, p. 206). Not all were so fortunate. In an early Italian manifestation of a now familiar problem, Daniele di Fazio Gallerani lamented in his 1480s tax returns: 'Io so doctore di legie canonica ch'a ssiena poco s'adopera et niente guadagnia. Non so condotto, èmi lo doctorato più presto charico che utile' (*Lira* 200, no foliation, 1481; he repeats the lament in *Lira* 212, no foliation, 1483-4, and *Lira* 221, no foliation, 1488). What precisely lay behind these statements is a matter for speculation. He had in fact taught in 1473-4 (*Gabella* 24, f. 56r, 5 May, payment for second terzaria of £33/6/8; *Conc.* 645, f. 26r-v, 27 Aug, ed. BAI, doc. 354, p. 350). He was offered a contract to teach canon law in 1475 for two years at the basic annual salary of 25 florins (*Conc.* 653, f. 23v, 28 Jun, ed. BAI. doc. 360, pp. 362-5), and there were further offers in 1485 (*Conc.* 712, ff. 18v-19r, 17 Jun, ed. FERRERI, doc. 219, pp. 184-5) and 1490 (*Conc.* 744, ff. 10v-11v, 12 Oct, ed. FERRERI, docs. 307-8, pp. 281-5; this time the salary was 80 florins), but in none of these cases was the invitation followed by any evidence that he taught or was paid.

5. *'Le consuetudini de' studenti'*[81]

From the perspective of this study, the least penetrable aspect of the world of students must be that of their everyday living conditions, their conduct, their preoccupations, their sense of identification and solidarity (or otherwise) with the various categories or groups to which by definition they belonged, and the tensions and resentments that accompanied such groupings.[82] Communal records tell us what is prescribed and proscribed, but only occasionally allow us glimpses of the reality behind the legislation. But to the standard difficulty of assessing such topics is added another. Students are even less visible than the rest of the population, because they were at one remove from communal jurisdiction; internal discipline was supposed to be dealt with by the rector, and if his judgments were ever recorded they certainly have not survived. We therefore only see the cases that got beyond him, for one reason or another. Most of these are either cases of serious crime, or cases involving relations between students and townspeople which, despite any claim to authority that the rector may have had in such matters, ended up before a higher body.[83] We therefore have to put out of our minds any idea that the surviving anecdotal evidence, however interesting in itself, can be taken as typical or used for generalisation, still less that it is capable of any kind of quantitative evaluation. The nature of the records and the parameters of the present investigation thus put it *hors de combat* in the discussion of issues that are currently most engaging social historians, such as the nature and level of crime, and group behaviour. What follows can do no more than give a flavour – with no claims to representativity – of the problems that exercised the authorities.[84]

The evidence regarding disciplinary matters relates almost entirely to individuals or at most small groups. Incidents between students and other individuals in Siena are, unsurprisingly, not unknown. The cases that ended up in front of the *Concistoro* may well have been those that were most difficult to resolve; certainly they tend to be the ones in which both sides to the story got heard. The prominent citizen Dino di Bertoccio di Marzi, fined for assaulting a student, Maestro Girolamo da Imola, in April 1430, claimed that he had acted in self-defence after Girolamo had first insulted him and then gathered 'molti e molti scolari compagni' who had attacked him and his family with weapons when they were returning home at night.[85] Another petitioner, the citizen Jacomo di Credi di Simone, also fined for violence against the officers of the *Capitano di Giustizia*, pleaded that he had been the victim of a provocative attack by foreign students, which the forces of law and order had not understood.[86] But the majority of the few cases that we have are ones in which the student is the victim,

---

[81] See below, nn. 98-9.

[82] See DENLEY, 'Communities within Communities', pp. 729-41, and 'Trasgressioni e rivolte studentesche'; also G. P. BRIZZI, 'L'identità dello studente tra medioevo ed età moderna', in *Identità collettive tra Medioevo ed età moderna*, eds. P. Prodi and W. Reinhard (Bologna, 2002), pp. 313-32.

[83] A systematic exploration of the records of the Sienese judiciary in the fifteenth century still awaits an intrepid future researcher (see above, n. 20).

[84] The situation becomes a little clearer for the sixteenth century, as evidenced by the work of CATONI, 'Il carnevale degli scolari', KOŠUTA, 'Documenti', Appendice III, pp. 569-78, and IDEM, 'Siena nella vita e nell'opera di Marino Darsa'. Dr Jonathan Davies is currently engaged in a comparative study of student violence in the Tuscan universities under the Medici.

[85] *Conc.* 2145, no. 59, 20 Nov 1433 (see above, p. 266). Later in life, in 1455, Dino was one of the *Savi dello Studio* (*CG* 405, f. 162r).

[86] The language is revealing: 'Magnifici Signori la verità è questa, che esso Iacomo non per fare alcuno dispiacere a persona ma per dilecto e piacere avendo il nome andavasi sollazzando e sonando e pigliando piacere come fanno e giovani innamorati. Et non si può né dire né trovare che lui facesse mai dispiacere a persone del mondo. Et così con certi altri andandosi dilectando e sonando, furono armata mano assaltati da certi scolari forestieri. Et essi essendo giovani e l'animo Iuvenile e non vile, diliberavano non fuggire ma mostrare a forestieri che giovani Senesi anno animo e ardere e non ultra. Et parevalo

such as the unnamed student allegedly killed in or before 1470 by Alessandro di Marchisi from the Valtellina,[87] and a similar fatality in 1492 involving a soldier from Piombino;[88] or Antonio da Rieti, student of medicine, whose possessions were stolen by Domenico di Angelo da Seggiano in 1417.[89]

Of course students regularly feature as transgressors. They are found on the streets at night, and breaking the regulations on carrying weapons, as has been seen.[90] In 1465 a group of Portuguese students were accused of sacrilege,[91] and in 1519 twelve *sapientini* were charged with having damaged the college's property.[92] Students are occasionally found guilty of attacking non-university people; though in the examples given above responsibility may be unclear, it is less so in the case of the *sapientini* who in 1472 attacked an official of the *podestà*.[93] They also, of course, fell out with each other, as in 1440 when two Spaniards and five Sicilians ended up in a fight which rendered at least one of the Sicilians unable to appear in person at the meeting to resolve the issue.[94] The *Savi* were charged with effecting a reconciliation in this and other cases.[95] Where this was not possible, or where the offence could not be overlooked, prison might follow,[96] and it is usually these cases that we hear about because of course that was a shocking predicament for aspirant professionals, and the student's patrons and relatives would hasten to try to get him out.[97] An unusually well documented example was Simone or Pier Simone da Ascoli, who was imprisoned in 1495 for stealing fish ('ad piliare tonine et sturioni salati fora de una botega de pizigaiollo')

---

che fusse non solamente poco honore ma grandissima vergogna che e giovani Senesi fussero assaltati e cacciati da forestieri. Et per questo deliberaro non ricevere né loro e la città vra. tanto vergogna da forestieri. Et essendo intra loro la pugna vi corse il cavaliere del capit. cola famiglia senza che lui ne sapesse alcuna cosa....' (*Conc.* 2151, no. 69, 11 May 1448). But not all such disturbances reflect tensions between Sienese and foreigners, or even a 'town/gown' split. Earlier that year a band which included five students, two citizens and three *forenses*, had been involved in a brawl (*Conc.* 492, ff. 29r-v, 3 Feb, and 30v-31r, 8 Feb). One of them was Battista da Recanati, who had been in trouble four years earlier (above, pp. 235 n. 34 and 266 n. 157). This time he was permanently expelled from the Sapienza.

[87] *Conc.* 2022, no. 9, 17 Mar 1470 (letter from Jacopo d'Appiano d'Aragona, *signore* of Piombino, on Alessandro's behalf).

[88] *Balìa* 548, no. 51 13 Jan (it is again the *signore* of Piombino who writes to the Sienese authorities: 'Non senza mio grande dispiacere ho inteso la morte successo di quello scolare al quale fu mossa la mano ad li giorni passati, et eo maxime perché intendo in tale scandalo essere intervenuto uno mio balestrieri chiamato gigante, quale intendo però essere costì in mano della iustitia').

[89] *CG* 208, f. 55v, and *Conc.* 2175, no foliation, 23 Dec 1417; Domenico petitions to be picked for the traditional practice of releasing prisoners at Christmas. The items stolen included two books on logic valued at 5 florins.

[90] Above, pp. 234-5.

[91] *Conc.* 594, ff. 36v-37r, Oct 1465.

[92] Below, p. 337; there is further discussion of the internal discipline of the Sapienza in the same chapter.

[93] Below, pp. 336 n. 93.

[94] MINNUCCI, 'Documenti', doc. III-227, pp. 196-7, 20 Aug, and see p. 24; also IDEM, Professori e scolari giuristi', pp. 115-6. Another example is Dns. Antonius Catelanus, 'personaliter detentus occasione cuiusdam risse per eum facte' (*Conc.* 477, f. 3r, 1 Jul 1445). That the *Savi* were charged with bringing about peace between him and his adversaries suggest that the latter were also students, as does the petition of the former student Lelio di Giusti da Verona requesting pardon for an offence in that period (*CG* 226, ff. 270v-271r, 27 Oct 1454). Further examples of such conflicts between *sapientini* are discussed below, pp. 336-7.

[95] See previous note.

[96] It is not always clear why a student is in prison. In 1421 the case of the medical student Mag. Tommaso 'greco' came before the *Concistoro* (*Conc.* 332, f. 9r, 11 May); the *Quattro Provveditori di Biccherna* were instructed 'quod faciant apotissa paupertatis' for him, suggesting he was in for debt. This may have been a fine for a brawl; on 13 Jun that year, Mariano di Nardi da Siena was fined 200 *lire* for his part in an argument with Tommaso that had taken place at the latter's house on 11 Mar 1420 (*CG* 209, ff. 125v-126r). In 1424 Magister Jacobus Gothfredi de Roma was freed by the *Concistoro* at the behest of, among others, the rector, who had earlier demanded his imprisonment (*Conc.* 351, f. 14r, 22 Jul 1424; and see above, p. 266).

[97] E.g. Hieronimo de Rasimo of Narni, on whose behalf the priors of that town wrote on 14 Feb 1495(=1496); he had been imprisoned, according to the letter, 'per certa suspitione nata per cascione del suo patrono, al quale sorviva per repetitore in casa' (*Balìa* 555, no. 35a).

together with other students who got away. A barrage of eminent petitioners, including three cardinals, immediately wrote in support.[98] They pleaded Simone's youth, the trivial nature of the offence, and the natural inclinations of students.[99] Simone was the son of a physician, Giovanni Antonio Alato, also named as 'de Petruciis', who the supplicants all described as a friend; perhaps it was also relevant to the Sienese authorities (although none of the letters mention the fact) that he had recently taught at Siena.[100] In any event, the episode does not seem to have done Simone's career any harm. In 1497 he was given a place in the Sapienza for two years as a substitute for another student,[101] and after that the *Concistoro* made strenuous efforts to get him a medical *condotta* in the subject town of Massa Marittima.[102]

A common solution to more intractable problems with non-citizen students was exclusion. Bartolomeo da Sicilia was banished from the city in 1443, 'consideratis multis malefitiis et facinoribus per eum commissis que pro meliori tacentur'.[103] Five Sapienza students were banished in 1461,[104] and several Portuguese in 1466;[105] Francesco da Sicilia and two others were banned from the city in 1469.[106] Antonio Griaca (or Sciacha) has the dubious distinction of having been excluded twice, in 1421 and again in 1429.[107]

A final aspect of communal attitudes should be mentioned. That the authorities thought of the students, a population of young males, many not citizens, as requiring special attention, has already been demonstrated.[108] As Zdekauer pointed out, their concern extended into the area of sexual *mores*, and is mentioned specifically in the context of measures concerning brothels. Sienese legislation, as that elsewhere, had sought to contain and regulate this aspect of urban life,[109] and the commune was itself a 'stakeholder', paying the rent of some prostitutes in each of the three *terzi* of the city. In 1338 the authorities closed two of the town's brothels and concentrated activities in the Val di Montone, at the

---

[98] *Balìa* 555, no. 90, 24 Mar (Bagarottus Grillis 'Silvestri Marchiae Locumtenens'); *Balìa* 552, no. 29, 30 Mar (the *Anziani* of Ascoli); *Conc.* 2075, no. 18, 30 Mar (the cardinal of S. Teodoro, who was another Marchesan, Federico da S. Severino; EUBEL, II, p. 78); *Conc.* 2075, no. 22, 9 Apr (Giulio Cesare da Varano da Camerino); *Balìa* 552, no. 78, 10 Apr (Sinolfo, of the *camera apostolica*); *Balìa* 553, no. 36B, 25 Apr (the cardinal of S. Giorgio); and *Conc.* 2075, no. 39, 26 Apr (the cardinal of Siena).

[99] 'le consuetudini de' studenti: li quali più presto per troppo ardore et licentia che per studio de peccare soleno comittere de simili delicti...' (the cardinal of S. Teodoro); 'errore che ve ne è proceduta da levita de' scolari' (Giulio Cesare da Varano).

[100] Above, p. 171. He was hired again in 1498 (*Balìa* 43, f. 266v, 6 Dec, and see f. 293r, 1 Feb 1499); and he was made a citizen in 1499 (f. 299r, 14 Feb).

[101] *Sale* 24, f. 154r, 15 Mar; cf. BCS, *ms.* A.XI.12, f. 73v, and in BONAFACCIA, 'La "Domus Sapientiae"', p. 114.

[102] *Conc.* 1708, no foliation, 27 Oct and 10 Dec 1499, and *Conc.* 1709, no foliation, 31 Jan 1500.

[103] *Conc.* 465, f. 12v, 23 Jul.

[104] See below, p. 336 and n. 96. The rector, Paolo da Prato, was accused of being the ringleader, and stripped of his office, before or after fleeing (above, p. 269). Letters petitioning on behalf of two of them, Benedetto and Angelo, both medical students from Camerino, are in *Conc.* 2001, no. 42, 21 Sept (from the cardinal of Siena, who states that the penalty was imposed 'ob certam controversiam inter scolares civesque exortam') and 23 Sept (from the cardinal of Spoleto).

[105] *Conc.* 2013, no. 41, 15 Jun; letter from the cardinal of Valencia on behalf of this group ('intelliximus expulsi certi scholares portugallenses ob certum maleficium'). The cardinal argues that they have the option of moving to Perugia, but would prefer to resume their studies at Siena. These may well be the same students who were accused of sacrilege a few months earlier (above, n. 291).

[106] *Conc.* 618, ff. 7r, 9 Sept, and 15r-v, 21 Sept. The charges included breaking into the house of a citizen, Rinaldo Angelini da Cortona, and raping his son. The *Concistoro* decided to make an example of Francesco, 'studentem seu in studio senen. commorantem', and banished him for life; his two accomplices, Mag. Johannes Jacobi franco de Sicilia and Mag. Melchior Juliani Pierozi de Aversa, were banished for three years (their titles suggest that they may have been students as well, but this is not stated).

[107] *Conc.* 331, f. 14v, 29 Mar 1421 (for the petition by teachers and students the following year to allow him to return, see above, pp. 252 and 278 n. 257), and *Conc.* 331, f. 14v, 29 Mar 1429 ('quia est homo malvole').

[108] Above, p. 233.

[109] E.g. the prohibition in the communal statutes of 1262 of prostitutes close to churches; L. ZDEKAUER, 'Il frammento degli ultimi due libri del più antico costituto senese (1262-1270)', *BSSP*, 2 (1894), pp. 131-54 (rubr. 24, p. 147).

southern extremity of the town, thus effectively turning this into the municipal brothel.[110] In 1415 – a year of revival for the *Studio* and of preparation for the launch of the Casa della Sapienza, as it happens – there was an attempt to move it, as its public location, 'drieto al palazo', was deterring young people from using it 'per vergogna di non essere veduti'. The stated purpose of the reform was to help reduce temptations of sodomy.[111] A deliberation of 18 February 1422 abolished the tax on prostitutes in order to attract a larger clientele and to protect the more respectable women of the town; the wording shows that one of the main targets was the scholars the town had attracted to the city 'che, come è noto, sono giovani e non possono, bollendole el sangue, avere quella continentia, che se fussero in più matura età'.[112] The frequenting of brothels by students was hardly a novelty in medieval universities,[113] but such explicit recognition by a government of their function and value to students is nonetheless unusual.

6. *Identities and collectivities*

Minor episodes aside, collectively the student population appears to have been peaceable. We can be reasonably sure that we would have heard of any major upheavals – 'political' as opposed to 'common'

---

[110] BALESTRACCI and PICCINNI, *Siena nel Trecento*, pp. 60-1; R. MUCCIARELLI, 'Igiene, salute e pubblico decoro', p. 66 and n. 101.

[111] *CG* 207, ff. 111v-112v, 23 Sept 1415; *Statuti* 25, f. 407, publ. in GAROSI, p. 521 (see also pp. 519-21, and BALESTRACCI and PICCINNI, *Siena nel Trecento*, pp. 60-1). Though this was at the opposite side of town from the Sapienza, there were clearly disreputable areas close to that building as well (below, p. 384). In Turin, which is unusual in having had a physical centre for its *Studio* from early on, this was located close to the two brothels of the town; A. FALCO, R. PLANTAMURA and S. RANZATO, 'Le istituzioni per l'istruzione superiore in Torino dal XV al XVIII secolo: considerazioni urbanistiche e architettoniche. L'Università e le residenze studentesche', *Bollettino storico-bibliografico subalpino*, 20 (1972), pp. 545-87 (p. 556, n. 29). On the topographical aspect of the management of prostitution see B. GEREMEK, *The Margins of Society in Late Medieval Paris* (tr. Cambridge, 1987), pp. 87-94, and, following that approach very specifically, D. C. MENGEL, 'From Venice to Jerusalem and Beyond: Milíč of Kroměříž and the Topography of Prostitution in Fourteenth-Century Prague', *Speculum*, 79 (2004), pp. 407-42.

[112] This decidedly pre-Bernardinian measure is found in *CG* 209, f. 191r-v; quoted in ZDEKAUER, pp. 105-6. The institution seems to have had its problems; on 11 August the tax was reinstated as the only effect had been to lower standards: 'Et etiamdio per essere la dicta cabella tolta via, non è meglio servito che prima fusse, però che la cosa buona e vantaggiata guadagna e può suplire a la cabella, e la cosa meno che buona non guadagna e non può suplire a la cabella: e pertanto el dicto luogo viene a essere peggio fornito che di prima, che così vi può stare la trista mercantia come la buona' (ZDEKAUER, loc. cit.). On a similar tax in Bologna, BELLOMO, *Saggio sull'Università*, p. 84 n. 11. For other points regarding the reputation of students, and particularly those of the Sapienza, in this respect, see below, p. 384 and n. 17.

[113] The theme is a commonplace of caricatures of students and student life, and emerges through anecdote. Legal writers mention students visiting prostitutes among the innumerable hypothetical cases they discuss (cf. THORNDIKE, *University Records*, doc. 174, esp. pp. 390-1); commentators and authorities tend to voice their disapproval of the juxtaposition of classroom and brothel (e.g. Jacques de Vitry's picture of schools and prostitutes sharing premises, quoted in J. RICHARDS, *Sex, Dissidence and Damnation. Minority Groups in the Middle Ages* [London, 1991], p. 116; cf. the 1358 Parisian decision to close the Rue de Fouarre at night; H. DENIFLE and A. CHATELAIN [eds.], *Chartularium Universitatis Parisiensis* [Paris, 1891-99, repr. Brussels, 1964], III, pp. 53-4; tr. THORNDIKE, *University Records*, doc. 85, pp. 241-2), and occasionally attempt to forbid students visiting brothels (e.g. Heidelberg, 1442; tr. THORNDIKE, *University Records*, doc. 141, pp. 332-3; though P. SCHUSTER, *Das Frauenhaus. Städtische Bordelle in Deutschland 1350 bis 1600* [Paderborn, 1992], pp. 118-20 argues that such embargoes are usually temporary and for exceptional reasons, for example in 1445, during the wedding of the Elector, so that the guests would not get an unfavourable idea of student life, and in 1460, during war, to avoid conflicts with the soldiers, whose need of the prostitutes was given priority). Despite this stereotype, no evidence has emerged to suggest that students were more inclined than other groups to use these facilities. The main surveys, to the limited extent that they focus on the clientele of prostitutes, do not even mention students; J. ROSSIAUD, *Medieval Prostitution* (tr. Oxford, 1988), pp. 38-42; M. S. MAZZI, *Prostitute e lenoni nella Firenze del Quattrocento* (Milan, 1991), pp. 354-65. I would be inclined to agree that this image is 'the distorted product of cautionary tales'; R. C. SCHWINGES, 'Student Education, Student Life', in *A History of the University in Europe*, I, pp. 195-243 (p. 224), quoted with approval by one of the leading authorities on the subject, T. DEAN, *Crime in Medieval Europe* (London, 2001), p. 114.

violence[114] – yet with two early exceptions, the reluctance of members of the *Studio* to return from Montalcino in 1420,[115] and the controversies over the system for electing a rector in 1429, which led to a delay in the start of the academic year,[116] there do not appear to have been any major incidents which disrupted either the *Studio* or its relations with the town in the fifteenth century.[117] This is in striking contrast to, for example, the sort of corporate unrest which periodically darkened the relationship of Pavia with its student community, and even brought temporary garrisons of troops from Milan in the late fifteenth century;[118] or indeed the endemic violence reported at late fifteenth-century Ferrara by a chronicler who was also one of the university's teachers.[119] Why was this so? It could be argued that it was a measure of the extent and success of communal control, and the consequent weakness of the student-university as an institution. The evidence also suggests that the elements within the student population were not strong, either institutionally or in practice. It has been seen that in Siena the *natio* remained a hazy concept in the period. There were of course rivalries over election procedures, but few instances of those of different geographical origins in open rivalry with each other on a group basis – at least, in what has survived.[120]

Another factor may have been that at Siena, students' needs to express identity were diverted into specific activities and directions that lowered the potential for the escalation of tension. This is a highly speculative area, but three possibilities suggest themselves as topics for further research. The first is carnival. The recent historiography of the culture and statecraft in early modern Europe has seen this tradition as an example of such deflection, an event into which social tensions could be channelled under controlled circumstances.[121] The records of the fifteenth-century Italian universities suggest that that interpretation may be optimistic or at least premature. In the long story of 'town-gown' unrest, carnival was more often than not the flashpoint;[122] controlling the 'world upside down' was always a

---

[114] The distinction made by P. ROSSO, 'Vicende studentesche pavesi nella seconda metà del Quattrocento', *Bollettino della Società Pavese di Storia Patria*, 45 (1993), pp. 37-66 (p. 40).

[115] Above, pp. 113-4.

[116] Above, p. 259.

[117] The same cannot be said of the following period, on which see the work of KOŠUTA, esp. 'Documenti', Appendice III, pp. 569-78, and also 'Siena nella vita e nell'opera di Marino Darsa'.

[118] VACCARI, *Storia dell'Università di Pavia*, pp. 91-2; cf. ROSSO, op. cit., and, among the many relevant works of the late A. SOTTILI, 'Le contestate elezioni rettorali di Paul von Baenst e Johannes von Dalberg all'Università di Pavia', *Humanistica Lovaniensia*, 31 (1982), pp. 29-75; repr. in his *Università e Cultura. Studi sui rapporti italo-tedeschi nell'età dell'Umanesimo*. Bibliotheca eruditorum. Internationale Bibliothek der Wissenschaften, 5 (Goldbach, 1993), pp. 272*-318*; and IDEM, 'Il palio per l'altare di Santa Caterina e il 'dossier' sul rettorato di Giovanni di Lussemburgo', *Annali di Storia Pavese*, 18-19 (1989), pp. 77-102.

[119] ZAMBOTTI, *Diario ferrarese*.

[120] This is, of course, not to say that such expressions of identity did not matter; but we are as likely to hear of them as of instances of students acting in support of a fellow-citizen outside the university. For example, in 1442 Genoese students supported the petition of a goldsmith, Benedetto di Mantica[?] 'del contado di Genova', who was being investigated on forgery charges: 'A la quale non solo luj exponente predicto ma Ancho tutti scolari genovesi che sono nello studio della vra. Mag.ca Città supplicano' (*Conc.* 2148, no. 23); in 1474, Domenico da Cortona was released from prison after the testimony of two fellow-Cortonese, one of whom was the civil law student Giovanni Battista di Agostino (*Conc.* 648, f. 37r, 31 Oct).

[121] Of the many studies, see the classic R. W. SCRIBNER, 'Reformation, Carnival, and the World Turned Upside-Down', *Social History*, 3 (1978), pp. 235-64; repr. in his *Popular Culture and Popular Movements in Reformation Germany* (London, 1987), pp. 71-101. A rich Italian case-study is G. CIAPPELLI, *Carnevale e quaresima. Comportamenti sociali e cultura a Firenze nel Rinascimento*. Temi e testi, n.s. 37 (Rome, 1997).

[122] A case in point is Pisa, where the correspondence of the Florentine officials shows countless episodes of carnival getting out of hand and disrupting the *Studio*; see VERDE, *Lo Studio fiorentino*, IV, pp. 46, 332, 656-8, 770-2, 792-3, 883, 1025, 1068, 1106-7, 1193 and 1424.

risky business. Yet it is interesting that student indiscipline in connection with carnival does not feature in the Sienese administrative records before the sixteenth century.[123] A second area, often closely linked to carnival, is theatre. The long tradition of student involvement with drama (certainly traceable back to early fifteenth-century Pavia)[124] again does not appear to have impinged in Siena in the fifteenth century, but as is well known, in the early sixteenth century the students of Siena made it very much their own.[125] A third issue, which undoubtedly does take us back into the fifteenth century, is the special role of the Casa della Sapienza. As a key but distinct element in the *Studio*, the Sapienza may well have acted as an alternative focus; membership of it was an ambition for many foreign students, and the more eminent and privileged in particular tended to succeed in that ambition. The college's prominence may well have helped keep the student community fragmented, or at least prevented it from coming together in threatening ways.

---

[123] G. CATONI, 'Il carnevale degli scolari. Feste e spettacoli degli studenti senesi dal XVI al XVIII secolo', in *Scritti per Mario delle Piane* (Naples, 1986), pp. 23-37. M. BATTISTINI, 'Una rissa tra frati e studenti dello Studio senese nel secolo XVI', *BSSP*, 25 (1918), pp. 111-12, on the carnival riots of 1565, refers to the 'antico costume degli scolari di andare a raccogliere dai dottori, e dai conventi della città, quella mercede che per antica usanza doveva servire a fare qualche festa'. Pre-1500 origins of this and other 'antichi costumi' (cf. KOŠUTA, 'Documenti', Appendice III, pp. 569-78) have not emerged in the course of the present research.

[124] E.g. *Repetitio Zanini de martulibus coqui*, in V. PANDOLFI and E. ARTESE (eds.), *Teatro goliardico dell'Umanesimo* (Milan, 1965), pp. 293-310; introduction by E. Artese pp. 289-91. The subject is brought together in M. CHIABÒ and F. DOGLIO (eds.), *Spettacoli studenteschi nell'Europa umanistica: convegno internazionale, Anagni 20-22 giugno 1997* (Rome, 1998), with extensive bibliographies of Italian (by C. FRISONE, pp. 219-42) and non-Italian (by A. BURLANDO, pp. 243-79) research.

[125] Among the many works, see esp. CATONI, op. cit.; L. G. CLUBB, 'Pre-Rozzi e pre-Intronati allo Studio di Siena', in *Umanesimo a Siena*, pp. 149-70; EADEM and. and R. BLACK, *Romance and Aretine Humanism in Sienese Comedy*. Bibliotheca Studii Senensis, 6 (Florence, 1993).

PART FOUR
THE CASA DELLA SAPIENZA

I

The Growth of a New Type of College

1. *Origins*

It would hardly be an exaggeration to say that the most distinctive feature of Siena's university in this period was the foundation of what soon became a college of a uniquely innovative kind. The Casa della Sapienza was famously described in a measure of 1437 as the 'membro principale' of the *Studio*,[1] and the rhetoric of many other communal documents has the college as its mainstay, the chief guarantor of its fame and stability,[2] as well as one of the glories of the city.[3] It was evident to contemporaries, as it is to posterity, that the continuity and floridity of the *Studio* dates quite closely from the time at which this college was launched.[4]

---

[1] *CG* 219, f. 117r, 25 Feb; cf. Catoni, 'Genesi', p. 175, and Idem, 'Il Comune di Siena e l'amministrazione della Sapienza', p. 122, both dating it 1438; the operation of conversion to modern dating appears to have been performed twice, but it has passed into the general literature in this form. The proposal first appears among 'Proposte generali' on 25 Feb 1437; *Conc.* 2114, f. 103r, ed. Shaw, 'Provisions following "Proposte generali"', doc. 18, p. 121, leaving the date in *stile senese*.

[2] E.g. 'et considerato essa casa essere l'ornato del vro. Mag.co Studio' (*CG* 221, f. 21v, 26 Jun 1441); 'la quale essendo bene governata, è potissima ragione di mantenere lo studio nella vra. città, et consequenter quando non s'abbi diligentia et cura in breve tempo mancharebbe in modo bisognarebbe serrarla' (*Balìa* 6, f. 152v, *Statuti* 40, f. 132r-v, 7 Feb 1458).

[3] 'la casa della sapientia è cosa honoratissima alla nostra città' (*Conc.* 2114, f. 78r, 28 Jan 1435); 'uno ornamento del vostro Regimento' (*CG* 227, f. 241r, 10 Sept 1456; = *Mis.* 1, f. 93r, and *Conc.* 2118, f. 111v); 'publicamente è noto che quanta utilità et honore la detta vra. sapientia sia stata et sia alla vra. città' (*Conc.* 2139, no. 106, f. 194r, probably 1497; see below, p. 377 n. 132). On the other hand, petitioners could be equally vocal about the shame that would befall the comune if the college failed; it would lead to 'grandissimo disonore e danno della città nostra' (loc. cit.). Such phrases were of course standard rhetoric among petitioners and in communal declarations generally – cf. the description of the *gabella*, in the statutes of their officials, 1300, as 'lumen et columpna pacifici status et tranquilli civitatis et comitatus sen.', ed. Bowsky, *Finance*, p. 114; Zarrilli, 'Amministrare con arte', p. 27, and the use of the very same term, 'principale membro' in the statutes of the *Regolatori* to describe the role of agriculture (*Regolatori* 1, f. 161r, 31 Oct 1427, ed. in G. Piccinni, *Il contratto di mezzadria nella Toscana medievale*, III. *Il Contado di Siena, 1349-1518* [Florence, 1992], doc. XXXIII, pp. 419-21, and cf. pp. 16-17) – but their thrust need not therefore be completely discounted.

[4] Cf. also the observations from the neighbouring and rival *Studio* of Florence, of approximately the same period, that a college 'è la cagione e 'l fondamento del mantenimento perpetuo delli Studii; e dove sono state queste Sapientie si vide mai li Studii vi son manchati, però che 'l numero certo delli scolari che sempre in quello luogho si governa, è cagione di tirare alla città gran quantità degli altri, sì per la compagnia di quelli, sì perchè comprehendono lo Studio in quelli luoghi essere durabile'; deliberation of the *Consiglio del Capitano del Popolo*, Florence, 15-18 March 1428(=1429), ed. Gherardi, *Statuti*, appendix, part 1, doc. 117, pp. 210-4 (p. 212). This was a period in which Florence was readily sending students to Siena; above, p. 237.

The chief peculiarity and pioneering feature of the Sienese college was its dependence from the outset on communal initiative. It has traditionally been assumed that the college emerged from the suggestion of the bishop of Siena, the Neapolitan Francesco Mormille, who in December 1393 wrote to the *Concistoro* suggesting that the *Consiglio Generale* appoint a committee to help him explore the possibility of recreating the *Studio* and founding a 'casa di Sapientia'. These explorations were to include discussion with the pope.[5] In fact the first mention of the idea comes in a resolution of the *Consiglio Generale* of 23 June 1388, five and a half years before the bishop's proposal, and one of a sequence of measures for the revival of the *Studio* following regime change in 1385.[6] Six *Savi* were to see to it that a 'domus Sapientie' be set up for poor students.[7] Mormille's initiative was clearly a belated response to that, but also perhaps to the fact that in the intervening period the *Studio*'s fortunes had not revived despite the reforming zeal of the new government.[8] A month after his proposal, on 12 January 1394, the advisory committee came up with a way to realise this ambition; the old and declining Casa della Misericordia, Siena's second-largest hospital, would be converted into a residential college.[9]

Church and state thus combined forces to create this radical institution. Giuliano Catoni, who has ably traced the details of the conversion of the Misericordia to the Sapienza, speculated that the bishop probably already had the Misericordia in mind when he made his suggestion, but was reluctant to be seen personally to be pulling the plug on that old caritative foundation.[10] The terms of this cooperation were, however, very one-sided. The 1388 resolution to create a Sapienza had stipulated that it should be 'sine aliqua expensa tam fienda pro comune'.[11] Mormille's 1393 offer respected that ('e certamente spero che cci si trovarà modo senza che 'l Comune vi metta alcuna cosa')[12] and the 1394 resolution spelt it out again ('sì veramente che 'l Comune di Siena non ci spenda alchuna cosa'). While the measure appointed the bishop and a panel of citizens to oversee the conversion and expansion of the institution, it also stipulated that this did not give the bishop any jurisdiction over it;[13] such jurisdic-

---

[5] 'mi sian dati ad compagnia quattro o vero sei cittadini, cogli quagli io abbia fare ad conferire e cierchare di modi, in Siena o di fuore, col Sancto Padre, per li quali esso Studio e casa di Sapientia si faccia in Siena' (ed. ZDEKAUER, doc. VII, pp. 147-8; the original is now in *Conc.* 2171, fasc. 42, for 1392). At the bottom of the letter the *Concistoro*'s decision to put the proposal to the *Consiglio Generale* is recorded, 'Die viii.a Decembris'; Zdekauer dates it as 1392 on the basis that that body's decision was taken on 12 Jan 1393. Since this is an error for 1394 (see below, n. 9), his dating of Mormille's letter also needs to be revised, to December 1393. The *Concistoro*'s decision is also recorded in *Conc.* 176, f. 16r, 9 Dec 1393.

[6] Above, pp. 50-1.

[7] 'quod in civitate senarum ordinetur et sit domus sapientie in qua morari possint pauperes'. *CG* 196, f. 67v, 23 Jun 1388. This was first noted by GAROSI, p. 195, but has not usually been mentioned in subsequent accounts. Cf. P. R. DENLEY, 'The Collegiate Movement in Italian Universities in the Late Middle Ages', *History of Universities*, 10 (Oxford, 1991), pp. 29-91 (pp. 43-44); and IDEM, 'Academic Rivalry', p. 202.

[8] See above, p. 51.

[9] *CG* 197, f. 188v, ed. ZDEKAUER, doc. VIII, pp. 148-9. See CATONI, 'Genesi', pp. 155-6, both giving the date as January 1393; account has not been taken of the *stile senese*. The correction is made in P. NARDI, 'Origini e sviluppo della Casa della Misericordia nei secoli XIII e XIV', in *La Misericordia di Siena*, pp. 65-93 (p. 93 n. 207). There is a copy of the resolution in *Conc.* 2111, f. 62r-v.

[10] CATONI, 'Genesi', p. 155; and see now P. BROGINI, 'La trasformazione', pp. 121-33.

[11] As n. 7.

[12] As n. 5.

[13] 'Non acquistando però per lo vescovado alchuno dominio nè giuriditione sopra la decta Casa'; as n. 9. I know of only one subsequent example of episcopal intervention in Sapienza affairs; in 1422, in return for additional assets he had acquired for the college, Antonio Casini was allowed to nominate students to places for the coming academic year (*Conc.* 337, f. 8, 10 Mar; cf. *Conc.* 1620, ff. 38v-39r, 12 Mar, and *Conc.* 1901, no. 6, 25 Apr 1422 for related correspondence). Casini, who as treasurer of pope Martin V was highly influential in Rome – a Sienese diplomat described him as 'lo altro papa' (W. BRANDMÜLLER, 'Casini Antonio', *DBI*, 21 (1978), pp. 351-2; see also MINNUCCI, 'Documenti', pp. 17-18 and 225-6) – as

tion remained, as had been the case with the Casa della Misericordia, with the commune.[14] This is perhaps understandable given the Sienese tradition of communal involvement with its caritative institutions,[15] but it must be stressed that for a college of students within a university it was highly unusual; most colleges, whether founded by ecclesiastics or by laymen, had an element of ecclesiastical supervision built into their constitutions.[16]

What made the Sienese authorities focus their attentions, at a time when their own and other academic institutions were experiencing so many problems, on the idea of establishing a college? As far as the timing of the initiative is concerned, it is worth looking at the activities of Siena's traditional competitors, especially Florence. Is it accidental that the 1388 initiative was taken at the height of the expansion of the Florentine *Studio*? Or that Bishop Mormille's letter and the commune's resolution to proceed with the Sapienza came only months after the Florentines had announced the construction of a substantial building for its *Studio*?[17] This can be no more than speculation. On the nature of the initiative, however, the position is much clearer, since Mormille's letter makes it explicit that he envisages 'una casa di Sapientia, come è ad Bolongna et a Perugia'. The Sienese were planning to build on existing Italian models.

While Italian universities are not as famed for their colleges as those of northern Europe, a movement clearly had taken root, with foundations preceding the Sienese at Bologna, Padua and Perugia.[18] The Bolognese tradition was the oldest, with French-influenced small foundations in the thirteenth and early fourteenth centuries (Collegio Avignonese, 1256, Collegio Bresciano, 1326), and a wave of foundations, some of them substantial, from the 1360s (especially the Collegio di Spagna, 1364, and the Collegio Gregoriano, 1370). The habit had also begun on a much smaller scale at Padua (Tornacense, 1363, Campi, 1369, Arquà, 1385). Closest to Siena, however, was the example of Perugia. The Collegio Gregoriano, founded in 1360,[19] was known informally as the 'domus Sapientie' since at least 1371;[20] its acquisition of this name may be connected with a still earlier project, since a 'domus Sapi-

---

well as being an important patron in his native city (cf. PERTICI, *La città magnificata*, p. 31), was later involved in the opening of the Sapienza Nuova at Perugia in 1431; L. MARCONI and M. A. PANZANELLI FRATONI, 'L'Università scopre le sue carte. I lavori di riordinamento dell'archivio storico dell'Università degli Studi di Perugia', *Bollettino della Deputazione di Storia Patrie per l'Umbria*, 98:2 (2001), pp. 459-84 (p. 463); G. NARDESCHI, 'Le costituzioni della "Sapienza Nuova" dell'Anno 1443'. Unpublished *tesi di laurea*, Università degli Studi di Perugia, Facoltà di Magistero, Anno Accademico 1971-2, pp. 46-8; ERMINI, *Storia*, I, p. 399.

[14] In 1415, when plans for the house were revived, these principles were reiterated; *CG* 206, f. 266v, *Mis.* 1, ff. 51v, 80v-81r, 1 Feb 1415; CATONI, 'Genesi', p. 165.

[15] See below, p. 303 n. 29.

[16] DENLEY, 'The Collegiate Movement', pp. 29-91 (p. 55). Another exception is the Collegio Engleschi at Padua, founded in 1446. This was a lay college, whose founder prescribed that the bishop was to have no relations with it; apart from daily prayers, 'sono assenti obblighi esteriori di carattere religioso'. E. VERONESE CESERACCIU, 'Il Collegio Engleschi nel Quattro e Cinquecento', in *Studenti, università, città nella storia padovana*, pp. 257-315 (p. 281).

[17] SPAGNESI, *Utiliter Edoceri*, pp. 149-52, 21 Aug 1392. On the competition with Florence see DENLEY, 'Academic Rivalry', pp. 201-3.

[18] For an overview, see DENLEY, 'The Collegiate Movement'.

[19] The date was correctly established by SEBASTIANI, 'Il collegio universitario', pp. 27-8; U. NICOLINI, 'La "Domus Sancti Gregorii" o "Sapienza Vecchia" di Perugia. Il periodo delle origini', in *I Collegi universitari in Europa tra il XIV e il XVIII secolo*. Atti del convegno di studi della Commissione Internazionale per la Storia delle Università, Siena-Bologna, 16-19 maggio 1988, eds. D. Maffei and H. de Ridder-Symoens. Orbis Academicus, Saggi e Documenti di Storia delle Università, 4 (Milan, 1991), pp. 47-52 (pp. 48-9). See now also G. ANGELETTI and A. BERTINI, *La Sapienza Vecchia* (Perugia, 1993), pp. 63-70.

[20] SEBASTIANI, 'Il collegio universitario', Appendix I, p. 29.

entie' is reported as having been in operation in Perugia in 1351.[21] As far as can be ascertained, the term remained unique to Perugia until its appearance in Siena in 1388, and the Sienese use of it – no other was ever suggested, and it became the official name for the college[22] – is arguably the clearest indication that the proposers had an eye on their Perugian neighbours and rivals.[23] More than that, the Gregoriano's role in Perugia must have been one of relative prominence; with fifty students it was easily the largest Italian foundation to date, and that in one of the smaller universities. Commentators have not ascribed that significant a role to it, but that may be because this is a period that has not attracted much study. Though there is no conclusive evidence, the Perugian experience may well have suggested to the Sienese the strategy of linking the future of their *Studio* with that of the projected new college. The constant and repeated pairing of the two is a striking feature of the documentation. In 1388 it is not yet explicit, though the resolution was part of a broader one reforming the *Studio*; but Mormille's letter makes the connection in unequivocal terms. His purpose is the health of the *Studio* ('o pensato che sia di necessità provedere che in Siena si faccia certo Studio') and the creation of a

---

[21] NICOLINI, 'La "Domus Sancti Gregorii"', pp. 50-1.

[22] The 1394 resolution proposed the term 'Casa de la Misericordia e Sapientia', but it was not incorporated formally into Gregory XII's bull, which established the 'Domus Sapientie civitatis et Studii Senensis'. The name of the Misericordia survived for some time into the fifteenth century, sometimes used in conjunction with 'Sapienza', occasionally – especially in matters to do with the administration of the estate – on its own (e.g. references to the 'camarlingus Misericordie', *Conc.* 2310, no foliation, n.d. but referring to Manno Vitaleoni who occupied the post from 1465 to 1468; *CG* 233, f. 108r, 4 Apr 1470, referring to Angelo Berti, *Camarlengo* of the Sapienza that year, *Regolatori* 9, f. 297v). There are instances of both usages in the same document, suggesting indifference (e.g. *CG* 242, f. 177r, 16 Jun 1527, where the 'savi dello studio et casa della misericordia' discuss the 'casa della sapientia et misericordia'; *Not.* 694, ff. 1r-1*bis* v, 22 Jun 1445, ed. MINNUCCI, 'Documenti', II-4, pp. 77-80, in which the term 'Misericordia' is used in all paragraphs relating to property matters, but 'casa della Misericordia et Sapienza', or variants of it, is used to denote the institution). Cf. also MINNUCCI, 'Documenti', pp. 30-31 n. 70 on the exchangeability of the terms.

The term Sapienza – presumably derived from Proverbs 9.1, 'Sapientia aedificavit sibi domum' – appears to have remained endemic and largely peculiar to central Italy until the late-fifteenth-century foundation of a *Domus Sapientie* in Freiburg im Breisgau. On the use of the term generally, Cf. P. R. DENLEY, 'The Vocabulary of Italian Colleges to 1500', in *Le Vocabulaire des collèges universitaires (XIII-XVIᵉ siècles). Actes du colloque Leuven 9-11 avril 1992*, ed. O. Weijers. CIVICIMA: Études sur le Vocabulaire Intellectuel du Moyen Age, 6 (Turnhout, 1993), pp. 70-7 (pp. 73-5); and A. ESPOSITO, 'I collegi universitari di Roma: progetti e realizzazioni tra XIV e XV secolo', loc. cit., pp. 80-89 (pp. 85-6). Other colleges which subsequently took the name, either formally or informally, include the Collegio Gerolimiano or Sapienza Nuova at Perugia, the Capranica and Nardini at Rome (cf. EADEM, 'Le "Sapientie" romane: i collegi Capranica e Nardini e lo "Studium Urbis"', in *Roma e lo Studium Urbis*, pp. 40-68), and the college at Pisa, for which plans went back to the Florentine proposal of 1429 (SPAGNESI, *Utiliter Edoceri*, pp. 69 *seq.*; DENLEY, 'Academic Rivalry', pp. 202-3; and the work of M. KIENE, esp. 'Der Palazzo della Sapienza – zur italienischen Universitätsarchitektur des 15. und 16. Jahrhunderts', *Römisches Jahrbuch für Kunstgeschichte*, 23/24 [1988], pp. 221-71 [esp. pp. 223-36]). Also of that period is the only northern Italian instance known to me of a proposal (1428) to found a 'domus Sapientiae', at Padua; D. GALLO, 'La "domus Sapientiae" di Pietro Donato: un progetto quattrocentesco per un collegio universitario', *Quaderni per la Storia dell'Università di Padova*, 33 (2000), pp. 115-30. The emergence of the term 'Sapienza' as synonymous with a *studio* as a whole can be traced later – via the late fifteenth-century project for a building of that name at Pisa, in which teaching rather than residential accommodation was the main purpose (KIENE, loc. cit.), and the end-of-century initiation of the construction of a Sapienza in Rome which was entirely given over to teaching (and which subsequently gave the name to the university); cf. ESPOSITO, 'Le "Sapientie" romane', p. 47 and n. 23.

[23] Without wishing to read too much into temporal coincidence, it is also worth pointing out that from the weeks before the commune's first proposal for a Sapienza there are three extant letters from a Perugian teacher to his Sienese counterpart referring to the Perugian 'domus Sapientie' and its rector; L. ZDEKAUER (ed.), *Tre lettere di M. Alberto Guidalotti, lettore allo Studio di Perugia a M. Bartolomeo di Biagio, lettore allo Studio di Siena (1388)*, per Nozze Petrucci-Sozzifanti, 30 agosto 1898 (Siena, 1898), and *BSSP*, 5 (1898), pp. 288-98. When the final push towards the creation of the Sienese college was made in 1415 it was to be 'ad instar domus Sapientie Perusine'; *CG* 206, f. 266v, 1 Feb 1415; *Mis* 1, f. 51v; *Statuti* 47, ff. 212v-213r (cf. CATONI, 'Genesi', p. 165, and below, pp. 325 *seq.*).

way of obviating the need for citizens to go elsewhere to study ('ad ciò che di gli uomini si facciano valenti, e chi vuole studiare e non può, per non andare per l'altrui terre'), the means is the Sapienza ('e veduto che neuna cosa può mantenere e perpetovare esso Studio, quanto sarebbe fare una casa di Sapientia').[24] The commune's resolution of 12 January 1394 echoes these points precisely: 'Et considerato che 'l mantenere lo Studio et fondamento d'esso sia avere principalmente ne la città di Siena una casa di Sapientia, dove gli scolari povari si possano riducere et abbino la vita loro necessaria…'.[25] The prescience of this belief (which the comune reiterated in many subsequent documents) is striking; in no other Italian case of the period did a college come to play such a pivotal role in the university.[26] The close interconnection of the two was enshrined in the college's formal title; in the foundation bull of 1408 Gregory XII declared that it should be called 'Domus Sapientie civitatis et Studii Senensis'.[27] If in due course the idea that colleges could play such a critical role became more widespread,[28] that is largely because of what the Sienese, and to a lesser extent the Perugians, achieved.

The history of the long and protracted birth of the Casa della Sapienza has been well described by Giuliano Catoni, and now by Paolo Brogini. The long-term decline of the Casa della Misericordia, now analysed in detail by Paolo Nardi, afforded an ideal opportunity. The hospital was situated close to the centre of the town, and its finances had effectively collapsed under the pressures of mounting debts, geographically haphazard and often inconvenient donations, and a dearth of personnel to keep it running. In 1363 it had lost its autonomy and come under communal control.[29] By 1391 it did not have enough brothers to form a chapter, and in the same year it petitioned the *Consiglio Generale* to be allowed to sell some of its possessions despite the prohibition of this by its statutes.[30] This reminder of

[24] See above, p. 300 n. 5.

[25] See above, p. 300 n. 9. The proposal is entirely consonant with the assumptions and ambitions of the time; cf. G. P. BRIZZI, 'Da "domus pauperum scholarium" a collegio d'educazione. Evoluzione e ruolo del collegio in Europa dal Medioevo all'età napoleonica', in *Università e collegi. Storia e futuro.* Atti del Convegno (7 marzo 1994) organizzato dal Collegio Universitario S. Caterina da Siena di Pavia, ed. M. P. Musatti. Fonti e studi per la storia dell'Università di Pavia, 22 (Bologna, 1994), pp. 17-46. A 'domus pauperum scolarium' is what is proposed in the 1370s for what became the Collège de Dormans-Beauvais in Paris; T. KOUAMÉ, *Le collège de Dormans-Beauvais à la fin du Moyen Age. Stratégies politiques et pouvoirs individuels à l'Université de Paris (1370-1485).* Education and Society in the Middle Ages and Renaissance, 22 (Leiden, 2005), p. 29.

[26] Perhaps the closest to it is indeed Perugia, where in 1395 the Sapienza is described as 'membrum singulare generalis Studii Perusini' in a petition to exempt it from certain taxes; SEBASTIANI, 'Il collegio universitario', p. 69 and appendix 1, doc. 13 (pp. 72-7 of appendix).

[27] *Mis.* 1, ff. 72r-78v (Latin), and 63r-64r (Italian; ed. BARDUZZI, *Documenti*, p. 24); CATONI, 'Genesi', p. 162.

[28] Cf. Leon Battista Alberti's plan to found one of those 'chollegi e sapienzie che sono il mantenimento degli Studii'; G. MANCINI, 'Il testamento di L. B. Alberti', *Archivio Storico Italiano*, 72:2 (1914), pp. 20-52 (p. 20); cf. DENLEY, 'The Collegiate Movement', p. 58.

[29] CATONI, 'Genesi', pp. 156-7; and *Pergamene*, p. 30; also COHN, *Death and Property*, esp. pp. 20-1. This increased control was the price exacted by the commune for rescuing the house from bankruptcy (p. 49); but Cohn also points out that the 1262 constitution of Siena already gave the *podestà* the right to oversee the administration of the house (p. 268 n. 43). Cf. also NARDI, 'Origini e sviluppo della Casa della Misericordia', pp. 70-2. On communal control over the hospital of S. Maria della Scala, see above, pp. 105-6. The commune's habit of helping out pious institutions is aptly illustrated in a petition of 1388 to place a hospital in Arcidosso under its protection. The proposers observe: 'E come sapete, signori, se'l comune di Siena non avesse posto le mani a l'Uopare Sancte Marie, allo spedale della Scala e ala casa dela Misericordia come le cose sarebbono ite' (CG 196, f. 81r-v, 18 Oct 1388; quoted in EPSTEIN, *Alle origini della fattoria toscana*, p. 25).

[30] *CG* 197, f. 22r-v, 24 Nov; NARDI, 'Origini e sviluppo della Casa della Misericordia', pp. 85-6; CATONI, loc. cit. Two years later the debts amounted to 3,000 florins (CG 197, f. 88v, 24 Oct 1393, and see BALESTRACCI and PICCINNI, *Siena nel Trecento*, p. 154). On the terminal problems of the Misericordia in the period see NARDI, 'Origini e sviluppo', pp. 79-86; also LIBERATI, 'Chiese, monasteri, oratori e spedali', *BSSP*, 68 (1960), pp. 158-9. The previous decade had seen a protracted lawsuit brought by the house against a member of the Malavolti family; M. ASCHERI, 'La decisione nelle corti giudiziarie

the Misericordia's plight came at a convenient moment; the change of use from hospital to college must have seemed a natural solution to two separate problems. In the event, over two decades elapsed between the first proposal for its conversion and the actual opening of the new institution. The same crises that affected the *Studio* as a whole repeatedly delayed action. From 1394, through the Visconti emergency, to the change of regime in 1403 nothing more is heard of the plan; in 1396 it had receded to the point that the Casa della Misericordia was one of the bodies expected (in a failed petition) to contribute funds towards the refounding of the *Studio*.[31] In neither this nor accounts of the regime's subsequent attempts to revive the *Studio* is any reference made to the conversion plan. In 1404 the new coalition or *regime tripartito*, wishing to revive the *Studio* and distance itself from the policies of its predecessor,[32] restored the budget and lectureships and returned to the issue of the Misericordia; on 21 November the *Consiglio Generale* ordered 'che nella Città di Siena sia da ora innanzi una casa della Sapientia la quale sia el luogo de lo spedale di S. Maria della Misericordia', giving the *Concistoro* the power to commandeer the resources of 'luoghi e spedali' it thought fit for this purpose.[33] Yet the Misericordia continued its existence and its caritative work,[34] disrupted only by an order in 1407 that the halls usually used for teaching be cleared for the doctors – virtually the only evidence that the house had previously been used as a venue for instruction.[35] In 1408 a series of bulls from Gregory XII finally decreed the conversion of the hospital to a college, and made the arrangements for the transfer of the house and its possessions, adding to the estate of the new institution several small hospitals in the dioceses of Siena, Massa and Grosseto.[36] The formal foundation had been put through; the documents were presented to the *Concistoro* by the new bishop, Antonio Casini, on 2 January 1409,[37] and a month later the *Savi dello Studio* were ordered to implement the new college.[38] This too was destined

italiane del Tre-Quattrocento e il caso della Mercanzia di Siena', in *Judicial Records, Law Reports, and the Growth of Case Law*, ed. J. H. Baker. Comparative Studies in Continental and Anglo-American Legal History, 5 (Berlin, 1989), pp. 101-22 (pp. 114-5); repr. as 'Giustizia ordinaria, giustizia di mercanti e la Mercanzia di Siena nel Tre-Quattrocento', in his *Tribunali, giuristi e istituzioni dal medioevo all'età moderna* (rev. ed. Bologna, 1995), pp. 23-54 (p. 36). On the agrarian crisis in Siena in the late fourteenth century, affecting Misericordia possessions, see PICCINNI, *Il contratto di mezzadria*, III, pp. 26-7.

[31] *Conc.* 2111, f. 126v, 23 Apr; above, p. 51.

[32] Above, p. 54.

[33] *CG* 201, f. 166r, 21 Nov, partially ed. GAROSI, pp. 526-7; copies in *Mis.* 1, ff. 50v-51r, *Statuti* 38, f. 23r; and see CATONI, 'Genesi', pp. 159-60 and n. 17, correcting Garosi's dating.

[34] CATONI, 'Genesi', pp. 160-1.

[35] *Conc.* 250, f. 21r, 24 Oct. See above, p. 117 and n. 64. The use of the Misericordia as a teaching venue does not imply a specific relationship; other venues, including churches, were used (above, pp. 113 *seq.*). There is also some evidence that the Misericordia itself organised teaching for its inmates or at least accommodated teachers. In 1316 Scabello del fu Chiavellino, a grammar teacher, was allocated a room in the house, together with some of its income; G. CATONI, 'Gli oblati della Misericordia. Poveri e benefattori a Siena nella prima metà del Trecento', in *La società del bisogno*, pp. 1-17 (p. 10) speculated that this may have been for the teaching of young inmates. In the mid-fourteenth-century the future notary Ser Cristofano di Gano di Guidino was sent to Siena by his grandfather to study with the teacher maestro Pietro dell'Ochio, 'che stava de la Misericordia'; G. CHERUBINI, 'Dal libro di ricordi di un notaio senese del Trecento', in his *Signori, contadini, borghesi. Ricerche sulla società italiana del basso medioevo* (Florence, 1974), pp. 393-425 (p. 397), and cf. CATONI, loc. cit. This was glossed by Cherubini as meaning the confraternity of S. Maria della Misericordia, but they were in essence the same entity; Catoni descibes the Misericordia as 'una confraternità laicale…divenuta ben presto…un importante istituto di carità, che fungeva anche da ospedale' (CATONI, 'Genesi', p. 156).

[36] Published in BARDUZZI, *Documenti*, pp. 24-34, and discussed in detail by BROGINI, 'La trasformazione', pp. 122-3, and CATONI, 'Genesi', pp. 161-3, with full references to other editions and literature.

[37] *Concistoro*, 258, f. 4r; CATONI, 'Genesi', p. 163; BROGINI, 'La trasformazione', p. 123. On Casini see above, pp. 48 n. 114, and 54; and on the payment for his services, p. 104 n. 100.

[38] *Concistoro*, 258, f. 19r, 1 Feb; CATONI, loc. cit.; BROGINI, loc. cit.

to be postponed, first by Siena's conflict with Ladislas of Durazzo in 1409 and then by plague in 1411,[39] and when the *Studio* reopened in 1412 there was once again no talk of a Sapienza.[40] Only in 1414 did the commune return to this project,[41] granting the *Savi dello Studio* full authority over the Misericordia on 1 February 1415.[42] The hospital was finally suppressed, others incorporated,[43] and the house officially reopened in its new capacity, with the first ten students being admitted in February 1416, another ten in October and a third batch of ten in February 1418.[44]

Attempts at collegiate foundations at moments of crisis or difficulty are not unusual. Colleges could be a visible, indeed physical, demonstration of continuity in adverse times, and in this sense have perhaps a special significance in a period when dedicated university buildings were not yet in evidence.[45] What is unique about the Sienese Sapienza is its communal roots; it is the only successful Italian example of a government-created college before the very end of the fifteenth century.[46] In these roots lies also the explanation for some of its more striking peculiarities.

2. *From* domus pauperum scholarium *to the charging of fees*

The radically different nature of this new foundation can nowhere be seen more clearly than in what happened to its stated purpose between the original foundation moves and its actual opening. The 1388 resolution expressed the conventional aim of creating a college for poor students, and the 1394 deliberation echoed this, stipulating also that places in the college would only be open to people from the town or *contado* of Siena.[47] Both sentiments were still evident in 1404, when it was also decided that the forty places envisaged would be divided equally between the town and the *contado*.[48] In the year in which the transformation of the Misericordia was finally effected, however, there was a sudden change in the geographical focus of the college. In August 1415 it was decided

> cum expediens sit, quod solum forenses in ea recipiantur, tum propter famam civitatis, et Studii ampliandum, tum propter bonificamentum, et augmentum Studii proseguendum, quod scolares forenses, et

---

[39] See above, p. 56.

[40] CATONI, 'Genesi', p. 164.

[41] *Conc.* 293, f. 9v, 14 Nov. Only a month earlier the *Concistoro* had decided to elect a new *Camarlengo* of the Misericordia in view of the many accusations that the house was being run badly (*Conc.* 2113, f. 35r, 10 Oct).

[42] *CG* 206, f. 266v; *Mis* 1, f. 51v (another copy ff. 80v-81r); *Statuti* 47, ff. 212v-213r. As late as 1412 people were making donations to the 'Misericordia'; CATONI, *Pergamene*, p. 47, n. 197.

[43] *CG* 207, f. 95v, 12 Aug 1415 (incorporation of the hospital of S. Andrea).

[44] *Conc.* 300, f. 40r, 22 Feb, and *Conc.* 304, f. 40r, 7 Oct 1416 (and see CATONI, 'Genesi', pp. 170-2); *Conc.* 312, f. 20r, 4 Feb 1418. The 1418 admissions were accompanied by the declaration that no others were to be allowed into the Sapienza unless they had been there before, which suggests (along with the gap between the second and the third batch of admissions) that the plague of 1417 may have had an impact on the college as well as on the *Studio* as a whole; cf. above, p. 113. A further two students were admitted on 27 June 1418 (*Conc.* 314, f. 23v). Since it is unlikely that at this early stage the authorities were already admitting numbers in excess of the places created, the implication is that at least two places had become vacant through students failing to return or dropping out.

[45] See below, p. 398.

[46] The Florentines attempted to emulate it but failed; SPAGNESI, *Utiliter Edoceri*, ch. 2; and DENLEY, 'Academic Rivalry', pp. 201-3.

[47] See p. 300 nn. 7 and 9.

[48] *CG* 201, f. 166r, and *Mis.* 1, ff. 50v-51r, *Statuti* 38, f. 23r, 21 Nov, ed. GAROSI, pp. 526-7.

de longinquis partibus venientes, quantum magis provecti sunt ... erunt causa manutentionis, et amplificationis dicti Studii ...[49]

The first twenty students to be admitted in 1416 reflected this change, coming from all over Italy and also including a Catalan. The regulation was soon refined; in 1418 an attempt was made to rule that only one student per town (and its *contado*) could be admitted,[50] and in 1422, when this was confirmed, it was added that the penalty for falsification was expulsion and the loss of the entrance fee.[51] In 1448 'foreign' was defined as a minimum of sixty *miglia* from Siena.[52]

These early changes were accompanied by a no less significant decision about the type of students to be admitted. Whereas in most Italian colleges the quotas of students admitted to study each subject were, at least initially, biased against civil law (the Sapienza Vecchia of Perugia initially allowed only four to six civilians 'quod advocationis officium maxime in partibus Italie danpnationis est anime',[53] and the Spanish College at Bologna admitted none at all),[54] in Siena no distinction was made between

---

[49] *CG* 207, f. 95r, and *Mis.* 1, ff. 51v-52r, 12 Aug. The reason for the sudden change must be a matter for speculation. Since there is a strong case for the argument that in the final stages of preparation for the opening of the new college the authorities turned particularly to the model of the Collegio Gregoriano in Perugia (see esp. below, pp. 325 *seq.*), it may be relevant to note that the original constitutions of its founder, Cardinal Niccolò Capocci, made the same stipulation 'quia non est de more in aliquo studio…quod recipiatur aliquis de loco proprio'; Biblioteca Comunale Augusta di Perugia, *ms.* 1239, const. 4, f. 7v, eds. SEBASTIANI, 'Il collegio universitario', appendix III, p. 213, and ANGELETTI and BERTINI, *La Sapienza Vecchia*, pp. 348-9.

[50] *Conc.* 2113, f. 127v (new foliation), 19 Aug, with the marginal annotation 'suspendatur de mandato dominorum', which is also recorded, less unambiguously, in the *repertorio* of measures in *CG* 478, f. 71v. Unlike the measure immediately preceding it, relating to the Scala's contribution (above, pp. 105-6), which was approved, this does not appear in the *Consiglio Generale* deliberations. But the unsuccessful *Conc.* 2113 measure proposes 'per gli ordini fatti per li savi primi dello studio del modo forma ordine et conditione degli scolari della casa della sapientia contiene infra l'altre cose che più che uno per terra non ve ne possa stare in uno medesimo tempo, né vi si possa mettare niuno di minore età d'anni vinti etc. s'osservino in tutto et per tutto…'. For possible reasons why this was not included, p. 330 below.

[51] *Mis.* 1, ff. 53v-54v, 14 Dec, ed. ZDEKAUER, doc. XIII, pp. 161-2 (from a later copy; see n. 55 below), and see pp. 96-7. The one-student-per-town rule was still in vigour in 1456, when an exemption from it was granted by the *Balìa* for two students of arts and medicine from Città di Castello (*Balìa* 1, ff. 95r, 12 Dec, and 109r, 29 Dec).

[52] *Mis.* 1, f. 61v, 22 Nov 1448. This was repeated in 1542 (*Studio* 110, f. 7r, 17 Feb 1542, ed. MARRARA, *Lo Studio di Siena*, p. 296, and KOŠUTA, 'Documenti', doc. IV, p. 361; and see CASCIO PRATILLI, *L'Università e il Principe*, p. 13 n. 5). The only exception to this (and to the quota) was that in the 1550s Montalcino was given the privilege of having two places in the Sapienza for its students. A privilege to this effect was granted on 4 Jul 1553 (*CG* 246, f. 183r). FALUSCHI, *Disordinate Memorie per formare la Storia dello Studio, e Università di Siena* (BCS, *ms.* E.VI.9, ff. 154r-55v) records two measures, a twenty-year privilege to this effect of 4 Jul 1553, subsequently changed to a privilege in perpetuity, without payment by the students, on 7 Dec 1555. Cf. S. LANDI, *Indice 1777 delle Filze, e Deliberazioni che sono nell'Armario dipinto coll'Arme della Sapienza* (1777-83; ASS, *ms.* C.51 *bis*, f. 1v). I have not found supporting evidence for this in original Sienese archival sources. The 1555 tradition is also recorded in GIGLI, *Diario Sanese*, part 2, p. 360, and in the *Libro dei Privilegi* for Montalcino; cf. P. G. MORELLI, S. MOSCADELLI and C. SANTINI (eds.), *L'Archivio Comunale di Montalcino. Inventario della sezione storica*, I (Siena, 1989), p. 86. The seventeenth-century compiler of the *Privilegi dello Stato Sanese* (BCS, *ms.* A.III.19) stated that the concession was given for a twenty-year period in 1505 (f. 101r); I have been unable to trace such a measure, and there is no sign of Montalcinese students in the list of entrants to the Sapienza in BCS, *ms.* A.XI.12 (on which see above, pp. 24-5), even in a period in which there was a marked increase in the proportion of Tuscan entrants. This is surely a further distortion of the 1555 tradition. Even less plausible is the early eighteenth-century claim of A. B. FANCELLI, *Origine dello Studio Sanese* (BCS, *ms.* A.XI.29, no foliation, copy in *Studio* 126, f. 20r) that ever since the plague of 1424 the town of Montalcino, which had hosted the *Studio* at the time, was entitled to send two students to the Sapienza free of charge. I have found no evidence, either in legislation or in practice, to support this.

[53] ROSSI, 'Documenti per la storia dell'Università di Perugia', doc. 100A, 20 Sept 1362; ERMINI, *Storia*, I, p. 395 (the college only admitted secular clerics). But six years later, twenty out of the fifty students were to be civilians; ROSSI, op. cit., doc. 101C, and ERMINI, *Storia*, I, p. 397.

[54] MARTI, *The Spanish College*, pp. 30, 128-32; this although laymen as well as clerics were admitted. The college insisted on this despite the difficulties in attracting Spaniards to other subjects (especially medicine, 'quia ab experto

canon and civil law. Both were considered attractive; no more than five inmates could be students of arts or medicine, because 'le Facultà di ragione canonica e di ragione civile sono quelle, che fanno venire in grande dignità e stato quelli che seguitano, e più honore riportano a la città che niuna altra Facultà in che l'uomo studi'.[55] This statement comes from the reform of 1422, but it was foreshadowed already in October 1416, when the second batch of ten students was admitted to the new institution; it was resolved that henceforth only lawyers were to be admitted, though others who had already been accepted could remain.[56]

The swift change of geographical orientation and the break with tradition over subject are indicative of a new pragmatic attitude, and it would not be an exaggeration to say that they set the tone and shape for the new institution. A logical but much more fundamental next step, adding commercial instincts to the pragmatism, was the abandonment of the caritative principle. As has been seen, the 1388 resolution spoke of a house for 'pauperes';[57] that of 1394 referred to 'quelli povari che anno volontà d'essere virtuosi et buoni, e che ne possa risultare utilità e honore a la città e contado di Siena';[58] the 1404 revival of the project repeated this aspiration;[59] Gregory XII's foundation bull of 1408 made it clear that the college was to be for poor students;[60] and the February 1415 resolution once again confirmed this intention.[61] As soon as the Sapienza got underway and foreigners were admitted, however, the emphasis on this aspect all but disappeared from the documents. From very early on there appears to have been an entrance fee;[62] two students admitted in June 1418 had to pay an unspecified amount,[63] as did three admitted in January 1421 'as usual'.[64] Later that year the fee is specified for the first time, as 50 *lire*.[65] The following year, in the first reforms to the system, the period of admission was raised from six to seven years and the fee doubled to 100 *lire*.[66] But this proved to be just the beginning. By 1434 the Sapienza was charging an en-

---

vidimus male haberi posse Hispanos volentes audire scienciam medicine'; op. cit., p. 142), very much in contrast to the Sienese attitude.

[55] *Mis.* 1, f. 53r-v, 14 Dec 1422. ZDEKAUER, doc. XIII, pp. 161-2, publishes the text from the seventeenth-century copy in BCS, *ms.* C.IV.26 (f. 192r), attributing it to *ms.* C.IV.6, f. 141. *Ms.* C.IV.26 is in turn apparently a transcription of the copy in *Mis.* 2 (f. 36v); all three have the error 'la Facultà ... sono' (see above, p. 123 n. 9).

[56] Cf. *Conc.* 304, f. 40v, 7 Oct 1416. The decision was not upheld in February 1418, when four of the ten students admitted were in arts (*Conc.* 312, f. 20r, 4 Feb), but as Table 6 below (p. 312) shows, in the early years of the college a bias towards law students was undoubtedly maintained.

[57] As p. 300 n. 7.

[58] As p. 300 n. 9.

[59] As p. 304 n. 33.

[60] As p. 304 n. 36.

[61] As p. 305 n. 42.

[62] This is the implication of the earliest 'ordini' which charge the rector with the task of screening out students who were too young and were therefore wasting their money: 'Item se alcuno fosse recevuto troppo iovinetto el quale scialacquasse desutelemente la sua pecunia, è disposto che prima sia admonito a la voluntà del rectore.' CATONI, 'Genesi', p. 181. But the date of these 'ordini' cannot be established; below, p. 325 n. 4.

[63] *Conc.* 314, f. 23v, 27 Jun (Dns. Andreas de Camerino and Mag. Bernardus de Venetiis).

[64] *Conc.* 330, f. 13v, 21 Jan (Dns. Andreas de Monterchio, Dns. Brandaglia de Aretio and Mag. Johannes Martino de Parma).

[65] *Conc.* 334, f. 9v, 12 Sept (admission of Dns. Johannes de Scotia).

[66] *Mis.* 1, f. 53r-v, 14 Dec 1422 (on ZDEKAUER's edition, doc. XIII, pp. 161-2, see above, n. 55). Payment of the entrance fee still had to be enforced; in legislation of 10 Feb 1424, students 'solverunt debitum mercedem pro introitu dicte domus' within two months, otherwise they would not be admitted or, if they had been, they were to be expelled (*Conc.* 348, f. 17v, 10 Feb 1424; variant in *Mis.* 1, f. 55r; and see CATONI, 'Genesi', p. 170). There are still cases of student admis-

trance fee of 40 florins,[67] and by 1437 this was raised to 50 florins, i.e. four times the original fee.[68] The justification for this rate was given in 1445, in a phrase that, in the directness of its logic, reveals much about how far the original purpose had been abandoned: 'cum manifeste videatur in dicta domo intromictuntur scolares divites, et non pauperes'.[69] The basic fee remained at that level until 1542, when it was fixed at 60 ducats.[70]

This change was not to be reversed. An attempt to return to the original principles in the mid-fifteenth century – 'acciò vi si mettino scolari bisognosi, et non per molte pregarie come si fa oggi' – was defeated.[71] If the idea that poorer students might gain a place was not entirely abandoned, it was certainly relegated to the position of an afterthought. Students applying for exemptions or concessions often claimed poverty as their grounds for doing so, and sometimes these requests were accepted.[72] One significant attempt was made to reopen the Sapienza to poor and local students; in 1512 a Paduan cleric, Bartolomeo Bolis, who had retired to the decanate of Siena cathedral after a curial career, gave 1,000 ducats to be invested in property, the income from which was to fund six free places for Sienese.[73] The will was contested by Bolis's disappointed relatives, and it is far from clear how quickly these places materialised and how regularly they were filled;[74] in the event, they were soon trans-

---

sions where payment is not mentioned; *Dipl., R. Università degli Studi*, 13 Dec 1424 (Michael Albrel[?] of the diocese of Tortosa, student in canon law; cf. *Conc.* 353, f. 16r, 13 Dec), in contrast to *Conc.* 353, f. 21r, 27 Dec 1424 (Lodovico di Magio da Volterra, also a student of canon law, document drawn up by the same notary and in other respects almost identical). Two students admitted in 1425 had to pay 100 *lire*; *Dipl., R. Università degli Studi*, 14 Sept 1425 (Guglielmo di Pietro Esguert from Barcelona, student in civil law; cf. *Conc.* 358, f. 12v, 14 Sept, where it is stated that the admission was subject to the usual conditions), and *Dipl., Archivio Generale*, 3 Oct 1425 (Niccolò Ghelde Pollacco, student in canon law; cf. *Conc.* 358, f. 24r, 3 Oct).

[67] *Mis.* 1, f. 56v, *Conc.* 413, f.13v, 17 Nov.

[68] *Mis.* 1, f. 85r, 29 May.

[69] *Mis.* 1, f. 57v, 18 Mar; ZDEKAUER, p. 35, n. 2, and CATONI, 'Genesi', p. 170 n. 68.

[70] *Studio* 110, f. 7r, 17 Feb, ed. MARRARA, *Lo Studio di Siena*, p. 296, and KOŠUTA, 'Documenti', doc. IV, p. 361.

[71] *Conc.* 2310, no foliation, n.d. but, on the basis of the rector it names, locatable between 1448 and 1452; see below, p. 346 n. 70. There was also an attempt, in 1451, to return to the original intentions; admissions were to be the domain of the *Concistoro* and *Savi dello Studio* 'ut immictant scolares pauperes et egeni' (*Conc.* 510, f. 40r, 16 Jun, and *CG* 225, f. 183r, 27 Jun). It is not clear whether the undated proposal and the 1451 measure are directly connected.

[72] E.g. the Portuguese student who in 1463 asked for a place 'per mezo tempo' 'perché impotente a pagare per tucto lo tempo' (*CG* 230, f. 68r-v, 23 Dec).

[73] P. PICCOLOMINI, 'Bartolomeo Bolis da Padova e la sua fondazione per lo Studio di Siena (24 luglio 1512)', *Archivio Storico Italiano*, ser. V, vol 36 (1905), pp. 143-152, publishing Bolis' proposal to the *Balìa* (copied in *Mis.* 36, f. 82 *seq.*) and other documents including the account of the episode by Tizio. (A codicil to his will, not affecting the bequest to the Sapienza, is in *Dipl., Arch. Generale*, 4 Apr 1514.) The places were to be allocated to two students in canon law, two in civil law and two in arts and medicine, chosen by a committee of the nine Sienese doctors 'più antichi nel doctorato', three from each of the disciplines. Pandolfo Petrucci was asked to nominate the first batch of students. He chose three; the other three were chosen by his son Borghese. As an incentive, these students were to receive a payment of 100 *lire* on taking their degrees. The income from two properties was hypothecated for this purpose. But FANCELLI, *Origine dello Studio Sanese* (BCS, *ms.* A.XI.29, no foliation; copy in *Studio* 126, ff. 17v-18v, and cf. *Studio* 127, filza XXI, nos. 2 and 3) suggests that these rents were not collected and that the practice was abandoned due to the fear of the cost implications if all six students decided to take their degrees at the same time.

[74] None of the six nominees of 1512 appear in the 'admissions register' in BCS, *ms.* A.XI.12. In the case of just one, Stefano di Giovanni, student in canon law, there is a possible identification with Stefanus Iohanninensis de Senis, who took a degree in civil law in 1519; MINNUCCI and MORELLI, *Lauree*, IV, pp. 24-5. Sienese names appear only rarely after that; one in 1535 (BCS, *ms.* A.XI.12, f. 142v; BONAFACCIA, 'La "Domus Sapientiae"', p. 170), two in 1536 (f. 143v; BONAFACCIA, pp. 170-1), and three in 1542 (ff. 162v-163r; BONAFACCIA, pp. 189-90).

formed into non-resident scholarships.[75] But this initiative never occupied more than a minor role in the history of the Sapienza, which, as will be seen, came to stand for something very different.

The significance of this change is difficult to exaggerate. Siena and Perugia seem to have been the first Italian colleges to charge an entrance fee, and Siena appears to have been the first to make it a condition for all students.[76] It is difficult to see this as anything other than opportunism, and the swift hike in the fee in the 1420s and 1430s should be viewed as a direct and indeed business-like response to demand; this was the moment of sudden Italian and indeed international attention on the Sienese *Studio* as an exciting and upcoming institution with an impressive roll-call of teachers.[77] What we can say is that it is an interesting reflection on the relationship between church and state in Siena that the commitment to places for poor students could be overturned so rapidly and apparently so effortlessly.[78] From the moment of fee-charging the Sienese Sapienza clearly became a much more obviously secular institution, with different functions and problems from others in Italy. If we look ahead to the end of the century this no longer seems unique; but that is largely because by then the success of the Sienese and Perugian experiments had prompted imitations.

What sort of deal were the Sienese offering? The entrance fee to the Sapienza entitled the student to board and lodging for first six, then seven years.[79] Full advance payment of 50 florins (as it soon became) was clearly out of the question for truly poor students. This is not, of course, to say that the Sapienza automatically became the equivalent of a luxury residence. Rather, it should be seen as a bid for students in a competitive environment. The Sapienza must have been an attractive proposition for those looking for affordable means of studying at university. In the 1450s the physician Maestro Marco di Maestro Antonio of Pistoia, contemplating sending his son Antonio to Bologna to study, decided that it would be cheaper to send him first to Florence and then to the Sapienza in Siena.[80] What we know of the membership of the Sapienza from the names that survive is not conclusive.[81] They show a sprinkling of eminent and obviously wealthy students, but for the majority we can be less sure. A

---

[75] GIGLI, *Diario Sanese*, vol. 2, p. 360, says 'convivevano questi al principio nella Sapienza, ma già da lungo tempo stannosene alle Case loro, e dalla Sapienza vengono proveduti di pane, vino, carne, e di qualche denaro ancora per le altre spese'. This might explain their absence from the register, but the implication of that line of argument is that the transformation into non-resident places was immediate. In the 1542 statutes there is another phenomenon which however does not appear to me to relate to these scholars: 'tucti quelli scolari dela Casa che vogliano stare fuore di Casa possino havere la parte et perdino le camere dela Casa' (*Studio* 110, f. 10v, 11 Mar, ed. KOŠUTA, 'Documenti', doc. IV, p. 364).

[76] The Perugian Sapienza introduced a charge for its law students in 1417; SEBASTIANI, 'Il collegio universitario', pp. 76-81, and appendix II, pp. 284-5; ANGELETTI and BERTINI, *La Sapienza Vecchia*, pp. 397-8. The charge was similarly 40 florins; the Sapienza had sixty students at the time. See also DENLEY, 'Collegiate Movement', p. 45. Given the extent to which the Sienese modelled their college on that of Perugia (see below, pp. 325 *seq.*), it is quite possible that this was imitative as well, but the documentation does not make it unequivocally clear which was the first to introduce fees.

[77] It also follows two years of heightened numbers of admissions (see Table 6 below, p. 312), presumably as the first batch of entrants completed their time and left.

[78] FIORAVANTI, 'Pietro de' Rossi', p. 130, saw this *volte-face* as the catalyst for the social direction in which the *Studio* as a whole was moving. Cf. also CATONI, 'Il Comune di Siena e l'amministrazione della Sapienza', p. 121.

[79] The six-year stipulation appears in the first 'ordini' of the house (*Mis.* 1, f. 49r, n.d.; on the date see below, p. 325 n. 4), and was amended in 1422, as the first batch of entrants were completing their term (*Mis.* 1, ff. 53r-54v, 14 Dec). See CATONI, 'Genesi', pp. 171, 181.

[80] PARK, *Doctors and Medicine*, p. 124. Maestro Marco estimated that sending his son to Bologna would cost 30 florins a year. Maestro Marco's other considerations were that his brother had ecclesiastical connections in Siena, and that 'students lived under the artful eyes of the university authorities' (PARK, loc. cit.).

[81] Such a list has been prepared for this study, but more prosopographical work is necessary before it will be ready for publication.

number of students who pleaded poverty were actually asking for longer to pay or for places for a shorter period of time. Many 'poor' students were well connected; in 1422 the request of the Genoese student Luca Stella for a place came in the form of no fewer than three letters of recommendation, including one from the *doge*, Tommaso Campofregoso.[82] And indeed the whole issue is clouded by the problem that, while contemporaries clearly used terms such as *pauper* in a variety of ways understood by them, they are less easy to pin down centuries later. The division of the student population into *nobiles*, *dives* and *pauperes* is not made formally in Italy (as it clearly was in, say, the matriculation lists of German universities) in this period, though it certainly becomes more evident from the end of the fifteenth century onwards.[83] Other colleges subscribed to the principle that places were for poor students, but it was somewhat attenuated in practice. For example, the statutes of the Collegio di Spagna at Bologna stipulated that no student with an income of over fifty florins should be admitted, and members of the college whose income rose above that level would have to leave within six months;[84] but we know that the College's system of recommendation soon helped to make it a training-ground for future elites.[85] The notion of caritative support for the well-born is well illustrated in mid-fifteenth-century Pavia; the 1458 will of the lawyer Catone Sacco (whose relations with Siena have been described above),[86] bequeathing funds for what was to become the *domus Catonis*, makes it clear that he had in mind a college for poor noble students.[87] Siena's departure from the principle that a college should be for poor students is significant, not just because it happened in practice – which is not so different from the experience in other *studi* – but because it was made explicit. This in turn hastened its implementation elsewhere.[88]

3. *Admission*

The way in which charges were introduced, and what the documents tell us about the thinking of the authorities, suggest a pragmatic, indeed businesslike approach. Catoni is surely right in explaining the

---

[82] *Conc.* 1900, nos. 59 and 60, 12 Mar; and n. 61, 13 Mar. The letters all refer to the twenty-four places available for poor students, suggesting imperfect information in Genoa.

[83] For a general overview, SCHWINGES, 'Student Education, Student Life', pp. 209-11; J. M. FLETCHER, 'Wealth and Poverty in the Medieval German Universities with Particular Reference to the University of Freiburg', in *Europe in the Late Middle Ages*, eds. J. Hale, R. Highfield and B. Smalley (London, 1965), pp. 410-36; R. N. SWANSON, 'Godliness and Good Learning: Ideals and Imagination in Medieval University and College Foundations', in *Pragmatic Utopias: Ideals and Communities, 1200-1630. In Honour of Barrie Dobson*, eds. S. Rees Jones and R. Horrox (Cambridge, 2001), pp. 43-59 (p. 49); for the issue of definition, see the survey of J. PAQUET, 'Recherches sur l'universitaire "pauvre" au Moyen Age', *Revue belge de philologie et d'histoire*, 56 (1978), pp. 301-53 (esp. pp. 306-7); for methodological discussions of the problem, also IDEM, 'L'universitaire "pauvre" au Moyen Age: problèmes, documentation, question de méthode', in *Les Universités a la fin du moyen âge*, eds. J. IJsewijn and J. Paquet (Louvain, 1978), pp. 399-425; and E. MORNET, '*Pauperes scolares*. Essai sur la condition matérielle des étudiants scandinaves dans les universités aux XIVᵉ et XVᵉ siècles', *Le Moyen Age*, 84 (1978), pp. 53-102.

[84] Statute 6; MARTI, *The Spanish College*, pp. 152-7.

[85] DENLEY, 'Collegiate Movement', p. 40.

[86] Pp. 152, 176 n. 247, 186 and 189.

[87] D. ZANETTI, 'Il primo collegio pavese per studenti stranieri', in *Studi in memoria di Mario Abrate* (Turin, 1986), vol. 2, pp. 789-812 (pp. 792 and 794, and cf. 797-8); repr. in his *Fra le antiche torri: scritti di storia pavese* (Pavia, 2000), pp. 135-61.

[88] But the Florentine plans for a Sapienza of 1429-30 were for poor students; GHERARDI, *Statuti*, appendix, part 1, doc. 117, pp. 210-4, 15-18 Mar 1428 (p. 213).

change from a house for poor students to one with paying 'guests' as connected to the outlook of the tripartite regime:

> Costoro erano per lo più gli eredi diretti…di quei banchieri, mercanti e proprietari terrieri che più di un secolo prima avevano imposto, con il governo dei Nove, una scelta decisiva per l'organizzazione politica senese: una scelta, cioè, 'mercantile', dove perdevano qualsiasi spessore ideologico termini come guelfo o ghibellino, nero o bianco, e dove l'obbiettivo principale era quello di evitare negative 'congiunture' e real-izzare i migliori profitti, non necessariamente personali, ma legati a quelli generali della città.[89]

The mentality described here pervades the whole administration of the Sapienza, which needs to be looked at in terms of market forces. Having opted for a fee-based institution, the authorities found themselves in the grip of such forces, and experienced frequent tensions between what they wanted to achieve in the Sapienza and what could actually be done in practice. This is immediately clear from an investigation of the terms of admission and the way in which they changed, seen through both legisla-tion and individual cases. For example, students were initially expected to pay the sum on entry,[90] as well as the sum of 2 florins 'per certa colazione' to the members of the Sapienza (later to be given to the chapel),[91] and at one stage a deposit for the furniture and items they received upon entering.[92] That these terms were on the stiff side is shown by a certain degree of relaxation which crept into the system. As early as 1434 some students were let in without prepayment, and their position was implic-itly regularised in a ruling which gave priority of choice of rooms to those who had paid up.[93] Exemp-tions were granted, sometimes involving delayed payment[94] or payment by instalments,[95] and some-times to the extent that the fee was partly or entirely waived.[96]

---

[89] CATONI, 'Il Comune di Siena e l'amministrazione della Sapienza', p. 122. Further reflections on this in BROGINI, 'La trasformazione', p. 124, quoting the same passage.

[90] *Conc.* 348, f. 17v, 10 Feb 1424 (= *Mis.* 1, f. 55r); any student who did not pay within two months of arrival was to lose his place. The provision is also listed in the late-fifteenth-century summary of the statutes of the Sapienza made for the Florentines in 1487; above, p. 27 n. 144.

[91] *Mis.* 1, f. 92v, 29 Oct 1451; ZDEKAUER, p. 105; and cf. *Conc.* 536, ff. 30v-31r, 12 Feb 1456.

[92] *Mis.* 1, f. 115r, 1491. From 1521 it sufficed to promise to return these goods on penalty of a maximum fine of 100 ducats (*Mis.* 1, f. 102r-v, 18 Nov).

[93] *Mis.* 1, f. 56r, 21 Oct. At the end of the fifteenth century the *Savi*'s complaints about the sorry state of the Sapienza include one about 'scolari intrati senza pagamento' (*Conc.* 2139, no. 104, f. 187r-v, n.d. but probably 1497; see below, p. 377 n. 132).

[94] For example Niccolò Jacopo de Griffis of Ferrara, who entered the Sapienza in 1456 and was given four months to pay (*Conc.* 536, ff. 30v-31r, 12 Feb).

[95] This appears to have been a late fifteenth-century innovation; examples in *Balìa* 33, ff. 44r and 84v, 5 Mar and 21 May 1485; *Sale* 23, ff. 92v and 93v, 24 Mar and 21 Apr 1496; *Sale* 24, ff. 164r, 13 Mar, 165r, 7 and 24 May 1498. In 1499 two students were admitted on the same day with different payment conditions (*Sale* 24, f. 171v, 15 and 19 Feb).

[96] E.g. the son of Benedetto da Volterra, a former rector of the Sapienza, was given seven free years in 1445 (*CG* 223, f. 78r-v, 14 Nov, and below, p. 323); in 1449 the commune petitioned the pope for the exemption of the fee of 'Dn.o Nico-lao francioso' (*Conc.* 503, f. 27v, 14 Dec; it is not made clear why this had to go to higher authority), and the same year the vice-rector of the *Studio*, Giovanni di Orlando de Sicilia, was effectively billeted on the Sapienza for six months without payment (*Conc.* 502, f. 15v, 20 Sept; the fact that this was free of charge is made explicit in *Conc.* 504, f. 54r, 24 Feb 1450). In 1493 the *Savi* reinstated a payment of four ducats despite the *Balìa*'s waiving of all fees for one student (*Studio* 2, f. 133r, 21 Feb). But the *Balìa* continued to make special cases; despite complaints that students were entering without paying (*Conc.* 2139, no. 104, Jan 1495), the *Savi* gave two students free places in 1496 on their instructions, one for a half period and one for the full period (*Sale* 23, ff 92v, 93r, 24 and 29 Mar). See also the emperor Frederick III's recommendation of Petrus Johel de Linsi in 1442 (below, p. 323) That there was a soft edge to the fee policy is also demonstrated by the deci-sion in 1456 that two *sapientini* who wanted to leave before their seven years were up could have a refund for the unused time (*Conc.* 540, f. 30r, 7 Oct), and by the petition of a grammar teacher, maestro Evangelista Riverio dall'Aquila, who of-fered to renounce his salary in exchange for a place in the Sapienza (*Conc.* 2309, no foliation, n.d.).

Table 6 – Known admissions to the Casa della Sapienza (first twenty-five years)

Year[1]	No. of admissions[2]	Cumulative 7-year total[3]	Law	Arts/Medicine	Italians	Ultramontanes	References
1416	20	20	17	3	18	2	*Conc.* 300, f. 40r; *Conc.* 304, f. 40r
1417	–	20	–	–	–	–	–
1418	12	32	1	5	12	–	*Conc.* 312, f. 20r; *Conc.* 314, f. 23v
1419	1	33	–	–	–	1	*Conc.* 323, f. 28v
1420	–	33	–	–	–	–	
1421	4	37	3	1	3	1	*Conc.* 330, f. 13v; *Conc.* 334, f. 9v
1422	–	37	–	–	–	–	
1423	12	29	7	3	4	1	*Conc.* 343, ff. 4v and 6r–v; *Conc.* 347, ff. 14r and 25v
1424	11	40	5	2	3	4	*Conc.* 348, f. 17v; *Conc.* 350, ff. 10v and 14v; *Conc.* 353, ff. 16v and 21r
1425	5	33	5	–	2	3	*Conc.* 358, ff. 12v and 24r; *Conc.* 359, ff. 34v and 49v
1426	3	35	3	–	3	–	*Conc.* 361, f. 15v
1427	10	45	7	2	7	2	*Conc.* 367, f. 4v; *Conc.* 370, f. 21v
1428	4	45	3	1	4	–	*Conc.* 372, ff. 6v and 35v; *Conc.* 374, f. 18r
1429	7	52	6	1	4	3	*Conc.* 377, f. 32v; *Conc.* 379, f. 22r; *Conc.* 380, f. 44v
1430	6	46	5	1	3	3	*Conc.* 383, f. 6r; *Conc.* 384, f. 37r; *Conc.* 387, f. 32v
1431	–	35	–	–	–	–	
1432	–	30	–	–	–	–	
1433	3	35	6	2	7	–	*Conc.* 405, f. 34r; *Conc.* 406, f. 37r; *Conc.* 407, f. 10v
1434	6	31	6	–	5	1	*Conc.* 410, f. 19r; *Conc.* 412, f. 58r; *Conc.* 413, f. 8v
1435	7	34	5	1	5	1	*Conc.* 415, ff. 10r and 29r; *Conc.* 417, f. 22r; *Conc.* 418, f. 15r; *Conc.* 419, f. 28v
1436	6	33	5	1	2	4	*Conc.* 424, f. 32r
1437	1	28	–	1	1	–	*Conc.* 429, f. 15r
1438	2	30	2	–	2	–	*Conc.* 434, f. 55v; *Conc.* 435, f. 19v
1439	11	41	9	2	3	2	*Conc.* 439, f. 54v; *Conc.* 440, ff. 17v and 20r; *Conc.* 441, f. 30r; *Conc.* 442, f. 32v; *Conc.* 443, f. 41r
1440	3	36	2	–	1	1	*Conc.* 444, f. 22r; *Conc.* 445, f. 35r; *Conc.* 449, f. 3r–v
Totals	139		97[4]	26[4]	89[5]	29[5]	

[1] The figures have been calculated for calendar rather than academic years since students were admitted at all stages of the year, usually with immediate effect.

[2] Figures include those granted a place at the first opportunity.

[3] This artificial statistic has been included to indicate what the student population of the Sapienza would have been if a) the surviving records represented a complete profile of admissions, and b) all students had remained for seven years. In 1441 there were thirty-eight students in the college (*CG* 221, ff. 21v–22r, 26 Jun), which is a clear indicator (unless a substantial number of students were staying for longer than seven years!) of missing evidence on a significant scale.

[4] In sixteen cases the discipline is not specified.

[5] In twenty-one cases the provenance is not specified. Of the ultramontanes, nine are Germans, seven Spaniards, four Portuguese, three Poles, two French and two Scots. It has not been possible to identify the provenance of the remaining two.

The main change to these original stipulations – which may or may not have had much to do with cost[97] – was the regularisation of shorter terms of residence. As has been seen, at the opening of the house students were admitted for six years, but in 1422, as that period came to an end for the original inmates, the period was extended to seven.[98] From an analysis of the (doubtless incomplete) figures it has been possible to compile of those admitted to the Sapienza in the first twenty-five years of its existence (Table 6), it is clear that from the earliest days the 'dropout rate' must have been significant,[99] and it was only a matter of time before the aspiration to a seven-year commitment began to weaken and the authorities started to admit students for shorter periods. There was, after all, a degree of tension between the seven-year principle and another requirement, namely that inmates should have already studied for a number of years.[100] The first example of shorter terms to have come to light is from 1440, when the *Concistoro* agreed to admit a student nominated by the count of Urbino, who would be entitled to stay for half of the usual period, paying *pro rata*.[101] In 1443 'Dns. Johannes Gigliachus de Francia' was admitted for six years (while paying the full fee),[102] and in 1467 Giovanni di Roberto degli Altoviti of Florence was admitted 'per mezzo tempo' on the recommendation of the Neapolitan orator.[103] The possibility was not just there for the well-recommended. From 1460 it became a regular feature,[104] and in 1462 eight out of nine applicants wanted to be admitted for a half-period.[105] In 1469 the majority of *sapientini*[106] were full-term, but there were complaints about the number of half-termers; the *Camarlengo* was instructed not to admit

---

[97] The German Peter Pront(?), a student in canon law, requested a place for half time in 1473 'essendo povaro homo e di bisogno sia aitato da li homini da bene' (*CG* 235, f. 20v, 21 Feb); and cf. the Portuguese case of 1463 referred to above (p. 308 n. 72). Martino di Pietro of Portugal, applying for a place in 1467, gave a different reason: 'Et pertanto havendo studiato circa ad sei anni in nel suo paese, et desiderando proficere et finire el suo studio ne le parti d'Italia...' (*CG* 232, f. 23v, 22 Oct). The proliferation of shorter-term ultramontane students and the insistence on their taking a degree in Siena suggest that this was a common motive.

[98] Above, p. 307 n. 55.

[99] In the first twenty-five years only three students are actually recorded as being given permission to leave early; Blasius de Narnia in 1426 (*Conc.* 361, f. 11v, 16 Mar; the Florentines had invited him to be *podestà*), an unnamed Portuguese student in 1435 (*Conc.* 418, f. 15r, 27 Sept; a quarter of his payment was however retained) and Antonio Gotto da Sicilia in 1437 (*Conc.* 428, f. 17v, 28 May). On the other hand one student who had left the Sapienza after five years of study was readmitted in 1433 for the rest of his time (*Conc.* 403, f. 48v, 24 Apr). There are cases of students not taking up places within the stipulated month and therefore forfeiting them (*Conc.* 415, f. 29r, 21 Apr 1435; three students are stripped of their places for this reason).

[100] This dates from 1422, when a minimum of three years was stipulated, soon altered to two years in the subject to be studied in the Sapienza, and subsequently changed again several times; see below, p. 319.

[101] *Conc.* 449, f. 3r-v, 2-3 Nov. The student was Piero de' Pegolotti of Verona; *Conc.* 1946, no. 18, 15 Sept 1440 (letter from Guidantonio da Montefeltro to the *Concistoro*).

[102] *Conc.* 464, f. 22v, 30 May.

[103] *CG* 231, f. 262v, 25 Mar, and see below, p. 322 n. 184.

[104] E.g. *CG* 228, f. 282r, 5 Sept (the first such admission for a while); *CG* 229, ff. 36v, 17 Mar, and 142v, 11 Dec 1461.

[105] *Balìa* 496, no. 18, 7 Mar (Angelo di Ser Luca of Piombino, recommended by Jacopo d'Appiano, *signore* of Piombino); *Conc.* 574, f. 22v, 26 May (and f. 54r, 29 Jun; Tommaso da Iesi); *CG* 229, f. 240r, 16 Jul (and *Conc.* 575, f. 16r and v, 14 and 15 Jul; Claudio de Burgundia, recommended by the cardinal of Arras); *CG* 229, f. 242r-v, 22 Jul (and *Conc.* 575, f. 22r-v, 21 Jul, and 33r-v, 1 Aug; 'Dominus Alvarus et Johannes Alfonsi de Regno Algarbie', recommended by cardinal Francesco Todeschini Piccolomini of Siena); *Conc.* 575, f. 31r, 30 Jul (the canonist Giovanni di Lorenzo da Roma – the only one to be admitted full time – also recommended by the cardinal of Siena); *Conc.* 575, f. 34v, 2 Aug and *Conc.* 576, f. 10r, 12 Sept (Pietro Parvo and Giovanni de Orliaco, recommended by the cardinal of Avignon). A ninth recommendation, by the cardinal of Bologna of an unnamed relative of his (*Conc.* 2003, no. 66, 20 May) may be identifiable with Tommaso da Iesi.

[106] The first mention I have found of this term is in *Sale* 24, f. 158v, 7 Nov 1497.

such students unless the *Consiglio del Popolo* ordered it.[107] In 1472 the *Consiglio del Popolo*'s monopoly over *mezzo tempo* admissions was reaffirmed, and it was stipulated that there was to be a blanket minimum fee of 30 florins.[108] By 1481 there are signs of a quota system – eight to ten members of the Sapienza could be half-termers at any moment[109] – and in the same year, in an opportunistic move, a group of five Germans were given half-term places in one batch.[110] Towards the end of the century there is evidence of yet more flexibility – more such entrants,[111] greater variety of lengths of stay[112] and of conditions, including the option of a second half-term,[113] or of returning to use up

---

[107] *CG* 232, f. 233r-v, 18 Feb. The complaints were not confined to this: 'Item acteso che li cam.o de la misericordia non observano li statuti nel ricievare li scolari ne la decta casa, Inperò che molti si ricievano in decta casa che secondo le nostre leggi non si possono ricievare, Et alcuni con mezo tempo alcuni co' famigli, alcuni che non danno la sicurità del doctorato…'. Any *camarlengo* found contravening these regulations would in future be admonished and have his name recorded in the *Libro della Balzanella*.

[108] *CG* 234, ff. 198v-199v, and *Mis.* 1, f. 101v, 25 Sept. The payment of two additional ducats, one to the *sacrestia* and one for *bombarde*, soon led to a form of inflation; sometimes one, sometimes the other was added to a base fee of 32 ducats (see *Conc.* 642, f. 16r-v, 3 Oct 1473; *Conc.* 645, f. 34v, 14 Apr 1474; *Conc.* 646, ff. 24v-25r, 3 Jun 1474; *Conc.* 647, f. 8r, 14 Jul 1474). The fee subsequently rose. In 1485 it was 36 ducats (*Balìa* 33, ff. 5v, 23 Mar, and 81r, 14 May, and *Balìa* 34, f. 30r, 7 Dec; cf. *Balìa* 37, f. 14r, 15 Jun 1492), and in 1495, 38 ducats (*Balìa* 40, f. 104v, 26 Dec). In 1518 it was back at 35 ducats (*Sale* 25, f. 81v, 1 Jul); in 1542 it was fixed at 40 ducats (*Studio* 110, f. 7r, 17 Feb 1542, published in MARRARA, *Lo Studio di Siena*, p. 296, and KOŠUTA, 'Documenti', p. 361).

[109] *CG* 238, ff. 238v-239r, 25 Sept, and 250v, 11 Nov.

[110] *CG* 238, f. 260r, 14 Dec. They were seduced by the prospect of more to come: 'Li vostri Servidori proveditori dello Studio con reverentia ricordano come passando di qua a questi giorni cinque scolari tedeschi e quali andavano a perugia, Et per li vostri Doctori col favore d'essi proveditori de lo studio si sonno facti fermare qui, Et desiderano essare messi ne la casa vostra de la sapientia per mezzo tempo, che considerato li temporali l'è paruto assai honore de la città: Et perche ne aspectano più loro compagni. Ricordarebbero che Infino a dieci più si potessero per essi Savi dello Studio mettare in essa casa connumerati essi cinque scolari tedeschi che certamente stimano essare utile et honore de la vostra città.' A few months later the *Consiglio del Popolo* was asked to give the place of one of these students, who 'li pare non esserli conforma e vorrebbe repatriare', to the brother of one of the others (*CG* 239, f. 25v, 29 Mar 1482; original petition *Conc.* 2139, no. 72, ff. 134r, 135v). On this episode see also above, p. 237 n. 50. On the phenomenon of student travel groups, see R. C. SCHWINGES, 'Studentische Kleingruppen im späten Mittelalter. Ein Beitrag zur Sozialgeschichte deutscher Universitäten', in *Politik, Gesellschaft, Geschichtsschreibung. Giessener Festgabe für František Graus zum 60. Geburtstag*, eds. H. Ludat and R. C. Schwinges. Beihefte zum Archiv für Kulturgeschichte, 18 (Cologne and Vienna, 1982), pp. 319-361; J. MIETHKE, 'Die Studenten', in *Unterwegssein im Spätmittelalter*. Zeitschrift für historische Forschung, Beiheft 1 (Berlin, 1985), pp. 49-70; and DENLEY, 'Communities within Communities', pp. 730-1 for further references.

[111] For example, 1489 saw four such admissions within a month, of two Germans and two Portuguese (*Balìa* 36, ff. 143v, 19 Jun, 148r, 26 Jun, and 155v, 13 Jul).

[112] In 1498 Mag. Cristoforo Astolfi of Spoleto was given a place for five and a half years (*Sale* 24, f. 162v, 21 Jan), and four others were given places for six years (ff. 164r, 13 Mar, Dns. Johannes Valascho, 164v, 29 Mar, Dns. Cesare M.i Cristofori de Fulignio, 165r, 24 Apr, Dns. Bernardinus [de Mendosis de Amelia: cf. *BCS*, *ms.* A.XI.12, f. 76r, and BONAFACCIA, 'La "Domus Sapientiae"', p. 117; he was placed on a waiting list] and loc. cit., 24 May, Dns. Henricus theutonicus), while another, Dns. Antonius de Mendosis de Amelia, was given the remaining three years and two months of a student who had left – suggesting that there was still a certain logic at work (f. 164v, 29 Mar). It appears to have been abandoned by 1540, when an unnamed German student was admitted 'da incominciarsi il tempo quel dì che comincia a mangiare in detta Casa intrando' (*Studio* 4, f 144v, 23 May, ed. KOŠUTA, 'Documenti', p. 380). The late fifteenth century sees the first examples of regulations being suspended to allow students to stay beyond their allotted seven years; two Germans were given an extra year at a cost of eleven ducats (*Sale* 24, ff. 168r, 3 Dec, the German Dns. Jacobus de ascetia and 169r, 14 Dec 1498, Johannes teutonicus, and see below, p. 320).

[113] On 11 Jul 1492 the *Balìa* gave places to two students (*Balìa* 37, f. 24v); 'Johannes Alvari' of Portugal, who had had a place for *mezzo tempo* three and a half years previously but had left after a year – he was allowed a second three-and-a-half-year term on payment of 30 ducats (he had entered on 13 Nov 1488; *BCS*, *ms.* A.XI.12, f. 52v; ZDEKAUER, doc. XXIII, p. 187, and BONAFACCIA, 'La "Domus Sapientiae"', p. 101, and see p. 257; *Not.* 694, f. 33r-v, ed. MINNUCCI, 'Documenti', doc. II-32, p. 99 [and see p. 270], however, suggests that he was in the Sapienza on 3 Jun); and 'Henricus Ienis [= Jena] de Sanxonia', who was to pay 36 ducats on entry and had until 11 November to pay the remaining 16 ducats for the full seven

unfinished time[114] – and by 1519 there is even a case of a Maestro Leonardo who was admitted for one year at the charge of one ducat per month.[115] When in 1525 the *Consiglio del Popolo* ruled out half-periods and reaffirmed that a seven-year stay was compulsory,[116] the applications to the Sapienza fell drastically and the *mezzo tempo* had to be reinstated.[117]

The transition to shorter terms appears to be an inevitable concomitant of the shift to fee-payers. The seven-year term was an ideal way of granting poor students the opportunity to go to university and to see a programme of study right through to completion. It was far less suitable for the kind of student who actually ended up in the Sapienza; the fashionable practice among students who went further afield than their nearest regional or official university was increasingly to 'shop around', and perhaps to do the 'academic grand tour'.[118] A shorter period of residence was much more suitable for this purpose. It also fitted better with the regulation that expected students to have completed some years of study before admission, and meant that effectively such students were coming in for the second part of their period of study – a feature that we can also see in the stipulation that *sapientini* were supposed to take their degree in Siena at the end of their stay. Three and a half years both offered a good deal and provided encouragement for mobile students to stay and to complete their studies in the city. But again, the issue should be looked at in terms of supply and demand. It is odd that the authorities still held out for seven years despite the fact that it seems not to have generated sufficient interest. In practice the *mezzo tempo*, which seems to be regarded as second best in the view of authorities, was much more popular. Full-term membership seems to have been upheld because it was a means of keeping something of the original aims of the enterprise – and perhaps of building a sense of collegiality and loyalty – while in practice the commercial and networking pressures to do otherwise proved irresistible. Actually, though, it is the compromise that in the event proves most characteristic.

By blending the long-term with the medium-term, the Sienese were also able to maximise demand and determine the proportions of the mix. Pressure on places appears – apart from the 1525-8 experiment with full-term admissions only – to have been relentless. From the start, the regulations about admission and the evidence of individual cases point to the continuous pressure of demand, which

---

years; if he failed to do so he would have three and a half years (not to be confused with 'Henricus Brystidde de Brunswick ex Sansonia', who appears as an entrant sometime between 15 Apr 1490 and 27 Sept 1492 in BCS, *ms.* A.XI.12, f. 59r; ZDEKAUER, doc. XXIII, p. 189, and BONAFACCIA, p. 108). In 1498 Martinus Luft was given a second half term (*Balìa* 43, f. 79r, 28 Feb. He was from Worms, and had entered on 27 Jun 1494; BCS, *ms.* A.XI.12, f. 67v; ZDEKAUER, doc. XXIII, p. 189, and BONAFACCIA, p. 110). A similar case is that of the Portuguese Martino Lópes Lobo in 1538 (*Studio* 4, f. 116r, 6 Mar, ed. KOŠUTA, 'Documenti', doc. VI, p. 378).

[114] This was conceded to Stefano Macri at the behest of the cardinal of Siena (*Sale* 24, f. 158v, 7 Nov 1497; on Macri cf. also *Not.* 694, f. 33r-v, 3 Jun 1492, ed. MINNUCCI, 'Documenti', doc. II-32, p. 98 [and see p. 310], and above, p. 285), and to the French student Benedetto who, like Macri, had left the Sapienza because of the outbreak of plague (f. 160r, 29 Dec 1497).

[115] *Studio* 3, f. 13v, 1519; he was obliged to take his degree that year. In the same year another student was admitted *per mezzo tempo* for 24 ducats (*Studio* 3, f. 2v, 10 Jan). In 1520 a student was admitted for three months (at one ducat per month) after which he got a place *per mezzo tempo* for 31 ducats (*Studio* 3, f. 21r, 1520).

[116] *CG* 242, f. 32r-v, 28 Jul.

[117] *CG* 243, ff. 11v-12r, 1 Dec 1528: 'doppo, che era stata innovata la deliberazione...non si trovava chi ci volesse tornare per essere troppo longo'. Only three months earlier, however, the *Savi* were still trying to get the seven-year rule enforced (*Studio* 260, no foliation, 13 Sept).

[118] Shorter terms also crept in at the Collegio Gregoriano at Perugia, where, in contrast to Siena, the authorities clamped down on the practice; Biblioteca Comunale Augusta di Perugia, *ms.* 1239, f. 45r-v, 29 Sept 1446, eds. SEBASTIANI, 'Il collegio universitario', appendix III, pp. 334-7 (and see 81-2), and ANGELETTI and BERTINI, *La Sapienza Vecchia*, pp. 433-4.

regularly outstripped the number of vacancies. Despite the plans of 1404 for forty places,[119] when the project was revived in February 1415 it was for twenty students.[120] This was raised in August to thirty,[121] and when the Sapienza opened in February 1416 it was officially to thirty students.[122] Since these places were all filled within two years, it is not surprising that by 1420 there was already a number of prospective applicants who could not be accommodated, and the authorities were trying to quash the practice of reservation of future places, because with such a waiting list 'si tolle la speranza a molti che verebbero ad stare a Siena con animo e intenzione di potere intrare nella detta casa.'[123] The maximum of thirty was stipulated again in 1441, when the *Concistoro* was told that there were forty-three students in the house, and that this was a major reason for its financial difficulties;[124] yet the authorities themselves seem to have been keeping up the pressure on places, for in 1442 the *Consiglio del Popolo*, repeating the quota, simultaneously resolved to choose three scholars for the first three vacancies to arise, suspending the ban on waiting lists,[125] and later that year one student was in fact placed in the Sapienza at the request of the emperor, despite the overcrowding.[126] In 1446 there were again forty-three students in the college,[127] and the thirty-place limit was repeated in 1447 and 1448.[128] Financial considerations of a more suspect kind were clearly behind a similar packing of the building in 1455, when the *Concistoro* ordered the *Savi* to choose and admit ten scholars for the full period; of their entrance fees, 200 ducats were to be loaned to the *Camarlengo di Biccherna*.[129] Reforms of Sep-

---

[119] Above, p. 304 n. 33.

[120] Above, p. 305 n. 42.

[121] Above, p. 305 n. 43.

[122] See p. 305 n. 44 above.

[123] *CG* 209, f. 28r, 9 Mar; *Statuti* 41, f. 246v, and *Statuti* 47, f. 245v. The practice of allocating places in advance nonetheless continued; see *Conc.* 372, f. 35v, 20 Apr 1428 (Dominus Paulus Ser Simonis Pauli de Florentia; cf. p. 237 n. 48 above); *Conc.* 379, f. 22r, 13 Jun 1429 (Dominus Henricus teutonicus); *Conc.* 380, f. 44r, 26 Aug 1429 (four students, to be admitted in order; Dominus Johannes de rufaldis de trapani de cicilia, Dominus Martinus? teutonicus, Dominus Pietrus guilelmi de catelonia and Dominus cristoforus de sermona); *Conc.* 412, f. 58r, 21 Oct 1434 (three students, Dominus Malatesta de Cattaneis de Burgo, Dominus Jacobus de Amandola and Dominus Matheus catelanus, were to be admitted, but there were only two available places; they would be ranked by scrutiny 'in presenti circulo' and the third would have to wait for the first available place. The outcome of the scrutiny is not known, but Malatesta certainly did enter the college and eventually became its rector; below, p. 343); *Conc.* 463, ff. 31v-32v, 28 Mar 1443 (Dominus Valerius Jacobi simonelli[?] de urbeveteri); *Conc.* 464, f. 22v, 30 May 1443 (Dominus Johannes Gigliachi de Francia, on whom see also below, p. 352).

[124] *Mis.* 1, ff. 87v-88r, *CG* 220, ff. 223v-224r, 3 Feb; cf. *CG* 221, ff. 21v-22r, 26 Jun 1441 (by which time the number had fallen to thirty-eight). The biographer of Angelo Geraldini, recording his entry in the house in 1436, describes it as having forty places; H. PETER, *Die Vita Angeli Geraldini des Antonio Geraldini. Biographie eines Kurienbischofs und Diplomaten des Quattrocento. Text und Untersuchungen* (Frankfurt-am-Main and New York, etc., 1993), p. 177. It is questionable, however, whether this can be taken as an accurate description of the Sapienza at the time; the entrance fee is given as 60 'aureos', and the college is described as for law students.

[125] *CG* 221, f. 144v, 5 Oct (*Conc.* 460, f. 25v, 30 Sept); two German students in 'artium liberalium', Johannes Cessor (Giesser) and Mag. Jacobus Sencho (Schrenk), both from Munich, were chosen on 12 Nov (f. 154v); the fuller record of the *Concistoro*, resolving to put the proposal to the *Consiglio del Popolo*, describes them as students of arts and medicine, and states that these admissions were to be over and above the ones resolved in September, and that they were to be made despite the fact that these students had not yet been in Siena for the minimum one year, and despite their ages (*Conc.* 461, f. 6v). For the recommendations of these two by the emperor, see below, p. 321 n. 181.

[126] Dns. Petrus Johel de Linsi; see below, p. 323.

[127] *Mis.* 1, f. 88v, 29 Dec.

[128] *CG* 223, f. 234v, *Mis.* 1, f. 60v, 13 Mar 1447 (if more were admitted the notary was to be punished); *Mis.* 1, f. 61v, 22 Nov 1448.

[129] *Conc.* 530, ff. 27v, 18 Jan, 71r-v, 12 Feb; and see below, p. 375.

tember 1456 show the extent to which things had got out of hand; since 'nella decta Casa de la Sapientia al presente sonno molti scholari entrati contro la forma degli statuti, et ordinamenti dessa, cioè
chi per mezo tempo, chi sotto nome di cherico, et chi di fameglio', there was to be a purge of all ille-
gals within fifteen days.[130] A month later, two students who had paid for *mezzo tempo* in good faith,
but who had now been thrown out, were given a choice between the rest of their time in the Sapienza
and a refund.[131] But in December of that year, contentious admissions were still occurring, apparently
for the same reasons as before; the *Balìa* ordered the admission of another four students, and authorised the *Tre sopra la Moneta* to enforce their reception.[132]

The pressure on places continued for much of the late fifteenth century. In 1460 the *Concistoro*
directed that the 52-ducat admission fee of Antonio di Maestro Matteo da Pescia be spent 'in acta-
mine dicte domus et maxime in construendo de novo plures cameras'.[133] In 1469 there was again a
waiting list; the brothers Giovanni and Soldano di Ser Jacopo di Ser Soldano da Piombino were giv-
en a single room and promised a second as soon as one became free.[134] More than three years later
they were still waiting.[135] In 1474-5 there were forty-seven students in the Sapienza,[136] and there
were overspill facilities; 'case nuovamente fatte nella Strada di S. Antonio' were used to house three
Roman students who had been admitted when there were no places for them.[137] In a deliberation of
the *Savi dello Studio* that can probably be dated around the same year, the officials proposed to convert one of the superfluous teaching rooms for residence.[138] Pressure on space clearly continued to be
an issue,[139] and may have spawned the plans for a new, rebuilt college, discussed below; the autumn
of 1481, the period in which the project was first mooted, saw the admission of twenty-eight students in two batches.[140] The consequences of this pressure from the authorities to admit more students than there were places are spelt out in documents of the 1490s. 1492 – the year in which the

---

[130] *CG* 227, f. 241r, and *Mis.* 1, f. 93r, 10 Sept (also *Conc.* 539, ff. 59r-60r, 24 Aug).

[131] *Conc.* 540, f. 30r, 7 Oct; *CG* 227, ff. 250v-251r, 8 Oct; *Conc.* 2138, no. 36, f. 55r. They were Giovanni di Pietro
Balle of Perpignan and Antonio di Ser Carluccio from Naples.

[132] *Balìa* 1, ff. 90r, 10 Dec, and 94v-95r, 12 Dec (also *Balìa* 1, f. 95r).

[133] *Conc.* 564, f. 14v, 26 Sept. On the pressure on space see also MINNUCCI, 'Documenti', pp. 30-1 and 'La vita nel collegio', pp. 26-7.

[134] *Conc.* 614, f. 13r, 19 Jan.

[135] Petition of their father, *Conc.* 2024, no. 18, 25 Nov 1470, and of Jacopo d'Appiano, *signore* of Piombino, *Conc.*
2028, no. 28, 1 May 1472. Soldano was found in 1474 to have appropriated a room without permission and ordered to return the keys (*Studio* 2, f. 12v, 7 Feb 1474, and cf. f. 35r, 2 Dec 1475). Giovanni became vice-rector of the *Studio* (*Conc.*
651, f. 45v, 30 Apr 1475), and appears to have gone on to make a career; MINNUCCI, 'Documenti', pp. 26-7 and 259.

[136] *Not.* 694, f. 2ra-rb, ed. MINNUCCI, 'Documenti', doc. II-34, pp. 100-1 (and see p. 27). He dates it by careful comparison with the names on the 'admissions register' of BCS, *ms.* A.XI.12 as published by ZDEKAUER, doc. XXIII, pp. 180-90.

[137] *Studio* 2, ff. 18v, 3 Nov 1474, 22v-23r, 4 Jan 1475; MINNUCCI, 'Documenti', p. 28 n. 62 (and cf. *Not.* 694, f. 23v, 3
Dec, no year, ed. IBID., doc. II-50, p. 121); ZDEKAUER, pp. 104-5. That this was a holding stage is clear from the fact that
these students entered the college proper on 13 April; *Studio* 2, f. 25r (and cf. 29v, 5 Jun? 1475, where two of them are
named as Mag. Bartolomeo de la Mandola and Dns. Johannes de Argentina; on the latter see below, pp. 337 and 348 n. 85).

[138] *Not.* 694, f. 4r, n.d., ed MINNUCCI, 'Documenti', pp. 101-2. It is not clear whether the conversion was carried out.
On the relationship of teaching rooms to residence, see below, Chapter IV.5.

[139] Two Spanish students were put on a waiting list in 1475 (*Conc.* 544, f. 13r, 16 Nov), two Italians in 1476 (*Conc.*
661, f. 33r, 31 Dec).

[140] *Conc.* 690, f. 39r, 23 Oct, and *Conc.* 691, f. 41r, 31 Dec 1481. That there was a shortage of space is again evidenced
by the provisional nature of the admission of three German students, Dns. Federichus chuzer, Dns. Georgius chreuz and
Dns. Urbanus vitore, in April 1484 (*Balìa* 31, f. 90r-v, 9 Apr), and a fourth, Dns. Massimianus, in May (*Balìa* 32, f. 8r, 24
May). On the new building see below, pp. 388 *seq*.

plans for a new Sapienza were revived – saw dramatic growth; forty-seven students are known to have sworn the oath on 3 June,[141] but over the following five months, fourteen new students were admitted.[142] A report by the *Savi dello Studio*, probably in January 1497, highlighted a financial crisis due at least partly to overcrowding; students had entered without paying, there were seventy mouths to feed, the harvest had been poor, and the *Savi* were having to chip in with their own funds. The *Savi* proposed a return to the limit of thirty students.[143] The *Balìa* recognised the severity of the crisis and appointed a commission to sell some of the Sapienza's property, but it only decided to reduce the number of students to forty,[144] and later in the year was again putting fresh students into the college.[145] The quota itself was only raised formally to forty in 1542,[146] but clearly the numbers exceeded the limit on many occasions previous to that.

If the number of students in the Sapienza was a factor with which the authorities allowed themselves considerable leeway, often to the detriment of order and the finances of the house, other regulations governing the admission of students often had a similar fate; and again, the frequency with which they had to be repeated, and with which abuses were dealt with (or, not uncommonly, allowed to continue) are evidence of this. A minimum age for entry in the Sapienza was not stipulated in the initial regulations,[147] but an attempt was made to establish it in 1418 as twenty.[148] The measure was repeated in 1441, 1448 and 1456.[149] In 1477 it was decided to evict 'tutti quelli, che fussero minori di anni venti' (their presence may have had something to do with a recent rector's alleged sexual inclinations).[150] Although the initial requirement (1415) that entrants should be 'proximi ad gradum doctoratus'[151] was soon abandoned in favour of longer periods of residence for stu-

---

[141] *Not.* 694, f. 33r-v, ed. MINNUCCI, 'Documenti', doc. II-32, pp. 98-99, and see pp. 27-9.

[142] *Balìa* 37, ff. 61r, 13 Jun, 14r, 15 Jun, 15r, 23 Jun, 18r, 30 Jun, 24v, 11 Jul (two students), 41r, 7 Aug, 67v, 12 Sept (two students), 70r, 19 Sept, 89r, 20 Oct, 92v and 93v, 29 Oct (three students).

[143] *Conc.* 2139, no. 104, f. 187r-v. The dating is suggested by comparison with the *Balìa*'s deliberation of 8 Feb, which is clearly a response to this report (the list of properties to be sold is identical). Cf. also nos. 105, f. 192r, and 106, f. 194r, n.d. On this crisis see below, p. 377.

[144] *Balìa* 41, f. 103v, 8 Feb.

[145] *Balìa* 41, f. 242v, 30 Oct, and 43, f. 12r, 30 Nov. We cannot of course be sure that this was not facilitated by turnover. However, the following year there was again a waiting list (*Sale* 24, f. 165r, 24 Apr 1498).

[146] *Studio* 110, f. 7r, 17 Feb, ed. MARRARA, *Lo Studio di Siena*, p. 296, and KOŠUTA, 'Documenti', doc. IV, p. 361. In June of that year the *Savi* reported that 'nela decta Casa ci si truovano circha ottanta boche'; *CG* 244, ff. 227v-230r, 25 Jun, ed. KOŠUTA, 'Documenti', doc. XVI-2, p. 459. WEIGLE, *Die Matrikel der Deutschen Nation in Siena*, stated in his description of BCS, *ms.* A.XI.12 (p. 24) that in 1546 the college had forty-eight rooms, some with more than one occupant. I have been unable to ascertain the source of this statement.

[147] Following those of the Collegio Gregoriano at Perugia (see below, pp. 325-30), the Sienese 'ordini' merely state that 'se alcuno fosse recevuto troppo iovinetto el quale scialacquasse desutelmente la sua pecunia, è disposto che prima sia admonito a la volonta del rectore' (*Mis.* 1, f. 49r, ed. CATONI, 'Genesi', p. 181). On these regulations see below, Chapter IV.2.2.

[148] *Conc.* 2113, f. 127v (new foliation), 19 Aug, with the marginal annotation 'suspendatur de mandato dominorum'; cf. *CG* 478, f. 71v; see above, p. 306 n. 50. CATONI, 'Genesi', p. 171 n. 73, pointed out that this was based on the statutes of the Collegio Gregoriano at Bologna.

[149] *Conc.* 450, f. 33r, 2 Feb, *Mis.* 1, ff. 87v-88r, *CG* 220, f. 232r, 3 Feb 1441; *Conc.* 497, f. 11r, 15 Nov, *Mis.* 1, f. 61v, *CG* 224, f. 187v, 22 Nov 1448; *Mis.* 1, f. 94v, *CG* 227, f. 242r, 10 Sept 1456. Angelo Geraldini was fourteen when he entered the Sapienza in 1436; J. PETERSOHN, *Ein Diplomat des Quattrocento. Angelo Geraldini (1422-86)* (Tübingen, 1985), p. 25; PETER, *Die Vita Angeli Geraldini*, p. 177.

[150] *Studio* 2, f. 54v, 7 Mar. For accusations against the rector see ZDEKAUER, doc. XXI, pp. 176-8.

[151] 12 Aug; as p. 306 n. 49 above.

dents,[152] it was still necessary that they had some experience. The first set of regulations governing the college provide for entrants to be examined in grammar 'a li scolari',[153] but no more is heard of this. In 1422, three years' study was initially stipulated, though later that year this was changed to a requirement of proof that the candidate had studied for two years in the subject in which they were intending to study while in the Sapienza.[154] In 1441, one year's previous study in Siena was required,[155] and in 1448 two years' study, of which one had to have been in Siena.[156] The student had to declare by public instrument that he satisfied these and the other requirements.[157]

Once accepted, the student faced further conditions. He had to promise not to leave in order to study elsewhere; if it was shown that he had done so he could not return.[158] Indeed, he had to ask permission to leave for any reason, and the only motive for which unauthorised leave could be validated retrospectively was plague in the city.[159] No substitution, exchange or selling of places was allowed,[160] though this was sometimes waived,[161] and there is even one case, in 1493, of a student being permitted to sell two of his five remaining years in the house.[162] As has been seen, no student of the Sapienza could hold a lectureship,[163] though this too was occasionally breached.[164] At the completion of his degree the student had one month in which to depart,[165] unless he decided to take another degree within the norms of academic progression (i.e. arts graduands could take medicine, civilians could take canon law and canonists civil law, but no other permutations were allowed).[166] Yet here too there were fre-

---

[152] But see the case of a student in arts who in 1443 was to be admitted to the Sapienza as soon as he had taken his degree (*Conc.* 465, f. 30r, 26 Aug 1443).

[153] *Mis.* 1, f. 49r, ed. Catoni, 'Genesi', p. 181.

[154] *Conc.* 338, f. 17r, 25 May, and *Mis.* 1, ff. 53r-54v, 14 Dec, ed. Zdekauer, doc. XIII, pp. 161-2 (on which see above, p. 306 n. 55), and cf. pp. 96-7.

[155] See p. 316 n. 124 above.

[156] *Mis.* 1, f. 61v, 22 Nov.

[157] Loc. cit.

[158] See the cases of Gaspar Turiglia and Bartolomeo di Ser Giovanni Ciosi da Pistoia, below, p. 338 and p. 320 n. 173 respectively.

[159] An example of such retrospective permission is in *Studio* 2, ff. 73r, 27 Apr, 75v, 13 Jul 1481. Sometimes such permission is given in advance, in the event of plague (*Balìa* 1, f. 95v, 13 Dec 1456; *Balìa* 4, f. 14v, 2 May 1457; *Balìa* 6, f. 147r, 1 Feb 1458). The authorities often made arrangements for *sapientini* during plague epidemics; in the epidemic of 1449 students from the Sapienza who followed the movements of the *Studio* were to receive 4 *lire* each from the *Camarlengo* for food (*Conc.* 498, f. 18v, 24 Jan), and in the plague of 1530 the *sapientini* were allowed to leave and would receive food subsidies if they stayed in the town; one was even given a subsidy for living in the Val di Strove (*Studio* 3, f. 80v, 10 Jun).

[160] *Mis.* 1, f. 62r, 22 Nov 1448; and cf. *Conc.* 2310, no foliation, n.d. (see above, p. 308 n. 71), which alleges that 'spesse volte li scolari vendono i loro luoghi segretamente ad altri'. The prohibition on the sale of places was repeated in 1497 (*Sale* 24, f. 152v, 9 Feb).

[161] Cf. p. 314 n. 110 above; and *Sale* 24, ff. 154r, 15 Mar 1497, 167r, 30 Oct 1498. One interesting suspension of the rule occurred in 1485; 'Dns. Theodericus discov alamannus' was permitted to take the place of another student, Dns. Eustachius, provided the latter remained in Siena (*Balìa* 33, f. 39v, 28 Feb). It appears that anything to increase the number of foreign students in Siena was considered acceptable.

[162] *Studio* 2, f. 136v, 19 Jun 1493. In 1542 the sale of rooms was allowed in some circumstances (*Studio* 110, f. 11r, 27 Apr, *ed.* Košuta, 'Documenti', doc. IV, pp. 364-5).

[163] *Conc.* 349, f. 14r, 24 Mar 1424; a *condotta* in philosophy is given to Mag. Giovanni di Martino on condition that he 'exeat de domo sapientie et nichil recipiat a domo predicta'.

[164] See above, p. 284.

[165] The reason given for the removal of a *sapientino* in 1483 (*Sale* 21, f. 212v, 22 Dec).

[166] *CG* 210, f. 61r; *Mis.* 1, f. 54r, 18 Aug 1423. This should be seen in the context of the quota system whereby only five out of the thirty in the Sapienza could be students of arts. Above, p. 307. The Collegio Engleschi, a Paduan college for student of arts and medicine, had five-year terms; Veronese Ceseracciu, 'Il Collegio Engleschi'.

quent breaches, as is shown by the need for a resolution by the *Consiglio del Popolo* in 1476 that the *Savi* had no power to extend the stay of any student after his time was up.[167] By the 1490s payment for an extra year was not unusual.[168]

The condition about which the authorities were most exercised was that students admitted to the Sapienza had to promise to take a degree in Siena.[169] As has been seen, this could be a very costly operation in Italian universities, and one which in all probability only a minority undertook.[170] The insistence on this commitment was therefore significant. Failure to honour this obligation was to lead to a fine of 50 florins,[171] or, in practice, confiscation of the student's property.[172] Again we encounter the usual difficulty of lack of documentation in the fifteenth century – there are few surviving degree certificates, and so it is impossible to say how strictly this was enforced – but the *Savi* were certainly on the lookout for such abuse, frequently making individual students find a guarantor who would pay the fine.[173] Unlike some of the regulations, it does not seem that attempts to enforce this were ever abandoned, though at one stage it was apparently softened to the stipulation that if the student took a degree it should be in Siena.[174] And again, Siena's lack of interest in poor students is reflected in the fact that it is most unusual for a college not to concede a number of free degrees to its poorer members.[175]

---

[167] *Mis.* 1, f. 103r, 3 Apr 1476. On the reluctance of some students to depart, ZDEKAUER, p. 105. Here too some flexibility was introduced in 1542 (*Studio* 110, f. 11r, 27 Apr, ed. KOŠUTA, 'Documenti', doc. IV, pp. 364-5).

[168] *Sale* 24, ff. 158v, 7 Nov 1497, 168r, 3 Dec 1498, 169r, 14 Dec 1498 (Stefano Macri; cf. p. 285 above).

[169] *Mis.* 1, f. 103v, 4 Apr 1476; *Conc.* 657, f. 31r-v, 4 Apr 1476, ed. FERRERI, doc. 9, p. 9.

[170] Above, pp. 288-9.

[171] The measure of 1422, as above, n. 55.

[172] *Mis.* 1, f. 103v, 4 Apr, and *Studio* 2, f. 38r, 12 Jan 1476.

[173] This was applied to Dns. Petrus de Francia in 1459 (*Conc.* 559, f. 16r, 20 Nov), and generally to all future entrants in 1469 (*CG* 232, f. 233r-v, 18 Feb); cf. *Studio* 2, ff. 38r, 12 Jan 1476, 52r, 4 Jan 1477, 75v-82v *passim*, 1481, 96r, 29 Nov 1483, 98v, 11 Mar 1484, 119v, Jan 1487, and 122v, 13 Jan 1488. On the other hand the condition had been waived earlier on when foreign students were obviously having difficulty in finding guarantors; it was determined that an oath on the sacraments would suffice (*Conc.* 345, f. 18r, 9 Aug 1423). The best documented case of a student who fell foul of this regulation is that of Bartolomeo di Ser Giovanni Ciosi da Pistoia. In 1474, after seven years in the college, he was forced to leave at the request of the Florentine authorities; he was threatened with a fine of 44 large ducats if he did not take his degree (*Studio* 2, f. 11r, 19 Jan). He left in June that year, promising to return and take his degree within three years, with the Sienese Ventura di Antonio Venturi as guarantor to the tune of 40 gold ducats (*Not.* 694, f. 20r, 8 Jun, ed. MINNUCCI, 'Documenti', doc. II-7, pp. 82-3), but he never returned, taking his degree indeed three years later, but in Pisa. VERDE, *Lo Studio fiorentino*, III.1, p. 133; MINNUCCI, 'Documenti', pp. 235, 35 n. 90, and cf. IDEM, 'La vita nel Collegio della Sapienza di Siena durante la seconda metà del XV secolo', in *I Collegi universitari in Europa*, pp. 23-32 (p. 27).

[174] The ten scholars to be admitted in October 1481 merely had to provide a guarantor 'de non doctorando se nisi in studio senensi' (*Conc.* 690, f. 39r, 23 Oct). A similar practice was adopted in Bologna in 1488, when a papal bull required students at four colleges, the Spanish College, the Ancarano, the Fieschi and the Reggiano, to swear not to take a degree elsewhere (TROMBETTI BUDRIESI, 'L'esame di laurea', pp. 169-70 n. 86). The Collegio Sacco in Pavia had what might be considered more realistic provisions; in 1492 it was decided that any student who had resided in the college for four years was not allowed to take his degree elsewhere (ZANETTI, 'Il primo collegio', p. 800).

[175] The Collegio di Spagna also helped students who could not otherwise afford it to take their degree (MARTI, *The Spanish College*, pp. 164-8), as apparently did the two Sapienze at Perugia (ERMINI, *Storia*, I, p. 488). The Collegio Castiglioni of Pavia won the privilege of free degrees for its students in 1462; A. L. VISINTIN, 'Il più significativo precedente del collegio Ghislieri: il collegio universitario Castiglioni (1429-1803)', in M. BENDISCIOLI *et al.*, *Il Collegio Universitario Ghislieri di Pavia* (Milan, 1966-70), 1, pp. 51-89 (p. 63 n. 52), and ROSSO, 'Presenze studentesche e collegi pavesi', p. 30; and the two Roman colleges, the Capranica and the Nardini, had similar privileges by 1525 (ESPOSITO, 'Le "Sapientie" romane', p. 40). On the Europe-wide practice of waiving graduation fees for poor students cf. PAQUET, 'Recherches sur l'universitaire "pauvre"', pp. 314-6.

All these regulations were designed to ensure a fair, stable and regular turnover of students. Yet the difficulty of enforcement was never overcome. Even the elaborate system of fines and other punishments, operating through the inevitable secret denunciations,[176] could not root out abuse when the chief offenders were often the authorities themselves, eager to maximise the potential of the Sapienza for diplomatic advantage. The process of recommendation, well illustrated by Zdekauer, Catoni and Minnucci,[177] worked directly against the order desired by the *Savi*, and the measure of 1420 prohibiting reservation of places was undermined by the actions of the highest bodies of the state.[178] Recommendations of individual students for places began to reach the authorities even before the college was opened,[179] and there was a steady stream of them in the first years, mostly of law students, and particularly from the civic authorities of other towns.[180] At that stage few of them appear to have been successful. In time, however, the standing of recommenders rises, and with that, unsurprisingly, so does the success rate. Over the fifteenth century supporters of supplicants for Sapienza places included an emperor,[181] a king,[182] several cardinals,[183] major

---

[176] *Mis.* 1, ff. 93r-95v, 10 Sept 1456 (93v-94r).

[177] ZDEKAUER, pp. 42-4, 100; CATONI, 'Genesi', p. 175 n. 87, and MINNUCCI, 'Documenti', esp. pp. 26-8; 'Il Collegio della Sapienza', pp. 24-9; 'La Casa della Sapienza', pp. 361 *seq.*

[178] See p. 316 n. 123 above.

[179] The earliest appears to be a letter from the authorities of Montefiascone, 'audito quod in civitate vestra erecta est domus sapientie', recommending Bartolomeo Stefani, currently studying in Bologna (*Conc.* 2305, fasc. 10, no. 18, 13 Nov; no year given, but from the indiction and the context dateable to 1415). No student of this name is recorded among the admissions of the early years.

[180] For example, in 1416 the priors of Spoleto recommended Matteo di Maestro Tommaso, a law student (*Conc.* 1887, no. 20, 15 May – filed in the Archivio di Stato as 1415, but the indiction shows it to be 1416); the recommendation was successful (reply in *Conc.* 1613, f. 68r, 27 May 1416; he was among the second batch of entrants, *Conc.* 204, f. 40r, 7 Oct 1416). On 20 Apr 1417 Braccio di Fortebraccio recommended Ser Jacopo di Montone, a student in civil law (*Conc.* 1891, no. 12); the *Concistoro* replied that he would be accepted when a place became available (*Conc.* 1614, f. 73v, 3 May. There is no indication in the sources that the student was eventually admitted, and the same is true of a further nominee of Braccio's, Antonio di Maestro Giovanni da Montemorello, *Conc.* 1901, no. 37, 29 Jun 1422). On 25 Jul 1417 the cardinal of S. Angelo, Pedro Fonseca, wrote to recommend the Roman Antonio de Casarellis, another student of law (*Conc.* 1891, no. 60); there is no evidence that he was put in, any more than was Crescimbene, a poor law student recommended by the *Conservatores pacis* of Orvieto (*Conc.* 1893, no. 70, 13 Sept 1418). The same is true of Bartolomeo di Maestro Antonio, recommended by the Pistoiese in 1422 (ASS, *ms.* C.19, recorded as in *filza* 21) and of the Genoese student Luca Stella with three letters of recommendation in 1422 (above, p. 310). A string of recommendations from other Tuscan towns in 1433 (Giovanni di Ser Donato, recommended by the Aretines, *Conc.* 1931, no. 1, 1 Oct; Bello di Goro, recommended by the Pistoiese, *Conc.* 1931, no. 20, 24 Oct, and cf. no. 13, 15 Oct, and two Florentine protégés, Ricciardo de' Ricciardi of Pistoia, *Conc.* 1930, no. 6, 26 Aug, and Domenico Buzichini da San Gimignano, *Conc.* 1930, no. 85, 16 Sept) also appear to have had no successful outcome; none of these names appear among the lists of those admitted (*Conc.* 406, f. 37v, 30 Oct, *Conc.* 407, f. 10v, 18 Nov).

[181] The emperor Frederick III recommended three German students for the Sapienza, all of whom were admitted, in 1442 (*Conc.* 461, ff. 4v, 6 Nov, 6v, 8 Nov, and 27r-v, 25 Nov; cf. *CG* 221, f. 154v [new foliation], 12 Nov, and 161r, 3 Dec; see also CATONI, 'Genesi', p. 175 n. 87). The letters are in *Conc.* 2177, no foliation, 8 Nov (two letters, recommending 'Mag.ro Johanne Giesser de Monaco and M.ro Jac.o Screncho Alamanie de Monacho, artium liberalium studentibus'; cf. *Conc.* 1952, no. 99, date unclear, on behalf of the latter). For the recommendation of the third student, Petrus de linsi, see below, p. 323 and n. 187).

[182] In 1424 the king of Aragon recommended Maestro Pietro di Stefano, student of arts and medicine; the *Concistoro* was happy to oblige him (*Conc.* 348, f. 17v, 10 Feb). In 1453 Afonso V of Portugal recommended Nuño Consalvi, student of civil law (*Conc.* 1976, no. 86, 7 Feb; cf. A. LISINI, *Sala della mostra nell'Archivio di Stato in Siena* [Siena 1889 edn.], p. 12).

[183] The cardinal of S. Angelo recommended a student in 1417 (above, n. 180); the cardinal of S. Ciriaco (Dionysius Széch, archbishop of Esztergom) recommended Guido de Francia in 1440 (*Conc.* 444, f. 22r, 27 Jan 1440; CATONI, 'Genesi',

powers and other eminent individuals.[184]

The practice of recommendation was not confined to outsiders, or to admission. It was not unknown for teachers to recommend or even to bargain for the right to nominate students.[185] One such, Giovanni Battista Caccialupi, succeeded in obtaining a place for his nephew.[186] As well as engineering the admission of a candidate, patrons might well secure preferential treatment in other respects; and the

[184] p. 175 n. 87); Cardinal Domenico Capranica recommended a student from Forlì in 1441 (*Studio* 19, no foliation, 21 Apr). 1462 saw a cluster of such recommendations (see above, p. 313 n. 105), as did 1466; two Pistoiese students, the civilian 'Dnus Guido Johannis ser Pieri de Forteguerris', and the canonist 'Dns. Simon Antonii Talini de Lanciano' were admitted for *mezzo tempo* on the recommendation of a relative of the former, Niccolò Forteguerri, the cardinal of Teano (*Conc.* 598, ff. 27v, 28v, 1 and 2 Jun; and cf. *CG* 231, f. 148r, and *Conc.* 2182, no foliation, 1 Jun. Forteguerri was himself a Sienese graduate; A. Esposito, 'Forteguerri, Niccolò', *DBI*, 49 [1997], pp. 156-9 [p. 156]); Jacopo Mariani of Fermo, student in civil law, was given a place *pro medietate temporis* at the request of the cardinal of Siena, Francesco Todeschini Piccolomini (*Dipl., Riformagioni*, 18 Jul 1466; cf. *CG* 231, f. 170v, *Conc.* 599, f. 10r, 9 Jul, and *Conc.* 2182, no foliation); and Angelo Capranica, cardinal of Rieti, successfully recommended Messer Bartolomeo of Milan for *mezzo tempo* in September of that year (*Conc.* 2014, no. 5, 15 Sept; approved in *Conc.* 600, f. 25r, and *Conc.* 2182, no foliation, 1 Oct), and another, Johannes de Petronibus de Nepi, also for *mezzo tempo*, the following spring (*Conc.* 2015, nos. 23, 15 Apr, and 80, 23 May, and see *Conc.* 604, ff. 5r, 5 May, 15r, 13 May, 20v-21r, 18 May 1467). In 1469 cardinal Jacopo Ammannati, the cardinal of Pavia (also a Piccolomini, and a most influential Sienese figure) recommended Pietro de' Fabritti, another student from Fermo, for the Sapienza so that he could complete his studies (*Conc.* 2021, no. 78, 19 Jul 1469, ed. I. Ammannati Piccolomini, *Lettere (1444-1479)*, ed. P. Cherubini. Pubblicazioni degli Archivi di Stato. Fonti, 25 [Rome, 1997], doc. 394, p. 1261; similar letter from Ammannati, of the same date, to the *Savi*, in *Studio* 19, no foliation. The same student was recommended for a teaching post in the same year by Bartolomeo Roverella, cardinal of S. Clemente; Zdekauer, p. 42). Cardinal Ammannati and Giovanni di Micheli, cardinal of S. Angelo, recommended Luís Teixeira for a place in the Sapienza in 1473 (Ammannati Piccolomini, *Lettere*, doc. 650, pp. 1695-6; Zdekauer, pp. 42-3; and below, pp. 323, 347 n. 81, 349-50 and 352; further letters in his favour to the *Savi* from them and from the cardinal of Siena in *Studio* 19, no foliation); in the same year the cardinal of Siena, writing directly to the *Savi dello Studio*, recommended 'Dns. Johanes Lylarde'[?] (*Conc.* 2306, fasc. 28, no. 26, 22 Apr 1473); in 1475 Cardinal Latino Orsini asked that Latino de' Regoli, already a *sapientino*, be allowed to have his attendant, Agostino, with him so that the latter could be educated as well (*Not.* 694, f. 37r-v, 18 Feb 1475, ed. Minnucci, 'Documenti', doc. II-19, p. 88, and cf. p. 27; see also below, p. 333 n. 81).

[185] [184] Examples are Malatesta de' Malatesti, who nominated a Dns. Nicolaus in a letter (which the applicant brought with him) of 15 Mar 1419 (*Conc.* 1894, no. 78); the *doge* of Genoa (above, p. 310); Guidantonio da Montefeltro, count of Urbino (*Conc.* 449, ff. 3r-v, 2-3 Nov 1440; cf. Catoni, 'Genesi', p. 175 n. 87; he asks for the right to nominate a student, and when he receives it, nominates him); Paola Colonna-Appiani, widow of the *signore* of Piombino, who recommended Messer Jacopo d'Andrea da Piombino (*Conc.* 466, f. 45r, 17 Oct 1443); Piero di Cosimo de' Medici, who together with Bishop Alvaro of Silva in Portugal successfully recommended Piero di Ferdinando, nephew of the bishop, for *mezzo tempo* (*CG* 231, f. 228v, and *Conc.* 2182, no foliation, 9 Nov 1466); and Antonio Cicinelli, orator of the king of Naples, recommending the Florentine Giovanni di Roberto degli Altoviti for *mezzo tempo* (*Conc.* 2182, no foliation, 15 Mar 1467; he was admitted, *CG* 231, f. 275v, and *Conc.* 603, f. 13r, 17 Mar). In 1462 Jacopo III d'Appiano, the *signore* of Piombino, made a recommendation (above, p. 313 n. 105), and in 1475 his successor, Jacopo IV d'Aragona d'Appiano, recommended Stefano of Piombino for a room vacated by another of his subjects, Giovanni (*Not.* 694, f. 38r-v, 31 Jan 1475, ed. Minnucci, 'Documenti', II-18, pp. 87-8, and cf. pp. 26-7. I have not found evidence that this petition was successful). There was of course nothing unique to Siena about all this, except perhaps the extent of the practice. On recommendations to the Castiglioni at Pavia, see Rosso, 'Presenze studentesche e collegi pavesi', pp. 31-3.

[185] E.g. *Conc.* 379, f. 22r, 13 Jun 1429 (Mag. Niccolò di Paolo d'Assisi is given a place at the recommendation of mag. Guasparre da Bologna); *Conc.* 427, f. 12v, 11 Mar 1437 (Piero de' Giovanetti accepts a lectureship on condition that he may have a student put in the Sapienza). At one point in the mid-1470s the *Savi* received a batch of requests from doctors (*Not.* 694, f. 22r, 17 Jan, no year, ed. Minnucci, 'Documenti', II-48, pp. 118-9, and see p. 28), though it is unclear whether they were for the admission of students to the Sapienza or just the allocation of specific rooms to students whose applications for places had already been approved. Three of the four requests appear in the 'admissions book' (BCS, *ms.* A.XI.12, and in the petition against Bernardino da Cortona [below, p. 350]) Other intellectual figures known to Siena might also intervene in this way; in 1537 two nominees of Giovanni Girgos, a Neapolitan *medico* at the court of the duke of Amalfi and a member of the *Intronati*, were accepted (*Studio* 4, f. 111r, 9 Apr 1537, ed. Košuta, 'Documenti', p. 377).

[186] *Conc.* 2156, no. 28, 23/28 Sept, *CG* 231, f. 201v, 28 Sept, *Dipl., Arch. Generale*, 6 Oct 1466.

favours granted to privileged students knew few bounds. Peter Johel of Linz, recommended by Frederick III, was admitted in 1442 despite the fact that the Sapienza was over-full and there was already a waiting-list for places; on top of that the entrance-fee was waived.[187] For Luís Teixera, a relative of the king of Portugal, the rector was made to vacate the best room; he was allowed a servant in the Sapienza and was made vice-rector.[188] But it was not necessary to be eminent; connections with the Sapienza could also be effective. One rector, Benedetto da Volterra, received particularly favourable treatment. After several terms of office in the 1430s, and some teaching in the same period,[189] Benedetto was able to secure the admission of his nephew Niccolò,[190] and in 1445, after his death, his son Antonio was admitted free for seven years because of his father's great services to the city.[191]

The value of these petitions to the commune is on the face of it self-evident. It is a form of currency, oiling the diplomatic wheels.[192] In the Sapienza the Sienese had found an attraction which could, in terms of exchange with other powers, be an equivalent to the culture and patronage of the courts with which they could not compete on even terms. The Sienese clearly appreciated the potential of this bargaining counter from the start. In reality, notwithstanding the status accorded the Sapienza within the commune's policy, it should be seen alongside other such assets.[193] The Sapienza places

---

[187] *CG* 221, f. 161v, and *Dipl., Arch. Gen.*, 3 Dec 1442 (and further copy in *Conc.* 2177, no foliation); ZDEKAUER, p. 43; and cf. *Conc.* 461, f. 27r-v, 25 Nov. The fact that he had not previously studied in Siena was also discounted. This must be (since there are no other candidates for the match) Peter Joel, from Linz on the Rhine, the brother of Johannes Ruysch and Jakob Joel, nephews of Tilmann Joel, doctor of canon law and eminent figure in Rhineland politics. On this family see SOTTILI, 'Le lettere di Johannes Ruysch', and ROSSO, 'Studenti di area germanica', pp. 43-8, with additional material and bibliography. Jakob took his uncle's surname, and from this document it is clear that Peter did the same. Peter had been in Siena previously, with Johannes, and it was he who reported on the unsatisfactory conditions there in 1434 (above, p. 238 n. 58). The three brothers studied at Pavia in the late 1430s, where Johannes became rector. Peter and Jakob moved to Bologna in 1439, both entering the *Natio Germanica* in 1439. Jakob took his degree there in 1442, and in the same year Peter became *procurator* of the nation. See FRIEDLÄNDER and MALAGOLA (eds.), *Acta Nationis Germanicae*, pp. 187-9, and G. KNOD, *Deutsche Studenten in Bologna (1289-1562): Biographischer Index zu den Acta nationis germanicae Universitatis Bononiensis* (Berlin, 1899), pp. 307-8. Peter died during his stay in the Sapienza, and was buried in S. Domenico on 18 Sept 1444; BCS, *ms. C.III.2 (Obituario S. Domenico, 1336-1596)*, f. 82r.

The entrance fee was also waived for Margaret of Austria's protégé, Paolo Zilango (*Studio* 4, f. 121r, 3 Jan 1539, ed. Košuta, 'Documenti', p. 378).

[188] The case of Teixeira is amply discussed in MINNUCCI, 'Documenti', pp. 283-5; also IDEM, 'Il Collegio', pp. 28-30, 'La Casa della Sapienza', pp. 368-9, and 'Studenti giuristi portoghesi', pp. 1482-4; see also A. MOREIRA DE SÁ, *Humanistas portugueses em Itàlia. Subsìdios para o estudo de Frei Gomes de Lisboa, des dois Luises Teixeiras, de João de Barros e de Henrique Caiado* (Lisbon, 1983), pp. 45-110.

[189] See p. 311 n. 96 above, and below, pp. 342-3 (also pp. 192 n. 87 and 284 n. 47).

[190] *CG* 218, ff. 71v-72r, 12 Oct 1434.

[191] *Conc.* 479, f. 5v, 5 Nov, and *CG* 223, f. 78r-v, 14 Nov; cf. CATONI, 'Il Comune di Siena e l'amministrazione della Sapienza', p. 123 n. 7.

[192] The admissions policy could have many nuances. On 23 Jun 1492 the *Balìa* admitted 'Dnus. Franciscus gentilis palavicinus Januensis' for the full seven years 'non obstantibus represalii contra Januenses' (*Balìa* 37, f. 15r).

[193] Another such was the spas within the Sienese territory, over which the commune had control. Petriolo was particularly famed, and the stream of prestigious visitors, as well as Siena's extravagant treatment of many of them, are illustrated by G. VENEROSI PESCIOLINI, 'I bagni senesi di Petriolo nel Medioevo', *La Diana. Rassegna d'arte e vita senese*, 6:2 (1931), pp. 110-35 (esp. pp. 121-3), and more recently by D. BOISSEUIL, *Le thermalisme en Toscane à la fin du Moyen Âge. Les bains siennois de la fin du XIII siècle au début du XVI siècle*. Collection de l'École Française de Rome, 296 (Rome, 2002), pp. 181-91; IDEM, 'Le paysage thermal siennois au début du XVI siècle, d'après le *De Urbis Senae origine* de Lucio Antonio Maynero', in *Scrivere il medioevo*, pp. 41-54; and V. BOYARSKY, 'Medical Baths and Bathing in the Renaissance with Special Reference to Tuscany', unpublished M.Phil. dissertation, The Warburg Institute, University of London, 1989. Baverio de' Bonetti da Imola, who taught briefly in Siena (see above, pp. 168 n. 185 and 188), was a keen advocate of baths (CHAMBERS, 'Spas', p. 22, BOYARSKY, 'Medical Baths', pp. 137-9, and STEFANUTTI, 'Bonetti, Baverio Maghinardo de', while Barto-

were a new element in an old game, but one which was developing rapidly with the growth of courtly culture. Recommendations were an avenue to many other appointments, both within the *Studio* (in the form of lectureships)[194] and in government and in administrative posts in the gift of the authorities; and the Sienese were not backward in making such requests themselves.[195] A full evaluation of its role would need to explore the dense patronage networks on which so much of public life and career development depended.[196]

The outcome of all the policies and negotiations is perhaps best measured by giving a flavour of the make-up of the Sapienza over the period. The membership of the Sapienza is better known to us than any other part of the student population. From the early 1470s we have a book in which entrants personally recorded their acceptance of the materials in their room; before that, we have the *Concistoro* records of decisions to admit students, which are detailed though clearly not complete. From these sources and others, a tentative profile can be drawn. The first twenty-five years inevitably saw a predominance of Italian entrants (eighty-nine, to twenty-four ultramontanes),[197] but by the second half of the fifteenth century the two groups were virtually in balance. A roll of members of the mid 1470s lists twenty-four ultramontanes and seventeen Italians as well as six of uncertain, but probably Italian, origin; of the ultramontanes, ten are Portuguese, eight German, three French, two Hungarians and one Spanish, of the Italians five are Roman, one is from Sicily, six are from the Papal States, four from Tuscany and one from Montferrat.[198] Perhaps more typical is the breakdown made by Zdekauer of the entrants to the Sapienza from about 1470 to 1496.[199] 138 of the names are Italian, 130 foreign; of the foreigners the Germans are easily the largest group, with seventy-four, followed by the Spanish and Portuguese with forty-two, and a handful only of others – four English,[200] three French, two Swedes, two Hungarians and three unidentified. And this rough balance between citramontanes and ultramontanes holds good as late as 1541, when of the forty *sapientini* electing their rector, nineteen are ascertainably ultramontanes and eighteen Italians.[201]

---

lo di Tura spent an increasing part of his old age in Petriolo, where he had property (cf. his petition in *CG* 236, ff. 3r-4r, 24 Oct 1474, ed. BOISSEUIL, *Thermalisme*, pp. 247-8) and also wrote about the virtues of the waters; L. ZDEKAUER, 'Un consulto medico data a Pio II', *BSSP*, 5 (1898), pp. 101-6 (pp. 104-5), and see WHITLEY, 'Concepts of Ill Health and Pestilence', pp. 193-4. On the cultural functions of spas generally, D. S. CHAMBERS, 'Spas in the Italian Renaissance', in *Reconsidering the Renaissance. Papers from the Twenty-First Annual Conference,* ed. M. A. di Cesare. Medieval and Renaissance Texts and Studies, 93 (Binghamton, New York, 1992), pp. 3-27, repr. in IDEM, *Individuals and Institutions*, ch. II; and K. PARK, 'Natural Particulars: Medical Epistemology, Practice, and the Literature of Healing Springs', in *Natural Particulars. Nature and the Disciplines in Renaissance Europe*, eds. A. Grafton and N. Siraisi (Cambridge, Ma., 1999), pp. 347-67.

[194] Above, pp. 177-8.

[195] E.g. Cardinal Ammannati's reply to the request for Domenico Biliotti to be made archdeacon of Siena, 10 Jan 1463 (AMMANNATI PICCOLOMINI, *Lettere*, letter 55, pp. 451-2).

[196] DENLEY, 'The Collegiate Movement', pp. 46-7.

[198] As p. 317 n. 136 above.

[197] See Table 6 above (p. 312).

[199] ZDEKAUER, doc. XXIII, pp. 180-90 (from BCS, *ms.* A.XI.12), and cf. BONAFACCIA, 'La "Domus Sapientiae", and WEIGLE, *Die Matrikel der Deutschen Nation in Siena*, p. 24. See also above, p. 244 on the Italians in this list.

[200] Against this must be placed the warning of MITCHELL, 'English Student Life', p. 63, that the *obituario* of S. Domenico often lists English students among the Germans buried there. But of course this is only one of many qualifications to be made about the minefield of identification of provenance.

[201] KOŠUTA, 'Siena nella vita e nell'opera di Marino Darsa', p. 70 n. 3.

II

LIFE IN THE COLLEGE

1. *Statutes and deliberations*

For information about the internal life and organisation of the Sapienza it would be natural to turn to statutes. All colleges either had, or aspired to have, such a corpus or rule; those founded by an individual often had statutes written by their founder, or left for the college in their will. Such statutes represent a formal moment in the life of the institution – usually early on in that life – and whereas they do not give us much information about the dynamics of the institution they do give us the idealised, or perhaps better the inspirational, view of what the founders or institutors wanted to achieve.[1]

With Siena this is as usual more complicated. There is a set of 'ordini del vivere'[2] – they are never called statutes[3] – which by comparison with what is known of the house can quite plausibly be narrowed down to the opening years of the college.[4] This is confirmed by the place they occupy in what soon came to be seen as the statute book of the college, the old statute book of the Casa della Misericordia;[5] they are the first entry after the statutes and other material relating to the old hospital. Their most significant feature must be their provenance. Catoni noted the influence of the Spanish College and the Collegio Gregoriano at Bologna, and the Collegio Gregoriano or Sapienza Vecchia at Perugia, on the creation of the Sienese Sapienza.[6] The relationship with the Bolognese colleges is a matter for

---

[1] On the creation of statutes as a process, cf. V. DAVIS, 'The Making of English Collegiate Statutes in the Later Middle Ages', *History of Universities*, 12 (1993), pp. 1-23.

[2] *Mis.* 1, ff. 47r-49v. These have been published by CATONI, 'Genesi', pp. 177-82.

[3] See below, p. 327.

[4] Catoni dates these to 1415/16 (op. cit., pp. 170-1), chiefly on the grounds that they stipulate a six-year period for the students, and in 1422, when the first batch of students had completed the six years for which they had been admitted, it was decided to extend the term for a further year (*Mis.* 1, f. 53r-v, 14 Dec; copy in BCS, *ms.* C.IV.26, f. 192r ed. ZDEKAUER, doc. XIII, pp. 161-2; see above, p. 307 n. 55). While this certainly puts the 'ordini' prior to 1422, I do not see that they must necessarily precede the opening of the college; indeed, a measure of 1418 could be construed as implying a later date: 'Quod sapientes studii habeant eam gubernare et regere, unde jam sit datus ordo de scolaribus actis ad studium ibidem retinendis, Et pro modo conservationis, et manutentionis dicte domus' (*CG* 208, f. 60v-61r, 8 Jan 1418; copies in *Mis.* 1, f. 81r, *Statuti* 41, f. 213r, and *Statuti* 47, f. 212r).

[5] *Mis.* 1; see above, pp. 25-7 for a description and discussion of this volume.

[6] CATONI, 'Genesi', pp. 170-1.

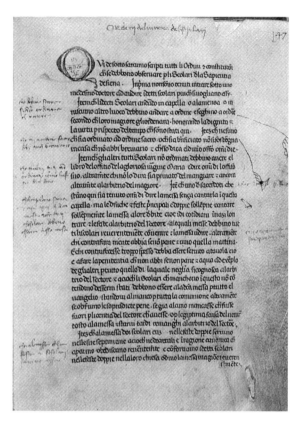

Fig. 14 – 'Ordini del vivere de li scholari', c. 1415-6
(Archivio di Stato di Siena, *Mis.* 1, f. 47r).

speculation,[7] but as far as concerns the Gregoriano at Perugia the case is conclusive. The circumstantial evidence adduced by Catoni for Perugian influence[8] is amply confirmed by a comparison of the Sienese 'ordini' with the first revised version of Niccolò Capocci's statutes for the Perugian college, apparently made immediately after his death in 1368.[9]

---

[7] The parallels are circumstantial; like the two Bolognese colleges the Sienese Sapienza was to have thirty places, and the minimum age of entry, twenty (found in subsequent legislation rather than in the 'ordini'; above, p. 318), is also found in the Gregoriano of Bologna (CATONI, 'Genesi', p. 171 n. 73). On the influence of the Gregoriano of Bologna on the Spanish College and the subsequent influence of the Spanish College further afield, MARTI, *The Spanish College*, esp. pp. 34-40 and 147-8, and DENLEY, 'The Collegiate Movement', esp. pp. 39-41 and 56-7; for a Pavian example A. L. VISINTIN, 'Due collegi universitari del tardo Medioevo', in M. BENDISCIOLI et al., *Il Collegio Universitario Ghislieri*, 2, pp. 299-311 (esp. pp. 308-11).

[8] CATONI, 'Genesi', p. 171 n. 78 drew attention to the earlier presence in the Sienese library of a copy of the statutes of the Gregoriano and the will of its founder; this according to an eighteenth-century inventory of the university library, *Studio* 108, p. 355. There is also a payment in 1415 of individuals sent on behalf of the *Studio* to Perugia (but also 'sive ad alias partes'); *Conc.* 295, f. 13v, 3 Apr 1415; cf. CATONI, 'Genesi', p. 170. To this one might also add that one of the teachers in Siena, Giovanni di Buccio da Spoleto, who by the time of the opening of the Sapienza had been lecturing there for twenty years, had been at the Gregoriano in Perugia as a student; ARBIZZONI, 'Giovanni da Spoleto', p. 227.

[9] In the Biblioteca Comunale Augusta di Perugia, *ms.* 1239, ff. 20r-27v, ed. SEBASTIANI, 'Il collegio universitario', appendix III, pp. 243-73, collating with a second version, in Archivio di Stato di Perugia, *Collegio della Sapienza Vecchia, Miscellanea* 1; and now ed. with Italian translation in ANGELETTI and BERTINI, *La Sapienza Vecchia*, pp. 369-87 (and facsimile reproduction on pp. 567-81).

The Sienese 'ordini' are a close copy, if not a verbatim translation, of the 1368 Gregoriano statutes. Comparison of the two reveals the following points (see Table 7). First, the Sienese copied the structure and sequence of the Perugian statutes rigidly. The parallels are truly point-for-point, down to the separation of clauses, with only a couple of instances of a clause being separated into two.[10] The substance and indeed the precise wording are also taken over in the great majority of cases, sometimes with some modification or reduction but for the most part verbatim, and in a handful of cases inappropriately. Given their derivation, there is little to be gained from examination of the structure of the 'ordini'; what is interesting is the variation. A number of clauses are shorter, omitting for the most part the preambles in which the Perugian constitutions give the moral justification for the measure.[11] Some omit levels of detail, particularly regarding the penalties stipulated by the Perugians,[12] and there are also a few changes in terminology – most obviously the use of the title of rector for the head of the college rather than, as at the Gregoriano, president,[13] but also to take account of the obviously different circumstances of the Sienese college.[14] By and large these differences, far from being substantial, leave one with the suspicion that the authorities were not trying very hard to create a systematic or comprehensive code. An odd case in point is the measure about 'founders' day'. The Perugian regulations, in common with most colleges, include a day on which their founder, Niccolò Capocci, was to be commemorated, and the Sienese took this over in abbreviated and generic form, stipulating 'Item si debba fare l'annovale omni anno per l'anima de colui che fece la Casa'.[15] Given that the College was founded by the commune, it is difficult to see who the drafters had in mind unless it were Andrea Gallerani, founder of the original Casa della Misericordia; but even then, a date would have been specified (as it was in the Perugian model). A more likely explanation is that this was a hasty rendering of the original into a neutral form, a suspicion confirmed by the absence of any subsequent references to the observance of such a practice. Another clause that is taken over but effectively never heard of again is that regarding the responsibility of the rector for the under-aged.[16] The characteristics of the manuscript also suggest the same *ad hoc* approach; only some of the clauses are prefaced with titles, and the text veers from one style of paragraphing to another. The fact that they are rendered in the vernacular (in Siena, as elsewhere at the time, this often indicates a less formal status) is also relevant.

---

[10] E.g. Perugian constitutions, clause 49 becomes two clauses in the Sienese version (3 and 4; my numbering, for convenience of reference; for full references see Table 7); the Perugian clause 59 becomes the Sienese clauses 14 and 15.

[11] E.g. 'Ordini', clauses 1, 9, 21, 24, 29, 37, 39, 40 and 44. An exception is clause 43, in which the preamble is present but shortened.

[12] E.g. clauses 22, 23, 25, 29, 30, 38 and 39.

[13] An exception is clause 32, in which the Sienese version contains the lapse 'cum licentia del presidente'. On the other hand the Perugian model for clause 33 has 'rectore' and 'presidentis' in the same sentence; and the statutes of 1391, repeatedly referring to 'Rector, seu Presidens', show that both terms were in use (ANGELETTI and BERTINI, *La Sapienza Vecchia*, pp. 472-7). 'President' is rarely used in Siena; see below, p. 340 n. 12.

[14] For example, in the Perugian constitutions permission to be absent had to be granted by 'presidentis et prioris monasterii sancte Marie de Monte Oliveti' (clause 79); the Sienese leave this to the rector (clause 31).

[15] Clause 20.

[16] Clause 28 (and see above, p. 318).

Table 7 – 'Ordini del vivere' of the Casa della Sapienza compared with 'Constitutiones' of the Collegio Gregoriano, Perugia

'Ordini del vivere' of the Casa della Sapienza, Siena[1]				'Constitutiones' of the Collegio Gregoriano, Perugia[2]				
No.[3]	Fol.[4]	Catoni p.[5]	Rubric/Summary[6]	No.[7]	Fol.[8]	Sebastiani p.[9]	Angeletti /Bertini p.[10]	Rubric
					20r-21r	243-6	369-71	Costitutiones Domus Sapience. [Preamble: places that could nominate students, and authorities within them; similar to Collegio di Spagna, Bologna]
1	47r	177	[As Gregoriano]	46	21r	246-7	371	De disposicione Domus.
2			[As Gregoriano]	47		247	371-2	In primis
3			[All clerics to have breviary and to say office]	48		247-8	372	De ordine scolarium
4			[Rest to have 'libro de l'offitio de la gloriosa Virgine Maria']	49	21r-v	248		De officio dicendo
5			[As Gregoriano]	50	21v	248-9	372-3	De missa in capella et eius observacione
6		178	[As Gregoriano]	51		249-50	373	De ministrando ad missam
7	47v		[As Gregoriano]	52		250	373-4	De confessione et comunione
8			[As Gregoriano]	53	22r	250-1	374	De Ieiuniis
9			De la vita di scolari	54	22r	251-2	374-5	De victu scolarium
10			[As Gregoriano]	55		252	375	De quantitate carnium [in festivitatibus]
11			[S. Maria di Septembre, 'principale festa di questa Casa']	56	22v	252-3		De festo Sancti Gregorii
12			[As Gregoriano]	57		253	376	De Refeccione in Carnisprivio
13			[As Gregoriano]	58		253-4		De qualitate carnium
14			[Holy Thursday]	59		254		De refectione in cena Domini in Parasceve die iovis sancto
15	48r	179	[Good Friday]					[Good Friday included in same clause]
16			[As Gregoriano]	60	22v-23r	254-5	376-7	De vigilia Nativitatis domini
17			[As Gregoriano]	61	23r	255	377	De Benedictione ad mensam
18			Del leggiere a la mensa	62		255-6		De legendo ad mensam
19			De le congregatione a la campana	63		256	377-8	De congregando se scolares ad sonum Campanelle
20			[As Gregoriano]	64	23r-v		378	De Anniversario celebrando
21	48r-v	179-80	De le ingiurie	65	23v	256-7		De verbis iniuriosis
22		180	Del deffenderse contro colui che l'ingiuria	66		257-8	378-9	De defendendo se contra iniuriante primo
23	48v		De pronumptiare sopra l'ingiuria	67		258		De pronunciando super iniuria
24			De colui che percote cum l'arme	68	24r	258-9		De percussore cum armis
25			De la pace infra l'ingiurianti etc.	69		259		De pace iniuriancium
				70		259-60	380	De iniuriarum denunciacione

Mis. 1 No.[3]	Mis. 1 fol.[4]	[7]	Mis. 1 rubric[6]	ms 1239 fol.[8]	No.	Catoni[5]	Sapienza[10]	Gregoriano rubric
26			Di stare honestamente specialmente in camera		71	260-1		De morando honeste et presertim in Camera
27			[As Gregoriano]	24v	72	261	380-1	De denunciatione fienda
28			[As Gregoriano]		73	261-2	381	De Iuramenta prestando
29	48v-49r	181	D'examinare quelli che saranno ricevuti in casa		74	262		De exsaminatione in primitivis
30	49r			24v-25r	75	262-3		De stando per sex annos
					76	263	382	De Custodia Iuvenum scolarium
					77	263-4		De Repetitore Noviciorum
					78	264		De Inscriptione in quaterno fienda
31			De la licentia de partirse	25r-v	79	264-5	382-3	De Licencia absentantis se
32			[As Gregoriano]	25v	80	265	383	De non pernoctando extra domum
33			[As Gregoriano]		81			De assignacione clavis camere
34			[As Gregoriano]		82			Ut nullus possit habere officium extra domum
35			[As Gregoriano]		83	266		Ne recipiatur ad pernoctandum forenses
					84		383-4	De Electione Camerarum
				26r	85	267	384	De dimicendis Cameris munitis
36			De conferendo fori del dormentorio e refectorio		86	267-8		De Conferendo extra dormitorium, et Refectorium
37			[As Gregoriano]		87	268	384-5	De mutuis serviciis prestandis
38	49r-v	182	[As Gregoriano]	26r-v	88	268-9	385	Ne quis Iudicem adeat extra domum
39	49v		[As Gregoriano]		89	269		De non comedendo per cameras
40			[As Gregoriano]		90	270	386	De singulariter comedendo
41			[As Gregoriano]		91			De discursu Camerarum
42			[As Gregoriano]	26v-27r	92	270-1		De non Residendo continuo ante portam
					93	271	386-7	De permansione superius
43			[As Gregoriano]		94	271-2	387	De non petendo contra constituciones istas
44					95	272		De numero scolarium

[1] Mis. 1, ff. 47r-49v (and various ms. copies; see above, p. 25 n. 134); ed. CATONI, 'Genesi', pp. 177-82. The 'Ordini' were drawn up at or near the opening of the house, between 1416 and 1418 (see p. 325 n. 4).

[2] Biblioteca Augusta, ms. 1239, ff. 20r-27r (another version in Archivio di Stato di Perugia, Collegio della Sapienza Vecchia, Miscellanea 1); eds. SEBASTIANI, 'Il collegio universitario', appendix III, pp. 243-73, and ANGELETTI and BERTINI, La Sapienza Vecchia, pp. 369-87 (with Italian translation, and on pp. 567-81 facsimile reproduction. The constitutions copied were those ordered by the executors of the will of the founder, cardinal Niccolò Capocci, d. 25 June 1368.

[3] The 'ordini' are not numbered in the ms. or in Catoni's edition; I have numbered them here for convenience of reference.

[4] Foliation of Mis. 1.

[5] Page numbers of the edition in CATONI, 'Genesi'.

[6] Only a few of the statutes have rubrics, which Catoni rendered as headings for whole sections. Where these exist they have been given; for the rest, a summary description of the theme of the statute has been given where it differs from that of the Perugian statutes.

[7] These numbers are later additions to the ms.

[8] Foliation of Perugia, Biblioteca Augusta, ms. 1239.

[9] Page numbers of edition in SEBASTIANI, 'Il collegio universitario'.

[10] Page numbers of edition in ANGELETTI and BERTINI, La Sapienza Vecchia.

Perhaps more significant are the omissions, most of which it would be safe to conclude were deliberate. The two exceptions are clauses in the Perugian constitutions concerning the obligation placed on students to denounce each other to the president for misdemeanours,[17] and forbidding servants from accessing the scholars' rooms upstairs unless they were carrying books.[18] There are possible explanations for the omission of these from the Sienese version, but none so compelling as to rule out the possibility of simple error. Such an explanation is much less likely for the remainder. The preamble of the Perugian constitutions, which lists those entitled to nominate students for places, and the first clause, 'De disposicione Domus', which fixes the name and purpose of the college and the number of poor students in theology and grammar to be admitted, are not copied; the Sienese Sapienza was to be a fundamentally different institution.[19] Also omitted are clauses providing for a *repetitor* for the benefit of new students (again an area in which the Sienese authorities demonstrated little interest),[20] requiring the admission of each student to be recorded in a book (a practice for which there is evidence in Siena only later),[21] regulating the election of the *Camarlengo*,[22] and finally stipulating the number of scholars to be admitted.[23] In the case of one clause, on what a student was to be given when he had been allocated a room,[24] the Sienese replaced the original with a substantially different regulation concerning the basis on which rooms were to be allocated.[25]

To sum up, the Sienese authorities borrowed their constitutions wholesale from their model and rival in Perugia. There are signs that this was done in some haste and without much clear thought about what was wanted; clauses that did not fit with what they had in mind, that encroached on Sienese practice, that pre-empted decisions about the college that had not yet been taken, or that implied a more caritative approach, were by and large omitted. It should be added that such an approach was possible not least because the Perugian constitutions, too, by and large avoided the critical areas that would have tied the hands of the communal authorities.[26] Specifically, they also said little about the choice of president. The Perugian arrangements regarding admission were simply not copied. The importation of these constitutions was acceptable because their primary focus was internal discipline, an area in which the Sienese had no experience and needed a model. The 'ordini del vivere' are just that; a disciplinary code for the internal life of the college.[27]

Given these problems, the value of these regulations is limited. They form a departure point for the

---

[17] Perugian constitutions, clause 72.

[18] Perugian constitutions, clause 93.

[19] Perugian constitutions, clause 46.

[20] Perugian constitutions, clause 77.

[21] Perugian constitutions, clause 78. Though the first surviving volume, BCS, *ms.* A.XI.12, begins only in the 1470s, the inventory of the Sapienza's archive compiled by abbot Sestigiani (ASS, *ms.* B.82, *Repertorio di strumenti della Sapienza* [1695]) gives five volumes starting in 1441; CATONI, *Pergamene*, p. 4, and see above, p. 24 n. 128.

[22] Perugian constitutions, clause 84. Again, the Sienese had their own established practices for this; see below, pp. 353 *seq.*

[23] Perugian constitutions, clause 95.

[24] Perugian constitutions, clause 85.

[25] 'Ordini', clause 36.

[26] It is interesting to note that arrangements concerning the rectorate were also codified in Perugia some time after the constitutions regarding internal discipline – coincidentally, at about the time of the Sienese 'importation'; reforms of the bishop of Perugia of 24 July 1417, Perugia, Biblioteca Augusta, *ms.* 1239, ff. 27r-30r, ed. SEBASTIANI, 'Il collegio universitario', Appendix III, pp. 273-90, and ANGELETTI and BERTINI, *La Sapienza Vecchia*, pp. 389-400.

[27] The studious avoidance of the term statutes may be relevant. The final clause (44) refers to 'i predecti capitoli e constitutioni' (a phrase also taken from the Perugian model).

fifteenth-century Sapienza, but given their imported nature, perhaps we need to be cautious about reading too much into them. They can be compared with the formal statutes of 1532 and after,[28] and with a further set promulgated in 1542;[29] for the period in between, the historian can draw on the measures taken by the authorities, particularly the *Savi* (whose deliberations have survived in fairly continuous sequence from the 1470s).[30] These also illuminate the constant flow of individual cases of infringement, which give a good picture of how these regulations were being enforced and which areas caused problems.

2. *Discipline and daily life*

The first concern of the original 'ordini' was the enforcement of regular religious functions on all the students in the Sapienza, whether clerics or not. All students had to say office daily – clerics from the breviary, the rest from the office of the Virgin. Mass, said on weekdays, sung on Sundays and holidays, was compulsory, and so that no scholar could claim to have been present when he was not, all had to stay for the Gospel and Communion unless they had been exempted, for good reason, by the rector. Those who missed mass were denied food and wine, and regular offenders had to do penance in public. Canon law students had to attend extra masses. Each student had, on pain of expulsion, to confess twice yearly to the priest of the Sapienza.[31]

The devotional stipulations are known to us through the statutes, but otherwise they make few appearances in the records. Apart from one case in which a false ducat was discovered in the collection and steps were taken to find the culprit,[32] and another case of a disagreement among the chaplains,[33] this side of Sapienza life does not feature in records of disciplinary matters. The sixteenth-century statutes saw a relaxation in the confession rule; one confession a year was now enough.[34] The only devotional regulations that are heard of frequently are those connected with fasting during religious holidays. Food looms large in the regular records of the Sapienza, and regulations about it reveal much about its importance. The first concern of the 'ordini' in this respect was to establish a standard of nutrition. Bread and wine were to be provided 'sufficientemente' both morning and evening, the wine to be diluted at the rector's discretion; each student was to be given eight ounces of meat, good *castrone*, and a pound on holidays, which were also marked by the giving of bread to the poor.[35] The deliberations of the *Savi*, which occasionally (and in the sixteenth century increasingly) deal with administrative arrangements properly under the control of the *Camarlengo*, show interesting examples of how these original provisions might be stretched according to the financial and other considerations of the times. In 1481 a 'Dnus. Leonardus teutonicus', who ate neither meat nor fish, 'habeat debitum suum

---

[28] *Studio* 109, ff. 2r-6r, 15 Feb 1532, with additions, 7v-10r, ed. Košuta, 'Documenti', doc. II, pp. 343-52 (and introduction, p. 342).

[29] *Studio* 110, ff. 1r-9r, 17 Feb 1542, with additions, 10v-12r, ed. Košuta, 'Documenti', doc. IV, pp. 355-65 (excerpts also ed. Marrara, *Lo Studio di Siena*, pp. 295-6), and see discussion by Cascio Pratilli, *L'Università e il Principe*, p. 13 n. 5.

[30] In the volumes of *Studio* 2 onwards, plus some in the archive of the *Quattro Maestri del Sale*. See above, pp. 20-1.

[31] 'Ordini', clauses 3-7.

[32] *Studio* 2, f. 123v, 13 Mar 1488. The student, Petrus de Viterbio, was given five days in which to produce a real ducat.

[33] *Studio* 2, f. 7v, 23 Dec 1473; and see p. 358.

[34] *Studio* 110, rubric III, ff. 1v-2r, 17 Feb 1542, ed. Košuta, 'Documenti', doc. IV, pp. 356-7.

[35] 'Ordini', clauses 9-13; and cf. Minnucci, 'Casa della Sapienza', p. 359.

circa victum'.[36] Relaxation of the regulations could get out of hand. In 1527 a *credenza* full of old bread was discovered; it was decided that until it had been finished the *Camarlengo* was not to buy any fresh bread.[37] The standard of provision could suffer from financial shortages. In 1492 the *Savi*, together with the *Nove Custodi*, reined in the rector's discretion over the amount of wine to be served with meals; it was to be limited to a *boccale*.[38] In 1528 it was decided that this quantity was to be halved; the students soon protested, however, when the quality deteriorated as well, and as a result of their protests a certain type of wine was stipulated.[39] Scholars also complained in 1495, to the *Balìa*, that they were not getting enough to eat.[40]

Meals were accompanied by readings from the Scriptures 'come fanno li Religiosi'.[41] Apart from this they were to be eaten in silence.[42] Great emphasis was laid on punctuality. A bell was to ring twice, with an interval, before each meal, and absentees or latecomers were not given food.[43] Anyone who missed Grace also went without, and a later measure ordered that anyone who had been deprived of their dining rights as a punishment was to come to table and sit through the meal all the same.[44] Various attempts were made to make meals compulsory. The original statutes were relatively liberal on this score; anyone wishing to eat alone could have bread and wine only in his room, although this was to be denied him if he demanded it too often.[45] In 1493 it was decided that this required the rector's permission,[46] and in 1496 that students could not eat Sapienza food 'in secundis tabulis' or in rooms;[47] in the 1532 statutes it was laid down that a student could only eat in his room if he was ill.[48] Yet the records repeat the instructions that students were to eat in the Sapienza – in 1438,[49] in 1484, when it was decided that no food would be provided unless the students ate together,[50] in 1493, when it was explicitly stated that the rector and the priests of the Sapienza had to eat with them,[51] and in 1520 and 1521.[52] There was of course the occasional exemption – one for example in 1483,[53] others

---

[36] *Studio* 2, f. 82r, 14 Dec.

[37] *Studio* 3, f. 65r-v, 3 Oct.

[38] *Not.* 694, f. 34r, 8 Jun, ed. MINNUCCI, 'Documenti', doc. II-33, pp. 99-100, and cf. p. 28.

[39] *Studio* 3, ff. 67r-v, 13 Jan 1528, and 79v, 3 May 1530.

[40] 'Intellectus etiam multis et variis lamentationibus scolarium existentium in Sapientia quod non habent comoditatem eorum victus in ipsa domo' (*Balìa* 40, f. 9v, 25 Aug).

[41] 'Ordini', clause 18; cf. *Studio* 109, rubric IV, f. 3r, 15 Feb 1532: ed. KOŠUTA, 'Documenti', doc. II, p. 345.

[42] 'Ordini', clause 18; cf. *Studio* 110, rubric VI, f. 3r, 17 Feb 1542, ed. KOŠUTA, 'Documenti', doc. IV, p. 357, when the whole meal was to be eaten 'con silentio et moderantia'.

[43] 'Ordini', clause 19; reiterations in *Mis.* 1, f. 85r, 10 May, and *Conc.* 428, ff. 16v-17r, 27 May 1437; also *Mis.* 1, f. 92v, 7 Nov 1452; cf. *Studio* 109, rubric VIII, f. 4r, 15 Feb 1532, ed. KOŠUTA, 'Documenti', doc. II, p. 345; and *Studio* 110, rubric V, f. 2v, 17 Feb 1542, ed. KOŠUTA, 'Documenti', doc. IV, p. 357.

[44] *Mis.* 1, f. 112v, 11 Oct 1483; also *Studio* 2, f. 92v, 27 May 1483.

[45] 'Ordini', clause 41.

[46] *Studio* 2, f. 131v, 5 Jan.

[47] *Sale* 23, f. 91r, 26 Jan; repeated f. 94r, 17 May.

[48] *Studio* 109, rubric X, f. 4v, 15 Feb, ed. KOŠUTA, 'Documenti', doc. II, p. 345.

[49] *Mis.* 1, ff. 86r-87v, 4 Jun.

[50] *Studio* 2, f. 99v, 11 Mar.

[51] *Studio* 2, f. 131v, 5 Jan.

[52] *Studio* 3, ff. 22v, 26 Oct, 23r, 13 Nov 1520, and 27r, 1521; cf. also *Studio* 110, rubric VI, f. 3r, 17 Feb 1542, ed. KOŠUTA, 'Documenti', doc. IV, pp. 357-8.

[53] *Studio* 2, f. 97r, 22 Dec.

in 1498,[54] and one in 1488 when a scholar was allowed to eat in his room because the mealtimes clashed with his lectures in *medicina pratica*.[55] But the frequency with which the instruction is repeated suggests that its enforcement was a problem. The same can be said of the practice of admitting guests to meals. The 'ordini' allowed guests on holidays at the discretion of the rector,[56] but from 1483 guests were certainly forbidden, as was the practice of sending others to meals in one's place.[57]

Students of the Sapienza were thus expected, as in other Italian colleges, to lead an institutional life which at least in some ways imitated the only real model for residential institutions, the religious houses. There were bound to be tensions, however, between on the one hand the community-orientated aspirations of the administrators, and on the other the individual needs and inclinations of adults who were mostly studying secular subjects for vocational or other reasons which were unlikely to include dedication to a semi-religious life-style. In particular, students needed privacy for study which was, despite contemporary projections and later romanticisations of the medieval student community, essentially an individual activity. To some extent the authorities recognised this and tried to maintain in the Sapienza an atmosphere conducive to study, insisting that disputations take place quietly and in areas away from the rooms.[58] When, however, they attempted to enforce discipline in the privacy of the scholar's rooms, problems were inevitable. Here too, standards were tightened rather than relaxed, but the frequency of disciplinary measures suggests mixed success. The 'ordini' made some concessions to the students. They were allowed to entertain a maximum of two scholars (to bread and wine),[59] and though they could not invite non-Sapienza students into their rooms or have them stay the night without the rector's permission, it is interesting that the possibility of such permission was even mentioned.[60] But in this respect the Perugian blueprint was soon modified. Already in 1437 students were forbidden on pain of expulsion to 'tenere ad sua Compagnia alcuno Scolajo scriptore compagno, o famiglo'.[61] In 1456 this was repeated and all guests staying the night were forbidden;[62] in 1488 it was

---

[54] *Sale* 24, ff. 165r, 24 May (for the rector), and 166r, 4 Jul. In both cases the students were not just exempted from the obligation to eat in the Sapienza, but given their provisions outside the house. In 1533 the rector was to receive more than the other students, particularly if he ate with them (*Studio* 4, f. 37r, 22 Aug, ed. KOŠUTA, 'Documenti', doc. VI-1, p. 374).

[55] *Studio* 2, f. 123v, 21 Mar.

[56] 'Ordini', clause 11.

[57] *Studio* 2, f. 92v, 27 May; see also *Studio* 3, ff. 23r, 26 Oct 1520, 27r, 15 Apr 1521, *Studio* 109, rubric XI, f. 4v, 15 Feb 1532 (ed. KOŠUTA, 'Documenti', doc. II, p. 345), and *Studio* 110, rubric XXVIII, f. 9r-v, 17 Feb 1542 (ed. KOŠUTA, 'Documenti', doc. IV, p. 363).

[58] 'Ordini', clause 37. Students in the Sapienza were obliged to attend lectures long before this obligation was placed on all members of the university (*Conc.* 341, f. 7r, 11 Nov 1422, ed. PIANIGIANI, doc. 57, p. 80); the rector was to see that they studied (below, p. 341 and n. 23), and in 1510 the penalty for repeated non-attendance was expulsion for a year, while anyone obstructing the teachers who used the Sapienza for lectures was to be fined 30 ducats 'in oro larghi' (PICCOLOMINI, 'Istruzioni di Giacomo Todeschini-Piccolomini al figlio Enea', pp. 115-6). But the instruction was not unique; see ESPOSITO, 'Le "Sapientie" romane', pp. 48-9.

[59] 'Ordini', clause 40.

[60] 'Ordini', clause 35.

[61] *Mis.* 1, f. 84v, 10 May. In 1475 Cardinal Latino Orsini requested that a *sapientino*, maestro Latino, be permitted to have 'uno mamolo nominato Agustino suo attinente' with him in the college 'per farlo imparare et dare a le lettere fine a tanto che el sirà in età perfecta da entrare ancora luy in epsa Sapienza' (*Not.* 694, f. 37r-v, 18 Feb 1475, ed. MINNUCCI, 'Documenti', doc. II-19, p. 88, and cf. pp. 27, 280, identifying him with the Latino de' Regoli who appears in BCS, *ms.* A.XI.12; ZDEKAUER, doc. XXIII, p. 183, and BONAFACCIA, 'La "Domus Sapientiae", p. 83 [and pp. 261-2, following Minnucci]). I have not found any evidence that permission was given (and the *Concistoro*'s replies to correspondence for that year have not survived). The ban on students having servants was repeated in 1483 (*Mis.* 1, f. 112v, 11 Oct).

[62] *Mis.* 1, f. 94v, 10 Sept.

emphasised that no guests of either sex could stay,[63] and in the 1542 statutes no women were allowed to enter the Sapienza at all.[64] The only official exceptions to these rules were in cases of illness,[65] but in practice exemptions were agreed. Important guests were sometimes allowed a servant, in one case at the Sapienza's expense,[66] and by the end of the fifteenth century this was quite normal.[67] The principle must have been compromised also by the occasional sharing of rooms during periods of heavy demand for places.[68]

The importance of the students' rooms, their only bastion of privacy, is reflected in the competition they caused.[69] We know little about the structure of the building,[70] but there must have been variations in the size, or at least in the position, of the rooms which made some more desirable than others. The original statutes allocated rooms on a basis of first come first served (to which was added, in 1434, the refinement that students who paid the full fee in advance had priority over the others),[71] although 'nientemeno el rectore considerata la qualità de la persona e legiptima cagione debba provedere'.[72] Twice in the early history of the house, changes or exchanges of rooms had to be prohibited,[73] and the 1542 statutes forbade the selling or renting of rooms which, as has been seen, was not unknown.[74] Each scholar was to be given 'fulcitam, lectica, bancis, et aliis massaritiis de lignamine'

[63] *Studio* 2, f. 122v, 14 Jan; see also f. 132r, 9 Jan 1493, and *Sale* 24, f. 152r, 9 Feb 1497; the stricture was 'sub pena privationis'.

[64] *Studio* 110, rubric XVII, f. 6r, 17 Feb, ed. KOŠUTA, 'Documenti', doc. IV, p. 360; cf. IDEM, 'Siena nella vita e nell'opera di Marino Darsa', p. 76 n. 2, seeing in this development the spirit of the Counter-Reformation. In the Engleschi at Padua women servants over the age of fifty were permitted; VERONESE CESERACCIU, 'Il Collegio Engleschi', p. 290 n. 2.

[65] E.g. in 1473 a sick student, Mag. Gaspar Turiglia, was allowed to keep a servant till he recovered (*Studio* 2, f. 5r, 19 Sept).

[66] *Studio* 2, f. 61r-v, 15 Oct 1479 (the student was Messer Gonsalvo, from Portugal, on whom see MINNUCCI, 'Documenti', p. 261).

[67] On 26 Jan 1496 the *Savi* forbade scholars from keeping a *famulus*, 'sub pena privationis' (*Sale* 23, f. 91r); on 16 Mar and 17 May two students were given permission to have servants. Thereafter the regulation was that students might not have 'famuli' or 'socii', 'servandi' or 'forenses' without permission (*Sale* 24, f. 163v, 17 Feb 1498, and 171r, 14 Jan 1499); such servants were conceded for a fee (f. 167v, 19 Nov 1498; one could stay for four months at a fee of one gold ducat per month, another was allowed retrospectively on payment of 10 *lire* a month to date and 8 *lire* a month henceforth; 169v, 22 Dec 1498, another at 8 *lire* a month; 171r, 14 Jan 1499, again at 1 ducat; this last was cancelled). The normality of the practice can be gauged by the deliberations of the *Balìa* in 1510 which include the stipulation that 'li garzoni, così delli scolari di Sapientia come di Nobilisti et scolari de l'Università' are to be punished by '4 tracti di corda' if they infringed any of these measures (P. PICCOLOMINI, 'Istruzioni di Giacomo Todeschini-Piccolomini al figlio Enea', p. 116).

[68] One case is that of Niccolò 'di Lonenborche della magna' (Lüneburg), who applied for *mezzo tempo*, paying the usual sum, but saying that there was no need for him to be given a room, as he would share a room and bed with his friend. He was admitted on this basis (*CG* 231, f. 267r-v, 12 Feb 1467, and *Conc.* 602, f. 28r, 16 Feb 1467; petition in *Conc.* 2138, clause 100, f. 165r, 31 Jan 1467; see CATONI, 'Il Comune di Siena e l'amministrazione della Sapienza', p. 127). In 1470 two brothers, who had been admitted on the basis that they would have to share a room until a second became available, petitioned for this (*Conc.* 2024, clause 18, 25 Nov); they were still waiting in 1472 (*Conc.* 2028, clause 28, 1 May).

[69] This privacy must surely have been the most important of the factors that made the house 'molto attuita allo studiare' (as described in the petition of Nicholas of Lüneburg for a place, above, n. 68); cf. CATONI, 'Il Comune di Siena e l'amministrazione della Sapienza', p. 127, quoting *Conc.* 2138, clause 100, 31 Jan 1467.

[70] See below, pp. 382 *seq*.

[71] Above, p. 311.

[72] 'Ordini', clause 36.

[73] *Mis.* 1, f. 82r, 19 Jun 1419; *Mis.* 1, f. 85v, 18 Apr 1438. This was repeated later in the century (e.g. *Sale* 24, f. 152v, 9 Feb 1497).

[74] *Studio* 110, rubric XIV, f. 5v, 17 Feb, ed. KOŠUTA, 'Documenti', doc. IV, p. 360; and above, p. 319.

and was not allowed any more in his room.[75] An inventory of 1459 shows that on the whole this simple prescription held good; the average room had little more than the barest essentials.[76] None of these items could be taken out of the house,[77] though this did occur in 1484, when some students moved out to rented accommodation and took some items with them.[78] To this end, in 1491 a deposit was expected of the students on entry, as has been seen.[79] Students' rooms were also lockable, though if members of the college were given permission to be away they had to leave their key with a colleague.[80]

As well as putting down a deposit for the material side of his stay, the new student had to swear that he would behave, and that he would report any wrongdoings that came to his attention.[81] In addition, anyone who took a fellow-student to court without permission was to be deprived of his board.[82] Students were expected to wear academic dress – 'veste lunga...a mezza gamba almeno'[83] – and according to the 1542 statutes could not wear 'cappe alla spagnuola' in the daytime.[84] The original statutes forbade excessive playing of the guitar or other instruments, and this and gaming were punishable at the discretion of the rector.[85] The latter measure is frequently repeated.[86] Swearing was forbidden in the later statutes;[87] 'sceleraggini e altre cose disoneste' were to be punished as the rector saw fit,[88] and

---

[75] *Mis.* 1, f. 57v, 18 Mar 1445; and see *Studio* 109, rubric VI, f. 3v, 15 Feb 1532, ed. KOŠUTA, 'Documenti', doc. II, p. 344. But a student who had a Sapienza place reserved for him in 1443 was allowed to spend extra money on furnishing his room (*Conc.* 463, ff. 31r-32v, 28 Mar).

[76] See below, pp. 384-6, ZDEKAUER, pp. 100-2, and esp. CATONI, 'Genesi', pp. 168-9, on the inconsistencies between this document (which he publishes, pp. 183-98) and other information we have. Cf. also CHŁEDOWSKI, *Siena*, II, p. 140; MITCHELL, *The Laurels and the Tiara*, p. 74; EADEM, *John Free*, pp. 26-7.

[77] *Studio* 3, f. 36r, 12 Feb 1524.

[78] *Studio* 2, f. 99r, 12 Mar.

[79] Above, p. 311.

[80] 'Ordini', clause 33.

[81] 'Ordini', clause 27; cf. *Studio* 109, rubric XIV, f. 5v, 15 Feb 1532, ed. KOŠUTA, 'Documenti', doc. II, p. 346, and *Studio* 110, rubric XXVI, f. 8v, 17 Feb 1542, ed. KOŠUTA, 'Documenti', doc. IV, p. 362. One example of a record of members of the Sapienza taking such an oath has come to light (*Not.* 694, f. 33r-v, 3 Jun 1492, ed. MINNUCCI, 'Documenti', doc. II-32, pp. 98-9). The emphasis on respect for authority and the rules is found also in a measure of 1483, in which five scholars were put under pressure to swear obedience (*Not.* 886, ff. 153r-154r, 6 Oct).

[82] 'Ordini', clause 39. The deprivation was for one month for civil actions and two months for criminal ones. Cf. also *Studio* 109, rubric XV, f. 5v, 15 Feb 1532, ed. KOŠUTA, 'Documenti', doc. II, p. 346.

[83] *CG* 218, f. 41v, 28 Jun 1434.

[84] *Studio* 110, rubric IV, f. 2r, 17 Feb, ed. KOŠUTA, 'Documenti', doc. IV, p. 357. Cf. ZDEKAUER, p. 82.

[85] 'Ordini', clause 26. Contrary to the claim of KOŠUTA, 'Siena nella vita e nell'opera di Marino Darsa', p. 82, there is no evidence that plays were put on in the Sapienza in the fifteenth century; his evidence, from MAZZI, *La Congrega de' Rozzi*, I, p. 54, refers to the performance of Pollastra's *Parthenio* by students in the Palazzo Comunale (see CATONI, 'Il carnevale degli scolari', p. 23, and L. G. CLUBB, 'Siena, Crucible of Theater', in CLUBB and BLACK, *Romance and Aretine Humanism*, pp. 11-37 (pp. 15-16).

[86] *CG* 210, f. 200r, 8 Jun 1425 (the 'statuti Bernardiniani'; above, p. 223 n. 108). The rector of the *Studio* and other authorities were to enforce this universal prohibition. See also *Mis.* 1, f. 89v, 7 Dec 1447, when dice and other 'giuochi prohibiti' were subject to the penalty of 10 *lire*; *Balìa* 38, f. 21v, 21 Dec 1492 – this matter now exercised the *Balìa*, which appointed two people to draw up provisions 'ad providendum quod in domo sapientie in cameris scolarium non retineatur ludus nec baractaria'; and *Studio* 110, rubric VIII, f. 3v, 17 Feb 1542, ed. KOŠUTA, 'Documenti', doc. IV, p. 358. On communal legislation see also BALESTRACCI and PICCINNI, *Siena nel Trecento*, p. 61, and MENGOZZI, *Il feudo del vescovado*, pp. 85-6.

[87] *Studio* 109, rubric II, f. 2v, 15 Feb 1532, ed. KOŠUTA, 'Documenti', doc. II, p. 343; *Studio* 110, rubric IX, f. 3v, 17 Feb 1542, ed. KOŠUTA, 'Documenti', doc. IV, p. 358.

[88] 'Ordini', clause 26.

the prohibition of arms was again frequently restated.[89] The penalties for more serious crimes of insulting or physically attacking fellow-students are finely graded in the original statutes. Anyone who uttered 'parole ingiuriose e infamie' was to be deprived of all food and company for one week and given only bread and wine the second (though only one week's punishment was meted out if the insults were in retaliation), the rector deciding what constituted such an offence. Violence without the use of weapons was punishable by one month's deprivation of food and company except for one meal of bread and water a week, taken on the floor; the rector could increase the penalties in serious cases. Any dispute between students which was still not settled after three warnings from the rector was to be punished by expulsion; and this was also the penalty for all violence which involved the use of arms.[90] In essence these provisions remained relatively unchanged in the sixteenth-century statutes.[91]

In practice the penalties for these offences could vary. Students were usually only expelled for acts of violence. The authorities seem to have been most concerned to clamp down when the victims were members of the Sapienza staff,[92] or people outside the Sapienza,[93] or when more than one student was involved. Two students from Viterbo were banned from the house for fighting between themselves in 1475.[94] There is a more complex case in or before 1460, when Antonio Cherubini de Urbe and Angelo Sabe dell'Anguillara petitioned against their expulsion for having wounded another student, Antonio da Velletri, outside the college. He had provoked them by writing infamous accusations on the doors of their rooms, calling them 'filios meretricium et sacerdotum', and had also been expelled, for sodomy and other crimes.[95] Group transgressions were dealt with briskly and firmly. In 1461 five students caught out at night with arms were expelled after public protest at their behaviour, which had previously included serious disturbances of the peace; two of them were given three hours, the others three days, to pack their belongings and leave Siena altogether.[96] By the late fifteenth and early sixteenth centuries temporary exclusion appears more frequent, even for serious offences, and there is legislation to prevent excluded students from being allowed back into the college.[97] In 1496 the German Goffredo was evicted for a year for 'insultis cum armis' and given a sort of banishment; he was not allowed within ten miles of the city, which suspended his studies as well as his residence in the

---

[89] 'Ordini', clause 26; *Mis.* 1, loc. cit., and f. 85v, 18 Apr 1438; *Studio* 2, f. 134r, 28 Mar 1493; *Studio* 110, rubric X, f. 4r, 17 Feb 1542, ed. KOŠUTA, 'Documenti', doc. IV, pp. 358-9.

[90] 'Ordini', clause 24.

[91] *Studio* 109, rubric XII, f. 5r, 15 Feb 1532, ed. KOŠUTA, 'Documenti', doc. II, p. 346; *Studio* 110, rubrics X-XII, ff. 4r-5r, 17 Feb 1542, ed. KOŠUTA, 'Documenti', doc. IV, p. 358-9. One difference is the addition of special penalties for assaults on staff; below, p. 359 n. 190.

[92] Below, p. 359 and n. 190.

[93] In 1472 the *Concistoro* ordered the *Savi* to find out which scholars had been responsible for insulting and wounding the servant of the *podestà*, and the 'iudex domus sapientie' (meaning the rector?) to see to it that *sapientini* did not bear arms (*Conc.* 569, f. 19r, 22 Jul).

[94] *Studio* 2, f. 30v, 3 Jul 1475. The measure does not name them, and gives Viterbo in the text but Orvieto in the margin. The wording is odd, and suggests that they may in fact not have been members of the college.

[95] *Conc.* 1998, clause 50, 15 Sept (petition on their behalf by the count of Anguillara; both the expelled students are described by him as from Anguillara), and *Conc.* 2138, clause 48, f. 78r, n.d. but dateable in the context of the earlier document; to which should be added the circumstantial evidence of a decision on 18 Oct 1460 to admit two students to the Sapienza in place of others who had been sacked (*Conc.* 564, f. 25r). Both petitions refer to Cardinal Colonna as the students' patron. The event is described on the basis of the second petition by CATONI, 'Genesi', pp. 173-4 n. 81, and cf. MINNUCCI, 'Documenti', p. 28 n. 64, and IDEM, 'La vita nel Collegio', p. 25.

[96] *Conc* 569, f. 19r, 22 Jul; see CATONI, 'Genesi', p. 198 n. 39, and see above, p. 292 n. 104.

[97] E.g. *Not.* 886, ff. 153r-154r, 6 Oct 1483, and *Mis.* 1, f. 112v, 11 Oct 1483.

Sapienza.[98] In 1525 a dispute between two students was punished by a two-month ban only.[99] A similarly light punishment was meted out in 1519 to a group of twelve students who had gone to the Sapienza's property in Sant'Ansano a Dofana where they had caused 'enormi danni' (one of the few reported cases of vandalism) and removed some property. They were to be banned for three months, and if they failed to observe this they would be expelled permanently.[100]

Disciplinary measures were not cast in stone. It was not uncommon for the authorities to relent,[101] and students with connections could be quick to get backup from their patrons. Matteo Malferit of Catania, excluded from the Sapienza for six months for an unspecified reason, took advantage of the presence of a number of luminaries in Florence to obtain three letters, including one from king Alfonso and another from a cardinal's nephew, all written on the same day, 27 February 1441, petitioning for him to be reinstated.[102] More generally, insistence on the disciplinary side of the authorities' jurisdiction over the *sapientini* can obscure its more constructive aspect, that of settling disputes and bringing about peace. This is a less obvious aspect because it is often not documented; indeed we only hear of it when it went beyond the rector. Between them the rector and the *Savi* tried to resolve differences whenever possible. For example in 1473, following 'ludis factis illicite in domo sapientie', a German, Giovanni da Alemagna, and a Spaniard, Gaspar Turiglia, each claimed the other owed him money; the *Savi* ordered both students to hand over the amount in dispute, to be spent on the college, and to make their peace.[103] In 1474 the *Savi* asked the rector to resolve a dispute over debts between two Portuguese students.[104] From roughly the same period there are statements concerning a violent incident between two German students which suggest a formal process, possibly instigated by the rector; that this does not reach the records of the *Savi* (which are extensive for the period to which this incident can be ascribed), and that one of the students, Giovanni d'Argentina (Strasbourg), subsequently became rector, suggest that the episode was resolved effectively.[105] The resolution of disputes could be effected through various means well-known to historians of peacemaking; removal of the chief means of inflicting violence, i.e. weapons,[106] requiring dissident or suspect students to take an oath of loyalty,[107] and/or threats of penalties for those who refused to resolve their differences.[108]

The final area over which the authorities sought to legislate was the students' freedom of movement, both in the Sapienza and out of it. The original statutes forbade loitering outside the main door

[98] *Sale* 23, f. 95v, 14 Aug.

[99] *Studio* 3, f. 47r, 11 Jun.

[100] *Studio* 3, f. 14v, 23 Dec; cf. *Sale* 25, f. 51r.

[101] Cf. the example of Filippo da San Miniato, who was reinstated on 6 Mar 1466 (*Conc.* 597, f. 13v).

[102] *Conc.* 1946, clause 98, from 'Johannes nepos Kardinalis de Comitibus', *Conc.* 2301, fasc. 17; *Conc.* 2305, fasc. 5 (from King Alfonso). These last two have only the day and the month. The outcome of these petitions is not known.

[103] *Studio* 2, f. 9r, 30 Dec. Gaspar Turiglia later absconded to Pisa; below, p. 388.

[104] *Not.* 694, f. 4r, 18 Dec, ed. MINNUCCI, 'Documenti', doc. II-14, pp. 85-6, and see pp. 29-30. The case involved the famous Luís Teixeira; see above, esp. p. 323.

[105] *Not.* 694, ff. 16r-17r, n.d., ed. MINNUCCI, 'Documenti', doc. II-44, pp. 113-5 (n. 155 on his reasons for suggesting a date between 13 April 1475 and early 1476), and see pp. 29 and 258-9 (also IDEM, 'Vita del Collegio', p. 25); on Giovanni d'Argentina see above, p. 317 n. 137, and below, p. 348 n. 85.

[106] In 1518 the *Savi*, 'attenta rissa et questiona est inter scolares dicte Sapientie', ordered that no arms, either offensive or defensive, be permitted in the college (*Sale* 25, f. 81r, 6 May).

[107] *Mis.* 1, f. 112v, 11 Oct 1483, and see p. 335 and n. 81 above.

[108] In 1498 two *sapientini* who were in dispute with the daughter of the previous *Camarlengo* were ordered by the *Savi* to pay her within eight days or face expulsion (*Sale* 24, f. 162v, 8 Jan). The threat had to be repeated several times (ff. 163r, 17 Feb, 163v, 14 Mar, and 164v, 13 Mar).

'a riguardare le vanitade e lascivie'.[109] A later measure decreed that this door was to be kept shut at night,[110] and a back door was eventually walled up 'per evitare gli scandali'.[111] The kitchen, larder and cellar were out of bounds.[112] Students were not allowed out at all in the evenings in winter, and only for two hours in summer.[113] No nights could be spent out without permission and good reason, and three months' unauthorised absence would cost a student his place (this was extended to six months in 1542).[114] Any student absent, with permission, for over a week had to leave the key to his room with another student, later with the *Camarlengo*.[115] The most unforgivable offence, of course, was for a *sapientino* to leave the *Studio* altogether; Gaspar Turiglia, who in 1474 was discovered to have gone to study at Pisa, was stripped of his place in the college, and an order was issued for his possessions to be confiscated should he ever return to Siena.[116]

---

[109] 'Ordini', clause 43.

[110] *Studio* 2, f. 132r, 9 Jan 1493. By 1540 this act had taken on a different complexion; the students had begun to shut and even lock the door, apparently to keep the *Camarlengo* out, and the *Balìa* and *Savi* were making various attempts to stop them (KOŠUTA, 'Documenti', doc. VI-1, pp. 379-80, and 382, and cf. pp. 319-20, n. 13).

[111] Cf. below, p. 350.

[112] *Mis.* 1, f. 87r, 1 Mar 1440 (and see CATONI, 'Genesi', p. 169 n. 64); *Studio* 3, f. 79v, 3 May 1530; *Studio* 109, f. 4r-v, 15 Feb 1532, ed. KOŠUTA, 'Documenti', doc. II, p. 345; *Studio* 110, f. 6r, 17 Feb 1542, ed. KOŠUTA, 'Documenti', doc. IV, p. 360.

[113] *Studio* 110, f. 7v, 17 Feb 1542.

[114] 'Ordini', clauses 31-2, and *Mis.* 1, ff. 52r-v, 21 Jan 1421; *Studio* 110, f. 10v, 11 Mar 1542, ed. KOŠUTA, 'Documenti', doc. IV, p. 364. Extended periods of leave were by no means unknown. The early years of the Sapienza saw two students being given a year's leave of absence (*Conc.* 344, f. 21v, 21 Jun 1423; *Conc.* 532, f. 125v, 30 Jun 1455), and four being given six months' leave (*Conc.* 434, f. 30r, 28 May 1438; *Conc.* 490, f. 27r, 9 Oct 1447). Cf. also p. 313 n. 99 above.

[115] 'Ordini', clause 33, and cf. *Mis.* 1, ff. 87r-v, 4 Jun 1438, *Mis.* 1, f. 89r, 29 Dec 1445, and *Studio* 110, f. 5v, 17 Feb 1542, ed. KOŠUTA, 'Documenti', doc. IV, p. 360.

[116] *Studio* 2, f. 19r, 28 Nov 1474, and cf. *Not.* 694, f. 25r, 28 Nov, no year, ed. MINNUCCI, 'Documenti', doc. II-52, p. 122, and cf. pp. 35-6 (also IDEM, 'La vita nel Collegio', p. 27).

III

ADMINISTRATION

1. *Layers of government: the commune and the* Savi dello Studio

The tensions over admissions discussed above[1] – the *Savi dello Studio* trying to keep a lid on numbers and the *Consiglio del Popolo*, the *Concistoro* and the *Balìa* insisting on putting in favoured students – are symptomatic of the problems that could arise at the top levels of decision-making. Early proposals – those of 1404 and 1415 – envisaged decisions regarding admissions as the responsibility of the *Concistoro* in conjunction with the *Savi*.[2] Sometimes the task was delegated to the *Savi*, occasionally in conjunction with the *Camarlengo* of the Sapienza who dealt with the formalities of entrance;[3] more often the *Consiglio del Popolo* claimed back the right to intervene, or the *Balìa* to override, sometimes at inauspicious moments.[4] As has been seen,[5] this is not untypical of the position of the *Savi* generally. Their overall responsibility for the Sapienza was affirmed in 1414 and 1415,[6] and again once the house had opened.[7] They were to oversee the internal management of the house, but in practice they usually referred major or contentious matters upwards to the *Concistoro*. A typical division of labour would be that the *Concistoro*, meeting with the *Savi*, would make substantial decisions and then leave the details for the *Savi* to resolve. The admission of students would be a major decision, but the rooms to be allocated to them would be left up to the *Savi*.[8] For much of the fif-

---

[1] Pp. 310 *seq.*

[2] See above, pp. 304-5.

[3] E.g. *Mis.* 1, f. 115r-v, 13 Jun 1491.

[4] The *Consiglio del Popolo* was responsible for adding to the overcrowding problems of 1441-2; see above, p. 316.

[5] Above, pp. 76 *seq.*

[6] *Conc.* 293, f. 9v, 14 Nov 1414; *Mis.* 1, f. 51v, 1 Feb 1415.

[7] *CG* 207, f. 222v, 23 Oct 1416. The position was spelt out formally in 1418 in a measure which, despite its temporary nature (it relates to the fact that the *Savi*'s period of office had expired and the house was 'sine Gubernatoribus') was copied into the various collections of statutes: 'Quod sapientes studii habeant eam gubernare et regere, unde jam sit datus ordo de scolaribus actis ad studium ibidem retinendis, Et pro modo conservationis, et manutentionis dicte domus' (*CG* 208, f. 60v-61r, 8 Jan 1418; copies in *Mis.* 1, f. 81r, *Statuti* 41, f. 213r, *Statuti* 47, f. 212r). The *Savi* were occasionally described as 'Savi dello Studio e della Sapienza', or even just 'Savi della Sapienza'; above, p. 80.

[8] E.g. *Conc.* 559, f. 16r, 20 Nov 1459 (Petrus de Francia was to be admitted; the *Savi* were to assign him a room); see also *Not.* 694, ff. 7-8, 7 Jun 1470-2, ed. MINNUCCI, 'Documenti', II-38, p. 109, and *Not.* 694, f. 22, n.d., ed. MINNUCCI, II-48, pp. 118-9.

teenth century the relationship between the two bodies has to be deduced from the records of the *Concistoro*, where we find petitions and issues raised by the *Savi* determined and then handed down again. This pattern is confirmed for the last part of the century by the deliberations of the *Savi*, which survive from 1473.[9]

These were still only the top tiers of authority. The college had two officers of its own, whose development and changing functions need to be examined in detail.

2. *The rector*

The central figure in the life of the Sapienza, as of any college, was its head, the rector. He was directly in authority over the students and responsible for their discipline. In the 'ordini del vivere de li scolari', which date from within two years of the house's opening,[10] this role emerges pragmatically rather than explicitly. The rector is repeatedly named as the arbiter in disciplinary matters; students not attending mass, or talking in rooms,[11] or wishing to request leave, are all referred to him, and in addition he is to use his discretion on matters as diverse as organising 'recreatione' on Christmas Eve and warning any students who have been admitted at too tender an age that they were wasting their money. The legislation of subsequent years helps to fill out the detail of this picture a little. Within the Sapienza his authority was wide-ranging, but its limits were carefully defined, as were his obligations. According to the first substantial reforms of the rectorate, of the 1440s,[12] it was for the first time spelt out that the rector was basically responsible for the good conduct of the scholars.[13] Clerical status was no exemption from his jurisdiction.[14] He had wide discretion over the suspension or expulsion of students for serious infringements.[15] Scholars had to swear to respect him and not to offend him,[16] and his jurisdiction over them was declared to be equivalent to that of the rector of the *Studio* over scholars outside the Sapienza.[17] Equally, of course, he was expected to set a good example, living in the

---

[9] See above, pp. 20-1.

[10] See above, p. 325 n. 4.

[11] 'Ordini', clause 42 (above, p. 329, Table 7).

[12] The following points are gleaned from a number of successive reforms over a five-year period. There is the complication that in this period the rectorate itself oscillated between foreign students and a Sienese appointment, and in one such reform (*Mis.* 1, ff. 88v-89v, 29 Dec 1445) the powers are ascribed not to the rector (who had resigned) but to a *Presidente*, clearly an interim figure who lacked the formal title. See below, pp. 343-4. It is likely that the powers of the head of the house were spelt out precisely because this temporary figure lacked the powers that would have been vested in a rector.

[13] 'Item che'l decto Rectore habbi sopra li scolari d'essa casa per li scandali et errori comettessero auctorità de poterli coregiare etiamdio provarli sel caso el meritasse quanta hanno e savii d'essa casa, non manchando per questo alchuna auctorità havesseno e savii sì come sempre s'è observato' (*CG* 224, f. 115v, 5 Apr 1448). This statement regarding his authority was only one of the seventeen clauses; the rest related to his election, appointment, duties and responsibilities. The measures were not transcribed into the 'statute book' (*Mis.* 1), possibly because they were soon superseded (below, pp. 345-6).

[14] *CG* 224, f. 188r, and *Mis.* 1, f. 62v, 22 Nov 1448; cf. ZDEKAUER, pp. 103-4 (erroneously giving 22 Dec).

[15] *Mis.* 1, f. 88v, 29 Dec 1445. Students had the right to appeal against such expulsion, but not to reside in the Sapienza or to eat there pending the appeal.

[16] *Mis.* 1, f. 89r, 29 Dec 1445. A notice to this effect was put up in 1493, which raises the question of whether his authority was being taken seriously (*Studio* 2, f. 131v, 5 Jan).

[17] *Mis.* 1, f. 89r, 29 Dec 1445. This was reported as one of the key features in Siena later in the century, in the Florentine summary of the practices of the Sienese *Studio* (above, p. 27 n. 144).

house,[18] wearing long robes and a cowl, and eating with the scholars.[19] Finally these principles were confirmed in the mid-sixteenth century in two statutes, of 1532 and 1542, which include the more conventional clauses on the authority of the rector that were so strikingly absent from the first redaction; the stipulation that students must swear an oath of obedience to him,[20] his duty to resolve conflicts between students,[21] the denial to students of the right of recourse to any other authority.[22] The 1542 statutes also charged the rector with the responsibility of seeing that the *sapientini* attended to their studies.[23]

The authorities supported the rector in his role. It is in the nature of the records of the *Savi*, the *Concistoro* and the *Balìa* that they record derogations and suspensions rather than the rector's normal execution of his functions; but it is clear from such documents that his authority over the members of the college, including the duty and right of arbitration between students, was being complemented, reinforced or occasionally overridden, but not questioned in principle.[24] The rector was sometimes authorised or deputed by the *Savi* or higher bodies to act on their behalf.[25] He could attend meetings of the *Savi* and speak on Sapienza matters,[26] and is once also recorded as jointly admitting a student along with the *Concistoro*.[27]

Who was the rector? The lack of definition of his mode of appointment in the early 'ordini' (or indeed in the later measures) is not accidental. It is a reflection of the main characteristic which was clear from the outset; in contrast to every other Italian college of the period, in which this post was democratically filled from among the students, in Siena the rector was a communal appointee.[28] For

---

[18] *CG* 222, f. 41v, 4 Aug 1443.

[19] 'debbi vestire de vestimente longhe e honeste per insino presso al dosso del pié de panno monachino et simil portare el capuccio honesto come se richiede a tal Rectorato.' *CG* 224, f. 115v, 5 Apr 1448.

[20] *Studio* 109, f. 5v, 16 Feb 1532, rubric XIV, ed. Košuta, 'Documenti', doc. II, p. 346; *Studio* 110, f. 8v, 17 Feb 1542, rubric XXVI, ed. Košuta, 'Documenti', doc. IV, p. 362. In the 'ordini' of the college, students of the Sapienza were forbidden to bring a fellow-student before a judge without the rector's permission. Civil action resulted in one month's denial of food; for a criminal action the penalty was doubled ('Ordini', clause 39).

[21] *Studio* 109, f. 5r-v, clause 13, ed. Košuta, 'Documenti', doc. II, p. 346; *Studio* 110, f. 5r, clause 13, ed. Košuta, doc. IV, p. 359.

[22] *Studio* 109, f. 5v, clause 15, ed. Košuta, 'Documenti', doc. II, p. 346; *Studio* 110, f. 8r-v, clause 25, ed. Košuta, doc. IV, p. 362.

[23] *Studio* 110, f. 6v, clause 18, ed. Košuta, 'Documenti', doc. IV, pp. 360-1; cf. Cascio Pratilli, *L'Università e il Principe*, p. 13 n. 5. He was to inspect the students' rooms at least once a month, warning delinquents up to three times before expelling them, 'perché tali scolari che non vogliano studiare, ruinano tutti li altri scolari'. This is an unusual measure for Italian college statutes; the only comparable examples of something similar before the Counter-Reformation come from Rome, in the fifteenth-century statutes of the Collegio Capranica and the Collegio Nardini, where students who did not attend lectures were to be deprived of their food; Esposito, 'Le "Sapientie" romane', pp. 48-9.

[24] Examples include the *Savi* ordering the expulsion of a Portuguese student if he did not settle his debt to the rector, a fellow Portuguese (*Not.* 694, f. 4r, 18 Dec 1474, ed. Minnucci, 'Documenti', doc. II-14, pp. 85-6, and see 29-30); and the arrangement of arbitration between two *sapientini* during a vacancy in the rectorate (*Conc.* 725, f. 34v, 21 Aug 1487).

[25] E.g. the *Savi* deputing arbitration between two students to the rector; *Studio* 2, f. 96r, and *Sale* 21, f. 212r, 16 Dec 1483.

[26] *CG* 224, f. 115v, 5 Apr. 1448.

[27] *Conc.* 597, f. 13v, 6 Mar 1466.

[28] Denley, 'The Collegiate Movement', pp. 55-6. After years of disturbances the Perugians eventually removed the right of the students in the Sapienza Vecchia to elect their own rector, giving it instead to the bishop and the prior of the monastery of Monte Morcino. Biblioteca Comunale Augusta di Perugia, *ms.* 1239, ff. 43r-45r, 26 Jul 1467, eds. Sebastiani, 'Il collegio universitario', appendix III, pp. 329-334 (and see pp. 94-5), and. Angeletti and Bertini, *La Sapienza Vecchia*, pp. 429-33.

the first three decades these appointments were made by the *Concistoro* or the *Consiglio del Popolo*, with no explanation in the documents of the criteria for selection. The appointments were all short-term, either for one year or at most two. The rectors were probably all members of the academic community, and almost all, as far as we can tell, were non-Sienese, suggesting that the authorities had accepted the notion that a community of foreign scholars should have a foreign scholar at its head, but not the usual corollary that the same community should therefore choose that individual. It also appears that they wanted the rector to be someone with a degree (or at least someone close to the end of his studies), who would therefore have some natural authority over the members of the Sapienza. The appointment did not, however, apparently have to be from within the ranks of the *sapientini*.[29] The first mention of a rector by name – Simone – is found in 1419;[30] the first recorded appointment, of Giovanni da Visso, dates from 1421.[31] Neither of these appears to have been a member of the college, and indeed it might have been difficult to appoint a student so soon after the opening of the house. The third rector known to us, Filippo da Lucca, appointed in 1424,[32] was probably the same Filippo di Andrea Balducci da Lucca who was admitted as a student in the first batch in February 1416;[33] he appears to have held the post for about four years, after two renewals.[34]

The issue of who should be rector began to be problematic, and eventually contentious, in the 1430s and 1440s, which saw a string of unsatisfactory or unenthusiastic candidates. In the 1430s the post was held several times by Benedetto da Volterra, an exile from his native city, who again does not appear to have been a member of the college prior to his appointment.[35] After his first term (1432-4) a student in the Sapienza, Giovanni d'Amelia, was given the job, but he soon renounced it because he was unwilling

---

[29] See below, nn. 31 and 35, and pp. 343-5. Also from this period, unfortunately not dateable, is a proposal to the *Concistoro* from the *Savi* that Giovanni Battista, collateral of the outgoing *podestà*, might be willing, for an appropriate salary, to accept both a lectureship and the rectorate of the *Sapienza*: 'et avendo la casa vostra della Sapienza necessario di provedersi Solo per lo governo et hordine delli Scolari d'un Sofficiente rectore forestiero per provedere a disordini di quella casa, a quali si no si ripara potrebbe seguitare qualche grande inconveniente…' (*Conc.* 2138, no. 15, f. 25r, n.d.). This is indicative of the fluidity of the terms of the rectorate. The position of this document in the volume (which is in clear chronological sequence) suggests 1442 as a possible date, which would fit; clearly the internal problems of the house were evident, but the *Savi* were not thinking at that stage of a citizen rector.

[30] He is named simply as Simone (*Conc.* 1616, f. 57v, 2 Apr 1419). Although he has the title *dominus*, there is no way of knowing whether he was a student, and there is no previous record of a student of this name being admitted. What happened to the rectorate in the transition from Misericordia to Sapienza is not known. It used to be thought that the last rector of the old Misericordia, Bencivenne di Gano, had conveniently died in 1416; but BCS, *ms.* A.IX.2, 'Elenco dei Rettori dell'antica Casa della Misericordia', ed. G. B. GUASCONI in *La Misericordia di Siena*, p. 119, demonstrates that he was still alive, though not necessarily rector, on 5 Jun of that year. (By 1418 he was dead, and his will was being contested; below, p. 363.)

[31] Appointed rector by the *Concistoro* on 24 May 1421, he was to appear in Siena by the end of September (*Conc.* 1619, f. 66v). He is described as 'legum isperitus', a term used for those who were not doctors, but he was also appointed to a *lectura* in civil law in the Sapienza. Another candidate, Filippo d'Amelia, recommended for the job by Tartaglia di Lavello, was clearly not appointed (*Conc.* 1619, f. 15v, 7 Feb 1421). Giovanni da Visso's term was renewed two years later (*Conc.* 345, f. 26r, 25 Aug 1423). Neither of these two appears to have been admitted to the Sapienza as a student.

[32] He was appointed on 28 Feb 1424, for a period of one year, beginning on 18 Oct of that year; *Dipl., Biblioteca Pubblica*, 28 Feb 1423(=1424).

[33] *Conc.* 300, f. 40r, 22 Feb.

[34] The first renewal was on 7 Mar 1425 (addition to *Dipl., Biblioteca Pubblica*, 28 Feb 1423(=1424); cf. *CG* 211, f. 44v, 6 Mar 1426 (end of his first term); *Conc.* 361, ff. 15v, 21 Mar, and 18r, 25 Mar 1426 (he was given a lectureship in addition, on condition that he remained rector); and *Conc.* 373, f. 28r, 2 Jun 1428 (a further lectureship).

[35] He was given a two-year appointment in 1432 (*Conc.* 400, f. 35r, 5 Oct). I have found no record of Benedetto having been admitted as a student. On Benedetto see ZDEKAUER, p. 99.

to accept the condition that he take his degree.[36] Benedetto was eventually re-hired for a further two years, subsequently renewed.[37] His third term was cut short by death.[38] His successor, Ercole de' Cataldini da Visso, asked to be excused after six months,[39] and the next incumbent, Malatesta de' Catanei da Borgo, a *sapientino* of four years' standing,[40] left after two months when he was given a lectureship.[41]

Benedetto's second tenure of the post had come after his acquisition of Sienese citizenship,[42] which must have raised the expectations of Sienese citizens that they might be eligible for the post, just as their eligibility for lectureships was formalised in this period.[43] This, and frustrations over the discontinuity of the post, appear to have prompted the first substantial reforms of the office, made in 1443, following the death of the incumbent.[44] The minute of this measure gives a most articulate evaluation of what was considered to be wrong with the management structure. Rapid turnover of officials at all levels, and lack of commitment and liaison, were identified as responsible for the difficulties of the college.[45] The solution was to be the elevation of the rectorate into an office of considerable and well-defined authority and status. The new 'rettore e governatore' was, first, to be a Sienese citizen, 'di buona conditione e fame'; and – an indication of his status – he was to be chosen by the *Consiglio del Popolo* from a shortlist of three names drawn up by the *Concistoro* and the *Savi*.[46] The appointment was to be for life.[47] While he did not have to be a cleric, he had to be without offspring.[48] His salary

---

[36] *Conc.* 412, f. 36, 28 Sept 1434 (his appointment as rector); this is presumably the same as Dns. Johannes Ser Ugolini de Amelia, admitted as a student in 1427, *Conc.* 367, ff. 4v-5r, 7 Mar). For his renunciation see *Conc.* 414, f. 17r, 28 Jan 1435 (and below, p. 347 on the issue of rectors taking degrees).

[37] He was appointed in January 1435 for a further two years, to begin in October (*Conc.* 414, f. 17r, 28 Jan 1435; cf. also *Conc.* 413, f. 4r, 4 Nov 1434); a scholar in the Sapienza, Giovanni di Frangano da Sicilia, took over for the rest of the academic year (*Conc.* 414, ff. 26r, 12 Feb, 30v, 19 Feb 1435), though later that year the post was held by Giovanni da Catalonia, who also became vice-rector of the *Studio* (*Conc.* 418, f. 8v, 14 Sept). Benedetto was given a fifth year in 1437 (*Conc.* 430, f. 25v, 12 Oct).

[38] BCS, *ms.* C.III.2 (*Obituario S. Domenico, 1336-1596*), f. 77v, 25 Dec 1437, ed. ZDEKAUER, p. 99 n. 2.

[39] *Conc.* 432, f. 28r, 21 Feb 1438 (appointment, for one year); *Conc.* 436, f. 21v, 2 Oct 1438.

[40] He appears to have been admitted in 1434; see above, p. 316 n. 125.

[41] *Conc.* 436, f. 21v, 2 Oct, and *Conc.* 437, f. 35v, 16 Dec 1438. NARDI, 'Una fonte inedita delle lauree senesi' is cautious about the possibility that this is the same Malatesta de Burgos who is found teaching in 1441 and 1443 (see above, pp. 153 n. 36 and 166 n. 174). A Marinus d. Raynerii Catanensis de Burgo Sancti Sepulcri, presumably a relative, also became a *sapientino*, then rector of the Sapienza and vice-rector of the *Studio* before taking his doctorate *in utriusque iuris* on 3 Jun 1500; MINNUCCI, *Lauree*, I, no. 99, p. 70 (and cf. *Conc.* 798, f. 10r, 30 Oct 1499).

[42] *Conc.* 415, f. 10r, 10 Mar 1435.

[43] Above, pp. 192-3. In 1440 it was reported in the *Consiglio del Popolo* that many Sienese officials were neglecting their jobs because they hoped to be given a lectureship or the rectorate of the Sapienza (*CG* 220, f. 178r, 21 Sept 1440).

[44] BCS, *ms.* C.III.2 (*Obituario S. Domenico*), f. 81v: 'Dnus. N. honorabilis rector scolarium domus sapientie sepultus fuit die 16 mensis Martii 1442[=1443].' A five-year gap in information about the rectorate is broken only by this notice.

[45] 'Anno considerato che el decto mancamento procede solamente per non avere una persona la quale abbi continua cura a le cose d'essa casa, Et che ve stia cum carità e amore e de dì e de notte perche stando così sotto il governo de' savi, E quali cum difficultà se ragunano et sotto el governo del camarlengo, che sta due anni, actendono ad avere per quello tempo honore quanto possono, parendo alloro assai avere satisfacto quando anno governato li scolari, Et cosi entrando ogni anno al governo dessa gente nuova, per forza e necessità seguita che non si possa usare quella diligentia che se rechiedarebbe' (*CG* 222, f. 48v [new foliation], 4 Aug 1443; copy in *Conc.* 2115, f. 82r, n.d.). Related to this, and making similar points, is the petition in *Conc.* 2115, f. 68v, n.d. but from its contents and position in the volume – which is chronological in sequence – probably 1442/43.

[46] On 30 Aug this was amended to a shortlist of six (*CG* 222, ff. 55v-56r).

[47] This is added in the margin of f. 48v.

[48] *CG* 222, f. 48v, 4 Aug 1443 (should he become a father during his tenure of the post he would have to leave). Cf. *CG* 224, f. 115r, 5 Apr 1448, and *CG* 236, f. 127v-128v, 28 Jun 1475, when the notion of a Sienese rector was revived. The condition was now more of an aspiration; the shortlist was to include nine citizens 'che la più parte o tutti non habbino figliuoli, se havere li potranno'.

was raised from 30 to 80 florins,[49] out of which sum he was to pay for at least two servants ('una fante e uno fameglio') and a horse with which he was to travel round the property of the Sapienza on tours of inspection. He did not have to 'prendere la dignità de la militia' or wear any other status symbols. He had to reside in the Sapienza. In conjunction with the *Savi*, he was to have the same authority over the Sapienza as the rector of the hospital of S. Maria della Scala had over that institution in conjunction with the *Savi de lo Spedale*. This was bolstered by other conditions; he was to be called *dominus*, he was to have priority at anatomical sessions,[50] and in the *Consiglio del Popolo* and the *Consilio Generale* he was to be seated before all doctors, following the *milites*.[51]

The new rectorate bears a number of resemblances (beyond the one made explicit) to the rectorate of the Scala, the appointment to which, like much of the hospital's administration, had come under communal control.[52] This was a position of honour and dignity in communal politics; a life appointment for an unmarried man, who became a *cavaliere* on taking office, and a member of the *Consiglio Generale*, and who was expected to leave his possessions to the hospital.[53] It was also a position which at times inevitably became politicised.[54] That this appears not to have happened with the Sapienza is largely because the replacement of an annual internal student appointee with a communal figure repeatedly proved unworkable, and although several attempts were made during the fifteenth century to revive it, it remained a last resort for what was perceived as an emergency situation. The first rector chosen under those regulations, the Sienese Pietro di Nanni Biringucci, an eminent citizen (though as far as we know not a university man),[55] who subsequently went on to a prominent diplomatic career,

---

[49] The 30-florin salary is known from a petition of only two years earlier; *CG* 221, f. 21v, 26 Jun 1441.

[50] This is the only element in the document that suggests that he might be an academic, though it might be that his attendance was ceremonial.

[51] These privileges were re-stated by the *Concistoro* at the moment of appointment (*Conc.* 466, f. 42r-v, 13 Oct 1443). The seat on the council is not declared to be *ex officio*.

[52] By 1404 the election to this post was in the hands of the *Consiglio del Popolo*, in reforms which 'trasformarono questa carica sostanzialmente in un ufficio pubblico'; G. CANTUCCI and U. MORANDI, 'Introduzione', *Archivio dell'ospedale di Santa Maria della Scala. Inventario*. 2 vols. (Rome, 1960-62), I, pp. VII-LXXX (p. XXIV, and cf. pp. IX-X, XIII). On the process of growing communal influence in the late fourteenth century, of which this was the culmination, see esp. ISAACS, 'Lo spedale di Santa Maria della Scala', pp. 25-6, EPSTEIN, *Alle origini della fattoria toscana*, pp. 22-7, and more generally PICCINNI and VIGNI, 'Modelli di assistenza', p. 159.

[53] As previous note. The rector's membership of the *Consiglio Generale* goes back to the communal statutes of 1262; ISAACS, 'Lo spedale di Santa Maria della Scala', p. 24. These characteristics were not all taken over for the new post for the Sapienza; for example, he was not compelled to take a knighthood (the reason this is mentioned is presumably to stress the distinction between this and the Scala rectorate). There is also no mention of an automatic seat in the *Consiglio Generale*. The provision that the lifelong rector should leave his possessions to the institution was also not copied for the Sapienza in 1443, though a watered-down version of it was introduced at the next attempt to make this a life appointment, in 1448; below, p. 345.

[54] Cf. the ousting of Niccolò di Galgano Bichi in 1435, on which Ascheri has unearthed fresh evidence demonstrating its political motivation, M. ASCHERI, 'Storia dell'Ospedale e/o storia della città', in *Spedale di Santa Maria della Scala*, pp. 65-71 (pp. 66-8); the removal and subsequent reinstatement of Salimbene de' Capacci during the political upheavals of 1480-82, L. BANCHI (ed.), *Statuto dello Spedale di Santa Maria a Siena, 1318-79*, in *Statuti senesi scritti in volgare ne' secoli XIII e XIV*, eds. F. L. Polidori and L. Banchi (Bologna, 1863-77), III (1877), pp. 274-5, 279); and the increasing politicisation of the office at the end of the fifteenth century, culminating in effective takeover by Pandolfo Petrucci after 1500, leading eventually to its downgrading to a fixed-term post, ISAACS, 'Lo spedale', p. 26, ASCHERI, loc. cit., and GALLAVOTTI CAVALLERO, *Lo Spedale di Santa Maria della Scala*, p. 265.

[55] The appointment of the new rector was made on 13 Oct 1443 (*Conc.* 466, f. 42r-v). The name of the appointee is not given – there is a gap in the *Consiglio Generale* volume for October 1443 – and has to be deduced from the documents of 1445 (below, n. 56). Biringucci was the son of a previous *Camarlengo* (below, p. 344 n. 138), and had received a knighthood earlier in the year (BCS, *ms.* P.III.4, *ad annum*).

relinquished his post with the permission of the *Consiglio del Popolo* after only two years.[56] His successor was again an academic and a non-citizen, Johannes de Gigliaco of Savoy, a student in civil law,[57] who within the year was also given a *condotta*.[58] Soon the authorities decided on a second major reform, in 1448.[59] This went into much more detail. Appointing – for life – another Sienese, Agapito d'Ambrogio,[60] who had been *Camarlengo*,[61] and who was neither a student nor a doctor, the *Consiglio del Popolo* added seventeen clauses describing the job. It represented a scaling down of the position of the rector. His salary was back to 30 florins, out of which he had to pay for his *famiglia*.[62] He could not hold any other communal office or run any business; he had to wear formal long dress,[63] and eat with the scholars. His authority was equal to that of the *Savi* – he could even expel students – and he could sit with the *Savi* when they were discussing Sapienza business. On the other hand he could not handle any money (this was the job of the *Camarlengo*), and could not authorise expenditure on repairs above 5 florins without the approval of the *Savi*.[64]

Agabito d'Ambrogio remained in office for four years. Although it was he who, on the instructions of the *Concistoro*, drew up an inventory of the house's possessions,[65] in other respects his tenure was not a success. At one stage the students of the Sapienza took the unprecedented step of writing a letter of complaint to the *Concistoro*, alleging that he had abused his office, that he would not eat with them, and that when plague came to Siena he had decamped to the Sapienza's property at Sant'Ansano a Dofana with his family and relatives, and was living there off Sapienza resources, leaving the scholars to run the house themselves.[66] On his resignation[67] there was disagreement about how to proceed. The *Savi* first recommended the appointment of a single figure who would combine the roles of rector, *Camarlengo* and *governatore* all in one (and at considerable saving).[68] In the event, after a

---

[56] *CG* 223, f. 41v, 13 Jul, *Conc.* 477, f. 18r, 26 Jul 1445. He had to stay until the end of December; *Conc.* 479, f. 6r, 6 Nov. Biringucci's connections with the Sapienza did not quite end there; in 1452 he was elected as one of three *provisionarii* to draw up proposals regarding the rectorate (*Conc.* 513, f. 53r, 18 Apr; cf. 45v-46r, 16 Apr).

[57] *Conc.* 481, f. 46r, 20 Apr 1446; he was already vice-rector of the Sapienza.

[58] *Conc.* 485, f. 38r, 19 Dec 1446.

[59] *CG* 224, ff. 115r-116v, 5 Apr.

[60] *Conc.* 493, f. 16v, 1 Apr.

[61] *Conc.* 487, f. 32v, 5 Apr 1447.

[62] He was allowed only one servant; the Sapienza would contribute a salary of 6 florins for him, but any extra expenditure was to come out of the salary of the rector. As this was the standard salary both before and after 1443, the suspicion must be that the 80 florins of that year were designed specifically for Biringucci.

[63] 'debbi vestire de vestimente longhe e honeste per insino presso al dosso del pié de panno monachino et simil portare el capuccio honesto come se richiede a tal Rectorato.'

[64] Other clauses included the reinforcement of the 1443 measure that he must not have children – if his wife died he was not to remarry – and the condition that, should the Sapienza return to being a hospital during his tenure of office, he had to leave property of his own, to the tune of 1,200 *lire*, to it.

[65] Ordered on 15 Nov 1448; *Conc.* 497, f. 11r; see CATONI, 'Il comune di Siena e l'amministrazione della Sapienza', p. 124, and on the inventory itself below, p. 363.

[66] *Conc.* 1967 no. 99, n.d. The letter has been archived under 1450, which is plausible; this and 1448 were both years of plague (above, p. 114).

[67] *Conc.* 513, f. 5r, 4 Mar 1452. The resignation was accepted on condition that he remained in office until May, to which he agreed. Although there was much criticism of his rectorate, this was not the end of his public career; the following year he was *podestà* of Casole, certainly a much less prestigious post but a post nonetheless (*Conc.* 1674, f. 206r, 5 Sept 1453).

[68] *Conc.* 513, ff. 45v-46r, 16 Apr, and 53r, 18 Apr 1452.

commission had investigated the matter,[69] the authorities did not go down this route.[70] Since the financial state of the Sapienza was the priority,[71] they first appointed the current *Camarlengo* to be *governatore* and *Camarlengo* together (with a substantial salary raise).[72] While they made no explicit decision about the rectorate, in fact it reverted to being an academic and foreigner's post, filled first by Bartolomeo da Massa, doctor of law (1452-5),[73] then by Nuño of Portugal (1455-6),[74] before a further measure[75] finally laid down the terms and conditions of this office in a form which remained stable for the rest of the century. Henceforth the office was to be annual; each October the *Savi* would choose three candidates to be put to the *Consiglio del Popolo* for scrutiny.[76] The candidates must be doctors or must take their doctorate within a month; one was to be the outgoing rector.[77]

[69] The commission was set up on 18 Apr 1452 (*Conc.* 513, f. 53r), and included the former rector Pietro di Nanni Biringucci.

[70] It is likely that the proposals of 'Certi Savi cittadini electi per li M.ci S. per auctorità del conseglio oportuni a fare provisioni a bene et mantenimento della casa della Sapientia', preserved in *Conc.* 2310, no foliation, is the report of this commission. The document is from the period of Agapito's rectorate, and from its content presumably the end of that period, but is not precisely dateable. The document denounces the abuses in frank and uncompromising language: 'li scolari vendono i loro luoghi segretamente'; scholars are admitted 'per molte pregarie'. The root of these ills is the lack of a figure of status at the head of the house: 'veduto una grande parte del mancamento di quella casa procedere dalla discordia delli Scolari per la poca ubidientia et reverentia hanno a quelli lo sono preposti per Rectori maxime non havendo alcuno grado o dignità'. The *Savi* proposed that the rectorate should revert to foreign scholars, 'distante dalla Città di Siena al meno miglia cinquanta'. The rector was to have had a law degree for at least three years; he would have authority over the students in the college but absolutely none over financial and estate matters, for which a *governatore* was to be appointed, who would have much of the status and qualities of the rector as defined in the previous reforms. The measure was narrowly defeated, but in many respects heralded the division of responsibility which was eventually adopted.

[71] 'come da poi che Agabito d'Ambrogio lassò el rectorato et governo de la decta casa truovano esserci grandissimi mancamenti et maximamente ne le possessioni per non esserci persona deputata sopra el governo d'esse possessioni' (*CG* 226, f. 2r, 12 Aug 1452; = *Conc.* 2138, no. 19, f. 29r).

[72] He was to be paid 35 florins per annum rather than the previous 20; he was not eligible for other offices. This was a recent appointment; since Agapito's elevation to the rectorate there had been at least two other *Camarlenghi*, Nanno di Cioni Fei (re-appointment in *Conc.* 499, f. 32r, 16 Apr 1449) and Angelo Guidoni (appointment in *Conc.* 505, f. 46v, 21 Apr 1450).

[73] I have found only the instructions for payment for this rector; the first is *Conc.* 518, f. 21r, 24 Jan 1453, ed. BAI, doc. 45, p. 40, the last *Conc.* 534, f. 19v, 19 Sept 1455, BAI, doc. 79, p. 65, i.e. covering the academic years 1452-5.

[74] *Conc.* 534, f. 19r, 19 Sept 1455 (his election); *Conc.* 535, f. 27v, Dec 1455, BAI, doc. 82, p. 68 (first payment). The candidate had been recommended by the king of Portugal in 1453 (above, p. 321 n. 182).

[75] *CG* 227, f. 241r (new foliation), 10 Sept 1456 (= *Mis.* 1, f. 93r). That this measure, in contrast to those of 1443, 1448 and 1452, was entered in the statute book of the Sapienza, is indicative. The reform also defined the role of the *Camarlengo*, here called *Fattore per lo governo delle possessioni* and clearly distinct in competency, and reasserted the *Savi*'s authority over all appointments to lesser functions within the house (chaplains, sacristans, clerics, the *canovaio* and others).

[76] Loc. cit. The first rector to be appointed under the new dispensation was Fabiano da Monte San Savino (*Conc.* 540, f. 30r, 7 Oct 1456). Sometimes an incomplete meeting of the *Savi* made the nominations, on one occasion as few as two. In 1477, three had been away because of an outbreak of plague; their decision was ruled valid by the *Consiglio del Popolo* (*CG* 237, f. 210r [new foliation], *Conc.* 666, f. 38r, ed. FERRERI, doc. 51, p. 45, and *Conc.* 2117, f. 202v, all 26 Oct 1477, and cf. *Conc.* 2187, 1477, n.d.). It is not always clear whether the *Savi* did this on their own and then had them confirmed by the *Concistoro*; on some occasions the text is explicit about it being the *Savi*'s decision, while on others it appears to be down to the *Concistoro* (e.g. *Conc.* 715, f. 9v, FERRERI, doc. 222, p. 187, 17 Nov 1485). By the end of the century, as with so many *Studio* matters, the *Balìa* took this function from the *Concistoro* (*Balìa* 38, f. 131r, 21 Jun 1493). In 1495 they authorised the *Concistoro* to do it; *Balìa* 40, f. 51v, 5 Nov (and *Conc.* 775, f. 2v, 7 Nov, ed. FERRERI, doc. 344, p. 348).

[77] The presence of the outgoing rector on the shortlist was not a frequent occurrence, perhaps unsurprisingly given that the office was designed to be held by students at the end of their time. One such instance was the 1478 election, in which the incumbent, Petrus de Portugallia (Pedro Vasques, on whom below, p. 348 n. 84), was re-elected (*Conc.* 673, f. 15r, 29 Dec). Acceptance of a second term was clearly part of a career strategy or at least progression; the following year he went on to become *Iudex curiarum domini collateralis et pupillorum* (*Conc.* 678, f. 15r, 10 Oct 1479), and by 1480 *giudice degli appelli* (MINNUCCI, 'Documenti', doc. III-245, p. 203, 30 Dec 1480, and see p. 304 for other references). On the other hand, the inclusion in the

With this measure the fluidity, tensions and experiments of the first forty years were resolved in an acceptable division. The requirement that the rector be an academic, a foreigner and a *sapientino*, were accepted;[78] the students had become resistant to anything else, and there are signs that even during the brief periods in which the college had a Sienese rector, a student head of some kind also existed.[79] The commune now set about using the new dispensation to advantage, exploiting the competition for the job while keeping control of it – it is significant that not even the drawing up of the shortlist was entrusted to the scholars.[80] After 1456 the position remained an annual one, but apart from this several of the earlier reforms remained in effect. The stipulation that the rector was to be a doctor, or if not to take his degree either before taking office or within a short time of taking office, remained, though it did not always prove easy to enforce.[81] His salary also remained at 30 florins, together with at least

scrutiny of the outgoing rector was no guarantee that he would be chosen. In 1469 the incumbent, Alvaro (below, p. 349 n. 90), lost out to Bretuldus de Alamannia (*Conc.* 618, f. 22v, 4 Oct). The same happened to Henricus Gelingh de Svevia, who lost to Filippo de' Scalandrini da Bracciano in 1496 despite the fact that the *Savi* had taken the unusual step of recommending him above the other two candidates who were only nominated for form's sake (*Conc.* 2139, no. 103, n.d., and cf. *Balìa* 41, f. 51v, 16 Nov). The *Savi* were proved right; the new man was not immediately available – Gelingh had his rectorate extended until Christmas to cover – and Filippo proved reluctant to take on the vice-rectorship of the *Studio* as well; by June 1497 a new rector, Conforto da Spoleto, the third candidate in the November shortlist, was appointed (*Conc.* 784, f. 17r-v, 25-26 Jun; cf. *Sale* 24, f. 157v, 18 Oct 1497), while Filippo's possessions were confiscated (*Sale* 24, f. 156v, 11 Aug 1497).

[78] There was one further attempt at resistance; in 1476, after the scandals of the rectorate of Bernardino of Cortona (below, p. 350), the *Concistoro* resolved again that the next rector should be a citizen, selected from a shortlist of six (*Conc.* 657, f. 31r-v, 4 Apr, ed. FERRERI, doc. 8, p. 8), and on 8 April Niccolò di Lorenzo di Niccolò, *ligrittiere*, was appointed 'pro Rectore sive Gubernatore et Camerario' (*Conc.* 657, f. 36r, ed. FERRERI, doc. 11, p. 10). By August they had reverted to a foreign academic (*Conc.* 659, f. 28v, 5 Aug, ed. FERRERI, doc. 20, p. 18). The reversion to a Sienese rector had been mooted the previous year; *CG* 236, f. 127v-128v, 28 Jun 1475 (see above, p. 343 n. 48, and below, p. 350).

[79] ZDEKAUER, pp. 98-99, stated that the Sapienza had two rectors, an administrator appointed by the comune and a student rector elected by the *sapientini*. Although, as the discussion above should make clear, this does not hold good for most of the period, and in the terms in which Zdekauer put it is a conflation of the two types of rector with which the comune experimented in the early decades of the college's existence, it is an accurate description at one stage and contains a grain of truth for others. On the implementation of the 1443 reform which established a Sienese 'rettore e governatore', the *Concistoro* declared that he was to have precedence over the 'Rector scolarium dicte domus Sapientie' (*Conc.* 466, f. 42r-v, 13 Oct 1443); and indeed shortly afterwards we hear that Dns. Jacobus thome de Savona, 'rector sapientie', was given a further term of a year (*Conc.* 467, f. 36r, 30 Dec 1443). By the time of Biringucci's renunciation his successor, Johannes de Gigliaco of Savoy, was already vice-rector (see pp. 345 and 352), and in 1488 the 'rettore e governatore generale' held office alongside the 'rettore forestiero' (below, pp. 356-7).

[80] The only exception I know of is an undated fragment of a document in which the scholars of the Sapienza appear to put forward two candidates for the office (*Studio* 127, filza 1, no. 9): 'Nos Scolares alme domus misericordie eligimus statuimus et ordinamus in Rectorem ac Gubernatorem nostrum Spectabilem Dominum Noe Germanum aut Dominum Adrianum Gratiosum de Marchia Anconitana, et ille intelligatur nos statuisse (ex iis superius dictis) qui ab amplissimo senen. Sena. Approbatus fuerit in quorum fide singuli manu propria indicabunt etc.' There are thirteen names on the fragment. The document is from the mid-sixteenth century; one of the signatories, Laurentius Wildhelm, took a degree in civil law in 1548 (MINNUCCI and MORELLI, *Lauree*, IV, p. 184).

[81] It was present from 1424, when Filippo da Lucca was to take his degree within a month – seven months before taking office; *Dipl., Biblioteca Pubblica*, 28 Feb 1423(=1424). In the early period the taking of a degree as precondition was the norm (e.g. also Giovanni d'Amelia in 1434; *Conc.* 412, f. 36v, 28 Sept). From early on it could be difficult to fill the post on these terms – in 1435, after the renunciation of Giovanni d'Amelia, no candidates who were doctors presented themselves and it was agreed that the *Concistoro* and *Savi* could use their discretion (*CG* 218, f. 131r [new foliation], 13 Feb 1435); a scholar in the Sapienza, Giovanni di Frangano da Sicilia, took over for the rest of the academic year (*Conc.* 414, ff. 26r, 12 Feb, 30v, 19 Feb 1435). In practice the majority of appointees in the late fifteenth century were students, and it often took some effort to persuade them to take their degree. The most famous example is Luís Teixeira, the relative of the king of Portugal whose entry into the Sapienza in 1473 was so ostentatiously gilded by his almost simultaneous appointment as vice-rector; MINNUCCI, 'Documenti', doc. II-5, pp. 81-2 (and on his dating see below, p. 352 n. 118). In August 1476 he was elected rector (*Conc.* 659, f. 28v, 5 Aug, ed. FERRERI, doc. 20, p. 18), and given two months (i.e. until just before the beginning of the academic year) in which to take his degree. Despite two extensions (*Studio* 2, ff. 48v, 31 Oct, and 49v, 15 Nov, when

some of the status he was to be accorded. His authority over the inmates of the Sapienza remained largely unaltered.

Who became rector, and why? The procedure envisaged doctors or students close enough to the completion of their degrees to be able to take them before or soon after taking office. Possession of a degree would give the incumbent authority – one of the complaints in the case of Agapito had been that he had not been respected – though it would also mean that the Sapienza maintained a certain distance from the more common practice elsewhere of having a student rector.[82] It also satisfied the intense Sienese desire to see students taking degrees, which was something of an *idée fixe*. On the other hand there is a paradoxical element too; why would someone wish to take on this appointment once they had completed their degree? The answer must be a combination of factors; the attractions of status, perhaps the salary (comparable to that for an initial lectureship),[83] and the fact that it could be a stepping-stone towards greater things, a rung on the career ladder. Rectors who acquitted themselves well could expect further patronage from the comune; some obtained appointments in the judiciary,[84] others received letters of recommendation for future patrons.[85] In this context it is perhaps un-

---

he was given ten days), he failed to do so; by 28 Nov he was removed from office and told he could only regain it by taking his degree within ten days (*Conc.* 661, f. 16v, ed. FERRERI, doc. 28, p. 25), and on 15 Dec he was replaced as rector (f. 26r, ed. FERRERI, doc. 29, p. 25, by a countryman, Martinus, who was possibly playing the role of placeman). On 23 Dec he was given a further two months before he faced expulsion (*Studio* 2, f. 51r). He appealed for reinstatement on condition that he took the degree within four months (*Conc.* 2303, fasc. 3, no. 24, n.d.), and the *Savi* accepted this (*Studio* 2, f. 53r, 9 Jan 1477) on the basis that failure to do so would entail renunciation of his remaining two and a half years in the Sapienza. In the meantime another rector, a German, was appointed (*Studio* 2, f. 53v, 5 Feb, and *Conc.* 662, f. 25r, 7 Feb, ed. FERRERI, doc. 36, p. 32) and given the rector's room (*Studio* 2, f. 54r, 7 Mar). Zdekauer stated (p. 100) that at this point 'con tutto il garbo possibile' the authorities gave Teixeira leave to return home; I know only of the deliberation of the *Concistoro* of 12 April – which certainly matches Zdekauer's description in its diplomacy – that he might have one of the houses owned by the Sapienza (*Conc.* 663, f. 33r, 12 Apr 1477, ed. FERRERI, doc. 41, pp. 35-6. The document refers just to 'Dominus Lodovicus', but the details make it clear that it refers to Teixeira). On Teixeira see also the work of Minnucci, as above, p. 323 n. 188.

There are other examples too. On one occasion the cajoling of the *Savi* that the rector, Pedro da Navarra, take his degree before going on leave is accompanied by the offer of an incentive, better furniture for his room when he took it (*Studio* 2, f. 140r, 2 Dec 1493, and cf. 139r, 18 Nov). One student appears to have got away with a flat refusal. Avianus de Coppis de Montefalco, elected on 28 Nov 1457 provided that he took his degree within a month (*Conc.* 547, f. 10r), refused to accept the condition; he was nonetheless appointed from the following March, with no further mention of a degree – he is again described as *iurisperitus* – and accepted on this basis (*Conc.* 547, f. 18r, 16 Dec).

[82] A not dissimilar example is the Collegio Gerolimiano or Sapienza Nuova at Perugia, where Angelo Geraldini, who had studied at Siena, became the first rector in 1443, taking his degree there in 1445 (PETERSOHN, *Ein Diplomat des Quattrocento*, p. 28). However, it should also be recognised that this is a grey area, as the very practice of appointing senior students and then insisting on their graduation bears out. 'Notions of student and professor [were] in many cases no longer clearly separable' (SCHWINGES, 'Student Education', p. 198).

[83] Above, p. 184. On the other hand, against that might have to be set the cost of graduation.

[84] See the example of Pedro Vasques of Portugal (on whose rectorate see above, n. 77, and below, n. 90), who went on to be collateral and *iudex pupillorum* and then *giudice degli appelli* (*Conc.* 678, f. 15r, 10 Oct 1479; *Balìa* 18, f. 4r, 2 Jan 1480; *Conc.* 682, ff. 19v-20r, 24 May, and 40r, 12 Jun 1480; *Conc.* 683, f. 6r, 15 Jul 1480; *Not.* 529, f. 70r, 30 Dec 1480, ed. MINNUCCI, 'Documenti', doc. III-245, p. 203), to which was added a lectureship (*Balìa* 23, f. 73v, 30 Apr 1481); cf. RAU, 'Italianismo na cultura jurídica', p. 188, and MINNUCCI, 'Documenti', p. 304 for other references. Sometimes rectors' expertise would be drawn on while they were still in post; in 1425 Filippo da Lucca was appointed, with another doctor, to judge a case with no *Studio* relevance (*Conc.* 2175, no foliation, 30 Oct. They declared themselves 'incompetentes').

[85] Giovanni Museler de Argentina (Strasbourg) received such an open letter, full of praise for his conduct, on his last day as rector, together with a specific one to the authorities of his home town (*Conc.* 1692, ff. 269r-70r, 30 Oct 1477; see also ZDEKAUER, pp. 183 and 105 n. 1, and MINNUCCI, 'Documenti', doc. II-44, p. 113 and n. 155. He appears to have been one of the students 'outhoused' in November 1474, possibly put in the main building in 1475). For another German rector, Tederigo, the *Concistoro* wrote a letter of recommendation to the bishop of Merseburg (*Conc.* 1700, 27 Oct 1488). Fi-

surprising that the prohibition on rectors of the Sapienza holding lectureships was undermined, and what had begun as an exception that required derogation ended up being offered, if not as a matter of course, at least without particular attention to the fact of double office.[86] Moreover, rectors, particularly eminent ones, might acquire honours and responsibilities during their tenure. Important individuals could also obtain preferential or more speedy advancement. Luís Teixeira was made vice-rector of the Sapienza on entry, and rector after only three years;[87] the Russian student Martinus was a candidate for the rectorate in 1485 after less than two years of residence.[88]

Within the house, the identity of the rector also became a matter of considerable interest. Status accrued both to the individual and to the 'group' to which he belonged. There was no formal student participation in the appointment of the rector, and no formal pattern was established to regulate rotation of the office between students of different disciplines or origins (unlike the rectorate of the university), but there are indications that at times these were issues. Divisions by subject do not appear to have been a controversial matter;[89] however, the geographical origin of the rector clearly could be. The rectorate oscillated between different 'nationalities' or regional groupings – Iberian, German and Italian above all, with rather fewer French – but without any specific pattern or ruling. Portuguese students are particularly strongly represented, and in the mid to late 1470s even achieved a near-continuous run of the office.[90] This is also the period in which the office began again to be plagued by recurrent problems. First we hear in 1475 that the election procedure for the rector was tightened up (it

nally ten years after the rectorate of Scipio d'Asti the *Concistoro* wrote to four cardinals on his behalf in an attempt to help him obtain a benefice (*Conc.* 1687, f. 226r, 29 Nov 1469).

[86] The *letture* granted to Giovanni da Visso (1421), Filippo da Lucca (1426) and Benedetto da Volterra (1435) (see above, p. 284 n. 47) were all before the prohibition. That it was intended to mean something is reflected in the *lettura* given to Scipio da Asti in 1458; it was on condition that, should he be elected rector of the Sapienza, he would receive no additional salary beyond the 45 florins of his *lettura* (*Conc.* 552, f. 32v, 21 Oct. He was in due course elected rector; *Conc.* 553, f. 10r, 15 Nov). *Letture* were subsequently given to Libertà da Lucca (*Conc.* 559, f. 16r, 20 Nov 1459, with a salary of only 15 florins because he already had the salary for his rectorate), Andrea da Genova (*Conc.* 565, f. 16v, 24 Nov 1460; he had been elected rector on 5 Oct, *Conc.* 564, f. 19r), Gonsalvo (*Conc.* 687, f. 26v, 17 Apr 1481; a *lettura morta*), Conforto da Spoleto (*Sale* 24, f. 157v, 18 Oct 1497; another *lettura morta*) and Alvaro (*Sale* 24, f. 166v, 30 Oct 1498; again, a *lettura morta*).

[87] Above, p. 347 n. 81.

[88] *Conc.* 715, f. 9v, 17 Nov 1485, ed. FERRERI, doc. 222, p. 187. Martinus had entered for the full seven-year term (*Balìa* 31, f. 32r, 14 Jan 1484). He was later involved in an internal Sapienza dispute (*Conc.* 725, f. 34v, 21 Aug 1487, ed. FERRERI, doc. 250, p. 213). However short a rector's previous residence, it seems that by the late fifteenth century he was always a *sapientino* (cf. the wording of *Not.* 879, no. 42, 13 Jun 1484: 'Sapientes debeant eligere tres scholares ex existentibus in domo sapientie'); Luís Teixeira's appointment on entry as vice-rector (above, p. 347 n. 81) is as far as this form of patronage might go.

[89] An unusual election took place in 1485; the three shortlisted candidates were a canonist, a civilian and a student of medicine (*Conc.* 715r, 17 Nov, ed. FERRERI, doc. 222, p. 187), but six days after the list was drawn up the medic was replaced without explanation by another civilian (13v, 23 Nov, ed. FERRERI, doc. 224, p. 189) who was subsequently chosen (17r, 6 Dec, ed. FERRERI, doc. 225, p. 190). Apart from this I have found no instance where the discipline of the student shows even the appearance of having been an issue.

[90] Portuguese rectors of the period include Giovanni (*Conc.* 589, f. 29r, 16 Dec 1464); Alvaro Alfonsi (elected in 1468 despite a mix-up with the ballot bags; *Conc.* 612, f. 35r-v, 19 Oct, and 613, f. 34v, 30 Dec; from a petition of Cardinal Rodrigo Borgia on his behalf, *Conc.* 2022, no. 3, 3 Sept 1469, and from a Sienese letter to the pope, *Conc.* 1687, ff. 201v-202r, 18 Oct 1469, it is clear that he is the nephew of the bishop of Evora; from EUBEL, II, p. 165 it can be speculated that it is his namesake, the late bishop, rather than the new incumbent); Giovanni di Giglio (*Conc.* 647, f. 29r, 26 Aug, and 32r, 31 Aug 1474); Ferdinandino (appointed as interim rector, *Studio* 2, f. 19r, 28 Nov 1474); Luís Teixeira (1476 – see above, p. 347 n. 81); Pedro Vasquez (*Conc.* 2117, f. 38v, 26 Oct 1477; again, there was doubt because only two *Savi* were involved [see above, p. 346 n. 76]; he was re-elected the following year; *Conc.* 673, f. 15r, 29 Dec 1478; on Vasques see above, p. 348 n. 84); Gonsalvo (*Conc.* 678, f. 21r, 21 Oct 1479).

was vacant) because of 'infiniti mancamenti' which, tantalisingly, 'come è quasi noto a ciascuno cittadino...tedio sarebbe a narrarli'.[91] The following year the rectorate of Bernardino of Cortona (elected August 1475) culminated in an anonymous petition to the *Concistoro* demanding that he be sacked.[92] The grounds given are, interestingly, mixed. The charge that he had presided over moral decline in the house ('dove e Casa di Sapientia, s'ingegnava che sia casa di Sodomia e di ogni altra dissolutione') appears to have exercised the petitioners less than the fact that he was a Florentine subject (and thus forbidden to hold public office in the commune).[93] Though he had been elected by an overwhelming vote,[94] he was now represented as an enemy of the Sienese republic, who had set out to destroy the Sapienza (he is described as its 'guastatore') by fomenting divisions, appointing a second and rival vice-rector,[95] sacking servants appointed by the *Savi* and defying their and the *Concistoro*'s orders, and it is hinted that the object of this behaviour was to boost the prospects of the newly transferred *Studio* at Pisa.[96] Bernardino's tenure came to an end by April 1476, when a Sienese was once again appointed 'Rectore sive Gubernatore et Camerario'.[97] The aftermath of this episode appears to bear out the charges levelled against him. In the spring of 1476 four students were expelled,[98] a door was ordered to be walled up 'ad scandala evitanda',[99] and the new rector was twice forbidden to admit anyone other than scholars[100] and told to dismiss all 'buchas superfluas'.[101] In August the authorities reverted to the appointment of a foreign scholar, the vice-rector Luís Teixeira.[102]

Though this is the best documented example of tensions over the rector and his origins, it is not the only one. In 1484 a dispute between German and Italian students in the college led to a ruling by the *Savi* that the German rector would remain in post to 5 December, but that at that point the

---

[91] *CG* 236, f. 127v; *Mis.* 1, f. 105r, 28 Jun.

[92] *Studio* 127, no foliation, n.d., ed. ZDEKAUER, doc. XXI, pp. 176-7 (and see p. 104).

[93] To this the petitioners added a further alleged breach of statutes; Bernardino had been in the Sapienza for nine years, not the maximum seven. This is true; he was admitted on 27 Oct 1467 (*Conc.* 606, f. 41r).

[94] 'Obtinuit infrascriptus per multos et multos lupinos' (*Conc.* 653, f. 36r, 21 Aug 1475). Bernardino had been one of the three shortlisted candidates the previous year (*Conc.* 647, f. 29r, 26 Aug 1474). All three of these became rector in turn; first Giovanni di Giglio da Portogallo, then Antonio da Lucca (*Conc.* 649, f. 20v, 9 Dec 1474) despite the recommendation of Bernardino by the priors of Cortona (*Conc.* 2033, no. 33, 21 Nov 1474). Antonio had also been recommended by the authorities of his home town (*Not.* 694, f. 39r-v, 19 Jul 1474, ed. MINNUCCI, 'Documenti', doc. II-10, p. 84, and see p. 27).

[95] 'che eran parechi anni che era inimico capitale del primo Vicerettore'; the original vice-rector being, presumably, still Luís Teixeira (above, p. 349). On the role of the vice-rector see below, pp. 352-3.

[96] 'Per chè possano stimare vostre Mag.ce Sig.rie, quanto premio conseguirebbe dalli suoi Signori Fiorentini, se per sua operatione lo Studio vostro ricevesse qualche diminutione, per chè serrebbe augumento di quello di Pisa, per la vicinità.' Despite the focus on this motive, Zdekauer was of the opinion that this was an internal Sapienza petition rather than something set up outside by Sienese. The notary who signed it appears to be foreign. The petition does, however, cite not only *sapientini* but also teachers, citizens and neighbours of the Sapienza as witnesses to Bernardino's reprehensible conduct.

[97] Niccolò di Lorenzo, *ligrittiere* (see above, p. 347 n. 78). Bernardino appears to have continued until roughly this period, as he was paid the usual amount for his second *terzaria* on 9 April (*Conc.* 657, f. 37v, ed. FERRERI, doc. 12, p. 12).

[98] *Studio* 2, ff. 43v-44r, 16 May (Johannes Albus, banned for six months for having wounded a servant), and 44r-v, 5 Jun (Guasparre de Portugallia; he was reinstated on 20 June; f. 45r; summary of case on f. 44v, 8 Jun). One, Gonsalvo, was reinstated on 16 June (f. 44v).

[99] *Studio* 2, f. 44r, 16 May; below, p. 384.

[100] *Studio* 2, f. 44r, 16 May, and 44v, 8 Jun.

[101] *Studio* 2, f. 45v, 6 Jul.

[102] *Conc.* 659, f. 28v, 5 Aug, ed. FERRERI, doc. 20, p. 18.

names to be shortlisted would all be Italian.[103] The dispute had been smouldering for a month (though we are given no details of its nature),[104] and a few weeks after the ruling the rector resigned.[105] This was clearly a bad patch. His successor, Hieronimo da Viterbo, was sacked.[106] In 1486 the rector again had to be given an ultimatum – twice – to take his degree.[107] The following year there appears to have been a vacancy,[108] and in 1488 it was decided to appoint a single individual as both rector and *Camarlengo*.[109] However, later that year the rector was again a student, the German Theodoricus, who resigned the post shortly after his term began.[110]

This bumpy ride suggests that it would be entirely wrong to see the history of the rectorate as one long struggle for possession by different factions or 'nations'. Sometimes, far from a contest, it was actually quite difficult to find a volunteer. As has been seen, by limiting the job to *sapientini* at the end of their period of study, the authorities had considerably narrowed the field of possible candidates. At least one potential rector saw a further drawback to the office; the Frenchman Benedetto d'Adamo 'fece alcuna resistentia di acceptare' because he would lose the remaining three years of his term if he did so; he was given the right to remain for a year after his rectorate.[111] Another obstacle was the stipulation that the rector obtain his doctorate before taking up office. Not only was this sometimes difficult to enforce, it could clearly also deter people from accepting the job. One rector, Achille di Ser Michele da Castiglione, negotiated an unusual way round the main obstacle, cost, in 1488; the *Balìa* agreed that instead of the usual salary for the rectorate he could take his degree free of charge.[112] The following year's appointment shows that cost was not the only problem; it was not a foregone conclusion that the candidate would receive his doctorate, and the *Balìa* deputed two of its members to put pressure on the college of doctors to ensure a successful outcome of the examination.[113]

The fifteenth-century documents abound in evidence of delays in rectors taking up appointments,[114]

---

[103] *Not.* 879, no. 42, 13 Jun 1484. A further controversy occurred in 1498, when the *Concistoro* had to rule that the election of Alvaro of Portugal was valid despite the voices that were questioning it (*Conc.* 790, f. 23r-v, 24 Jun). We have no information about what was behind this discontent, but it is interesting that there had previously been a recommendation of a Spoletan, Gabriel Lottus, to the post (*Balìa* 43, f. 154r, 11 May 1498). Had this been successful it would have given the Sapienza two Spoletan rectors in a row (the previous rector being Mag. Confortus; *Sale* 24, ff. 157v, 18 Oct, 161r, 30 Dec 1497, and 164r, 29 Mar 1498; by 24 May 1498 he was living outside the Sapienza but with the right to meals, 165r). The *Balìa* had referred the recommendation to the *Consiglio del Popolo*. The following year he was recommended for the post of *iudex pupillorum* by the cardinal of S. Maria in Trastevere (*Balìa* 560, no. 49, 17 Mar 1499).

[104] *Balìa* 32, f. 7r-v, 19 May. The *Regolatori* are ordered not to allow the students' legal case against the rector to proceed without the *Balìa*'s permission, and the *Savi* are instructed to take the matter in hand.

[105] *Balìa* 32, f. 28r, 28 Jul.

[106] *Studio* 2, ff. 109r, 17 May 1485. A Mag. Hieronimus de Verreschis de Viterbio was admitted on 17 Oct 1481; ZDEKAUER, p. 184.

[107] *Conc.* 716, ff. 28v, 18 Feb, and 30v, 24 Feb, ed. FERRERI, docs. 227, p. 193, and 229, p. 194.

[108] *Conc.* 725, f. 34v, 21 Aug 1487, ed. FERRERI, doc. 250, p. 213.

[109] *CG* 240, ff. 175v, 15 May (petition in *Conc.* 2139, no. 84, f. 154r-v). On the appointee see below, p. 376.

[110] *Balìa* 36, f. 43v, 1 Nov 1488. On the relationship between the two see below, pp. 356-7.

[111] *CG* 238, f. 255r, 30 Nov 1481. From a deliberation of 1484 it appears that a student's period as rector did not count towards his time; the resignation of a rector is accepted on condition that he pays what he would have had to pay had he not held the office (*Balìa* 32, f. 28r, 28 Jul).

[112] *Balìa* 36, f. 66v, December 1488.

[113] *Balìa* 36, f. 87r, 22 Jan 1489; on the position of the authorities on degrees, see above, p. 289.

[114] *Studio* 2, f. 103r, 12 July 1484.

premature resignations,[115] periods of absence and vacancies.[116] It is therefore not surprising to find the authorities having recourse to a fall-back, the appointment of a vice-rector. It may be significant that the first mention of such a figure is the case of Johannes de Gigliaco, a student who was appointed vice-rector in 1446, after the rectorate of the Sienese Pietro di Nanni Biringucci.[117] The second and more intensive use of the office came in the 1470s. In the well-known case of Luís Teixeira, who was made vice-rector soon after entry (probably at the end of 1473),[118] this was not an honorific title; the rectorate was vacant at the time. Information about the office becomes more frequent during the continued vacancy. During Teixeira's absence from Siena[119] a fellow Portuguese, Ferdinandino, was twice appointed to the job, the second time pending the imminent election of a rector.[120] When the new rector, Antonio da Lucca, failed to materialise, Teixeira was reconfirmed as vice-rector;[121] as such he was obliged to read the statutes to the scholars,[122] and later that year his jurisdiction was made equal to that of a full rector.[123] At no stage, to my knowledge, were norms for such appointments laid down. They seem to have begun, and continued, as a pragmatic solution to a temporary problem (and, of course, a way round the degree rule). Vice-rectors for the most part just appear in the records; sometimes we hear of their appointment by the *Savi* or a higher authority, and indeed the Bernardino da Cortona episode suggests that such a figure could even be appointed by the rector himself.[124] By this time it is clear that the office had become more than a way of filling a vacancy, since rectors and vice-rectors regularly held office simultaneously. Occasionally the vice-rectorate could be a stepping-stone to the rectorate;[125] on one occasion it was the opposite, when an outgoing rector accepted the vice-rectorate.[126] The office might afford some flexibility, but this is unlikely to have compensated for the lack of a rector, and a student appointed on a temporary basis did not start out in a promising position as an impartial upholder of discipline. On one

---

[115] *Balìa* 32, f. 28r, 28 Jul 1484, and *Balìa* 36, ff. 43v, 1 Nov, and 66v, Dec 1488 in addition to the cases mentioned on pp. 342, 345 and 351.

[116] *Conc.* 725, f. 34v, 21 Aug 1487, and examples on pp. 349-50.

[117] See above, pp. 344-5 and n. 57.

[118] *Not.* 694, f. 26r, ed. MINNUCCI, 'Documenti', doc. II-5, pp. 81-2, dating it, on the basis of the year and the indiction, between Sept 1473 and Mar 1474; this is probably the full version of the deliberation of *Not.* 694, f. 10r, 20 Dec, ed. MINNUCCI, 'Documenti', doc. II-40, p. 110, which he speculates is also from 1473 on the basis of its relationship with the fuller document.

[119] See MINNUCCI, 'Documenti', p. 283.

[120] *Studio* 2, f. 14r, 24 Mar 1474. Two days later Teixeira was given the previous rector's room (loc. cit.). The suggestion is that there was no hostility between the two; yet there was subsequently a dispute between Ferdinandino and one Ludovicus de Portugallia over a debt, in which the *Savi* intervened, in December 1474 (*Not.* 694, f. 4r, 18 Dec, ed. MINNUCCI, 'Documenti', doc. II-14, pp. 85-6). The second appointment of Ferdinandino was on 28 Nov 1474; *Not.* 694, f. 25r, ed. MINNUCCI, 'Documenti', doc. II-52, p. 122, no year given, but dateable through comparison with the 'official' record in *Studio* 2, f. 19r, which is almost identical ('actento quod in domo sapiente non est rector qui dictum Domum gubernet, d.nus ferdinandinus de portugallia intelligatur et sit vicerector quousque de novo rectore ipsius domus providbeatur').

[121] *Studio* 2, f. 22v, 4 Jan 1475; *Not.* 694, ff. 12r and 14r, 4 Jan 1475, ed. MINNUCCI, 'Documenti', docs. II-16 and II-17, pp. 86-7; and cf. f. 18r, n.d., ed. MINNUCCI doc. II-45, pp. 115-6. Antonio da Lucca had been recommended for nomination as rector by the Anziani of Lucca; f. 39r-v, ed. MINNUCCI, doc. II-10, p. 84, 19 Jul 1474.

[122] *Studio* 2, f. 22v, 4 Jan 1475; *Not.* 694, f. 12r 4 Jan 1475, ed. MINNUCCI, 'Documenti', doc. II-16, pp. 87.

[123] *Studio* 2, f. 31r, 3 Jul 1475.

[124] Above, p. 350.

[125] The example of Johannes de Gigliaco, above, p. 345.

[126] *Sale* 23, f. 98r, 14 Nov 1496. He is not named here but is Henricus Gelingh de Svevia; above, p. 346 n. 77. Two days later his successor was appointed but his period of office as rector was extended until Christmas (*Balìa* 41, f. 51v, 16 Nov).

occasion a dispute between the vice-rector and the *sapientini* ended with the *Concistoro* intervening on behalf of the latter, instructing the vice-rector to apportion rooms fairly.[127]

3. *The* Camarlengo

Whatever the position with regard to a citizen or a foreign rector, one respect in which communal control over the Sapienza was never in doubt was responsibility for finances. This fell to the *Camarlengo*, a post which may initially have been less prestigious than the rectorate but which was certainly no less important. This office has very different origins and a less visible but more successful history. An administrator of finances, in terms of both housekeeping and estate management, was a *sine qua non* for such an institution, and here the Sienese could draw on their rich experience. There appears to have been direct continuity with the Casa della Misericordia; the Sapienza inherited not only its possessions but also the administrative mechanisms for its governance. Initially, and indeed for a long time, the office drew on both the Misericordia tradition and the standard practices for the administration of Siena's many pious institutions. Significantly, it is likely that the last *Camarlengo* to be appointed to the old Misericordia was the same individual who held the office for its first two years as the Sapienza.[128]

The role of the *Camarlengo* was defined early on – much sooner than that of the rector – and underwent relatively few changes. The method of election varied little. The commune had a standard system for the selection of *camarlenghi* of pious institutions, in use previously for the Casa della Misericordia, and this remained the basic one for the *Camarlengo* of the Sapienza – at least until the office began to change. It was an 'extraordinary' office;[129] the candidates' names were selected from a *bossolo* of names of candidates for a group of such offices.[130] The candidates were not just Sienese citizens but *riseduti*, i.e. people already in the political caste, and thus to be considered loyal and fit for communal office.[131] In 1424 it was stated that the *Camarlengo* might, but need not, be in regular orders;[132] later measures stipulated that he had to be aged between twenty-five and sixty.[133] He could not hold any other communal post,[134] except in some cases that of prior, i.e. member of the *Concis-*

---

[127] *Conc.* 690, f. 24r, 3 Oct 1481, ed. FERRERI, doc. 226, p. 108. The vice-rectorate of the Sapienza should not be muddled with that of the university, which, confusingly, came to be held by the rector of the Sapienza. Above, pp. 270-1.

[128] It was decided to elect a *Camarlengo* for one year beginning 1 Jan 1415 (*CG* 206, f. 206r, and *Conc.* 2113, ff. 34v-35r, 7 Oct 1414) 'conciosiacosa che molte querele sieno che la casa de la misericordia sia male guidata…'. The audits of the *Regolatori* show that this office was held by Nofrio d'Ambrogio from 1 Jan 1415 to 9 Oct 1417 (*Regolatori* 6, ff. 363r-4r, 1 Dec 1417, and 389r, 7 Jun 1418).

[129] *Statuti* 44, f. 4r, 23 Feb 1433(=1434), eds. CAMBI and QUARTESAN, 'Gli uffici', p. 125 (= *Statuti* 45, f. 3v, and copy in *Conc.* 2395, f. 12r). I thus read the first passage differently from ASCHERI, 'Presentazione', in op. cit., p. XIV. On the meaning of the term, see above, pp. 71-2.

[130] *Statuti* 44, f. 6r, eds. CAMBI and QUARTESAN, 'Gli uffici', p. 128. The names for these scrutinies were drawn from the *cerna minore*; f. 25v (1465).

[131] CATONI, 'Il comune di Siena e l'amministrazione della Sapienza', p. 126, makes the point that the regime changes are reflected in the names of the *Camarlenghi*, 'che viene sempre scelto fra persone esperte e fedeli'.

[132] *Conc.* 352, f. 12r-v, 18 Sept.

[133] *CG* 239, ff. 32v-33r, and *Mis.* 1, f. 110v, 30 Apr 1482; *Conc.* 707, ff. 16v-17r, 3 Aug 1484.

[134] *Mis.* 1, ff. 87v-88v, 3 Feb 1441, and *Statuti* 44, ff. 12v (eds. CAMBI and QUARTESAN, 'Gli uffici', p. 139), and cf. 21v. A specific ban was added on a *Camarlengo* being related to any of the *Savi dello Studio*; f. 22r (18 Feb 1457), and cf. *Statuti* 45, ff. 20r and 33r, and *Conc.* 2395, ff. 37r-v. The bar from civic office was reduced in 1482 to a bar from salaried office 'di dentro' (*CG* 239, ff. 32v-33r, *Mis.* 1, f. 111r, 30 Apr).

toro.[135] The *Concistoro* and *Savi* decided when it was necessary or advisable to make a new appointment (when an incumbent's term was up, when he resigned or when the authorities decided to sack him).[136] At the moment of transition from hospital to college the office was for a fixed term of one year;[137] shortly afterwards the authorities experimented briefly with an open term, 'ad vita o vero ad beneplacito',[138] before the office settled down to shorter periods of one to three years.[139] The regulations appear to have been enabling rather than restricting, since many appointees had their terms of office renewed. In the early years the Sapienza benefited from a series of long-serving *camarlenghi*. Best known to posterity is Ser Mariano di Jacopo detto il Taccola, the influential engineer and inventor, who held the post from 1424 to 1433, and whose connections within the university included Mariano Sozzini, and outside it the emperor Frederick III.[140] After him Niccolò d'Antonio Foscherani held the office for eight years (1433-41);[141] Melchior di Agostino di Maestro Antonio for seven (1458-65)[142] and Manno di Bartolomeo Vitaleoni for three (1465-8).[143] In 1468 the authorities reverted to an annual appointment,[144] but after less than a decade life appointments, or three-

---

[135] This condition was one of the terms of appointment of Chimento di Niccolò di Jacopo Rinaldi (*Conc.* 324, f. 17v, 3 Feb 1420, and *Dipl., Università*, 6 Feb 1419[=1420]), at his own request, and reappears in the reforms of 1458 (*Balìa* 6, f. 152v, *Statuti* 40, f. 132r-v, 7 Feb).

[136] *Statuti* 44, f. 12v, eds. CAMBI and QUARTESAN, 'Gli uffici', p. 139.

[137] Above, n. 128.

[138] *Statuti* 40, f. 15r-v; *Statuti* 41, f. 54r-v; and *Statuti* 47, f. 54r-v, dateable through marginal annotations to 19 Jun 1419. Flexibility was the order of the day; in December that year a scrutiny for a new *Camarlengo* was annulled and the incumbent, Nanni di Pietro Biringucci, was offered another term or, if he wished it, the post 'ad vitam' (*Conc.* 323, f. 28v, 28 Dec 1419). He must have rejected the offer, as this is soon followed by the election of Chimento di Niccolò di Jacopo Rinaldi (above, n. 135), the terms of which included that he would leave his possessions to the Sapienza.

[139] The first change from a one-year term was the biennial appointment of 1441; *Statuti* 44, ff. 12v and 21v, 3 Feb. By 4 Aug 1443 it was back to annual (loc. cit.), though appointments could be renewed, as was that of Nanni di Cione di Feio in 1447 (*Conc.* 2121, no. 49, 22 Feb 1446=7). In reforms of 1458 the office was for the first time to be for three years, with the upgrading of the office to 'governatore et bonificatore' (*Balìa* 6, f. 152v, *Statuti* 40, ff. 131v-132v, 7 Feb 1458). The appointee, Melchior di Agostino di Maestro Antonio (*CG* 227, f. 270r, 19 Feb, *Balìa* 6, f. 166r, 26 Feb 1458), was reconfirmed for another three years in 1461 (*CG* 229, f. 19r, 6 Feb), then for a two-year period after some opposition (*CG* 229, f. 343r, 28 Mar 1463), before finally losing his job to another three-year appointee, Manno Vitaleoni (cf. *CG* 230, ff. 280r, and 282r, *Conc.* 592, ff. 8v and 14r, and *Conc.* 2311, no foliation, 8 and 12 May 1465).

[140] J. H. BECK, 'The Historical "Taccola" and Emperor Sigismund in Siena', *Art Bulletin*, 50 (1968), pp. 309-20, esp. p. 310, tr./rev. in his edition of MARIANO DI JACOPO DETTO IL TACCOLA, *Liber Tertium de ingeneis ac edifitiis non usitatis* (Milan, 1969), pp. 11-25; F. D. PRAGER and G. SCAGLIA, *Mariano Taccola and his book De ingenuis* (Cambridge, Ma., 1972), esp. Chapter 1; CATONI, 'Genesi', p. 167 n. 58; NARDI, *Mariano Sozzini*, p. 71. Taccola had had previous experience of such work; he had been the rector and *spedaliere* of the hospital of S. Andrea (*Dipl., Arch. Gen.*, 7 Feb 1413[=1414], and *Not.* 292, ff. 182v-185v, ed. MINNUCCI, 'Documenti', doc. III-147, p. 168, and pp. 286-7 for further references), which was incorporated into the Sapienza estate in 1415 (below, p. 362), and he later rented property from the Sapienza (below, p. 358 n. 184). It will be evident from what is said in these pages that I consider the tradition in the Taccola literature that the Sapienza post was a sinecure that allowed him the peace and time to write and use his college contacts (e.g. KUCHER, *The Water Supply System of Siena*, pp. 8-9, 15-16) to be an underestimate of the burdens of the office.

[141] His office was scrutinised closely by the *Regolatori* and was found to be prudent; the expenses of the house dropped significantly (*Regolatori* 8, ff. 37v-38v, accounts for 1 Aug 1433 to 17 Jan 1435, approved 23 Nov 1436; cf. CATONI, 'Il Comune di Siena e l'amministrazione della Sapienza', pp. 126-7).

[142] *Regolatori* 9, ff. 9r-10r (1 Apr 1464-1 Apr 1465). The series is interrupted for the previous years.

[143] *Regolatori* 9, ff. 43v-44r (May 1465-May 1466), 114r-116r (May 1466-May 1467), 145r-146r (May 1467-May 1468).

[144] *Regolatori* 9, ff. 192v-193v (accounts of 1468-9; the *Camarlengo* is Antonio Scarpi), 232r-v (1469-70; Jacopo d'Antonio Corti), 297v-298v (1470-71; Agnolo di Berto Altesi), 327v-329r (1471-72; Biliotto di Domenico di Biliotto), 372r-373r (1472-73; 'Lorenzo d'Agnolo di m.° Merigo et Jacopo suo figliuolo'. Lorenzo became ill and had his son take over, *Conc.* 2139, no. 26, f. 47r, 19 Oct 1472; they presented accounts together), 421r-422r (1473-74; Lorenzo di Meo Griffoli),

year periods which could be renewed only by the *Consiglio del Popolo*, reappeared.[145] The three-year term remained the standard, though regulations continued to be rough approximations of pragmatic reality; some *camarlenghi* left office prematurely, others returned for a subsequent term.[146] For much of the period the authorities appear to have stuck strictly to the principle of rotation between *monti*,[147] and this may have contributed to the relative absence of controversy over appointments.[148]

The many descriptions of the *Camarlengo*'s duties and responsibilities repeat several key features. He was in charge of all financial aspects of the Sapienza; in 1448 it was expressly stated that all financial transactions were to be effected by him and that the rector was not to have any control over finance.[149] He had to render annual accounts,[150] to both the *Savi* and the *Regolatori*, the commune's chief auditors, which has

465v-466r (1474-75; Battista di Cecco de Rondine), 497r-498r (1475-76; Guasparre di Martino di Niccolò). See also *CG* 407, f. 386r, and *CG* 408, f. 127r (lists of communal officials).

[145] Life appointments were made in 1476 ('ad vitam seu beneplacitum', according to *CG* 408, f. 127r; the appointee was Niccolò di Lorenzo, *Regolatori* 9, ff. 451v-542r, and see above, p. 347 n. 78) and 1488, but these are of figures who combine the role with that of rector (see above, pp. 350-1). In 1482 a *Camarlengo et governatore* was appointed 'ad sua vita, et a bene-placito sempre del Consiglio del Popolo' (*CG* 239, ff. 32v-33r, and *Mis.* 1, f. 110v, 30 Apr). In 1491 a 'gubernator et camerar-ius' was appointed for life, but requiring confirmation after three years (*Mis.* 1, f. 114r-v, 13 Jun); in 1493 the appointment was again for the standard three years (*Balìa* 38, f. 51r, and *Mis.* 1, f. 116r, 29 Jan); and see the documents relating to the office in 1533-41, ed. KOŠUTA, 'Documenti', docs. VII-1 to VII-10, pp. 384-9. The 'life' appointments were always qualified by be-ing 'ad beneplacitum'; a *Camarlengo* could always resign or be dismissed. A resigning *Camarlengo* had to give six months' notice (*CG* 239, ff. 32v-33r, *Mis.* 1, ff. 110v-111r, 30 Apr 1482); cf. the resignation, 'secundum formam sui stantiamenti', of 'Alfonso di Ser Lorenzo Giusa' (*Conc.* 754, f. 14v, 17/18 Jun 1492, ed. FERRERI, doc. 322, p. 301, and *Conc.* 2139, no. 123, f. 224r).

[146] Alfonso di Lorenzo Guisa or Giusa held the office for a total of four years, from 1482 to 1484, when he renounced the job, and from 1491 to 1492, when he renounced it again (see previous note); Pietro piovano della Pieve di Pacina held it for three years (September 1488 to May 1491); Niccolò di Bartolomeo di Domenico cartario, who was appointed in Al-fonso's place in 1484 (*Conc.* 707, ff. 16v-17r, 3 Aug, and 22r, 22 Aug 1484; there is no mention of the period of office), was appointed again in 1493, for three years (*Balìa* 38, f. 51r, and *Mis.* 1, f. 116r, 29 Jan).

[147] This is evidenced in the sequence of appointments from 1442 to 1445 (*CG* 403, f. 330r) and 1458 to 1476 (see n. 139 above); this despite the decision by the *Balìa* in 1458 that the office was to be filled 'non avendo rispecto ad monti' (*Balìa* 6, f. 152v, *Statuti* 40, f. 132r-v, 7 Feb 1458). The practice appears to have been abandoned, at least temporarily, by the 1480s (see below, p. 356 and n. 158). On the *monti* see above, p. 219.

[148] There were exceptions. There is a gap in our knowledge of the office from 1447 to 1457, but at the end of that peri-od problems had clearly arisen. An attempt to get the *Consiglio del Popolo* to sack the incumbent and return the office to an annual one rotating *per monte* failed (*Conc.* 2118, f. 112r, 10 Sept 1456), but succeeded early the following year, when the *Balìa* terminated the tenure of Giovanni di Francesco, ordered his accounts to be audited by a special panel of *revisores*, and declared the office to be annual and drawn from the *bossolo della cerna minore* (*Balìa* 2, f. 172v, 7 Feb, and 189v, 18-20 Feb 1457; also *Balìa* 3, ff. 165r -166r and 188r-v, *Statuti* 40, f. 17r, and *Statuti* 44, f. 22r). Giovanni's successor, Melchior di Agostino di Maestro Antonio, was in fact appointed for three years, and renewed for a further two years in 1461, but there was controversy over his reappointment for another two years, in 1463, and by 1465 he had lost out to a rival, Manno Vita-leoni (see above, n. 139). In 1541 the *Consiglio del Popolo* repeatedly refused to renew the appointment of Giovanni Battista Umidi despite the pleas of the *Concistoro* and the *Savi dello Studio*; eventually, after a petition from the rector and students of the Sapienza, a fresh appointment was made (KOŠUTA, 'Documenti', docs. VII-4 to VII-9, pp. 386-9, 2 Jun to 6 Jul).

[149] *CG* 224, f. 115r-v, 5 Apr.

[150] E.g. *Statuti* 40, f. 15r-v, 19 Jun 1419 (= *Statuti* 41, f. 54v, and *Statuti* 47, f. 54r-v); *Conc.* 352, f. 12r-v, 18 Sept 1424; *CG* 222, f. 49r, 4 Aug 1443; *CG* 227, f. 241r, 10 Sept 1456 (= *Mis.* 1. f. 93r, and *Conc.* 2118, f. 112r-v); *CG* 239, ff. 32v-33r, *Mis.* 1, ff. 110v-111r, 30 Apr 1482. Other arrangements were occasionally made to scrutinise the accounts of this official; in 1437 they were to be checked by the *riveditori del bossolo* in 1437 (*CG* 219, f. 147v, and *Mis.* 1, f. 85r, 10 May) and in 1446 by the *Camar-lengo dell'Opera* (*Conc.* 481, f. 33v, 4 Apr). In 1455 special *revisores* were appointed to examine his books (*CG* 405, f. 156v). Dis-crepancies were found in the accounts of at least three *Camarlenghi* (described in CATONI, 'Il comune di Siena e l'amministrazione della Sapienza', p. 126). The accounts of Taccola's last year in office included a shortfall of £124/8/9, which he owed to the house (*Regolatori* 8, f. 249r; accounts for 1432-33); the same with Biliotto di Domenico in 1472 (360 *lire* were not correctly explained; *Regolatori* 9, ff. 328v-329r; he had petitioned unsuccessfully for a second term of office, *Conc.* 633, f. 27r, 8 Apr 1472), and in

left us with good summary accounts of the college's finances for most of the fifteenth century. He was responsible for the management of the estates[151] (though he had to refer significant decisions to the *Savi*, and they in turn had to obtain approval for major ones from the *Concistoro* or even the *Consiglio del Popolo* or the *Balìa*), and for the supply of victuals to the house itself, as well as being personally in charge of actually receiving students who had been granted a place,[152] allocating them a room (in which task he might receive directions or interference from the *Savi* or a higher authority, as has been seen),[153] giving them bedding and furniture and getting them to sign for them, and chasing them for payment of their debts.[154]

The real changes to the *Camarlengo*'s job are best seen in relation to changes in the rectorate. The lowest point came with the 1443 decision to appoint a Sienese rector; the job of *Camarlengo* was explicitly downgraded at this point. However, as has been seen, this was short-lived because of the resistance from students, and despite several other attempts the comune in the end accepted the desirability of a student rector.[155] The compensation for this was to reallocate effective power, moving it away from the rector and in favour of the *Camarlengo*. There are several indications of the growing importance of this office. One is the significance attached to his election, which in the 1480s became a matter of increasing attention; in 1482 it was stipulated that this had to be held in the *Consiglio del Popolo* with a quorum of 200 members.[156] In that year's election, twenty-seven names, nine per *monte*, were shortlisted,[157] and there were subsequent modifications to the method of election which bear the imprint of the political changes of the decade.[158] Another indicator is his salary. The first salary of a Sapienza *Camarlengo* to be specified, that for Chimento di Niccolò di Jacopo Rinaldi in 1420, was 50 gold florins.[159] In 1424 it was 30 florins.[160] Between then and 1443 it must have risen again; that year, which saw the first appointment of a citizen as rector and therefore less responsibility for the *Camarlengo*, it was downgraded from 42 florins to 20.[161] It gradually rose again,[162] and in 1491 it was increased to 60 florins, twice that of the rector.[163]

1476 Guasparre di Martino was found guilty of various errors, fined 25 florins on top of the order of restitution, and suspended for two years from all communal offices (*Regolatori* 9, f. 498r, 9 Aug 1476). Guasparre had held office during a year of multiple crises in the house (above, p. 350), and it is possible that this harsh punishment was part of the overall process of tightening up; on 12 Jan 1477, pleading poverty, he successfully petitioned for the suspension to be annulled (*Conc.* 2160, no. 14, 14 Feb).

[151] This included the obligation to pursue debtors (*Conc.* 2115, f. 69v, n.d. but from its position in the volume probably 1442/3). The *Camarlengo* was to place the names of all those who owed money to the house 'a lo spechio' within fifteen days.

[152] E.g. *CG* 232, f. 233r-v, 18 Feb 1469.

[153] Above, pp. 339-40, and cf. *Not.* 694, f. 12r, 4 Jan 1475, ed. Minnucci, 'Documenti', doc. II-16, p. 87; the *Camarlengo* may not allocate rooms without the permission of the *Savi*.

[154] E.g. *Not.* 694, f. 8r, 26 Aug, no year, ed. Minnucci, 'Documenti', doc. II-38, p. 109, suggesting 1470-72.

[155] Above, pp. 343-51.

[156] *CG* 239, ff. 32v-33r, *Mis.* 1, f. 110v, 30 Apr.

[157] *Conc.* 694, f. 9v, 14 May, ed. Ferreri, doc. 146, pp. 123-4.

[158] In 1484 the shortlist contained thirty names, ten from each *terzaria* (*Conc.* 707, ff. 16v-17r, 3 Aug; the names are listed); in 1487, thirty-five, this time apportioned according to *monte*; nine each from the *Nove*, the *Popolo* and the *Riformatori*, four each from the *Nobili* and the *Dodici* (*Conc.* 626, f. 25r, 10 Oct, ed. Ferreri, doc. 253, p. 216).

[159] *Conc.* 324, f. 17v, 3 Feb, and *Dipl., Università*, 6 Feb 1419(=1420).

[160] *Conc.* 352, f. 12r-v, 18 Sept.

[161] 'Item perché essendovi el decto Rectore non bisogna fare sì grande spesa nel cam.o come si fa al presente che a de salario fl. xlii. Et basta solamente uno che tenga le intrate e l'uscite e facci le scripture appartenenti a la casa' (*CG* 222, f. 49r, 4 Aug).

[162] In 1446 it was still 20 florins (*Conc.* 481, f. 33v, 4 Apr); in 1457, 100 *lire* (*Balìa* 6, f. 44v, =*Balìa* 7, f. 48v, *Statuti* 40, f. 128r, 10 Nov); in 1458, 30 florins (*Balìa* 6, f. 152v, *Statuti* 40, f. 132r-v, 7 Feb).

[163] *Mis.* 1, ff. 114r-115v, 13 Jun. It appears to have remained at that level.

The decisive moment for this office came with a major reform of 1488, which established a 'rettore et governatore generale'.[164] This official was to combine all the economic and administrative functions of the *Camarlengo*, whom it explicitly replaced,[165] together with some of the disciplinary powers over the students traditionally ascribed to the rector.[166] These latter were subsidiary to those of the student rector who is described as the *rectore forestiero*,[167] and were in fact removed three years later, when the office was retitled as 'governatore et camarlengo', which most accurately describes the post.[168] Between them these two reforms define the role of the *Camarlengo* in clear and fresh terms, making it clear that he was now the officer of principal interest to the authorities. Perhaps most significantly, in 1488 he obtained the right to sit with the *Savi* on all matters pertaining to the Sapienza,[169] while in 1491 he was actually made a full member of the 'collegio dei Savi dello Studio', with full voting rights and even the right to become its 'prior';[170] he was also authorised to make decisions with them on the admission of students.[171] His salary was established as 60 florins, and he was allowed 'una Cavalcatura a costo, et spese di decta Casa', presumably for the purposes of inspecting the Sapienza's property.[172]

With these measures we see a decisive shift. They did not remain permanently in effect – for example, the *Camarlengo* was by no means always present at meetings of the *Savi* – but the general impact does appear to have lasted; the status of the *Camarlengo* as in practice the most important figure in the Sapienza seemed assured. In additions to the 1532 statutes of the Sapienza, the *Camarlengo* and the *Savi* were between them in charge of most of the Sapienza's affairs.[173]

4. *Other personnel*

The other staff of the Sapienza are soon described. These were all normally appointed by the *Savi*,[174] though sometimes higher authorities intervened in such matters.[175] Like the students, they had to be

---

[164] *Conc.* 730, ff. 13r-16r, 29 May, ed. FERRERI, doc. 278, pp. 238-44.

[165] 'in locum Camerarii et pro Camerario dicte Domus' (*Conc.* 730, f. 13v; FERRERI, p. 238).

[166] The new official is permitted, in conjunction with the *Savi*, to 'corregiare, punire et gastigare tutti li scolari' as well as any of the other inmates of the college, and to expel any scholars or others who did not obey the statutes (f. 14r-v; FERRERI, p. 240).

[167] 'in qualunche acto avesse ad intervenire debbi andare doppo lo rectore forestiere di detta casa etiam quando avesse ad intervenire co li savi predicti e quando non intervenisse lo rectore forestieri sega doppo el priore di detti savi' (ff. 15v-16r; FERRERI, p. 243).

[168] *Mis.* 1, ff. 114r-115v, 13 Jun 1491.

[169] *Conc.* 730, ff. 15r; FERRERI, p. 242. There was a precedent; in 1483 the *Camarlengo* took the place of one of the *Savi* who was absent (*Balìa* 30, f. 18r, 19 Aug). For the *Camarlengo* to act or petition in conjunction with the *Savi*, for example on property matters, was normal; cf. *Conc.* 2137, no. 22, f. 35r, 17 Dec 1434.

[170] *Mis.* 1, f. 114v, 13 Jun. In emergency provisions of 1527, reining in the powers of the *Camarlengo*, his right to become prior of the *Savi* was expressly removed (*CG* 242, f. 177v, 15-16 Jun; on this measure see below, p. 378).

[171] *Mis.* 1, f. 115r-v. This was incorporated in the 1532 statutes (*Studio* 109, rubric VI, f. 3v, 15 Feb 1432, ed. KOŠUTA, 'Documenti', doc. II, p. 344).

[172] *Mis.* 1, f. 114r. An earlier example of such an exercise, in which the *Camarlengo* was given two assistants for the expedition, is *Not.* 694, f. 9r, 21 Jun (no year, but from its position in the volume presumably mid-1470s), ed. MINNUCCI, 'Documenti', doc. II-39, p. 110.

[173] *Studio* 109, ff. 8r-v, eds. MARRARA, *Lo Studio di Siena*, pp. 298-302, and KOŠUTA, 'Documenti', doc. II, pp. 348-50. The additions were made on 17 Dec 1533.

[174] In 1456 it was declared that 'non si possano per lo advenire mettare cappellani, sagrestano, cherici, canovajo, ne altri servi de la casa, se non saranno approvati per li savi dello studio' (*CG* 227, f. 241r, 10 Sept; = *Mis.* 1, f. 92v).

[175] For example, in 1457 the *Balìa* authorised the *Savi* and *Camarlengo* to appoint a 'rector ecclesie Misericordie', *Balìa* 6, f. 44v, 10 Nov.

at least twenty years old.[176] Along with the church (the present Chiesa di S. Pellegrino alla Sapienza), the house had its own religious officials; at least one chaplain, and a sacristan. There were several of them at once[177] – a list of Sapienza members, probably from 1474-5, has five[178] – and at one stage there was even a waiting list.[179] Their duties were to say mass daily on work days and to sing it on feast days, and to hear confession. They might get involved with other administrative tasks for the Sapienza.[180] Chaplains and sacristans had the same call on accommodation as students, and rooms were allocated between them apparently without distinction.[181] They were subject to the discipline of the college and the authority of the rector (even if he was a secular), just as were the other members, and it is possible that the post did not always attract candidates of the highest moral calibre; there are several examples of them being punished or dismissed for misdemeanours.[182] Some appointments proved to be short-term; others, such as that of Ser Bartolommeo di Matteo da Radicofani, lasted for many years.[183] Chaplains, in other words, could play an integral part of the life of the institution.[184]

A list of members of the Sapienza from around 1474/5 gives eight 'familiares' in addition to four *capellani*. One is a 'chierico', clearly of inferior rank to the chaplains. The others include a 'famiglio', a 'famiglio di sala', the rector's own servant, the cook, the cook's servant (*guattaro*) and a *fattore*.[185] Another important figure (who does not feature in this particular list) was the *canovarius*, who was responsible for the supply and distribution of food and wine.[186] Servants of the Sapienza (as opposed to those of the rector or of students) were also appointed by the *Savi*,[187] but all servants came under the same jurisdiction and had to swear obedience to the statutes of the house.[188] If we focus on a short pe-

---

[176] *CG* 227, f. 242v, 10 Sept 1456 (= *Mis.* 1, f. 94v).

[177] In the 1470s there was an apparent flood of appointments; *Studio* 2, ff. 4r (13 Aug 1473), 24r (6 Mar 1475; two elected), 29r (5 Jun 1475), 35v (2 Dec 1475), 41r (3 Apr 1476), 49v (15 Nov 1476), 54v (17 Mar 1477; election of a sacristan), 57r (14 Jan 1478). This suggests a rapid turnover, but should probably also be seen in connection with the scandal of 1476 in which accusations of abuse, and an excess of personnel, were made.

[178] *Not.* 694, f. 2r, ed. MINNUCCI, 'Documenti', doc. II-34, pp. 100-1.

[179] *Sale* 24, ff. 163r, 21 Jan, and 169v, 19 Dec 1498 (also 165v, 6 Jun).

[180] *Studio* 2, f. 9v, 29 Dec 1473; Ser Bartolomeo is involved with the refurbishment of a mill on the Sapienza's property at Sant'Ansano a Dofana (cf. also f. 3r, 27 Jul).

[181] *Studio* 2, f. 12r, 7 Feb 1474; Bartolomeo Gatti, a Sicilian student, is allocated a room previously occupied by Pietro di Bartolomeo, a *presbiter*, and another chaplain, Paolo, gets Bartolomeo's room.

[182] E.g. Ser Petrus Silvestri Jacobi of Trequanda (appointed 'cum salario et emolumentis consuetis', *Sale* 24, f. 162v, 21 Jan 1498), disciplined for an unspecified contravention (f. 171v, 15 Feb 1499). Another chaplain was actually sacked in 1527 for not doing his job (*Studio* 3, f. 60v, 3 Jun).

[183] In 1479 he completed seven years of service; in June 1480 the *Savi*, expressing their appreciation in fulsome terms, appointed him for a further seven-year period (*Studio* 2, f. 67r-v, 7 Jun). Gaps in the records of the deliberations of the *Savi* mean that it has not been possible to follow his career beyond that point.

[184] In 1462 Cosimo del Mosca, the *sacrestano* for life of the Sapienza, requested the house of the late Taccola, next to the Sapienza on the road to S. Domenico; he was given it on condition that he spent 50 florins on its repair as well as donating two florins to the sacristy. *CG* 229, ff. 249v-250r, 6 Aug (= *Conc.* 2138, no. 55, f. 89r, n.d.), and cf. *Conc.* 575, f. 35v, 3 Aug; also CATONI, 'Genesi', p. 168 n. 59.

[185] *Not.* 694, f. 2r, ed. MINNUCCI, 'Documenti', doc. II-34, pp. 100-1.

[186] E.g. *Sale* 24, f. 168v, 13 Dec 1498; Antonio Ribaldini is elected *canovarius* following the resignation of Ser Antonio di Angelo.

[187] E.g. *Studio* 2, ff. 60v, 20 Sept 1479 (Galganus Caterini, appointed for a year at the usual salary of 24 *lire*; see above, p. 85 n. 182); *Sale* 24, f. 163r, 21 Jan 1498 (Lazzaro Pellegrini of Parma is appointed at a salary of 4 *lire* per month and the usual emoluments). Payment of their salaries was also authorised by the *Savi* (e.g. *Studio* 2, ff. 60v, 20 Sept, 62v, 20 Dec 1479).

[188] E.g. *Studio* 2, f. 64r, 5 Jan 1480.

riod at the end of the fifteenth century, for which records of the deliberations of the *Savi* are preserved, it is clear that the cases in which servants were punished or dismissed for indiscipline[189] were easily outnumbered by those in which they appear as victims of abuse by students.[190] Finally there are occasional references to other officials who seem not to have a permanent existence. In the mid-1470s there is mention of a *fattore*,[191] and in 1496 of an *exactor*, subsequently called *vice-camerarius*.[192] There are also isolated references to a *notaio della Sapienza*[193] and, perhaps more unusually, a *bidello della Sapienza*.[194] One feature of the personnel is striking. The resident chaplains, servants and other minor officials known to us by name are overwhelmingly non-Sienese, and many of them are non-Italians. This must have further sharpened the distinction between those in the house and the surrounding area, and perhaps done something to enhance the feeling of community and purpose, even if there does not appear to have been much solidarity between the students and the staff, who after all were of different occupational, and usually different social, status.

[189] E.g. in 1473 a servant, Federico, was sacked for having facilitated gaming in the house (*Studio* 2, f. 9v, 29 Dec). In 1496 the *canovarius*, Domenico di Francesco of Piacenza, nicknamed 'lo strologo', was imprisoned for stealing bread from the Sapienza (*Sale* 23, f. 95v, 14 Aug); in 1498 Georgius, a German *famulus sapientie*, was sacked for the same offence (*Sale* 24, f, 164v, 29 Mar). In 1476 the *Savi* ordered the rector to exclude Niccolò, his *famulus*, for eight days (*Studio* 2, f. 38v, 26 Jan). Chaplains were not immune from misdemeanour and punishment. In 1499 Ser Pietro was removed from the Sapienza for an undisclosed offence, though he was allowed his ration of food (*Sale* 24, f. 171v, 15 Feb). In the 1470s Ser Vincenzo was excluded for offending a fellow chaplain (*Studio* 2, f. 7v, 23 Dec 1473), reinstated (11v, 20 Jan 1474) and then sacked definitively for an unspecified reason (23v, 6 Mar 1475).

[190] In 1476 Johannes albus was excluded for six months for having wounded one of the Sapienza's servants 'cum sanguis effusionis' (*Studio* 2, f. 43v, 16 May); in 1496 Blasius of Portugal was excluded for having attacked and wounded a servant (*Sale* 23, f. 92r, 16 Mar); in 1497 five scholars were excluded for having beaten a chaplain (*Sale* 24, f. 154v, 17 Apr); in 1498 'Vedericus [*sic*] scolarus teutonicus' was excluded for a month for attacking 'dominicum magistrum collegii' (f. 164v, 29 Mar); and in 1535 the Sicilian Angelo Pandolfi was deprived of his board during carnival because he had hit the cook (*Studio* 4, f. 70v, ed. Košuta, 'Documenti', doc. VI-1, p. 377). The 1542 statutes stipulated special penalties for 'scolares vapulantes et percutientes servitores' (*Studio* 110, f. 11v, 3 Jul 1542).

[191] *Not.* 694, f. 4r, n.d. but probably *c*. 1474, ed. Minnucci, 'Documenti', doc. II-35, pp. 102 (102); the *Savi* recommended to their successors 'che si facci uno factore contadino che habbi cura a le possessioni di fuore'.

[192] *Sale* 23, ff. 94r, 17 May, and 94v, 13 Jun 1496.

[193] *Scala* 177, f. 124v, 21 Mar 1484 refers to 'Ser Francesco di Domenico da Torrita notaio de la Sapienza'.

[194] *Studio* 2, f. 40r, 1 Mar 1476, mentions 'Ser Jacobus bidellus sapientie' (giving him leave for a month provided he puts in a substitute, who is Ser Filippus Angeli Pietri notarius); *Sale* 21, f. 208r, 28 Jul 1483 refers to 'Ser Filippus bidellus sapientie'. But these are the same figures as the *bidelli* of the *Studio* (above, pp. 82-3). I am not aware of bedels in Italian university colleges. The existence of such a figure in the Sapienza of Pistoia (A. S. Zmora, 'The *Pia Casa di Sapienza* of Pistoia: A Charitable Foundation and the Promise of Education in a Late Renaissance Community', unpublished Ph.D. dissertation, University of Maryland, 1995, pp. 86-8) is perhaps the exception that proves the rule; the Pistoiese foundation was a pre-university college, with no institutional affiliation, and the bedel performed many of the tasks of a university bedel elsewhere.

IV

THE ESTATE: FINANCE

1. *From Misericordia to Sapienza: the estate*

The foundation of the Casa della Sapienza has traditionally been seen as the key to the *Studio*'s financial stability.[1] The process began with the clutch of bulls issued by Gregory XII on 7 May 1408. Eight bulls were issued in all, of which four concern specifically the Sapienza. One of these instituted the Sapienza in the old Casa della Misericordia, assigning to it all the property owned by the house.[2] A second instructed the bishops of Siena, Grosseto and Massa to pass to the Sapienza a total of 6,000 florins worth of *incerti* and *maltolti* (the proceeds of usury and other profits defined as 'ill-gotten') from their dioceses.[3] A third united to the administration of the Sapienza all hospitals in those dioceses that were not functioning,[4] while a fourth offered five years' indulgence to all who left something to the Sapienza in their will.[5]

Notwithstanding the comprehensive nature of the pope's measures, the process of transfer of property was gradual and not without complication. While the administrators of the Sapienza could count on the property of the Misericordia itself – the perception that it was 'under new management' was barely noticeable, as evidenced by the continued use of the term 'Misericordia', above all in documents relating to the estate[6] – the additional measures could encounter obstacles. Some institutions were in no hurry to be amalgamated, and there were other signs of resistance. The first test came in the year after the issue of the bulls. It is not clear under which of Gregory's headings the commune was moved to act against the Canonica di San Sano (Sant'Ansano a Dofana, 7 km east of Siena), but in February 1409 the *Concistoro* empowered the rector of the Misericordia to take charge of it 'vigore

---

[1] CATONI, 'Genesi', p. 175; and ZDEKAUER, p. 33 ('Questa trasformazione della Casa della Misericordia in un collegio con rendite sue proprie è il punto di partenza per la formazione di un patrimonio indipendente dell'Università di Siena'). Cf. PRUNAI, III, p. 82.

[2] *Mis.* 1, f. 72r-v, Italian version ff. 63r-64r, ed. BARDUZZI, *Documenti*, pp. 24-5.

[3] *Mis.* 1, ff. 73r-74r, Italian version ff. 64r-65v, ed. BARDUZZI, *Documenti*, pp. 25-7. On the role of *incerti* and *maltolti* in Sienese bequests, COHN, *Death and Property*, pp. 51-3.

[4] *Mis.* 1, ff. 74r-75r, Italian version ff. 65v-67v, ed. BARDUZZI, *Documenti*, pp. 27-9.

[5] *Mis.* 1, ff. 75v-76r, Italian version ff. 67v-68r, ed. BARDUZZI, *Documenti*, pp. 29-30. On 11 Mar 1410 the bishop of Massa wrote to the *Concistoro* promising to do what he could to find the required funds; *Conc.* 1874, no. 57.

[6] Cf. p. 302 n. 27 above.

bulle apostolice concordate'.[7] The incumbent resisted. The case was taken to a doctor of canon law, Paolo di Castro, who ruled that the Sapienza had ownership but the incumbent retained life tenancy.[8] Yet provisions of 1441 for Sant'Ansano made no reference at all to the Sapienza or its officials.[9] As late as 1448 a *breve* of Pope Nicholas V ruled that Sant'Ansano was to be united to the Sapienza and its *cappellano* given a pension of 50 ducats out of the Sapienza's funds.[10] The property does appear in the inventory of the Sapienza's possessions made in 1451,[11] but it was not until the 1470s that the *Savi* showed any signs of attempting to make something of this important possession.[12] There are other examples. The bull making over defunct hospitals envisaged rectors handing over hospitals or, failing that, that the Sapienza would take possession when they died. The first and most important instance of either of these things happening is the absorption in 1415 of the hospital of S. Andrea with its not inconsiderable estate;[13] but in 1422 the commune was seeking a further bull from Martin V to effect the promised transfers. The Sienese documentation has not revealed the outcome of this request, but by 1451 S. Andrea appears in the pages of the Sapienza's inventory.[14] Whatever his reactions to this request, Martin did issue a bull granting the Sapienza 6,000 florins of *incerti* and *maltolti*.[15] It is quite possible that this is in fact a reiteration of Gregory's bull rather than a further sum, as there is no evidence – admittedly in a decade in which the Sapienza is less richly documented than subsequently – that the initial sum had been paid. A further attempt to secure the sums ordered by the pope was made in 1424,[16] and an initiative in 1434 to obtain a fresh concession of five years' worth of *incerti*

---

[7] *Conc.* 258, f. 28v, 21 Feb. For attempts in the same year to regain Misericordia property, *Conc.* 260, ff. 12r, 11 May, 20v, 23 May.

[8] Paolo di Castro's ruling is in *Conc.* 261, f. 38r, 23 Aug 1409 (and see CATONI, 'Genesi', p. 163 no. 34); cf. also *Conc.* 260, ff. 25v, 31 May, 40r, 14 Jun, 43r, 17 Jun, 44v, 18 Jun; *Conc.* 261, f. 31r, 10 Aug; *Conc.* 262, ff. 19r, 20 Sept, 23v, 26 Sept 1409; *CG* 205, ff. 135v-136r, 28 Jun 1412; and CATONI, *Pergamene*, p. 34.

[9] *Conc.* 453, f. 29v, 10 Aug; *Conc.* 455, f. 36r, 14 Dec.

[10] *Dipl., Università degli Studi*, 10 Dec 1448; cf. *Conc.* 497, f. 18v, 28 Nov, *Studio* 126, ff. 14v-15r, and *Studio* 127, no foliation, insert in the hand of Sestigiani reporting that 'per ottenere tal concessione, et unione vi andò Ambasciatore Ambrogio d'Antonio Rettore di detta Casa'. This mysterious figure may be a mistranscription for Agapito di Ambrogio (above, p. 345).

[11] *Mis.* 36, ff. 23v-24r. On this inventory see below, p. 363 n. 20.

[12] In 1475 the *Consiglio del Popolo* approved a proposal to restore the baths for public use, 'in modo si potesse per li vostri cittadini e forestieri usare. E quando fusse commodo a li povari e richi havere questo bagno, si può dire nella città' (*CG* 236, ff. 12tr-128v, 23-28 Jun 1475, ed. BOISSEUIL, *Le thermalisme*, dossier 1, doc. 17, pp. 296-7; copy in *Mis.* 1 f. 105r, 28 Jun 1475; see also *Studio* 2, ff. 28r, 30 May 1475). Of all the baths in Sienese territory this was easily the closest to the city. On the *Savi*'s interest in Sant'Ansano see also *Studio* 2, ff. 3r, 27 Jul, 4v, 26 Aug, and 8v, 23 Dec 1473; 13r, 8 Mar, and 13v-14r, 14 Mar 1474; 29r, 5 Jun, 30r, 3 Jul, and 31v, 21 Aug 1475; 52r-v, 31 Dec 1476; 74r, 19 Jun, and 83r-v, 31 Dec 1481; 92v, 10 Jun 1483; 103v, 23 Aug 1484; 120r, 26 Feb 1487; and 136r, 10 Jun 1493.

[13] *CG* 207, f. 94v; *Mis.* 1, f. 52r, 12 Aug.

[14] *Conc.* 338, f. 3v, 5 May. On its estate see below, pp. 365 and 369. The hospital of S. Maria della Stella, also known as the Spedale de' Salimbeni, passed some of its possessions to the Sapienza between 1414 and 1420 (*Mis.* 36, f. 3v); an inventory of its contents was made in 1459 as part of the process of listing the contents of the Sapienza (*Studio* 128, f. 5r; below, pp. 384-5). The Sapienza's *grancia* at Grosseto included the defunct hospital of S. Giovanni della Misericordia (*Mis.* 36, f. 39r), and the hospital of Vignone passed to the Sapienza possibly in 1420 (*Mis.* 36, f. 28r). The 'Spedale di Sta. Caterina nel popolo di San Mamiliano fuori de la porta nuova' was also listed in the 1451 inventory (*Mis.* 36, f. 1v, index), but that part of the document has not survived.

[15] *Dipl., Università degli Studi*, 23 Apr 1422; copy in PECCI, *Zibaldone* (BCS, ms. B.IV.28), ff. 37v-38r (new foliation).

[16] On 30 Dec 1424 the deadline for payment of 2,000 florins from the estate of the moneylender Zeno di Chiarasco da Soncino was lifted by the bishop's representative (addition to *Dipl., Università degli Studi*, 16 Dec 1424). On this (Christian) moneylender see BOESCH GAJANO, 'Il Comune di Siena', pp. 199-200.

from Eugenius IV appears to have come to nothing.[17] Even bequests to the house might be contested, as was that of the last rector of the Casa della Misericordia, Bencivenne di Gano, in 1418.[18] It would be wrong, therefore, to assume that Gregory XII's bulls had immediate effect.

Since almost all the estate-books of the Sapienza have disappeared (they were weeded out and destroyed to make space in 1790),[19] its history can be traced only fitfully through what survives and through the main communal sources. However one document, an inventory made in 1451 at the orders of the *Consiglio del Popolo*,[20] is fairly detailed and provides a good opportunity for comparison with the fourteenth-century estate of the Casa della Misericordia for which documentation is richer, or at least more compact. The basic source for the fourteenth century is the 1318 *Tavola delle Possessioni*, Siena's register of the owners of property in town and *contado*, in which an extensive and detailed declaration of the Casa della Misericordia's possessions appears.[21] This was analysed by a team of students under the guidance of Giuliano Catoni, who also traced subsequent developments in the fourteenth century, principally through a late seventeenth-century register of contracts.[22] By the fifteenth century this register gives out, but there are other means of comparison. Almost from its inception, the Sapienza was protected by a measure forbidding the alienation of its possessions.[23] Any such alienation thereafter needed the sanction of the *Consiglio del Popolo* and is therefore likely to appear in its archive. Acquisitions, on the other hand, can often be traced through the 1451 inventory, which gives quite detailed accounts of the history of each possession and is in many ways a conspectus of the estate books available to the compilers at the time, but now vanished. In 1448 the *Consiglio Generale*

---

[17] *Conc.* 413, f. 13v, 17 Nov 1434. Bartolomeo Borghesi was entrusted with the negotiations, and the summary of the *Concistoro*'s letters to him (*Conc.* 1643, ff. 76r, 20 Nov, 85r, 5 Dec, and 87v, 12 Dec; his replies have not survived) make it clear that this was a lost cause. On 28 Jan 1435 a proposal to the *Consiglio del Popolo* to revive the committee of three with responsibility for the pursuit of *incerti* owed to the Sapienza was resoundingly defeated, suggesting that the issue was now dead in the water (*Conc.* 2114, f. 77r).

[18] *Dipl., Università degli Studi*, 2 Sept 1418; three of the six *Savi* (the others being absent) appointed a procurator to pursue the matter. Bencivenne's will is in *Dipl., Università degli Studi*, 5 Jun 1416.

[19] See above, p. 17. An inventory of the Sapienza's archive, made at the end of the seventeenth century (ASS, *ms.* B.82) gives a detailed list of 304 volumes of financial and administrative records, of which forty-nine pertain to the fifteenth century. The list is summarised in CATONI, *Pergamene*, pp. 4-5.

[20] The inventory is in *Mis.* 36, and is the main surviving estate book of the house (see above, p. 24). According to the preamble (f. 1r), the order of the *Consiglio del Popolo* was apparently given in April 1447, although it does not appear in that body's records. An identical order does appear in the *Concistoro*'s records for 1448 (*Conc.* 497, f. 11v, 15 Nov), subsequently put to and approved by the *Consiglio del Popolo* on 22 Nov: 'item acciochè i contracti de la Casa, et sue scripture, si trovino al bisogno, e non s'abbino a cercare dalla longa, providero, che per lo innanzi qualunque Notajo de Savi sara rogato d'alcuno contracto della Casa, o compro, o vendita, o Allogagione, o altro Contracto subitamente el debba scrivere publico in uno libro da ordinarsi per lo Rectore…' (*CG* 224, ff. 180r-181r, and *Mis.* 1, f. 61r-62r; and cf. *Conc.* 497, f. 11v, 15 Nov). The inventory is headed 1450 but was completed by the *Savi* who took office on 1 January 1451 (cf. *Mis.* 36, f. 1r with *CG* 225, f. 84v, 16 Nov 1450), and must therefore have been started in early 1451 (1450 *stile senese*). Hence the mislabelling in the inventories. It contains measures as late as December 1451, the end of their period of office (*Mis.* 36, f. 25v). See CATONI, 'Genesi', pp. 167 *seq.*

The 1451 inventory is in fact the second one we know of from the institution's incarnation as Casa della Sapienza. An inventory was made in 1443, but is now lost, though we do have Sestigiani's *spoglio* of it, in ASS, *ms.* B.82, ff. 149v-154r. Cf. CATONI, 'Introduzione' to *Archivio Storico dell'Università di Siena*, p. XVI and n. 10.

[21] On the *Tavola delle Possessioni* in general, CHERUBINI, *Signori, contadini, borghesi*, pp. 231-311, and IDEM (ed.), 'I proprietari di beni immobili e di terre a Siena intorno al 1320 (dalla "Tavola delle Possessioni")', *Ricerche Storiche*, 5 (1975), pp. 357-510; introduction, pp. 37-63.

[22] CATONI, *Pergamene*. The inventory is in the same *ms.*, B.82 (see n. 19 above).

[23] *CG* 209, f. 102r, and *Mis.* 1, f. 51r, 27 Feb 1421.

also instructed that in future the notary of the *Savi* was to record all contracts pertaining to the house's possessions in a book, probably the book since bound together with the 1451 inventory;[24] and comparison with the later records of the *Savi* suggests that this operation was regularly carried out. It would be a mistake to assume, at least for the period 1408-51, that this combination of circumstance has left us with a complete record of all movements of Sapienza property. *Lacunae* are inevitable, and besides, the 1451 inventory does not give valuations of the property and is often haphazard about listing the size of the various *appezzamenti*.[25] But if the scope for precise, unit-by-unit comparison is limited, the overall picture given by the inventory yields some general indications of how the estate had altered, while the records of purchases and sales, and the accompanying justifications, give some idea of the changing financial position.

According to Catoni's team,[26] in 1318 the Casa della Misericordia owned 315 *appezzamenti* in the *contado* of Siena covering a total of 701.9 hectares and valued at 22,983.6 florins. This represented 92% of its total assessed wealth. The remaining 8% consisted of thirty possessions in Siena itself, valued at 2,151.4 florins. This is a higher than average proportion of country to town possessions for Siena.[27] With a total assessment of 25,134.9 florins the Casa della Misericordia, it was concluded, ranked among the most important landowning bodies in Siena, following only the hospital of S. Maria della Scala, the bishopric, and the monastery of S. Galgano.[28] The remainder of the fourteenth century saw significant changes to this 'portfolio'. Catoni's research seminar found 213 donations, forty-eight purchases and forty-six sales between 1315 and 1404.[29] This under-represents the activity of the last decade of the century,[30] but it is nonetheless clear that there was a substantial drop in the level of transactions after the Black Death. Cohn has shown that this is consistent with the overall pattern for Siena, a pat-

---

[24] See n. 20 above. The book may have been kept by either the *Balìa* or the *Concistoro* (above, p. 80 n. 138).

[25] It has not even survived in its entirety, though the index at the beginning shows that only three pages out of forty-three are missing.

[26] CATONI, *Pergamene*, pp. 18-22. My calculations from their summary table yield 311 possessions, covering 699 hectares, value 21,909 florins. Their spatial calculations are on the basis that one Sienese *staioro* was equal to 1,300.75m² (CATONI, *Pergamene*, p. 42 n. 87; cf. CHERUBINI, *Signori, contadini, borghesi*, p. 232 n. 5), and I have followed their example. Obviously there are dangers in interpreting measurements too precisely. See BOWSKY, *Finance*, pp. xx and 24 n. 27.

[27] CHERUBINI, 'I proprietari di beni immobili', p. 360 concludes that for private and institutional owners the proportion is 80% : 20% on average.

[28] CATONI, *Pergamene*, p. 18, IDEM, 'Gli oblati', p. 10, and CHERUBINI, *Signori, contadini, borghesi*, pp. 251-2. Only 4.8% of all landowners had more than 65 hectares (CHERUBINI, 'I proprietari di beni immobili', p. 361). It was clearly a long way behind S. Maria della Scala. Precise comparisons are not possible because some of the volumes of the *Tavola delle Possessioni* relating to the Scala do not survive. Moreover the territory of the *Vescovado* was excluded from the exercise, as was the monastery of S. Galgano, as a rural landowner. An evaluation of the Misericordia in comparison with other property owners in the parish of S. Donato a lato dei Montanini is given by C. MANDRIANI, 'I proprietari delle "Libre" di San Donato a lato dei Montanini, San Donato a lato della Chiesa, San Donato di Sopra e San Donato di Sopra', in CHERUBINI, 'I proprietari di beni immobili', pp. 357-510 (pp. 439-54, esp. p. 440).

[29] Extrapolated from CATONI, *Pergamene*, diag. A, facing p. 27. The twelve years following the 1318 evaluation saw acquisitions by the Casa della Misericordia from individuals to the taxable value of 3,833 *lire*, and sales to individuals worth only 914 *lire*; CHERUBINI, *Signori, contadini, borghesi*, p. 305. (The Casa della Misericordia was the only public institution in the parish of S. Donato a lato dei Montanini, which makes it possible to deduce these figures from the table he gives.) Cherubini is at pains to point out (p. 308) that many of the sales recorded might well be 'vendite fittizie, portate a termine per sottrarre le ricchezze alle imposizioni fiscali'. Almost all the acquisitions are from citizens. On the expansion and rationalisation of the town possessions of the Misericordia in the fourteenth century, and on its various *sedi*, BALESTRACCI and PICCINNI, *Siena nel Trecento*, pp. 153-4.

[30] Their estimates are based on a trawl of later *spogli*. Comparison with the contents of *Mis.* 36 suggests that there are omissions for the last decade.

tern bucked only by the Scala, which increasingly became the main focus of hospital donation at the expense of the Misericordia and others.[31] By the end of the century, as has been seen, despite these donations (and possibly also because of the strain they placed on the administration of the estate), the house was in considerable financial difficulty, which culminated in bankruptcy in 1391[32] and led eventually to the proposal that it be converted into a Sapienza for students. Thereafter there were far fewer bequests; although the status of the house remained one of pious institution, and donations continue to be important in principle, in practice it appears that the secular nature of the Sienese Sapienza made it a less obvious beneficiary of pious bequests than the more conventional ones.

Compared (to the extent that it is possible to do so) with the assessment of 1318, the 1451 inventory presents a rather different picture. The document first lists twenty-four possessions in the town, of which one is known to have been acquired in the fourteenth century after 1318, and three in the fifteenth century.[33] There follow two lists, respectively of the town and *contado* possessions of the hospital of S. Andrea which passed to the Sapienza in 1415; the former lists twenty-seven possessions, the latter twenty-three.[34] Finally the bulk of the document consists of a listing of the Sapienza's possessions in the *contado*.[35] There are 577 items in this incomplete list, of which 107 are buildings mentioned independently of land; in other words, to use the criterion of Catoni *et al.* for the sake of comparison (admittedly a less than satisfactory method), there are 470 *appezzamenti*. What is most striking about this list, however, is the lack of correspondence with the 1318 assessment. By no means all of the items in the 1451 list mention the date or mode of acquisition. For many there is no information; in other cases the date of first mention is given, or it is simply stated that the property appears in a specific estate book (and it is often possible to establish the date of these through the seventeenth-century inventory). Of the 107 houses listed separately, however, it is clearly stated of thirty-three that they were acquired after 1318, and of the 470 *appezzamenti* no fewer than 298 were acquired after that date. A location-by-location analysis shows an even more acute divergence. Only six locations are common to the two lists; and even in these cases the books have by no means remained static. At Bibbiano Guiglieschi an area of woodland is registered which may correspond to that of 1318;[36] at Montagutolo Giuseppi four *appezzamenti* correspond more precisely.[37] For San Mamiliano we know from the index that some property was still held there in 1451, but the details are missing;[38] at Sant'Agnati di Vignano and Lucignano d'Asso it is clear that the properties listed in 1451 were not those listed in 1318.[39] Only in the case of Monticchiello in

---

[31] COHN, *Death and Property*, pp. 17-24.

[32] Above, p. 303; CATONI, *Pergamene*, p. 33; BALESTRACCI and PICCINNI, loc. cit.

[33] *Mis.* 36, ff. 2r-5v.

[34] *Mis.* 36, ff. 6r-12v. On the *botteghe* of the hospital of S. Andrea, BALESTRACCI and PICCINNI, *Siena nel Trecento*, pp. 137-8.

[35] Mis 36, ff. 13r-40v.

[36] *Mis.* 36, f. 16v; CATONI, *Pergamene*, p. 19.

[37] *Mis.* 36, f. 22r; CATONI, *Pergamene*, loc. cit.

[38] *Mis.* 36, f. 1v; CATONI, *Pergamene*, p. 20.

[39] *Mis.* 36, ff. 22v and 36v-38v respectively; CATONI, *Pergamene*, p. 19. This method of comparison also hides properties that were acquired since 1318 and given up before 1451; for example, around 1400 the Misericordia owned a substantial *albergo* in Lucignano d'Arbia (M. TULIANI, *Osti, avventori e malandrini. Alberghi, locande e taverne a Siena e nel suo contado tra Trecento e Quattrocento* [Siena, 1994], p. 102), which appears in neither the 1318 nor the 1451 listings for the institution under that locality.

the Val d'Orcia, the largest concentration of property in both lists, can continuity be established on a significant scale. Sixty-five items are listed in 1318 and 157 in 1451, of which fifty-nine are stated to have been acquired after 1319.[40]

The substantial change in the possessions of the house cannot be explained simply by reference to the series of acquisitions and sales over the fourteenth and early fifteenth centuries. Coupled with the post-1408 amalgamations this series would, as has been seen, have produced a much larger estate. It is legitimate to conclude that during the period of crisis in the late fourteenth century many possessions must have slipped from the Misericordia's control. A spread of possessions such as that of the 1318 assessment – which Catoni's team emphasised as a feature[41] – could only be maintained by strict surveillance, regular collection of rents or the landowner's share of the produce, sanctions against debtors and eviction of illegal occupiers. Whereas such effective control was being exercised in the early fourteenth century there is evidence, particularly in the years following the Black Death, of illegal occupation of Misericordia property and thereafter of incompetence on the part of the administrators.[42] There is no way of telling, therefore, exactly what the Sapienza did inherit, but one can assume from the bankruptcy of 1388 and the terminal difficulties of the Misericordia that the worst of the damage was done before the transfer.

This loss of property is also one explanation for the second striking feature of the 1451 inventory, namely the marked concentration of property in fewer but larger areas. Thirty-five locations appear in the 1451 inventory as opposed to sixty-eight in 1318. If the size of estates is measured by the number of *appezzamenti* per *podere* or group of *poderi*, it is indisputable that there has been a significant shift towards the larger unit (see Fig. 15). This is clearly a very crude form of measurement; the potentially decisive evidence here, actual area, is inadequate, as only some *appezzamenti* are listed with any indication of size, although those that are point towards the same conclusion (see Tables 8a and 8b). This concentration of property, and the abandonment of small, individual, isolated holdings, were encouraged by some of the authorities. There is evidence of concentrated buying in areas such as the Val di Strove, Monticchiello and Lucignano ad Asse in the mid-fourteenth century, as well as of rationalisation by the *Savi* and the *Consiglio del Popolo* in the mid and late fifteenth century.[43] Undoubtedly, though, it also owed a great deal to natural events. The abandonment of remote or individual properties which seems to have occurred in the late fourteenth century was compensated by donations which added chiefly to property in existing areas. It seems likely that, particularly in the three areas mentioned above, the presence of the Casa della Misericordia as landowner in an area encouraged donations in that same area, perhaps more than where the house had no property. Gradual simplification of the structure of the house's possessions, then, seems to have taken place, but this was only partly a matter of deliberate policy.

---

[40] *Mis.* 36, ff. 29r-35r; Catoni, *Pergamene*, p. 19.

[41] Catoni, *Pergamene*, p. 20.

[42] Catoni, *Pergamene*, pp. 16, 17, 28-30. This last phase of the Misericordia's existence includes the correspondence relating to property at Monte Oliveto Maggiore which was published, and brilliantly analysed, by G. Piccinni, '*Seminare, fruttare, raccogliere'. Mezzadri e salariati sulle terre di Monte Oliveto Maggiore (1374-1430)* (Milan, 1982), ch. 6 and appendix.

[43] Below, pp. 372-5.

Table 8a – The largest Casa della Misericordia properties in 1318

Location	Total area in hectares	No. of *appezzamenti*
Monticchiello	216.3	65
Orgia	58.4	20
Castiglione Benzetti	52.0	1
Montagutolo Giuseppi	42	5
Brenna	33.3	31
Certano	32.3	7

Table 8b – The largest Casa della Sapienza properties in 1451

Location	Total area in hectares	No. of *appezzamenti* giving area	Total no. of *appezzamenti*[1]
Monticchiello	241.4	102	137[2]
Val d'Orcia	82.9	15	22[3]
Grosseto	61.4	32	50
Val di Strove	32.7	31	74
Petroio	28.7	8	34
Vico di Montechiano	17.9	11	12

[1] The incompleteness of the evidence suggests that the total area for these – and other – possessions was substantially greater than the figures indicate. Only figures given in *staiori* have been included. See p. 364 n. 26.

[2] In addition, two *appezzamenti* are measured in *moggiate* (they yield 8, or about 200 bushels; see p. 377 n. 122.

[3] There are in addition nine appezzamenti yielding 34 *moggiate*, and four vineyards with 264 vines.

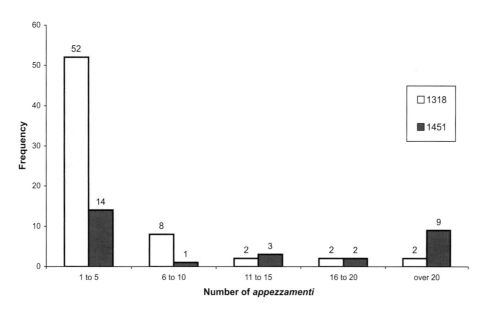

Fig. 15 – Concentration of Casa della Misericordia/Casa della Sapienza property.

A more complex question still is that of the quality of the lands owned, without which information the statistics about area remain fairly meaningless. Catoni's students found that in the 1318 assessment the overwhelming proportion of *appezzamenti*, 86%, was cultivated while 8.9% was mixed and 5.1% uncultivated, and that this was probably the explanation of the high value of the estate.[44] The 1451 inventory is again reticent on this matter; 54.6% of the *appezzamenti* are not described at all, but it may be significant that of the remainder only 61% are described as cultivated; 14.5% were mixed and 24.4% uncultivated. But again these figures, based on *appezzamenti* rather than area, deny us the most useful information. It may be more profitable to compare the uses to which land was put. In 1318, of the 315 *appezzamenti* listed, sixty-three are described as *lavorativi* with *vigne* and eleven were actual *vigne* – in other words, vines were present in 23% of them. Only four, or 1.3%, had any olives.[45] In 1451 these proportions may well have been greater. Of the 213 *appezzamenti* which are described, seventy-nine, or 37.1%, include vines, and twenty-two, or 10.3%, include olives. The proportion of buildings in the *contado* to the total number of *appezzamenti* – a figure for which the 1451 inventory can be assumed to be reliable – has remained virtually the same; 22.5% in 1318, 22.8% in 1451.[46] They are, however, spread more evenly, and large properties with few buildings – such as that of Monticchiello in 1318, which led Catoni's students to suppose that this was an example of land farmed with hired labour[47] – no longer feature.[48] Very few indications are given of the sort of buildings owned. Apart from five mills and four *romitori*, only twenty-five of the 123 entries mentioning buildings in 1451 run to any description beyond the words *casa*, *casina* etc. They include ten *chiostri*, seven *columbai*, one *forno*, one *aia* and fifteen *capanne*; two are described as *palazzi* and one as a 'belissimo casamento e case assai'.

The proportion of properties with buildings gives at least a clue to an important but elusive aspect, mode of tenure. The sources are least helpful on the question of forms of land tenure, a particularly regrettable omission in view of the amount of interest that this has recently attracted. The *Tavola delle Possessioni* gives incomplete information, since the records for the Misericordia are among those for which this detail is frequently omitted. Catoni's team worked on the basis that properties with buildings were likely to be held by *mezzadri* (sharecroppers), since residence was a prerequisite for this form of tenure, and those with no buildings were likely to be rented out or farmed by paid non-resident labour, usually journeymen. This must now be considered too crude a criterion, given the detailed studies of Ginatempo and Piccinni (the latter demonstrating that even in the fifteenth century it was far from automatic that *mezzadri* would live exclusively or even at all on the *podere*).[49] The position is not much better for the 1451 inventory, which, being primarily a register of possessions, was compiled for the purpose of proving ownership rather than describing tenancy, and therefore also tends to omit this information. A number of properties including a building are explicitly described as rented, suggesting that it would be dangerous to apply *tout court* the criteria used by Catoni's team. Overall

---

[44] Catoni, *Pergamene*, p. 21.

[45] Loc. cit.

[46] Catoni, *Pergamene*, pp. 18-20. On the difficulties in categorising land, because of the considerable variety of description, Cherubini, *Signori, contadini, borghesi*, p. 263.

[47] Catoni, *Pergamene*, p. 21.

[48] The holdings at Monticchiello had two buildings in 1318, over thirty-five in 1451. Of the other large estates, that of Grosseto included at least fifteen buildings, that of the Val di Strove at least twenty-two. Of the others, only that of the Val d'Orcia may have had less than one building per ten hectares, and this estate is known to have had a high proportion of uncultivated land.

[49] Ginatempo, *Crisi di un territorio*; Piccinni, *Il contratto di mezzadria*, III, esp. pp. 34-6, 54, 112, 117.

the proportion of properties with buildings is virtually identical to that of the 1318 'portfolio', but other indicators suggest a move towards sharecropping; a larger number of entries, especially in the larger units, are described as *poderi*,[50] and many now include buildings.[51] We are little better informed on land rented out in 1451; details are given in only a handful of cases.[52] Rents in the late twelfth century ranged from 10 to 80 *lire*, averaging around 20 to 30;[53] isolated references in the 1451 inventory and also in later contracts only rarely exceed the 30-*lira* figure and were often lower than 10 *lire*. On the other hand these small figures could rapidly add up; twenty-one of the twenty-three *contado* possessions of the hospital of S. Andrea listed in the inventory state the rent due, and the total is £299/18/4.[54] Rents in town were often higher; thirteen of the twenty-four possessions of the Sapienza in Siena brought in £266/7/0.[55] Even these rents vary enormously, of course, not only according to the size and value of the property but also according to the terms of the contract and the conditions under which it had come into the Sapienza's possession.

[50] However, PICCINNI, op. cit., pp. 104-5 points out that the existence of a *podere* was not automatically an indicator of sharecropping.

[51] An especially good example is the institution's holdings at Monticchiello. In 1318 these included sixty-five *appezzamenti* but only two buildings (CATONI, *Pergamene*, p. 19); the 1451 the fifty-nine *appezzamenti* were mostly subsumed into *poderi* which included nine buildings (*Mis.* 36, ff. 29r-31r). This fits with the observation that *mezzadria* farming only reached this area in the early fifteenth century; G. PICCINNI, 'Ambiente, produzione, società della Valdorcia nel tardo medioevo', in *La Val d'Orcia nel medioevo e nei primi secoli dell'età moderna*. Atti del convegno internazionale di studi storici, Pienza, 15-18 settembre 1988, ed. A. Cortonesi (Rome, 1990), pp. 33-58 (p. 41). CHERUBINI, *Signori, contadini, borghesi*, pp. 296 and 299, shows that public institutions went in for mixed forms of tenure, unlike the private Sienese owners who showed a marked preference for *mezzadria* – a generalisation for Tuscany partly modifiable for Siena (PICCINNI, *Il contratto di mezzadria*, III, pp. 118-9). On the extent of *mezzadria* and its intimate connection with the process of *appoderamento*, CHERUBINI, *Signori, contadini, borghesi*, pp. 295-301; IDEM, 'La mezzadria toscana delle origini', in *Contadini e proprietari nella Toscana moderna. Atti del Convegno di Studi in onore di Giorgio Giorgetti*. Vol. 1. *Dal medioevo all'età moderna*. Unione Regionale delle Province Toscane. Biblioteca di Storia Toscana Moderna e Contemporanea. Studi e Documenti, 19 (Florence, 1979), pp. 131-152; P. J. JONES, 'From Manor to Mezzadria: A Tuscan Case-Study in the Medieval Origins of Modern Agrarian Society', in *Florentine Studies*, ed. N. Rubinstein (London, 1968), pp. 193-241; L. A. KOTEL'NIKOVA, 'Rendita in natura e rendita in denaro nell'Italia medievale (secoli IX-XV)', in *Storia d'Italia. Annali 6. Economia naturale, economia monetaria*, eds. R. Romano and U. Tucci (Turin, 1983), pp. 94-112; PICCINNI, *Il contratto di mezzadria*, III, and for a detailed case study, EADEM, 'Seminare, fruttare, raccogliere', esp. ch. 1.
Appoderamento at Montichiello was probably also linked to demographic decline, particularly marked there in the first half of the fifteenth century; efforts were made to repopulate it in 1413 and 1436, when there were only seventy males, and the dimensions of the encircling wall had to be reduced. Eventual success is noted just after the transfer of property from the Sapienza to the Scala. In 1469 the Scala, which had '70 paia di buoi' in the area, was instructed to build a *grancia*, using the castle of Monticchiello, which was in need of restoration, as its main depository; in the 1480s a colony of immigrants, the only one in Sienese territory outside the Maremma, was established; by 1532 the community was in rude demographic health, with 750-800 inhabitants in 156 households, of which twenty were *poderai*. GINATEMPO, *Crisi di un territorio*, esp. pp. 201-2 n. 85, 214 n. 121, 328 n. 172, 432-3, 441, 459, 514 n. 18, 513, though she also warns against too rigid assumptions of cause and effect (pp. 206-8); EADEM, 'Il popolamento della Valdorcia alla fine del medioevo (XV-XVI secolo)', in *La Val d'Orcia nel medioevo*, pp. 113-53 (pp. 130-1).

[52] Eleven land rents are listed under the possessions of the Sapienza proper; four are cash rents, five involve payment in kind and two are a mixture of both. For an example of a proposed rent in kind, *Not.* 694, f. 32r, ed. MINNUCCI, 'Documenti', doc. II-57, p. 125, n.d. but among documents from the 1470s.

[53] CATONI, *Pergamene*, p. 15.

[54] *Mis.* 36, ff. 9v-12v.

[55] *Mis.* 36, ff. 2r-5v. Cf. BALESTRACCI and PICCINNI, *Siena nel Trecento*, pp. 133-5 on urban rents in the fourteenth century.

2. *The commune and the finances of the Sapienza*

The best way to view the Sapienza's income and expenditure is through the annual summaries of the accounts drawn up and approved by the *Regolatori*. Since so much of its income was in kind – the produce, whether from sharecropping or rents in kind, which supplied most of the needs of the house's inmates – no simple statistics are possible. Cash rents were clearly secondary in importance. The Sapienza's other source of income, of course, was the not inconsiderable entrance fee paid by the students. With thirty students in the house, paying 50 florins for a seven-year stay (and proportionately slightly more for shorter stays), the administration could under normal circumstances expect 214 florins per year from this source – though as will be seen, circumstances were not often 'normal'.[56] Out of these sources the Sapienza had to run and maintain[57] the house, feed the students and pay the salaries of the rector, *Camarlengo* and servants;[58] it also had to pay annuities to those who had made property over to the house for the remainder of their lives, for which again no total is possible.

The commune oversaw, participated in and regulated the management of the estate with varying degrees of interest and intensity. These can be gauged through its legislation, with the usual proviso that for a balanced picture the extent of its control has to be assessed also in relation to the activities of the *Savi* – for which we know more for the later part of the century – and the *Camarlengo*, much of whose work is hidden from view. With these cautions, the history of the Sapienza's finances in our period can be characterised in four phases. In the first half of the fifteenth century the authorities attempted to establish the position of the estate, legislated in favour of the Sapienza's rights, and ordered improved mechanisms of assessment and control. In the mid-fifteenth century this culminated in a brief but effective programme of permutations and purchases which rationalised the Sapienza's holdings, particularly through a series of property deals with the hospital of S. Maria della Scala. In the third quarter of the century the authorities developed a new approach, milking the institution – which was now evidently in good financial health – for its own purposes. Finally the burgeoning number of *sapientini*, together with economic difficulties of Siena generally, led to a steady worsening of its finances and a clear descent into crisis, evident from the last quarter of the fifteenth century and continuing into the first third of the sixteenth, when it threatened to overwhelm the institution.

Communal measures were taken above all in response to need; most of them were passed by the *Consiglio del Popolo* or the *Concistoro* at the suggestion of the *Savi*, often in conjunction with the *Camarlengo*. Many are *ad hoc* reactions to particular situations or crises; for example, in November 1432 the Sapienza was in urgent need of grain, so the *Concistoro* decreed that it be given 8 *moggia*, for which a loan was arranged, to be repaid by the feast of S. Maria the following August.[59] The most frequent type of measure is support for the Sapienza in its perennial efforts to chase up debts. This could take the form of the pursuit of specific debts, such as payments for property sold to institutions (in-

---

[56] Below, esp. pp. 376 *seq.*

[57] An explicit example of a connection between income and expenditure in this respect is the decision that the 52-florin entrance fee of 'Dominus Johannes Brensset theotonicus' be used 'pro bancis reficiendis conficiendis et murandis in scolas' (*Conc.* 605, f. 20v, 24 Jul 1467).

[58] Above, pp. 347-8 and 356.

[59] *Conc.* 401, f. 12r, 9 Nov 1432. An attempt to build on this precedent was made in or around 1443, though it appears not to have been approved; the *Savi* asked that the *Camarlengo del Sale* be obliged to provide 12 *staiora* of salt annually, and that the *Biccherna* be obliged to hand over all fines deducted from teachers' salaries to the Sapienza (*Conc.* 2115, f. 118v, n.d.).

cluding the state itself),[60] or general legislation to enforce payment (e.g. of rents) by threatening to in-
scribe debtors in the *libro dello specchio*.[61] Other measures are managerially more proactive, such as the
ordering of inventories and recording of contracts,[62] the placing on the Sapienza of the obligation to
maintain a reserve of 60 *moggia* of grain each year,[63] and steps taken to monitor expenditure; despite
the fact that the *Regolatori* conducted an annual audit of the *Camarlengo*'s accounts, on several occasions the *Concistoro* ordered specially appointed *revisores* to check his books as well.[64]

The main concern of the authorities was of course the stability of the Sapienza's finances, which
depended above all on the maintenance of the integrity of the estate and on its productivity. The renting out of Sapienza property and the effective collection of those rents was critical for this, and since
issues of fairness and competition arose it was one which also interested the authorities. The letting of
property was controlled to prevent abuses; in 1437 a detailed measure laid down a public procedure
by which a vacant property had to be advertised before it could be let, and the practice of advance
reservation was forbidden except in time of war.[65] In 1452 the *Consiglio del Popolo* went further and
declared that all property in the areas of S. Ansano a Dofana, Montaperti, Vico di Montechiano and
the Val di Strove could only be let with its permission,[66] though it does not seem that this order was
followed to the letter. These measures were not merely attempts at control; they attempted to protect
the Sapienza from corruption or incompetence on the part of its administrators. Similar considerations inform the repeated insistence on redress of irregularities in rents, and the demand that tenants
whose contracts were not legitimate return their property.[67] One issue of particular concern was the
length of tenancies. Lifelong tenancies reduced the Sapienza's room for manoeuvre, and it is thus unsurprising to find legislation to outlaw lifetime or indefinite contracts; a package of reforms passed by
the *Consiglio del Popolo* in 1448 included the imposition of a maximum length of six years.[68]

The most substantive and contentious issue repeatedly brought before the *Concistoro* and *Consiglio
del Popolo* concerned the integrity of the estate. Given the institution's status as a charitable body, to
which legacies had been made on that basis, the starting point always had to be the inalienability of

[60] E.g. *CG* 228, f. 168v, and *Mis.* 36, f. 55v, 26 Oct 1459 (the Sapienza's property at Monticchiello had been sold in
1454, but the purchase price had not yet been paid); and cf. the pursuit of *incerti*, discussed above, pp. 361-2.

[61] E.g. *Conc.* 312, f. 6r, 7 Jan 1418; *CG* 217, f. 81v, 19 Sept 1433 (= *Mis.* 1, f. 55v, and *Conc.* 2114, f. 32r); *Conc.* 2115,
f. 69v, n.d. but from collocation probably 1443; same batch as 68v which is probably 1442/3, concerning the rector. The
Savi routinely pursued debtors; *Studio* 2, ff. 11r, 10 Jan 1474 (a specific case), 39r, 26 Jan 1476 (a general *bando*) and 49v,
15 Nov 1476 (general), 138r, 11 Aug 1493 (a debtor is in jail; his release is ordered provided he gives surety); *Studio* 3, ff.
3v, 11 Mar 1519, 72 (an individual case). Only in times of war or plague were tenants of the house exempted from paying
their rent, and I have found only one instance in which this was stated (*Studio* 2, f. 67r, 7 Jun 1480).

[62] *CG* 224, f. 180r-v, *Mis.* 1, f. 61v, 22 Nov 1448; and see above, p. 363 n. 20.

[63] *CG* 232, f. 72v, 20 Feb 1468: 'per conservatione dessa casa'. The hospital of S. Maria della Scala was obliged to maintain a reserve of 300 *moggia* (f. 72r-v).

[64] *Conc.* 338, f. 2v, 4 May 1422; *Conc.* 370, f. 18v, 2 Dec 1427; *Conc.* 377, f. 4v, 4 Jan 1429; *Mis.* 1, f. 85r, 19 May
1437 (the task is given to the *riveditori del bossolo*); *Conc.* 481, f. 33v, 4 Apr 1446 (the accounts were to be checked by the
camerarius operae); and cf. *Studio* 3, f. 59r-v, 16 May 1527, when the *Savi* elected the *revisores*. See above, p. 355.

[65] *Mis.* 1, f. 84r-v, 19 May; *Conc.* 2114, f. 134v (proposed 29 Apr). A measure of 1448 confirmed this and declared all
illegal lettings invalid (*CG* 224, f. 180r; *Mis.* 1, f. 61r, 22 Nov).

[66] *CG* 225, f. 260r; *Mis.* 1, f. 92v, 10 Jan. These were the chief remaining rural properties after the decisions of the previous year to sell or exchange substantial clusters of property.

[67] E.g. *Conc.* 504, f. 46v, 16 Feb, and *CG* 224, f. 334r, 20 Feb 1450 (= *Mis.* 1, f. 90r-v); *CG* 236, ff. 127v-128r, and
Mis. 1, f. 105r-v, 28 Jun 1475.

[68] *CG* 224, f. 180r, *Mis.* 1, f. 61v, 22 Nov.

property. This was made explicit in 1421, when the *Savi* were forbidden to alienate any part of the estate.[69] Repeatedly the *Savi* came forward with proposals to alter this policy, and repeatedly they were rebuffed. The saga reveals much about the problems with the estate, and the eventual change of heart is also instructive. There appear to have been two driving factors; financial difficulties – to which the rise in Sapienza numbers was clearly contributing – and the growing perception that the haphazard configuration of bequests, many far-flung, was an inefficient basis for maximising revenue. The first proposal was made in 1434. Though the decision had been appropriate at the time, the *Savi* argued, war and 'gattivi temporali' had reduced the majority of houses owned by the Sapienza to ruin. Two-fifths of all revenue was needed for repairs; yet the annual income of 1,000 *lire* was only enough to provide food for the members of the college. If the income could be brought up to 300 florins (i.e. 1,200 *lire*) a mill in the Val d'Orcia could be repaired, which would yield 10 or more *moggia*, a considerable enhancement. The *Savi* proposed a public *bando* or auction to sell off some property, the money from which could be reinvested in *bottighe* in Siena.[70] The proposal was defeated.[71] Another attempt was made in 1437, this time stressing the number of possessions which yielded little or nothing; again, without success.[72] Alarm bells continued to ring; in 1441 the *Savi* reported that the revenue was inadequate and the possessions were in poor condition, and that it was difficult to provide for the thirty-eight scholars in the college.[73] Other proposals from the same period refer to the same problems,[74] as well as pointing out how many of the least productive properties were in distant and scattered areas,[75] how much of the rent due to the Sapienza was simply not being collected,[76] and how properties which did not include a building were particularly prone to rapid abandonment.[77] By this period the *Savi* of the time were estimating that two-thirds of revenue needed to be spent on repairs.[78]

In 1443, the year in which an inventory of possessions was compiled,[79] a *bando* for the sale of Sapienza property was finally authorised, though it does not appear to have had an immediate or significant impact.[80] What seems to have unblocked the situation much more effectively was the prospect of exchanges of property with another pious institution, the hospital of S. Maria della Scala.

---

[69] *CG* 209, f. 102r, *Mis.* 1, f. 51r, 27 Feb. According to a measure of 1434 (*Conc.* 2137, no. 22, f. 35r, 17 Dec) this was repeated in 1426. I have been unable to trace this. In this respect there was supposedly a significant divergence between *enti* and private citizens, though again PICCINNI, *Il contratto di mezzadria*, III, pp. 118-22, esp. 122, points out how little difference there was in practice.

[70] *Conc.* 2137, no. 22, f. 35r, 17 Dec. The *Concistoro* decided to put the proposal to the *Consiglio del Popolo*.

[71] *Conc.* 2114, f. 78r, 28 Jan.

[72] *Conc.* 2114, f. 135r, 29 Apr. This was the only one of a batch of *Studio* and Sapienza measures not to be approved; cf. *CG* 219, ff. 146v-147v; *Mis.* 1, ff. 83r-85r; *Statuti* 41, ff. 255v-256r; some edited in ZDEKAUER, doc. XVIII, pp. 169-71.

[73] *CG* 221, ff. 21v-22r, 26 Jun.

[74] E.g. *Conc.* 2115, f. 68v, n.d. but presumably 1442 or 1443 judging from its position in the volume and since the proposal is for a 'rectore e governatore cittadino'; see above, p. 343.

[75] *Conc.* 2138, no. 14, f. 24r, n.d.; filed between documents of 1442 and 1452. The properties referred to are in the Val d'Orcia, Sant'Angelo in Colle, Lucignano ad Asso and elsewhere. The proposal is to sell them in exchange for '*butighe* o possessioni più presso a la vra. città'. The same diagnosis is evident in proposals of sale of 1460 (see below, pp. 373-4); 'et molte cose spezzate e disutili si potranno convertire in cose utili e più in Siena' (*CG* 228, ff. 289v-290v [290r], 18 Oct).

[76] *Conc.* 2115, f. 69v, n.d. but in the same batch as a document (f. 68v) which appears to relate to others of 1442-3.

[77] *CG* 222, f. 43r-v, 7 Jul 1443.

[78] *CG* 222, ff. 48v-49r, 4 Aug 1443; = *Conc.* 2115, f. 82r.

[79] Above, p. 363 n. 20.

[80] *CG* 222, f. 43r-v, 7 Jul. The *Consiglio del Popolo* had authorised the operation, and the *Savi* reported that so far the interest generated led them to recommend only one sale, of a property in Capraia; they were awaiting further bids.

The first mention of this scheme is in June 1445, when an inventory and valuation of the Sapienza's possessions in Val d'Orcia was actually drawn up by the *Savi dello Studio* and agreed between the two institutions with the intention that they be sold to the Scala or exchanged for other property.[81] The *Concistoro* forwarded the proposal – emanating from the rectors of both institutions – to the *Consiglio del Popolo* in August, where it appears not to have been approved,[82] but the idea – which emerged during the period of office of the first known Sienese rector of the Sapienza, Pietro di Nanni Biringucci – was to prove to be the way forward. The need for urgent action was becoming ever more pressing. In January 1447 the Sapienza's circumstances were reported to be such that 'con grande fatica a pena si può reggiare li scolari, che so nela casa'.[83] In April of that year a full inventory of all the Sapienza's possessions was ordered (it materialised in 1451).[84] In November 1448 the *Consiglio del Popolo* tightened up on all aspects of estate management with a 'package' of rulings – no alienation of property without permission, return of property illegally alienated, no lettings for over six years, redress of irregularities in the books, recording of all contracts.[85] With the completion of the inventory the way forward was clear. A proposal from the *Savi* to sell the Val d'Orcia possessions was lost,[86] but by the end of 1451 the *Consiglio del Popolo* had approved a proposal to sell off most of the Sapienza's remoter estates: the possessions in Lucignano Val d'Asso and the Val d'Orcia, and the *grancia* in Grosseto. The Scala, which appears to have lost interest since the original proposal of 1445, was offered the Val d'Orcia estate; the proceeds of any sale were to be invested by the comune, with the Sapienza receiving interest.[87] The measure was only put into effect in stages. Nothing appears to have happened until 1454, when possessions in Monticchiello were sold to the Scala for 2,200 florins.[88] The Sapienza was still chasing up the income due to it from the sale, with the help of the authorities, five years later.[89] In 1460 the plans to sell off outlying properties were revived; the *Consiglio del Popolo* approved the announcement of an auction, 'come si costuma fare de le cose de lo spedale di Sc.a Maria', of a number of scattered properties as well as the possessions at Lucignano Val d'Asso, and an exchange with the Scala which would give it the *grancia* of Grosseto; both of these holdings were reported to be in seri-

---

[81] *Not.* 694, f.1r-v, 22 Jun, ed. MINNUCCI, 'Documenti', doc. II-4, pp. 77-80, and see p. 26.

[82] *Conc.* 477, f. 23v, 3 Aug.

[83] *Conc.* 2121, no. 52, 25-28 Jan; cf. TURRINI, *"Per honore et utile"*, pp. 143-4.

[84] See above, p. 363 n. 20.

[85] *CG* 224, f. 180v, *Mis.* 1, f. 61r, 22 Nov. That this had some impact is demonstrated by the fact that in the inventory of 1451 there are two examples of sales which had been effected in violation of this standing order, and which were nullified after its reiteration in 1448; *Mis.* 36, ff. 2v and 4v.

[86] *Conc.* 2118, f. 19r-v, 2 Sept 1451.

[87] *CG* 225, ff. 240v-241r, 30 Nov-14 Dec, and *Mis.* 1, ff. 90v-91r, 14 Dec.

[88] *Conc.* 526, ff. 14v-15v, May; the full contract is in *Scala* 72, ff. 345r-351r, with an inaccurate later heading describing it as the contract for the Grosseto estate. The issue had been reactivated in April, when the *Concistoro* and *Balìa* gave the rector discretion to sell property at Asciano; for the Val d'Orcia property, however, it imposed a commission of three to conclude the agreement with the Scala, adding that it could not be sold for less than 2,000 florins (*Conc.* 525, f. 61r-v, 16 Apr). The valuation of the property proposed for sale in 1445 had been 1,750 florins (above, n. 81). The inventory of the property sold (*Scala* 1423, ff. 62r-74r) is much more detailed but appears to cover the same items that were listed in the 1445 valuation.

[89] *CG* 228, f. 168v, and *Mis.* 36, ff. 55v, 26 Oct 1459, and 56r, 9 Feb 1460. In 1457 the *Balìa* attempted to give the process of selling off Sapienza property a push. The reason stated is that it wanted 1,200 florins from the proceeds for military expenditure, but behind that is the fact that three months earlier the Sapienza had bought property in Val di Strove to that value (25 Jun; *Mis.* 36, no. 14, ff. 54r-55v; *Balìa* 4, f. 63r; *Balìa* 5, f. 71r, blocking payment, 27 Jun). The individual concerned is Blasius d.ni Francisci (*Balìa* 4, ff. 72r, 12 Jul, 78v, 16 Jul, 80v-81r, 19 Jul, 88r, 27 July, 111v, 18 Aug, 132v, 3 Sept 1457; copies in *Balìa* 5, ff. 80r, 86v, 88r-v, 95r, 118v, 137v).

ous decline, with many houses in Grosseto collapsing and its hospital lacking a roof. The condition was made that all proceeds were to be spent on 'cose stabili', i.e. property.[90] The *permuta* with the Scala was authorised again and negotiations begun in January 1463,[91] and eventually completed in 1467; the *grancia* of Grosseto passed to the Scala in exchange for three *butighe* in Siena.[92]

The logic of the rationalisation of the Sapienza's estates was inescapable; exchange of large, outlying estates which had fallen into disrepair (as well as the sale of smaller, scattered and isolated properties) for other more productive forms of investment, whether the *monte* or urban holdings. The only question is why it took so long. Finding buyers or, in the case of the Scala, exchange partners, could take time, especially if the intention was to maintain the latent efficiency of larger-scale agriculture embodied in the concentration of property at Monticchiello and Grosseto. In addition, it seems possible that there was continued resistance to the idea of selling off property donated to a pious institution. When it did become more common, this was perhaps not least because the practice had become accepted for the Scala itself. But purchase by the Scala (Monticchiello), or *permuta* with it (Grosseto) was the best solution for all. The Scala had maintained, indeed expanded, its rural hegemony during the crisis years of the fourteenth century, acquiring more property from the other pious institutions that merged with it, steadily consolidating its system of granges, fortifying them and streamlining them. The acquisition of these two major swathes of property from the Misericordia/Sapienza fitted well with their existing portfolio, being adjacent to some of the largest of their own holdings, and they immediately acted to integrate the new acquisitions.

For its part, the Sapienza could then concentrate on two strategies. First, a more efficient pattern of holdings, closer to Siena and therefore easier to access for the collection of produce (and rent). It is notable that after 1413 no property in the *contado* is recorded as having been bought which was not in an area where the Sapienza already owned extensive property. This was henceforward the pattern; only two further purchases in the *contado* are recorded in that century, both in the vicinity of Sant'Ansano, the one area – much nearer to Siena than those sold off – in which the *Savi* took a serious interest.[93] Secondly, an increased emphasis on urban holdings, both rents and shops. These had been a comparatively small part of the estate, but always an important one. Again, the first priority had to be for the institution to divest itself of unprofitable holdings which required prohibitive investment. Various houses in the vicinity of the Albergo del Gallo, one of the largest and best-known *alberghi* in Siena, just around the corner from the Sapienza and briefly owned by it,[94] were sold in 1434 and 1439.[95] The Gallo itself

---

[90] *CG* 228, ff. 289v-290v, 18 Oct.

[91] *Scala* 24, ff. 133v-134r, 18 Jan; and see *Scala* 523, f. 159r.

[92] *Mis.* 36, ff. 67v-69v, and *Scala* 72, ff. 141r-143v, 23 Mar; see also *Scala* 24, f. 176r, 21 Mar. An inventory was made of what was passed over, in 1469 (*Scala* 1406, ff. 30r-35v, 25 Nov; copy 36r-43r). This is the hospital's initial assessment. The Sapienza's inventory of the property as passed over is in *Scala* 1407, ff. 3r-5v, a list of items 'ritratte de libro del catasto de le chose da detta chasa' (almost certainly literally 'ritratte', as such a list no longer exists in *Mis.* 36). These can be compared with the Sapienza's inventory of its Grosseto possessions made in 1442 (*Dipl., Spedale di S. Maria della Scala*, 1442).

[93] Purchases in 1481 and 1483, as in p. 362 n. 12 above.

[94] It was in what is now the Via dei Termini, at the junction with the Vicolo della Rosa; see Turrini, *"Per honore et utile"*, pp. 141-4; and Balestracci and Piccinni, *Siena nel Trecento*, p. 151. It is not clear when the Albergo del Gallo came into the possession of the Sapienza. In the 1318 *Tavola delle Possessioni* it is still listed as privately-owned (Balestracci and Piccinni, loc. cit.). By 1434 it belonged to the Sapienza, on whose behalf the authorities opposed a claimant to a house which formed an essential part of it (*CG* 217, ff. 138v-139r, and *Conc.* 2137, no. 18, f. 27r-v, 6 and 18 Jan; see also Tuliani, *Osti, avventori e malandrini*, pp. 124-5, Nardi, *Mariano Sozzini*, p. 76 n. 24, and Bargagli, *Bartolomeo Sozzini*, p. 54 and n. 20). Turrini, loc. cit., believes it was acquired by the Sapienza around 1430.

[95] *CG* 217, ff. 138v-139r, 18 Jan 1434; *Mis.* 1, ff. 86v-87r, 13 Feb 1439.

was in poor condition, and in 1447 it was decided that the necessary repairs were so prohibitive that it would be better to sell the *albergo* itself[96] (it went to Mariano Sozzini for 900 florins).[97] After the sales of the large rural holdings, the focus of property purchases was overwhelmingly urban. Apart from Sant'Ansano, all other purchases were in Siena, the most extreme example being the purchase in 1493 of *scorticatoi* behind the Sapienza at a cost of 1,600 florins,[98] to pay for which the *Savi* sold (after the event) no fewer than twenty-two scattered possessions in the *contado*.[99]

It seems, in short, that the 1451 inventory, as well as furnishing the authorities with a profile of the Sapienza's holdings, at the same time offered indications of what should be done given the new function of the Sapienza; and the considerable programme of realisation of some assets, and concentration and rationalisation of others, over a period of about forty years is evidence of this. However prolonged, this rationalisation appears to have paid off. There is a comparative lull of about twenty years in the litany of complaints about shortfalls. This new situation offered the comune a new opportunity; to treat the Sapienza like any other pious institution and exploit it. Whatever the reason, the temptation proved difficult to resist, and it soon became clear that communal support for the Sapienza was not entirely altruistic. It has already been seen how the comune could muscle in, insisting that the proceeds of the Val d'Orcia sale be invested by the comune, with the Sapienza getting a fixed amount of interest.[100] It has also been seen that in 1455 the college was made to loan the *Camarlengo di Biccherna* part of the entrance fee of ten scholars.[101] In 1457 the *Balìa* ordered the sale of 1,200 florins' worth of property, money it required for the payment of mercenaries.[102] In 1463, when Pius II's crusading ambitions left Siena with the obligation of a *presta* towards the campaign, the Sapienza took its place among the *luoghi pii* expected to contribute a total of 2,000 florins.[103] It was also obliged to contribute towards the cost of civic or diplomatic occasions such as the honouring of the Prince of Calabria in 1468 (400 *lire*)[104] and the funerary expenses of the wife of the Count of Urbino in 1472.[105] From 1471 it was obligated towards the programme of urban regeneration, contributing 100 florins annually.[106] By 1473 this appears to have been modified to an obligation to build two houses each year for ten years.[107] By this stage the burden had been compounded; with the foundation of the *Monte di Pietà* in 1472, the

---

[96] *CG* 223, f. 224v, and *Mis.* 1 ff. 89v-90r, 15 Feb; the proposal was put late January, *Conc.* 2121, no. 52; cf. TURRINI, loc. cit. The Sapienza finances are described as such that 'con grande fatica a pena si può reggiare li scolari, che so nela casa'.

[97] *Mis.* 36, ff. 48v-50r, 29 May.

[98] *Mis.* 36, ff. 80v-81r, 16 Apr 1493.

[99] *Studio* 2, ff. 134v-141r, 12 Apr to 4 Dec, *passim.* This must have been related to plans for expansion (below, pp. 388 *seq.*).

[100] Above, p. 373.

[101] Above, p. 316.

[102] Above, p. 373 n. 89.

[103] *Conc.* 2118, ff. 180r-182r and 196r-197r; on this episode see M. GINATEMPO, *Crisi di un territorio*, pp. 49-51, and O. MALAVOLTI, *Dell'historia di Siena* (Venetiis, 1599, repr. Bologna, 1968), III, pp. 67-8. The Sapienza's share in 1464 was 641 *lire* (*Conc.* 585, f. 13v, 14 Mar). Shortly after this decision the pope ordered the restitution to the clergy and pious institutions of funds raised (*Conc.* 1771, ff. 33r-34v, 27 Apr).

[104] *Conc.* 611, f. 36v, 9 Aug.

[105] *Conc.* 635, f. 24r-v, 27 Jul.

[106] *CG* 233, ff. 308v-309r, 21 Jun. The hospital was to contribute 400 florins and the *Monte di Pietà* 1,000 florins. Cf. also PERTICI, *La città magnificata*, p. 140. Pertici points out that the tax went back to 1469, and was to be annual from 1471.

[107] *Mis.* 1, f.101v, 22 Mar (= *Conc.* 2139, no. 21, ff. 37r and 38v); cf. CATONI, 'Il Comune di Siena e l'amministrazione della Sapienza', p. 126.

Sapienza was obliged to contribute 300 florins as a four-year loan.[108] This was no more than an extension of the *ad hoc* practice of calling on institutions that could afford it to help out with communal initiatives, a practice of from which both the *Studio* and the Sapienza had previously benefited[109] – except perhaps for the scale of the loan, which made quite an impact.

Despite the extent of its possessions and the help of the commune, the Sapienza's history from the mid-fifteenth century is one of a slow slide towards insolvency. In the last quarter of the century the commune was more directly involved in helping the Sapienza out. This pattern is already evident before. From 1479 the financial crisis of the Sapienza was frequent, almost continuous. That year, hail and harvest failure, and the consequent shortage of provisions for the *sapientini*, led to the *Savi* asking for the return of the house's 300-florin loan to the *Monte di Pietà*.[110] The request was repeated the following year, this time on the grounds that, because of plague and wars, the *mezzaiuoli* had been exempted from paying their contributions.[111] It was half successful; in July 1480 the *Balìa* ordered the *Camarlengo* of the *Monte* to pay the Sapienza 150 florins.[112] There is evidence of continued retrenchment through the 1480s, with sales of property. In the mid-1480s there are instances of the salaries of the *bidello* and the servants of the Sapienza being paid by the *Camarlengo di Biccherna*.[113] It is not clear whether these payments amount to a subsidy or are the repayment of a loan.[114] The petition of 1488 for the appointment of a rector/*governatore* was justified entirely on financial grounds. The house was almost destitute, owing 400 florins in food bills alone, and had exhausted its possibilities of credit; the produce from its farms was sufficient to feed the inmates for only four months per year, and at least 500 florins' worth of investment in oxen and other animals was urgently needed; the present *Camarlengo* had resigned, and it was difficult to find anyone wishing to take on the office.[115] By appointing a *religioso*, Pietro d'Antonio, as rector and *governatore* for life,[116] the authorities hoped to shore up the house's management problems (not least because he was obliged to leave it 300 florins from his own estate),[117] though further measures were also necessary. That year the Sapienza was given

[108] *CG* 234, f. 99v, 6 Mar; CATONI, loc. cit. The loan was payable within a year in four instalments; but the Sapienza did not oblige so quickly. In March 1473 the *Savi* asked for permission to look to their debtors to respond to the strains these obligations were putting on them (as n. 107); in October that year they had still not paid, and were instructed to put the entrance fees of three students to this use (*Conc.* 642, ff. 16r-v, 3 Oct, and 17r-v, 6 Oct 1473).

[109] E.g. in 1468 the *Camarlengo* of the Sapienza was instructed to lend the *Camarlengo di Biccherna* 100 ducats so that he could pay the expenses of Niccolò Severini, the Sienese orator in Rome (*Conc.* 608, f. 43r, 16 Feb, and 46r, 17 Feb); in 1470 he had to lend the same official 10 ducats towards payment for a painting of Monte Vasone undertaken by Francesco di Giorgio Martini for a location in the Val di Strove (*Conc.* 624, ff. 36v-37r, 16 Oct 1470). The payment is ordered on f. 43r, 25 Oct, ed. C. ZARRILLI, 'Francesco di Giorgio pittore e scultore nelle fonti archivistiche senesi', in *Francesco di Giorgio e il Rinascimento a Siena 1450-1500*, ed. L. Bellosi (Milan, 1993), pp. 530-38 (p. 530).

[110] *Conc.* 2139, no. 62, f. 117r, 29 May.

[111] *Studio* 2, f. 67r, 7 Jun 1480. On the sequence of crises (famine, plague, war) of the late 1470s see GINATEMPO, *Crisi di un territorio*, pp. 330-5.

[112] *Balìa* 20, f. 52v, 29 Jul.

[113] *Studio* 2, ff. 105r, 13 Sept 1484, and 109r, 21 Apr 1485.

[114] The *Biccherna* may have been given the proceeds of the sales of the 1450s. That was certainly the intention of the 1451 sale; see p. 373 n. 87 above.

[115] *CG* 240, f. 175v, 15 May (= *Conc.* 2139, no. 84, ff. 154r-v, 155v); cf. also *Conc.* 2139, no. 90, f. 164r; n.d. but probably a preliminary version of this petition.

[116] *Conc.* 730, ff. 13r-16r, 29 May 1488, ed. FERRERI, doc. 278, pp. 238-44.

[117] If he remained in office for less than three years he only had to leave the equivalent of his salary; doc. cit., f. 15r-v; FERRERI, p. 242.

a five-year exemption from *gabelle* on the movement of goods,[118] and a five-year annual subsidy of 80 florins from the *Camarlengo dei salmi*;[119] in 1489 the *Camarlengo* of the *Monte di Pietà* was ordered to make an annual payment to the Sapienza;[120] in 1491 the house was exempted from all *gabelle* and *gravezze*, and forever freed from payment of any rent to the commune;[121] in 1493 the exemptions were confirmed and the house was given, for ten years, a subsidy of 40 *staia* of salt from Grosseto,[122] as well as 50 *moggia* of grain from six other designated communities;[123] and later that year, 'veduta la povertà della Casa della Sapienza', the *Savi* authorised the recall of 600 *lire*'s worth of another loan, to the *Monte del Sale*.[124] In 1495 a further 100 *moggia* of grain were found for the house.[125]

Unsurprisingly, none of these measures, most of which were *ad hoc* and small in scale, appears to have made much difference to the long-term position. In 1495 the students were complaining about shortages of food,[126] and a committee was appointed[127] – the first of five in just over a year[128] – to deal with the problem. Remedies attempted in this period included the provision of more grain,[129] the cashing in of *monte* credits,[130] and the sale of property.[131] A petition from the *Savi* of this period[132] highlights both the extent and the nature of the problem. The debts now amounted to 1,200 florins; the *Savi* had been making good the shortfall from their own pockets, since the alternative was closure of the college. Students were being admitted without payment, and larger amounts of produce were urgently needed to feed the seventy members of the college. One of the proposed measures[133] urged return to a maximum of thirty students prescribed 'anticamente' by the statutes of the house, but, far from acting on this, the authorities continued to admit students,[134] even seeing their entrance fees as the short-term palliative for the resolution of immediate debts, or – on one occasion – earmarking a student's entrance fee to pay the butcher's bill.[135]

---

[118] *Conc.* 730, f. 39r-v, 25 Jun 1488, ed. Ferreri, doc. 283, p. 252.

[119] *Conc.* 733, ff. 12v-13r, 27/28 Nov 1488, ed. Ferreri, doc. 289, p. 258.

[120] *Balìa* 36, f. 88r, 23 Jan.

[121] *Mis.* 1, f. 115r, 13 Jun 1491.

[122] *Mis.* 1, f. 116r-v, 29 Jan. Cf. also *Mis.* 36, ff. 93r-95r, 27 Dec 1538. A Sienese *staio* was approximately equivalent to a bushel; 24 *staia* equalled one *moggio*. Bowsky, *Finance*, pp. xx and 41 n. 92. Cf. Balestracci, '"Li lavoranti non cognosciuti", p. 71 n. 14 for a full list of measurements.

[123] *Balìa* 412, ff. 8v-9r, 1 Feb.

[124] *Studio* 2, f. 138v, 30 Aug.

[125] *CG* 240, f. 285v, 23 Mar (= *Conc.* 771, f. 6r, 15 Mar, ed. Ferreri, doc. 346, p. 340).

[126] *Balìa* 40, f. 9v, 25 Aug.

[127] *Balìa* 40, ff. 96v-97r, 17 Dec; and cf. f. 103r, 26 Dec.

[128] E.g. *Balìa* 40, f. 40r, ff. 125r-v, 126r, 13 Jan 1496; *Sale* 23, f. 90r, 9 Jun and 6 Sept 1496; *Balìa* 41, ff. 4v, 6 Sept, and 52r, 16 Nov 1496; *Balìa* 41, ff. 84v-85r, 5 Jan 1497.

[129] *Balìa* 41, ff. 84v-85r, 5 Jan 1497.

[130] *Balìa* 40, f. 40r, ff. 125v-126r, 13 Jan 1496. The *Savi* were allowed to redeem 200 ducats' worth of credits.

[131] *Sale* 23, f. 90r, 9 Jun and 6 Sept 1496 (the *Savi* were allowed to sell 150 ducats' worth of property); *Balìa* 41, ff. 4v, 6 Sept, and 52r, 16 Nov 1496 (the sum is now 200 florins); further sales in *Balìa* 41, f. 103v, 8 Feb 1497, and *Not.* 1042, ff. 82r, 83r-v, 19 Jul 1499.

[132] This petition survives in three draft forms; *Conc.* 2139, nos. 104-106, ff. 187r-194r. Since it does not appear in the records of the *Consiglio Generale* or the *Balìa* it is not possible to date them precisely (though they appear in *Conc.* 2139, which is in reasonably precise chronological order, between documents of March 1495 and 1497).

[133] *Conc.* 2139, no. 104, at f. 187v.

[134] Two students were given free places, in the middle of the crisis, on the order of the *Balìa* (*Sale* 23, ff. 92v, 24 Mar 1496, 93r, 29 Mar 1496).

[135] *Sale* 24, ff. 168r, 3 Dec, 168v, 14 Dec, and 169r, 19 Dec 1498.

Given this attitude (and of course the darkening financial situation of the republic as a whole during the years of war), it is not surprising that the atmosphere of crisis continued. In 1512 Bartolommeo Bolis left the house 1,000 ducats with which to provide for six scholars,[136] and although this is an indication that some still believed in and were working for the house's future, since the bequest was earmarked for fresh places it did not lead to any improvement in the overall situation. In 1514 the house faced its biggest crisis to date. A measure of the *Balìa* reported that the Sapienza was 'in declinazione'; it had debts of 1,800 florins, to offset which the *Savi* were authorised to sell off as much property as necessary. Several subventions were granted; 25 *staia* of salt per annum from the *Camarlengo del Monte del Sale*, 60 florins per annum from the *Gabella delle Parti*, and 80 *moggia* of grain and 215 *some* of wine per annum from two hospitals and eight religious houses.[137] Yet another crisis followed in 1526-7, and this time the *Savi's* memorandum to the *Consiglio del Popolo* makes it clear that it affected both the Sapienza and the *Studio* as a whole. Earlier interruptions had led to gaps in teaching provision; students were threatening to leave. Those in the Sapienza had the additional disadvantage of being inadequately provided with food and wine, and were alleging breach of contract.[138] The house's debt again (or still) amounted to almost 1,800 florins.[139] The council's response, a donation of 200 florins 'pro charitate et ipsius necessitatibus',[140] made little impression on the problem and the *Savi* were back the following year reporting deteriorating accounts and with worse news. Fire had destroyed a number of the house's possessions,[141] and legal action was being threatened by creditors.[142] This time the *Consiglio del Popolo* accepted the need for drastic measures. The *Savi* were authorised to sell property to the value of 1,200 to 1,500 florins, or to make over individual properties to that value to creditors,[143] but there was also an important new element; the commune gave the Sapienza the goods confiscated from two rebels, Belisario Bulgarini and Ippolite Bellarmati, valued at 5,000 florins.[144]

The financial problems of the Sapienza run parallel to those of the commune and of Sienese agriculture generally.[145] Yet they are perhaps still puzzling in the context of the considerable estates with which it began its existence. The patchiness of the surviving evidence does not help us to clarify the picture. Some tentative suggestions, however, do emerge from the predominantly anecdotal material. One is that a number of abuses, or potential abuses, against which the commune had to legislate

---

[136] Above, pp. 308-9.

[137] *Mis.* 1, ff. 117v-118r, 26 Jan. A *soma* was equal to two *barili* of wine or about 91 litres. BALESTRACCI, loc. cit.

[138] 'Apreso si expone come la casa della sapientia si trova havere assai debito et mancamento delle cose necessarie al vivere et precipue per non vi essere vino sono guasto, et per defetto de denari è impossibile ad quanto faria di bisogno a provedere per il che li scolari non havendo el debito et conveniente victo oltre al mancamento delle lettioni fanno intendere volersi partire, protestando de fide non servata, La quale cosa saria non senza preiudicio et grave infamia della vostra città.' *CG* 242, ff. 98v-100r, 3 Apr 1526 (f. 99r).

[139] 1,200 florins of this amount were owed to the *Camarlengo*. The memorandum includes a breakdown of the debt (f. 99r).

[140] *CG* 242, ff. 99v-100r.

[141] *CG* 242, ff. 168v-169v, 28 Mar 1527; cf. *Mis.* 36, ff. 63v-64r.

[142] *CG* 242, f. 177r, 16 Jun 1527.

[143] Loc. cit. The *Savi's* orders of sale are in *Studio* 3, ff. 60v-61r, 21 Jun, and assignations of properties to creditors on f. 65r, 30 Oct 1527.

[144] *Conc.* 963, f. 18r-v, and *Mis.* 36, f. 87r, 28 Mar 1527; and see *Studio* 3, f. 67r, 1 Jan 1528.

[145] A. K. ISAACS, 'Le campagne senesi tra Quattro e Cinquecento: regime fondiario e governo signorile', in *Contadini e proprietari nella Toscana moderna*, 1, pp. 377-403, esp. pp. 377-8; HOOK, *Siena*, ch. 9, esp pp. 176-9.

stemmed from the intrinsic weakness of the system by which the Sapienza was administered. There was no guarantee that the rector or the *Camarlengo*, often appointed for short periods, would put aside their personal interests in favour of those of the Sapienza; nor that the *Savi*, who were engaged even more fleetingly, would give due weight to long-term priorities in estate management as well as those of college discipline and the recruitment of good teachers. Finance and estate management might have been the speciality of many of these individuals, but they were remote from the other aspects of the running of a *Studio*. On the other hand, the fact that the authorities often got bogged down in problems of funding and administration should not detract from their ultimate success in running affairs. The financial problems of the early sixteenth century were after all not least due to the expansion of the Sapienza to house more students; and if in the process the old financial arrangements broke down under the strain, this does not alter the fact that the commune did support the *Studio* by extra subsidies and subventions.

At the same time it is much harder to conclude that the Sapienza contributed to the stability of the *Studio* in financial or organisational terms. In the early days there were instances of the Sapienza's resources being used to pay for the return of the *Studio* from Montalcino, in 1417, or advancing money for the sending of messengers to negotiate with a teacher, but within a very short time the position had been reversed, the commune helping with supplies of grain to the *sapientini* and paying the salary of the rector.[146] The contribution to success was rather in providing an immense attraction for students, an attraction which for example Florence, Siena's fiercest rival, could not offer; and beyond that in providing a centre for the *Studio* which gradually became more important. Only after the fall of the republic did the resources of the Sapienza, bolstered by bequests and scholarships for its students, provide the financial stability to which the developments of this period were a costly and often cumbersome prelude.

---

[146] CATONI, 'Genesi', pp. 174-5; Conc. 401, f. 12r, 9 Nov 1432, and above, pp. 376-7.

V

BUILDINGS AND PROJECTS

1. *The buildings*

Compared with the mass of information on other aspects of the life of the college, little is known about the buildings of the Sapienza, as inherited from the Casa della Misericordia and as used or modified through the period. It stood on the site currently occupied by the present Biblioteca Comunale degli Intronati, the Istituto Statale d'Arte 'Duccio di Boninsegna', and the church of S. Pellegrino alla Sapienza which was in fact the church of the Misericordia (Figs. 16 and 17).[1] To be more accurate, it occupied the northern and eastern part of the block currently bounded to the north by the main route from the centre to the church of S. Domenico, the Via della Sapienza (known at the time as Chiaravalle), to the east by the Via delle Terme, to the south by what is now known as the Via dei Pittori, and to the west by the Costa di S. Antonio.[2] What reconstruction is possible derives from a sequence of 'snapshots in time', with an element of projection backwards in time from later descriptions and ground plans. As far as the heritage of the Casa della Misericordia is concerned, the *Tavola delle*

---

[1] LIBERATI, 'Chiese, monasteri, oratori e spedali senesi', esp. *BSSP*, 64 (1957), pp. 186-201. Despite reconstruction in 1767 it has undergone the least change of all the Sapienza's buildings; Touring Club Italiano, *Guida d'Italia: Toscana* (4th ed., Milan, 1974), p. 543. Its boundaries were and are the corner of Via della Sapienza and Via delle Terme, with an entrance on the former. In the eighteenth century it was intercommunicating with the Sapienza; Pecci writes in 1731 of 'la Porta, per la quale s'entra nell'Androne che conduce alle pubbliche scuole dalla porte della strada' (G. A. PECCI, *Raccolta universale di tutte le iscrizioni, arme e altri monumenti, sì antichi, come moderni, esistenti nel terzo di Camollia fino a questo presente anno MDCCXXXI. Libro Terzo*; ASS, *ms.* D.6, p. 129r), while Faluschi's description of the church refers to a 'scala per andare nelle stanze degli Studenti' (G. FALUSCHI, *Breve relazione delle cose notabili della Città di Siena* [Siena, 1784], p. 219; rev. edn. [Siena, 1815], p. 177). The church contains tombs and inscriptions of scholars (PECCI, op. cit., pp. 125v-142v); most of three are sixteenth century or later, but they do include an inscription to Peter Bart von Oppenheim, student of canon law, who died on 20 Aug 1474; op. cit., p. 128v, and cf. A. LUSCHIN VON EBENGREUTH, 'I sepolcri degli scolari tedeschi in Siena', *BSSP*, 3 (1896), pp. 9-21, 299-326, 5 (1898), pp. 52-62; repr. in *I tedeschi nella storia*, pp. 105-47 (p. 108). From the sixteenth century German scholars were buried in S. Domenico; LUSCHIN, op. cit., and O. VON MÜLLER, 'I sepolcri di studenti tedeschi in San Domenico di Siena', *Rivista Araldica*, 4 (1906), pp. 13-16, 74-7, 146-9, 219-21; repr. in *I tedeschi nella storia*, pp. 149-57; and A. BRILLI, 'L'Università e la presenza degli stranieri', in *L'Università di Siena. 750 anni*, pp. 541-57 (pp. 547-8 esp.).

[2] It certainly did not occupy all of the southernmost, and perhaps the westernmost, part of that block. This is clear from the proposals for a new Sapienza which entailed the purchase of more property within these boundaries; below, p. 391. The full extent of the northernmost part was part of the complex by 1679; see the plan in *Governatore*, 1049, published in M. CIAMPOLINI, 'Casa della Sapienza', p. 315, and reproduced here, Fig. 19 below.

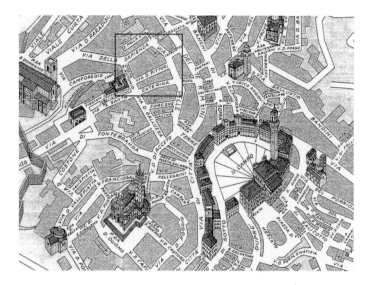

Fig. 16 – Plan of central Siena.

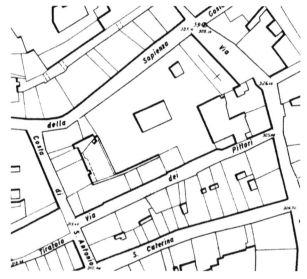

Fig. 17 – Ground plan of the Sapienza area.

Possessioni of the early fourteenth century gives a summary description.[3] Of the twenty-four houses owned or part-owned by the Sapienza at the time, several were adjacent to the hospital itself; the *Tavola* indicates a group of seven buildings 'retro domos veteres Misericordie',[4] which is clearly distinct from what is termed the 'domus magna'.[5] It is a reflection of the gaps in our records that we can say very little about these buildings in the fifteenth century, even whether the 'domus veteres' continued to be used and what relationship they had to the main building. The main evidence must be architectural, and centres on the *loggiato* or quadrangle that is now at the centre of the Biblioteca Co-

---

[3] *Estimo* 131, ff. 217v-220r; the above follows the analysis of Balestracci and Piccinni, *Siena nel Trecento*, pp. 153-4.

[4] *Estimo* 131, f. 219r. At least one other house belonging to the Misericordia was in the same street, Chiaravalle (f. 217v).

[5] *Estimo* 131, ff. 218r.

Fig. 18 – The Casa della Sapienza in 1595. From Francesco Vanni, *Pianta di Siena*, as engraved by Pieter De Jode (University of Siena, Rettorato).

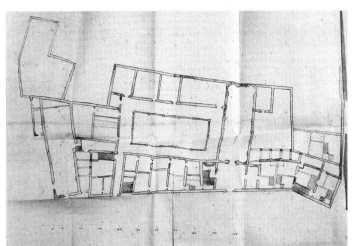

Fig. 19 – Groundplan of the Casa della Sapienza c. 1679 (Archivio di Stato di Siena, *Governatore*, 1049).

munale, and which on stylistic grounds has been dated to the mid-fifteenth century.[6] This was a large, two-storey rectangular edifice; it was reduced in the nineteenth century, but a seventeenth-century ground plan (Fig. 19) shows it to have been not much smaller than the church. It has been speculated that this central building must have formed the focal point for lectures and therefore the academic heart for the college, and that the alterations made in the fifteenth century reflect this, placing the *loggiato* in the same category as that of the Spanish College in Bologna and (later) the Sapienza at Pisa.[7] This makes much sense, even if it unfortunately cannot be borne out by administrative documents re-

---

[6] CIAMPOLINI, 'Casa della Sapienza', p. 313, and now IDEM, 'La Domus Misericordiae', p. 139.

[7] CIAMPOLINI, ' Casa della Sapienza', p. 313.

lating to its rebuilding. The only such reference to have emerged relates to the ordering of new *cattedre* for 'scolis novis sapientie' in 1441.[8]

Information about the surrounding buildings is also sparse. The inventory of 1451, drawn up on orders of the *Consiglio Generale* in 1448,[9] though tantalisingly saying virtually nothing about the main buildings of the Sapienza and its church, does give more precise information about the Sapienza's other possessions, including a description of the borders and position of each entry, though not in a form that allows us to be unambiguously specific about topographical detail.[10] We learn from this that behind the *loggiato* there was 'uno horto con piaze et citerna',[11] and it also lists two small *piazze* on the western side of the block,[12] as well as four houses[13] and five shops.[14] All of these were occupied or rented out to people extraneous to the Sapienza,[15] so we can conclude that the college possessed much of the block, and possibly all of the northern side of it, but was operating these adjacent properties commercially rather than using them for residential or academic purposes. However, the fact of their existence raises the possibility that, although the main entrance was on the then Via di Chiaravalle, there may well have been others. In 1344 the Casa della Misericordia, having acquired property across a narrow street called Chiasso Fastelli, which had a reputation as a rough spot, requested and received from the *Concistoro* permission to build over it, constructing a 'pellegrinaio'.[16] The area behind the institution appears to have continued to be a problem. In 1457 the Compagnia di S. Donato al lato a Montanini di S. Giglio requested and obtained permission to open up public access to the college's fountain, forcing the Sapienza to bear half the cost of the work. Two reasons were cited, in a petition full of resentment: the need for rapid access, in case of fire, to what was the only fountain in the *contrada* ('e bisongna bussare due hore prima che sia aperto'), and the infamous morals of the house which made it shameful that citizens had to enter it to obtain water.[17]

If we know disappointingly little about the buildings, there is rather more (if still incomplete) evidence regarding their contents. An inventory was drawn up in 1459, possibly again in response to criticisms of maladministration.[18] Almost half of the document concerns the contents of the sacristy

---

[8] *Conc.* 454, f. 50v, 16 Oct.

[9] *Mis.* 36; see above, p. 363 n. 20.

[10] *Mis.* 36, ff. 2r-5v. The following summary draws on Catoni's in his 'Genesi', pp. 167-9.

[11] *Mis.* 36, f. 4v.

[12] 'in sul chanto del fondacho di sancto antonio' (*Mis.* 36, f. 5r). This and at least one of the houses and one *bottega* appear to indicate that the Sapienza's possessions extended to the Costa di S. Antonio, though it is not clear how much of the block it occupied.

[13] *Mis.* 36, f. 2r-v.

[14] *Mis.* 36, f. 3r-v.

[15] One of the houses, adjacent to the *spedale* and its *loggia*, was granted 'a vita' to the former *Camarlengo*, Ser Mariano di Iacopo detto il Taccola, and his wife (f. 2r), and was subsequently rented out. Above, p. 358 n. 184.

[16] BALESTRACCI and PICCINNI, *Siena nel Trecento*, p. 154.

[17] 'Essendo noto chome può essere quasi a buona parte della Città la disonesta le brutture e li scellerati modi che si tengano nelle stantie della misericordia luogo sacro e dedicato a hopere piatose e sancte, et hora essendo divenuto uno pu[bli]co postribulo, perchè non è quello di drietro al palazo pelle schiave e altre povere persone che de necessità vanno per l'aqqua a quella fonte che sarebbe cosa di sommo obbobrio a enarrale alle S.V. quello che vi si fa pelli scolari e altre genti di quella chasa' (*Balìa* 2, ff. 234v-235r, and *Balìa* 3, ff. 220v-221r, 29 Mar 1457).

[18] The inventory is in *Studio* 128, ff. 1r-4v, and has been published by CATONI, 'Genesi', pp. 183-97, and further discussed by CIAMPOLINI, 'La Domus Misericordiae', p. 139. Catoni speculated (p. 169) that this inventory may have been compiled in response to the fierce reform measures of 10 Sept 1456, which railed against the 'disonestà e mancamenti in questa Casa', describing its governance as 'una infamia…in disonore di Idio, del mondo e del Reggimento vostro' (*CG* 277,

and the body of the church, after which the inventory covers the *cantina e cielliere*, the kitchen, the *chanova* or pantry, the *biccherna* or administrative room, the residences of the *Camarlengo* and the *canovaio*, and finally twenty-nine rooms for students, four of whom are named. There follows an inventory of the *ospedaletto* of S. Maria della Stella, a property belonging to the Sapienza, and there is thus no manuscript indication that the inventory is incomplete, which raises the disturbing question of why there is no mention of a refectory, or of any teaching rooms, both of which are mentioned in other documents.[19] One possible explanation – and it is only a tentative suggestion, perhaps not to be preferred over error or missing pages – is that the inventory was not intended to cover public areas; all the rooms described were either private in the sense that they were occupied by individuals or were the responsibility of individuals, or were rooms to which access was controlled or forbidden to the unauthorised. The inventory appears more concerned with light and movable items of property than with furniture,[20] and it may well be that the refectory, and such teaching areas as there may have been at this stage in the college's development, simply did not contain anything of significance other than basic tables, desks and benches. These were also rooms which were in almost constant public use (public in the sense that *sapientini* used the refectory, and scholars from the whole university attended lectures). The only other 'public' chamber was the church, whose contents were clearly of such value as to require listing, and which in any case would not have remained permanently unlocked. The most detailed lists are those pertaining to the church and the kitchen, and it is therefore perhaps unsurprising that these are the two areas for which subsequent inventories are also found.[21] A further possibility is that teaching rooms were excluded from the inventory because they were not considered the province of the Sapienza, but rather of the *Studio*. This is certainly the implication of the *Concistoro*'s order of 1427 that the *bidello* of the *Studio* make an inventory of the benches and *cattedre* 'in scolis sapientie',[22] though soon after the compilation of this inventory the distinction became blurred, with a student's entrance fee being used 'pro bancis reficiendis conficiendis et murandis in scolas',[23] and even a proposal to convert some teaching rooms into students' rooms.[24] These are also problemat-

---

ff. 241r-242v; *Mis.* 1, ff. 93r-95r). As has been seen, this and further controversy and reform in the following two years led to the appointment in 1458 of a *Camarlengo* for three years, and it is possible that this official, Melchior or Marchionne di Agostino di Maestro Antonio, ordered the inventory to be made. It was compiled by Lodovico Benassai, whose name does not otherwise appear in records pertaining to the Sapienza. Above, p. 358.

[19] The refectory is mentioned in the early 'ordini' (clause 37), though not, to my knowledge, after that. On this point CATONI, 'Genesi', p. 168 n. 61, followed by MORETTI, 'L'architettura delle sedi universitarie', pp. 278-82, mentions references in 1437 (*CG* 219, ff. 146v-147v, 10 May; = *Mis.* 1, ff. 83v-85r, and *Statuti* 41, ff. 255v-256r, and ed. ZDEKAUER, doc. XVIII, pp. 169-71) and 1456 (*CG* 227, f. 241v, 10 Sept), but these regulate communal eating arrangements without mentioning the refectory. On teaching rooms see pp. 117-8 and 398 *seq.*

[20] For example, it omits any references to chairs in the kitchen, and lists only one in the *biccherna*; and there is no mention of any tables or chairs in students' rooms (though beds do feature); CATONI, 'Genesi', pp. 168-9. A number of the fabric items bear the emblem of the house; op. cit., pp. 185-6, and see BORGIA and FUMI CAMBI GADO, 'I sistemi emblematici', pp. 566-7.

[21] BCS, *ms.* A.XI.12, ff. 91r-93r is a detailed inventory of the church made on 30 Dec 1510; a further one was made on 5 Nov 1529 (f. 123r). A list of all the items given by the *Camarlengo* to the cook was made on 21 Aug 1518 (f. 104v). The kitchen was out of bounds to students at all times (*Mis.* 1, f. 87r, 1 Mar 1440, ed. CATONI, 'Genesi', p. 169 n. 64).

[22] *Conc.* 370, f. 19v, 4 Dec; cf. CATONI, 'Genesi', p. 168. The inventory was to be kept by a *Camarlengo* of the comune.

[23] *Conc.* 605, f. 20v, 24 Jul 1467.

[24] *Not.* 694, f. 4r, n.d. but among documents of the 1470s, ed. MINNUCCI, 'Documenti', doc. II-35, pp. 101-2. The reasons for the suggestion, which appears in a note made by outgoing *Savi* for their successors, are a greater number of students than there are rooms, and excess capacity of teaching rooms ('essendo stanze di sopra di superchio per leggere'). If the idea was taken up it has not left traces in the documentation.

ic; the inventory makes no mention of desks or chairs, though earlier measures spelling out what each student's room should contain make it clear that these were to be provided, and it is inconceivable that they were not.[25] The actual items given to each scholar can be studied further through one other important source; from the 1470s we have the *Camarlengo*'s register in which each *sapientino* was to sign for all the items, including furniture, with which he was issued on entry, and again on return of those items on departure. This has mostly been treated as a sort of 'admissions register', but it thus also gives considerable information about the lifestyle of the members of the college.[26]

2. *A library?*

The completeness or otherwise of the inventory is important in relation to another issue, namely the total absence of any reference in the period to a library in the Sapienza. This is really quite significant given the minute level of detail to which the documents so frequently descend. Minnucci has tentatively suggested that an inventory found in the records of the notary Lorenzo di Lando Sborgheri, who was notary of the *Studio* from 1474 to 1475 and quite possibly beyond, was that of the Sapienza library. The inventory (which he published and analysed)[27] is of a collection of academic texts, clearly comes from within a university ambience, and would have been a splendid basis for the Sapienza's intellectual activity; moreover, it appears among a collection of documents that are otherwise all indisputably connected to the *Studio*, and most of them to the *Savi dello Studio*. This is the main argument that Minnucci puts forward for his hypothesis, to which he adds others; the significant number of duplicated items, the fact that there are many unbound volumes, the thematic structure of the list (which corresponds to the traditional divisions of university teaching), and the range of disciplines covered, which makes it most unlikely to have been an inventory of the library of any single teacher. But while none of these points can be disputed (except perhaps the last),[28] the identification of this list with the Sapienza raises substantial problems. That a room housing books should be left out of an evi-

---

[25] In 1435 the *Savi* determined that students were to have 'una lettiera rossa, con saccone pieno di pagl[i]a, uno letto di penna, con uno capezale, una coltre da dosso con uno tappeto, ovvero panno rosso, uno bancho, una bancha et una lucerna, e tutte queste chose debino per inventario esser segnate del segno dela casa' (*Mis.* 1, f. 82r, 17 Sept 1435); in 1445 they were to have 'fulcitam lecticam, bancis et aliis necessariis massaritiis de lignamine tantum, et plus petere vel habere non possint' (*Mis.* 1, f. 57v, 18 Mar 1445); both ed. CATONI, 'Genesi', pp 168-9.

[26] BCS, *ms.* A.XI.12; see above, pp. 24-5.

[27] *Not.* 694, f. 5r, ed. MINNUCCI, 'Documenti', II-37, pp. 103-9, and cf. 31-3; and 'Il Collegio', pp. 31-2. The document has since also been published with corrections and additions, including previously illegible elements enhanced with a Wood lamp, by Enzo Mecacci in BASTIANONI et al., *Lo Studio e i testi*, pp. 55-8. Mecacci shares the reservations expressed below about Minnucci's suggestion; 'Lo Studio e i codici', in op. cit., pp. 17-38 (pp. 34-5 n. 17). He also makes a salient point about its date (p. 55); another document in the same file bears the same watermark, and is dated 8 Jun 1492.

[28] In his argument that the libraries of individual teachers do not, by and large, have interdisciplinary breadth, Minnucci adduces comparisons with inventories of fifteenth-century intellectuals from Siena and Naples (pp. 32-3 n. 76). One of these, Lodovico Petrucciani, has precisely such a mix; the great majority of the 362 entries are classical writings but there are also sixteen legal and two medical texts. In the *Not.* 694 inventory, 112 of the 126 items are legal (twenty canon, ninety-two civil), and there are six works of philosophy and medicine, two 'in humanitate' and two 'in arte notarie'. A much broader range than either is demonstrated by the library of Filippo Beroaldo il Vecchio; F. PEZZAROSSA, '"Canon est litterarum". I libri di Filippo Beroaldo', in *Libri, lettori e biblioteche dell'Italia medievale (secoli XI-XV). Fonti, testi, utilizzazioni del libro*. Atti della tavola rotonda italo-francese (Roma, 7-8 marzo 1997), eds. G. Lombardi and O. Nebbiai dalla Guardia (Rome, 2000), pp. 301-48. For a rich overview of this subject, T. PESENTI, 'Gli inventari delle biblioteche dei professori', in *La storia delle università italiane*, pp. 251-69.

dently incomplete inventory of the college's contents is one thing;[29] for it never to get mentioned at all is another. Even if the Sapienza acquired or established a library after the middle of the fifteenth century, it is difficult to imagine how, in a period so rich in the documentation of every other aspect of the institution's life, this could have escaped attention so completely. In the records of the *Savi*, not to mention those of higher authorities, no regulations feature at any stage in the fifteenth century about access to a library, the use or borrowing of books, supervision, donations or purchases; and there are no references anywhere to books that belonged to the college (as opposed to the many referring to the books of individual students or teachers). It is as unlikely that such a library could have been put together under the noses of the authorities without a mention[30] as it is that the old Casa della Misericordia might have had such a collection – and the inventory lists 126 items, which would have had to be housed and maintained. Of course, arguments from silence tend to be inadequate, and by definition always provisional. A more decisive point must be that there is a clear explanation of why the Sapienza might not have been given or acquired a library, namely the same characteristic that made it unique in Italian collegiate history at the time; it had not been privately founded.[31] Most college founders left their own libraries to their colleges,[32] collections which were sometimes augmented by subsequent donations.[33] The records have left no such traces for the Sapienza until the donation of the library of Sallustio Bandini in 1758, a gift which became the basis for the present Biblioteca Comunale.[34]

These observations hardly advance our understanding of the inventory first published by Minnucci, which must surely be of significance to the *Studio*. If it does not relate to the Sapienza, what does it represent? Could this be telling us about an early attempt at a university library? But this is not a con-

[29] The compiler of the 1459 inventory of the Sapienza had no problem describing and even valuing the twenty-seven books in the sacristy (*Studio* 128, ff. 1v-2r, ed. Catoni, 'Genesi', pp. 187-8, and see p. 168 n. 60).

[30] Contrast for example the regulations about the founder's library in the statutes of the Spanish College at Bologna (Statutes 24 and 32, ed. Marti, *The Spanish College*, pp. 256-7, 282-3) and the Gregoriano at Perugia (statute 39 of the Gregoriano; see Table 7, p. 329 above, and cf. Sebastiani, 'Il collegio universitario', pp. 50-58); or the detailed regulations about the use of the library of that college passed by the commune in 1422 when a substantial bequest, of the library of the lawyer Angelo Baglioni, was added; Ermini, *Storia*, I, pp. 464-5; and below, n. 32.

[31] The only other example of a state foundation is that of Florence, with its intermittent attempts at a college during the fifteenth century and eventual success in the shape of the Sapienza at Pisa at the end of the century. Denley, 'Collegiate Movement', pp. 48-9, and idem, 'Academic Rivalry', pp. 201-3.

[32] Gargan, 'Libri, librerie e biblioteche', esp. pp. 242-5, has demonstrated how this was integral to Italian collegiate foundations in the fourteenth century, to which can be added some fifteenth-century examples such as the Sapienza Nuova at Perugia (Ermini, I, p. 465; Nardeschi, 'Le costituzioni della "Sapienza Nuova"', p. 91). It was not just the larger foundations which benefited. Giovanni de Grassi, founder of the Collegio Grassi in Turin, stipulated in his will that his books were to be placed in a dedicated room, the 'libraria, cum banchis et cathenis', from which they were not to be removed, ed. T. Vallauri, *Storia delle Università di Piemonte* (Turin, 1845-6, repr. 1945), vol. 1, pp. 318-25 (see p. 320), and cf. Falco et al., 'Le istituzioni per l'istruzione superiore in Torino', p. 566. Giovanni Matteo Ferrari da Grado's eponymous foundation at Pavia (after his death in 1472) included a bequest of 150 or so books which has been studied by M. L. Grossi Turchetti, 'La dotazione libraria di un collegio universitario del Quattrocento', *Physis*, 22 (1980), pp. 463-75.

[33] Cf. the addition to the Sapienza Vecchia at Perugia of the books of Angelo Baglioni in 1422 (though it has to be said that it is unclear what the college possessed before that). Gargan, op. cit., pp. 243-4; Ermini, *Storia*, I, p. 464; R. Belforti, 'Le librerie di due dottori in leggi del secolo XV', *Bollettino della R. Deputazione di Storia Patria per l'Umbria*, 17 (1911), pp. 617-22.

[34] Faluschi, *Breve relazione*, pp. 174-6; G. A. and P. Pecci, *Giornale Sanese (1715-1794)*, eds. E. Innocenti and G. Mazzoni (Siena, 2000), pp. 184, 187-9. The library was opened in 1759. Inventories of its contents at the time are in *Studio* 102 and 103. See also C. Bastianoni and G. Catoni, 'La Biblioteca comunale', in *Storia di Siena*, II. *Dal Granducato all'Unità*, eds. R. Barzanti, G. Catoni and M. De Gregorio (Siena, 1996), pp. 365-84.

cept known in Italy before the seventeenth century.[35] A public library, along the model established in Florence?[36] The texts are far too legally orientated, and indeed too close to the university syllabus, for this. If the contents of this document, and its archival collocation, undoubtedly place it in the world of the *Studio*, it is much more likely to have been a stationer's list, i.e. related to the private enterprise side of university life about which, in Siena as elsewhere, we still know very little. This would also be a better explanation for the high proportion of unbound works in the list, which would make items suitable for borrowing on a *pecia*-like basis,[37] but highly unsuitable for an institutional library from the security point of view, and unlikely for a private collection which was much more likely to have only, or mainly, bound volumes. The format of the list – 350 x 490 mm, or significantly larger than modern A3, and written on one side only – also suggests this; like university *rotuli*, it was probably intended for public display rather than for administrative purposes. As a stationer's list it would still have the eccentricity that there are no indications of value or price, for either purchase or hire, though it would appear not to be unique in this respect.[38] The issue is unresolved.

3. *Plans for a new college*

A final aspect of the Sapienza's physical history that must be discussed is the plan at the end of the fifteenth century to build a second college. Though it came to nothing, the proposal tells us much about both the thinking in Siena and the state of collegiate architecture at the time. The project dates back to 1481, though there are hints of discussions even earlier.[39] On 11 Nov 1481 the *Consiglio del Popolo* approved a proposal from the *Savi* to plan for a second Sapienza, to accommodate forty to fifty scholars.[40] It was unambiguously stated that this should complement rather than replace the existing college,[41] 'perché sempre lo Studio vostro havarebbe di queste due case scolari cento almanco forestieri, oltre a li altri che stessero sopra di sé e a dozzina'. As to the means of achieving this ambition, the pro-

[35] T. Pesenti Marangon, *La Biblioteca universitaria di Padova dalla sua Istituzione alla fine della repubblica veneta (1629-1797)*. Contributi alla Storia dell'Università di Padova, 11 (Padua, 1979), esp. p. 5.

[36] B. L. Ullman and P. A. Stadten, *The Public Library of Renaissance Florence: Niccolo Niccoli, Cosimo de' Medici and the Library of San Marco*. Medioevo e Umanesimo, 10 (Padua, 1972).

[37] A point acknowledged by Minnucci, 'Documenti', p. 33. On the predominance of unbound volumes for sale (and the gradual growth of the practice of binding such books at the end of the fifteenth century), A. Nuovo, *Il commercio librario nell'Italia del Rinascimento* (Milan, 1998), p. 169.

[38] One such is published by A. Nuovo, *Il commercio librario a Ferrara tra il XV e XVI secolo. La bottega di Domenico Sivieri*. Storia della tipografia e del commercio librario, 3 (Florence, 1998), pp. 180-273; and see esp. her analysis of the possible functions of the inventory, pp. 149-53.

[39] In June 1480, shortly before the regime change, the *Savi* made modest proposals for the expansion of the *Studio*, suggesting an increase in expenditure and reforms to teachers' appointments. The preamble may be significant: 'che essendo la città con la gratia di dio in pace et sana, si giudica per ognuno che ama lo honore et utile di quella che una de le principali provisioni si possa fare utile et honorevole sarebbe di reformare et ampliare el vostro studio, a la quale cosa ne sete confortati etiam dal summo pontifice. Et molti R.mi Car.li che hanno studiato nel vostro studio, Et etiam da la M.tà del Re come publicamente è stato referato per li vostri ambasciadori.' *Conc.* 2123, f. 19r (approved 20v, 2 Jun 1480). On this document see p. 89 n. 24 above; on the political context, Isaacs, 'Cardinali e "spalagrembi"', pp. 1013-20.

[40] *CG* 238, f. 250r, 11 Nov, ed. G. Chironi, 'Appendice documentaria', in *Francesco di Giorgio architetto*, a cura di F. P. Fiore & M. Tafuri (Milan, 1993), pp. 400-11 (p. 403).

[41] *Pace* Ciampolini, 'Casa della Sapienza', whose description (p. 13) rests on the assumption that the plan was to rebuild the old Sapienza (and see now Idem, 'La Domus Misericordiae', p. 141). Catoni, 'Genesi', p. 167 makes the same point, which is discussed below, p. 390 n. 49.

posal indicated a route very similar to that taken with the first house a century earlier. It was recognised that building such a college and providing it with adequate revenues would be a substantial undertaking in the current climate.[42] The authorities would therefore look to the acquisition and rationalisation of 'luoghi religiosi' which were understaffed but rich in income. For this, of course, the pope's consent would be necessary, but the petition points out that the cardinal of Siena, who was well disposed to the project, would shortly be leaving for Rome and could be approached if the *Balìa* approved the initiative.[43]

The involvement of the cardinal – Francesco Todeschini Piccolomini, nephew of Pius II and himself destined to become pope Pius III in 1503[44] – is highly significant. The fifteenth century had seen the development of a long tradition of cardinals sponsoring or founding colleges in Italy; it was becoming one of the pious activities expected of them, and a standard type of legacy.[45] By 1492, when the project reappeared before the *Balìa* in more concrete form, the cardinal of Siena was described as the 'fondatore' of the new college; his five appointed representatives had chosen the site, and three officials were to be appointed to support them by negotiating the terms of the necessary (and compulsory) purchases.[46] The designs of Giuliano da Sangallo for the building (Fig. 20a below) bear the title 'SAPIENZA PER CHARDINALE DI SIENA', though no record of a formal commission has been adduced.[47] It is also interesting to note the location chosen; after earlier discussions of the possibility of 'lo locho delli Umiliati' (in the Terzo di Camollia),[48] the 1492

---

[42] 'ad volere hedificare di nuovo ex publico una tale casa et darle l'entrate convenienti per lo governo di detti scolari saria spesa grande et da non potersi fare per la Republica vostra attesa la qualità de tempi' (as n. 40).

[43] On the cardinal's Sienese sojourn of 1482 see A. A. STRNAD, 'Francesco Todeschini Piccolomini: Politik und Mäzenatentum im Quattrocento', *Römische historische Mitteilungen*, 8-9 (1964-66), pp. 101-425 (p. 354). There is no mention of this project (see below, n. 47).

[44] On his key political role in Siena, ISAACS, 'Cardinali e "spalagrembi"', p. 1023; A. L. JENKENS, 'Pius II's Nephews and the Politics of Architecture at the End of the Fifteenth Century in Siena', *BSSP*, 106 (1999), pp. 68-114 (pp. 81-2, 84).

[45] DENLEY, 'Collegiate Movement', pp. 50-1; cf. P. CORTESI, *De Cardinalatu libri tres* (Casa Cortese, 1510), f. ciii.

[46] *Balìa* 37, ff. 6v-7r, 13 Jun; cf. H. BURNS, 'Progetti per la nuova casa della Sapienza, Siena', in *Francesco di Giorgio architetto*, pp. 296-301 (pp. 296-7).

[47] *Taccuino* of Giuliano da Sangallo (below, pp. 391-2). FALUSCHI, *Breve relazione*, p. 173 states 'pensò nel 1492 il Card. Francesco Piccolomini…a crescerle in amplissima forma, con disegno, e Pianta di Giuliano da S. Gallo'. From ZDEKAUER (p. 79) onwards it has been received wisdom that the cardinal commissioned the plans. But no documentary trace of this has been found by any of the scholarly work on Giuliano da Sangallo, nor does Strnad's exhaustive biography of the cardinal so much as mention the project. The cardinal's involvement with the Sienese *Studio* was limited to the conventional, notwithstanding his role (as bishop of Siena) as its chancellor (see BARGAGLI, *Bartolomeo Sozzini*, p. 150 n. 5). Indeed, there is more evidence of his sympathies with Perugia, where he may have been a student, and for which he appears to have done more; STRNAD, 'Francesco Todeschini Piccolomini', pp. 137-8 and esp. n. 111.

[48] This emerges from a letter of 1484 from Giovanni Battista Caccialupi, now *advocatus concistorialis* in Rome, to the *Concistoro*, informing it about a similar proposal for Perugia of which he had learnt through his old friend and former classmate Angelo Geraldini, the bishop of Suessa. The bishop asked whether the Sienese project had a site in mind; Caccialupi reported that he had replied 'gia era stato ragionamento de farla nello locho delli humiliati' (*Conc.* 2056, no. 53, 1 Oct 1484). On this letter see NARDI, 'Giovanni Battista Caccialupi a Siena', pp. 121-3, and for a fuller summary, and comments on what the document reveals about the operation of 'educational circles', cf. DENLEY, 'Collegiate Movement', p. 47. The Umiliati church of S. Tommaso was to the east of the Via di Camollia; there remains today a Vicolo degli Umiliati, and the former Piazza degli Umiliati is now the Piazza del Sale; more precise detail in P. ANGELUCCI, 'Gli Umiliati a Siena e la chiesa del borgo franco di Paganico', in *Chiesa e società dal secolo IV ai nostri giorni. Studi storici in onore del P. Ilarino da Milano*, I (Rome, 1979), pp. 261-89 (pp. 265-72, esp. 267), and V. LUSINI, 'Notizie storiche sulla topografia di Siena nel secolo XIII', *BSSP*, 28 (1921), pp. 239-341 (esp. pp. 335-6). The church was modified in the 1460s (F. J. D. NEVOLA, '"Per Ornato Della Città": Siena's Strada Romana and Fifteenth-Century Urban Renewal', *Art Bulletin*, 82 [2000], pp. 26-50 [p. 40]), but it is not clear how the proposed college would have fitted with its position.

measure opted for a site which appears to be contiguous with, and probably in the same block as, the old Sapienza.[49] The building of the new Sapienza would be a big operation, necessitating con-

[49] The site is described as 'Nel terzo di Kamollia in loco decto Aringhieri, cioè la casa de' Capacci per infino a la strada che va a San Domenico e da la strada che passa dinanti a la porta de la Sapientia et va nell'arte de la lana fino el chiasso che volta et entra nel chiasso socto la volta et casa de Capacci' (as n. 40). Scholars have not managed to agree on the exact location and orientation of the building. Kiene, on the basis of the Sangallo designs, the second and more precise set of which (Fig. 20b, below) has an angular lower end which could correspond with the angle of the Via dei Pittori, argues for a rectangular site with the entrance on the Via della Sapienza; M. Kiene, 'I progetti di Giuliano da Sangallo per l'Università di Siena', in *L'Università di Siena. 750 anni*, pp. 525-6); Idem, 'La sede del sapere. I progetti per la Casa della Sapienza da Giuliano da Sangallo a Francesco di Giorgio Martini', in *Le dimore di Siena. L'arte dell'abitare nei territori dell'antica Repubblica dal Medioevo all'Unità d'Italia*, ed. G. Morolli (Florence, 2002), pp. 139-44 (p. 141), and Idem, 'Der Palazzo della Sapienza', p. 240. He does not speculate on the relationship of the new building to the existing Sapienza. H. Burns, 'Progetti', examining the Magliabechiano drawings assumed to be the work of an associate of Francesco di Giorgio Martini (Figs. 20a-d, below), notes that the entrance is described as on the 'strada maestra' and that the right hand side of the building gives onto the Sapienza, and concludes, puzzlingly, that the site 'si trovava subito a sud della vecchia Sapienza…con il suo ingresso principale sulla continuazione dell'attuale via della Sapienza, non appena questa sale verso piazza Salimbeni' (p. 297), which I am unable to reconcile either internally or with the basic topography. It is difficult to find an explanation for these inconsistencies. The two architects may have been planning for different sites within the block, though the fact that the two sets of designs are for buildings of pretty much the same size (see below, n. 60) makes this unlikely. The hypothesis that the Magliabechiano designs were a revised version of Francesco di Giorgio Martini's original design, now in the Uffizi (Fig. 23 below), also works against this notion; that was for a significantly wider building (see below, pp. 392-3 and n. 58), and the logical explanation would be that Francesco's original concept had to be adapted to a specific site which was the same as that worked on by Sangallo.

If we agree that both architects' detailed plans were drawn up with a specific site in mind, where exactly was it? Here I differ from Ciampolini, 'Casa della Sapienza', p. 313, and 'La Domus Misericordiae', p. 140 about the relationship of the projected new college to the existing one. The easiest way to reconcile the topography with the Sangallo designs in particular would be to accept his view that the building was in fact intended to replace the old Sapienza. To do this one would have also to conclude that the 1481 plan, which explicitly refers to a second and additional Sapienza, had been abandoned. But there are problems with this hypothesis. First, it implies a late change in intentions, since two colleges were certainly still in the frame at the time when the site was being decided in 1492 (see letter to the cardinal in *Balìa* 411, ff. 119r-121v, 14 Jun; f. 119v). Second, it is difficult to reconcile it with the inclusion of references to the existing Sapienza in the specification of the location of the proposed new building. To this non-specialist at least, it seems illogical to embellish designs with pointers ('intrata inverso la sapienza', 'logia inverso la sapienza', 'intrata a mezo chamino inverso la sapienza') to buildings which will have to be demolished to make way for the new project. Finally, and perhaps more substantially, it flies in the face of common sense. By replacing the old college, at immense cost, the authorities would certainly have gained some teaching rooms, but only by dramatically reducing the number of residential places (see the evaluation below, p. 401).

If that assumption is correct, the possibilities within this block – which still seems the most likely location, though others close by should perhaps also be investigated – appear to me to be three: A) The north-west corner of the block, with the main entrance on the Via della Sapienza. This fits closely with the dimensions of the Sangallo plans, and accords with Kiene's observations about the angle of the lower end, but contrasts with the Magliabechiano plans which explicitly have the 'Sapienza' (which must surely mean the existing college) to the right of the building as one enters. Could this be a mistake on the part of Francesco's assistant? Francesco himself, a Sienese, would have been most unlikely to get wrong such a basic detail of a major cultural landmark, even if, as is possible, he created his original design *in absentia* (Burns, 'Progetti', p. 297). An assistant might well not have been familiar with the site and could perhaps have copied erroneously. On the other hand, the plans are full of precise detail (apart from the tantalisingly generalised references to the 'strada maestra'), in contrast, according to Burns, to the idealised (though precisely measured) initial plan in the Uffizi ('Progetti', p. 297). It seems unlikely that such a fundamental error would have survived uncorrected, although Kiene stresses that the Magliabechiano plans are full of corrections, freehand additions, pencil and differently coloured annotations ('La sede del sapere', p. 142; and 'I progetti', p. 529). B) The north-east corner of the block, again with the main entrance on the Via della Sapienza. This fits both the main sets of designs (though the degree of descent of the current site is nothing like as steep as envisaged in at least the Magliabechiano plans, in which the entrance to the building is on the upper floor), but meets the apparently unanswerable objection that it would have entailed the demolition of the church; there does not appear to be room for a building of such width between it and the old Sapienza. No suggestion that such a major step was being contemplated appears in the documents. C) The south-east corner of the block, with the main entrance on the Via delle Terme, and the length of the building running south-westwards. This is

siderable preparation and outlay. It was taken in hand in 1493-4; in 1493 the *Savi* sold twenty-two possessions in the *contado* in order to raise 1,600 florins for the purchase of *scorticatoi* behind the Sapienza,[50] and in 1494 the cardinal purchased the house of Ser Alessandro di Niccolò della Grammatica for 1,400 florins 'pro construenda nova Sapientia ex auctoritate eis concesso a Dominis Officialibus Balie'.[51]

The multiple crises of 1494 and thereafter appear to have ensured that nothing came of the project. There is no mention of it in communal documents after 1494.[52] All that remains of it is a number of designs for the buildings, actually in some proliferation for a project that never passed the planning stage. Two of the most eminent architects of the day appear to have been involved, though we have no documentation about when they were asked or when they produced their plans.[53] Best known is the design of the Florentine Giuliano da Sangallo, who included in his *Taccuino senese* both an early, ide-

compatible with the descriptions on the Magliabechiano drawings, and is also in descent. One of the Magliabechiano drawings (Fig. 24c below) also has the lower end of the building looking onto the 'logia inverso la sapienza', which would be consistent with this location and orientation. A building of the dimensions planned would not have fitted into the present block without partial demolition of the church, but there is another possibility, namely that it was to extend over the present Via dei Pittori. The *scorticatoi* purchased in 1493 'super plano fontis brande' (below, n. 50) may well have included this alley (though equally they may be others. The *Hinterland* of the Sapienza had previously included some back alleys of dubious repute; see above, p. 384).

I am of course not qualified to judge these issues from an architectural point of view, nor was this the object of this excursus. However, for what it is worth, and in case Sienese topographical experts can make more of such evidence, other indications should be noted. One of the Magliabechiano drawings (Fig. 24d below) has the left hand side of the building 'verso l'ostaria dela rosa' (not one of those mentioned by TULIANI, *Osti, avventori e malandrini*). The main plot purchased for the new building was the house of Ser Alessandro Grammatica, 'qual casa era situata nel Terzo di Camollia luogo d. Volta de' Corsieri' (BCS, *ms.* P.II.22, entry under Sapienza, no foliation, 5 Nov 1493; and see below, n. 51). Anyone who can establish the location of these, and indeed the 'loco decto Aringhieri' and the 'volta et casa de Capacci' mentioned in the 1492 resolution, will have come closer to solving this conundrum.

[50] *Balìa* 38, f. 90r, 29 Mar (original decision to buy the *scorticatoi*); *Mis.* 36, ff. 80v-81r, 16 Apr (purchase of the *scorticatoi*; cf. also *Not.* 968, no foliation, 15 and 16 Apr, and 9 Dec 1493); *Balìa* 39, ff. 27r, 16 Aug (sales authorised), 42v, 21 Sept (the sales are explicitly for the construction of the new Sapienza), 50v, 26 Oct (estimators appointed to make compulsory purchase orders); and cf. *Studio* 2, ff. 134r-141r, 28 Mar to 4 Dec, *passim*, for the sales. The new Sapienza was not the only driving force for these; one such sale is made 'visa paupertate dicta domus et visa necessitate vini pro scolaribus dicte domus' (*Studio* 2, f. 138v, 11 Aug).

[51] *Not.* 682, no foliation, 12 Jun (preliminary contract, in draft). There is a copy of the final contract in BCS, *ms.* B.VI.15, no. 191, ff. 290v-291v, 20 Aug. The price was fixed by the estimators on 5 Nov 1493, along with that for the house of Donato d'Antonio Guelfi, valued at 250 florins (according to the *spoglio* of documents in BCS, *ms.* P.II.22, no foliation).

[52] The last reference to the sale-and-purchase operation I have found is dated 6 Dec 1494; *Not.* 968, no foliation (deliberation of the *Savi* concerning payments; it does not refer to the new Sapienza). BURNS, 'Progetti', p. 297 refers to the appointment of commissioners to direct 'l'opera della Sapienza', citing *Conc* 769, f. 12v, 13 Jan 1494, and *CG* 240, f. 274r, 18 Dec 1494. The first reference is misdated for 18 Dec; the two refer to the same decision, the routine appointment of *Savi*, first for the *Studio* and subsequently for the hospital of S. Maria della Scala and the Opera del Duomo. There is no mention of the new building; the elements of the minute have erroneously been conflated.

[53] The first floor plan of the first Sangallo drawing (below, Fig. 20a and n. 54) has the date 1492 on it, but this is in the hand of Pecci, and is the only specific evidence to link it with that date. Kiene has speculated that, given that the proposal for a new Sapienza is now known to go back to 1481, at least the first set of Sangallo designs – which, for example, do not appear to be as site-specific – could be pre-1492 and thus from an earlier period in his repertoire ('I progetti', p. 525). BURNS, 'Progetti', p. 296, doubts whether Francesco di Giorgio was involved at that stage, and it must be said that the dimensions of both of Sangallo's sets of designs, as well as their closeness to those of the Magliabechiano set, not to mention the upper-storey entrance of the latter, all suggest that they were done with a specific site in mind, arguing for a later date, probably 1492.

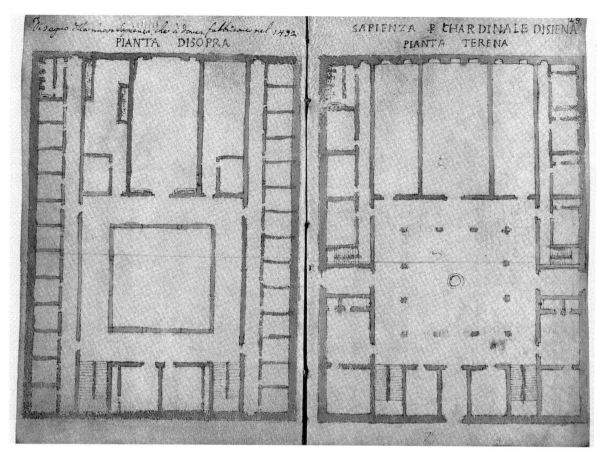

Fig. 20a – Giuliano da Sangallo, first designs for a Casa della Sapienza, in *Taccuino Senese* (BCS, ms. S.IV.8, ff. 28v-29r).

alised plan (Fig. 20a),[54] and what appears to be a subsequent and more detailed one (Fig. 20b).[55] This has long been known in the Sienese literature, and we have additional drawings elaborating on this design by his nephew Giovanni Battista da Sangallo, 'Il Gobbo' (Fig. 21),[56] and subsequently by Giovanni Antonio Pecci in the eighteenth century (Fig. 22).[57] Secondly, there is a design in the hand of the Sienese architect Francesco di Giorgio Martini, in the Uffizi collection (Fig. 23), which is thought by some to be for the Sienese Sapienza; its dimensions fit less well with the other designs (though they are close enough to have given rise to the attribution), and it is more generic; it has received less atten-

[54] BCS, *ms.* S.IV.8, ff. 28v-29r, ed. L. ZDEKAUER, *Il Taccuino Senese di Giuliano da San Gallo* (Siena, 1902, repr. Bologna, 1979. The 1902 edition appeared under the name of R. Falb, the owner of the studio which reproduced the manuscript; the 1979 attribution of authorship reflects the fact that the introduction was written by Zdekauer), Tav. 29; KIENE, 'I progetti', p. 532; BURNS, 'Progetti', p. 300 fig. XVI.1.6.

[55] BCS, *ms.* S.IV.8, ff. 20v-21r, ed. ZDEKAUER, *Il Taccuino Senese*, Tav. 21; KIENE, 'I progetti', p. 532; BURNS, 'Progetti', p. 300, fig. XVI.1.6.

[56] Florence, Galleria degli Uffizi, Gabinetto dei Disegni e delle Stampe, 1666A, ed. KIENE, 'I progetti', p. 533.

[57] BCS, *ms.* S.IV.8, f. 52v; it has been bound together with Giuliano's *Taccuino senese*. (above, n. 54). Cf also G. A. PECCI, *Ristretto delle cose più notabili della città di Siena a uso dei forestieri* (Siena, 1759, repr. 1761), pp. 163-4 of 1761 edn.

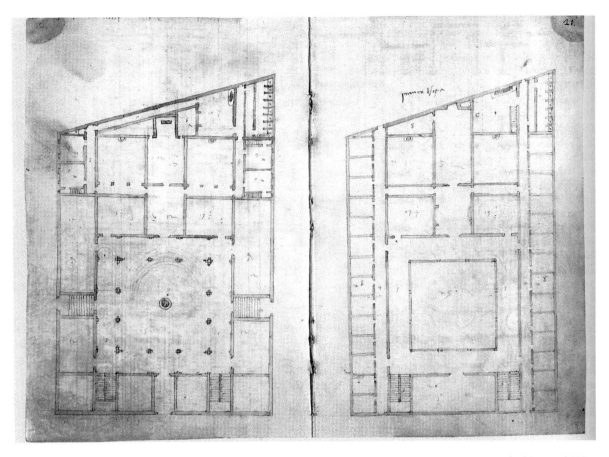

Fig. 20b – Giuliano da Sangallo, more detailed designs for a Casa della Sapienza, in *Taccuino Senese* (BCS, ms. S.IV.8, ff. 20v-21r).

tion from scholars, as it will here.[58] Finally there is a set of four drawings, with more detailed elaborations but different overall proportions, bound together with drawings of Francesco di Giorgio in a volume of the Magliabechiano collection but actually in the hand of an assistant (Figs. 24a-d).[59] The

---

[58] Florence, Galleria degli Uffizi, Gabinetto dei Disegni e delle Stampe, U 318 Av; published by M. MORRESI, 'Francesco di Giorgio e Bramante: osservazioni su alcuni disegni degli Uffizi e della Laurenziana', in *Il disegno di architettura. Atti del convegno* (Milano, 15-18 febbraio 1988), eds. P. Carpeggiani and L. Patetta (Milan, 1989), pp. 117-24 (p. 118), and EADEM, 'Bramante, Enrico Bruno e la parrocchiale di Roccaverrano', in *La piazza, la chiesa e il parco*, ed. M. Tafuri (Milan, 1991), pp. 96-165 (p. 130 and cf. pp. 138-9), who takes up the speculation of Corrado Maltese, based on similarities of dimension, that it might be for the Sienese Sapienza; FRANCESCO DI GIORGIO, *Trattati di architettura, ingegneria e arte militare*, ed. C. Maltese, 2 vols. (Milan, 1967), I, pp. LVI-II. This tentative attribution is adopted without reservation by BURNS, 'Progetti', pp. 296-7; Kiene by contrast does not discuss the design even in his most recent article on the new Sapienza, 'La sede del sapere'. The design is for a building of about 55 x 49 metres (if the measurements are in *braccia senesi*; this is Burns's assumption, p. 297. The dimensions of 45 x 49 metres given in MORRESI, 'Francesco di Giorgio', p. 117 appear to be a misprint).

[59] Biblioteca Nazionale di Firenze, cod. Magliabechiano II.I.140, ed. KIENE, 'I progetti', pp. 530-1, and BURNS, 'Progetti', p. 299. For clarity I follow Burns, who numbers them. They are: ff. 249v-250r (Burns Fig. XVI.1.1), a plan of the lower floor; ff. 249v-250r (Burns Fig. XVI.1.2), a plan of the upper floor, including the main entrance; ff. 245v-246r (Burns Fig. XVI.1.3) and ff. 247v-248r (Burns Fig. XVI.1.4), both variant designs for the upper floor.

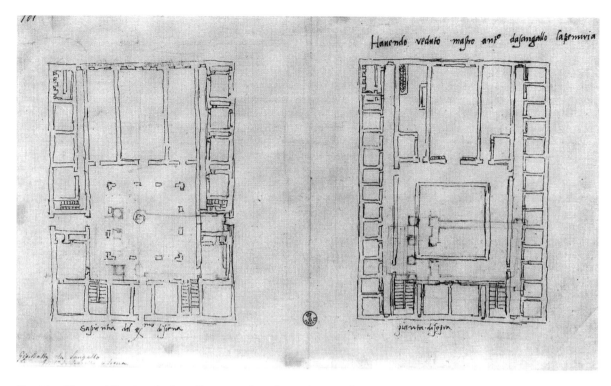

Fig. 21 – Giovanni Battista da Sangallo, copy of Giuliano da Sangallo's designs (Florence, Galleria degli Uffizi, Gabinetto dei Disegni e delle Stampe, disegno 1666a).

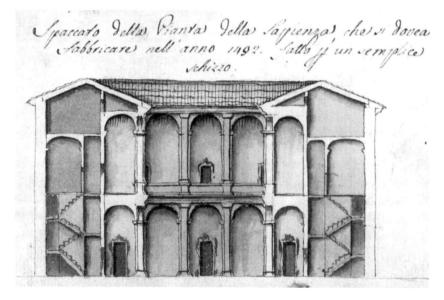

Fig. 22 – G. A. PECCI, cross-section of Giuliano da Sangallo's design, in *Taccuino Senese* (BCS, *ms.* S.IV.8, f. 52v).

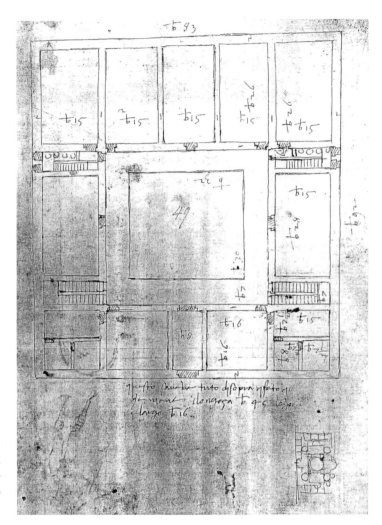

Fig. 23 – Francesco di Giorgio Martini, possible design for a Casa della Sapienza in Siena (Florence, Galleria degli Uffizi, Gabinetto dei Disegni e delle Stampe, disegno U 318 Av).

Sangallo 'set' and the Magliabechiano elaborations (though not the Uffizi design) have recently been published and discussed by Kiene, and subsequently by Burns. The first Sangallo designs and the Magliabechiano plans are broadly similar in dimensions, which adds to the complexity of the issues of sequence and attribution,[60] and they are also comparable in their basic scheme of a rectangular basis of the building constructed around a large central *cortile* (a feature of the Uffizi design as well), though beyond that they are substantially different in conception, layout, purpose and detail. Kiene and Burns have not only disagreed on the involvement of Francesco di Giorgio; they have offered substan-

---

[60] Burns calculates the dimensions of the Magliabechiano designs to be approximately 55 x 42 metres (p. 297), and those of the original Sangallo design to be 55.5 x 42.8 metres; those of the revised Sangallo design are calculated as 48.5 metres long on one side, 58.5 metres long on the other, and 38.6 metres wide (p. 298).

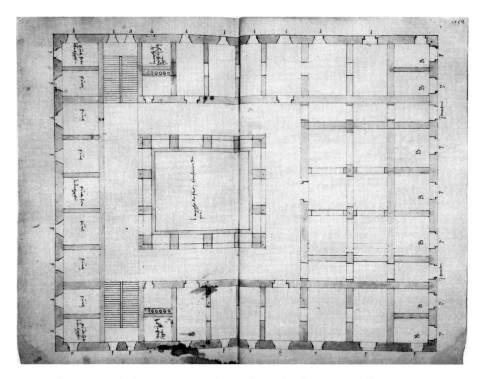

Fig. 24a – Assistant of Francesco di Giorgio Martini, lower-floor plan for a Casa della Sapienza (Florence, Biblioteca Nazionale, Magl. II.I.140, ff. 251v-252r).

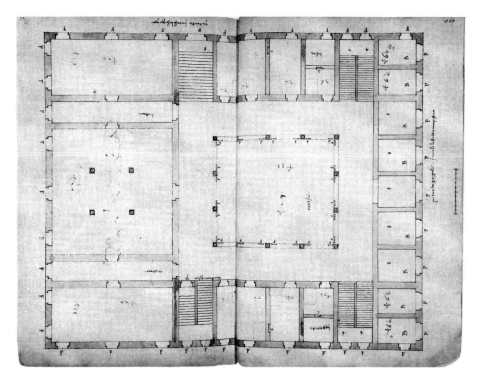

Fig. 24b – Assistant of Francesco di Giorgio Martini, upper-floor plan for a Casa della Sapienza (Florence, Biblioteca Nazionale, Magl. II.I.140, ff. 249v-250r).

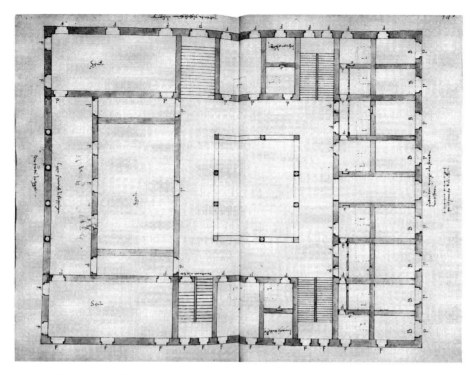

Fig. 24c – Assistant of Francesco di Giorgio Martini, variant upper-floor plan for a Casa della Sapienza (Florence, Biblioteca Nazionale, Magl. II.I.140, ff. 245v-246r).

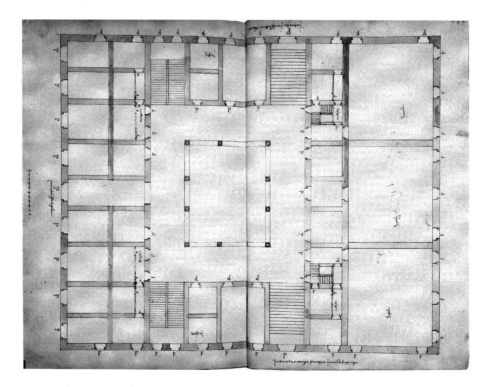

Fig. 24d – Assistant of Francesco di Giorgio Martini, variant upper-floor plan for a Casa della Sapienza (Florence, Biblioteca Nazionale, Magl. II.I.140, ff. 247v-248r).

tially different interpretations of both sets of plans.[61] The state of research has been comprehensively surveyed by Ciampolini.[62]

My purpose here is not to make technical observations, still less to intrude on the expertise of architectural historians, but rather to glean from the designs what information we can of relevance for the history of the old Sapienza and indeed the *Studio* as a whole. In this context what commands attention is the interrelationship between ideals and practice, and between architectural traditions and local exigencies. Both Kiene and Burns have rightly stressed that the involvement of such distinguished architects is more than an indicator of the prestigious nature of the project (and, in the case of Sangallo, of Siena's good relations with Lorenzo de' Medici);[63] it draws attention to the fact that the building would take its place in a growing architectural tradition of such *palazzi*. Kiene, who has researched extensively the *palazzi della sapienza* of the period, has placed both sets in a comparative context and argued that the focusing of the building around a grand *loggiato* is typical of central Italian *sapienza* design of the period, as well as of colleges which incorporated teaching elsewhere;[64] and he stresses that Sangallo had also been involved in the slow-maturing plans to build a *sapienza* in Pisa.[65] The central *cortile* plan is of course an emerging characteristic of colleges not just as residential units but as academic communities, in which residence and learning are combined, and in which the Vitruvian ideal of *logge* as places for scholarly debate is given visual and spatial centrality.[66] Both Kiene and Burns emphasise that the Sangallo designs make the relationship between teaching and living spaces, and the separation of public and private, exceptionally clear.[67]

What would such a building have given the Sienese *Studio*? This is a less straightforward matter. From the institutional point of view a key aspect is the addition of teaching areas. This is the first instance in Siena of a plan to construct, *ex novo*, a building and an institution in which residence and teaching would be integrated. These functions had been combined in the old Sapienza, but as a result of chance rather than planning; a building was inherited which had space in which teaching could be and was conducted, even before the conversion of the Misericordia to a Sapienza, in the same way that churches were used for this purpose.[68] Teaching had never been a declared function of the first Sapienza when it was planned, nor was it mentioned in either of the two key deliberations (1481 and 1492) regarding the new one. This fits the Italian pattern; the growth of a teaching dimension within the colleges, far from being explicit, was almost casual. The Spanish College at Bologna and the Collegio Gregoriano at Perugia, both repeatedly held up as specific models for Siena, initially made provision only for the teaching of

---

[61] Kiene, who does not consider the Francesco di Giorgio drawing in the Uffizi, sees little to tie the Magliabechiano drawings to him and instead sees them as later elaborations of Sangallo's design ('I progetti', pp. 529-30; 'La sede del sapere', p. 142); Burns relates the Magliabechiano designs to the Uffizi drawing which he considers to be in Francesco's hand, and therefore argues that they must be more detailed elaborations of it ('Progetti', p. 297). Kiene published the Magliabechiano drawings for the first time ('I progetti', pp. 530-1). He has also been more selective than Burns in his use of the labels on these drawings, preferring the approach of reconciliation with what he considers to be the earlier Sangallo schemes.

[62] Ciampolini, 'La Domus Misericordiae', pp. 140-3.

[63] Burns, 'Progetti', p. 298.

[64] Kiene, 'I progetti', esp. pp. 524-5; 'La sede del sapere', p. 142; 'Der Palazzo della Sapienza', esp. pp. 241-2.

[65] Kiene, 'I progetti', pp. 520-1.

[66] See esp. Kiene, 'I progetti', pp. 523, 532-3, and 'Der Palazzo della Sapienza', p. 236; taken up by A. Bedon, *Il palazzo della Sapienza di Roma* (Rome, 1991), pp. 22-3.

[67] Kiene, 'I progetti', p. 529; Burns, 'Progetti', p. 298; and cf. Moretti, 'L'architettura delle sedi universitarie', p. 282.

[68] See above, pp. 115 *seq.*

their own students; the Gregoriano merely provided for a *repetitor*,[69] and theology teaching at the Spanish College was opened up to other students almost as an afterthought.[70] The suggestion that Niccolò da Uzzano's projected Sapienza at Florence (1430) might have had a dual function of residence for members and teaching for the *Studio*[71] has not yet been substantiated; certainly no such role was envisaged either by the founder or by the authorities whose deliberations preceded his offer.[72] The Sapienza project at Pisa, perhaps the most direct comparator because of its chronological and geographical proximity to, and competition with, the plans for a new Sapienza in Siena[73] (not to mention the involvement of Giuliano da Sangallo in both schemes), is an example of a different route rather than a straightforward model; the proposal (and Sangallo's drawing for it) clearly prioritised teaching, with fourteen *aule* (subsequently reduced to eleven), and accommodation for forty students on the upper floor which, however, had certainly not been completed by 1494.[74] The Pisan Sapienza should also be seen in the context of another gradually emerging trend, that towards dedicated teaching accommodation. Such a building was commissioned in Florence in 1392, though virtually nothing is known about its subsequent history.[75] In Turin in 1443 a building was converted to become the seat of the *studium generale*, with three lecture rooms, a 'scuola grande', a 'scuola degli artisti' and a 'scuola dei legisti'.[76] The idea was later taken up in Padua, where conversion of the Palazzo del Bo into a teaching centre was begun in 1493,[77] and in Rome, where Alexander VI's building, begun in 1497, was intended for teaching only.[78]

---

[69] Cf. the statutes, Cost. 17, ed. ROSSI, 'Documenti per la storia dell'Università di Perugia', doc. 107; fuller editions in SEBASTIANI, 'Il collegio universitario', pp. 206 *seq.* (p. 221, and see p. 35), and ANGELETTI and BERTINI, *La Sapienza Vecchia*, pp. 343-67 (p. 353).

[70] Statute 27, ed. MARTI, *The Spanish College*, pp. 268-73. The college was built with a lecture room (KIENE, 'Der Palazzo della Sapienza', p. 234); the design of the building ensured that non-members only got as far as the entrance wing (KIENE, op. cit., p. 235). On the issue of teaching in Italian colleges see DENLEY, 'Collegiate Movement', pp. 58-9.

[71] KIENE, op. cit., pp. 223-6, 'I progetti', pp. 518-9, 'La sede del sapere', p. 140, quoting both Wackernagel's reference to Vasari, who speaks of 'una Sapienza ovvero Studio' (*Le vite de' più eccellenti pittori scultori ed architettori*, ed. G. Milanesi, 9 vols [Florence, 1878-1885], vol. 2, p. 54), and L. F. DEL MIGLIORE, *Zibaldone Istorico* BNF, Magl. XXV, 415, f. 20r, saying that the Sapienza 'prese le funzioni di università, in quanto vi venivano insegnate tutte le scienze'. (I have not been able to locate this statement in that volume.) Neither of these seems to me conclusive evidence for an otherwise unsupported claim.

[72] GHERARDI, *Statuti*, appendix, part 1, doc. 117, pp. 210-4 (communal deliberation of 15-18 March 1428=9) and 230-9 (will of Niccolò da Uzzano, 27 Dec 1430). Nor is there any trace of the dual function in the documents examined in the most recent study, DAVIES, *Florence and its University*, pp. 17-18. The suggestion appears to be a conflation of Uzzano's proposal with the construction of a building for teaching which was ordered in 1392 (see below, n. 75).

[73] DENLEY, 'Academic Rivalry', pp. 201-3, and IDEM, '*Signore* and *Studio*, pp. 213-4.

[74] KIENE, 'I progetti', pp. 520-1.

[75] SPAGNESI, *Utiliter Edoceri*, pp. 31-5, and 149-52 (edition of the contract, dated 21 August 1392). Spagnesi presents the evidence for it having been built (though it is not clear when it was completed). The deduction of DAVIES, *Florence and its University*, pp. 16-17, from subsequent exemptions that it became the usual place for teaching may be true by extension; but Spagnesi himself speculates that teaching may have continued in previously used locations, which tended all to be in the same street as the new building, a street already known as the Via dello Studio by the time of the 1392 contract (pp. 32, 150).

[76] FALCO et al., 'Le istituzioni per l'istruzione superiore in Torino', pp. 556-8. The authors stress that the accommodation was in a far from suitable or salubrious area, close to the market and the town's two brothels; that the dedication of this building to the *Studio* was a reluctant response of the *comune* to the insistence by the duke of Savoy in 1412 that such a building be provided; and that it continued to be necessary to use other venues for university activities, especially events which involved a large number of participants, and degree ceremonies for which the *sede* was not considered sufficiently prestigious. Nonetheless this was 'il primo edificio italiano, che abbia ospitato in modo continuo una sede universitaria'.

[77] L. MONTOBBIO, *Splendore e utopia nella Padova dei Carraresi* (Padua, 1989), pp. 277-9.

[78] CHAMBERS, 'Studium Urbis and the *Gabella Studii*', p. 83; A. BEDON, *Il palazzo della Sapienza di Roma* (Rome, 1991), pp. 15-16. Bedon ascribes the lack of interest in building a combined institution, then and previously, to the modest scale of the Roman *Studio* and the existence of the Collegio Capranica (pp. 14-15). A similar point could be made

So were the Sienese making a programmatic statement with their new plans? They appear rather to have been taking a rational decision about the expansion of accommodation for non-Sienese students and, at the same time, of teaching space. It is less easy to come to a conclusion about the balance between the two, since the various plans point in different directions. The Sangallo drawings are unclear about the purpose of many of the rooms, and it is necessary to resort to speculation. Sangallo's first set of plans (Fig. 20a) include six long rooms at the far end of the building, three on each floor; the central room on the lower floor may have been intended as a chapel (it was in the second set of drawings), and the room directly above it as a refectory.[79] There are also a number of medium-sized rooms, some of which have vestibules or ante-chambers, and Kiene, like Zdekauer, sees at least some of these as classrooms (in the designs for the Pisan Sapienza, such rooms are classrooms with ante-rooms for the teachers),[80] though it has to be said that these are unusually small for teaching purposes, as well as being distributed somewhat haphazardly throughout the building.[81] The revised and more specific second set of plans (Fig. 20b) no longer has rooms with vestibules, but there are four large rectangular rooms, all giving onto the *loggiato*, which it is difficult to imagine as anything other than *aule*. If Kiene is right, then Sangallo's first, general plans have a somewhat *ad hoc* distribution of classrooms, while the second set of plans make the clear separation of public and private areas for which the design has been praised.[82] Teaching rooms are also more centrally placed in the Magliabechiano drawings, which by and large give fuller explanations of the purpose of each area; however, two of the variant ground-plans for the upper, entrance-level floor (Figs. 24c and 24d) have only three rooms explicitly designated as *scuole*.[83] None of these variants[84] compare to the eleven teaching rooms of the Pisan project, but of course there was no need for that, since they would have been additions to the existing teaching rooms in the old Sapienza (it is still not known how many of these there were, though the references to them are in the plural), as well as provision elsewhere in the city. Taking these various designs together, one can say that the authorities appear to have been contemplating a significant shift towards concentration of the *Studio*'s teaching activities on one site, though given the number of simultaneous classes required this would still have fallen short of catering for all instruction.

about the *Studio* and building of Turin, which did not yet aspire to international competition and whose function was basically the training of local lawyers and doctors of medicine; Falco et al., 'Le istituzioni per l'istruzione superiore in Torino', p. 545.

[79] The suggestion of Zdekauer, p. 80.

[80] Kiene, 'I progetti', p. 526; Zdekauer, p. 80 and Idem, *Ill Taccuino Senese*, p. 21, positing a total of twelve such rooms, five along each side and a further two at the front upstairs.

[81] Of the rooms with ante-chambers the two largest, on the left and right sides near the entrance on the ground floor, can be calculated (on the assumption that the measures given on the diagrams are in Florentine *braccia*) as just over 7m x 6m; the four smaller ones at the far end of the ground floor, on the right, are 5.1m x 4m, and the two first-floor rooms above the entrance are 6.m x 5.8m. Compare these with the sizes of what appear to be *aule* in U 318A, 26 x 15 *braccia senesi* or *c*. 15.6m x 9m, or what are explicitly labelled *scuole* in the Magliabechiano designs, 26 x 15 and 28 x 15 *braccia senesi*. The dedicated teaching rooms of the Pisan Sapienza and the Spanish College of Bologna are also much closer to this latter size. It would certainly be interesting if such small teaching rooms were contemplated.

[82] Above, n. p. 398.

[83] Kiene, 'I progetti', p. 531, believing these to be subsequent versions of the original Sangallo plans, sees this reduction as an indication of adaptation to economic reality.

[84] Francesco di Giorgio Martini's Uffizi drawing (Fig. 23) – whose relationship to the Sienese project is, as has been seen, unproven – consists entirely of large and public rooms.

The Sangallo designs add substantially to Siena's provision of student accommodation; the first set provides for twenty-six student rooms, the second for twenty-eight.[85] The Magliabechiano drawings are more problematic in this respect. Two of the three schemes for the upper, entrance-level floor have small rooms in which beds are indicated; one (Fig. 24b) has eight, the other (Fig. 24c) twelve. The third (Fig. 24d) has no such labels, though there are small rooms that could have been used for that purpose. There is similar ambiguity about the lower floor (Fig. 24a), because a number of rooms are not labelled on the plan, and while twelve of them are on the sides of the building and have windows, several do not have independent doors, so it is far from clear that they were intended for students. Indeed, if they were, they would have been incongruous; the rest of the floor, for which the plan does have clear labels, is entirely given over to storage (to a degree that suggests catering for much more than a small number of residents), the water facilities, and at the far end of the building, where it comes out at ground level, a row of *butighe* which give onto the street. Two of the upper-level designs (Figs. 24b and 24c) also have shops on either side of the main entrance, while on the third, less generously labelled plan (Fig. 24d) these rooms still have doors opening onto the street. Burns comments that this is consonant with other work of Francesco di Giorgio;[86] it is interesting that, in a purpose-built major college building, commercial activities were to be awarded an important place, much as indeed they had had in the estate of the old Sapienza which, as can be seen from the 1451 *catasto*, included a number of shops and workshops that were rented out by the college.[87] It might be concluded that in the plans for their new academic institution, commercial factors were never far from Sienese minds; equally, though, the presence of shops can be portrayed as an example of continued integration of 'town and gown'.[88] One could go further. The three designs for the upper, entrance-level floor all emphasise the formal and public aspects of the institution much more than the private and residential. In this respect the Magliabechiano designs, too, would have given the building a public and centralised focus above all, and one which it is legitimate to speculate would have readily formed a basis for the administration of more than the college itself – perhaps providing storage facilities for the old Sapienza as well, or indeed for many of the functions of the *Studio*. It is not impossible that the new building was being considered as the 'flagship' for the university, much as at Pisa. At the very least, the juxtaposition of the new and the old college, focusing a good proportion of the *Studio*'s teaching in one place, would have represented a substantial move in the direction of a physical centre for the *Studio*. None of this is announced or envisaged in any of the documentation; all we have to go on is these mysterious sets of unrealised designs. But Kiene is surely right in pointing out their significance for collegiate architecture at the moment of their creation,[89] even if their interpretation remains a matter of controversy.

In view of the financial situation of the existing Sapienza – let alone the events of 1494 and after – it is hardly surprising that this venture did not get off the ground. Yet the authorities cannot be

---

[85] KIENE, 'I progetti', p. 526.

[86] BURNS, 'Progetti', p. 298.

[87] Above, p. 384; and compare with Turin, where the converted university building also had *botteghe* downstairs; FALCO et al., 'Le istituzioni per l'istruzione superiore in Torino', p. 564.

[88] A point stressed by KIENE, 'La sede del sapere', p. 143: 'come già ai tempi di Ambrogio Lorenzetti, nemmeno adesso l'Università disdegnava di integrarsi nella vita della città. Diversamente dagli ordini monastici e conventuali, essa non si ritirò in chiostri separati e non accessibili, ma si insediò in palazzi sfruttati economicamente e collocati nel mezzo della città.' Earlier (p. 139) the point is made that the role of the teacher in Lorenzetti's *Good Government* is similarly integrated; p. 139.

[89] KIENE, 'La sede del sapere', p. 139.

blamed for trying. The first Sapienza had also begun in the least promising of periods, and ended up transforming the fortunes of the *Studio* itself. Ciampolini goes further, arguing that, although the documentation is poor, the influence of Francesco di Giorgio's plans can be seen in the modifications that were eventually made in the early sixteenth century to the Sapienza complex, assisting its 'passaggio da collegio a palazzo universitario'.[90] Even though it never materialised, the new Sienese Sapienza should be seen as part of the city's long and proud record of attempting to shape and manage the built environment of the community[91] as well as its intellectual, cultural and professional life – and indeed, perhaps as an original attempt to bring aspects of the two together.

---

[90] CIAMPOLINI, 'La Domus Misericordiae', p. 143.

[91] For examples from this period see esp. PERTICI, *La città magnificata*; TURRINI, *"Per honore et utile"*; F. J. D. NEVOLA, 'Siena nel Rinascimento: sistemi urbanistici e strutture istituzionali (1400 circa – 1520)', *BSSP*, 106 (1999), pp. 44-67; IDEM, '"Per Ornato Della Città"'; IDEM, 'Creating a Stage for an Urban Elite: the Re-development of the Via del Capitano and Piazza Postierla in Siena (1487-1520)', in *The World of Savonarola. Italian Elites and Perceptions of Crisis*. Papers from the Conference held at the University of Warwick, 24-31 May 1998, to mark the fifth centenary of the death of Fra Girolamo Savonarola, eds. S. Fletcher and C. Shaw. Warwick Studies in the Humanities (Aldershot, 2000), pp. 182-93; IDEM, 'Revival or Renewal: Defining Civic Identity in Fifteenth-Century Siena', in *Shaping Urban Identity in the Middle Ages*, eds. P. Stabel and M. Boone (Leuven/Apeldoorn, 2000), pp. 109-35.

Conclusion

The Sienese surrender of power to the Medici in 1557 was followed, despite the duke's assurances,[1] by an initial sharp decline in the fortunes of the *Studio*.[2] Cosimo I saw Pisa as the principal Tuscan university, and made no alteration to the law making it the obligatory destination for all Florentine subjects who wished to study. The extent to which Sienese hopes on this score were frustrated can be measured by the fact that in 1564 the *Studio* had only thirteen teachers on the payroll.[3] Under Francesco I there was a significant revival; his commitment first to financial support of the *Studio*, and then by the 1570s to making Siena the principal Tuscan university at the expense of Pisa, brought about a resurgence in the numbers of students and of lecturers (fifty by 1587-8).[4] The rule of Ferdinand I began with two major reforms, the first, in 1589, regulating the terms of, and instituting competition for, lectureships (the only major innovation in the university organisation of the period), and the second, in 1591, reinstating the rector of the *Studio* as a figure distinct from that of the Sapienza.[5] In a little over thirty years, both had been abandoned. The system of appointments to lectureships, though arguably a fairer method, and one which ensured tenure for successful candidates, had killed all hope of attracting non-Sienese teachers,[6] and the reinstatement of the rectorate, a concession to the ultramontanes, proved as unworkable as it had done in the fifteenth century; it first degenerated into a Sienese office and then lapsed altogether.[7]

---

[1] PRUNAI, III, pp. 81-2.

[2] For a survey, see CATONI, 'Le riforme del Granduca'; NARDI, 'Lo Studio di Siena nell'età rinascimentale', pp. 264-5; TRAPANI, 'Statuti senesi'. The change was of course not an abrupt transformation; the Medici influence had been growing before, with repercussions for the *Studio*; cf. NARDI, 'Note sulla scuola giuridica senese'. On the dangers of assuming discontinuity and seeing the fall of the republic in monochrome, ASCHERI, 'Siena senza indipendenza', pp. 10-14.

[3] CASCIO PRATILLI, *L'Università e il Principe*, pp. 16-21.

[4] CASCIO PRATILLI, *L'Università e il Principe*, pt. I, ch. II, esp. pp. 39 *seq.*, 46-7, 53 *seq.*, and 68 *seq.*

[5] MARRARA, *Lo Studio di Siena*; CASCIO PRATILLI, *L'Università e il Principe*, pt. I, ch. III; ZDEKAUER, *Documenti*, part I, doc. I, pp. 13-23; and see CATONI, 'Le riforme del Granduca', p. 54. Marrara should be read in the light of Cascio Pratilli's re-evaluation. On the transitional period see also P. NARDI, 'Note sulla scuola giuridica senese negli anni della caduta della Repubblica', *Studi senesi*, 87 (1975), pp. 195-220. The work of Jonathan Davies on the universities in central Italy in the sixteenth century will revisit these issues.

[6] CASCIO PRATILLI, *L'Università e il Principe*, pp. 88, 92; MARRARA, *Lo Studio di Siena*, ch. I, and p. 149; PRUNAI, III, pp. 101 *seq.* (but cf. pp. 83-93, 122, showing that there were great difficulties in making foreign appointments before this experiment).

[7] CASCIO PRATILLI, *L'Università e il Principe*, pp. 101-5: PRUNAI, III, p. 118: MARRARA, *Lo Studio di Siena*, pp. 132 *seq.*,

The post-republican developments can be summarised as further centralisation (albeit with the ultimate decisions made at one remove), and in consequence provincialisation.[8] But in institutional terms, nearly all the developments of the period had been foreshadowed in the fifteenth and early sixteenth centuries. The concentration of power in the hands of the *Quattro Deputati sullo Studio* is very similar to that of the *Quattro Deputati sopra le condotte*, established in 1533,[9] with a separate magistrature continuing to oversee the Sapienza.[10] The rise of the *Camarlengo* of the Sapienza continued, to the point where he replaced its rector and inherited his title.[11] The rectorate of the university remained almost completely in abeyance till its revival in 1591, at which point the arrangements made bear a strong resemblance to those of the republican period. With its eventual extinction went virtually all the other trappings of the student-university.[12] Other features, such as the academic organisation of the *Studio*, also underwent little change, the only substantial novelty being the foundation of chairs of simples, the Pandects, and, for German students only, *lingua toscana*.[13] But the institutional similarities went much deeper than this. The ground for central direction had been well laid in the republican period; it was the removal of that direction to non-Sienese overlordship, and above all the exposure of Siena not to a Tuscan 'catchment area', as had been hoped, so much as to Tuscan competition, which transformed the *Studio*.[14]

Where does the Sienese experiment fit into the story of the development of universities? What is typical, and what distinctive? In the fifteenth century the Italian *studi*, by now a long way beyond the early stages of evolution, were increasingly 'domesticated', utilitarian, and government-controlled. A number of classificatory schemes have been proposed for them.[15] In particular, university historians have played their part in the debate about the different forms of state in renaissance Italy, and specifically the growth of the territorial state, a dominant theme in the decades since Philip Jones began to

153. Marrara published the list of rectors from 1590 to 1623 (pp. 343-4) from ASS, *mss.* A.119 and A.123). Florence of course had had citizens as rectors since the fifteenth century (SPAGNESI, *Utiliter Edoceri*, p. 28, VERDE, *Lo Studio fiorentino*, I, p. 270). The disappearance of the rectorate in Siena follows that of Bologna (1609; RASHDALL, I, p. 187), and the Perugian rector had disappeared by 1627 (ERMINI, *Storia*, I, pp. 351 *seq.*). In each case, lack of candidates was the reason.

[8] CASCIO PRATILLI, *L'Università e il Principe*, pp. 113-5.

[9] See above, p. 80.

[10] CASCIO PRATILLI, *L'Università e il Principe*, pp. 36, 67; MARRARA, *Lo Studio di Siena*, pp. 105-6; CATONI, 'Le riforme del Granduca', p. 46.

[11] CASCIO PRATILLI, *L'Università e il Principe*, p. 65; MARRARA, *Lo Studio di Siena*, pp. 108, 129, 131; CATONI, loc. cit..

[12] CASCIO PRATILLI, *L'Università e il Principe*, pp. 106 *seq.*; MARRARA, *Lo Studio di Siena*, pp. 91 *seq.*: PRUNAI, III, pp. 116 *seq.*; CATONI, 'Le riforme del Granduca', pp. 54-6.

[13] CASCIO PRATILLI, *L'Università e il Principe*, pp. 79 *seq.*, 93; PRUNAI, III, pp. 97-8, 108; CATONI, 'Le riforme del Granduca', p. 51. The latter two add mathematics as a new chair, but there had been a chair in this in the *rotoli* of 1539-40 and 1545-6 (see Table 3 above, pp. 127-8).

[14] Again, it would be wrong to portray this as coming out of the blue. The proximity of the two *Studi* of Siena and Pisa, and the political relationship between the two states, had led to cooperation as well as rivalry in the past, long before the absorption of Siena into the Grand Duchy; see esp. above, pp. 179-82 and 246 n. 117.

[15] One such is an attempt to see a 'Mediterranean model', to which the royal foundation of Naples belonged; D. PRYDS, '*Studia* as Royal Offices: Mediterranean Universities of Medieval Europe', in *Universities and Schooling in Medieval Society*, eds. W. J. Courtenay and J. Miethke. Education and Society in the Middle Ages and Renaissance, 10 (Leiden, 2000), pp. 83-99. Another is an elaborate seven-fold system distinguishing universities in the first instance according to location (in political capitals or subject towns) and then by other criteria: type of government for those in capitals (royal, papal, ducal, state/patrician – the classification for Siena), relationship to state for those in subject towns ('parachuted', peripherical, provincial). P. DEL NEGRO, 'Il Principe e l'Università in Italia dal XV secolo all'età napoleonica', in *L'università in Italia fra età moderna e contemporanea. Aspetti e momenti*, eds. G. P. Brizzi and A. Varni (Bologna, 1991), pp. 11-27 (p. 14).

shift attention from the ideology-laden antithesis between 'communes' and 'despots' to the issue of size.[16] Silvano's investigation of the *studi* of the three major northern territorial states (Padua, Pavia, Pisa) concludes that the key development of the period was their 'statalizzazione'. But despite not being a 'territorial state' on the same scale as the major powers, as founders and administrators of a *studio* the Sienese authorities demonstrate many of the same characteristics as their larger rivals. All major aspects of the *Studio* were under their aegis. The appointment of the executive officers of the *Studio* (the *Savi*) and the key officers of the Sapienza was firmly within the framework of the local political system. Decision-making was brought more and more closely under the control of the regime (the *Balìa*, and in the sixteenth century the *Quattro Deputati sopra le condotte*). Student power and representation was strictly limited and controlled in the form of extensive intervention in the election and functions of the rector. Teachers, as communal employees, were on a tight leash, and had the terms of their *condotte* repeatedly regulated; they might be prestigious figures, but they had no opportunity for collective action; more to the point, their increasingly close identification with the political elite meant that by and large they had no need or desire to take such action.[17] Administrative procedures such as those for the hiring and payment of teachers were streamlined over time, the Sapienza estates were rationalised and the length of stay for students in the college was made more flexible. And in the endless search for fresh resources, Siena, by taxing the clergy and the hospital of S. Maria della Scala, set an early example which was later emulated by Florence.

These examples are not, of course, senses in which Siena's extensive control of its *Studio* was 'advanced' (a misleadingly teleological way of looking at the issue); they derive largely from the fact that the *Studio* had begun as a communal initiative, and indeed was never anything else. But it should in any case not be surprising to find a commune engaging in the same practices and policies as the larger states. The universities were all locked into the same competitive system, in which no individual institution could afford to step seriously out of line. The parameters of academic convention were much more influential than local particularities.[18] In the end the critical feature of the large territorial states was indeed size, and it was to this that Siena eventually fell victim. In the fifteenth century, however, not being in that league was no obstacle to the running of a *Studio*. The smaller-scale operation in Siena was clearly attractive to many, and if the financial clout of Florence, as wielded for example by a determined Lorenzo de' Medici in his relaunch of the *Studio* in Pisa, could outstrip that of its smaller neighbour when it came to salaries and prestige, over the century this was effectively counterbalanced by the persistence demonstrated by Siena, and the continuity with which that persistence was rewarded.

---

[16] P. J. JONES, 'Communes and Despots: the City-State in Late Medieval Italy', *Transactions of the Royal Historical Society*, 5th ser., 15 (1965), pp. 71-96; for a conspectus of research see J. KIRSHNER (ed.), *The Origins of the State in Italy 1300-1600* (Chicago, Il., 1995).

[17] This summation does not imply acceptance of the whole 'social control' theory as caricatured and attacked by B. DOOLEY, 'Social Control and the Italian Universities: From Renaissance to Illuminismo', *Journal of Modern History*, 61 (1989), pp. 205-39.

[18] It is worth observing that there has also been a discussion in German university historiography about the differences between civic and princely foundations, coming to conclusions very similar to the above. H. KOLLER, 'Stadt und Universität im Spätmittelalter', in *Stadt und Universität*, pp. 9-26; R. SCHMIDT, 'Kräfte, Personen und Motive bei der Gründung der Universitäten Rostock (1419) und Greifswald (1456)', in *Beiträge zur pommerschen und mecklenburgischen Geschichte. Vorträge der wissenschaftlichen Tagungen "Pommern – Mecklenburg" 1976-1979, veranstaltet von der Historischen Kommission für Pommern*, ed. R. Schmitt (Marburg/Lahn, 1981), pp. 1-33, repr. in his *Fundatio et Confirmatio Universitatis*, pp. 215*-47* (esp. p. 220*); and H. BOOCKMANN, *Wissen und Widerstand. Geschichte der deutschen Universität* (Berlin, 1999), pp. 92 *seq.*

The type of government did of course make a difference. No prince meant no figurehead, no individual fount of authority, no direct personal patronage from the top, and no court. Fioravanti has suggested that one consequence of this was a lower priority in the *Studio* for humanistic studies,[19] and, drawing on the example of Siena, Avellini has pointed out that the preoccupation of republics with the traditional professions meant that they were less ready to incorporate these 'new' disciplines into their universities.[20] This may be true; but it is also a matter of nuance. Humanistic studies remained a minority element of Italian university curricula, peripheral and less well paid than the traditional subjects. For decades the essential activities of the humanists had been conducted predominantly outside the structured framework of teaching institutions, so it is unsurprising that this continued to be the case, in Siena as well as in the more obvious centres, and particularly those with a court. Siena did have humanists teaching within the *Studio*, though after Filelfo it relied overwhelmingly on local teachers (as in other disciplines) more than on outsiders. But criticism of the fact that the Sienese did not accord humanists a higher profile within their *Studio* is misplaced in another sense. The key to an understanding of the problem lies not with the authorities, nor with the teachers, but with the students. The 1533 matriculation list shows a clear distinction between the mixed population of those who were studying the traditional subjects of law and arts/medicine, and the overwhelmingly Sienese, and for that matter patrician, students enlisted for *humanitas*.[21] Very similar conclusions can be drawn from an analysis of the students who attended poetry and rhetoric lectures in Florence after the traditional university subjects had been relocated to Pisa.[22] The humanistic disciplines did not constitute a degree subject in fifteenth-century Italy. So Siena's modest but continuous provision of lectures in such subjects was clearly aimed in a different direction. Law and arts/medicine were the subjects that drew students, especially ultramontanes, from elsewhere; and humanistic studies was one area in which it would have been difficult for Siena to mount serious competition to other centres. From the point of view of the well-being of the *Studio*, the policy was entirely logical.

What accounts for the success of this institution? What the Sienese were offering was a medium-sized, compact, well-organised and closely supervised university in a relatively peaceful city. The *Studio* occupied a prominent place in the town, was valued culturally and economically by the authorities and by citizens, and given privileges and protection in accordance with that esteem. Its size and location afforded opportunities for the cultivation of relations and friendships among fellow-students or fellow-teachers, and across categories, between teachers, students and other residents – what we now call networking. It was an institution run by authorities who were and remained firmly committed to it, who paid tireless attention to detail, exercised sound pragmatic judgment, and were unafraid to innovate and exploit opportunities. The feature that encapsulates this best is the Casa della Sapienza. The Sapienza really was a college for its time. Like the *Studio* itself, it was the product of the persistent and pragmatic aspirations of its sponsors. From its *ad hoc* beginnings, with borrowed statutes and

[19] FIORAVANTI, 'Alcuni aspetti della cultura umanistica senese', pp. 166-7.

[20] 'Il "ritardo" o la precarietà dell'affermazione universitaria umanistica nei cosidetti regimi popolari – rispetto invece alla precoce e pacifica alleanza fra letterati e monarchi – non è frutto di sordità culturale, ma di una permanenza ideologica che mantiene subalterna l'area disciplinare non coincidente con le "professioni", concrete del giurista e del medico.' AVELLINI, 'Università e umanesimo', p. 29, also contrasting Siena's refusal to give the humanist Francesco Filelfo the pay rise which would have retained him, while going to unprecedented lengths in this respect for the lawyers Niccolò Tedeschi and Francesco Accolti.

[21] See Table 5 above, p. 240, and see p. 245.

[22] Above, p. 245 n. 109.

quick reversals of purpose, it rapidly became a cornerstone of government relations with others in the diplomatic and cultural spheres. In terms of patronage, there is a sense in which the Sapienza, almost more than the *Studio*, can be described as Siena's answer to the courts of the *signori*. The Sapienza is also Siena's lasting contribution to university history. The new institution does not really fit into any of the categories of college that have been defined to date.[23] Taking resources and its original framework from pious institutions, like the majority of foundations, it soon 'turned secular', as the charging of entrance fees gave it an increasingly elitist flavour. This innovation proved influential; by end of the century, others had begun to imitate it, and the whole trend can be seen as an antecedent of the phenomenon of the 'aristocratisation' of the universities most visible in the sixteenth century. The Sapienza was also unique in its relationship to the *Studio* as a whole. While it began as a new element, administered by the town authorities in the same way as the university but without reference to it, by the late fifteenth century it had become a natural focus for teaching and eventually for the university as a whole; its rector started to assume the vice-rectorship of the *Studio*, and by the 1530s this role was enshrined constitutionally in the method of election of the student rector. Elsewhere, the relationship between colleges and universities could be complex, and sometimes fraught;[24] in Siena, the process whereby the college reached this unusually dominant position appears to have been a natural and a largely harmonious one, again largely thanks to the fact that the authorities were responsible for both institutions and kept them under such close supervision.

These two features, constant communal control and the Casa della Sapienza, were Siena's particular contribution to the process of the development of universities, away from their conflictual roots, and towards a state-run, utilitarian system. The Sienese example also reminds us that this process goes well back in time, crossing the chronological boundaries of those pernicious labels 'medieval' and 'renaissance' with which we seem to be lumbered, and moreover challenging, at least in some respects, the conceptual distinctions that these terms are supposed to represent.

[23] See J. M. FLETCHER, 'The History of Academic Colleges: Problems and Prospects', in *I Collegi universitari in Europa*, pp. 13-22.

[24] Perceptive comments on the complexities of the relationship between colleges and universities are in A. SEIFERT, 'Die Universitätskollegien – eine historisch-typologische Übersicht', in *Lebensbilder deutscher Stiftungen, 3: Stiftungen aus Vergangenheit und Gegenwart* (Tübingen, 1974), pp. 355-72, esp. p. 357.

BIBLIOGRAPHY

1. *Archival and manuscript sources*

BOLOGNA, Archivio di Stato

Assunteria di Studio: Riformatori dello Studio: Appuntazioni dei Lettori, 1465-1512

FLORENCE, Archivio di Stato

Signoria, Dieci di Balìa, Otto di pratica: Legazioni e Commissarie, Missive e Responsive 27
Studio Fiorentino e Pisano, 1357-1568 (formerly *Repubblica: Ufficiali dello Studio*) 7

FLORENCE, Biblioteca Nazionale Centrale

ms. Magl. XXV, 415 (L. F. DEL MIGLIORE, *Zibaldone Istorico*)

PAVIA, Biblioteca Civica 'Bonetta'

ms. II.39 (R. MAIOCCHI, *Regesto e trascrizione di documenti universitari pavesi del secolo XV*)

PERUGIA, Archivio di Stato

Collegio della Sapienza Vecchia, Miscellanea I

PERUGIA, Biblioteca Augusta

ms. 1239 (*Le costituzioni della casa degli Scolari di San Gregorio*)

Siena, Archivio Arcivescovile

101-8 (*Bollari*, 1408-99)
4420 (*Notai e cancellieri della curia:* Protocollo dei rogiti di ser Antonio di Gandino da Calci, 1409-23)
6435-8 (*Protocolli degli atti di laurea*, 1484-1557)
6508-10 (*Spogli e Regesti*)

Siena, Archivio di Stato

Archivio Sergardi-Biringucci, ms. A.II
Balìa
    1-45 (Deliberazioni, 1455-1500)
    253 (Appendice alle Deliberazioni, 1496-1516)
    396-416 (Copialettere, 1455-99)
    488-560 (Carteggio, 1455-1501)
Biccherna
    1-3 (Statuti, 1298-1500)
    238-347, 369-70 (Entrate e uscite, 1358-1495)
    416-56 (Memoriali, 1364-1425)
    457-79 (Significazioni, 1376-1472)
    591-611 (Misture, 1360-1429)
    694-97 (Ufficiali, 1360-64)
    736 (Banditi e carcerati, 1385-1430)
Capitoli 5 ('*Caleffetto*'), 19, 28, 107, 124-27, 159, 194
Casa della Misericordia
    1-2 (Statuti, 1318-1521)
    31 (Processi, 1306-1492)
    36 (Possessioni, 1444-1538)
Concistoro
    11-805 (Deliberazioni, 1358-1500)
    1595-1709 (Copialettere, 1363-1500)
    1770-72 (Copiarii, 1400-83)
    1774-2078 (Carteggio, 1355-1515)
    2111-18 (Scritture Concistoriali, Proposte di Savi, 1295-1483)
    2119-24 (Scritture Concistoriali, Ufficiali del Comune, 14th century -1485)
    2136-39 (Scritture Concistoriali, Luoghi Pii e Studio, 14th century -1499)
    2140-61 (Scritture Concistoriali, Particolari, 1299-1483)
    2171-93 (Scritture Concistoriali, Scritture Concistoriali, 1272-1499)
    2301-7 (Lettere senza data, 14th - 17th centuries)
    2308 (Cifrari, 14th - 16th centuries)
    2309-14 (Carte varie, 14th - 17th centuries)
    2315-16 (Riformagioni, 1244-1718)
    2357 (Statuto sulle precedenze, 1514-1608)
    2395 (Statuto delle vacazioni, 1384-16th century)
Consiglio Generale
    161-246 (Deliberazioni, 1358-1524)
    428, 434, 438 (Libri dei Bossoli, 1466-80)
    726, 768

Diplomatico, Archivio Generale, 16 May 1401, 13 May 1404, 7 Feb 1413(=1414), 27 Apr 1413, 5 Dec 1413, 8 Dec 1413, 6 Apr 1421, 3 Dec 1442, 17 Jul 1451, 15 Dec 1453, 22 Jan 1461(=1462), 11 Jun 1462, 9 Sept 1466, 6 Oct 1466, 17 Mar 1466(=1467), 22 Oct 1467, 6 Sept 1468, 8 Dec 1468, 17 Jun 1469, 13 Nov 1471, 26 Dec 1473, 20 Dec 1475, 17 Jun 1476, 3 Oct 1481, 7 May 1482, 9 Dec 1489, 25 Jun 1496, 11 Feb 1509(=1510), 21 Aug 1514, 26 Jun 1517, 18 Aug 1517, 1 Dec 1519, 27 Jan 1527(=1528), 25 Sept 1532, 19 Jul 1549

Diplomatico, Biblioteca Pubblica, 28 Feb 1423(=24), 31 May 1430, 19 Feb 1437(=38), 13 Aug 1549, 26 Nov 1553

Diplomatico, Pergamene Bichi-Borghesi, 31 (1477), 33 (20 Oct 1480), 41 (1474)

Diplomatico, Opera Metropolitana, 27 Sep 1440, 14 Oct 1463

Diplomatico, Convento di S. Domenico, 1 Feb 1428(=1429), 24 May 1364, 1 Feb 1429

Diplomatico, Riformagioni, 11 Dec 1399, 18 Oct 1426, 14 Jul 1447, 18 Jul 1466, 10 Jul 1468 (in 'Busta 5')

Diplomatico, Riformagioni Leone, 29 Sep 1433

Diplomatico, S. Agostino di Siena, 8 Sep 1450

Diplomatico, Spedale di S. Maria della Scala, 1442 (see Arch. Generale), 24 Nov 1448, 24 Nov 1448, 28 Nov 1448

Diplomatico, Tolomei, 11 Aug 1440

Diplomatico, Università degli Studi, 2 Sept 1418, 8 Oct 1418, 6 Feb 1419(=1420), 18 Mar 1419(=1420), 23 Apr 1422, 13 Dec 1424, 16 Dec 1424 (=30 Dec 1424), 27 Dec 1424, 23 Jul 1428, 26 Aug 1429 (2 docs.), 29 Apr 1430 (2 docs.), 19 Jul 1441, 10 Dec 1448, 18 Jun 1465 (=28 Jun), 12 Oct 1486

Estimo 131 (Tavola delle Possessioni, 1318-20: San Donato a lato dei Montanini, including possessions of the Casa della Misericordia)

Gabella dei Contratti

    4, 9 (Statuti e tariffe, 1388-1585)

    24 (Entrata e uscita, 1473-80)

Governatore

    929 (Rescritti e ordini sovrani 1790: *Relazione Sopra Lo Spurgo de'Libri d'Amministrazione dell'Università*)

    1048 (Ordini Relativi all'Università della Sapienza, 1590-1784)

Lira

    12-15, 19-21, 24-28, 32-33, 35-37, 39-54, 56-66, 68-72, 74-79, 82-86, 88-94, 97-104, 106-110 (Libri della Lira, 1366-1508)

    136-49, 151-64, 166-80, 182-209, 211-33 (Denunzie, 1453-98)

    411, 414 (Preste per lo Studio, 1405, 1416)

Mercanzia 690 (late 15th century)

Notarile ante-cosimiano

    220-26 (Bartolomeo di Giacomo da Radicondoli, 1381-1429)

    266 (Angelo di ser Guido d'Orlando da Siena, 1396-98)

    285-87 (Giovanni di Bindo di Piero da Rapolano, 1420-28)

    292 (Antonio di Guido da Calci, 1412-14)

    311 (Giovanni di Benedetto Giannelli da Casole d'Elsa, 1442-45)

    383-84 (Filippo di ser Giuliano Cantoni da Casole, 1455-65)

    478 (Bartolomeo di Rigoccio Lambardi da Siena, 1440-84)

    583-84 (Francesco di Antonio di Niccolò da Siena, 1461-83)

    589 (Bartolomeo di Filippo Ballati da Siena, 1462-69)

    600 (Cristoforo di ser Filippo Cantoni da Siena, 1465-75)

    652-53, 655, 657-60, 662, 667 (Benedetto di Stefano Biliotti da Siena, 1468-1519)

    681-82, 691, 694 (Lorenzo di Lando Sborgheri da Siena, 1471-98)

698, 703 (Bernardino di Pietro Politi da Siena, 1471-81)

713, 715 (Bartolomeo di Leonardo Pieri da Grosseto, 1472-1513)

799 (Leonardo di Antonio Gesti da Volterra, 1476-93)

800-801 (Francesco di Giacomo Carnevali da Montalcino, 1476-1512)

856, 858 (Feliciano di ser Neri Nerini da Sarteano, 1452-1518)

879-80, 886 (Alessandro di Niccolò Grammatica da Siena, 1480-1514)

908 (Gabriele di Sensio di Paolo da Siena, 1482)

967-68 (Cristoforo di Bartolomeo Fungai da Siena, 1484-96)

1018-20 (Matteo di Gaspero Andreucci da Siena, 1487-1510)

1042 (Magio di Taddeo Bargagli da Siena, 1488-1522)

1053 (Tommaso di Guido da Casole, 1488-1502)

1060 (Giacomo di Benvenuto Tolosani da Siena, 1488-1502)

1137 (Lorenzo di Simone da Siena, 1491-1523)

1138 (Mattia di Cristoforo Selva da Montefollonico, 1491-96)

2207 (Anton Maria di Cesare Mariotti da Asciano, 1531-36)

2720 (Persio di Mariotto Mariotti da Siena, 1546-50)

Ospedale di S. Maria della Scala

20-25 (Deliberazioni, 1379-1551)

72, 93, 105, 109 (Contratti e Protocolli, 14th - 15th centuries)

177 (Ricordi e Memorie, 15th century)

515-17 (Libri a Ricogliare e Bilanci, 1354-1412), 523 (1460s)

852-53 (Entrata e Uscita di Denari, 1385-1416)

1406-7 (Grancia di Grosseto, 1309-1778)

1423 (Memorie, 15th century)

5931-36 (Annali, 1364-1500)

Patrimonio dei Resti Ecclesiastici 2189, 3536-37

Quattro Maestri del Sale 6 ('Libro dele boche'), 20-5 (Deliberazioni)

Regolatori

1 (Statuto)

2-13, 16 (Revisioni, 1362-1537)

58-59, 63-64 (Deliberazioni, 1487-94)

Spedaletti Soppressi

48 (Spedale di S. Andrea de'Salimbeni, 1380)

55 (Grosseto, Spedale della Misericordia, 1388)

Statuti di Siena

25 (1334-1472), 30 (1354-92), 31 (1355-67), 32 (1355-1410), 33 (1355-98), 34 (1357-67), 35 (1369-71), 36 (1382-8), 37 (1385-6), 38 (1403-9), 39 (1412-66), 40 (1419-59), 41 (1422-44), 42 (mid 15th century), 43 (end 15th century), 44 (1433-80), 45 (1435), 46 (1433-60), 47 (14th-15th centuries)

Università degli Studi

2-6, 16 (Deliberazioni, 1473-1552, 1779-93)

17 (Bastardelli di deliberazioni, 1533-41)

19 (Lettere ai Savi, 1441-1569)

20-22 (Otto sopra la Condotta, 1535-1788)

36-39 (Repertori)

40 (1565-1777: copies of earlier documents)

41 (Collegio dei Giureconsulti, 1418)

100 (Collegio germanico, 15th-16th centuries)

108 (Libreria Pubblica, Inventario)

109-10 (Casa della Sapienza, Statuti, 1531-42)

126-28 (Casa della Sapienza, Carte varie)

260 (Miscellanea)

mss.

A.119: G. BICHI, *Catalogo de Rettori della Casa della Misericordia* (1725)

A.140: G. BICHI, *Ruolo di Dottori Leggenti nella Sapienza di Siena. Parte Prima – dall'Anno 1513 all'Anno 1625*

B.16-20: *Repertorio Generale delle Scritture Esistenti nelle Quattro Casse del Cassone dell'Illustrissimo Collegio di Balìa* (1725)

B.22: spoglio Diplomatico, Riformagioni

B.31-33: A. SESTIGIANI, *Spoglio de' Contratti esistenti nell'Archivio della Sapienza...* (1695-99)

B.40: spoglio Diplomatico, Opera Metropolitana

B.43: spoglio Diplomatico, Spedale di S. Maria della Scala

B.55: spoglio Diplomatico, Patrimonio Resti Ecclesiastici: Convento di S. Domenico

B.66-67: *Spoglio di Contratti Spettanti alla Casa della Misericordia* (1700-1804)

B.74-76: spoglio delle pergamene Bichi-Borghesi

B.82: A. SESTIGIANI, *Repertorio di Strumenti Antichi della Sapienza* (1695)

B.91-94: spoglio Diplomatico, Archivio Generale

B.96 *ter*: spoglio Diplomatico, Biblioteca Pubblica

B.98: spoglio Casa della Misericordia, contratti

C.10-12 *bis*: spoglio Concistoro

C.16: spoglio Balìa et al. (incl. Sapienza)

C.18: spoglio Balìa

C.19: *Spoglio di Lettere scritte alla Repubblica*

C.51: *Statuti et Ordini per la Casa della Misericordia. Et Ordini e Costituzioni per li Scolari della Sapienza*. Transcription by T. Mocenni (1725)

C.51 *bis*: S. LANDI, *Indice 1777 delle Filze, e Deliberazioni che sono nell'Armario dipinto coll'Arme della Sapienza* (1777-83)

C.51 *ter*: A. SESTIGIANI, *Indice di Libri diversi spettanti alla pia Casa della Misericordia, dal 1300, al 1587*

D.6: G. A. PECCI, *Raccolta universale di tutte le iscrizioni, arme e altri monumenti, sì antichi, come moderni, esistenti nel terzo di Camollia fino a questo presente anno MDCCXXXI. Libro Terzo*

D.64: *Forma dell'Elezione de Rettori dello Studio. 1613*

D.88: *Miscellanea di cose spettanti alla Città, e Stato di Siena* (1725)

D.107-111: G. MACCHI, *Memorie*

D.131: *Attinenze d'Antichità*

SIENA, Biblioteca Comunale

mss.

A.III.19: *Relazione di tutti i privilegi, ch'è stato concesso dell'excelso Concistoro sanese à tutti i Castelli...della Città, e Stato di Siena dall'anno MCCC. in quà.*

A.III.33: *Raccolta degli Autori Senesi*

A.V.1: *Miscellanea istorica*

A.VI.24: *Memorie antiche di Siena e di Colle*

A.VII.1: A. SESTIGIANI, *Spogli delle pergamene dell'archivio della Casa della Sapienza di Siena, 1195-1695* (copy)

A.VII.11-14: *Spogli delle Deliberazioni del Consiglio Generale*

A.VII.23: *Spoglio delle Deliberazioni del Concistoro*

A.IX.2: G. A. PECCI, *Rettori dello Spedale della Misericordia, Rettori dello Studio, e della Casa della Sapienza dal 1273 al 1757*

A.XI.1: *Collegio Teologico dell'Università di Siena. Libri delle incorporazioni e delle deliberazioni, 1472-1737*

A.XI.12: *Inventario dei mobili che si consegnavano a i giovani studenti che convivevano nella Casa o Collegio dello Studio di Siena dal 1478 al 1547*

A.XI.29: A. B. FANCELLI, *Origine dello Studio Sanese*

B.IV.28: G. A. PECCI, *Zibaldone per la Storia dell'Università di Siena* (1749)

B.VI.15: *Spoglio di Strumenti dal 988 al 1550*

C.III.2: *Obituario S. Domenico, 1336-1596*

C.IV.6, C.IV.26, C.V.7, C.V.16: *Benvoglienti Miscellanee*

E.VI.9: G. FALUSCHI, *Disordinate Memorie per formare la Storia dello Studio, e Università di Siena* (collected by Ettore Romagnoli, 1835)

E.VI.19: G. FALUSCHI, *Spoglio di Archivi per Materia, O-Z*

L.V.14: *Notizie de' Pittori Sanesi*

P.II.22: BORGHESI, *Notizi dei Luoghi e delle Cose di Siena*

S.IV.8: A. DI SAN GALLO, *Taccuino*

VATICAN CITY

Reg. Lat. 131

2. Published historiographical and literary sources

This list includes the historiographical and literary sources consulted. Because of the profusion in this field of works combining edition and analysis, books and articles containing edited historical documents have been included among secondary works.

AGNOLO DI TURA DEL GRASSO, *Cronaca Senese*, in *Rerum Italicarum Scriptores*², vol. XV, part VI (Bologna, 1933-5), pp. 255-564.

ALIOTTI, HIERONYMUS, *Epistolae et opuscola*, 2 vols. (Arezzo, 1769).

ALLEGRETTI, A., *Diari scritti da Allegretto Allegretti delle Cose Sanesi del suo Tempo*, in *Rerum Italicarum Scriptores*, XXIII (Milan, 1733), cols. 767-860.

AMMANNATI PICCOLOMINI, I., *Lettere (1444-1479)*, ed. P. Cherubini. Pubblicazioni degli Archivi di Stato. Fonti, 25 (Rome, 1997).

Annali Sanesi (1385-1422), in *Rerum Italicarum Scriptores*, XIX (Milan, 1731), coll. 387-428.

BANDINI, F. T. (Francesco Tommaso di Giovanni Bandini de' Bartolomei), *Historia Senensis*, in *Rerum Italicarum Scriptores*, XX (1731), cols. 23-26.

BANDINI, G., *Historia senensis ab anno MCCCCII usque ad annum MCCCCXXII, auctore Johanne Bandino de Bartholomeis....* in *Rerum Italicarum Scriptores*, XX (Milan, 1731), cols. 5-64.

BARNABA DI NANNI, *Barnaba Senese, Epistolario*, ed. G. Ferraù (Palermo, 1979).

BENZI, U., *Scriptum de somno et vigilia*, eds. G. Fioravanti and A. Idato. Università degli Studi di Siena; Bibliotheca Studii Senensis, 3 (Florence, 1991).

BERNARDINO DA SIENA, *Le prediche volgari di San Bernardino. Predicazione a Siena, 1425*, ed. C. Cannarozzi, 2 vols. (Florence, 1958).

–, *Prediche Volgari sul Campo di Siena, 1427*, ed. C. Delcorno, 2 vols. (Milan, 1989).

BRACCIOLINI, POGGIO, *Lettere*, II. *Epistolarum familiarorum libri*, ed. H. Harth (Florence, 1984).

CACCIALUPI, G. B., *Modus studendi in utroque iure*. Intr/tr. S. di Noto Marrella (Parma, 1995).

–, *De modo studendi et vita doctorum tractatus* (Venetiis, 1472).

CORTESI, P., *De Cardinalatu libri tres* (Casa Cortese, 1510).

DATI, A., *Opera* (Senis, 1503).

DEI, A., *Chronicon Senense Italice scriptum ab Andrea Dei, et ab Angelo Turae continuatum…* in *Rerum Italicarum Scriptores*, XV (Milan, 1729), cols. 11-294.

ERASMUS, D., *Collected Works of Erasmus; Letters* (Toronto, 1974-).

FABRONI, A., *Laurentii Medicis magnifici vita* (Pisa, 1784).

FALUSCHI, G., *Breve relazione delle cose notabili della Città di Siena* (Siena, 1784, rev. 1815).

FARULLI, G., *Notizie Istoriche dell'Antica e Nobile Città di Siena* (Lucca, 1722, repr. Bologna, 1975).

FECINI, T., *Cronaca senese di Tommaso Fecini (1431-1479)*, in *Rerum Italicarum Scriptores²*, vol. XV, pt. VI (Bologna, 1939).

GERALDINI, A., *Vita Angeli Geraldini* see PETER, *Die Vita Angeli Geraldini des Antonio Geraldini*.

GIGLI, G., *Diario Sanese* (Lucca, 1723).

MALAVOLTI, O., *Dell'historia di Siena* (Venetiis, 1599, repr. Bologna, 1968).

MEDICI, LORENZO DE', *Lettere*, VIII, ed. H. Butters (Florence, 2001).

MONTAURI, T., *Cronaca Senese*, in *Rerum Italicarum Scriptores²*, vol. XV, part VI (Bologna, 1933-5), pp. 689-835.

MÜLLNER, K. (ed.), *Reden und Briefe italienischer Humanisten: ein Betrag zur Geschichte der Pädagogik der Humanismus* (Vienna, 1899, repr. Munich, 1970, ed. B. Gerl, Humanistische Bibliothek. Abhandlungen und Texte).

PECCI, G. A., *Memorie storico-critiche della Città di Siena che servono alla Vita Civile di Pandolfo Petrucci* (Siena, 1755-60, repr. 1988).

–, *Ristretto delle cose più notabili della città di Siena a uso dei forestieri* (Siena, 1759, repr. 1761).

–, *Storia del vescovado della città di Siena* (Lucca, 1748).

– and P. PECCI, *Giornale Sanese (1715-1794)*, eds. E. Innocenti and G. Mazzoni (Siena, 2000).

PETRUCCI, A., *Epistole* see Pertici (ed.), *Tra politica e cultura nel primo Quattrocento senese*.

PICCOLOMINI, E. S., *Enee Silvii Piccolomini, postea Pii PP II, De viris illustribus*, ed. A. van Heck. Biblioteca Apostolica Vaticana, Studi e Testi, 341 (Vatican City, 1991).

Repetitio Zanini de martulibus coqui, in PANDOLFI and ARTESE, *Teatro goliardico*, pp. 293-310.

Sanctiones reformatae collegii theologorum senensis universitatis (Siena, 1651).

TIZIO, S., *Historiae Senenses*. vol. I.I.I ed. M. Doni Garfagnini, *Rerum Italicarum Scriptores Recentiores*, 6 (Rome, 1992); vol. I.II.I ed. G. Tomasi Stussi, *RISR*, 10 (Rome, 1995), and vol. III.IV ed. P. Pertici, *RISR*, 12 (1998).

VASARI, G., *Le vite de' più eccellenti pittori scultori ed architettori*, ed. G. Milanesi, 9 vols. (Florence, 1878-1885).

ZAMBOTTI, B., *Diario ferrarese dall'anno 1476 sino al 1504*, a cura di G. Pardi, in *Rerum Italicarum Scriptores²* (Bologna, 1928-1937), t. XXIV, parte VII.

ZAZZERA, F., *Della Nobiltà dell'Italia*, 2 vols. (Naples, 1615-28).

3. Published documentary sources and secondary works

This list includes all works referred to in the text, most of the Sienese material consulted, and a selection only of works consulted on university history generally.

ANON, 'Arti esercitate in Siena nel 1311', *Miscellanea storica senese*, 4 (1896), pp. 57-9.

ANON, 'Barzi, Benedetto', *DBI*, 7 (1965), pp. 20-5.

ANON, 'Benzi, Ugo', *DBI*, 8 (1966), pp. 720-3.

ANON, 'Biglia, Andrea', in *DBI*, 10 (1968), pp. 413-5.

ANON, 'Elenco nominativo dei giustiziati in Siena dall'anno 1476 al 1491', *BSSP*, 29 (1922), pp. 100-111.

ABBONDANZA, R., 'Bartolini, Onofrio', *DBI*, 6 (1964), pp. 617-22.

Acta Graduum Academicorum Gymnasii Patavini: 1406-1450, eds. G. Zonta and G. Brotto (Padua, 1922, repr. 1970); *1451-60*, ed. M. P. Ghezzo (Padua, 1990); *1461-70*, ed. E. Martellozzo Forin (Padua, 1969-82); 1471-1500, ed. E. Martellozzo Forin, 4 vols. (Rome-Padua, 2001).

ADAMI, F. E., 'L'insegnamento del diritto canonico nello Studio di Ferrara tra il XV e il XVI secolo', *Annali di storia delle università italiane*, 8 (2004), pp. 37-60; repr. in *Per una storia dell'Università di Ferrara* (Bologna, 2004), pp. 11-34.

ADAMS, N., 'The Life and Times of Pietro dell'Abaco, a Renaissance Estimator from Siena (active 1457-1486)', *Zeitschrift für Kunstgeschichte*, 48 (1985), pp. 384-95.

ADORNI BRACCESI, S. and M. ASCHERI see *Politica e cultura nelle repubbliche italiane.*

A Ennio Cortese. Scritti promossi da D. Maffei e raccolti a cura di I. Birocchi, M. Caravale, E. Conte and V. Petronio, II (Rome, 2001).

ALTMANN, W. (ed.), *Die Urkunden Kaiser Sigmunds (1410-1437)*, in *Regesta Imperii*, ed. J. F. Böhmer, XI, 2 vols. (Innsbruck, 1897-1900).

ANGELETTI, G. and A. BERTINI, *La Sapienza Vecchia* (Perugia, 1993).

ANGELUCCI, P., 'Gli Umiliati a Siena e la chiesa del borgo franco di Paganico', in *Chiesa e società dal secolo IV ai nostri giorni. Studi storici in onore del P. Ilarino da Milano*, I (Rome, 1979), pp. 261-89.

Antica Legislazione della Repubblica di Siena, ed. M. ASCHERI (Siena, 1993).

AQUARONE, B., *Gli ultimi anni della storia repubblicana di Siena (1551-1555)* (Siena, 1869).

ARBESMANN, R., 'Andrea Biglia Augustinian Friar and Humanist', *Analecta Augustiniana*, 28 (1965), pp. 154-218.

ARBIZZONI, G., 'Giovanni da Spoleto (Giovanni di ser Buccio da Spoleto)', *DBI*, 56 (2001), pp. 227-30.

ARCHIVIO DI STATO DI SIENA, *Archivio del Consiglio Generale del Comune di Siena. Inventario.* Pubblicazioni degli Archivi di Stato, 9 (Rome, 1952).

–, *Archivio della Biccherna del Comune di Siena. Inventario.* Pubblicazioni degli Archivi di Stato, 12 (Rome, 1953).

–, *Archivio del Concistoro del Comune di Siena. Inventario.* Pubblicazioni degli Archivi di Stato, 10 (Rome, 1952).

–, *Archivio di Balìa. Inventario.* Pubblicazioni degli Archivi di Stato, 26 (Rome, 1957).

–, *Guida-Inventario dell'Archivio dello Stato.* Pubblicazioni degli Archivi di Stato, 5 (vol. I, Rome, 1951), 6 (vol. II, Rome, 1951), 92 (vol. III, Rome, 1977).

ARRIZABALAGA, J., 'Tradició medieval i cultura humanista: la medicina universitària: les activitats editorials de Francesc Argilagues i Guillem Caldentei per a les premses italianes de les acaballes del segle XV', in *Al tombant de l'edat mitjana. Tradició medieval i cultura humanista.* XVIII Jornales d'Etudis Históricis Locals, ed. M. Barceló Crespi (Palma de Mallorca, 2000), pp. 175-87.

–, GARCIA-BALLESTER, J. and SALMÓN, F., 'A propósito de las relaciones intelectuales entre la Corona de Aragón e Italia (1470-1520): los estudiantes de medicina valencianos en los estudios generales de Siena, Pisa, Ferrara y Padua', *Dynamis. Acta Hispanica ad Medicinae Scientiarumque Historiam Illustrandam*, 9 (1989), pp. 117-47.

ASCHBACH, J., *Geschichte Kaisers Sigmund's*, 4 vols. (Hamburg, 1838-45).

ASCHERI, M. see *Antica Legislazione della Repubblica di Siena.*

–, 'Assemblee, democrazia comunale e cultura politica: dal caso della Repubblica di Siena (secc. XIV-XV)', in *Studi in onore di Arnaldo d'Addario*, ed. L. Borgia, F. De Luca, P. Viti and R. M. Zaccaria (Lecce, 1995), IV/I, pp. 1141-55; repr. with minor changes in *Contributi alla storia parlamentare europea (secoli XIII-XX)*, ed. M. S. Corciulo. Atti del 43° Congresso ICHRPI, Camerino, Palazzo Ducale 14-17 Luglio 1993. Studies presented to the International Commission for the History of Representative and Parliamentary Institutions, 78 (Camerino, 1996), pp. 77-99.

M. ASCHERI, 'I "consilia" dei giuristi: una fonte per il tardo Medioevo', *Bullettino dell'Istituto Storico Italiano per il Medio Evo*, 105 (2003), pp. 305-34.

–, 'Il *consilium* dei giuristi medievali', in *Consilium. Teorie e pratiche del consigliare nella cultura medievale*, eds. C. Casagrande, C. Crisciani and S. Vecchio. Micrologus' Library, 10 (Florence, 2004), pp. 243-58.

–, *Dedicato a Siena* (Siena, 1989).

–, 'La decisione nelle corti giudiziarie italiane del Tre-Quattrocento e il caso della Mercanzia di Siena', in *Judicial Records, Law Reports, and the Growth of Case Law*, ed. J. H. Baker. Comparative Studies in Continental and Anglo-American Legal History, 5 (Berlin, 1989), pp. 101-22; repr. as 'Giustizia ordinaria, giustizia di mercanti'.

–, 'Le fonti e la flessibilità del diritto comune: il paradosso del *consilium sapientis*', in *Legal Consulting in the Civil Law Tradition*, eds. M. Ascheri, I. Baumgärtner and J. Kirshner. Studies in Comparative Legal History (Berkeley, Ca., 1999), pp. 11-53.

–, 'Giuristi, umanisti e istituzioni del Tre-Quattrocento. Qualche problema', *Annali dell'Istituto Storico italo-germanico in Trento*, 3 (1977), pp. 43-73.

–, 'Giustizia ordinaria, giustizia di mercanti e la Mercanzia di Siena nel Tre-Quattrocento', in his *Tribunali, giuristi e istituzioni dal medioevo all'età moderna* (rev. ed. Bologna, 1995), pp. 23-54.

–, 'Introduzione: Lo Statuto del Comune di Siena del 1337-1339', introduction to CIAMPOLI, *Il Capitano del popolo*, pp. 7-21.

–, 'Un invito a discutere di oligarchia: in margine al governo di Siena nel Tre-Quattrocento', in *Esercizio del potere e prassi della consultazione*, eds. A. Ciani and G. Diurni. 8° colloquio internazionale ronanistico-canonistico (10-12 maggio 1990). 'Utrumque ius'. Collectio Pontificiae Universitatis Lateranensis, 21 (Vatican City, 1991), pp. 263-72.

–, 'Istituzioni e governo della città', in *Storia di Siena*, I, pp. 327-40.

–, 'Legislazione, statuti e sovranità'; see 'Statuti, legislazione e sovranità: il caso di Siena', below.

–, 'Nicola "el monaco" consulente, con edizione di due suoi pareri olografi per la Toscana', in *Niccolò Tedeschi (abbas panormitanus) e i suoi Commentaria in Decretales*, ed. O. Condorelli (Rome, 2000), pp. 37-68.

–, 'La nobiltà dell'Università medievale nella Glossa e in Bartolo da Sassoferrato', in *Sapere e/è potere*, III, pp. 239-68.

–, 'Le novelle: una fonte per la storia di Siena', in CEPPARI RIDOLFI, JACONA and TURRINI, *Schiave ribaldi e signori*, pp. 201-10.

–, 'Dalla prima istanza all'appello: atti originali della Rota di Siena (sec. XVI)', in *Case Law in the Making. The Techniques and Methods of Judicial Records and Law Reports*, ed. A. Wijffels. Comparative Studies in Continental and Anglo-American Legal History, 17/2 (Berlin, 1997), pp. 215-31.

–, *Renaissance Siena (1355-1559)* (Siena, 1993).

–, 'Repubblica, principato e crisi del diritto comune a Firenze. Dalla motivazione delle sentenze all'edizione delle Pandette', *Annali della Facoltà di Lettere e Filosofia dell'Università di Siena*, 6 (1985), pp. 117-40.

–, 'La Rota della Repubblica di Siena nel secolo XVI', in *Case Law in the Making. The Techniques and Methods of Judicial Records and Law Reports*, ed. A. Wijffels. Comparative Studies in Continental and Anglo-American Legal History, 17/1 (Berlin, 1997), pp. 183-97.

–, 'Scheda di due codici giuridici senesi', *Studi senesi*, 83 (1971), pp. 125-46.

–, 'La scuola giuridica senese in età moderna', in *L'Università di Siena. 750 anni*, pp. 131-44.

–, 'Siena centro finanziario, gioiello della civiltà comunale italiana', in *Le Biccherne di Siena*, pp. 14-21.

–, 'La Siena del "Buon Governo" (1287-1355)', in *Politica e cultura nelle repubbliche italiane*, pp. 81-107.

– see *Siena e il suo territorio nel Rinascimento III*.

–, *Siena e la città-stato del medioevo italiano* (Siena, 2004).

–, 'Siena in the Fourteenth Century: State, Territory, and Culture', in *The "Other Tuscany". Essays in the History of Lucca, Pisa, and Siena during the Thirteenth, Fourteenth and Fifteenth Centuries*, eds. T. W. Blomquist and M. F. Mazzaoui (Kalamazoo, Mi., 1994), pp. 163-97.

–, *Siena nella storia* (Milan, 2000).

–, 'Siena nel primo Quattrocento: un sistema politico tra storia e storiografia', in *Siena e il suo territorio, I*, pp. 1-53.

–, 'Siena nel rinascimento: dal governo di "popolo" al governo nobiliare', in *I ceti dirigenti nella Toscana del Quattrocento*, pp. 405-30; expanded version in his *Siena nel Rinascimento. Istituzioni e sistema politico* (Siena, 1985), pp. 9-108.

–, *Siena nel Rinascimento. Istituzioni e sistema politico* (Siena, 1985).

–, 'Siena senza indipendenza: Repubblica continua', in *I libri dei leoni: la nobiltà di Siena in età medicea, 1557-1737*, ed. M. Ascheri (Siena, 1996), pp. 9-69.

–, 'Statuti, legislazione e sovranità: il caso di Siena', in *Statuti, città, territori in Italia e Germania tra Medioevo ed età moderna*, eds. G. Chittolini and D. Willoweit. Annali dell'Istituto storico italo-germanico, Quaderni, 30 (Bologna, 1991), pp. 145-94; repr. as 'Legislazione, statuti e sovranità', in *Antica Legislazione della Repubblica di Siena*, pp. 1-40.

–, 'Storia dell'Ospedale e/o storia della città', in *Spedale di Santa Maria della Scala*, pp. 65-71.

– (ed.), *L'ultimo statuto della Repubblica di Siena (1545)*. Accademia Senese degli Intronati, Monografie di storia e letteratura senese, 12 (Siena, 1993).

–, 'Un trittico da Siena nel Quattrocento', in *Excerptiones iuris. Studies in Honor of André Gouron*, eds. B. Durant and L. Mayali. Studies in Comparative Legal History (Berkeley, Ca., 2000), pp. 17-34.

– and D. CIAMPOLI see *Siena e il suo Territorio nel Rinascimento I and II*.

– and P. PERTICI, 'La situazione politica senese del secondo Quattrocento (1456-1479)', in *La Toscana al tempo di Lorenzo*, III, pp. 995-1012.

– and P. TURRINI see *La Misericordia di Siena*.

– and P. TURRINI, 'La storia della Misericordia e la Pietà dei laici a Siena', in *La Misericordia di Siena*, pp. 15-49.

AVELLINI, L, 'Università e umanesimo', in *L'Università in Europa dall'Umanesimo ai Lumi*, pp. 20-35.

BACCETTI, B. see *Cultura e Università a Siena*.

BAGGIOLINI, E., *Lo Studio Generale di Vercelli nel Medio Evo* (Vercelli, 1888, repr. Bologna, 1976).

BAI, C., 'Documenti per la storia dello Studio senese dal 1450 al 1475', unpublished *tesi di laurea*, Università degli Studi di Siena, Facoltà di Giurisprudenza, anno accademico 1993-94, relatore P. Nardi.

BALESTRACCI, D., 'Appunti per una storia del "Bullettino Senese di Storia Patria": la metodologia e i contenuti', *BSSP*, 84-85 (1977-8), pp. 290-319.

–, '"Li lavoranti non cognosciuti". Il salariato in una città medievale (Siena 1340-1344)', *BSSP*, 82-83 (1975-6), pp. 67-157.

–, 'The Regulation of Public Health in Italian Medieval Towns', in *Die Vielfalt der Dinge. Neue Wege zur Analysa mittelalterliche Sachkultur. Internationaler Kongress Krems an der Donau, 4. bis 7. Oktober 1994. Gedenkschrift In Memoriam Harry Kühnel* (Vienna, 1998), pp. 345-57.

– et al., *I bottini. Acquedotti medievali senesi* (2nd ed. Siena, 1985).

–, D. LAMBERINI and M. CIVAI, *I bottini medievali di Siena* (Siena, n.d.).

– and G. PICCINNI, 'L'ospedale e la città', in D. GALLAVOTTI CAVALLERO, *Lo Spedale di Santa Maria della Scala*, pp. 21-42.

– and G. PICCINNI, *Siena nel Trecento. Assetto urbano e struttura edilizia* (Florence, 1977).

BANCHI, L., 'Alcuni documenti che concernono la venuta in Siena nell'anno 1321 dei lettori e degli scolari dello Studio bolognese', *Giornale Storico degli Archivi Toscani*, 5 (1861), pp. 237-47, 309-31.

–, *Di un recente opuscolo del D. F. C. Carpellini* (Siena, 1861).

–, 'Provvisioni della Repubblica di Siena contro la peste degli anni 1411 e 1463', *Archivio Storico Italiano*, ser, 4, 14 (1884), pp. 325-32.

– (ed.), *Statuti de la Casa di Santa Maria della Misericordia di Siena volgarizzati circa il 1331 ed ora editi da Luciano Banchi* (Siena, 1886).

– (ed.), *Statuto dello Spedale di Santa Maria a Siena, 1318-79*, in *Statuti senesi scritti in volgare ne' secoli XIII e XIV*, eds. F. L. Polidori and L. Banchi (Bologna, 1863-77), III (1877).

BARBIERI, N., 'Note di cronologia: le ore a Siena dal XIV al XVIII secolo', *BSSP*, 90 (1983), pp. 148-51.

BARDUZZI, D., 'Brevi notizie sulla R. Università di Siena', *Monografie delle Università e degli Istituti Superiori*, 1 (Rome, 1911), pp. 469-80 (repr. Siena, 1912).

–, *Documenti per la storia della R. Università di Siena* (Siena, 1900).

–, *Sul patrimonio della R. Università di Siena* (Siena, 1899).

BARGAGLI, R., *Bartolomeo Sozzini giurista e politico (1436-1506)*. Quaderni di 'Studi senesi', 92 (Milan, 2000).

–, 'Bartolomeo Sozzini, Lorenzo de' Medici e lo Studio di Pisa (1473-1494)', in *La Toscana al tempo di Lorenzo*, III, pp. 1165-71.

–, 'Documenti senesi per la biografia di Bartolomeo Sozzini (1436-1506)', *BSSP*, 99 (1992), pp. 266-323.

BARSANTI, P., *Il pubblico insegnamento in Lucca dal sec. XIV alla fine del sec. XVIII* (Lucca, 1905).

BARTALINI, R., 'Goro di Gregorio e la tomba del giurista Guglielmo da Ciliano', *Prospettiva. Rivista di storia dell'arte antica e moderna*, 41 (1985), pp. 120-38.

BARZANTI, R., G. CATONI and M. DE GREGORIO see *Storia di Siena*, I.

BASCAPÈ, G., 'Sigilli Universitari Italiani', in *Studi Storici in Memoria di Mons. Angelo Mercati*, Fontes Ambrosiani, 30 (Milan, 1956), pp. 43-72; repr. in his *Sigillografia: il sigillo nella diplomatica, nel diritto, nella storia, nell'arte*, 3 vols. (Milan, 1969-94), I, pp. 303-42.

BASTIANONI, C., and G. CATONI, 'La Biblioteca comunale', in *Storia di Siena*, II. *Dal Granducato all'Unità*, eds. R. Barzanti, G. Catoni and M. De Gregorio (Siena, 1996), pp. 365-84.

–, and G. CATONI, *Impressum Senis. Storie di tipografi, incunaboli e librai* (Siena, 1988).

– et al., *Lo Studio e i testi. Il libro universitario a Siena (secoli XII-XVII). Catalogo della mostra coordinato da Mario Ascheri, Siena, Biblioteca Comunale, 14 settembre – 31 ottobre 1996* (Siena, 1996).

BATTAGLIA, F., *Enea Silvio Piccolomini e Francesco Patrizi, due politici senesi del '400* (Siena, 1936).

BATTISTINI, M., 'Francesco Accolti d'Arezzo e un suo credito coi senesi per l'insegnamento suo nello Studio', *BSSP*, 24 (1917), pp. 69-70.

–, 'Una rissa tra frati e studenti dello Studio senese nel secolo XVI', *BSSP*, 25 (1918), pp. 111-12.

BAUMGÄRTNER, I., 'De privilegiis doctorum. Über Gelehrtenstand und Doktorwürde im späten Mittelalter', *Historisches Jahrbuch*, 106 (1986), pp. 298-332.

–, *Martinus Garatus laudensis. Ein italienischer Rechtsgelehrter des 15. Jahrhunderts*. Dissertationen zur Rechtsgeschichte, 2 (Cologne and Vienna, 1986).

–, 'Stadtgeschichte und Consilia im italienischen Spätmittelalter', *Zeitschrift für historische Forschung*, 17 (1990), pp. 129-54.

BECK, J. H., 'The Historical "Taccola" and Emperor Sigismund in Siena', *Art Bulletin*, 50 (1968), pp. 309-20, tr./rev. in his edition of MARIANO DI JACOPO DETTO IL TACCOLA, *Liber Tertium de ingeneis ac edifitiis non usitatis* (Milan, 1969), pp. 11-25.

BECKER, R., 'Bildungskarrieren im Süden. Italienische Studienwege bayerische Bischöfe in der frühen Neuzeit (1448-1648)', *Römische Quartalschrift für christliche Altertumskunde und Kirchengeschichte*, 97 (2002), pp. 301-22.

BEDON, A., *Il palazzo della Sapienza di Roma* (Rome, 1991).

BEINHOFF, G., *Die Italiener am Hof Kaiser Sigismunds (1410-1437)* (Frankfurt, 1995)

BELFORTI, R., 'Le librerie di due dottori in leggi del secolo XV', *Bollettino della R. Deputazione di Storia Patria per l'Umbria*, 17 (1911), pp. 617-22.

BELLOMO, M., *I fatti e il diritto. Tra le certezze e i dubbi dei giuristi medievali (secoli XIII-XIV)*. I libri di Erice, 27 (Rome, 2000).

– (ed.), *Die Kunst der Disputation. Probleme der Rechtsauslegung und Rechtsverwendung im 13. und 14. Jahrhundert*. Schriften des Historischen Kollegs, 38 (Munich 1997).

–, *Saggio sull'Università nell'Età del Diritto Comune* (Catania, 1979).

–, 'Scuole giuridiche e università studentesche in Italia', in *Luoghi e metodi di insegnamento*, pp. 121-40.

–, 'Studenti e "populus" nelle città universitarie italiane dal secolo XII al XIV', in *Università e società*, pp. 61-78.

BELLONE, E., 'I primi decenni della Università di Torino: 1406-1436', *Studi piemontesi*, 12 (1983), pp. 351-69.

–, 'L'Università di Torino a Chieri (1427-1434) e a Savigliano (1434-1436)', *Studi piemontesi*, 14 (1985), pp. 23-33.

BELLONI, A., 'Giovanni Dondi, Albertino da Salso e le origini dello studio pavese', *Bollettino della Società Pavese di Storia Patria*, 82 (1982), pp. 17-47.

–, 'L'insegnamento giuridico nelle università italiane', in *Luoghi e metodi di insegnamento*, pp. 143-52.

–, *Professori giuristi a Padova nel secolo XV. Profilo bio-bibliografico e cattedre.* Ius commune, Sonderhefte, 28 (Frankfurt a. M., 1986).

–, 'Signorolo Omodei e gli inizi della scuola giuridica pavese', *Bollettino della Società Pavese di Storia Patria*, 85 (1985), pp. 29-39.

BENDISCIOLI, M., et al., *Il Collegio Universitario Ghislieri di Pavia* (Milan, 1966-70).

BÉNÉ, C., 'Échanges universitaires dans l'Europe humaniste: l'exemple de la Croatie', in *Les échanges entre les universités*, pp. 269-80.

BERNARDINELLO, S., 'Le orazioni per i santi protettori dell'Università di Padova', *Quaderni per la storia dell'Università di Padova*, 19 (1986), pp. 17-86.

BERNOCCHI, M., *Le Monete della Repubblica Fiorentina* (Florence, 1974-78).

BERTAGNA, M., 'Memorie Bernardiniane, I. Glorificazione senese di S. Bernardino', *BSSP*, 71 (1964), pp. 5-50.

BERTI, L., 'I capitoli "De vestibus mulierum" del 1460, ovvero "status" personale e distinzioni sociali nell'Arezzo di metà Quattrocento', in *Studi in onore di A. D'Addario*, eds. L. Borgia, F. De Luca, P. Viti and R. M. Zaccaria (Lecce, 1995), IV, pp. 1171-214.

BERTONI, L., 'Il "Collegio" dei teologi dell'Università di Siena e i suoi statuti del 1434', *Rivista di Storia della Chiesa in Italia*, 21 (1968), pp. 1-56.

BIAGIOLI, M., 'The Social Status of Italian Mathematicians, 1450-1600', *History of Science*, 27 (1989), pp. 41-95.

BIANCHI, R., 'Cultura umanistica intorno ai Piccolomini fra Quattro e Cinquecento. Antonio da San Severino e altri', in *Umanesimo a Siena*, pp. 29-88.

Le Biccherne di Siena. Arte e finanza all'alba dell'economia moderna, ed. A. Tomei (Bergamo, 2002).

BIDEAUX, M., and M.-M. FRAGONARD see *Les échanges entre les universités européennes*.

BILLANOVICH DAL ZIO, M., 'Bidelli, cartolai e miniatori allo Studio di Padova nel secolo XV', *Quaderni per la Storia dell'Università di Padova*, 6 (1973), pp. 59-72.

BINGEN, N., 'Les étudiants de langue française dans les universités italiennes à la Renaissance: mise à jour du recensement et analyse des données', in *Les échanges entre les universités*, pp. 25-43.

BINI, V., *Memorie Istoriche della Perugina Università degli Studi* (Perugia, 1816, repr. Bologna, 1977).

BLACK, R., *Benedetto Accolti and the Florentine Renaissance* (Cambridge, 2005).

–, 'Education and the Emergence of a Literate Society', in *Italy in the Age of the Renaissance*, ed. J. M. Najemy (Oxford, 2004), pp. 18-36.

–, 'Higher Education in Florentine Tuscany: New Documents from the Second Half of the Fifteenth Century', in *Florence and Italy*, pp. 209-222.

–, *Humanism and Education in Medieval and Renaissance Italy: Tradition and Innovation in Latin Schools from the Twelfth to the Fifteenth Century* (Cambridge, 2001)

–, *Studio e scuola in Arezzo durante il medioevo e il Rinascimento* (Arezzo, 1996).

BOEHM, L., 'Libertas Scholastica und Negotium Scholare. Entstehung und Sozialprestige des akademischen Standes im Mittelalter', in *Universität und Gelehrtenstand 1400-1800*, eds. H. Rössler and G. Franz. Deutsche Führungsgeschichte in der Neuzeit, 4 (Limburg/Lahn, 1970), pp. 15-61; repr. in *Geschichtsdenken, Bildungsgeschichte, Wissenschaftsorganisation. Ausgewählte Aufsätze von Laetitia Boehm anläßlich ihres 65. Geburtstag*, eds. G. Melville, R. A. Müller and W. Müller. Historische Forschungen, 56 (1996), pp. 607-46.

BOESCH GAJANO, S., 'Il Comune di Siena e il prestito ebraico nei secoli XIV e XV', in *Aspetti e problemi della presenza ebraica nell'Italia centro-settentrionale (secoli XIV e XV)*. Quaderni dell'Istituto di Scienze Storiche dell'Università di Roma, 2 (Rome, 1983), pp. 177-225.

BOISSEUIL, D., 'Le paysage thermal siennois au début du XVIᵉ siècle, d'après le *De Urbis Senae origine* de Lucio Antonio Maynero', in *Scrivere il medioevo*, pp. 41-54.

–, *Le thermalisme en Toscane à la fin du Moyen Âge. Les bains siennois de la fin du XIIIᵉ siècle au début du XVIᵉ siècle*. Collection de l'École Française de Rome, 296 (Rome, 2002).

BONAFACCIA, M., 'La "Domus Sapientiae" di Siena ed i suoi studenti nei secoli XV-XVI', unpublished *tesi di laurea*, Università degli Studi di Siena, Facoltà di Giurisprudenza, anno accademico 1988-89, relatore P. Nardi.

BONELLI-GANDOLFO, C., 'La legislazione suntuaria senese negli ultimi centocinquant'anni della Repubblica', *Studi senesi*, 35 (1919), pp. 243-75, 334-98.

BONOLIS, G., 'Lodovico Zdekauer', *Atti e memorie della R. Deputazione di Storia Patria per le Marche*, ser. 4, III/1 (1925), pp. 105-9.

BOOCKMANN, H., *Wissen und Widerstand. Geschichte der deutschen Universität* (Berlin, 1999).

BORELLI, G., '"Doctor an miles": aspetti della ideologia nobiliare nell'opera del giurista Cristoforo Lanfranchini', *Nuova Rivista Storica*, 73 (1989), pp. 151-68.

BORGIA, L., and F. FUMI CAMBI GADO, 'I sistemi emblematici e le Università europee con particolare riferimento all'Ateneo senese', in *L'Università di Siena. 750 anni*, pp. 559-73.

BORSETTI, F., *Historia almi Ferrariae Gymnasii* (Ferrara, 1735).

BORST, A., 'Crisis and Reform in the Universities of the Late Middle Ages', in his *Medieval Worlds. Barbarians Heretics and Artists* (tr. Cambridge, 1991), pp. 167-81.

BOSKOVITS, M., *Tuscan Paintings of the Early Renaissance* (tr. Budapest, 1968).

BOWSKY, W. M., 'The *Buon Governo* of Siena (1287-1355): a Medieval Italian Oligarchy', *Speculum*, 37 (1962), pp. 368-81.

–, *The Finance of the Commune of Siena, 1287-1355* (Oxford, 1970).

–, 'The Impact of the Black Death upon Sienese Government and Society', *Speculum*, 39 (1964), pp. 1-34.

–, 'Medieval Citizenship: the Individual and the State in the Comune of Siena', *Studies in Medieval and Renaissance History*, 4 (1967), pp. 195-243.

–, *A Medieval Italian Commune. Siena under the Nine, 1287-1355* (Berkeley and Los Angeles, Ca., 1981)

–, 'A New *Consilium* of Cino of Pistoia (1324): Citizenship, Residence and Taxation', *Speculum*, 42 (1967), pp. 431-41.

BOYARSKY, V., 'Medical Baths and Bathing in the Renaissance with Special Reference to Tuscany', unpublished M.Phil. dissertation, The Warburg Institute, University of London, 1989.

BRAMBILLA, E., 'Genealogie del sapere. Per una storia delle professioni giuridiche nell'Italia padana (secoli XIV-XVI)', *Schifanoia*, 8 (1989), pp. 123-50, and in *Forme ed evoluzione del lavoro in Europa: XIII-XVIII secc. Atti della 'Tredicesima Settimana di Studio', 2-7 maggio 1981*, ed. A. Guarducci. Istituto Datini di Prato (Florence, 1991), pp. 733-86.

–, *Genealogie del sapere. Università, professioni giuridiche e nobiltà togata in Italia (XIII-XVII secolo). Con un saggio sull'arte della memoria*. Early Modern: Studi di storia europea protomoderna, 19 (Milan, 2005).

BRANDMÜLLER, W., 'Casini Antonio', *DBI*, 21 (1978), pp. 351-2.

–, *Das Konzil von Pavia-Siena 1423-4*, 2 vols. Vorreformationsgeschichtliche Forschungen, 16; Vol. I, *Darstellung* (Münster, 1968), 2nd ed. in the series *Konziliengeschichte*, Reihe I: Darstellungen, ed. W. Brandmüller (Paderborn etc., 2002), tr. as *Il Concilio di Pavia-Siena 1423-1424. Verso la crisi del conciliarismo* (Siena, 2004); Vol. II, *Quellen* (Münster, 1974).

–, 'Die Römischen Berichte des Pietro d'Antonio De'Micheli an das Concistoro von Siena im Frühjahr 1431', *BSSP*, 73-75 (1966-8), pp. 146-99.

–, 'Siena und das Basler Konzil – die Legation des Battista Bellanti', in *Studien zum 15. Jahrhundert. Festschrift für Erich Meuthen*, eds. J. Helmrath and H. Muller (Munich, 1994), pp. 207-29.

–, 'Der Übergang vom Pontifikat Martins V. zu Eugen IV.' *Quellen und Forschungen aus italienischen Archiven und Bibliotheken*, 47 (1967), pp. 596-629.

BRILLI, A., 'L'Università e la presenza degli stranieri', in *L'Università di Siena. 750 anni*, pp. 541-57.

BRIZIO, E., 'L'elezione degli uffici politici nella Siena del Trecento', *BSSP*, 98 (1991), pp. 16-62.

–, 'L'elezione della Signoria: provvedimenti inediti (1371-1398)', in *Antica Legislazione della Repubblica di Siena*, pp. 136-59.

–, 'Leggi e provvedimenti del Rinascimento (1400-1542): Spoglio di un registro archivistico (*Statuti di Siena 40*)', in *Antica Legislazione della Repubblica di Siena*, pp. 161-200.

BRIZZI, G. P., 'Da "domus pauperum scholarium" a collegio d'educazione. Evoluzione e ruolo del collegio in Europa dal Medioevo all'età napoleonica', in *Università e collegi. Storia e futuro*. Atti del Convegno (7 marzo 1994) organizzato dal Collegio Universitario S. Caterina da Siena di Pavia, ed. M. P. Musatti. Fonti e studi per la storia dell'Università di Pavia, 22 (Bologna, 1994), pp. 17-46.

–, 'Da "domus pauperum scholarium" a collegio d'educazione: università e collegi in Europa (secoli XII-XVIII)', in *Disciplina dell'anima, disciplina del corpo e disciplina della società tra medioevo ed età moderna*, ed. P. Prodi. Annali dell'Istituto storico italo-germanico, Quaderno 40 (Bologna, 1984), pp. 809-30.

–, 'Una fonte per la storia degli studenti: i "libri amicorum"', in *Studenti, università, città*, pp. 389-401.

–, 'L'identità dello studente tra medioevo ed età moderna', in *Identità collettive tra Medioevo ed età moderna*, eds. P. Prodi and W. Reinhard (Bologna, 2002), pp. 313-32.

–, 'Studenti in età moderna', in *Studenti, università, città*, pp. 745-53.

–, 'Le università italiane', in *Le Università dell'Europa: dal Rinascimento alle riforme religiose*, eds. G. P. Brizzi and J. Verger (Milan, 1991), pp.21-53; repr. as 'Le università italiane tra Rinascimento ed età moderna', in *Il pragmatismo degli intellettuali*, pp. 175-200.

–, and A. DE BENEDICTIS, 'Le università italiane', in *L'Università in Europa dall'Umanesimo ai Lumi*, pp. 36-72.

–, and A. I. PINI see *Studenti e Università*.

–, and A. ROMANO see *Studenti e dottori*.

–, and A. VARNI see *L'università in Italia*.

–, and J. VERGER see *Le Università dell'Europa*.

–, and J. VERGER see *L'Università in Europa dall'Umanesimo*.

–, and J. VERGER see *Le università minori*.

BROGI, M. see *Il diritto a studiare*.

BROGINI, P., 'Per una prosopografia dell'Università di Siena (1247-1500)', *Annali di storia delle Università italiane*, 4 (2000), pp. 234-6.

–, 'La trasformazione della Casa della Misericordia in Casa della Sapienza', in *La Misericordia di Siena*, pp. 121-33.

BRONZINO, G. (ed.), *Notitia doctorum sive catalogus doctorum qui in collegiis philosophiae et medicinae bononiae laureati fuerunt ab anno 1480 usque ad annum 1800*. Universitatis Bononiensis Monumenta, IV (Milan, 1962).

BROWN, A., *Bartolomeo Scala, 1439-1497, Chancellor of Florence. The Humanist as Bureaucrat* (Princeton, N.J., 1979).

BRUCKER, G., 'A Civic Debate on Florentine Higher Education (1460)', *Renaissance Quarterly*, 34 (1982), pp. 517-33; repr. in his *Renaissance Florence*, pp. 207*-223*.

–, 'Florence and its University, 1348-1434', in *Action and Conviction in Early Modern Europe*, eds. T. K. Rabb and J. E. Seigel (Princeton, 1969), pp. 220-36; repr. in his *Renaissance Florence*, pp. 189*-205*.

–, *Renaissance Florence: Society, Culture and Religion* (Goldbach, 1994).

–, 'Renaissance Florence: Who Needs a University?', in *The University and the City: From Medieval Origins to the Present*, ed. T. Bender (New York, 1988), pp. 47-58; repr. in his *Renaissance Florence*, pp. 225*-236*.

BRUNI, F., 'Provocazioni sulla politica culturale di Federico II', in *Nel segno di Federico II. Unità politica e pluralità culturale del Mezzogiorno*. Atti del IV Convegno Internazionale di Studi della Fondazione Napoli Novantanove (Napoli, 30 settembre-1 ottobre 1988) (Naples, 1989), pp. 93-109; repr. in his *Testi e chierici del Medioevo* (Genoa, 1991), pp. 71-89.

BUCK, A., 'Die "studia humanitatis" im italienischen Humanismus', in *Humanismus im Bildungswesen des 15. und 16. Jahrhunderts*, ed. W. Reinhard. Deutsche Forschungsgemeinschaft: Mitteilung XII der Kommission für Humanismusforschung (Wenheim, 1984), pp. 11-24.

BULLETTI, E., 'Angelo Salvetti (c. 1350-1423) in documenti dell'Archivio di Stato di Siena', *Archivum Franciscanum Historicum*, 54 (1961), pp. 26-93.

BULST, N., 'La législation somptuaire d'Amédée VIII', in *Amédée VIII – Felix V premier duc de Savoie et pape (1385-1451. Colloque international, Ripaille-Lausanne, 23-26 octobre 1990*, eds. B. Andenmatten and A. Paravicini Bagliani (Lausanne, 1992), pp. 191-200.

BURKE, P., 'Decentering the Renaissance: the Challenge of Postmodernism', in *At the Margins. Minority Groups in Premodern Italy*, ed. S. Milner (Minneapolis, Mn., 2005), pp. 36-49.

BURNS, H., 'Progetti per la nuova casa della Sapienza, Siena', in *Francesco di Giorgio architetto*, a cura di F. P. Fiore and M. Tafuri (Milan, 1993), pp. 296-301.

BUZZETTI, D., 'La Faculté des arts dans les universités de l'Europe méridionale. Quelques problèmes de recherche', in *L'enseignement des disciplines à la Faculté des arts (Paris et Oxford, XIIIᵉ-XVᵉ siècles). Actes du colloque international*, eds. O. WEIJERS and L. HOLTZ. Studia Artistarum: Études sur la Faculté des arts dans les Universités médiévales, 4 (Turnhout, 1997), pp. 457-66.

BUZZI, F., 'La teologia tra Quattro e Cinquecento. Istituzione scolastica, indirizzi e temi', *Cheiron. Materiali e strumenti di aggiornamento storiografico. Rivista semestrale del Centro di ricerche storiche e sociali Federico Odorici*, 33 (2000), pp. 17-78.

BYLEBYL, J. J., 'The School of Padua: Humanistic Medicine in the Sixteenth Century', in *Health, Medicine and Mortality in the Sixteenth Century*, ed. C. Webster (Cambridge, 1979), pp. 335-70.

CAFERRO, W., *Mercenary Companies and the Decline of Siena* (Baltimore, Md., and London, 1998).

CAGLIARITANO, U., *Storia di Siena* (Siena, 1977).

CAMBI, M. A., and M. QUARTESAN (eds.), 'Gli uffici del Comune di Siena e le incompatibilità, 1433', in *Siena e il suo Territorio, II*, pp. 121-49.

CAMMAROSANO, P., *Tradizione documentaria e storia cittadina. Introduzione al 'Caleffo Vecchio' del Comune di Siena* (Siena, 1988).

CANTUCCI, G., review of GAROSI, *Siena nella storia della medicina*, BSSP, 65 (1958), pp. 179-81.

–, and U. MORANDI, 'Introduzione', *Archivio dell'ospedale di Santa Maria della Scala. Inventario*. 2 vols. (Rome, 1960-62), I, pp. VII-LXXX.

CAPITANI, O., see *Cultura universitaria e pubblici poteri*.

–, see *L'Università a Bologna*.

CAPUTO, V., 'Gli statuti del collegio ferrarese dei dottori utriusque iuris (sec. XV), *Annali dell'Università di Ferrara. Sezione di scienze giuridiche*, 2 (1952-3), pp. 1-99.

–, and R. CAPUTO, *L'Università degli Scolari di medicina e d'arte dello Studio ferrarese* (Ferrara, 1990).

CARPELLINI, C. F., *Risposta al Signor Luciano Banchi, intorno alle sue Osservazioni sull'opuscolo 'Dell'origine nazionale ...'* (Siena, 1862).

–, *Sulla origine nazionale e populare delle Università di studi in Italia, e particolarmente della Università di Siena* (Siena, 1861).

CASANOVA, E., *Archivistica* (2nd. ed. Siena, 1926), available in *La biblioteca di ARCHIVI*, http://archivi.beniculturali.it.

–, 'La donna senese del Quattrocento nella vita privata', *BSSP*, 8:1 (1900), pp. 3-93.

CASCIO PRATILLI, G., *L'Università e il Principe. Gli Studi di Siena e di Pisa tra Rinascimento e Controriforma*. Accademia Toscana di Scienza e Lettere 'La Colombaria', Studi, 38 (Florence, 1975).

CASTELLANO, I., 'Religiosità e cultura universitaria a Siena', in *Cultura e Università a Siena*, pp. 71-80.

CASTELLI, P. see *La rinascita del sapere*.

CATONI, G., 'L'alchimia dei Monti', in *Repubblica di Siena (1400-1507)* (Milan, 2002).

–, 'Il carnevale degli scolari. Feste e spettacoli degli studenti senesi dal XVI al XVIII secolo', in *Scritti per Mario delle Piane* (Naples, 1986), pp. 23-37.

–, 'Il Comune di Siena e l'amministrazione della Sapienza nel secolo XV', in *Università e società*, pp. 121-29.

–, 'La faziosa armonia', in A. Falassi and G. Catoni, *Palio* (Siena, 1982), pp. 225-72.

–, 'Genesi e ordinamento della Sapienza di Siena', *Studi senesi*, 85 (1973), pp. 155-98.

–, 'Introduzione' to *Archivio Storico dell'Università di Siena. Inventario della Sezione storica* (Siena, 1990), pp. XI-XXV.

–, 'L'inventario dell'archivio storico dell'Università di Siena', in *La storia delle università italiane*, pp. 103-7.

–, 'Gli oblati della Misericordia. Poveri e benefattori a Siena nella prima metà del Trecento', in *La società del bisogno*, pp. 1-17.

–, 'I privilegi degli scolari nella Siena medievale e moderna', in *Il diritto a studiare: residenze universitarie a Siena tra passato e futuro. Atti del convegno, Siena, 6-7 dicembre 1991*, ed. M. Brogi (Siena, 1995), pp. 9-18.

–, 'I "Regolatori" e la giurisdizione sui contabili nella repubblica di Siena', *Critica Storica*, 12 (1975), pp. 46-70.

–, 'Relazioni culturali fra la città di Siena e l'Ungheria nei secoli 14. e 15.', estr. from '*Ungheria d'oggi*'. *Atti del Convegno italo-ungherese di studi rinascimentali, Spoleto, 9-10 ottobre 1964*, pp. 1-4.

–, 'Le riforme del Granduca, le "serre" degli scolari e i lettori di casa', in *L'Università di Siena. 750 anni*, pp. 45-66.

–, 'Il Sigillo dell'Università di Siena', *Studenti &/a Siena. Periodico d'informazione della Azienda Comunale diritto allo Studio Universitario*, II:1 (15 gennaio 1991), p. 2.

– (ed.), *Statuti Senesi dell'Arte dei Giudici e Notai del Secolo XIV*. Fonti e studi del *Corpus membranarum italicarum*, 8 (Rome, 1972).

– and G. PICCINNI, 'Alliramento e ceto dirigente nella Siena del Quattrocento', in *I ceti dirigenti nella Toscana del Quattrocento*, pp. 451-61.

– and G. PICCINNI, 'Famiglie e redditi nella *Lira* senese del 1453', in *Strutture familiari, epidemie, migrazioni nell'Italia medievale*, eds. R. Comba, G. Piccinni and G. Pinto (Naples, 1984), pp. 291-304.

– et al., *Le Pergamene dell'Università di Siena e la 'Domus Misericordiae'. Seminario di Archivistica* (Siena, 1975-6).

CAVALLAR, O., '*Ledere Rem Publicam*. Il trattato "*De portacione armorum*" attribuito a Bartolo di Sassoferrato e alcune *quaestiones* di Martino da Fano', *Ius Commune*, 25 (1998), pp. 1-38.

–, S. DEGENRING and J. KIRSHNER, *A Grammar of Signs: Bartolo da Sassoferrato's "Tract on Insignia and Coats of Arms"*. Studies in Comparative Legal History (Berkeley, 1994).

– and J. KIRSHNER, '"Licentia navigandi… prosperis ventibus aflantibus". L'esenzione dei "doctores" e delle loro mogli da norme suntuarie', in *A Ennio Cortese*, I, pp. 204-27.

CAVAZZA, F., *Le scuole dell'Antico Studio bolognese* (Milan, 1896).

CECCHINI, G. *Archivio di Stato di Perugia. Archivio Storico del Comune di Perugia. Inventario*. Pubblicazioni degli Archivi di Stato, 21 (Rome, 1956).

–, 'Pagamenti effettuati dalla Camera degli Officiali dell'Abbondanza a lettori e a personale dello Studio', *Bollettino della R. Deputazione di Storia Patria per l'Umbria*, 58 (1961), pp. 129-38.

– and G. PRUNAI (eds.), *Chartularium Studii Senensis* (Siena, 1942).

CENCETTI, G., 'Il foro degli scolari negli studi medievali italiani', *Atti e Memorie della R. Deputazione per l'Emilia e la Romagna*, 5 (1940), pp. 163-88; repr. in his *Lo Studio di Bologna*, pp. 95-112.

–, 'La laurea nelle università medievali', *Studi e Memorie per la Storia dell'Università di Bologna*, 16 (1943), pp. 247-73; repr. in his *Lo Studio di Bologna*, pp. 77-93.

–, *Lo Studio di Bologna. Aspetti Momenti e Problemi (1935-1970)*, eds. R. Ferrara, G. Orlandelli and A. Vasina (Bologna, 1989).

–, 'Studium fuit Bononie', *Studi Medievali*, ser. 3, 7 (1966), pp. 781-833, repr. in *Le origini delle Università*, ed. G. Arnaldi (Bologna, 1974), pp. 101-51 and in his *Lo Studio di Bologna*, pp. 29-73.

CEPPARI RIDOLFI, M. A., 'La signoria di Gian Galeazzo Visconti', in *Storia di Siena*, I, pp. 315-26.

–, 'Il sindacato degli ufficiali del Comune di Siena nel Trecento', in *Scrivere il medioevo*, pp. 77-94.

–, E. JACONA and P. TURRINI, *Schiave ribaldi e signori a Siena nel Rinascimento* (Siena, 1994).

– and P. TURRINI, *Il mulino delle vanità. Lusso e cerimonie nella Siena medievale* (Siena, 1993).

CESSI, R., 'La biblioteca di Prosdocimo de' Conti', *Bollettino del Museo Civico di Padova*, 12 (1909), pp. 140-8; repr. in his *Padova Medioevale*, II, pp. 729-42.

–, 'L'invasione degli Ungari e lo Studio di Padova (1411-1413)', *Atti e Memorie, R. Accad. Di Scienze, lettere ed arti in Padova*, n.s., 27 (1910-11), pp. 237-55; repr. in his *Padova Medioevale*, II, pp. 665-80.

–, *Padova Medioevale. Studi e Documenti*, collected and re-edited by D. Gallo, 2 vols. Scritti Padovani, 2 (Padua, 1985).

I ceti dirigenti nella Toscana del Quattrocento. Atti del V e VI Convegno: Firenze, 10-11 dicembre 1982; 2-3 dicembre 1983 (Florence, 1987).

I ceti dirigenti nella Toscana tardo comunale. Atti del III Convegno: Firenze, 5-7 dicembre 1980 (Florence, 1983).

CHAMBERS, D. S., 'Studium Urbis and the *Gabella Studii*', in *Cultural Aspects of the Italian Renaissance*, ed. C. Clough (Manchester, 1976), pp. 68-110; repr. in his *Individuals and Institutions in Renaissance Italy* (Aldershot, 1998), ch. II.

– and T. DEAN, *Clean Hands and Rough Justice. An Investigating Magistrate in Renaissance Italy* (Ann Arbor, Mi., 1997).

CHANG, K., 'From Oral Disputation to Written Text: the Transformation of the Dissertation in Early Modern Europe', *History of Universities*, 19/2 (2004), pp. 129-87.

Chartularium Studii Bononiensis, 15 vols. (Bologna, 1909-88).

CHERUBINI, G., 'Dal libro di ricordi di un notaio senese del Trecento', in his *Signori, contadini, borghesi*, pp. 393-425.

–, 'I mercanti e il potere a Siena', in *Banchi e mercanti di Siena* (Rome, 1987), pp. 161-220; repr. in his *Scritti toscani. L'urbanesimo medievale e la mezzadria* (Florence, 1991), pp. 71-115.

–, 'La mezzadria toscana delle origini', in *Contadini e proprietari*, pp. 131-52.

–, (ed.), 'I proprietari di beni immobili e di terre a Siena intorno al 1320 (dalla "Tavola delle Possessioni")', *Ricerche storiche*, 5 (1975), pp. 357-510.

–, *Signori, contadini, borghesi. Ricerche sulla società italiana del basso medioevo* (Florence, 1974).

CHIABÒ, M., and F. DOGLIO (eds.), *Spettacoli studenteschi nell'Europa umanistica: convegno internazionale, Anagni 20-22 giugno 1997* (Rome, 1998).

CHIAPPELLI, A., 'Medici e chirurgi a Pistoia nel Medio Evo. Contributi alla Storia delle Arti Mediche in Italia, con documenti', *Bullettino Storico Pistoiese*, 8 (1906), pp. 9-46, 121-52; 9 (1907), pp. 186-235; 10 (1908), pp. 1-42, 133-43.

CHIAPPELLI, L., 'Lodovico Zdekauer', *Archivio Storico Italiano*, 82 (1924), pp. 159-74.

CHIELLINI, S., 'Contributo per la storia degli insegnamenti umanistici dello studio ferrarese', in *La rinascita del sapere*, pp. 210-45.

CHIRONI, G., 'Nascita della signoria e resistenze oligarchiche a Siena: l'opposizione di Niccolò Borghesi a Pandolfo Petrucci (1498-1500)', in *La Toscana al tempo di Lorenzo*, III, pp. 1173-95.

–, 'Repertorio dei documenti riguardanti Mariano di Jacopo detto il Taccola e Francesco di Giorgio Martini', in *Prima di Leonardo. Cultura delle Macchine a Siena nel Rinascimento*, ed. P. Galluzzi (Milan, 1991), pp. 471-82.

–, 'La signoria breve di Pandolfo Petrucci', in *Storia di Siena*, I, pp. 395-406.

–, 'Il testo unico per l'ufficio dei Regolatori, 1351-1533', in *Siena e il suo Territorio, II*, pp. 183-220.

CHŁĘDOWSKI, C., *Siena* (Berlin, 1913).

CHRISTIANSEN, K., 'Painting in Renaissance Siena', in CHRISTANSEN ET AL, *Painting in Renaissance Siena*, pp. 3-32.

–, L. B. KANTER and C. B. STREHLKE, *Painting in Renaissance Siena 1420-1500* (New York, 1988).

CIAMPOLI, D., *Il Capitano del popolo a Siena nel primo Trecento*. Documenti di Storia, 1 (Siena, 1984).

–, 'Una raccolta di provvisioni senesi agli albori del XV secolo: il "libro della catena"', *BSSP*, 86 (1979), pp. 243-83.

–, 'Le raccolte normative della seconda metà del Trecento', in *Antica Legislazione della Repubblica di Siena*, pp. 121-36.

CIAMPOLINI, M., 'Casa della Sapienza', in *L'Università di Siena. 750 anni*, pp. 312-5.

–, 'La Domus Misericordiae dalle origini ai giorni nostri: vicende costruttive e decorazione', in *La Misericordia di Siena*, pp. 135-55.

CIAPPELLI, G., *Carnevale e quaresima. Comportamenti sociali e cultura a Firenze nel Rinascimento*. Temi e testi, n.s. 37 (Rome, 1997).

CIONI, E., *Il Sigillo a Siena nel Medioevo. Catalogo della mostra di Siena 25 febbraio – 19 marzo 1989* (Siena, 1989).

–, and D. Fausti see *Umanesimo a Siena*.

Cipolla, C. M., *Studi di Storia della Moneta,* I. *I movimenti dei cambi in Italia dal secolo XIII al XV* (Pavia, 1948).

City and Countryside in Late Medieval and Renaissance Italy: Essays Presented to Philip Jones, eds. T. Dean and C. Wickham (London, 1990).

Clubb, L. G., 'Pre-Rozzi e pre-Intronati allo Studio di Siena', in *Umanesimo a Siena*, pp. 149-70.

–, 'Siena, Crucible of Theater', in Clubb and Black, *Romance and Aretine Humanism*, pp. 11-37.

–, and R. Black, *Romance and Aretine Humanism in Sienese Comedy*. Bibliotheca Studii Senensis, 6 (Florence, 1993).

Cobban, A. B., 'Elective Salaried Lectureships in the Universities of Southern Europe in the Pre-Reformation Era', *Bulletin of the John Rylands University Library of Manchester*, 67 (1984-85), pp. 662-87.

–, *The Medieval Universities: their Development and Organisation* (London, 1975).

–, 'Medieval Student Power', *Past and Present*, 53 (1971), pp. 28-66.

Cohn, S. K., Jr., *Death and Property in Siena, 1205-1800* (Baltimore, Md., 1988).

Coing, H. (ed.), *Handbuch der Quellen und Literatur der neueren europäischen Rechtsgeschichte*, vol. I. *Mittelalter (1100-1500)* (Munich, 1973).

I Collegi universitari in Europa tra il XIV e il XVIII secolo. Atti del convegno di studi della Commissione Internazionale per la Storia delle Università, Siena-Bologna, 16-19 maggio 1988, eds. D. Maffei and H. de Ridder-Symoens. Orbis Academicus, Saggi e Documenti di Storia delle Università, 4 (Milan, 1991)

Colli, V., 'Cattedre minori, letture universitarie e collegio dei dottori di diritto civile a Bologna nel secolo XV', in *Sapere e/è potere,* III, pp. 135-55.

Collino, G., 'La guerra veneto-viscontea contro i Carraresi nelle relazioni di Firenze e di Bologna col Conte di Virtù', *Archivio Storico Lombardo*, 37 (1909), pp. 5-58, 315-86.

Colombini, P., *Cenni Storici sulla Università di Siena* (Siena, 1891).

Contadini e proprietari nella Toscana moderna. Atti del Convegno di Studi in onore di Giorgio Giorgetti. Vol. I. *Dal medioevo all'età moderna.* Unione regionale delle Province Toscane. Biblioteca di Storia Toscana Moderna e Contemporanea, Studi e Documenti, 19 (Florence, 1979).

Coppi, E., *Le Università Italiane nel Medioevo* (2nd edn., Florence, 1880).

Corso, C., 'Araldi e canterini nella Repubblica Senese del '400', *BSSP*, 62-63 (1955-56), pp. 140-60.

–, 'Francesco Accolti d'Arezzo lettore di diritto nello Studio di Siena', *BSSP*, 62-63 (1955-56), pp. 22-78.

–, 'L'Ilicino (Bernardo Lapini)', *BSSP*, 64 (1957), pp. 3-108.

–, 'Il Panormita in Siena e l'Ermafrodito', *BSSP*, 60 (1953), pp. 138-88.

Cortese, E., *Il diritto nella storia medievale*, II (Rome, 1995, repr. 1999).

–, 'Legisti, canonisti e feudisti: la formazione di un ceto medievale', in *Università e società*, pp. 195-281.

Cortonesi, A. see *La Val d'Orcia*.

Coselschi, F., and D. Caporali, 'Appunti biografici e bibliografici sui giureconsulti senesi', *Studi senesi*, 1 (1884), pp. 81-96, 204-18 and 321-6, and 2 (1885), pp. 141-51 and 335-41.

Courtenay, W. J., 'The Effects of the Black Death on English Higher Education', *Speculum*, 55 (1980), pp. 676-714.

Cremascoli, G., 'La facoltà di teologia', in *Luoghi e metodi di insegnamento*, pp. 83-99; repr. in *Il pragmatismo degli intellettuali*, pp. 181-200.

Cultura e Università a Siena. Epoche, argomenti, protagonisti, ed. B. Baccetti (Siena, 1993).

Cultura universitaria e pubblici poteri a Bologna dal XII al XV secolo. Atti del 2° convegno, Bologna, 20-21 maggio 1988, ed. O. Capitani (Bologna, 1990).

Cséfalvay, P. (ed.), *Christian Museum Esztergom* (tr. Budapest, 1993).

D'Accone, F. A., *The Civic Muse. Music and Musicians in Siena during the Middle Ages and the Renaissance* (Chicago, 1997).

d'Alatri, M., 'Panorama geografico, cronologico e statistico sulla distribuzione degli *Studia* degli ordini mendicanti: Italia', in *Le Scuole degli ordini mendicanti (secoli XIII-XIV)*. Convegni del Centro di Studi sulla Spiritualità Medievale, 17 (Todi, 1978), pp. 49-72.

DALLARI, U., *I Rotuli dei Lettori legisti e artisti dello Studio di Bologna dal 1384 al 1799* (Bologna, 1888-1924), 4 vols.

D'AMELIO, G., 'Castro, Paolo di', in *DBI*, 22 (1979), pp. 227-33.

DAVIDSOHN, R., 'Documenti del 1240 e 1252 relativi allo studio senese', *BSSP*, 7 (1900), pp. 168-70.

DAVIES, J., 'Elites and Examiners at Italian Universities during the Late Middle Ages', *Medieval Prosopography*, 21 (2001), pp. 191-209.

–, *Florence and its University during the Early Renaissance* (Leiden, 1998).

–, 'A "Paper University"? The *Studio lucchese*, 1369-1487', *History of Universities*, 15 (1997-9), pp. 261-306.

–, 'Studio, Stato and State: the University of Florence and the Medici from Party Bosses to Grand Dukes', paper to the International Commission of the History of Universities session at the 19th International Congress of Historical Sciences, Oslo, 6 to 13 August 2000 (www.oslo2000.uio.no/A10/A1016/group-2/Davies.pdf, downloaded on 7 April 2004).

DAVIS, V., 'The English Medieval Clergy Database and University History', in *Computing Techniques and the History of Universities*, ed. P. R. Denley. Halbgraue Reihe zur historischen Fachinformatik, A30 (St. Katharinen, 1996), pp. 60-64.

–, 'The Making of English Collegiate Statutes in the Later Middle Ages', *History of Universities*, 12 (1993), pp. 1-23.

DEAN, T., *Crime in Medieval Europe* (London, 2001).

– and C. WICKHAM see *City and Countryside*.

DE ANGELIS, L., *Biografia degli Scrittori Sanesi* (Siena, 1824, repr. Bologna, 1976).

–, *Discorso storico sull'Università di Siena ai Signori Commissari per 1'Organizzazione della Pubblica Istruzione nei Dipartimenti Francesi Cisalpini* (Siena, 1831, repr. 1840).

DE BENEDICTIS, A., 'Luoghi del potere e Studio fra Quattrocento e Cinquecento', in *L'Università a Bologna*, pp. 205-27.

–, *Repubblica per contratto. Bologna: una città europea nello Stato della Chiesa*. Annali dell'Istituto storico italo-germanico, Monografie, 23 (Bologna, 1995).

–, 'Retorica e politica: dall'*Orator* di Beroaldo all'ambasciatore bolognese nel rapporto tra *respublica* cittadina e governo pontificio', in *Sapere e/è potere*, III, pp. 411-38.

DE COSTER, A., 'La mobilità dei docenti: Comune e Collegi dottorali di fronte al problema dei lettori non-cittadini nello Studio bolognese', in *Studenti e dottori*, pp. 227-41.

–, 'Vreemde docenten en burgerschapsverlening te Bologna (15de eeuw)', *Bulletin van het Belgisch Historisch Instituut te Rome / Bulletin de l'Institut historique Belge de Rome*, 70 (2000), pp. 59-143.

DE FEO CORSO, L., 'Il Filelfo in Siena', *BSSP*, 47 (1940), pp. 181-209, 292-316.

DE FREDE, C., 'Un docente di diritto civile nel Rinascimento: Antonio Giordano da Venafro', in *Sodalitas. Scritti in onore di Antonio Guarino* (Naples, 1984), 8, pp. 3805-16.

DE GREGORIO, M., 'Giordano, Antonio', *DBI*, 55 (2000), pp. 258-9.

DEL GUERRA, G., *Rustichello da Pisa* (Pisa, 1955).

DEL NEGRO, P., 'Il Principe e l'Università in Italia dal XV secolo all'età napoleonica', in *L'università in Italia*, pp. 11-27.

DENIFLE, H., *Die Entstehung der Universitäten des Mittelalters bis 1400* (Berlin, 1885).

–, 'Die Statuten der Juristen-Universität Bologna vom Jahre 1317-47 und deren Verhältniß zu jenen Paduas, Perugias, Florenz', *Archiv für Literatur- und Kirchengeschichte des Mittelalters*, 3 (1887), pp. 196-408.

–, 'Die Statuten der Juristen-Universität Padua vom Jahre 1331', *Archiv für Literatur- und Kirchengeschichte des Mittelalters*, 6 (1892), pp. 309-562.

– and A. CHATELAIN (eds.), *Chartularium Universitatis Parisiensis* (Paris, 1891-99, repr. Brussels, 1964).

DENLEY, P. R., 'Academic Rivalry and Interchange: the Universities of Siena and Florence', in *Florence and Italy*, pp. 193-208.

–, 'Career, Springboard or Sinecure? University Teaching in Renaissance Italy', *Medieval Prosopography*, 12:2 (Autumn 1991), pp. 95-114.

–, 'The Collegiate Movement in Italian Universities in the Late Middle Ages', *History of Universities*, 10 (Oxford, 1991), pp. 29-91.

–, 'Communities within Communities: Student Identity and Student Groups in Late Medieval Italian Universities', in *Studenti, università, città*, pp. 721-44.

–, 'Dal 1357 alla caduta della repubblica', in *L'Università di Siena. 750 anni*, pp. 27-44.

–, 'Governments and Schools in Late Medieval Italy', in *City and Countryside*, pp. 93-108.

–, 'Medieval and Renaissance Italian Universities and the Role of Foreign Scholarship', *History of Universities*, 19/1 (2004), pp. 159-81.

–, 'Recent Studies on Italian Universities of the Middle Ages and Renaissance', *History of Universities*, 1 (1981), pp. 193-205.

–, '*Signore* and *Studio*: Lorenzo in a Comparative Context', in *Lorenzo the Magnificent: Culture and Politics*, eds. M. Mallett and N. Mann (London, 1996), pp. 203-216.

–, 'The Social Function of Italian Renaissance Universities: Prospects for Research', in *Town and Gown: the University in Search of its Origins. CRE-Information* (Quarterly published by the Standing Conference of Rectors, Presidents and Vice-Chancellors of the European Universities), 62 (Geneva, 1983), pp. 47-58.

–, 'Students in the Middle Ages', in *Universitates e Università*. Atti del Convegno, Bologna 16-21 novembre 1987 (Bologna, 1995), pp. 119-24; translated and modified version 'Trasgressioni e rivolte studentesche', in *Le Università d'Europa*, pp. 81-103.

–, 'The University of Siena, 1357-1557', unpublished D.Phil. thesis, University of Oxford, 1981.

–, 'The Vocabulary of Italian Colleges to 1500', in *Le Vocabulaire des collèges*, pp. 70-77.

– and C. M. ELAM see *Florence and Italy*.

DE RIDDER-SYMOENS, H. see *A History of the University in Europe*, I.

–, 'Rich Men, Poor Men: Social Stratification and Social Representation at the University (13th-16th Centuries)', in *Showing Status: Representations of Social Positions in the Late Middle Ages*, eds. W. Blockmans and A. Janse. Medieval Texts and Cultures of Northern Europe, 2 (Turnhout, 1999), pp. 159-75.

DE ROSA, S., 'Studi sull'Università di Pisa. I, Alcune fonti inedite: Diari, lettere e rapporti dei bidelli (1473-1700)', *History of Universities*, 2 (1982), pp. 97-125.

DE SANDRE, G., 'Dottori, Università, Comune a Padova nel '400', *Quaderni per la Storia dell'Università di Padova*, 1 (1968), pp. 15-47.

DE SOUSA COSTA, A. D., 'Portugueses no Colégio de S. Clemente de Bolonha durante o século XV', in *El Cardenal Albornoz y el Colegio de España*, ed. E. Verdera y Tuells, III. Studia Albornotiana, 13 (Bologna, 1973), pp. 211-415.

–, *Portugueses no Colégio de S. Clemente e Universidade de Bolonha durante o século XV*. Studia Albornotiana, 56 (Bologna, 1990).

DE VERGOTTINI, G., 'Lo Studio di Bologna, l'Impero, il Papato', in *Studi e Memorie per la storia dell'Università di Bologna*, n. s., 1 (1956), pp. 19-95; repr. in his *Scritti di storia del diritto italiano*, ed. G. Rossi. Seminario giuridico della Università di Bologna, 74 (Milan, 1977), vol. II, pp. 695-792.

DI BERNARDO, F., *Un vescovo umanista alla corte pontificia: Giannantonio Campano (1429-1477)* (Rome, 1975).

DIENER, H., 'Die Hohen Schulen, ihre Lehrer und Schüler in den Registern der päpstlichen Verwaltung des 14. und 15. Jahrhunderts', in *Schulen und Studium*, pp. 351-74.

DI NOTO MARRELLA, S., *Doctores. Contributo alla storia degli intellettuali nella dottrina del diritto comune*, 2 vols. Pubblicazioni della Facoltà di Giurisprudenza, Università degli Studi di Parma, n.s. 18-19 (Padua, 1994).

DIONISOTTI, C., 'Jacopo Tolomei fra umanisti e rimatori', *Italia medioevale e umanista*, 6 (1963), pp. 137-76.

DI STOLFI, L., 'De S. Bernardini Senensis formatione scientifica', *Antonianum*, 20 (1945), pp. 245-66.

DI TORO, P., and R. DI PIETRA, *Amministrazione e contabilità nel XV e XVI secolo. Lo Spedale senese del Santa Maria della Scala attraverso i libri contabili*. Storia delle Istituzioni e del Pensiero Ragioneristico, 4 (Padua, 1999).

DOHRN-VAN ROSSUM, G., *History of the Hour. Clocks and Modern Temporal Orders* (tr. Chicago, Il., 1996).

DOMINICI, P., 'La misura del tempo. Storia delle ore del giorno in Italia: dalle horae temporariae romane alle ore attuali di tempo universale coordinato', *Sapere*, 51:12 (Dec 1985), pp. 29-39.

DONATI, D., *L'idea di nobiltà in Italia. Secoli XIV-XVIII* (Rome, 1988).

DONATI, F., 'Provvisioni della Repubblica sopra i matrimoni', *Miscellanea Storica Senese*, I (1893), pp. 167-8.

DONATO, M. M., 'Ancora sulle "fonti" nel *Buon Governo* di Ambrogio Lorenzetti: dubbi, precisazioni, anticipazioni', in, pp. 43-79.

–, 'La "bellissima inventiva": immagini e idee nella Sala della Pace', in *Ambrogio Lorenzetti. Il Buon Governo*, ed. E. Castelnuovo (Milan, 1995), pp. 23-41.

–, 'Il princeps, il giudice, il "sindacho" e la città. Novità su Ambrogio Lorenzetti nel Palazzo Pubblico di Siena', in *Imago urbis. L'immagine della città nella storia d'Italia*, eds. F. Bocchi and R. Smura (Rome, 2003), pp. 389-416.

DOOLEY, B., 'Social Control and the Italian Universities: From Renaissance to Illuminismo', *Journal of Modern History*, 61 (1989), pp. 205-39.

DORATI DA EMPOLI, M. C., 'I lettori dello Studio e i maestri di grammatica a Roma da Sisto IV ad Alessandro VI', *Rassegna degli Archivi di Stato*, 40 (1980), pp. 98-147.

DOTZAUER, W., 'Deutsches Studium in Italien unter besonderer Berücksichtigung der Universität Bologna. Versuch einer vorläufigen Zusammenstellenden Überschau', *Geschichtliche Landeskunde*, 14 (1976), pp. 84-130.

–, 'Deutsches Studium und deutsche Studenten an Europäischen Hochschulen (Frankreich, Italien) und die nachfolgende Tätigkeit in Stadt, Kirche und Territorium in Deutschland', in *Stadt und Universität*, pp. 112-41.

DUPUIGRENET DESROUSSILLES, F., 'L'Università di Padova dal 1405 al Concilio di Trento', in *Storia della cultura veneta*, 3:2 (Vicenza, 1980), pp. 607-47.

Les échanges entre les universités européennes à la Renaissance, eds. M. BIDEAUX and M.-M. FRAGONARD (Geneva, 2003).

EDGERTON, S. Y., *Pictures and Punishment: Art and Criminal Prosecution during the Florentine Renaissance* (Ithaca, N.Y., 1985).

ELSHEIKH, M. S. (ed.), *Il costituto del Comune di Siena volgarizzato nel MCCCIX-MCCCX* (Siena, 2002).

EPSTEIN, S. R., *Alle origini della fattoria toscana. L'ospedale della Scala e le sue terre (metà '200 – metà '400)* (Florence, 1986).

ERMINI, G., *Storia dell'Università di Perugia* (Florence, 1971 edn. in 2 vols.).

ESPOSITO, A., 'I collegi universitari di Roma: progetti e realizzazioni tra XIV e XV secolo', in *Le Vocabulaire des collèges*, pp. 80-89.

–, 'Forteguerri, Niccolò', *DBI*, 49 [1997], pp. 156-9.

–, 'Le "Sapientie" romane: I collegi Capranica e Nardini e lo "Studium Urbis"', in *Roma e lo Studium Urbis*, pp. 40-68.

EUBEL, K., *Hierarchia Catholica Medii Aevi*, I-II (Monasterii, 1913-14).

FACCIOLATI, I., *Fasti Gymnasii Patavini* (Padua, 1757).

FALCO, A., R. PLANTAMURA and S. RANZATO, 'Le istituzioni per l'istruzione superiore in Torino dal XV al XVIII secolo: considerazioni urbanistiche e architettoniche. L'Università e le residenze studentesche', *Bollettino storico-bibliografico subalpino*, 20 (1972), pp. 545-87.

FALLETTI-FOSSATI, C., *Costumi senesi nella seconda metà del secolo XIV* (Siena, 1881, repr. Bologna, 1980).

Fälschungen im Mittelalter. Internationaler Kongreß der Monumenta Germaniae Historica, München, 16. – 19. September 1986. Teil I: Kongreßdaten und Festvorträge, Literatur und Fälschung. Monumenta Germaniae Historica, Schriften, 33.i (Hannover, 1988).

FASOLI, G., 'I bidelli: sotto la cattedra c'erano anche loro', *Saecularia Nona. università di Bologna 1088-1988*, 3 (1988), pp. 50-53.

–, 'La composizione del falso diploma Teodosiano', *Studi e memorie per la storia dell'Università di Bologna*, n.s. 3 (1961), pp. 77-94, repr. in her *Scritti di storia medievale*, eds. F. Bocchi, A. Carile and A. I. Pini (Bologna, 1974), pp. 583-608.

–, 'Il falso privilegio di Teodorico II per lo Studio di Bologna', in *Fälschungen im Mittelalter*, pp. 627-41.

–, *Per la storia dell'Università di Bologna nel Medioevo* (Bologna, 1970).

–, 'Università, città, principe, poteri ecclesiastici nei secoli XI-XV', in *Universitates e Università*. Atti del Convegno, Bologna 16-21 novembre 1987 (Bologna, 1995), pp. 39-45.

– and G. B. PIGHI, 'Il privilegio teodosiano. Edizione critica e commento', *Studi e memorie per la storia dell'Università di Bologna*, n.s., 2 (1961), pp. 55-94.

FAVALE, S., 'Siena nel quadro della politica viscontea nell'Italia centrale', *BSSP*, n.s., 7 (1936), pp. 315-82.

FAVARO, A., 'Contribuzioni alla storia dello Studio di Padova intorno alla metà del secolo XIV', *Atti dell'Accademia di scienze, lettere ed arti in Padova*, 36 (1920), pp. 31-40.

–, 'Nuovi documenti intorno all'emigrazione dei professori e degli scolari dello Studio di Bologna avvenuta nel 1321', *Atti e Memorie, R. Deputazione di Storia patria per le Provincie di Romagna*, ser. 3, 10 (1892), pp. 313-23.

FEDELI, C., *I documenti pontifici riguardanti l'Università di Pisa* (Pisa, 1908).

FEDERICI VESCOVINI, G., 'Medicina e filosofia a Padova tra XIV e XV secolo: Jacopo da Forlì e Ugo Benzi da Siena (1380-1430)', in her *"Arti" e filosofia nel sec. XIV* (Florence, 1983), pp. 231-78.

FELDGES-HENNING, U., 'The Pictorial Programme of the Sala della Pace: a New Interpretation', *Journal of the Warburg and Courtauld Institutes*, 35 (1972), pp. 145-62.

FERRARI, H.-M., *Une chaire de médicine au XV⁰ siècle. Un professeur à l'Université de Pavie de 1432 a 1472* (Paris, 1899).

FERRERI, T., 'Documenti per la storia dello Studio senese dal 1475 al 1500', unpublished *tesi di laurea*, Università degli Studi di Siena, Facoltà di Giurisprudenza, anno accademico 1995-96, relatore P. Nardi.

FILIPPINI, F., 'L'esodo degli studenti da Bologna nel 1321 e il "Polifemio Dantesco"', *Studi e Memorie per la storia dell'Università di Bologna*, 6 (1921), pp. 105-85.

FIORAVANTI, G., 'Alcuni aspetti della cultura umanistica senese nel '400', *Rinascimento*, 19 (1979), pp. 117-67, repr. in his *Università e città*.

–, 'Le "arti liberali" nei secoli XII-XV', in *L'Università di Siena. 750 anni*, pp. 255-71.

–, 'Classe dirigente e cultura a Siena nel '400', in *I ceti dirigenti nella Toscana del Quattrocento*, pp. 473-84.

–, 'Formazione e carriera di un domenicano nel '400: l'autobiografia di Simone Bocci da Siena (1438-1510)', in *Studio e studia: le scuole degli ordini mendicanti tra XIII e XIV secolo*. Atti del XXIX convegno internazionale, 'Società Internazionale di Studi Francescani di Assisi' e del 'Centro Interuniversitario di Studi Francescani', n.s., 12 (Spoleto, 2002), pp. 339-64.

–, 'Maestri di grammatica a Siena nella seconda metà del Quattrocento', *Rinascimento*, 33 (1993), pp. 193-207; repr. in *Umanesimo a Siena*, pp. 11-27.

–, 'Pietro de' Rossi: Bibbia ed Aristotele nella Siena del '400', *Rinascimento*, 20 (1980), pp. 87-159, repr. in his *Università e città*.

–, 'Polemiche antigiudaiche nell'Italia del Quattrocento: un tentativo di interpretazione globale', in *Atti del VI Congresso internazionale dell'Associazione Italiana per lo Studio del Giudaismo* (Rome, 1988), pp. 75-91.

–, *Università e città. Cultura umanistica e cultura scolastica a Siena nel '400* (Florence, 1981).

FIORELLI, P., 'Una data per l'Università di Firenze', in *Le vie della ricerca. Studi in onore di Francesco Adorno*, ed. M. S. Funghi (Florence, 1996), pp. 491-6.

FLETCHER, J. M., 'The History of Academic Colleges: Problems and Prospects', in *I Collegi universitari*, pp. 13-22.

–, 'Wealth and Poverty in the Medieval German Universities with Particular Reference to the University of Freiburg', in *Europe in the Late Middle Ages*, eds. J. Hale, R. Highfield and B. Smalley (London, 1965), pp. 410-36.

Florence and Italy. Renaissance Studies in Honour of Nicolai Rubinstein, eds. P. R. Denley and C. M. Elam. Westfield Publications in Medieval Studies, 2 (London, 1989).

FOLCHI, M., 'Tomba di Guglielmo di Ciliano e Niccolò Aringhieri' in *L'Università di Siena. 750 anni*, pp. 334-6.

FOLIN, M., 'Studio e politica negli stati estensi fra Quattro e Cinquecento: dottori, ufficiali, cortigiani', in *Giovanni e Gianfrancesco Pico. L'opera e la fortuna di due studenti ferraresi*, ed. P. Castelli (Florence, 1998), pp. 59-90.

FRANCHI, F. C., and G. COSCARELLA, 'Le grance dello Spedale di Santa Maria della Scala nel contado senese', *BSSP*, 92 (1985), pp. 66-92.

FREEDBERG, D., 'Infamy, Justice, and Witchcraft: Explanation, Sympathy, and Magic', in his *The Power of Images: Studies in the History and Theory of Response* (Chicago & London, 1989), pp. 246-82, 480-85.

J. FRIED see *Schulen und Studium*.

FRIEDLÄNDER, E., and C. MALAGOLA (eds.), *Acta Nationis Germanicae Universitatis Bononiensis* (Berlin, 1887, repr. Bologna, 1988).

FROVA, C., 'Crisi e rifondazione nella storia delle piccole università italiane durante il medioevo', in *Le università minori*, pp. 29-47.

–, 'L'Europa vista dai centri universitari italiani', in *Europa e Mediterraneo tra Medioevo e prima età moderna: l'osservatorio italiano*, ed. S. Gensini. Centro di studi sulla civiltà del tardo medioevo di San Miniato, 4 (Pisa, 1992), pp. 375-93.

–, 'Martino V e l'università', in *Alle origini della nuova Roma: Martino V (1417-1431)*, eds. M. Chiabò, G. D'Alessandria, P. Piacentini and C. Ranieri (Rome, 1992), pp. 187-203 (p. 194).

–, 'Nazioni e culto dei santi nelle università medioevali', in *Comunità forestiere e 'nationes' nell'Europa dei secoli XIII-XVI*, ed. G. Petti Balbi (Naples, 2001), pp. 11-22.

–, 'L'università e la città: elementi per una discussione', in *L'università e la sua storia*, pp. 15-28.

–, 'Università italiane nel medioevo: nuovi orientamenti per una periodizzazione', *Annali di storia delle università italiane*, 1 (1997), pp. 213-8.

–, 'L'Università di Roma in età medievale e umanistica con una nota sulle vicende istituzionali in età moderna', in *L'Archivio di Stato di Roma*, ed. L. Lume (Florence, 1992), pp. 247-61.

– and M. MIGLIO, '"Studium Urbis" e "Studium Curiae" nel Trecento e nel Quattrocento: linee di politica culturale', in *Roma e lo Studium Urbis*, pp. 26-39.

FRUGONI, C., *A Distant City* (tr. Princeton, 1991).

–, 'Il governo dei Nove a Siena e il loro credo politico nell'affresco di Ambrogio Lorenzetti', *Quaderni Medievali*, 7 (1979), pp. 14-42, and 8 (1979), pp. 71-103 (revised version in her *A Distant City*.

FUSAI, L., *La Storia di Siena dalle origini al 1559* (Siena, 1987).

GABRIEL, A. L., '*Translatio Studii*. Spurious Dates of Foundation for some Early Universities', in *Fälschungen im Mittelalter*, pp. 601-26.

GALLAVOTTI CAVALLERO, D., *Lo Spedale di Santa Maria della Scala in Siena. Vicenda di una committenza artistica* (Pisa, 1985).

GALLO, D., 'La "domus Sapientiae" di Pietro Donato: un progetto quattrocentesco per un collegio universitario', *Quaderni per la Storia dell'Università di Padova*, 33 (2000), pp. 115-30.

–, 'Lauree inedite in diritto civile e canonico conferite presso lo Studio di Padova (1419-1422, 1423, 1424, 1428)', *Quaderni per la Storia dell'Università di Padova*, 20 (1987), pp. 1-50.

–, *Università e signoria a Padova dal XIV al XV secolo* (Trieste, 1998)

GARCÍA Y GARCÍA, A., 'Los difíciles inicios (siglos XIII-XIV)', in *La Universidad de Salamanca*, ed. M. Fernández Alvarez et al., 3 vols. (Salamanca, 1989-90), I. Trayectoria histórica y proyecciones, pp. 13-34.

GARCÍA Y GARCÍA, A. and P. WEIMAR see *Miscellanea Domenico Maffei dicata*.

GARFAGNINI, G. C., 'Città e Studio a Firenze nel XIV secolo: una difficile convivenza', *Critica storica*, 25 (1988), pp. 182-201, and in *Luoghi e metodi di insegnamento*, pp. 101-20.

GARGAN, L., 'L'enigmatico "conduxit". Libri e dogana a Padova fra Tre e Quattrocento', *Quaderni per la Storia dell'Università di Padova*, 16 (1983), pp. 1-41.

–, 'Libri, librerie e biblioteche nelle università italiane del Due e Trecento', in *Luoghi e metodi di insegnamento*, pp. 221-46.

–, 'Le note "conduxit". Libri di maestri e studenti nelle Università italiane del Tre e Quattrocento', in *Manuels, programmes de cours et techniques d'enseignement dans les universités médiévales*. Actes du Colloque international de Louvain-la-Neuve (9-11 septembre 1993), ed. J. Hamesse. Université Catholique de Louvain, Publications de l'Institut d'Études Médiévales, Textes, Études, Congrès, 16 (Louvain-la-Neuve, 1994), pp. 385-401.

– and O. LIMONE see *Luoghi e metodi di insegnamento*.

GAROSI, A., 'Alcuni documenti sulla vita di Ugo Benzi', in *Atti del IV Congresso Nazionale della Società Italiana di Storia delle Scienza Mediche e Naturali (Roma, 1933)* (Siena, 1934), pp. 89-135.

–, 'I codici di medicina del maestro Alessandro Sermoneta', *Rivista di Storia delle Scienze Mediche e Naturali*, 28 (1937), pp. 225-32.

–, *Inter artium et medicinae doctores* (Florence, 1963).

–, *Siena nella storia della medicina, 1240-1555* (Florence, 1958).

–, 'La vita e l'opera di Francesco Casini Archiatro di sei papi', *BSSP*, 42 (1935), pp. 277-378.

GAROSI, G. (ed.), *Inventario dei manoscritti della Biblioteca Comunale di Siena*, 3 vols. (Florence, 1978-86).

GASPARRI, S., *I 'milites' cittadini. Studi sulla cavalleria in Italia*. Istituto Storico Italiano per il Medioevo. Nuovi Studi Storici, 19 (Rome, 1972).

GATTONI DA CAMOGLI, M., *Pandolfo Petrucci e la politica estera della Repubblica di Siena (1487-1512)* (Siena, 1997).

GENNARO, C., 'Borghese, Borghese', *DBI*, 12 (1970), pp. 583-4.

GEREMEK, B., *The Margins of Society in Late Medieval Paris* (tr. Cambridge, 1987).

GHERARDI, A., *Statuti della Università e lo Studio Fiorentino* (Florence, 1881).

GHEZZO, M. P. see *Acta Graduum Academicorum Gymnasii Patavini*.

GIEYZSTOR, A., 'Management and Resources', in *A History of the University in Europe*, I, pp. 108-43.

GILLI, P., *La Noblesse du droit. Débats et controverses sur la culture juridique et le rôle des juristes dans l'Italie médiévale (XIIe-XVe siècles)*. Études d'histoire médiévale, 7 (Paris, 2003)

GILMORE, M. P., 'Pius II and Mariano Sozzini 'De Sortibus'', in *Enea Silvio Piccolomini: Papa Pio II*. Accademia Senese degli Intronati: Atti del Convegno per il Quinto Centenario della morte e altri scritti raccolti da Domenico Maffei (Siena, 1968), pp. 187-194.

–, '*Studia Humanitatis* and the Professions in Fifteenth Century Florence', in *Florence and Venice: Comparisons and Relations*. Acts of two conferences at Villa I Tatti in 1976-77 (Florence, 1979), I, pp. 27-40.

GINATEMPO, M., *Crisi di un territorio. Il popolamento della Toscana senese alla fine del medioevo* (Florence, 1988).

–, 'Motivazioni ideali e coscienza della "crisi" nella politica territoriale di Siena nel XV secolo', in *I ceti dirigenti nella Toscana del Quattrocento*, pp. 431-50; expanded version in *Ricerche Storiche*, 14 (1984), pp. 291-336.

–, 'Il popolamento della Valdorcia alla fine del medioevo (XV-XVI secolo)', in *La Val d'Orcia*, pp. 113-53.

–, 'Potere dei mercanti, potere della città: considerazioni sul "caso" Siena alla fine del medioevo', in *Strutture del potere ed élites economiche nelle città europee dei secoli 12-16*, ed. G. Petti Balbi (Naples, 1996), pp. 191-221.

–, *Prima del debito. Finanziamento della spesa pubblica e gestione del deficit nelle grandi città toscane (1200-1350 ca.)*. Biblioteca Storica Toscana, 38 (Florence, 2000).

GIORGI, A., 'Il carteggio del Concistoro della Repubblica di Siena (Spogli delle lettere: 1251-1374)', *BSSP*, 97 (1990), pp. 193-573.

GIRGENSOHN, D., 'Per la storia dell'insegnamento giuridico nel Quattrocento: risultati raggiunti e ricerche auspicabili', *Quaderni per la storia dell'Università di Padova*, 22-23 (1989-1990), pp. 311-9.

–, 'Studenti e tradizione delle opere di Francesco Zabarella nell'Europa centrale', in *Studenti, università, città*, pp. 127-76.

GLORIA, A., 'Antichi statuti del collegio padovano dei dottori giuristi', *Atti del Reale Istituto Veneto di Scienze, Lettere e Arti*, s. VI.7 (1889), pp. 355-402.

–, 'I sigilli della Università di Padova dal 1222 al 1797. Nota con documenti', *Atti del Reale Istituto Veneto di Scienze, Lettere e Arti*, s. VI.7 (1889), pp. 932-86.

–, *Monumenti della Università di Padova (1318-1405)*, 2 vols. (Padua, 1888, repr. Bologna, 1972).

GOLDBRUNNER, H. M., 'Die Mailändische Herrschaft in Perugia (1400-1403)', *Quellen und Forschungen aus italienische Archiven und Bibliotheken*, 45 (1972), pp. 397-475.

–, 'Die Übergabe Perugias an Giangaleazzo Visconti (1400)', *Quellen und Forschungen aus italienische Archiven und Bibliotheken*, 42/43 (1964), pp. 285-369.

GOLDTHWAITE, R. A., *The Building of Renaissance Florence. An Economic and Social History* (Baltimore, Md., 1980)

GOURON, A., 'La crise des Universités françaises à la fin du XIVᵉ siècle', in *Atti del Simposio Internazionale Cateriniano-Bernardiniano*, Siena, 17-20 aprile 1980, eds. D. Maffei and P. Nardi (Siena, 1982), pp. 907-15.

–, 'A l'origine d'un déclin: les universités méridionales au temps du Grand Schisme', in *Genèse et débuts du Grand Schisme d'Occident*. Colloques internationaux du C.N.R.S, 586 (Paris, 1980), pp. 175-84.

–, 'The Training of Southern French Lawyers during the Thirteenth and Fourteenth centuries', in *Post Scripta. Essays on Medieval Law and the Emergence of the European State in Honor of Gaines Post*, eds. J. R. Strayer and D. E. Queller. Studia Gratiana, 15 (1972), pp. 217-27.

GRAFTON, A. and L. JARDINE, *From Humanism to the Humanities: Education and the Liberal Arts in Fifteenth- and Sixteenth-Century Europe* (London, 1986).

GRAMSCH, R., *Erfurter Juristen im Spätmittelalter: Die Karrieremuster und Tätigkeitsfelder einer gelehrten Elite des 14. und 15. Jahrhunderts* (Leiden, 2003).

GRECI, R., 'L'associazionismo degli studenti dalle origini alla fine del secolo XIV', in *Studenti e Università*, pp. 15-44.

– see *Il pragmatismo degli intellettuali*.

–, 'Professioni e "crisi" bassomedievali: Bologna tra Due e Quattrocento', in *Disuguaglianze: stratificazione e mobilità sociale nelle popolazioni italiane dal secolo 14. agli inizi del secolo 20.: relazioni e comunicazioni presentati da autori italiani al 2. Congré 'Hispano Luso Italià' de demografia històrica: Savona, 18-21 novembre 1992* (Bologna, 1997), pp. 707-29.

GRENDLER, P. F., *The Universities of the Italian Renaissance* (Baltimore, Md., 2002).

–, 'The Universities of the Renaissance and Reformation', *Renaissance Quarterly*, 57 (2004), pp. 1-42.

GRIGUOLO, P., 'Antonio Mincucci da Pratovecchio e il Monastero della Vangadizza', *Quaderni per la Storia dell'Università di Padova*, 36 (2003), pp. 101-8.

GUALAZZINI, U., *Corpus Statutorum Almi Studii Parmensis* (Milan, 1978 edn.).

GUERRINI, M., 'Provvedimenti congiunturali 1385-1386', in *Siena e il suo territorio, II*, pp. 71-97.

GUIDI BRUSCOLI, F., *Benvenuto Olivieri. I* mercatores *fiorentini e la camera apostolica nella Roma di Paolo III Farnese (1534-1549)* (Florence, 2000).

HANKINS, J., 'The Invention of the Platonic Academy of Florence', *Rinascimento*, 41 (2001), pp. 3-38.

–, 'The Myth of the Platonic Academy of Florence', *Renaissance Quarterly*, 44 (1991), pp. 429-75.

HANLON, G., 'The Decline of a Provincial Military Aristocracy: Siena 1560-1740', *Past and Present*, 155 (May 1997), pp. 64-108.

HAUSMANN, F. R., 'Campano, Giovanni Antonio', *DBI*, 17 (1974), pp. 424-9.

HICKS, D. L., 'The Sienese Oligarchy and the Rise of Pandolfo Petrucci, 1487-97', in *La Toscana al tempo di Lorenzo*, III, pp. 1051-72.

–, 'Sienese Society in the Renaissance', *Comparative Studies in Society and History*, 2 (1959-60), pp. 412-20; tr. as 'Caratteristiche socio-economiche delle famiglie senesi aggregate ai monti tra 400 e 500', in *La caduta della Repubblica di Siena*, ed. E. Pellegrini (Siena, n.d.), pp. 53-60.

–, 'The Sienese State in the Renaissance', in *From the Renaissance to the Counter-Reformation. Essays in honour of Garrett Mattingly*, ed. C. H. Carter (London, 1966), pp. 75-94.

–, 'Sources of Wealth in Renaissance Siena: Businessmen and Landowners', *BSSP*, 93 (1986), pp. 9-42.

A History of the University in Europe, I. *Universities in the Middle Ages*, ed. H. DE RIDDER-SYMOENS (Cambridge, 1992).

HOOK, J., 'The Search for an Ideology in Sixteenth-Century Siena', *The Italianist*, 4 (1984), pp. 73-92.

–, *Siena. A City and its History* (London, 1979).

HÜLSEN-ESCH, A. VON, 'Gelehrte als *uomini famosi* in Oberitalien im 14. und 15. Jahrhundert', *Jahrbuch für Universitätsgeschichte*, 5 (2002), pp. 69-86.

–, 'Kleider machen Leute. Zur Gruppenrepräsentation von Gelehrten im Spätmittelalter', in *Die Repräsentation der Gruppen. Text – Bilder – Objekte*, ed. O. G. Oexle (Göttingen, 1998), pp. 225-57.

HUMPHREYS, K. W., *The Library of the Franciscans of Siena in the Late Fifteenth Century* (Amsterdam, 1978).

HUNT, A., *Governance of the Consuming Passions* (Basingstoke, 1996)

HYDE, J. K., *Padua in the Age of Dante* (Manchester and New York, 1966).

–, 'Universities and Cities in Medieval Italy', in *The University and the City: From Medieval Origins to the Present*, ed. T. Bender (New York, 1988), pp. 13-21.

IANZITI, G., *Humanist Historiography under the Sforzas. Politics and Propaganda in Fifteenth-Century Milan* (Oxford, 1988)

ILARDI, A., 'Ordinamenti del magistrato di Balìa di Siena ai lettori del pubblico studio', in *Atti del XXI congresso internazionale di storia della medicina, Siena (Italia), 22-28 settembre 1968* (Rome, 1969), pp. 164-70.

Il diritto a studiare: residenze universitarie a Siena tra passato e futuro. Atti del convegno, Siena, 6-7 dicembre 1991, ed. M. Brogi (Siena, 1995), pp. 9-18.

IRRGANG, S., *Peregrinatio Academica. Wanderungen und Karrieren von Gelehrten der Universitäten Rostock, Greifswald, Trier und Mainz im 15. Jahrhundert*. Beiträge zur Geschichte der Universität Greifswald, 4 (Stuttgart, 2002).

ISAACS, A. K., 'Le campagne senesi tra Quattro e Cinquecento: regime fondiario e governo signorile', in *Contadini e proprietari*, pp. 377-403.

–, 'Cardinali e "spalagrembi". Sulla vita politica a Siena fra il 1480 e il 1487', in *La Toscana al tempo di Lorenzo*, III, pp. 1013-50.

–, 'Impero, Francia e Medici: orientamenti politici e gruppi sociali a Siena nel primo Cinquecento', in *Firenze e la Toscana dei Medici nell'Europa del '500* (Florence, 1983), pp. 249-70.

–, 'Magnati, comune e stato a Siena nel Trecento e all'inizio del Quattrocento', in *I ceti dirigenti nella Toscana tardo comunale*, pp. 81-96.

–, 'Politica e giustizia agli inizi del Cinquecento: l'istituzione delle prime Rote', in *Atti di convegni di grandi tribunali e rote nell'Italia di antico regime*, eds. M. Sbriccoli and A. Bettoni. Pubblicazioni della Facoltà di Giurisprudenza, Università di Macerata, 4 (Milan, 1993), pp. 341-86.

–, 'Popolo e monti nella Siena del primo Cinquecento', *Rivista Storica Italiana*, 82 (1970), pp. 32-80; repr. in *La caduta della Repubblica di Siena*, ed. E. Pellegrini (Siena, n.d.), pp. 61-78.

–, 'Lo spedale di Santa Maria della Scala di Siena nell'antico stato senese', in *Spedale di Santa Maria della Scala*, pp. 19-29.

JENKENS, A. L., 'Pius II's Nephews and the Politics of Architecture at the End of the Fifteenth Century in Siena', *BSSP*, 106 (1999), pp. 68-114.

JONES, P. J., 'Communes and Despots: the City-State in Late Medieval Italy', *Transactions of the Royal Historical Society*, 5th ser., 15 (1965), pp. 71-96.

–, *Economia e società nell'Italia medievale* (Turin, 1980).

–, *The Italian City-State. From Commune to Signoria* (Oxford, 1997).

–, 'From Manor to Mezzadria: A Tuscan Case-Study in the Medieval Origins of Modern Agrarian Society', in *Florentine Studies*, ed. N. Rubinstein (London, 1968), pp. 193-241.

KAGAN, R. L., 'Universities in Italy, 1500-1700', in *Les Universités européens du XVIe au XVIIIe siècle: histoire sociale des populations étudiantes*, eds. D. Julia, J. Revel and R. Chartier, vol. 1 (Paris, 1986), pp. 153-86.

KAUFMANN, G., 'Die Universitätsprivilegien der Kaiser', *Deutsche Zeitschrift für Geschichtswissenschaft*, 1 (1889), pp. 118-65.

KIBRE, P., *The Nations in the Medieval Universities* (Cambridge, Ma., 1948).

–, *Scholarly Privileges in the Middle Ages. The Rights, Privileges, and Immunities, of Scholars and Universities at Bologna, Padua, Paris, and Oxford* (London, 1962).

KIENE, M., 'Die Bautätigkeit in den italienischen Universitäten von der Mitte des Trecento bis zur Mitte des Quattrocento', *Mitteilungen des Kunsthistorischen Institutes in Florenz*, 30:3 (1986), pp. 433-92.

–, 'Die Grundlagen der europäischen Universitätsbaukunst', *Zeitschrift für Kunstgeschichte*, 46 (1983), pp. 63-114.

–, 'Die italienischen Universitätspalast vom 14. Bis 18. Jahrhundert als Mittel der Politik', in *Stadt und Universität*, ed. H. Duchhardt (Cologne, etc., 1993), pp. 51-82.

–, 'Der Palazzo della Sapienza – zur italienischen Universitätsarchitektur des 15. und 16. Jahrhunderts', *Römisches Jahrbuch für Kunstgeschichte*, 23/24 (1988), pp. 221-71.

–, 'I progetti di Giuliano da Sangallo per l'Università di Siena', in *L'Università di Siena. 750 anni*, pp. 517-37.

–, 'La sede del sapere. I progetti per la Casa della Sapienza da Giuliano da Sangallo a Francesco di Giorgio Martini', in *Le dimore di Siena. L'arte dell'abitare nei territori dell'antica Repubblica dal Medioevo all'Unità d'Italia*, ed. G. Morolli (Florence, 2002), pp. 139-44.

KIRSHNER, J., 'Civitas sibi faciat civem: Bartolus of Sassoferrato's Doctrine on the Making of a Citizen', *Speculum*, 48 (1973), pp. 694-713.

–, 'Paolo di Castro on Cives ex Privilegio: a Controversy over the Legal Qualifications for Public Office in Early Fifteenth-Century Florence', in *Renaissance Studies in Honor of Hans Baron*, eds. A. Molho and J. A. Tedeschi (Florence, 1971), pp. 227-64.

– (ed.), *The Origins of the State in Italy 1300-1600* (Chicago, Il., 1995).

KNOD, G., *Deutsche Studenten in Bologna (1289-1562): Biographischer Index zu den Acta nationis germanicae Universitatis Bononiensis* (Berlin, 1899).

KOHL, B., 'Conti, Prosdocimo' in *DBI*, 28 (1983), pp. 463-5.

KOLLER, H., 'Stadt und Universität im Spätmittelalter', in *Stadt und Universität*, pp. 9-26.

KOŠUTA, L., 'Aonio Paleario et son groupe humaniste et réformateur à Sienne (1530-1546)', *Lias*, 7 (1980), pp. 18-21.

–, 'Documenti per la Storia dello Studio senese dal 1531 al 1542', in MINNUCCI and KOŠUTA, *Lo Studio di Siena*, pp. 315-578.

–, 'Siena nella vita e nell'opera di Marino Darsa (Marin Držić)', *Ricerche slavistiche*, 9 (1961), pp. 67-121.

KOTEL'NIKOVA, L. A., 'Rendita in natura e rendita in denaro nell'Italia medievale (secoli IX-XV)', in *Storia d'Italia. Annali 6. Economia naturale, economia monetaria*, eds. R. Romano and U. Tucci (Turin, 1983), pp. 94-112.

KOUAMÉ, T., *Le collège de Dormans-Beauvais à la fin du Moyen Age. Stratégies politiques et pouvoirs individuels à l'Université de Paris (1370-1485)*. Education and Society in the Middle Ages and Renaissance, 22 (Leiden, 2005).

KOUDELKA, V. J., O.P., 'Spigolature dal Memoriale di Niccolò Galgani O.P. († 1424)', *Archivum Fratrum Praedicatorum*, 29 (1959), pp. 111-47.

KOVESI KILLERBY, C., 'Practical Problems in the Enforcement of Italian Sumptuary Law, 1200-1500', in *Crime, Society and the Law in Renaissance Italy*, eds. T. Dean and K. J. P. Lowe (Cambridge, 1994), pp. 99-120.

–, *Sumptuary Law in Italy 1200-1500* (Oxford, 2002).

KRISTELLER, P. O., 'The Curriculum of the Italian Universities from the Middle Ages to the Renaissance', in *Proceedings of the Patristic, Medieval and Renaissance Conference*, IX, 1984 (1986), pp. 1-16; repr. in his *Studies in Renaissance Thought and Letters*, IV (Rome, 1996), pp. 75-96.

–, *Die italienischen Universitäten der Renaissance*. Schriften und Vorträge des Petrarca-Instituts Köln, 1 (1953); repr. in his *Studies in Renaissance Thought and Letters*, IV (Rome, 1996), pp. 97-113.

KUBOVÁ, M., 'University založené Karlem IV. (Die von Karl IV. gegründeter Universitäten)', *Acta Universitatis Carolinae – Historia Universitatis Carolinae Pragensis*, 11 (1971), pp. 7-31.

KUCHER, M. P., *The Water Supply System of Siena, Italy. The Medieval Roots of the Modern Networked City* (New York and London, 2005).

LANDI, A., *Il papa deposto (Pisa 1409). L'idea conciliare nel grande schisma* (Turin, 1985).

LAURIOUX, B., and L. MOULINIER-BROGI see *Scrivere il medioevo*.

LAZZARINI, V., 'Crisi nello Studio di Padova a mezzo il Quattrocento', *Atti dell'Istituto Veneto di Scienze Lettere ed Arti, Classe di Scienze Morali e Lettere*, 109 (1950-51), pp. 201-11.

LEE, E., 'Humanists and the "Studium urbis", 1473-1484', in *Umanesimo a Roma nel Quattrocento*, eds. P. Brezzi and M. De Panizza Lorch (Rome, 1984), pp. 127-46.

–, *Sixtus IV and Men of Letters* (Rome, 1978).

LE GOFF, J., 'Alle origini del lavoro intellettuale in Italia. I problemi del rapporto fra la letteratura, l'università e le professioni', in *Letteratura italiana*, I. *Il letterato e le istituzioni* (Einaudi, Turin, 1982), pp. 649-79.

–, 'Dépenses universitaires a Padoue', *Mélanges d'Archéologie et d'Histoire, École Française de Rome*, 68 (1956), pp. 377-95, tr. as 'Academic Expenses at Padua in the Fifteenth Century' in his *Time, Work, and Culture in the Middle Ages* (Chicago, Il., 1980), pp. 101-6, 309-18.

–, *Les intellectuels au moyen âge* (Paris, 1957), tr. as *Intellectuals in the Middle Ages* (Cambridge, Ma., and Oxford, 1993).

–, 'Les universités et les pouvoirs publics au moyen âge et a la Renaissance', *XIIe Congrès International des Sciences Historiques, Vienne, 29 Août – 5 Septembre 1965. Rapports, III: Commissions* (Vienna, n. d.), pp. 189-206, tr. as 'The Universities and the Public Authorities in the Middle Ages and the Renaissance' in his *Time, Work, and Culture in the Middle Ages* (Chicago, Il., 1980), pp. 135-49, 321-4.

LEICHT, P. S., 'Discorso inaugurale per l'inizio del VIII centenario della R. Università', in *Senarum universitatis ...ineunte octavo vitae suae saeculo* (Siena, 1942).

–, 'Il primo tentativo di costituire un'Università nella Venezia orientale', *Memorie Storiche Forogiuliesi*, 6 (1910), pp. 1-14.

–, 'Sull'Università di Cividale', *Memorie Storiche Forogiuliesi*, 8 (1912), pp. 311-3.

LEONCINI, A., 'I simboli dell'Università di Siena', *Annali di Storia delle Università italiane*, 4 (2000), pp. 123-38; rev. vn. 'I simboli dell'Università di Siena dal XIV al XX secolo', in *Siena e il suo territorio, III*, pp. 235-58.

LIBERATI, A., 'Chiese, monasteri, oratori e spedali senesi (Ricordi e notizie)', *BSSP*, 46-68 (1939-61), esp. 64 (1957), pp. 186-201.

–, 'Lucignano di Val d'Arbia. Ricordi e documenti', *BSSP*, 45 (1938), pp. 48-67.

LINES, D., *Aristotle's Ethics in the Italian Renaissance (ca. 1300-1650): The Universities and the Problem of Moral Education* (Leiden, 2002)

–, 'Natural Philosophy in Renaissance Italy: the University of Bologna and the Beginnings of Specialization', *Early Science and Medicine*, 6 (2001), pp. 267-323.

LIOTTA, F., 'Barbazza, Andrea', in *DBI*, 6 (1964), pp. 146-8.

LISINI, A., 'Papa Gregorio XII e i senesi', *La Rassegna Nazionale*, 91 (1 Sept. 1896), pp. 97-117, 280-321.

–, 'Le leggi prammatiche durante il governo dei Nove, 1287-1355', *BSSP*, 37 (1930), pp. 41-70.

LOCKWOOD, D. P., *Ugo Benzi, Medieval Philosopher and Physician, 1376-1439* (Chicago, Il., 1951).

LUCHAIRE, J., *Documenti per la storia dei rivolgimenti politici del Comune di Siena dal 1354 al 1369* (Lyons, 1906).

Luoghi e metodi di insegnamento nell'Italia medioevale (secoli XII-XIV), eds. L. Gargan and O. Limone (Galatina, Lecce, 1989).

LUSCHIN VON EBENGREUTH, A., 'I sepolcri degli scolari tedeschi in Siena', *BSSP*, 3 (1896), pp. 9-21, 299-326, 5 (1898), pp. 52-62; repr. in *I tedeschi nella storia*, pp. 105-47.

–, review of ZDEKAUER, *Studio*, *Göttingische gelehrte Anzeige*, n.s. 12 (1895), pp. 965-71.

LUSINI, V., 'Notizie storiche sulla topografia di Siena nel secolo XIII', *BSSP*, 28 (1921), pp. 239-341.

LUZZATI, M., 'Dottorati in medicina conferiti a Firenze nel 1472 da Judah Messer Leon da Montecchio a Bonaventura da Terracina e ad Abramo da Montalcino', in *Medicina e salute nelle Marche dal Rinascimento all'età napoleoica. Atti del Convegno, Ancona – Recanati, 28-30 maggio 1992*. Atti e Memorie per la storia Patria delle Marche, 97 (Ancona, 1994), pp. 41-53.

Maestri e scolari a Siena e Perugia, 1250-1500. Una prosopografia dinamica del corpo accademico e studentesco. ricerche di prosopografia elettronica curate da Carla Frova, Paolo Nardi, Paolo Renzi, at www.unisi.it/docentes.

MAFFEI, D., 'Un documento spagnolo sulla ricettività studentesca senese nel Cinquecento', in *Scritti dedicati ad Alessandro Raselli*, 2 (Milan, 1971), pp. 953-58.

–, 'Giovanni Battista Caccialupi biografo', *Zeitschrift der Savigny-Stiftung für Rechtsgeschichte. Kanonistische Abteilung*, 83 (1997), pp. 392-400.

–, *Gli inizi dell'umanesimo giuridico* (Milan, 1956).

–, 'Una nuova fonte per la biografia di Benedetto Barzi da Perugia (1379 ca. – 1459). Con precisazioni su Benedetto da Piombino', *Index. Quaderni camerti di studi romanistici / International Survey of Roman Law*, 22: Omaggio a Peter Stein (1994), pp. 511-28; repr. in his *Studi di storia delle università e della letteratura giuridica* (Goldbach, 1995), pp. 235*-252*.

–, 'Il trattato di Martino Garati per la canonizzazione di San Bernardino da Siena', *Studi senesi*, 100 (1988), pp. 580-603 repr. in his *Studi di storia delle università e della letteratura giuridica* (Goldbach, 1995), pp. 253*-276*.

–, 'Un trattato di Bonaccorso degli Elisei e i più antichi statuti dello Studio di Bologna nel manoscritto 22 della Robbins Collection', *Bulletin of Medieval Canon Law*, 5 (1975), pp. 73-101; repr. in his *Studi di storia delle università e della letteratura giuridica* (Goldbach, 1995), pp. 23*-51* with additions pp. 524*-526*.

– and P. MAFFEI, *Angelo Gambiglioni giureconsulto aretino del Quattrocento* (Rome, 1994).

– and H. DE RIDDER-SYMOENS see *I Collegi universitari*.

– et al. see *A Ennio Cortese*.

– et al. (eds.), *I codici del Collegio di Spagna di Bologna*. Orbis Academicus. Saggi e Documenti di Storia delle Università, 5 (Milan, 1992).

MAIERÙ, A., 'Ancora sugli atti scolastici nelle università italiane', in *Studi sulle società e le culture del Medioevo per Girolamo Arnaldi*, eds. L. Gatto and P. Supino Martini (Florence, 2002), pp. 307-26.

–, 'Gli Atti scolastici nelle Università italiane', in *Luoghi e metodi di insegnamento*, pp. 247-87; English tr. as Chapter 2 of his *University Training*.

–, 'Tecniche di insegnamento', in *Le scuole degli Ordini Mendicanti (secoli XIII-XIV). Convegno del Centro di Studi sulla Spiritualità Medievale, XVII, 11-14 ottobre 1976* (Todi, 1978), pp. 307-52; ; English tr. as Chapter 1 of his *University Training*.

–, 'La terminologie de l'universitè de Bologne de médecine et des arts: "facultas", "verificare"', in *Vocabulaire des écoles et des méthodes d'enseignement au moyen âge*. Actes du colloque Rome 21-22 octobre 1989, ed. O. Weijers. Études sur le vocabulaire intellectuel du moyen âge, 5 (Turnhout, 1992), pp. 140-56; repr. in *Miscellanea Domenico Maffei dicata*, 2, pp. 393-409; English tr. as Chapter 3 of his *University Training*.

–, *University Training in Medieval Europe*, tr./ed. D. N. Pryds (Leiden, 1994).

MAIOCCHI, R., *Codice diplomatico dell'Università di Pavia* (Pavia, 1905-15).

MALAGOLA, C., *Statuti delle Università e dei Collegi dello Studio bolognese* (Bologna, 1888).

MANCINI, G., 'Il testamento di L. B. Alberti', *Archivio Storico Italiano*, 72:2 (1914), pp. 20-52.

MANDRIANI, C., 'I proprietari delle "Libre" di San Donato a lato dei Montanini, San Donato a lato della Chiesa, San Donato di Sopra e San Donato di Sopra', in CHERUBINI (ed.), 'I proprietari di beni immobili', pp. 439-54.

MANTEGNA, C., *Lo* Studium Urbis *nei* Diversa Cameralia *dell'Archivio Segreto Vaticano. Nuova edizione di documenti universitari romani (1425-1517)* (Rome, 2000).

MARCONI, L., and M. A. PANZANELLI FRATONI, 'L'Università scopre le sue carte. I lavori di riordinamento dell'archivio storico dell'Università degli Studi di Perugia', *Bollettino della Deputazione di Storia Patrie per l'Umbria*, 98:2 (2001), pp. 459-84.

MARI, P., 'Buonguglielmi, Sallustio', *DBI*, 15 (1972), pp. 237-41.

MARIOTTI, G., *Memorie e documenti per la storia dell'Università di Parma nel Medio Evo* (Parma, 1888).

MARLETTA, F., 'Un episodio della vita di Andrea Barbazza', *Archivio Storico Messinese*, 40-49 (1939-48), pp. 23-34.

–, 'Note all'Epistolario del Panormita', *La Rinascita*, 5 (1942), pp. 516-26.

–, 'Per la biografia di Porcelio Pandoni (Note e Documenti)', *La Rinascita*, 3 (1940), pp. 842-81.

–, 'Philelphiana', *La Rinascita*, 5 (1942), pp. 122-34.

MARONGIU, A., 'Protezionismi scolastici e problemi universitari di ieri e oggi', *Archivio giuridico* (1943); repr. in his *Stato e scuola*, pp. 283-312.

–, 'Protezionismi scolastici e stipendi professoriali', in *Studi in onore di Amintore Fanfani*, 6 vols. (Milan, 1942), VI, pp. 313-28; repr. in his *Stato e Scuola*, pp. 251-65.

– *Stato e scuola. Esperienze e problemi della scuola occidentale* (Milan, 1974).

MARRARA, D., 'I magnati e il governo del Comune di Siena dallo statuto del 1274 alla fine del XIV secolo', in *Studi per Enrico Fiumi* (Pisa, 1979), pp. 239-76.

–, *Riseduti e nobiltà. Profilo storico-istituzionale di un'oligarchia toscana nei secoli XVI-XVIII*. Biblioteca del 'Bollettino Storico Pisano', Collana Storica, 16 (Pisa, 1976).

–, *Lo Studio di Siena nelle riforme del granduca Ferdinando I (1589 e '91)* (Milan, 1970).

MARTELLOZZO FORIN, E. see *Acta graduum academicorum gymnasii patavini*.

MARTI, B. M., *The Spanish College at Bologna in the Fourteenth Century* (Philadelphia, Pa., 1966).

MARTINES, L., *Lawyers and Statecraft in Renaissance Florence* (Princeton, N.J., 1968).

–, *Power and Imagination: City-States in Renaissance Italy* (London, 1980).

–, *The Social World of the Florentine Humanists, 1390-1460* (London, 1963).

MASCHKE, E., and J. SYDOW see *Stadt und Universität*.

MATSCHINEGG, I., 'Student Communities and Urban Authorities', *Medium Aevum Quotidianum*, 48 (2003), pp. 29-36.

MATSEN, H. S., 'Alessandro Achillini (1463-1512) as Professor of Philosophy in the "Studio" of Padua (1506-1508)', *Quaderni per la Storia dell'Università di Padova*, 1 (1968), pp. 9l-109.

–, 'Students' "Arts" Disputations at Bologna around 1500 Illustrated from the Career of Alessandro Achillini (1463-1512)', *History of Education*, 6 (1977), pp. 169-181.

MAZO KARRAS, R., 'Separating the Men from the Beasts: Medieval Universities and Masculine Formation', ch. 2 of her *From Boys to Men. Formations of Masculinity in Late Medieval Europe* (Philadelphia, Pa., 2003).

MAZZI, C., 'Alcune leggi suntuarie senesi del secolo XIII', *Archivio Storico Italiani*, se. 4, 5 (1880), pp. 133-44.

–, 'La biblioteca di messer Nicolò di Messer Bartolomeo Borghesi ed altre in Siena nel Rinascimento', *Rivista delle Biblioteche e degli Archivi*, 6 (1895), pp. 120-25, 150-59.

–, *La casa di maestro Bartalo di Tura* (Siena, 1900).

–, *La Congrega de' Rozzi di Siena nel secolo XVI*, 2 vols. (Florence, 1881).

–, 'Lo studio di un medico senese del secolo XV', *Rivista delle Biblioteche e degli Archivi*, 5 (1894), pp. 27-48.

MAZZI, M. S., *Prostitute e lenoni nella Firenze del Quattrocento* (Milan, 1991).

MECACCI, E., *La biblioteca di Ludovico Petrucciani docente di diritto a Siena nel Quattrocento*. Quaderni di 'Studi senesi', 50 (Milan, 1981).

–, 'Contributo allo studio delle biblioteche universitarie senesi (Alessandro Sermoneta – Giorgio Tolomei – Domenico Maccabruni)', *Studi senesi*, 97 (1985), pp. 125-78.

–, 'Lo Studio e i codici', in C. BASTIANONI et al., *Lo Studio e i testi. Il libro universitario a Siena (secoli XII-XVII). Catalogo della mostra coordinato da Mario Ascheri, Siena, Biblioteca Comunale, 14 settembre – 31 ottobre 1996* (Siena, 1996), pp. 17-38.

MELIS, F., 'Sul finanziamento degli allievi portoghesi del Real Collegio de España di Bologna nel XV secolo', *El Cardenal Albornoz y el Colegio de España*, ed. E. Verdera y Tuells, III. Studia Albornotiana, 13 (Bologna, 1973), pp. 417-34; repr. in *I mercanti italiani nell'Europa medievale e rinascimentale*, ed. L. Frangioni (Florence, 1990), pp. 19-33.

MENCHELLI, M., 'Agostino Dati traduttore del greco', in *Umanesimo a Siena*, pp. 89-110.

MENGEL, D. C., 'From Venice to Jerusalem and Beyond: Milíč of Kroměříž and the Topography of Prostitution in Fourteenth-Century Prague', *Speculum*, 79 (2004), pp. 407-42.

MENGOZZI, G., 'Lodovico Zdekauer', *BSSP*, 30 (1923), pp. 240-2.

MENGOZZI, N., *Il feudo del vescovado di Siena* (Siena, 1911, repr. 1980).

–, 'La crise religieuse du XV siècle – Martino V ed il concilio di Siena (1418-1431)', *BSSP*, 25 (1918), pp. 247-314.

–, 'Il pontefice Paolo II e i senesi', *BSSP*, 21 (1914), pp. 141-74, 197-288, 455-530; 22 (1915), pp. 253-302; 24 (1917), pp. 37-68, 85-130, 205-60; 25 (1918), pp. 3-75.

MERCER, R. G. C., *The Teaching of Gasparino Barzizza, with Special Reference to his Place in Paduan Humanism.* Modern Humanities Research Association, Texts and Dissertations, 10 (1979).

MEYER-HOLZ, U., *Collegia Iudicum. Über die Form sozialer Gruppenbildung durch die gelehrten Berufsjuristen im Oberitalien des späten Mittelalters, mit einem Vergleich zu Collegia Doctorum Iuris.* Fundamenta iuridica, 6 (Baden-Baden, 1989).

–, 'Die *Collegia Iudicum* und ihre Bedeutung für die Professionalisierung der Juristen', *Zeitschrift für Historische Forschung*, 28 (2001), pp. 359-84.

MEYHÖFER, M., 'Die kaiserlichen Stiftungsprivilegien für Universitäten', *Archiv für Urkundenforschung*, 4 (1912), pp. 291-418.

MIETHKE, J., 'Die Studenten', in *Unterwegssein im Spätmittelalter.* Zeitschrift für historische Forschung, Beiheft 1 (Berlin, 1985), pp. 49-70.

MILANI, G., 'Bologna's two Exclusions and the Power of Law Experts', in press (*Europäisches Forum junger Rechtshistorikerinnen und Rechtshistoriker (Osnabrück, 22-25 May 2002)*); and online on "Reti Medievali".

–, 'La memoria dei *rumores*. I disordini bolognesi del 1274 nel ricordo delle prime generazioni: note preliminari', in *Le storie e la memoria. In onore di Arnold Esch*, eds. R. Delle Donne and A. Zorzi (Florence, 2002), pp. 271-93.

MILLER, M. C., 'Participation at the Council of Pavia-Siena, 1423-1424', *Archivum historiae pontificiae*, 22 (1984), pp. 389-406.

MINNUCCI, G., 'Bibliografia sulla storia dello Studio senese dalle origini fino al XVI secolo', in *I tedeschi nella storia*, pp. 159-65.

–, 'La Casa della Sapienza', in *Storia di Siena*, I, pp. 357-70.

–, 'La Chiesa e le istituzioni culturali senesi tra Medioevo e Rinascimento', in *Chiesa e vita religiosa a Siena dalle origini al Grande Giubileo. Atti dei Convegno di studi (Siena 25-27 ottobre 2000)*, eds. A. Mirizio and P. Nardi. Istituto Storico Diocesano di Siena, Testi e Documenti, 4 (Siena, 2002), pp. 217-28.

–, 'Il conferimento dei titoli accademici nello Studio di Siena fra XV e XVI secolo. Modalità dell'esame e provenienza studentesca', in *Università in Europa. Le istituzioni universitarie*, pp. 213-26; revised version in MINNUCCI and MORELLI, *Le lauree dello Studio senese nel 16. secolo: regesti degli atti dal 1573 al 1579*, pp. ix-xxviii.

–, 'Documenti per la Storia dello Studio senese (Secoli XIV-XVI)', in MINNUCCI and KOŠUTA, *Lo Studio di Siena*, pp. 9-314.

–, 'La laurea in diritto civile di Lancelotto Politi', *BSSP*, 88 (1981), pp. 254-5.

–, *Le lauree dello Studio senese alla fine del secolo XV.* Quaderni di 'Studi senesi', 51 (Milan, 1981).

–, *Le lauree dello Studio senese all'inizio del secolo XVI (1501-1506)* and *II (1507-1514).* Quaderni di 'Studi senesi', 55 and 56 (Milan, 1984 and 1985).

–, 'Professori e scolari giuristi nello Studio di Siena dalle origini alla fine del XV secolo', in *L'Università di Siena. 750 anni*, pp. 111-30.

–, 'Rassegna bibliografica sulla storia dello Studio senese dalle origini fino alla prima metà del Cinquecento', *Studi senesi*, 93 (1981), pp. 425-45.

–, 'San Bernardino patrono dell'Università di Siena', *L'Osservatore romano*, 148 (28 Jun 1984), p. 7.

–, 'Siena e l'Europa. Studenti stranieri a Siena fra XV e XVII secolo', in *Cultura e Università a Siena*, pp. 27-34.

–, 'A Sienese Doctorate in Canon Law from 1389', in *The Two Laws. Studies in Medieval Legal History Dedicated to Stephan Kuttner*, eds. L. Mayali and S. A. J. Tibbetts. Studies in Medieval and Early Modern Canon Law,

1 (Washington, 1990), pp. 202-8; Italian version, with additions and revisions, 'Una laurea senese in diritto canonico del 1389', *Annuario dell'Istituto Storico Diocesano di Siena* (1994-5), pp. 151-60.

–, 'La storia delle Università italiane nel medio Evo. Prospettive di ricerca', *Studi senesi*, 107 (1995), pp. 145-64, repr. as 'La storia delle università medievali. Ricerche e prospettive', in *La storia delle università italiane*, pp. 293-309.

–, 'Studenti boemi laureati a Siena fra XV e XVII secolo', in *Siena in Praga*, pp. 54-58.

–, 'Studenti giuristi portoghesi a Siena nella seconda metà del XV secolo', in *Amicitiae pignus. Studi in onore di Adriano Cavanna*, eds. A. Padoa Schioppa, G. di Renzo Villata and G. P. Massetto, 3 vols. (Milan, 2003), pp. 1477-88.

– see *I tedeschi nella storia dell'Università di Siena* (Siena, 1988).

–, 'La vita nel Collegio della Sapienza di Siena durante la seconda metà del XV secolo', in *I Collegi universitari*, pp. 23-32.

– and L. KOŠUTA, *Lo Studio di Siena nei secoli XIV-XVI*. Orbis Academicus, Saggi e Documenti di Storia delle Università, 3/Saggi e Documenti per la Storia dell'Università di Siena, 1 (Milan, 1989).

– and P. G. MORELLI, *Le lauree dello Studio senese nel XVI secolo. Regesti degli atti dal 1516 al 1573*. Bibliotheca Studii Senensis, 5 (Siena, 1992)

– and P. G. MORELLI, *Le lauree dello Studio senese nel 16. secolo: regesti degli atti dal 1573 al 1579*. Università degli Studi di Siena, Dipartimento di Scienze Storiche, Giuridiche, Politiche e Sociali: Istituto Storico Diocesano di Siena (Siena, 1998)

Miscellanea Domenico Maffei dicata: historia, ius, studium, eds. A. García y García and P. Weimar (Goldbach, 1995).

La Misericordia di Siena attraverso i secoli. Dalla Domus Misericordiae all'Arciconfraternita della Misericordia, eds. M. ASCHERI and P. TURRINI (Siena, 2004).

MITCHELL, R. J., 'English Student Life in Early Renaissance Italy', *Italian Studies*, 7 (1952), pp. 62-81.

–, *John Free. From Bristol to Rome in the Fifteenth Century* (London, 1955).

–, *The Laurels and the Tiara. Pope Pius II, 1458-1464* (London, 1962).

MOCENNI, A., 'Pene ai traditori', *Miscellanea Storica Senese*, 1 (1893), pp. 23-4.

MOLHO, A., *Florentine Public Finances in the Early Renaissance, 1400-1433* (Cambridge, Ma., 1971).

–, 'The State and Public Finance: a Hypothesis Based on the History of Late Medieval Florence', in *The Origins of the State in Italy 1300-1600*, ed. J. Kirshner (Chicago, Il., 1995), pp. 97-135.

MONDOLFO, G., 'Il ruolo dello Studio Senese del 16 ott. 1500', *BSSP*, 4 (1897), pp. 412-17.

MONFRIN, J., 'Etudiants italiens a la fin du XIVᵉ siècle', *Mélanges d'Archéologie et d'Histoire, École Française de Rome*, 63 (1951), pp. 195-280.

MONTOBBIO, L., *Splendore e utopia nella Padova dei Carraresi* (Padua, 1989).

MORANDI, U., 'L'Ufficio della Dogana del Sale in Siena', *BSSP*, 3rd s., 22 (70) (1963), pp. 62-91.

MOREIRA DE SA, A., *Humanistas portugueses em Itàlia. Subsìdios para o estudo de Frei Gomes de Lisboa, des dois Luises Teixeiras, de João de Barros e de Henrique Caiado* (Lisbon, 1983).

MORELLI, G., 'I Collegi di Diritto nello Studio di Bologna fra XIV e XVII secolo. Considerazioni preliminari', *Il Carrobbio*, 8 (1982), pp. 248-58.

MORELLI, P. G., S. MOSCADELLI and C. SANTINI (eds.), *L'Archivio Comunale di Montalcino. Inventario della sezione storica*, ed., I (Siena, 1989).

MORETTI, I., 'L'architettura delle sedi universitarie', in *L'Università di Siena. 750 anni*, pp. 275-300.

MORIANI, L., *Notizie sulla Università di Siena* (Siena, 1873).

MORNET, E., '*Pauperes scolares*. Essai sur la condition matérielle des étudiants scandinaves dans les universités aux XIVᵉ et XVᵉ siècles', *Le Moyen Age*, 84 (1978), pp. 53-102.

MORONI, M., *Lodovico Zdekauer e la storia del commercio nel medio Adriatico*. Quaderni monografici di "Proposte e ricerche", 22 (Ancona, 1997).

MORRESI, M.. 'Bramante, Enrico Bruno e la parrocchiale di Roccaverrano', in *La piazza, la chiesa e il parco*, ed. M. Tafuri (Milan, 1991), pp. 96-165.

–, 'Francesco di Giorgio e Bramante: osservazioni su alcuni disegni degli Uffizi e della Laurenziana', in *Il disegno di architettura. Atti del convegno* (Milano, 15-18 febbraio 1988), eds. P. Carpeggiani and L. Patetta (Milan, 1989), pp. 117-24.

MORRISSEY, T. E., 'Padua in Crisis and Transition Around 1400', paper for International Congress of the Historical Sciences, Oslo 2000, published on www.oslo2000.uio.no/A10/A1016/group-2/Morrissey.pdf (downloaded on 7 April 2004).

MOSCADELLI, S., 'Apparato burocratico e finanze del Comune di Siena sotto il Dodici (1355-1368)', *BSSP*, 89 (1982), pp. 29-118.

–, 'Oligarchie e Monti', in *Storia di Siena*, I, pp. 267-78.

–, 'Recenti studi su Siena medievale', *Archivio Storico Italiano*, 145 (1987), pp. 81-98.

MUCCIARELLI, R., 'Igiene, salute e pubblico decoro nel Medioevo', in R. MUCCIARELLI, L. VIGNI and D. FABBRI, *Vergognosa immunditia. Igiene pubblica e privata a Siena dal medioevo all'età contemporanea* (Siena, 2000), pp. 13-84.

MÜNSTER, L., *Baverio Maghinardo de' Bonetti, medico imolese del Quattrocento: la vita, i tempi, il pensiero scientifico* (Imola, 1956).

MUZZARELLI, M. G., 'Bologna', in *La legislazione suntuaria secoli XIII-XVI. Emilia-Romagna*, ed. M. G. Muzzarelli. Pubblicazioni degli Archivi di Stato, Fonti 41 (Rome, 2002), pp. 1-262.

–, '"Contra mundanas vanitates et pompas": aspetti della lotta contro i lussi nell'Italia del XV secolo', *Rivista di Storia della Chiesa in Italia*, 40 (1986), pp. 371-90.

–, 'La disciplina delle apparenze. Vestiti e ornamenti nella legislazione suntuaria bolognese fra XIII e XV secolo', in *Disciplina dell'anima, disciplina del corpo, disciplina della società tra medioevo ed età moderna*, ed. P. Prodi (Bologna, 1994), pp. 757-84.

–, *Gli inganni delle apparenze. Disciplina di vesti e ornamenti alla fine del Medioevo* (Turin, 1996).

–, 'Le leggi suntuarie', in *Storia d'Italia, Annali 19: La moda*, eds. C. M. Belfanti and F. Giusberti (Turin, 2003), pp. 185-220.

– (ed.), *La legislazione suntuaria secoli XIII-XVI. Emilia-Romagna*. Pubblicazioni degli Archivi di Stato, Fonti 41 (Rome, 2002).

–, 'Prestigio, vesti e "discernenza di persone"', in *I giochi di prestigio. Modelli e pratiche della distinzione sociale*, ed. M. Bianchini; Special issue of *Cheiron: materiali e strumenti di aggiornamento storiografico*, 31-32 (1999), pp. 171-86.

NARDESCHI, G., 'Le costituzioni della "Sapienza Nuova" dell'Anno 1443'. Unpublished *tesi di laurea*, Università degli Studi di Perugia, Facoltà di Magistero, Anno Accademico 1971-2.

NARDI, P., 'Appunti sui maestri e gli studi giovanili di San Bernardino da Siena', *Istituto Storico Diocesano di Siena. Annuario 1992-93* (Siena, 1993), pp. 201-222.

–, 'Carlo IV di Boemia e l'Università di Siena', in *Siena in Praga*, pp. 50-53.

–, 'La carriera accademica di Lodovico Zdekauer storico del diritto nell'Università di Siena (1888-1896)', *Studi senesi*, 100 (1988), Suppl. II, pp. 751-81.

–, 'Comune, Impero e Papato alle origini dell'insegnamento universitario in Siena (1240-1275)', *BSSP*, 90 (1983), pp. 50-94.

–, 'Contributo alla biografia di Federico Petrucci con notizie inedite su Cino da Pistoia e Tancredi da Corneto', *Scritti di storia del diritto offerti dagli allievi a Domenico Maffei*, ed. M. Ascheri. Medioevo e Umanesimo, 78 (Padua, 1991), pp. 153-80.

–, 'Dalle origini al 1357', in *L'Università di Siena. 750 anni*, pp. 9-26.

–, 'Dalle *Scholae* allo *Studium generale*; la formazione delle università medievali', in *Studi di storia del diritto medioevale e moderno*, ed. F. Liotta (Bologna, 1999), pp. 1-32.

–, 'Docci, Tommaso', in *DBI*, 40 (1991), pp. 339-44.

–, 'Enea Silvio Piccolomini, il cardinale Domenico Capranica e il giurista Tommaso Docci', in *Studi in memoria di Mario E. Viora*. Biblioteca della Rivista di storia del diritto italiano, 30 (Rome, 1990), pp. 539-47.

–, 'Una fonte inedita delle lauree senesi nel secolo XV: i libri di amministrazione dell'Opera del Duomo', *Annali di storia delle Università italiane*, 10 (2006, forthcoming).

–, 'Giovanni Battista Caccialupi a Siena: Giudice delle Riformagioni e docente nello Studio', *Studi senesi*, 109 (1997), pp. 83-124.

–, *L'insegnamento superiore a Siena nei secoli XI-XIV*. Orbis Academicus, Saggi e Documenti di Storia delle Università, 6/Saggi e Documenti per la Storia dell'Università di Siena, 2 (Milan, 1996).

–, 'Introduzione ad una ricerca sulle origini dello Studio di Siena', *Studi senesi*, 94 (1982), pp. 348-61.

–, '*Licentia ubique docendi* e Studio generale nel pensiero giuridico del secolo XIII', in *Studi senesi*, 112 (2000), pp. 554-65; and in *A Ennio Cortese*, II, pp. 471-77.

–, 'Maestri e scolari: alle origini dello Studio', in *Storia di Siena*, I, pp. 141-54.

–, *Mariano Sozzini giureconsulto senese del Quattrocento*. Quaderni di 'Studi senesi', 32 (Milan, 1974).

–, 'Note sulla scuola giuridica senese negli anni della caduta della Repubblica', *Studi senesi*, 87 (1975), pp. 195-220.

–, 'Note sui rapporti tra *studia* e pubblici poteri nei secoli XII-XIII', in *Cristianità ed Europa. Miscellanea di studi in onore di Luigi Prosdocimi*, ed. C. Alzati (Rome – Freiburg – Vienna, 1994), vol. 2, pp. 609-33.

–, 'Le origini del concetto di "Studium generale"', *Rivista internazionale di diritto comune*, 3 (1992), pp. 47-78; also in *L'università e la sua storia*, pp. 29-58.

–, 'Le origini dello Studio senese', *Studi senesi*, 104 (1992), pp. 284-303.

–, 'Origini e sviluppo della Casa della Misericordia nei secoli XIII e XIV', in *La Misericordia di Siena*, pp. 65-93.

–, 'A proposito di recenti studi sulle Università di Pisa e Siena nel Cinquecento', *Studi senesi*, 90 (1978), pp. 104-14.

–, 'Relations with Authority', in *A History of the University in Europe*, I, pp. 77-107.

–, 'Siena e la Curia pontificia nel 1378', in *La Roma di santa Caterina da Siena*, ed. M. G. Bianco. Quaderni della Libera Università 'Maria SS. Assunta', 18 (Rome, 2001), pp. 49-66.

–, 'Lo Studio di Siena nell'età rinascimentale: appunti e riflessioni', *BSSP*, 99 (1992), pp. 249-65; also as 'Lo Studio di Siena nell'età rinascimentale', in *Cultura e Università a Siena*, pp. 19-26 (without notes).

–, 'Umanesimo e cultura giuridica nella Siena del Quattrocento', *BSSP*, 88 (1981), pp. 234-53.

–, with collaboration by G. MINNUCCI and M. BROGI, 'Siena', in *Charters of Foundation and Early Documents of the Universities of the Coimbra Group*, eds. J. M. M. Hermans and M. Nelissen (Groningen, 1994), pp. 24-5.

NASALLI ROCCA DI CORNELIANO, E., *Il trasferimento dello Studio visconteo di Pavia a Piacenza dal 1398 al 1402* (Milan, 1927).

NEGRUZZO, S., 'Les réguliers et la chaire. La mobilité des maîtres dans l'Italie du nord aux XVᵉ et XVIᵉ siècles', in *Les échanges entre les universités*, pp. 93-102.

NEVOLA, F. J. D., 'Cerimoniali per santi e feste a Siena a metà Quattrocento. Documenti dallo Statuto di Siena 39', in *Siena e il suo territorio, III*, pp. 171-84.

–, 'Creating a Stage for an Urban Elite: the Re-development of the Via del Capitano and Piazza Postierla in Siena (1487-1520)', in *The World of Savonarola. Italian Elites and Perceptions of Crisis*. Papers from the Conference held at the University of Warwick, 24-31 May 1998, to mark the fifth centenary of the death of Fra Girolamo Savonarola, eds. S. Fletcher and C. Shaw. Warwick Studies in the Humanities (Aldershot, 2000), pp. 182-93.

–, '"*Lieto e trionphante per la città*": Experiencing a Mid-Fifteenth-Century Imperial Triumph along Siena's *Strada Romana*', *Renaissance Studies*, 17:4 (2003), pp. 581-606.

–, '"Per Ornato Della Città": Siena's Strada Romana and Fifteenth-Century Urban Renewal', *Art Bulletin*, 82 (2000), pp. 26-50.

–, 'Revival or Renewal: Defining Civic Identity in Fifteenth-Century Siena', in *Shaping Urban Identity in the Middle Ages*, eds. P. Stabel and M. Boone (Leuven/Apeldoorn, 2000), pp. 109-35.

–, 'Siena nel Rinascimento: sistemi urbanistici e strutture istituzionali (1400 circa – 1520)', *BSSP*, 106 (1999), pp. 44-67.

–, 'Urbanism in Siena (*c*.1450-1512). Policy and Patrons: Interactions between Public and Private', unpublished Ph.D. thesis, University of London, 1998.

NICOLAJ, G., 'Forme di Studi medioevali. Spunti di riflessione dal caso aretino', in *Miscellanea Domenico Maffei dicata*, 3, pp. 183-217; repr. in *L'università e la sua storia*, pp. 59-91.

NICOLINI, U., 'La "Domus Sancti Gregorii" o "Sapienza Vecchia" di Perugia. Il periodo delle origini', in *I Collegi universitari*, pp. 47-52.

–, 'Dottori, scolari, programmi e salari alla Università di Perugia verso la metà del sec. XV', *Bollettino della Deputazione di Storia Patria per l'Umbria*, 58 (1961), pp. 139-59.

NORMAN, D., *Painting in Late Medieval and Renaissance Siena* (New Haven, Ct., and London, 2003).

NUOVO, A., *Il commercio librario a Ferrara tra il XV e XVI secolo. La bottega di Domenico Sivieri*. Storia della tipografia e del commercio librario, 3 (Florence, 1998).

–, *Il commercio librario nell'Italia del Rinascimento* (Milan, 1998).

NUTTON, V., 'Continuity or Rediscovery? The City Physician in Classical Antiquity and Mediaeval Italy', in *The Town and State Physician in Europe from the Middle Ages to the Enlightenment*, ed. A. W. Russell. Wolfenbütteler Forschungen, 17 (Wolfenbüttel, 1981), pp. 9-46.

NYGREN, E., 'Ericus Olais och andra svenskars stidiebesök i Siena', *Kyrkohistorisk årsskrift*, I:19 (1918), pp. 118-26.

OHL, R., 'The University of Padua, 1405-1509: an International Community of Students and Professors', unpublished Ph.D. dissertation, University of Pennsylvania, 1980.

ORVIETO, P., 'Siena e la Toscana', in *Letteratura italiana. Storia e geografia*, II.2 (Turin, 1987-9), pp. 203-34.

PACE, G., 'Nuovi documenti su Hinrich Murmester, *rector iuristarum* dello Studio di Padova nel 1463. Con un *consilium* di Angelo degli Ubaldi', *Quaderni per la Storia dell'Università di Padova*, 32 (1999), pp. 223-38.

PACETTI, D., 'La necessità dello studio: predica inedita da S. Bernardino', *Bullettino di Studi Bernardiniani*, 2 (1936), pp. 301-21.

PADOA SCHIOPPA, A., 'Sul ruolo dei giuristi nell'età del diritto comune: un problema aperto', in *Il diritto comune e la tradizione giuridica europea. Atto del convegno di studi in onore di Giuseppe Ermini, Perugia, 30-31 ottobre 1976*, ed. D. Segolini. Università degli Studi di Perugia, Annali della Facoltà di Giurisprudenza, n.s., 6/1 (Perugia, 1980), pp. 155-66.

PAGNIN, B., 'Collegi universitari medievali', in *I quattro secoli del Collegio Borromeo di Pavia. Studi di storia e d'arte pubblicati nel IV centenario dellafondazione 1561-1961* (Milan, 1961), pp. 229-42.

PAJORIN, K., 'Enea Silvio Piccolomini ed i primi umanisti ungheresi', in *Rapporti e scambi: tra umanesimo italiano ed umanesimo europeo*, ed. L. Rotondi Secchi Tarugi. Istituto di Studi Umanistici Francesco Petrarca, Mentis Itinerarium, Caleidoscopio, 10 (Milan, 2001), pp. 649-56.

PALMER, R., 'Physicians and the State in Post-Medieval Italy', in *The Town and State Physician in Europe from the Middle Ages to the Enlightenment*, ed. A. W. Russell. Wolfenbütteler Forschungen, 17 (Wolfenbüttel, 1981), pp. 47-61.

PAGNI, L., and S. VACCARA, 'Un Magistrato scomodo: il Maggior Sindaco nello statuto del 1422', in *Siena e il suo territorio, I*, pp. 251-336.

PANDOLFI, V., and E. ARTESE (eds.), *Teatro goliardico dell'Umanesimo* (Milan, 1965).

PAOLINI, L., 'La laurea medievale', in *L'Università di Bologna*, pp. 133-55.

PAQUET, J., 'Bourgeois et universitaires a la fin du Moyen Age', *Le Moyen Age*, ser. 4, 16 (1961), pp. 325-40.

–, 'Coût des études, pauvreté et labeur; fonctions et métiers d'étudiants au Moyen Âge', *History of Universities*, 2 (1982), pp. 15-52.

–, 'Recherches sur l'universitaire "pauvre" au Moyen Age', *Revue belge de philologie et d'histoire*, 56 (1978), pp. 301-53.

–, 'L'universitaire "pauvre" au Moyen Age: problèmes, documentation, question de méthode', in *Les Universités a la fin du moyen âge*, eds. J. IJsewijn and J. Paquet (Louvain, 1978), pp. 399-425.

PARAVICINI BAGLIANI, A., 'La fondazione dello "Studium Curiae": una rilettura critica', in *Luoghi e metodi di insegnamento*, pp. 57-81; repr. in his *Medicina e scienze della natura alla corte dei Papi nel Duecento*. Centro italiano di Studi sull'alto medioevo (Spoleto, 1991), pp. 363-90, and in *Il pragmatismo degli intellettuali*, pp. 125-45.

PARDI, G., 'Atti degli scolari dello Studio di Perugia dall'anno 1497 al 1515', *Bollettino della R. Deputazione di Storia Patria per l'Umbria*, 4 (1890), pp. 487-509.

–, *Titoli dottorali conferiti dallo Studio di Ferrara nei secc. XV e XVI* (Lucca, 1900, repr. Bologna, 1970).

–, 'Titoli dottorali conferiti nello Studio di Lucca nel sec. XV', *Studi Storici*, 8 (1899), pp. 3-14.

PARDUCCI, P., 'L'incontro di Federigo III imperatore con Eleonora di Portogallo', *BSSP*, 13 (1906), pp. 297-379; 14 (1907), pp. 35-96.

PARK, K., 'The Criminal and the Saintly Body: Autopsy and Dissection in Renaissance Italy', *Renaissance Quarterly*, 47:1 (1994), pp. 1-33.

–, *Doctors and Medicine in Early Renaissance Florence* (Princeton, N.J., 1985).

–, 'Natural Particulars: Medical Epistemology, Practice, and the Literature of Healing Springs', in *Natural Particulars. Nature and the Disciplines in Renaissance Europe*, eds. A. Grafton and N. Siraisi (Cambridge, Ma., 1999), pp. 347-67.

–, 'The Readers at the Florentine Studio according to Comunal Fiscal Records (1357-1380, 1413-1446)', *Rinascimento*, 20 (1980), pp. 249-310.

PARSONS, G., *Siena, Civil Religion and the Sienese* (Aldershot, 2004).

PATON, B., *Preaching Friars and the Civic Ethos: Siena, 1380-1480* (London, 1992).

PAZDEROVÁ, A., and L. BONELLI CONENNA see *Siena in Praga*.

PELLEGRINI, E., 'La pianta di Siena eilevata da Francesco Vanni e i luoghi dello Studio senese', in *L'Università di Siena. 750 anni*, pp. 575-84.

PERTICI, P., *La città magnificata. Interventi edilizi a Siena nel Rinascimento. L'ufficio dell'Ornato (1428-1480)* (Siena, 1995).

–, 'Una "coniuratio" del reggimento di Siena nel 1450', *BSSP*, 99 (1992), pp. 9-47.

–, 'La furia delle fazioni', in *Storia di Siena*, I, pp. 383-94.

– (ed.), *Tra politica e cultura nel primo Quattrocento senese. Le epistole di Andreoccio Petrucci (1426-1443)* (Siena, 1990).

PESENTI, T., 'Arti e medicina: la formazione del curriculum medico', in *Luoghi e metodi di insegnamento*, pp. 155-77.

–, *La Biblioteca universitaria di Padova dalla sua Istituzione alla fine della repubblica veneta (1629-1797)*. Contributi alla Storia dell'Università di Padova, 11 (Padua, 1979).

–, 'Gli inventari delle biblioteche dei professori', in *La storia delle università italiane*, pp. 251-69.

–, *Marsilio Santasofia tra Corti e università. La carriera di un 'Monarcha medicinae' del Trecento*. Contributi alla Storia dell'Università di Padova, 35 (Treviso, 2002).

–, *Professori e promotori di medicina nello studio di Padova dal 1405 al 1509. Repertorio bio-bibliografico*. Contributi alla Storia dell'Università di Padova, 16 (Trieste, 1984).

PESSINA LONGO, H., *Georgius de Russia, rettore a Bologna nel XV secolo*. Memorie e documenti dello Studio bolognese, 2 (Bologna,1988).

PETER, H., *Die Vita Angeli Geraldini des Antonio Geraldini. Biographie eines Kurienbischofs und Diplomaten des Quattrocento. Text und Untersuchungen* (Frankfurt-am-Main and New York, etc., 1993).

PETERSOHN, J., *Ein Diplomat des Quattrocento. Angelo Geraldini (1422-86)* (Tübingen, 1985).

PETTI BALBI, G., '*Felix Studium viguit*: l'organizzazione degli studenti e dei dottori a Parma del Quattrocento', in *Università in Europa. Le istituzioni universitarie*, pp. 37-50.

PEZZAROSSA, F., '"Canon est litterarum". I libri di Filippo Beroaldo', in *Libri, lettori e biblioteche dell'Italia medievale (secoli XI-XV). Fonti, testi, utilizzazioni del libro*. Atti della tavola rotonda italo-francese (Roma, 7-8 marzo 1997), eds. G. Lombardi and O. Nebbiai dalla Guardia (Rome, 2000), pp. 301-48.

PIANA, C., *La facoltà teologica dell'Università di Firenze nel Quattro e Cinquecento*. Spicilegium Bonaventurianum, 15 (1977).

–, *Il "Liber Secretus Iuris Caesarei" dell'Università di Bologna, 1451-1500*. Orbis Academicus. Saggi e Documenti di Storia delle Università, 1 (Milan, 1984).

–, *Il "Liber Secretus Iuris Pontificii" dell'Università di Bologna, 1451-1500*. Orbis Academicus. Saggi e Documenti di Storia delle Università, 2 (Milan, 1989).

–, *Nuovi documenti sull'Università di Bologna e sul Collegio di Spagna*. Studia Albornotiana, 26 (1976).

–, 'Scritti polemici fra Conventuali e Osservanti a metà del '400 con la partecipazione di giuristi secolari', *Archivum Franciscanum Historicum*, 72 (1979), pp. 37-105.

–, 'Il traduttore e commentatore della Divina Commedia fra Giovanni Bertoldi da Serravalle O.F.M. baccalario a Ferrara nel 1379 ed altri documenti per la storia degli Studi francescani', *Analecta Pomposiana. Studi di storia religiosa delle diocesi di Ferrara e Comacchio*, 7 (1982), pp. 131-83.

PIANIGIANI, A., 'Documenti per la storia dello Studio senese nella prima metà del Quattrocento', unpublished *tesi di laurea*, Università degli Studi di Siena, Facoltà di Giurisprudenza, anno accademico 1991-92, relatore P. Nardi.

PICCINNI, G., 'Ambiente, produzione, società della Valdorcia nel tardo medioevo', in *La Val d'Orcia*, pp. 33-58.

–, *Il contratto di mezzadria nella Toscana medievale*, III. *Il Contado di Siena, 1349-1518* (Florence, 1992).

–, 'Cultura, società, Università a Siena nel Medioevo', in *Cultura e Università a Siena*, pp. 11-17.

–, 'L'Ospedale di Santa Maria della Scala di Siena. Note sulle origini dell'assistenza sanitaria in Toscana (XIV-XV secolo)', in *Città e servizi sociali nell'Italia dei secoli XII-XV. Dodicesimo convegno di studi*. Centro Italiano di Storia e d'Arte, Pistoia (Pistoia, 1990), pp. 297-324.

–, *'Seminare, fruttare, raccogliere'. Mezzadri e salariati sulle terre di Monte Oliveto Maggiore (1374-1430)* (Milan, 1982).

–, 'Tra scienza ed arti: lo Studio di Siena e l'insegnamento della medicina (secoli XIII-XVI)', in *L'Università di Siena. 750 anni*, pp. 145-58.

–, 'La strada come affare. Sosta, identificazione e depositi di denaro di pellegrini (1382-1446)', in G. PICCINNI and L. TRAVAINI, *Il Libro del Pellegrino (Siena 1382-1446). Affari, uomini, monete nell'Ospedale di Santa Maria della Scala* (Napoli, 2003), pp.1-81.

– and L. VIGNI, 'Modelli di assistenza ospedaliera tra Medioevo ed Età Moderna. Quotidianità, amministrazione, conflitti nell'ospedale di Santa Maria della Scala di Siena', in *La società del bisogno*, pp. 131-74.

PICCOLOMINI, P., 'Bartolomeo Bolis da Padova e la sua fondazione per lo Studio di Siena (24 luglio 1512)', *Archivio Storico Italiano*, ser. V, vol 36 (1905), pp. 143-52.

–, 'Istruzioni di Giacomo Todeschini-Piccolomini al figlio Enea (1499-1500) e Calendario dello Studio Senese nel 1510', *BSSP*, 10 (1903), pp. 107-16.

–, *La vita e l'opera di Sigismondo Tizio, 1458-1528* (Siena, 1903).

PIERINI, M., *L'arca di San Cerbone* (Massa Marittima, 1995).

PILTZ, A. (ed.), *Studium Upsalense, Specimens of the Oldest Lecture Notes Taken in the Medieval University of Uppsala*. Acta Universitatis Upsaliensis. Skrifter rörande Uppsala Universitet. C., Organisation och historia, 36 (Uppsala, 1977).

PINI, A. I., 'Federico II, lo Studio di Bologna e il "Falso Teodosiano"', in *Federico II e Bologna*. Deputazione di Storia Patria per le Province di Romagna: Documenti e Studi, 27 (Bologna, 1996), pp. 27-60; repr. in *Il pragmatismo degli intellettuali*, pp. 67-89.

–, 'I maestri dello Studio nell'attttività amministrativa e politica del Comune bolognese', in *Cultura universitaria e pubblici poteri*, pp. 151-78.

–, 'Il mondo universitario: professori, studenti, bidelli', in *Ceti, modelli, comportamenti nella società medievale (secc. XIII – metà XIV)* (Pistoia, 2001), pp. 123-45.

–, 'Le "nationes" studentesche nel modello universitario bolognese del medio evo', in *Studenti e dottori*, pp. 21-9.

–, 'La presenza dello Studio nell'economia di Bologna medievale', in *L'Università a Bologna*, pp. 85-111.

–, 'Per una storia sociale dell'università: i bidelli bolognesi nel XIII secolo', *Annali di storia delle università italiane*, 1 (1997), pp. 43-75.

PINTO, G., 'Signori della finanza: le grandi compagnie bancarie', in *Storia di Siena*, I, pp. 69-78.

–, '"Honour" and "Profit": Landed Property and Trade in Medieval Siena', in *City and Countryside*, pp. 81-91.

–, 'I mercanti senesi e la terra', in *Banchi e mercanti di Siena* (Rome, 1987), pp. 221-90; repr. in his *Città e spazi economici nell'Italia comunale* (Bologna, 1996), pp. 139-84.

–, see *La società del bisogno*.

PIOVAN, F., and L. SITRAN REA see *Studenti, università, città*.

Politica e cultura nelle repubbliche italiane dal Medioevo all'Età moderna. Firenze – Genova – Lucca – Siena – Venezia, eds. S. Adorni Braccesi and M. Ascheri. Annuario dell'Istituto storico italiano per l'età moderna e contemporanea, 53-4 (Rome, 2001).

POLVERINI FOSI, I., '"La comune, dolcissima patria": Siena e Pio II', in *I ceti dirigenti nella Toscana del Quattrocento*, pp. 509-21.

POLZER, J., 'Ambrogio Lorenzetti's *War and Peace* Murals Revisited: Contributions to the Meaning of the *Good Government Allegory*', *Artibus et historiae. Rivista internazionale di arti visive e cinema*, 45 (2002), pp. 63-105.

POPPI, A., 'Il dibattito sull'esclusione della teologia dal ruolo universitario nello Studio di Padova (1363-1806). Un aggiornamento', in IDEM, *Ricerche sulla teologia e la scienza nella scuola padovana del Cinque e Seicento*. Saggi e testi, n.s. 1 (27) (Soveria Mannelli, Catanzaro, 2001), pp. 7-22.

–, *Statuti dell'"Universitas theologorum" dello Studio di Padova (1385-1784)*. Contributi per la Storia dell'Università di Padova, 36 (Treviso, 2004).

PRAGER, F. D. and G. SCAGLIA, *Mariano Taccola and his book De ingenuis* (Cambridge, Ma., 1972).

Il pragmatismo degli intellettuali. Origini e primi sviluppi dell'istituzione universitaria, ed. R. Greci (Turin, 1996).

PROMIS, D., *Monete della repubblica di Siena* (Turin, 1868).

PRUNAI, G., 'Bandini, Bartalo (Bartolo di Tura)', *DBI*, 5 (1963), pp. 106-7.

–, 'I notai senesi del XIII e XIV secolo e l'attuale riordinamento del loro archivio', *BSSP*, 60 (1953), pp. 78-109.

–, 'Lo studio di Siena dalle origini alla "migratio" bolognese (sec. XIII-1321)', *BSSP*, 56 (1949), pp. 53-79.

–, 'Lo studio senese dalla "migratio" bolognese alla fondazione della "Domus Sapientiae" (1321-1408)', *BSSP*, 57 (1950), pp. 3-54.

–, 'Lo studio senese nel primo quarantennio del principato Mediceo', *BSSP*, 66 (1959), pp. 79-160.

– and S. DE' COLLI, 'La Balìa dagli inizi del XIII secolo fino alla invasione francese (179)', *BSSP*, 65 (1958), pp. 33-96.

PRYDS, D., '*Studia* as Royal Offices: Mediterranean Universities of Medieval Europe', in *Universities and Schooling in Medieval Society*, eds. W. J. Courtenay and J. Miethke. Education and Society in the Middle Ages and Renaissance, 10 (Leiden, 2000), pp. 83-99.

PUCCINOTTI, F., *Storia della Medicina* (Florence, 1870).

RASHDALL, H., *The Universities of Europe in the Middle Ages*, eds. F. M. Powicke and A. B. Emden, 3 vols. (Oxford, 1936 edn.).

RAU, V., 'Alguns estudantes e eruditos portugueses em Italia no século XV', *Do Tempo e da Historia*, 5 (1972), pp. 29-99; Italian tr. 'Studenti ed eruditi portoghesi in Italia nel secolo XV', *Estudios Italiános em Portugal*, 36 (1973), pp. 7-73.

–, 'Italianismo na cultura jurídica portuguesa do século XV', *Revista Portuguesa de História*, 12 (1969) (= Homenagem ao Doutor Paulo Merêa, I), pp. 185-206.

RENZI, P., '"Ché più si spara et dimenticha in uno dì che non se impara in dieci": Arezzo, lo *Studio* che abbiamo perduto', *Nuova Rivista Storica*, 85 (2001), pp. 39-60.

–, '*Studium Generale*: aurea mediocritas? Riflessioni sul caso senese', *Nuova Rivista Storica*, 79 (1995), pp. 303-20.

– see *L'università e la sua storia*.

Repertorium Germanicum, VIII. *Verzeichnis der in den Registen und Kameralakten Pius' II. vorkommenden Personen, Kirchen und Orte des Deutschen Reiches, seiner Diözesen und Territorien, 1458-1464*, 2 vols., eds. D. Brosius and U. Scheschkewitz (Tübingen, 1993).

REXROTH, F., *Deutsche Universitätsstiftungen von Prag bis Köln. Dir Intentionen des Stifters und die Wege und Chancen ihrer Verwirklichung im spätmittelalterlichen Territorialstaat*. Beischrifte zum Archiv für Kulturgeschichte, 34 (Cologne – Weimar – Vienna, 1992).

RICCIARELLI, F., 'Propaganda politica e rituali urbani nella Arezzo del tardo Medioevo', *Archivio storico italiano*, 162 (2004), pp. 233-58.

RICHARDS, J., *Sex, Dissidence and Damnation. Minority Groups in the Middle Ages* (London, 1991).

RIEDL, P. A., and M. SEIDEL (eds.), *Die Kirchen von Siena* (Munich, 1985-).

RIGONI, E., 'Il tribunale degli scolari dell'Università di Padova nel medioevo', *Memorie della R. Accademia di scienze, lettere ed arti i Padova*, n.s., 59:3 (1942-3), pp. 19-34.

RIGONI, M. P., 'Una conferma in ruolo a metà del XV secolo: il notaio e il bidello generale dell'Università giurista', *Quaderni per la Storia dell'Università di Padova*, 6 (1973), pp. 163-7.

La rinascita del sapere. Libri e maestri dello studio ferrarese, ed. P. CASTELLI (Venice, 1991).

ROEST, B., *A History of Franciscan Education (c.1210-1517)* (Leiden, 2000).

ROGGERO, M., 'I collegi universitari in età moderna', in *L'università in Italia*, pp. 111-33.

Roma e lo Studium Urbis. Spazio urbano e cultura dal Quattro al Seicento. Atti del convegno, Roma, 7-10 giugno 1989. Pubblicazioni degli Archivi di Stato, Saggi, 22 (Roma, 1992).

ROMANO, A. (ed.), *Dall'Università degli Studenti all'Università degli Studi* (Messina, 1991).

– see *Università in Europa. Le istituzioni universitarie*.

– and J. VERGER (eds.), *I poteri politici e il mondo universitario (XIII-XX secolo)*. Atti del Convegno Internazionale di Madrid 28-30 Agosto 1990 (Messina, 1994).

ROSSI, A., 'Documenti per la storia dell'Università di Perugia', *Giornale di Erudizione Artistica*, 4 (1875), pp. 26-32, 51-64, 87-96, 122-8, 153-60, 185-92, 250-6, 279-88, 319-28, 349-52, 377-82; 5 (1876), pp. 50-64, 120-8, 175-92, 304-20, 353-82; 6 (1877), pp. 49-64, 110-28, 161-92, 229-56, 288-320, 367-76.

ROSSI, G., '"Universitas scholarium" e Comune', *Studi e Memorie per la storia dell'Università di Bologna*, n. s., 1 (1956), pp. 173-266.

ROSSI, P., 'Carlo IV di Lussemburgo e la Repubblica di Siena (1355-1369)', *BSSP*, 37 (1930), pp. 5-39, 179-242.

–, 'Fredo Tolomei rettore della Università dei legisti citramontani dello Studio bolognese nel 1301. Documenti e notizie', *Studi senesi*, suppl. to 5 (1888), pp. 187-204.

–, 'La "Lectura Dantis" nello Studio Senese: Giovanni da Spoleto maestro di rettorica e lettore della "Divina Commedia" (1396-1445)', *Studi giuridici dedicati ed offerti a Francesco Schupfer nella ricorrenza del XXV anno del suo insegnamento, II. Studi di Storia del diritto italiano* (Turin, 1898, repr. anast. Rome, 1975), pp. 153-74.

ROSSIAUD, J., *Medieval Prostitution* (tr. Oxford, 1988).

ROSSO, P., 'Catone Sacco. Problemi biografici. La tradizione delle opere', *Rivista di Storia del Diritto Italiano*, 73 (2000), pp. 237-338.

–, 'Presenze studentesche e collegi pavesi nella seconda metà del Quattrocento', *Schede umanistiche*, n.s. (1994), n. 2, pp. 25-42.

–, 'Problemi di vita universitaria pavese nella seconda metà del Quattrocento: i professori', *Bollettino della Società Pavese di Storia Patria*, 45 (1993), pp. 67-93.

–, 'I "Rotuli" dell'Università di Pavia nella seconda metà del Quattrocento: considerazioni sull'entità degli stipendi assegnati al corpo docente', *Schede umanistiche*, 10:1 (1996), pp. 23-49.

–, 'Studenti di area germanica presso l'Università di Torino nel Quattrocento', *Schede umanistiche*, 15:2 (2001), pp. 35-55.

–, 'Vicende studentesche pavesi nella seconda metà del Quattrocento', *Bollettino della Società Pavese di Storia Patria*, 45 (1993), pp. 37-66.

ROTZOLL, M., 'Appunti su un "magister" del secondo Quattrocento: Alessandro Sermoneta da Siena', *Quaderni del raggruppamento tosco-umbro-emiliano di storia della medicina* (1987), pp. 87-99.

RUBINSTEIN, N., 'Le allegorie di Ambrogio Lorenzetti nella Sala della Pace e il pensiero politico del suo tempo', *La Diana. Annuario della Scuola di Specializzazione in Archeologia e Storia dell'Arte dell'Università degli Studi di Siena*, I (1995), pp. 33-46 (without notes); full version in *Rivista Storica Italiana*, 109 (1997), pp. 781-802; repr. in his *Studies in Italian History*, I, pp. 347-64.

–, 'The Place of the Empire in Fifteenth-Century Florentine Political Opinion and Diplomacy', *Bulletin of the Institute of Historical Research*, 30 (1957), pp. 125-35.

–, 'Political Ideas in Sienese Art: the Frescoes by Ambrogio Lorenzetti and Taddeo di Bartolo in the Palazzo Pubblico', *Journal of the Warburg and Courtauld Institutes*, 21 (1958), pp. 179-207; repr. in his *Studies in Italian History*, I, pp. 61-98.

–, 'I primi anni del Consiglio Maggiore a Firenze (1494-1499)', *Archivio Storico Italiano*, 112 (1954), pp. 151-94, 321-47.

–, *Studies in Italian History in the Middle Ages and the Renaissance*, ed. G. Ciappelli, 3 vols. (Rome, 2004-).

–, 'Die Vermögenslage florentiner Humanisten im 15. Jahrhundert', in *Humanismus und Ökonomie*, ed. H. Lutz. Mitteilungen der Kommission für Humanismusforschung, 8 (Weinheim, 1983), pp. 107-19.

RUTIGLIANO, A., *Lorenzetti's Golden Mean. The Riformatori of Siena, 1368-1385* (New York, 1991).

SABATTANI, A., *De vita et operibus Alexandri Tartagni de Imola*. Quaderni di Studi senesi, 27 (Milan, 1972).

SABBADINI, R., 'Andrea Biglia milanese, frate agostiniano del secolo XV', *Rendiconti del R. Instituto Lombardo di Scienze e Letteratura*, 39 (1906), pp. 1087-1102.

SALOMON, R., 'Eine vergessene Universitätsgründing', *Neues Archiv der Gesellschaft für ältere deutsche Geschichte*, 37 (1912), pp. 810-7 and additional note, 879-80.

SANESI, G., 'Rassegna bibliografica dei documenti per la storia della Università di Siena', *Archivio Storico Italiano*, ser. 5, 27 (1901), pp. 376-87.

Sapere e/è potere. Discipline, dispute e professioni nell'Università medievale e moderna. Il caso bolognese a confronto, 3 vols. (Bologna, 1990): I. *Forme e oggetti della disputa delle arti*, ed. L. Avellini; II. *Verso un nuovo sistema del sapere*, ed. A. Cristiani; III. *Dalle discipline ai ruoli sociali*, ed. A. De Benedictis.

SATTA MEUCCI, A., 'Per un'interpretazione di due lettere di Enea Silvio Piccolomini', *BSSP*, 81-82 (1975-6), pp. 393-404.

SAVIGNY, F. C. VON, *Geschichte des Römischen Rechts im Mittelalter*, 6 vols (Heidelberg, 1815-31).

SBARAGLI, F., '"I tabelloni" degli Intronati', *BSSP*, 49 (1942), pp. 177-213, 238-67.

SCAGLIA, G., *Francesco di Giorgio: Checklist and History of Manuscripts and Drawings in Autographs and Copies from ca. 1470 to 1687 and Renewed Copies (1764-1839)* (London, 1992).

SCALI, M., A. LEONCINI and N. SEMBOLONI, 'L'Archivio dell'Università di Siena', *Annali di Storia delle Università italiane*, 3 (1999), pp. 231-3.

SCHMIDT, R., 'Begründung und Bestätigung der Universität Prag durch Karl IV. und die kaiserliche Privilegiering von Generalstudien', in *Kaiser Karl IV., 1316-1378. Forschungen über Kaiser und Recht*, ed. H. Patze (Neustadt/Aisch, 1978), and *Blätter für deutsche Landesgeschichte*, 114 (1978), pp. 695-719; repr. in his *'Fundatio'*, pp. 1*-25*.

–, *'Fundatio et confirmatio universitatis'. Von den Anfängen deutscher Universitäten* (Goldbach, 1998).

–, 'Kräfte, Personen und Motive bei der Gründung der Universitäten Rostock (1419) und Greifswald (1456)', in *Beiträge zur pommerschen und mecklenburgischen Geschichte*. Vorträge der wissenschaftlichen Tagungen "Pommern – Mecklenburg" 1976-1979, veranstaltet von der Historischen Kommission für Pommern, ed. R. Schmitt (Marburg/Lahn, 1981), pp. 1-33; repr. in his *Fundatio'*, pp. 215*-47*.

–, 'Päpstliche und kaiserliche Universitätsprivilegien im späten Mittelalter', in *Das Privileg im europäischen Vergleich*, II, eds. B. Dolemayer and H. Mohnhaupt. Ius Commune, Sonderhefte, 93 (Frankfurt, 1997), pp. 143-54.

SCHMITT, C. B., *The Aristotelian Tradition and Renaissance Universities* (London, 1984).

–, 'The Faculty of Arts at Pisa at the Time of Galileo', *Physis*, 14 (1972), pp. 243-72; repr. in his *Studies in Renaissance Philosophy and Science* (London, 1981), Ch. IX.

–, 'Filosofia e scienza nelle università italiane del XVI secolo', in *Il Rinascimento: interpretazioni e problemi* (Bari, 1979), pp. 353-98, tr. as 'Philosophy and Science in Sixteenth-Century Italian Universities', in *The Renais-*

sance. Essays in Interpretation to Eugenio Garin (London and New York, 1982), pp. 297-336 and repr. in his *The Aristotelian Tradition*, ch. XV.

–, 'Science in the Italian Universities in the Sixteenth and Seventeenth Centuries', in *The Emergence of Science in Western Europe*, ed. M. P. Crosland (London, 1975), pp. 35-56; repr. in his *The Aristotelian Tradition*, ch. XIV.

–, 'Thomas Linacre and Italy', in *Linacre Studies*, ed. F. Maddison (Oxford, 1977), pp. 36-75; repr. in his *The Aristotelian Tradition*, ch. XII.

–, 'The University of Pisa in the Renaissance', *History of Education*, 3 (1974), pp. 3-17; repr. in his *Reappraisals in Renaissance Thought* (London, 1989), Ch. IX.

SCHUBERT, E., *König und Reich. Studien zur spätmittelalterlichen deutschen Verfassungsgeschichte* (Göttingen, 1979).

Schulen und Studium im sozialen Wandel des hohen und späten Mittelalters, ed. J. Fried. Vorträge und Forschungen / Konstanzer Arbeitskreis für mittelalterliche Geschichte, 30 (Sigmaringen, 1986).

SCHUSTER, P., *Das Frauenhaus. Städtische Bordelle in Deutschland 1350 bis 1600* (Paderborn, 1992).

SCHWINGES, R. C., 'Student Education, Student Life', in *A History of the University in Europe*, I. *Universities in the Middle Ages*, ed. H. De Ridder-Symoens (Cambridge, 1992), pp. 195-243.

–, 'Studentische Kleingruppen im späten Mittelalter. Ein Beitrag zur Sozialgeschichte deutscher Universitäten', in *Politik, Gesellschaft, Geschichtsschreibung. Giessener Festgabe für František Graus zum 60. Geburtstag*, eds. H. Ludat and R. C. Schwinges. Beihefte zum Archiv für Kulturgeschichte, 18 (Cologne and Vienna, 1982), pp. 319-361.

SCRIBNER, R. W., 'Reformation, Carnival, and the World Turned Upside-Down', *Social History*, 3 (1978), pp. 235-64; repr. in his *Popular Culture and Popular Movements in Reformation Germany* (London, 1987), pp. 71-101.

Scrivere il medioevo. Lo spazio, la santità, il cibo. Un libro dedicato a Odile Redon, eds. B. Laurioux and L. Moulinier-Brogi (Rome, 2001).

Le Scuole degli Ordini Mendicanti (secoli XIII-XIV). Convegni del Centro di Studi sulla Spiritualità Medievale, 17 (Todi, 1978).

SEBASTIANI, M., 'Il collegio universitario di San Gregorio in Perugia detto la Sapienza Vecchia', unpublished *tesi di laurea*, Università degli Studi di Perugia, Facoltà di Lettere e Filosofia, Anno Accademico 1966-67.

SECCO-SUARDO, G., 'Lo Studio di Ferrara a tutto il secolo XV', *Atti della Deputazione Ferrarese di Storia Patria*, 6 (1894), pp. 11-294.

SEIBT, F., *Karl IV. Ein Kaiser in Europa 1346 bis 1378* (Munich, 1978).

SEIDEL, M., *Dolce vita. Ambrogio Lorenzettis Porträt des Sieneser Staates*. Vorträge der Aeneas-Silvius-Stiftung an der Universität Basel, 33 (Basel, 1999); it. tr. in IDEM, *Arte italiana del Medioevo e del Rinascimento* (Venice, 2003).

SEIFERT, A., 'Die Universitätskollegien – eine historisch-typologische Übersicht', in *Lebensbilder deutscher Stiftungen*, 3: *Stiftungen aus Vergangenheit und Gegenwart* (Tübingen, 1974), pp. 355-72.

SENIGAGLIA, Q., 'Lo statuto dell'Arte della Mercanzia senese (1342-1343)', *BSSP*, 16:1 (1909), pp. 211-71, and 16:2, pp. 67-290.

SHAW, C., *L'ascesa al potere di Pandolfo Petrucci il Magnifico, Signore di Siena (1487-1498)* (Siena, 2001).

–, 'Counsel and Consent in Fifteenth-Century Genoa', *English Historical Review*, 116 (2001), pp. 834-62.

–, 'The French Invasions and the Establishment of the Petrucci *Signoria* in Siena', in *The World of Savonarola. Italian Elites and Perceptions of Crisis*. Papers from the conference held at the University of Warwick, 29-31 May 1998, to mark the fifth centenary of the death of Fra Girolamo Savonarola, eds. S. Fletcher and C. Shaw (Aldershot, 2000), pp. 168-81.

–, 'Memory and Tradition in Sienese Political Life in the Fifteenth Cenntury', *Transactions of the Royal Historical Society*, 6th ser., 9 (1999), pp. 221-31.

–, 'Political Elites in Siena and Lucca in the Fifteenth Century', *Bulletin of the Society for Renaissance Studies*, 14:1 (1996), pp. 8-12.

–, 'Politics and Institutional Innovation in Siena, 1480-1498', *BSSP*, 103 (1996), pp. 9-102, and 104 (1997), pp. 194-307.

–, 'Provisions following "Proposte generali" 1436 and 1456', in *Siena e il suo territorio, III*, pp. 109-52.

–, 'Rome as a Centre for Italian Political Exiles in the Later Quattrocento', in *Roma capitale (1447-1527)*, ed. S. Gensini. Centro di Studi sulla Civiltà del Tardo Medioevo, 5/Pubblicazioni degli Archivi di Stato, Saggi, 29 (Pisa, 1994), pp. 273-88.

Siena e il suo territorio nel Rinascimento, I. Documenti raccolti da M. Ascheri and D. Ciampoli. Documenti di Storia, 4 (Siena, 1986).

Siena e il suo Territorio nel Rinascimento, II. Documenti raccolti da M. Ascheri and D. Ciampoli. Documenti di Storia, 5 (Siena, 1990).

Siena e il suo territorio nel Rinascimento / Renaissance Siena and its Territory III, ed. M. ASCHERI (Siena, 2000).

Siena in Praga. Storia, arte, società... Catalogo della mostra, eds. A. Pazderová and L. Bonelli Conenna (Prague, 2000).

SILVANO, G., 'Stato, territorio e istituzioni: lo Studio generale a Padova, Pavia e Pisa al tempo di Lorenzo il Magnifico', in *La Toscana al tempo di Lorenzo*, III, pp. 981-94.

SIMIONI, A., *Storia di Padova dalle Origini alla fine del secolo XVIII* (Padua, 1968).

SIRAISI, N., *Arts and Sciences at Padua* (Toronto, 1973).

–, *Taddeo Alderotti and his Pupils. Two Generations of Italian Medical Learning* (Princeton, 1981).

SITRAN REA, L. see *La storia delle università italiane*.

SKINNER, Q., 'Ambrogio Lorenzetti: the Artist as Political Philosopher', *Proceedings of the British Academy*, 72 (1986), pp. 1-56; briefer version in *Malerei und Stadtkultur in der Dantezeit. Die Argumentation der Bilder*, eds. H. Belting and D. Blume (Munich, 1989), pp. 85-103; abridged and revised version as '*Il Buon Governo* di Ambrogio Lorenzetti e la teoria dell'autogoverno repubblicano', in *Politica e cultura nelle repubbliche italiane*, pp. 21-42; revised version as 'Ambrogio Lorenzetti and the Portrayal of Virtuous Government', in his *Visions of Politics*, pp. 39-92.

–, 'Ambrogio Lorenzetti's *Buon Governo* Frescoes: Two Old Questions, Two New Answers', *Journal of the Warburg and Courtauld Institutes*, 62 (1999), pp. 1-28; revised version as 'Ambrogio Lorenzetti on the Power and Glory of Republics', in his *Visions of Politics*, pp. 93-117.

–, *Visions of Politics*, II (Cambridge, 2002).

La società del bisogno. Povertà e assistenza nella Toscana medievale, ed. G. Pinto (Florence, 1989).

SOLERTI, A., 'Documenti riguardanti lo Studio di Ferrara nei Secoli XV e XVI conservati nell'Archivio Estense', *Atti della Deputazione Ferrarese di Storia Patria*, 4.ii (1892), pp. 7-65.

SORBELLI, A. (ed.), *Liber Secretus iuris caesarei dell'Università di Bologna*, 2 vols. Universitatis Bononiensis Monumenta, 2-3 (Bologna, 1938-42).

–, *Storia dell'Università di Bologna* (Bologna, 1940), vol. 1.

SOTTILI, A., '*Aemulatio*: la concorrenza tra i professori all'Università di Pavia nel Quattrocento', in *'Parlar l'idiom soave'. Studi di filologia, letteratura e storia della lingua offerti a Gianni A. Papini*, ed. M. M. Pedroni (Novara, 2003), pp. 107-19.

–, 'Le contestate elezioni rettorali di Paul von Baenst e Johannes von Dalberg all'Università di Pavia', *Humanistica Lovaniensia*, 31 (1982), pp. 29-75; repr. in his *Università e Cultura*, pp. 272*-318*.

– (ed.), *Documenti per la storia dell'Università di Pavia nella seconda metà del '400, I. (1450-1455)*. Fonti e studi per la storia dell'Università di Pavia, 21 (Milan, 1994).

– (ed.), *Lauree Pavesi nella seconda metà del '400*, I (1450-1475) and II (1476-1490). Fonti e studi per la storia dell'Università di Pavia, 25 and 29 (Milan, 1995 and 1998).

–, 'Le lettere di Johannes Ruysch da Chieri e Pavia nel contesto dei rapporti tra umanesimo italiano e umanesimo tedesco', *Annali della Scuola Normale Superiore di Pisa*, Classe di Lettere e Filosofia, ser. 3, 19:1 (1989), pp. 323-412.

–, 'Il palio per l'altare di Santa Caterina e il 'dossier' sul rettorato di Giovanni di Lussemburgo', *Annali di Storia Pavese*, 18-19 (1989), pp. 77-102.

–, '"Sunt nobis Papie omnia iucunda": il carteggio tra Konrad Nutzel ed Anton Kress, prevosto di San Lorenzo a Norimberga', in *Filologia umanistica per Gianvito Resta*, eds. V. Fera and G. Ferraú. Medioevo e Umanesimo, 96 (Padova 1997), III, pp. 1729-1765.

–, 'Università e Umanesimo', in *Acta conventus neo-latini Abulensis. Proceedings of the Tenth International Congress of Neo-Latin Studies (Avila, 4-9 August 1997)*, eds. R. Green et al. Arizona Center for Medieval and Renaissance Studies, Medieval Texts and Studies, 227 (Tempe, Az., 2000), pp. 603-10.

–, *Università e cultura. Studi sui rapporti italo-tedeschi nell'età dell'Umanesimo*. Bibliotheca eruditorum. Internationale Bibliothek der Wissenschaften, 5 (Goldbach, 1993).

–, 'Zum Verhältnis von Stadt, Staat und Universität in Italien im Zeitalter des Humanismus, dargestellt am Fall Pavia', in *Die Universität in Alteuropa*, eds. A. Patschovsky and H. Rabe. Konstanzer Bibliothek, 22 (Konstanz, 1994), pp. 43-67.

– and P. Rosso (eds.), *Documenti per la storia dell'Università di Pavia nella seconda metà del '400, II. (1456-1460)*. Fonti e studi per la storia dell'Università di Pavia, 38 (Milan, 2002).

Spagnesi, E., 'I documenti costitutivi dalla provvisione del 1321 allo statuto del 1388', in *Storia dell'Ateneo Fiorentino. Contributi di Studio,* I (Florence, 1986), pp. 109-45.

–, *Utiliter Edoceri. Atti Inediti degli Ufficiali dello Studio Fiorentino (1391-96)* (Milan, 1979).

Spedale di Santa Maria della Scala. Atti del Convegno Internazionale di Studi, 20-22 novembre 1986 (Siena, 1988).

Spufford, P., *Handbook of Medieval Exchange*. Royal Historical Society Guides and Handbooks, 13 (London, 1986).

Stadt und Universität im Mittelalter und in der früheren Neuzeit. 13. Arbeitstagung in Tübingen, 8.-10. 11. 1974, eds. E. Maschke and J. Sydow. Stadt in der Geschichte. Veröffentlichungen des Südwestdeutschen Arbeitskreises für Stadtgeschichtsforschung, 3 (Sigmaringen, 1977).

Starn, R., 'The Republican Regime of the "Room of Peace" in Siena, 1338-40', *Representations*, 18 (1987), pp. 1-32; revised version in R. Starn and L. Partridge, *Arts of Power: Three Halls of State in Italy, 1300-1600* (Berkeley and Los Angeles, Ca., 1992), Part I, pp. 9-80.

Stefanutti, U., 'Bonetti, Baverio Maghinardo de', *DBI*, 11 (1969), pp. 792-4.

Steffen, W., *Die studentische Autonomie im mittelalterlichen Bologna. Eine Untersuchung über die Stellung der Studenten und ihrer Universitas gegenüber Professoren und Stadtregierung im 13./14. Jahrhundert* (Bern, 1981).

Stelling-Michaud, S., 'Quelques remarques sur l'histoire des universités à l'époque de la renaissance', in *Les Universités Européennes du XIVe au XVIIIe siècle. Actes du Colloque International à l'occasion du VIe Centenaire de l'Université Jagellonne de Cracovie, 6-8 Mai 1964*. Commission Internationale pour l'Histoire des Universités, Etudes et Travaux, 1 (Geneva, 1967), pp. 71-83.

Stelzer, W., 'Zum Scholarenprivileg Friedrich Barbarossas (Authentica "Habita")', *Deutsches Archiv für Erforschung des Mittelalters*, 34 (1978), pp. 123-65.

Sticco, M., *Pensiero e poesia in S. Bernardino da Siena* (Milan, 1945 edn.)

Stopani, R., *La Via Francigena. Una strada europea nell'Italia del Medioevo* (Florence, 1988).

La storia delle università italiane. Archivi, fonti, indirizzi di ricerca, ed. L. Sitran Rea. Contributi alla Storia dell'Università di Padova, 30 (Trieste, 1996).

Storia dell'Università di Pisa, I. *1343-1737* (Pisa, 1993).

Storia di Siena, I. *Dalle origini alla fine della repubblica*, eds. R. Barzanti, G. Catoni and M. De Gregorio (Siena, 1995).

Strehlke, C. B. 'Art and Culture in Renaissance Siena', in K. Christansen, L. B. Kanter and C. B. Strehlke, *Painting in Renaissance Siena 1420-1500* (New York, 1988), pp. 33-60.

Strnad, A. A., 'Francesco Todeschini Piccolomini: Politik und Mäzenatentum im Quattrocento', *Römische historische Mitteilungen*, 8-9 (1964-66), pp. 101-425.

Studenti e dottori nelle università italiane (origini – 20. secolo: atti del Convegno di studi, 25-27 novembre 1999, eds. G. P. Brizzi and A. Romano (Bologna, 2000).

Studenti e Università degli Studenti dal XII al XIX secolo, eds. G. P. Brizzi and A. I. Pini. Studi e Memorie per la Storia dell'Università di Bologna, n.s., 7 (1988).

Studenti, università, città nella storia padovana. Atti del convegno di studi, 6-8 febbraio 1998, eds. F. Piovan and L. Sitran Rea (Padua, 2001)

SWANSON, R. N., 'Godliness and Good Learning: Ideals and Imagination in Medieval University and College Foundations', in *Pragmatic Utopias: Ideals and Communities, 1200-1630. In Honour of Barrie Dobson*, eds. S. Rees Jones and R. Horrox (Cambridge, 2001), pp. 43-59.

–, *Universities, Academics and the Great Schism* (Cambridge, 1979).

SZABÓ-BECHSTEIN, B., 'Die Sieneser Urkunden der Staatsbibliothek Preussischer Kulturbesitz Berlin (12.-18. Jh.). Die Fonds S. Leonardo al Lago, S. Salvatore di Lecceto, S. Maria del Carmine und Piccolomini', *Quellen und Forschungen aus Italienischen Archiven und Bibliotheken*, 55-6 (1976), pp. 159-99.

TABACCO, G., 'Gli intellettuali nel medioevo nel giuoco delle istituzioni e delle preponderanze sociali', in *Storia d'Italia, Annali 4: Intellettuali e potere* (Turin, 1981), pp. 5-47.

TALBOT, C. H., 'Medicine', in *Science in the Middle Ages*, ed. D. C. Lindberg (Chicago, 1978), pp. 391-428.

TANGHERONI, M., 'L'età della Repubblica (dalle origini al 1406)', in *Storia dell'Università di Pisa*, I. *1343-1737* (Pisa, 1993), pp. 5-32.

–, 'Le origini dello studio pisano (1338-1406)', in *Le università minori*, pp. 95-102.

TARRAGLIA, N. F., *Storia della lotta tra Alfonso V d'Aragona e Renato d'Angiò* (Chianciano, 1908).

I tedeschi nella storia dell'Università di Siena, ed. G. Minnucci (Siena, n.d.).

TEGA, W. (ed.), *Lo Studio e la Città. Bologna 1888-1988* (Bologna, 1987).

TERVOORT, A., *The 'iter italicum' and the Northern Netherlands. Dutch Students and Italian Universities and their Role in the Netherlands' Society (1426-1575)*. Education and Society in the Middle Ages and the Renaissance, 21 (Leiden, 2005).

TERZANI, T., 'Siena dalla morte di Gian Galeazzo Visconti alla morte di Ladislao d'Angiò Durazzo', *BSSP*, 67 (1960), pp. 3-84.

TERZIANI, R., *Il Concistoro della Repubblica di Siena 1498-1525*. www.storia.unifi.it/_pim/scriptorium/terziani.htm

–, *Il governo di Siena dal Medioevo all'Età moderna. La continuità repubblicana al tempo dei Petrucci (1487-1525)*. Documenti di Storia (Siena, 2002).

–, 'L'instaurazione del regime oligarchico-signorile (1487-1488)', in *Siena e il suo territorio, III*, pp. 195-208.

THOMSON, S. H., 'Learning at the Court of Charles IV', *Speculum*, 25 (1950), pp. 1-20.

THORNDIKE, L., *University Records and Life in the Middle Ages* (New York, 1944).

TODERI, G., 'Le Monete della repubblica di Siena (1180-1559)', in B. PAOLOZZI STROZZI, G. TODERI and F. VANNEL TODERI, *Le monete della repubblica senese* (Cinisello Balsamo, 1992), pp. 283-403.

TOGNETTI, S., '"Fra li compagni palesi et li ladri occulti". Banchieri senesi del Quattrocento', *Nuova Rivista Storica*, 88 (2004), pp. 27-102.

TOMEI, A. see *Le Biccherne di Siena*.

La Toscana al tempo di Lorenzo il Magnifico. Politica economia cultura arte. Convegno internazionale di Studi, Firenze, Pisa, Siena 5-8 novembre 1992 (Pisa, 1996), 3 vols.

TRAPANI, L., 'Docenti senesi dalla fondazione dello Studio generale all'istituzione della facoltà teologica (1357-1408)', *Annali di storia delle Università italiane*, 10 (2006, forthcoming).

–, 'Statuti senesi concernenti lo Studio', in *Gli statuti universitari: tradizione dei testi e valenze politiche*. Convegno Internazionale di Studi, Messina, 14-17 aprile 2004 (in press).

TREXLER, R. C., '*Ne fides comunis diminuatur*. Papal Authority and Communal Sovereignty at Florence and Siena, 1345-1380', *Rivista di Storia della Chiesa in Italia*, 39 (1985), pp. 448-501, and 40 (1986), pp. 1-25; repr. in his *Church and Community 1200-1600. Studies in the History of Florence and New Spain* (Rome, 1987), pp. 357-439.

TRIO, P., 'Financing of University Students in the Middle Ages: a New Orientation', *History of Universities*, 4 (1984), pp. 1-24.

TROMBETTI BUDRIESI, A. L., 'Andrea Barbazza tra mondo bolognese e mezzogiorno d'Italia', in *Scuole, diritto e società nel mezzogiorno medievale d'Italia*, ed. M. Bellomo. Settimana di Studio Erice, 1983, 1 (Catania, 1985), pp. 289-324.

–, 'L'esame di laurea presso lo Studio bolognese. Laureati in diritto civile nel secolo XV', in *Studenti e università*, pp. 137-91.

–, *Gli statuti del collegio dei dottori, giudici e avvocati di Bologna (1393-1467) e la loro matricola (fino al 1776)*. Deputazione di Storia Patria per le Province di Romagna. Documenti e Studi, 23 (Bologna, 1990).

TULIANI, M., 'Il Campo di Siena. Un mercato cittadina in epoca comunale', *Quaderni medievali*, 46 (Dec 1998), pp. 59-100.

–, *Osti, avventori e malandrini. Alberghi, locande e taverne a Siena e nel suo contado tra Trecento e Quattrocento* (Siena, 1994).

TURNAU, I., *European Occupational Dress* (Warsaw, 1994).

TURRINI, P., 'Le cerimonie funebri a Siena nel basso Medio evo: norme e rituale', *BSSP*, 110 (2003), pp. 53-102.

–, 'Lodovico Petroni, diplomatico e umanista senese', *Interpres*, 16 (1997), pp. 7-59.

–, *"Per honore et utile de la città di Siena". Il comune e l'edilizia nel Quattrocento* (Siena, 1997).

–, 'Lo Stato senese e l'edilizia pubblica e privata nel '400: un'introduzione archivistica', in *Siena e il suo territorio, III*, pp. 185-94.

UGINET, F.-C., 'Casini, Francesco', *DBI*, 21 [1978], pp. 356-9.

UGURGIERI AZZOLINI, I., *Le Pompe Sanesi o vero relazione degli huomini e donne illustri di Siena e suo Stato* (Pistoia, 1649).

ULLMAN, B. L., and P. A. STADTEN, *The Public Library of Renaissance Florence: Niccolo Niccoli, Cosimo de' Medici and the Library of San Marco*. Medioevo e Umanesimo, 10 (Padua, 1972).

Umanesimo a Siena. Letteratura, Arti Figurative, Musica, eds. E. Cioni and D. Fausti. Bibliotheca Studii Senensis, 9 (Siena, 1994).

L'Università a Bologna. Personaggi, momenti e luoghi dalle origini al XVI secolo, ed. O. CAPITANI (Milan, 1987).

L'Università di Siena. 750 anni di storia (Milan, 1991).

L'università e la sua storia. Origini, spazi istituzionali e pratiche didattiche dello Studium *cittadino*. Atti del Convegno di Studi (Arezzo, 15-16 novembre 1991), ed. P. Renzi (Siena, 1998).

L'Università e le istituzioni culturali di Siena (Siena, 1935).

Le Università dell'Europa: Gli uomini e i luoghi, eds. G. P. Brizzi and J. Verger (Milan, 1993).

Università e società nei secoli XII-XVI, Pistoia 20-25 sett. 1979. Centro italiano di Studi di Storia e d'Arte: Nono Convegno Internazionale (Pistoia, 1982).

L'Università in Europa dall'Umanesimo ai Lumi, eds. G. P. Brizzi and J. Verger (Milan, 2002).

Università in Europa. Le istituzioni universitarie dal Medio Evo ai nostri giorni. Strutture, organizzazione, funzionamento. Atti del Convegno Internazionale di Studi, Milazzo 28 Settembre – 2 Ottobre 1993, ed. A. Romano (Messina, 1995).

L'università in Italia fra età moderna e contemporanea. Aspetti e momenti, eds. G. P. Brizzi and A. Varni (Bologna, 1991).

Le università minori in Europa (secoli XV-XIX). Convegno Internazionale di Studi, Alghero, 30 Ottobre – 2 Novembre 1996, eds. G. P. Brizzi and J. Verger (Soveria Mannelli, Catanzaro, 1998).

Universitates e Università. Atti del Convegno, Bologna 16-21 novembre 1987 (Bologna, 1995).

VACCARI, P., *Storia dell'Università di Pavia* (Pavia, 1957 edn.).

La Val d'Orcia nel medioevo e nei primi secoli dell'età moderna. Atti del convegno internazionale di studi storici, Pienza, 15-18 settembre 1988, ed. A. Cortonesi (Rome, 1990).

VALLAURI, T., *Storia delle Università di Piemonte* (Turin, 1845-6, repr. 1945), 3 vols.

VALLERANI, M., 'The Generation of the "Moderni" at Work: Jurists between School and Politics in Medieval

Bologna (1270-1305)', in press (*Europäisches Forum junger Rechtshistorikerinnen und Rechtshistoriker (Osnabrück, 22-25 May 2002)*); and online on "Reti Medievali".

VAN DAMME, S., 'Enseignants et société (XIII*e*-XIX*e* siècle). Problèmes posés par la construction des identités "professionnelles"', *Cahiers d'histoire. Révue d'histoire critique*, 71 (1998), pp. 5-12.

VARANINI, G. M., 'Come si progetta uno *Studium generale*. Università, società, comune cittadino a Treviso (1314-1318)', in *L'Università medievale di Treviso* (Treviso, 2000), pp. 11-46.

VASINA, A., 'Bologna nello Stato della Chiesa: autorità papale, clero locale, Comune e Studio fra XIII e XIV secolo', in *Cultura universitaria e pubblici poteri*, pp. 125-50.

–, 'Lo "studio" nei rapporti colle realtà cittadine e il mondo esterno nei secoli XII-XIV', in *L'Università a Bologna*, pp. 29-59.

VENEROSI PESCIOLINI, G., 'I bagni senesi di Petriolo nel Medioevo', *La Diana. Rassegna d'arte e vita senese*, 6:2 (1931), pp. 110-35.

VERDE, A., *Lo Studio fiorentino 1473-1503*, 1 and 2 (Florence, 1973), 3 (Pistoia, 1977), 4 (Florence, 1985), 5 (Florence, 1994).

VERESS, E., *Olasz egyetemeken járt magyarországi tanulók anya könyve és iratai, 1221-1864 (Matricula et acta Hungarorum in universitatibus Italiae studentium)*. Olaszországi magyar emlékek, 3 (Budapest, 1941).

VERGER, J., *Men of Learning in Europe at the End of the Middle Ages* (tr. Notre Dame, In., 2000).

–, 'La politica universitaria di Federico II nel contesto europeo', in *Federico II e le città italiane*, eds. P. Toubert and A. Paravicini Bagliani (Palermo, 1991), pp. 129-43.

–, 'Le rôle social de l'Université d'Avignon au XV*e* siècle', *Bibliothèque d'Humanisme et Renaissance*, 33 (1971), pp. 489-504.

–, 'Les universités entre pouvoirs universels et pouvoirs locaux au Moyen Age', in *Universitates e Università*. Atti del Convegno, Bologna 16-21 novembre 1987 (Bologna, 1995), pp. 29-38.

–, 'Les universités européennes à la fin du XV*e* siècle', in *Les échanges entre les universités*, pp. 11-22.

VERONESE CESERACCIU, E., 'Il Collegio Engleschi nel Quattro e Cinquecento', in *Studenti, università, città*, pp. 257-315.

–, 'Spagnoli e portoghesi all'Università di Padova nel ventennio 1490-1510', *Quaderni per la Storia dell'Università di Padova*, 11 (1978), pp. 39-83.

VIAN, P., 'Garofoli, Gabriele', *DBI*, 52 (1999), pp. 368-70.

VISCONTI, A., 'De nobilitate doctorum legentium in studiis generalibus', in *Studi di storia e diritto in onore di Enrico Besta per il 40. anno del suo insegnamento* (Milan, 1939), III, pp. 219-41.

–, *Storia dell'Università di Ferrara* (Bologna, 1950).

VISINTIN, A. L., 'Due collegi universitari del tardo medioevo', in BENDISCIOLI et al., *Il Collegio Universitario Ghislieri*, 2, pp. 299-311.

–, 'Il più significativo precedente del collegio Ghislieri: il collegio universitario Castiglioni (1429-1803)', in BENDISCIOLI et al., *Il Collegio Universitario Ghislieri*, 1, pp. 51-89.

*Le Vocabulaire des collèges universitaires (XIII-XVI*e* siècles)*. Actes du colloque Leuven 9-11 avril 1992, ed. O. Weijers. CIVICIMA: Études sur le Vocabulaire Intellectuel du Moyen Age, 6 (Turnhout, 1993).

VORBRODT, G. W., and I. VORBRODT, *Die akademischen Szepter und Stäben in Europa. Corpus Sceptrorum*, I.1 (Heidelberg, 1971), p. 232.

WAINWRIGHT, V. L., 'Conflict and Popular Government in Fourteenth Century Siena: il Monte dei Dodici, 1355-1368', in *I ceti dirigenti nella Toscana tardo comunale*, pp. 57-80.

–, 'The Testing of a Popular Sienese Regime. The *Riformatori* and the Insurrections of 1371', *I Tatti Studies*, 2 (1987), pp. 107-70.

WALEY, D. P., *The Italian City-Republics* (3rd edition London, 1988).

–, *Siena and the Sienese in the Thirteenth Century* (Cambridge, 1991).

–, and P. DENLEY, *Later Medieval Europe 1250-1520* (3rd edn. Harlow, 2001).

WALSH, K., '"Böhmens Vater – Des Reiches Erzstiefvater?" Gedanken zu einem neuen Bild Kaiser Karls IV.', *Innsbrucker Historische Studien*, 3 (1980), pp. 189-210.

WALTHER, H. G., 'Die Anfänge des Rechtsstudiums und die kommunale Welt Italiens im Hochmittelalter', in *Schulen und Studium*, pp. 121-62.

–, 'Learned Jurists and their Profit for Society – Some Aspects of the Development of Legal Studies at Italian and German Universities in the Late Middle Ages', in *Universities and Schooling in Medieval Society*, eds. W. J. Courtenay and J. Miethke (Leiden, 2000), pp. 100-26.

WATT, D. E. R., *A Biographical Dictionary of Scottish Graduates to AD 1410* (Oxford, 1977).

–, 'University Clerks and Rolls of Petitions for Benefices', *Speculum*, 34 (1959), pp. 213-29.

WEBB, D., 'Eloquence and Education: a Humanist Approach to Hagiography', *Journal of Ecclesiastical History*, 31:1 (1980), pp. 19-39.

WEBER, C. F., '*Ces grands privilèges*: The Symbolic Use of Written Documents in the Foundation and Institutionalization Processes of Medieval Universities', *History of Universities*, 19/1 (2004), pp. 12-62.

WEIGLE, F., 'Deutsche Studenten in Italien, I. Die Deutsche Nation in Perugia', *Quellen und Forschungen aus italienischen Archiven und Bibliotheken*, 32 (1942), pp. 110-88.

–, 'Deutsche Studenten in Italien, II. Die Deutschen Doktorpromotionen in Siena, 1485-1804', *Quellen und Forschungen aus italienischen Archiven und Bibliotheken*, 33 (1944), pp. 199-251.

–, *Die Matrikel der Deutschen Nation in Siena, 1573-1738*. Bibliothek des Deutschen Historischen Instituts in Rom, 22-3 (Tübingen, 1962).

WEIJERS, O., *La "disputatio" dans les Facultés des arts au Moyen Age* (Turnhout, 2002).

–, *Terminologie des universités au XIIIe siècle*. Lessico Intellettuale Europeo, 39 (Rome, 1987).

– see *Le Vocabulaire des collèges*.

WHITLEY, A., 'Concepts of Ill Health and Pestilence in Fifteenth-Century Siena', unpublished Ph.D. thesis, Warburg Institute, University of London, 2005.

WIDDER, E., *Itinerar und Politik. Studien zur Reiseherrschaft Karls IV. südlich der Alpen*. Forschungen zur Kaiser- und Papstgeschichte des Mittelalters, Beihefte zu J. F. Böhmer, *Regesta Imperii*, 10 (Cologne/Weimar/Vienna, 1993).

WIERUSZOWSKI, H., 'Arezzo as a Centre of Learning', *Traditio*, 9 (1953), pp. 321-91, repr. in her *Politics and Culture in Medieval Spain and Italy* (Rome, 1971), pp. 387-474.

WILSON TORDI, A. (ed./tr), *La festa et storia di Sancta Caterina. A Medieval Italian Religious Drama*. Studies in the Humanities: Literature – Politics – Society, 25 (New York, 1996).

WRETSCHKO, A. VON, 'Universitäts-Privilegien der Kaiser aus der Zeit von 1412-1456', in *Festschrift Otto Gierke zum siebzigsten Geburtstag* (Weimar, 1911), pp. 793-816.

–, *Die Verleihung gelehrter Grade durch den Kaiser seit Karl IV* (Weimar, 1910).

ZANETTI, D., *Fra le antiche torri: scritti di storia pavese* (Pavia, 2000).

–, 'Il primo collegio pavese per studenti stranieri', in *Studi in memoria di Mario Abrate* (Turin, 1986), vol. 2, pp. 789-812; repr. in his *Fra le antiche torri*, pp. 135-61.

–, 'A l'Université de Pavie au XVe siècle: les salaires des professeurs', *Annales: Economies, Sociétés, Civilisations*, 17 (1962), pp. 421-33; Italian tr. in his *Fra le antiche torri*, pp. 103-17.

ZANNINI, A., 'Stipendi e status sociale dei docenti universitari. Una prospettiva storica di lungo periodo', *Annali di storia delle università italiane*, 3 (1999), pp. 9-39.

ZARRILLI, C., 'Amministrare con arte. Il lungo viaggio delle Biccherne dagli uffici al Museo', in *Le Biccherne di Siena*, pp. 22-34.

ZDEKAUER, L., 'Il Constituto dei Placiti del Comune di Siena', *Studi senesi*, 6 (1889), pp. 152-206, and 'Il Constituto dei consoli del Placito del Comune di Siena. II Parte', *Studi senesi*, 9 (1892), pp. 35-75.

–, 'Un consulto medico data a Pio II', *BSSP*, 5 (1898), pp. 101-6.

– (ed.), *Il Constituto del Comune di Siena del 1262* (Milan, 1897).

–, *Documenti per servire alla Storia dello Studio di Siena, 1240-1789* (Siena, 1896); extract from *L'Unione universitaria*, 3 (1896).

–, 'Lettere volgari del rinascimento senese', *BSSP*, 4 (1897), pp. 237-86.

–, *The Life of Old Siena* (Siena, 1914) (translation of *La vita privata dei senesi nel dugento*, Siena, 1896, and *La vita pubblica dei senesi nel dugento*, Siena, 1897).

–, *Il mercante senese nel dugento* (Siena, 1900).

–, 'Dai protocolli d'uno scriba *Universitatis Studii Senensis*, 1437-41', *BSSP*, 12 (1905), pp. 318-26.

–, *Lo Studio di Siena nel Rinascimento* (Milan, 1894, repr. Bologna, 1977).

–, *Sulle Origini dello Studio Senese* (Siena, 1893).

– (ed.), *Il Taccuino Senese di Giuliano da San Gallo* (Siena, 1902, repr. Bologna, 1979).

– (ed.), *Tre lettere di M. Alberto Guidalotti, lettore allo Studio di Perugia a M. Bartolomeo di Biagio, lettore allo Studio di Siena (1388)*, per Nozze Petrucci-Sozzifanti, 30 agosto 1898 (Siena, 1898), and *BSSP*, 5 (1898), pp. 288-98.

–, *La vita privata dei senesi nel dugento* (Siena, 1896; repr. Bologna, 1973).

–, *La vita pubblica dei senesi nel dugento* (Siena, 1897; repr. Bologna, 1973).

ZEILLINGER, K., 'Das erste roncaglische Lehensgesetz Friedrich Barbarossas, das Scholarenprivileg (Authentica Habita) und Gottfried von Viterbo', *Römische Historische Mitteilungen*, 26 (1984), pp. 191-217.

ZMORA, A. S., 'The *Pia Casa di Sapienza* of Pistoia: A Charitable Foundation and the Promise of Education in a Late Renaissance Community', unpublished Ph.D. dissertation, University of Maryland, 1995.

ZOLLER, I., 'I medici ebrei laureati a Siena negli anni 1543-1695', *La rivista israelitica* (1913-15), pp. 60-70, 100-10.

ZONTA, C., 'La presenza degli slesiani nelle università europee e italiane dal XVI al XVIII secolo', in *Studenti, università, città*, pp. 403-23.

–, *Schlesische Studenten an italienischen Universitäten. Eine prosopographische Studie zur frühneuzeitlichen Bildungsgeschichte*. Neue Dorschungen zur Schlesischen Geschichte, 10 (Cologne – Weimar – Vienna, 2004).

–, 'Studenti stranieri in Italia: gli slesiani nell'età moderna', in *Studenti e dottori*, pp. 31-40.

ZONTA, G., and A. BROTTO see *Acta graduum academicorum gymnasii patavini*.

– and A. BROTTO, *La facoltà teologica dell'Università di Padova (secoli XIV e XV)* (Padua, 1922).

ZORZOLI, M. C., 'Alcune considerazioni sui collegi dei giuristi nella Lombardia dall'antico regime', *Annali di storia moderna e contemporanea*, 7 (2001), pp. 449-75.

–, 'Il Collegio dei giudici di Pavia e l'amministrazione della giustizia (Le basi normative, dallo Statuto visconteo alle Nuove Costituzioni', *Bollettino della società pavese di storia patria*, 81 (1981), pp. 55-90.

–, 'Interventi dei Duchi e del Senato di Milano per l'Università di Pavia (secoli XV-XVI)', *Studi senesi*, 92 (1980), pp. 128-49.

–, *Università, dottori giureconsulti. L'organizzazione della "facoltà legale di Pavia nell'età spagnola* (Pavia, 1986).

Index of Personal Names

Historical figures of the period are listed by first name. They have normally been listed in the form and language in which their names appear in the text; please cross-refer for variants. Dates that appear in the index refer only to the documentation quoted, and are included in order to help with orientation and identification; they are *not* intended as a full guide to the individual's presence or activity in the *Studio*.

ABBONDANZA, R., 176n

Abramo da Montalcino (doctorate in arts and medicine in Florence, 1472), 247n

ABRATE, M., 310

Abroardus de Camerino (teacher of law, 1437), 164n

Accolti *see* Benedetto, Francesco

Achille di Ser Michele da Castiglione (student of arts and medicine and rector of the Sapienza, 1488), 207n, 351

ADAMI, F., 137n

ADAMS, N., 169n

ADORNI BRACCESI, S., 17n

ADORNI, G., 43n

ADORNO, F., 37n

Adovardus de Anglia (student of arts/medicine, *sapientino* in 1481), 243n

Adrianus Gratiosus de Marchia Anconitana (law student, candidate for rectorate of the Sapienza, 16th century), 347n

Afonso V (king of Portugal), 321n, 346n

Agapito d'Ambrogio (rector of the Sapienza, 1448-52), 345, 346n, 348, 362n

Agapito di Matteo da Perugia (teacher of law, n.d.), 170n

Agliotti *see* Girolamo

Agnolo di Berto Altesi (*Camarlengo* of the Sapienza, 1470-1), 354n

Agnolo di Messer Grifolo (Sienese representative at 'parlamento' in Florence, 1321), 37n

AGNOLO DI TURA DEL GRASSO, 41n, 206n

Agostino (servant of the *sapientino* Latino de' Regoli, 1475), 321n, 333n

Agostino Curradi of Alessandria (student of law, 1463), 151n

Agostino Dati (teacher of rhetoric and poetry, and chancellor of the republic, 1450-74), 9, 22n, 61, 111, 118n, 215, 226n, 264n

Agostino da Viterbo (rector of the *Studio*, 1438), 269n

Agostino di Martino di Conte (notary), 273n

Agostino di Niccolò Borghesi (*Savio dello Studio*, 1435, 1444, 1446, 1458), 73

Alamanni *see* Filippo Boccaccini

Alato *see* Giorgio, Giovanni Antonio

Albert, duke of Saxony, 236

Alberti *see* Leon Battista

Alberto de Sinibaldo Cattani of Bologna (teacher of law, 1466-8), 152, 156-7, 168n

Albizzeschi *see* Bernardino

Albrel *see* Michael

Albus *see* Johannes

Alessandro Aringhieri (teacher of law, 1470), 169n

Alessandro Borghesi (*Savio dello Studio*, 1489), 72n

Alessandro da Bologna, O.P. (teacher, 1471), 116n, 156

Alessandro da S. Gimignano, O.S.A. (teacher, 1476), 161n

Alessandro da Siena (doctor of arts and medicine, 1462), 281n

Alessandro de' Tommasi (teacher of law, 1474), 142n

Alessandro del Antella of Florence (hired to teach law, 1363), 48n

Alessandro di Marchisi from the Valtellina (killed a student, *c.*1470), 291

Alessandro di Niccolò della Grammatica (notary of the *Studio*, 1483; sells property to new Sapienza project, 1494), 21n, 390n, 391

Alessandro Petrucci (teacher of law, 1495-1514), 118n, 141n, 193

Alessandro Sermoneta (teacher of medicine, 1473-85), 61, 89n, 132, 134n, 152, 153n, 156, 161n, 171n, 181, 183n

Alessandro Tanci de' Tanci (doctor of arts/medicine, 1511), 206n

Alessandro Tartagni da Imola (teacher of law at Bologna), 138n

Alexander VI, pope, 399

Alexander, son of King James of Scotland (studied in Siena, 1508-9), 243n

Alfonso V, king of Aragon/Naples, 165n, 175n, 186n

Alfonso, duke of Calabria, 261n, 265n

Alfonso di Ser Lorenzo Giusa/Guisa (*Camarlengo* of the Sapienza, 1482-4 and 1491-2), 355n

Alighieri *see* Dante

Almaçán *see* Juan

Almerico di Filippo Corsini of Florence (degree in law, 1410), 199n

Altesi *see* Agnolo di Berto

ALTMANN, W., 42n

Altoviti *see* Giovanni di Roberto

Alvaro Alfonsi of Portugal (rector of the *Studio*, 1469), 346n, 349n

Alvaro da Silva, bishop, 322n

Alvaro of Portugal (student of law and vice-rector of the *Studio*, 1497-8), 267n, 284n, 349n, 351n

Alvarus de regno algarbie (student of law and applicant for the Sapienza, 1462), 313n

Ambrogio d'Antonio (rector of the Sapienza? *see* Agapito d'Ambrogio), 362n

Ambrogio da Lucca (rector of the *Studio*, 1480-1), 262n

Ambrogio Lorenzetti (frescoes in the Sala della Pace, 1338-9), 4, 40, 68-9, 144n, 401n

Ambrogio Luti (teacher of law, 1478-83), 171

Ambrosius de Ungaria (student of canon law, admitted to the Sapienza in 1474), 125n, 243n

Ambrosius ser priami de cechinis (student lectureship, 1498), 285n

Ammannati *see* Jacopo

AMMANNATI PICCOLOMINI, I., 321n, 324n

ANDENMATTEN, B., 225n

Andrea Barbazza (law teacher, 1445-56), 153-4, 157n, 179n, 187, 190

Andrea Benzi (teacher of medicine in Florence, 15th century), 181n

Andrea Biglia of Milan, O.S.A. (teacher of philosophy and theology, 1429-35), 111, 135n, 140n, 180-1

Andrea da Genova (rector of the Sapienza, 1460), 349

Andrea di Maestro Bartolomeo (teacher of medicine, 1440-4), 204n, 211n, 246n

Andrea di Francesco Marretta (teacher of medicine, 1487-98), 211n

Andrea di Giusto (notary of the *Riformagioni*, 1395-8), 93

Andrea florentino (paid for negotiations with Lancilotto Decio, 1483), 151n

Andrea Gallerani (founder of the Casa della Misericordia), 327

Andreas de Camerino (law student, admitted to the Sapienza in 1418), 307n

Andreas de Monterchio (law student, admitted to the Sapienza in 1421), 307n

Andreucci *see* Giorgio

Andrew of Hawyk (canon law student, rector of the *Studio* 1423-4), 58-9, 243n

Andromacus (teacher of Greek, 1478), 137

Angelelli *see* Valentius

ANGELETTI, G., 301n, 306n, 309n, 315n, 326-7nn, 329-30nn, 341n, 399n

Angelo Baglioni (law teacher at Perugia; bequest of 1422), 387n

Angelo Berti (*Camarlengo* of the Sapienza, 1470), 302n

Angelo Capranica, cardinal of Rieti (1466), 321n

Angelo d. Iovannachi (rector of the *Studio*, 1390; *see* Angelo Malavolti), 252n

Angelo da Camerino (student of medicine, 1461), 292n

Angelo da Perugia (teacher of law, 1419), 210n

Angelo degli Ubaldi of Perugia (teacher of canon law, 1456, 1460), 157n, 169n, 170-1, 178-9, 181, 190

Angelo di Felice de' Narducci da Perugia (teacher of law, 1436-8), 164n, 202n

Angelo di Francesco Bruogi da San Gimignano (degree in philosophy and arts, 1409), 203n, 287n

Angelo di Jacopo da Amelia (student of law, 1435), 285n

Angelo di Ser Luca of Piombino (applicant for the Sapienza, 1462), 313n

Angelo di Paolo da Gubbio (rector of the *Studio*, 1451), 267n, 284n

Angelo di Paolo da Narni (student in civil law and *sapientino*, 1434-6), 285n

Angelo di Pietro da Gubbio (student lectureship *in artibus*, 1449; *see* Angelo di Paolo da Gubbio), 284n

Angelo Fondi (teacher of poetry and rhetoric, and chancellor of the republic, 1495-9), 72n, 142n, 215-6

Angelo Geraldini of Amelia (entered the Sapienza in 1436; first rector of the Sapienza Nuova in Perugia, 1443; bishop of Suessa, 1484), 316n, 318n, 348n, 389n

Angelo Guidoni (*Camarlengo* of the Sapienza, 1450), 346n

Angelo Malavolti (rector of the *Studio*, 1390), 252n

Angelo Pandolfi of Sicily (*sapientino*, 1535), 359n

Angelo Sabe dell'Anguillara (*sapientino*, *c*.1460), 336

Angelo Salvetti, O.F.M. (teacher of theology and philosophy, 1420), 58n, 135n, 137n, 155n

ANGELUCCI, P., 389n

Angelus Andree Bernardini de Guidonibus of Perugia (degree in law, 1419), 59n

Antella *see* Alessandro

Antimo degli Ugurgieri (Sienese teaching at Padua, 1357), 42n

Antonini *see* Cipriano

Antonio Beccadelli, 'il Panormita' (recommendation, 1426), 74

Antonio Berti, Camaldolese, abbot of S. Maria della Rosa (teacher of canon law, 1470s to 16th century), 135n, 140n, 167n, 173, 203n, 214, 278n

Antonio Bichi (oration, 1450s), 63n

Antonio Campani (*depositarius*, 1490s), 173n

Antonio Casini (bishop of Siena), 48n, 54, 104n, 236n, 300n, 304

Antonio Cesso da Sicilia (rector of the *Studio*, 1424), 253

Antonio Cherubini de Urbe (*sapientino*, *c*.1460), 336

Antonio Cicinelli (orator of king of Naples, 1467), 322n

Antonio da Amelia (teacher of law, 1400), 53n

Antonio da Arezzo (teacher of grammar, 1425), 164n, 170n

Antonio da Batignano (doctor of law, 1419), 210n

Antonio da Fermo (recommended for office, 1436), 246n

Antonio da Lucca (elected rector of the Sapienza, 1474), 350n, 352

Antonio da Rieti (student of medicine, 1417), 291

Antonio da Velletri (*sapientino*, *c*.1460), 336

Antonio de Caputis da Castello (collateral of the *Capitano di Giustizia*, 1465), 216n

Antonio de Casarellis from Rome (student of law, recommended for the Sapienza in 1417), 321n

Antonio de' Guazzi/Guacci da Mantova (student of arts, contemplates transfer to Siena before 1394), 51n, 238

Antonio di Angelo (*canovaio* of the Sapienza, 1498), 358n

Antonio di Bastiano Tinellocci (teacher of law, 1474), 142n

Antonio di Ser Carluccio from Naples (*sapientino*, 1456), 317n

Antonio di Benedetto da Volterra (admitted to the Sapienza, 1445), 323

Antonio di Maestro Francesco (vice-rector of the *Studio*, 1415), 262n, 270n

Antonio di Francesco di Bartolomeo Petrucci, 74

Antonio di Gandino da Calci (notary of the chancery, early 15th century), 22, 199n, 287n

Antonio di Giovanni da Grosseto (notary of the *Studio*, 1447-8), 273n

Antonio di Giovanni da Itri (student of arts/medicine, rector of the *Studio*, 1428-9), 258n, 262n

Antonio di Maestro Giovanni da Montemorello (recommended for the Sapienza, 1417), 321

Antonio di Giovanni Roselli da Arezzo (doctor of arts/medicine and teacher of medicine, 1409-34), 78n, 177n, 180, 187n

Antonio di Lorenzo Lanti (teacher of civil law, 1427), 141n, 184

Antonio di Maestro Marco di Maestro Antonio of Pistoia (student, 1450s), 309

Antonio di Maestro Matteo da Pescia (admitted to the Sapienza, 1460), 317

Antonio di Niccolò Santi da Arezzo (teacher of grammar, 1428), 164n

Antonio di Pietro de' Micheli (*Savio dello Studio*, 1449), 72n

Antonio di Rosello Roselli da Arezzo (teacher of civil law, 1423-39), 61, 164n, 180, 188-9, 194n, 203n, 288n

Antonio di Ser Salvi da S. Gimignano (teacher of grammar, 1395), 123n

Antonio Giordano da Venafro (teacher of law, 1486-16th century), 118n, 145n, 161n, 172, 205, 214, 220

Antonio Gotto da Sicilia (student of law and *sapientino*, 1434-7), 285n, 313n

Antonio Mincucci da Pratovecchio (teacher of law, 1435-40), 78n, 202-3

Antonio Pace de' Carapelli d'Aquila (degree in civil law, 1409), 199

Antonio Ribaldini (*canovaio* of the Sapienza, 1498), 358n

Antonio Scarpi (*Camarlengo* of the Sapienza, 1468-9), 354n

Antonio 'Sciacha'/Griacha de Sicilia (student, 1421-9), 252, 278n, 292

Antonio Tani da Chianciano (teacher of canon law, 1399), 52n, 159n

Antonius basilij, O.S.A. (teacher of theology, 1445), 118n

Antonius Catelanus (student, 1445), 291n

Antonius de Mendosis de Amelia (*sapientino*, 1498), 314n

Antonius magistri Jacobi Vite de Senis (*medico condotto*, 1463), 211n

Antonius Cristophori Petri dni. Johannis Cristophori (doctor of medicine, 1511), 206n

Antonius de Drepano (Trapani) (rector of the *Studio*, 1422), 253n

Antoniusmaria Bandini de Ptomasis (student lectureship, 1498), 285n

AQUARONE, B., 223n

ARBIZZONI, G., 52n, 326n

Arcangelo di Giovanni di Domenico (teacher of medicine, 1483-93), 133n, 161n, 181n, 193, 207n

Arcangelo Toti (teacher, 1482-8), 171n

Arigus de Bramante de Alamania (cadaver requested for anatomy, 1446), 133n

Aringhieri, family, 390n, and *see* Alessandro, Niccolò

ARNALDI, G., 143n

Arnaldo de Via, cardinal, 59n

Arrighini *see* Tommaso

ARRIZABALAGA, J., 241n

ARTESE, E., 295n

ASCHBACH, J., 42n

ASCHERI, M., XII, 1-4n, 15n, 17n, 19-20nn, 26n, 38n, 40-2nn, 54n, 59n, 65n, 68n, 71-4nn, 76-7nn, 80n, 121n, 154n, 166n, 185n, 193n, 199n, 215n, 217-8nn, 223-6nn, 233n, 241n, 255n, 258n, 270-1nn, 303n, 344n, 353n, 403n

Astolfi *see* Cristoforo

Augustinians, 126

Aurispa *see* Giovanni

AVELLINI, L., 2n, 406

Avianus de Coppis de Montefalco (rector of the Sapienza, 1457), 347n

Avicenna, 38

Azel *see* Johannes von

BACCETTI, B., 1n

Baccio (cadaver granted for anatomy, 1498), 133n

Bagarottus Grillis (recommendation, 1495), 292n

Baglioni *see* Angelo, Niccolò, Rodolfo

BAI, C., XIII, 14n, 60n, 62n, 78n, 82n, 84n, 98n, 111n, 116n, 118n, 122-3nn, 129n, 142-4nn, 151-4nn, 156-7nn, 160-1nn, 166-7nn, 169n, 171n, 174n, 176n, 189-90nn, 193n, 201n, 211n, 215-6nn, 222n, 262n, 267n, 282n, 284-5nn, 346n

BAKER, J., 303n

Baldaccio/Baldinaccio degli Ubaldi of Gubbio (teacher of *notaria*, 1363), 48n, 132n

Baldassare Vettori (lawyer, 1435), 202n, 223n

Baldo Bartolini da Perugia ('Baldo Novello') (teacher of law, 1447), 61, 178, 181

Baldo degli Ubaldi of Perugia (jurist, 14th century), 179, 205n, 261n

Balducci *see* Filippo di Andrea di Antonio

BALESTRACCI, D., 3n, 11n, 41n, 107n, 115n, 168n, 183n, 293n, 303n, 335n, 364-5nn, 369n, 374n, 377-8nn, 382n, 384n

Ballati *see* Bartolomeo di Filippo

Balle *see* Giovanni di Pietro

BALTASARI *see* Mateolo

BANCHI, L., 11n, 37n, 225n, 344n

BANDINI, F., 58n

Bandini *see* Antoniusmaria, Bartolo di Tura, Giovanni, Sallustio

BANDINI, G. *see* Giovanni Bandini

Bandino d'Arezzo (teacher of grammar, 1287-96 and 1302-8), 36n

Banghen *see* Corrado

Barbazza *see* Andrea

Barbetta (teacher, 1476), 161n

BARBIERI, N., XII, 139

BARCELÒ CRESPI, M., 241n

Bardassini *see* Giorgio

BARDUZZI, D., 25n, 26n, 33, 42n, 55n, 104n, 106n, 122-3nn, 131n, 232n, 303-4nn, 361n

Bargagli *see* Magius, Mino

BARGAGLI, R., 13-n, 59n, 65n, 78n, 98n, 111n, 114n, 139n, 152n, 156-7nn, 162n, 167n, 170n, 174n, 176n, 178n, 219n, 222, 223n, 231n, 236n, 246n, 253n, 279n, 285n, 374n, 389n

Barnaba di Nanni (humanist, *Savio dello Studio* in 1438), 73, 75n, 152

Baroccino Barocci (tried for heresy, 1321), 206n

BARSANTI, P., 45n, 280n

Bart *see* Peter

BARTALINI, R., 39n, 226n

Bartolini *see* Baldo, Onofrio

Bartolo da Perugia (degree in canon law, 1389), 199n, 252n

Bartolo da Sassoferrato (jurist, 14th century), 178, 226n, 261n

Bartolo di Tura Bandini (teacher of logic, philosophy and medicine, 1428-68), 9n, 22n, 61, 132, 134n, 164-5nn, 185, 211n, 323n

Bartolomeo (vicar of the bishop of Siena and teacher of canon law, 1401), 53n

Bartolomeo Bellanti (teacher of law, 1440), 118n

Bartolomeo Bolis (benefactor of the Sapienza, 1512), 289n, 308

Bartolomeo Borghesi (student of civil law in 1425, teacher 1427-35), 114n, 141n, 164n, 184-5, 246n, 363n

Bartolomeo Compagnini (teacher, 1487), 161n

Bartolomeo da Genova (rector of the *Studio*, 1456-9), 260n, 262n

Bartolomeo da Massa (student of law, rector of the Sapienza 1452-3), 346

Bartolomeo da Milano (recommended for the Sapienza, 1466), 321n

Bartolomeo da Sicilia, O.P. (teacher, 1496-9), 118n, 171, 227n

Bartolomeo de Herculanis of Bologna (accepted *condotta* in 1459), 157n, 179n

Bartolomeo de la Mandola (*sapientino*, 1475), 317n

Bartolomeo della Grazia (recommended Benedetto Accolti, 1440), 177n

Bartolomeo di Antonio da Perugia (case heard by Sienese college, 1443), 199n

Bartolomeo di Maestro Antonio of Pistoia (recommended for the Sapienza, 1422), 321n

Bartolomeo di Checho di Binduccio da Asciano (*bidello*, 1428-49), 82

Bartolomeo di Cola da Castiglione Aretino (teacher of canon law, 1400-1), 53n

Bartolomeo di Cristoforo da Arezzo (teacher, 1420s), 180n

Bartolomeo di Filippo Ballati (notary of the *Studio*, 1472), 273n

Bartolomeo di Ser Giovanni Ciosi da Pistoia (*sapientino*, 1467-74), 319-20nn

Bartolomeo di Matteo da Radicofani (chaplain of the Sapienza from 1472), 358

Bartolomeo di Pier Antonio (applicant for post of *puntatore*, 16th century?), 160n

Bartolomeo di Tofo Sansedoni (teacher of law, 1474-88), 142n, 161n, 171n

Bartolomeo Gatti of Sicily (*sapientino*, 1474), 358n

Bartolomeo Petrucci (landlord, 1469), 280n

Bartolomeo Roverella, cardinal of S. Clemente (recommendation for a teaching post, 1469), 321n

Bartolomeo Salimbeni (teacher, 1447, 1466), 164n, 207n

Bartolomeo Scala (letter to Siena, 1472), 175n

Bartolomeo Sozzini (teacher of law from 1459), 13, 61, 139, 152, 156-7, 167n, 172n, 174n, 176n, 180, 181-2, 184-5nn, 219, 221-3, 231n, 236, 285n

Bartolomeo Stefani (recommended for the Sapienza, 1415), 321n

BARZANTI, R., 1n, 387n

Barzi *see* Benedetto

BASCAPÉ, G., 201n, 276

BASTIANONI, C., 38n, 281-2nn, 386-7nn

Battista da Fabriano, O.P. (teacher of theology and philosophy, 1438-40), 77n, 143n, 176n

Battista di Maestro Giovanni da Recanati (cleric and *sapientino*, 1444-8), 235n, 266n, 290n

Battista de' Bellanti (teacher of law from 1427; *Savio dello Studio* in 1471), 72n, 131, 141n, 167n, 177n, 184-5

Battista di Cecco de Rondine (*Camarlengo* of the Sapienza, 1474-5), 354n

BATTISTINI, M., 295n

BAUMGÄRTNER, I., 50n, 151n, 205n, 218n, 224n

Baverio de' Maghinardi de' Bonetti (teacher of medicine, 1443-9), 168n, 188, 323n

Beccadelli *see* Antonio

BECK, J., 354n

BECKER, R., 242n

BEDON, A., 399n

BELFANTI, C., 224n

BELFORTI, R., 387n

Belisario Bulgarini (confiscated goods assigned to the Sapienza, 1527), 378

Bellanti family, 194, and *see* Bartolomeo, Battista, Francesco di Giovanni, Giovanni di Francesco, Lutio, Pietro, Ugo di Battista

Bellarmati *see* Ippolite

Bello di Goro of Pistoia (recommended for the Sapienza, 1433), 321n

BELLOMO, M., 4n, 32n, 109n, 113n, 136n, 138n, 143n, 154n, 159n, 189n, 196n, 201n, 233n, 249n, 277n, 279n, 282n, 287-8nn, 293n

BELLONE, E., 90n, 113n

BELLONI, A., 47n, 52n, 54n, 56n, 137-40nn, 143n, 154n

BELLOSI, L., 376n

BELTING, H., 68n

Benassai *see* Lodovico

Bencivenne di Gano (last rector of the Casa della Misericordia, 1416-8), 342n, 363

BENDISCIOLI, M., 320n, 326n

BENÉ, C., 243n

Benedetti *see* Niccolò di Ser Lazaro

Benedetto (French *sapientino*, 1497), 315n

Benedetto Accolti (negotiations for an appointment, 1440 and 1456), 177n, 190

Benedetto Barzi (teacher of civil law, 1425-35 and 1448-54), 61, 78n, 131, 141n, 162, 175n, 178, 179n, 180-1, 183n, 186-7, 202, 252n, 267n

Benedetto Capra da Perugia (teacher of law, offered *condotta* in 1458), 190

Benedetto d'Adamo (French student and rector of the Sapienza in 1481), 351

Benedetto da Camerino (student of medicine, 1461), 292n

Benedetto da Cingoli (teacher of grammar and rhetoric, 1456, 1488), 119n, 161n, 166n

Benedetto da Lucca (collateral of the *Capitano di Giustizia*, 1445), 216n

Benedetto da Piombino (member of college of doctors of law, 1390), 51n, 162n

Benedetto da Volterra (rector of the Sapienza, 1432-4 and 1435-7; lectureship in 1435), 192n, 284n, 311n, 323, 342-3, 349n

Benedetto di Ser Lazaro (teacher of medicine, 1450-7), 211n

Benedetto di Mantica, del contado di Genova (goldsmith, 1442), 294n

Benedict XII, pope (and the *Studio* of Bologna, 1338), 41n

Benedictus de Farano in terris Rome (student lectureship *in artibus*, 1445), 284n

Benvoglienti family, 194

BENVOGLIENTI, UBERTO, 10, 25n, 252n

Benzi *see* Andrea, Sozzino, Ugo

Berengarius de Comitibus de Catelonia (rector of the *Studio* of Perugia, n.d.), 175n

Bernabò Visconti (siege of Bologna, 1361), 47

BERNARDINELLO, S., 276n

Bernardino (teacher and *Capitano del Popolo*, 1472), 167n

Bernardino da Cortona (*sapientino* 1467-76, and rector of the Sapienza 1475-6), 181n, 322n, 347n, 350, 352

Bernardino da Lucignano Val di Chiana (doctor of law, claimed right to membership of college, 1487), 203n

Bernardino da Siena, O.CARM. (teaching 1480, 1488), 126n, 161n

Bernardino degli Albizzeschi da Siena, St., 52n, 87, 103, 152, 226, 233, 264, 276, 293n

Bernardino de Mendosis de Amelia (admitted to the Sapienza, 1498), 314n

Bernardino Guelfi (teacher, 1520), 161n

Bernardino Luti (teacher of law, 1472-8), 118n, 142, 161n

Bernardino Tommasi (oration at opening of *Studio*, 1475), 111n

Bernardinus pauli aurifici (student lectureship, 1498), 285n

Bernardo di Pietro Lapini, 'l'Ilicino' (teacher of medicine and philosophy, 1460s-70s; prior of college of doctors of medicine and arts, 1464), 134-5nn, 143n, 205

Bernardo Politi (letter to *Balìa*, 1484), 236n

Bernardus de Venetiis (student of arts/medicine, admitted to the Sapienza, 1418), 307n

Beroaldo *see* Filippo

BERTAGNA, M., 227n

BERTI, L., 225n

Berti *see* Angelo, Antonio, Guasparre, Mariano di Paolo

BERTINI, A., 301n, 306n, 309n, 315n, 326n, 327n, 329n, 330n, 341n, 399n

Berto Ildebrandi (chancellor of the republic, 1440), 177n

BERTONI, L., 14n, 55n, 104n, 109n, 126n, 135n, 206n, 246n

Bery *see* John

BESTA, E., 224n

BETTONI, A., 217n

Biagio da Castro (student, 1438), 151n

Biagio Montanini (teacher of law, early 14th century), 44

Biagio Smeraldi (teacher of medicine from 1498), 211n

BIAGIOLI, M., 212n

BIANCHINI, M., 224n

BIANCO, M., 48n

Bichi, Firmano, 10n

BICHI, GALGANO, 10, 25n, 270n

Bichi *see* Antonio, Niccolò di Galgano

BIDEAUX, M., 67n

Biglia *see* Andrea

Biliotti *see* Domenico

Biliotto di Domenico di Biliotto (*Camarlengo* of the Sapienza, 1471-2), 354-5nn

BILLANOVICH DAL ZIO, M., 81n

Bindi *see* Bindo di Ser Giovanni, Hieronimus Johannis Vici

Bindino di Tommaso (teacher of law, 1495), 161n

Bindo di Ser Giovanni Bindi (teacher of law, 1443-4), 166n, 177n

BINGEN, N., 244n

BINI, V., 45n

Biringucci *see* Nanni di Pietro, Pietro di Nanni

BIROCCHI, I., 35n

BLACK, R., XII, 36n, 43n, 45n, 113n, 135n, 177n, 295n, 335n

Blasius de Narnia (*sapientino*, 1426), 313n

Blasius d.ni Francisci (sold property to the Sapienza, 1457), 373n

Blasius of Portugal (*sapientino*, 1496), 359n

BLOCKMANS, W., 224n

BLUME, D., 68n

Boccaccini de Alamannis *see* Filippo

Boccaccio *see* Giovanni

BOCCHI, F., 34n, 68n

Bocci *see* Simone

BOEHM, L., 58n

BÖHMER, J., 42n

BOESCH GAJANO, S., 100n, 362n

BOISSEUIL, D., 323n, 362n

Bolis *see* Bartolomeo

Bonaccorso Bonaccorsi of Florence (teacher of law, 1321), 38

BONAFACCIA, M., 15n, 24n, 281n, 292n, 308n, 314n, 324n, 333n

Bonazini *see* Pietro di Ser Antonio

BONELLI CONENNA, L., 42n

BONELLI-GANDOLFO, C., 224-6nn

Bonetti *see* Baverio de' Maghinardi

Bonifazio, O.S.M. (student lectureship, 1470-1), 284n

BOOCKMANN, H., 405n

BOONE, M., 402n

Borchardus de Anderten (licence in canon law, 1460), 22n

BORELLI, G., 224n

Borghese di Agostino Borghesi (teacher of law, 1461-90), 79n, 153n, 161n, 162, 167n, 191n, 207n, 213, 217n, 264

Borghese di Pandolfo Petrucci (chooses *sapientini*, 1514), 308n

Borghesi family, 72n, 194, and *see* Agostino di Niccolò, Alessandro, Bartolomeo, Borghese di Agostino, Francesco, Galgano di Agostino, Niccolò di Andrea, Niccolò di Bartolomeo, Simone

BORGIA, L., 17n, 201n, 276n, 385n

Borgia *see* Rodrigo

BORGOGNI, M., 47n

Born *see* Johannes

BORSETTI, F., 67n, 265n

Borso d'Este, *marchese* of Ferrara (patient of Ugo Benzi, 1451), 221

BORST, A., 46n

Boscoli *see* Giovanni

BOSKOVITS, M., 115n

BOWSKY, W., 19n, 37n, 41-2nn, 46n, 67n, 69n, 73n, 89, 90n, 99n, 168n, 183n, 198n, 210n, 218n, 223-5nn, 232-3nn, 235n, 299n, 364n, 377n

BOYARSKY, V., 323n

Bracali *see* Polidoro

Braccino da Pistoia (teacher of medicine, 1306), 36n

Braccio Baglioni of Perugia (recommendation, 1462), 164n

Braccio di Fortebraccio (recommendation, 1417), 321n

Bracciolini *see* Poggio

BRAMBILLA, E., 38n, 138n, 184n, 196-8nn, 224n, 283n

Brandaglia de Aretio (admitted to the Sapienza, 1421), 307n

BRANDMÜLLER, W., 58-9nn, 114n, 165n, 300n

Brensset *see* Johannes

Bretuldus de Alamannia (rector of the Sapienza, 1469), 346n

BREZZI, P., 170n

Brillet *see* Guillelmus

BRILLI, A., 381n

BRIZIO, E., 50n, 71n

BRIZZI, G. P., XII, 2n, 5n, 46n, 132n, 138n, 184n, 249n, 290n, 303n, 404n

BROCKLISS, L., XII

BROGI, M., 15n, 42n

BROGINI, P., 104n, 300n, 303, 304n

BRONZINO, G., 286n

BROSIUS, D., 22n

BROTTO, A., 206n, 286-7nn

BROWN, A., 280n

BRUCKER, G., 46n, 55n, 57n, 87n, 90n, 105n, 181n, 237n, 262n

BRUNI, F., 31n

Bruni *see* Lisabetta

Bruogi *see* Angelo di Francesco

Brystidde *see* Henricus

Buccius quondam Nicolay de Collestefano, O.S.B. (degree in canon law, 1390), 199n

BUCK, A., 136n

Bulgarini *see* Belisario, Bulgarino, Gheri

Bulgarino Bulgarini (teacher of law, 1467-98), 153n, 156, 161n, 171, 172n, 181, 193, 217n, 219

BULLETTI, E., 137n, 155n

BULST, N., 225n

Buonguglielmi *see* Sallustio

Buoninsegna Buoninsegni (teacher of arts/medicine, 1488-99), 172n, 177-8nn, 181, 207n

Buoninsegni family, 194, and *see* Buoninsegna, Guidantonio

Buonriposi *see* Francesco de Mansuetis

Burgi *see* Giovanni

BURKE, P., 2n

BURLANDO, A., 295n

BURNS, H., XII, 389-93nn, 394, 398, 401

BUTTERS, H., 177n, 216n

Buvalello de' Buvalelli da Bologna (teacher of civil law, 1369), 49, 210

Buzichini *see* Domenico

BUZZETTI, D., 122n

BUZZI, F., 135n

BYLEBYL, J., 133n, 138n

Caccialupi *see* Giovanni Battista

Cadichio *see* Francesco

CAFERRO, W., 20n, 47n, 105n

CAGLIARITANO, U., 47n

Calci *see* Antonio di Gandino

Caltararis *see* Nicolaus olim Benedicti

CAMBI, M., 19n, 72n, 353-4nn

Cambioni *see* Niccolò

CAMMAROSANO, P., 3n, 13n

Campani *see* Angelo

Campano *see* Giannantonio

Campofregoso *see* Tommaso

CANNAROZZI, C., 87n

Cannucciari *see* Lorenzo

Cantalicio (Giovanni Valentini, detto il) (hired to teach grammar, 1475), 153

Cantoni *see* Cristoforo di Ser Filippo

CANTUCCI GIANNELLI, G., 14n, 344n

Capacci family, 390n, and *see* Salimbene

CAPITANI, O., 196n, 198n

Capocci *see* Niccolò

CAPORALI, D., 12n

Capra *see* Benedetto

Capranica *see* Angelo, Domenico

Caputi *see* Antonio

CAPUTO, R., 253n

CAPUTO, V., 201n, 253n

Carapelli *see* Antonio Pace

CARAVALE, M., 35n

Carboni *see* Gianfrancesco

CARILE, A., 34n

Carlo of Pavia (medical practitioner, 1448), 238n

Carolus Augustini de Pinis (doctor of arts/medicine, 1511), 206n

CARPEGGIANI, P., 393n

CARPELLINI, C., 11n, 33

Carusi *see* Jacomo

CASAGRANDE, C., 218n

CASANOVA, E., 10n, 224n

Casarelli *see* Antonio

CASCIO PRATILLI, G., 13n, 80n, 163, 306n, 331n, 341n, 403-4nn

Casini *see* Antonio, Francesco

Castellano Utinelli (*Savio dello Studio*, 1412), 73

CASTELLI, P., 131n

CASTELLINI, A., 233n

Castello *see* Jacomo

CASTELNUOVO, E., 68n

Castiglione *see* Cristoforo

Cataldini *see* Ercole

Catani *see* Giovanni di Filippo

Catherine of Alexandria, St., 201n, 274n, 276, 288n

Catone Sacco (teacher of law; Sienese attempts to hire, 1438-42), 75n, 152, 176n, 179n, 186, 189, 310

CATONI, G., XII-XIII, 1n, 10n, 13n, 15-6, 17n, 20n, 24n, 25, 26n, 47n, 54-7nn, 66n, 70n, 73n, 83n, 104-5nn, 112n, 117n, 149n, 172n, 194, 198n, 232-3nn, 239n, 243n, 275-6nn, 281n, 282-3nn, 290n, 295n, 299n, 300, 301-2nn, 303, 304-5nn, 307-9nn, 310-11, 318-9nn, 321, 322-3nn, 325-6, 329-30nn, 334-6nn, 338n, 345n, 353-5nn, 358n, 362n, 363-6, 368, 369n, 375-6nn, 379n, 384-8nn, 403-4nn

Cattani *see* Alberto de Sinibaldo, Malatesta, Marinus d. Raynerii

Cavalcanti *see* Roberto

CAVALLAR, O., 224-6nn, 235n

Cavallo *see* Niccolò

CAVAZZA, F., 15n

CAVINA, M., 130n, 184n

Cecchi *see* Giorgio di Tommaso

CECCHINI, G., 13, 18-9nn, 69n, 76n

Cecchini *see* Ambrosius ser priami, Pietro di Giovanni

Cecci di Bernardo di Matteo di Salvi (notary of the *Studio*, 1472), 84n, 273n

Celli *see* Jacopo

Cellolo *see* Guglielmo

CENCETTI, G., 217n, 265n

Cennino di Maestro Niccolò (teacher of law, 1498), 161n

CEPPARI RIDOLFI, M., XII, 53n, 214n, 217n, 224-5nn

Cerretani family, 194

Cerretano de' Cerretani (Sienese teacher of canon law in Florence, 1359), 47, 180

Cesare m.i Cristofori de Fulignio (admitted to the Sapienza, 1498), 314n

CESSI, R., 56n

Cesso *see* Antonio

CHAMBERS, D., 87n, 100n, 136n, 217n, 323n, 399n

CHANG, K., 143n

Charles IV, emperor (charters to universities, 1348-69), 8, 25n, 42, 43n, 44-69, 55, 117, 123, 129, 191, 245

CHATELAIN, A., 293n

CHERUBINI, G., 47n, 50n, 304n, 363-4nn, 368-9nn

CHERUBINI, P., 321n

Cherubini *see* Antonio

CHIABÒ, M., 57n, 295n

CHIAPPELLI, L., 11n

CHIELLINI, S., 131n

Chimento di Niccolò di Jacopo Rinaldi (*Camarlengo* of the Sapienza, 1420), 354n, 356

CHIRONI, G., 20n, 71-2nn, 89n, 220n, 388n

CHITTOLINI, G., 19n

CHŁEDOWSKI, C., 133n, 226n, 335n

Chreuz *see* Georgius

CHRISTIANSEN, K., 2n

Chrysoloras *see* Emanuel

Chuzser *see* Federicus

CIAMPOLI, D., 19n, 54n, 56n, 199n, 233n

CIAMPOLINI, M., 15n, 381-2nn, 384n, 388n, 390n, 398, 402

CIAPPELLI, G., 68n, 294n

Cicinelli *see* Antonio

Cienni di Francesco Salviati (notary of the *Studio*, 1473), 273n

Cino da Pistoia (jurist, early 14th century), 36n, 38, 210

CIONI, E., 14n, 15n, 201n

Ciosi *see* Bartolomeo di Ser Giovanni

CIPOLLA, C., 88n

Cipriano Antonini da Foligno (recommended for office, 1485), 216n

Cipriano di Simone da Radicondoli (teacher of medicine, 1445-50), 211n

Ciprianus de Marcialla comitaus pisanorum (student lectureship in philosophy, 1442), 284n

Ciscar *see* Guglielmo

CIVAI, M., 3n

Claudio de Burgundia (recommended for the Sapienza, 1462), 313n

CLOUGH, C., 87n

CLUBB, L., 295n, 335n

COBBAN, A., 167n, 234n, 239n, 278n

COHN, S., 56n, 303n, 361n, 364-5

Cola da Gaeta (medical practitioner, 1464), 157

Cola da Sicilia (student, then teacher of logic, 1428-9), 152n, 188, 285n

COLLI, V., 196n, 197n

COLLINO, G., 53n

COLOMBINI, P., 12n

COMBA, N., 20n

Compagnini *see* Bartolomeo

CONDORELLI, O., 59n

Conforto da Spoleto (rector of the Sapienza, 1497), 284n, 346n, 351n

Consalvi *see* Nuño

CONTE, E., 35n

Conte di Costantino (admitted to the college of doctors of law, 1435), 202n

Conti *see* Berengarius, Prosdocimo

COPPI, E., 4n

Coppi *see* Avianus

Coppoli *see* Francesco di Bettolo

CORCIULO, M., 17n

Corradino di Marchese (rector of the *Studio*, 1362), 251

Corrado Banghen (doctorate in canon law, 1489), 257n, 264n, 275n, 288

Corsini *see* Almerico di Filippo, Tommaso

CORSO, C., 114n, 135n, 211n

CORTESE, E., 56n, 209n, 224n, 225

CORTESI, P., 389n

Corti *see* Jacopo d'Antonio

CORTONESI, A., 369n

COSELSCHI, F., 12n

Cosimo I de' Medici, 246n, 403

Cosimo del Mosca (sacristan in the Sapienza, 1462), 358n

Cosma da Arezzo (student lectureship, 1493), 283-4nn

COURTENAY, W., 46n, 209n, 404n

Covoni *see* Tommaso

CREMASCOLI, G., 125n

Crescimbene (law student recommended for Sapienza, 1418), 321n

CRISCIANI, C., 218n

Cristofano di Gano di Guidino (studied in Siena, 14th century), 304n

Cristoforo Astolfi of Spoleto (student of arts/medicine, admitted to the Sapienza in 1498), 314n

Cristoforo Castiglione (teacher of civil law, 1418), 168n

Cristoforo da Chianciano (teacher of astrology, 1497), 171-2

Cristoforo d'Andrea (chancellor of the republic 1404-19, *Savio dello Studio* in 1415), 73

Cristoforo di Ser Domenico (teacher of arts/medicine, 1474-9), 143n, 211n

Cristoforo di Ser Filippo Cantoni (notary of the *Studio*, 1471), 273n

Cristoforus de Sermona (student of law, given a place in the Sapienza, 1429), 316n

Cristoforus Zbengh (German student, 1498), 267n

CROSLAND, M., 134n

CROUZET-PAVAN, E., 235n

Csanády, T., 11n

CSÉFALVAY, P., 115n

Curradi *see* Agostino

D'ACCONE, F., 105n, 114n, 167n, 183n, 264n

D'ADDARIO, A., 17n, 225n

D'ALATRI, M., 125-6nn

D'ALESSANDRIA, G., 57n

DALLARI, U., 12n, 61n, 110n, 131-2nn, 144n, 155n, 176n

D'AMELIO, G., 54n

Daniele di Fazio Gallerani (canonist, 1474-90), 289n

Dante Alighieri, 52, 136, 137n, 144n

Dardi *see* Niccolò

Darsa *see* Marin

Dati *see* Agostino, Mariano

DAVIDSOHN, R., 32n, 33, 233n

DAVIES, J., XII, 2n, 13n, 45n, 52n, 61n, 71n, 73n, 90n, 105n, 110n, 131n, 140n, 180n, 182n, 196n, 198n, 201n, 246n, 260n, 273n, 279n, 290n, 399n, 403n

DAVIS, V., 243n, 325n

DEAN, T., 1n, 217n, 293n

DE ANGELIS, L., 11, 25n

DE BENEDICTIS, A., 2n, 132n, 196n, 209n, 224n

Decio *see* Lancilotto, Filippo

DE' COLLI, S., 13n, 18n, 80n, 194

DE COSTER, A., 170n, 184n, 283n

DE FEO CORSO, L., 114n, 137n, 187n

DE FREDE, C., 214n, 220n

DEGENRING, S., 226n

DE GREGORIO, M., 1n, 214n, 387n

DEI, A., 252n

DELCORNO, C., 87n, 103n

DEL GUERRA, G., 280n

DELLE DONNE, R., 32n

DEL MIGLIORE, L., 399n

DEL NEGRO, P., 404n

DE LUCA, F., 17n

DENIFLE, H., XIII, 4n, 12n, 31n, 32-3, 35, 38n, 41-3nn, 45n, 69n, 124n, 143n, 250n, 261n, 293n

DENLEY, P., 4-5nn, 7n, 12-3nn, 36-8nn, 43n, 46-7nn, 57n, 81n, 105n, 110n, 112n, 124-5nn, 144n, 156n, 190n, 243n, 246n, 249n, 268n, 271n, 273n, 278n, 290n, 300n, 301-3nn, 305n, 309-10nn, 314n, 324n, 326n, 341n, 387n, 389n, 399n

DE PANIZZA LORCH, M., 170n

DE RIDDER-SYMOENS, H., 44n, 224n, 301n

DE ROSA, S., 67n, 81n

DE SANDRE, G., 100n, 190n, 197n

Desiderius Erasmus, 243n

DE SOUSA COSTA, A., 242n

Dethardus Sleter (doctorate, 15th century), 22n

DE VERGOTTINI, G., 33

DI BERNARDO, F., 238n

DI CESARE, M., 323n

DIENER, H., 43n

Dino del Garbo (teacher of medicine, in Siena 1306-9 and from 1321), 36n, 38, 132, 180

Dino di Bertoccio di Marzi (Sienese citizen in case against a student, 1430; *Savio dello Studio* in 1455), 266, 290

DI NOTO MARRELLA, S., 143n, 194n, 224n, 282n

Dionysius Széch, archbishop of Esztergom and cardinal of S. Ciriaco (recommendation, 1440), 321n

DIONISOTTI, C., 213n

DI PIETRA, R., 107n

DIPLOVATATIUS, T., 36n

DI RENZO VILLATA, G., 241n

Discov *see* Theodoricus

DI STOLFI, L., 87n

DI TORO, P., 107n

DOBSON, B., 310

Docci family, 194, and *see* Tommaso

Dodonis *see* Johannes

DOGLIO, R., 295n

DOHRN-VAN ROSSUM, G., 139n

DOLEMAYER, B., 44n

Domenico Biliotti (request for archdiaconate of Siena, 1463), 324n

Domenico Buzichini da San Gimignano (applicant for the Sapienza, 1433), 321n

Domenico Capranica, cardinal (recommendations/correspondence, 1435-58), 175-6nn, 321n

Domenico da Arezzo (teacher of grammar, 1417), 168n

Domenico da Chianciano (physician, 1365), 168n

Domenico da Cortona (in prison, 1474), 294n

Domenico da Ragusa (teacher of medicine, 1425), 204

Domenico di Angelo da Seggiano (imprisoned for theft, 1417), 291

Domenico di Francesco (*bidello* of the *Studio*, 1388), 81-3nn

Domenico di Ser Francesco (teacher of law, 1468), 167n

Domenico di Francesco of Piacenza, 'lo strologo' (*canovarius* of the Sapienza, 1473), 359n

Domenico Mentebona da Roma (rector of the *Studio*, 1475-7), 260n, 262n

DOMINICI, P., 139n

Dominici *see* Giovanni

Domperus of Sicily (student, 1470), 280n

DONATI, D., 224n

DONATI, F., 224n

DONATO, M., 68n

Donato d'Antonio Guelfi (sold house to new Sapienza project, 1493), 391n

DONI GARFAGNINI, M., 9n

DOOLEY, B., 405n

DOTZAUER, W., 242

Držić *see* Marin

DURANT, B., 154n

EDGERTON, S., 154n

Edward *see* Adovardus de Anglia

ELAM, C., XII, 37n

Eleonora, princess of Portugal (visit to Siena, 1452), 112n, 227n

Elias of Pavia (teacher of medicine, 1448-9), 211n, 238n

ELSHEIKH, M., 35n, 184n, 216n, 232n

Emanuel Chrysoloras (teaching in Florence, 1396), 52n

Emanuel of Portugal, O.F.M. (teacher of theology, late 15th century), 178n

EMDEN, A., XIV, 1n

Emmanuele, O.S.M. (teacher, 1498), 156n

Enea Silvio Piccolomini (student at Siena, early 15th century; relationship to *Studio* as Pope Pius II, 1459-63), 9, 25n, 59n, 101n, 104n, 186n, 194n, 239n, 375, 389

ENGAMMARRE, M., 2n

Enzo, king, 32n, 33

EPSTEIN, S., 105-7nn, 303n

Erasmus *see* Desiderius

Ercolani *see* Bartolomeo

Ercole de' Cataldini da Visso (rector of the Sapienza, 1438), 343

ERMINI, G., 43n, 45n, 53n, 69n, 80-1nn, 90n, 109-10nn, 112n, 122-3nn, 136n, 140n, 143n, 153n, 155n, 178n, 207n, 209n, 213n, 233n, 237-9nn, 261n, 265n, 266n, 273n, 278n, 281-2nn, 287n, 289n, 300n, 306n, 320n, 387n, 403n

ESCH, A., 32n

ESPOSITO, A., 302n, 320-1nn, 333n, 341n

Este *see* Borso, Leonello, Niccolò

EUBEL, K., XIII, 292n, 349n

Eugenius IV, pope, 59n, 175-6nn, 196, 362-3

Eustachius (student of law and *sapientino*, 1485), 319n

Evangelista da Camerino (rector of the *Studio*, 1435-7), 244n, 268-9

Evangelista Riverio dell'Aquila (teacher of grammar and applicant for the Sapienza, n.d.), 311n

Faba *see* Guido

Fabiano d'Antonio da Monte San Savino (recommended for lectureship in law, 1450), 177n

Fabiano da Monte San Savino (rector of the Sapienza, 1456), 346n

Fabiano del Monte (degree, 1445-6), 177n

FABRETTI, A., 237n

Fabritti *see* Pietro

Fabrizi *see* Gabriele

FABRONI, A., 139n

Faccalume *see* Jacopo di Galgano

FACCIOLATI, I., 56n

FAHY, E., 115n

FALASSI, A., 47n

FALB, R., 392n

FALCO, A., 293n, 397n, 399n, 401n

FALLETTI-FOSSATI, C., 223n, 233n

FALUSCHI, G., 10, 48n, 306n, 381n, 387n, 389n

FANCELLI, A., 10n, 306n, 308n

FANFANI, A., 175n

Farfalla *see* Filippo

FASOLI, G., 34n, 81n

FAUSTI, D., 14-5nn

FAVALE, S., 53n

FAVARO, A., 37n, 41n

FEDELI, C., 43n

FEDERICI VESCOVINI, G., 220n

Federico (servant of the Sapienza, 1473), 359n

Federico da S. Severino, cardinal of S. Teodoro (recommendation, 1495), 292n

Federico P. of Rocca Val d'Orcia (student lectureship, 1496), 285n

Federico Petrucci (teacher of canon law, early 14th century), 40-1, 174n, 178n, 210

Federicus chuzer (German student of law, given provisional place in the Sapienza, 1484), 317n

Federicus Johannes Corradi of Nürnberg (cleric, detained 1447), 104n

Federicus scolarus teutonicus (*sapientino*, 1498), 359n

FELDGES-HENNING, U., 68n

Felice da Pieve di Cadore (teacher of medicine, 1475), 144n

Felice di Giovanni de' Tagoni of Castello della Pieve (Sienese graduate, placed in college of doctors of arts and medicine in 1478), 204-5nn

Feliciano di Ser Neri (notary of the *Studio*, 1480), 22-3, 27n, 273n

Felino Sandei (teacher of law at Pisa, 1476), 144

Feliziano *see* Matteo

FERA, V., 271n

Ferdinand I, Grand Duke of Tuscany, 235, 403

Ferdinandino da Portogallo (interim rector of the Sapienza, 1474), 349n, 352

Ferdinando da Portogallo (rector of the *Studio*, 1470-4), 260n

FERNÁNDEZ ALVAREZ, M., 102n

Fernandino of Cordoba (theologian, visited Siena in 1446), 145n

Ferrandus of Portugal (teacher of surgery, 1473), 161n

FERRARA, R., 217n

FERRARI, H.-M., 187n

Ferrari *see* Giovanni Matteo

FERRAÚ, G., 271n

FERRERI, T., XIII, 14n, 60n, 62n, 65n, 71n, 75n, 78-80nn, 89n, 98n, 112n, 135n, 137-8nn, 141n, 143n-5nn, 150-1nn, 153n, 156-7nn, 160-2nn, 164n, 167-71nn, 177-8nn, 193n, 201n, 211n, 214-8nn, 243n, 253n, 260n, 262n, 264n, 267-8nn, 271n, 283n, 285n, 289n, 320n,

346n, 347n, 349-51nn, 353-4n, 356-7nn, 376-7nn

Ffabri *see* Nicolaus

Filelfo *see* Francesco

FILIPPINI, F., 37n

Filippo Beroaldo il Vecchio (Bolognese humanist), 386n

Filippo Boccaccini de Alamannis da Firenze (rector of the *Studio*, 1465-8), 260n, 262-3nn

Filippo d'Agnolo da Prato (*ricercatore*, 1465), 160n

Filippo d'Amelia (candidate for rectorate of the Sapienza, 1421), 342n

Filippo d'Antonio (*bidello* of the *Studio* from 1495), 82n, 83

Filippo d'Antonio del Frignano (degree in civil law, 1412), 199n

Filippo da S. Miniato (*sapientino*, 1466), 337n

Filippo Decio (teacher of law, 1484-7 and 16th century), 61, 140n, 178n, 180

Filippo de' Scalandrini da Bracciano (rector of the Sapienza, 1496-7, vice-rector of the *Studio*, 1497-8), 163n, 270n, 346n

Filippo di Andrea di Antonio Balducci da Lucca (*sapientino* from 1416, rector of the Sapienza 1424-8, degree in civil law 1424, teaching 1426-44), 59n, 141n, 175n, 180n, 181, 188-9, 202-3nn, 284n, 287n, 342, 347-9nn

Filippo di Angelo/Agnolo di Pietro (substitute *bidello* in 1476; *bidello* of the *Studio*, 1478 or 1481 to 1488), 81n, 82-3, 173n, 359n

Filippo di Sinibaldo de' Lazzari da Pistoia (teacher of law, 1435-43), 118n, 164n, 180, 187, 281n

Filippo Farfalla (teacher of canon law, 1470), 155n

Filippo Francesconi (teacher of law, 1475-6), 161n, 167n

Filippo Villani (*lectura Dantis* in Florence from 1392), 52n

Filippo Maria Visconti, duke of Milan, 176n, 186n

FINESCHI, S., XII

FIORAVANTI, G., 7, 8n, 14, 57n, 62n, 66-7nn, 74n, 111n, 122n, 126n, 134-5nn, 137, 143n, 145n, 172n, 181n, 185n, 187n, 211n, 218n, 221n, 246n, 264n, 281n, 309n, 406

FIORE, F., 388n

FIORELLI, P., 37n

FLETCHER, J., XII, 310n, 407n

FLETCHER, S., 402n

Floriano Sampieri (teacher of law, 1423-4), 157, 170n, 176-7

FOLCHI, M., 226n

Fondi *see* Angelo, Pietro

Fonseca *see* Pedro

Fontano *see* Guasparre

Forteguerri *see* Guido Johannis Ser Pieri, Niccolò

Foscherani *see* Niccolò d'Antonio

FRAGONARD, M.-M., 2n, 67n

Francesco I de' Medici, 403

Francesco Accolti (teacher of law, 1451-84), 61, 78n, 101n, 145, 156, 161n, 169n, 170-1, 175n, 180-1, 183n, 189-90, 217n, 219, 406n

Francesco Borghesi (teacher of law, 1482-98), 141n, 171n

Francesco Cadichio dell'Aquila (rector of the *Studio*, 1477-9), 262n, 264-5

Francesco Casini (teacher of medicine, 1366-1409), 48, 50n, 54, 134n, 165n, 178n

Francesco da Abbadia S. Salvatore (surgeon, 1364), 168n

Francesco da Catalonia (student of canon law and rector of the *Studio*, 1405), 54n, 258

Francesco da Ciglione (teacher of arts/medicine, 1488), 161n

Francesco da Crema (teacher of civil law, 1462), 190n

Francesco da Nardò, O.P. (teacher, mid-15th century), 172n

Francesco da Sicilia (student, 1469), 292

Francesco da Urbino (rector of the *Studio*, 1464), 262n

Francesco da Vergelle (teacher of law, 1474-88), 143n, 181-2

Francesco de Filippis da Montefalco (rector of the *Studio*, 1482-4), 260n, 265

Francesco de Mansuetis or de' Buonriposi of Perugia (teacher of civil law, 1433), 153n, 178

Francesco della Rovere da Savona, O.F.M. (later pope Sixtus IV) (teacher, 1459), 172n

Francesco di Antonio da Pescia (student of civil law, recommended for the Sapienza in 1428), 237m

Francesco di Bartolomeo Petrucci, 'Checcho Rosso' (*Savio dello Studio*, 1426), 73-4

Francesco di Bartolomeo (Sienese teacher in Florence from/after 1359), 180

Francesco di Bettolo Coppoli da Perugia (teacher of law, 1363-5), 48n, 116-7nn

Francesco di Domenico (notary of the *Savi*, 1451), 84n

Francesco di Domenico da Torrita (notary of the Sapienza, 1484), 359n

Francesco di Giorgio Martini (architect, 1480s/90s), 376n, 390n, 391n, 392-3, 395-7, 400n, 401-2

Francesco di Giovanni di Bellanti, bishop of Grosseto († 1417), 247n

Francesco di Giovanni (servant of the *Studio*, 1428-30), 274n

Francesco di Ser Jacopo di Ser Mino di Tura (teacher of medicine, 1460-1), 211n

Francesco di Jacopo Tolomei (*Savio dello Studio* in 1445, teacher of canon law, 1450), 72n

Francesco di Ser Matteo da San Miniato (degree in civil law, 1410, and vice-rector of the *Studio*), 199n, 270n

Francesco di Meo Peri (teacher of logic and philosophy, 1459-67), 161n, 285n

Francesco di Neri Gherardini da Rapolano (teacher of law, 1372), 49, 168n

Francesco di Sante/Santi da Roma (teacher of medicine, 1439-44), 118n

Francesco Filelfo (teacher of rhetoric, Greek and Latin, 1434-8), 61, 111, 114n, 137, 158n, 180-1, 188, 406

Francesco Franci, O.S.A. (recommended for a lectureship, 1433), 126n

Francesco Marretta (*Savio dello Studio*, 1483), 72n

Francesco Mormille, bishop of Siena (1393), 52n, 66n, 105, 300-2

Francesco Nini/di Ser Nini/Sernini (teacher of medicine, 1401-29), 53n, 211n

Francesco Nini/de' Nini (teacher of medicine, 1478-89), 164n, 171, 181-2, 193

Francesco Patrizi (teacher, 1441), 213n

Francesco Pontano (teacher of arts and rhetoric, 1422), 164, 181, 278n

Francesco Sforza, duke of Milan (correspondence, 1459), 170

Francesco Tegrini da Pisa (teacher of law, 1363), 48n

Francesco Todeschini Piccolomini, cardinal of Siena (1474-92), 177n, 389

Francesconi *see* Filippo

Franci *see* Francesco

Franciscus Gentilis palavicinus Januensis (student of law, admitted to Sapienza, 1492), 323n

Franco di Stefano di Vanno (notary of the *Studio*, 1428-9), 273n

Franco *see* Johannes Jacobi

FRANGIONI, L., 242n

FRANZ, G., 58n

Frederick I Barbarossa, emperor (Authentic *Habita*, 1155), 34, 52n, 174n, 232, 235, 266

Frederick II, emperor (relations with Bologna, Naples and Siena, 1224-40s), 31-2, 34n, 45n

Frederick III, emperor (recommendations, 1442; visit to Siena, 1452), 112n, 227n, 311n, 316n, 321n, 323, 354

Frederick of Antioch, king (relations with Bologna and Siena, 1246), 31, 33, 34n

Fredo Tolomei (Sienese rector of the citramontane university of jurists at Bologna, 1301), 36n

FREEDBERG, D., 154n

FREY, B., 45n

FRIED, J., 43n, 209n

FRIEDLÄNDER, E., 12n, 236n, 323n

FRIGERIO, A., 194n

FRISONE, C., 295n

FROVA, C., 6n. 25, 15n, 43n, 46n, 54n, 57n, 67n, 163n, 271n, 277n

FRUGONI, C., 68n

FUBINI, R., 181n

Fulgosio *see* Raffaele

FUMI CAMBI GADO, F., 201n, 276n, 385n

FUNGHI, M., 37n

FUSAI, L., 47n

GABRIEL, A., 34n

Gabriel de Macerata (student of civil law and candidate for the rectorate of the *Studio*, 1439), 269n

Gabriel Lottus of Spoleto (recommended for rectorate of the Sapienza, 1498), 351n

Gabriele da Spoleto, O.S.A. (teacher of theology and natural philosophy, 1426-9), 61, 126n, 135n, 163n, 168n, 177n

Gabriele Fabrizi da Perugia (teacher of law, 1463-6), 168n, 267

Gabrielli *see* Hieronimo di Cristoforo

Galgano de' Galgani (Sienese teacher of philosophy and theology at Pisa from 1490), 181

Galgano di Agostino Borghesi (teacher of law, 1443-60), 164n, 166-7nn

Galgano di Caterino 'Rotellino' (servant of the *Studio*, 1471-92), 85n, 160n, 358n

GALLAVOTTI CAVALLERO, D., 107n, 344n

Gallerani family, 73n, and *see* Andrea, Daniele di Fazio

GALLO, D., 56n, 69n, 154n, 197n

Garati *see* Martino

GARCIA-BALLESTER, J., 241n

GARCÍA Y GARCÍA, A., 56n, 102n, 123n

GARFAGNINI, G., 46n

GARGAN, L., 32n, 84n, 234n, 387n

GAROSI, A., XIII, 1n, 14, 42n, 48n, 50n, 54n, 56n, 65n, 70-1nn, 76-9nn, 88-9nn, 102n, 106n, 109-

10nn, 113-4nn, 130n, 132-5nn, 139-41nn, 149n, 151-3nn, 155n, 165n, 168-9nn, 176n, 185n, 187n, 191n, 193n, 204n, 211n, 218n, 220-1nn, 231n, 238n, 282n, 284n, 293n, 300n, 304-5nn

GAROSI, G., 10n, 24n

Gaspar Turiglia of Spain (*sapientino*, 1473-4), 319n, 334n, 337-8

GASPARRI, S., 224n

Gattamelata, *condottiere* (patient of Bartolo di Tura, 1440), 165n

Gatti *see* Bartolomeo

GATTO, L., 143n

GATTONI DA CAMOGLI, M., 222n

Gelingh *see* Henricus

GENNARO, C., 213

GENSINI, S., 271n

Gentile da Foligno (teacher of medicine, 1320s), 38, 132

Georgius chreuz of Germany (German student of law, given provisional place in the Sapienza, 1484), 317n

Georgius of Germany (servant of the Sapienza, 1498), 359n

Geraldini *see* Angelo

Gerardo dell'Abbaco (teacher of *abbaco*, 1312), 212n

GEREMEK, B., 293n

GERL, B., 111n

Germonia *see* Jacopo

Gesti *see* Leonardo di Antonio

Ghelde *see* Niccolò

GHERARDI, A., 12n, 43n, 45n, 47n, 52n, 57n, 62n, 66n, 69n, 105n, 143n, 154n, 186-8nn, 221n, 253n, 265n, 279n, 299n, 310n, 399n

Gherardi *see* Giovanni

Gherardini *see* Francesco di Neri

Gheri Bulgarini (*Savio dello Studio*, 1473, 1478 and 1481), 73

Giacomo Aretino (teacher, 1474-5), 143n

Giacomo Nuccino (notary of the chancery, 1427-8, and of the *Studio*, 1435), 22, 84n

Gianfrancesco Carboni da Santa Vittoria (degree in civil law, 1489), 202, 203n

Giangaleazzo Visconti, duke of Milan (relations with Siena and Perugia, 1389-1402), 51, 53, 88, 90n, 175n

Giannantonio Campano (humanist, 1452-9), 238

Giason del Maino (teacher of law at Pavia, 1484), 144n

Giesser *see* Johannes

GIEYZSTOR, A., 253n, 254n

GIGLI, G., 9n, 219n, 306n, 309n

Gigliaco *see* Johannes

Gilio dell'Abbaco (teacher of *abaco*, 1395-1414), 93, 155n, 169n

Gilio di Pietro (*bidello* of the *Studio*, 1490-3), 82n

GILLI, P., 224n

GILMORE, M., 185n

GINATEMPO, M., 18n, 20n, 56n, 74n, 90, 105n, 368, 369n, 375-6nn

Giordano da Bergamo, O.P. (teacher, mid-15th century), 172n

Giordano *see* Antonio

GIORGI, A., 49n

Giorgio alamanno (rector of the *Studio*, 1462), 262n

Giorgio Andreucci (student, 1436; chancellor of the republic, 1448), 207n, 215, 218n

Giorgio Bardassini (*promotor* at a degree examination, 1441), 207n

Giorgio d'Alato (recommended for office, 1438; collateral of *Capitano di Giustizia*, 1441), 216n

Giorgio di Tommaso Cecchi (student of civil law, 1408), 246n

Giorgio of Catalonia (degree in canon law, 1434), 289n

Giovanelli *see* Giovanni di Urbano

Giovannetti *see* Pietro

Giovanni Antonio Alato da Ascoli (teacher of law, 1493-9), 171, 292

Giovanni Antonio di Nastoccio Saracini (teacher of rhetoric and *humanitas*, 1487-90, and chancellor of the republic, 1487-8), 215-6

Giovanni Antonio di Paolo (teacher of law, 1477), 177n

Giovanni Aurispa (humanist; moves to appoint to a lectureship, 1426), 74

Giovanni Bandini Tommasi (teacher of law, 1399-1418), 52n, 57n, 158n, 159n, 200, 252n

Giovanni Battista (collateral of *podestà*, considered for the rectorate of the Sapienza and a lectureship, *c.*1442), 342n

Giovanni Battista Caccialupi da San Severino (teacher of law and *Giudice delle Riformagioni*, 1451-84), 61, 78n, 79n, 84, 89n, 100n, 145, 156, 164n, 167-9nn, 171, 181, 190, 193-5, 214, 216, 217n, 277n, 282, 322, 389n

Giovanni Battista da Lucca (*sapientino* and student lecturer, 1496-7), 284-5nn

Giovanni Battista da Sangallo (architect, 16th century), 392, 394

Giovanni Battista da San Gimignano (student, 1476), 234n

Giovanni Battista de' Malavolti (degree at Bologna, 1494), 247n

Giovanni Battista di Agostino da Cortona (student of civil law, 1474), 294n

Giovanni Battista Santi (teacher, 1482-98), 171-2nn

Giovanni Battista Umidi (teacher, 1541), 355n

Giovanni Boccaccio (*lectura Dantis* at Florence, 1373), 52

Giovanni Boscoli (teacher of law, 1420s), 180n

Giovanni Burgi (offered a lectureship, 1447), 153n

Giovanni da Alemagna (*sapientino*, 1473), 337

Giovanni da Barbanza de Alamania (rector of the *Studio*, 1431-3), 112n, 260n, 267n, 284n

Giovanni da Catalonia (rector of the Sapienza and vice-rector of the *Studio*, 1435), 262n, 270n, 343n

Giovanni da Chianciano (teacher, 1431), 165n

Giovanni da Montalcino (teacher, 1476), 161n

Giovanni da Napoli (*puntatore*, 1443), 160-1

Giovanni da Prato (degree in canon law, 1428), 59n, 202

Giovanni da San Gimignano (teacher of canon law, 1460), 140n

Giovanni da Sermoneta (teacher of medicine, 1416-42), 155n, 165n, 181, 187, 211n

Giovanni da Sicilia (teacher of canon law, 1433), 153n

Giovanni da Visso (rector of the Sapienza, 1421), 342, 349n

Giovanni de Grassi (founder of the Collegio Grassi at Turin), 387n

Giovanni de' Guasconi da Bologna (teacher of civil law, 1430), 187

Giovanni de Orliaco (recommended for the Sapienza, 1462), 313n

Giovanni di Antonio (teacher of law, 1474-5), 143n

Giovanni di Maestro Antonio da Pistoia (student of civil law, recommended for the Sapienza, 1428), 237n

Giovanni di Bartolomeo (Sienese teacher in Florence from/after 1359), 180

Giovanni di Bindo (notary of the *Studio*, 1425), 273n

Giovanni di Ser Buccio da Spoleto (teacher of Dante, grammar, rhetoric and *auctores*, 1396-1446), 52, 53n, 93, 136-7, 164n, 167-8, 188, 223n, 326n

Giovanni di Cristoforo (*notaio delle riformagioni*, 1401-7), 93-4

Giovanni di Domenico (teacher of medicine, 1440-67), 165n, 211n

Giovanni di Ser Donato da Arezzo (student of arts and medicine, recommended for the Sapienza, 1433; admitted 1435; teacher of medicine, 1449-86), 118v, 161n, 163n, 180, 211n, 282n, 321n

Giovanni di Filippo de' Catani da Milano (student of arts/medicine, 1452), 265n

Giovanni di Francesco Bellanti (teacher of civil law, 1395-1406), 51, 52-3nn, 164n, 167n, 191n

Giovanni di Francesco Nini (teacher of medicine, 1444-56), 211n

Giovanni di Francesco (*Camarlengo* of the Sapienza to 1457), 355n

Giovanni di Frangano da Sicilia (*sapientino* and rector of the Sapienza, 1435), 343n, 347n

Giovanni di Giglio of Portugal (rector of the Sapienza, 1474), 349-50nn

Giovanni di Guccio da Rapolano (teacher of law, 1387-1402), 158, 210n

Giovanni di Jachomo (servant of the *Savi*, 1489), 85n

Giovanni di Ser Jacopo di Ser Soldano da Piombino (admitted to the Sapienza, 1469), 317

Giovanni di Lorenzo da Roma (student of canon law, admitted to the Sapienza, 1462), 313n

Giovanni di Lorenzo de' Giustini da Roma (surgeon and teacher of surgery, 1465-74), 99n, 156, 211n

Giovanni di Ser Mariano (notary of the *Studio*, 1459, and the *Savi*, 1472), 84n, 273n

Giovanni di Mariano di Ser Bindotto (teacher, 1467), 161n

Giovanni di Martino of Parma (admitted to the Sapienza, 1421; given lectureship in philosophy, 1424), 307n, 319n

Giovanni di Matteo, O.S.A. (teacher, 1438), 126n

Giovanni di Michele Contugio da Volterra (teacher of medicine, 1480-90), 205

Giovanni di Micheli, cardinal of S. Angelo (recommendation, 1469), 321n

Giovanni di Neri Pagliaresi (teacher of law, 1333-65), 40, 48n, 116-7nn, 174-5nn, 178n

Giovanni di Niccolò di Mino Vincenti (*advocatus comunis* and teacher of civil law, 1371-82), 49-50, 210

Giovanni di Orlando da Sicilia (vice-rector of the *Studio*, 1448), 270n, 311n

Giovanni di Pietro (painter), 115n

Giovanni di Maestro Pietro da Arezzo (student of civil law, recommended for the rectorate of the *Studio* in 1428), 237n, 258n

Giovanni di Pietro Balle of Perpignan (*sapientino*, 1456), 317n

Giovanni di Roberto degli Altoviti of Florence (admitted to the Sapienza, 1467), 313, 322n

Giovanni di Ser Ugolino d'Amelia (admitted to the Sapienza, 1427; rector, 1434-5), 342-3, 347n

Giovanni di Urbano Giovanelli (teacher of law, 1427-35), 141n, 184-5

Giovanni Dominici, O.P., cardinal (relations with Siena, 1409), 154n

Giovanni Gherardi da Prato (*lectura Dantis* at Florence after 1412), 52n

Giovanni Girgos of Naples (*medico*, nominates students to the Sapienza in 1537), 322n

Giovanni Malpaghini (*lectura Dantis* at Florence, 1412), 52n

Giovanni Matteo Ferrari da Grado (teacher of medicine at Pavia; negotiations for a contract at Siena, 1451; founder of Pavian college), 16n, 187n, 387n

Giovanni Mignanelli (teacher of law, 1431-43), 165n, 167n, 177n, 180, 213n

Giovanni Milanesi da Prato (rector of the *Studio*, 1418), 269n

Giovanni Minocci (teacher of canon law, 1434-6), 175n, 289n

Giovanni Museler d'Argentina (Strasbourg) (*sapientino*, 1474-8), 317n, 337, 348n

Giovanni Nicoletti da Imola (teacher of law, 1405-10), 54, 56, 168n, 194, 278

Giovanni of England (teacher of grammar, 1297-1301), 36n

Giovanni of Piombino (recommended for the Sapienza, 1475), 322n

Giovanni of Portugal (rector of the Sapienza, 1464), 349n

Giovanni Pensio (vice-rector and then of the *Studio*, 1469-70; knighted and made *Capitano di Giustizia*, 1471), 260-2nn, 264

Giovanni Polo da Parma (cadaver used for anatomy, 1476), 133n

Giovanni Riczari (degree in civil law, 1428), 59n

GIRGENSOHN, D., XII, 43, 56n, 111n, 137n, 141n

Girgos *see* Giovanni

Girolamo Agliotti (student, early 15th century), 194n, 239n

Girolamo da Imola (student, 1430), 266, 290

Girolamo da San Miniato (teacher, 1424-5), 141n, 180n

Girolamo di Andrea del Marretta (doctorate in arts, 1464, and teacher, 1474-5), 72n, 143n, 206

Girolamo Piccolomini (teacher, 1474-5), 143n

Girolamo Sergardi (teacher, 1498), 141n

Girolamo Torti (Pavia, † 1484), 144n

Giuliano da Sangallo (architect, 1480s-92), 389, 390n, 391-4, 398-401

Giuliano di Ser Lorenzo di Giuliano Tani from Prato (student, 1494-6), 246n

Giulio Cesare da Varano, signore of Camerino (recommendations, 1485-95), 216n, 292n

Giusa *see* Alfonso di Ser Lorenzo

GIUSBERTI, F., 224n

Giustini *see* Giovanni di Lorenzo

GLORIA, A., 12n, 40n

Gobboli *see* Perus

Goffredo of Germany (*sapientino*, 1496), 336

GOLDBRUNNER, H., 53n, 178n

GOLDTHWAITE, R., 183n

Gonsalvo d'Aragona (offered rectorate or vice-rectorate of the *Studio*, 1420), 270n

Gonsalvo Mendes de Silveira of Portugal (*sapientino*, 1476; rector of the Sapienza, 1479, and vice-rector of the *Studio*, 1480; student lectureship, 1481), 270n, 334n, 349n, 350n

Gori *see* Marianus Crescentii Petri

Goro di Gregorio (sculptor, 14th century), 39

Goro Lolli (teacher of law, 1448-56), 165n, 177n

Gotto *see* Antonio

GOURON, A., 46n, 244n

GRAFTON, A., 2n, 324n

Grammatica *see* Alessandro di Niccolò

GRAMSCH, R., 242n

Gratiosi *see* Adrianus

GRECI, R., 34n, 223n

Gregory XII, pope (relations with Siena, 1407-8), 25, 54-8, 104n, 106n, 121, 123, 126, 131n, 232n, 234, 302n, 303-4, 307, 361-3

GREEN, R., 2n

Gregorio d'Alessandria (teacher of medicine, 1464-92), 167-8nn, 204n, 205, 211n

Gregorio da Spoleto, O.S.A. (teacher of philosophy, 1459), 126n, 172n

GRENDLER, P., 2n, 4n, 35n, 43n, 61n, 110n, 134-5, 163n, 174n, 209n

Griacha *see* Antonio

Griffi *see* Niccolò Jacopo

Griffoli *see* Jacopo di Nanni di Jacopo, Lorenzo di Meo

GRIGUOLO, P., 78n

Grilli *see* Bagarottus

GROSSI TURCHETTI, M., 387n

GUALAZZINI, U., 207n, 253n, 261n, 273n, 277n, 288n

GUARDUCCI, A., 38n

GUASCONI, G., 342n

Guasconi *see* Giovanni, Zanobi

Guasparre Berti (teacher of logic, 1490-8), 211n

Guasparre de Portugallia (*sapientino*, 1476), 350n

Guasparre di Martino di Niccolò (*Camarlengo* of the Sapienza, 1475-7), 354-5nn

Guasparre Fontano da Modena (recommended for office of *Giudice de' Pupilli*, 1471), 216n

Guasparre Pelliciai da Valentia (rector of the *Studio*, 1455-6), 269

Guasparre Sighicelli da Bologna (teacher of law, 1427-9), 61, 154, 164, 176, 181

Guazzi/Guacci *see* Antonio

Guelfi *see* Bernardino, Donato d'Antonio

Guelphs, 32-3, 43

GUERRINI, M., 19n, 50n

Guglielmo Ciscar de Valentia (candidate for degree in law, 1441), 207n

Guglielmo di Cellolo da Perugia (teacher of canon law, 1388), 50, 51n

Guglielmo di Ciliano (teacher of law, 1321-4), 39-40, 226n

Guglielmo di Pietro Esguert from Barcelona (student of civil law, admitted to the Sapienza in 1425), 307n

Guicciardo di Bondo da Bologna (teacher of grammar, 1306-15), 36n

Guidantonio Buoninsegni (teacher of civil law, 1467-82), 153n, 161n, 167n, 171, 213

Guidantonio da Montefeltro, Count of Urbino (recommendations, 1440-1), 140, 177n, 313n, 322n

GUIDI BRUSCOLI, F., 100n

Guido de Francia (recommended for the Sapienza, 1440), 321n

Guido Faba (teacher of rhetoric, 1240s), 36n

Guido Johannis Ser Pieri de Forteguerris of Pistoia (student of civil law, recommended for the Sapienza in 1466), 321n

Guidone de Capranica (student *in artibus*; student lectureship, 1459), 283n

Guidoni *see* Angelo, Angelus Andree Bernardini, Niccolò di Ser Angelo

Guidotto da Bologna (teacher of grammar, 1278-82), 36n

Guilielmus Anglius (teacher of arts/medicine, 1407), 177n

Guillelmus Brillet (rector of the Roman *Studio* and member of the Council of Pavia-Siena, 1423-4), 58n

Guisa *see* Alfonso di Ser Lorenzo

HAMESSE, J., 234n
HANKINS, J., 201n, 219n
HANLON, G., 10n
HARTH, H., 178n
HAUSMANN, F., 238n
Henricus Brystidde de Brunswick ex Sansonia (admit-
  ted to the Sapienza between 1490 and 1492),
  314n
Henricus de Sylberberg (vice-rector of the *Studio*,
  1488-91), 256, 262-3nn, 265, 275n
Henricus Gelingh de Svevia (rector of the Sapienza,
  1495-6), 346n, 352m
Henricus Ienis (Jena) de Sanxonia (admitted to the
  Sapienza, 1492), 314n
Henricus teutonicus (allocated a place in the Sapien-
  za, 1429), 316n
Henricus teutonicus (admitted to the Sapienza,
  1498), 314n
HERMANS, J., 42n
HICKS, D., 80n, 219n
Hieronimo de Rasimo of Narni (student and *repetitor*,
  1496), 280n, 291n
Hieronimo di Cristoforo Gabrielli (student, 1497),
  234n
Hieronimus de Foligno (student of arts/medicine,
  1488), 238n
Hieronimus de Verreschis de Viterbio (student of
  arts/medicine, admitted to the Sapienza in 1481,
  and rector of the Sapienza, 1485), 351n
Hieronimus Johannis Vici de Bindis (doctor of medi-
  cine, 1511), 206n
HIGHFIELD, R., 310n
HOLTZ, L., 122n
Honorius III, pope (bull *Super Speculam*, 1219), 234
HOOK, J., 2n, 144n, 166n, 214n, 378n
HORROX, R., 310n
HUMPHREYS, K., 281n
HUNT, A., 224n
HYDE, J., 213n, 231-2, 249n

IACOMETTI, F., 53n
IANZITI, G., 238n
IDATO, A., 221n
ILARDI, A., 78n, 80n, 83n, 89n, 109n, 131n, 138n,
  141n, 145n, 158n, 233n, 257n, 280n, 283n
Ildebrandi *see* Berto
Ingerardus de allamania (doctor of arts, given student
  lectureship, 1430), 283n

Innocent IV, pope (privilege of 1252), 32, 45n, 104n,
  233, 235; use of term *facultas*, 125n
Innocent VII, pope (and reform of *Studium Urbis*,
  1406), 54n
Innocent VIII, pope (letter to the rector of the *Studio*,
  1489), 257n, 289n
INNOCENTI, E., 387n
Ippolite Bellarmati (confiscated goods assigned to Sa-
  pienza, 1527), 378
Ippolito di Ser Niccolò da San Gimignano (degree in
  medicine, 1414), 203n, 287n
IRRGANG, S., 242n
ISAACS, A., 70n, 88n, 107n, 217n, 218-20nn, 226n,
  344n, 388-9nn

JACKSON, P., 220n
Jacoba di Mariano (daughter of *bidello*, 1494-9), 83n
Jacobus de Amandola (student of law, to be admitted
  to the Sapienza, 1434), 316n
Jacobus de ascetia (student of law and *sapientino*,
  1498), 314n
Jacobus Gothfredi de Roma (student of arts/medici-
  ne, imprisoned in 1424), 266n, 291n
Jacobus Schrenck Allamanus de Monacho (student of
  arts and medicine, admitted to the Sapienza in
  1442), 316n, 321n
Jacobus thome de Savona (rector of the Sapienza,
  1443), 347n
Jacomo Carusio of Utrecht (student of arts and medi-
  cine, and rector of the *Studio*, 1437), 243n, 268n
Jacomo Castello da Brescia (communal official, 15th
  century), 216n
Jacomo da San Gimignano (teacher of logic, 1440),
  77n
Jacomo da Ongaria (rector of the *Studio*, 1321), 243n
Jacomo di Benedetto (notary of the *Studio*, 1492),
  273n
Jacomo di Credi di Simone (Sienese citizen in case in-
  volving students, 1448), 290
JACONA, E., 214n
Jacopo Ammannati, cardinal of Pavia (recommenda-
  tions, 1463-9), 321n, 324n
Jacopo Celli (*bidello* of the *Studio*, 1452-84), 81n, 82,
  84, 359n
Jacopo d'Andrea da Piombino (student of law, recom-
  mended for a place in the Sapienza, 1443), 322n
Jacopo d'Antonio Corti (*Camarlengo* of the Sapienza,
  1469-70), 354n
Jacopo III d'Appiano of Piombino (recommendations, 1462-70), 291n, 313n, 317n, 322n

Jacopo IV d'Aragona d'Appiano of Piombino (recommendation, 1475), 322n

Jacopo da Forlì (teacher of medicine, 1405), 54, 187

Jacopo de Fornaria (teacher of canon law, 1428), 78n

Jacopo del Germonia (teacher of law, 1483-97), 79n, 161n, 281n

Jacopo di Bastiano Tinellocci (teacher of law, 1477), 161n

Jacopo di Belviso (jurist, 14th century), 36n

Jacopo di Filippo da Sinalunga (teacher of medicine, 1465-06), 173n, 211n

Jacopo di Galgano Faccalume (teacher of medicine, 1459-91), 133n, 156-7, 170n, 173n, 211n

Jacopo di Giovanni d'Arezzo (teacher of medicine, 1478), 157n

Jacopo di Lippo da San Miniato (teacher of law, 1328), 168n

Jacopo di Lorenzo d'Agnolo di m.° Merigo (*Camarlengo* of the Sapienza, 1472-3), 354n

Jacopo di Montone (student in civil law, recommended for the Sapienza in 1417), 321n

Jacopo di Nanni di Jacopo di Griffolo (teacher of law, 1427-9), 141n, 184

Jacopo di Pietro Tolomei (teacher of law, 1435-42), 202n, 213n

Jacopo Mariani of Fermo (student of civil law, admitted to the Sapienza in 1466), 321n

Jacopo of Valencia (student at Bologna, executed 1321), 37

Jacopo Pagliaresi (lawyer, 13th century), 39n

Jacques de Vitry, 293n

Jakob Joel, of Linz on the Rhine (student at Bologna, 1439-42), 323n

JANSE, A., 224n

JARDINE, L., 2n

JENKENS, A., 389n

Jodocus Jungmair (licence in canon law, 1491; doctorate in 1503), 288

Joel *see* Jakob, Tilmann

Johannes Albus (*sapientino*, 1476), 350n, 359n

Johannes Alfonsi e Regno Algarbie (recommended for the Sapienza, 1462), 313n

Johannes Alvari of Portugal (*sapientino*, 1488-92), 314n

Johannes Arrighi de Alamannia (candidate for the rectorate of the *Studio*, 1439), 269n

Johannes Born (rector of the *Studio*, 1435), 260n

Johannes Brensset (admitted to the Sapienza, 1467), 117n, 370n

Johannes de Alamannia (servant of a student, 1444), 266n

Johannes de Gigliaco of Savoy (admitted to the Sapienza in 1443; vice-rector and then rector in 1446), 151n, 313, 316n, 345, 347n, 352

Johannes de Lysura (student, 1434), 281n

Johannes de Messchede (licence *in utriusque iuris* in 1494, doctorate in 1500), 288

Johannes de Petronibus de Nepi (admitted to the Sapienza, 1467), 321n

Johannes de Rufaldis de Trapani de Cicilia (student of law, allocated a place in the Sapienza in 1429), 316n

Johannes de Scotia (student of law, admitted to the Sapienza in 1421), 307n

Johannes de Weissenbach (doctorate, 15th century), 22n

Johannes Dodonis of Rotterdam (degree in medicine, 1412), 203n, 243n, 287n

Johannes Giesser of Munich (student of arts and medicine, admitted to the Sapienza in 1442), 316n, 321n

Johannes Jacobi franco de Sicilia (student?, 1469), 292n

Johannes Lylarde (recommended for the Sapienza, 1473), 321n

Johannes Mancini de Sicilia (student lectureship in canon law, 1445), 284n

Johannes Naddi (notary, 1321), 70

Johannes nepos Kardinalis de Comitibus (petition on behalf of a student, 1441), 337n

Johannes Ruysch (student at Siena and Pavia, 1430s), 238n, 323n

Johannes teutonicus (*sapientino*, 1498), 314n

Johannes Valascho (admitted to the Sapienza, 1498), 314n

Johannes von Azel (teacher of canon law, 1423-5), 58

Johel *see* Petrus

John XXI, pope *see* Pietro Ispano

John XXII, pope (intervention in favour of Bologna, 1322), 44n

John XXIII, pope (bull of 1414), 103n

John Bery, O.S.A. (student between 1419 and 1423), 243n

JONES, P., XII, 1n, 67n, 226n, 369n, 404-5

Jordanus (teacher of arts/medicine, 1473), 161n

Juan Almaçán from Sagunto (student of medicine; at Council of Pavia-Siena, 1423-4), 59n

Julianus de Squaquaris de Gaeta (student lectureship in law, 1438), 284n

Jungmair *see* Jodocus

Jurij Kotermak of Drogobyč (rector at Bologna, 15th century), 243n

KANTER, L., 2n
KAUFMANN, G., 42n
KAVKA, F., 45n
KIBRE, P., 38n, 234n
KIENE, M., XII, 302n, 390-3nn, 394, 398, 399n, 400-1
KIRSHNER, J., 20n, 168n, 218n, 224-6nn, 405n
KNOD, G., 323n
KOHL, B., 56n
KOLLER, H., 405n
KOŠUTA, L., XIn. 1, XII-XIV, 9n, 13, 18n, 21n, 26-7nn, 65-6nn, 72n, 80n, 89n, 110n, 113n, 140-1nn, 162-4nn, 173-4nn, 178n, 239n, 241n, 243n, 270n, 272-3nn, 277, 278n, 290n, 294-5nn, 306n, 308-9nn, 314n, 318-20nn, 322n, 324n, 331-6nn, 338n, 341n, 355n, 357n, 359n
KOTEĽNIKOVA, L., 369n
Kotermak *see* Jurij
KOUDELKA, V., 281n
KOVESI KILLERBY, C., 224-5nn
KRISTELLER, P., 2n, 125n
KUBOVÁ, M., 45n
KUCHER, M., 3n, 354n
KUTTNER, S., 51n

Ladislas of Durazzo, Anjou and Naples (invasion of Sienese territory, 1409), 56, 305
LAMBERINI, D., 3n
Lancilotto Decio (teacher of law, 1483), 61, 100n, 151n, 178n, 180, 190
LANDI, A., 54n, 55n
LANDI, S., 16-7nn, 25n, 306n
Lanti *see* Antonio di Lorenzo, Lorenzo
Lapini, Bernardo di Pietro, Pietro di Bernardo
Latino de' Regoli (*sapientino*, 1475), 321n, 333n
Latino di Niccolò de' Ranuccini (admitted to the college of doctors of arts and medicine, 1481), 204-5nn
Latino Orsini, cardinal (recommendation, 1475), 321n, 333n
Laurentius Wildhelm (degree in civil law, 1548), 347n
LAURIOUX, B., 217n
Lazzari *see* Filippo di Sinibaldo
LAZZARINI, V., 162n
Lazzaro Pellegrini of Parma (servant of the Sapienza, 1498), 358n

LEE, E., 136n, 170n, 183n
LE GOFF, J., 6n, 224n, 288n
LEICHT, P., 33n, 45n
Lelio di Giusti da Verona (student, 1445-54), 291n
Leon Battista Alberti (plan to found a college in Florence), 303n
Leonardo, O.P. (teacher of astrology, 1459), 285n
Leonardo (student of arts/medicine, admitted to the Sapienza in 1519), 315
Leonardo da San Miniato (physician, 1360), 168n
Leonardo da Perugia, O.P. (theologian, 1458), 176n
Leonardo di Antonio Gesti (notary of the *curia*, 1489-93), 22n
Leonardo Roselli da Arezzo (teacher of medicine, 1424), 141n, 180n
Leonardus teutonicus (*sapientino*, 1481), 331
LEONCINI, A., 17n, 73n, 201n, 206n, 274n, 276n
Leonello d'Este (petitioned for re-foundation of the Ferrarese *Studio*, 1442), 67n
Leonora *see* Eleonora
LEVI, G., 235n
Liazari *see* Paolo
LIBERATI, A., 114n, 115n, 303n, 381n
Libertà da Lucca (rector of the Sapienza and student lecturer, 1459), 349n
LIMONE, O., 32n
LINES, D., 90n, 154n
LIOTTA, F., 35n, 154n
Lisabetta, wife of Cecco di Jacopo di Ser Francesco Bruni (case against a student, 1452), 265n
LISINI, A., 19n, 50n, 53-5nn, 224n, 321n
Lobo *see* Martino Lópes
LOCKWOOD, D., 14n, 202n, 220-1nn
Lodovico Benassai, 384n
Lodovico da Gubbio (teacher of medicine from 1498), 211n
Lodovico da Spoleto (student lectureship in logic, 1442; teacher of medicine, 1449-82), 144n, 161n, 168n, 204-6, 207n, 211n, 226n, 284n
Lodovico di Magio da Volterra (student of canon law, admitted to the Sapienza in 1424), 307n
Lodovico of Barcelona (student, 1444), 235n, 266n
Lodovico Petroni (member of college of doctors of law, 1476), 207n
Lodovico Petrucciani da Terni (teacher of law, 1436-50), 151n, 157n, 386n
Lodovico Pontano of Rome (teacher of law, 1428-36), 61, 152n, 154n, 162, 175n, 176, 180-1, 186, 188n, 189, 202n, 238n, 278n
Lolli *see* Goro

LOMBARDI, G., 386n

Lorenzetti *see* Ambrogio

Lorenzo Cannucciari (teacher of law, 1484), 281n

Lorenzo d'Agnolo di M.º Merigo (*Camarlengo* of the Sapienza, 1472-3), 354n

Lorenzo d'Arezzo (teacher of canon law, 1419-22), 164n, 177n

Lorenzo da Casole (Sienese teacher of surgery at Padua, 15th century), 247n

Lorenzo de' Medici (relations with the Sienese *Studio* and that of Florence/Pisa, 1472-85), 7n, 139, 152, 177n, 181, 216n, 219, 222, 398, 405

Lorenzo di Lando Sborgheri (notary of the *Studio*, 1470s), 21, 386

Lorenzo di Meo Griffoli (*Camarlengo* of the Sapienza, 1473-4), 354n

Lorenzo di Simone (notary of the *Studio*, 1487-8), 273n

Lorenzo Lanti (teacher of law and chancellor of the republic, 1474-82), 165n, 216

Lorenzo Luti (teacher of law, 1493), 281n

Lotti *see* Gabriel

Luca, O.F.M. (teacher of theology, 1424), 163n

Luca (doctor of arts/medicine, 1492), 207n

Luca da Perugia (teacher of medicine, 1434), 177

Luca de Callio (student, then teacher of civil law, 1441-3), 130n, 140, 177n, 188

Luca di Cristoforo da Asciano (student lectureship, 1496), 285n

Luca di Niccolò Martini (teacher of law, 1484), 281n

Luca Stella of Genova (recommended for the Sapienza, 1422), 310, 321n

Lucas dominici presbitero de Asciano (student lectureship, 1498), 285n

LUCHAIRE, J., 47n

LUDAT, H., 314n

Luft *see* Martinus

Luigi d'Aversa (controversy over election as collateral of *Capitano di Giustizia*, 1440), 216n

Luís Teixeira (admitted to the Sapienza and made vice-rector, 1473; rector, 1476-7), 241, 280n, 321n, 323, 347n, 349-50, 352

LUME, L., 54n

Lupi *see* Mattia

Lupo of Portugal, 283n

LUSCHIN VON EBENGREUTH, A., 11n, 381n

LUSINI, V., 389n

Luti family, 194, and *see* Ambrogio, Bernardino, Lorenzo, Luti, Pietro

LUTI, A., 10n

Lutio Bellanti (teacher of arts/medicine, 1487-92), 100n, 156, 171

Lutio Luti (teacher of law, 1483), 161n

LUTZ, H., 88n

LUZZATI, M., 247n

Lylarde *see* Johannes

Maccabruni family, 194

MACCHI, G., 116n

Macri *see* Stefano

MADDISON, F., 133n

MAFFEI, D., XII, 35n, 40n, 46n, 54n, 56n, 109n, 113n, 123-4nn, 145n, 151n, 157n, 162n, 185n, 187n, 194n, 241n, 249n, 301n

MAFFEI, P., 54n, 56n

Maghinardi *see* Baverio

Magius Bargagli (notary of the *Sudio* and the *Savi*, 1496-8), 84n, 273n

MAIERÙ, A., 123-5nn, 137n, 143-4n

MAIOCCHI, R., 12-3nn, 45n, 47n, 81n, 113n, 184n, 186n, 286n, 287n

MALAGOLA, C., 12n, 124n, 138n, 143n, 236n, 253n, 282n, 323n

Malatesta de' Cattani di Burgo (admitted to the Sapienza in 1434; rector, 1438; appointed to teach canon law, 1438), 130n, 284n, 316n, 343

Malatesta dei Malatesti (recommendations, 1419-24), 178, 322n

Malatesta di Borgo (teacher of canon law, 1441-3), 153n, 166n, 343n

Malavolti family, 73n, 194, 303n, and *see* Angelo, Giovanni Battista

MALAVOLTI, O., 375n

Malferit *see* Matteo

Malpaghini *see* Giovanni

MALTESE, C., 393n

MANCINI, G., 303n

Mancini *see* Johannes

MANDRIANI, C., 364n

Manni *see* Mariano di Ser Jacopo

Manno di Bartolomeo Vitaleoni (*Camarlengo* of the Sapienza, 1465-8), 302n, 354-5nn

Mansueti *see* Francesco, Mansueto

Mansueto Mansueti of Perugia (teacher of law, 1462-5), 84, 157n, 162, 164n, 170, 178, 190

MANTEGNA, C., 100n, 234n

Manuel of Catalonia (teacher of canon law, 1433), 153n

Manuele, O.F.M. (teacher of arts/medicine, 1499), 161n

Marchionne *see* Melchior

Marchisi *see* Alessandro

Marco di Maestro Antonio of Pistoia (father of a student, 1450s), 309

Marco di Giovanni (*Savio dello Studio*, 1387, and teacher of medicine, 1387-1400), 72n, 176n

MARCONI, L., 300n

Marescotti family, 73n

Margaret of Austria (recommendation, 1539), 323n

Mariani *see* Jacopo

MARIANO DATI, 227n

Mariano de' Vecchiani da Pisa (rector of the *Studio*, 1453), 269

Mariano di Jacopo (son of a *bidello* of the *Studio*, 1496), 82n

Mariano di Jacopo, detto il Taccola (*Camarlengo* of the Sapienza, 1424-33; documentation 1414-62), 354, 355n, 358n, 384n

Mariano di Nardi da Siena (in argument with a student, 1420), 291n

Mariano di Paolo Berti (teacher of law, 1482), 169n, 171n

Mariano di Ser Jacopo Manni (teacher of medicine, 1401-36), 53n, 211n, 226n

Mariano Sozzini (teacher of law, 1425-65), 9n, 13, 59n, 61, 78n, 114n, 118n, 131, 140-1nn, 145, 162, 165n, 167n, 170n, 175-6nn, 179n, 184-5, 194, 218n, 221-2, 267n, 282, 284n, 354, 375

Marianus Crescentii Petri de Goris (doctor of arts/medicine, 1511), 206n

Marianus quondam Eustachii de Ubertinis de Senis (studied at Bologna, 1436; degree at Ferrara, 1441), 247n

Marianus spoletanus (candidate for the rectorate of the *Studio*, 1480), 268n

Marin Držić (Marino Darsa) (rector of the Sapienza and vice-rector of the *Studio*, 1541-2), 243n

Marinus d. Raynerii Catanensis de Burgo Sancti Sepulcri (*sapientino*, rector of the Sapienza, vice-rector of the *Studio*; degree *in utriusque iuris*, 1500), 343n

MARIOTTI, G., 12n

Mariotto da Assisi (teacher of logic, 1459), 285n

MARLETTA, F., 111n, 118n, 135-6nn, 151n

MARONGIU, A., 175n, 244-5nn

MARRARA, D., 13n, 26n, 70n, 73n, 138n, 185n, 258n, 264n, 270n, 306n, 308n, 314n, 318n, 331n, 357n, 403-4nn

Marretta *see* Andrea di Francesco, Francesco, Girolamo di Andrea

Marsilio Santasofia (teacher of medicine, 1388-9), 50-1, 180, 194, 238n

MARTELLOZZO FORIN, E., 263n

MARTI, B., 287n, 306n, 310n, 320n, 326n, 387n, 399n

Martin V, pope (bull requested by the Sienese, 1422), 104n, 126n, 300n, 362

MARTINES, L., 183n, 213n, 279n, 288n

Martini *see* Francesco di Giorgio, Luca di Niccolò

Martino da Genova (rector of the *Studio*, 1389), 251-2

Martino di Pietro of Portugal (requested a place in the Sapienza, 1467), 66n, 231n, 313n

Martino Garati da Lodi (teacher of law, 1445), 151n

Martino Lópes Lobo of Portugal (*sapientino*, 1538), 314n

Martino of Russia (*sapientino*, 1484-8; candidate for the rectorate, 1485), 243, 349

Martinus Luft of Worms (*sapientino*, 1498), 314n

Martinus of Portugal (rector of the Sapienza, 1476), 347n

Martinus? teutonicus (to be admitted to the Sapienza, 1429), 316n

Marzi *see* Dino di Bertoccio

MASCHKE, E., 242n

MASSETTO, G., 241n

Massimianus of Germany (student of law, admitted to the Sapienza, 1484), 317n

Mateolo de Baltasaris (teacher of arts at Perugia, 1412), 176n

Matheus catelanus (student of law, to be admitted to the Sapienza, 1434), 316n

MATSCHINEGG, I., 5n

MATSEN, H., 163n, 283n

Matteo da Grosseto (teacher, 1476), 161n

Matteo da Matera (rector of the *Studio*, 1493), 261, 263

Matteo da Rocca Contrada (student of law, 1480), 238n

Matteo da Siena, O.S.A. (recommended for a lectureship, 1432), 126n

Matteo di Cione of Siena (student at Bologna, 1415), 238n

Matteo di Maestro Tommaso of Spoleto (admitted to the Sapienza, 1416), 321n

Matteo Feliziano (to be admitted to the college of doctors of law, 1434), 202n, 203n

Matteo Malferit of Catania (*sapientino*, 1441), 337

Matteo mei francisci (notary of the *Studio*, 1443), 273n

Matteo Ugurgieri (teacher of law, 1498), 141n

Mattia Lupi of San Gimignano (teacher of grammar and poetry, 1423), 168n

Mattiolo Mattioli da Perugia (teacher of medicine, 1447-56), 177n, 178, 190, 211n

MAYALI, L., 51n, 154n

MAZZI, C., 219n, 224-5nn, 335n

MAZZI, M., 293n

MAZZONI, G., 387n

MECACCI, E., 13n, 38n, 151-2nn, 386n

Medici, 403 and *see* Francesco I, Lorenzo, Piero di Cosimo

Melchior (or Marchionne) di Agostino di Maestro Antonio (*Camarlengo* of the Sapienza, 1458-65), 354, 355n, 384n

Melchior Juliani pierozi de Aversa (student?, 1469), 292n

MELIS, F., 242n

MELVILLE, G., 58n

Menci *see* Pasquino

Mendes *see* Gonsalvo Mendes de Silveira

Mendosi *see* Antonius, Bernardinus

MENGEL, D., 293n

MENGOZZI, N., 58-9nn, 104-5nn, 178n, 335n

Mentebona *see* Domenico

MERCATI, A., 201n

MERCER, R., 136n

MERÊA, P., 242n

MEYHÖFER, M., 42n, 45n

Michael Albrel? of Tortosa (student of canon law, admitted to the Sapienza in 1424), 307n

Micheli *see* Pietro d'Antonio, Pietro

MIETHKE, J., 209n, 314n, 404n

MIGLIO, M., 43n

Mignanelli *see* Giovanni, Mignanello di Leonardo

Mignanello di Leonardo Mignanelli (teacher of civil law and *notaria* 1399-1419), 52-3nn, 158, 200, 210n, 253n

MILANESI, G., 399n

MILANI, G., 32n, 209n

MILLER, M., 58-9nn

Mincucci *see* Antonio

MINNUCCI, G., XIn, XII-XIV, 9n, 14, 2-3, 27n, 40n, 42n, 47-52nn, 54n, 57-9nn, 71n, 73n, 79n, 80-4nn, 104n, 110-2nn, 116-7nn, 123n, 125n, 133n, 135n, 138n, 143-4nn, 156-7nn, 163n, 165n, 167n, 169n, 171n, 177n, 182n, 185n, 189n, 193n, 199n, 200n, 202-3nn, 205-6nn, 211n, 213n, 216n, 219-20nn, 238n, 240n, 241, 242-3nn, 243n, 245, 246n, 252-3nn, 258n,

263n, 267n, 271n, 273-4nn, 276n, 281n, 285n, 286, 287n, 288, 289n, 291n, 300n, 302n, 308n, 314-5nn, 317-8nn, 320n, 321, 322-3nn, 331-9nn, 341n, 346-8nn, 350n, 352n, 354n, 356-9nn, 373n, 385n, 386-7, 388n

Mino Bargagli (*Savio dello Studio*, 1452-7), 73

Mino Vincenti (*Savio dello Studio* and teacher of law, 1387), 72n

Minocci *see* Giovanni

MIRIZIO, A., 42n

MITCHELL, R., 24n, 114n, 243n, 324n, 335n

MOCENNI, T., 25n, 154n

MOHNHAUPT, H., 44n

MOLHO, A., 20n, 66n, 168n

MONDOLFO, G., 166n, 193n, 220n

MONFRIN, M., 238n

Montanini *see* Biagio

MONTOBBIO, L., 399n

MORANDI, U., XII, 13n, 21n, 194, 242n, 344n

MOREIRA DE SA, A., 323n

MORELLI, G., 7n, 196n, 198n

MORELLI, P., XIV, 14n, 22, 23n, 83-4nn, 306n, 308n, 347n

Moreschi *see* Pietro

MORETTI, I., 115n, 116n, 385n, 398n

MORIANI, L., 11n, 42n

Mormille *see* Francesco

MOROLLI, G., 390n

MORONI, M., 11n

MORRESI, M., 393n

MORRISSEY, T., 46n

MOSCADELLI, S., 20n, 47, 48n, 70-1nn, 76n, 100n, 306n

Moscato da Spoleto (*sapientino*, 1487), 243n

MOULINIER-BROGI, L., 217n

MUCCIARELLI, R., 225n, 293n

MÜLLER, R., 58n

MÜLLER, W., 58n

MÜLLNER, K., 111n

MÜNSTER, L., 168n, 188n

MUSATTI, M., 303n

Museler *see* Giovanni

MUZZARELLI, M., 224-5nn

Naddi *see* Johannes

Naldo da Colle (physician, 1304), 168n

Nanni di Pietro Biringucci (*Camarlengo* of the Sapienza, 1419, and *Savio dello Studio*, 1423-7), 73, 354n

Nanni Ranucci (estate in debt to commune, 1409), 101n

Nanno di Cioni di Feio (*Camarlengo* of the Sapienza, 1447-9), 346n, 354n

NARDESCHI, G., 300n, 387n

NARDI, P., XIn. 2, XII-XIV, 8n, 11-12nn, 13-14, 15n, 22, 31-3nn, 34-5, 36-46nn, 48n, 52-3nn, 55n, 59n, 68n, 70n, 73-6nn, 78-9nn, 82n, 87n, 109n, 113-5nn, 117n, 123n, 135n, 137n, 140-1nn, 152n, 154n, 156n, 161n, 163n, 165n, 167-9nn, 174n, 176n, 177n, 184-6nn, 189-92nn, 195, 210n, 214n, 216n, 218n, 220-1nn, 222, 223n, 227n, 232n, 241n, 243-5nn, 251, 282n, 286, 289, 300n, 303, 343n, 354n, 374n, 389n, 403n

Narducci *see* Angelo di Felice

NASALLI ROCCA DI CORNELIANO, E., 113n

Natimbene de' Valenti da Trevi (recommended for office, 1463), 216n

NEBBIAI DALLA GUARDIA, O., 386n

NELISSEN, M., 42n

Neri Pagliaresi (teacher of law, 1321), 39

Nerio de Monte Piscario (teacher of grammar, 1498), 177n

NEVOLA, F., XII, 19n, 144n, 227n, 389n, 402n

Niccolò (recommended for lectureship in philosophy, 1474), 177n

Niccolò (servant of the rector of the Sapienza, 1476), 359n

Niccolò Aringhieri da Casole (lawyer, 14th century), 39, 40, 226n

Niccolò Baglioni of Perugia, prior of Gerosolimitans (doctor of canon law, recommended for a lectureship, 15th century), 177n

Niccolò Capocci, cardinal (founder of Collegio Gregoriano at Perugia, † 1368), 306n, 326-7

Niccolò Cavallo de Sicilia (student of law, 1445), 152n

Niccolò d'Andrea Borghesi (chancellor of the republic, 1492-3), 215n

Niccolò d'Angelo da Siena (accepted a contract on behalf of Francesco Accolti, 1466), 157n

Niccolò d'Antonio Foscherani (*Camarlengo* of the Sapienza, 1433-41), 354

Niccolò Dardi (chancellor of the republic and *Savio dello Studio*, 1423-30), 73

Niccolò da Pistoia (teacher of law, 1443), 166n

Niccolò da Recanati (student, 1463), 267

Niccolò da San Miniato (teacher, 1380s), 180

Niccolò da Sirmione (teacher of medicine, 1456-9), 190

Niccolò da Uzzano of Florence (proposed a Sapienza in Florence, 1430), 399

Niccolò da Volterra (admitted to the Sapienza, 1434), 323

Niccolò de' Cambioni da Prato (teacher of law, 1366-7), 48n, 180, 210

Niccolò d'Este, *marchese* of Ferrara (patient of Ugo Benzi, 1430s), 221n

Niccolò di Ser Angelo Guidoni (teacher of law, 1472), 167n

Niccolò di Bartolomeo Borghesi (teacher of rhetoric, *humanitas* and moral philosophy, and chancellor of the republic, 1467-95), 118n, 164n, 167, 215-6, 220, 226n

Niccolò di Bartolomeo di Domenico (*Camarlengo* of the Sapienza, 1484-96), 355n

Niccolò di Ser Galgano (notary of the *Studio*, 1447), 273n

Niccolò di Galgano Bichi (rector of the hospital of S. Maria della Scala to 1435), 344n

Niccolò di Giglio da Città di Castello (teacher of grammar, 1387), 170n

Niccolò di Ser Lazaro Benedetti (teacher of law, 1468-73), 143n, 167n

Niccolò di Lonenborche (Lüneburg) (admitted to the Sapienza, 1467), 231n, 334n

Niccolò di Lorenzo di Niccolò (rector, *gubernator* and *Camarlengo* of the Sapienza, 1476), 347n, 350n, 355n

Niccolò di Nanni de' Piccolomini (recruiting teachers of law, 1483), 151n

Niccolò di Nanni Severini (teacher of law, *Savio dello Studio*, and ambassador, 1441-79), 63n, 72n, 207n, 213n, 285n, 376n

Niccolò di Paolo d'Assisi (student of arts/medicine, admitted to the Sapienza, 1429), 322n

Niccolò Forteguerri, cardinal of Teano (recommendation, 1466), 321n

Niccolò Ghelde of Poland (student of canon law, admitted to the Sapienza in 1425), 243n, 307n

Niccolò Jacopo de Griffis of Ferrara (admitted to the Sapienza, 1456), 311n

Niccolò Sozzini (teacher of canon law, 1399-1400), 52n, 53n, 122n, 158, 164n, 253n

Niccolò Tedeschi/de Tudeschis, 'abbate Panormitano' (teacher of canon law, 1419-34), 16n, 59, 61, 111n, 131, 167n, 178n, 185, 186n, 194, 200, 210n, 238n, 264n, 266, 406n

Nicholas, St. (patron of lawyers, honoured by the *universitas scholarium*, 1440 and 1511), 201n, 207n, 274n, 276n, 288-9n

Nicholas V, pope (*breve* of 1448; reforms for Bologna, 1448-50), 104n, 130n, 184n, 362

Nicholaus alamannus (substitute for vice-rector of the *Studio*, 1487), 262n

Nicholaus de Anglia (teacher of philosophy, 1278-82), 36n

NICOLAJ, G., 249n

Nicolao Francioso (student of law and *sapientino*, 1449), 311n

Nicolaus (student of law, recommended for the Sapienza in 1419), 322n

Nicolaus de Montefalco (student of law and substitute rector of the *Studio*, 1484), 267n

Nicolaus Ffabri of Žagan (degree in medicine, 1412), 203n, 243n, 287n

Nicolaus olim Benedicti de Caltararis, O.S.B. (degree in canon law, 1390), 199n

Nicoletti *see* Giovanni

NICOLINI, U., 278n, 301-2nn

Nini *see* Francesco, Giovanni di Francesco

Noe Germanus (student in law and *sapientino*, candidate for the rectorate of the Sapienza, 16th century), 347n

Nofrio (teacher of grammar, 1392-5), 93, 188n

Nofrio d'Ambrogio (*Camarlengo* of the Casa della Misericordia/Sapienza, 1415-17), 353n

NORMAN, D., 2n

Nuccino *see* Giacomo

Nuño of Portugal (rector of the Sapienza, 1455-6), 346

Nuño Consalvi (student of civil law, recommended for the Sapienza in 1453), 321n

NUOVO, A., 388n

NUTTON, V., 211n

NYGREN, E., 243n

Oddone di Petruccio of Viterbo (recommended for the rectorate of the *Studio*, 15th century), 258n

Odofredo (jurist, 13th century), 109n

OEXLE, O., 224n

OHL, R., 278n

Oldrado da Ponte (jurist, early 14th century), 36n

Oliverius Pisanelli (teacher of arts and medicine, 1490), 143n

Oliviero di Michele (teacher of medicine, 1468), 161n

Oliviero di Michele (Sienese teacher of philosophy and logic at Pisa, 1492-1502), 181

Onesto di Bartolomeo da Montepulciano (doctor of medicine, 1317-26), 168n

ONGARO, G., 133n

Onofrio Bartolini da Perugia (teacher of law, 1408-9), 56, 131, 168n, 176, 178

ORIGO, I., 87n

ORLANDELLI, G., 217n

Orsini *see* Latino

ORVIETO, P., 137n

PACE, G., 23n

Pace da Ascoli (student of law, admitted to the Sapienza in 1433), 152n, 285n

PACETTI, D., 87n

PADOA SCHIOPPA, A., 209n, 241n

Pagliaresi *see* Giovanni di Neri, Jacopo, Neri

PAGNI, L., 199n, 264n

PAJORIN, K., 243n

Pallavicini *see* Franciscus Gentilis

PALMER, R., 211n

PANDOLFI, V., 295n

Pandolfi *see* Angelo

Pandolfo Petrucci (involvement with the *Studio* esp. 1489-1512), 8, 152, 172n, 173, 214, 220, 222n, 308n, 344n

Pandoni *see* Porcelio

Panunzio (teacher of medicine, 1448), 284n

PANZANELLI FRATONI, M., 300n

Paola Colonna-Appiani of Piombino (recommendation, 1443), 322n

PAOLINI, L., 198n

Paolo (*capellano* of the Sapienza, 1474), 358n

Paolo da Pisa (student, 1473), 234n

Paolo da Prato (rector of the *Studio*, 1460-1), 260n, 262n, 269, 292n

Paolo da Venezia/Paolo Veneto (teacher of theology and philosophy, 142os), 61, 114, 134n

Paolo dei Liazari da Bologna (teacher of canon law, 1321), 38, 154n

Paolo di Antonio (admitted to college of doctors of law, 1435), 202n

Paolo di Castro (teacher of law, 1405-19), 54, 56n, 131, 168n, 180-1, 194, 210n, 278, 362

Paolo di Martino (teacher of law, 1442), 213n

Paolo di Pietro (notary of the *Studio*, 1475-6), 273n

Paolo di Ser Simone di Paolo of Florence (student of civil law, recommended for the Sapienza in 1428), 237n, 316n

Paolo Peri (student, 1469), 234n

Paolo Zilango (admitted to the Sapienza, 1539), 323n

PAOLOZZI STROZZI, B., 88n

PAQUET, J., 5n, 310n, 320n

PARAVICINI BAGLIANI, A., 31n, 125n, 225n

PARDI, G., 9n, 12n, 239n, 244n, 261-2nn, 272-3nn

PARDUYCCI, P., 227n

PARK, K., 98n, 110n, 133n, 183n, 186n, 247n, 262n, 309n, 323n

PARSONS, G., 4n

PARTRIDGE, L., 68n

Parvo *see* Pietro

Pasquino di Simone (teacher of *notaria*, 1399), 52n

Pasquino Menci (*ricercatore* of the *Studio*, 1467), 160n

PATETTA, L., 393n

Patrizi *see* Francesco

PATSCHOVSKY, A., 2n

PATZE, H., 44n

Paulus de Danetria/Daventria or Deventer (*sapientino*, 1492), 243n

Paulus de Eversa (student of arts, 1495), 267n

Paulus de Plenzi de civitate competinensi de partibus alamanie alte (student of law, 1493), 281n

Paulus Pontanus de Urbe (student lectureship in law), 284n

PAZDEROVÁ, A., 42n

PECCI, G.A., 9n, 10, 42n, 220n, 223n, 362n, 381n, 387n, 391n, 392, 394

Pecci *see* Pietro

Pedro da Navarra (rector of the Sapienza, 1493), 347n

Pedro Fonseca, cardinal of S. Angelo (recommendation, 1417), 321n

Pedro Vasques, of Portugal (rector of the Sapienza, 1477-8; teacher of law and communal official, 1479-80), 214, 346n, 348-9nn

PEDRONI, M., 142n

Pegolotti *see* Piero

PELLEGRINI, E., 219n

Pellegrini *see* Lazzaro

Pelliciai *see* Guasparre

Pensio *see* Giovanni

Peri *see* Francesco di Meo, Paolo

PERTICI, P., 3n, 9n, 41n, 55n, 72n, 219n, 227n, 300n, 375n, 402n

Perus Gobboli of Portugal (student, 1498), 267n

PESENTI, T., 51n, 53n, 57n, 135n, 247n, 386n, 388n

PESSINA LONGO, H., 243n

PETER, H., 316n

Peter Bart von Oppenheim (student of canon law, † 1474), 381n

Peter of Perpignan (student of medicine, 1423-4), 59n

Peter Pront (student in canon law, application to the Sapienza in 1473), 313n

Peter Ruysch (letter from Siena, 1434), 238n, 323n

PETERSOHN, J., 318n, 348n

Petroni *see* Johannes, Lodovico

PETRONIO, V., 35n

Petrucci *see* Alessandro, Antonio di Francesco di Bartolomeo, Bartolomeo, Borghese di Pandolfo, Federico, Francesco di Bartolomeo, Pandolfo

Petrucciani *see* Lodovico

Petrus (Sienese teacher of arts/medicine in Perugia, n.d.), 175n

Petrus de Francia (student of law, admitted to the Sapienza in 1459), 320n

Petrus de Michelibus de Cathelonia (student lectureship, 1445), 283n

Petrus de Viterbio (*sapientino*, 1488), 331n

Petrus Johel de Linsi/Linz (admitted to the Sapienza in 1442, † 1444), 311n, 316n, 321n, 323

Petrus Silvestri Jacobi of Trequanda (chaplain in the Sapienza, 1498-9), 358n

PETTI BALBI, G., 73n, 74n

PEZZAROSSA, F., 386n

PIACENTINI, P., 57n

PIANA, C., 49n, 56n, 126n, 134-5nn, 154n, 179n, 206n, 234n, 238n, 247n, 264n, 280n, 282n, 286n

PIANIGIANI, A., XIV, 14n, 53-4nn, 56n, 74-6nn, 78-9nn, 88-9nn, 98n, 100-1nn, 103n, 109n, 111-2n, 114n, 118n, 123n, 130n, 132n, 135-6nn, 140-1nn, 143n, 153-5nn, 157-8nn, 162n, 166-8nn, 170n, 175-7nn, 184-9nn, 191-3nn, 202-5nn, 211n, 220n, 238n, 252n, 262n, 282-5nn, 333n

PICCINNI, G., 1n, 3n, 20n, 23n, 25n, 41n, 49n, 56n, 62n, 65n, 105n, 107, 115n, 132-3nn, 168n, 176n, 280n, 293n, 299n, 303n, 335n, 344n, 364-6nn, 368, 369n, 374n, 382n, 384n

Piccolomini family, 194, and *see* Enea Silvio, Francesco Todeschini, Girolamo, Niccolò di Nanni

PICCOLOMINI, P., 9n, 112-3nn, 122n, 272n, 308n, 333-4nn

Pier Ieronimo (*bidello* of the *Studio*, 1488), 83n

Pier Simone da Ascoli; *see* under Simone

PIERINI, M., 226n

Piermarino da Foligno (teacher of oratory, 1497), 142n

Piero da Pisa (degree in law, 1428), 289n

Piero de' Pegolotti of Verona (admitted to the Sapienza, 1440), 313n

Piero di Cosimo de' Medici (recommendations, 1461-6), 269n, 322n

Piero di Fernando of Portugal (admitted to the Sapienza, 1466), 322n

Piero di Francesco di Tagliacozzo (cadaver granted for anatomy, 1457), 133n

Pierozzi *see* Melchior Juliani

Pietro (chaplain in the Sapienza, 1499), 359n

Pietro Bellanti (teacher of canon law, 1493), 171

Pietro d'Ancarano (teacher of canon law, 1387-90), 50-1, 131

Pietro d'Antonio (rector and *governatore* of the Sapienza, 1488), 376

Pietro d'Antonio de' Micheli (teacher of law, 1421-48; *Savio dello Studio* in 1448), 58, 72n, 164n, 165, 166n, 185, 236n

Pietro da Capranica (student lectureship in civil law and communal official, 1496-8), 285

Pietro da Pisa (teacher of Greek, 1490), 137

Pietro de' Fabritti of Fermo (recommended for the Sapienza, 1469), 321n

Pietro de' Pecci (teacher of law, 1413-33), 61, 131, 141n, 165n, 166n, 167, 185, 194, 200, 210n, 226

Pietro de' Rossi (teacher of philosophy and theology, 15th century), 9n, 61

Pietro de' Spinelli (teacher of law, 1476), 161n

Pietro dell'Ochio (teacher in the Casa della Misericordia, 14th century), 304n

Pietro di Ser Antonio Bonazini (teacher of *notaria*, 1401-30), 53n, 101n, 106n, 132n, 164n, 166n

Pietro di Bartolomeo (priest in the Sapienza, 1474), 358n

Pietro di Bastiano Tinellocci (teacher of arts/medicine, 1469), 169n

Pietro di Bernardo Lapini (teacher of medicine, early 15th century), 132, 176n, 194

Pietro di Chello (teacher of grammar, 1369), 50, 170n

Pietro (di Giglio) dell'Abbaco (teacher of *abaco*, 1425-39), 155n, 212n

Pietro di Giovanni Cecchini (on mission to hire teachers, 1412), 151n

Pietro di Lorenzo (notary of the university of students, 1425), 273n

Pietro di Nanni Biringucci (rector of the Sapienza, 1443-5, *Savio dello Studio* in 1461), 73, 344, 345-7nn, 352, 373

Pietro di Stefano (student of arts/medicine, recommended for the Sapienza in 1424), 321n

Pietro Fondi (teacher of poetry and rhetoric, and chancellor of the republic, 1464-77), 215-6

Pietro Giovannetti of Bologna (teacher of medicine, 1423-39), 61, 165n, 168n, 176n, 188, 203n, 204, 278n, 322n

Pietro Ispano (teacher of medicine, 13th century), 36, 132

Pietro Luti (teacher of law, 15th century), 189

Pietro (Moreschi) dell'Abbaco (teacher of *abaco*, 1468), 169n

Pietro Parvo (recommended for the Sapienza, 1462), 313n

Pietro piovano della Pieve di Pacina (*Camarlengo* of the Sapienza, 1488-91), 355n

Pietro Sacco da Verona (teacher of philosophy, 1443-4, and medicine, 1458-74), 156, 161n, 169n, 170-1, 175-6nn, 190

Pietrus guilelmi de catelonia (student of law, to be admitted to the Sapienza, 1429), 316n

PIGHI, G., 34n

PILTZ, A., 243n

PINI, A., 34n, 80, 82-3nn, 138n, 196n, 209n

Pini *see* Carolus Augustini

PINTO, G., 1n, 20n, 47n, 107n

PIOVAN, F., 5n

Pisanelli *see* Oliverius

Pius II, pope; *see* Enea Silvio Piccolomini

Pius III, pope; *see* Francesco Todeschini Piccolomini

Placido di Aldello de' Placidi (teacher of law, 1467-83), 143n, 161n, 177n, 219, 237n

PLANTAMURA, R., 293n

Plenz *see* Paulus

Pocci *see* Simone di Bartolomeo

Poggio Bracciolini (recommendation, 1440), 177n

POLIDORI, F., 344n

Polidoro Bracali (degree in medicine, 1449), 22n

Politi *see* Bernardo

Polo da Lucca (candidate for a lectureship in medicine, 1428), 78n

Polo *see* Giovanni

POLZER, J., 41n

Pontano *see* Francesco, Lodovico, Paulus

POPPI, A., 125n

Porcelio de' Pandoni (teacher of grammar, 1447-8), 118n, 136-7

POWICKE, F., XIV, 1n

PRAGER, F., 354n

PREMUDA, L., 133n

PRODI, P., 224n

Pront *see* Peter

Prosdocimo Conti (Paduan teacher of law, early 15th century), 56n

Prospero (teacher of arts/medicine, 1474-5), 143n

PRUNAI, G., XII, XIV, 11n, 13, 18n, 31n, 32n, 33, 35n, 37n, 41-3nn, 47n, 49n, 51-2nn, 65-6nn, 80n, 113n, 115-7nn, 121n, 141n, 150n, 154n, 168n, 176n, 185n, 194, 198n, 210n, 233n, 235n, 245-6nn, 250n, 265n, 276n, 278n, 288n, 361n, 403-4nn

PRYDS, D., 123n, 404n

PUCCINOTTI, F., 78n, 80n, 83n, 89n, 109n, 131n, 138n, 141n, 145n, 158n, 233n, 257n, 280n, 283n

QUAGLIONI, D., 44n

QUARTESAN, M., 19n, 72n, 353-4nn

QUELLER, D., 244n

RABB, T., 46n

RABE, H., 2n

Raffael catalanus/de cathelonia (student lectureship in canon law, 1442-5?), 283-4nn

Raffaele Fulgosio (teacher of law, 1408), 56, 131

Rainaldo da Camerino (teacher of law, negotiating *condotta* in 1425), 154n

Rainaldo da Sicilia (vice-rector of the *Studio*, 1420), 270n

RANIERI, C., 57n

Ranucci *see* Nanni

Ranuccini *see* Latino di Niccolò

RANZATO, S., 293n

RASHDALL, H., XIV, 1n, 4n, 32, 35, 43n, 45n, 65, 69n, 102n, 124n, 138n, 233n, 261n, 270n, 403n

Rasimo *see* Hieronimo

RAU, V., 242n, 348n

REDON, O., 217n

REDONDO, A., 2n

REES JONES, S., 310n

Regoli *see* Latino

REINHARD, W., 136n

RENZI, P., 2n, 3n, 15n, 43-4nn, 46n, 67n

REXROTH, F., 41n, 45n

Ribaldini *see* Antonio

RICCI, S., 2n

Ricciardo de' Ricciardi of Pistoia (recommended for the Sapienza, 1433), 321n

Ricciardus de Fonte (teacher of law, 1429), 155n

RICCIARELLI, F., 227n

RICHARDS, J., 293n

Rico Richi (teacher of law, 1483), 156

Riczari *see* Giovanni

RIEDL, P., 115n

RIGONI, E., 267n

RIGONIO, M., 82n

Rinaldi *see* Chimento di Niccolò di Iacopo

Rinaldo Angelini da Cortona (Sienese victim of student violence, 1469), 292n

Riverio *see* Evangelista

Roberto Cavalcanti of Florence (rector of the *Studio*, 1427, and teacher of law, 1427-8), 141n, 180, 188, 202n, 284n

Rodolfo Baglioni (letter to Lorenzo de' Medici, 1474), 139

Rodrigo Borgia, cardinal (recommendation, 1469), 349n

ROEST, B., 126n

ROMAGNOLI, E., 10n

ROMANO, A., 4n, 184n, 277n

ROMANO, R., 369n

Roselli *see* Antonio di Giovanni, Antonio di Rosello, Leonardo

ROSSI, A., 12n, 45n, 140n, 239-40nn, 273n, 306n, 399n

ROSSI, G., 33, 56n

ROSSI, P., 36n, 42n, 52n, 137n, 168n

Rossi *see* Pietro

ROSSIAUD, J., 293n

ROSSO, P., 81n, 152n, 174n, 184n, 187n, 242n, 281n, 294n, 320n, 322-3nn

RÖSSLER, H., 58n

ROTONDI SECCHI TARUGI, L., 243n

ROTZOLL, M., 152n

Rovere *see* Francesco

Roverella *see* Bartolomeo

Rubertis *see* Scipio

RUBINSTEIN, N., XII, 37n, 42n, 68n, 75n, 88n, 369n

Ruffaldi *see* Johannes

RUSSELL, A., 211n

RUTIGLIANO, A., 48n, 90n

Ruysch *see* Johannes, Peter

SABATTANI, A., 138n

SABBADINI, R., 111n

Sabe *see* Angelo

Sacco *see* Catone, Pietro

Salimbene de' Capacci (rector of the hospital of S. Maria della Scala, 1480-2), 344n

Salimbeni *see* Bartolomeo

Sallustio Bandini (donation of library, 1758), 387

Sallustio Buonguglielmi of Perugia (teacher of law,

1419-28), 61, 141n, 175-6nn, 178, 181, 187, 202n, 210n

SALMÓN, F., 241n

SALOMON, R., 45n

Salvetti *see* Angelo

Salviati *see* Cienni di Francesco

Sampieri *see* Floriano

Sandei *see* Felino

SANESI, G., 33

Sangallo *see* Giovanni Battista, Giuliano

Sansedoni *see* Bartolomeo di Tofo

Santasofia *see* Marsilio

Santi *see* Antonio di Niccolò, Francesco, Giovanni Battista

SANTINI, C., 306n

Saracini *see* Giovanni Antonio di Nastoccio

SATTA MEUCCI, A., 185n

SBARAGLI, F., 219n

SBRICCOLI, M., 217n

Scabello del fu Chiavellino (teacher of grammar, 1316), 304n

SCAGLIA, G., 281n, 354n

Scala *see* Bartolomeo

Scalandrini *see* Filippo

SCALI, M., 17n

Scarpi *see* Antonio

SCHESCHKEWITZ, U., 22n

SCHMIDT, R., 44n, 45n, 405n

SCHMITT, C., XII, 125n, 133-5nn, 138-9nn, 240n

SCHMITT, J.-C., 235n

Schrenck *see* Jacobus

SCHUBERT, E., 45n

SCHUCHARD, C., 58n

SCHUPFER, F., 52n

SCHUSTER, P., 293n

SCHWINGES, R., 293n, 310n, 314n, 348n

Sciacha *see* Antonio

Scipio d'Asti (lecturer and rector of the Sapienza, 1458-9; recommended by the *Concistoro* in 1469), 348-9nn

Scipio de Rubertis of Ferrara (recommendation, 1471), 216n

Scipione di Jacopo (son of *bidello*, 1494), 82n

SCRIBNER, R., 294n

SEBASTIANI, M., 237n, 301n, 303n, 306n, 309n, 315n, 326n, 329-30nn, 341n, 387n, 399n

Secchi Tarugi family, 23n

SECCO-SUARDO, G., 154n

SEGOLONI, D., 209n

SEIBT, F., 45n

SEIDEL, M., 68n, 115n, 154n

SEIFERT, A., 407n

SEIGEL, J., 46n

SEMBOLONI, N., 17n

SENIGAGLIA, Q., 232n

Serafino da Camerino (rector of the *Studio*, 1446-7; teacher of medicine, 1451-3), 211n, 244n, 284n, 289n

Sergardi *see* Girolamo

Sermini/Sernini family, 285n, and *see* Francesco, Ugo di Battista

Sermoneta *see* Alessandro

Sernini *see* Francesco

Sestigiani, Antonio (archivist, 17th century), 10, 25n, 330n

Severini *see* Niccolò di Nanni

Sforza dynasty of Milan, 7n. 27 and *see* Francesco

SHAW, C., 18n, 65n, 76n, 114n, 215n, 220n, 222-3nn, 299n, 402n

Sighicelli *see* Guasparre

Sigismund, emperor (charter of 1433), 42n

Sigismund of Germany (rector of the *Studio*, 1488), 262n

SILVANO, G., 7n, 81n, 90n, 105, 197n, 245n

Silvestro (teacher of law, 1425), 155n

Simon Antonii Talini de Lanciano of Pistoia (student of canon law, admitted to the Sapienza, 1466), 321n

Simone (rector of the Sapienza, 1419), 342

Simone Bocci, O.P. (teacher of arts, 1470s), 122n, 142-3, 145, 172n

Simone Borghesi (teacher of law, 1498), 141n

Simone/Pier Simone da Ascoli (student of medicine, 1495-7), 291-2

Simone da Campiglia (teacher of grammar, 1365), 168n

Simone di Bartolomeo Pocci (notary of the *Studio*, 1453), 273n

Simone di Iacomo di Ghieri da Radicondoli (notary of the *Studio*, 1451), 84n, 273n

Simone di Neri (*bidello* of the *Studio*, 1362-3), 81n

Simonelli *see* Valerius Jacobi

Simonetto di S. Lupidio (teacher of logic and philosophy, 1430), 123n

Sinibaldo di Maestro Bartalaccio of Montalcino (teacher of medicine, 1429-44), 211n, 213n

Sinolfo (Sienese orator to Rome, 1482-95), 236-7nn, 292n

SIRAISI, N., 38n, 133-4nn, 136n, 138n, 324n

SITRAN REA, L., 5n, 16n

SKINNER, Q., 68n

Sleter *see* Dethardus
SMALLEY, B., 310n
Smeraldi *see* Biagio
SMURA, R., 68n
Soldano di Ser Jacopo di Ser Soldano da Piombino (admitted to the Sapienza, 1469), 317
SOLERTI, A., 12n
SORBELLI, A., 132n, 139n, 286-7nn, 288n
SOTTILI, A., 2n, 142, 144n, 152n, 174n, 238n, 242n, 245n, 271n, 277n, 281n, 283n, 287n, 294n, 323n
Sozzini family, 194, and *see* Bartolomeo, Mariano, Niccolò
Sozzino Benzi (teacher of medicine at Florence, 15th century), 181n
SPAGNESI, E., 37n, 51-2nn, 81n, 115n, 175n, 281n, 301n, 305n, 399n, 403n
Spinelli *see* Pietro
SPUFFORD, P., 88n
Squaquaris *see* Julianus
STABEL, P., 402n
STADTEN, P., 388n
STARN, R., 68n
Stefani *see* Bartolomeo
Stefano d'Arezzo (recommended for a lectureship in canon law, 1485), 177n
Stefano da Piombino (recommended for a room in the Sapienza, 1475), 322n
Stefano di Giovanni (student of canon law, nominated for Bolis scholarship in the Sapienza, 1512), 308n
Stefano Macri of Savoy (student of law and *sapientino*, 1497; appointed to lectureship and office of *Giudice delle Appellagioni*, 1499; degree in 1500), 285, 315n, 320n
Stefanus de trentis de luccha (student of civil law, candidate for rectorate of the *Studio*, 1439), 269n
Stefanus Iohanninensis de Senis (degree in civil law, 1519), 308n
STEFANUTTI, U., 188n, 323n
STEFFEN, W., 249n
Stella *see* Luca
STELLING-MICHAUD, S., 67n
STELZER, W., 34n
STICCO, M., 87n
STOPANI, R., 3n
STRAYER, J., 244n
STREHLKE, C., 2n
STRNAD, A., 389n
Strozzi family, 199

SUPINO MARTINI, P., 143n
SWANSON, R., 58n, 310n
SYDOW, J., 242n
Sylberberg *see* Henricus
SZABÓ-BECHSTEIN, B., 126n
Széch *see* Dionysius

T. de Mutina (cadaver granted for anatomy, 1490), 133n
Taddeo di Giovanni da Firenze (teacher in Siena, 15th century), 180n
TAFURI, M., 388n, 393n
Tagoni *see* Felice di Giovanni
TALBOT, C., 133n
Talini *see* Simon Antonii
Tanci *see* Alessandro
TANGHERONI, M., 43n, 46n, 253n
Tani *see* Antonio, Giuliano di Ser Lorenzo di Giuliano
Tantucci family, 194
TARRAGLIA, N., 175n
Tartaglia di Lavello (recommendation, 1421), 342n
Tartagni *see* Alessandro
Tarugio di Bernardino Tarugi da Montepulciano (degree *in utroque iuris*, 1507), 23n
TÁTRAI, V., 115n
Tebaldus, 32n, 251
TEDESCHI, J., 168n
Tedeschi *see* Niccolò
TEGA, W., 12n
Teixeira *see* Luís
Teodorico di Piemonte (teacher of medicine, 1449), 153
TERVOORT, A., 243n
TERZANI, T., 54n, 56-7nn
TERZIANI, R., 18n, 75n, 78n, 215-6nn
Theodorico da Spagna (*sapientino*; student lectureship in civil law, 1439), 283-4nn
Theodoricus discov alamannus (admitted to the Sapienza, 1485; rector of the Sapienza, 1488), 319n, 348n, 351
Theodosius, emperor (false privilege of 423), 34n
THOMSON, S., 45n
THORNDIKE, L., 67n, 293n
TIBBETTS, S., 51n
Tilmann Joel (canonist, 15th century), 323n
Timoteo da Pistoia (teacher of philosophy, 1423-5), 180n, 188, 204
Tinellocci *see* Antonio di Bastiano, Jacopo di Bastiano, Pietro di Bastiano
Tizio, Sigismondo (16th-century history of Siena), 9

TODERI, G., 88n

Todeschini Piccolomini *see* Francesco

TOGNETTI, S., 1n, 242n

Tolomei family, 73n, 194, and *see* Francesco di Jacopo, Fredo, Jacopo di Pietro

TOMASI STUSSI, G., 9n

TOMEI, A., 3n

TOMMASI, G., 218n

Tommasi family, 285n, and *see* Alessandro, Antoniusmaria Bandini, Bernardino, Giovanni Bandini

Tommaso Battista di Maestro Andrea da Pisa (student, 1462), 281n

Tommaso Campofregoso, *doge* of Genova (recommendation, 1422), 310

Tommaso Corsini (teacher of civil law, 1320s), 180

Tommaso da Amelia (teacher of law, 1399), 52n

Tommaso da Bordello of Perugia, vicar general to the bishop of Arezzo (*Concistoro* appeal to him for help, 1418), 103n

Tommaso da Ficecchio (rector of the *Studio*, 1357), 251

Tommaso da Iesi (recommended for the Sapienza, 1462), 313n

Tommaso de' Arrighini da Pontremoli, bishop of Brugnato (recommended for a lectureship in canon law, 1427), 177n

Tommaso de' Covoni of Florence (teacher of civil law, 1387-90), 50-1, 188

Tommaso Docci (teacher of law, 1423-55), 9n, 61, 131, 141n, 164n, 165, 177n, 184-5, 192, 213n, 218, 278, 282n

TOMMASO FECINI, 226n, 227n

Tommaso 'greco' (student in arts/medicine, 1421), 291n

TOMMASO MONTAURI, 53n, 57-8nn

Torti *see* Girolamo

Toti *see* Arcangelo

TOUBERT, P., 31n

TRAPANI, L., XII, 13n, 47n, 76n, 186n, 210n, 232n, 403n

TRAUTZ, F., 45n

TRAVAINI, L., 62n

Trenti *see* Stefano

TREXLER, R., 102n

TRIO, P., 280n

TROMBETTI BUDRIESI, A., 5n, 25n, 138n, 154n, 184n, 198n, 279n, 286-9nn, 320n

TUCCI, U., 369n

Tudeschis *see* Niccolò

TULIANI, M., 144n, 365n, 374n, 390n

Turiglia, Gaspar

TURNAU, I., 224n

TURRINI, P., XII, 15n, 41n, 57n, 65n, 133n, 214n, 219n, 224-6nn, 373-5nn, 402n

Ubaldi *see* Angelo, Baldaccio, Baldo

Ubertini *see* Marianus quondam Eustachii

UGINET, F.-C., 178n

Ugo Benzi (teacher of medicine, 1405-51), 132, 134n, 154n, 164n, 176-7nn, 180, 181n, 191, 220-1

Ugo di Battista Bellanti (teacher of law, 1472-81), 167n, 213

Ugo Sermini (teacher of medicine, 1496-8), 172n, 285n

Ugolino di Piero da Siena (medical student at Florence, 1417), 247n

Ugurgieri family, 73n, 194, and *see* Antimo, Matteo

UGURGIERI AZZOLINI, I., 9n, 10n, 252n

ULLMAN, B., 388n

Umidi family, 194, and *see* Giovanni Battista

Urbanus vitore (German student of law, given provisional place in the Sapienza, 1484), 317n

Utinelli *see* Castellano

VACCARA, S., 199n, 264n

VACCARI, P., 113n, 239n, 244n, 273n, 294n

Valascho *see* Johannes

Valenti *see* Natimbene

Valentini, Giovanni *see* Cantalicio

Valentius Angelelli of Narni (degree in law, 1421), 59n

Valerius Jacobi simonelli? de Urbeveteri (student of law, allocated a place in the Sapienza, 1443), 316n

VALLAURI, T., 387n

VALLERANI, M., 209n

VAN DAMME, S., 196n

VAN HECK, A., 59n

VAN LIERE, K., 102n

VANNEL TODERI, F., 88n

VANNI, F., 383

VARANINI, G., 32n

VARNI, A., 404n

VASARI, G., 399n

VASINA, A., 217n

VASOLI, C., 2n

Vasques *see* Pedro

Vecchiani *see* Mariano

Vecchietta, 115n, 116

VECCHIO, S., 218n

VENEROSI PESCIOLINI, G., 323n

Ventura di Antonio Venturi (Sienese guarantor of a student, 1474), 320n

Ventura son of Tebaldo (teacher of grammar, *c.*1261), 68n

VERDE, A., 27n, 61-2nn, 66n, 74-5nn, 88n, 90n, 105n, 110-3nn, 131n, 138n, 142n, 144n, 151n, 163n, 169n, 174n, 178n, 181, 182n, 214n, 239, 242n, 245-6nn, 253n, 261n, 266n, 272n, 279n, 284n, 294n, 403n

VERDERA Y TUELLS, E., 242n

VERESS, E., 243n

Vergelle *see* Francesco

VERGER, J., 2n, 5n, 46n, 67n, 209n, 223n, 249n, 287n

VERONESE CESERACCIU, E., 242n, 301n, 319n, 334n

Verreschi *see* Hieronimus

Vettori *see* Baldassare

VIAN, P., 163n

VIGNI, L., 107n, 344n

Villani *see* Filippo

Vincenti *see* Giovanni di Niccolò di Mino, Mino

Vincenzo (chaplain in the Sapienza, 1473-5), 359n

VIORA, M., 165n

Visconti dynasty of Milan, 7n, 304, and *see* Bernabò, Filippo Maria, Giangaleazzo

VISCONTI, A., 224n, 265n

VISINTIN, A., 320n, 326n

Vitaleoni *see* Manno di Bartolomeo

VITI, P., 17n

Vitruvius (treatise on architecture), 398

Vivianus of Pordenone (*professor* of civil law, recommended for office, 1384), 216n

VON HÜLSEN-ESCH, A., 224n

VON MÜLLER, O., 381n

VON SAVIGNY, F., 109n, 138n, 139n

VORBRODT, G., 274n

VORBRODT, I., 274n

WACKERNAGEL, M., 399n

WAINWRIGHT, V., 47n

WALEY, D., XII, 18n, 23n, 36n, 69n, 73n, 209, 234n, 268

WALSH, K., 45n

WALTHER, H., 209n

WATT, D., 59n

WEBER, C., 34n, 67n

WEIGLE, F., 24n, 240n, 242n, 243n, 287n, 318n, 324n

WEIJERS, O., 122n, 123n, 143n, 302n

WEIMAR, P., 123n

WHITLEY, A., 14n, 52n, 113n, 152n, 206, 211n, 323n

Whittick, Christopher, 23n

WICKHAM, C., 1n

WIDDER, E., 46n

WIERUSZOWSKI, H., 36n

WIJFFELS, A., 217n

Wildhelm *see* Laurentius

Wilhelmus de Reichenau (degree, 1464), 22n

WILLOWEIT, D., 19n

WILSON TORDI, A., 276n

WRETSCHKO, A. VON, 42n, 226n

ZACCARIA, R., 17n

ZAMBOTTI, B., 9n, 294

ZANETTI, D., 16n, 61n, 90n, 174n, 183-5nn, 223n, 310n, 320n

ZANNINI, A., 183-4nn,

Zanobi Guasconi (degree and *condotta* in law, 1425), 180

Zanobio (degree in law, 1425), 289n

ZARRILLI, C., 19n, 299n, 376n

ZAZZERA, F., 200n, 252n

Zbengh *see* Cristoforus

ZDEKAUER, L., XIV, 6n, 8n, 11-2, 22, 23n, 25n, 31, 32n, 33, 34n, 36n, 38n, 42-3nn, 47-8nn, 50n, 52-3nn, 55-6nn, 58-9nn, 62n, 66n, 70-1nn, 77n, 83n, 88n, 99-100nn, 102n, 104-6nn, 109-11nn, 114n, 116n, 118n, 123n, 125n, 130n, 132-3nn, 139n, 144n, 150n, 154n, 155, 157-8nn, 159, 168n, 174n, 177n, 181n, 185-7nn, 191-4nn, 198-9nn, 202-3nn, 210n, 212-3nn, 217-8nn, 221n, 226n, 233n, 235-6nn, 239n, 241n, 243n, 244, 250-2nn, 254n, 255, 256-9nn, 261n, 264-6nn, 267-8, 269n, 274n, 278n, 280-2nn, 283, 284-6nn, 289n, 292, 293n, 300n, 302n, 306-8nn, 311n, 314n, 317-20nn, 321, 323n, 324-5nn, 333n, 335n, 340n, 342-3nn, 347-8nn, 350-1nn, 361n, 372n, 385n, 389n, 392n, 400, 403n

ZEILLINGER, K., 34n

Zeno di Chiarasco da Soncino (moneylender; estate, 1424), 362n

Zilango *see* Paolo

ZMORA, A., 359n

ZOLLER, I., 100n

ZONTA, C., 242n

ZONTA, G., 206n, 286-7nn

ZORZI, A., 32n

ZORZOLI, M. C., 87n, 163n, 186n, 193n, 197n, 202n

INDEX OF PLACE NAMES AND INSTITUTIONS

The *Studio* of Siena, its components and the Sienese magistracies concerned with it have not been indexed on account of their ubiquity in the text.

Abbadia S. Salvatore *see* Francesco

Aberdeen, 59n

Alessandria *see* Agostino Curradi, Gregorio

Amalfi, duke of, 322n

Amelia *see* Angelo di Jacopo, Angelo Geraldini, Antonio, Antonius de Mendosis, Bernardinus de Mendosis, Filippo, Giovanni di Ser Ugolino, Tommaso

Amendola *see* Bartolomeo de la Mandola, Jacobus

Ancarano *see* Pietro

Ancona, 199, and *see* Adrianus Gratiosus

Anderten *see* Borchardus

Anguillara, students from, 336n, and *see* Angelo Sabe

Aquila *see* Antonio Pace de' Carapelli, Evangelista Riverio, Francesco Cadichio

Aragon *see* Gonsalvo

Arcidosso, 303n

Arezzo, 225n, 321n, and *see* Antonio, Antonio di Giovanni Roselli, Antonio di Niccolò Santi, Antonio di Rosello Roselli, Bandino, Bartolomeo di Cristoforo, Benedetto Accolti, Brandaglia, Cosma, Domenico, Francesco Accolti, Giovanni di Ser Donato, Giovanni di Maestro Pietro, Jacopo di Giovanni, Leonardo Roselli, Lorenzo, Stefano

–, University of, 4n, 36-n, 43, 45, 67n

Asciano, 100, 103n, 114n, 171n, 172n, 192, 373n, and *see* Bartolomeo di Checho di Binduccio, Luca di Cristoforo

Ascoli, 292n, and *see* Giovanni Antonio Alato, Pace, Simone

Assisi, 280n, and *see* Mariotto, Niccolò di Paolo

Asti *see* Scipio

Augustinian order, 126, and *see* Alessandro da S. Gimignano, Andrea Biglia, Antonius basilij, Francesco Franci, Gabriele da Spoleto, Giovanni di Matteo, Gregorio da Spoleto, John Bery, Matteo da Siena

Austria *see* Margaret

Aversa *see* Luigi, Melchior Juliani pierozi, Paulus

Avignon, University of, 57n, 287n

Barcelona *see* Guglielmo di Pietro Esguert, Lodovico

Basel, University of, 67n

Batignano *see* Antonio

Bergamo *see* Giordano O.P.

Bibbiano Guiglieschi, 365

Bohemia, students from, 243

Bologna, 34n, 36n, 43, 44n, 47, 82n, 176n, 177n, and *see* Alberto de Sinibaldo Cattani, Alessandro O.P., Bartolomeo de Herculanis, Buvalello de' Buvalelli, Filippo Beroaldo il Vecchio, Floriano Sampieri, Giovanni de' Guasconi, Guasparre Sighicelli, Guicciardo di Bondo, Guido Faba, Guidotto, Paolo dei Liazari, Pietro Giovannetti of Bologna

–, University of, 4, 7-8, 9n, 12, 25n, 27, 31-3, 34n, 36-8, 40-1, 43, 46, 50, 52n, 57n, 61-2, 63n, 66n, 67n, 80-1, 82n, 87n, 88, 109n, 110, 113n, 115n, 121-2, 123n, 124, 125n, 126, 130n, 131-2, 133n, 134, 136n, 138n, 139, 143n, 144, 149n, 152n, 154n, 155n, 157n, 158-9, 163, 168n, 170n, 173-5nn, 176, 177n, 179, 184n, 190, 192-3nn, 196, 198, 201n, 205n, 209n, 210, 221n, 223n, 225, 232, 234n, 236n, 237n, 238, 242, 243n, 246n,

247n, 249-51, 253n, 256, 264, 265n, 270n, 279n, 280n, 282, 283n, 285n, 286n, 288n, 289n, 301, 309, 321n, 323n, 403n

–, –, Collegio Ancarano, 320n

–, –, Collegio Avignonese, 301

–, –, Collegio Bresciano, 301

–, –, Collegio Fieschi, 320n

–, –, Collegio Gregoriano, 301, 325, 326n

–, –, Collegio Reggiano, 320n

–, –, Collegio di Spagna, 242n, 301, 306, 310, 320n, 325, 326n, 383, 387n, 398-9, 400n

Borgo San Sepolcro *see* Malatesta de' Cattani, Malatesta, Marinus d. Raynerii Catanensis

Bracciano *see* Filippo de' Scalandrini

Brenna, 367

Brescia *see* Jacomo Castello

Brunswick *see* Henricus Brystidde

Burgundy *see* Claudio

Calabria *see* Alfonso (duke)

Camaldolese order *see* Antonio Berti

Cambridge, University of, 4

Camerino *see* Abroardus, Andreas, Angelo, Benedetto, Evangelista, Giulio Cesare da Varano, Rainaldo, Serafino

Campiglia *see* Simone

Candia, 133n

Capraia, 372n

Capranica *see* Angelo, Domenico, Guidone, Pietro

Carmelite order, 126, and *see* Bernardino da Siena

Casole, 114n, 345n, and *see* Lorenzo, Niccolò Aringhieri

Castello *see* Antonio de Caputis

Castello della Pieve *see* Felice di Giovanni de' Tagoni

Castiglione *see* Achille di Ser Michele

Castiglione Aretino *see* Bartolomeo di Cola

Castiglione Benzetti, 367

Castro *see* Biagio, Paolo

Catalonia, students from, 271n, 306, and *see* Antonius Catelanus, Berengarius de Comitibus de Catelonia, Francesco, Giorgio, Giovanni, Guglielmo di Pietro Esguert, Lodovico da Barcelona, Manuel, Matheus, Matteo Malferit, Petrus de Michelibus, Pietrus guilelmi, Raffael

Certano, 367

Ciglione *see* Francesco

Chianciano *see* Antonio Tani, Cristoforo, Domenico, Giovanni

Chieri, 113n, 238n

Ciliano *see* Guglielmo

Cingoli *see* Benedetto

Città di Castello, 211n, 306n, and *see* Niccolò di Giglio

Cividale, University of, 45

Colle Val d'Elsa, 280n, and *see* Naldo

Collestefano *see* Buccius quondam Nicolay O.S.B.

Constance, Council of, 57

Cordoba *see* Fernandino

Corsignano, 10n, 114, 241

Cortona, 350n, and *see* Bernardino, Domenico, Giovanni Battista di Agostino, Rinaldo Angelini

Crema *see* Francesco

Croatia, students from, 243, and *see* Marin Držić

Deventer *see* Paulus de Danetria

Dominican order, 125 and *see* Alessandro da Bologna, Bartolomeo da Sicilia, Battista da Fabriano, Francesco da Nardò, Giordano da Bergamo, Giovanni Dominici, Leonardo, Leonardo da Perugia, Simone Bocci

Drogobyč *see* Jurij Kotermak

England, students from, 243, 324; and *see* Adovardus, Giovanni, Guilielmus, John Bery O.S.A., Nicholaus

Fabriano *see* Battista da Fabriano, O.P.

Fermo *see* Antonio, Jacopo Mariani, Pietro de' Fabritti

Ferrara, 1, 165n, 216n, and *see* Borso d'Este, Felino Sandei, Leonello d'Este, Niccolò Jacopo de Griffis, Scipio de Rubertis

–, Council of, 59n, 176n

–, University of, 27, 59n, 63n, 131, 149n, 154n, 176n, 187, 189, 201n, 221-2, 236n, 247n, 253n, 265n

Florence, 1, 3, 11, 37-8, 54, 62, 87n, 183n, 201n, 210, 215n, 220-1, 238n, 244, 247n, 258n, 269n, 313n, 321n, 337, 350, 388, 403, and *see* Alessandro del Antella, Almerico di Filippo Corsini, Andrea florentino, Bartolomeo Scala, Bonaccorso Bonaccorsi, Filippo Boccaccini de Alamannis, Cosimo I de' Medici, Dante Alighieri, Emanuel Chrysoloras, Filippo Villani, Francesco I de' Medici, Giovanni Boccaccio, Giovanni di Roberto degli Altoviti, Giovanni Malpaghini, Leon Battista Alberti, Lorenzo de' Medici, Niccolò da Uzzano, Niccolò d'Este, Paolo di Ser Simone di Paolo, Piero di Cosimo de' Medici, Roberto Cavalcanti, Taddeo di Giovanni, Tommaso Corsini, Tommaso de' Covoni, Zanobi Guasconi

–, Platonic Academy, 219n

–, Sapienza, 399

–, University of (to 1472), 12n, 27, 43, 45, 46n, 47, 51, 55, 57n, 59n, 62n, 66n, 69n, 81n, 87, 88n, 90, 105, 110n, 115n, 131, 140n, 143n, 154n, 163n, 164, 175n, 176, 177n, 179-82, 186-8, 192n, 201n, 220, 221n, 237, 238n, 246-7nn, 251n, 253, 260n, 262n, 265n, 278-9nn, 281n, 299n, 301, 305n, 310n, 320, 379, 387n, 399, 403n

Florence/Pisa, University of (from 1472), 27, 61-2, 73-5nn, 87, 88n, 90n, 105, 110n, 112-3nn, 125n, 131, 139, 144, 151n, 152, 163n, 169n, 171, 174n, 176n, 178n, 180-2, 185n, 222, 236, 238n, 239, 240n, 242n, 244, 245-6nn, 253n, 261n, 266n, 272n, 294n, 311n, 338, 340n, 350, 403, 404n, 405-6

–, Sapienza, 302n, 383, 387n, 398-401

Foligno *see* Cesare m.i Cristofori, Cipriano Antonini, Gentile, Hieronimus, Piermarino

Forlì, 247n, and *see* Jacopo

Fornaria *see* Jacopo

France, 222; students from, 244-5, 272n, 312, 324, and *see* Guido, Nicolao, Petrus

–, universities of, 167n

Francigena, Via, 3n

Franciscan order, 124-5, 137n, 155n, 206n, and *see* Angelo Salvetti, Emanuel of Portugal, Francesco della Rovere of Savona, Luca, Manuele

Freiburg im Breisgau, *Domus Sapientie*, 302n

Frignano *see* Filippo d'Antonio

Fucecchio *see* Tommaso

Gaeta *see* Cola, Julianus de Squaquaris

Geneva, University of, 45

Genoa, 233, 310; students from, 244, 294; and *see* Andrea, Bartolomeo, Benedetto di Mantica, Franciscus Gentilis palavicinus, Luca Stella, Lucas dominici presbitero, Martino, Tommaso Campofregoso

Germany: copyists from, 281n; students from, 241-5, 272n, 281n, 312, 314, 324, 349-50, 381n; and *see* Albert duke of Saxony, Arigus de Bramante, Bretuldus, Federicus, Federicus chuzer, Georgius chreuz, Georgius, Giorgio, Giovanni, Giovanni da Barbanza, Giovanni Museler, Goffredo, Henricus Gelingh de Svevia, Henricus Ienis de Sanxonia, Henricus, Ingerardus, Jodocus Jungmair, Johannes Arrighi, Johannes Born, Johannes, Johannes de Lysura, Johannes de Weissenbach, Johannes

Ruysch, Johannes, Johannes von Azel, Laurentius Wildhelm, Leonardus, Martinus, Massimianus, Nicholaus, Noe, Paulus de Plenzi, Peter Pront, Peter Ruysch, Sigismund, Theodoricus discov, Urbanus vitore

–, universities of, 310

Gerosolimitan order *see* Niccolò Baglioni

Graz, Universitätsbibliothek, 11n

Grosseto, 100n, 177n, 247n, 267n, 304, 361, 362n, 367, 368n, 373, 374, and *see* Antonio di Giovanni, Matteo

–, S. Giovanni della Misericordia, hospital, 362n

Gubbio *see* Angelo di Paolo, Angelo di Pietro, Baldaccio/Baldinaccio degli Ubaldi, Lodovico

Heidelberg, University of, 293n

Hungary, students from, 243, 324; and *see* Ambrosius, Dionysius Széch, Jacomo

Iberia, students from, 241-2, 244, 349, and *see* Johannes Valascho

Iesi *see* Tommaso

Imola, 37, 70, and *see* Alessandro Tartagni, Giovanni Nicoletti, Girolamo

Itro *see* Antonio di Giovanni

Jena *see* Henricus

Kalamazoo, 2n

Leeds, 2n

Lewes, East Sussex Record Office, 23n

Linz am Rhein *see* Jakob Joel, Petrus Johel, Tilmann Joel

Lodi *see* Martino Garati

Lombardy, 75n, 151n, 165n; students from, 235-6

Low Countries, students from, 243; and *see* Desiderius Erasmus, Jacomo Carusio, Johannes Dodonis, Paulus de Danetria

Lucera, 177n

Lucca, 175n, 352n; students from, 244, 280; and *see* Ambrogio, Antonio, Benedetto, Filippo di Andrea di Antonio Balducci, Giovanni Battista, Libertà, Polo, Stefanus de trentis

–, University of, 45, 197n

Lucignano d'Arbia, 365n

Lucignano d'Asso, 365-6, 372n, 373

Lucignano Val di Chiana, 114, 203n, 213n, 243n, and *see* Bernardino

Lüneburg *see* Niccolò di Lonenborche

Macerata, 11; students from, 244; and *see* Gabriel

Magliano, 165n

Mantua, 1, 217n, and *see* Antonio de' Guazzi/Guacci

Marche, 11; students from, 244-5, 272n; and *see* Adrianus Gratiosus

Marcialla (Pisa) *see* Ciprianus

Maremma, 166n, 369n

Massa Marittima, 113n, 292, 304, 361

Massa *see* Bartolomeo

Matera *see* Matteo

Meschede *see* Johannes

Milan, 1, 7n, 220, 294, and *see* Andrea Biglia, Bartolomeo, Bernabò Visconti, Filippo Decio, Filippo Maria Visconti, Francesco Sforza, Giangaleazzo Visconti, Giovanni di Filippo de' Catani, Lancilotto Decio

Modena *see* Guasparre Fontano

Montagutolo Giuseppi, 365, 367

Montalcino, 113, 114, 135n, 166n, 171n, 207n, 294, 306n, 379, and *see* Abramo, Bernardo di Pietro Lapini, Giovanni, Sinibaldo di Maestro Bartalaccio

Montaperti, 371

Montefalco *see* Avianus de Coppis, Francesco de Filippis, Nicolaus

Montefeltro *see* Guidantonio, Count of Urbino

Montefiascone, 321n

Montemorello *see* Antonio di Maestro Giovanni

Monte Oliveto Maggiore, 366

Montepescali *see* Nerio

Montepulciano *see* Onesto di Bartolomeo, Tarugio di Bernardino Tarugi

Monterchio *see* Andreas

Monte San Savino *see* Fabiano d'Antonio, Fabriano

Monte Vasone, 376n

Montferrat, student from, 244, 324

Monticchiello, 36-8, 369n, 371n, 373-4

Montpellier, University of, 57n

Munich, 11, and *see* Jacobus Schrenck, Johannes Giesser

Naples, 1, 238, 386n; Aragonese court, 186; king of, 321n; orator of, 313; queen of, 49; students from, 244; and *see* Alfonso V, Antonio di Ser Carluccio, Giannantonio Campano, Giovanni, Giovanni Girgos

–, University of, 4n, 31-2nn, 34n, 45n, 57n, 67n, 250n, 404n

Narni *see* Angelo di Paolo, Blasius, Hieronimo de Rasimo, Valentius Angelelli

Navarre *see* Pedro

Nepi *see* Johannes de Petronibus

Nürnberg *see* Federicus Johannes Corradi

Oppenheim *see* Peter Bart

Orange, University of, 45

Orbetello, 100n, 171n, 172n

Orgia, 367

Orvieto, 321n, and *see* Valerius Jacobi simonelli

–, students from, 336n

Oxford, University of, XI, 4, 38

Pacina *see* Pietro

Padua, 87n, and *see* Bartolomeo Bolis, Marsilio Santasofia, Prosdocimo Conti

–, University of, 7n, 9n, 12n, 27, 32n, 34n, 37n, 38, 40, 42n, 46, 47n, 50, 61, 67n, 69n, 81n, 82n, 100, 110n, 114n, 125n, 133n, 138-40nn, 143n, 144, 151n, 152, 154n, 170-1nn, 175n, 179, 183n, 190n, 197, 201n, 206n, 213n, 221-2nn, 234n, 236-7nn, 242, 247n, 253n, 263n, 265n, 267n, 278n, 280n, 286n, 399

–, –, Collegio Arquà, 301

–, –, Collegio Campi, 301

–, –, Collegio Engleschi, 301n, 319n, 334n

–, –, Collegio Tornacense, 301

–, –, 'domus Sapientiae', 302n

–, –, Palazzo del Bo, 399

Paganico, 100n, 171n

Papal State, 43; students from, 244, 324

Paris, University of, 32n, 38, 57n, 58, 122, 126, 232n, 249, 293n

–, –, Collège de Dormans-Beauvais, 303n

Parma *see* Giovanni di Martino, Giovanni Polo, Lazzaro Pellegrini

–, University of, 73n, 207n, 220, 221n, 237n, 253n, 261n, 273n

Pavia, 238n, and *see* Carlo, Catone Sacco, Elias, Giason del Maino, Giovanni Matteo Ferrari da Grado

–, University of, 7n, 13n, 27, 45-6, 51, 57n, 61, 81n, 90, 110-11nn, 113n, 138n, 144n, 152n, 163n, 174n, 176n, 179, 184, 185n, 186, 193, 197, 202n, 221n, 236n, 239, 244n, 273n, 277n, 286n, 294-5, 323n

–, –, Collegio Castiglioni, 320n, 322n

–, –, Collegio Ferrari da Grado, 387n

–, –, Collegio Sacco, 310, 320n

Pavia-Siena, Council of, 58-9, 115n

Perpignan *see* Giovanni di Pietro Balle, Peter

Perugia, 47, 53, 176, 199n, 233, and *see* Agapito di Matteo, Angelo, Angelo Baglioni, Angelo degli

Ubaldi, Angelo di Felice de' Narducci, Angelus Andree Bernardini de Guidonibus, Baldo Bartolini, Baldo degli Ubaldi, Bartolo, Bartolo da Sassoferrato, Bartolomeo di Antonio, Benedetto Barzi, Benedetto Capra, Braccio Baglioni, Francesco de Mansuetis or de' Buonriposi, Francesco di Bettolo Coppoli, Gabriele Fabrizi, Guglielmo di Cellolo, Leonardo O.P., Luca, Mansueto Mansueti, Mateolo de Baltasaris, Mattiolo Mattioli, Niccolò Baglioni, Onofrio Bartolini, Rodolfo Baglioni, Sallustio Buonguglielmi, Tommaso da Bordello

–, Monte Morcino, monastery of, 341n

–, S. Maria di Monte Oliveto, 327n

–, University of, 27, 37n, 40, 43, 45-6, 50, 53, 57n, 63n, 70n, 80n, 82n, 84n, 90, 100, 109n, 110n, 112n, 115, 122n, 133n, 140n, 143n, 149n, 153n, 155, 174-7nn, 178, 192n, 201n, 207n, 213n, 236n, 237-9, 240n, 244, 246n, 251n, 261n, 262n, 265-6nn, 269, 272-3nn, 278n, 280-2nn, 289n, 292n, 301-2, 303n, 326n, 389n, 403n

–, –, Collegio Gregoriano or Sapienza Vecchia, 25n, 53n, 301-2, 306, 309, 315, 318n, 320n, 325-30, 333, 341n, 387n, 398-9

–, –, Collegio Gerolimiano or Sapienza Nuova, 302n, 320n, 348n, 387n

Pescia *see* Antonio di Maestro Matteo, Francesco di Antonio

Petriolo, Bagni di, 164n, 165n, 323n

Petroio, 367

Piacenza, 113n, and *see* Domenico di Francesco, Raffaele Fulgosio

Piedmont *see* Teodorico

Pieve di Cadore *see* Felice

Piombino, 291, and *see* Angelo di Ser Luca, Benedetto, Giovanni di Ser Jacopo di Ser Soldano, Giovanni, Jacopo Andree, Jacopo III d'Appiano, Jacopo IV d'Aragona d'Appiano, Paola Colonna-Appiani, Soldano di Ser Jacopo di Ser Soldano, Stefano

Pisa, 39, 43, 46n, 62, 113n, 280, and *see* Ciprianus de Marcialla, Francesco Tegrini, Mariano de' Vecchiani, Paolo, Piero, Pietro, Tommaso Battista di Maestro Andrea

–, University of (to 1472; thereafter *see* under Florence/Pisa), 7n, 27, 43, 46n, 57n, 125n, 176n, 197n, 253, 265n

Pistoia, 11, 52n, 113n, 115n, 187n, 321n; students from, 244; and *see* Antonio di Maestro Marco di Maestro Antonio, Bartolomeo di Maestro Antonio, Bartolomeo di Ser Giovanni Ciosi, Bello di

Goro, Braccino, Cino, Filippo di Sinibaldo de' Lazzari, Giovanni di Maestro Antonio, Guido Johannis ser Pieri de Forteguerris, Marco di Maestro Antonio, Niccolò, Niccolò Forteguerri, Ricciardo de' Ricciardi, Simon Antonii Talini de Lanciano, Timoteo

–, Pia Casa di Sapienza, 359n

Poland, students from, 243, 312, and *see* Niccolò Ghelde, Nicolaus Ffabri of Žagan

Pontremoli *see* Tommaso de' Arrighini

Pordenone *see* Vivianus

Portugal, students from, 241-2, 291-2, 308n, 312, 314n, 324, 341n, 349; and *see* king Afonso V, Alvaro, Alvaro Alfonsi, Alvarus de regno algarbie, Blasius, princess Eleonora, Emanuel O.F.M., Ferdinando, Ferdinandino, Ferrandus, Giovanni di Giglio, Giovanni, Gonsalvo Mendes de Silveira, Guasparre, Johannes Alfonsi, Johannes Alvari, Luís Teixeira, Lupo, Martino di Pietro, Martino Lópes Lobo, Martinus, Nuño, Nuño Consalvi, Pedro Vasques, Perus Gobboli, Piero di Fernando (*see* also under Iberia)

Prague, 11

–, University of, 43

Prato, 113n, 246n, 269n, 280, and *see* Filippo d'Agnolo, Giovanni, Giovanni Gherardi, Giovanni Milanesi, Giuliano di Ser Lorenzo di Giuliano Tani, Niccolò de' Cambioni, Paolo

Pratovecchio *see* Antonio Mincucci

Radicofani, 165n, and *see* Bartolomeo di Matteo

Radicondoli, 114n and *see* Cipriano di Simone, Simone di Iacomo di Ghieri

Ragusa *see* Domenico

Rapolano *see* Francesco di Neri Gherardini, Giovanni di Guccio

Recanati *see* Battista di Maestro Giovanni, Niccolò

Reichenau *see* Wilhelmus

Rieti *see* Antonio

Rocca Contrada *see* Matteo

Rocca Val d'Orcia *see* Federico P.

Rome, 1, 3, 11, 54, 82n, 175n, 216n, 231, 236-7nn, 285n, 300n; students from, 244, 272n, 324; and *see* Antonio Cherubini, Antonio de Casarellis, Benedictus de Farano, Domenico Mentebona, Francesco di Sante/Santi, Giovanni di Lorenzo de' Giustini, Giovanni di Lorenzo, Jacobus Gothfredi, Lodovico Pontano, Paulus Pontanus

–, University of, 4n, 27, 43n, 54, 57-8nn, 67n, 87, 100, 136n, 152n, 163n, 177n, 234n, 243n, 399n

–, –, Collegio Capranica, 302n, 320n, 341n, 399n
–, –, Collegio Nardini, 302n, 320n, 341n
–, –, Sapienza, 302n, 387n, 399
Roncaglia, Diet of, 34n
Rotterdam *see* Johannes Dodonis
Russian, students from, *see* Jurij Kotermak, Martino

Sagunto *see* Juan Almaçán
Salamanca, University of, 102n
Salerno, University of, 4n
Sant'Agnati di Vignano, 365
Sant'Angelo in Colle, 372n
Sant'Ansano a Dofana, 337, 345, 361-2, 374-5
San Galgano, 364
San Gimignano *see* Alessandro O.S.A., Angelo di Fran-
    cesco Bruogi, Antonio di Ser Salvi, Domenico Bu-
    zichini, Giovanni Battista, Giovanni, Ippolito di
    Ser Niccolò, Mattia Lupi
San Giovanni in Persiceto *see* Guasparre Sighicelli
San Lupidio *see* Simonetto
San Mamiliano, 365
San Miniato *see* Filippo, Francesco di Ser Matteo, Gi-
    rolamo, Jacopo di Lippo, Leonardo, Niccolò
San Quirico, 171n
San Severino *see* Federico, Giovanni Battista Caccia-
    lupi
Santa Vittoria *see* Gianfrancesco Carboni
Sarteano, 281n
Sarzana, 247n
Sassoferrato *see* Bartolo
Savigliano, 113n
Savona *see* Francesco della Rovere, Jacobus thome
Savoy, 225, and *see* Johannes de Gilliacho/Gigliaco,
    Stefano Macri
Scandinavia, students from, 243
Scotland, students from, 243, 312; and *see* Alexander,
    son of King James, Andrew of Hawyk, Johannes
Seggiano *see* Domenico di Angelo
Sermoneta *see* Alessandro, Cristoforus, Giovanni
Servite order, 126, and *see* Bonifazio, Emmanuele
Sicily, students from, 241n, 244-5, 272n, 291, 324;
    and *see* Andrea Barbazza, Angelo Pandolfi, Anto-
    nio Becadelli, Antonio Cesso, Antonio Gotto, An-
    tonio 'Sciacha'/Griacha, Bartolomeo da Sicilia,
    O.P., Bartolomeo Gatti, Cola, Domperus, Frances-
    co, Giovanni, Giovanni Aurispa, Giovanni di
    Frangano, Giovanni di Orlando, Giovanni Pensio,
    Giovanni Riczari, Johannes Jacobi franco, Johan-
    nes Mancini, Niccolò Cavallo, Niccolò Tedeschi,
    Rainaldo

Siena:
–, areas and locations:
–, –, Aringhieri, 'loco decto degli', 390n
–, –, Camollia, Terzo di, 389, 390n
–, –, Camollia, Via di, 389n
–, –, Campo, Piazza del 87n, 103, 119, 144, 154,
    227
–, –, Capacci, 'casa de', 390n
–, –, Chiaravalle, Via, 381, 382n, 384
–, –, Corsieri, 'Volta de', 390n
–, –, Costarella, 143n
–, –, Fastelli, Chiasso, 384
–, –, Montone, Val di, 292
–, –, Pittori, Via dei, 381, 390n
–, –, Rosa, Vicolo della, 374n
–, –, Sale, Piazza del, 389n
–, –, Salimbeni, Piazza, 390n
–, –, S. Antonio, Costa di, 381, 384n
–, –, S. Antonio, Strada di, 317
–, –, S. Donato a lato dei Montanini, parish, 364n
–, –, Sapienza, Via della, 381, 390n
–, –, Terme, Via delle, 381
–, –, Termini, Via dei, 374n
–, –, Tolomei, Piazza, 115n, 116, 154
–, –, Umiliati, Piazza degli, 389n
–, –, Umiliati, Vicolo degli, 389n
–, churches:
–, –, S. Agostino, 114n
–, –, S. Cristoforo, 115-6
–, –, S. Desiderio, 116n, 206
–, –, S. Domenico, 323-4nn, 358n, 381
–, –, S. Maria (cathedral), 281
–, –, S. Pellegrino della Sapienza, 358, 381
–, –, S. Pietro d'Ovile, 115-6, 117n
–, –, S. Tommaso (Umiliati), 389
–, –, S. Vigilio, 115, 118n
–, –, S. Vincenti, 115
–, hospitals:
–, –, S. Andrea, 205n, 354n, 362, 365, 369, 371
–, –, S. Caterina nel popolo di San Mamiliano, 362n
–, –, S. Maria della Scala, 10n, 25n, 27, 50, 51, 56,
    62n, 75n, 88, 102-3, 104n, 105-7, 133, 158,
    210n, 211, 226-7nn, 258n, 264, 280-1nn, 303n,
    304, 306, 344, 364, 369n, 370, 371n, 372-4,
    375n, 391n, 405
–, –, S. Maria della Stella/de' Salimbeni, 362n, 385
–, other institutions
–, –, Archivio di Stato, 16-17
–, –, Archivio Arcivescovile, 16
–, –, Biblioteca degli Intronati, 381, 382-3, 387

–, –, Compagnia di San Donato al lato a Montanini di San Giglio, 384

–, –, Confraternity of S. Maria della Misericordia, 304n

–, –, Gallo, albergo del, 374-5

–, –, Istituto Statale d'Arte 'Duccio di Boninsegna', 381

–, –, *Monte di Pietà*, 169n, 375-7

–, –, Opera del Duomo, 75n, 82n, 84, 104n, 106n, 286, 288n, 391n

–, –, Palazzo Pubblico/Comunale, 4, 68, 111

Sinalunga *see* Jacopo di Filippo

Sirmione *see* Niccolò

Soncino *see* Zeno di Chiarasco

Sovana, 213

Spain, students from, 241, 245, 291, 306n, 312, 317n, 324; and *see* Alfonso V, Gaspar Turiglia, Theodorico (*see* also under Aragon, Catalonia, Iberia, Valencia)

–, universities of, 167n

Spoleto, 321n, and *see* Conforto, Cristoforo Astolfi, Gabriel Lottus, Gabriele O.S.A., Giovanni di Ser Buccio, Gregorio O.S.A., Lodovico, Marinus, Matteo di Maestro Tommaso, Moscato

Staggia, 269n

Strasbourg *see* Giovanni Museler

Swabia *see* Henricus Gelingh

Sweden, students from, 243n, 324

Tagliacozzo *see* Piero di Francesco

Terni *see* Cantalicio, Lodovico Petrucciani

Torrita *see* Francesco di Domenico

Tortosa *see* Michael Albrel

Toulouse, University of, 34n, 57n

Trapani *see* Antonius de Drepano, Johannes de Rufaldis

Trequanda *see* Petrus Silvestri Jacobi

Trevi *see* Natimbene de' Valenti

Treviso, University of, 32n, 197n

Turin, University of, 90n, 114n, 238n, 293n, 399, 401n

–, Collegio Grassi, 387n

Tuscany, 11, 31, 244, 369n, 403-4; students from, 244-5, 272n, 324

Urbino, 1, 313, and *see* Francesco

Utrecht *see* Jacomo Carusio

Val d'Orcia, 238, 366-7, 368n, 372-5

Val di Strove, 366-7, 368n, 371, 373n, 376n

Valencia *see* Guasparre Pelliciai, Guglielmo Ciscar, Jacopo

Valtellina *see* Alessandro di Marchisi

Velletri *see* Antonio

Venafro *see* Antonio Giordano

Venice, 1, 7n, 11, 197, 199, 264n, and *see* Bernardus, Paolo

Vergelle *see* Francesco

Verona, student from, 244; and *see* Lelio di Giusti, Piero de' Pegolotti, Pietro, Pietro Sacco

Vescovado di Siena/di Murlo, 364n

Vico di Montechiano, 367, 371

Vienna, 11

–, University of, 176, 221

Vignone, Bagno, 171n, 207n

–, hospital, 362n

Visso *see* Ercole de' Cataldini, Giovanni

Viterbo, 258n; students from, 336; and *see* Agostino, Hieronimus de Verreschis, Oddone di Petruccio, Petrus

Vitry *see* Jacques

Volterra *see* Antonio di Benedetto, Benedetto, Giovanni di Michele Contugio, Lodovico di Magio, Niccolò

Worms *see* Martinus Luft

Žagan *see* Nicolaus Ffabri

Centro interuniversitario per la storia delle università italiane

Studi

1. Gian Paolo Brizzi, Andrea Romano (a cura di), *Studenti e dottori nelle università italiane (origini - XX secolo)*. Atti del Convegno di studi. Bologna, 25-27 novembre 1999

2. Sabino Cassese (a cura di), *Il testo unico delle norme sull'Università*. Introduzione di Andrea Romano

3. Gian Paolo Brizzi, Roberto Greci (a cura di), *Gesuiti e università in Europa (secoli XVI-XVIII)*. Atti del Convegno di studi. Parma, 13-15 dicembre 2001

4. Ariane Dröscher, *Le facoltà medico-chirurgiche italiane (1860-1915)*. Repertorio delle cattedre e degli stabilimenti annessi, dei docenti, dei liberi docenti e del personale scientifico

5. Antonio I. Pini, *Studio, università e città nel medioevo bolognese*

6. Giuliana Mazzi (a cura di), *L'Università e la città. Il ruolo di Padova e degli altri Atenei italiani nello sviluppo urbano*. Atti del Convegno di studi. Padova, 4-6 dicembre 2003

7. Peter Denley, *Commune and Studio in Late Medieval and Renaissance Siena*